In Praise ⸤
Making Sense of Beliefs and Values

Fabulous book! It's really timely, because contemporary developments all over the world make the need to "make sense of beliefs and values" more pressing than ever before, I think. It's the only way our humanity can rise again. The book is a trailblazer in that critical sense, and is the most compelling response to the age-old quandary that is captured in a pithy observation made by Ian McKellen in the new film, Mr. Holmes, *about human nature being a mystery that "logic alone could not illuminate." This is a book that must be read by all – the elite and those on the streets alike.*

Akwasi Aidoo, PhD
Senior Fellow
Humanity United

In Making Sense of Beliefs and Values, *Craig Shealy and colleagues take on the herculean task of calling our collective attention to that which is generally ignored yet routinely practiced in our lives – namely the construction, adoption, and enactment of values and beliefs as a dominant sociopolitical force. Focusing on these foundational matters is akin to exposing the pervasive HTML codes lurking behind the user interfaces that are blithely operated with the push of a button or a swipe across a touchscreen. Based on substantial research and presented in detailed eloquence,* Making Sense of Beliefs and Values *admirably draws out the autonomic nature of our belief systems for closer scrutiny, and perhaps ultimately, for more intentional advancement of our collective efforts to engage the issues of the day.*

Randall Amster, JD, PhD
Executive Director, Peace and Justice Studies Association
Director, Program on Justice and Peace, Georgetown University
Author of *Peace Ecology* (2014)

Making Sense of Beliefs and Values *advances a goal of "cultivating the globally sustainable self" – being a greater capacity to simultaneously care for self, others and the wider world – and is committed to education systems that create the circumstances through which people can look beyond their own views of reality and the confines of their own parochialism, to reach out to those who are far away and with whom, whether they like it or not, they must share this planet. This is a laudable collection espousing a more than worthy cause.*

Jo Beall, PhD
Director of Education and Society and Executive Board Member
British Council, London

With his understanding of the constant interaction of cultural, religious and political diversity, Craig Shealy investigates ideas and ideologies that cause prejudice, racism, acts of violence and abuse of power. This collapse of social texture is not the result of indifference, as it provides evidence of intransigence. Making Sense of Beliefs and Values: Theory, Research, and Practice *proposes the urgent need to develop personal and communal new skills of reflection and the building of a methodology that will enhance respect and awareness using sustainable educational models, scholarship, and policy-making towards the acquisition of empathy.*

Claudia Bernardi, Hon DFA, MFA
Founding Director, School of Art and Open Studio
Professor, California College of the Arts

This book comprehensively and articulately describes how and why we make sense of beliefs and values. This interdisciplinary book is a must read for all – educators, scholars and practitioners. It gives us not only an overview but also a practical application and a strong conceptual framework.

Yoshie Tomozumi Nakamura, EdD
Director of Organizational Learning and Research
Columbia Business School

This is a highly sophisticated and scholarly treatment of values and beliefs with wide ranging implications for the promotion of personal, interpersonal, organizational, community and global well-being. Through a combination of conceptual integration and applied projects, the authors distill the implications of values and beliefs for a more peaceful, sustainable, caring, and just world. This is a wonderful integration of theory and practice.

Isaac Prilleltensky, PhD
Mautner Chair in Community Well-Being
Dean and Professor
School of Education and Human Development
University of Miami

Why do we as humans continue to think and behave in ways that support a world, locally and globally, that is framed around inequalities and a predisposition for self-interest and self-destruction? Why do we keep doing this to ourselves? The study of beliefs and values is central to making sense of such a world. All credit to Craig Shealy and his colleagues for tackling this complex and underdeveloped field as a way of advancing our thinking and behaviour. This book offers a very accessible framework and tools that can be applied across all disciplines. Given that values are at the heart of what we all do, this is a reference for everybody.

Gary Shaw
International Education Division
Department of Education and Early Childhood Development
East Melbourne, Victoria

When working in the international sector, we are taught to understand and manage cultural differences. This is not enough. Making Sense of Beliefs and Values: Theory, Research, and Practice *provides both theoretical and practical background on understanding how people work at a core level, regardless of their cultural background. Combining an understanding of cultural knowledge (macro) with individuals' beliefs (micro) is essential for effectively working in global and multicultural organizations. This book should be a must-read for all those leading people and groups.*

Christopher Shirley, MBA
Director, MEPI, CAYA, Business Development, CIED
Center for Intercultural Education and Development (CIED)
Georgetown University

In educating our children, we as a society put great emphasis on knowledge and abstract analytical thinking. Our instruction and even our assessments, including standardized tests, weigh these factors heavily. But if you look at what moves a society and changes it, you don't find knowledge and abstract analytical thinking having much to do with it. Rather, you find that societies move forward, and too often, backward, on the basis of the beliefs and values of their citizens and their leaders. This book will help you understand how those beliefs and values come to be, how they are organized, and how they translate into the actions that make our world either a better, or a worse place in which to live.

Robert J. Sternberg, PhD
Past President, American Psychological Association
Professor of Human Development
Cornell University

For those with an eye to addressing the presently inexorable trend towards increasing social injustice, religious intolerance and its associated conflict, environmental degradation, and international, as well as intra-national, aggression, this is essential reading. Not only does it show how systems of beliefs and values feed into such disharmony but also it maps out realistic ways of rectifying the situation.

Ron Toomey, PhD
Conjoint Professor of Education (Ret.), University of Newcastle
Consulting Researcher, Educational Transformations

This important book presents an interdisciplinary roadmap for understanding the practical importance of beliefs and values in today's increasingly global society. It is essential reading for all of us engaged in the work of global education.

Brian Whalen, PhD
President and CEO
Forum on Education Abroad

The book Making Sense of Beliefs and Values: Theory, Research, and Practice *is a must read for anyone concerned about the world we live in . . . from unprecedented violence to growing inequalities to more insistent and vitriolic rhetoric. While the magnitude of the problems (or potential for future problems) may seem overwhelming, the clarity of this book is soothing even while it invites us, indeed challenges us, to transform ourselves, more deeply understand the human condition, and cultivate our ability to intervene for positive change. The text outlines a wide-range of theories and research findings, culminating in a new theoretical and empirically-grounded framework for understanding our beliefs, needs, and ourselves. The book is extremely well-written and engaging, and it is frankly inspiring. Read it and then give it to others to read!*

Elizabeth Nutt Williams, PhD
Professor of Psychology and Department Chair
Director of Matriculation and Academic Planning
St. Mary's College of Maryland, the Public Honors College

MAKING SENSE OF BELIEFS AND VALUES

Craig N. Shealy, PhD, is the executive director of the International Beliefs and Values Institute (IBAVI; www.ibavi.org) and professor of graduate psychology at James Madison University. Dr. Shealy works with the IBAVI's executive board to coordinate activities and initiatives such as *Cultivating the Globally Sustainable Self*, a research-to-practice summit series (www.jmu.edu/summitseries).

Dr. Shealy's research on the etiology, maintenance, and transformation of beliefs and values has been featured in a wide range of national and international publications and scholarly forums, and the Forum BEVI Project (www.forumea.org/research-bevi-project). Drs. Shealy and Merry Bullock, senior director of American Psychological Association's (APA's) Office of International Affairs, co-edit *Going Global: How Psychology and Psychologists Can Meet a World of Need*, a forthcoming volume from APA Books, which presents the work of leading psychologists in the United States and internationally.

A licensed clinical psychologist, Dr. Shealy is 2016 president elect of the APA's Division of International Psychology, a recipient of the Early Career Award from the APA's Division of Psychotherapy, a Madison Scholar at James Madison University, a Nehru Chair at the Maharaja Sayajirao University of Baroda, India, and a National Register Legacy of Excellence Psychologist.

MAKING SENSE OF BELIEFS AND VALUES

THEORY, RESEARCH, AND PRACTICE

Craig N. Shealy, PhD

Editor

SPRINGER PUBLISHING COMPANY
NEW YORK

Springer Publishing Company, LLC
11 West 42nd Street
New York, NY 10036
www.springerpub.com

Acquisitions Editor: Nancy S. Hale
Composition: Exeter Premedia Services Private Ltd.

ISBN: 978-0-8261-0452-6
e-book ISBN: 978-0-8261-0453-3

15 16 17 18 / 5 4 3 2 1

Unless otherwise stated, the opinions expressed in this book are those of the individual authors and do not represent the official position of the Department of Veterans Affairs, Department of Defense, U.S. Government, or any specific VA facility or program.

The editor, publisher, and authors of this Work have made every effort to use sources believed to be reliable to provide information that is accurate and compatible with the standards generally accepted at the time of publication. The editor, publisher, and authors shall not be liable for any special, consequential, or exemplary damages resulting, in whole or in part, from the readers' use of, or reliance on, the information contained in this book. The publisher has no responsibility for the persistence or accuracy of URLs for external or third-party Internet websites referred to in this publication and does not guarantee that any content on such websites is, or will remain, accurate or appropriate.

Library of Congress Cataloging-in-Publication Data

Names: Shealy, Craig N., editor.
Title: Making sense of beliefs and values : theory, research, and practice /
    [edited by] Craig N. Shealy.
Description: New York : Springer Pub. Company, LLC, 2015.
Identifiers: LCCN 2015028128 | ISBN 9780826104526
Subjects: LCSH: Belief and doubt. | Values.
Classification: LCC BF773 .M295 2015 | DDC 153.4—dc23
LC record available at http://lccn.loc.gov/2015028128

Special discounts on bulk quantities of our books are available to corporations, professional associations, pharmaceutical companies, health care organizations, and other qualifying groups. If you are interested in a custom book, including chapters from more than one of our titles, we can provide that service as well.

For details, please contact:
Special Sales Department, Springer Publishing Company, LLC
11 West 42nd Street, 15th Floor, New York, NY 10036-8002
Phone: 877-687-7476 or 212-431-4370; Fax: 212-941-7842
E-mail: sales@springerpub.com

Printed in the United States of America by McNaughton & Gunn.

For Lee and Sophie,
my love and light.

CONTENTS

PART III: MAKING SENSE OF BELIEFS AND VALUES THROUGH PRACTICE: ASSESSMENT, EDUCATION, FORENSICS, LEADERSHIP, AND PSYCHOTHERAPY

PART IV: IMAGINING A WORLD WHERE BELIEFS AND VALUES MAKE SENSE

CONTRIBUTORS

Kris Acheson, PhD, Lecturer and Director, Undergraduate Program in the Department of Applied Linguistics & ESL, Georgia State University, Atlanta, Georgia

Tamara Baldwin, MSc, Associate Director, International Service Learning, University of British Columbia, Vancouver, British Columbia, Canada

Brad Baltensperger, PhD, Research Professor of Geography, Michigan Technological University, Houghton, Michigan

Timothy W. Brearly, PsyD, MIRECC Advanced Psychology Fellow, W. G. Hefner VA Medical Center, Salisbury, North Carolina

Lindy Brewster, MSc, BA, President, OR Consulting Inc., Reston, Virginia

Brian Brubaker, MBA, IES Abroad, Carol Stream, Illinois

Sam Cochran, PhD, Professor Emeritus, University of Iowa, Iowa City, Iowa

Molly Coates, PsyD, Primary Care Psychologist, Pediatrics and Family Medicine, Healthcare Network of Southwest Florida, Naples, Florida

Jared Cozen, PsyD, LMFT, Psychology Assistant, Kaiser Permanente Mental Health Department, Antioch, California

Kelly Dyjak-LeBlanc, MA, Doctoral Candidate, C-I Psychology Program, James Madison University, Harrisonburg, Virginia

Adam J. Edmunds, PsyD, Psychological Counselor, Haverford College, Haverford, Pennsylvania

Christopher M. Federico, PhD, Professor of Psychology and Political Science, Department of Psychology, University of Minnesota, Minneapolis, Minnesota

Barry Glick, PhD, NCC, ACS, LMHC, LPCC, G + G Consultants, Rio Rancho, New Mexico

RT Good, EdD, Associate Dean and Professor of Management, Harry F. Byrd, Jr. School of Business, Shenandoah University, Winchester, Virginia

Steve Grande, PhD, Executive Director, Spencer Center for Civic and Global Engagement, Mary Baldwin College, Staunton, Virginia

William Hanson, PhD, Associate Professor, Coordinator, Counselling Psychology Program Department of Educational Psychology, University of Alberta, Edmonton, Canada

Vesna Hart, PsyD, Project Coordinator, International Network of Universities, Assistant Professor, Graduate Psychology, James Madison University, Harrisonburg, Virginia

Jenna Holt, PsyD, Assistant Professor of Psychology, Mary Baldwin College, Staunton, Virginia

Chitra Iyer, PsyD, School Psychologist, Bellevue, Washington

Sarah Jones, PsyD, Director, Center for Cadet Counseling and Office of Disabilities Services, Virginia Military Institute, Lexington, Virginia

Shagufa Kapadia, PhD, Professor and Chair, Department of Human Development and Family Studies, Director, Women's Studies Research Center, Faculty of Family and Community Sciences, The M.S. University of Baroda, Gujarat, India

Jennifer Kelly, PhD, Assistant Professor, Michigan State University, East Lansing, Michigan

Lisa Legault, PhD, Assistant Professor of Psychology, Clarkson University, Potsdam, New York

Wenjuan Ma, Consultant, Center for Statistical Training and Consulting, Michigan State University, East Lansing, Michigan

Lauren Mays, PsyD, Postdoctoral Fellow, Center for Counseling and Psychological Health, University of Massachusetts Amherst, Amherst, Massachusetts

Usha Nayar, Tata Chair Professor and FMR Deputy Professor, Tata Institute of Social Science, Mumbai, Maharashtra, India

Hajime Nishitani, PhD, MJur, Vice-President (International), Professor, Faculty of Law, Hiroshima University, Hiroshima, Japan

Victor Nolet, PhD, Professor, Woodring College of Education, Western Washington University, Bellingham, Washington

Rituma Patel, PsyD, Affiliate and Webmaster, International Beliefs and Values Institute, Harrisonburg, Virginia

Christen Pendleton, PsyD, Psychologist, Department of Pediatric Psychiatry, New York Presbyterian/Columbia University Medical Center, New York, New York

John Poston, PhD, Assistant Professor, Rosemead School of Psychology, Biola University, La Mirada, California

Dawn T. Psyarchik, PhD, Professor, Department of Advertising and Public Relations, Michigan State University, East Lansing, Michigan

Jarrod Reisweber, PsyD, Licensed Clinical Psychologist, Richmond, Virginia

Doug B. Samuel, PhD, Assistant Professor of Clinical Psychology, Department of Psychological Sciences, Purdue University, West Lafayette, Indiana

Seth Schwartz, PhD, Professor, Department of Public Health Sciences, Leonard M. Miller School of Medicine, University of Miami, Florida

Craig N. Shealy, PhD, Professor of Graduate Psychology, James Madison University, and Executive Director, International Beliefs and Values Institute, Harrisonburg, Virginia

Sandra L. Shullman, PhD, Managing Partner, Columbus Office, Executive Development Group, Columbus, Ohio

Jessica Spaeth, PsyD, MSc, Licensed Psychologist, Coastal Carolina Neuropsychiatric Center, Jacksonville, North Carolina

Lee G. Sternberger, PhD, Associate Provost, Academic Affairs, Executive Director, Office of International Programs, Professor, Graduate Psychology, James Madison University, Harrisonburg, Virginia

Mary Tabit, PsyD, Postdoctoral Resident, Assessment and Evaluation Center, Warren E. Smith (WES) Health Center, Philadelphia, Pennsylvania

Charlene Tan, PhD, Associate Professor, Policy and Leadership Studies Academic Group, National Institute of Education, Nanyang Technological University, Singapore

Kees van den Bos, PhD, Professor of Social Psychology and Professor of Empirical Science, Utrecht University, The Netherlands

Kayan Phoebe Wan, PsyD, Licensed Psychologist, Student Health Center, University of Missouri-Columbia, Columbia, Missouri

Elizabeth Wandschneider, PhD, Assistant Director for Program Management, Office of Study Abroad, Michigan State University, East Lansing, Michigan

Felix Wang, MBA, Associate Executive Director, Office of International Programs, James Madison University, Harrisonburg, Virginia

Marlana Webster, PsyD, Staff Psychologist, Primary Care Mental Health Integration, Hampton Veterans Affairs Medical Center, Hampton, Virginia

Randall P. White, PhD, Principal, Executive Development Group, Greensboro, North Carolina

FOREWORD

Why do people do what they do? Or more to the point, what makes us want to do what we do? In understanding what guides our actions, individually and collectively, *Making Sense of Beliefs and Values* is an extraordinary and essential book. However, when asked to write the foreword for this volume, I hesitated not because I questioned its basic perspectives or findings, but because I really wasn't sure how to begin. On the one hand, a casual flip through this tome will reveal the enormity of its scope, not just because of the comprehensive reviews of literature or the detailed nature of results, but because this book is a genuinely fascinating read. The initial conceptual framework, the Equilintegration or EI model, is as riveting as it is revealing in terms of why we human beings become who we are. More specifically, the first part of this book offers a powerful theoretically and empirically grounded framework for understanding the linkage between core human needs, the beliefs and values we call our own, how these constructs live within us, and how they are expressed in the wider world. As an educator and administrator by background, I can confirm that this perspective alone has the potential to shape how we understand who we are as human beings, including why we believe what we believe, and equally important, why we behave as we do.

For many years, this understanding of what shapes our action, or lack thereof, has been the core concern of my own life's work, and that of so many others around the globe with whom I collaborate in our shared quest for a more sustainable world. It is through this lens of seeking and creating a more sustainable future for all that I delved into *Making Sense of Beliefs and Values*, which is not a book on sustainability, but rather a framework and insightful way of understanding human behavior that can be so useful in a plethora of contexts. I deeply recommend this book, as it can help us, as it helped me, understand who we are, why we do what we do, and what might be done to create more sustainable societies, structures, and selves. However, I reiterate, on a theoretical basis alone I can foresee immense usefulness well beyond my own sphere of addressing sustainability.

In addition to this important conceptual foundation, what further distinguishes *Making Sense of Beliefs and Values* is that it seeks, and succeeds, in matters of application. Not only do we learn about why we are who we are, and what that means for our potential as a species, we encounter a comprehensive psychological measure, the Beliefs, Events, and Values Inventory or BEVI, in development for over 20 years, that demonstrates in an understandable manner how these complex processes emerge in the real world. That is no small feat, for in my experience, it is one thing to offer deep propositions about the nature of reality. It is quite another to test and demonstrate the validity of such propositions in empirical terms that are comprehensible by people like me, who are not statisticians. We all are among those whom researchers ultimately want to reach if their theories and findings are to influence policies and practices. From my perspective, the fact that this erudite volume remains true to the deepest principles of sound scholarship, while translating concepts and data into a form that nonempiricists are likely to experience as meaningful, is the single greatest triumph of *Making Sense of Beliefs and Values*. Bridging the chasm between research and practice—as this book certainly does—should be applauded in its own right, for until we bring both of these communities together, in respectful and ongoing dialogue with each other, we will not address the "wicked problems" of our day, such as climate change, access to education, religious and ethnic conflict, or human rights, which populate headlines on a daily basis around the world.

Following presentation of the EI model and BEVI method, *Making Sense of Beliefs and Values* tackles these essential issues of research and practice head on, through a series of authoritative chapters: on *research*—culture, development, environment, gender, politics, and religion; and on *practice*—assessment, education, forensics, leadership, and psychotherapy. Because the final chapter of this book provides a concise summary of each chapter, along with compelling reflections on future directions, I won't offer specifics here, except to say that my sense is, whether you are an established advocate, educator, practitioner, or scholar in one or more of these topical areas, a student just starting out, or an engaged member of the public at large, you will experience these chapters as meaningful, captivating, and poignant. This is unusual to say about a scholarly book that joins together sophisticated analyses, convincing literatures, and compelling applications, which brings me to some final reflections on this book.

In my life, I have spent the last five decades trying to help us understand both the realities and possibilities of living on earth in the way that we do. I have done so because we have good reason to believe that our actions now are determining the kind of world that we are leaving behind, not only for our children, but for their children as well. Such a statement is based upon a well-grounded sense of my own human experience combined with thousands of analyses by top scholars around the world. I have witnessed anthropocentric-induced changes to the planet. I feel that what we are doing to our planet must be corrected. Issues such as biodiversity loss, water and soil degradation, and social issues such as racism and exclusion are all either created by humans or exacerbated by humans.

Climate change is a globally felt example of the many human-centered wicked problems we are creating and imposing, so let me work with this. Here, the mystery remains. Now that we know, why don't we act? The average European citizen emits as much carbon in 11 days as the average Bangladeshi in an entire year. The average North American citizen emits as much carbon in 7 days as the average Bangladeshi in an entire year. Yet it is the government and the people of Bangladesh who are expected to pay for the escalating costs of storm-proofing this low-lying country. This is not addressing a city such as New Orleans, Bangkok, or even Venice, but an entire coastline of one of the world's poorest yet most populous countries. If we are a major cause, what is our role?

By pumping tons of carbon and other gases into our atmosphere day after day, we are changing the very chemistry, and therefore, the very reality, of our living physical world, its flora and fauna, and the human civilizations that depend upon a particular atmospheric ratio of elements that have allowed humans to establish dominion over the earth, as we most certainly have. As stated in the opening chapter of *Making Sense of Beliefs and Values*, it is not hyperbolic to conclude that *we already have changed this chemistry*—that is not a matter of conjecture, upon which "nonscientist" politicians routinely comment, but an empirical fact for anyone who dispassionately examines the data, from ice cores, migration patterns, and growing seasons, to the changing intensity, range, and scope of weather events around the globe.

As UNESCO Chair on Reorienting Teacher Education to Address Sustainability—and as one who has traveled literally around the world more than 50 times over many years to discuss these issues and advocate for change—what has been bewildering to me is why we stubbornly insist upon ignoring, minimizing, or denying what is by now overwhelming evidence that we already have altered the chemical makeup of our atmosphere. This alteration has, not surprisingly, begun to affect environmental systems around the globe. As a summary report from the National Aeronautics and Space Administration (NASA) concludes, "Multiple studies published in peer-reviewed scientific journals show that 97 percent or more of actively publishing climate scientists agree: Climate-warming trends over the past century are very likely due to human activities" (see climate.nasa.gov/scientific-consensus/). If I stretch myself to the point of incredulity, I possibly could imagine how some individuals could seize upon phrases in the above NASA report such as "very likely due" or "97 percent" to make the case that "we don't know for sure." From a scientific perspective, and in the strictest sense, that is true. We cannot be 100 percent sure that the "3 percent" of scientists who are not in agreement are definitely wrong, just as we cannot be 100 percent sure that "human activities" definitely are causing climate change, only that such changes are "very likely due" to what we humans are doing.

All that said, what is more bewildering to me is, even if I potentially and grudgingly grant such uncertainties—which always is the case with honest science—it still doesn't explain why we would hedge our bets on matters of such enormous and potentially irreversible consequence, which would profoundly affect our children and theirs, OR why we would so stubbornly deny such a monumental and global scientific consensus on these matters. In other words, even if the "97 percent" of scientists were wrong, as a matter of self-preservation at least, doesn't it stand to reason that we still should take actions to ameliorate what we "hypothetically" are doing to affect our climate in ways that are of such monumental consequence? In what other realm of human existence do we have such overwhelming data and consensus, and still find reasons within us to question, to doubt, to dismiss? Heavens knows, we implement profound, costly, often unpopular, and comprehensive policies all the time—in our judicial, educational, economic, health, and welfare systems—that have far less scientific consensus than we do around climate change. Racial profiling leading to mass incarceration, denial of schooling to girls, predatory lending, abstinence-only sex education, or regressive tax policies that exacerbate poverty, are only a smattering of examples among hundreds of possible candidates. Routinely, we develop, enforce, and fund such policies with very little scientific evidence, and even worse, do so when our scientific evidence concludes that such policies actually are wrong or even harmful in terms of outcomes. So why do we do support policies that directly are in opposition to that which we convincingly can demonstrate empirically?

To answer such questions, we have to go beyond, far beyond, the veneer of rationality, which—as *Making Sense of Beliefs and Values* points out time and time again—is an illusion in any case. Rather, we must go on a journey deep into the human mind and heart—and blaze a new path, illuminated not just by the light of the hard sciences—which are absolutely necessary, but also, are by no means totally sufficient. To fully move from understanding to informed and effective action we also must see by the light of the social sciences and humanities. I firmly believe that beliefs, values, ethics, and morality are crucial components in building the concerted global efforts we need to assuage these issues.

Put plainly, as one who has spent his life trying to facilitate change in the realm of awareness raising and educating for sustainability, I submit that we will not solve the wicked problem of sustainability only by a hard-nosed examination of physical facts in our material world. Instead, we must understand that we are "believing and needing selves," who think, feel, and act in ways that are driven by highly complex processes. These processes often are unknown to us, even though they are in fact largely knowable already or in the near future if we have the right lamps to light our way. This book—*Making Sense of Beliefs and Values: Theory, Research, and Practice*—provides such light. If we see by it, a thicket of incomprehension will be cleared, and the sorely needed, more sustainable path forward will be illuminated. We need science for solutions to the "wicked" physical issues, but we also need the social sciences and humanities to move people to act upon the issues that we can solve. That inability to build informed collective action might itself be the greatest "wicked issue" we are facing.

In this spirit, I invite you to immerse yourself in this deeply readable and timely book, which not only describes why we humans create the wicked problems we do, but how we may solve them. Equally as important, *Making Sense of Beliefs and Values: Theory, Research, and Practice* could help societies learn to mobilize humanity to act effectively together, for ourselves here and now, and for future generations who will reap what we sow, for better or worse.

Charles Hopkins
UNESCO Chair
Reorienting Teacher Education Towards Sustainability
York University, Toronto

PREFACE

Contemplating a book that strives to "make sense of beliefs and values" is one matter; putting one together represents a qualitatively different leap of faith, evidenced in part by the fact that this volume has been in development for the past seven years, and is based upon well over two decades of scholarly and applied work. An undoubtedly feeble attempt to thank all who have participated in this process is made in the acknowledgment section. Here, some orienting perspective is provided so that readers of various backgrounds might encounter the material presented in this book in a way that is maximally meaningful and relevant.

At the outset, it should be noted that *Making Sense of Beliefs and Values* is written to be accessible for an engaged and educated public, regardless of background; at the same time, this book is intended as an appeal of sorts to the broader interdisciplinary, academic, and professional community. That is because the central goal of this volume—*making sense of beliefs and values*—is of considerable interest to us all, by dint of being human, but of specific relevance to those of us who spend our lives trying to understand these complex processes, and translate and apply what we learn to a myriad of real world issues, populations, settings, and contexts.

In terms of organizational structure, this book is divided into four interrelated parts. Part I consists of four chapters, which focus on the meaning, etiology, and assessment of beliefs and values. Specifically, Chapter 1 provides big picture context regarding how and why it is imperative that we "make sense of beliefs and values," given their ubiquity across multiple aspects of human functioning, and clear relevance to local and global actions, policies, and practices. Chapter 2 provides an in-depth examination of theory, data, and application related to three constructs—beliefs, needs, and self—that are integral to "Equilintegration" (EI) Theory, which seeks to explain how, why, and under what circumstances beliefs and values are acquired, maintained, and transformed. Chapter 3 continues this focus, but does so through the EI Self, a pictographic framework that illustrates how the interaction between our core needs (e.g., for attachment, affiliation) and formative variables (e.g., caregiver, culture) results in beliefs and values about self, others, and the world at large that we internalize over the course of development and across the life span. Taken together, Chapters 2 on EI Theory and 3 on the EI Self comprise the EI model, which is the major explanatory and interpretive framework through which we endeavor to "make sense of beliefs and values" in this book. Part I concludes with Chapter 4, which provides a detailed description and explanation of the Beliefs, Events, and Values Inventory (BEVI), an assessment measure that has been used to evaluate the hypotheses and principles of the EI model, and is applied in a wide range of settings and contexts. Analyses presented in later research and practice chapters are drawn directly from the use of the BEVI with multiple populations in the real world.

Part II of this book—*Research*—essentially describes all that we have learned thus far through examination of the EI model and BEVI method across six separate chapters, which explore *culture, development, environment, gender, politics,* and *religion*. Part III—*Practice*—follows a similar approach, but focuses instead on the actual application of the BEVI in five separate domains: *assessment, education, forensics, leadership,* and *psychotherapy*. Although the demarcation between research and practice will become evident, we sought throughout the development of this book to include an emphasis on the "other side of the aisle" in each chapter. That is, research chapters strive to offer applied implications of the theory and data that are presented; practice chapters include data-based findings as well as considerations of areas for future research. In this way, we wished to recognize that research and practice on "beliefs and values" are inextricably linked and mutually informing. This overall commitment is reflected in other features of these chapters, including the comprehensive scope and nature of literature reviews, which attempt to situate each topic within a depth- and breadth-based milieu. Rounding out this book, Part IV consists of a single comprehensive and integrative chapter, which focuses on future directions and further reflections by envisioning how the world might look, feel, and be if we were to adopt a habit of "making sense of beliefs and values" as a matter of course.

Although the question of "audience" was touched upon earlier, some additional explication may be in order to help would-be readers navigate this material in a way that is most likely to be accessible. Of course, readers of all stripes are encouraged to complete the entire book as such an undertaking is most likely to illustrate the *what, why,* and *how* of beliefs and values in the deepest and widest sense. That said, some of the chapters (particularly those of a research and assessment nature) do include information, such as statistical analyses and psychometric information, which may be a bit daunting to the unversed. Nonetheless, regardless of focus, all chapters include relevant literature, accessible interpretations of findings and/or real world applications, clear summaries of fundamental points, and specific recommendations for future research and practice. In short, the material throughout this book— although complex at times—is presented in a manner that is meant to be maximally comprehensible and engaging, regardless of one's point of entry.

All that said, for readers who wish to know exactly what they are getting into, here is some guidance regarding what to expect before wading into any uncharted waters. First, if you are just beginning to think about why we believe what we believe—or want to reflect more deeply upon such matters—the introductory chapter offers a good overview of why we can and must do a much better job of "making sense of beliefs and values," both locally and globally. If you wish to go further, and delve deeply into a range of captivating literatures that bear directly on the nature, etiology, and dynamics of beliefs and values, Chapter 2 is an essential read, with Chapter 3 to follow in order to help translate such content into real world form. If the BEVI is your primary focus (i.e., you want to learn more about what the BEVI is and what it assesses), there can be no substitute for a thorough read of Chapter 4.

Moving from Part I into Parts II and III, it should be emphasized that research and practice chapters deliberately have been written in a way that allows each to "stand alone." So for example, if you are a scholar who is interested in matters of culture, development, ecology, gender, politics, or religion—or a practitioner working in the area of assessment, education, forensics, leadership, or therapy—it should be possible to gain sufficient understanding of the implications and applications of the EI model and BEVI method for one or more of these topical areas simply by reading whatever chapters fall within your purview.

Finally, although I probably should not say so, in sympathy for all of the students (bright and motivated juniors and seniors in high school, undergraduates, and graduate/professional students) who are most fortunate to be offered the "invitation" to engage with the material in this tome, "CliffNotes" of sorts are included in Part IV, the final chapter, which provides an overview of major recommendations from each of the research and practice chapters as well as an in-depth discussion of "future directions" and "further reflections." Fair warning, though—there is a lot of content in this book, and any instructor worth his or her salt could easily extract a nugget or two from one or more chapters in order to separate the diligent sheep who have read from the slacker goats who have not.

In the final analysis, the most important goal of this book is to provide relevant findings and meaningful applications for serious researchers and practitioners who wish to consider how and why "making sense of beliefs and values" may enrich and extend their work. On the other hand, we also want to reach additional devotees of the human condition—including, but not limited to, organizational leaders, educators, and students, to journalists, policy makers, and the clergy—as well as the intrigued public at large, who all desire to be that much more informed about these most pressing issues of our day. That is because the overarching quest here—to "make sense of beliefs and values"—is and should be a matter of deep importance to all thinking and feeling human beings, regardless of educational level, disciplinary background, or professional affiliation.

Hopefully, this preface offers a measure of guidance for such diverse audiences to encounter the material from this book in a way that meets them where they are, rather than the other way around. It is in this spirit, then, that we heed the wisdom of Laozi, who declared the following over two millennia ago: *A journey of a thousand miles begins with a single step.* So let us take a deep breath and begin at the beginning, by examining the whys and wherefores of our "belief in belief," as we step forth on a fascinating journey that is of profound relevance to us all.

Craig N. Shealy
James Madison University
International Beliefs and Values Institute

ACKNOWLEDGMENTS

In a book that represents well over 20 years of work, it both is inevitable and lamentable that individuals who played an important role along the way will not specifically be mentioned in these acknowledgments. For such inadvertent omissions, I offer heartfelt apologies in advance, and only can ask you to know that I am thankful for your contributions, even if they are not consciously accessible as I write these words. To be sure, the material essence of this book incubated for decades, and was nurtured throughout by the contributions of countless teachers, friends, and colleagues, from the distant and recent past, and across the interdisciplinary spectrum. To all of you, I owe the greatest debt for your kind encouragement, stellar discernments, and captivating contributions, which showed me time and again how the world could and would be, if we would but make sense of beliefs and values, a hope that lives at the very heart of this entire volume.

I remember (weirdly, I'm sure) finding myself entranced during my own scholarly journey over the years by the contributions of luminaries including Kurt Geisinger, Paul Meehl, and Samuel Messick, for their unparalleled advancements regarding assessment, validity, and psychometrics; to the brilliantly accessible work of Elliot Aronson, John Dirkx, Riane Eisler, Stephen Jay, Alice Miller Gould, Robert Sternberg, and Margaret Wheatley; to the penetrating insights on the human self, systems, and conduct, from Heinz Kohut and Margaret Mahler, to Dante Cicchetti, Michael Rutter, and Alan Sroufe, to Murray Bowen, Carl Rogers, Hans Strupp, and B.F. Skinner, to Carl Jung and Ken Wilbur, to Jean Piaget and Robert Kegan, to Mark Leary, June Tangney, Abraham Tesser, and Drew Weston, to Mary Ainsworth and John Bowlby; to the fundamental conceptual infrastructure and global implications of human values pioneered by Norman Feather, Ronald Inglehart, Milton Rokeach, and Shalom Schwartz as well as the vital scholarship on human needs from Edward Deci, Abraham Maslow, Henry Murray, and Richard Ryan, among so many others who regrettably are not mentioned above, but nonetheless are integral to this book.

Like Ricky Bobby and his kin, if you are "full of wonderment" as I am about our existence here on earth (see *Talladega Nights* . . . really), it is essential first and foremost to acknowledge our debt to thought leaders who are of deep personal consequence, such as the inchoate roster I offer above. If you are a scholar who dares to place your ideas out there in the public sphere, and you question periodically the impact of your intellectual labors, I can tell you from the depths of my being that your thinking and writing matter, enormously, as there is no thrill quite like discovering a pivotal theoretical concept, ingenious research design, impressive empirical finding, demonstrably substantive intervention, or astute final conclusion, which illuminates not only how to apply such theory, research, and findings effactually in the real world, but also where to go from here. So, taking a lead from Isaac Newton who stated as much in 1676, to all of the giants on whose shoulders I stand—those noted herein and so many kindred others—I thank you.

Next, I must thank my students, beginning with the University of Maryland programs in Asia and Europe, who reviewed the early versions of the BEVI, and pondered aloud with me the nature and meaning of "beliefs and values" as we went about our lives in countries and communities that originally were not our own, until we made them more so. And, to my students at James Madison University (JMU), I only can offer my profound appreciation to all of you who lent your kind support, thought, and assistance as we cleared brush and burrowed down into a veritable village of interconnected rabbit holes, over so many years of discussions, presentations, and dissertations, contemplating the meaning of this factor analysis or that correlation matrix. You have been sojourners with me along the way, and I always will be grateful for your abiding engagement with the theory, research, and practice described in this book. I hope our work together—exemplified by the multiple chapters that follow, on which many of you serve as authors—was enriching and meaningful for you, as it most certainly has been for me. Thank you all.

Likewise, to my faculty colleagues, what can I say? My heartfelt thanks go out first to my comrades-in-arms in the Combined-Integrated Doctoral Program in Clinical and School Psychology at JMU, superbly led by my good friend and respected colleague, Gregg Henriques, and joined in solidarity by the incomparable Ken Critchfield, Elena Savina, Anne Stewart, Trevor Stokes, and the late, great Harriet Cobb, who would be so pleased that this book *finally* is completed, as well as my friends and colleagues in the inimitable Department of Graduate Psychology and Madison International Learning Committee, and in so many other departments and divisions across JMU, exemplified most recently by the Summit Council and Host Committee in support of the Cultivating the Globally Sustainable Self Summit Series, which is highlighted within this book. And, to the many core advisors, teachers, and mentors during my own intellectual path—including Jerry Beker, W. D. Blackmon, Barry Burkhart, Paul Companik, Randall Flory, Jean Goldsmith, Diane Koch, George Ledger, Elissa Lewis, Phil Lewis, James Miller, Marie Sanders, Joan Solie, Rick Weinberg, and Paul Woods, to highlight only a few—I thank you for your support and nurturance of my fledgling intellectual self when I needed it most.

To my administrator colleagues, again there are too many to mention, but I'll note several who simply must be recognized. To Bill Walker, who thankfully headed the search committee that brought me to JMU, along with other key administrators and leaders—Jon Alger, Robin Anderson, Jerry Benson, Doug Brown, Harriet Cobb, Maggie Burkart Evans, Pamela Fox, Linda Halpern, Sharon Lovell, Kate O'Connell, Ronald Reeve, Sheena Rogers, Linwood Rose, Lee Sternberger, Heather Ward, and Phil Wishon—all of you lent historic support at key points in time and/or continue to provide essential assistance as we contemplate derivative implications of this and allied work from colleagues at JMU as well as our regional, national, and international partners. Although you may never receive such due in public accolades, I hope you recognize that we faculty simply could not accomplish what we do without your ability and willingness to subordinate ego in the service of supporting sustained programs of inquiry and practice, such as the 2003 Consensus Conference or, most recently, the Cultivating the Globally Sustainable Self Summit Series. Such activity is, and should be, at the heart of the academy, creating "enlightened citizens who lead productive and meaningful lives," as JMU nobly aspires to do and be.

To my splendid friends who serve with me on the executive board of the International Beliefs and Values Institute—Devi Bhuyan, Jennifer Coffman, Steve Grande, Fletcher Linder, Roderic Owen, David Owusu-Ansah, Lee Sternberger, and Teresa Harris, who also works so ably as managing director of IBAVI, and has provided indispensable support and guidance on countless occasions—I thank you for your thoughtfulness, guidance, creativity, humor, and investment over so many years now in our shared conviction that there is great merit in "making sense of beliefs and values," and how they are linked to actions, policies, and practices around the world. I could not have done my part without all of you. Thank you for believing in me.

Likewise, to all who have joined the Summit Series, as we grapple with issues that are highly resonant with the chapters and themes in this book, I thank you all for the gracious gift of your time, inspiration, and self. We've already envisioned and pursued so much of merit, and I look forward to all we will learn and accomplish together in the years to come.

To my esteemed collaborators who have served helpfully and selflessly on allied papers, presentations, dissertations, or committees, including Robin Anderson, D. Lee Beard, Harriet Cobb, Eric Cowan, Ken Critchfield, Michele Estes, Teresa Harris, Gregg Henriques, Cara Meixner, Carol Lena Miller, Renee Staton, Anne Stewart, Lee Sternberger, Tim Thomas, and Phil Wishon, and so many other valued colleagues at JMU; to the many distinguished coauthors in the United States and internationally who lent their time and expertise to one or more chapters in this book; to Nancy Hale and the superlative folks at Springer Publishing Company for their excellent efforts and steadfast support; to Brian Whalen, the Forum-IBAVI Working Group, and the Forum on Education Abroad, for their crucial and constructive collaboration on the multiyear, multisite Forum BEVI Project; to the legion of statisticians and programmers who have played a key role at various phases of this process—and let me give a singular shout out to Wenjuan Ma and Craig Salee, gifted statistician and programmer, respectively. I thank all of you not only for me, but on behalf of all involved. We could have not accomplished what we did without your extraordinary skill, commitment, and perspective over so many years.

Within the American Psychological Association (APA)—particularly APAGS (the American Psychological Association of Graduate Students) lo so many years ago, Division 29 (Psychotherapy), Division 52 (International Psychology), Merry Bullock and the Office of International Affairs, and APA writ large—I have such respect for all you are and do. Thank you to those who kindly served as mentors and supporters (you know who you are), for believing in me, and for giving me spaces and places to explore ideas, pursue initiatives, surmount challenges, and to witness what it means to provide transformative leadership that matters in the real world, all of which shaped the letter and spirit of this book. For all of the warm hospitality I have received, and venues where I have had the good fortune to contribute and serve, I have been forever changed, and I thank you for the honor of knowing and working with you all.

No set of acknowledgments would be complete without expressing gratitude to the hundreds of psychotherapy and assessment clients I have been privileged to know and care for over the years. So much of what I have learned about life and living, I have learned from all of you. Your courage and capacity to grow and develop—even in the face of odds that so often seemed insurmountable to us all—have been deeply humbling, instructive, and affirming as I have striven to forge my own life path. I have learned as much from you as ever I instilled through thousands of hours of work together over the past 25 years. I hope this book provides a measure of richly deserved tribute to all that you've taught, given, and been to me.

To my iconoclast parents, and my sibs, thank you for raising me under such a colorful big top, which no doubt was formative in my trying to understand why we believe what we believe in the first place. To our beloved Wilhelm clan, I am grateful for your good-natured forbearance each time I stole away to hammer a particularly vexing chapter into submission. Quidditch and other nutty antics have been deeply restorative, and I thank you for being there for us over so many memorable years together.

To my wonderful friends—you also know who you are—thank you for your faith in me, and for enduring countless gabby hours with good humor regarding this or that point or process, which undoubtedly was orbiting out of some arcane belief/need/self space. To take but one example of such indulgence, to Jennifer and Tom Zitt, as I promised then, I am thanking you now for allowing me to toil away on a perfectly sunny afternoon in a Sicilian sand cave, so I could make some bloody deadline for this book, on what otherwise was a grand romp across Italy. As Clarence declares in the final moments of *It's a Wonderful Life*, "No man is a failure who has friends." I understand and value those words, thanks to all of you.

Finally, and in closing, this book would not exist if not for the enduring love and support of my brilliant and beautiful wife, Lee Sternberger. Lee, I cannot express the wonder and appreciation I have for all you have been and done over the 22 years of our remarkable journey together thus far. This book, and its EI model and BEVI method, have grown up together with us both, much to your dismay I am sure at times, although you have borne this process with grace and our trials with grit. Without your beliefs and values—in me and all I have been trying to do and say over these past two decades—*Making Sense of Beliefs and Values* simply would not and could not have happened. And to our lovely and gifted daughter, Sophie, I thank you for entering our world with such wisdom, humor, and spirit, and for tolerating my all-consuming obsession with this endeavor. Your presence and perspective have profoundly inspired me, this work, and its ultimate message of faith, hope, and love for you and yours in the decades to come. For these reasons, and so many more, I dedicate this book to you both with gratitude beyond measure and love beyond words.

MAKING SENSE OF BELIEFS AND VALUES: THE MEANING, ETIOLOGY, AND ASSESSMENT OF BELIEFS AND VALUES

Craig N. Shealy   1

OUR BELIEF IN BELIEF

The world we see that seems so insane is the result of a belief system that is not working.

—William James

Open a web browser, turn on a radio or television, or pick up a newspaper any-where in the world and one ineluctable fact immediately becomes clear: Beliefs and values are at the very heart of why we humans do what we do—and who we say we are—to ourselves, others, and the world at large. From politics, religion, educa-tion, and the arts, to marriage, family, gender, and sexuality, what arguably is most interesting about the varying opinions we express on such topics is not whether this belief is "right," or that value is "wrong." Much more important is understand-ing the complex interactions (e.g., among affect, cognition, context, culture, and development) that culminate in a unique constellation of beliefs and values for every human being, as well as how and why these different versions of reality inevitably are linked to the actions, practices, and policies of individuals, groups, organizations, governments, and societies all over the world. Why? Because our lack of knowledge regarding this linkage is placing us at increasing risk of causing negative and potentially irreversible consequences for societies around the world, humanity as a whole, and planet Earth.

At one level, these considerations regarding human nature and society are as old as recorded history, which can be read as nothing more or less than a catalog of causes and campaigns that were justified on the basis of beliefs and values, and fit a unique time and place. However, it might also be argued that matters have become much more complicated of late, for if the past century and the beginning of the present one teach us anything, it is that we now have the means to express our beliefs and values in ways that decimate entire ethnic or religious communities, undermine economic stability around the world, or damage the global environ-mental systems necessary to sustain life. By way of orientation to this basic prem-ise, consider the belief-based implications of "dirty bombs," just one of many exemplars we will explore in this book, ranging from the acceptance, or not, of cli-mate change, to arguments regarding a "tough-on-crime" agenda, to the role and impact of "hyper-partisanship," to our beliefs regarding what makes a "great teacher" or a "bad leader."

For decades, radioactive materials have been used in millions of applications, from industry, medicine, and research. Such materials could be combined with traditional explosives to create a "dirty bomb" (e.g., Medalia, 2011). Now, any group with the motives and means to acquire and detonate just one such bomb in a strategically selected capital city somewhere in the world could cause social, economic, political, and military havoc across the entire globe. How likely is such a scenario? An article from the *New Scientist* offers the following perspectives:

> A terrorist attack using a dirty bomb is "a nightmare waiting to happen," says Frank Barnaby, a nuclear consultant who used to work at the UK's atomic weapons plant in Aldermaston in Berkshire. "I'm amazed that it hasn't happened already". . . [and] Eliza Manningham-Buller, director-general of the UK's counter-intelligence agency MI5, said a crude attack against a major western city was "only a matter of time." (Risk of radioactive "dirty bomb" growing, 2004)

Although we may be able to develop regulatory and containment strategies that will limit unauthorized access to these materials (and global efforts in this regard have long been under way), technology is silent on motive. That is, such measures, even if effective for some indeterminate period of time, will not address the underlying issue of *why* particular individuals and groups would be motivated to engage in such horrific actions in the first place.

Of course, the historical record is clear that we humans always have had varying motives for the destruction of others and the larger world, either as an explicit objective or an unintended consequence of our actions (e.g., Bongar, Brown, Beutler, Breckenridge, & Zimbardo, 2007; Staub, 2013). What distinguishes the contemporary era is our unprecedented means for doing so. From terrorism and genocide, to global warming and the degradation of our natural resources, the challenges we now face as a species are of unparalleled scope and scale. As such, it is neither unreasonable nor alarmist to conclude that the single most important lesson from the past century—and the beginning of this one—that is within our collective purview and relevant to a more peaceful and sustainable 21st century, is the need to understand the central mediating role of beliefs and values across the entire range of human functioning, from the private and public justifications we harbor for the perpetration of violence against others, to the way we treat and regard cultures, religions, and species different from our own, to our attitude and subsequent actions vis-à-vis the protection and sustenance of planet Earth.

BELIEFS, VALUES, AND VERSIONS OF REALITY

The human tendency and apparent need to legitimize or defend actions, policies, and practices such as these—on the basis of beliefs and values that are held to be self-evident—suggests an active but not necessarily conscious attempt to convince self or others about the "truth" or "goodness" of what may be called a particular "version of reality" (VOR).[1] Theoretically, one's VOR could refer to the entire range of human

---

[1] Selected aspects of chapters in this book include content that has been authored by Shealy for the International Beliefs and Values Institute and Cultivating the Globally Sustainable Self websites as well as adapted and/or excerpted from the following publications: (a) Shealy (2015); (b) Shealy (2014); (c) Shealy, Bhuyan, & Sternberger (2012); (d) Shealy (2005); (e) Shealy (2004).

expression, conduct, and existence, from the way in which one presents self to others, to opinions about how the world and people within it should function or be structured, to deeply held convictions about who one is, and the degree to which one's thoughts, feelings, or actions are internally consistent with this core sense of self. Fundamentally, then, one of the basic propositions of this book is that we humans are designed and inclined to assure ourselves and others regarding the validity and integrity of our own beliefs and values, which is to say, that our personal worldview or VOR is correct, defensible, and good (e.g., Aronson, 2012; Moskowitz, 2005). As Newberg and Waldman (2006) observe,

> Beliefs govern nearly every aspect of our lives. They tell us how to pray and how to vote, whom to trust and whom to avoid; and they shape our personal behaviors and spiritual ethics throughout life. But once our beliefs are established, we rarely challenge their validity, even when faced with contradictory evidence. Thus, when we encounter others who appear to hold differing beliefs, we tend to dismiss or disparage them. (p. 5)

In short, the beliefs and values that comprise one's VOR function as a lens or filter through which self, others, and the world at large are experienced and interpreted (Shealy, Bhuyan, & Sternberger, 2012).

This perspective suggests a fundamental paradox in that two human beings are capable of asserting diametrically opposed VORs while simultaneously declaring with complete certitude that one's own VOR is true and good whereas the other's is not. In doing so, individuals who express diametrically opposed VORs appear often to seek out a basis for justifying why their particular VOR is not only good or true, but also better or superior to another's. And one of the most striking and defining characteristics of such processes is the demonstrable absence of awareness of the basic constructivist insight that one's own beliefs and values may, in the end, be nothing more or less than that . . . one's own (e.g., Aronson, 2012; Gergen, 1998, 1999; Gerhardt & Stinson, 1995; Kuchel, 2003; Martin & Sugarman, 2000; Neimeyer & Raskin, 2000; Panepinto, Domenici, & Domenici, 2012; Raskin, 2012). To be sure, human beings will claim that their beliefs and values are right or superior to those of others because they are derivative of, congruent with, or prescribed by a larger system of thought or practice (e.g., political or religious), which has declared itself to be "right" or "true." But, if there is no clear and credible way to ascertain whether claims about the inherent "truth" or "rightness" of one's beliefs and values are "more" valid than another's, then there is no external means by which support for such claims can reliably be mustered. *None of this is to say that specific beliefs and values are not or cannot be true, right, or better than others*, only that such claims may not be justifiable on the basis of empirical evidence and/or universal opinion.

FROM AURORA AND BOSTON TO FALWELL AND ROBERTSON: CASE STUDIES IN VERSIONS OF REALITY

Believing something to be "the real truth"—even vehemently—has no more power to make it so than nonbelief has the power to make it not so. That is because there is no inherent and necessary linkage between that which is or is not believed and that which is or is not "truth" in any absolute sense. Belief exists in a realm that may or may not be aligned with "reality" or "truth," despite the fact that human beings behave as though there is a direct and inviolable linkage between what they believe and what might, in fact, be real or true (e.g., Aronson, 2012; Moskowitz, 2005; Newberg & Waldman, 2006; Shealy, 2004). This phenomenon is apparent especially in subjective spheres such as politics and religion. One need only tune in to "talk radio" or political "talk shows" on television in the United States, where even under the best circumstances—when respectful listening, honest dialogue, and an open exchange of perspectives actually occur—devotees of the major political parties will argue for the inherent goodness or rightness of their particular beliefs and values, which may be expressed in the form of preferred and often diametrically opposed perspectives regarding particular sociopolitical events, proposals, or policies. Such "debates" often appear to unfold on the basis of a priori assumptions about reality that (a) are designed to identify and present confirmatory rather than disconfirmatory evidence and (b) do not appear to recognize how such VORs become internalized (i.e., claimed as one's own) in the first place. Instead, the mere fact that such VORs are *held to be true* often appears to be all that is necessary and sufficient to contend that such VORs *are in fact true.*

These paradoxical processes often become deeply apparent in the sphere of religion. For example, at the most basic level, contrast person A who believes that the only way to "get to heaven" is to believe in X, with person B who believes that the only way to "get to heaven" is to believe in Y. The rather ironic and disturbing fact that both belief systems cannot be true—if the validity of X is predicated on the invalidity of Y (and vice versa)—seems often lost on persons A and B. In short, at the level of expressed conviction and certitude in politics and religion, at least, these tautologies often do not appear to be recognized as such.

At a deeper level, consider the role of religious beliefs vis-à-vis the rash of mass killings in the United States and around the world over the past decade. Although any horrific exemplar could be cited, let us focus on the Aurora, Colorado theater shootings of on July 20, 2012 as well as the Boston Marathon bombings on April 15, 2013 as they typify a fundamental challenge we face collectively in "making sense of beliefs and values." First, ponder the observations of Rob Brendle,[2] founding pastor of Denver United Church, written shortly after the Aurora, Colorado theater shootings, in which 12 people were killed and 70 injured.

> There are at least four influences on human events: God's will, to be sure; but also the will of Satan, our adversary; peoples' choices, for better or for worse; and natural law (gravity, collision, combustion, and the like). It is difficult to know which force causes the circumstances that devastate us. But it is enough to know that God need not be responsible for them.

Next, regarding the Boston marathon bombings, in which 3 people died and an estimated 264 others were injured, consider first the view of Brandon Levering, pastor of Westgate Church in Weston, Mass: "As our city quakes from the effects of sin in this world — the evil, the violence, the injuries and loss of life — we pray that your holy and healing presence would be made known."[3] Along related lines, the Very Reverend Gary Hall, dean of the National Cathedral in the United States, reflected upon the Boston bombings as follows:[4]

---

[2] Retrieved from http://religion.blogs.cnn.com/2012/07/28/my-take-this-is-where-god-was-in-aurora

[3] Grossman, C.L. (2013). Boston Marathon blast puts same question on everyone's lips: Why? The News Leader, Staunton, VA, Section A, Page 6, Wednesday, April 17, 2013.

[4] Retrieved from www.npr.org/player/v2/mediaPlayer.html?action=1&t=1&islist=false&id=167399098&m=167399089

In a tragedy, there really isn't much to say aside from just being with the people who are suffering. The problem of evil, and the problem of why God allows suffering, is probably the major religious problem for all religious traditions. And no tradition really finally gives a satisfactory answer. Almost every tradition just holds it up finally as a mystery. So, in the face of that, it seems to me that people of faith are called not so much as to try to explain why something happened, as to simply stand with, and put our arms around, and care for people as they go through tragedy.

What unites these perspectives? Aside from the tragic nature of these events—which rightly calls upon us all for deep and abiding compassion and care—what is most striking from the standpoint of "making sense of beliefs and values" are (a) the genuine sense of bewilderment expressed by eminent spiritual leaders about *why* these terrible killings occurred and (b) the causal explanations that are offered regarding why these events happened (e.g., "God's will," "the will of Satan," "peoples' choices," "natural law," "sin").

So, at the outset of this book—and with genuine respect—it seems worth asking if the preceding reactions (e.g., bewilderment) and explanations (e.g., "the will of Satan") to these terrible events are really the best we can do? For example, might additional or alternative factors more parsimoniously explain these events? Why cannot we—why should not we—"try to explain why something happened," if we have a theoretically and empirically grounded basis for doing so? For instance, consider the following rudimentary observations regarding the nature of mass killers since 1982: "Forty four of the killers were white males. Only one of them was a woman. . . A majority were mentally troubled—and many displayed signs of it before setting out to kill" (Follman, Aronsen, & Pan, 2014, p. 1). So, it would appear that being male, White, and unstable are correlated positively with a killing propensity whereas mirror attributes (e.g., female, non-White, and stable) are not.[5, 6]

But for present purposes, the larger question is: What possible benefit is there in throwing "God's will"—or Satan's for that matter—into the mix? Unless God or Satan is preternaturally hostile toward White males who are emotionally disturbed—and kindly inclined toward stable females of whatever hue—it simply makes no sense to indict these entities as plausibly playing a leading role in the occurrence of such tragedies. Worse still, rather than bringing all we know and could learn in order to illuminate *why* these terrible events occur, invoking God or Satan as causally salient serves inadvertently to obfuscate. Are we well served by a shared shrug—however reverent—regarding the fundamental question of why we believe what we believe, and do what we do (i.e., must these tragedies be—and remain—"mysteries")? Surely the victims of such crimes—and the rest of us who vicariously are victimized—deserve better.

The next time one of these tragedies occurs, and there will be many, would it not be refreshing to hear religious leaders pair their call for God's consolation, which clearly has deep meaning to so many—with a simultaneous plea for redoubled efforts to understand how and why relatively few males become filled with such profound

---

[5] Of course, "highly correlated" should not be confused with "highly causal" since the vast majority of White, unstable, males do not engage in killing sprees.

[6] The question of why such variables are predictive indeed is relevant and worthy of study (e.g., see Chapter 8, on gender, for an in-depth discussion of how boys are socialized as well as the attendant negative implications for access to emotion in self and other; see Chapter 13 for the role of "beliefs and values" in our criminal justice system, which focuses largely on punishment over prevention or rehabilitation).

hate that the only recourse imaginable to them is to visit their vitriol upon self and other—and what to do about this lamentable phenomenon? For example, while never condoning such acts, perhaps it would be useful to listen—deeply—to the explanations such killers sometimes offer for what they believe, and why they do what they do, even if we rightly find their "explanations" to be disturbed at best, if not abhorrent (e.g., see Garbarino, 2015)?[7] Would not such an approach ultimately provide greater insight and understanding than well-intentioned bromides regarding "God's will?" In addition to demonstrating that religion and science need not be in opposition, this tack also might provide an antidote to dropping attendance and weakening fidelity to church doctrine, particularly by young people, who tend to see less need for animosity between religion and science, or competing religious creeds, and instead are seeking pragmatic and meaningful solutions to our challenges in society and in life (e.g., America's Changing Religious Landscape, 2015; Dickerson, 2012).

Although the examples of religious beliefs and values vis-à-vis mass killings in Aurora and Boston have their own complexities, adherents to such etiological paradigms clearly are approaching these matters with deep compassion as well as an earnest desire to be of service to people who have been traumatized deeply. Contrast the perspectives of such religious leaders with some of their brethren. Here we have a news account of comments by the Reverend Jerry Falwell and religious broadcaster Pat Robertson, which occurred 2 days after the terrorist attacks of September 11, 2001 in the United States.

Robertson and Falwell: God Gave Us "What We Deserve"[8]

The Associated Press

The Rev. Jerry Falwell and religious broadcaster Pat Robertson said Tuesday's terrorist attacks happened because Americans have insulted God and lost the protection of heaven.

"We have imagined ourselves invulnerable and have been consumed by the pursuit of . . . health, wealth, material pleasures and sexuality," Robertson wrote in a four-page statement issued Thursday by the Christian Broadcasting Network.

Terrorism, he said, "is happening because God Almighty is lifting his protection from us."

---

[7] For a glimpse into "the mind" of such an individual, consider the beliefs that James Holmes articulated for his mass killings in Aurora, Colorado: www.cnn.com/2015/06/05/us/james-holmes-theater-shooting-trial/index.html. In doing so, review the sources of scholarly and applied information that Holmes reportedly investigated in an attempt to understand his own self-recognized disturbance, which apparently were grounded substantively in a "neuroscience" perspective. As recorded in a notebook he kept, which emerged during his trial, "So always, that's my mind," he wrote. "It is broken. I tried to fix it. . .Neuroscience seemed like the way to go but it didn't pan out. In order to rehabilitate the broken mind, my soul must be eviscerated. I could not sacrifice my soul to have a 'normal' mind." Unfortunately, worthy and relevant as it is, "neuroscience" in its current and foreseeable state, simply cannot, by itself, explain much less "fix" this type and level of mental disturbance, despite the fact that Holmes apparently sought a curative explanation from this field, and was receiving psychiatric treatment. Consistent with a number of themes and findings presented throughout this book, the fact that Holmes was deeply motivated to seek an explanation and cure for his ills through the paradigm of neuroscience should compel substantive contemplation by all of us in the mental health field. More specifically, as scholars, educators, practitioners, and leaders, we all should reflect upon the "treatment-based" implications and applications of the epistemologically and values-based explanatory frameworks we endorse for "why people believe what they believe" and "do what they do" as well as how our preferred "treatments" are justified by such frameworks (e.g., see Coates, Hanson, Samuel, Webster, & Cozen, 2016; Cozen, Hanson, Poston, Jones, & Tabit, 2016).

[8] Robertson and Falwell: God gave us 'what we deserve.' (2001, September 15). *The News Leader*, p. A2.

Falwell, a Baptist minister and chancellor of Liberty University in Lynchburg, Virginia, said Thursday on Robertson's religious program "The 700 Club" that he blames the attacks on pagans, abortionists, feminists, homosexuals, the American Civil Liberties Union, and the People For the American Way.

"All of them have tried to secularize America, I point the finger in their face and say, 'You helped this happen,'" Falwell said.

He added later, "God continues to lift the curtain and allow the enemies of America to give us probably what we deserve." "Jerry, that's my feeling," Robertson responded. "I think we've just seen the antechamber to terror. We haven't even begun to see what they can do to the major population."

Elizabeth Birch, executive director of the Human Rights Campaign, a gay rights organization, said Friday the comments of Falwell and Robertson "were stunning. They were beyond contempt. They were irresponsible at best, and a deliberate attempt to manipulate the nation's anger at worst."

Robertson, who founded the Christian Coalition and unsuccessfully ran for the 1988 Republican presidential nomination said in his statement that Americans have insulted God by allowing abortion and "rampant Internet pornography." He also chided the U.S. Supreme Court for, among other things, limiting prayer in public schools.

"We have a court that has essentially stuck its finger in God's eye," Robertson wrote. "We have insulted God at the highest level of our government. Then, we say, 'Why does this happen?'"

Robertson was among leaders on the religious right who backed President Bush in last year's election. A White House official called the remarks "inappropriate" and added, "The president does not share those views."

Falwell said Friday that he did not mean to blame any one group.

"But I'd say this is a wake up call from God," Falwell told The Associated Press. "I feel our spiritual defenses are down. If we don't repent, then more events might happen in the future."

Bill Leonard, dean of the Wake Forest University Divinity School in Winston-Salem N.C. compared Falwell and Robertson's comments with militant Islamic rhetoric that has been condemned worldwide.

"It trivializes theology. It trivializes the dead," Leonard said. "It suggests that God was somehow protecting us more than other countries—Britain, Israel—that had terrorist attacks in the past."

"This is not a time to be blaming anyone, but to huddle together. To lament and cry out."

Asked to comment on Falwell and Robertson's comments, a spokesman for the American Civil Liberties Union said, "We are not dignifying it with a response."

As indicated, if one is disinclined toward such beliefs, reactions may range from outright dismissal ("not dignifying [them] with a response"), to objections on logical grounds (Does the fact that terrorists could successfully attack other nations—Britain, Israel—imply God has not been providing them protection?), to outrage (such comments were "stunning," "beyond contempt," "irresponsible at best, and a deliberate attempt to manipulate the nation's anger at worst"). Moreover, as one commentator notes, the stark and unequivocal tone of such remarks seems strikingly similar to those of the late Osama bin Laden and his followers, in that a problem is identified (e.g., Americans are "consumed by the pursuit of . . . health, wealth, material pleasures, and sexuality"), which has effects (i.e., "God Almighty is lifting his protection from us"), and which in turn has a solution (e.g., "If we don't repent, then similar events might happen in the future").

But apart from one's personal reaction to these statements, such comments actually seem to reflect refreshing candor on the part of Falwell and Robertson, in that they were giving full and open voice—in the heat of the moment (i.e., two days after the attacks)—to deeply held beliefs that seemed entirely justified, defensible, and internally consistent to them; in fact, from their VORs, as men who have represented the views of millions of Americans and seek to "lead" others in matters spiritual, they perhaps felt obliged to offer this perspective, since not doing so would violate their duty to lead others, and the nation, toward their concept of a better end for all of us.

In the quest to make sense of beliefs and values, it is important first to move beyond personal and emotional reactions to comments like these, understandable though they are, and consider basic questions of etiology. That is, how is it that people who witness the same event can hold such radically different beliefs about why it occurred? Moreover, why is it that people who witness the same event are compelled to focus on such radically different aspects of it? For Falwell and Robertson, these attacks provide "data" about causal dynamics and processes at a metaphysical level that, from their perspective, clearly are operative in our three-dimensional world: God has been "insulted" and angered by our profligate and secular ways, and has therefore decided to "lift the protection" that apparently has shielded us from such horrific events historically. Although absurd, illogical, and offensive to many, such beliefs suggest a complex but largely mechanistic and deterministic VOR in which events, outcomes, and processes on Earth may be determined by an omnipotent and omniscient entity who is capable of being enraged by our actions and impelled to "teach us a lesson" that will set us on the correct path once again.

If you do not share this VOR, imagine for a moment what it would be like to see things in these terms: all of your own behavior and that of others, all events in the world, natural and otherwise, ultimately are under the potential control of an inscrutable yet all-powerful and capricious entity who seems strikingly human (e.g., this entity appears to think, perceive, feel, and behave) and could, at any moment, lash out at us or create a long-term plan for our demise if it concludes that we are sufficiently disobedient or in opposition to its idea of who we should and must be. On the other hand, presumably, if we demonstrate appropriate deference to and congruence with its idea of whom we should and must be, protection and intercession become our just reward. An adherent to such a VOR certainly would remain vigilant to evidence about where we stood as individuals and as "a nation," and rightly would fear and decry signs that we were straying from this prescribed "path" as a harbinger of bad things to come. And of course, since such individuals appear to believe that they articulate a rendering of the Christian faith that is sovereign, literal, and true, such fears and concerns arguably are well founded (e.g., can certainly be supported by a source document, the Bible, that such individuals believe directly communicates this entity's perspective on things). From all of this, then, the link for such individuals between, say, the destruction of Sodom and Gomorrah in the Old Testament and the destruction of the World Trade Center Towers in New York City is logical and inevitable, since such destruction is permitted and/or caused by a God who is capable of insult and outrage, and inclined toward violent retribution as a corrective measure, particularly when our collective "sin" (e.g., tolerance and promotion of homosexuality, feminism, and pornography, and disavowal of prayer in schools) is experienced by this entity as rampant, unyielding, or simply too much to bear. The point is not to validate or invalidate such thinking, but to note that even if we experience another's beliefs as personally "unbelievable," it still is the case that to the adherent, such beliefs often are experienced as (a) internally consistent, (b) a logical outgrowth of a larger system of thought, (c) a crucial element in legitimizing, justifying, or making sense of events in the world, and (d) an ineluctable part of being human, in that it simply is not possible to be completely void of "belief."

To contemplate this reality from a more universally accessible viewpoint, consider that we live in a probabilistic universe where many phenomena and events are mysterious, debatable, not entirely predictable, or subject still to discovery; where the meaning and purpose of life cannot unequivocally be confirmed by all; and where reality often cannot be tested against some inviolable and absolute standard that is clear and agreed upon by everyone across time and place. In such a milieu, it simply is not possible to avoid having to accept some things on "faith," even if that faith is limited to an implicit conviction that oxygen still will be accessible the moment you complete this sentence. Even then, with probabilities so high as to be virtually certain, they are not entirely so, and we cannot be completely sure. That is because in truth, we simply do not know what the next moment will bring, at any level. Having no good alternative, we tend to accept such uncertainties "on faith" and do not think much about them, occupying ourselves with other matters over which we seem to have some control.

If such processes are operative even within the temporal and material realm, imagine how much more equivocal matters become around issues of political ideology or religious faith. Here, it seems (current and historical evidence suggests, in fact) that "anything goes," that anyone can come to believe anything about anyone or anything. In this subjective realm, it can seem that there are no rules, no boundaries, no universally agreed upon sense of what is right and what is wrong. Because that is the nature of this level of reality, it indeed is the case that within oneself, one's own convictions may be experienced as correct, defensible, and good even if, theoretically, the entire human race expressed a heartfelt and diametrically opposed belief. For example, even if the entire species believed, to a person save one, that the Earth was round, it is still possible that one individual among us could believe differently. True, such an obstinate person may be persuaded to believe as we do, or we could beat or torture that individual until he or she recanted or even came to share our belief. But the mere expression of belief typically does not in itself have the power to eliminate or invalidate the mental space in another where a contrary belief may continue to exist.[9] Anyone who has ever felt compelled to assert or argue for the legitimacy of one's own beliefs and values (and who has not?), but in the end, does not convince others, knows how frustrating this reality of being human can be, which also is why the weakest form of evidence for the validity of one's own beliefs is to cite the beliefs of another.

The fact that human beings appear capable of believing just about anything, is a quite separate matter from the fact that the processes by which beliefs and values are acquired, maintained, and modified are knowable, albeit imperfectly and

---

[9] Indeed, Charles K. Johnson, the late president of the International Flat Earth Research Society, maintained for nearly 30 years until his death in 2001 that "people with a great reservoir of common sense. . .don't believe idiotic things such as the Earth spinning around the sun. Reasonable, intelligent people have always recognized that the earth is flat." Retrieved June 3, 2014, from www.lhup.edu/~dsimanek/fe-scidi.htm

incompletely. That is, while we may not be able to alter the fact that we are built to believe in just about anything (and probably would not want to), we do know something about why people come to believe and value that which they do, and the forces and dynamics that tend to be associated with such processes and outcomes (e.g., Aronson, 2012; Feather, 1995; Newberg & Waldman, 2006; Rokeach & Ball-Rokeach, 1989; Schwartz, 2012; Shealy et al., 2012). Such knowledge is no small thing, because with it we also know something about how to apprehend and potentially shape what actually is held to be true.

OUR BELIEF IN BELIEF: 9/11 AND BEYOND

As a dramatic exemplar of such processes, consider again the terrorist attacks of September 11, 2001. These malignant and iniquitous acts were distinctive at a number of levels: the coordination of attacks in broad daylight in major metropolitan areas; the indiscriminant killing of as many people as possible, most of whom were civilians with no involvement in military operations or affairs; the calculated use of airliners as weapons of mass destruction, and the deliberate selection of planes filled to capacity with fuel for long flights; the apparent willingness and desire of the terrorists, several of whom are purported to have strong family ties, to sacrifice their own lives in pursuit of their larger objectives; and perhaps most striking, the vainglorious justification for all of this in the name of Islam and the Muslim people.

If these attacks appear unprecedented, however, it is because of the brazen intent and graphic magnitude of their impact, rather than because the beliefs and behaviors of their principle agents are unknown to us. Certainly, the varied and concomitant justifications for the destruction of others are manifest in our recent collective history as a species, from Nazi Germany and the Holocaust to more recent ethnic cleansing in Bosnia and Rwanda; to the enslavement of millions of Africans and subsequent lynching of thousands more in the United States; to practices of footbinding, suttee, and genital mutilation that have been perpetrated against millions of women; to contemporary bombings and killings that all are justified in one way or another by governments, organizations, and the individuals who represent or comprise them across the entire ideological, economic, sociocultural, and geopolitical landscape (e.g., Aronson, 2012; Bongar et al., 2007; Staub, 2013).

Of course, destructive justifications that emanate from the human psyche are apparent on a less massive scale. In our recent past, for example, consider Matthew Shepherd, the gay male from Wyoming who was beaten, tied to a fence, and left to freeze to death on the grounds that he had made sexual advances toward two men in a bar. Or, James Byrd, Jr., the Black man from Jasper, Texas who, for racially motivated reasons, was beaten, chained to the rear of a pickup truck, and dragged to his death. And of course, these are just a few national "exemplars." Click on the news or pick up a paper any day of the week. There, you will see evidence for more of the same—more or less dramatic perhaps, in terms of scope or detail—but not qualitatively different in terms of the intrapsychic dynamics that compel people to behave in these ways toward other living beings, and certainly no less traumatic for those who bear the consequences.

How should we respond to such events? What can we claim legitimately in terms of knowledge or expertise about how, why, and under what circumstances human beings are compelled to commit and subsequently justify such acts? As will be discussed throughout this book, answers to questions like these likely depend upon one's point of departure: our life histories, backgrounds, and aspirations, which culminate in the beliefs, identities, and roles to which we ascribe. As such, the chapters that follow are written in a way that should be accessible to an engaged and educated public, regardless of background; at the same time, they are also intended as an appeal of sorts to the broader interdisciplinary, academic, and professional community. That is because the central goal of this book—*making sense of beliefs and values*—is of considerable interest to us all, by dint of being human, but of specific relevance to those of us who spend our lives trying to understand these complex processes, and translate and apply what we learn to a myriad of real world issues, populations, settings, and contexts.

Within the broader academic community, in particular, it is worth asking how we might further such understanding, both explicitly and deliberately? For example, as scholars and practitioners, how do we heed Phillip Zimbardo's post-9/11 call ". . . to act, to apply everything we know about human nature" (Murray, 2002, p. 24)? More specifically, how would we go about the business of applying "everything we know about human nature" to a topic as vast and multidetermined as understanding why, how, and under what circumstances individuals will commit and justify violent and destructive acts toward other human beings? Since so many interacting forces and factors are likely to influence the timing and nature of events like these, does not the inherent complexity of such phenomena suggest that our scholarly reach will exceed our grasp? After all, our theories are imperfect, and our methods imprecise. Only in the past several decades have we begun to gain sufficient capacity—from a measurement and statistical standpoint—to examine and predict the complex interactions among behavior, cognition, affect, biology, development, society, culture, and life circumstances, while simultaneously seeking to comprehend the religious and spiritual forces that provide meaning and motive to so many people all over the world.

And yet, with all of these limitations and caveats, we do know something—quite a bit actually—about how and why people come to believe and value what they do. For example, we have evidence to suggest that economic and political factors are certainly relevant if not necessary to the construction of ideologies like those of the Third Reich, or the Taliban, for that matter. In this regard, consider the observations of former U.S. President Jimmy Carter about global conditions:

> Nearly a billion people are illiterate. More than half the world's people have little or no healthcare and less than two dollars a day for food, clothing, and shelter; some 1.3 billion live on less than *one* dollar a day. At the same time, the average household income on an American family is more than $55,000 a year with much of the industrialized world enjoying the same, and in some cases an even higher, standard of material blessings. . .The nations of the European Union have set a public goal of sharing four-tenths of one percent of their GNP with the developing word. But the United States and most other rich nations fall short of this goal. (Carter, n.d., pp. 1–2)

When such disproportionate inequities are juxtaposed with the perception—right or wrong—that the United States often is indifferent to views other than its own, or the effects of its policies on the rest of the world, it is easier to understand why extremist ideologies are directed at us (e.g., Consider this America, 2002; Fisher, 2013; White, 2002).

Nonetheless, economic and political factors—crucial though they are—do not explain either the "complex psychological reasons [that] give rise to the terrorist impulse, which is to purge through a spasm of violence a soul that feels corrupted by the modern world" (Ignatius, 2001, p. B7), or why so few people exposed to these debilitating conditions ever resort to violence, terrorist or otherwise. In short, otherwise valuable analyses that attempt to explain extremism only or primarily on economic or political grounds will inevitably lack a measure of depth, because the crucible for these dark forces is—and must be—the human psyche. Although nonpsychological factors certainly do facilitate the emergence of extremist beliefs (indeed, all beliefs), such "states" ultimately are mental and biological as much as they are economic or political; for those who are motivated to harm or annihilate others often find ways to justify such conduct, which implies internalization of, or receptivity to, beliefs about who "others" are and what "they" deserve (e.g., Altemeyer & Hunsberger, 1992; Aronson, 2012; Bongar et al., 2007; Moskowitz, 2005; Newberg & Waldman, 2006; Shealy, 2005; Staub, 1996, 2003, 2013).

MAKING SENSE OF BELIEFS AND VALUES: THE VITAL ROLE OF EDUCATORS, SCHOLARS, AND PRACTITIONERS

We humans are nowhere near as free to discern and control intrapsychic forces and dynamics as we fancy ourselves to be. Rather, as discussed throughout the various chapters of this book, abundant evidence suggests that what we believe and value as good or true is a function—at least in part—of our unique developmental, life, and contextual experiences, which interact with powerful affective and attributional processes that are neurobiologically mediated, and of which we may have little awareness (e.g., Aronson, 2012; Feather, 1995; Newberg & Waldman, 2006; Rokeach & Ball-Rokeach, 1989; Schwartz, 2012; Shealy, 2005; Wegner, 2002). Therefore, a plausible strategy could find us striving to identify extant and emerging programs of inquiry that logically are aligned with the larger task of understanding these complex phenomena. Psychology certainly would play a key role in the construction of such a framework. Toward that end, and a true integration of our "scientist–practitioner" ideal (e.g., Gaudiano & Statler, 2001; Henriques, 2011; Magnavita & Achin, 2013), it would be necessary for us to consider perspectives and contributions that derive from a range of different epistemologies, activities, and subfields—from abnormal, biological, clinical, cognitive, cultural, developmental, family, personality, political, and social psychology—abandoning along the way our unfounded prejudices about who is and is not qualified to comment on such complicated matters.

But our active presence and collective contribution, though necessary, would not be sufficient. Other perspectives from allied fields of inquiry and practice are also needed, including, but not limited to, anthropology, biology, economics, journalism, philosophy, political science, religious studies, and sociology, not to mention rich and compelling theory, data, and analyses that transcend any specific domain. As Braithwaite and Scott (1991) have observed, "The study of values is central to and involves the intersection of interests of philosophers, anthropologists, sociologists, and psychologists" (p. 661) (for a sampling of interdisciplinary perspectives and approaches, see Boudon, 2001; Gioseffi, 1993; Inglehart, Basáñez, & Moreno, 1998; Inglehart, Basáñez, Díez-Medrano, Halman, & Luijkx, 2004; Kelley & De Graaf, 1997; Leuty, 2013; Mays, Bullock, Rosenzweig, & Wessells, 1998; McElroy, 1999; Newberg & Waldman, 2006; Ryan, Curren, & Deci, 2013; Sargent, 1995; Schwartz, 2012).

As educators, scholars, and practitioners with demonstrable interests and expertise in such matters, we are positioned well to offer compelling data and theory that can help make sense of beliefs and values to policy makers and the public at large. Collectively, we have access to a wide range of theoretical, empirical, and applied subfields with direct relevance to an understanding of these constructs[10]; we also possess the methodological sophistication and research tools necessary to measure and evaluate a myriad of relevant hypotheses and applications. This area of inquiry also offers extraordinary opportunities for interprofessional collaboration across a range of disciplines (e.g., Arredondo, Shealy, Neale, & Winfrey, 2004; Association for International Studies, 2014; Center for the Study of Interdisciplinarity, 2014; International Network of Inter- and Transdisciplinarity, 2014; Johnson, Stewart, Brabeck, Huber, & Rubin, 2004). As Milton Rokeach, the eminent social psychologist and pioneer in the study of beliefs and values declared over four decades ago,

> . . . the value concept, more than any other, should occupy a central position across all of the social sciences—sociology, anthropology, psychology, psychiatry, political science, education, economics, and history. More than any other concept, it is an intervening variable that shows promise of being able to unify the apparently diverse interests of all the sciences concerned with human behavior. (Rokeach, 1973, p. 3)

Nonetheless, despite the demonstrable global need to explicate how actions, policies, and practices are mediated by the implicit and explicit beliefs and values of individuals, groups, governments, and societies around the world—and the vast analytic capacity of the international academic community to meet this need—formal theories and models of beliefs and values remain relatively rare. As Fiedler and Bless (2000) note, "In all the huge and wide-spread literature on the psychology of cognition and emotion, there is almost no reference to research on beliefs" (p. 144). Likewise, Musek (1998) observes that, "Despite the growing interest in the study of values. . .no great attention has been devoted to individual values in relation to political and religious orientation" (p. 47). Similarly, Grube, Mayton, and Ball-Rokeach (1994) comment that "very little research" has been conducted on promising belief/value frameworks such as "belief system theory and value self-confrontation"; as such, "our understanding of how people organize their cognitive lives and the implications this organization has for behavior remains unfulfilled" (p. 172). From an applied perspective, Kuchel (2003) reports that "very few studies have examined the role of values in. . .clinical decision-making and diagnosis" (p. 24). Finally, as Leuty (2013) observes, "The lack of research on values and needs has led to great misunderstanding of the definition and importance of these constructs." (p. 363)

A central thesis of this book is that scholarship focusing explicitly on human beliefs and values has not progressed further due to a lack of definitional clarity and conceptual explication regarding: (a) what beliefs and values are and are not; (b) the ontological and contextual factors and processes that are relevant to the etiology, maintenance, and transformation of beliefs and values; (c) the relationship between beliefs and values and other biopsychosocial mechanisms and processes that must concurrently be defined and articulated (e.g., needs and self); (d) theoretical frameworks that optimally may contain and/or account for the interaction among all of these constructs; and (e) methodologies for measuring and evaluating various hypotheses and principles that would be predicted by such frameworks.

---

[10] As defined by Hubley and Zumbo (2013), a "*construct* may be conceived of as a concept or a mental representation of shared attributes or characteristics, and it is assumed to exist because it gives rise to observable or measurable phenomena" (p. 3).

This book attempts to address these issues by offering (a) a theoretical model, Equilintegration or EI Theory, that specifies a number of testable hypotheses regarding the relationship between needs, values, and self, and suggests further areas of inquiry; (b) a pictographic framework, the Equilintegration or EI Self, that illustrates how and why the beliefs and values we call our own are the functional result of an expression of adaptive potential and core need, which are mediated by a complex interaction among developmental processes and formative variables; and (c) an assessment method called the Beliefs, Events, and Values Inventory or BEVI that has been used in a wide range of research and applied contexts, and also is designed to evaluate and further develop EI Theory and the EI Self (Shealy, 2004, 2005; Shealy et al., 2012). In addressing such matters, first, we must describe and define in sufficient detail the three core components of this explanatory system: *beliefs*, *needs*, and *self*. As such, relevant literatures and emerging definitional and explanatory guidelines for each of these "construct components" are explicated next, followed by an overview of EI Theory, the EI Self, and the BEVI, which attempt to integrate these component parts into a coherent whole.

REFERENCES

Altemeyer, B., & Hunsberger, B. E. (1992). Authoritarianism, religious fundamentalism, quest, and prejudice. *International Journal for the Psychology of Religion*, 2(2), 113–133.

America's changing religious landscape. (2015). *Pew Research Center: Religion & Public Life.* Retrieved from http://www.pewforum.org/2015/05/12/americas-changing-religious -landscape/

Aronson, E. (2012). *The social animal* (11th ed.). New York, NY: Worth Publishers.

Arredondo, P., Shealy, C., Neale, M., & Winfrey, L. (2004). Consultation and interprofessional collaboration: Modeling for the future [Special Series]. *Journal of Clinical Psychology, 60*(7), 787–800.

Associated Press. (2001, September 15). The Rev. Jerry Falwell and religious broadcaster Pat Robertson. Robertson and Falwell: God gave us 'what we deserve'. *The News Leader*, p. A2.

Association for International Studies. (2014). Retrieved on May 7, 2014, from www.units .miamioh.edu/aisorg/

Bongar, B., Brown, L. M. Beutler, L. E., Breckenridge, J. N., & Zimbardo, P.G. (Eds.). (2007). *The psychology of terrorism*. New York, NY: Oxford University Press.

Boudon, R. (2001). *The origin of values: Sociology and philosophy of beliefs*. London: Transaction Publishers.

Braithwaite, V. A., & Scott, W. A. (1991). Values. In J. P. Robinson, P. R. Shaver & L. S. Wrightsman (Eds.), *Measures of personality and social psychological attitudes* (pp. 661–753). San Diego, CA: Academic Press.

Carter, J. (n.d.). *A tale of two worlds*. Retrieved June 3, 2014, from www.cartercenter.org/ documents/1541.pdf

Coates, M., Hanson, W., Samuel, D. B., Webster, M., & Cozen, J. (2016). The Beliefs, Events, and Values Inventory (BEVI): Psychological assessment implications and applications. In C. N. Shealy (Ed.), *Making sense of beliefs and values* (pp. 371–406). New York, NY: Springer Publishing.

Cozen, J., Hanson, W., Poston, J., Jones, S., & Tabit, M. (2016). The Beliefs, Events, and Values Inventory (BEVI): Implications and applications for therapeutic assessment and intervention. In C. N. Shealy (Ed.), *Making sense of beliefs and values* (pp. 575–621). New York, NY: Springer Publishing.

Center for the Study of Interdisciplinarity. (2014). Retrieved July 26, 2014, from http://www .csid.unt.edu/

Consider this America . . . Nine Views from Around the World. (2002, January 6). *The Washington Post*, pp. B2–B3.

Dickerson, J. S. (2012, December 16). The decline of evangelical America. *Sunday Review*, p. 5.

Feather, N. T. (1995). Values, valences, and choice: The influence of values on the perceived attractiveness and choice of alternatives. *Journal of Personality and Social Psychology, 68*(6), 1135–1151.

Fiedler, K., & Bless, H. (2000). The formation of beliefs at the interface of affective and cognitive processes. In N. A. Frijda, A. S. Manstead, & S. Bem (Eds.), *Emotions and beliefs: How thoughts influence feelings* (pp. 144–170). Cambridge, UK: Cambridge University Press.

Fisher, M. (2013, January). *Who loves and hates America: A revealing map of global opinion toward the U.S.* Retrieved June 3, 2014, from http://www.washingtonpost.com/blogs/worldviews/wp/2013/01/11/who-loves-and-hates-america-a-revealing-map-of-global-opinion-toward-the-u-s/

Follman, M., Aronsen, G., & Pan, D. (2014). *A guide to mass shootings in America.* Retrieved from http://www.motherjones.com/politics/2012/07/mass-shootings-map

Garbarino, J. (2015). *Listening to killers: Lessons learned from my twenty years as a psychological expert witness in murder cases.* Oakland, CA: University of California Press.

Gaudiano, B. A., & Statler, M. A. (2001). The scientist-practitioner gap and graduate education: Integrating perspectives and looking forward. *The Clinical Psychologist, 54*(4), 12–18.

Gergen, K. J. (1998). From control to construction: New narratives for the social sciences. *Psychological Inquiry, 9*, 101–103.

Gergen, K. J. (1999). Psychological science in a postmodern context. *American Psychologist, 56*(10), 803–813.

Gerhardt, J., & Stinson, C. S. (1995). "I don't know": Resistance or groping for words? The construction of analytic subjectivity. *Psychoanalytic Dialogues, 5*(4), 619–672.

Gioseffi, D. (Ed.). (1993). *On prejudice: A global perspective.* New York, NY: Anchor Books.

Grube, J. W., Mayton, D. M., & Ball-Rokeach, S. J. (1994). Inducing change in values, attitudes, and behaviors: Belief system theory and the method of value self-confrontation. *Journal of Social Issues, 50*(4), 153–174.

Henriques, G. (2011). *A new unified theory of psychology.* New York, NY: Springer.

Ignatius, D. (2001, October 28). The psyche of Bin Laden. *The Washington Post*, p. B7.

Inglehart, R., Basáñez M., & Moreno, A. (1998). *Human values and beliefs: A cross-cultural sourcebook.* Ann Arbor, MI: The University of Michigan Press.

Inglehart, R., Basáñez, M., Díez-Medrano, J., Halman, L. & Luijkx, R. (2004). *Human beliefs and values: A cross-cultural sourcebook based on the 1999–2002 values surveys.* Mexico: Siglo XXI Editores.

International Network of Inter- and Transdisciplinarity. (2014). Retrieved May 7, 2014, from http://www.inidtd.org/

Johnson, C. E., Stewart, A. L., Brabeck, M. M., Huber, V. S., Rubin, H. (2004). Interprofessional collaboration: Implications for combined-integrated doctoral training in professional psychology. *Journal of Clinical Psychology, 60*(10), 995–1010.

Kelley, J., & De Graaf, N. D. (1997). National context, parental socialization, and religious belief: Results from 15 nations. *American Sociological Review, 62*, 639–659.

Kuchel, S. (2003). *Individualism and collectivism: A study of values and inferencing in psychotherapy* (Unpublished doctoral dissertation). McGill University, Montreal.

Leuty, M. E. (2013). Assessment of needs and values. In K. F. Geisinger (Ed.), *APA handbook of testing and assessment in psychology* (pp. 363–377). Washington, DC: American Psychological Association.

Magnavita, J. & Achin, J. (2013). *Unifying psychotherapy: Principles, methods, and evidence from clinical science.* New York, NY: Springer Publishing.

Martin, J., & Sugarman, J. (2000). Between the modern and the postmodern: The possibility of self and progressive understanding in psychology. *American Psychologist, 55*(4), 397–406.

Mays, V. M., Bullock, M., Rosenzweig, M. R., & Wessells, M. (1998). Ethnic conflict: Global challenges and psychological perspectives. *American Psychologist, 53*(7), 737–742.

McElroy, J. H. (1999). *American beliefs: What keeps a big country and a diverse people united.* Chicago, IL: Ivan R. Dee, Publisher.

Medalia, J. (2011). *"Dirty bombs": Technical background, attack prevention and response, issues for congress.* Retrieved June 24, 2014, from http://www.fas.org/sgp/crs/nuke/R41890.pdf.

Moskowitz, G. B. (2005). *Social cognition: Understanding self and others.* New York, NY: The Guildford Press.

Murray, B. (2002, January). 'Mr. Psychology' has a message for America. *Monitor on Psychology, 33*(1), 24–27.

Musek, J. (1998). Political and religious adherence in relation to individual values. *Studia Psychologica, 40*(1–2), 47.

Neimeyer, R., & Raskin, J. (2000). *Constructions of disorder.* Washington, DC: American Psychological Association.

Newberg, A., & Waldman, M. R. (2006). *Why we believe what we believe: Uncovering our biological need for meaning, spirituality, and truth.* New York, NY: Free Press.

Panepinto, A. R., Domenici, D. J., & Domenici, V. A. (2012). An introduction to the special issue on creatively construing constructivism. *Journal of Constructivist Psychology, 25*(3), 181–183.

Raskin, J. D. (2012). Evolutionary constructivism and humanistic psychology. *Journal of Theoretical and Philosophical Psychology, 32*(2), 119–133.

Risk of radioactive "dirty bomb" growing. (2004, June 2) Retrieved August 7, 2006, from https://www.newscientist.com/article/dn5061-risk-of-radioactive-dirty-bomb-growing/

Rokeach, M. (1973). *The nature of human values.* New York, NY: Free Press.

Rokeach, M., & Ball-Rokeach, S. J. (1989). Stability and change in American value priorities. *American Psychologist, 44*(5), 775–784.

Ryan, R. M., Curren, R. R., & Deci, E. L. (2013). What humans need: Flourishing in Aristotelian philosophy and self-determination theory. In A. S. Waterman (Ed.), *The best within us: Positive psychology perspectives on eudaimonia* (pp. 57–75). Washington, DC: American Psychological Association.

Sargent, L. T. (Ed.). (1995). *Extremism in America.* New York, NY: New York University Press.

Schwartz, S. H. (2012). An Overview of the Schwartz Theory of Basic Values. *Online Readings In Psychology and Culture, 2*(1), 1–20. Retrieved from http://dx.doi.org/10.9707/2307-0919.1116

Shealy, C. N. (2004). A model and method for "making" a C-I psychologist: Equilintegration (EI) Theory and the Beliefs, Events, and Values Inventory (BEVI). *Journal of Clinical Psychology, 60,* 1065–1090.

Shealy, C. N. (2005). Justifying the Justification Hypothesis: Scientific-Humanism, Equilintegration (EI) Theory, and the Beliefs, Events, and Values Inventory (BEVI). [Special Series]. *Journal of Clinical Psychology, 61*(1), 81–106.

Shealy, C. N. (2014). Education for sustainability research: Why it matters. In D. Sobel, S. J. Gentile, & P. Bocko (Eds.), *A national blueprint for education for sustainability* (pp. 27–28). Boston, MA: Houghton Mifflin Harcourt.

Shealy, C. N. (2015). *The Beliefs, Events, and Values Inventory (BEVI): Overview, implications, and guidelines.* Test manual. Staunton, VA: Author.

Shealy, C. N., Bhuyan, D., & Sternberger, L. G. (2012). Cultivating the capacity to care in children and Youth: Implications from EI Theory, EI Self, and BEVI. In U. Nayar (Ed.), *Child and adolescent mental health* (pp. 240–255). New Delhi, India: Sage Publications.

Staub, E. (1996). Cultural-societal roots of violence. The examples of genocidal violence and of contemporary youth violence in the United States. *American Psychologist, 51*(2), 117–132.

Staub, E. (2003). Notes on cultures of violence, cultures of caring and peace, and the fulfillment of basic human needs. *Political Psychology, 24*(1), 1–21.

Staub, E. (2013). Building a peaceful society: Origins, prevention, and reconciliation after genocide and other group violence. *American Psychologist, 68*(7), 576–589.

Wegner, D. M. (2002). *The illusion of conscious will.* Cambridge, MA: The MIT Press.

White, B. (2002, February 3). Elite cast debates poverty at forum. *The Washington Post,* p. A3.

BELIEFS, NEEDS, AND SELF: THREE COMPONENTS OF THE EI MODEL

Frisbeetarianism is the belief that when you die, your soul goes up on the roof and gets stuck.

—George Carlin

I will never forget my initial session with Elaine, who offered an illuminating study in hope, perseverance, and the transformation of self.[1] When I met her—in a homeless shelter—my first impression was of a loud and brash human being, who would not ever be defined by me, whatever credentials I presumed to possess. Immediately suspicious that I would try to "change" her religion, she was able—over the course of several sessions—to release her defensive posture and grant that I just might be telling the truth when uttering that I had no desire to "take away" her religious convictions, which included fidelity to a local sect in what may be referred to as "hollers" in the rural and mountainous Shenandoah Valley. Among other precepts, my understanding of her religious convictions included the belief that women were to submit to and obey their husbands (as commanded by Paul of the Biblical *Corinthians*), and to avoid any ostentatious displays of femininity that might call her commitment to husband and family into question.

From this point of departure, in the months to come, a torrent of detail and pain flowed forth: the untenable situation she and her family (Evan, her husband, along with two boys and two girls, ranging in age from 4 to 14) endured in a humiliating family shelter; the condemnation she experienced from her extended family, which had never accepted Evan, because of his checkered employment history and transient ways (the family had moved frequently since they were married); and, the chronic conflict with her kin, who were consumed with a colorful array of hopelessly muddled disputes over, well, just about everything, which mostly boiled down to whom was "to blame" for the mess of their lives (Elaine occupied a privileged position near the top of the heap). These roiling intra- and extra-familial dynamics extended far into the surrounding community, manifesting in chronic and unrelenting dysfunction within each of Urie Bronfenbrenner's nested systems, and

---

[1] The de-identified presentation of assessment or clinical material and results in this chapter and book are informed by the March 2012 Special Section of the journal *Psychotherapy*, entitled "Ethical Issues in Clinical Writing," Volume 49, Issue 1, pp. 1–25, as well as the Health Insurance Portability and Accountability Act (HIPAA) regulations, American Psychological Association (APA) ethical guidelines, and other best practices for reporting such information. In this regard, although all assessment and report results are consistent with original patterns and profiles, key information may have been modified on occasion (e.g., specific scores) in order to ensure the anonymity of respondents and/or consistency across the long and short versions of the Beliefs, Events, and Values Inventory (BEVI).

reverberating in screams and tears within what originally amounted to a concrete bunker in the homeless shelter, echoing later within a three-bedroom refuge that my doctoral students and I managed to secure for them, with the crucial assistance of a small army of social service administrators and staff.

As the months went by, and Elaine and I continued to meet—sometimes alone, sometimes with Evan, sometimes with children, and across all manner of clinical configurations—a subtle but powerful transformation unfolded among us, which typically is understood in terms of the "therapeutic alliance," but really boiled down to the fact that Elaine, and her family, had begun to trust me and the other doctoral students whom I had integrated into various aspects of this complex process of treatment. For example, Evan began to understand and ultimately embrace greater responsibility in his roles of father and husband. The high octane tempo of parent/child conflict ratcheted slowly but inexorably downward, as the parents became less crabby with one another, less punitive from a disciplinary standpoint, and more united in terms of a firm but nurturing approach toward their kids. For Elaine, what were barely perceptible rivulets morphed over time into jetting spouts through a breaching dam, as she launched a guilty and wracking process of confessing more and more of what she really felt and really wanted: to complete her education; her doubts about the religious leader and system to which they had committed; her longing for stability within the home; her wish for greater connection within her marriage; and most of all, an overarching and ineffable desire to be, and feel, like she was known and respectable to herself, others, and the larger world. This process was curvilinear, to say the least, zigging here and there as the process unfolded over months of anger, angst, and ultimately, hope.

From my perspective at least, one key moment in our process remains fixed in my mind as epochal of all we were attempting to understand, pursue, and achieve together. In this particular session, Elaine was engaged in an affectively laden exposition on multiple aspects of self: her spiritual path, educational hopes, and longings for her own life and her family. As her own emotional pitch increased, the dam gave forth altogether and found her on the floor in shrieks and tears, screaming in fear about the devil, who apparently had joined us in the room, and the wrongness of all she was thinking, feeling, and wanting. I got down on the floor with her, spoke calmly and softly, telling her just to breathe, to hold on, to quiet herself, and to talk with me. Through her sobs that still evoke resonance in me so many years later, she confessed her deepest fear that she was becoming something she was not permitted to be, even as she neither knew what such a "self" was nor how she ever could become again the obeisant wretch of her prior incarnation. I listened as hard as I could, straining with everything in me to hear and speak to the part of her that was experiencing such exquisite pain and dissent at the deepest levels of self.

As she calmed herself and emerged from what might clinically be characterized as a brief psychotic episode, she spoke with extraordinary lucidity about a profound schism she had felt within her, between these internalized notions about all she was supposed to be (e.g., dutiful believer, wife, mother) and all that she longed to become (e.g., educated and strong woman who was stable, independent, and fulfilled). In the process that followed between us, for the months afterwards that we continued to work together, the overarching theme ultimately was about how she was coming to encounter who she really was, and perhaps always had been, despite the fact that such realities for her had become encrusted with layer upon layer of belief regarding whom she was supposed be rather that what she was, a potential that she desperately wanted to pursue, but had been compelled to bury within the deepest recesses of self.

So, how to explain the phenomenology of this especially fateful session, variations of which I have observed on innumerable occasions since seeing my first client over 25 years ago? *From my perspective, on that particular day, the self-structure which had contained her deepest aspirations within an armored shell of self-abnegating beliefs, cracked apart, and was no longer able to constrain what was a rush of affectively mediated need.* The subjective sequelae of this process—referred to as "disequilintegration" from an Equilintegration (EI) perspective—were experienced by Elaine as "coming apart," a point at which her self-structure no longer was bound together in its previous form. Such a state literally does feel "crazy" because the human being in the midst of experiencing it has no way to make sense of what is happening, since the attendant rending of previously fused affect and cognition is much bigger than one's capacity to apprehend and assimilate such powerful intrapsychic forces in real time.

IMPETUS AND RATIONALE FOR EI THEORY AND THE EI SELF

Note three constructs in particular from that which has been presented thus far—*beliefs, needs,* and *self* —as they are core to everything discussed next and really, throughout this entire book. When beginning to collect verbal utterances of clients, students, and other notable public figures in the early 1990s, I did not have in mind the development of Equilintegration Theory or the EI Self—which together comprise the EI Model—or an accompanying measure called the Beliefs, Events, and Values Inventory (BEVI), all of which are discussed in this chapter and those that follow. Instead, I simply was trying to make sense of how and why human beings could become so deeply and unquestioningly invested in a version of reality whose origins seemed unknown to them. Only later did it become clear that an optimal and essential construct for describing such utterances was that of "belief." And yet, the mere explication of even a very large list of such beliefs (over 500 at the outset) did not really explain much of anything; it appeared that these "belief statements" were simply a final manifestation of highly complex processes that occurred over a long period of time. Ultimately, the fact that such belief statements often were held rigidly and intensively meant that they were emanations of something much deeper, which I came to understand ultimately as core human needs. Early in my own training, aspects of this connection were revealed while working with adolescent males, in a residential facility, who were legally removed from their homes after experiencing abuse and neglect. Deeply poignant, it was very common for these youth to defend vehemently their own caregivers, even while simultaneously acknowledging the experience of seriously disturbed and disturbing behavior directed at them. As noted on the basis of this experience at the time, and attendant immersion in the literature,

> The deep attachments between human beings are not interchangeable, but person specific. That is one reason why children and youth who were neglected, abused, or exploited by a parent or parents, and were subsequently placed out of home, often continue to yearn for reunification with them. (Shealy, 1995, p. 577)

The faith these young people continued to have—manifesting verbally in the unstinting belief in the inherent "goodness" of their caregivers, and often in accompanying belief statements about their own concomitant "badness" (e.g., *I caused them to treat me that way*)—seemed in fact to be a desperate attempt to cling to a hope for what they needed most—to be loved, cared for, and valued—by the human beings who mattered most of all. Put in other terms, to *disbelieve* in the inherent goodness of one's own caregivers is intolerable to the developing self; it is easier to believe that the reason for abusive or neglectful conduct by one's caregivers has to do with deficiencies in one's own conduct or character, which therefore was under one's own control (e.g., *If I just do better, they will love me*). To give up on the hope that one can "win over" one's own parents or caregivers—despite all evidence to the contrary—is to resign oneself to a lack of control over one's life, and ultimately, to give up on one's own self; the subsequent rage, hurt, and grief that accompany such a state of defeat often lead to a life of destruction toward self and others, which may require years to work through therapeutically, if such resolution even is attempted (Shealy, Bhuyan, & Sternberger, 2012). In any case, as became clear over time in my own work as a clinician, this last point represented a final dimension that needed to be apprehended as well, since one's needs did not just emerge in disembodied form, but lived within and emanated from a larger regulatory and organizational system called the "self."

The problem was, the literature on all three of these constructs (beliefs, needs, self) seemed to be all over the place, which represented a challenge and opportunity to grapple with these literatures across eight interrelated levels of analysis—definitional, relational, disciplinary, etiological, experiential, communal, integrative, and application—as described next. Engagement with these issues ultimately led to the development of the Equilintegration or EI theoretical framework, which attempts to account for the complexity described in the preceding observations, while illuminating many of the findings of the BEVI. At this point, then, it seems important to explicate what these eight levels of analysis are in order to apprehend better the impetus for the EI model and BEVI method that are discussed throughout this book.

An Eightfold Impetus for the *Equilintegration* or EI Model

1. *Definitional.* Overall, scholars and practitioners often used terms such as beliefs, values, attitudes, schemas, opinions, biases, prejudices, and so forth interchangeably in reference to similar or even identical events or phenomena. So, it is difficult to know whether and what is and is not meant by specific terms (i.e., Is there any difference at all?).

2. *Relational.* When distinctions among constructs were articulated, the full relationship among them (e.g., as with Rokeach's explication of values and needs) was not always specified in sufficient detail. So, it was difficult to make sense theoretically of how and why these constructs related to each other and under what circumstances.

3. *Disciplinary.* At times, scholars and practitioners from specific subdisciplines did not seem aware of each other's literatures, much less the perspectives of scholars and practitioners working outside of one's field. For example, the attitudinal concept from social psychology shows great complementarity to the schema concept from depth-based approaches in clinical and developmental psychology. And yet, such complementarity was not often noted. Likewise, philosophers have grappled with "values" literally for millennia (e.g., from an ethical and epistemological perspective), but their insights were not often referenced even theoretically within mainstream academic discourse in psychology, and vice versa.

4. *Etiological.* Questions of why there are differences between individuals in the beliefs and values that are declared to be one's own——and the implications of such developmental processes for why we experience self, others, and the larger world as we do—seemed relatively neglected in favor of nomothetic analyses that focus on mean-based belief/value differences between various groups (i.e., aggregated analyses tend to emphasize mean-based or average differences between groups even though within group differences may be greater than between group differences). Although highly relevant, of course, the reasons why individual human

beings acquire the beliefs and values they do in the first place—and how these etiological factors and forces play out in terms of real world behavior and within-group variation—would seem to be an equally valid level of analysis.

5. *Experiential*. There is no question that programmatic research, particularly in sub-fields such as social and developmental psychology, has influenced profoundly our understanding of the nature of "beliefs and values," broadly defined. Certainly, the fundamental underpinnings of EI Theory presented in the following discussion—as well as a number of chapters that follow—are informed greatly by theories and data within these and other scholarly subfields. But one of the arguments advanced throughout this book is that much also may be learned by the actual experience of "beliefs and values," when seen through a theoretically and methodologically rigorous lens. For example, the experience of beliefs and values in real time via psychotherapy and psychological assessment offers a powerful applied milieu in which to see up close how life history and events interact with core needs (e.g., for attachment, affiliation) and extant contingencies (e.g., what is reinforced in real time) to influence how we humans experience self, others, and the larger world. As later chapters attest, much can be learned by grappling with such beliefs and values as therapists and assessors, as we are in the privileged position of testing our theories in real time in order to determine how to create change and transform lives. And of course, there certainly are other ways to examine these constructs experientially—up close and in real time as teachers, leaders, advocates, and the like (e.g., Coates, Hanson, Samuel, Webster, & Cozen, 2016; Cozen, Hanson, Poston, Jones, & Tabit, 2016; see also Cranton, 2006; Dirkx, 2012; Kuh, 2008; Mezirow & Taylor, 2009). In addition to quantitative methods, approaches that are well suited to such engagement (e.g., qualitative assessment) also may illuminate what "is happening" thematically. But the bottom line is, the complex, interacting, and very human nature of "beliefs and values" means that scholars and practitioners who wish to understand them may be well served by balancing empirical strategies for doing so with person-close interventions that allow them to encounter their own "selves" even as they seek to apprehend the "other." Through such real world engagement with "beliefs and values," subsequent theory, research, and practice may have a greater likelihood of capturing the true nature and depth of these constructs in a manner that is generalizable, meaningful, and valid across cultures and contexts.

6. *Communal*. Ultimately, differences in beliefs and values seem to be more a matter of degree than kind. That is to say, there is little reason to believe that processes leading to the beliefs and values we declare to be true about matters that are defined within a clinical domain are qualitatively different from those that are associated with what we believe and value in any other realm. In other words, although the content of our beliefs and values—and the attendant manifestations regarding how we experience self, others, and the larger world—may differ, there is no reason to believe that all things being relatively equal, "believers" around the world are fundamentally different in terms of how and why we function as we do vis-à-vis beliefs, needs, and self. Thus, although the assessment work described in this book began in a clinical domain—which allowed for in-depth observation and understanding of how and why these complex and interacting processes manifest as they do—our focus still includes, but has progressed far beyond that sphere. As the research and applied chapters later in this book illustrate, there is every reason to believe that this "deep level" of analysis can illuminate why we do what we do in a nonclinical realm, since such distinctions between "clients" and "the rest of us" may largely be spurious in terms of the acquisition and expression of beliefs and values (e.g., Anmuth et al., 2013; Horwitz, 2002). In short, one of the basic

postulates of the work presented here is that we humans are more alike than different, and that the differences that do emerge among us—at the level of beliefs and values—are due to "formative variables" rather than fundamental differences in our basic design as *Homo sapiens sapiens* (e.g., Tabit et al., 2012).

7. *Integrative.* As is discussed later in this chapter, the "I" of EI Theory refers in part to the integrative nature and intent of this perspective as it juxtaposes interrelated constructs—such as beliefs, needs, and self—and seeks to illustrate their inextricable relationship to one another. In doing so, multiple disciplinary perspectives are brought to bear on such processes as well as insights that may be gleaned from both science and practice. In short, the "I" of EI serves as a reminder that "to make sense of beliefs and values," the interactions among multiple concepts, disciplines, and ways of knowing are best apprehended simultaneously as an integrated gestalt rather than isolable "parts" (i.e., the explication of "parts" is necessary but not sufficient to make sense of the larger "whole").

8. *Application.* Finally, there are much broader implications of beliefs and values for making sense of actions, policies, and practices in the larger world, beyond "the individual," to include why groups, organizations, societies, and nations behave as they do. In other words, there is a real need to illustrate how and under what circumstances belief/value processes at the individual level play out in dynamics among human beings at a larger level. To take but two examples of thousands, how are policy decisions about the need to educate girls affected by underlying beliefs and values regarding the "proper" role of females in society? Or, how, why, and under what circumstances does one's life history and context mediate the tendency to accept, or deny, climate change? Ultimately, the goal here is to link these fundamental intrapsychic processes (e.g., how beliefs and values are internalized) with their manifestation in the "real world" (e.g., actions, policies, and practices) in order to illuminate the relationship between these micro- and macrolevels of analysis (e.g., How and why are our policy preferences determined, in no small part, by the ways in which we were treated during our own processes of development?) (Cultivating the Globally Sustainable Self, 2015).

In many ways, then, to "make sense of beliefs and values," we need to recognize and address all eight of these interrelated levels of analysis in order to (a) illuminate what these constructs are, (b) understand the relationships among them, (c) appreciate the perspectives of multiple disciplines and subdisciplines, (d) ascertain the role of etiology and individual differences, (e) apprehend how a "deep" encounter with such processes in both experiential and applied terms may enrich our understanding of these constructs, (f) grapple with the fact that there may be greater within than between group differences, culturally and otherwise, (g) appreciate why an integrative framework helps in the explication of these phenomena, and (h) remember that in the final analysis, research on beliefs and values has implications for how theory and data can and should inform what we "do" in the real and larger world.

Rationale for the *Equilintegration* or EI Term

Finally, in light of the preceding eight points, it may be helpful to provide additional explication regarding the term "equilintegration" in order to understand the rationale for its selection. Essentially, this term is composed of the prefix, "equi" from the Latin *aequare*, meaning "to make equal" and the noun "integration," meaning "the process of coordinating and unifying disparate elements into a whole" (Reber, Allen, & Reber,

2009, p. 390). This term seems appropriate since a wide range of "disparate elements"—in both a scholarly and applied sense—have informed the development of the Equilintegration or EI Model over the years. These terminological elements include (a) the need to address the impetus for this model as described in the eight components noted above (i.e., definitional, relational, disciplinary, etiological, experiential, communal, integrative, and application); (b) the overarching goal of integrating three key literatures—beliefs, needs, and self—in order to develop a model of sufficient breadth and depth for the task at hand (i.e., "making sense of beliefs and values"); (c) the seminal contributions of Jean Piaget and his formulation of *equilibrium*, which, in deference to his genius, account (in part) for the appendage of the letter "l" to "equi"; (d) a goal to strive explicitly for "equal" treatment of these "disparate elements" via the phonetic prompt of *equal*—again, via the addition of "l"—as in *equal— integration*); (e) a burgeoning theoretical and applied consensus that "integration" represents an optimal state of identity or condition of the self (i.e., as will be discussed, "integration" is seen as an optimally calibrated psychological state that once grasped tentatively, is doggedly pursued over the course of one's life); (f) a recognition that deep-level understanding and change vis-à-vis the human condition is done well through an "integrative" approach to assessment, therapy, education, and training; and finally, (g) the related and ultimate goal of adopting an integrative approach (e.g., to include interdisciplinary, interprofessional, and international perspectives) when seeking (a) to *evaluate and facilitate social transformation*, both locally and globally (e.g., via relevant scholarly models and methods of research, assessment, and intervention that seek to translate their perspectives into maximally accessible forms) across (b) *"big picture" movements* (e.g., conflict resolution, human rights, sustainability, global education, religious and cultural understanding) that are (c) *pursuing complementary missions*, whether there is or is not deliberate awareness that one is doing so (e.g., Cultivating the Globally Sustainable Self, 2015). With the impetus and rationale for the EI Model and term now described, let us focus first on trying to understand what we mean by these three overarching and interrelated constructs of beliefs, needs, and self, which are considered the three primary components of EI Theory.

We begin with the first of these, by describing the "basics of belief," which includes, but is not limited to, the seminal contributions of Milton Rokeach, Shalom Schwartz, and Norman Feather. Next, we turn to fundamental aspects of how beliefs and values are acquired, maintained, and modified, beginning with the essential discoveries of Jean Piaget, and moving from there to what we have learned about related processes, including but not limited to attachment-based working models and schemas to theoretical, empirical, and applied work with "openness to experience" and "therapeutic resistance." To illustrate the centrality of the "belief" construct to research, we then discuss two fundamental programs of scholarship—on authoritarian personality and attribution theory—before turning to three practice-based examples of beliefs and values vis-à-vis leadership, education, and mental health. Finally, on the basis of all that has been considered, we conclude our discussion by offering a working definition of *belief* along with related implications.

EI COMPONENT I: BELIEF

In considering how the social sciences in general and psychology in particular formally have studied "beliefs" and "values" over the years, one first must determine how wide a scholarly net to cast. From an explicit standpoint—that is, those who declared that they were studying "beliefs" or "values"—there are a few pioneers who contributed substantially to our understanding of these issues, including Milton Rokeach, Norman Feather, Shalom Schwartz, and Abraham Maslow (e.g., Feather, 1992, 1994, 1995; Maslow, 1954, 1964, 1968, 1971; Rokeach, 1956, 1960, 1973; Rokeach & Ball-Rokeach, 1989; Schwartz, 1992, 2012; Schwartz & Bilsky, 1987, 1990), among other scholars and practitioners highlighted in this chapter and those that follow. Aside from such seminal figures, formal theories of beliefs and values, along with accompanying methodology and data, are uncommon, as noted in the opening chapter of this book. On the one hand, these omissions are striking because human beings so often invoke their own beliefs and values to explain or justify what they do. On the other hand, abundant evidence suggests that "beliefs and values" are, in fact, at the very heart of some of the most significant programs of scholarship in our field, but not always in an explicit manner; their "omission," therefore, may be due to semantics as much as substance. For example, if Aronson (2012) is correct in asserting that social psychology may be defined in terms of "the influences that people have upon the beliefs, feelings, and behavior of others" (p. 6), then it becomes clear how central the construct of "belief" is to this rich and compelling field of inquiry. Or, consider clinical and counseling psychology: Even therapeutic systems that strive for or claim neutrality (e.g., toward issues of "normality" for example) are doing so in relation to the beliefs (e.g., the worldview, narrative) that clients convey. From developmental psychology, one might argue that the fundamental process of learning about the world in which one lives (e.g., as an infant) is concerned with the burgeoning belief in the relative predictability and consistency of that world, as evidenced, for example, in Erik Erikson's first stage of psychosocial development—trust versus mistrust. Or from a behavioral perspective, what is "learned helplessness" (in dogs or humans) but the erroneous belief, acquired through experience, that one's behavior has no effect upon one's circumstances? The point of this momentary glance across the scholarly and applied landscape within psychology is not to claim that we are all basically just studying beliefs and values, and should acknowledge that fact. The point rather is that beliefs and values, although variously defined and understood, are at least peripherally if not centrally relevant to a wide spectrum of phenomena, issues, and topics that are of demonstrable interest to scholars and practitioners. Therefore, it seems relevant to consider not only direct approaches to the study of beliefs and values, but programs of scholarship where "beliefs" and "values" have a virtual and ineluctable presence.

Basics of Belief

In this regard, there is perhaps no better point of departure than Milton Rokeach, who designed and built a durable theoretical and methodological bridge between these explicit and implicit realms. Rokeach sought to describe the ontological and etiological relationship among beliefs, values, and attitudes—constructs that theretofore had lacked sufficient differentiation. According to Rokeach (1979), "humans have thousands of attitudes but only dozens of values. . .values are deeper as well as broader than attitudes. . .values are standards of 'oughts' and 'shoulds' whereas attitudes are not [and]. . .values are determinants rather than components of attitudes" (p. 272). Rokeach (1973) also had much to say about the relationship between beliefs and values, defining a value as "an enduring belief that a specific mode of conduct or end-state of existence is personally or socially preferable to an opposite or converse mode of conduct or end-state of existence" (p. 5). Ultimately, Rokeach was interested in understanding how beliefs emerged from and inextricably were linked to core aspects of the self, a theme that will emerge throughout this book. More specifically, as summarized by Braithwaite and Scott (1991), Rokeach theorized that value systems were:

> Part of a functionally integrated cognitive system in which the basic units of analysis are beliefs. Clusters of beliefs form attitudes that are functionally and cognitively connected to the value system. Rokeach further postulated classes of beliefs concerned with self-cognitions representing "the innermost core of the total belief system, and all remaining beliefs, attitudes and values can be conceived of as functionally organized around this innermost core" (1973, p. 216). . . beliefs are not just cognitions in Rokeach's conceptual schema, but predispositions to action capable of arousing affect around the object of the belief. (pp. 662–663)

Over the years, Rokeach and colleagues investigated the interactions and properties emergent from this general framework through The Values Survey (Rokeach, 1967) as well as allied programs of research. Among many other findings, this research illustrated that values, as conceptualized by Rokeach, were "significantly related to variations in socioeconomic status, age, gender, race, religion, and lifestyle. . .[and] significant predictors of many social attitudes and behaviors, including consumer behavior," addiction, political and economic tendencies (e.g., fascist, capitalist, socialist, and communist) as well as conservative and liberal ideologies (Rokeach & Ball-Rokeach, 1989, p. 776).

Building upon Rokeach's seminal work, Shalom Schwartz and Norman Feather in particular have extended our understanding of the nature of values at multiple levels of analysis. Specifically, Schwartz both has consolidated Rokeach's original formulation of instrumental and terminal values into 10 "value types" along with a circumplex model, which demonstrates the dialectical relationship of similar and different values to one another. Schwartz's 10 value types are presented next; each bolded value is defined in terms of specific values, listed in parentheses (e.g., Schwartz, 2012).

> **Power:** Social status and prestige, control or dominance over people and resources (authority, social power, wealth, preserving my public image)
>
> **Achievement:** Personal success through demonstrating competence according to social standards (ambitious, successful, capable, influential)
>
> **Hedonism:** Pleasure or sensuous gratification for oneself (pleasure, enjoying life, self-indulgent)
>
> **Stimulation:** Excitement, novelty, and challenge in life (daring, a varied life, an exciting life)
>
> **Self-direction:** Independent thought and action—choosing, creating, exploring (creativity, freedom, independent, choosing own goals, curious)
>
> **Universalism:** Understanding, appreciation, tolerance, and protection for the welfare of all people and for nature (equality, social justice, wisdom, broadminded, protecting the environment, unity with nature, a world of beauty)
>
> **Benevolence:** Preservation and enhancement of the welfare of people with whom one is in frequent personal contact (helpful, honest, forgiving, loyal, responsible)

Tradition: Respect, commitment, and acceptance of the customs and ideas that traditional culture or religion provides (devout, respect for tradition, humble, moderate)

Conformity: Restraint of actions, inclinations, and impulses likely to upset or harm others and violate social expectations or norms (self-discipline, politeness, honoring parents and elders, obedience)

Security: Safety, harmony, and stability of society, of relationships, and of self (family security, national security, social order, clean, reciprocation of favors)

Over the years, Schwartz and colleagues have produced an impressive array of analyses, which have focused in large part on demonstrating value-based differences and similarities around the world, using both the Schwartz Values Survey and alternative Portrait Values Questionnaire (e.g., Schwartz, 1992, 2012; Schwartz & Bilsky, 1987, 1990). For present purposes, what is most salient about Schwartz's work is his perspective on the theoretical nature of values vis-à-vis allied constructs. In particular, he posits "six main features" of values that are "implicit in the writings of many theorists." A consolidated adaptation and excerpting of these is as follows: "(a) values are beliefs linked inextricably to affect; (b) values refer to desirable goals that motivate action; (c) values transcend specific actions and situations; (d) values serve as standards or criteria; (e) values are ordered by importance relative to one another; and, (f) the *relative* importance of multiple values guides action" (see pp. 3–4). As he further notes,

> The above are features of *all* values. What distinguishes one from another is the type of goal or motivation that it expresses. The values theory defines ten broad values according to the motivation that underlies each of them. These values are likely to be universal because they are grounded in one or more of three universal requirements of human existence with which they help to cope. These requirements are needs of individuals as biological organisms, requisites of coordinated social interaction, and survival and welfare needs of groups. Individuals cannot cope successfully with these requirements of human existence on their own. Rather, people must articulate appropriate goals to cope with them, communicate with others about them, and gain cooperation in their pursuit. (Schwartz, 2012, pp. 3–4)

As another exemplar, Norman Feather also has done much to explicate the nature of values in a manner that, like Schwartz, is highly complementary to the present approach. Building again on Rokeach as well as Schwartz's scholarship, Feather observed relatively early in his own work that "it is necessary to distinguish between values and valences." Specifically,

> *values* can be conceived as abstract structures that involve the beliefs that people hold about desirable ways of behaving or about desirable end states. These beliefs transcend specific objects and situations, and they have a normative, or oughtness, quality about them. They have their source in basic human needs and in societal demands. They are relatively stable but not unchanging across the life span. They are assumed to function as criteria or frameworks against which present experience can be tested. Values vary in their relative importance for the individual, and they are fewer in number than the many specific beliefs and attitudes that people possess. Thus they are

more abstract than attitudes, and they are hierarchically organized in terms of their importance for self. They are not affectively neutral. People usually feel strongly about their central values. . .*valences* refer to the subjective attractiveness or aversiveness of specific objects and events within the immediate situation. The emphasis here is on the goal properties of potential actions and outcomes as perceived by the person at a given moment. . .Valences are linked to a specific context and to a present time frame. In contrast, values are properties of persons, they are more abstract and general, and they maintain some stability across a wider time frame. . .Values may also be considered not only as generalized beliefs about what is or is not desirable but also as motives. I have assumed that they function like needs to influence goal-directed behavior. (Feather, 1995, p. 1135)

Both before and after this theoretical explication, Feather has presaged several aspects of the current approach of this book through his career, by focusing for example on the relationship of values to macrolevel phenomena such as conservative ideology (Feather, 1979), gender identity (Feather, 1984), the justice system and its intersection with ethnicity (Feather, 1994; Feather & Souter, 2002), and authoritarianism (Feather & McKee, 2012).

Acquiring Beliefs and Values

On the basis of the preceding discussion (i.e., the "basics of belief"), the "E" or Equilibrium half of EI Theory now may be explicated further, which—in deference to Jean Piaget, the Swiss psychologist and philosopher—seeks to describe process-based aspects of how and why beliefs and values are acquired, maintained, and modified, for whom, and under what circumstances. Although all three components of the EI Model—*beliefs*, *needs*, and *self*—must be considered in this regard, one key element of this model is derived from Piaget, who was interested in how and under what conditions knowledge about the larger world was organized mentally and emotionally, and the processes by which these organizational structures developed (e.g., Kegan, 1982; McLeod, 2009; Piaget, 1976, 1977). Piaget's robust observations are highly relevant to an understanding of beliefs and values because "according to Rokeach (1973, 1979), values are central to a person's *cognitive* organization" (Dollinger, Leong, & Ulicni, 1996, p. 25). Moreover, as will become clear later, Piaget's framework "fits for the special insight gained in therapy" in that "insight affords a qualitatively different perspective, an altered state" (Peake, VanNoord, & Albott, 1979, p. 100). Along these lines, Kegan observes the following:

> if the Piagetian framework has traditionally seemed to have little to say to counseling and clinical psychology, its root metaphors and premises may actually make it better equipped to deal with the very issues central to these psychologies which have been the most influential to the therapeutic enterprise. (p. 7)

As will be emphasized throughout the research and applied chapters of this book, neo-Piagetian perspectives such as Kegan's illuminate the nature of change processes overall as well as how beliefs and values are acquired, maintained, and modified, which should be of great relevance not only to clinicians and trainers, but to change agents more generally (Cultivating the Globally Sustainable Self, 2015; Shealy & Bullock, in press).

Piaget perhaps is best known for his four stages of cognitive/affective development: sensorimotor operations, preoperational, concrete operations, and formal operations. Briefly, the sensorimotor stage (birth through 18–24 months) finds the infant, then toddler, experimenting with the three-dimensional world, learning ultimately, that some objects have "permanence" (i.e., they continue to exist even if they cannot be seen), while also developing basic language capacities, which indicates the beginning of symbolic meaning making (e.g., words can stand for, or represent, people, places, and things). During the preoperational stage (toddlerhood, from 18–24 months through early childhood, at age 7), language use and symbolic thinking become more developed. Temporal awareness expands (i.e., there is a past, present, and future), which when combined with increased memory capacity, leads to a rich interior life of imagination and make-believe. In concrete operations (ages 7–12), children begin to realize that their own perspectives on self and the larger world may not be shared by others. They likewise begin to demonstrate basic capacities of logic and reason, including the ability to perform reversible mental operations (e.g., they can count, add, and subtract). Finally, individuals who reach formal operations (adolescence through adulthood) are able to think in hypothetical, "if/then" relations, which means there is a capacity to work with abstraction (i.e., they are able to contemplate interactions among multiple variables, which may lead to multiple outcomes) as well as complex constructs, such as what is meant by, and what are the conditions that demonstrate, "truth" or "justice." Interestingly, based upon the experimental procedures designed to measure this stage of development, Piaget observed that only half of the population (at least in the West) ever achieved formal operations (e.g., Bernstein, 2011; Wadsworth, 1996).

In addition to these stages, Piaget found that the developing child "naturally" groups together information or objects in the world on the basis of likeness or kind, even if such categorizations violate or ignore more subtle and fine-grained distinctions that readily are apprehended by an adult. Piaget called this process *assimilation*. The resulting "schemata" are comprised, in part, of information and rules about how objects and information are to be organized; they are "the cognitive and mental structures by which individuals adapt to and organize the environment" (Wadsworth, 1996, p. 14; see also McLeod, 2009). However, with development and acquisition of additional knowledge about the way in which the world is organized, existing schemas either must be modified, or new ones created, a process Piaget referred to as *accommodation* (Wadsworth, 1996, p. 17). These schemas may be defined as "the cognitive or mental structures by which individuals intellectually adapt to and organize the environment. As structures, schemata are the mental counterparts of biological means of adapting. . .They are inferred to exist and are properly called hypothetical constructs" (p. 14). Finally, Piaget emphasized that cognitive change and growth results from a dialectic tension between these processes, successive resolutions of which culminate in an increasingly complex, interwoven, and variegated cognitive structure. Piaget's term for the synergic relationship between assimilation and accommodation was *equilibration*, the "state of balance between assimilation and accommodation" whereas *disequilibrium* is the "state of imbalance between assimilation and accommodation. *Equilibration* is the process of moving from disequilibrium to equilibrium" (Wadsworth, 1996, p. 19; see also Dollinger et al., 1996; Kegan, 1982; McLeod, 2009; Peake et al., 1979; Piaget, 1976, 1977). Finally, although these processes and precepts continue to receive deserved scholarly and applied attention, it should also be noted that aspects of Piaget's approach have been criticized (e.g., the linearity of his stages of development; issues of measurement and methodology; not attending sufficiently to sociocultural processes that affect development) (e.g., Hopkins, 2011; Matusov & Hayes, 2000).

As this brief review of Piagetian theory and research suggests, some of the more intriguing questions vis-à-vis cognitive development in general—and beliefs and values in particular—have as much to do with *content* (e.g., what actually is believed or valued) as they do with matters of *process* (e.g., how and under what circumstances beliefs and values are acquired) as well as *structure* (e.g., how, indeed "where" beliefs and values are "stored," in what cognitive–affective configuration, and in what relationship to overarching aspects of personality or "self") (see also Harter, 1999, 2012). Again, in complex considerations of this sort, it is necessary to apprehend the landscape of our larger field, and observe that many different scientific and practice subfields currently are describing similar processes and phenomena, albeit with different theoretical precepts, terminologies, and methodological tools (e.g., Aronson, 2012; Auerbach, 1998; Bach, 1998; Curtis, 1991; Ferrari & Sternberg, 1998; Kohut & Wolf, 1978; Leary & Tangney, 2012; Muran, 2001; Newberg & Wadlman, 2006; Roth & Kulb, 1997; Ryan, Curren, & Deci, 2013). For example, from an analytic perspective, Adler and Bachant (1998) observe that

> Modification of fundamental structure is the highest aspiration . . .Freud's (1905/1953b) initial formulation of the self-preservation drive, Kohut's (1971, 1977, 1984) focus on the development of the self (including his principle of the primacy of preserving the self), and Winnicott's (1960) description of the protective function of the false self, each represents an important contribution to the analyst's understanding of the ways in which the individual actively strives to preserve the cohesive dynamic and representational structures that anchor a sense of secure identity. (pp. 459–460)

Notably, John Bowlby (1973), the psychoanalytically trained "father" of attachment theory, likewise maintained that affective development was similarly regulated, through a series of dyadic and intrapsychic processes that cohered around sets of "working models of attachment figures and of self" (p. 203) (see also Bowlby, 1969, 1980). Implicit in this attachment-based frame is the notion that such processes must be grounded in a neurobiological substrate. In other words, we do not form the attachments we do without an underlying neurobiological basis for them. That is not to say that a neurobiological level of analysis is sufficient for understanding the acquisition of beliefs and values, but undoubtedly is necessary, since it is hard to imagine how beliefs and values could exist without brain-based activity, which includes a neurobiological dimension. Few have done more to advance our understanding of such processes than Andrew Newberg.[2] The work of Newberg and colleagues has identified brain-based differences that are associated with various "states" of belief (e.g., atheists, Buddhists, nuns, Pentacostals, etc.) via brain blood flow/imaging techniques (e.g., functional magnetic resonance imaging or fMRI). Importantly, Newberg allows for—in fact insists upon—a recognition that multiple factors interact in the acquisition of beliefs and values, including aspects of perception, cognition, social consensus, and emotional value. Specifically,

> these four interacting spheres of influence. . .allow us to identify, explore, evaluate, and compare a wide variety of beliefs, from our most mundane evaluations

---

[2] For current perspective regarding the work of Newberg and colleagues, see www.andrewnewberg.com

of the world to the most extraordinary visions that illuminate our purpose in life. These influences affect the strength, power, and relative truth of a specific belief. Each circle of influence has a "volume control," and the greater the overall volume, the more real and truthful that belief becomes (Newberg & Waldman, 2006, p. 22).

Regarding such acquisitional processes, and consistent with the EI Self described in Chapter 3, Newberg further maintains that the origins of our beliefs are determined heavily by the familial and sociocultural context in which we are raised, noting

> . . .we have no choice but to believe. From the moment we are born, we depend on others to teach us about the world. As children, we are given a specific language, a particular religion, and a taste of science, and we unconsciously assume that we are learning facts about the world. We are not. We are simply being told what to believe. (p. 25)

At an applied level, such perspective is resonant with the lived experience of Elaine, described at the outset of this chapter, who reportedly was "told"—among other "truths"—that girls and women were to be subordinated to boys and men, a "truth" she perhaps had no "choice" but to believe until such beliefs no longer were reconcilable with her emerging experience of self, others, and the larger world.

For Elaine and all of us, then, what is the basis for this "specific language" we are given? As Bugental, Johnston, New, and Silvester (1998) observe,

> Parents' early social experiences, primarily with their own parents, form the basis for knowledge structures concerning caregiving and child behavior that are stored schematically . . .Such knowledge structures act as chronically accessible schemas that are easily retrieved in response to relevant events. (p. 462)

Although the nature of how and why beliefs and values come to be structured as they are remains a vital point of inquiry, more has been noted about the variables that tend to be associated with aspects of structural stasis or change. Here, both researchers and practitioners agree that structure, once established, often is quite stable, if not immutable. That is, once beliefs and values are internalized, the tendency is to resist efforts or evidence that might contradict or compromise their integrity, a reality that will be immediately familiar to clinicians, educators, policy makers, and other change agents, broadly defined. Scholarship on resistance, closedness, and openness speaks directly to these maintenance or preservation processes, which are key to EI Theory and considered next.

Maintaining Beliefs and Values

Adler and Bachant (1998) note that "resistance" is nothing less than a client's attempt to preserve and protect his or her intrapsychic world from being seen, known, or altered, even as the client may recognize that this structure is not congruent with his or her own life goals and objectives. At the same time, as analysts (and other therapists as well as clinical supervisors) have recognized the "everyday" nature of resistance, so too do they understand that resistance is "an inevitable and even healthy phenomenon. It guards psychic equilibrium in dangerous—though archaically conceived—circumstances, until an improved situation can be substituted" (p. 456). Although often conceptualized in "defensive" terms, resistance—for "clients" and humans writ large—basically serves a self-preservation function in that it "attempts to reestablish homeostatic equilibrium in response to disruptive tensions clinically identifiable as anxiety, depression, shame, and guilt, and the emotional states that give warning of potentially traumatic psychic threat" (p. 456). As Castonguay (2000) observes, ". . .because the exploration of emotions and the challenge of long-standing beliefs and interpersonal patterns are by definition threatening, client's resistance is viewed as part of the therapeutic process, not as a detrimental element" (p. 272). Furthermore, it should be noted that the phenomenon of resistance is not limited to "adults," as Sommers-Flanagan, Richardson, and Sommers-Flanagan (2011) document vis-à-vis therapeutic work with adolescents. As they comment, "More recent resistance formulations depathologize client resistance, no longer locating it within the psyche of the client and noting that psychotherapists themselves may be responsible for resistance" (p. 70). Moreover, such "resistance" processes operate at multiple levels—from the individual, to the group, to the societal, as Beier (1984) prophetically recognized via his "application of a model of psychotherapy to world problems," particularly the rise of fundamentalist thought. As he noted three decades ago, "Resistance to change is at least one base to the understanding of a fundamentalist philosophy. Resistance can be defined as a wish to stay with the problems one knows rather than the ones dictated by existential demands" (p. 1281).

In trying to apprehend the specific elements of resistance, consider the perspective of Pomerantz, Chaiken, and Tordesillas (1995), who identified "embeddedness" (the degree to which an attitude or issue is linked to an individual's overarching "self-concept, value system, and knowledge structure") and "commitment" (the relative degree or strength of "one's commitment to a particular position") as two factors associated with the relative strength of various attitudes/beliefs as well as resistance to attitude/belief change. According to these scholars,

> when individuals are highly committed to their position, they may be motivated to defend their attitude and associated beliefs, even at the cost of accuracy . . . this dimension may be indicative of attitudes that are strongly set in a larger cognitive structure encompassing values, identities, and knowledge. (p. 417)

Kruglanski and Webster focused on an allied aspect of cognitive–affective equilibration: namely, the human need to minimize ambiguity and the attendant loss of certitude about what "is" and "is not" real or true in the individual case. As they note, "cognitive closure refers to individuals' desire for a firm answer to a question and an aversion toward ambiguity" and exists "along a continuum anchored at one end with a strong need for closure and at the other end with a strong need to avoid closure" (Kruglanski & Webster, 1996, p. 264). Although focused primarily on the social psychological realm, and offering compelling data in support of this framework, such processes also are immediately recognizable to the clinical supervisor or practitioner—or change agent, for that matter—and descriptive of the central dilemma many students experience during education and training, clients encounter in therapy, and advocates encounter in the "real world"—namely, the motivation to "close one's mind," "seize" upon a particular explanation of a presenting problem, and reject alternative perspectives on the issue at hand, typically when such "knowledge" is freighted with implications for one's own self.

In this regard, Openness to Experience—one of the "Big Five" factors of personality—perhaps comes closest to the sort of applied end point that many supervisors attempt to inculcate in their student trainees, and psychotherapists attempt to discern and facilitate in their clients.[3] As typically understood and defined, Openness to Experience "describes imaginative, curious, and exploratory tendencies as opposed to rigid, practical, and traditional tendencies" (McCrae & Costa, 2013, p. 16) and is "a broad and general dimension, seen in vivid fantasy, artistic sensitivity, depth of feeling, behavioral flexibility, intellectual curiosity, and unconventional attitudes" (McCrae, 1996, p. 323).

Informing so much of the research in this larger area, the seminal contributions of Milton Rokeach remain salient. As McCrae (1996) summarized, Rokeach argued in his 1960 volume, *The Open and Closed Mind*, that

> regardless of ideological content, a rigid cognitive organization of attitudes and values leads to predictable social consequences, including prejudice and authoritarian submission. He also showed that dogmatism was related to a wide range of psychological variables (e.g., aesthetic sensitivity), thus anticipating later conceptions of the dimension of Openness. (p. 325)

Perhaps the most explicit clinical consideration of such processes vis-à-vis Piagetian theory was articulated by Wachtel (1981, 2008), who derived a linkage between the Freudian concept of "transference" with Piagetian notions of assimilation and accommodation. His compelling account of how schemas activated by the transference relationship involve "affect" as well as "defense" was not explicitly addressed by Piaget, but can help account for why schemas are so often resistant to modification in the context of the therapeutic relationship, a key consideration of EI Theory (see also McLeod, 2009).

From a more applied perspective, Heller and Northcut (1998) describe the interactions among such "equilibration" processes and the concomitant implications for assessment and intervention. For example, Heller and Northcut maintain that a careful evaluation of schemas and attributions,

> when completed as part of a general ego psychological assessment, engages the client, facilitates the integration of historical and current affects and events, and offers a means of systematically exploring and challenging motivating beliefs and assumptions about how the world operates. (pp. 185–186)

To conduct such evaluations, it is necessary not only to identify historical events that may have etiological relevance but also to consider the functional consequences of such experiences, and the meaning associated with them, at multiple levels. This assessment activity is directed toward an understanding of the specific schemas and attributions that comprise a client's larger worldview of self, other, and the world as well as how this worldview affects perception of past, present, and future.

In the context of the aforementioned research and theory as well as attendant applications, it would appear that beliefs and values are acquired, maintained, and modified vis-à-vis powerful, often nonconscious, interactions among developmental, affective, and attributional processes that become "stored" in memory to be sure, but

---

[3] As Dollinger et al., (1996) note, however, the therapeutic understanding of openness, which refers to "an individual's self-disclosive tendencies or lack of defensiveness . . . are not necessarily implicated by the concept of openness to experience (McCrae, 1994)" (p. 24).

also in constitutive aspects of personality or what has been variously described as "self."[4] Given the embedded nature of beliefs and values, it also should be of no surprise that their alteration would be resisted or that—in extreme cases—aspects of one's external world could be experienced as so threatening to the stability of one's sense of self to be worthy of destruction. Depending upon their strength, and the sociocultural context in which they evolved and preponderate, the beliefs and values people claim as their own are far more than idiosyncratic artifacts of different life histories that may be modified or removed like software code; they rather are akin to living, nervous tissue, the potential loss of which is extremely threatening to the human organism.[5]

In addition to the expositional aspects of the preceding theoretical frameworks, and the implication that such beliefs and values are acquired during socialization and adaptation to a prevailing sociocultural context, the relationship of "beliefs and values" to other allied conceptual frameworks and major programs of research, such as authoritarianism and attribution theory, may be evident as well. For example, prior to development of The Values Survey (Rokeach, 1967) noted earlier, Rokeach (1956) developed a measure of authoritarianism called *The Dogmatism (D) Scale*, which has been researched extensively as a measure of general authoritarianism, and is "designed to measure individual differences in open versus closed belief systems" particularly in relation to politics and religion (Christie, 1991, p. 560). At a more general level, Rokeach recognized also that beliefs and values were, in a very real sense, causal attributions about reality, in that believing something to be true about oneself, others, or entities/systems within the larger world, implied something about the way in which an individual made causal meaning. For example, relevant to this discussion, and prescient of the September 11, 2001 terrorist attacks in the United States, Rokeach (1979) noted that:

> Generally neglected in theories of beliefs, attitudes, and values, and neglected also in attribution theories, is an analysis of the extent to which existential and causal beliefs are implied whenever we say a person has an attitude, a philosophy of life, a belief system, a political ideology, or a religious or scientific outlook. In all such instances existential attributions as well as causal attributions are made and the two are so closely tied to one another, and tied also to evaluative and prescriptive–proscriptive beliefs, that it is difficult to sort out chicken from egg. Racists, for example, account for the impoverished conditions and performance of Blacks by first attributing the existence of certain attributes to them, such as lack of effort or laziness, and by then making causal attributions to explain the existential attributions, such as inferior genes, or God having decreed it that way (p. 276). . .Humans will engage in conflict with one another and even go to war with one another not so much over whether attributions are internal [attributed to genes, free will, etc.] or external [attributed to Zionism, God, etc.], but over which attributions are the more valid. Perhaps more to the

---

[4] Sources that are especially relevant to this perspective include Aronson, 2012; Baumeister and Vohs, 2012; Cross and Gore, 2012; Csikszentmihalyi, 1990; de Laszlo, 1959; Ferrari, 1999; Flapan and Fenchel, 1987; Harter, 1999, 2012; Kagan, 1982; Kohut and Wolf, 1978; Leary, 2002; Leary and Tangney, 2012; Levinson, 1978; Manstead and Hewstone, 1999; Margolis, 1998; Morf and Mischel, 2012; Oyserman, Elmore, and Smith, 2012; Reber, Allen, and Reber, 2009; Tesser, Stapel, and Wood, 2002; Weston, 1992; and, Wilber, 2000.

[5] Sources that are especially relevant to this perspective include Aronson, 2012; Feather, 1992, 1994, 1995; Emery, Wade, and McLean, 2009; Feather and McKee, 2012; Frijda, Manstead, and Bem, 2000; Kuchel, 2003; Maslow, 1954, 1964, 1968, 1971; Newberg and Waldman, 2006; Rokeach, 1956, 1960, 1973; Rokeach and Ball-Rokeach, 1989; Schwartz, 1992, 2012; Schwartz and Bilsky, 1987, 1990; and Schwartz and Boehnke, 2004.

point, wars have been fought over *whose* rather than *which* existential and causal attributions are the more valid. (p. 279)

From this perspective, beliefs and attributions are inextricably linked, in that an attribution is nothing less than a *belief* about etiology. In short, these two exemplars of belief scholarship—authoritarianism and attribution theory—not only are aligned closely with the seminal contributions of value-based scholars including Rokeach, Schwartz, and Feather, such vibrant programs of research are at the very heart of what we know about the acquisition and expression of beliefs and values in general. More to the point, the voluminous research on authoritarianism and attribution theory illustrates much about how such beliefs are acquired in the first place, and as such, speaks directly to issues of socialization and development, processes which must be accounted for—from the standpoint of the Equilintegration or EI Model—if we are to understand not only what human beings believe and value, but why.

EI Exemplar 1: Authoritarian Beliefs and Values

As a construct, authoritarianism is well established with roots within the social sciences extending back to the 1930s (Christie, 1991). However, it was not until the publication of Adorno, Frenkel-Brunswik, Levinson, and Sanford's (1950) *The Authoritarian Personality* that the construct received widespread attention. This program of research produced the well-known California F Scale, which was "one of the most widely used scales" during the second half of the twentieth century (Christie, 1991, p. 501). In essence, the F Scale (which stands for prefascist tendencies) assesses the tendency toward obedience to authority, nationalism, anti-intellectualism, and other ethnocentric beliefs; and indeed, the F Scale and its many derivatives over the years have continued to demonstrate that measures of authoritarianism, though variously defined and not without criticism, are associated with a range of issues including

> . . . attitudes toward contemporary social issues such as AIDS (Cunningham, Dollinger, Satz, & Rotter, 1991; Witt, 1989), the environment (Schultz & Stone, 1994), violence against women (Walker, Rowe, & Quinsey, 1993), feminism (Duncan, Peterson, & Winter, 1997; Haddock & Zanna, 1994), and the success and failure of current political leaders (Feather, 1993; McCann, 1991; McCann & Stewin, 1987). (in Peterson, Smirles, & Wentworth, 1997, p. 1202)

Most recently, the work of Robert Altemeyer and colleagues has invigorated such research by carefully examining the statistical properties of various items and constructs from the original F Scale, and retaining only those that could be justified strongly on empirical grounds. Specifically, Altemeyer's Right Wing Authoritarianism (RWA) scale "can be defined usefully as the covariation of authoritarianism, submission, authoritarian aggression, and conventionalism," and shows consistency across a range of cultures (Altemeyer & Hunsberger, 1992, p. 114; see also Ekehammar, Akrami, & Gylje, 2004; Mirels & Dean, 2006; Feather & McKee, 2012).

Considerable theory and data indicate that such authoritarian beliefs—like beliefs and values in general—are acquired throughout development and socialization processes variously described as "identification," "imitation," "internalization," "introjection," and "reinforcement," among related constructs (e.g., Aronson, 2012; Cummings, Davies, & Campbell, 2000; Dalhouse & Frideres, 1996; Ekehammar et al., 2004; Fonagy, 1996; Kaslow, Celano, & Dreelin, 1995; Kirkpatrick & Shaver, 1990;

Koestner, Losier, Vallerand, & Carducci, 1996; Mirels & Dean, 2006; Moskowitz, 2005; Myers, 1996; Simon, 1996; Snyder, Velasquez, Clark, & Means-Christensen, 1997; Zeller, 1991). This notion—that family and parental environments are key to the "transmission" of beliefs and values—is by no means new, as many scholars have described the nature and impact of such acquisitional processes across contexts and cultures (e.g., Baumrind, 1971; Cummings et al., 2000; Duncan & Stewart, 1995; Newberg & Waldman, 2006; Peritti & Statum, 1984).

One of the more innovative programs of research relevant to the acquisition and expression of authoritarian beliefs and values has been conducted by Bill Peterson and colleagues, who have studied the dialectical relationship between authoritarianism, as initially conceptualized by Adorno and others, with Erikson's seminal work on generativity, a construct closely aligned with "openness." Among other implications, Peterson, Smirles, and Wentworth (1997) found that "those who scored high on authoritarianism were closed minded and uninterested in creative pursuits, whereas those who scored high on generativity were open minded and interested in imaginative endeavors." As the authors note, "These results are consistent with Rokeach's (1960) ideas about dogmatism" (p. 1212) among other perspectives regarding Factor 5, Openness to Experience (see McCrae & Costa, 2013). Congruent with an overarching theme of this book, Peterson and colleagues conclude that "In a time when rejectivity of people on the basis of ethnic and racial similarities continues to flare up around the globe, it is important to understand how authoritarianism can be tempered with the tolerance that is often part of generativity" (p. 1214) (e.g., Peterson, Kim, McCarthy, Park, & Plamondon, 2011).

EI Exemplar 2: The Belief *in* Attribution

Fritz Heider, the "father of attribution theory," was the first to recognize explicitly that human beings actively "strive to make sense of their perceptions of behavior" as "naïve psychologist[s]" (Goddard & Miller, 1993, p. 84). Since Heider's initial observations, and as "the earliest topic in social-cognition applied to clinical psychology" (Kowalski & Leary, 1999, p. 5), attribution theory has come to be one of the most widely researched and important areas of inquiry within psychology (e.g., Aronson, 2012; Blanchard-Fields, Hertzog, & Horhota, 2011; Miller, 1995; Manusov & Harvey, 2001; Moskowitz, 2005). Why a particular attribution is preferred is key, because (as with authoritarianism), if we know why certain beliefs about etiology are valued more than others, we know something about the forces that construct ideology.

Much of the relevant research indeed has focused on understanding whether and how parental beliefs about causation may affect the development and functioning of offspring, and mediate parental behavior vis-à-vis the implicit rationalizing, interpretive, and justification functions that attributions serve (e.g., Aronson, 2012; Bugental et al., 1998; Blanchard-Fields et al., 2011; Dix, 1993; Manusov & Harvey, 2001; Miller, 1995; Moskowitz, 2005). Considerable evidence suggests that attributional processes in families (e.g., attributions made about children by parents) can have "positive" and "negative" effects on offspring, regardless of the "accuracy" or validity of the attribution itself (e.g., Cummings et al., 2000). If the effects of such processes were limited to the realm of subjective perception only (i.e., if what people believed about causation had no effect on anyone or anything else), then interest in attribution theory would probably not be as robust as it is. Such is not the case, however, since the attribution of characteristics or motives to others can affect not only the perception of self and others, but developmental and functional processes as well. Such realities become apparent in research on parental attributions toward children as we have known for decades. For example, as Dix (1993) observed over 20 years ago,

> attributing dispositions to children is important, not only because it alters parents' emotions and disciplinary behavior, but because, by expressing which dispositions they think children possess, parents directly influence children's views of who they are and how they should act. A principal hypothesis about attribution and socialization is that adults' attributions about children influence children's internalization of values and views of themselves. When told that they are clean, competitive, or altruistic, children do subsequently display behavior that is cleaner, more competitive, and more altruistic than when adults do not express these attributions. (p. 640)

As with the content of authoritarian beliefs and values, other factors also influence the types of attributions made. For example, parental mood or emotion seems to be a particularly salient mediator (e.g., Cummings et al., 2000). Moreover, different contexts and cultures may "provide parents with beliefs about children's fundamental nature or inherent dispositions—for example, beliefs about whether infants are fragile, social, and able to learn" as well as "values that specify which dispositions are important and which are trivial" (Dix, 1993, p. 634). Finally, researchers have convincingly demonstrated that the attributions spouses make about each other's conduct have implications for the spousal relationship and larger family system (e.g., Blanchard-Fields et al., 2011; Manusov & Harvey, 2001; Moskowitz, 2005).

The preceding discussion illustrates that many of the key beliefs and values people claim as their own (e.g., about the proper approach to child rearing, or why people do what they do) are a function, at least in part, of the kinds of beliefs and values that were "transmitted" to them during their own development; such beliefs and values are not mere artifacts of individual history, but may have a profound impact on their own development, behavior, and relations with others. Moreover, as cross-cultural evidence suggests, beliefs and values may differ in *content* as a function of different contexts, but the processes by which they are acquired seem relatively invariant—in other words, *what* we believe and value may differ; *that* we believe and value as a result of interacting affective, attributional, and developmental processes, does not (e.g., Wandschneider et al., 2016).

Transforming Beliefs and Values: The 7Ds

Thus far, we have described the "basics of belief" vis-à-vis key figures such as Rokeach, Schwartz, and Feather, before discussing how beliefs and values are acquired, maintained, and modified, including two major literatures—authoritarian personality and attribution theory—which exemplify what the Equilintegration or EI Model seeks to understand vis-à-vis research on beliefs and values. But in the final analysis, such research ultimately should illuminate phenomena that matter in the real world, however far our investigatory machinations may seem to reside from this destination. And in fact, many scholars—often the most hard-nosed—are deeply concerned about the world in which we live and what our children, and theirs, will inherit. These concerns are not mawkish affectations, but deadly serious and data-based, as the clearest thinkers in our midst get it, deeply: they apprehend the implications of our current trajectories for the well-being of our species and all living things, irrespective of whether local and global policy makers are able or willing to see and act upon the realities that we collectively face. Juxtaposed at that level, any singular effort—including the present hope to make sense of beliefs and values—is "less than a drop in the great blue motion of the sunlit sea." Even so, what choice do we have but to forge on in the hope that we might listen eventually to "the better angels of our nature?"[6]

One such effort—described in the final chapter of this book—is called *Cultivating the Globally Sustainable Self*. This research-to-practice summit series brings together "leaders from a range of big picture movements—conflict resolution, human rights, sustainability, global education, and religious and cultural understanding—in order to "learn from each other's missions, methods, goals, and activities." By

> bringing together local and global researchers, educators, students, advocates, leaders, and policy makers, we seek to understand better why and how transformation occurs, for whom, and under what circumstances. Ultimately, we intend to learn how to cultivate a more globally sustainable way of living, knowing, and being, and translate our findings into practical solutions for the enhancement of teaching, training, and learning (see Cultivating the Globally Sustainable Self, 2015).

By design, many models and methods will inform the deliberations of this assembly, including results from a multiyear, multi-institution initiative—the *Forum BEVI Project*—which was designed to assess the processes and outcomes of international, multicultural, and transformative learning (www.forumea.org/research-bevi-project.cfm). A collaboration between the International Beliefs and Values Institute (www.ibavi.org) and Forum on Education Abroad (www.forumea.org), one fundamental conclusion of this project was the "7Ds" (Shealy, 2014), which help explain why "beliefs and values" do or do not change, to what degree, for whom, and under what circumstances as a result of exposure to a change-oriented intervention. Specifying the variables that empirically seem to be associated with the degree of belief/value transformation that does—or does not—occur, the 7Ds are as follows: (a) *duration* (i.e., how long the intervention occurs); (b) *difference* (i.e., how different the experience of the intervention is from what the "self" of the experiencer is accustomed); (c) *depth* (i.e., what is the capacity of the learner to experience all that the intervention is able to convey); (d) *determine* (i.e., through formal and informal assessment, how well does the intervener understand his or her audience); (e) *design* (i.e., based upon knowledge of the audience and careful deliberation and development, what is the quality of the intervention); (f) *deliver* (i.e., how able is the intervener to fulfill the transformative potential of the intervention); and, (g) *debrief* (i.e., before, during, and after the intervention, how deeply does the intervener assess the nature of what has been experienced, and use such feedback to improve future interventions). As is illustrated in the following, these 7Ds may apply to a wide range of contexts.

---

[6] These quotes are excerpted respectively from the final scene of *Camelot* (1967), the musical, and Abraham Lincoln's first inaugural address in 1861. Despite the betrayal and disillusionment he experienced, Arthur knights young "Pelly" in the hope that he might realize again the "one brief shining moment that was known as Camelot." Lincoln, of course, was beseeching southerners in the United States—futilely, it turned out—to join in a process of reconciliation rather than war. Such quotes seem to capture the hope, and frustration, felt by those educators, scholars, and practitioners who seek to "make sense of beliefs and values" as well as the change agents among us, who inevitably must grapple with the implications of beliefs and values—for better or worse—on a daily basis.

For example, recall, from the outset of this chapter, the actual process by which Elaine appeared to experience transformation, and that several of these "Ds" seemed directly applicable in her case, including the first three: duration, difference, and depth. Certainly, our work together (well over a year) was of sufficient *duration* to allow the possibilities for change to emerge in what was a highly complex and rigidly held self-structure, which was embedded further with a larger family/sociocultural system that also was highly resistant to change. Moreover, the *difference* Elaine experienced across various psychotherapeutic milieus (from individual, to couples, to family, to in-home) was radically different from anything she had experienced before, compelling her over time to engage in an internal dialogue regarding the nature of what was "real" or "true" in her own life. Finally, although often fatiguing and burdensome, Elaine also clearly was able to experience the *depth* of what was unfolding within her—in terms of conflictual thoughts, deep feelings, and unmet needs—and therefore was able to access the transformative potential of the therapeutic process in order to make meaningful and substantive changes. The point is, these "7Ds" theoretically apply not just to "learning," per se, but to attendant processes of growth and development across a wide range of settings and populations, as described next via the following practice-based examples.

EI Exemplars in Practice

As noted, the first two "EI Exemplars" included well-established research literatures: authoritarian personality and attribution theory. But by design, the EI Model seeks to makes sense of beliefs and values across the domains of research and practice. In this regard, the "7Ds" apply to multiple attempts to transform beliefs and values as the following three exemplars illustrate, from what we call for in future leaders, to our approach toward international/multicultural education, to the training of mental health practitioners.

EI Exemplar 3: Leadership

As our first example of beliefs and values in practice, consider the work of Dyjak-LeBlanc, Brewster, Grande, White, and Shullman (2016) vis-à-vis leadership and organizational development. As they observe,

> a complex interaction among core needs (e.g., for attachment, affiliation) and formative variables (e.g., life history, culture) culminates in the beliefs and values we hold to be true, which subsequently impact how and why we experience self, others, and the larger world as we do. Such theory and data offer a complementary emphasis to the traditional focus on *who* good leaders are and *what* good leadership is. In the larger literature, much less attention has been devoted to questions of *why* leaders differ as they do in their experience of self, others, and the larger world as well as *how* to translate such understanding into effective strategies for leadership and organizational development. (p. 534)

To address such matters, Dyjak-LeBlanc et al. report on a comprehensive model of leadership and its belief/value implications and applications in a real world organization. Among other implications, on the basis of findings that were presented, analysis of small group process content, and workshop feedback, Dyjak-LeBlanc et al. offer four concluding points, which have additional implications for research and practice.

1. *First, leadership models matter.* As the authors note: "From the standpoint of leaders and leadership, the type of model to which we are drawn likely says a great deal about what we believe human beings are as well as why we do what we do" (p. 562).

2. *Second, beliefs and values are integral to leaders and leadership.* As the authors note: "An overarching strength and benefit from the leadership workshop was the importance of how it helped the participants gain a greater understanding of how beliefs and values develop in individuals, how differences and similarities emerge among leaders and the led, and ultimately how and why people function as they do" (p. 563).

3. *Third, leadership assessment reveals what is and is not working, and why.* As the authors note: ". . .the pattern of findings presented here suggests the need, opportunity, and benefits of more such reflection and subsequent actions along these lines in collaboration between executive and lower levels of leadership" (p. 565).

4. *Fourth, leadership models and assessment methods provide a road map for change.* As the authors note: ". . .if our assessment processes. . .are translated into flexible road maps that lead toward leadership and organizational growth, we and the people who work for and with us, will be the beneficiaries (p. 568).

EI Exemplar 4: Education
As another example of beliefs and values "in practice," Wandschneider et al. (2016) report the implications from the aforementioned Forum BEVI Project: a multi-institution, multiyear assessment of international, multicultural, and transformative learning initiative. Consider, for example, Implication 2, which was based upon a wide range of empirical and practice-based findings both in the classroom and in the field, locally and globally.

Implication 2. Education, broadly defined, is associated with—and likely causes—change in beliefs and values
Abundant quantitative and qualitative evidence from different types of learning experiences assessed by the Forum BEVI Project (e.g., study abroad, multicultural coursework, general education) indicate that students are likely to see and experience themselves, others, and the larger world differently following such experiences.

Among other empirically derived observations relevant to the preceding implications, the authors note the following:

> critical thinking as defined by the BEVI should be understood not only in terms of the relative attributional sophistication of human beings (e.g., the ability to understand the complexities of why we think, feel, and do what we do or why events happen as they do in the larger world). At a more complex level, it also appears that such capacities and inclinations may in fact be associated with our life histories, since a *higher degree* of Negative Life Events and Needs Closure appears to be associated with a *lower degree* of critical thinking as defined by the BEVI. . .In any case, the most basic finding here is that the relative sophistication and complexity of attributional tendencies about why people do what they do, or why events happen in the world as they do, increases with the more years of college or university that people experience. . .such results suggest that repeated exposure to complex concepts combined with multiple experiences in which one is required to understand, reflect upon, and justify the

rationale for beliefs and values in self, others, and the larger world may in fact be associated with the acquisition of more sophisticated attributional frameworks over time. (p. 430)

EI Exemplar 5: Mental Health

In addition to leadership and education, a final example that has long recognized the inextricable linkage between beliefs and values and real world practice is in the realm of mental health assessment and therapy, which in addition to the process for Elaine, also are addressed by respective chapters later in this book (Coates et al., 2016; Cozen et al., 2016). Although some scholars and practitioners have focused explicitly on the role of "belief" vis-à-vis mental health functioning (e.g., Aaron Beck, Albert Ellis), an overarching professional precept has been as follows: competent and ethical practitioners know what they and their clients believe and value, and why, and understand the potential impact of their own beliefs and values on clients, trainees, and others. In this space, it is not possible to do justice to all of the cogent findings and perspectives that speak to these issues, but several exemplars should provide sufficient context. In this regard, the first two theses in Allen Bergin's (1980) seminal article are particularly instructive: (a) "Values are an inevitable and pervasive part of psychotherapy" and (b) "Not only do theories, techniques, and criteria reveal pervasive value judgments, but outcome data comparing the effects of diverse techniques show that non-technical, value-laden factors pervade professional change processes" (p. 97). In a powerful call to address these issues, Bergin wrote,

> If we are unable to face our own values openly, it means we are unable to face ourselves, which violates a primary principle of professional conduct in our field. Since we expect our clients to examine their perceptions and value constructs, we ought to do likewise. The result will be improved capacity to understand and help people, because self-deceptions and role playing will decrease and personal congruence will increase. (p. 102)

Bergin's perspective over 30 years ago (see also Bergin, 1991) was by no means the first of its kind, but his view was prophetic and highly influential, and numerous studies have since supported his theses and basic premise regarding the "generality" of these issues to therapeutic processes and outcomes (e.g., Emery, Wade, and McLean, 2009; Hall & Hall, 1997; Harris, 1998; Kuchel, 2003; Picchioni, 1995; Shealy et al., 2012; Stern, 1996; Tjeltveit, 1999).

The problem here is not only or primarily with the clinical act, but rather with the lack of awareness of the epistemological underpinnings that legitimize that act (e.g., Kuchel, 2003; Shealy, 2004; Tjeltveit, 1999). That is, practitioners too often behave as though what they do somehow exists apart from an underlying system of thought that justifies or gives credence to that which they do. Because there is insufficient awareness or appreciation that all clinical activity is epistemologically grounded, clinicians may behave as though their interventions are beyond reproach, as though controversies have been sufficiently settled or are irresolvable or irrelevant. And of course, the history of the "helping professions" is littered with the wreckage of many different views of how humans work, how they are best described, what causes them to do what they do, what "abnormality" looks like, and how behavioral, emotional, and mental "health" or "adjustment" should be promoted. From phrenology and eugenics, to the contemporary and reductionistic inveiglement of "bad genes" and "chemical imbalances in the brain," it sometimes is comical and often tragic to reflect on our history in this regard (e.g., Aronson, 2012; Deacon, 2013; Horwitz, 2002; Staub, 2013).

On the other hand, putative nostrums that beliefs and values are "bad" or to be "rooted out" and disregarded lest they contaminate the therapeutic enterprise, are not only simplistic and unrealizable, they miss the point entirely. It certainly is the case that the beliefs and values of practitioners may harm clients, but such risks are attenuated substantively if practitioners understand what they believe and value and why, and endeavor to do the same with their clients. The key, then, is not to eliminate beliefs and values (as if that were possible, or desirable), but to understand the processes by which they are acquired, and the attendant ethical implications for practice and training (e.g., Bergin, 1980, 1991; Emery et al., 2009; Hall & Hall, 1997; Harris, 1998; Kuchel, 2003; Picchioni, 1995; Shealy et al., 2012; Stern, 1996; Tjeltveit, 1999). Ultimately, such perspectives are consistent with a constructivistic and postmodern view. From this stance, attempts to classify human behavior or characteristics, without recognizing the fluid continuum among cognitive, emotional, behavioral, and spiritual manifestations of human "distress," are likely to do as much harm as good, mainly because such categorical organizational systems underestimate subjective and contextual influences on such seemingly "objective" processes, insufficiently capture the dynamic interplay among these variables, and only dimly inform the inherent complexities of clinical practice (e.g., Deacon, 2013; Gergen, 1998, 1999; Gerhardt & Stinson, 1995; Horwitz, 2002; Neimeyer & Raskin, 2000; Raskin, 2012).

All that said, it is not as though we are just discovering that assessment and therapy may be a force for good as well as ill. As Gartner et al. (1990) summarized from the literature 25 years ago, ". . .therapists with rigid ideologies tend to evaluate their patients more harshly than those with less rigid beliefs. Clinicians who are ethnocentric and authoritarian were more likely than the other clinicians to discriminate against ethnic minorities and lower class patients" (p. 99). Similarly and more recently, Kuchel (2003) observes that,

> factors such as cultural beliefs and values have been given relatively little attention. That is surprising, given evidence suggesting that factors such as cultural beliefs and values strongly impact the diagnosis and treatment of mental illness. . .values, in particular, would appear to play a pivotal role in the clinical judgment process, in that it has been shown that therapists do not remain value free, even when they intend to. (pp. 11–12)

Ultimately, to address these complex matters in a systematic and comprehensive manner, there is a need for more compelling methods and approaches through which the beliefs and values of practitioners, supervisors, trainees, and clients may be evaluated, a point that has long been emphasized by many scholars, and is a key implication of the EI model and BEVI method described in this book (e.g., Coates et al., 2016; Cozen et al., 2016).

For example, as Beutler (1979) concluded even before Bergin's (1980) seminal article, therapists are obliged to engage in a ". . .detailed evaluation of their inner beliefs which they have heretofore kept carefully protected from external observation. . . Inspection of these values and their role is both ethically and practically required" (p. 438). Madell (1982) also observed over 30 years ago that "investigations need to focus on values specifically related to psychotherapy issues rather than on measures that suggest only general value similarity. . . Perhaps a new, more robust measure of values needs to be developed. . .before more striking relationships will emerge between values and possible therapeutic efficacy" (p. 60). A decade later, Vachon and Agresti (1992) noted that, "It is now an accepted fact that psychotherapy is a value-laden enterprise. . .Few authors, however, have offered ways of helping therapists to become aware of these values or even how to work with them." (p. 509). Also in the 1990s, McLeod and Machin (1998) contended that "academics and researchers need to provide the concepts and tools through which context can be measured, deconstructed and explained," and provide methods by which "a better understanding of factors involved in achieving the best fit between counsellor, counselling approach and counselling" can be ascertained (p. 335). As a final example, yet another decade later, Emery, Wade, and McLean (2009) concluded that specific and unhelpful therapists beliefs,

> have been found to contribute to therapist stress, including the need to work at peak efficiency over all situations with all clients; attitudes of rigidity, inflexibility and dogmatism with respect to the application of therapeutic models and process; the need to appear knowledgeable; a low tolerance for ambiguity; the need for emotional and therapeutic control, and an intolerance for client emotionality. . . .[thus] it has been suggested that the active identification and challenging of unhelpful beliefs in therapist training and supervision, with a view to developing more adaptive, helpful alternative beliefs, may be important in maintaining therapist mental health. This may be of particular importance for trainee or inexperienced therapists who appear to be more susceptible to the symptoms of intrusion and avoidance. (p. 84)

Fortunately, it appears that the mental health field in general, and the profession of psychology in particular, are beginning to recognize the central mediating role of beliefs and values across all phases and levels of clinical practice and functioning. For instance, the Council of Chairs of Training Councils (CCTC)—the umbrella organization of doctoral, internship, and postdoctoral training associations in professional psychology—developed a document dealing explicitly with such matters. Specifically, its consensus-based policy document entitled *Comprehensive Evaluation of Student-Trainee Competence in Professional Psychology Programs* recognizes the need to evaluate student and trainee competency in areas such as:

> . . .interpersonal and professional competence (e.g., the ways in which student-trainees relate to clients, peers, faculty, allied professionals, the public, and individuals from diverse backgrounds or histories) [as well as] self-awareness, self-reflection, and self-evaluation (e.g., knowledge of the content and potential impact of one's own beliefs and values on clients, peers, faculty, allied professionals, the public, and individuals from diverse backgrounds or histories) (see Council of Chairs of Training Councils, 2004; see also Coates et al., 2016; Cozen et al., 2016).

Defining Belief and Values

At this point then, informed by the research and practice literatures and exemplars that now have been described, it is possible to offer a working definition of "belief," which essentially represents a psychometric and statistical default, by (a) examining how beliefs cluster together empirically, (b) illustrating the relationship of beliefs to allied constructs (e.g., values, schemas, attitudes, worldviews), and (c) reconciling this empirical reality with theoretical convention and real world practice. In the first place, recall for Rokeach that value systems were "part of a functionally integrated cognitive system in which the basic units of analysis are beliefs. Clusters of beliefs form attitudes that are functionally and cognitively connected to the value system" (Braithwaite & Scott, 1991, p. 662). Because Rokeach was interested in how these value systems were associated with a range of predictable processes and outcomes, much of his research and measurement work occurred at this level of analysis even as he clearly contended that "beliefs" were the "basic units of analysis." As noted, Rokeach was not alone in this regard as other pioneers also granted the legitimacy of this key point. Schwartz (2012), for example, observes that "values are beliefs linked inextricably to affect" (p. 3). Likewise, Feather (1995) maintains that

> *values* can be conceived as abstract structures that involve the beliefs that people hold about desirable ways of behaving or about desirable end states. These beliefs transcend specific objects and situations, and they have a normative, or oughtness quality about them. (p. 1135)

Consistent with other belief/value scholars, Newberg and Waldman (2006) also conclude that "our values and ethics are clearly beliefs" (p. 27). Moreover, beginning with the *Oxford English Dictionary*—which defines beliefs in terms of (a) a feeling that something exists or is true, especially one without proof; (b) a firmly held opinion; (c) trust or confidence in; and (d) religious faith—Newberg and Walman conclude from a biological and neuropsychological perspective that "a belief can be defined as any perception, cognition, or emotion that the brain assumes, consciously or unconsciously, to be true" (pp. 20–21). As a final exemplar, Leuty (2013) observes that "most definitions contend that values (a) are beliefs, (b) relate to desirable end states or behaviors, (c) are consistent across situations, (d) guide choice and evaluation of behavior and events, and (e) are ordered by relative importance" (p. 363).

Despite such consensus, however, the logical relationship of "belief" to other constructs (e.g., values, schemas, attitudes, worldviews, etc.) still seems unclear. That is because if beliefs are the most basic building blocks, it stands to reason that other conceptual entities that are constructed from beliefs must be composed of them. In other words, whatever structural features or characteristics there may be of the belief "building block," it follows that other emergent constructs would at least have to account for these underlying features and characteristics of "belief" in their own functioning or dynamics. In short, it does not make sense to disconnect this most basic material—belief—from other constructs that are built from them. Consider this supposition from a metaphorical perspective. If you are building a house from brick, it would not be advisable to ignore the properties of a brick when laying the foundation, constructing the rooms that comprise the first floor, or a second story that is placed atop that floor, or the larger house that ultimately emerges from the assemblage of these bricks. Of course, the physical dynamics of the overarching house are going to include interactions among a wide range of variables that likely could not be understood only by understanding the properties of the brick. And yet, without knowing the properties of the brick, it would not be possible to calculate the properties or apprehend the dynamics of the larger house. In short, understanding the brick is necessary but not sufficient for understanding the house. That is to say, the house cannot be understood if the brick is not understood, but the house will not be understood only by understanding the brick.[7]

So it is with beliefs and their derivatives, which include—in the present framework—*values, schemas, attitudes,* and *worldviews.* Consistent with Rokeach's (1973) original proposition and the consensus that followed, the most basic unit of analysis for the EI model and BEVI method presented in later chapters is at the "belief" level. Expanding upon the preceding discussion, there are five specific advantages to this approach.

1. *Understanding Terminology.* By deliberately recognizing that a "belief" is the most basic unit of analysis, we avoid the confusion in the literature by the indiscriminant swapping of terms (e.g., beliefs, values, opinions, attitudes, worldviews) as though they are equivalent levels of analysis. They are not. Like the brick parts that comprise the whole house, our collective conflation of such terminology in writing and practice has obscured substantive similarities and differences among these levels of analysis, which further has impeded our ability to understand these constructs and communicate clearly with one another from a common point of departure.

2. *Understanding Individual Differences.* Because values rightly are composed of beliefs as Rokeach (1973), Schwartz (2012), and Feather (1995) aver, when we do not explicate this foundational component, we inadvertently sacrifice the ability to understand microlevel interactions among beliefs, which are essential to understanding individual differences. Individuals do differ in the "values" they hold, but because values represent a second level of analysis, which builds upon the most "basic unit of analysis," the belief-level variance that is there to be ascertained is collapsed into value-level variance, which essentially aggregates differences among individuals in order to make group-based comparisons.

3. *Understanding Values Composition.* From the standpoint of ecological validity, human beings typically do not reveal the "values" they hold through singular statements of belief. Instead, constellations of belief statements lead to our conclusions about the values we and others hold (e.g., about freedom, equality, etc.). If our focus only is on the aggregated beliefs that comprise values—instructive as this level of analysis is—we minimize the complex interactions that occur at a belief level, which may lead to differences in how and to what degree values are in fact maintained by two individuals, who both may endorse the same "value," but do so for different belief-based reasons, and to varying degrees (e.g., it may be that differences in value-based commitments are due to different combinations of belief-based commitments). Only by considering belief as the basic "unit of analysis," at the level of terminology and measurement, do we avoid the inadvertent attenuation of very real interactions that may be occurring at the individual level.

4. *Understanding Etiology.* A more fine-grained analysis, which adopts beliefs as the "basic unit of analysis," also allows us to examine matters of etiology, a crucial but relatively neglected dimension of such scholarship and practice. More specifically, it is highly relevant to understand *what* the differences are between individuals, groups, and societies in terms of belief/value-based preferences; as important, however, is understanding *why* such differences manifest in the first place. In this regard, theory helps us distinguish between *descriptive* and *interpretive* levels of analysis. That is, we need to examine *what* constitutes change (e.g., how we know it is happening), a descriptive level of analysis, as well as *why* it is occurring

---

[7] Of course, the work of Rokeach, Schwartz, and Feather—among other theorists—has done a great deal to explicate what these additional value-based properties are, which emerge from the combining together of "beliefs," the most basic building block.

(e.g., the rationale for why the changes we observe are in fact occurring), an interpretive level of analysis. We may be wrong or incomplete in our conclusions, but there can be no substitute for engaging in an ongoing interpretation or explanation of why we observe the changes—or lack thereof—that we do. The importance of attending to these complementary but different levels of analysis—between descriptive (*what*) and interpretive (*why*)—cannot be overemphasized when striving to "make sense of beliefs and values." Regarding *what* macrolevel factors (e.g., gender, ethnicity, education) differentiate and predict different belief/values profiles, there is no better exemplar than the exhaustive and longitudinal work of Ronald Inglehart and international colleagues through the World Values Survey and European Values Study Surveys, which allow for a highly detailed analysis of the beliefs and values of peoples from 81 different societies around the world (see Inglehart, Basáñez, & Moreno, 1998; Inglehart, Basáñez, Díez-Medrano, Halman, & Luijkx, 2004). Among other analytic possibilities, their sourcebook

> enables the reader to compare the responses to hundreds of questions across societies from all over the world covering the full spectrum of economic, political, and cultural variation. It also enables the reader to examine the differences between the responses of men and women in each society; and to examine generational differences; and differences linked with education and income, and according to whether the respondent has "Materialistic," "Mixed," or "Postmaterialist" values. . . . (Inglehart et al., 2004, p. 2)

Such a compendium not only provides a wealth of descriptive information vis-à-vis beliefs and values—the *what*—it also offers insight into the *why* of beliefs and values, mainly because belief statements around the world are comparable across a wide range of demographic/background variables (e.g., the role of gender, education, income, etc.). In this way, the association of such background/demographic variables to belief/value content may be ascertained as well in a manner that is consistent with multiple analyses in later chapters of this book (i.e., by contributing substantially to our understanding of etiology).

By extension then, as we move from macro- to microlevel analyses (i.e., from societies to individuals), it behooves us to structure our measurement and research in a way that allows for a fine-grained examination of *why* individual A has internalized X versus Y value systems—a process that should take biopsychosocial processes into account (e.g., affect, cognition, context, development, need). By doing so, we may apprehend the interacting complexity of these processes as they occur in real time, across development, and for real human beings. Although macrolevel observations regarding the relative role of values in shaping aspects of behavior are highly useful, the primary focus on values may be an artifact of various subfields within psychology playing a dominant role in the explication of what "values" are and how they should be studied. Again, there is no question that such a deductive focus has increased immeasurably our understanding of the central role that values play in human affairs. But more deliberate inclusion of scholars and practitioners who encounter and work with beliefs and values on the basis of deep immersion in the psychological life of individual human beings (e.g., advocates, clinicians, educators) may, at the very least, inform our understanding of what is happening at this deeper, idiographic level of the human condition. From this inductive process, which is aligned with a case study methodology, we may illuminate further depth-based principles and processes through which human beings develop the beliefs, values, attitudes, and worldviews that they do.

5. *Understanding Hierarchical and Definitional Distinctions.* In the final analysis, by starting with "belief" as the most basic level of analysis—and specifying its hierarchical relationship to values, schemas, attitudes, and worldviews—we are able simultaneously to differentiate and juxtapose these constructs in order to clarify their relationship to one another. From the perspective of the BEVI, discussed in Chapter 4, such clarification means that these constructs may be identified and studied empirically, in a manner that is informed psychometrically via factor analysis, and its attendant hierarchical organization. Specifically, a *"belief"* is akin to a single BEVI item, such as "Shame can be a good motivator for children." A *"value"* is akin to a subscale (i.e., a subfactor), which essentially is a clustering of beliefs that are differently worded but occupy similar statistical and conceptual space. A *"schemattitude"* (from "schema" and "attitude" scholarship, typically engaged in by clinical practitioner scholars and social psychology researchers, respectively) is akin to a scale, such as Sociocultural Openness on the BEVI, which is composed of two or more subfactors, which may be differentiated statistically and conceptually, but also are correlated sufficiently as to "load" on the same scale. A *"worldview"* is akin to all that is represented by the assessment instrument as a whole; using the BEVI, for example, someone's worldview includes the sum total of all scales taken together, which collectively represents (i.e., samples) the "big picture" of how an individual sees self, others, and the world at large. Because "belief" is the most basic building block of this system, it is defined in detail; the remaining three constructs (values, schemattitudes, worldview) are derivative terms that also are empirically (i.e., statistically) verifiable.

In summary, then (and integrative of additional perspectives discussed later in this chapter), from a definitional standpoint, a *belief*:

1. is an internalized and discrete version of reality (i.e., a mental representation about self, others, or the world at large) that can influence and mediate the experience and expression of needs, feelings, thoughts, and behaviors;
2. can vary along dimensions of cognitive complexity and affective intensity;
3. is subjectively experienced to be relatively "true" or "false" and/or "good" or "bad";
4. may or may not be empirically verifiable (i.e., the believer may not be able to prove or reliably demonstrate that a belief is true or false);
5. may or may not be consciously accessible (i.e., the believer may not be aware of his or her belief);
6. if consciously accessible, is typically verbalized in relativistic terms as a "truth" or "goodness" statement about self, others, and/or the world at large;
7. typically exists in a synergistic relationship to other beliefs in that a belief stated in one direction often is matched by one or more counterparts that exist in relative degrees of opposition to it;
8. may be characterized by four interrelated "dimensions of belief"—favorability, veracity, intensity, and congruency—and four "points of self-access"—hard structure, soft structure, crack in the structure, and space in the structure;
9. manifests along a "continuum of belief," ranging from "committed certitude" to "noncommitted skepticism"; and,
10. exists in the service of core human needs—appetitive, attachment, affective, acknowledgment, activation, affiliative, actualizing, attunement, and awareness—and emerges from an interaction among four levels of self—endoself, mesoself, ectoself, and exoself.

By definitional extension, then, a *value* is the clustering of two or more beliefs that are distinguishable but correlated within the same affective, cognitive, and conceptual space. A *schemattitude*—from schema and attitude—is the clustering of two or more values that are distinguishable but correlated within the same affective, cognitive, and conceptual space. A *worldview* is the gestalt of internalized beliefs, values, and schemattitudes through which self, others, and the larger world are experienced and explained.

Definitional Implications

A number of implications emerge from the preceding definition: (a) the relationship of beliefs to values, schemas, attitudes, and worldviews; (b) the need to explicate what is meant by the "four dimensions of belief" and "four points of self-access," which exist along a "Continuum of Belief"; (c) the fact that we cannot make sense of beliefs and values unless we understand them as manifesting from core human needs and interacting levels of self; and (d) the observation that "nonbelief" is still "belief." As we conclude our discussion of "EI Component I"—*belief*—each of these final implications is considered in turn.

The Relationship of Beliefs to Values, Schemas, Attitudes, and Worldviews

As may be evident, there are a number of implications of the "belief" definition that has just been presented, which will manifest throughout the chapters that follow. In the first place, the preceding definition of belief is consistent with, and informed by, the preceding definition and accompanying literature of what is meant by the term, "value," which is a higher order level of analysis. As we have done for decades now, it is very possible and useful to observe what happens when we combine beliefs into one or more *values*, which again, "(a) are beliefs, (b) relate to desirable end states or behaviors, (c) are consistent across situations, (d) guide choice and evaluation of behavior and events, and (e) are ordered by relative importance" (Leuty, 2013, p. 363). Hopefully, by taking "belief" as the most basic level of analysis, our observations of "what happens" at the level of "value"—and how, why, for whom, and under what circumstances—may be better understood, predicted, and studied. In other words, by deliberating accounting for the fundamental characteristics, features, and dynamics of "belief" from a definitional standpoint, we are more likely to "make sense of" the values, schemas/attitudes, and worldviews that are composed of these belief building blocks.[8]

---

[8] To elaborate further, as noted in the "brick" metaphor, nothing in this perspective should be construed to mean that "values" do not possess properties beyond those of individual beliefs. In fact, as various analyses illustrate later in this book, subfactors on the BEVI, which represent the statistical assemblage of related items as part of a larger scale, capture more from an attributional and affective standpoint than a single belief, by virtue of the fact that the singular contributions of individual beliefs are now combined together into a more encompassing construct. By extension, the same conceptual and empirical phenomena apply to larger levels of analysis—schemas, attitudes, and worldviews. Ultimately, though, as multiple scholars beginning with Rokeach have observed, beliefs are the most basic building blocks. Other constructs are composed of them. The present approach attempts to acknowledge and account for such theoretical, empirical, and applied considerations in a way that is consistent with, and draws upon, theory and research at these successive levels of analysis: beliefs, values, schemas, attitudes, worldviews.

Four Dimensions of Beliefs

As a second implication, some additional definitional "unpacking" may be helpful at this point in order to provide further context for the empirical findings and applied applications that follow. Consider first the observation that a single belief statement may be endorsed differentially by different believers, who all may share a similar conviction, but do so in markedly different ways from one another. This defining characteristic of belief is represented by Table 2.1, which explicates the "Four Dimensions of Belief."

These four dimensions essentially describe the ways in which beliefs may be "held"—as relatively good or bad (favorability); true or false (veracity); strongly or weakly (intensity); or consistently or inconsistently (congruency). Thus, all four of these dimensions must be considered in order to understand what, how, and why we believe as we do.

Four Points of Self-Access

At a complementary level, as is discussed next and in Chapter 3 via the EI Self, it should also be noted that access to one's beliefs (i.e., the degree to which one's own beliefs are known or knowable by one's own self or by others) may depend upon whether such beliefs are experientially organized in terms of *Hard Structure* (rigidly fixed and strongly held), *Soft Structure* (susceptible to change and loosely held), *Crack in the Structure* (two or more beliefs that are experienced in relatively contradictory terms), and *Space in the Structure* (a psychological space where no beliefs have been internalized).

The Continuum of Belief

Note also from the preceding definition that beliefs may be held along a "continuum of belief," ranging from "committed certitude" to "noncommitted skepticism." What do we mean by such an observation? Consider Figure 2.1, which provides three examples that illustrate the nature and dynamics of the Continuum of Belief.[9]

TABLE 2.1
Four Dimensions of Belief

Favorability:	Whether a belief is considered to be good or bad
Veracity:	Whether a belief is experienced as true or false
Intensity:	Whether a belief is held strongly or weakly
Congruency:	Whether a belief is experienced as consistent or inconsistent with other beliefs

---

[9] I appreciate the conceptual contribution of Tim Brearly, lead author on the religion chapter in this book, for his suggestion to use the term "investment," which helped to clarify the nature of "belief" vis-à-vis this continuum.

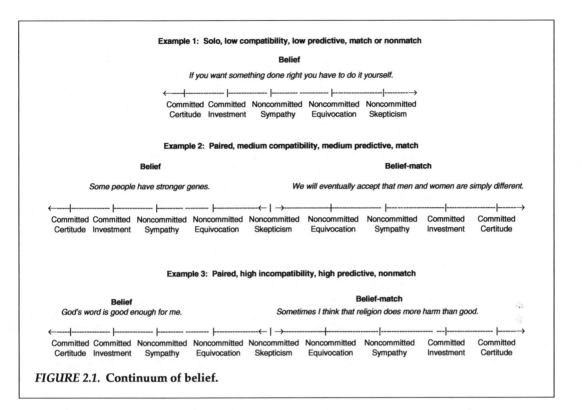

FIGURE 2.1. **Continuum of belief.**

Focus first on Example 1. As noted, this belief is described as "solo, low compatibility, low predictive, match or nonmatch." What does such a designation mean? Essentially, this belief statement—*If you want something done right you have to do it yourself*—is not paired in this example with a counterpart belief (thus it is "solo"). Moreover, the designation of "low compatibility" means that this belief statement, both theoretically and empirically, is less likely to be paired readily with a similar or dissimilar counterpart given the nature of the belief statement, regardless of any attempt to "match" this belief statement with its counterpart. In other words, at a construct level, it tends to stand more "alone" statistically and conceptually than other belief statements (i.e., items), as the following examples may help illustrate. Note also that from a conceptual standpoint, the end points along this continuum are, respectively, "Committed Certitude" and "Noncommitted Skepticism." That is, from the standpoint of the Continuum of Belief, greater skepticism than "Noncommitted Skepticism" regarding the first belief leads—of necessity—to potential engagement with the first belief's "belief match" along the Continuum of Belief (i.e., a belief that represents, statistically and conceptually, the opposite belief of the belief in question). This dynamic is illustrated in both Examples 2 and 3.

By way of contrast with Example 1, then, consider Example 2, which compares the following two items: (a) *Some people have stronger genes* and (b) *We will eventually accept that men and women are simply different*. As is noted above, this juxtaposition is designated as a "paired, medium compatibility, medium predictive, match."

Following the framework presented in Example 1, these two items do in fact represent—from a statistical standpoint—a compatible pairing with each other (i.e., they are positively and moderately correlated with one another), which means that a response on one item (e.g., agree or disagree) tends to be predictive of the response to the other item (i.e., if you agree to one, you will tend—statistically—to agree with the other). These items thus are matched, positively, in this case, and therefore are referred to as a "belief" and its "belief match."

Finally, consider Example 3, which represents an example of two beliefs that are matched strongly, but in the opposite direction, from one another. These two items—*God's word is good enough for me* and *Sometimes I think that religion does more harm than good*—also are "belief matches," but in the opposite direction. That is to say, these items are "paired, high incompatibility, high predictive, and nonmatch" meaning that these items are statistically highly paired (i.e., correlated) but negatively so, such that an agree response on the belief is highly likely to be associated with a disagree response on its belief match. These items are matched, but oppositely so, and in a manner that would be highly predictive of the other.

In short, from the standpoint of the Continuum of Belief, then (and as noted in definitional point 7), beliefs typically exist in a synergistic relationship to one another in that a belief stated in one direction often is matched by one or more counterpart beliefs that exist in relative degrees of opposition to it. Moreover, each belief may be designated as (a) solo or paired (i.e., indicating whether an opposite match has been demonstrated statistically); (b) predictive at the high, medium, or low level (i.e., essentially indicative of correlative strength in the positive or negative direction); and (c) predictive of a match or nonmatch (i.e., whether two beliefs, and two or more individuals holding them, are likely to be "compatible—matched" or "incompatible—nonmatched"—in terms of worldview).

But there is a final feature of the Continuum of Belief that also should be considered. As noted in the preceding definition, beliefs may be held along "Four Dimensions of Belief"[10]: (a) whether a belief is considered to be good or bad (favorability); (b) whether a belief is experienced as true or false (veracity); (c) whether a belief is held strongly or weakly (intensity); and (d) whether a belief is experienced as consistent or inconsistent with other beliefs (congruency). From the standpoint of the EI model and BEVI method, the interaction among these four dimensions results in where a belief statement for an individual falls along the Continuum of Belief. So, as Example 1 illustrates, a solo belief may be held along a continuum ranging from (a) "*Committed Certitude*" (completely committed to the belief with no consciously experienced or expressed doubts) to (b) "*Committed Investment*" (strongly inclined toward the belief, but open to the possibility that other beliefs also may have validity) to (c) "*Noncommitted Sympathy*" (sympathetically inclined toward the belief, but very open to alternative or even contradictory beliefs) to (d) "*Noncommitted Equivocation*" (has no stated preference for the belief and/or experiences a sense of ambivalence vis-à-vis its putative validity) to (e) *Noncommitted Skepticism* (disinclined toward the belief but unwilling to reject the belief completely at present).

However, note also from Example 3 that paired beliefs may be held along this same continuum, with virtually no difference between them (i.e., both beliefs are held with "Noncommitted Equivocation") or as differently as possible (i.e., both beliefs are held with "Committed Certitude").

---

[10] To examine these four points of self-access, please see the EI Self discussed in Chapter 3.

EXAMPLE 1: Solo, low compatibility, low predictive, match or nonmatch

Belief

If you want something done right you have to do it yourself

←----|-------------- |-------------- |--------- --------- |------------------|----------→
Committed   Committed   Noncommitted   Noncommitted   Noncommitted
Certitude   Investment   Sympathy   Equivocation   Skepticism

---

Revelatory of individual differences among us, and by way of explication, consider Example 3 in relation to the hypothetical "Huan," "Eleanor," and "Ana." Recall that the two beliefs of Example 3 are correlated strongly and negatively

---

EXAMPLE 3: Paired, high incompatibility, high predictive, nonmatch

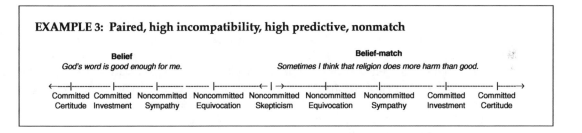

(i.e., Zpaired, but highly incompatible and highly predictive of a nonmatch between two different believers). Let us say Huan strongly agrees with the belief, *God's word is good enough for me*. Statistically speaking, Huan therefore is highly likely to disagree strongly with the belief, *Sometimes I think that religion does more harm than good*. Likewise, now consider "Eleanor," who represents the mirror opposite of Huan, strongly disagreeing that *God's word is good enough for* me and strongly agreeing that *Sometimes I think that religion does more harm than good*. On the Continuum of Belief, if other item pairings follow this same pattern, which is statistically predicted, both Huan and Eleanor likely would fall under "Committed Certitude" on opposite ends of the Continuum of Belief. Now consider a third example from "Ana," who disagrees that *God's word is good enough for me* AND disagrees that *Sometimes I think that religion does more harm than good*. Where would Ana fall along the Continuum of Belief? Probably not under "Committed Certitude," and more likely under "Noncommitted Equivocation." Consistent with BEVI data presented later (e.g., correlation matrix and structural equation modeling), the fact that Ana appears to hold complexity in this way—disagreeing that "God's word is good enough" BUT also disagreeing that "religion does more harm than good"—suggests that she is grappling with fundamental questions regarding her own beliefs vis-à-vis religion and spirituality, and remains open to a range of possible "truths."

Another key feature of the Continuum of Belief should be emphasized at this point via the distinction between "committed" and "noncommitted." From this perspective, individuals who experience self as in a state of "commitment" to a belief system may be contrasted with individuals who experience self in a state of "noncommitment" to that same belief system. The latter individuals—falling in one of three designations of *Noncommitted Sympathy*, *Noncommitted Equivocation*, or *Noncommitted Skepticism* —may be considered from the standpoint of the Continuum of Belief to be "agnostic," at relative degrees of commitment. Note in this regard that the word "agnostic" was coined by Thomas H. Huxley, the 19th century British scientist, and included but extended beyond the domain of religious belief. In current usage, agnosticism may be used as either a noun or adjective, as follows.[11]

Agnosticism as Noun:

1a. One who believes that it is impossible to know whether there is a God
1b. One who is skeptical about the existence of God but does not profess true atheism
2.   One who is doubtful or noncommittal about something

Agnosticism as Adjective:

1. Relating to or being an agnostic
2. Doubtful or noncommittal

Of these elements, the "noncommittal" aspect of this definition allows for the greatest degree of flexibility in application. So, one may be *sympathetically noncommitted* (i.e., inclined to believe but ultimately noncommittal), *equivocally noncommitted* (i.e., inclined neither to believe nor disbelieve but ultimately noncommittal), or *skeptically noncommitted* (i.e., inclined to disbelieve but ultimately noncommittal). From the standpoint of the Continuum of Belief, then, "agnostic" encompasses any of the "noncommitted" designations, which is consistent with the scope and intent of the term, "agnostic," meaning "without" ("a") "knowledge" ("gnosis"). *Thus, to declare oneself agnostic is to concede the inability to assert unequivocally the certainty of knowledge.*

Nonbelief is belief

As we conclude this discussion of Component I of the EI Model—*belief*—one final definitional point along these lines warrants explication. From the standpoint of the Continuum of Belief, a belief in nonbelief is still belief. In other words, a declaration that one "does not believe" is a declaration of belief in nonbelief. In this regard, I am in full accord with De Waal (2013) who, in *The Bonobo and the Atheist*, observes that

> Over the past few years, we have gotten used to a strident atheism arguing that God is not great (Christopher Hitchens) or is a delusion (Richard Dawkins). The neo-atheists call themselves "brights," thus implying that believers are not as bright. They have replaced Saint Paul's view that nonbelievers live in darkness by its opposite: nonbelievers are the only ones to have seen the light. Urging trust in science, they wish to root ethics in the naturalistic worldview. I do share their skepticism regarding religious institutions and their "primates"—popes, bishops, megapreachers, ayatollahs, and rabbis—but what good could possibly come from insulting the many people who find value in religion? And more pertinently, what alternative does science have to offer? Science is not in the business of spelling out the meaning of life and even less in telling us how to live our lives. (pp. 18–19)

---

[11] Copyright © 2014 by Houghton Mifflin Harcourt Publishing Company. Adapted and reproduced by permission from *The American Heritage Dictionary of the English Language, Fifth Edition.* See www.thefreedictionary.com/agnostic.

Do I hear an "Amen?"

In the final analysis, although considerations such as these typically manifest in the realm of religious belief, the status of "nonbelief as belief" may be applied to all manner of phenomena. For example, to state, "I do not believe in politics" is to say "I believe that it is not worthwhile to believe in politics." Likewise, regarding the matter of atheism, to say "I do not believe in God" is to say "I believe that there is no basis for believing in God." To be clear then, as a belief state, atheism is not nonbelief. That is because it is no more provable that there is a God than it is provable that there is not. In short, on matters that cannot unequivocally be proven empirically, belief is inevitable.

As may be clear by now, we cannot make sense of beliefs and values unless we apprehend them as manifesting from interactions among interconnected aspects of human experience. In particular, to preclude another lamentable instance of conceptual disembodiment, it should be recognized that beliefs are inextricably derivative of two other fundamental constructs: needs and self. So, at this point, with the basics of belief described, let us turn to the second component of the EI Model—the nature of core human need.

EI Component II: Need

The concept of human "need" has a long history within the social and behavioral sciences, as a number of theorists and researchers have offered accountings of what human needs are and are not, and how such putative needs are associated with various aspects of human functioning and conduct. In addition to Clark Hull (1943), who emphasized innate physiological needs (e.g., food and sex), the two most prominent needs-based theorists historically included Henry Murray (1938), who developed an extensive listing of needs, and Abraham Maslow (1954), who attempted to address both physiological and psychological levels of analysis in his well-known "hierarchy of needs." These theorists offer a number of observations regarding the definition and nature of needs, which are quite instructive when taking a big picture view of these issues.

In *Proposals for a Theory of Personality*, for example, Murray (1938) defines need as "a hypothetical process the occurrence of which is imagined in order to account for certain objective and subjective facts" (Schneidman, 1981, p. 137). Cognizant of the strong behavioral emphases of his time, but inclined more toward dynamic-organismic formulations of personality and self, Murray extrapolated backwards from behavior in which human organisms engage to the underlying need that the exhibition of the behavior reveals. Thus, a need referred to the ". . .organic potentiality or readiness to respond in a certain way under given conditions. In this sense a need is a latent attribute of an organism" (p. 142). Although a "hypothetical construct" in the sense that a need could not be directly observed—only its effects—Murray was clear that ". . .the need process must be placed in the brain" (p. 143). In addition to providing a number of arguments for the salience of "need" in explaining human behavior, Murray ultimately explicated multiple primary "viscerogenic" (e.g., air, water, food, sex) and secondary "psychogenic" (e.g., acquisition, achievement, affiliation) needs.

Abraham Maslow (1971) shared with Murray an interest in specifying the criteria under which a human "need" could be designated as "instinctoid" (i.e., innate). To take the first two such criteria,[12] Maslow contended that:

> . . .a need is instinctoid if. . .the chronic lack of the satisfier [that which meets the need] produces pathology, especially if this lack occurs early in life. . .[and if] deprivation at a critical period can cause the total and permanent loss of the desire and/or need, possibly never to be relearned or reinstated; the person is thereby permanently diminished and has lost a defining characteristic of the human species; he is no longer fully human. (p. 382)

Maslow's (1971) framework in this regard is detailed and specific. For example, and consistent with a humanistic framework in general, Maslow contended that the "real" need could emerge if it were ". . .uncovered, accepted, approved of, and strengthened by insight therapy, uncovering therapy (or by increase in health in general), (or by 'good conditions' in society), i.e., by the lifting of defenses, controls, fears" (p. 386). Congruent with this perspective, and a major theme of Maslow's work, was that human needs should neither be conceptualized as primitive, selfish, and potentially destructive (e.g., as "idinal" impulses) nor reduced to contingency-based paradigms, which erroneously attempted to "define human instinct in behavioral terms" (p. 380). As his well-known "hierarchy of needs" illustrates, Maslow's core contention was that human need is experienced at five levels: (a) physiological (e.g., biological needs for food, water, etc.); (b) safety (e.g., for security and predictability); (c) love, affection, and belongingness (e.g., being part of a community, giving/receiving love and affection); (d) esteem (e.g., to value others and be valued for who one is); and (e) self-actualization (e.g., to fulfill one's innate potential, to become all one was meant to be) (Maslow, 1954). Although more speculative, Maslow also contended that human beings experienced "higher needs" as well (e.g., for understanding, spiritual connectedness). For Maslow, these needs existed in hierarchical relationship to one another, such that each need must be sufficiently satisfied in turn. As he noted,

> A person who is lacking food, safety, love, and esteem would most probably hunger for food more strongly than for anything else. If all the needs are unsatisfied, and the organism is then dominated by the physiological needs, all other needs may become simply nonexistent or be pushed into the background. (p. 82)

Although aspects of Maslow's approach have been challenged (e.g., the linearity of this approach and its underlying suppositions regarding that homeostatic nature of the human organism) (e.g., Fox, 1982; Geller, 1982; Neher, 1991), Maslow's seminal contribution to needs-based theory ultimately helped facilitate a great deal of scholarship and application in a wide array of contexts (e.g., see Ryan et al., 2013; Staub, 2003).

For much of the 20th century, particularly during the behavioral era, an explicit focus on "human need" within psychology largely was confined to theorists such as Murray and Maslow. However, in the recent past, there has been a "renewed interest in the concept of need" within the broader academic community (Ward & Stewart, 2003, p. 132; see also Leuty, 2013). In summarizing this broader literature, Moskowitz

---

[12] In the *Farther Reaches of Human Nature* (1971), Maslow specifies 26 major and subcriteria for demonstrating that a need had an "instinctoid" basis.

(2005) identifies a range of physical needs (e.g., for food, reproduction, shelter from harm) as well as three "basic" psychological needs that help explain "why people act the way they do":

(1) Feeling as if we are approved of/loved and belong to a group of others that is larger than ourselves (affiliation needs)
(2) Having positive self-regard (self-esteem needs)
(3) Understanding and deriving meaning from the actions of others in a manner that is sufficient to allow us to plan our own behavior and interact in an appropriate manner (epistemic needs) (p. 5)

Often subsumed under the rubric of "motivation" (e.g., Manstead & Hewstone, 1999), Moskowitz offers the following semantic clarification among needs, motives, incentives, and goals; note that "need" is foundational, as these other constructs essentially are derivative of "need":

> A *need* is a drive state, usually conceived as arising from a physical (tissue) deficit of some sort. For example, hunger is a drive state that results from the body's requiring sustenance, and it results in the need to reduce that feeling of hunger or else the physical being will suffer (if not perish). A *motive* may be conceived of as a quasi-need, in that while there may be no tissue deficit, a similar process of being driven to reduce some perceived discrepancy between the current state of the organism and some desired state of the organism exists. In this case, it is a psychological deficit that impels people to reduce the discrepancy. . .*Incentives* are those people/things in the environment that will reduce the drive (the tension state) associated with a need/motive. Finally, *goals* are the end states people seek to attain by having pursued an incentive and addressed a need/motive. (p. 96)

Although a number of academic researchers and theorists are pursuing this line of inquiry again, the most far-reaching and empirically grounded is that of Edward Deci and Richard Ryan, who have developed a theory- and data-based framework of need, entitled self-determination theory or SDT (e.g., Deci & Ryan, 2000; Ryan et al., 2013; Ryan & Deci, 2008). By way of overview,

> SDT is a broad theory of optimal functioning and motivation. The theory's roots lie in organismic thinking—that is, the view that living things have an organizational nature, moving developmentally in a direction of greater autonomy— of greater coherence and integration in functioning. With regard to human psychological development, SDT looks to three fundamental needs as underlying our inherent tendency toward integrated growth and development. To function optimally, an individual must experience competence (efficacy and sense of control), relatedness (social significance and connection), and autonomy (volition and self-endorsement of behavior). Autonomy, competence, and relatedness describe the natural, intrinsic functionalities whose satisfaction predicts both high-quality motivation and well-being—in short, full, thriving functioning. (Ryan et al., 2013, p. 61)

Arguably, the most significant issue for any needs-based theorists is definitional, as such parameters presumably clarify what is and is not meant by the construct of need. In the context of SDT, Deci and Ryan define "needs" as:

innate psychological nutriments that are essential for ongoing psychological growth, integrity, and well being. . .a psychological need can be identified by observing that positive psychological consequences results from conditions that allow its satisfaction and negative consequences accrue in situations that thwart it. (Deci & Ryan, 2000, p. 229)

Although Deci and Ryan (2000) go to considerable lengths to clarify how their concept of need does and does not differ from other related theories (e.g., physiological, drive-based, motivational, goal-directed), their fundamental contention is that these three psychological needs (competence, relatedness, autonomy) are evident across cultures and are "linked to or catalyzed by our psychological design" as human beings (p. 232) (see also Ryan et al., 2013; Ryan & Deci, 2008). And it is on this basic and decades old point—that some psychological needs are innate—that a number of contemporary scholars of different backgrounds and emphases would appear to agree (e.g., Kramer & Akhtar, 1994; Anderson, Chen, & Carter, 2000; Baumeister, Brewer, Tice, & Twenge, 2007; Baumeister, Dale, & Muraven, 2000; Krapp, 2005; Leuty, 2013; Staub, 2003; Taylor, 2003; Ward & Stewart, 2003).

Definitional Dialectics Among Needs and Values

A number of needs-based theorists recognize a relationship between values and needs, although this connection—which is crucial to making sense of beliefs and values—has often lacked sufficient explication. As Leuty (2013) observes when addressing "needs and values" vis-à-vis assessment, "A basic understanding of the terminology is required before delving into the history and assessment of needs and values, especially given frequent confusion over their description" (p. 363). In this regard, consider the perspective of Murray, who noted that his own term, "sentiments" was being replaced in the early 1900s "by the favored term [of] value" (Schneidman, 1981, p. 28). However, he also emphasized the linkage between values and needs in maintaining that "personality is largely revealed in the objects that it cathects (values or rejects)" and that "one can often guess what needs are dominant in an individual by knowing the objects of his positive and negative sentiments" (i.e., values) (Schneidman, 1981, p. 176; see also Kluckhohn & Murray, 1953).

Although widely recognized as a "needs theorist," Maslow also expended a great deal of intellectual thought on values, clearly observing a common orbit between these two constructs. For example, in his preface to *New Knowledge in Human Values*, Maslow maintained that,

. . .we need a validated, usable system of human values, values that we can believe in and devote ourselves to because they are true rather than because we are exhorted to "believe and have faith." And for the first time in history, many of us feel, such a system—based squarely upon valid knowledge of the nature of man, of his society, and of his works—may be possible. (Maslow & Sorokin, 1959, p. viii)

Moreover, in *Religions, Values, and Peak Experiences*, Maslow (1964) linked the "need for transcendence" (p. xiv) to the release of ". . .one's own credo, or system of values, or system of beliefs" (Maslow, 1971, p. 279). Similarly, in *Motivation and Personality*, Maslow (1954) observes that, there are real psychological and operational differences between those needs called "higher" and those needs called "lower." This is done in order to establish that the organism itself dictates hierarchies of values. . .a greater value is usually placed upon the higher need than upon the lower by those who have been gratified in both. (pp. 146–148)

As the final exemplar of this linkage, Milton Rokeach (1973) directly articulated an inextricable relationship between human needs and values, contending that:

Values are the cognitive representations and transformations of needs, and man is the only animal capable of such representations and transformations. This proposition is not the whole story however: Values are the cognitive representations not only of individual needs but also of societal and institutional demands. . .The cognitive representation of needs as values serves societal demands no less than individual needs. Once such demands and needs become cognitively transformed into values, they are capable of being defended, justified, advocated, and exhorted as personally and socially desirable. For example, the need for sex which is so often repressed in modern society may be cognitively transformed as a value for love, spiritual union, or intimacy. . .Needs may or may not be denied, depending upon whether they can stand conscious personal and social scrutiny, but values need never be denied. Thus, when a person tells us about his values he is surely also telling us about his needs. (p. 20)

Although Rokeach maintains that values are the "cognitive representations and transformations of needs," he does not specify what these needs are or their defining characteristics, a problematic omission given that values ultimately are derivative of needs (see also Grube, Mayton, & Ball-Rokeach, 1994). Instead, Rokeach focuses the vast portion of his work on the explication and measurement of values as though the underlying needs from which values are derived simply are implied by these expressed values. But if values are the representational vinculum between "needs" on the one hand and "societal and institutional demands" on the other, it stands to reason that both levels of analysis—underlying needs and external demands, and the relationship between them—must be explicated in order to make sense of what beliefs and values are, and how, indeed where or in what context, they are internalized in the first place. Rokeach says little about the interacting needs-based, contextual, developmental, intrapsychic, and internalization mechanisms and processes that would seem to be implied by his own framework. Thus, although extraordinarily illuminating, his analysis largely is descriptive and predictive rather than interpretive or explanatory. As noted, such a focus on "what" and "who" is highly relevant and necessary, but not sufficient, as we also must answer questions of "why" and "how" if we are to make sense of beliefs and values as they relate to the interdependent functioning of real human beings. In other words, the complex etiological, ontological, and contextual interactions among beliefs, values, and needs cannot be understood if they are examined in isolation from each other or as abstractions that exist in disembodied form "out there." Beliefs, values, and needs are among the most human of constructs, and they require an ecologically valid framework that is sufficient to encompass this real world complexity.

Along these lines, it should be noted that both Schwartz and Feather concur with Rokeach—and the present EI Model—that beliefs and values ultimately are derivative of need. However, they each provide further explication about the nature of need as well as the relationship of needs to values. For Feather (1995), values

> have their source in basic human needs and in societal demands. . .Values may also be considered not only as generalized beliefs about what is or is not desirable but also as motives. I have assumed that they function like needs to influence goal-directed behavior. . .However, needs and values also have distinctive characteristics. An important difference relates to the fact that values are tied to a normative base involving a dimension of goodness and badness, whereas no necessary connection exists between needs and evaluations of goodness and badness (Feather, 1982b, 1990, 1992). McClelland (1985) described other differences between needs and values. In his analysis, values are seen as more easily verbalized and closer to conscious awareness than needs (see also Biernat, 1989). Subsequently, Weinberger and McClelland (1990) categorized needs as belonging to the class of implicit motives. They assumed that implicit motives are acquired early in life; are measured by indirect means, such as fantasy productions; and are built largely on nonverbal affective experiences (pp. 1135–1136).

Although the preceding exposition is instructive, by attempting to clarify the relationship between values and needs, the question of what these putative needs are is not yet specified. Of these values theorists, Schwartz (2012) offers the most direct explication of what these "needs" are. Again, as he notes, the distinguishing feature among different values,

> is the type of goal or motivation that it expresses. The values theory defines ten broad values according to the motivation that underlies each of them. These values are likely to be universal because they are grounded in one or more of three universal requirements of human existence with which they help to cope. These requirements are needs of individuals as biological organisms, requisites of coordinated social interaction, and survival and welfare needs of groups. Individuals cannot cope successfully with these requirements of human existence on their own. Rather, people must articulate appropriate goals to cope with them, communicate with others about them, and gain cooperation in their pursuit. Values are the socially desirable concepts used to represent these goals mentally and the vocabulary used to express them in social interaction. (p. 4)

So for Schwartz, needs are "grounded in one or more of three universal requirements of human existence," which include "needs of individuals as biological organisms, requisites of coordinated social interaction, and survival and welfare needs of groups." As may be clear, this helpful articulation of need is both similar and different from those presented by the needs theorists presented earlier, particularly Deci and Ryan. One can see, for example, that the SDT construct of "relatedness" may well be indicated by Schwartz's emphasis on "coordinated social interaction." But, the level of analysis appears to be different. Deci and Ryan are focusing on fundamental organismic variables of the individual human whereas Schwartz seems to be emphasizing broader goal-based social aspirations of human beings, particularly in a group-based context, even though he likely would endorse the organismic paradigm of Deci and Ryan. As will be contended next, these different levels of analysis are not irreconcilable, and are in fact, quite complementary if not compatible, if one takes an inclusive view of "need" based upon clear definitional and inclusion/exclusion criteria that explicate "needs" along a physiological–psychological continuum.

An Ecumenical Operationalization of Need

As may be evident, the differences that do emerge among needs-based theorists appear to result from differences among levels of analysis (e.g., physiological versus psychological), disciplinary and epistemological backgrounds (e.g., developmental psychology versus social psychology), construct focus (e.g., needs versus values), methodology implemented (e.g., controlled versus clinical settings), and evidentiary criteria employed (e.g., the threshold at which a "need" is said to exist). Thus, in an attempt to address the source of these differences, and based upon the historic and contemporary scholarship referenced earlier, it may be helpful to "operationalize need" by explicating (a) *questions to be answered*, (b) *parameters to be addressed*, (c) *core criteria to be met* in the development and evaluation of needs-based theories, (d) a *definition of "core need"* that seeks to be mindful and inclusive of the perspectives presented above, and (e) *a proposed continuum of physiological and psychological need* based upon the contributions of historically and currently prominent needs-based theorists, clinicians, and researchers. Although the following perspective across these five areas emerged during the development of the EI Model over the past 20 years, no inviolable claims are made here. Quite frankly, in seeking to understand the role of "needs" vis-à-vis the two other "components" of this model (*beliefs* and *self*), these five areas— *questions, parameters, criteria, definition,* and *continuum*—emerged out of necessity during the process of clarifying what "needs" were as well as the relationship of this construct to these other concepts that comprised the larger EI Model. In short, these five areas are intended neither to be exhaustive nor definitive, but simply to provide additional guidelines for consideration by scholars who are interested in the development, refinement, and evaluation of needs-based theories.

*First, the following 15 **questions** are among those that may be helpful to answer in the development, refinement, or evaluation of needs-based theories:*

1. By which definitional and empirical criteria may the presence or absence of a "need" be evaluated?
2. How many needs best represent the spectrum of what innate physiological and psychological needs might be?
3. What is the relationship between physiological and psychological needs?
4. What is the relationship between needs and other capacities and predispositions that also are assumed to be innate?
5. On what grounds may reliable distinctions be drawn among constructs that often are synonymous with need, such as "motive," "goal," "interest," and "desire," and how do we address the semantic difficulties that are inherent to such considerations?
6. In what human context or construct do these needs exist, and how do needs relate to other aspects of "self?"
7. How are needs related to the cognitive/affective representation of those needs, and via which mediational and regulatory processes?
8. How and under what circumstances are such cognitive/affective representations of need internalized, modified, and assessed?
9. How and when do these needs manifest in the context of maturation and development?
10. How do cultural, contextual, and environmental factors and processes influence the experience and expression of human need?
11. How, why, and under what circumstances is need expressed at the level of action?

12. Are there individual differences in "need strength?"
13. How are these needs and representations of needs expressed across the adaptive and functional continuum?
14. To what degree does any needs-based framework have ecological validity for both scholars and practitioners?
15. To what degree does any needs-based framework comport with the lived experience of being human?

Second, as noted, a central preoccupation of needs-based theorists from Murray (1938), to Maslow (1971), to Deci and Ryan (2000) has been the articulation of criteria by which a "need" may or may not be designated as "core": to have some causal, innate, and universal source, without which the human organism could not function or be recognized as such. Toward such means and ends, *the following 10 **parameters** are among those that might be considered in the development, refinement, or evaluation of a needs-based theory*:

1. Articulate the theoretical infrastructure (e.g., the self) in which these needs exist.
2. Specify how basic needs are and are not related to the cognitive/affective representations of those needs as well as any relevant process-based and mediational variables.
3. Account for the interaction between needs and developmental/maturational processes as well as how life experiences and external context interact with and are etiologically related to these cognitive/affective representations and needs.
4. Offer a theoretical explanation as to how and where these cognitive/affective representations are stored and modified.
5. Account for individual and cultural differences in the experience and expression of "need."
6. Provide a way to assess or measure these cognitive/affective representations of need.
7. Demonstrate relevance to the human condition across the functional and adaptive realm as well as ecological validity to scholars and practitioners alike.
8. Comport with lived experience by real human beings (i.e., laypersons).
9. Be grounded in relevant theory and available data.
10. Avoid Cartesian dichotomies between physiological and psychological processes.

Third, based upon the overview of "need," *the following four **criteria** may be considered "core" to the development or evaluation of needs-based theories*:

1. The putative need has clear adaptive significance for the human organism across cultures, contexts, and time.
2. Insufficient internal or external responsiveness to the need typically results in subjective feelings of distress and/or demonstrable impairment at a physiological, developmental, behavioral, emotional, cognitive, social, or existential level.
3. Sufficient internal or external responsiveness to the need typically results in subjective feelings of well-being and/or demonstrable enhancement at a physiological, developmental, behavioral, emotional, cognitive, social, or existential level.
4. The putative need has significant and demonstrable capacity to explain fundamental aspects of human functioning or conduct.

Fourth, on the basis of the overview of needs theories, questions, parameters, and criteria, the following **definition** *of "core need" is offered.* From the standpoint of the "self" discussed next and in Chapter 3, via the EI Self, beliefs and values exist in the service of *core human needs*, which:

1. motivate or drive the human organism throughout the life span to achieve fulfillment of the core needs to a degree that is subjectively experienced as sufficient for each human being (including the appetitive, attachment, affective, acknowledgment, activation, affiliative, actualizing, attunement, and awareness needs);
2. exist along a physical and psychological continuum that encompasses the whole of human experience;
3. are derived from our history of evolutionary adaptation and therefore are core to our existence and defining characteristics as a species;
4. are expressed through the adaptive potential that is unique for each human being;
5. are shaped in expressive form by developmental processes and formative variables that are unique to each human being; and,
6. are evidenced nonverbally through various physiological and behavioral indexes and/or expressed verbally through our stated beliefs and values about self, others, and the world at large.

Finally, although certainly subject to modification (i.e., no claims are made about the definitive nature of this proposed list of needs), an ecumenical reading of the beliefs/values- and needs-based literature noted previously as well as empirical and applied scholarship on "the self" presented next and in Chapter 3, suggests that *"core human needs" may exist along a* **continuum** *of nine interdependent levels:*[13]

- Level I = *Appetitive Needs* (hunger, evacuation, release, stasis);
- Level II = *Attachment Needs* (merger, touch, warmth, bonding, security, nurturance, responsiveness, predictability);
- Level III = *Affective Needs* (expression, reception, reciprocal empathy, regulation);
- Level IV = *Acknowledgment Needs* (mirroring, recognition, resonance);
- Level V = *Activation Needs* (stimulation, novelty seeking, causal relations, learning, efficacy);
- Level VI = *Affiliative Needs* (belongingness, connection, interdependence, relatedness, social exchange);
- Level VII = *Actualizing Needs* (potentiality, differentiation, achievement, influence, consistency, congruence, coherence, esteem, identity);
- Level VIII = *Attunement Needs* (composed of two subdimensions, including *attunement to the human condition*: altruism, community, compassion, fairness, justice, protection, responsiveness, self–other, truthfulness; and, *attunement to the natural world*: balance, sustainability, interconnectedness, living things, living systems, cosmos), and
- Level IX = *Awareness Needs* (openness, reflection, life place, life purpose, meaning making, existential, mortality, essence, finite–infinite, transcendence, transformation).

---

[13] The selection of words beginning with "A" to describe each of these levels was a heuristic, recognizing that the choice of term or label always has an element of judgment (as with factor analysis). At the same time, however, these terms were selected obviously to encompass specific types of needs that manifest under each of these nine levels (in parentheses). See the following discussion of "self" as well as the EI Self in Chapter 3 for additional perspective regarding the nature and real world expression of these needs.

Of course, core human needs—like beliefs and values—are (depending upon their theoretical and empirical status) hypothetical constructs that should have explanatory relevance and/or are intervening variables that statistically are demonstrably predictive of real world phenomena. Along these lines, it is not advisable to conceptualize such putative "needs" in a vacuum, but rather to apprehend them as existing within a larger affective, cognitive, contextual, and developmental space. As noted vis-à-vis the "operationalization" of need, a central problem in theoretical deliberations of this nature and its empirical specification statistically (e.g., through predictive models) is that "need" is contemplated as somehow separate, apart, or wholly distinguishable from other aspects of human functioning. As any depth-based clinical practitioner will attest, the ecological validity of "need" as a salient construct or variable is enhanced substantially if we apprehend it in relation to associated psychological phenomena. That is to say, need is fundamental to, but encompassed by, another organizing structure. Although other candidates might be selected (e.g., personality, mind, soul)—as hopefully will be demonstrated in the following—the paradigmatic framework that seems best to encompass, explain, and organize our other two components of the EI Model—*beliefs* and *needs*—is that of the human *self*.

EI Component III: Self

As may be clear from the preceding discussion of beliefs and needs, one of the fundamental challenges for theorists, researchers, and practitioners has been a lack of specification regarding "where" these constructs actually interact and "have their being." That is, what is "the thing" that encompasses and organizes these construct parts into a coherent whole? By asking such a question, we deliberately are granting primacy to the proposition that scholars and practitioners who focus on the nature of the human condition are obliged to think deeply about how their putative constructs relate to other constructs, and in what superstructure these constructs reside and are organized in relation to each other. This problem—of not attempting to specify the relationship of specific constructs to others that logically could encompass them—arguably limits the generalizability of various theoretical approaches, which otherwise, have much to offer in terms of illuminating why we humans function as we do. For present purposes, such an organizing and cohering framework, which clarifies the relationship between the two other constructs emphasized here—*beliefs* and *needs*—is that of the human *self*.

Although there are, at times, radical differences in emphasis, most theorists and researchers of the self probably would resonate deeply with the view of Krech and Crutchfield (1948), articulated over 60 years ago, that:

> . . .the self is the most important structure in the psychological field, and it is likely, under normal conditions to be one of the strongest structures. It has, therefore, a role of unparalleled significance in the determination of the organization of the field. (Markus & Sentis, 1982, pp. 41–42)

As evidence for the durability of this conviction, consider Kowalski and Leary's (1999) contention that:

> The self has been a central topic in personality and clinical psychology for many years and has regained respectability within mainline social psychology in the

past couple of decades. Recent theory and research on self and identity is truly voluminous, and much of it has clear implications for understanding and treating psychological problems. (p. 21)

Likewise, in their authoritative *Handbook of Self and Identity*, Leary and Tangney (2012) observe the following:

Major advances in sciences often occur when the work of a large number of researchers begin to converge on a single unifying construct. . .Since the 1970s, one such unifying construct within psychology and other social and behavioral sciences has been the self, as hundreds of thousands of articles, chapters, and books have been devoted to self-related phenomena. (p. 1)

Such perspective is borne out further by a review of the literature, which reveals that "self" is one of the most widely invoked constructs within the discipline and profession of psychology. In fact, a search of PsycINFO in July of 2014 resulted in 108,259 references with the world "self" in the title alone. Emergent references readily reveal the diverse applications of this term: "self-handicapping," "self-reporting," "self-presentations," "self-efficacy," "pro-self-component," "self-concept," "self-monitoring," and "self-esteem," to mention only a few. A concomitant search of the PsycINFO Thesaurus reveals no less than 54 specific terms with the prefix "self" (beginning with "self-acceptance" and ending with "self-talk"). Based upon a similar analysis by Greenwald in 1979, self was used ". . .as the first part of the combination with 18 different nouns" (Greenwald, 1982, p. 153); thus, it would appear that the pairing of "self" with a wide range of psychological constructs and phenomena has approximately tripled over the past three decades. The proliferation of self-related terms and research has not gone without notice. For example, Tesser, Stapel, and Wood (2002) noted that "the amount of psychological research on the self has grown tremendously over the past few decades. . .about 20 in 1 publications in 1970 were related to the self, and fully 1 in 7 publications in 2000 were related to the self" (p. ix). Likewise, Leary and Tangney (2012) found via a review of PsycINFO "over 260,000 abstracts that contained a hyphenated *self* term, and this did not include other central *self* terms as ego and identity!" (p. 9).

But what is this thing called "self?" Given the ubiquity of this term within the psychological literature, one would think that a common definition would have been established, or at the very least, that the basic dimensions of "self" would have been explicated so that we all had a common point of departure before invoking this construct in theory, research, or practice. By and large, that is not the case. As Leary and Tangney (2012) observe,

Although psychologists and sociologists often have had difficulty agreeing how to define and conceptualize their constructs, "self" has been particularly troublesome. Not only have we lacked a single, universally accepted definition of "self," but also many definitions clearly refer to distinctly different phenomena, and some uses of the term are difficult to grasp no matter what definition one applies. (p. 4)

And indeed, despite its omnipresence, finding a common definition of "self" proved elusive, either through a keyword search of psychological terminology or through "definition of self" by title. Although there are a few dictionary- and encyclopedia-based attempts to define or describe the self, scholars who discuss self in their work—sometimes as a core or central construct—differ greatly on which aspects they do and do not include or emphasize. Albert Bandura, whose well-known concept of "self-efficacy" is among the most referenced of "self" concepts, stated the essential problem thusly: "The self is a subject about which much has been written, although it is often ill-defined as to mystify what it embodies" (Bandura, 1982, p. 3). The net effect of this state of affairs is that one's notion of self appears to say as much if not more about the disciplinary, epistemological, or theoretical "self" of the scholar than about the construct of self.

Perhaps the central challenge in defining "self" is its sheer complexity and potential scope. As Manstead and Hewstone (1999) observe in their *Encyclopedia of Social Psychology*:

> A full understanding of self must encompass the physical body, the socially defined identity (including roles and relationships), the personality, and the person's knowledge about self (i.e., the self-concept). Self is also understood as the active agent who makes decisions and initiates actions. . .Still, this multiplicity should not be overstated. The very definition of self entails unity and continuity over time. Attributes, roles, motivations, and subjective states may change frequently, but they are all understood as belonging to one and the same self. The notion of self is thus best understood as embodying a fundamental unity with a diverse aggregate of attributes and facets. (p. 496)

One overarching implication of this perspective is that any comprehensive definition or formulation of self should specify the "parts," but also explicate the relationship between them as well as the "whole" gestalt into which they coherently are integrated. Contrast this standard with the definitions that are available within common reference materials. Let us start with a common or layperson's definition of self. Although it takes the prize with 138 terms preceded by "self" (from "self-abasement" to "self-worth"), Merriam-Webster (2004) does not seem especially informative about this widely cited construct, defining self as "1: the essential person distinct from all other persons in identity. 2: a particular side of a person's character. 3: personal interest: SELFISHNESS" (p. 653).

Given the central preoccupation of psychiatrist scholars with the self over many decades, perhaps a reference source from this field of inquiry would provide a definition of self that includes both the necessary parts in a sufficiently whole manner. Although Campbell's (2009) *Psychiatric Dictionary* does reference a wide array of "self" related terms (43 total), ranging from "self-absorption" to "self-talk," the concomitant definition is short on specifics, defining self simply as "the psychophysical total of the person at any given moment, including both conscious and unconscious attributes" (p. 886).

A quite comprehensive definition of self is articulated by Reber, Allen, and Reber in their (2009) *Dictionary of Psychology*. An adapted excerpt of this definition may be instructive, as it recognizes the vast sweep of this construct and attempts to explicate some of the common themes (see p. 716):

> One of the more dominant aspects of human experience is the compelling sense of one's unique experience, what philosophers have traditionally called the issue of personal identity or of the *self*. Accordingly, this term finds itself rather well represented in psychological theory, particularly in the areas of social and developmental psychology, the study of personality and the field of psychopathology. . .the following are what appear to be the six primary intentions of the users of the term *self*: [as. . .]

1. inner agent or force with controlling and direction functions over motives, fears, needs, etc.;
2. an inner witness to events;
3. the totality of personal experience and expression, self as living being;
4. synthesis, self as an organized, personalized whole;
5. consciousness, awareness, personal conception; self as identity;
6. abstract goal or end point on some personalistic dimension. . .the achievement of self thus being the final human expression of spiritualistic development.

Finally, in full recognition of the complexity such definitional processes evoke, Leary and Tangney (2012) provide a helpful framework for thinking about "self" through the identification of "five distinct ways in which behavioral and social scientists commonly use the world *self* and its compounds" (p. 4). These include the following: (a) *Self as the Total Person* (i.e., using self as "more or less synonymous with person, which also seems to be common in everyday language"); (b) *Self as Personality* (i.e., referring to self as "all or part of an individual's personality"); (c) *Self as Experiencing Subject* (i.e., "the self as subject, or 'I,' is the psychological process that is responsible for self awareness and self-knowledge. . .the 'self as knower' to distinguish it from the 'self as known'. . .This use of self is reflected in the phenomenology of selfhood. Most people have the sense that there is an experiencing 'thing' inside their heads that registers their experiences, thinks their thoughts, and feels their feelings"); (d) *Self as Beliefs About Oneself* (i.e., the *Me self*, which refers to "perceptions, thoughts, and feelings about oneself—the various answers that one might give to questions such as 'Who am I?' and 'What am I like?'"); and (e) *Self as Executive Agent* (i.e., the self is "a decision maker and doer, as the agentic 'ghost in the machine' that regulates people's behavior") (pp. 4–5).

As these definitions suggest, the "self"—like *beliefs* and *needs*—is among the most complex of constructs. Yet, such complexity has not prevented a very wide range of theorists, researchers, and clinicians from invoking the "self" concept in an effort to account for various phenomena and findings. In attempting to identify core dimensions of self, a cross-section of exemplars may prove instructive.

The Subjective and Objective Self

Flapan and Fenchel (1987) nicely summarize the following historical antecedents of scholarship on the self, as follows:

> In 1890, William James wrote that, "In its widest possible sense, a man's self is the sum total of all that he can call his." Some years later, Cooley (1902) conceptualized the "looking glass self," which referred to seeing oneself as reflected by others, as though the others were mirrors. In a somewhat different vein, Mead (1934) wrote about the "I" and the "me," the "I" being one's spontaneous, non-reflective action, and the "me" being the reflective looking back on one's own actions, and "taking the role of the other" toward oneself. Many years later, Chein (1972) stated that the self is the object of many enduring, interrelated, and interdependent concerns and motives that are always fueled in the serve of adaptation for self-preservation. . .Hartman (1964) referred to the self as the ego's mental representation of who we are and saw this as a way of defining and expressing ourselves, while Jacobson (1964) distinguished among the ego

as a topographical mental structure, the self as the totality of the psychic and bodily person, and self-representations as self-images based on momentary feelings of pleasure or unpleasure. (pp. 31–32)

As will become apparent, many of these historic emphases and themes resonate with more contemporary accountings as well. For example, as a prelude to his comprehensive discussion of various self theories both past and present, and as a nod in the direction of William James, Levin (1992) grapples with the self-explication challenge as follows:

The self is the ego, the subject, the I, or the me, as opposed to the object, or totality of objects—the *not me*. *Self* means "same" in Anglo-Saxon (Old English). So *self* carries with it the notion of identity, of meaning the selfsame. It is also the *I*, the personal pronoun, in Old Gothic, the ancestor of Anglo-Saxon. Thus, etymologically *self* comes from both the personal pronoun, *I*—exist, I do this and that—and from the etymological root meaning "the same"—it is the same I who does this, who did that. (p. 2)

Along similar lines, Ferrari (1999) observes that:

. . .the self-system is often considered to include two key structural aspects of the self. The "I" refers to the self as subject, with its own experience and sense of agency; the "me" refers to the self as object, as captured through self-concept and autobiographical stories (James, 1890/1950; Mead, 1934). Thus, the "I" stands for the author; the "me" for the actor or character of the narrative drama (Hermanys & van Gilst, 1991). (Ferrari, 1999, 398; see also Harter, 1999, 2012)

The concept of self as both subject and object is predicated upon a capacity for self-reflection and self-consciousness that appears to be uniquely human, in that we are the only animal (insofar as we know) that is aware of, or at least imagines, the existence of its own self. As Leary (2002) observes, these cognitive–affective aspects of self are necessary for human beings to

engage in abstract, symbolically mediated thought about themselves. . .This ability to take oneself as the object of one's own attention and to think consciously about oneself in complex ways is perhaps the cardinal psychological trait that distinguishes human beings from all other animals. . .This apparatus lies at the heart of what we are referring to when we use the term *self* and its variations. (p. 120)

The Encompassing Self

This central idea that the "self" encompasses and organizes the totality of processes associated with human consciousness and lived experience has been echoed over the years by a wide range of theorists, who may focus on particular features or aspects of self-structure or functioning, but do so in the context of a larger integrative system in which these components exist. For example, in his pioneering work on the "seasons of a man's life," Daniel Levinson (1978) emphasizes the synergic relationship between internal and external experiences and representations of self, and how processes of self-development are inextricably linked to the larger contextual forces in which the individual is embedded. Specifically, Levinson contends that:

> The self includes a complex pattern of wishes, conflicts, anxieties and ways of resolving or controlling them. It includes fantasies, moral values and ideals, talents and skills, character traits, modes of feeling, thought and action. Part of the self is conscious; much is unconscious; and we must consider both parts...An essential feature of human life is the *interpenetration* of self and world. Each is inside the other. Our thinking about one must take account of the other. . .the external world is an intrinsic part of the self. We cannot grasp the full nature of the self without seeing how diverse aspects of the world are reflected and contained within it. (p. 42, pp. 46–48)

Implicit within Levinson's definition is the notion that the self "is not a passive, indifferent, or unresponsive entity. Rather, the self is active, involved, and responsive, intentionally engaging in volitional processes to change, alter, or modify its thoughts, feelings, responses, and behaviors" (Baumeister & Vohs, 2012, p. 180). Thus, any encompassing definition of the self, includes these self-control and self-regulation aspects as well as ". . .each person's subjective awareness of his or her stable attributes—beliefs, moods, intentions, actions, and acute changes in feeling. These phenomena define the consensual, sense meaning of self among contemporary Western scholars" (Kagan, 1998, p. 137).

From a very different theoretical and applied standpoint, Mihaly Csikszentmihalyi (1990) draws a similar conclusion vis-à-vis the self from his work on *flow*—"the state in which people are so involved in an activity that nothing else seems to matter; the experience itself is so enjoyable that people will do it even at great cost, for the sheer sake of doing it" (p. 4). On the basis of this work, Csikszentmihalyi contends that:

> The self. . .contains everything else that has passed through consciousness: all the memories, actions, desires, pleasures, and pains are included in it. And more than anything else, the self represents the hierarchy of goals that we have built up, bit by bit, over the years. . .however much we are aware of it, the self is in many ways the most important element of consciousness, for it represents symbolically all of consciousness's other contents, as well as the pattern of their interrelations. (p. 34)

The Transcendent Self

As may be evident already, self-theorists often circle around recurrent and dichotomous themes, such as objectivity versus subjectivity (e.g., Leary, 2002) and consciousness versus unconsciousness (e.g., Levinson, 1978), or explicate continua that range from the physical and material to the metaphysical or spiritual self (e.g., Wilber, 2000). Ultimately, any ecumenical and pluralistic accounting of "self" must grant potential legitimacy to the full spectrum of scholarly views, ranging from putative mechanistic structures of the self to more esoteric dimensions, which are considered "transcendent" or even "spiritual." William James, for example, freely speculated about such matters, maintaining that:

> . . .the spiritual self refers to "a man's inner or subjective being, his psychic faculties or dispositions," that is, to what is most intimate and enduring in one's

self. . .The spiritual self thus corresponds to our every impulse toward psychic advancement, be it intellectual, moral, or religious. (Ferrari, 1999, p. 395; see also Levin, 1992; James, 1956)

Consider also Carl Jung's transcendent and encompassing "Self," in which ". . .the ego is only the subject of my consciousness, while the Self is the subject of my totality: hence it also includes the unconscious psyche. In this sense the Self would be an (ideal) factor which embraces and includes the ego" (Jung, 1959, p. 247). As de Laszlo (1959) explicates, Jung contended that the Self includes

. . .the totality of conscious plus its unconscious components. . .The *self* by definition comprises the full scope of a personality from its most individual traits to its most generic attitudes and experiences, actual as well as potential. Hence, it transcends the existing personality. (de Laszlo, 1959, pp. xxii–xxiii)

As another example of the "metaphysical school," Margolis's (1998) self is composed of three "types": "The Exchanger," the "Obligated Self," and the "Cosmic Self." In this formulation, "The Exchanger . . . .strives for emotional control; it appears to be perpetually balancing the quid pro quos of life" (p. 8). The Obligated Self recognizes that quid pro quo relations ". . .are not enough; human survival requires a continual and unconditional transfer of life's necessities from person to person and from generation to generation" (p. 10). The Cosmic Self "answers a critical human need. . .to imbue life with higher meaning" and give "life and death their explanations and their value"; thus, the Cosmic Self represents "an inmost essence of a higher, spiritual order" (p. 87).

Finally, although Wilber (2000) correctly would contend that his "integral" framework of self could help inform other "types" of self described here—a general point that could well apply to multiple theorists, researchers, and practitioners that are highlighted—a fair reading of Wilber's work arguably would find him occupied prominently with matters that fall within the "transcendental" realm. From his perspective, for example,

The *overall self*, then, is an amalgam of all of these "selves" insofar as they are present in you right now: the proximate self (or "I"), the distal self (or "me"), and at the very back of your awareness, that ultimate Witness (the transcendental Self, antecedent Self, or "I-I"). All of these go into your sensation of being a self in this moment, and all of them are important for understanding the development or evolution of consciousness. (p. 34)

As he further observes,

The ancient sages taught us that, precisely because reality is multi-layered—with physical, emotional, mental, and spiritual dimensions—reality is not simply a one-level affair lying around for all and sundry to see: you must be *adequate* to the level of reality you wish to understand. The soul is not running around out there in the physical world; it cannot be seen with microscopes or telescopes or photographic plates. If you want to see the soul, you must turn within. You must develop your consciousness. You must grow and evolve in your capacity to perceive the deeper layers of your Self, which disclose higher levels of reality: the great within that is beyond; the greater the depth, the higher the reality. (p. 188)

The Constructed Self

In contrast to such transcendent or spiritual propositions, which appear to represent relatively invariant theoretical attributes of the self that manifest uniquely for individual human beings, a number of scholars emphasize that self should be understood within its particular context through a developmental/contextual lens; in this view, changes in self follow changes in context across time and place. Congruent with the basic epistemologies of constructivist and narrative schools, the central contention here is articulated by Ferrari (1999) as follows:

> . . .I tend to conceive of the self as involving narratives that are constructed and change over time. However, I also believe it is important to consider individual differences, such as differences in level of cognitive development or cognitive style, that influence the type of narrative one can or prefers to tell. . .While the ability to tell and appreciate any human narrative reflects our evolutionary heritage and our biology, I find the most meaningful dimension of self is precisely that it grounds our experience in the world in ways that both individuate us and bind us to our community. (Ferrari, 1999, p. 415)

From this perspective, the self is an active, creative, unfolding, and organic structure that is ". . .not something just 'there' but, rather, something constructed out of sense and memory by acts of imagination" (Bruner & Kalmar, 1999, p. 308). A core aspect of Morf and Mischel's (2012) "psycho-social dynamic processing model of the self" seems resonant with this perspective, by noting that "the self is an interpersonal self-construction system" (p. 27). More specifically, the self "emerges through a process of self-construction that involved continuum reciprocal interaction between the dynamics of the system and the demands and affordances of the particular situation and context" (p. 33).

Kegan's (1982) "evolving self" offers a highly integrative and dynamic construction of self, which is conceptualized as a "helix of evolutionary truces," to include "incorporative," "impulsive," "imperial," "interpersonal," "institutional," and "interindividual" developmental progressions. Given its comprehensive and integrative nature, it is challenging to offer a crisp summary of this compelling model. Basically, Kegan focuses upon developmental meaning making, conceptualizing this process as an ongoing dialectic between yearnings for autonomy and fusion as the self inexorably engages with "the other" over the course of a lifetime.

Oyserman, Elmore, & Smith (2012) also speak to the embeddedness of "self" in an "other" context, when noting that,

> Self and identity theories converge in grounding self and identity in social context. Contextual effects on the self may be distal—parenting practices, schooling, the culture, the time and place in which one lives, the experiences one has had early in life. Contextual effects on the self also may be proximal—the psychological implications of the immediate situations one is in. (p. 76)

Along similar constructivist lines, and reminiscent of several historical exemplars noted previously (e.g., Flapan & Fenchel, 1987), different contexts may call for the cultivation and expression of different selves. For example, Snyder and Campbell (1982) maintain that some individuals ". . .tailor their social behavior to fit situational and interpersonal specifications of appropriateness" (i.e., the "Pragmatic Self"), while others ". . .may regard themselves as rather principled beings who value congruence between their actions in social situations and relevant underlying attitudes, feelings, and dispositions" (i.e., the "Principled Self") (pp. 186–187). Nonetheless, these selves "in action" must be interpreted through the various contextual domains through which they are expressed (e.g., cognitive, behavioral, interpersonal, sociocultural). As Cross and Gore (2012) note regarding future scholarship on these constructs of self, both locally and globally,

> We look forward to the day that research expands to include African, Latin American, or Aboriginal models of self. In addition, we look forward to the day that this research on cultural models has more impact on social issues and processes. The possible linkages between self-construal and mental or physical health, educational practices, intergroup relations, and other areas of applied research are ripe for examination. Regarding research on culture and self, we are confident that the best is yet to come. (p. 605)

The Gestalten Self

In contrast to such "multiple self" perspectives, other theorists have focused on the interaction among parts to create a larger whole. Consider, for example, two schools of thought that focus on different halves of the same self: the clinical-developmental (C-D) school, which is primarily psychodynamic, and the social-cognitive-developmental (S-C-D) school, which is primarily experimental (Weston, 1992). From a C-D perspective, perhaps the most widely known exemplar is the work of Heinz Kohut, the father of "self psychology," who conceptualized the self as an encompassing and overarching vessel for various affective and cognitive processes and phenomena. More specifically, for Kohut, the self is a:

> . . .*supraordinate* constellation, with the drives and defenses (the central ingredients of classical psychoanalytic conceptions of psychic functioning) subsumed as constituents of the self. This is the view of what is called the bipolar self, in which, with maturation, normally self-assertive ambitions crystallize as one pole and attained ideals and values as the other—the two poles then being connected by a tension arc of talents and skills (Wallerstein, 1999, pp. 223–224).

Here, the self is conceptualized in holistic terms, in which "parts and functions are built into the self [but] self is more important than and transcends the sum of its parts" (Rowe & Isaac, 1989, p. 60; see also Kohut & Wolf, 1978; Kramer & Akhtar, 1994). At the same time, the empathy-based features of Kohut's framework also should be recognized, because the self develops, for better or worse, in relation to the primary caregiver ". . .who becomes the empathic selfobject, anticipating and administering to the infant in a timely, sensitive manner" (Flapan & Fenchel, 1987, p. 32).

As prototypes of the social-cognitive-developmental perspective—and informing the "schema" half of the "schemattitude" construct described in Chapter 3 as the EI Self—Markus and Sentis (1982) conceptualize the self as ". . .a system of *self-schemata*," which are ". . .knowledge structures developed by individuals to understand and explain their own social experiences. They serve to integrate a wide range of stimulus information about the self." Ultimately, the self is emergent from these "structures of knowledge about the self" (p. 45). Along similar but expanded lines, consider Harter's (1999) definition of self, which explicates the structural–process continuum within a broader regulatory, cognitive, developmental, and contextual system, which also references elements of constructivism, noted previously. Here, the self is

> . . .both a cognitive and a social construction. In examining the self as a cognitive construction, attention focused on those cognitive-developmental processes that result in changes in the *structure* of the self-system, namely, how self-representations are organized. This approach provides an account of normative, developmental change, and emphasizes the *similarities* among individuals at a given stage of development. In treating the self as a social construction, attention turns to those socialization processes that reflect how children are treated by caregivers, interactions that primarily impact the *evaluative* content of self-representations. (p. 10)

Emphasizing these developmental processes throughout the life span, Harter (2012) further observes that "as cognitive processes undergo normative developmental change, so will the very *structure* and organization of self-representations. Thus, the particular advances, as well as limitations, of each developmental period dictate the features of the self-portrait that are crafted" (p. 680).

One of the more extensive attempts in the literature not only to specify parts in the context of the whole self—but to do so across the C-D and S-C-D schools noted previously—has its impetus in a 1992 target article by Drew Weston, which attempted to identify areas of commonality between the clinical-analytic and social-cognitive perspectives on self. As interesting as his initial formulation was, the 20 responses Weston received illustrate the inherent complexities in trying to bring together (indeed, even introduce) the ideas of these two communities, not to mention the epistemologically divergent scholars who comprise them. Preferring the term "self-representation" as a euphemism for "self," Weston identifies five dimensions that are common to various psychoanalytic formulations of self-representations, which are: (a) multidimensional, (b) affect-laden, (c) integral to "self in relation to other," (d) conscious and unconscious, and (e) relevant to an understanding of "other representations and to wishes and fears" (p. 3). From a social-cognitive perspective, Weston contends that initial conceptualizations saw the self as ". . .a schema, concept, or prototype. . .that is, an organized knowledge structure that aids processing of information about a given domain" (p. 3). Regarding the putative "common ground" from both of these traditions, Weston maintains that:

> Like psychoanalytic theorists, contemporary social-cognitive theorists view the self as affective, multidimensional, and interpersonal. Also like psychoanalytic theorists, they tend to distinguish momentarily activated from more enduring or "core" representations. Like social-cognitive theorists, psychoanalytic theorists view the self as a system of associatively connected representations. Psychoanalytic theorists have also, like social-cognitive developmental researchers, attempted to describe the development of representations from poorly differentiated and bodily self-representations to a complex sense of identity. (p. 4)

The Epistemology of Self

As may now be evident, one's view of the self may be influenced both by the underlying epistemology or disciplinary bent of the theorist's own "self" as well as the construct as it "actually exists" in nature. However, it is perhaps an emerging point of consensus that whatever formulation one prefers, the self must be conceptualized in comprehensive and integrative terms (e.g., Leary & Tangney, 2012; Reber, et al., 2009). For example, if parts of the self are specified, it is important that they may be summed together into a coherent and synergistic whole. That is, although the "parts" can and must be identified, a comprehensive and ecologically valid formulation of self (that would be recognizable by both the research and practice communities—as well as real human beings) must specify the interdependent relationships among these "parts." As Tesser, Stapel, and Wood (2002) likewise note,

> The self, like most psychological entities, consists of an organized set of beliefs, feelings, and behaviors. Psychologists' attempts to understand the self from a scientific perspective have tended, in different historical periods, to emphasize behavioral processes, cognitive processes, or affective and motivational processes. . .It has always been clear, however, that a complete understanding would necessarily involve all aspects of the self. (pp. 10–11)

Thus, as noted at the outset of this discussion, it is incumbent upon theorists and researchers of the self to clarify whether they are focusing on the parts, the whole, or both, and how, as each level of analysis is illuminating and necessary (e.g., Leary & Tangney, 2012; Tesser et al., 2002). Self-theorists may speak as though they are dealing with the "whole" self, when in fact the primary emphasis of their work may be on specifying formative, regulatory, contextual, or perceptual variables and phenomena. A related problem is the lack of definitional commitments to selected terminology in the context of a given formulation. For example, to talk of "wishes," "needs," "fears," and "beliefs" of the self, without attempting to define what is meant by these constructs, places a burdensome demand upon the reader, who is asked to take much more on faith than is reasonable for such a complex and demanding topic. In addition to a lack of definitional specificity, the tendency to assume that a whole and integrated self is apparent or implied, when the focus is really on selected aspects or facets of self (e.g., parts, mechanisms, structures, processes, levels) has been a—if not the—primary impediment to theoretical and conceptual clarity in this broad area of inquiry.

In the final analysis, depending upon one's own idiosyncratic position along Kimble's (1984) empiricist–humanist continuum, it is easy to become either overwhelmed or enthralled by the rich metaphorical language that theorists of the self so often invoke when attempting to explicate this construct. Perhaps that is because we are trying to explain something that "by definition" encompasses us, rather than the converse, which makes it difficult to observe the self with necessary objectivity and sufficient perspective. Or put in cognitive-developmental terms, the infrastructure of our own self is formed before we have the capacity to take perspective on it. Maybe that is why so many self-theorists resort to metaphorical levels of analysis in an attempt to explicate the nature and parameters of the self. Along these lines, it might be said that the fundamental dilemma for a self-theorist is seeing the forest while living in the trees. Although we may map the terrain, study various subsystems, and observe the relationships among them (i.e., the parts of the self), the challenge is imagining a bird's eye view of the entire, interdependent, living forest as it functions in real time and space (i.e., the whole self).

Dimensions of Self

Ultimately, the goal of this overview was not necessarily to explicate philosophical considerations, interesting though they are, as the intended end point. Moreover, the preceding perspective is neither exhaustive, nor intended to be so, since the plethora of compound nouns referencing "self" may well defy a definitive review. Instead, the more pragmatic hope was that such an overview could reveal definitional components and dimensions that a comprehensive and integrated theory of self might wish to address, including the EI Self that is presented in Chapter 3. Although certainly subject to review and modification, the preceding perspectives suggest the following working definition of self, which is illustrated further in Table 2.2.

The human self:

1. is a highly complex and interdependent system that is derivative of our acquisition of consciousness (e.g., awareness of our own existence) as a species;
2. is experienced by each human being in both subjective (I) and objective (me) terms;
3. encompasses and organizes all aspects of human experience and functioning (e.g., needs, feelings, thoughts, behaviors); and,
4. consists of at least six interacting dimensions, which all must be accounted for in any comprehensive framework of self:
   a) formative = the etiology and development of the self (i.e., as innate and/or constructed);
   b) regulatory = the functioning and organization of the self (i.e., its structures and/or processes);
   c) contextual = the level of analysis at which the self is described and experienced (i.e., as internal and/or external);
   d) perceptual = the self's awareness of its own existence, structures, and functions (i.e., as unconscious and/or conscious);
   e) experiential = whether the self is experienced as existing within a three-dimensional and empirical or transcendent and "spiritual" world (i.e., as physical and/or metaphysical); and,
   f) integrative = how, whether, and to what degree the individual components of the self are integrated into a coherent gestalt (i.e., as parts and/or whole).

TABLE 2.2
The Six Dimensions of Self

		SUBJECT SELF = I		OBJECT SELF = ME
I.	Formative:	innate	↔	constructed
II.	Regulatory:	structure	↔	process
III.	Contextual:	internal	↔	external
IV.	Perceptual:	unconscious	↔	conscious
V.	Experiential:	physical	↔	metaphysical
VI.	Integrative:	parts	↔	whole

THE "I" OF EI THEORY

Integrating the Component Parts of Beliefs, Needs, and Self Into a Coherent Whole

At this point, we have described and reviewed each of the three components of the EI Model—*beliefs, needs,* and *self*—while concluding with a working definition of these constructs. But from an interpretive and explanatory standpoint, the remaining task is to engage in a deliberate process of integration across these concepts for purposes of clarity and coherence, theoretically, empirically, and in applied terms. Toward such means and ends, it is important to explicate the "I" or "integrative" aspect of the "Equilintegration" or EI Model. And in fact, throughout the development of the BEVI method and EI Model, the relevance of an integrative perspective has become abundantly clear via three interrelated scholarly and applied considerations: (a) *integration and the self*: from this perspective, integration represents an optimal state of identity or condition of the self, which is achieved only on the basis of prolonged expenditure of psychological "energy" that must persistently be allocated (i.e., "integration" is an optimally calibrated psychological state that once grasped tentatively, is doggedly pursued over the course of one's life) (e.g., Hammer, 2012; Kegan, 1982; Mahler, 1972; Morf & Michel, 2012; Wadsworth, 1996; Wilber, 2000); (b) *integration and human change*: deep-level understanding and transformation vis-à-vis the human condition may be facilitated via an "integrative" approach to assessment, therapy, education, and training; and finally (c) *integration and interdisciplinarity*: disciplinary and professional integration are essential to understanding and addressing the big picture, values-based issues of our day, both locally and globally (e.g., conflict resolution, human rights, sustainability, global education, religious and cultural understanding) (e.g., Coffman, Hopkins, & Ali, 2009; Center for the Study of Interdisciplinarity, 2014; Cultivating the Globally Sustainable Self, 2015; International Network of Inter- and Transdisciplinarity, 2014; Shealy & Bullock, in press). Each of these perspectives on "integration" is considered next.

Integration and the Self

Most fundamentally, the deliberate integration of these three literatures—on *beliefs, needs,* and the *self* —vis-à-vis the EI Model reflects an overarching recognition that "making sense of beliefs and values" requires immersion in multiple and complementary perspectives. Often implicit and sometimes explicit in the preceding theory and data—as well as the research and applied chapters that follow—"integration" is seen as an optimal end point of human development that is integral to more consolidated ways of relating to self, others, and the larger world. Further explication of several exemplars may be illustrative in this regard. Consider first Kegan's (1982) "constructive-developmental" framework of the self, described previously which is informed by a range of neo-Piagetian findings and perspectives. In describing the first two years of development—in which the infant and toddler begin to explore the contours of separateness from caregivers, both psychologically and physically—we see "the beginning of a history of transformations, each of which is a better guarantee to the world of its distinct integrity, a history of successive emergence from it (differentiation) in order to relate to it (integration)" (p. 31) (see also Mahler, 1972). In summarizing the Piagetian framework in relation to his own model of the "evolving self," Kegan comments that,

I have been trying in this rendering of Piaget's discoveries to make two points: first, that each of his stages is plausibly the consequence of a given subject-object balance, or evolutionary truce; and second, that the process of movement is plausibly the evolutionary motion of differentiation (or emergence from embeddedness) and reintegration (relation to, rather than embeddedness in, the world). That is, the rebalancing that 'moves' the action-sensing of the infant from subject to object leads to the first equilibrium (the preoperational), an equilibrium that makes one's meaning-making *subject to* the perceptions which coordinate action-sensing. . . . (p. 39)

Resonant with Kegan's (1982) framework, but seeking to integrate multiple "waves of being" from both eastern and western philosophical, research, and applied traditions, Wilber's (2000) "integral psychology" is one of the more far-reaching efforts to articulate an integrative perspective regarding the human condition. Essentially, spanning the spectrum from physiology to metaphysics, Wilber drew upon multiple perspectives from developmental research,

along with dozens of other modern theorists, and attempted to integrate it with the best of the perennial philosophers, to arrive at a master template of a *full-spectrum developmental space*, reaching from matter to body to mind to soul to spirit. . .these are the basic waves of being and knowing through which the various developmental streams will flow, all of which are balanced and (ideally) integrated by the self in its remarkable journey from subconscious to self-conscious to superconscious. (p. 90)

From a quite different level of analysis, consider another exemplar of the "integrative" perspective vis-à-vis psychological development and functioning in the form of the Developmental Model of Intercultural Sensitivity (DMIS) (e.g., Bennett, 2004; Hammer, 2012). The DMIS model contends that intercultural development occurs via six primary stages of increasing sensitivity to difference, including Denial, Defense, Minimization, Acceptance, Adaptation, and Integration. Used to guide the interpretation of results from the Intercultural Development Inventory (IDI), this theoretical framework essentially contends that human beings progress through stages from denial (in which differences between cultures are neither recognized nor acknowledged) to—in the final stage—integration (in which individuals do not have a primary investment in any one culture, but are able to move fluidly and empathically within and between them). In a revision to this original framework—the Intercultural Development Continuum (IDC)—Hammer (2012) observes that "integration" represents the "final stage" in the development of intercultural sensitivity and is "concerned with the construction of an intercultural identity rather than the development of intercultural competence" (p. 119).

As a final exemplar of the "integrative" perspective vis-à-vis psychological functioning and development—and as a bridge between the literature and working definition of "self" and the following description of the Equilintegration or EI Self—consider Morf and Mischel's (2012) observation that scholarship on the self,

. . .is scattered across diverse subfields and disciplines that often operate in isolation, impervious to developments just across the boundaries. As a result, integration and the growth of a cumulative science of self are exceedingly difficult, making it essential to cross those boundaries to obtain a comprehensive understanding of the self. (p. 21)

With a goal to "build on these developments to construct a more integrative framework for understanding the self" (p. 21), Morf and Mischel offer a Psycho-Social Dynamic Processing System, "as an effort to integrate diverse contributions that already exist—it is a system that rests on, and is intended to reflect, decades of cumulative contributions from many sides of our science" (p. 22). As they conclude,

> the study of the self now seems perched at the intersect—indeed the hub—between areas that include personality processes and dynamics, social cognition, emotion-motivation, developmental psychology, interpersonal behavior, clinical-health psychology-behavioral medicine, and cultural psychology. This expanded, integrative view influences how the science of the self organizes itself (e.g., in terms of conferences and journals), trains its students, and shapes its research projects. A curriculm for the training of the "complete self researcher" ideally needs to span virtually every area of psychological science. . .this expanded, yet integrated view of the self impacts on the type of conceptual framework needed to capture the complexities and scope of self-relevant phenomena and processes with the depth they deserve. (p. 42)

Against this conceptually aspirational backdrop regarding the importance of integration vis-à-vis the development and functioning of the self, consider a quintessential illustration of why integration is relevant in applied terms, via change-based processes within the field and profession of mental health.

Integration and Human Change

Although expressions of the integrative impulse have manifested in the mental health realm via theory and technique, its empirical foundation is grounded in the observation that it has been exceedingly difficult to identify a single theoretical perspective that facilitates change "better" for all or even most people all or most of the time. Rather, factors that are *common* across therapies and techniques (e.g., acceptance, congruence, empathy, encouragement, understanding, warmth) tend to be associated with the perception and experience of healing and growth irrespective of the theoretical framework through which they are expressed (e.g., Castonguay, 2000; Norcross, 2002). But from an EI perspective, there is another reason that exposure to such relational contexts is key: Just as human beings tend to thrive from exposure to such healing environments that are skillfully created and maintained, so does abundant evidence suggest that human beings suffer and experience developmental and functional impairment to the degree they are exposed to contexts and relational environments that are antithetical to that which would characterize an optimal therapeutic milieu. Such environments include chronic or intense exposure to anger, blurred or inappropriate boundaries, hostility or criticism, emotional rigidity, inflexibility, avoidance of affect, coercion, and so forth (e.g., Brewin, MacCarthy, Duda, & Vaughn, 1991; Cummings et al., 2000; Shealy, 1995; Sroufe, 2009; Toth & Cicchetti, 2013). In short, all aspects of development and functioning may be affected by the relative degree, intensity, and duration of exposure to such disparate contexts. As such, the "I" of EI theory maintains that many different subfields in psychology, and all major therapeutic schools and professions, have something of import to impart, and that interacting levels of analysis—biological, intrapsychic, individual, interpersonal, contextual, sociocultural, transcendent—may shape and be shaped by these contextual processes, and therefore are relevant to training, theory, research, and practice from an integrative perspective (e.g., Shealy, Cobb, Crowley, Nelson, & Peterson, 2004).

Complementary to this point, it also is necessary to contemplate what sort of "professional identity" we wish to inculcate in ourselves and our students. As may be clear, although occupying similar intellectual space, the place where these respective research and practice emphases reside remains a house divided. On the one hand, this split-level focus is emblematic of the chronic disconnect between researchers and practitioners in our larger field (e.g., Gaudiano & Statler, 2001; Henriques, 2011; Magnavita & Achin, 2013). In the case of beliefs and values, for example, researchers have largely been concerned with developing broad-based, nomothetic theories that can help explain behavior at a general level, even across contexts and cultures. For example, social psychologists have demonstrated powerfully that our attitudes and actions are shaped by potent social and situational forces (e.g., to conform), even though we tend to underestimate or minimize the impact of such forces on our own behavior (e.g., Aronson, 2012; Kowalski & Leery, 1999; Moskowitz, 2005). As Staub (1996, 2003, 2013) illustrates, such theory and research has been particularly salient for understanding genocide and other cultural–societal "roots" of violence.

Although typically familiar to practicing clinicians, it often is not clear how to translate and apply such information to the individual case (e.g., Kowalski & Leery, 1999). For example, if you are a clinical psychologist engaged in the process of evaluating the killers of Matthew Shepherd or James Byrd Jr. (see Chapter 1), theory and data on prejudice—a key emphasis in social psychology—might provide a theoretical backdrop against which specific assessment material could be juxtaposed. However, from a clinical and forensic standpoint, such theory does not provide the level of specificity that is necessary for practitioners, or the judiciary for that matter. Instead, to make sense of why people do what they do, practitioners have tended to draw upon theories and methods that are grounded ultimately in the individual case; such perspectives often focus on diagnostic, intrapsychic, and developmental psychopathological processes and dynamics (e.g., Cozen et al., 2016; Cummings et al., 2000; Horwitz, 2002; Shealy, 1995; Sroufe, 2009; Storr, 1991). For nonclinical, experimental researchers, such concepts and findings may seem poorly conceptualized and abstruse at best and/or not readily generalized beyond "case study" methodologies. The consequence of this "cultural clash" (e.g., Kimble, 1984) is that neither side gets a fair hearing, nor appreciates the powerful contributions and epistemologies of the other. Minds close, and the two (or more) "cultures" walk away from each other.

This unfortunate tendency is perhaps one reason why scientists and practitioners have followed such divergent paths vis-à-vis beliefs and values. Ironically, however, as Rokeach (1973) originally suggested, beliefs and values may epitomize the need and opportunity for greater "unification" in our field (e.g., Henriques, 2011; Magnavita & Achin, 2013; Shealy, 2005; Sternberg & Grigorenko, 2001), mainly because these phenomena intersect at the point where the individual psyche and the surrounding context meet; thus, our ability to offer a coherent and ecologically valid explanation for such processes and dynamics will require awareness and integration of both levels of analysis. In short, the fact that beliefs and values are acquired, maintained, and under specific circumstances, transformed, suggests that they function as a mediational and dialectic vinculum between the contextual and intrapsychic realms.

Thus, to derive a more comprehensive and unified approach to these issues, it is necessary to speak to the interests and concerns of both researchers and practitioners regardless of subfield or predilection, and provide theory and methods that can promote dialogue and collaboration across these two levels of analysis (e.g., Henriques, 2011; Magnavita & Achin, 2013; Sternberg & Grigorenko, 2001). For one, plausible theory is needed to account for the acquisition, maintenance, and transformation of beliefs and values across a wide but representative spectrum of what can be believed, from the sort of extreme religious and political ideology that can justify terrorist attacks, to basic beliefs about etiology that lead one to prefer a particular way of intervening with clients. That is, theory is needed to account for processes and dynamics that are relevant to understanding and investigating the acquisition, maintenance, and transformation of beliefs and values in general, regardless of their specific manifestation. Moreover, reliable and valid methods are needed to test such theory, in order to determine the degree to which its fundamental propositions are robust and relevant to real world events, circumstances, and processes. That is, if we are to try and understand and address the implications of values and beliefs (writ large) in a way that is epistemologically relevant and ecologically valid, our methods should be useful not only for matters of theoretical development, but to those who must contend with and make predictions about beliefs and values in the real world (e.g., practitioners, clients, training faculty, educators, policy makers). In addition to the two perspectives noted previously—on the importance of an integrative perspective for understanding the psychological development/functioning of the self as well as how the mental health field facilitates change—such integrative aspirations are well exemplified by the burgeoning movement to embrace a truly interdisciplinary approach to inquiry and practice.

Integration and Interdisciplinarity

As should be evident by now, to "make sense of beliefs and values" we cannot apprehend, much less address, highly complex phenomena (e.g., such as human nature or why we do what we do) without an appreciation that multiple disciplinary and professional frameworks may have perspectives that are worthy of consideration. This general philosophical and epistemological stance is known by a number of interrelated terms, but perhaps the most fundamental is that of "interdisciplinarity," which has—by some accounts—ancient roots in the acknowledgment that the more complex the issue at hand, the more necessary it becomes to include a wide swath of disciplinary perspectives, theoretically, empirically, and in applied terms. Multiple movements, organizations, and scholarly forums have arisen in support of this proposition (e.g., see Center for the Study of Interdisciplinarity, 2014; International Network of Inter- and Transdisciplinarity, 2014). At a more focused level—within the realm of health care/mental health care—frameworks such as "interprofessional education" and "interprofessional collaboration" are noteworthy as well (e.g., see Arredondo, Shealy, Neale, & Winfrey, 2004; Interprofessional Education Collaborative, 2014).

Likewise, any durable attempt to "make sense of beliefs and values" must grapple with the fact that *H. sapiens* lives all over the planet, and although is one species, often expresses "different" beliefs and values. From an EI perspective, this fact is most parsimoniously explained not by positing fundamental differences in the way we are built (e.g., the underlying affective, attributional, biological, developmental, and contextual processes that interact throughout our life span), but rather by differences in what is available for acquisition as well as the prevailing contingencies regarding what is and is not reinforced. As such, one of the fundamental propositions of EI Theory is that although that which is believed and valued may not transcend a given time or place, the human capacity and need for an organizing worldview is an etic derivative of the self. In other words, although the content of our beliefs and values may vary as a function of what is available for acquisition (e.g., in a given culture, time, and place), the processes (e.g., developmental, affective, attributional) by which beliefs and values are acquired are determined by constitutive dimensions of the self as noted in the preceding definition (e.g., formative, regulatory, contextual, perceptual, experiential, integrative). From an empirical standpoint, many findings presented in the research and practice chapters that follow offer support for this fundamental proposition that we are—in the end (e.g., in biopsychosocial terms)—fundamentally "the same" as a species, even if our beliefs and values about self, others, and the larger world differ.

In conclusion then, the "I" of EI Theory seeks to translate theory and data from multiple disciplines and perspectives into research and applied form that may credibly address the most pressing issues of our day. There can be no question that such a pursuit is ambitious and fraught with all manner of epistemological, methodological, and contextual peril. But do we have a choice? The "wicked issues of our day" require us to bring our collective expertise, wisdom, and energy to bear upon such matters (e.g., Coffman, Hopkins, & Ali, 2009). To not do so implies resignation in the face of the extraordinary complexities we encounter, locally and globally. The good news is, we now have the conceptual sophistication, methodological capacity, and interdisciplinary commitments to work together toward these shared means and ends. Ultimately, it is hoped that the research and practice described in this book offer one way to translate that which is abstruse and opaque—the etiology and nature of beliefs and values—into a form that is more accessible and actionable, in order to investigate what might be called, "belief studies," while simultaneously learning how to "cultivate the capacity to care" in self, others, and the larger world (Cultivating the Globally Sustainable Self, 2015; Shealy et al., 2012).

SUMMARY OF EI THEORY

Definitions and Principles

Because we have covered a lot of ground in this chapter, it may be helpful to provide a concluding set of definitions and principles, representing the essence of all that has been considered vis-à-vis Equilintegration or EI Theory, which—with the EI Self (discussed in Chapter 3)—comprise the EI Model. The below summary consists of three primary definitions (Belief, Need, Self) and six principles of EI Theory (Etiological, Mediational, Constitutive, Explicative, Resistance, Transformational).

I. Summary of EI Theory Definitions

A. Belief

A *belief*:

1. is an internalized and discrete version of reality (i.e., a mental representation about self, others, or the world at large) that can influence and mediate the experience and expression of needs, feelings, thoughts, and behaviors;
2. can vary along dimensions of cognitive complexity and affective intensity;
3. is subjectively experienced to be relatively "true" or "false" and/or "good" or "bad";
4. may or may not be empirically verifiable (i.e., the believer may not be able to prove or reliably demonstrate that a belief is true or false);
5. may or may not be consciously accessible (i.e., the believer may not be aware of his or her belief);

6. if consciously accessible, is typically verbalized in relativistic terms as a "truth" or "goodness" statement about self, others, and/or the world at large;

7. typically exists in a synergistic relationship to other beliefs in that a belief stated in one direction is often matched by one or more counterparts that exist in relative degrees of opposition to it;

8. may be characterized by four interrelated "dimensions of belief"—favorability, veracity, intensity, and congruency—and four "points of self-access"—hard structure, soft structure, crack in the structure, and space in the structure;

9. manifests along a "Continuum of Belief," ranging from "committed certitude" to "noncommitted skepticism"; and,

10. exists in the service of core human needs—appetitive, attachment, affective, acknowledgment, activation, affiliative, actualizing, attunement, and awareness—and emerges from an interaction among four levels of self—endoself, mesoself, ectoself, and exoself.

B. Need

Core human needs:

1. motivate or drive the human organism throughout the life span to achieve fulfillment of the core needs to a degree that is subjectively experienced as sufficient for each human being (including the appetitive, attachment, affective, acknowledgment, activation, affiliative, actualizing, attunement, and awareness needs);

2. exist along a physical and psychological continuum that encompasses the whole of human experience;

3. are derived from our history of evolutionary adaptation and therefore are core to our existence and defining characteristics as a species;

4. are expressed through the adaptive potential that is unique for each human being;

5. are shaped in expressive form by developmental processes and formative variables that are unique to each human being; and,

6. are evidenced nonverbally through various physiological and behavioral indexes and/or expressed verbally through our stated beliefs and values about self, others, and the world at large.

C. Self

The human self:

1. is a highly complex and interdependent system that is derivative of our acquisition of consciousness (e.g., awareness of our own existence) as a species;

2. experienced by each human being in both subjective (I) and objective (me) terms;

3. encompasses and organizes all aspects of human experience and functioning (e.g., needs, feelings, thoughts, behaviors); and,

4. consists of at least six interacting dimensions, which all must be accounted for in any comprehensive framework of self:

   a) *formative* = the etiology and development of the self (i.e., as innate and/or constructed);

   b) *regulatory* = the functioning and organization of the self (i.e., its structures and/or processes);

c) *contextual* = the level of analysis at which the self is described and experienced (i.e., as internal and/or external);

d) *perceptual* = the self's awareness of its own existence, structures, and functions (i.e., as unconscious and/or conscious);

e) *experiential* = whether the self is experienced as existing within a three-dimensional and empirical or transcendent and "spiritual" world (i.e., as physical and/or metaphysical); and,

f) *integrative* = how, whether, and to what degree the individual components of the self are integrated into a coherent gestalt (i.e., as parts and/or whole).

II. Summary of EI Theory Principles

Based upon all that has been discussed throughout this chapter, the following summary strives to explicate the essential principles of EI Theory across six interrelated levels of analysis: etiological, mediational, constitutive, explicative, resistant, and transformational. Against the backdrop of this chapter, these principles may also provide helpful context for the Equilintegration or EI Self and BEVI, discussed respectively in Chapters 3 and 4.

1. *Etiological.* Our beliefs and values are not necessarily correct or superior because they are ours. Rather, the beliefs and values we hold to be relatively good and true or bad and false are culminating artifacts of an interaction among (a) adaptive potential (e.g., genetic predispositions), (b) core need (e.g., attachment, affiliation), (c) formative variables (e.g., care givers, life history), and (d) extant contingencies (e.g., that which is and is not reinforced in a specific time and place).

2. *Mediational.* Beliefs and values are central mediating processes for behavior at individual and societal levels, but they may or may not be "known" (i.e., may be implicit or nonconscious), and are not necessarily rational or logically grounded.

3. *Constitutive.* Although that which is believed and valued may not transcend a given time or place, the human capacity and need for an organizing worldview is an etic derivative of the self. Thus, although the content of our beliefs and values may vary as a function of what is available for acquisition, the processes (e.g., developmental, affective, attributional) by which beliefs and values are acquired are determined by constitutive aspects of the self (i.e., formative, regulatory, contextual, perceptual, experiential, and integrative dimensions).

4. *Explicative.* When combined with sufficient knowledge about important life experiences and events, belief and value statements often provide (a) a great deal of information about the hypothetical structure and organization of personality or "self" and (b) a relatively accessible point of entry to issues and phenomena that are meaningful in a wide range of settings and contexts.

5. *Resistant.* Although they can and do change, beliefs and values are not easily modified because they represent the culmination of an interaction among (a) core needs (e.g., attachment, affiliation), (b) mediational processes (e.g., attribution, filtering), and (c) external contingencies (e.g., that which is reinforced), which are codified (ultimately at a physiological level) in personality and "self."

6. *Transformational.* Because human beings balance the desire for equilibrium and stasis against the inevitable internal and external pressures for development and growth, changing beliefs and values often means accessing underlying needs and reconfiguring their alignment to beliefs and values, which changes self-structure (and vice versa); this process of understanding how self-structure came to be

inevitably involves an emotionally charged and not-always-conscious examination of how one's needs may be better met with attendant implications for what one believes and values about self, others, and the world at large. Ultimately, whether or not and the degree to which beliefs and values "change" depends upon the "7Ds" (i.e., duration, difference, depth, determine, design, deliver, debrief).

So, at this point, we have considered three core constructs—*beliefs, needs*, and *self*—which represent the fundamental components of Equilintegration Theory. But this framework emerged over two decades, and in truth, was a highly organic process, informed through (a) immersion in a wide range of literatures regarding the nature of these constructs, (b) the gradual development of the BEVI since the early 1990s, and (c) use of this measure in a wide range of applied contexts and practice settings. On the basis of multiple presentations and discussions over the years, it has proven helpful to try and explain this theoretical framework—all that has been discussed throughout this chapter—in applied terms. The medium for doing so is the EI Self, described next in Chapter 3. Taken together, EI Theory and the EI Self comprise the EI Model, which seeks to explain and illustrate how and why "core need" (e.g., attachment, affiliation) interacts with "formative variables" (e.g., life history, demographics) to result in the "beliefs and values" we ultimately call our own.

REFERENCES

Adler, E., & Bachant, J. L. (1998). Intrapsychic and interactive dimensions of resistance: A Contemporary perspective. *Psychoanalytic Psychology, 15*, 451–479.

Adorno, T. W., Frenkel-Brunswik, E., Levinson, D. J., Sanford, R. N. (1950). *The authoritarian personality*. New York, NY: Harper.

Altemeyer, B., & Hunsberger, B. E. (1992). Authoritarianism, religious fundamentalism, quest, and prejudice. *International Journal for the Psychology of Religion, 2*(2), 113–133.

Anderson, S. M., Chen, S., & Carter, C. (2000). Fundamental human needs: Making social cognition relevant. *Psychological Inquiry, 11*(4), 269–275.

Anmuth, L. M., Poore, M., Cozen, J., Brearly, T., Tabit, M., Cannady, M., . . . Staton, R. (2013, August). *Making implicit beliefs explicit: In search of best practices for mental health clients, clinicians, and trainers*. Poster presented at the annual meeting of the American Psychological Association, Honolulu, HI.

Aronson, E. (2012). *The social animal* (11th ed.). New York, NY: Worth Publishers.

Oakland University. (2014). Association for Interdisciplinary Studies. Retrieved May 7, 2014 from http://www.units.miamioh.edu/aisorg/

Arredondo, P., Shealy, C., Neale, M., and Winfrey, L. (2004). Consultation and interprofessional collaboration: Modeling for the future. [Special Series]. *Journal of Clinical Psychology, 60*(7), 787–800.

Auerbach, J. S. (1998). Dualism, self-reflexivity, and intersubjectivity: Commentary on paper by Sheldon Bach. *Psychoanalytic Dialogues, 8*(5), 675–683.

Bach, S. (1998). Two ways of being. *Psychoanalytic Dialogues, 8*(5), 657–673.

Bandura, A. (1982). The self and mechanisms of agency. In J. Suls (Ed.), *Psychological perspectives on the self* (pp. 3–39). Hillsdale, NJ: Lawrence Erlbaum Associates.

Baumeister, R. F., Dale, K. L., & Muraven, M. (2000). Volition and belongingness: Social movements, volition, self-esteem, and the need to belong. In S. Stryker, T. Owens & R. White (Eds.), *Self, identity, and social movements* (pp. 239–251). Minneapolis, MN: University of Minnesota Press.

Baumeister, R. F., Brewer, L. E., Tice, D. M., & Twenge, J. M. (2007). Thwarting the need to belong: Understanding the interpersonal and inner effects of social exclusion. *Social and Personality Psychology Compass, 1*(1), 506–520.

Baumeister, R. F., & Vohs, K. D. (2012). Self-regulation and the executive function of the self. In M. R. Leary & J. P. Tangney (Eds.), *Handbook of self and identity* (2nd ed., pp. 180–197). New York, NY: The Guilford Press.

Baumrind, D. (1971). Current patterns of parental authority. *Developmental Psychology*, 4(1, Pt. 2), 1–103.

Beier, E. G. (1984). The application of a model of psychotherapy to world problems. *Journal of Clinical Psychology, 40*, 1278–1281.

Bennett, M. J. (2004). Becoming interculturally competent. In J. Wurzel (Ed.), *Towards multiculturalism: A reader in multicultural education* (2nd ed., pp. 62–77). Newton, MA: Intercultural Resource.

Bergin, A. E. (1980). Psychotherapy and religious values. *Journal of Consulting and Clinical Psychology, 46*(1), 95–105.

Bergin, A. E. (1991). Values and religious issues in psychotherapy and mental health. *American Psychologist, 46*(4), 394–403.

Beutler, L. E. (1979). Values, beliefs, religion and the persuasive influence of psychotherapy. *Psychotherapy: Theory, Research and Practice, 16*, 432–440.

Blanchard-Fields, F., Hertzog, C., & Horhota, M. (2011). Violate my beliefs? Then you're to blame! Belief content as an explanation for causal attribution biases. *Psychology and Aging*, 27(2), 324–337

Bowlby, J. (1969). *Attachment and loss: Vol. 1. Attachment*. New York, NY: Basic Books.

Bowlby, J. (1973). *Attachment and loss: Vol. 2. Separation: Anger and anxiety*. New York, NY: Basic Books.

Bowlby, J. (1980). *Attachment and loss: Vol. 3. Loss: Sadness and depression*. New York, NY: Basic Books.

Braithwaite, V. A., & Scott, W. A. (1991). Values. In J. P. Robinson, P. R. Shaver, & L. S. Wrightsman (Eds.), *Measures of personality and social psychological attitudes* (pp. 661–753). San Diego, CA: Academic Press.

Brewin, C. R., MacCarthy, B., Duda, K., & Vaughn, C. E. (1991). Attribution and expressed emotion in the relatives of patients with schizophrenia. *Journal of Abnormal Psychology, 100*, 546–554.

Bruner, J., & Kalmar, D. A. (1999). Narrative and metanarrative in the construction of self. In M. Ferrari & R. J. Sternberg (Eds.), *Self-awareness: Its nature and development* (pp. 308–331). New York, NY: The Guilford Press.

Bugental, D. B., Johnston, C., New, M., & Silvester, J. (1998). Measuring parental attributions: Conceptual and methodological issues. *Journal of Family Psychology, 12*(4), 459–480.

Campbell, R. J. (2009). *Psychiatric dictionary* (9th ed.). New York, NY: Oxford University Press.

Castonguay, L. G. (2000). A common factors approach to psychotherapy training. *Journal of Psychotherapy Integration, 10*, 363–382.

Center for the Study of Interdisciplinarity. (2014). Retrieved from July 27, 2014 http://www.csid.unt.edu/

Christie, R. (1991). Authoritarianism and related constructs. In J. P. Robinson, P. R. Shaver & L. S. Wrightsman (Eds.), *Measures of personality and social psychological attitudes* (pp. 501–571). San Diego, CA: Academic Press.

Coates, M., Hanson, W., Samuel, D. B., Webster, M., & Cozen, J. (2016). The Beliefs, Events, and Values Inventory (BEVI). Psychological assessment implications and applications. In C. N. Shealy (Ed.), *Making sense of beliefs and values* (pp. 371–406). New York, NY: Springer Publishing.

Coffman, J. E., Hopkins, C., & Ali, I. A. (2009). Education for Sustainable Development: Halfway through the Decade of ESD and a long way from sustainability. *Beliefs and Values, 1*(2), 142–150.

Council of Chairs of Training Councils. (2004). Retrieved November 3, 2015 from http://www.cctcpsychology.org/wp-content/uploads/2014/08/NCSPP-CCTC-model-Student-Competency.pdf

Cozen, J., Hanson, W., Poston, J., Jones, S., & Tabit, M. (2016). The Beliefs, Events, and Values Inventory (BEVI): Implications and applications for therapeutic assessment and intervention. In C. N. Shealy (Ed.), *Making sense of beliefs and values* (pp. 575–621). New York, NY: Springer Publishing.

Cross, S. E., & Gore, J. S. (2012). Cultural models of the self. In M. R. Leary & J. P. Tangney (Eds.), *Handbook of self and identity* (2nd ed., pp. 587–614). New York, NY: The Guilford Press.

Csikszentmihalyi, M. (1990). *Flow: The psychology of optimal experience*. New York, NY: Harper & Row.

Cultivating the Globally Sustainable Self. (2015, March). Retrieved November 3, 2015 from www.jmu.edu/summitseries

Cummings, E. M., Davies, P. T., & Campbell, S. S. (2000). *Developmental psychopathology and family process: Theory, research, and clinical implications*. New York, NY: Guilford Press.

Cranton, P. (Ed.). (2006). *Understanding and promoting transformative learning: A guide for educators of adults*. San Francisco, CA: Jossey Bass.

Curtis, R. C. (1991). *The relational self: Theoretical convergences in psychoanalysis and social psychology*. New York, NY: The Guilford Press.

Dalhouse, M., & Frideres, J. S. (1996). Intergenerational congruency: The role of the family in political attitudes of youth. *Journal of Family Issues, 17*(2), 227–248.

Deacon, B. J. (2013). The biomedical model of mental disorder: A critical analysis of its validity, utility, and effects on psychotherapy research. *Clinical Psychology Review, 33*, 846–861.

De Laszlo, S. V. (Ed.). (1959). *The basic writing of C. G. Jung*. New York, NY: The Modern Library.

De Waal, F. (2013). *The bonobo and the atheist*. New York, NY: W. W. Norton and Company.

Deci, E. L., & Ryan, R. M. (2000). The "what" and "why" of goal pursuits: Human needs and the self-determination of behavior. *Psychological Inquiry, 11*(4), 227–268.

Dirkx, J. M. (2012). Self-formation and transformative learning: A response to "Calling transformative learning into question: Some mutinous thoughts," by Michael Newman. *Adult Education Quarterly, 62*(4), 399–405

Dix, T. (1993). Attributing dispositions to children: An interactional analysis of attribution in socialization. *Personality and Social Psychology Bulletin, 19*(5), 633–643.

Dollinger, S. J., Leong, F. T. L., & Ulicni, S. K. (1996). On traits and values: With special reference to openness to experience. *Journal of Research in Personality, 30*, 23– 41.

Duncan, L. E., & Stewart, A. J. (1995). Still bringing the Vietnam War home: Sources of contemporary student activism. *Personality and Social Psychology Bulletin, 21*(9), 914–924.

Dyjak-LeBlanc, K., Brewster, L., Grande, S., White, R., & Shullman, S. (2016). The EI Leadership Model: From theory and research to real world application. In C. N. Shealy (Ed.), *Making sense of beliefs and values* (pp. 531–574). New York, NY: Springer Publishing.

Ekehammar, B., Akrami, N., & Gylje, M. (2004). What matters most to prejudice: Big five personality, social dominance, or right-wing authoritarianism. *European Journal of Personality, 18*(6), 463–482.

Emery, S., Wade, T. D., & McLean, S. (2009). Associations among therapist beliefs, personal resources and burnout in clinical psychologists. *Behaviour Change, 26*(2), 83–96.

Feather, N. T. (1979). Value correlates of conservatism. *Journal of Personality and Social Psychology, 37*(9), 1617–1630.

Feather, N. T. (1984). Masculinity, femininity, psychological androgyny, and the structure of values. *Journal of Personality and Social Psychology, 47*(3), 604–620.

Feather, N. T. (1992). Values, valences, expectations, and actions. *Journal of Social Issues, 48*(2), 109–124.

Feather, N. T. (1994). Human values and their relation to justice. *Journal of Social Issues, 50*(4), 129–152.

Feather, N. T. (1995). Values, valences, and choice: The influence of values on the perceived attractiveness and choice of alternatives. *Journal of Personality and Social Psychology, 68*(6), 1135–1151.

Feather, N. T., & McKee, I. (2012). Values, right-wing authoritarianism, social dominance orientation, and ambivalent attitudes toward women. *Journal of Applied Social Psychology, 42*(10), 2479–2504.

Feather, N. T., & Souter, J. (2002). Reactions to mandatory sentences in relation to the ethnic identity and criminal history of the offender. *Law and Human Behavior, 26*(4), 417–438.

Ferrari, M. (1999). Being and becoming self-aware. In M. Ferrari & R. J. Sternberg (Eds.), *Self-awareness: Its nature and development* (pp. 387–422). New York, NY: The Guilford Press.

Ferrari, M., & Sternberg, R. J. (Eds.). (1998). Self-awareness: Its nature and development. New York: Guilford Press.

Flapan, D., & Fenchel, G. H. (1987). *The developing ego and the emerging self in group therapy.* Northvale, NJ: Jason Aronson.

Fonagy, P. (1996). The significance of the development of metacognitive control over mental representations in parenting and infant development. *Journal of Clinical Psychoanalysis, 5*(1), 67–86.

Fox, W. M. (1982). Why we should abandon Maslow's need hierarchy theory. *Journal of Human Counseling, Education & Development, 21*(1), 29–32.

Frijda, N. H., Manstead, A. S., & Bem, S. (2000). The influence of emotions on beliefs. In N. H. Frijda, A. S. Manstead, & S. Bem (Eds.), *Emotions and beliefs: How thoughts influence feelings* (pp. 1–9). Cambridge, UK: Cambridge University Press.

Gartner, J., Harmatz, M., Hohmann, A., Larson, D., & Gartner, A. F. (1990). The effect of patient and clinician ideology on clinical judgment: A study of ideological countertransference. *Psychotherapy, 27*(1), 98–106.

Gaudiano, B. A., & Statler, M. A. (2001). The scientist-practitioner gap and graduate education: Integrating perspectives and looking forward. *The Clinical Psychologist, 54*(4), 12–18.

Geller, L. (1982). The failure of self-actualization theory: A critique of Carl Rogers and Abraham Maslow. *Journal of Humanistic Psychology, 22*(2), 56–73.

Gergen, K. J. (1998). From control to construction: New narratives for the social sciences. *Psychological Inquiry, 9,* 101–103.

Gergen, K. J. (1999). Psychological science in a postmodern context. *American Psychologist, 56*(10), 803–813.

Gerhardt, J., & Stinson, C. S. (1995). "I don't know": Resistance or groping for words? The construction of analytic subjectivity. *Psychoanalytic Dialogues, 5*(4), 619–672.

Goddard, H. & Miller, B. (1993). Adding attribution to parenting programs. *Families in Society, 74*(2), 84–92.

Greenwald, A. G. (1982). Is anyone in charge? Personalysis versus the principle of personal unity. In J. Suls (Ed.), *Psychological perspectives on the self* (pp. 151–181). Hillsdale, NJ: Lawrence Erlbaum Associates.

Grube, J. W., Mayton, D. M., & Ball-Rokeach, S. J. (1994). Inducing change in values, attitudes, and behaviors: Belief system theory and the method of value self-confrontation. *Journal of Social Issues, 50*(4), 153–174.

Hall, M. E., & Hall, T. W. (1997). Integration in the therapy room: An overview of the literature. *Journal of Psychology and Theology, 25*(1), 86–101.

Hammer, M. (2012). The Intercultural Development Inventory: A new frontier in assessment and development of intercultural competence. In M. Vande Berg, R. M. Paige, & K. H. Lou (Eds.), *Student learning abroad* (Ch. 5, pp. 115–136). Sterling, VA: Stylus Publishing.

Harris, S. M. (1998). Finding a forest among trees: Spirituality hiding in family therapy theories. *Journal of Family Studies, 4*(1), 77–86.

Harter, S. (1999). *The construction of the self: A developmental perspective.* New York, NY: The Guilford Press.

Harter, S. (2012). Emerging self-processes during childhood and adolescence. In M. R. Leary & J. P. Tangney (Eds.), *Handbook of self and identity* (2nd ed., pp. 680–715). New York, NY: The Guilford Press.

Henriques, G. (2011). *A new unified theory of psychology.* New York, NY: Springer.

Heller, N. R., & Northcut, T. B. (1998). Assessment of cognitive schemas and attributions in psychodynamic treatment. *Smith College Studies in Social Work, 68,* 185–202.

Hopkins, J. R. (2011, December). The enduring influence of Jean Piaget. Retrieved September 21, 2014 from http://www.psychologicalscience.org/index.php/publications/observer/2011/december-11/jean-piaget.html

Horwitz, A. (2002). *Creating mental illness.* Chicago, IL: University of Chicago Press.

Hull, C. L. (1943). *Principles of behavior: An introduction to behavior theory.* New York, NY: Appleton-Century-Crofts.

Inglehart, R., Basáñez, M., Díez-Medrano, J., Halman, L., & Luijkx, R. (2004). *Human beliefs and values: A cross-cultural sourcebook based on the 1999-2002 values surveys.* Mexico: Siglo XXI Editores.

Inglehart, R., Basáñez, M., & Moreno, A. (1998). *Human values and beliefs: A cross-cultural sourcebook.* Ann Arbor, MI: The University of Michigan Press.

International Network of Inter- and Transdisciplinarity. Retrieved May 7, 2014 from http://www.inidtd.org/

Interprofessional Education Collaborative. Retrieved May 7, 2014 from https://ipecollaborative.org/

James, W. (1956). *The will to believe and other essays in popular philosophy.* New York, NY: Dover Publications.

Kagan, J. (1998). Is there a self in infancy? In M. Ferrari & R. J. Sternberg (Eds.), *Self-awareness: Its nature and development* (pp. 137–147). New York, NY: The Guilford Press.

Kaslow, N. J., Celano, M., & Dreelin, E. D. (1995). A cultural perspective on family theory and therapy. *The Psychiatric Clinics of North America, 18*(3), 621–633.

Kegan, R. (1982). *The evolving self.* Cambridge, MA: Harvard University Press.

Kimble, G. A. (1984). Psychology's two cultures. *American Psychologist, 39*(8), 833–839.

Kirkpatrick, L. A., & Shaver, P. R. (1990). Attachment theory and religion: Childhood attachments, religious beliefs, and conversion. *Journal for the Scientific Study of Religion, 29*(3), 315–334.

Kluckhohn, C., & Murray, H. A. (1953). *Personality in nature, society, and culture.* New York, NY: Alfred A. Knopf.

Koestner, R., Losier, G. F., Vallerand, R. J., & Carducci, D. (1996). Identified and introjected forms of political internalization: Extending self-determination theory. *Journal of Personality Processes and Individual Differences, 70*(5), 1025–1036.

Kohut, H., & Wolf, E. S. (1978). The disorders of the self and their treatment: An outline. *International Journal of Psychoanalysis, 59,* 413–425.

Kowalski, R. M., & Leary, M. R. (Eds.). (1999). *The social psychology of emotional and behavioral problems: Interfaces of social and clinical psychology.* Washington, DC: American Psychological Association.

Kramer, S., & Akhtar, S. (Eds.). (1994). *Mahler and Kohut: Perspectives on development, psychopathology, and technique.* Northvale, NJ: Jason Aronson.

Krapp, A. (2005). Basic needs and the development of interest and intrinsic motivational orientations. *Learning and Instruction, 15,* 381–395.

Krech, D., & Crutchfield, R. S. (1948). Theory and problems of social psychology. New York: MacGraw-Hill.

Kruglanski, A. W., & Webster, D .M. (1996). Motivated closing of the mind: "Seizing" and "freezing." *Psychological Reports, 103,* 263–283.

Kuchel, S. (2003). *Individualism and collectivism: A study of values and inferencing in psychotherapy.* (Unpublished doctoral dissertation). McGill University, Montreal (Dissertation Abstracts International, *63,* 34–77).

Kuh, G. D. (2008). *High-impact educational practices: What they are, who has access to them, and why they matter.* Washington, DC: Association of American Colleges and Universities. Retrieved from http://secure.aacu.org/store/detail.aspx?id=E-HIGHIMP

Leary, M. R. (2002). When selves collide: The nature of the self and the dynamics of interpersonal relationships. In A. Tesser, D. A. Stapel, & J. V. Wood (Eds.), *Self and motivation: Emerging psychological perspectives* (pp. 119–146). Washington, DC: American Psychological Association.

Leary, M. R., & Tangney, J. P. (2012). The self as an organizing construct in the behavioral and social sciences. In M. R. Leary & J. P. Tangney (Eds.), *Handbook of self and identity* (2nd ed., pp. 1–8). New York, NY: The Guilford Press.

Leuty, M. E. (2013). Assessment of needs and values. In K. F. Geisinger (Ed.), *APA handbook of testing and assessment in psychology* (pp. 363–377). Washington, DC: American Psychological Association.

Levin, J. D. (1992). *Theories of the self.* Washington, DC: Hemisphere Publishing Corporation.

Levinson, D. J. (1978). *The seasons of a man's life.* New York, NY: Ballantine Books.

Madell, T. O. (1982). The relationship between values and attitudes toward three therapy methods. *Counseling & Values, 27*, 52–61.

Magnavita, J., & Achin, J. (2013). *Unifying psychotherapy: Principles, methods, and evidence from clinical science.* New York, NY: Springer Publishing.

Mahler, M. S. (1972). On the first three phases of the separation-individuation process. *International Journal of Psychoanalysis, 53*, 333–338.

Manstead, A. S., & Hewstone, M. (Eds.). (1999). *The Blackwell encyclopedia of social psychology.* Oxford, UK: Blackwell Publishers.

Manusov, V., & Harvey, J. H. (Eds.). (2001). *Attribution, communication behavior, and close relationships.* New York, NY: Cambridge University Press.

Margolis, D. R. (1998). *The fabric of self.* London, UK: Yale University Press.

Markus, H., & Sentis, K. (1982). The self in social information processing. In J. Suls (Ed.), *Psychological perspectives on the self* (pp. 41–70). Hillsdale, NJ: Lawrence Erlbaum Associates.

Maslow, A. H. (1954). *Motivation and personality.* New York, NY: Harper & Brothers.

Maslow, A. H. (1964). *Religions, values, and peak-experiences.* Columbus, OH: Ohio State University Press.

Maslow, A. H. (1968). *Toward a psychology of being.* New York, NY: D. Van Nostrand Company.

Maslow, A. H. (1971). *The farther reaches of human nature.* New York, NY: The Viking Press.

Maslow, A. H., & Sorokin, P. A. (1959). *New knowledge in human values.* New York, NY: Harper & Brothers, Publishers.

Matusov, E., & Hayes, R. (2000). Sociocultural critique of Piaget and Vygotsky. *New Ideas in Psychology, 18*, 215–239.

McCrae, R. R. (1996). Social consequences of experimental openness. *Psychological Bulletin, 120*, 323–337.

McCrae, R. R., & Costa, P. T. (2013). Introduction to the empirical and theoretical status of the Five-Factor Model of Personality Traits. In T. A. Widiger & P. T. Costa (Eds.), *Personality disorders and the five-factor model of personality* (pp. 15–27). Washington, DC: American Psychological Association.

McLeod, J., & Machin, L. (1998). The context of counseling: A neglected dimension of training, research and practice. *British Journal of Guidance & Counseling, 26*(3), 325–336.

McLeod, S. A. (2009). Jean Piaget. Retrieved from http://www.simplypsychology.org/piaget.html

Merriam-Webster. (2004). *The Merriam-Webster dictionary.* Springfield, MA: Merriam-Webster, Inc.

Mezirow, J., & Taylor, E. W. (Eds.). (2009). *Transformative learning in practice: Insights from community, workplace, and higher education.* San Francisco, CA: Jossey-Bass.

Miller, S. A. (1995). Parents' attributions for their children's behavior. *Child Development, 66*, 1557–1584.

Mirels, H. L., & Dean, J. B. (2006). Right-wing authoritarianism, attitude salience, and beliefs about matters of fact. *Political Psychology, 27*(6), 839–866.

Morf, C. C., & Mischel, W. (2012). The self as a psycho-social dynamic processing system: Toward a converging science of selfhood. In M. R. Leary & J. P. Tangney (Eds.), *Handbook of self and identity* (2nd ed., pp. 21–49). New York, NY: The Guilford Press.

Moskowitz, G. B. (2005). *Social cognition: Understanding self and others.* New York, NY: The Guildford Press.

Muran, J. C. (Ed.). (2001). *Self-relations in the psychotherapy process.* Washington, DC: American Psychological Association.

Murray, H. A. (1938). *Explorations in personality.* New York, NY: Oxford University Press.

Myers, S. M. (1996). An interactive model of religiosity inheritance: The importance of family context. *American Sociological Review, 61*, 858–866.

Neher, A. (1991). Maslow's theory of motivation: A critique. *Journal of Humanistic Psychology, 31*(3), 89–112.

Neimeyer, R., & Raskin, J. (2000). *Constructions of disorder*. Washington, DC: American Psychological Association.

Newberg, A., & Waldman, M. R. (2006). *Why we believe what we believe: Uncovering our biological need for meaning, spirituality, and truth*. New York, NY: Free Press.

Norcross, J. C. (Ed.). (2002). *Psychotherapeutic relationships that work: Therapist contributions and responsiveness to patients*. New York, NY: Oxford University Press.

Oyserman, D., Elmore, K., & Smith, G. (2012). Self, self-concept, and identity. In M. R. Leary & J. P. Tangney (Eds.), *Handbook of self and identity* (2nd ed., pp. 69–104). New York, NY: The Guilford Press.

Peake, T. H., VanNoord, R. W., & Albott, W. (1979). Psychotherapy as an altered state of awareness: A common element. *Journal of Contemporary Psychotherapy, 10*, 98–105.

Peritti, P. O., & Statum, J. A. (1984). Father-son inter-generational transmission of authoritarian paternal attitudes. *Social Behavior and Personality, 12*(1), 85–90.

Peterson, B. E., Kim, R., McCarthy, J. M., Park, C. J., & Plamondon, L. T. (2011). Authoritarianism and arranged marriage in Bangladesh and Korea. *Journal of Research in Personality, 45*(6), 622–630.

Peterson, B. E., Smirles, K. A., & Wentworth, P. A. (1997). Generativity and authoritarianism: Implications for personality, political involvement, and parenting. *Journal of Personality and Social Psychology, 72*(5), 1202–1216.

Piaget, J. (1976). *The grasp of consciousness: Action and concept in the young child*. Cambridge, MA: Harvard University Press.

Piaget, J. (1977). *The development of thought: Equilibration of cognitive structures*. New York, NY: Viking Press.

Picchioni, A. (1995). Searching for psychological truth: Some moral and philosophical problems. *TCA Journal, 23*(1), 28–40.

Pomerantz, E. M., Chaiken, S., & Tordesillas, R. S. (1995). Attitude strength and resistance process. *Journal of Personality and Social Psychology, 69*, 408–419.

Raskin, J. D. (2012). Evolutionary constructivism and humanistic psychology. *Journal of Theoretical and Philosophical Psychology, 32*(2), 119–133.

Reber, A. S., Allen, R., & Reber, E. S. (2009). *Dictionary of psychology* (4th ed.). London, England: Penguin Books.

Rokeach, M. (1956). Political and religious dogmatism: An alternative to the authoritarian personality. *Psychological Monographs: General and Applied, 70*, 1–43.

Rokeach, M. (1960). *The open and closed mind*. New York, NY: Basic Books.

Rokeach, M. (1967). Values survey. In J. P. Robinson, P. R. Shaver, & L. S. Wrightsman (Eds.), *Measures of personality and social psychological attitudes* (pp. 661–753). San Diego, CA: Academic Press.

Rokeach, M. (1973). *The nature of human values*. New York, NY: Free Press.

Rokeach, M. (1979). Some unresolved issues in theories of beliefs, attitudes, and values. *Nebraska Symposium on Motivation, 27*, 261–304.

Rokeach, M., & Ball-Rokeach, S. J. (1989). Stability and change in American value priorities. *American Psychologist, 44*(5), 775–784.

Roth, C. H., & Kulb, S. D. (1997). *The multiple facets of therapeutic transactions*. Madison, WI: International Universities Press.

Rowe, C. E., & Isaac, D. S. (1989). *Empathic attunement: The technique of psychoanalytic self-psychology*. Northvale, NJ: Jason Aronson.

Ryan, R. M., Curren, R. R., & Deci, E. L. (2013). What humans need: Flourishing in Aristotelian philosophy and self-determination theory. In A. S. Waterman (Ed.), *The best within us: Positive psychology perspectives on eudaimonia* (pp. 57–75). American Psychological Association.

Ryan, R. M., & Deci, E. L (2008). A self-determination theory approach to psychotherapy: The motivational basis for effective change. *Canadian Psychology, 49*(3), 186–193.

Schneidman, E. S. (Ed.). (1981). *Endeavors in psychology: Selections from the personology of Henry A. Murray.* New York, NY: Harper & Row Publishers.

Schwartz, S. H. (1992). Universals in the content and structure of values: Theoretical advances and empirical tests in 20 countries. In M. P. Zanna (Ed.), *Advances in experimental social psychology* (pp. 1–65). New York, NY: Academic Press.

Schwartz, S. H. (2012). An overview of the Schwartz Theory of basic values. *Online Readings In Psychology and Culture, 2*(1). Retrieved from http://dx.doi.org/10.9707/2307-0919.1116

Schwartz, S. H., & Bilsky, W. (1987). Toward a psychological structure of human values. *Journal of Personality and Social Psychology, 53,* 550–562.

Schwartz, S. H., & Bilsky, W. (1990). Toward a theory of the universal content and structure of values: Extensions and cross-cultural replications. *Journal of Personality and Social Psychology, 58*(5), 878–891.

Shealy, C. N. (1995). From Boys Town to Oliver Twist: Separating fact from fiction in welfare reform and out-of home placement of children and youth. *American Psychologist, 50*(8), 565–580.

Shealy, C. N. (2004). A model and method for "making" a C-I psychologist: Equilintegration (EI) theory and the Beliefs, Events, and Values Inventory (BEVI). *Journal of Clinical Psychology, 60,* 1065–1090.

Shealy, C. N. (2005). Justifying the justification hypothesis: Scientific-humanism, Equilintegration (EI) Theory, and the Beliefs, Events, and Values Inventory (BEVI) [Special Series]. *Journal of Clinical Psychology, 61*(1), 81–106.

Shealy, C. N. (2014, September). *Effective campus internationalisation: Implications and applications from the Forum BEVI Project.* Symposium panel presentation at the annual meeting of the European Association of International Educators, Prague, Czech Republic.

Shealy, C. N., Bhuyan, D., & Sternberger, L. G. (2012). Cultivating the capacity to care in children and youth: Implications from EI theory, EI self, and BEVI. In U. Nayar (Ed.), *Child and adolescent mental health* (pp. 240–255). New Delhi, India: Sage Publications.

Shealy, C. N., & Bullock, M. (Eds.). (in press). *Going global: How psychology and psychologists can meet a world of need.* Washington, DC: APA Books.

Shealy, C. N., Cobb, H. C., Crowley, S. L., Nelson, P. D., & Peterson, G. W. (2004). Back to our future? The consensus conference and combined-integrated (C-I) model of doctoral training in professional psychology [Special Series]. *Journal of Clinical Psychology, 60*(9), 893–909.

Simon, L. A. (1996). The nature of the introject and its implications for gestalt therapy. *The Gestalt Journal, 19*(2), 109–130.

Snyder, D. K., Velasquez, J. M., Clark, B. L., & Means-Christensen, A. J. (1997). Parental influence on gender and marital role attitudes: Implications for intervention. *Journal of Marital & Family Therapy, 23*(2), 191–201.

Snyder, M., & Campbell, B. H. (1982). Self-monitoring: The self in action. In J. Suls (Ed.), *Psychological perspectives on the self* (pp. 185–207). Hillsdale, NJ: Lawrence Erlbaum Associates.

Sommers-Flanagan, J., Richardson, B. G., & Sommers-Flanagan, R. (2011). A multi-theoretical, evidence-based approach for understanding and managing adolescent resistance to psychotherapy. *Journal of Contemporary Psychotherapy, 41,* 69–80.

Sroufe, A. L. (2009, December). The concept of development in developmental psychopathology. *Child Development Perspectives, 3*(3), 178–183.

Staub, E. (1996). Cultural-societal roots of violence. The examples of genocidal violence and of contemporary youth violence in the United States. *American Psychologist, 51*(2), 117–132.

Staub, E. (2003). Notes on cultures of violence, cultures of caring and peace, and the fulfillment of basic human needs. *Political Psychology, 24*(1), 1–21.

Staub, E. (2013). Building a peaceful society: Origins, prevention, and reconciliation after genocide and other group violence. *American Psychologist, 68*(7), 576–589.

Stern, D. B. (1996). The social construction of therapeutic action. *Psychoanalytic Inquiry, 16*(2), 265–294.

Sternberg, R. J., & Grigorenko, E. L. (2001). Unified psychology. *American Psychologist, 56*(12), 1069–1079.

Storr, A. (1991). *Human destructiveness*. New York, NY: Grove Weidenfeld.

Tabit, M., Hart, V., Brearly, T., Shealy, C. N., Staton, R., & Sternberger, L. G. (2012, August). *Creating prejudice through anti-prejudice pedagogy? Empirical evidence from the* Forum BEVI Project. Poster presented at the annual meeting of the American Psychological Association, Orlando, FL.

Taylor, A. J. (2003). Justice as a basic human need. *New Ideas in Psychology, 21*(3), 209–219.

Tesser, A., Stapel, D. A., & Wood, J. V. (Eds.). (2002). *Self and motivation: Emerging psychological perspectives*. Washington, DC: American Psychological Association.

Tjeltveit, A. C. (1999). *Ethics and values in psychotherapy*. New York, NY: Routledge.

Toth, S. L., & Cicchetti, D. (2013). Developmental psychopathology perspective on child maltreatment. *Child Maltreatment, 18*(3), 135–139.

Vachon, D. O., & Agresti, A. A. (1992). A training proposal to help mental health professionals clarify and manage implicit values in the counseling process. *Professional Psychology: Research and Practice, 23*(6), 509–514.

Wachtel, P. L. (1981). Transference, schema, and assimilation: The relevance of Piaget to the psychoanalytic theory of transference. *The annual of psychoanalysis, 8*, 59–76. New York: International Universities Press

Wachtel, P. S. (2008). *Relational theory and the practice of psychotherapy*. New York, NY: Guilford.

Wadsworth, B. J. (1996). *Piaget's theory of cognitive and affective development: Foundations of constructivism*. White Plains, NY: Longman Publishers USA.

Wallerstein, R. S. (1999). *Psychoanalysis: Clinical and theoretical*. Madison, WI: International Universities Press.

Wandschneider, E., Pysarchik, D. T, Sternberger, L. G., Ma, W., Acheson-Clair, K., Baltensperberger, B., . . . Hart, V. (2016). The Forum BEVI Project: Applications and implications for international, multicultural, and transformative learning. In C. N. Shealy (Ed.), *Making sense of beliefs and values* (pp. 407–484). New York, NY: Springer Publishing.

Ward, T., & Stewart, C. (2003). Criminogenic needs and human needs: A theoretical model. *Psychology: Crime & Law, 9*(2), 125–143.

Weston, D. (1992). The cognitive self and the psychoanalytic self: Can we put our selves together? *Psychological Inquiry, 3*(1), 1–13.

Wilber, K. (2000). *Integral psychology: Consciousness, spirit, psychology, therapy*. Boston, MA: Shambhala Publications.

Zeller, S. K. (1991). A devastating righteousness: The story of a patient and her introjected god. *Psychotherapy Patient, 7*, 103–117.

Craig N. Shealy

3

THE EI SELF:
REAL WORLD IMPLICATIONS AND
APPLICATIONS OF EI THEORY

Hope is the thing with feathers that perches in the soul—and sings the tunes without the words—and never stops at all.

—Emily Dickinson

Why are we compelled to change? How do we know we are changing? What is it in us that changes? These are among the most fundamental questions we may ask of ourselves and each other, since any student of the human condition—and who isn't?—is bound to grapple with them to varying degrees on a daily basis, and over the course of a lifetime. I ask such questions of my own doctoral students each year, and am surprised as much by the answers as I am by the difficulty we encounter when posing such questions. That probably is because the questions themselves beg so many more questions that it is difficult to know precisely where or how to enter the waters from which they flow. The goal of this pedagogical exercise is to ask us to reflect upon the deepest levels of our experiential selves and to apprehend what actually is happening "within us," and in others, vis-à-vis change. In the spirit of such inquiry, consider what is, I believe, the most basic of these questions: What is it in us that changes?

When I ask my students to reflect upon this question in light of how they have changed over time and experience, responses typically range from, "Well, I see things differently" or "I don't think in the way that I used to." Alternatively, they may resort to observations about stages of change, juxtapositions among different theories of human behavior and development, or neurobiological alterations. When I press them to "go deeper"—beyond the observation that they learn new information, develop more sophisticated understandings of phenomena, or that synaptic modifications would be associated with such change—the struggle begins in earnest, and may prompt more questions still. When I ask them how they know change is happening within them—or in their partners, friends, or families—they may, in exasperation, finally declare, "I don't know how I know; I just do." From my perspective at least, this question—"What is it in us that changes?"—is difficult to answer in any definitive way because we emanate from its source, which encompasses us and is "bigger" than we are.

In offering this proposition, I am not insisting that our origins are metaphysical in any traditional religious or spiritual sense, although I personally am entirely open to that possibility, if liberated from the theocratic baggage that has encumbered our inclination to encounter these putative aspects of the human condition. What I am trying to convey is that the nascent unfolding of our human potential from an onto-logical perspective existed before we were aware of, or could speak to, its existence. We derive from and are defined by it, whatever "It" may be. So actually, this question is one of what "It" is. And that is a hard question to know how to ask, much less answer. But it is an essential question with which to grapple if you wish to "make sense of beliefs and values," or are involved in bending human nature as a "change agent" in one form or another—advocate, educator, leader, parent, policy maker, or therapist—by whatever means, for whatever ends, as I hope to illustrate by returning to Elaine and her family.

ELAINE ENCOUNTERS SELF: A CASE STUDY IN BELIEFS, VALUES, AND NEEDS

Recall Elaine from Chapter 2, the homeless woman who was grappling with funda-mental aspects of self, her family, her past, and her future. There are many ways to explain the processes my students and I experienced with this client and her family, and from an Equilintegration (EI) perspective, many have potential merit. However, what was most intriguing—and perhaps at the heart of our quest to "make sense of beliefs and values"—is how the constellation of belief statements that frequently were declared at the outset of the therapeutic process changed over the course of our work together. A number of exemplars could be highlighted, from her initial stance, which maintained that the lot of women was to be subordinate to men, to her active questioning and ultimate rejection of these beliefs, to her husband's evolution from passivity and resignation to active engagement in his roles as husband and father. Such transformation is fascinating and deeply moving to facilitate and behold, but in the final analysis, a singular focus on changes in stated beliefs from Time A to Time B does not explain *why* such change occurs in the first place or begin to account for the underlying sequelae—the collage of confusing thoughts and intense feelings typi-cally accompanying such processes—that clients experience and attempt to express and understand as one session folds into the next. The belief content characterizing each of these phases may indeed be mapped and tracked from session to session; most clinicians are engaged in such processes implicitly at the very least, and often explicitly, as they seek to understand whether, how, and to what degree "change" is occurring. At a complementary level, it is also worth asking *why* a client would place him or herself in a situation where his or her beliefs and values about self, others, and the world at large would be scrutinized and evaluated by someone who—at the out-set of the therapeutic process at least—is a stranger at best. To ask a question that is more than rhetorical, why in the world would someone "willingly" place him or herself in such a vulnerable position? At the most basic level, clients do so because they are suffering and do not know what else to do except seek help from those that society has deemed qualified to alleviate such suffering.

In entering that fray, therapists who value and work in depth-based approaches, variously defined, find few meaningful answers from practitioners who are episte-mologically insistent upon the exclusive veracity of constructs such as "bad genes" or "chemical imbalances in the brain" or dismiss the question of "why we suffer" as irrelevant, since the modification of "disordered thoughts" or "external contingen-cies" is all that is necessary to "treat symptoms." That said, such approaches (e.g., psychotropic medications; addressing disordered thoughts and problematic contin-gencies) have their rightful place if the interventionist—of whatever stripe—avoids unhelpful dichotomies regarding human nature (e.g., we are *only* "biological," "cognitive," "emotional," "relational," or "spiritual" creatures, rather than an interactive gestalt among all of these "parts") (e.g., Anmuth et al., 2013; Castonguay, 2000; Deacon, 2013; Henriques, 2011; Horwitz, 2002; Lambert, 2001; Magnavita & Achin, 2013; Norcross, 2002, 2005; Wachtel, 1997, 2008; Wampold, 2010).

Such integrative, relational, and depth-based work is neither easy nor simple—as was the case throughout with Elaine—since too many complex and interacting variables are at play to risk über confidence. Recall from Chapter 2, for instance, that we endeavored at every turn to create the conditions wherein she and her family would have the opportunity to encounter "need" in self and other, to learn from and make meaning of their experiences, and in the process discover both causes and cures for the original distress. What is most salient in this regard is first, the inherent linkage between what Elaine said she believed and valued at the outset of therapy; second, the profound emotional distress she expressed at the same time; third, her stated fear about engaging in a therapeutic process with a psychologist who might (for all she knew) be hostile toward her beliefs and values (e.g., her strong religious convictions); fourth, how her fear of the entire therapeutic enterprise gave way over time to a freer and more open focus upon her own internal and external experience; fifth, how the nature of this internal experience simultaneously became more nuanced, complex, and mysterious to her as she began to report thoughts and feelings that were experienced to be in conflict with deeply held beliefs and values (e.g., resulting, at one point, in what might be described as a "psychotic episode" where she felt possessed by the devil); and sixth and finally, how she came, over time, to move at a fundamental level in her receptivity toward and appreciation of a whole range of thoughts, feelings, and, most importantly, needs, that simply were not and could not be experienced at the outset of therapy. Interestingly, Elaine did not know what was happening to her as it happened; and as her primary therapist, although I sought to understand and facilitate what seemed to be a flight toward health, I had no way to know where her specific trajectory would lead. I could only hope, and believe, that the evocation of feelings and needs within her over time would lead us both toward a deeper encounter and sustainable engagement with her own true self.

In grappling with these levels of reality over the years as a clinician, the working formulation that seems to have the greatest ecological validity for me is the idea that deep therapeutic work occurring in the context of a safe and caring relationship allows for previously blocked "core needs" to be felt and experienced again. To be sure, thousands of articles, chapters, and books have been written in an attempt to account for the inner psychological processes by which healing occurs, and any number of incisive sources across the spectrum of theoretical and applied approaches to therapeutic growth could be cited in this regard (e.g., Castonguay, 2000; Henriques, 2011; Lambert, 2001; Magnavita & Achin, 2013; Norcross, 2002, 2005; Wachtel, 1997, 2008; Wampold, 2010). However, if our quest is to "make sense of beliefs and values"—how, why, for whom, and under what circumstances they are or are not likely to change—we have to consider the relationship between three components of *beliefs*, *needs*, and *self*, as described in Chapter 2. We do so via the EI Self.[1]

---

[1] As an aid to the reader, terminology has been italicized; it will also be helpful to reference the EI Self figure (Figure 3.1) in order to see the interrelationship between various structures, processes, and levels.

UNDERSTANDING THE EI SELF

To begin, as a derivative of EI Theory, the Equilintegration or EI Self seeks to represent in pictographic form the integrative and synergistic processes by which beliefs and values are acquired, maintained, and modified as well as how these are linked to the *Formative Variables* (FoVs), *Core Needs* (CoNes), *and Adaptive Potential* (AP) of the self. By way of orientation, look first at the EI Self as it is pictured in Figure 3.1. You will notice first that there are three circular structures, which increase in complexity, from left to right. Underneath these circles, you will see columns of text, which help provide explanatory information useful in interpreting and understanding various aspects of this framework. At the most basic level, it should be emphasized that the EI Self is a developmental model, in that it seeks to represent the processes by which beliefs and values are acquired, maintained, and modified across the life span. Thus, two basic characteristics of the EI Self should be noted at the outset: first, moving from left to right, the three circles represent increasing development and complexity of the same "self" over the course of a lifetime, from infancy, to childhood/adolescence, to adulthood; second, because we are working in two-dimensional space on paper, what we are able to represent is akin to a cross-section of each "self," rather than a more apt three-dimensional sphere, which is implied by the parts comprising the whole of the EI Self.

Next, turn your attention to the third circle at the right of the page (with "Adult" underneath it). Note that the diagram includes four *Levels of Self*: (a) *Endoself* (Core Self), (b) *Mesoself* (Mediational Self), (c) *Ectoself* (Shell Self), and (d) *Exoself* (External Self). Each of these Levels of Self plays an interdependent and indispensable role vis-à-vis the processes and structures by which beliefs and values are internalized and expressed across the life span. For example, as conceptualized, the beliefs and values that human beings internalize at the Ectoself (Shell Self) level are those that are available for acquisition at the Exoself (External Self) level; in other words, belief/value content (i.e., the beliefs and values that a human being holds to be self-evident about self, others, and the world at large) largely is a function of those beliefs and values that predominate in the primary cultures and contexts in which that human being develops and lives.

As EI Theory maintains, we tend to acquire the beliefs and values that are available for acquisition. Of course, we are speaking in the aggregate here; many Formative Variables (FoVs) interact with other processes to create each person's unique constellation of beliefs and values; nonetheless, the fact that members of a particular culture often share a common set of beliefs and values (e.g., Inglehart, Basáñez, Díez-Medrano, Halman, & Luijkx, 2004; Inglehart, Basáñez, & Moreno, 1998; Schwartz, 1992, 2012) supports the contention that the most parsimonious explanation for such similarity is the simple fact that exposure to common beliefs and values tends to be associated with an endorsement of common beliefs and values at the individual level. Why, for example, do approximately 71% of Americans describe themselves as "Christian" (Pew Forum on Religion and Public Life, 2015) whereas nearly all (i.e., approximately 100%) of Saudi Arabians describe themselves as Muslim (International Religious Freedom Report, 2004)? Despite occasional claims to the contrary on various sides of religious aisles, the fact that people who live and work like oneself are, on average, in possession of similar religious beliefs and values says little about the inherent "truth" or "goodness" of such religious beliefs, but a great deal about the FoVs that are associated with the acquisition and maintenance of beliefs and values. As described in Chapters 1 and 2, and as any student of the social sciences realizes,

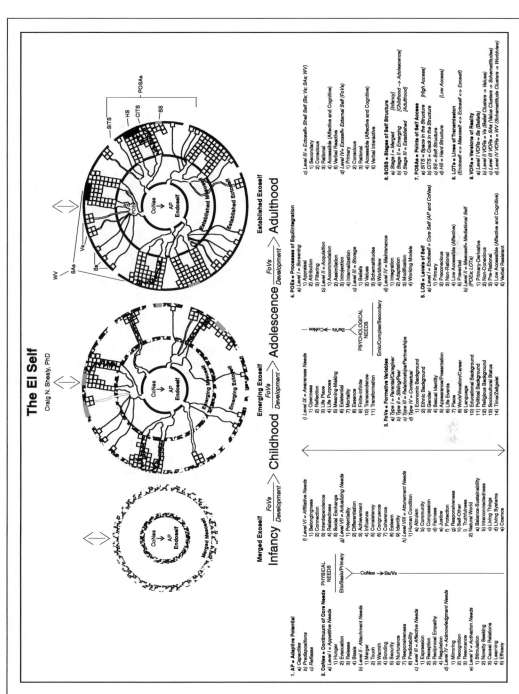

FIGURE 3.1. The EI Self.

many complex and interacting variables ultimately are responsible for "shaping" why we believe and value that which we do (e.g., Cummings, Davies, & Campbell, 2000; Feather, 1992, 1994, 1995; Rokeach & Ball-Rokeach, 1989; Schwartz, 1992, 2012; Sroufe, 2009; Toth & Cicchetti, 2013).

The Exoself

So, let us start beyond the boundaries of the circles in the EI Self, by examining the *Exoself* (External Self). Consistent with various aspects of "self" noted in Chapter 2, the EI Self recognizes both from a developmental and experiential level, that "the self" is not confined to the three-dimensional and physical human, but extends far into the larger field in which the physical self "lives and has its being," to include interpersonal, social, contextual, and cultural dimensions. As "social animals" (Aronson, 2012), humans constantly are engaged in processes of adapting to their external environment even as they seek to adapt their environment to them, a hallmark of intelligence, according to Sternberg (1985). As noted in Chapter 2, nearly all subfields within psychology recognize that human behavior cannot be understood without accounting for the interface between the individual human "separate and alone" and the external field in which we all are ineluctably embedded; and in fact, we simply cannot "make sense of beliefs and values" without accounting for this essential interaction between that which is psychologically "internal" and that which is socially "external" (e.g., Cummings et al., 2000; Shealy, Bhuyan, & Sternberger, 2012; Sroufe, 2009; Toth & Cicchetti, 2013).

In recognition of this interaction vis-à-vis the internalization and expression of beliefs and values, the Exoself level attempts to represent the major sources of external influence over the content of our beliefs and values. More specifically, and in full recognition that a definitive accounting of all such factors likely will remain elusive, the EI self posits four types of FoVs that are operative at the Exoself level: Type I = Parental/Caregiver (i.e., those who bear primary responsibility for child rearing); Type II = Sibling/Peer (i.e., individuals who live with and/or spend substantial time interacting with the individual, especially during formative years through late adolescence/early adulthood); Type III = Relationships/Partnerships (i.e., the type and nature of an individual's relationships or partnerships with others, including intimate and friendship relationships); and Type IV = Contextual (i.e., variables that generally are recognized to mediate or moderate human functioning and development) (e.g., Cummings et al., 2000; Shealy et al., 2012; Sroufe, 2009; Toth & Cicchetti, 2013). These "FoVs" include, but are by no means limited to, Economic Background, Ethnic Background, Gender, Sexual Identity, Appearance/Presentation, Life Events, Place, Work/Vocation/Career, Language, Educational Background, Political Background, Religious Background, Sociocultural Status, and Time/Zeitgeist. In short, taken as a whole, the FoVs listed in the EI Self, and operative at the Exoself level, are nothing more—or less—than the gestalt of factors that influence or shape "who we are" and "how we see the world," including our beliefs, values, schemas, attitudes, and worldviews. Metaphorically, such variables comprise the "air we breathe" and "the water in which we swim"; we are encompassed by—and immersed within—them from birth through death so wholly that we often do not consciously realize, without substantive and prolonged reflection, how fundamental such FoVs are to how and why we come to experience self, others, and the larger world as we do.

The Ectoself

But if the Exoself represents the "external" forces and factors that influence or shape what we believe and value, where in the EI Self do these putative beliefs and values actually "reside?" In obvious recognition that we are working at a construct level of analysis—and as EI Theory specifies, these belief/value constructs ultimately must be codified within (although are not wholly reducible to) a neurobiological sub-strate—the EI Self contends that beliefs and values are "stored" at the *Ectoself* or Shell Self level. As noted in Chapter 2, the relationship between beliefs, values, schemattitudes, and worldview are juxtaposed in a hierarchical manner (i.e., beliefs → values → schemattitudes → worldview). As represented within the Ectoself, moving from infancy, through childhood and adolescence, and ultimately into adulthood, beliefs (represented by individual "squares") cluster into values (clusters of beliefs), which further group into "schemattitudes" (clusters of values). The Ectoself taken as a whole—beliefs, values, and schemattitudes—may be considered an individual's "worldview." And as will be discussed next in Chapter 4, these different versions of reality (VORs) may be ascertained via a valid and sufficiently comprehensive measure, such as the Beliefs, Events, and Values Inventory (BEVI) (Shealy, 2004; Shealy et al., 2012).

Note that the beliefs, values, and schemattitudes within the Ectoself are differentiated via a range of distinct structural features (e.g., solid black blocks, lightly shaded areas). Consistent conceptually with the definition of "belief" as noted in Chapter 2 (e.g., the "continuum of belief")—and empirically with a range of findings illustrating how beliefs cluster together as they do—such characteristics are included in order to denote that aspects of the Ectoself may be relatively open and permeable (as in *Soft Structure* or *Space in the Structure*), closed and impermeable (as in *Hard Structure*), or structurally unsound (as in *Crack in the Structure*). In short, as will be discussed throughout the chapters that follow, these designations are derivable statistically since various clusters of beliefs and values can be shown to be held along these same dimensions (e.g., strong versus weak; contradictory), as indicated by the "four dimensions of belief" described in Chapter 2.

At this point, to enliven these pictographic elements, a second "case study" may be helpful, this time not from a clinical realm as with Elaine, but rather from the standpoint of educational processes, via intrapsychic dynamics among two students in a doctoral program. To wit, consider the curious difference between Abhay, a male Indian and practicing Hindu who has never been outside of his home state of Kerala, located on the southwestern coast of India, and Alice, a female agnostic Caucasian from Washington, D.C. Early in their first semester in the same graduate program, Alice offers to take Abhay to a local supermarket so that he may stock up on food for his apartment. In the car on the way home, Abhay finds himself feeling irritated and then angry about the experience. Sensing something is wrong, Alice asks, and Abhay explains that he is appalled by the fact that an entire aisle in this huge supermarket is devoted exclusively to food for pets. In his home village, an aisle of that length and breadth might contain the contents of an entire store, and enough to feed everyone. Alice ponders the implications of this perspective about American excess with mixed emotions—agreeing somewhat, but nowhere near as stridently—as Abhay observes further that he cannot understand the "obsession people here have with their pets." Back home, such animals not only were disallowed inside the house, but generally were considered unclean.

A lifelong city dweller, Alice not only had no pets while growing up, she rarely had encountered animals in any sort of setting, aside from dogs and squirrels in the park or occasional visits to the zoo during her childhood. If asked, Alice officially would be neutral regarding these issues, never having contemplated the proper role or place of animals in or out of one's domicile. Abhay's agitation is genuinely puzzling to Alice, who wonders why he is making such a "big deal" of this issue. Her private belief/value narrative runs something like, "What does it matter? Who cares? He should just let it be." Abhay meanwhile is experiencing a range of affectively loaded beliefs, such as how "greedy and materialistic" Americans seemed to be while wondering at the meaning of their intimate connection with their pets. The emptiness Abhay has also felt in his social encounters with Americans, who are all smiles but seem relatively superficial (e.g., "They always ask how you are but don't really care to hear any answer other than 'fine'"), must be compensated for somehow by these animals, who require nothing from their owners, a concept in itself that feels further alien to him (i.e., the human ownership of animals that subsequently are called pets).

How does all of this map onto the EI Self? In the case of Abhay and Alice, the black "Hard Structure" pictured in the Ectoself would be represented by Abhay's deeply held belief that "animals belong outside" or "Americans are greedy and materialistic." Essentially, as suggested by the "four dimensions of belief," "Hard Structure" beliefs are rigidly fixed and strongly held. From her perspective, Alice never has pondered the role and place of animals in the home; never having thought about this issue, she has no "belief" one way or another. That is what is meant by Space in the Structure: an issue about which no beliefs have been internalized. On the other hand, during her upbringing, Alice's parents made her aware of her relative privilege in the world, both at home and abroad. She understands differences at the level of economic class, and knows that her relative advantages in this regard automatically allow her access to opportunities and resources that simply are not available to many others. At the same time, Alice has a long history of "giving back" to the surrounding community through service and resources; she believes it is her duty to do so. She is also aware of the general spirit of charity and care that so many others in her world share toward those who are less fortunate. So, to Abhay's assertion about American excess, Alice is inclined to agree on the one hand, but not completely, and certainly not with the level of certitude expressed by him. In terms of the Ectoself, her beliefs in this regard would be characterized as "Soft Structure," that is, beliefs that are held loosely and are susceptible to change.

This encounter led to further discussion—sometimes heated—between Abhay and Alice in the months to come. One evening, they joined some classmates at a local restaurant for dinner. As often was the case, discussion turned to issues of politics and culture, with a particular focus on recent attempts to restrict access to abortion services. Most at the table were strongly pro-choice and deeply resented state interference with abortion rights. Listening to all of this, Abhay observed that abortion, from his perspective, was a violation of the sanctity of life, a contention that provoked heated debate all around. After some time, Abhay asked, "How many of you are in favor of the death penalty?" Everyone who answered said "no," and most rather emphatically. "Well," Abhay replied, "How can you be both pro-choice and anti-death penalty at the same time? Isn't there an inherent contradiction between these beliefs, in that one allows for the destruction of human life and the other does not?"

Essentially, Abhay's argument went as follows. Because both issues concerned matters of "life and death," if one is generally predisposed against abortion, a common rationale for being so is that "abortion kills a beating heart." Thus, if one objects to abortion because one opposes "killing an unborn child," would it not follow that one opposes any sort of killing of a human being? Interestingly, from the standpoint of how beliefs tend to be organized, the contradiction that Abhay has identified is illustrated by the fact that individuals on the "right" or more conservative side of the aisle tend to oppose abortion but support the death penalty whereas those on the "left" or more liberal side of the aisle tend to support a "pro-choice" stance vis-à-vis abortion while generally being more likely to oppose the death penalty (e.g., Costello, 2014). One need not be a logician to apprehend such paradoxes. And in fact, adherents for one stance or another often will point out this inconsistency to members of the opposing side, as in "If you're pro-life, how can you support the death penalty?" In short, the possibility for tension (i.e., disequilintegration from an EI perspective) between these two beliefs is high, as any instructor who has ever opened this issue up for discussion will attest.

In making his argument, Abhay encountered stiff resistance from the group (e.g., "the two instances aren't equivalent"; "the death penalty doesn't work"; "a fetus that cannot survive outside of the womb may not be granted full human status," etc.). For her part, as the conversation progressed, Alice felt a vague sense of unease, since she reluctantly found herself believing that Abhay's point made some sense. She was pro-choice, having negotiated a scare with pregnancy many years ago, and seeing the impact of too many unwanted children in the world. However, she viewed abortion as a necessary evil, which could be avoided if only we provided better sex education and greater access to birth control. Regarding the death penalty, she remembered all too well the terror inflicted in her home community by John Allen Muhammad and Lee Boyd Malvo, the "DC Snipers," who killed ten people and injured three others during 3 weeks in October 2002. She was a distant acquaintance of one of the people killed, and remembers wishing guiltily that Muhammad and Boyd would both be put to death for these heinous acts. At the same time, Alice knew and agreed with all the main anti-death penalty arguments; however, she still felt that perhaps some acts were so egregious, the death penalty might in fact be warranted. Unlike what she apprehended in her peers at the table, Alice felt genuine conflict between her two beliefs. She also experienced Abhay's argument as quite reasonable, and found herself in silent agreement that it was illogical for someone to be for the destruction of life in one circumstance, but not in the other. From the perspective of the Ectoself, Alice was experiencing a "Crack in the Structure," the subjective experience of relative contradiction between two or more correlated beliefs. Just why a feeling of discomfort occurs in the first place, is a point to which we turn next, in our discussion of the Mesoself (Mediational) level of the EI Self.

The Mesoself

Return now to Elaine, the homeless wife and mother from Chapter 2 who experienced what appeared to be an acute psychotic episode during one especially intense session of psychotherapy. At the outset of our work together, and frequently throughout, recall that Elaine experienced a range of complex and competing feelings about her participation in therapy. At the very beginning, her concerns largely were about whether or not I would attempt to challenge her religious beliefs (I would not and did not). As the process unfolded, she expressed feelings of deep guilt and fear about whether the process of therapy was changing her in ways that were not in line with her church's teachings, and whether "the devil" might work through this process in ways that harmed her spiritually. Sometimes, her thoughts and feelings were not shrouded in any mystery at all, even though she experienced guilt when she became aware of them. Wanting to go back to school and obtain a GED (General Education Diploma), for example, was experienced both as deeply desired as well as selfish and potentially antagonistic to what the role of a "wife and mother should be." When expressing such wishes, she often chided herself for doing so, or voiced the overarching beliefs that such goals were not realistic or attainable in any case. From an intrapsychic perspective, how we do make sense of such conflicts in Elaine, others, and ourselves?

To do so, it first should be recalled—as discussed in Chapter 2—that the processes through which beliefs and values ultimately are internalized and "made part of" the Ectoself are neither affectively neutral nor cognitively passive. Instead, from the standpoint of the EI Self, they are nonconsciously mediated vis-à-vis *Lines of Transmission* (LOTs) within the *Mesoself*. Obviously, as with all of these heuristic constructs, such abstractions (e.g., "LOTs") are not intended to map reality's terrain with empirically observable precision, at least with present technology. Rather, we are attempting to illustrate how and why relatively consciously accessible "beliefs" and "values" are tethered to underlying "needs" via processes that actually have been examined quite deeply in clinical, empirical, and theoretical literature via aspects of attribution, defense, dissonance, resistance, and so forth (see Chapter 2). The point here is that as we sink more deeply into self—below the "beliefs and values" that humans experience as consciously accessible and internally rationale—we encounter processes that are charged affectively and largely outside of our conscious awareness; likewise, our vaunted sense of "choice" and "free will" are not really operative at this level of reality, which occurs more or less automatically in response to the interaction between core (Endoself) and external (Exoself) levels of self (e.g., Aronson, 2012; Newberg & Waldman, 2006; Wegner, 2002). Theoretically, this process occurs at the "mediated" or Mesoself level, through (at least) four *Processes of Equilintegration* (POEs):

1. Level I = Screening (appraisal, attribution, and filtering)
2. Level II = Acquisition (accommodation, assimilation, introjection, and internalization)
3. Level III = Storage (beliefs, values, schemattitudes, and worldview)
4. Level IV = Maintenance (integration, adaptation, modification, and working models)

To illustrate how this process operates in real world terms, let us turn again to the experience Elaine seemed to be having in therapy. In our first few sessions, for example, Level I POEs predominated, in that her entire psychological apparatus was engaged in evaluating (a) whether or not the therapeutic milieu was safe and in her best interest (appraisal); (b) evaluating issues of motive on my part as well as trying to make sense of why I was saying what I was saying and why she was feeling what she was feeling (attribution); and (c) what thoughts and feelings were and were not acceptable or tolerable for her to experience (filtering). As a collective, from the standpoint of the Mesoself, such POEs are designed to "screen" in or out beliefs and values that are expressed by others, including but by no means limited to therapists. In fact, from an EI perspective, much of our mental life is consumed by such screening processes. The ubiquitous encounter with "beliefs and values" (e.g., via the Internet, reading newspapers, commentary by public figures, attending lectures, reading books, or simply relating with other human beings across a myriad of interpersonal forms) means we constantly are in a state of evaluating whether and to what degree we agree or disagree with the "beliefs and values" that we encounter.

To take but one of countless potential examples, consider the following actual excerpt from a government committee in India, entitled *Report on Introducing Sex Education in School, 2009*:

> According to the Committee, "adolescence education program" is a cleverly used euphemism whose real objective was to impart sex education to school-children and promote promiscuity. The Committee recommends that there should be no sex education in schools. Messages should appropriately be given to schoolchildren that there should be no sex before marriage, which is immoral, unethical, and unhealthy. Students should be made aware of the marriageable age, which is 21 years in the case of boys and 18 years in the case of girls, and that indulging in sex outside the institution of marriage is against the social ethos of India. (Khanna, 2010, p. 17)

From an EI perspective, take a moment to become aware of what your reactions are to the preceding report. Do you agree? Do you disagree? Are you undecided? How do you know what you think and feel about what you have just read (what information "within you" tells you what your reaction is)? Why do you believe that which you do (i.e., where do your beliefs regarding these issues come from or why do you have them)?

Generally, we do not engage in this sort of focused reflection upon encountering such belief/value stimuli. If we did so, it would be difficult to get through our day much less each passing moment mainly because we are surrounded if not bombarded with such stimuli on a constant basis. The automaticity of our reactions to such stimuli—where we have and register our experience internally, without necessarily being aware of, or attending to, the fact that we are doing so—is what is meant by "screening" from an EI perspective. From the perspective of this model, remember also that that which is being "screened" is an experience that begins at the level of the "Exoself" (e.g., the report that you read previously—an external stimulus), which is relatively more or less aligned with the organizational structure of your own "Ectoself" (e.g., beliefs and values that already have been internalized, which exist in a relative degree of congruence or incongruence with the beliefs that are conveyed through the given report from India). In fact, the function and purpose of Level I Screening POEs are to evaluate (e.g., appraise, attribute, filter) (a) the degree to which experiences at the Exoself level are consistent with the extant structure of the Ectoself (i.e., the "Shell Self") and (b) the degree to which experiences at the Exoself level have the potential to meet Core Needs at the level of the Endoself (i.e., "Core Self"), a point to which we will return.

So, if the Mesoself is in the business of screening content at the External Self level, how is it that beliefs and values get "laid down" as part of the Ectoself? From an EI perspective, Level II "Acquisition" POEs (Processes of Equilintegration)—including (but not necessarily limited to) accommodation, assimilation, introjection, and internalization—are among the theoretical constructs from extant scholarship that essentially are describing these sorts of processes. Accommodation and assimilation, for example, are well known Piagetian perspectives, described as part of EI Theory in Chapter 2 (e.g., Kegan, 1982; McLeod, 2009; Piaget, 1976, 1977). Introjection and internalization, on the other hand, are constructs derived primarily from psychodynamic, schema-based, and cognitive-developmental literatures, which describe the process by which human beings come to "internalize" various "VORs" (e.g., how people or relationships work; what is "normal" and "appropriate"; what the definition of a "good person" is) (e.g., Bruck, Winston, Aderholt, & Muran, 2006;

Carr, Szymanski, Taha, West, & Kaslow, 2014; Shealy, 2004; Taubner, Zimmerman, Kächele, Möller, & Sell, 2013). In general, beliefs/values are "laid down" over a long period of time via exposure to FoVs that predominate for a given individual. As the EI Self indicates, the foundation of one's worldview (again, defined as *the gestalt of internalized beliefs, values, and schemattitudes through which self, others, and the larger world are experienced and explained*) is established before one understands that such a process actually is occurring, especially throughout early development, but also throughout the life span; that is, fundamental beliefs and values become part of the self without the self necessarily possessing the capacity (early in life) or inclination (later in life) to reflect upon the occurrence of such internalization processes.

That is why it typically is difficult to answer the question, "Why do I believe what I believe?" with clarity or specificity, because the fact of the matter is, Level II Acquisition POEs largely occur outside of our conscious awareness that these processes are occurring, especially from infancy through early adulthood (i.e., the first two circles, from left to right, in the EI Self), but also throughout life. In other words, we "end up with"—and embrace—our beliefs and values, but typically do not know why. What is most intriguing about such a process is, we are basically disinclined to ask such a deconstructing question, precisely because of the "disequilintegration" to the self-structure that such a reflective process can evoke (Shealy, 2005).[2]

As a result of specific experiences that typically last a long time in a given culture and context, Level III "Storage" POEs result in the "beliefs," "values," "schemattitudes," and "worldview" that become the primary self-referencing content of the Ectoself. In other words, when we talk to ourselves and others about who we, they, and the larger world are—or should be—we are really doing so in relation to the content that has been stored at the level of the Ectoself. That is, we are describing, and often defending, the belief/value content that already has been internalized by us at this level of self, which is our VOR, without really knowing (must less acknowledging) how such content came to be "ours" in the first place.

To be clear then, our experience of self, others, and the larger world is mainly determined by (a) the content that has been stored at the Ectoself level interacting with (b) the degree to which our stored beliefs and values are or are not likely to meet Core Needs. As in the experience you may have had when reading the committee report from India, this process tends to be largely nonconscious, in that the thoughts and feelings we experience, on the basis of exposure to particular belief/value stimuli at the Exoself (External Self), are not "selected by us" as thoughts and feelings that we *will ourselves* to experience, but largely are a determined outcome of a lifelong developmental interaction between the Ectoself (Shell Self) and Endoself (Core Self), which is mediated by the Mesoself (Mediational Self), within a particular context at a given moment in time. That is one reason why our belief in "free will" or "choice" largely is illusory, since we really do not have access to "choices" that are not already available to us (e.g., Aronson, 2012; Newberg & Waldman, 2006; Wegner, 2002). In other words, at any given moment in time, it is hard to imagine how we could "choose" to think or feel in ways that are different from the possibilities that already are established by, for, within, and around us. That being said, clinical, educational, and other evidence from experiences that are designed to "transform" how people experience self, others, and the larger world suggests that we may *free will* over time, essentially through a process of disentangling previously internalized

---

[2] Of course, a primary purpose of education writ large, and higher education in particular, is to facilitate such reflection upon one's own beliefs and values about self, others, and the world at large (e.g., see Wandschneider et al., 2016).

belief from the underlying core need to which it is associated (e.g., Shealy et al., 2012). In other words, as with Elaine, our "will" is "freed," if by "will" we mean the powerful aspirational drive associated with meeting core need through our unique Adaptive Potential (AP), as evidenced by the fact that over many months of work, Elaine became much *less likely* to revisit her former self or behave in ways that emanated from, and were determined by, her previous experience of what and who she "must be."

By extension, then, the typically entrenched natures of beliefs and values should not imply that they cannot or do not change over time; they can and do as the "7Ds" from Chapter 2 specify. From an EI perspective, these Level IV "Maintenance" POEs consist of integration, adaptation, modification, and working models of the self. Note that "integration"—the I half of the EI model—is the first and primary function of belief/value maintenance. That is because the complex and interwoven network of beliefs and values that is internalized at the Ectoself level is designed—to the degree an individual human organism has the capacity to effect such an outcome—to be integrated. In fact, the final purpose of the self is to seek integration, regardless of whether and to what degree the content to be integrated readily lends itself to this fundamental task, which is at the heart of self-coherence (or the lack thereof) as discussed via the "I" of EI Theory in Chapter 2. Any practicing clinician lives this reality on a daily basis with clients, all of whom present—from an EI perspective—in a relatively integrated or "dis-integrated" state. As educators, we too grapple with this dynamic constantly, via the relative capacity and inclination of our students to integrate information that they receive into their existing belief/value structures. In fact, all of us are change agents to the degree that we exert influence on how and why other humans experience self, others, and the larger world as they do (Shealy & Bullock, in press; Cultivating the Globally Sustainable Self, 2015). Oftentimes, the conflict or resonance we experience in relation to others has to do with the relative degree of alignment between our respective "Ectoselves" (i.e., we experience connection, or the lack thereof, with others to the degree to which we experience alignment or misalignment at this level), which is in the service of meeting need within the Endoself or "Core Self," a process that is discussed in the next section.

Like all human beings, then, clients typically do not have the luxury of "choosing" which content they will internalize, especially during infancy, childhood, and much of adolescence. Again, we become as integrated as our innate capacity for integration allows, which interacts further with that which is available for acquisition, which further is delimited by the degree to which such acquisitive content aligns with our Core Needs. As such, by the time that clients, students, employees—or any other role state that human beings assume—come before us as adults, we are experiencing the end result of that integrative process up until the point at which we first encounter them. From a clinical standpoint then, our "assessments" and "interventions" are all about understanding what happened to create a specific integrative structure, and therefore, what is needed by the client in order to become less "dis-integrated" and more coherent and whole (i.e., in order to facilitate the pursuit of their Core Needs) in the context of their unique AP and FoVs (e.g., Coates et al., 2016; Cozen et al., 2016). From the standpoint of the intervener, such a gestalt of competencies has been referred historically to *the person of the therapist* (Aponte et al., 2009), and could rightly be extended to the person of the assessor as well. By extension then, as has been the case with *therapy common factors*—"those aspects of treatment that are associated with positive or negative outcomes across all therapies or therapists" such as empathy, acceptance, and understanding (Shealy, 1995, p. 567)— perhaps it is possible to identify *assessment common factors* through an integrative

Psychological Assessment as a Therapeutic Intervention (PATI) lens (Finn, 2007; Finn & Tonsager, 1997; Poston & Hanson, 2010). Such possibilities are explored more fully in Chapters 11 (assessment) and 15 (therapy) of this book.

In any case, the corresponding cascade of Level IV "Maintenance" POEs that are part and parcel of "integration"—namely, Adaptation, Modification, and Working Models—all are different phases and facets of the integrative process. New beliefs and values that are "allowed to pass" Levels I, II, and III POEs of screening, acquisition, and storage are dynamically and simultaneously adapted and modified into extant structure at the Ectoself level. Ultimately, they become what scholars have described as "working models" of the self (e.g., Ainsworth, 1990; Bethell, Hung-Chu, & McFatter, 2013; Bowlby, 1969, 1973, 1980; Wachtel, 2008)—relatively automatic frameworks by the self, of the self, and about the self—that are mediated largely by the nature and quality of our attachment-based relationships. It also should be noted that by extension, the Ectoself has illustrative compatibility with what we are understanding about synaptic processes at a neuronal level more generally in terms of their extraordinarily interconnected nature. Again and of course, as EI Theory maintains, all beliefs and values have a neurophysiological basis (i.e., they must be "laid down" at a brain-based level, and have underlying neurochemical correlates), even if they may not be reducible to, or readily apprehended at, this substrate level of analysis (e.g., Newberg & Waldman, 2006; Schacter, Gilbert, & Wegner, 2011), which leads us to the Endoself, the most basic level of analysis, and theoretically at the core of who we human beings are, and have the capacity to become.

The Endoself

As the EI Self illustrates, the POEs of the Mesoself occur between the Ectoself (Shell Self, which is described in the previous discussion) and the Endoself (Core Self), which consists of the self's Adaptive Potential (AP) (i.e., each individual's genetically mediated and unique capacities, predispositions, and reflexes) and a *Continuum of Core Needs* (CoNes) as noted in Chapter 2 (i.e., Appetitive, Attachment, Affective, Acknowledgment, Activation, Affiliative, Actualizing, Attunement, and Awareness). As may be evident, this continuum spans Level I (Appetitive Needs) to Level IX (Awareness Needs); here, the Core Needs on the "left" side of this continuum are seen as basic, primary, and foundational (Etic Needs), emerging immediately at birth and in less variant expressive form whereas those on the "right" side of this continuum are seen as aspirational, complex, and secondary (Emic Needs), emerging gradually through early development and in more variant expressive form. For example, and more specifically, Appetitive Needs (e.g., food, water) are relatively fixed and invariant defining characteristics of the human condition whereas Awareness Needs (e.g., meaning making, life purpose) ultimately may be expressed in highly variant form depending upon the FoVs (e.g., language, religion, culture) that predominate at the Exoself (External Self) level.

Among other implications, the EI Self suggests that the beliefs and values that human beings acquire and maintain are a functional result of the interaction between developmental/FoVs (which effectively establish the naturalistic or real world parameters for what may be acquired in the form of beliefs and values about self, others, and the world at large) and the Adaptive Potential and Core Needs of the self (which are realized along a continuum, based upon the relative congruence with, facilitation of, and/or receptivity toward this potential and need at the Exoself level). And, these beliefs and values are not just about others or the "world out there," but also about one's own self; in other words, they are experienced and expressed *by the self*—to the self, others, and the larger world—*as the self*. In this regard, *identity, as the self's narrative about itself, may productively be understood as a representation of the individual's beliefs about self to self, others, and the larger world, which manifests at any moment in time as the most recent culmination of a complex interaction between core needs, formative variables, and external contingencies.*

Consider the experiences of Elaine along these lines. Basically, her work in therapy may be understood as a process by which she learned to allow herself to feel and experience, and ultimately consciously articulate, core needs that previously had been negated by her toward her, without consciously recognizing that she was doing so. Of course, this process was aided and abetted by how such needs in her were experienced by others, namely her primary caregivers and sociocultural context, throughout her development and life, which came over time to determine how she experienced her own core needs. For example, her stated desire for education, to be recognized as important and credible, to have warmer and more connected relations with her husband and children, and to make betters sense of herself, all map directly onto multiple Core Needs from an EI perspective, including at least the following:

- *Level III = Affective Needs* (expression, reception, reciprocal empathy, regulation)
- *Level IV = Acknowledgment Needs* (mirroring, recognition, resonance)
- *Level V = Activation Needs* (stimulation, novelty seeking, causal relations, learning, efficacy)
- *Level VII = Actualizing Needs* (potentiality, differentiation, achievement, influence, consistency, congruence, coherence, esteem, identity)
- *Level IX = Awareness Needs* (openness, reflection, life place, life purpose, meaning making, existential, mortality, essence, finite–infinite, transcendence, transformation)

In many ways, the apparent effectiveness of therapy resulted from the subjectively experienced reality on her part that these needs not only became consciously recognizable to her, but were actively and successfully pursued. By her own assessment, in other words, she knew she was "better" at the conclusion of our time together because these needs had been increasingly able to be apprehended and subsequently accessed by her. The fact that she felt "more alive" testifies, from a clinical standpoint, to the phenomenological outcome of meeting these Core Needs. Of course, as described at the outset of Chapter 2, the means for getting to such ends were extremely "disequilintegrating" for her, which makes sense from an EI perspective, and brings us full circle in our understanding of the interaction among these different levels of self. For example, harkening back to the "7Ds" of transformation as noted in Chapter 2, by finding herself in a therapeutic environment, the FoVs to which she was accustomed suddenly were dramatically *different* (D1) from those to which she now was exposed. Moreover, the *duration* (D2) of our work together—over a year—was of adequate length to modify her beliefs about self, others, and the larger world. Finally, Elaine happened to have a necessary and sufficient capacity and inclination for *depth* (D3), which allowed her to experience the process of therapy at a very deep level of self.

Ultimately, as discussed previously, the self-protecting processes of the Mesoself (e.g., appraisal, attribution, filtering) were attenuated sufficiently through the therapeutic alliance such that the Core Needs that always were there no longer could be "contained" by the existing belief/value structure of the Ectoself. The ensuring "cracks" at that level—during her experience, which appeared consistent with a brief psychotic episode—led to a fundamental realignment between the Ectoself and Endoself, allowing her much greater and more immediate capacity to feel and attend to the pursuit of her Core Needs, which previously had been "off limits," as they were associated with an Ectoself that was organized in a way to prohibit their expression. Why? Because, as with all humans, the organizational structure and content of her Ectoself were a functional results of the Formative Variables (FoVs) to which she had been exposed at the Exoself level throughout her life, which were reinforced further by the religious "sect" and all its vestiges. Implied by such analysis, and returning to a question that was asked at the outset of this Chapter—"What is it in us that changes?"—a great ally to any practicing clinician or another change agent (e.g., teacher, parent, leader, etc.) is that a persistent longing for any human being, at least from an EI perspective, is to meet one's own Core Needs. This overarching motive, a legacy of our adaptive history as described in Chapter 2, drives us forward throughout our life span in a quest to meet such needs. To the degree that the capacity to feel and esteem such needs in ourselves, others, and the larger world is cultivated within us by others who care for us, we are that much better able and willing to understand why human functioning and development unfolds as it does, and respond accordingly throughout our lives, for better or worse. In this sense, we truly do reap what we sow, from micro (i.e., family) to macro (societal) levels of analysis. In other words, the degree to which we *sow* alignment between the Core Needs that are, and become, our human legacy—and the FoVs that are relatively attuned and responsive, or not, to them—is the degree to which we will *reap* a greater degree of fulfillment of our true human potential, on an individual and collective basis (e.g., Cultivating the Globally Sustainable Self, 2015; Shealy et al., 2012). In short, among many other sequelae of long-term exposure to relatively attuned alignment between our own Core Needs, and how the caregiving contexts in which we are embedded respond to them, is the degree to which we become that much more likely to experience and express the capacity and inclination to live according to the "golden rule" (e.g., to do onto others as we would have done onto self), as advocated by the great religious traditions of our world.

From a clinical standpoint, it is a rather straightforward proposition, actually. In the case of Elaine, by knowing, feeling, seeing, and respecting that her fundamental process really was an epic struggle to encounter self—to have and to hold her own Core Needs—we cocreated a space and a place for realignment to occur, between her Ectoself (her beliefs and values, now transmuted, regarding who she was, could be, and become) and Endoself (her deepest yearnings and capacities, which no longer were to be denied or suppressed). The benefits for her world and those in it were profound, as she tearfully described in a spontaneous phone call many months after our work had concluded. Mainly, she called just to say "thank you" to all of us who had listened to and cared for her and her clan. In addition to expressing heartfelt delight on behalf of the entire team, I also thanked her. Truly, as any change agent who is privileged to engage in transformative work with other human beings will attest—despite the angst, confusion, and fatigue that inevitably accompany such a process—when we care deeply for others we gain more than we give, by learning about ourselves and how the world could be, if we would but understand who we are and meet what we need.

REFERENCES

Ainsworth, M. (1990). Some considerations regarding theory and assessment relevant to attachments beyond infancy. In M. Greenberg, D. Cicchetti, & E. M. Cummings (Eds.), *Attachment during the preschool years: Theory, research, and intervention* (pp. 463–489). Chicago, IL: University of Chicago Press.

Anmuth, L. M., Poore, M., Cozen, J., Brearly, T., Tabit, M., Cannady, M., . . . Staton, R. (2013, August). *Making implicit beliefs explicit: In search of best practices for mental health clients, clinicians, and trainers*. Poster presented at the annual meeting of the American Psychological Association, Honolulu, HI.

Aponte, H. J., Powell, F. D., Brooks, S., Watson, M. F., Litzke, C., Lawless, J., & Johnson, E. (2009). Training the person of the therapist in an academic setting. *Journal of Marital and Family Therapy, 35*(4), 381–394.

Aronson, E. (2012). *The social animal* (11th ed.). New York, NY: Worth Publishers.

Bethell, L., Hung-Chu, L., McFatter, R. (2013). Embarrassment and empathy before helping: How internal working models come into play. *Motivation and Emotion, 38*(1), 131–139.

Bowlby, J. (1969). *Attachment and loss: Vol. 1. Attachment*. New York, NY: Basic Books.

Bowlby, J. (1973). *Attachment and loss: Vol. 2. Separation: Anger and anxiety*. New York, NY: Basic Books.

Bowlby, J. (1980). *Attachment and loss: Vol. 3. Loss, Sadness and depression*. New York, NY: Basic Books.

Bruck, E., Winston, A., Aderholt, S., & Muran, C. J. (2006). Predictive validity of patient and therapist attachment and introject styles. *American Journal of Psychotherapy, 60*(4), 393–406.

Carr, E., Szymanski, D., Taha, F., West, L., & Kaslow, N. J. (2014). Understanding the link between multiple oppressions and depression among African American women: The role of internalization. *Psychology of Women Quarterly, 38*(2), 233–245.

Castonguay, L. G. (2000). A common factors approach to psychotherapy training. *Journal of Psychotherapy Integration, 10*, 263–282.

Coates, M., Hanson, W., Samuel, D. B., Webster, M., & Cozen, J. (2016). The Beliefs, Events, and Values Inventory: Psychological assessment implications and applications. In C. N. Shealy (Ed.), *Making Sense of Beliefs and Values* (pp. 371–406). New York, NY: Springer Publishing.

Costello, C. (2014). *Can you be pro-life and pro-death penalty?* Retrieved May 17, 2014 from http://www.cnn.com/2014/05/14/opinion/costello-pro-life-pro-death-penalty/

Cozen, J., Hanson, W., Poston, J., Jones, S., & Tabit, M. (2016). The Beliefs, Events, and Values Inventory (BEVI): Implications and applications for therapeutic assessment and intervention. In C. N. Shealy (Ed.), *Making Sense of Beliefs and Values* (pp. 575–621). New York, NY: Springer Publishing.

Cultivating the Globally Sustainable Self (2015). Retrieved from www.jmu.edu/summitseries

Cummings, E. M., Davies, P. T., & Campbell, S. S. (2000). *Developmental psychopathology and family process: Theory, research, and clinical implications*. New York, NY: Guilford Press.

Deacon, B. J. (2013). The biomedical model of mental disorder: A critical analysis of its validity, utility, and effects on psychotherapy research. *Clinical Psychology Review, 33*, 846–861.

Feather, N. T. (1992). Values, valences, expectations, and actions. *Journal of Social Issues, 48*(2), 109–124.

Feather, N. T. (1994). Human values and their relation to justice. *Journal of Social Issues, 50*(4), 129–152.

Feather, N. T. (1995). Values, valences, and choice: The influence of values on the perceived attractiveness and choice of alternatives. *Journal of Personality and Social Psychology, 68*(6), 1135–1151.

Finn, S. E. (2007). *In our client's shoes: Theories and techniques of therapeutic assessment*. New York, NY: Routledge.

Finn, S. E., & Tonsager, M. E. (1997). Information-gathering and therapeutic models of assessment: Complementary paradigms. *Psychological Assessment, 9*(4), 374–385.

Henriques, G. (2011). *A new unified theory of psychology*. New York, NY: Springer.

Horwitz, A. (2002). *Creating mental illness*. Chicago, IL: University of Chicago Press.

Inglehart, R., Basáñez, M., Díez-Medrano, J., Halman, L., & Luijkx, R. (2004). *Human beliefs and values: A cross-cultural sourcebook based on the 1999-2002 values surveys*. Mexico: Siglo XXI Editores.

Inglehart, R., Basáñez, M., & Moreno, A. (1998). *Human values and beliefs: A cross-cultural sourcebook*. Ann Arbor, MI: The University of Michigan Press.

International Religious Freedom Report. (2004). *U.S. State Department*. Aggregates compiled by NationMaster. Retrieved from http://www.nationmaster.com/country-info/stats/Religion/Islam/Percentage-Muslim

Kegan, R. (1982). *The evolving self*. Cambridge, MA: Harvard University Press.

Khanna, R. (2010). Sexual rights are human rights: Lessons from community action in India. *Beliefs and Values, 2*(1), 16–26.

Magnavita, J., & Achin, J. (2013). Unifying psychotherapy: Principles, methods, and evidence from clinical science. New York, NY: Springer Publishing.

McLeod, S. A. (2009). Jean Piaget. Retrieved from http://www.simplypsychology.org/piaget.html

Newberg, A., & Waldman, M. R. (2006). *Why we believe what we believe: Uncovering our biological need for meaning, spirituality, and truth*. New York, NY: Free Press.

Norcross, J. C. (Ed.). (2002). *Psychotherapeutic relationships that work: Therapist contributions and responsiveness to patients*. New York, NY: Oxford University Press.

Norcross, J. C. (2005). A primer on psychotherapy integration. In J. C. Norcross & M. R. Goldfried, (Eds.), *Handbook of psychotherapy integration* (pp. 3–23). New York, NY: Oxford University Press, Inc.

Pew Forum on Religion and Public Life. (2015, May). *America's changing religious landscape*. Retrieved from http://www.pewforum.org/2015/05/12/americas-changing-religious-landscape/

Piaget, J. (1976). *The grasp of consciousness: Action and concept in the young child*. Cambridge, MA: Harvard University Press.

Piaget, J. (1977). *The development of thought: Equilibration of cognitive structures*. New York, NY: Viking Press.

Poston, J. M., & Hanson, W. E. (2010). Meta-analysis of psychological assessment as a therapeutic intervention. *Psychological Assessment, 22*(2), 203–212.

Rokeach, M., & Ball-Rokeach, S. J. (1989). Stability and change in American value priorities. *American Psychologist, 44*(5), 775–784.

Schwartz, S. H. (1992). Universals in the content and structure of values: Theoretical advances and empirical tests in 20 countries. In M. P. Zanna (Ed.), *Advances in experimental social psychology* (pp. 1–65). New York, NY: Academic Press.

Schwartz, S. H. (2012). An overview of the Schwartz theory of basic values. *Online Readings in Psychology and Culture, 2*(1). Retrieved from http://dx.doi.org/10.9707/2307-0919.1116

Schacter, D. L., Gilbert, D. T., & Wegner, D. M. (2011). *Psychology* (2nd ed.). New York, NY: Worth Publishers.

Shealy, C. N. (1995). From Boys Town to Oliver Twist: Separating fact from fiction in welfare reform and out-of home placement of children and youth. *American Psychologist, 50*(8), 565–580.

Shealy, C. N. (2004). A model and method for "making" a C-I psychologist: Equilintegration (EI) theory and the Beliefs, Events, and Values Inventory (BEVI). *Journal of Clinical Psychology, 60*, 1065–1090.

Shealy, C. N. (2005). Justifying the justification hypothesis: Scientific-humanism, Equilintegration (EI) theory, and the Beliefs, Events, and Values Inventory (BEVI) [Special Series]. *Journal of Clinical Psychology, 61*(1), 81–106.

Shealy, C. N., Bhuyan, D., & Sternberger, L. G. (2012). Cultivating the capacity to care in children and youth: Implications from EI theory, EI self, and BEVI. In U. Nayar (Ed.), *Child and adolescent mental health* (pp. 240–255). New Delhi, India: Sage Publications.

Shealy, C. N., & Bullock, M. (in press). *Going global: How psychology and psychologists can meet a world of need*. Washington, DC: APA Books.

Sroufe, A. L. (2009, December). The concept of development in developmental psychopathology. *Child Development Perspectives, 3*(3), 178–183.

Sternberg, R. J. (1985). *Beyond IQ: A triarchic theory of human intelligence*. New York, NY: Cambridge University Press.

Taubner, S., Zimmerman, J., Kächele, H., Möller, H., & Sell, C. (2013). The relationship of introject affiliation and personal therapy to trainee self-efficacy: A longitudinal study among psychotherapy trainees. *Psychotherapy, 50*(2), 167–177.

Toth, S. L., & Cicchetti, D. (2013). Developmental psychopathology perspective on child maltreatment. *Child Maltreatment, 18*(3), 135–139.

Wachtel, P. L. (1997). *Psychoanalysis, behavior therapy, and the relational world.* Washington, DC: American Psychological Association.

Wachtel, P. S. (2008). *Relational theory and the practice of psychotherapy.* New York, NY: Guilford.

Wampold, B. E. (2010). The research evidence for common factors models: A historically situated perspective. In B. L. Duncan & S. D. Miller (Eds.), *The heart and soul of change: Delivering what works in therapy* (2nd ed., pp. 49–81). Washington, DC: American Psychological Association.

Wandschneider, E., Pysarchik, D. T, Sternberger, L. G., Ma, W., Acheson-Clair, K., Baltensperberger, B., . . . Hart, V. (2016). The Forum BEVI Project: Applications and implications for international, multicultural, and transformative learning. In C. N. Shealy (Ed.), *Making sense of beliefs and values* (pp. 407–484). New York, NY: Springer Publishing.

Wegner, D. M. (2002). *The illusion of conscious will.* Cambridge, MA: The MIT Press.

4

BELIEFS, EVENTS, AND VALUES INVENTORY (BEVI)

Oh, everyone believes
From emptiness to everything
Oh, everyone believes
And no one's going quietly

Belief
—John Mayer

I still remember the careful and precise way in which Diana, the mother of my client, sat down in the chair across from me awaiting her "informing," the final phase of a comprehensive psychological evaluation in which assessment results and conclusions are presented and discussed in summary form by the testing psychologist. Having finished my internship, I was completing my residency year between a university-based department of pediatrics and a psychiatric hospital, absorbing the richness of these diverse experiences and applying my newfound knowledge across a wide range of fascinating presentations. As anyone practicing in the early 1990s will recall, Attention Deficit Disorder (ADD) was swiftly becoming the diagnosis du jour (du décennies, it turned out), receiving sustained and prominent national attention in the popular press.[1]

A striking women in her late 30s, Diana had already determined that Michael, her 10-year-old child, "had ADD," informing me as such during the initial clinical interview; from her perspective, and that of her family physician who had referred her to our clinic, all of the evidence pointed in this direction. Michael had difficulty concentrating in the classroom, was noncompliant at home, and generally seemed distractable and agitated. The department of pediatrics in which I worked actually had quite a progressive and interdisciplinary team at hand, including clinical psychology, developmental psychology, neurology, nursing, psychiatry, and social work, along with considerable access to other specialty areas with expertise bearing upon the presentations we

---

[1] Despite continued controversy, ADD (and its variants) has become one of the most common diagnoses assigned to children, youth, and even adults, rising from 7.8% of children aged 3 to 17 in 2003 to 11.0% of children in 2011, and increasing an average of 5% per year from 2003 to 2011. As of 2012, 9.5% of U.S. children aged 3 to 17—approximately 5.9 million children—had received a diagnosis of Attention Deficit Hyperactivity Disorder (ADHD). Interestingly, and presaging the chapter on gender later in this book (Pendleton, Cochran, Kapadia, & Iyer, 2016), 13.2% of children receiving an ADHD diagnosis are boys and 5.6% are girls (Centers for Disease Control and Prevention, 2014). Overall, these trends raise a number of questions, including but not limited to issues of diagnostic reliability and validity, the factors and forces that may facilitate such dramatic increases in this diagnosis over time, as well as the putative "genetic basis" for this condition (e.g., Anmuth et al., 2013; Coates et al., 2016; Cozen et al., 2016; Cummings, Davies, & Campbell, 2000; Deacon, 2013; Horwitz, 2002).

encountered. In that sense, Diana and Michael probably were receiving about the best level and scope of care available at the time. Indeed, a typical psychological assessment might include perspectives from psychology, neurology, nursing, social work, and psychiatry, thus exemplifying the best aspects of interprofessional collaboration (e.g., Arredondo, Shealy, Neale, & Winfrey, 2004; Interprofessional Education Collaborative, 2014; Johnson, Stewart, Brabeck, Huber, & Rubin, 2004). So it was with this young man, who was tested with a comprehensive battery, including continuous performance and other measures for ADD, along with additional instrumentation and assessment processes, including a thorough intake interview. The results of this process? None of us saw evidence for ADD, although other matters of concern readily were apparent. In particular, during the intake interview, Diana hesitatingly recounted a pattern of intense conflict in the home between herself and her husband, which mainly involved verbal altercations between them on a daily basis along with a general feeling of tension and disconnection. How long had this pattern prevailed? "Years," was Diana's airy reply, which was accompanied by the hasty disclaimer that such conflict was completely irrelevant from the standpoint of Michael's difficulties, which also had occurred ever since he had attended school. After sustained consultation, and several preliminary drafts, a final version of the psychological evaluation was presented to Diana for her review. Essentially, our collective diagnostic conclusion did not find evidence for ADD, although we agreed with Diana that Michael was emotionally distressed, perhaps in part because of the unrelenting conflict that he witnessed, which was confirmed to us during our interview with him.

I vividly recall Diana's reaction to this feedback, which was presented as gently and hypothetically as I could as a beginning clinician. To my observation that "perhaps the ongoing conflict between you and your husband are affecting Michael's ability to concentrate," Diana's jaw dropped, her breathing became rapid, and she declared, "My arm has gone numb." I stopped, leaned forward, and said something like, "It's okay. Just take a moment. We have physicians here. Should I get one?" She paused, for what seemed like forever, and said, "No. I'm okay." Her arm had feeling again, but her face had fallen, and I thought she might cry. Some inner resolve kicked in with a vengeance. Her features stiffened. She regarded me coldly, and declared, "There's nothing wrong with us that's affecting Michael." I assured her that I was *not* stating at any absolute or factual level that such was the case, only that both she and Michael had reported things were not happy in the home, and that Michael himself quietly had acknowledged that he felt badly about things in his family, wondering if there was something about him (e.g., his grades, his school problems) that was causing his parents to fight. Diana paused to take all this in. Eventually, she said, "There's nothing we can do about all of that," to which I replied that we might be able to help, if she would like to talk more. She had softened a bit by then, but was not yet sold. "I need to think what to do" she said, before thanking me and leaving the office. Although I moved on professionally soon after, and do not know if she ever followed up with our recommendations, I have thought about this session over the years, mainly because it was one of many that prompted me to begin work on the assessment measure and accompanying theoretical framework that is the focus of this book.

BEVI Impetus and Overview

In fact, I have long been fascinated by the origins, nature, and impact of "beliefs and values," no doubt due to their salience during my own upbringing, which certainly was characterized by perspectives on the world that were unconventional to say the least. And, I have likewise been captivated by an attendant idea, presented by a professor long ago, that we could in fact discover "lawfulness in nature," if our approach to methods and measures was sufficiently rigorous. With indulgence from my master's adviser, my thesis, in fact, sat squarely in the middle of these interests—beliefs, values, and assessment—by asking whether or not soap opera viewers differed from nonviewers in their "irrational beliefs," according to the *Jones Irrational Beliefs Test* (they did, to a degree). Given such preoccupations, it may not be surprising that I not only attended closely to what my clients said they believed about all manner of phenomena (e.g., why they and others did what they did), but began to jot down such "belief" statements as they emerged, right as I was completing my internship and postdoctoral training years, and continuing on during the process of conducting therapeutic interventions and graduate student training overseas through the University of Maryland system, which ultimately led to my running a counseling center in a small, highly internationalized campus in Germany. There, I was privileged to encounter beliefs and values about self, others, and the larger world from individuals all over the globe. My notes on belief statements kept growing as I continued a parallel process of researching all that we knew about the etiology and measurement of beliefs and values, which ultimately culminated in the "three components" of *belief*, *needs*, and *self* discussed in Chapter 2 as well as the fundamental dynamics that are illustrated via the EI (Equilintegration) Self of Chapter 3. From that process, an early version of the *Beliefs, Events, and Values Inventory* (BEVI) emerged, eventually winnowed down to 494 items, which represented the first full version of this measure. Twenty years later, there are two versions—long and short—of the BEVI, consisting of 336 and 185 items respectively. Anyone involved in test development knows that the process of developing a valid, reliable, and web-based measure is intensive and demanding, to say the least, in terms of time, energy, and resources, as so many different sources of expertise are involved, from theoretical and empirical to statistical and programming.

Over 20 years in, with dozens of studies and real world applications, hundreds of analyses, and thousands of administrations, I and the many researchers and practitioners who have participated in various phases of the BEVI's development, implementation, and evaluation—a number of whom are featured in later chapters—are about as confident as we can be that the measure described in this chapter is illuminating various manifestations of "lawfulness in nature" in a valid and reliable manner. However, in truth, the process of test development, analysis, and refinement never concludes. This chapter essentially describes what the BEVI is, why and how it emerged as it did, relevant psychometrics and scale descriptions, and key aspects of usage and interpretation. The research and practice chapters that follow provide further perspective and findings regarding all of these points. Finally, it should be noted that some of the following material addresses various statistical aspects of this measure for purposes of understanding its underlying psychometric properties. Individuals who are not familiar with such information are encouraged not to become overwhelmed, but instead to focus either on the "big picture" aspects of this measure (e.g., what is measures via specific scales; how it is used in the real world; the nature and application of individual, group, and organizational reports) and/or to learn more about such test development processes through further reading, coursework, and consultation in a range of relevant areas (e.g., test development and design; issues of reliability and validity; psychometrics and statistics).

So what is the BEVI? At the most basic level, it is a measure of psychological functioning, broadly defined. That is to say, like most psychological measures, it presents a series of questions that a respondent (i.e., test taker) may answer according to a set of response options, ranging in the case of the BEVI, from Strongly Agree, Agree, Disagree, and Strongly Disagree. But the BEVI takes another step, by seeking simultaneously to assess not only *what* and *how* the respondent is experiencing his or her own "Version of Reality," but *why*. That is because the BEVI deliberately includes what in clinical parlance is known as an "intake interview"[2]—an amalgamation of many such interview questions actually—seeking to ascertain core life experiences that may have impacted *why* one's sense of self, others, and the larger world is what it is. Moreover, the BEVI also asks the respondent to clarify the nature and form of such life experiences for them (i.e., comprising the "Events" of the BEVI, as in the Beliefs, *Events*, and Values Inventory), by including a comprehensive Background Information section, which queries about a very wide range of Formative Variables (as noted in the Chapter 3 discussion of the EI Self). For example, test takers are asked about their age, gender, ethnicity, where they were raised, their religious and political inclinations, and so forth. In this way, the BEVI was designed to be used with a very wide range of populations—from students, educators, and clinicians to leaders, clients, and inmates, among other individuals and groups—as the following chapters illustrate. Ultimately, the BEVI is relevant to an array of contexts since it seeks to ask and answer the following questions that are of broad interest and impact: (a) Why do we experience self, others, and the larger world as we do? (b) What are the implications of our experience of self, others, and the larger world on multiple aspects of human functioning? (c) How may such information be used to facilitate a range of processes and outcomes in the real world (e.g., greater awareness, growth, and development)? More specifically, usage of the BEVI tends to fall in one or more of eight areas of inquiry and practice:

1. *Evaluating learning experiences* (e.g., study abroad, multicultural courses, general education, training programs/workshops, service learning, etc.)
2. *Understanding learning processes* (e.g., who learns what and why, and under what circumstances)
3. *Promoting learning objectives* (e.g., increased awareness of self, others, and the larger world)
4. *Enhancing teaching and program quality* (e.g., which experiences, courses, programs, etc. have what impact, and why)
5. *Facilitating growth and development* (e.g., of individuals, groups, and organizations)
6. *Conducting research* (e.g., how, why, and under what circumstances people become more "open" to different cultures)
7. *Addressing organizational needs* (e.g., staff/leadership development)
8. *Complying with assessment and accreditation requirements* (e.g., linking objectives to outcomes)

---

[2] As any mental health clinician is aware, the "intake interview" is conducted early in a process of assessment or therapy, typically in the first session or two, and includes a wide range of questions regarding life history as well as thoughts, feelings, and behaviors that may bear upon the referral question—why they are there—as well as the "symptoms" they experience and possible processes or recommendations regarding the clinical intervention that follows. From the standpoint of the EI model and BEVI method—and as multiple analyses attest in various chapters of this book—such Formative Variables impact how all human beings experience self, others, and the larger world, not just individuals who may be seeking mental health services.

Development of the BEVI Long Version

In accordance with appropriate psychometric standards and processes (e.g., Downing & Haladyna, 1997; Geisinger, 2013; Hubley & Zumbo, 2013; Robinson, Shaver, & Wrightsman, 1991, 1999), the BEVI has been in development since the early 1990s. Although three phases may be identified to characterized its development—(a) Item Development and Literature Review; (b) Development, Usage, and Evaluation of the Long Version; and (c) Development, Usage, and Evaluation of the Short Version—the process is understood better along an evolutionary continuum than as discrete and separable stages, mainly because all that is learned from one "phase" of test development is linked inextricably to the next. In any case, to track how the BEVI arrived at its current incarnation, it may be helpful to document key aspects of its developmental trajectory.

The early process of BEVI development began with the realization that the "belief statements" uttered by clients—and later by students, and later still, by individuals in the public sphere (e.g., politicians and other public figures)—seemed to loom large for human beings vis-à-vis why and how they "made meaning" as they did. For the most part, these "belief statements" manifested in the form of verbal (and sometimes written) one-sentence assertions regarding why we humans do what we do and/or why the world works as it does. Mainly, I simply started to keep track of (i.e., began to write down) what people said on such matters, because I was intrigued by the trifold reality that (a) such statements were often expressed with complete certitude (i.e., there seemed to be no question in the asserter's mind that the belief statement was valid); (b) generally, there seemed to be not great awareness that the most parsimonious explanation for their own strongly held beliefs was that they were massively shaped if not determined by their own life histories and circumstances (i.e., the unique "Formative Variables" that characterized their own development were highly correlated with what they declared to be good or bad and true or false); and (c) such belief statements were invoked directly to explain or justify why they—and others—did what they did, with all manner of implications for acts of omission and commission in the real world (e.g., what they did and did not do in relation to self, others, and the larger world). In short, I was, and am, fascinated by the fact that we humans may live out our lives, for better or worse, on the basis of beliefs about the nature of reality that have not been identified, examined, or understood. And of course, in many cases—particularly in a clinical realm, but ultimately, at every level of reality (e.g., individual, group, organizational, societal, national, global)—these beliefs were not mere abstractions, but explicitly were cited as *the reason why* a specific action, policy, or practice was or was not deemed to be good and true or bad and false. As observed earlier, the historical record is clear in that regard, from the rationale for persecuting specific religious groups in antiquity, to the fundamental justification for the "final solution" of the Holocaust in the 20th century, to current "climate change denial," to invoke only a few of countless exemplars from the past, present, and undoubtedly, the future. In short, the fundamental observation—that we may be living our lives and impacting others according to beliefs that we acquired under circumstances and in situations of which we are unaware—was, and is, remarkable because so much of our existence, regard, and treatment of one another is traced directly to our apparent faith in such unexamined beliefs.

Of course, countless individuals have been drawn to such matters in one way or another through their lives and work, perhaps most notably beginning with Socrates's bold assertion that *The unexamined life is not worth living*. But at least two fundamental advances over the past century have allowed us to explore Socrates's proposition empirically and in applied terms. First, thanks to powerful statistical methodologies that painstakingly have been developed over the past century—and informed theoretically and empirically by a range of interdisciplinary scholarly and applied perspectives and technologies—we are able to demonstrate the real world etiology, impact, and transformation of "beliefs and values" in a reliable and valid manner. Second, decades of research on psychotherapy processes and outcomes as well as allied fields of inquiry (e.g., cognitive and developmental psychology; aspects of neurobiology), have allowed us to begin apprehending how the "self"—broadly defined—becomes structured as it does as well as why and under what circumstances various aspects of "self" may be transformed vis-à-vis therapeutic relationships and related change-oriented interventions (e.g., Henriques, 2011; Magnavita & Achin, 2013; Newberg & Waldman, 2006; Norcross, 2005; Wachtel, 2008; Wampold, 2010; see also Chapters 2 and 3). Of course, many other fields also contribute to this process of illuminating why we humans think, feel, and behave as we do—and many of these perspectives are integral to the EI Model. The implications of such scientific and applied advances cannot be overestimated for scholars, practitioners, educators, students, and policy makers who wish to illuminate why we humans do what we do, and how we might "cultivate our capacity to care" in a way that is demonstrably more sustainable over the short and the long term (e.g., Cultivating the Globally Sustainable Self, 2014; Shealy, Bhuyan, & Sternberger, 2012; Shealy & Bullock, in press). The trick of course is translating such high minded sentiment into concrete form. Here resides the intensive, long-term, and resource-extensive process of test development, evaluation, and refinement as well as programmatic and assessment-based research.

At the outset then, beginning in the early 1990s, an extensive review began of research and theory relevant to specific BEVI constructs, which culminated in the "three components" of *beliefs*, *needs*, and *self*, and continues to this day (e.g., Anmuth et al., 2013; Atwood, Chkhaidze, Shealy, Staton, & Sternberger, 2014; Bolen, Shealy, Pysarchik, & Whalen, 2009; Brearly, Shealy, Staton, & Sternberger, 2012; Hill et al., 2013; Isley, Shealy, Crandall, Sivo, & Reifsteck, 1999; Hayes, Shealy, Sivo, & Weinstein, 1999; Patel, Shealy, & De Michele, 2007; Pysarchik, Shealy, & Whalen, 2007; Shealy, 2004, 2005, 2015; Shealy, Burdell, Sivo, Davino, & Hayes, 1999; Shealy, Sears, Sivo, Allessandria, & Isley, 1999; Shealy et al., 2012; Spaeth, Shealy, Cobb, Staton, & Sternberger, 2010; Sternberger, Whalen, Pysarchik, & Shealy, 2009; Tabit et al., 2011; Williams & Shealy, 2004).

Concretely, as noted, preliminary items were developed from actual belief–value statements (e.g., from adolescent/adult clients and student trainees, students, and political/public figures), and reviewed and revised through multiple processes over the past 20-plus years (e.g., several Subject Matter Expert [SME] panel reviews; multiple Institutional Review Board processes; review processes via scholarly presentations/publications). From a statistical standpoint, five separate statisticians have participated in the evaluation of various iterations of the BEVI, including early exploratory factor analytic work, which culminated in 10 "process scales" for the 494-item version of the BEVI (e.g., Shealy, 2004). As indicated in Table 4.1, the majority of reliability and stability (i.e., 3-month test–retest) estimates for this version of the BEVI were .80 or higher.

TABLE 4.1
*Preliminary Reliability and Stability (3 Month Test–Retest)
Estimates for BEVI Scales[3]*

	RELIABILITY	STABILITY
Basic Openness	.86	.87
Negative Life Events	.90	.85
Naïve Determinism	.68	.85
Sociocultural Closure	.87	.90
Authoritarian Introjects	.68	.81
Religious Traditionalism	.95	.95
Need for Control	.62	.78
Emotional Attunement	.75	.65
Self Access	.70	.72
Separation Individuation	.83	.78
Gender Stereotypes	.86	.88

Initial evidence of validity is indicated by a number of studies demonstrating that the BEVI is able to predict group membership across a wide range of demographic variables, including gender, ethnic background, parental income, political orientation, and religious orientation (e.g., Anmuth et al., 2013; Atwood et al., 2014; Brearly et al., 2012; Hayes et al., 1999; Hill et al., 2013; Isley et al., 1999; Patel et al., 2007; Pysarchik et al., 2007; Shealy, 2004, 2005, 2015; Shealy et al., 2012; Tabit et al., 2011). For example, in a study comparing Mental Health Professionals and Evangelical Christians on the BEVI, Hayes (2001) found that ". . .the instrument accurately classified Evangelical Christians and Mental Health Professionals, with 95% of originally grouped cases correctly classified, which strongly suggests that the BEVI can validly discriminate between these two groups" (p. 102).[3]

In another study examining environmental beliefs and values in general and the reported degree of concern about global warming, Patel (2008) found the following:

> . . .women, Democrats, and atheists or agnostics with a lower "need for control," lower "self access," and a relatively lower degree of "separation-individuation" are most likely to express environmental concerns whereas Republican men who are Christians with a higher "need for control," higher "self access," and a relatively higher degree of "separation-individuation" are the least likely to express environmental concerns. . . .EI theory, the EI Self, and the BEVI offer a promising theoretical framework, model, and method for predicting and explaining who is and is not concerned about the environment by illuminating the underlying affective, attributional, developmental, and contextual processes that mediate and moderate why such belief/value processes and outcomes occur in the first place. (pp. 43, 46–47)

---

[3] *Note.* These estimates are based upon an initial sample of 648 participants of undergraduate psychology students.

As a final example, in a study comparing the BEVI and the Intercultural Development Inventory (IDI), Reisweber (2008) concluded the following:

> . . .it is both compelling and consistent with an EI framework that the BEVI was able to identify in advance which students would be more or less likely to increase their intercultural awareness by the end of that academic year. Specifically, students who reported lower Naïve Determinism and more Gender Stereotypes at the beginning of the academic year were statistically more likely to demonstrate an increase in intercultural awareness after living for nine months in an international residence hall. Furthermore, students with a higher degree of Negative Life Events (NLE) and Emotional Attunement, as measured by the BEVI, also demonstrated greater and more accurate intercultural sensitivity, as measured by the IDI. (pp. 79–80)

The Forum BEVI Project: Initial Findings and Implications

Beginning with Patel (2008) and Reisweber (2008), the Forum BEVI Project—a 6-year, multi-institution assessment of learning project—offered an ideal opportunity to examine and refine further the underlying psychometric properties of this measure, while also conducting a wide range of studies to understand the complex interactions among various BEVI scales (and subscales) as well as real world implications and applications (see Forum BEVI Project, 2015). As such, one of the major substantive outcomes of this initiative was further analysis of what was by then (following additional factor analytic work) a 415-item version of the BEVI in an attempt to lower the number of items on this measure, clarify further its underlying factor structure, and examine a wide range of mediators and moderators of learning. As reported in over 20 publications (e.g., articles, chapters, dissertations), 50 presentations (e.g., symposia, papers, posters), and hundreds of separate analyses from 2007 to 2014, a range of colleges, universities, and study abroad providers administered the BEVI to successive waves of participants including an initial sample of nearly 2,000 participants in the United States and internationally. Working from this 415-item version of the BEVI, statistical analysis narrowed the original number of factors on the BEVI from 40 to 18; nearly 60 items also were eliminated during the subsequent review process. Norms then were established for each of these "scales" (i.e., factors) with most reliabilities above 0.80 or 0.90 (no scale had a reliability of less than 0.75). Three new qualitative items also were integrated into the BEVI prior to the pilot phase, which allowed for complementary types of analyses.

Based upon factor analytic and correlation matrix data, the 18 scales of the BEVI—in what was now a 336-item, "long version"—were organized in a manner that corresponds with the basic EI theoretical framework of this measure. In an attempt to reduce further the number of factors, a Schmid–Leiman transformation (i.e., essentially, a factor analysis of a factor analysis) was conducted (Schmid & Leiman, 1957). Although six primary factors (PF) were in fact extractable from the larger Exploratory Factor Analysis (EFA), approximately half of the variance accounted for by the EFA was not accounted for by the six factors that were retained via Schmid–Leiman. Thus, in consultation with the project statistician, it was determined at that phase of the project to report out both "PF" (from Schmid–Leiman) and secondary factors ("SF") from the EFA as well as the order in which factors were extracted. A correlation matrix then was conducted (i.e., a correlation matrix is a statistical procedure by which all factors on a measure are correlated with each other in order to demonstrate the magnitude and direction of their correlative relationship to each other). As a whole, this information—combined with relative loadings of specific items on each factor—further illuminated both the nature of each factor (i.e., what it was measuring) as well as how—and perhaps why—such factors were related to each other as they were.

Consider, for example, the following correlation matrix data for two scales of the long version of the BEVI, Needs Closure and Emotional Attunement.[4] For interpretive purposes, the numbers listed in parentheses are the respective reliabilities for each scale; the "PF" and "SF" designations and the accompanying numbers refer to whether the scale was extracted as a "primary" or "secondary" factor, and in which order of extraction. The descriptive information listed for each scale corresponds to the type of content assessed by the items that load on each scale. The scales that are listed underneath each numbered scale are presented in descending order of magnitude from correlation matrix findings (e.g., the correlation of each scale by all other scales).

Scale 2. Needs Closure (0.88, PF 1)
(challenging life circumstances, odd explanations for why things are the way they are, ambivalent or distant relationship with core needs in self and/or others)

    Socioemotional Convergence (–0.93)
    Sociocultural Openness (–0.90)
    Emotional Attunement (–0.85)
    Identity Closure (0.84)
    Negative Life Events (0.81)
    Basic Closedness (0.78)
    Ecological Resonance (–0.72)
    Divergent Determinism (0.65)
    Hard Structure (0.53)
    Socioreligious Traditionalism (0.31)

Scale 10. Emotional Attunement (0.87, SF 17)
(highly emotional, highly sensitive, highly social, needy affiliative, undifferentiated, values emotional expression)

    Needs Closure (–0.85)
    Socioemotional Convergence (0.84)
    Basic Closedness (–0.77)
    Sociocultural Openness (0.77)
    Ecological Resonance (0.64)
    Identity Structure (–0.63)
    Negative Life Events (–0.62)
    Hard Structure (–0.59)
    Divergent Determinism (–0.58)
    Socioreligious Traditionalism (–0.20)

---

[4] This section is adapted and/or excerpted with permission from Shealy, C. N., Bhuyan, D., & Sternberger, L. G. (2012). Cultivating the capacity to care in children and youth: Implications from EI Theory, EI Self, and BEVI. In U. Nayar (Ed.), *Child and Adolescent Mental Health* (pp. 240–255). New Delhi, India: Sage Publications. See also the Forum BEVI Project at www.forumea.org/research-bevi-project.cfm

From the standpoint of the EI model and BEVI method, such findings illustrate (a) how the degree to which we believe our core needs were met is associated with how we experience ourselves, others, and the larger world and (b) how such processes are associated with our capacity to resonate emotionally with self and others. Needs Closure (the first of the "Primary Factors" or PF) is composed of items that indicate whether a respondent reports that his or her childhood was "happy," the degree to which basic needs were or were not met in a "good enough" way, and subjectively held explanations for why people or the world work as they do. In considering the interrelationship among Needs Closure and its three most highly correlated scales, note that the relationship between the reported experience of a "bad childhood" is associated with: (a) relative difficulty holding complex, equally plausible, and sometimes contradictory realities simultaneously in the mind (i.e., Socioemotional Convergence); (b) a relative lack of openness to beliefs and practices that are different from one's own (i.e., Sociocultural Openness); and (c) a relative difficulty with, or indifference toward, the "emotional world" of self or others (i.e., Emotional Attunement). How do we understand and interpret such findings?

As discussed in Chapters 2 and 3, abundant evidence suggests that what we believe and value as good or true is partly a function of our unique Family Variables (e.g., family, culture, context, life, and contextual experiences), which interact with powerful core needs (such as attachment, affiliation, actualization, etc.) to mediate affective and attributional processes of which we often have little awareness. Among other relevant fields, developmental psychopathology provides important insights about the variables that shape pathways to adaptation or maladaptation, by examining the interactions among genetic, biological, psychosocial, and familial domains in order to understand developmental processes and outcomes from infancy to adulthood. More specifically, this interdisciplinary field of inquiry examines the etiology and interactions among a wide range of processes that causally are associated with variation in human conduct and functioning, ranging from "disturbed" or "maladaptive" to "healthy" or "optimal" (e.g., Cummings, Davies, & Campbell, 2000; Sroufe, 2009; Toth & Cicchetti, 2013). Highly consistent with the Needs Closure intercorrelations from the BEVI, findings cited previously indicate that poor parenting, insecure attachment, abuse, and neglect are associated negatively with the capacity in children and youth to experience care for self and others (e.g., Shealy, 1995; Shealy et al., 2012). Among related explanations for such outcomes, perhaps the most parsimonious is that children and youth who were not well cared for themselves tend to be preoccupied by their own emotional, cognitive, and behavioral struggles, which are compounded by an impaired capacity for self-care as well as poor or inadequate support from caregivers.

Note also from the preceding correlation matrix data that Needs Closure is the most highly negatively correlated scale with Emotional Attunement. How might such findings be interpreted? Essentially, it appears that the degree to which individuals report that their core needs were *not* met in a "good enough" manner is associated with a *lack* of capacity and inclination to attend to emotional processes in self and other, and vice versa. Such findings do receive support from extant literature. For example, Garner, Dunsmore, and Southam-Gerrow (2008) examined the conversations of mothers regarding the explanation of emotion and emotional knowledge vis-à-vis the relational and physical aggression and pro-social behavior in their children. Essentially, children with mothers who explained emotion were more likely to engage in pro-social behavior. The authors hypothesize that such discussions facilitate the development of emotional capacity and skill, by validating their children's emotions and helping them to be aware of and sensitive to emotional cues in self and in others. Grounded in attachment theory, emotional security is mediated by the relative capacity to regulate one's own emotions (Cummings & Davies, 1996). Children living in homes characterized by domestic violence have significant challenges in safeguarding their security in the presence of unpredictable and volatile behaviors, posing considerable challenges to their adjustment (Davies, Winter, & Cicchetti, 2006; Shealy, 1995). Furthermore, McCoy, Cummings, and Davies (2009) found that how parents handled conflict (constructively or destructively) was associated with their children's emotional security and their relative likelihood to engage in pro-social behavior. Such findings rightly have influenced a wide range of interventions, including values-based curricula, which emphasizes the importance of attending to emotional experiences in self and others as well as other pro-social behaviors, all of which are designed to enhance a capacity and inclination to care (e.g., Singh, 2009; Toomey & Lovat, 2009). In short, these findings suggest that warm and engaged parenting is an important variable in positive mental health outcomes for children, which in turn yields a higher likelihood that children will engage in pro-social behaviors. Likewise, as the BEVI correlational matrix data illustrate, the degree to which we report the experience of "warm parenting" is highly associated with our attendant capacity and inclination toward "emotional attunement" in self and other (Shealy et al., 2012). In any case, for present purposes, findings such as those presented previously were among the first to emerge from the Forum BEVI Project. Ultimately, the hundreds of analyses that followed—including dozens of BEVI reports, which were used in a range of applied settings—are presented in the various research and practice chapters that follow later in this book.

Development of the BEVI Short Version

Despite such findings, a number of institutions/organizations still desired a shorter version of the BEVI for a number of reasons. First, within the context of higher education in particular, assessment demands already were high and student/faculty time was short. Second, although each scale on the long version of the BEVI assessed different constructs, these were interdependent with one another (i.e., by design, and consistent with the interconnected nature of beliefs, the "oblique" nature of factor rotation parameters allowed items to load on more than one factor). Information gleaned from separate EFAs during its development did much to illuminate how and why specific "beliefs, events, and values" were associated together as they were. However, we long had recognized the need to move beyond EFA in order to determine by Confirmative Factor Analysis (CFA) if and how the EFA structure of the measure held upon administration to a new and separate sample, and to understand the relationship among more parsimonious versions of each scale construct. Thus, from 2011 to 2013, we undertook the process of creating a "short version" of the BEVI. The overarching goal was to determine if a shorter version of the BEVI, with substantially fewer items, could be developed in a manner that did not compromise the fundamental integrity of the measure (i.e., a "short version" would continue to illuminate how and why "beliefs, events, and values" were interrelated as they seemed via multiple analyses). As any psychometrician will attest, this process was highly painstaking and intensive.[5] Following a data-scrubbing process (e.g., ensuring that duplicated or incomplete cases were removed from the database), we identified a sample of 2,331 cases to be used in conducing the CFA.

---

[5] An initial version of this section—on development of the short BEVI—was documented by Wenjuan Ma, a statistician for the Forum BEVI Project.

This first phase was much more doable than the next, which required multiple steps to determine which items could be eliminated without sacrificing the integrity of the measure. First, we confirmed which items were loading on which specific scale. Because a number of the long version scales were measuring higher order constructs, it was necessary again to identify smaller subsets of items (i.e., subfactors) that comprised the larger construct. Through Cronbach's alpha, items were selected that could be removed safely without significantly impacting the consistency of a particular factor (i.e., scale) or its subfactors (i.e., subscales). We then used analytic methods aligned with item response theory (IRT) to identify the relative contribution of each item to each scale. Again, the overarching goal of this step was to ensure that the short BEVI extracted information about respondents that was similar to the information extracted on the long BEVI.[6] Although the analyses for this process were relatively straightforward, the challenge lay in the sheer volume of data as well as the need to examine all possible permutations among all items and all scales. Ultimately, we automated these procedures via a "python program," which would stop and output results whenever the Cronbach's alpha coefficient was equal to 0.7 and allow us to compare the respective shape of the information curve for each scale of the BEVI. In other words, to preserve the integrity of the BEVI, items loading on the short version needed to evidence a similar capacity to identify the same types of respondents as did the longer version (e.g., regardless of whether someone strongly agreed or strongly disagreed to the items on a particular scale, the short BEVI needed to be able to identify such individuals with a degree of sensitivity that was equivalent to that of the longer version). The end result of this process was the identification of candidate items for retention and deletion in the development of the short BEVI.

But despite this fundamental step forward, we were not done yet. That is because the python program often "spat out" different multiple item combinations of various short BEVI scales. To figure out which combination was best for each scale, we used structural equation modeling (SEM) to test all of these possible combinations based upon theoretical propositions that had emerged over time to explain "what" specific BEVI scales were assessing and "why." This process was also highly iterative, involving a great deal of back-and-forth dialogue between theoretical and statistical perspectives on this measure. Ultimately, we were able to settle on final solutions for all scales that had good statistical and sound theoretical properties. At the conclusion of this process, 40 demographic and background variables (from 65), 185 items (from 336), and 17 scales (from 18) were retained in the short BEVI.[7] Table 4.2 summarizes core information regarding these scales.[8]

---

[6] Since most institutions, organizations, and settings are now using the "short version" of the BEVI, and because of the extensive analytic process that resulted in this version, it seems likely as of this writing that the "short version" of the BEVI will become the primary version of the BEVI.

[7] It should be noted that we retained one scale—Identity Diffusion—that did not meet this .70 threshold (it had an alpha of .61). Also, a few items progressing through the first steps did not survive SEM, but were retained nonetheless. Our reasons for doing so were to identify specific combinations of items for the short version of the BEVI that had the best reliability while also retaining as much fidelity as possible to the longer BEVI. One scale—Global Engagement— appeared to be a subfactor of a newly named factor, called Meaning Quest, which explains why the short version of the BEVI has one less scale than the long version. Extensive review of item combinations resulted in the renaming of several scales in order to better represent the apparent meaning of each factor. Finally, in addition to the statistical analyses of the 336 items from the long version, another round of SME review of the demographic/background items was conducted as well, which resulted in the elimination of 25 such items.

[8] Note that although scale names for the BEVI short version remain the same, the scale orders in Tables 4.2 and 4.3 are different from the final numbering of scales for purposes of theoretical alignment. Such differences were due to factor extraction and other analytic processes during scale/item review. Please see "Describing and Interpreting BEVI Scales" for the final linkages between scale numbers and names.

TABLE 4.2
BEVI Scale Summaries

	MEAN	STANDARD DEVIATION	CRONBACH'S ALPHA	NUMBER OF ITEMS
Negative Life Events	2.889	0.610	0.862	9
Needs Closure	2.646	0.290	0.712	25
Needs Fulfillment	1.892	0.342	0.882	24
Identity Diffusion	2.791	0.322	0.610	13
Basic Openness	2.108	0.417	0.809	12
Basic Determinism	2.887	0.355	0.755	16
Ecological Resonance	2.248	0.524	0.760	6
Self Certitude	2.122	0.357	0.761	13
Religious Traditionalism	2.705	0.782	0.903	5
Emotional Attunement	2.175	0.421	0.814	13
Physical Resonance	2.200	0.429	0.719	7
Self Awareness	1.855	0.358	0.810	12
Socioemotional Convergence	1.908	0.286	0.877	36
Sociocultural Openness	2.058	0.287	0.798	26
Global Resonance	1.719	0.469	0.828	6
Gender Traditionalism	2.275	0.472	0.828	11
Meaning Quest	1.873	0.317	0.831	19

As noted, to explore scale structure, we used SEM to test the relationships between the items and constructs, a process that was highly iterative. Table 4.3 summarizes the final model fit information, which indicates that (a) these scales have a relatively good model fit and (b) these scales sufficiently approximated the underlying theory.

Finally, it is important to demonstrate the emergent factor/subfactor structure for each scale. This information is provided in the following figures for each of the 17 scales (Figures 4.1–4.17) of the BEVI.[9]

---

[9] As of this writing, most subfactors have not formally been named. Initials listed in association with many subfactors were based upon an early EFA conducted on the BEVI (e.g., nfc = Need for Control). Also, in a few cases, subfactor names were emergent and have not yet been assigned. Although we have reasonable confidence in the higher order structure of each factor, with items associated significantly with their corresponding subfactors, further research is needed to understand the meaning and nature of all subfactors comprising each construct. For interpretive purposes, see Figure 4.1 as an example. Here, NLE is a one-dimensional construct with nine items. All nine items have relatively strong associations with the latent construct. As another example, consider Figure 4.2, Needs Closure. As is evident, there are five subfactors under the Needs Closure construct. All subfactors were associated significantly with Needs Closure, and all items were associated significantly with their corresponding subfactors.

TABLE 4.3
Model Fit Information for BEVI Scales

	CHI-SQUARE	DF	*P* VALUE	CFI	RMSEA
Negative Life Events	428.612	27	0.000	0.977	0.080
Needs Closure	2993.316	225	0.000	0.911	0.073
Needs Fulfillment	2855.248	248	0.000	0.912	0.067
Identity Diffusion	28.973	2	0.000	0.983	0.076
Basic Openness	619.225	54	0.000	0.956	0.067
Basic Determinism	536.465	41	0.000	0.927	0.072
Ecological Resonance	456.526	9	0.000	0.967	0.147
Self Certitude	634.634	62	0.000	0.937	0.064
Religious Traditionalism	166.821	9	0.000	0.995	0.087
Emotional Attunement	654.891	62	0.000	0.960	0.064
Physical Resonance	40.557	2	0.000	0.984	0.091
Self Awareness	598.360	54	0.000	0.948	0.066
Socioemotional Convergence	3523.339	369	0.000	0.901	0.061
Sociocultural Openness	2596.628	225	0.000	0.935	0.067
Global Resonance	93.898	14	0.000	0.994	0.050
Gender Traditionalism	765.686	44	0.000	0.948	0.084
Meaning Quest	836.661	61	0.000	0.925	0.074

In summary, to develop the BEVI short version, we progressed through a series of procedures. First, we used Cronbach's alpha to determine which items could be deleted without significantly influencing the reliabilities of the scales. Then, we used IRT to compute the information level of the items. A python program allowed us to compare the respective shapes of the information curve for each version of the BEVI, while SEM facilitated a deep understanding of constructs, which were in fact highly congruent with the EFA version of the measure. In the end, we had a short version BEVI (185 items), which was consistent with the essential structure of the long BEVI (336 items), but with substantially fewer items. Of course, further research is ongoing and will continue on this measure over time (e.g., to evaluate the temporal dimension; continue to assess reliability/validity across different groups, including non-English speakers).

Describing and Interpreting BEVI Scales

Although both "long" and "short" versions of the BEVI are in use, the short version seems preferred mainly due to time savings, as noted. Therefore, the following overview of BEVI scales is based upon the "short version," which overlaps substantially with the "long version" as indicated previously. Essentially, the BEVI consists of

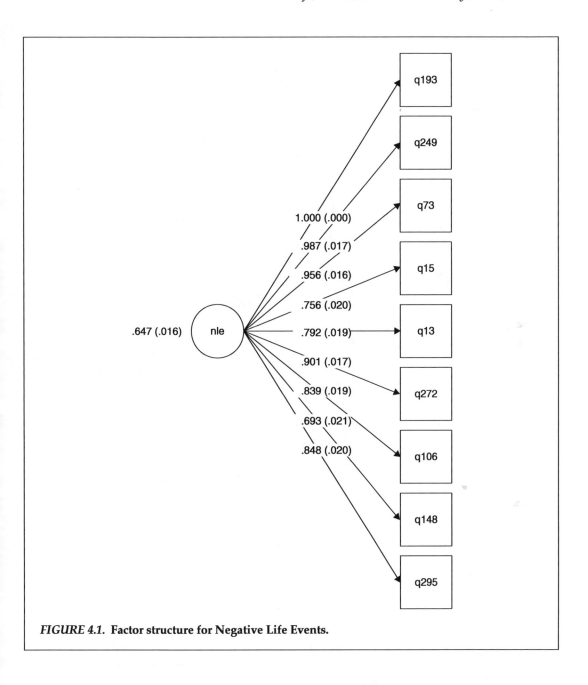

FIGURE 4.1. Factor structure for Negative Life Events.

2 validity and 17 process scales. Although there are many ways to present scale scores, they typically are presented as a series of colored bars along with a number within each bar (bars are presented here in shades of gray, not color). The number within each colored bar corresponds to the percentile score between 1 to 100 that an individual—or a group—has been assigned on each scale based upon his or her over-all response to the items that statistically load on each BEVI scale (i.e., "loading" refers to which items have been shown statistically to cluster together on a specific "construct" or scale of the BEVI, and therefore comprise the items on that scale). The resulting scores are standardized based upon the means and standard deviations for

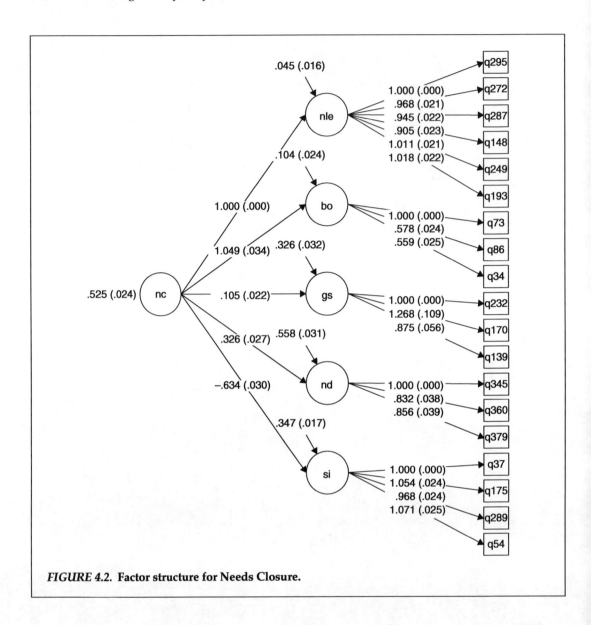

FIGURE 4.2. Factor structure for Needs Closure.

each scale (see Table 4.2). For group reports, the score is called "aggregate" because it represents the average score for all individuals in the group on a specific scale. BEVI results are presented under nine different domains. A description of each of the BEVI scales, under their respective domains, also is provided along with sample items for each scale (in parentheses).[10] In reviewing the following information, remember that by design, items may load statistically on a given scale in either a negative or positive direction. Thus, if sample items seem to be the opposite of one another, that is both expected and appropriate in terms of the psychometrics of inventories such as the BEVI (i.e., positively and negatively loading items both may comprise a given scale).

---

[10] The BEVI is a copyrighted instrument. BEVI items, item content, scales, or reports may not be modified, copied, disseminated, or published, in whole or part, without the written and express permission of Craig N. Shealy, PhD.

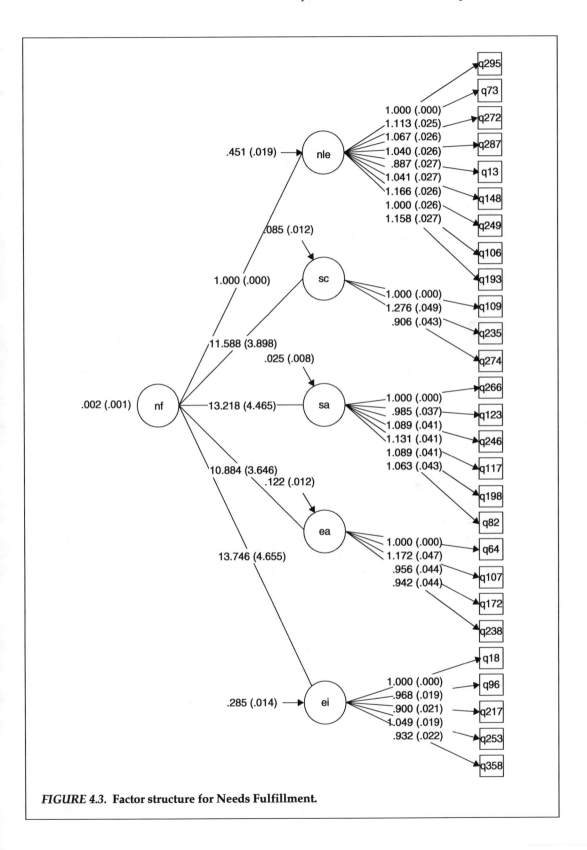

FIGURE 4.3. Factor structure for Needs Fulfillment.

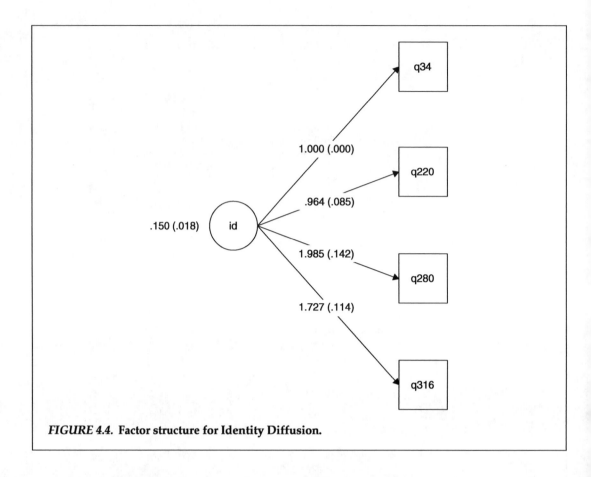

FIGURE 4.4. **Factor structure for Identity Diffusion.**

I. *Validity Scales*
   - *Consistency*: the degree to which responses are consistent for differently worded items that are assessing similar or identical content (e.g., *People change all the time; People don't really change*)
   - *Congruency*: the degree to which response patterns correspond to that which would be predicted statistically (e.g., *I have real needs for warmth and affection; I take my own feelings very seriously*)

II. *Formative Variables*
   - *Demographic/Background Items*: gender, educational level, ethnicity, political/religious orientation, income, and so on (e.g., *What is your gender? What is your ethnic background?*)
   - *Scale 1. Negative Life Events*: bad childhood; parents were troubled; life conflict/struggles; many regrets (e.g., *I have had a lot of conflict with one or more members of my family; My family had a lot of problems with money*)

III. *Fulfillment of Core Needs*
   - *Scale 2. Needs Closure*: challenging life circumstances, odd explanations for why things are the way they are, ambivalent or distant relationship with core needs in self and/or others (e.g., *I had a wonderful childhood; Some numbers are more lucky than others*)

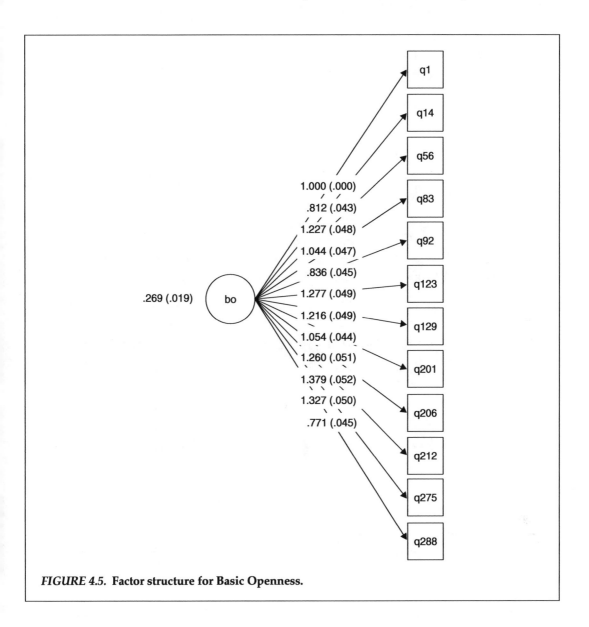

FIGURE 4.5. Factor structure for Basic Openness.

- *Scale 3. Needs Fulfillment*: open to experiences, needs, and feelings; deep care/ sensitivity for self, others, and the larger world (e.g., *We should spend more money on early education programs for children; I like to think about who I am*)
- *Scale 4. Identity Diffusion*: indicates painful crisis of identity; fatalistic regarding negatives of marital/family life; feels "bad" about self and prospects (e.g., *I have gone through a painful identity crisis; Even though we expect them to be, men are not really built to be faithful in marriage*)

IV. *Tolerance of Disequilibrium*
- *Scale 5. Basic Openness*: open and honest about the experience of basic thoughts, feelings, and needs (e.g., *I don't always feel good about who I am; I have felt lonely in my life*)

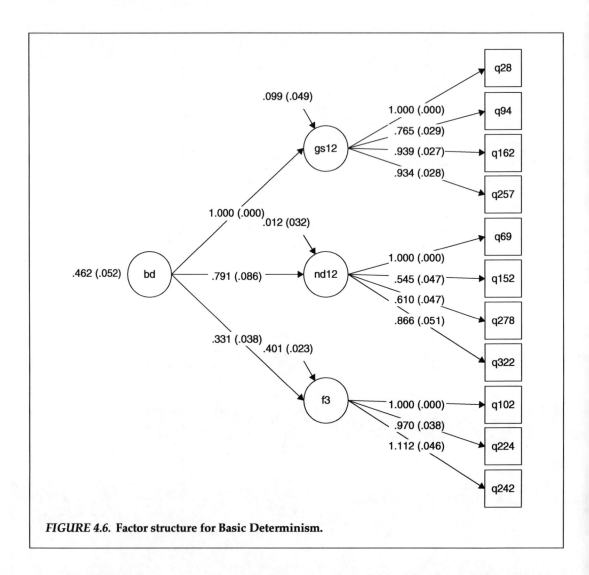

FIGURE 4.6. Factor structure for Basic Determinism.

- *Scale 6. Self Certitude*: strong sense of will; impatient with excuses for difficulties; emphasizes positive thinking; disinclined toward deep analysis (e.g., *You can overcome almost any problem if you just try harder; If you play by the rules, you get along fine*)

V. *Critical Thinking*
- *Scale 7. Basic Determinism*: prefers simple explanations for differences/behavior; people do not change/strong will to survive; troubled life history (e.g., *AIDS may well be a sign of God's anger; It's only natural that the strong will survive*)
- *Scale 8. Socioemotional Convergence*: open, aware of self/other, larger world; thoughtful, pragmatic, determined; sees world in shades of gray, such as the need for self-reliance while caring for vulnerable others (e.g., *We should do more to help those who are less fortunate; Too many people don't meet their responsibilities*)

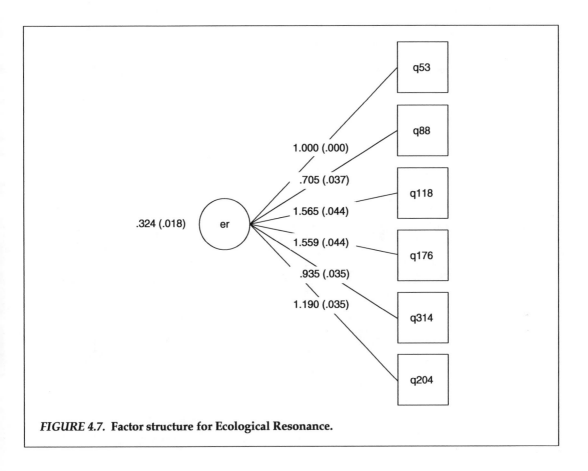

FIGURE 4.7. **Factor structure for Ecological Resonance.**

VI. *Self Access*
- *Scale 9. Physical Resonance*: receptive to corporeal needs/feelings; experientially inclined; appreciates the impact of human nature/evolution (e.g., *I am a free spirit; My body is very sensitive to what I feel*)
- *Scale 10. Emotional Attunement*: emotional, sensitive, social, needy, affiliative; values the expression of affect; close family connections (e.g., *I don't mind displays of emotion; Weakness can be a virtue*)
- *Scale 11. Self Awareness*: introspective; accepts complexity of self; cares for human experience/condition; tolerates difficult thoughts/feelings (e.g., *I am always trying to understand myself better; I have problems that I need to work on*)
- *Scale 12. Meaning Quest*: searching for meaning; seeks balance in life; resilient/persistent; highly feeling; concerned for less fortunate (e.g., *I think a lot about the meaning of life; I want to find a better sense of balance in my life*)

VII. *Other Access*
- *Scale 13. Religious Traditionalism*: highly religious; sees self/behavior/events as mediated by God/spiritual forces; one way to the "afterlife" (e.g., *Without religion there can be no peace; There is one way to heaven*)
- *Scale 14. Gender Traditionalism*: men and women are built to be a certain way; prefers traditional/simple views of gender and gender roles (e.g., *Women are more emotional than men; A man's role is to be strong*)

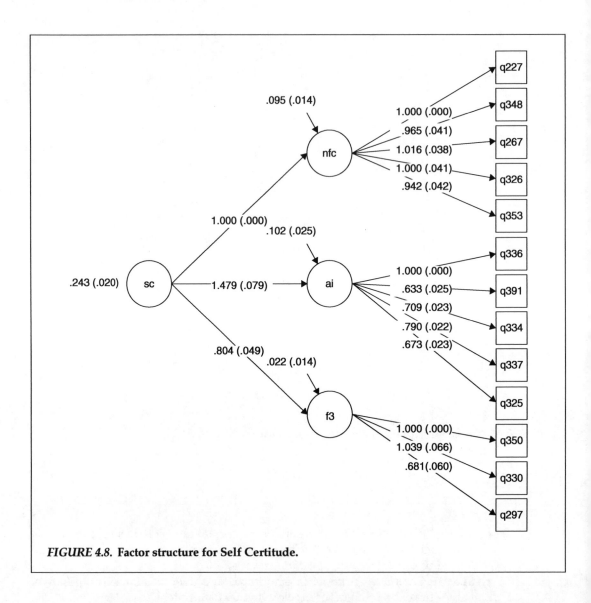

FIGURE 4.8. Factor structure for Self Certitude.

- *Scale 15. Sociocultural Openness*: progressive/open regarding a wide range of actions, policies, and practices in the areas of culture, economics, education, environment, gender/global relations, politics (e.g., *We should try to understand cultures that are different from our own; There is too big a gap between the rich and poor in our country*)

VIII. *Global Access*
- *Scale 16. Ecological Resonance*: deeply invested in environmental/sustainability issues; concerned about the fate of the earth/natural world (e.g., *I worry about our environment; We should protect the land no matter who owns it*)
- *Scale 17. Global Resonance*: invested in learning about/encountering different individuals, groups, languages, cultures; seeks global engagement (e.g., *It is important to be well informed about world events; I am comfortable around groups of people who are very different from me*)

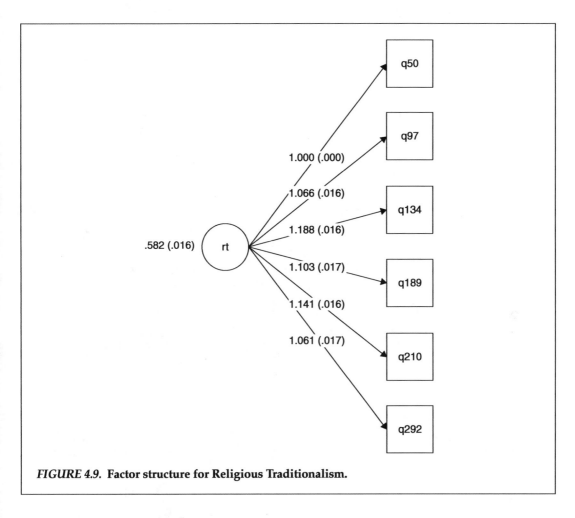

FIGURE 4.9. **Factor structure for Religious Traditionalism.**

IX. *Experiential Reflection Items*

The BEVI is a "mixed methods" measure in that both quantitative (i.e., Likert-scaled items) and qualitative (i.e., free response) questions are asked during administration and used for purposes of interpretation (e.g., Coates, Hanson, Samuel, Webster, & Cozen, 2016; Cozen, Hanson, Poston, Jones, & Tabit, 2016). The following three qualitative Experiential Reflection Items are included in the BEVI, and completed in written format at the conclusion of administration. *First, please describe which aspect of this experience has had the greatest impact upon you and why? Second, is there some aspect of your own "self" or "identity" (e.g., gender, ethnicity, sexual orientation, religious or political background, etc.) that has become especially clear or relevant to you or others as a result of this experience? Third, what are you learning or how are you different as a result of this experience?*

Understanding the BEVI's Design

By design, the BEVI essentially is an objective measure that functions in a projective manner. Although respondents "project" their own meaning onto items that are meant to elicit a response, the BEVI officially is neutral in regard to the nature of the response that is elicited. To understand the implications of this core feature of the

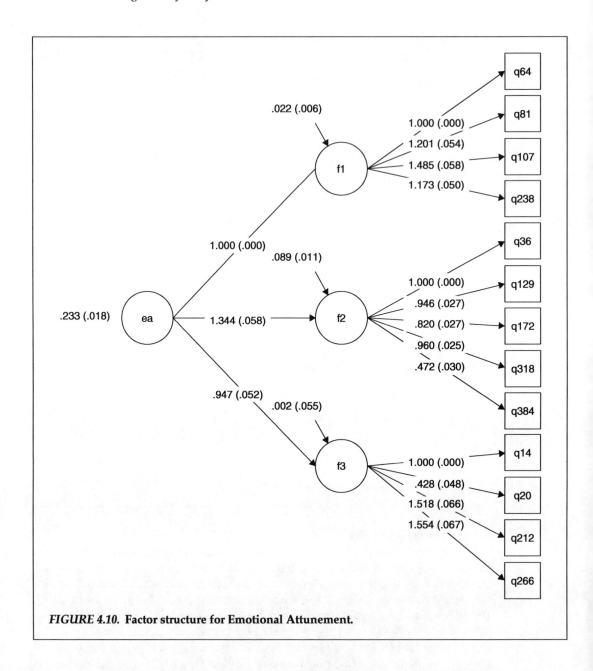

FIGURE 4.10. **Factor structure for Emotional Attunement.**

BEVI, it may be helpful to examine how items and responses on the BEVI are organized, and why such a structure is relevant to issues of statistical analysis and interpretation. The BEVI consists of a series of background information questions followed
by specific items covering a very wide range of issues, which are presented in the
form of statements about beliefs, values, and life events. At the most basic level, the
"power" of the BEVI is derived from the fact that items on the BEVI interact with each
individual's unique beliefs, values, life experiences, and overall worldview, to produce a particular response, which is coded on the following four-point scale: Strongly
Agree, Agree, Disagree, and Strongly Disagree. Although very different people may
have very different reactions to the very same items, it should be appreciated that the

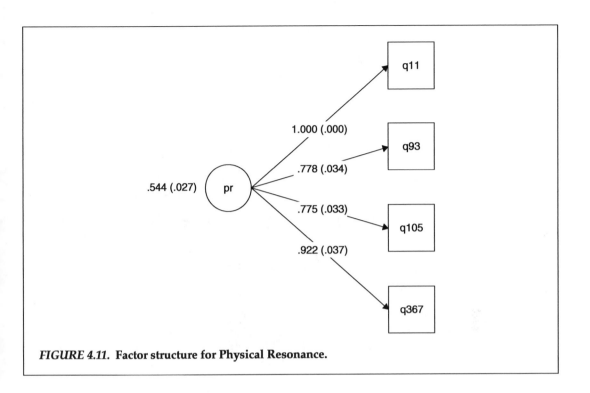

FIGURE 4.11. **Factor structure for Physical Resonance.**

BEVI takes no position on the "rightness" or "wrongness" of any item.[11] What it does do is offer a series of stimuli that different people will react to in different ways; depending upon the context, culture, and population at hand, reactions may range from very mild to very strong. For example, consider four highly predictive items on the BEVI from Scale 13, Religious Traditionalism, and Scale 15, Sociocultural Openness, respectively:

Sample Religious Traditionalism Items
God's word is good enough for me.
Sometimes I think that religion does more harm than good.
Sample Sociocultural Openness Items
Racism is no longer a big problem in our country.
We should do more to help minority groups in our country.

---

[11] Of course, all assessment measures—including the BEVI—are a product of "their time." Even though painstaking efforts have been devoted to ensuring that the BEVI is "valid" for usage in different sociocultural settings and contexts (e.g., statistically, in terms of item review, and in actual usage with diverse individuals and groups), such processes are and must be ongoing. Along these lines, it is important to appreciate that from a statistical and psychometric perspective, one core aspect of validity essentially refers to whether it is possible to predict "from" and "to" a range of variables and processes on the basis of appraising one's "beliefs and values" via the BEVI (e.g., do BEVI scales reliably predict specific background or demographic variables, such as gender, ethnicity, income, education, life events, and/or political/religious orientation; accounting for individual differences, do response patterns on the BEVI to various scales and indexes follow statistically expected patterns and trends). In this regard, as documented in various research and practice chapters of this book, the BEVI does seem to exhibit very good reliability and validity, across a range of settings, contexts, and populations. Nonetheless, the BEVI inevitably will be refined further on the basis of additional statistical analysis and real world application.

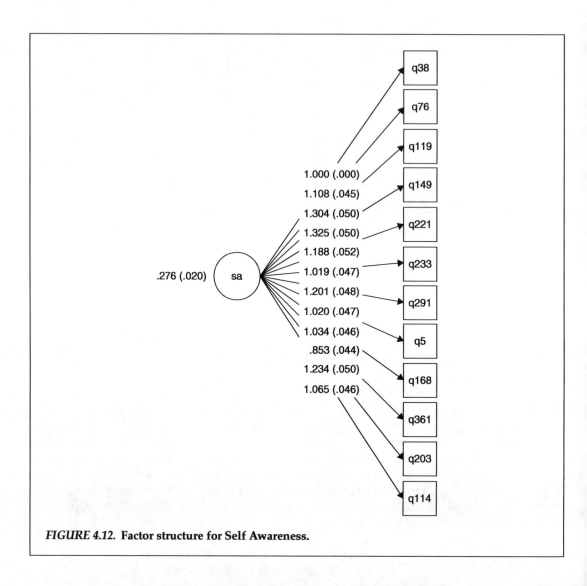

FIGURE 4.12. **Factor structure for Self Awareness.**

Such items illustrate a number of interrelated points, which all are key to understanding what the BEVI is and is not, and how and why it is structured and designed as it is.

First, at the most basic level, note that each of the preceding items essentially is a statement of "belief," which may be defined in part as "an internalized and discrete version of reality that can influence and mediate the experience and expression of needs, feelings, thoughts, and behaviors" (Shealy, 2015, p. 35). As a relatively accessible point of entry into the basic structure of personality or self, beliefs such as those listed are powerful phenomena for a number of interrelated reasons, as the following points that are derivative of EI Theory illustrate:

- We believe and value as we do for reasons that are often unknown to us.
- We are inclined toward particular beliefs and values because of a complex interaction among affective, attributional, and developmental processes that typically occurred over a long time in a specific context.

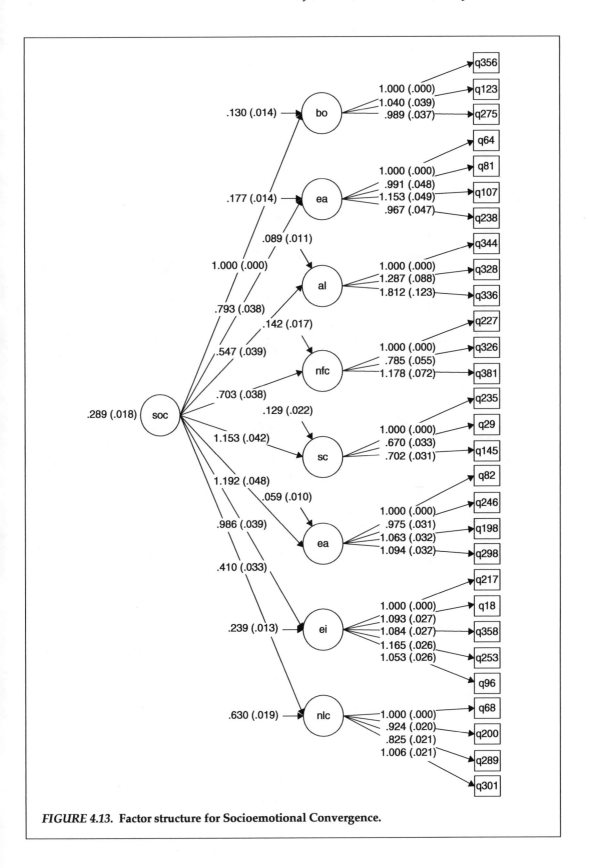

FIGURE 4.13. Factor structure for Socioemotional Convergence.

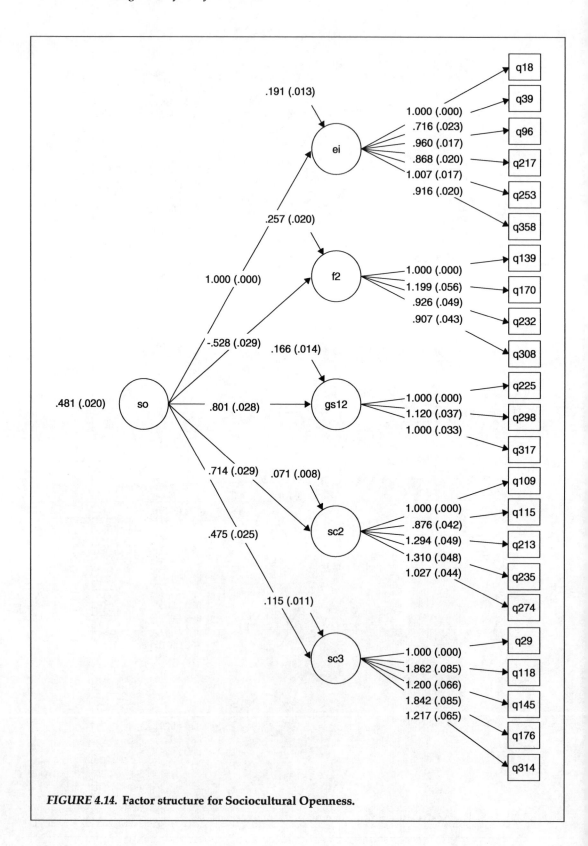

FIGURE 4.14. **Factor structure for Sociocultural Openness.**

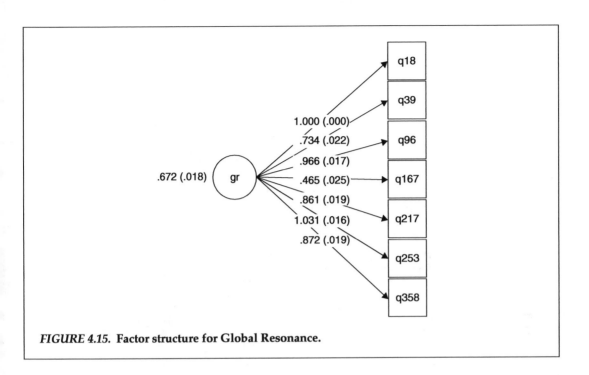

FIGURE 4.15. **Factor structure for Global Resonance.**

- We exist *in* our beliefs and values, and are *subject*—not object—to them; they innervate the deepest aspects of self and personality; they are—in no small part—who and what we say we are.
- Our beliefs and values may evolve vis-à-vis the experiences of our lives, but without substantial and sudden contradiction—or a deliberate and prolonged process of self-exploration—such evolution is likely to be quantitative not qualitative, and retain congruence with the basic cognitive structures and affective templates that represent constituent aspects of self and personality.
- Like the spoken language we learn, we tend to acquire the dominant beliefs and values of our context and culture; they become part of the "real" us, and we cannot call them into question without some parallel deconstruction of self.
- The fact that we all possess beliefs and values is not in itself sufficient to confer legitimacy upon them; that is to say, beliefs and values are not necessarily true, right, or better simply because they are held to be so (Shealy, 2005, pp. 101–102).

In other words, as discussed in Chapters 2 and 3, the beliefs we "hold to be self-evident" often suggest much more about us—what our history, culture, and context have been—than they do about some putative "reality" of "others" and "the world out there." Thus, knowing what we believe reveals a great deal about who we are, particularly if such information is combined with sufficient information about relevant historical events and contextual factors (e.g., Anmuth et al., 2013; Atwood et al., 2014; Brearly et al., 2012; Hayes et al., 1999; Hill et al., 2013; Isley et al., 1999; Patel et al., 2007; Pysarchik et al., 2007; Shealy, 2004, 2005, 2015; Shealy et al., 2012; Tabit et al., 2011).

Because constellations of beliefs, values, and life events effectively mediate the experience that people have of self, others, and the world at large, the BEVI is able to identify and predict significant differences and similarities among individuals and

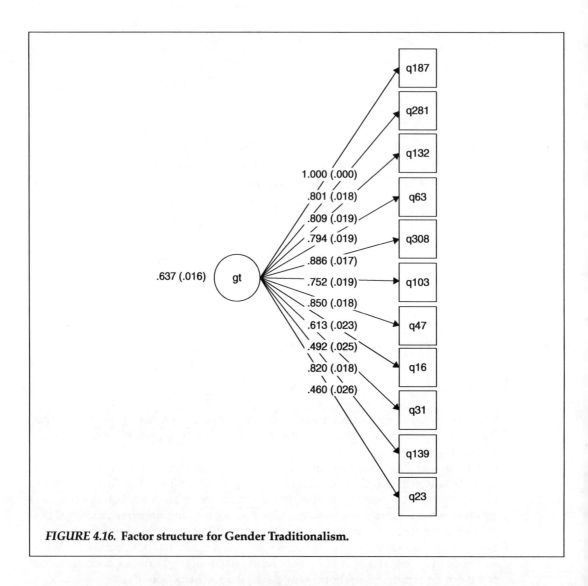

FIGURE 4.16. Factor structure for Gender Traditionalism.

groups; that is why the BEVI—in conjunction with its underlying EI theoretical framework—may provide information relevant to who learns what and why, and under what circumstances. That is also why the BEVI is not the Beliefs and Values Inventory, but the Beliefs, *Events*, and Values Inventory. Thousands of studies have demonstrated the impact that life events may have on individuals, and how such experiences interact with various affective, cognitive, contextual, and developmental processes; the entire field of developmental psychopathology is essentially concerned with such issues and outcomes (e.g., Cummings et al., 2000; Sroufe, 2009; Toth & Cicchetti, 2013).

Consider one BEVI study that examined the interaction between Scale 1, Negative Life Events (NLE), and religious orientation. Here, self-described Christians differed significantly from self-described atheists or agnostics on a number of items (Isley et al., 1999). For example, the Christian group was relatively likely to agree with the statement, *I have lost someone who was close to me* whereas the atheist/agnostic group was likely to disagree with this same statement. Although the potential interpretation

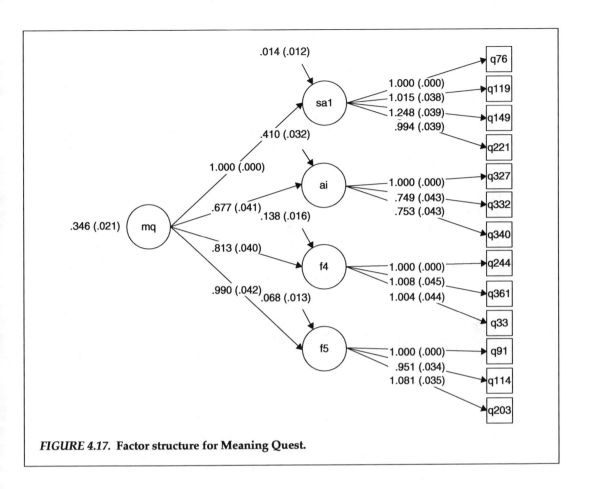

FIGURE 4.17. Factor structure for Meaning Quest.

of such a finding should be considered in the context of a larger response pattern—while also avoiding correlation/causation confusion—the point is that many reported life events were associated with differences in religious orientation (i.e., overall, Christians strongly differed from atheists/agnostics on a number of reported life events[12]). What are the implications of findings like these? To take but one example, in trying to understand complex processes or phenomena such as "international or multicultural learning," different groups may experience international or multicultural learning very differently for reasons that have nothing to do with the learning experience per se. For example, life events that participants have experienced may significantly influence who learns what and why, and under what circumstances, and how beliefs, values, and life experiences interact with such learning processes. In fact, evidence from the Forum BEVI Project suggests that "who someone is" prior to an "international learning experience" may significantly moderate or mediate (i.e., influence or shape) the nature or degree of international learning that an individual is able to experience or willing to demonstrate (e.g., Wandschneider et al., 2016). Such variables, which are

[12] Of course, as Brearly, van de Bos, and Tan (2016) document in their chapter on religious certitude, even though self-report categories such as "Christian" or "atheist" may, on the whole, be statistically predictive of a range of variables (e.g., gender, education), it is a mistake to conclude that all self-reported "Christians," "atheists," or any other group always responds in a similar manner on the BEVI. Such a conclusion is core to their chapter (i.e., avoid stereotyping and look more deeply into a range of interacting variables) as it is to multiple chapters in this book.

assessed by the BEVI, may be more important to the learning that actually occurs than the learning experience itself, a plausible interaction that cannot be evaluated if such variables are not assessed (e.g., Cummings et al., 2000).

Second, a basic criterion by which an instrument such as the BEVI is evaluated, is the degree to which it is "face valid," that is, the degree to which its goal or intent can be ascertained simply by examining the instrument at face value. If an average respondent can tell what an instrument is trying to assess simply by looking at it, the susceptibility of that instrument to conscious or nonconscious manipulation or "malingering" (i.e., faking) may be unacceptably high; likewise, the "social desirability" of particular responses or need to present one's self in a maximally favorable light is a well-documented phenomenon in the social sciences (e.g., Aronson, 2012). An instrument that is face valid may be prone to such psychological and social psychological processes because a respondent easily can "tell" what the instrument is trying to assess, and therefore can adjust his or her responses in an attempt to create the desired impression. The lack of attention to these issues in the design and execution of assessment instruments and assessment research may introduce a serious confound (i.e., an unintended and unrecognized source of error), which may adversely impact validity—the degree to which an instrument is measuring what it purports to measure (e.g., Campbell & Stanley, 2005; Geisinger, 2013; Mertens, 1998). Face valid measures also may neglect the "deeper" affective and attributional processes that interact to produce particular responses, by erroneously assuming that what people say they think or feel is actually what they do think or feel. Abundant evidence suggests that such assumptions are unwarranted at best, particularly when the implications of particular beliefs—were they to be freely and genuinely expressed—could have very real and largely negative consequences, socially and otherwise (e.g., Aronson, 2012; Bargh & Chartland, 1999; Frijda, Manstead, & Bem, 2000; Shealy, 2005). In short, face validity typically is *not* a desirable characteristic of measures that are designed to access or tap into psychological phenomena and emotional dynamics that are readily susceptible to cognitive screening and impression management processes.

Formal evaluation of the BEVI suggests it is not face valid (Shealy, 2004, 2015). Although the basic themes of the BEVI may be identified, the underlying structure and purpose of the instrument cannot. When the average participant is asked, "What is the BEVI getting at?" the typical response is, "Well, there were a lot of questions about politics, or religion, or family background." But, the interaction among such variables—and how they fit into a larger explanatory and predictive system—typically is not discernible. Interestingly, the lack of face validity to the BEVI, although a highly desirable feature, could also be a source of consternation on occasion, since the reason particular questions are being asked is by no means clear. If there are those who are puzzled by the content of various items, there is no way around this conundrum, except to include a discussion of what the BEVI is actually tapping in the context of a competently administered debriefing or follow-up session that occurs after the BEVI is administered and/or a research or assessment project is completed (e.g., Aita & Richer, 2005; Brody, Gluck, and Aragon, 1997, 2000; McShane, Davey, Rouse, Usher, & Sullivan, 2014; Mertens, 1998).

Third, items on the BEVI are worded in both the affirmative and negative, and are designed to tap "affective" and "nonconscious" processes. Any administrator of the BEVI should understand that the direction of the wording of BEVI items is irrelevant from the standpoint of item content (i.e., what the item assesses and the factor or scale on which the item is loaded), for two basic reasons: (a) respondents may indicate their agreement or disagreement to each item, thus indicating their particular "belief" in the "correctness" or "truth" of a given item; (b) for purposes of factor loading and various analyses (e.g., whether particular items, clusters of items, scales, or grouping of scales are predictive of other variables, measures, or outcomes), a correlation of −.30 is the same as a correlation of +.30 (i.e., it does not matter whether an item is worded in the affirmative or negative because disagreement conveys as much information as agreement). Although multiple factors are considered in the development, review, and evaluation of items (e.g., Downing & Haladyna, 1997; Weiss, 2013), from a psychometric and test design perspective, one reason to include both affirmative and negative items is to lower the face validity of the instrument (i.e., to make it more difficult to determine, *accurately*, what the BEVI is, and is not, designed to assess simply by reviewing the items).

Two related points also deserve emphasis. As noted, the BEVI is answered on a four-point scale, ranging from "Strongly Agree" to "Strongly Disagree"; there is no option of "undecided" or "neutral." This "forced choice" method is deliberate, and may even be essential to the BEVI, as many people likely would avoid committing to various beliefs if given the opportunity to do so. By "choosing" responses on one side or another, a respondent may access basic affective and nonconscious (i.e., "gut level") processes, which theoretically tap more than a simple cognitive or rational appraisal of whether an item is "true" or "false."

Could someone simply "fake" their responses in an attempt to mask their "true" thoughts and feelings? As with any inventory, the short answer is, "yes." However, from an analysis and psychometric perspective, the most important question is not the ability to "fake" responses, but rather to "fake" responses in a way that is not detectable. The BEVI contains two separate validity measures—Consistency and Congruency—along with a series of other internal validity checks (e.g., amount of time for completion), which are designed to appraise the degree to which a respondent is answering truthfully, consistently, and in a manner that would statistically be predicted. From the standpoint of BEVI reports (individual, group, organizational as described next), BEVI administrations that do not meet these validity thresholds ultimately are flagged from the standpoint of interpretation (i.e., are considered invalid). In short, multiple "checks" have been incorporated into the BEVI in order to identify individuals who may be attempting to "fake out" the BEVI; moreover, the fact that the BEVI shows good evidence of reliability, stability, and validity, suggests that the vast majority of respondents are answering BEVI items in a consistent manner.

Fourth, from a test design and statistical perspective, note that many BEVI items are worded in a way that is designed to elicit an opposite response even as they are "tapping" the same underlying construct. For example, an average respondent who disagrees with the item, *Racism is no longer a big problem in our country* is statistically likely to agree that, *We should do more to help minority groups in our culture;* likewise, an average respondent who agrees with the item, *God's word is good enough for me,* is statistically likely to disagree with the item, *Sometimes I think religion does more harm than good.* In each pair, these sample items strongly "load" (i.e., are correlated) on the same factor (i.e., scale), even though the correlation between them is negative, as discussed in Chapter 2 regarding the "Continuum of Belief." Of course, across thousands of administrations, this pattern will not (and should not) hold for everyone, but from a statistical standpoint, the degree to which such a pattern does hold is at the core of the reliability of any measure. In any case, what an item appears to assess—including "the way it is worded"—is not nearly as germane as whether or not it actually is predictive (presuming of course that basic quality indexes have been addressed in the development and review of items as noted previously). In any case, it is very important to understand this fundamental point, particularly with an instrument like the BEVI, which includes a number of items that deliberately are ambiguous.

Ultimately, we may never know why a particular item "clusters" with other items and/or tends to predict specific processes or outcomes. For example, if we included a rather absurd item such as, "Old shoes just feel better" on the BEVI, it is likely that strong agreement or strong disagreement with this "belief" would in fact be associated with other items on the BEVI, and would even predict specific outcomes or phenomena. Why? Although the answer to that question has occupied assessment theorists and psychometricians for decades (e.g., Nichols, 2004; Weiss, 2013), a common scholarly response has been, "It doesn't matter *why* it does, just *that* it does," a perspective that has been referred to as "dustbowl empiricism" (e.g., Freedheim, 2003). At another level, it makes intuitive sense that an item such as "Old shoes just feel better" might covary with items that also load on a scale such as "Emotional Attunement" on the BEVI, which assesses "receptivity and attitude toward a range of feelings, emotional experiences/behaviors, and affect in general, for oneself and others" (Shealy, 2005, p. 100). In the final analysis, whether or not this item or any other item is predictive in the real world can only be answered via statistical analysis. Thus, it really does not matter whether or not an item "seems" to make sense; ultimately, presuming appropriate processes of item and instrument development and review have been followed (e.g., Downing & Haladyna, 1997; Geisinger, 2013; Robinson et al., 1991, 1999; Weiss, 2013), the most relevant question is as follows: Is the item strongly and reliably associated with other items that demonstrably measure the same construct? If the answer is yes, a psychometrician may well wish to retain "Old shoes just feel better" even though the face validity of such an item is nil.

Fifth and finally, depending upon personal background, life history, and context (among other factors), reactions to BEVI items may occur at differing degrees (e.g., from mild to strong) and at multiple levels (e.g., from emotional to intellectual). Consider two studies of the BEVI that compared responses of different groups. In one study, the responses of Caucasian students to items on the BEVI were compared to those of ethnic minority students (defined for this analysis as African American, American Indian, Asian, or Hispanic) (Shealy et al., 1999); in a separate study, the responses of self-identified "Christian" students were compared with those of self-identified "atheists" and "agnostics" (Hayes et al., 1999). In both studies, very sharp differences emerged between these groups on the BEVI.

Now imagine that a random sample of individuals from each of these groups were put together in the same room and asked to "debate" questions such as, *We should do more to help minority groups in our culture* or *Without religion there can be no peace.* What might happen if the debating groups comprised only those individuals who expressed "strong agreement" or "strong disagreement" with the strongly differentiating items (excluding those who merely expressed "agreement" or "disagreement")? Further imagine that the BEVI as a whole were used to identify groups that were maximally different from one another, and we put these extremely divergent groups together to debate various issues? The ensuing "discussion" could well become heated at the very least.

The point is, at this level, all of the items on the BEVI are "biased" because there will be—by design—wide variability in how items are perceived or experienced by different groups and individuals. Different people and groups will have different perceptions and experiences of the BEVI, ranging from strong and mild disagreement, to mild and strong agreement. What these differences do NOT demonstrate is that one group is "right" and the other group is "wrong," or that the BEVI is "biased toward" or "biased against" one group or the other. The BEVI provides a set of stimuli (i.e., items) that have been carefully identified, developed, reviewed, and subjected to multiple statistical analyses to which different individuals and groups may react in different ways. Individual responses or profiles may well be deemed "right" or "wrong," but such value judgments are made by individuals and groups within a particular sociocultural context, not the BEVI.[13] Along similar lines, although the BEVI is used in a wide array of settings and contexts (see "BEVI Impetus and Overview"), it is officially "neutral" regarding such usage. At the very least, all usage of the BEVI (e.g., individual, group, course, program, institutional, organizational) should be conducted in a manner that is consistent with "best practices," a topic that is integral to the BEVI training and certification process.

Although a full explication of these and related issues exceeds the scope of this discussion (e.g., see Campbell & Stanley, 2005; Downing & Haladyna, 1997; Geisinger, 2013; Hong & Roznowski, 2001; Mertens, 1998; Robinson et al., 1991, 1999; Weiss, 2013), one definition of "test bias" is whether or not an assessment measure adversely impacts an identifiable group in a particular context (e.g., assessment of aptitude, employment screening) or is responded to differentially by various populations in a way that skews results. With an instrument such as the BEVI, respondents inevitably will, and by design, react to such items by agreeing or disagreeing, sometimes strongly. But the fact that someone agrees or disagrees with an item, even if such agreement or disagreement applies to a vast portion of the BEVI, or even all of it, says nothing in itself about the "bias" of the BEVI. To one individual or group, the BEVI may seem biased in one direction whereas to another person or group, the BEVI may seem biased in the other direction. That is the point of this instrument. An emotional reaction to any instrument—should it occur—says nothing in itself about the "rightness," "wrongness," or even "bias" of actual items on that instrument. Rather, "a reaction" to one or more items on a particular measure—and the similarities and differences among individuals and groups in the nature and strength of their reactions—is precisely the phenomenon that the BEVI is designed to assess.

In the final analysis, when using the BEVI, it must never be forgotten that many of the items on the BEVI were developed on the basis of actual statements from real people in a diverse array of contexts and settings. The ecological (i.e., real world) validity of BEVI items accords the BEVI its potential to evoke strong reactions for some individuals in particular contexts, in part because various items[14] may "tap" or interact with the beliefs, values, and real life experiences of a respondent; that is what is meant by the preceding observation that the BEVI is an objective measure that functions in a projective manner. Over the past two decades, various iterations of the BEVI have been administered to thousands of individuals without incident; the typical reaction to the BEVI ranges from humorous, to puzzlement, to thoughtfulness, to indifference. However, these facts should never be taken for granted or assumed for everyone, which is a main reason why all phases of BEVI administration must be conducted in an appropriate manner, the voluntary nature of the BEVI emphasized, and informed consent given (e.g., Aita & Richer, 2005; Brody, Gluck, & Aragon, 1997, 2000; Geisinger, 2013; McShane et al., 2014).

---

[13] Of course, the BEVI has been, and will continue to be, evaluated vis-à-vis reliability and validity in different sociocultural contexts. See footnote 11 from this chapter for additional perspective in this regard.

[14] For more information about the nature and origins of BEVI items, please see "BEVI Impetus and Overview."

Usage of the BEVI's Report System

As illustrated in later chapters of this book, the BEVI has been used for a wide range of purposes. Research-focused chapters explain how the EI model and BEVI method increase our conceptual sophistication and methodological capacity across an array of areas: culture, development, environment, gender, politics, and religion. Practice-oriented chapters demonstrate how the BEVI is used in the real world across a range of applied domains: assessment, education, forensics, leadership, and psychotherapy. These implications and applications of the BEVI are illuminated by a variety of statistical analyses (e.g., analysis of variance, regression, structural equation modeling) as well as the BEVI report system. From an applied standpoint, the underlying software for the BEVI produces three types of reports—individual, group, and organizational—which may be modified depending upon specific needs and goals.

Individual reports have multiple applications and are designed to facilitate thoughtful and substantive reflection on self, others, and the world at large. Through the underlying software that drives the report system, individual reports consist of a seven- to nine-page narrative, which includes both common text that everyone receives (e.g., explaining the nature and implications of beliefs and values) as well as individually tailored content based upon responses to the background information section of the BEVI along with scores on specific BEVI scales. More specifically, based upon each individual's responses, a report is generated under the following headings, which correspond to the "BEVI structure," which is as follows:

1. *Introduction*
   Provides an overview of the BEVI.
2. *The Foundation: "Formative Variables" and "Core Needs"*
   Provides an indication of what the respondent reports about his or her own life history relative to others.
3. *Tolerance of Disequilibrium*
   Describes whether the respondent sees him or herself as "very clear" or "not sure" about who he or she and others "are" under the auspices of how "confident" or "questioning" the respondent appears to be.
4. *Making Sense of Why We Do What We Do*
   Indicates attributional tendencies in general (e.g., how and why people do what they do and why events happen as they do).
5. *Access to Yourself and Your Thoughts, Feelings, and Needs*
   Describes how the individual deals with his or her own emotions as well as his or her interest in and predilection toward introspection and reflection upon "the self."
6. *Access to the Thoughts and Feelings of Others*
   Describes how the person tends to regard and experience issues that are of consequence at a sociocultural level (e.g., beliefs about politics, religion, gender, or the way society "should be structured").
7. *Access to the Larger World*
   Indicates one's perspectives on "big picture" issues of the environment (e.g., the degree to which one is or is not concerned about ecological issues) and global engagement (e.g., the degree to which we should or should not be concerned about, or invested in, what is happening outside of our own country, culture, and context).
8. *Conclusion*
   Provides context for the report and offers closing thoughts to consider.

As noted, reports are individualized based upon one's unique pattern of scores. How does such a process work? Essentially, the underlying software uploads bolded text that corresponds with BEVI scale scores, and integrates that text into the over-arching narrative that each individual receives (i.e., at least three bolded narratives have been developed for each scale from the individual report, corresponding with whether the scale score falls in the bottom, middle, or upper third of the profile). In this way, respondents receive an in-depth but accessible "primer" on the nature and role of "beliefs and values" under the headings noted previously, but through a framework that corresponds with their unique BEVI profile (i.e., the bolded text relates to their unique scores). The following sample individual report excerpt from "Access to Yourself and Your Thoughts, Feelings, and Needs" illustrates the interplay between an individual's unique scores (reflected in the bolded text) and the general text from all individual reports.

Access to Yourself and Your Thoughts, Feelings, and Needs

You probably have noticed that some people tend to be more emotional and sensitive while also valuing the expression of needs or feelings more deeply than others. Such a description seems less descriptive of how you approach your own feelings and those of others, in that you may tend to be puzzled and even irritated at times by what you experience as excessive displays of emotion or vulnerability in other people. If that is the case for you, it may be helpful to reflect again on the fact that our backgrounds and life experiences may make us much more likely—or much less likely—to be able and willing to "access" deep needs and feelings. Only you can be the judge of whether your background and experiences were such that you were discouraged in general from feeling too deeply or needing too much from others. If that was your experience, it's important to think about the possible impact of such processes for you in your life, in your relationships with others, and in how you experience people, situations, and relationships, which may be difficult to handle, at least at first, particularly when they are new. Think for a moment about how central emotions are to human existence. The ability to feel what you feel, while accurately interpreting and understanding the feelings of others—what some have referred to as "emotional intelligence"—is key to navigating every aspect of life, from your personal relationships to the world of work. Without emotions, it would be very difficult to understand what we like and who others are, and who we want to be.

So, in this excerpt from a BEVI individual report, the bolded text would correspond with an individual's score that fell in the lower third on Emotional Attunement of the BEVI. A great deal of attention by SME panels was devoted to such language in order to promote the developmental/growth-oriented nature of these reports (i.e., the over-arching goal is not to point out "pathology," per se, but rather to offer opportunities for reflection on how and why individuals experience self, others, and the larger world as they do). At the same time, it should be noted that in some contexts (e.g., clinical, forensic, leadership) the individual report system does include a mechanism for reporting out individual scores via a profile along with "Critical Items" (e.g., those that are marked as "Strongly Agree" or "Strongly Disagree") as well as full scale and other domain scale scores. Usage of this feature of the individual report system requires the administrator to be authorized (e.g., via training) to interpret such scores and indexes in an appropriate manner. In short, the default setting for individual reports is an individualized narrative, although much greater scale/index specificity may also be obtained when appropriate.

Group reports are designed for cohorts of 10 or more, and may be used with appropriate oversight by qualified administrators in a wide range of group-based contexts and forums. These reports aggregate the data from a group of participants in order to produce the following components: (a) **descriptive information** about the group (e.g., gender, ethnicity); (b) **profiles** which include, in bar graph form, both the average scores for each of the 17 BEVI scales along with distribution data to show the variation among the group across the scales; (c) multiple **index and table scores**, which illustrate a wide range of phenomena regarding how the group sees self, others, and the larger world as well as the similarities and differences within the group; (d) **qualitative data**, from across the three "experiential reflective" questions of the BEVI, so that the group report administrator can get a sense of how participants are reacting—in their own words—to a particular experience; and (e) **an aggregate report**, which averages the individual scores to produce a single report of the group as a whole.

Finally, *organizational reports* are designed for administrators or other leaders to use in multiple applications including but not limited to (a) **assessment purposes** (e.g., to assess overall learning and belief/value change processes within their institution or organization); (b) **comparing and contrasting cohorts** over time; (c) **evaluating outcomes** across specific programs or experiences; (d) **enhancing and improving learning, growth, and development experiences** (e.g., interventions, programs, courses); and (e) **meeting assessment needs and requirements** (e.g., accreditation; program review; quality assurance). In addition to many of the features for group level reports (i.e., aggregated background variables; table and index scores; qualitative responses), organizational reports also include the option of acquiring customized analyses. For example, administrators and/or leaders within an institution or organization may wish to review the interaction between particular demographic variables and scale scores, or focus in on more detailed analyses of learning, growth, or development experiences or programs, in order to examine processes or outcomes that are of particular relevance within a specific context (e.g., to see who learns what and why and under what circumstances). It is also possible to compare BEVI results with other sources of data and/or measures that are of interest to an institution or organization. By specifying which analyses are wanted, these customized reports may be tailored to meet the different assessment goals and needs at an institution or organizational level.

It should be noted that one difference between an individual report narrative and a group/organizational report narrative is that the group/organizational report narrative takes the average score of all members of the group and uses that score to determine which bolded text is uploaded and integrated into the report (i.e., the group report uses the average score of the group to determine which bolded text is to be uploaded into the report for the group as a whole). Such group/organizational narrative reports help the group—and individuals who are in various leadership roles (e.g., course instructors, program directors, managers, group facilitators, administrators)—get "a feel" for how the group as a whole is experiencing self, others, and the larger world.

Additional questions that commonly appear to be asked and answered via the report system include the following: (a) How would you describe the group, organization, or institution overall in terms of the most striking findings? (b) How is the group most different and most similar to itself? (c) Which findings are most surprising, and how can you make sense of such results on the basis of data that are provided (e.g., from Background–Domain information)? (d) Which findings were expected, and what do they suggest about your group, organization, or institution? (e) Which findings would be most relevant or interesting to a particular group or your overall organization/institution, and why? (f) How could findings inform or shape group-based discussions and processes (e.g., in class, during program orientation/debriefing processes, as part of training)? (g) What do findings suggest in terms of a particular course, program, or learning experience (e.g., where might areas of consensus or conflict occur over time; how might patterns interact with a learning, growth, or development experience in terms of overarching goals)? (h) What might findings suggest about the effectiveness of a particular learning, growth, or development experience? (i) How might findings be used to facilitate the development of new or improved learning, growth, or development experiences? (j) How might findings be used to track changes over time? Again, there are many other questions to be asked of such report results. Overall, we have learned that it is very important for users to take the time to review and reflect upon reports in order to ascertain which tables, indexes, or specific findings are most relevant for their specific goals and purposes.

Juxtaposing Individual and Group Reports

As later chapters in this book illustrate, a common usage of the report system is to combine individual and group reports. Specifically, individuals are offered the opportunity to receive their own individual report, which they, and only they, read (although that provision may vary when appropriate across different settings). Then, the group as a whole reviews a group report—typically facilitated by the leader of the experience (e.g., course instructor, program director, workshop coordinator, etc.)—that had been developed on the basis of the aggregate scores from these individuals (e.g., all of the individual members from a group of which they are a part), typically via projection onto a screen. In this way, individuals are able to reflect upon (in private) their own BEVI results in the form of a narrative by juxtaposing it with the indexes and other scale information from the BEVI group report (in public). This dialectic process between private and public reflection seems to be integral to the sort of awareness, insight, and discussion (e.g., regarding self, others, and the larger world) that participants frequently report from this process (e.g., "It helped to think about why I am who I am"; "It helps me appreciate why others believe what they do"; "I now understand better why we have the dynamics we do in our group").

At another level, group reports help interventionists, program directors, course instructors, workshop facilitators, and so forth understand better the differences and similarities of life histories or worldviews by the members of their group. For example, we often encounter bimodal distributions on various scales (e.g., Gender Traditionalism; Religious Traditionalism), which when combined with the breakdown of scale scores by profile, permits the interventionist, leader, or administrator to understand better the makeup of a group even before the group experience begins. From an applied standpoint, such results may be used productively by showing group-based results and asking for volunteers to discuss "why they believe what they believe," a process which leads very often to rich dialogue and reflection by participants.

Finally, as noted, group and organizational reports are helpful in understanding "big picture" processes that characterize a larger system (e.g., the worldviews of entering students; prominent expectations of self/other in an organizational context). Such information may be very helpful not only in understanding the basic profile of an institution's or organization's members, but also where resources might productively be directed for a wide range of purposes (e.g., outreach and engagement to specific subgroups; to see how worldviews shift over time; to appraise the relative effectiveness of specific experiences in promoting learning and growth).

Finally, all three report types—individual, group, and organizational—may also be reported out longitudinally for purposes of mapping change processes and outcomes over time. More specifically, T1 reports refer to the report from the original administration of the BEVI to a specific group. T1/T2 reports refer to the report that examines how groups change from one administration of the BEVI to the next. And it should be noted, that T1/T2/T3, and so on, reports may be derived, and are recommended in terms of tracking trends over the long term. The primary difference between T1 and T1/T2 reports is that a few indexes only may be developed on the basis of comparisons between groups from Time 1 to Time 2 (e.g., Worldview Shift).

BEVI Tables and Indexes

Both group and organizational reports—and selected aspects of the individual reports in specific contexts—contain a wide range of tables and indexes, which are essential for processes of interpretation. Although training processes offer much more depth as well as hands-on usage, a brief explication of these tables and indexes may be helpful at this point.

Background–Domain Contrast illustrates how different or similar the group is at the level of background information and domain scores by the lowest 30%, middle 40%, and highest 30% of full scale scores.[15] Background–Domain Contrast is "key" to understanding whether and to what degree group characteristics (e.g., background variables such as gender, ethnicity, etc.) and domain scores (e.g., differences in Critical Thinking, Self Access, etc.) are different or similar across these different full scale levels. For example, particular background variables may be associated with low, medium, or high full scale scores on the BEVI, which may be helpful in understanding how such variables are associated with a relative degree of group predilection toward or against a specific learning, growth, or development experience.

Profile Contrast illustrates how different and similar the group is across all 17 BEVI scales via the lowest 30%, middle 40%, and highest 30% of full scale scores. Profile Contrast is "key" to interpreting whether and to what degree groupings by low, medium, and high full scale scores are associated with different elevations on specific BEVI scales. For example, such information may be helpful in interpreting the variability within a specific group, which may range from minimal to substantial. Profile Contrast may also help users apprehend how and why subgroups within the larger group show changes in similar and different directions in the context of learning, growth, and development experiences. Thus, this index is considered a more robust and nuanced measure of the differential impact of specific learning experiences than are aggregated indexes, which may obscure subgroup differences or cancel out changes that are in fact occurring among subsets of the larger group.

Lowest Optimal Background–Domain presents aggregated background information and domain scores for the 1st to 30th percentile of full scale scores. It is "key" to interpretation and intervention because this subgroup weights the bottom 30% of the overall group (i.e., this subgroup likely could benefit most from "change" in a

---

[15] The full scale score is summative of scores from the seven domains of the BEVI under which the 17 process scales are clustered: (a) Formative Variables; (b) Fulfillment of Core Needs; (c) Tolerance of Disequilibrium; (d) Critical Thinking; (e) Self Access; (f) Other Access; and (g) Global Access (see www.thebevi.com).

direction that probably would be consistent with key goals of the learning, growth, or development experience in which such individuals are participating).

Lowest Optimal Profile presents aggregated background information and domain scores for the 1st to 30th percentile of full scale scores across all 17 process scales of the BEVI. In other words, this profile represents the Aggregate Profile of those individuals who scored "lowest" on the full scale score of the BEVI. It is "key" to interpretation and intervention because this subgroup weights the bottom 30% of the overall group (i.e., this subgroup likely could benefit most from "change" in a direction that probably would be consistent with key goals of the learning, growth, or development experience in which such individuals are participating).

Aggregate Background–Domain presents aggregated background information and domain scores for the full scale scores of the entire group (i.e., 1st–100th percentile). It is most useful for Time 1 assessment (i.e., understanding where the overall group is at the outset of a learning, growth, or development experience) and to track group results over time (i.e., from year to year). However, it generally should not be used alone to determine if a learning, growth, or development experience is or is not effective (e.g., at Time 2 assessment) mainly because it may obscure subgroup differences and/or "cancel out" changes that actually are occurring within various subsets of the larger group. The best index to determine what is happening in this regard (i.e., between the lowest 30%, middle 40%, and highest 30% of full scale scorers) is Profile Contrast.

Aggregate Profile presents aggregated background information and domain scores for the full scale scores of the entire group (i.e., 1st–100th percentile). It is most useful for Time 1 assessment (i.e., understanding where the overall group is at the outset of a learning, growth, or development experience) and to track group results over time (i.e., from year to year). However, it generally should not be used alone to determine if a learning, growth, or development experience is or is not effective (e.g., at Time 2 assessment) mainly because it may obscure subgroup differences and/or "cancel out" changes that actually are occurring within various subsets of the larger group. The best index to determine what is happening in this regard (i.e., between the lowest 30%, middle 40%, and highest 30% of full scale scorers) is Profile Contrast.

Decile Profile illustrates how scores for group participants cluster across deciles (i.e., from the lowest 10% that individuals may score on each BEVI scale to the highest 10%—and everything in between—in "chunks" of 10%). For example, on a BEVI group report for 40 people, if 10% of the group falls within the "first decile," that means that 4 people (i.e., 4 out of 40 = 10%) scored in the lowest 10% that can be scored on a particular BEVI scale. This profile is particularly useful in observing the dispersion of the larger group across all BEVI scales (e.g., it helps illustrate if a group clusters at one or both ends of a scale or is scattered throughout the entire scale).

Aggregate Profile by Country of Origin compares the scores of participants who report that they were raised primarily in one country (the target country of origin) versus those who report that they were raised primarily in countries other than the target country across all 17 process scales of the BEVI.[16]

---

[16] It should be noted that these "Aggregate Profile by. . ." tables are not meant to capture the full complexity of all that is happening on any given variable for a specific group (e.g., ethnicity, politics, religion). Other individual and group report indexes (e.g., Profile Contrast; Decile Profile) should be juxtaposed with these Aggregate Profiles to help explicate similarities and differences within a particular cohort. However, these "Aggregate Profiles by. . ." may well illuminate the relative salience of specific variables within a larger group, thus clarifying underlying processes or dynamics that may be worthy of further exploration. Finally, because these "Aggregate Profiles by. . ." tables are, by necessity, generated from self-reported identifications, it is important to keep such processes in mind when reviewing various results (e.g., to ascertain how the individual members of the larger cohort are self-identifying).

Aggregate Profile by Gender compares the scores of females and males across all 17 process scales of the BEVI.

Aggregate Profile by Education compares the scores of participants at the lowest 30% of educational attainment versus the highest 30% of educational attainment across all 17 process scales of the BEVI.

Aggregate Profile by Ethnicity compares the scores of participants who report that they are Caucasian to those who report that they are non-Caucasian across all 17 process scales of the BEVI.

Aggregate Profile by Income compares the scores of participants who report at the lowest 30% of household income compared to those who report at the highest 30% of household income across all 17 process scales of the BEVI.

Aggregate Profile by Interest compares the scores of participants who report at the lowest 30% of interest in participating in a learning, growth, or development experience to those who report at the highest 30% of such interest across all 17 process scales of the BEVI.

Aggregate Profile by Politics compares the scores of participants who report overall as "liberal" or overall as "conservative" across all 17 process scales of the BEVI.

Aggregate Profile by Religion compares the scores of participants who report a religious affiliation to those who report no religious affiliation (e.g., as "atheist" or "agnostic") across all 17 process scales of the BEVI.

Aggregate Profile by Satisfaction compares the scores of participants who report at the lowest 30% of satisfaction upon completing a learning, growth, or development experience to those who report at the highest 30% of such satisfaction across all 17 process scales of the BEVI.

Full Scale Shift provides background and domain score information for the top 30% of individuals who (a) move from higher to lower, (b) do not move substantially, or (c) move from lower to higher on their full scale scores from Time 1 to Time 2 administrations of the BEVI. More specifically, Negative Full Scale Shift represents the top 30% of the overall group that goes from higher to lower on their full scale scores. Neutral Full Scale Shift represents the top 30% of the overall group that shows the least amount of change from Time 1 to Time 2. Positive Full Scale Shift represents the top 30% of the overall group that goes from lower to higher on their full scale scores. Full Scale Shift may be helpful in understanding which background variables and domain scores seem to be most and least associated with changes in anticipated and/or unanticipated directions across different administrations of the BEVI.

Worldview Shift is an aggregate index that illustrates how a group moves higher or lower on each of the 17 scales on the BEVI from the initial to subsequent administrations of the BEVI. It is most useful for tracking group results over time (i.e., from year to year), but generally should not be used alone to determine if a learning, growth, or development experience is or is not effective, mainly because it may obscure subgroup differences and/or "cancel out" changes that actually are occurring within various subsets of the larger group. The best index to determine what is happening in this regard (i.e., between the lowest 30%, middle 40%, and highest 30% of full scale scorers) is Profile Contrast. However, Worldview Shift may be especially useful if the overall group demonstrates movement in desired directions across many or all scales of the BEVI, mainly because such results suggest that a learning, growth, or development experience may be having a similar impact across most if not all subgroups within the larger group.

Worldview Intensity indicates the degree to which individuals tend to endorse Strongly Agree or Strongly Disagree—versus Agree or Disagree—on the items for each of the 17 process scales of the BEVI (e.g., a higher degree of Worldview Intensity is associated with a greater tendency to endorse response options of Strongly Agree or Strongly Disagree).

Worldview Convergence indicates the degree to which the group is responding similarly or differently from itself across each of the 17 process scales of the BEVI (e.g., a lower degree of Worldview Convergence is associated with less variation by members of the group with each other on a given scale).

Experiential Reflection Items. The BEVI is a "mixed methods" measure in that both quantitative (i.e., Likert-scaled items) and qualitative (i.e., free response) questions are asked during administration and used for purposes of interpretation. The following three qualitative Experiential Reflection Items are included in the BEVI. *First, please describe which aspect of this experience has had the greatest impact upon you and why? Second, is there some aspect of your own "self" or "identity" (e.g., gender, ethnicity, sexual orientation, religious or political background, etc.) that has become especially clear or relevant to you or others as a result of this experience? Third, what are you learning or how are you different as a result of this experience?* In the development of group reports for the BEVI, up to 20 responses are selected randomly from the range of responses that are available and uploaded under each of these questions. In doing so, a response under question 1 is drawn from the same participant as are questions 2 and 3 (e.g., response number 14 under each of the three questions is from the same person). In this way, it is possible to consider how qualitative aspects of learning, growth, or development are experienced by a random sample of individuals from the larger group through subjective reflections on one's own experience in one's own words. Because the T1/T2/T3, and so on, feature of the report system also allows for the juxtaposition of qualitative responses across time, it becomes possible to compare and contrast—at a qualitative level—learning, growth, and development before, during, and after the experience, and in the respondent's own words. Oftentimes, such information may be juxtaposed productively with quantitative scale scores to understand in a deeper manner what the experience of a group is or has been.

Narrative Reports are developed at individual, group, and organizational levels, typically are between seven and nine pages in length,[17] and consist of written text in two different forms: (a) general information regarding the nature of beliefs and values (e.g., their etiology, how they change) as well as the role of life experiences and events in influencing why we experience self, others, and the larger world as we do; (b) bolded text within these reports, which corresponds to where the individual or group scores on each scale of the BEVI. The underlying software for the BEVI uploads and integrates bolded text into the narrative, which corresponds to the actual scores that an individual—or an overall group—produces on the BEVI.

---

[17] Group and organizational reports may be substantially longer depending upon the number of tables/indexes that are accessed during the review of such reports (i.e., there is a provision for opening or closing additional indexes depending upon which are of greatest relevance for purposes of review).

The Report System in Practice: Five Examples

To illustrate how various components of the BEVI report system work, five examples are offered next (multiple chapters later in this book also illustrate such usage). These include: (a) *Sample Narrative Report, Aggregate Profile, and Decile Profile*[18]; (b) *Background–Domain Contrast*[19]; (c) *Time 1/Time 2 Comparisons Across BEVI Scales*; (d) *Time 1/Time 2 Comparisons Across Formative Variables*; and (e) *Longitudinal Assessment via Time 1/Time 2/Time 3 Analysis*.

Example 1: Narrative Report and Aggregate/Decile Profiles.

First, consider one project involving a learning community at James Madison University, called Madison International, which brings together U.S. and international students as part of a living and learning community, which completes coursework and participates in other experiences together during their first year in the university (see www.jmu.edu/international/mip). The subsequent example of individual/group report usage focuses on a subset of these students (N = 22), who completed a course called *Making Sense of Beliefs and Values: A Guided Tour for Global Citizens*. After providing consent and completing the BEVI, individual reports were provided (in a sealed envelope) to each student in the course, who had the opportunity to read their report privately (a process that typically requires approximately 10 minutes). Although additional information about the structure of individual reports is provided, recall that these basically consist of a seven- to nine-page narrative, which contains common information presented to all report recipients along with individualized content, which is bolded throughout the report, and which is uploaded into the report based upon each student's unique scores on the BEVI. By way of context, the first page of such a report is similar to the excerpt from Figure 4.18.

After each student has read his or her full individual report in private, the BEVI trained coordinator of the process then reviews the group report with all members of the cohort. As noted, both group and organizational reports include a range of different sections, all of which may or may not be emphasized depending upon the goals of a particular BEVI workshop. In the case of Madison International, most of the focus centered on the three components of the group report, which include (a) *Background Information* (i.e., which provides descriptive information regarding how the group "breaks down" across a range of different demographic variables); (b) the *Aggregate Profile* (i.e., provides the aggregate scores for participants across all BEVI scales); and (c) *Decile Profile* (i.e., breaks down the aggregate scores across each scale in increments of 10%, in order to illustrate how the members of a group are dispersed across each of the BEVI scales). Figures 4.19 to 4.22 illustrate these three components of the BEVI Group Report for the Madison International Learning Community.

How were the three components of the BEVI group profile used with the Madison International Learning Community? Essentially, after reviewing the background characteristics of the group (e.g., highlighting areas of similarity and difference), the bulk of this session focused on explaining and discussing the results from the Aggregate Profile and Decile Profile. To highlight a number of these scales, note overall that

---

[18] This example is excerpted and/or adapted from Chapter 12 in this book. BEVI reports typically are presented in color, but are printed here in black and white.

[19] The full scale score is summative of scores from the seven domains of the BEVI under which the 17 process scales are clustered: (a) Formative Variables; (b) Fulfillment of Core Needs; (c) Tolerance of Disequilibrium; (d) Critical Thinking; (e) Self Access; (f) Other Access; and (g) Global Access (see www.thebevi.com).

Beliefs, Events, and Values Inventory

You and Your Worldview

A Personal Report from the
Beliefs, Events, and Values Inventory (BEVI)™

User: 9389488   **Date of Test: 8/29/2012**

Introduction

Pick up a newspaper or turn on a radio or television anywhere in the world and one fact becomes immediately clear: beliefs and values are integral to the human experience. People have strong opinions about topics from politics, religion, education and the arts, to marriage, family, gender, and sexuality. However, whether a specific belief is "right" or "wrong" is arguably less important than understanding the complex interaction among thoughts, feelings, behavior, life history, and context that results in a unique version of reality for each human being. Such understanding is important because beliefs and values influence the actions, policies, and practices of individuals, groups, organizations, governments, and societies all over the world. The BEVI provides a way for us to explore these complex issues at the individual level, by helping each of us to make sense of why we hold certain beliefs and values, while also examining why other people may see the world in similar and different ways. At the outset, however, it is very important to emphasize that the BEVI takes no position on whether one set of beliefs and values is "right," "wrong," "better," or "worse" than any other set of beliefs and values.

So, let's take a closer look at what you seem to believe and value, while also offering some possibilities about why you believe what you believe. In addition to explanatory information throughout this report, your unique responses to the BEVI are highlighted in bold. Admittedly, these "what" and "why"...

FIGURE 4.18. **Sample introductory page from the BEVI individual report.**

the group as a whole reports relatively positive life histories (e.g., Negative Life Events, Needs Closure); is quite open to basic thoughts/feelings that characterize the typical experience for most human beings (e.g., Basic Closedness); demonstrates a moderate degree of attributional complexity regarding why human beings do what they do and why events in the world happen as they do (e.g., Basic Determinism); evidences a moderate degree of religiosity (e.g., Socioreligious Traditionalism); is highly self and emotionally aware (e.g., Emotional Attunement, Self Awareness); appears to possess a high capacity to experience self and other in shades of gray rather than in dichotomous terms (e.g., Socioemotional Convergence); is very open to cultural beliefs and practices that are different from one's own (e.g., Sociocultural Openness); is concerned about the environment and natural world (e.g., Ecological

Beliefs, Events, and Values Inventory

BEVI Group Report

Madison International

N = 22

Background

Ethnic Group

Black and White	4.55%
Black/African-American	13.64%
Hispanic/Latino	9.09%
Scandinavian	4.55%
White	68.18%

Gender

Female	63.64%
Male	36.36%

Political Orientation

Democrat	31.82%
Independent	31.82%
Philosophical Anarchist	4.55%
Republican	27.27%
Social Democrat (mostly Democratic)	4.55%

Religious Orientation

FIGURE 4.19. **Introductory excerpt from the background information section of the group report for the Madison International Learning Community.**

Resonance); and is deeply interested in making a difference in the world (e.g., Global Engagement). In many ways, such a profile would perhaps be consistent with a group of individuals who have self-selected to be part of an international living and learning community. However, as noted, it is very important to go beyond aggregate results in order to understand areas of difference and similarity by the group as a whole. To do so, let us focus on one of the BEVI scales, Socioreligious Traditionalism, from the Decile Profile, particularly because this scale prompted a great deal of reflection and discussion by community members. As illustrated in Figure 4.22, note first

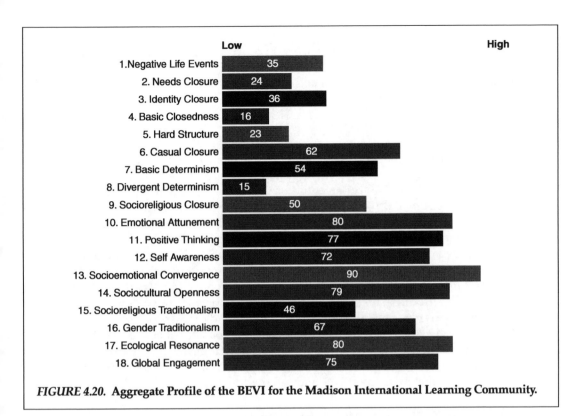

FIGURE 4.20. **Aggregate Profile of the BEVI for the Madison International Learning Community.**

Deciles	1	2	3	4	5	6	7	8	9	10
1. Negative life events	18%	14%	23%	5%	9%	0%	14%	9%	5%	5%
2. Needs closure	23%	14%	23%	18%	23%	0%	0%	0%	0%	0%
3. Identity closure	23%	5%	5%	23%	36%	5%	0%	0%	0%	5%
4. Basic closedness	45%	9%	5%	23%	14%	5%	0%	0%	0%	0%
5. Hard structure	32%	18%	5%	9%	18%	0%	9%	5%	5%	0%
6. Casual closure	9%	0%	18%	0%	5%	27%	14%	0%	9%	18%
7. Basic determinism	5%	9%	18%	14%	9%	9%	18%	0%	5%	14%
8. Divergent determinism	32%	18%	32%	5%	5%	5%	0%	0%	0%	5%
9. Socioreligious closure	18%	5%	9%	5%	5%	18%	5%	9%	23%	5%
10. Emotional attunement	0%	0%	5%	0%	5%	14%	5%	18%	27%	27%
11. Positive thinking	5%	0%	9%	9%	9%	9%	9%	9%	14%	27%
12. Self awareness	14%	9%	0%	9%	5%	5%	0%	9%	14%	36%
13. Socioemotional convergence	0%	0%	0%	0%	0%	5%	9%	18%	27%	41%
14. Sociocultural openness	0%	0%	0%	0%	0%	14%	14%	23%	32%	18%
15. Socioreligious traditionalism	23%	5%	9%	14%	0%	0%	0%	32%	9%	9%
16. Gender traditionalism	5%	5%	9%	0%	14%	9%	9%	14%	23%	14%
17. Ecological resonance	0%	0%	0%	0%	5%	27%	9%	14%	14%	32%
18. Global engagement	5%	9%	0%	14%	5%	5%	14%	9%	18%	23%
Deciles	1	2	3	4	5	6	7	8	9	10

FIGURE 4.21. **Decile Profile of the BEVI for the Madison International Learning Community.**

15. Socioreligious traditionalism	23%	5%	9%	14%	0%	0%	0%	32%	9%	9%

FIGURE 4.22. **The Socioreligious Traditionalism scale from Decile Profile of the BEVI for the Madison International Learning Community.**

the extraordinary dispersion by the group across this scale, which essentially results in a bimodal distribution. That is, approximately 50% of the learning community falls between the 1st and 40th percentile of the scale whereas the remaining 50% falls between the 70th and 100th percentile (no respondents fall between the 41st and 69th percentile). Note further that approximately one quarter of the community occupies the lowest 10th percentile on this scale (i.e., approximately 25% of the community essentially is disavowing religion and religious belief). The presentation of this finding sparked a great deal of dialogue by the group (along with other scales, where dispersion was especially noteworthy, such as Negative Life Events, Self Awareness, and Gender Traditionalism). From a thematic perspective, the group engaged deeply in discussions regarding the fact that such profound differences existed among them. Moreover, the meaning of the larger issues was considered as well, such as the purpose of existence, where beliefs and values come from, and why such considerations should—or should not—matter to us as individuals and as a society, particularly in a community that juxtaposed U.S. and international students (Iyer, 2013).

Example 2: Background–Domain Contrast

The preceding conclusion is bolstered further by another dimension of the reporting system, which distinguishes among "high," "medium," and "low" full scale scores among subgroups. As noted previously, various indexes and tables on the reporting system examine this issue, including Background–Domain Contrast, which illustrates how different or similar the group is at the level of background information and domain scores by the lowest 30%, middle 40%, and highest 30% of full scale scores (i.e., again, full scale scores represent an amalgamation of BEVI scores—organized under the seven main domains of the BEVI, from Formative Variables through Global Access, as illustrated in Tables 4.4 and 4.5—in order to obtain an overall profile of where an individual is according to the BEVI as a whole). Specifically, consider the following excerpts of T1/T2 Group Report results from a sample of university participants (N = 101) from one of the Forum BEVI Project partners on Background–Domain Contrast. Of other highlights that might be emphasized, note from Tables 4.4 and 4.5 that individuals who, at the outset of a learning experience, are at the low, middle, or high end of the "full scale" continuum (i.e., are, relative to each of these subgroups, the least, neutral, or most inclined toward a learning experience from the standpoint of their full scale score), demonstrate specific profile characteristics, either in terms of "background" variables (e.g., age, gender, education) or "domain" variables (i.e., one of the seven areas under which BEVI scales are clustered). To take just a few examples, for this sample, students who are most versus least inclined toward an international, multicultural, or transformational learning experience would appear to be older (average age = 27 versus 19); approximately twice as likely to be female; more likely to come from a less wealthy family ($70,000 versus $85,000); and more likely to have experienced a greater number of years of education (7 versus 2). Moreover, as would be expected given differences in full scale scores across high (71), medium (58), and low (41) respondents, these subgroups

TABLE 4.4
Sample Findings from the Background Information Section of Background–Domain Contrast:
Lowest Full Scale (N = 31), Middle Full Scale (N = 37), and Highest Full Scale (N = 31)

BACKGROUND INFORMATION	BACKGROUND INFORMATION	BACKGROUND INFORMATION
Average Age: **19**	Average Age: **22**	Average Age: **27**
Males: **15** Females: **16**	Males: **11** Females: **26**	Males: **11** Females: **20**
Caucasians: **25** Non-Caucasians: **6** ➢ Details:	Caucasians: **26** Non-Caucasians: **11** ➢ Details:	Caucasians: **20** Non-Caucasians: **11** ➢ Details:
Raised in the United States: **31** Not raised in the United States: **0** ➢ Details:	Raised in the United States: **37** Not raised in the United States: **0** ➢ Details:	Raised in the United States: **29** Not raised in the United States: **2** ➢ Details:
Average Years of Education: **2**	Average Years of Education: **3**	Average Years of Education: **7**
Average Parental/Household Income: **$85,484**	Average Parental/Household Income: **$77,162**	Average Parental/Household Income: **$70,161**

TABLE 4.5
Sample Findings from the Domain Section of Background—Domain Contrast

FULL SCALE: 41	FULL SCALE: 58	FULL SCALE: 71
III. Formative Variables • Negative Life Events: **40** • See Background Information	III. Formative Variables • Negative Life Events: **64** • See Background Information	III. Formative Variables • Negative Life Events: **51** • See Background Information
IV. Fulfillment of Core Needs: **27**	IV. Fulfillment of Core Needs: **69**	IV. Fulfillment of Core Needs: **82**
V. Tolerance of Disequilibrium: **36**	V. Tolerance of Disequilibrium: **52**	V. Tolerance of Disequilibrium: **68**
VI. Critical Thinking: **35**	VI. Critical Thinking: **51**	VI. Critical Thinking: **73**
VII. Self Access: **57**	VII. Self Access: **76**	VII. Self Access: **78**
VIII. Other Access: **30**	VIII. Other Access: **55**	VIII. Other Access: **78**
IX. Global Access: **32**	IX. Global Access: **54**	IX. Global Access: **78**

show substantial differences on nearly all domain scores as indicated in Table 4.5 (e.g., 36, 52, and 68 on Tolerance of Disequilibrium; 35, 51, 73 on Critical Thinking; 30, 55, 78 on Other Access; 32, 54, and 78 on Global Access).

As may be clear, such report-based findings illustrate again that groups may be substantially different from one another at the level of both background (e.g., age, gender) and domain (e.g., various clusters of BEVI scales) characteristics before they have even begun to engage in a learning experience together, which may influence not only whether they are inclined toward, or against, participation in such an experience at the outset, but the degree to which they are likely to express satisfaction about the experience once it has concluded (i.e., as noted, we are able to predict such satisfaction even before they have engaged in it) (e.g., Wandschneider et al., 2016).[20]

Example 3: Time 1/Time 2 Scale Comparisons

Regarding the overarching issue of what we may learn about learning processes and outcomes from Time 1 to Time 2, consider the following comparisons of Aggregate Profile and Profile Contrast results across two BEVI scales for one of the Forum BEVI Project partners: Negative Life Events (NLE) and Identity Diffusion (ID) (N = 36). To facilitate interpretation, the Aggregate Profile Time 1/Time 2 scale scores are followed by the Profile Contrast Time 1/Time 2 scores, and then by an explanation of salient points regarding this juxtaposition.

At least two observations are worth noting from the preceding contrast. In the first place, note that the Aggregate Profile for NLE goes up from the 48th to the 55th percentile on the Aggregate Profile. However, on Profile Contrast, the lowest 30% and middle 40% (70% of the overall sample) actually go down from Time 1 to Time 2 on NLE. A basic and overarching conclusion from such results is that Profile Contrast is a much more robust and nuanced analysis of what is actually happening within a group than is the Aggregate Profile. So, we must be very careful in our interpretation of Time 1/Time 2 findings on any measure—including but not limited to the BEVI—in order to ensure that we are apprehending what actually is happening within subsets of the overall group, as such subgroups may actually be responding very differently from one another in the context of an international, multicultural, or transformative learning experience. Note the very interesting finding—observed across multiple group report analyses in the larger project—that the perception of one's life history and background may differentially be affected by one's point of departure prior to engaging in an international, multicultural, or transformative learning experience. This observation is highly congruent with a narrative framework that how we experience ourselves, others, and the larger world is mediated strongly by the life experiences we have and may not "exist" in absolute or inviolable terms (as noted in Chapters 2 and 3). In other words, our memory and experience of our "past" is highly dependent upon events that occur in the present and future. And yet, this process may unfold differently for individuals depending upon their point of departure (i.e., how they are "organized" affectively or cognitively prior to the learning experience). For example, as Figure 4.23 illustrates, individuals who report a greater degree of "NLE" at Time 1 subsequently show a decrement in such a report at Time 2 (3–4 months after the international/multicultural learning experience) whereas individuals who report a lesser degree of "NLE" at Time 1 subsequently show an increase in such a report at Time 2. What do such findings suggest? Although we emphasize that such findings are common but not universal, such outcomes suggest that prolonged exposure to radically different "Formative Variables" (e.g., a different culture, context, language, religion, etc.) interacts with "who we were" at the outset of the experience to produce a sort of "progression to the mean" effect. Such findings imply further that those who experienced their past

---

[20] Many other examples of variations on BEVI reports as well as varying aspects of analysis, interpretation, and usage are described in later chapters of this book. See in particular Chapter 12 by Wandschneider et al., which summarizes the implications of the Forum BEVI Project along with accompanying data and profiles. By way of example, the following section regarding Negative Life Events and Identity Diffusion was excerpted and/or adapted from Chapter 12.

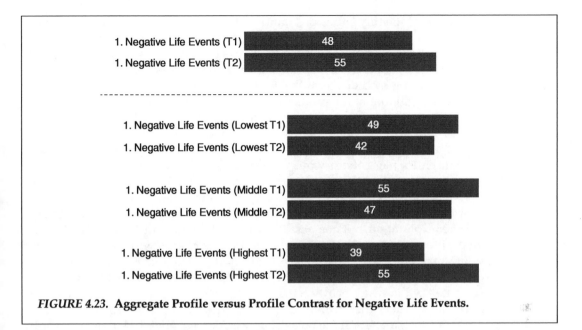

FIGURE 4.23. **Aggregate Profile versus Profile Contrast for Negative Life Events.**

as especially "negative" or "positive" are not so sure that was the case following the completion of this intensive learning experience (i.e., relative to what they experienced, their past may have been "better" or "worse" than what they believed after being exposed to a culture and context that was radically different from that which they were accustomed). Along related lines, next consider Figure 4.24. From an interpretive standpoint, the Aggregate Profile and Profile Contrast results on Identity Diffusion amplify the preceding point.

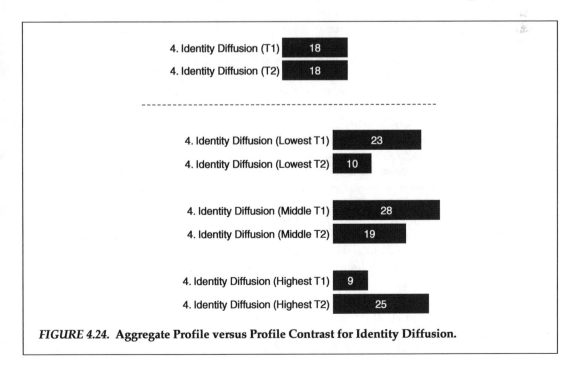

FIGURE 4.24. **Aggregate Profile versus Profile Contrast for Identity Diffusion.**

Recall that "Identity Diffusion" indicates the degree to which individuals report a "painful crisis of identity," and are "fatalistic regarding negatives of marital/family life," and "feel 'bad' about one's self and prospects." If we only review the Time 1/Time 2 Aggregate Profile (which takes the average of all participants), we would conclude that no change occurred on this fundamental aspect of how one experiences self from the beginning to the conclusion of the experiences (i.e., the Time 1/Time 2 Aggregate Report remains at the 18th percentile). Such a conclusion would be ill-advised as there are clear differences between subgroups on this core construct of the BEVI, as indicated by the Profile Contrast results for this scale. Specifically, the lowest and middle "full scale" cohorts would appear to become substantially clearer on who they are and where they are going in life, whereas those who believed they were the clearest on such aspects of self at the beginning of the experience report markedly less clarity by the conclusion of this experience. The reasons for such findings warrant further exploration, but one possibility is that by dint of their exposure to a context and culture that is substantially different from what they were accustomed, each subgroup may "balance" what they previously believed and valued against what they saw in terms of the realities that others faced. Such a process may differentially be associated with greater clarity for those who were relatively unclear about who they were and where they were going versus those who, relatively speaking, felt clearer about such matters at the outset, but became less convinced of their clarity by the end of the experience.

Example 4. Time 1/Time 2 Formative Variable by Scale Comparisons

Likewise, note also that such differences manifest not only between different subgroups with a larger group on the basis of low, medium, or high full scale scores on the BEVI. Differences also emerge on the basis of single variables, a point that is expanded upon substantially in the forthcoming chapters. There are many such variables, but for illustrative purposes, a couple of examples may suffice. Consider the role of gender and religious orientation on two BEVI scales—Religious Traditionalism and Gender Traditionalism (from a university-wide T1/T2 report from one of the Forum BEVI Project partners). In Figures 4.25 and 4.26, we see that not unexpectedly perhaps, individuals who self-report as having a religious affiliation (N = 85) receive substantially higher scores on Religious Traditionalism at Time 1 and Time 2 than do individuals who report no religious affiliation (e.g., as atheists or agnostics, N = 26). Likewise, individuals who self-report as males (N = 43) also show substantially higher scores on Gender Traditionalism at Time 1 and Time 2 than do females (N = 77). What is most interesting and relevant, from an interpretive perspective, are the interactions that seem to emerge. Note, for example, that individuals who report a religious affiliation also achieve a substantially higher score on Gender Traditionalism at Time 1 and Time 2. Moreover, note interestingly that women in this sample tend to achieve a substantially higher score on Religious Traditionalism at Time 1 and Time 2 than do men. Finally and perhaps most intriguing, note that both Religious Traditionalism and Gender Traditionalism decrease for all four subgroups in this particular group report—religious, nonreligious, male, and female. Whether such outcomes are "good," "bad," or "indifferent" really is a matter for the institution/organization and its members to determine based upon their goals and the nature of the intervention(s) that were introduced between Time 1 and Time 2 of BEVI administration. For present purposes, then, the most salient points are that (a) different demographic variables are often associated with different response patterns on BEVI

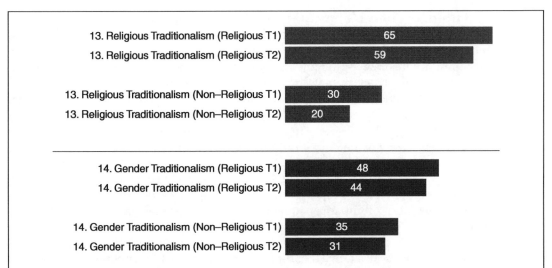

FIGURE 4.25. The association of religious orientation to Religious Traditionalism and Gender Traditionalism on the BEVI.

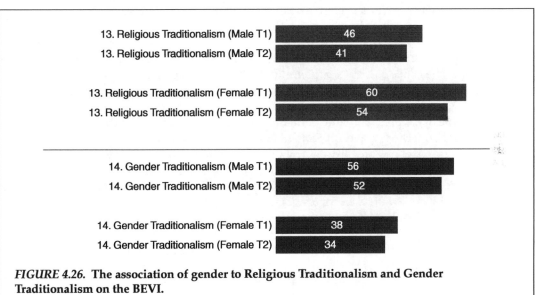

FIGURE 4.26. The association of gender to Religious Traditionalism and Gender Traditionalism on the BEVI.

profiles; (b) interpretation of the BEVI requires that we examine such interactions to understand what "really is happening" within the larger group; (c) change at the level of beliefs and values appears not only to occur and be measurable across time, but may show underlying patterns that help us evaluate the effectiveness of the intervention that we have implemented; and d) with the BEVI—and arguably any assessment measure—we should not simply look at overall results to determine what is happening for a group, since powerful mediators and moderators of subgroup change may in fact be driving what we see an aggregated or overall level.

Example 5: Time 1/Time 2/Time 3 Group Reports and the "7Ds."
Although many more findings, implications, and applications from the BEVI and its report system are presented in subsequent chapters, one final profile comparison may be helpful to illustrate a fundamental point that has been emphasized in Chapter 2. Although relatively immutable over the short term, beliefs and values may well change as a function of exposure to Formative Variables that meet specific criteria, such as duration, difference, and depth (e.g., the "7Ds" as noted previously); as such, it is wise to adopt a longitudinal approach to assessment and measurement whenever possible, as the true nature and form of belief/value "transformation" may be detectable best over the long term. Consider, in this regard, Figure 4.27, which consists of T1/T2/T3 comparisons for the same group of study abroad students (N = 20) with one of the Forum BEVI Project partners. As this figure illustrates, although some aspects of the T1/T2 comparison move in a direction that presumably would be desirable at the conclusion of a study abroad experience (e.g., Self Certitude drops from the 42nd to the 28th percentile; Gender Traditionalism drops from the 38th to the 27th percentile), other scales move in a direction that presumably would not be desirable, given the goals of the study abroad experience (e.g., Needs Fulfillment drops from the 54th to the 39th percentile; Self Awareness drops from the 78th to the 63rd percentile; and Sociocultural Openness drops from the 76th to the 62nd percentile). As noted in Figure 4.27, T1/T2 administrations occurred between 3 and 4 months after initial administration of the BEVI at the beginning of the study abroad experience. So, what happens if we let at least half a year pass before assessing these same students again? Here we see a highly intriguing flip on a number of key scales. For example, in Figure 4.27, consider the three scales noted previously that presumably went in the "opposite direction" of what reasonably could be anticipated (or at least hoped for) at Time 2: (a) *Scale 3. Needs Fulfillment* (which measures openness to experiences, needs, and feelings; deep care/sensitivity for self, others, and the larger world); (b) *Scale 11: Self Awareness* (which measures a tendency toward introspection, acceptance of self-complexity, cares for the human experience/condition, and tolerates difficult thoughts/feelings); and (c) *Scale 15. Sociocultural Openness* (which measures progressiveness/openness regarding a wide range of actions, policies, and practices in the areas of culture, economics, education, environment, gender, global relations, and politics). As illustrated in Figure 4.27, on all three of these scales (among others that might be reviewed as well), results now solidly are in the direction of what might be anticipated (or hoped for) at the conclusion of a study abroad experience. How do we explain such findings? As discussed in Chapters 2 and 3, from an Equilintegration or EI perspective, the "7Ds" of belief/values transformation explicitly acknowledge that multiple factors interact simultaneously to determine how, for whom, and under what circumstances "change" occurs. Moreover, the greater the discrepancy between one's original "Formative Variables" and those to which one is next exposed, the greater the degree of potential "affective/cognitive shut down" that occurs, as the "self" strives essentially to protect "its self" from the intensely experienced shock of such exposure, which may in qualitative and subjective terms be described as "amazing," but nonetheless may exert a toll on the self, which simply needs time and space to consolidate and "make sense of beliefs and values" once again. Thus, we see a Time 3 profile that is, in many ways, a mirror image of Time 2, and in some ways, is a poignant reminder of what the human self endures as we all go about the business of living, which is felt that much more dramatically when experiencing "high impact" and "transformative" learning, such as study abroad (e.g., Cranton, 2006; Dirkx, 2012; Kuh, 2008; Mezirow & Taylor, 2009). From the standpoint of the BEVI and its report system, the basic point

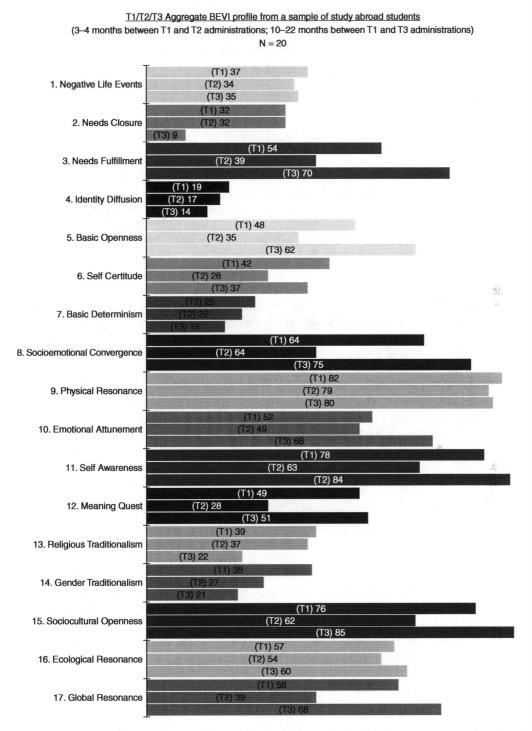

FIGURE 4.27. Comparison of T1/T2/T3 BEVI group report results for the same group of study abroad students.

here is to keep in mind that the interface between the complexities of being human and the complexities of assessment requires us to adopt measurement strategies that do not wag the dog; meaning let us first be who we are, and then and only then, seek to capture the meaning of our experience vis-à-vis assessment (e.g., by assessing such evolving human phenomenology over time, rather than "just once"), as such an approach is more likely to allow for our human complexity to be apprehended as it manifests naturally in the real world.

Usage of the BEVI Report System: Summary

In the final analysis then, as we conclude this chapter on the BEVI, the implications of the preceding report-based findings should be clear.

First, differences within groups should not be underestimated, but expected (e.g., we should assume that groups may well have important differences at multiple levels, from different Formative Variables—the *events* component of the BEVI to how they experience self, others, and the larger world—to the *beliefs* and *values* components of the BEVI).

Second, for those who are leading learning, growth, or development experiences, reviewing such differences may be very helpful in understanding the nature of the group with which they will be interacting throughout the learning experience.

Third, for appropriately trained and skilled facilitators, it may be helpful to share some or all such results with participants in order to sensitize them to such differences and similarities among them (e.g., to highlight the fact that there may be very good reasons for why participants react as they do to the experiences they are about to have, as illustrated on several occasions through various projects reported herein and in subsequent chapters).

Fourth, such findings may help at the level of interpretation (e.g., the role of the instructor/leader and/or learning/growth experience should be appraised accurately in terms of relative impact) since most likely, there will be multiple interactions occurring simultaneously that affect learning, growth, and development processes and outcomes.

Fifth, and finally, from the standpoint of the BEVI and its report system, it is important to keep in mind that the interface between the complexities of being human and the complexities of assessment requires us to adopt measurement strategies that do not wag the dog. That is to say, let us allow ourselves first to be who we are, and then and only then, seek to capture the meaning of our experience vis-à-vis an ecologically valid assessment of such evolving human phenomenology over time, rather than "just once" (i.e., such an approach is more likely to allow for our complexity to be apprehended as it really exists). In short, by reviewing such report-based results, more reflective and skillful assessment, research, and learning interventions may be developed, implemented, and appraised. That is because we will have a legitimate basis for understanding *why* and *how* learning, growth, and development processes and outcomes unfold as they do, for whom, and under what circumstances.

The BEVI in Conclusion: Over 20 Years in and 20 Years Hence

We have covered a lot of ground in this chapter, which may not be surprising as the goal essentially was to describe over 20 years of work on this measure. Recall that we began with a discussion of Diana, who was convinced that her son "had ADHD," which prompted a comprehensive evaluation process to try and ascertain whether that diagnosis best fit the circumstances (it did not, as far as we could tell). This clinical anecdote was offered by way of introduction to the fundamental impetus for the BEVI: to understand why, how, and under what circumstances individuals became committed, often deeply, to particular beliefs and values regarding self, others, and the larger world. The trajectory of BEVI development was then traced, beginning with an amalgamation of actual belief statements by clients, students, and public figures over the years along with accompanying immersion in various literatures that were relevant to these constructs. The original "long version" of the BEVI that emerged in the early 1990s eventually culminated in a range of statistical analyses, to include multiple factor analyses along with examination of psychometric properties of the overall measure, its scales, and items (e.g., factor structure, stability, reliability).

The next phase of development occurred under the auspices of the Forum BEVI Project, a multiple-site, multiyear assessment of international, multicultural, and transformative learning initiative over a period of 6 years (from 2007 to 2013), which resulted in hundreds of analyses as well as a range of publications and presentations (e.g., see Forum BEVI Project, 2015). To illustrate some of these findings, we focused next on correlation matrix data and their implications from two sample scales of the BEVI—Needs Closure and Emotional Attunement.

Another major development during the Forum BEVI Project was that of the short version of this measure, which occurred over a period of several years (N = 2331), and included a variety of statistical procedures (e.g., from IRT to SEM). Ultimately, we narrowed the demographics to 40 (from 65), items to 185 (from 336), and scales to 17 (from 18). After reporting scale summaries (e.g., means, standard deviations, Cronbach's alpha), model fit information (e.g., CFI, RMSEA), and factor/subfactor structure for each of the 17 scales, information was offered regarding the description and interpretation of all BEVI scales, including the three "experiential reflection items," before explicating the BEVI's design (e.g., meaning and role of "belief statements"; the issue of face validity; the rationale for item wording and positive/negative loadings; basic aspects of administration).

Next, we discussed the BEVI's report system, including the structure and usage of individual, group, and organizational reports (e.g., for assessment, outcome evaluation, enhancing learning, growth, and development, meeting assessment needs) before reviewing a range of BEVI tables and indexes, from Background–Domain Contrast and Profile Contrast to Aggregate and Decile Profiles. Finally, we concluded with five examples of the report system in practice, including (a) Narrative Reports and Aggregate/Decile Profiles; (b) Background–Domain Contrast; (c) what can be learned both from Time 1/Time 2 comparisons at the scale level as well as (d) interactions between Formative Variables and specific BEVI scales; and last, (e) the role of longitudinal assessment including the "7Ds" of belief/value transformation (who learns what and why and under what circumstances).

Hopefully, the information presented throughout this chapter provides an accessible overview of what the BEVI is, why and how it emerged as it did, relevant psychometrics and scale descriptions, and key aspects of usage and interpretation. Along with theoretical considerations presented in Chapters 2 and 3, the research and practice chapters that follow provide additional information on all of these points. In the final analysis, we know from much experience now that there is no substitute for real world immersion in BEVI data, scales, and reports as well as ongoing consultation with other users. In fact, many of the most enjoyable and intriguing discussions over the years have been from users "in the field" who have run a myriad of analyses and creatively experimented with various approaches to usage, interpretation, and the like. Although we are over 20 years in, it still feels like we are just getting started. It will be interesting indeed to see all we will have discovered, developed, and implemented in 2035, two decades hence.

REFERENCES

Aita, M., & Richer, M. C. (2005). Essentials of research ethics for healthcare professionals. *Nursing and Health Sciences, 7,* 119–125.

Anmuth, L. M., Poore, M., Cozen, J., Brearly, T., Tabit, M., Cannady, M., . . . Staton, R. (2013, August). *Making implicit beliefs explicit: In search of best practices for mental health clients, clinicians, and trainers.* Poster presented at the annual meeting of the American Psychological Association, Honolulu, HI.

Aronson, E. (2012). *The social animal* (11th ed.). New York, NY: Worth Publishers.

Arredondo, P., Shealy, C., Neale, M., & Winfrey, L. (2004). Consultation and interprofessional collaboration: Modeling for the future [Special Series]. *Journal of Clinical Psychology, 60*(7), 787–800.

Atwood, K., Chkhaidze, N., Shealy, C. N., Staton, R., & Sternberger, L. G. (2014, August). *Transformation of self: Implications from the Forum BEVI Project.* Poster presented at the annual meeting of the American Psychological Association, Washington, DC.

Bargh, J. A., & Chartrand, T. L. (1999). The unbearable automaticity of being. *American Psychologist, 54*(7), 462–479.

Bolen, M., Shealy, C. N., Pysarchik, D., & Whalen, B. (2009, February). *Present applications and future implications of the "Forum BEVI Project."* Presentation delivered at the annual meeting of the Forum on Education Abroad, Portland, OR.

Brearly, T., Shealy, C. N., Staton, R., & Sternberger, L. G. (2012, August). *Prejudice and religious and non-religious certitude: An empirical analysis from the Forum BEVI Project.* Poster presented at the annual meeting of the American Psychological Association, Orlando, FL.

Brody, J. L., Gluck, J. P., & Aragon, A. S. (1997). Participants understanding of the process of psychological research: Informed consent. *Ethics & Behavior, 7*(4), 285–298.

Brody, J. L., Gluck, J. P., & Aragon, A. S. (2000). Participants understanding of the process of psychological research: Debriefing. *Ethics & Behavior, 10*(1), 13–25.

Campbell, D. T., & Stanley, J. C. (2005). *Experimental and quasi-experimental research.* Boston, MA: Houghton Mifflin.

Center for Disease Control and Prevention. (2014). Attention-Deficit/Hyperactivity Disorder. Retrieved June 10, 2014 from http://www.cdc.gov/ncbddd/adhd/data.html

Coates, M., Hanson, W., Samuel, D. B., Webster, M., & Cozen, J. (2016). The Beliefs, Events, and Values Inventory (BEVI). Psychological assessment implications and applications. In C. N. Shealy (Ed.), *Making sense of beliefs and values* (pp. 371–406). New York, NY: Springer Publishing.

Cozen, J., Hanson, W., Poston, J., Jones, S., & Tabit, M. (2016). The Beliefs, Events, and Values Inventory (BEVI): Implications and applications for therapeutic assessment and intervention. In C. N. Shealy (Ed.), *Making sense of beliefs and values* (pp. 575–621). New York, NY: Springer Publishing.

Cranton, P. (Ed.). (2006). *Understanding and promoting transformative learning: A guide for educators of adults.* San Francisco, CA: Jossey Bass.

Cultivating the Globally Sustainable Self. (2015). Retrieved from http://www.jmu.edu/summitseries/

Cummings, E. M., & Davies, P. (1996). Emotional security as a regulatory process in normal development and the development of psychopathology. *Development and Psychopathology, 8,* 123–139.

Cummings, E. M., Davies, P. T., & Campbell, S. S. (2000). *Developmental psychopathology and family process: Theory, research, and clinical implications.* New York, NY: Guilford Press.

Davies, P. T., Winter, M. A., & Cicchetti, D. (2006). The implications of emotional security theory for understanding and treating childhood psychopathology. *Development and Psychopathology, 18*(3), 707–735. doi:10.1017/S0954579406060354

Deacon, B. J. (2013). The biomedical model of mental disorder: A critical analysis of its validity, utility, and effects on psychotherapy research. *Clinical Psychology Review, 33*, 846–861.

Dirkx, J. M. (2012). Self-formation and transformative learning: A response to "Calling transformative learning into question: Some mutinous thoughts," by Michael Newman. *Adult Education Quarterly, 62*(4), 399–405

Downing, S. M., & Haladyna, T. M. (1997). Test item development: Validity evidence from quality assurance procedures. *Applied Measurement in Education, 10*(1), 61–82.

Forum-BEVI Project. (2015). Retrieved from http://www.forumea.org/research-bevi-project.cfm

Freedheim, D. J. (Ed.). (2003). *Handbook of psychology, Vol 1: History of psychology*. Hoboken, NJ: John Wiley & Sons.

Frijda, N. H., Manstead, A. S., & Bem, S. (2000). The influence of emotions on beliefs. In N. H. Frijda, A. S. Manstead, & S. Bem (Eds.), *Emotions and beliefs: How thoughts influence feelings* (pp. 1–9). Cambridge, UK: Cambridge University Press.

Garner, P. W., Dunsmore, J. C., & Southam-Gerrow, M. (2008). Mother-child conversations about emotions: Linkages to child aggression and prosocial behavior. *Social Development, 17*(2), 259–277. doi:10.1111/j.1467-9507.2007.00424.x

Geisinger, K. F. (Ed.). (2013). *APA handbook of testing and assessment in psychology*. Washington, DC: American Psychological Association.

Hayes, D. J. (2001). A comparison of evangelical Christians and mental health professionals on the Beliefs, Events, and Values Inventory (BEVI) (Unpublished doctoral dissertation, James Madison University). *Dissertation Abstracts International, 62*, 1577.

Hayes, D. J., Shealy, C. N., Sivo, S. A., & Weinstein, Z. C. (1999, August). *Psychology, religion, and Scale 5 (Religious Traditionalism) of the BEVI*. Poster session presented at the meeting of the American Psychological Association, Boston, MA.

Henriques, G. (2011). *A new unified theory of psychology*. New York, NY: Springer.

Hill, C., Johnson, M., Brinton, C., Staton, R., Sternberger, L., & Shealy. (2013, August). *The etiology of economic beliefs and values: Implications and applications from the Forum BEVI Project*. Poster presented at the annual meeting of the American Psychological Association, Honolulu, HI.

Hong, S., & Roznowski, M. (2001). An investigation of the influence of internal test bias on regression slope. *Applied Measurement in Education, 14*(4), 351–368.

Hubley, A. M., & Zumbo, B. D. (2013). Psychometric characteristics of assessment procedures: An overview. In K. F. Geisinger (Ed.), *APA handbook of testing and assessment in psychology*. (Vol. 1, pp. 3–19). Washington, DC: American Psychological Association.

Interprofessional Education Collaborative. (2014). *Connecting health professions for better care*. Retrieved May 7, 2014 from https://ipecollaborative.org

Isley, E. B., Shealy, C. N., Crandall, K. S., Sivo, S. A., & Reifsteck, J. B. (1999, August). *Relevance of the BEVI for research in developmental psychopathology*. Poster presented at the meeting of the American Psychological Association, Boston, MA.

Iyer, C. (2013). *Assessing and engaging beliefs and values in a learning community of U.S. and international students: Implications and applications from the Forum BEVI Project* (Unpublished doctoral dissertation). James Madison University, Harrisonburg, VA.

Johnson, C. E., Stewart, A. L., Brabeck, M. M., Huber, V. S., & Rubin, H. (2004). Interprofessional collaboration: Implications for combined-integrated doctoral training in professional psychology. *Journal of Clinical Psychology, 60*(10), 995–1010.

Kuh, G. D. (2008). *High-impact educational practices: What they are, who has access to them, and why they matter*. Washington, DC: Association of American Colleges and Universities. Retrieved from https://www.aacu.org/leap/hips

Magnavita, J., & Achin, J. (2013). *Unifying psychotherapy: Principles, methods, and evidence from clinical science*. New York, NY: Springer Publishing.

McCoy, K., Cummings, E. M., & Davies, P. T. (2009). Constructive and destructive marital conflict, emotional security and children's prosocial behavior. *The Journal of Child Psychology and Psychiatry, 50*(3), 270–279. doi:10.1111/j.1469-7610.2008.01945.x

McShane, K. E., Davey, C. J., Rouse, J., Usher, A. M., & Sullivan, S. (2015). Beyond ethical obligation to research dissemination: Conceptualizing debriefing as a form of knowledge transfer. *Canadian Psychology/Phychologie canadienne, 56*(1), 80–87.

Mertens, D. M. (1998). *Research methods in education and psychology: Integrating diversity with quantitative and qualitative approaches.* Thousand Oaks, CA: Sage Publications.

Mezirow, J., & Taylor, E. W. (Eds.). (2009). *Transformative learning in practice: Insights from community, workplace, and higher education.* San Francisco, CA: Jossey-Bass.

Newberg, A., & Waldman, M. R. (2006). *Why we believe what we believe: Uncovering our biological need for meaning, spirituality, and truth.* New York, NY: Free Press.

Nichols, D. S. (2004). Giving the self a voice for MMPI self report: Jerry Wiggins and the Content Scales. *Multivariate Behavioral Research, 39*(2), 155–165.

Norcross, J. C. (2005). A primer on psychotherapy integration. In J. C. Norcross & M. R. Goldfried (Eds.), *Handbook of psychotherapy integration* (pp. 3–23). New York, NY: Oxford University Press, Inc.

Patel, R. (2008). *Environmental beliefs, values, and worldviews: Etiology, maintenance, and transformation* (Doctoral dissertation). James Madison University, Harrisonburg, VA.

Patel, R., Shealy, C. N., & De Michele, P. (2007, August). *Environmental beliefs and values: Etiology, maintenance, and transformation.* Poster presented at the annual meeting of the American Psychological Association, San Francisco, CA.

Pendleton, C., Cochran, S., Kapadia, S., & Iyer, C. (2016). Understanding the gendered self: Implications from EI Theory, EI Self, and the BEVI. In C. N. Shealy (Ed.), *Making sense of beliefs and values* (pp. 261–302). New York, NY: Springer Publishing.

Pysarchik, D. I., Shealy, C. N., & Whalen, B. (2007, February). *Antecedents to Outcomes-Based International Learning: A New Psychometric Assessment Approach.* Symposium presented at the annual meeting of the Association of International Education Administrators, Washington, DC.

Reisweber, J. R. (2008). *Beliefs, values, and the development of intercultural awareness* (Doctoral dissertation). James Madison University, Harrisonburg, VA.

Robinson, J. P., Shaver, P. R., & Wrightsman, L. S. (Eds.). (1991). *Measures of personality and social psychological attitudes.* San Diego, CA: Academic Press.

Robinson, J. P., Shaver, P. R., & Wrightsman, L. S. (Eds.). (1999). *Measures of political attitudes.* San Diego, CA: Academic Press.

Schmid, J., & Leiman, J. N. (1957). The development of hierarchical factor solutions. *Psychometrika, 22*, 53–61.

Shealy, C. N. (1995). From Boys Town to Oliver Twist: Separating fact from fiction in welfare reform and out-of home placement of children and youth. *American Psychologist, 50*(8), 565–580.

Shealy, C. N. (2004). A model and method for "making" a C-I psychologist: Equilintegration (EI) Theory and the Beliefs, Events, and Values Inventory (BEVI) [Special Series]. *Journal of Clinical Psychology, 60*(10), 1065–1090.

Shealy, C. N. (2005). Justifying the justification hypothesis: Scientific-Humanism, Equilintegration (EI) Theory, and the Beliefs, Events, and Values Inventory (BEVI) [Special Series]. *Journal of Clinical Psychology, 61*(1), 81–106.

Shealy, C. N. (2015). *The Beliefs, Events, and Values Inventory (BEVI): Overview, implications, and guidelines* [Test manual]. Staunton, VA: Author.

Shealy, C. N., Bhuyan, D., & Sternberger, L. G. (2012). Cultivating the capacity to care in children and youth: Implications from EI Theory, EI Self, and BEVI. In U. Nayar (Ed.), *Child and adolescent mental health* (pp. 240–255). New Delhi, India: Sage Publications.

Shealy, C. N., & Bullock, M. (Eds.). (in press). *Going global: How psychology and psychologists can meet a world of need.* Washington, DC: APA Books.

Shealy, C. N., Burdell, L. L., Sivo, S. A., Davino, D. F., & Hayes, D. J. (1999, August). *Men, masculinity, and Scale 10 (Gender Stereotypes) of the BEVI*. Poster presented at the meeting of the American Psychological Association, Boston, MA.

Shealy, C. N., Sears, J. L., Sivo, S. A., Alessandria, K. P., & Isley, E. B. (1999, August). *Intercultural psychology and Scale 3 (Sociocultural Closure) of the BEVI*. Poster presented at the meeting of the American Psychological Association, Boston, MA.

Singh, K. (2009). Learning values for living together. *Beliefs and Values, 1*(1), 90–93. doi:10.1891/1942-0617.1.1.90

Spaeth, J., Shealy, C. N., Cobb, H. C., Staton, R. A., & Sternberger, L. G. (2010, August). *Life events, identity development, and the construction of self: Preliminary results from the "Forum BEVI Project."* Poster presented at the annual meeting of the American Psychological Association, San Diego, CA.

Sroufe, A. L. (2009). The concept of development in developmental psychopathology. *Child Development Perspectives, 3*(3), 178–183.

Sternberger, L. G., Whalen, B., Pysarchik, D. I., & Shealy, C. N. (2009, November). *Cultural learning and the Forum BEVI Project: Who learns what, where, and why?* Symposium presented at the annual meeting of the Council on International Education Exchange, Istanbul, Turkey.

Tabit, M. B., Cozen, J., Dyjak, K., Pendleton, C., Shealy, C. N., Sternberger, L. G., & Staton, R. (2011, August). *Sociocultural impact of denial: Empirical evidence from the Forum BEVI Project*. Poster presented at the annual meeting of the American Psychological Association, Washington, DC.

Toomey, R., & Lovat, T. (2009). Values education, quality teaching, and service learning: The harmony of a new pedagogy? *Beliefs and Values, 1*(2), 220–229. doi:10.1891/1942-0617.1.2.220

Toth, S. L., & Cicchetti, D. (2013). Developmental psychopathology perspective on child maltreatment. *Child Maltreatment, 18*(3), 135–139

Wachtel, P. S. (2008). *Relational theory and the practice of psychotherapy*. New York, NY: Guilford.

Wampold, B. E. (2010). The research evidence for common factors models: A historically situated perspective. In B. L. Duncan & S. D. Miller (Eds.), *The heart and soul of change: Delivering what works in therapy* (2nd ed., pp. 49–81). Washington, DC: American Psychological Association.

Wandschneider, E., Pysarchik, D. T., Sternberger, L. G., Ma, W., Acheson-Clair, K., Baltensperberger, B., . . . Hart, V. (2016). The Forum BEVI project: Applications and implications for international, multicultural, and transformative learning. In C. N. Shealy (Ed.), *Making sense of beliefs and values* (pp. 407–484). New York, NY: Springer Publishing.

Weiss, D. J. (2013). Item banking, test development, and test delivery. In K. F. Geisinger (Ed.), *APA handbook of testing and assessment in psychology* (Vol. 1, pp. 185–200). Washington, DC: American Psychological Association.

Williams, E. A., & Shealy, C. N. (April, 2004). *How aware are you of how aware you are? A real world examination of self-awareness*. Paper presented at the meeting of the Virginia Psychological Association, Roanoke, Virginia.

PART II

MAKING SENSE OF BELIEFS AND VALUES THROUGH RESEARCH: CULTURE, DEVELOPMENT, ENVIRONMENT, GENDER, POLITICS, AND RELIGION

Mary Tabit, Lisa Legault, Wenjuan Ma, and
Kayan Phoebe Wan

5

IN SEARCH OF BEST PRACTICES FOR MULTICULTURAL EDUCATION: EMPIRICAL EVIDENCE FROM THE FORUM BEVI PROJECT

If we are to achieve a richer culture, rich in contrasting values, we must recognize the whole gamut of human potentialities, and so weave a less arbitrary social fabric, one in which each diverse human gift will find a fitting place.

—Margaret Mead

As of 2010, 308.7 million people resided in the United States (U.S. Census Bureau, 2011). Of these, 72% of the total population reported their race as White, 13% reported Black or African American, 5% reported Asian, 0.9% reported American Indian or Alaskan Native, and 0.2% reported Native Hawaiian or Other Pacific Islander. In addition, 3% of the total population responded by indicating more than one race, and 6% reported "Some Other Race," which includes "multiracial, mixed, interracial, or a Hispanic or Latino group" (U.S. Census Bureau, 2011, p. 3). More than half of the growth in the total population was attributed to an increase in individuals from Hispanic origin (U.S. Census Bureau, 2011). Moreover, current projections indicate that non-White residents will become the majority of the population by 2042 (U.S. Census Bureau, 2008). Such trajectories are illustrated by the fact that in 2009, 43% of students in elementary through high school belonged to a minority population (U.S. Department of Commerce, 2011).

Despite such dramatic demographic shifts, kindergarten through twelfth grade (K-12) teachers remain remarkably homogeneous. For example, according to a survey of public school teachers in the United States conducted by the National Center for Education Information (NCEI), 84% of K-12 teachers are Caucasian; of these individuals, 85% are female. Out of all individuals surveyed, 22% are under the age of 30 (Feistritzer, 2011). As Gay (2010) observes, "Teacher education continues to be dominated by European American students and instructors, but the children to be taught in public schools are radically different in both aspiration and actuality" (p. 143). An examination of postsecondary school enrollment reveals that from 1976 to 2009, the percentage of minority students enrolled in U.S. colleges and universities increased significantly from 3% to 12% for Hispanic students, 9% to 14% for Black students, and 2% to 7% for Asian/Pacific Islander students. At the same time, the percentage of White students enrolled in postsecondary education decreased from 83% to 62% (National Center for Education Statistics, 2011). In addition, from 2009 to 2010 approximately 60% of graduate degrees were awarded to international students residing in the United States. Although China, India, South Korea, Taiwan, and Canada are the top five countries of origin for international graduate students in the United States, China, India, and South Korea account for half of all non-U.S. citizens attending American graduate schools (Council of Graduate Schools, 2012). In terms of college and university faculty as of 2009, 7% of total faculty surveyed identified themselves as Black, 6% as Asian/Pacific Islander, 4% Hispanic, 1% American Indian/Alaskan Native, and 79% as White (National Center for Education Statistics, 2011). Consistent with these data, the postsecondary education student body continues to diversify while the faculty demographics remain predominately the same. Engberg (2004) argues that "the history of intergroup relations on college and university campuses is deeply embedded in the changing demographic composition of the postsecondary student body" (p. 473). As such, White (2004) contends that "the classroom must become a meeting ground of cultures, where the worldviews of students meet those of their teachers and the institutions in which they teach" (p. 113).

Such data provide a compelling portrait of rapidly expanding diversity within U.S. society. More to the point, from an educational perspective, student demographics are not congruent with the characteristics of those who are charged with educating them, at least in terms of ethnic background. Extant research has demonstrated that demographic matches between students and teachers could affect educational outcomes such as academic achievement (Steele & Aronson, 1995) and teachers' perceptions of their students (Dee, 2005). Based on the National Education Longitudinal Study of 1988, Dee found that both White and minority (i.e., Black and Hispanic) students are more likely to be perceived as disruptive by a teacher who does not share the student's racial traits. At a larger level, emerging trends offer a window into a future that will look and sound far more diverse than anything we ever have experienced as a nation (U.S. Census Bureau, 2011). Thus, as the composition of the United States continues to become more diverse, a corresponding need exists to facilitate understanding and positive relations among individuals from different backgrounds. The promotion of positive intergroup relations is important because increased diversity means we must work across as well as within our own social group, which not only increases our interdependence, but may be associated with inevitable cross-group tension (Lopez & Sabudeco, 2007). Indeed, the reduction and resolution of intergroup conflict is a crucial undertaking that has received substantial attention in research and practice.

A recent report from the Higher Education Research Institute at the University of California at Los Angeles found that minority students attending school at a low diversity campus face more stereotyping, harassment, and other forms of discrimination when compared to majority students (Hurtado & Ruiz, 2012). Although there are many reasons for such prejudicial processes and tensions (e.g., relative access to economic and political resources, social categorization and stereotyping, ethnocentrism and prejudice, systematic privilege and inequality), one substantive source of conflict derives from different worldviews, which influence the ways in which humans from diverse racial groups understand and relate to each other. If by worldview, we mean "the gestalt of internalized beliefs, values, and schemattitudes through which self, others, and the larger world are experienced and explained" (Shealy, 2016, p. 47), then one's worldview may include preconceived notions regarding individuals of other cultural backgrounds, including prejudices and stereotypes (Aronson, 2012). Many disciplines, including psychology, sociology, and education have attempted to understand why prejudice and stereotyping occur, identifying factors such as social categorization, parental influence, interaction with peers, media influence, heritability of attitudes, individual differences in authoritarianism or social dominance orientation, previous personal experiences, and extant contingencies, which may sanction individuals and groups differently depending upon personal characteristics such as ethnicity (Brown, 2010; Stangor, 2009). Likewise, multiple interventions have attempted to promote positive intercultural relations such as multicultural education in schools, intergroup contact/dialogue (Allport, 1954; Pettigrew & Tropp, 2006), and transformative learning experiences (Gorski, 2006).

The following literature reviews the values-based nature of "multicultural education," as well as its underlying goals and methodologies. Factors that appear to influence the effectiveness of such educational interventions (e.g., instructor characteristics, instructional methodology, multicultural curricula) as well as behaviors and attributes of individuals who conduct them (e.g., current beliefs and values, experiences that mediate worldview) are considered. To examine the potential perils of attempting to teach tolerance, literature related to student resistance strategies and theories of cultural identity change also are discussed. Then, findings are presented from a multiyear, multi-institution initiative—the Forum BEVI Project—which examine the processes and outcomes of international, multicultural, and transformative learning (e.g., see Chapter 4 and www.ibavi.org/content/featured-projects). Implications of this project are juxtaposed with questions for consideration that are at the heart of the rationale for developing and implementing such programs and courses. Such questions include: How is the formation of worldviews affected by Formative Variables (e.g., demographic characteristics; life history)? What is the etiological basis of human belief systems? If and when our capacity to reflect upon our own worldview is exceeded by the experiential demands placed upon us, what are the consequences in terms of learning? The theoretical framework for answering these questions will be grounded in the Equil-integration (EI) model, which seeks to explain ". . . the processes by which beliefs, values, and worldviews are acquired and maintained, why their alteration is typically resisted, and how and under what circumstances their modification occurs" as well as the Beliefs, Events, and Values Inventory (BEVI) method, which is "designed to identify and predict a variety of developmental, affective, and attributional processes and outcomes that are integral to EI Theory" (Shealy, 2004, p. 1075) (see also www.ibavi.org/content/featured-projects).

THE ORIGINS AND PRINCIPLES OF MULTICULTURAL EDUCATION

Multicultural education has been described as ". . .an idea or concept, an educational reform movement, and a process" as well as a method of improving intercultural awareness and a central component in the reduction of prejudice and racism among diverse groups (Banks, 2005, p. 3; see also Bennett, 2003). Sleeter and Grant (1987) further describe multicultural education as a reform movement aimed at modifying both the content of education and the processes by which it occurs. In terms of goals, Banks (1993) contends multicultural education should:

> . . .help students to understand how knowledge is constructed. Students should be given opportunities to investigate and determine how cultural assumptions, frames of references, perspectives, and the biases within a discipline influence the ways the knowledge is constructed. Students should also be given opportunities to create knowledge themselves and identify ways in which the knowledge they construct is influenced and limited by their personal assumptions, positions, and experiences. (p. 11)

In the United States, multicultural education likely has its clearest origins in response to the Civil Rights Movement, which eventually developed into the Black Power movement, and later evolved to encompass the needs and agendas of many other minority groups, such as women (Bennett, 2001). At the same time, although the 1954 *Brown v. Board of Education* decision by the U.S. Supreme Court marked the official end of segregation in schools, children and youth from minority backgrounds continued to be denied equal access to education for reasons that seemed often arbitrary at best, if not wantonly prejudicial. As Bennett further documents, the K-12 curricula reflected these biases in its codification of an Anglo-European American worldview across the entire spectrum of academic content.

Multicultural education had its genesis in response to such historical and sociocultural factors, culminating by the 1970s into a burgeoning set of core values and principles. Even so, many scholars contend that a unifying definition of what multicultural education is, and should be, is lacking (Bennett, 2001). As such, Gorski (2006) examined conceptualizations offered by leading multicultural education pioneers such as Nieto (2000), Sleeter (1996), Grant and Sleeter (1998), and Banks (2004) in order to identify principles that define the field. His analysis yielded the following five overarching commonalities (p. 165):

1. Multicultural education is a political movement and process that attempts to secure social justice for historically and presently underserved students.
2. Multicultural education recognizes that, while some individual classroom practices are consistent with multicultural education philosophies, social justice is an institutional matter and as such, can be secured only through comprehensive school reform.
3. Multicultural education insists that comprehensive school reform can be achieved only through critical analysis of systems of power and privilege.
4. The underlying goal of multicultural education—the purpose of this critical analysis—is the elimination of educational inequities.
5. Multicultural education is good education for all students.

Historically and currently, despite its good intentions, research suggests that actual multicultural education practice tends to fail in its realization of these principles at multiple levels (Gorski, 2006). For example, using qualitative content analysis, Gorski (2009) evaluated 45 syllabi from multicultural teacher education courses taught within the United States. His focus was on the ways in which multicultural education is outlined in course descriptions, goals, and objectives. Findings suggest that although the majority of the courses included in his analysis were intended to prepare teachers with "cultural sensitivity, tolerance, and multicultural competence"

(p. 316), only 26.7% were designed in a way that was consistent with the defining principles of multicultural education.

> In other words, most of the syllabi failed to frame multicultural education as a political movement concerned with social justice, as an approach for comprehensive reform, as a critical analysis of power and privilege, or as a process for eliminating educational inequities. (p. 316)

Along similar lines, Banks (1996) proposed that five types of knowledge should be taught in multicultural curriculum: personal/cultural, popular, mainstream academic, transformative academic, and school knowledge. Specifically, personal or cultural knowledge refers to the influence of personal experiences across diverse environments that contribute to the types of interpretations and explanations that students hold. Popular knowledge consists of concepts, interpretations, and beliefs that are depicted by and through the mass media, including movies and television. Mainstream academic knowledge refers to the traditional "Western-oriented canon" (p. 14), such as that seen in the social and behavioral sciences. Transformative academic knowledge has to do with challenging current paradigms and mainstream academic knowledge in such a way that current theories and explanations are able to be reviewed and revised. Last, school knowledge encompasses facts that are present in student texts, instructor lectures, and other media forms (Banks, 1996).

Multicultural Education in Learning Institutions

Bennett (2001) contends that curricular reform activities are highly salient to the goals of multicultural education since such efforts have resulted in an emphasis on contributions made by ethnic minorities and women, which further have led to scholarly revisions (e.g., of world and U.S. histories). Such research likely has its most significant impact upon university-level curricula, subsequently resulting in novel courses, academic departments, and programs. Many higher education institutions actually have implemented formal diversity experiences into their curricula (e.g., courses addressing issues of diversity). Based upon the most recent identified survey of diversity requirements in higher education published by the Association of American Colleges and Universities (2000), 62% of colleges and universities either currently have a diversity requirement or were in the process of developing one (54% had a diversity requirement in place, and 8% were in the process of developing one at the time they were surveyed). According to this same survey, however, of those institutions that have a requirement in place, 12% exempt certain students from the requirement (for unarticulated reasons), and 44% allow students to fulfill the requirement without having to address issues of diversity within the United States (e.g., through courses that address diversity outside the United States or non-Western culture courses).

From the standpoint of specific disciplinary emphases, a number of professional organizations have promulgated diversity requirements at the level of curricula or programs. As only one example, Wyatt-Nichol and Antwi-Boasiako (2008) evaluated the National Association of Schools of Public Affairs and Administration (NASPAA) standards—*Diversity Across the Curriculum*—which now require master's degree programs in public affairs, policy, and administration to include a diversity focus in their program activities and curricula. The researchers were interested both in determining the extent to which diversity training is included in these programs, as well as the perception of the standard itself according to program administrators. Results suggest that although administrators who responded to the researchers' survey felt that it was important for graduate programs to promote diversity awareness, the majority of training opportunities were limited to courses that assimilated diversity issues into existing courses. In addition, 68% of those surveyed indicated that they did not intend to increase the number of stand-alone diversity courses offered in the program. In examining administrator perceptions, two themes emerged: lack of clarity in terms of how such standards should be implemented as well as the need for flexibility in terms of standard implementation. The research of Wyatt-Nichol and Antwi-Boasiako succinctly demonstrates the divide between diversity education theory and practice (e.g., although administrators felt that diversity education was important, few seemed inclined or able to create novel opportunities).

Self Awareness and Multicultural Education

Despite limitations at the level of implementation, multicultural educators often emphasize the crucial role that educational institutions across the spectrum play in bolstering—or hindering—intra- and intergroup awareness in students (Banks, 2005). As Camicia (2007) observes, schools "have the potential to be effective agents of social change" (p. 225) by providing students with the necessary tools to deconstruct prejudice through comprehensive examination of conventional narratives across subject areas. Given the increased focus on multicultural education, related questions arise regarding the nature of training in the development and dissemination of such curricular material. For example, how do we prepare teaching faculty—from K-12 through higher education—to teach multicultural educational materials in a way that is appropriate? What practices currently are recommended and how do we know they are effective? What is the role of the multicultural educator in facilitating the overall goals of multicultural education? As Feistritzer (2011) contends, "Who teachers are, where they are coming from and what they think are of great interest to every segment of society" (p. viii), particularly within the diverse and value-laden field of multicultural education. Along these lines, Sfeir-Younis (1993) describes three basic principles that apply to all multicultural education: (a) an individual's race, gender, ethnicity, and cultural background influence his or her worldviews, as well as the experience he or she has in the classroom and understanding of course content; (b) power dynamics in the classroom influence student participation, their ability to trust and feel safe in the classroom environment, and the interactions in which they engage; and (c) the educational experience should be approached in such a way that all students in the classroom are able to benefit through the recognition and validation of diverse student experiences.

Adherence to such principles requires specific skills in order to address the needs of all students in an individualized but equitable manner while validating the relevance of diverse cultures and worldviews (Bennett, 2003). However, other scholars suggest that training in cultural competency typically is limited to courses that incorporate diversity issues into existing courses or stand-alone diversity courses (Wyatt-Nichol & Antwi-Boasiako, 2008). Brown (2004a, 2004b) argues that in limiting student experience to stand-alone diversity courses, preexisting stereotypical perceptions by students of self and other may inadvertently be reinforced. If and when they occur, such antithetical outcomes could be due to many different factors. For example, Brown (2004a, 2004b) points to student resentment of, or resistance to, multicultural education resulting from insufficient preclass preparation, reluctance to engage in course-related activities and discussion, and a lack of overall commitment to cross-cultural engagement. Along these lines, Mildred and Zuniga (2004) found that student resistance is demonstrated via a lack of awareness of the relevancy of diversity issues, lack of acknowledgment in terms of the need to self-reflect, and minimizing or undermining classroom activities—consciously or unconsciously—that are designed to address these issues. In addition, Brown (2004b) contends that:

> . . .student resistance is further exacerbated by the lack of opportunity to: build and sustain a class community, facilitate postclass peer interaction and support, augment student/expert dialogues, develop interdisciplinary connections, and monitor preclass preparation and comprehension. Finally, the race, ethnicity, and/or gender of an instructor, may also influence resistance. (p. 537)

On the potential consequences of student resistance, Whitehead and Wittig (2005) note that ". . .if students reject the messages of an intervention, fail to recognize its value and actively participate in it, then it is unlikely that the intervention will achieve its desired results" (p. 4).

Not surprisingly then, one best practice for teaching multicultural content is for educators to engage in a systematic evaluation of their own backgrounds and histories, understanding how such processes may have influenced their own personal beliefs and values as well as their subsequent experience of and interactions with individuals from other cultures (Shealy, 2004). Such self-examination may not only facilitate the effective sharing of multicultural content, but also enhance the receptivity of those who are exposed to such material. As Banks (1994) contends:

> Because the teacher mediates the messages and symbols communicated to the students through the curriculum, it is important for teachers to understand their own personal and cultural values and identities in order for them to help students from diverse racial, ethnic, and cultural groups to develop clarified identities and relate positively to each other. (p. 250)

Likewise, Gay (2010) also recommends a focus on increasing self awareness, to include apprehending one's own beliefs and values, since such factors may significantly impact how content is developed and conveyed. In addition to self-appraisal, it is also important for multicultural educators to acquire specific knowledge about why multicultural education is necessary in the first place. As Bennett (2003) notes,

> Teaching aimed at reducing prejudice and discrimination can be difficult as well as rewarding. It requires an understanding of the prevalence and nature of prejudice, as well as clarity about key concepts such as prejudice, stereotype, discrimination, racism, and sense of racial or ethnic identity. (pp. 73–74)

Therefore, multicultural educators would be well-advised to engage in regular evaluations of self as well as teacher–student dynamics in the classroom, and evaluate how these processes may be impacting the effectiveness of their educational interventions.

Theories of Cultural Identity Change

Consistent with the preceding prescriptions and proscriptions, it may be helpful to highlight leading theoretical propositions regarding the nature of change vis-à-vis multicultural education. Here, we focus on three such models in order to illustrate the types of perspectives that are relevant to an understanding of *why* change may, or may not, occur (see McAllister & Irvine, 2000). First, Helms's (1990) model of White racial identity development consists of six stages, and focuses upon relations and interactions between Black and White individuals. White individuals enter the first stage, *contact*, when they encounter "the idea or the actuality of Black people" (p. 55). During this stage, White individuals either are curious or fearful of Blacks depending upon their familial environment and an "inconsistent awareness of being White" (p. 55). Behaviors characteristic of this stage include limited interactions with Black individuals; when they do occur, such encounters are marked by cognitive comparisons of such individuals to racial stereotypes. The second stage, *disintegration*, typically is marked by feelings of anxiety as White individuals become consciously aware of their ethnicity and its associated privilege, with concomitant feelings of dissonance resulting from "moral dilemmas associated with being White" (p. 58). During the third stage, *reintegration*, individuals acknowledge their White identity and retreat back into White culture through avoidance or overt discrimination, while also experiencing reactive anxiety and anger perpetuated by feelings of White superiority and Black inferiority. During the *pseudo-independence* stage, White individuals begin to redefine their Caucasian identity in more positive ways. Here, Whites start to question the idea that Blacks are inherently inferior, and acknowledge their role in a racist society. This "racist identity" causes discomfort, propelling the individual to self-reflect on his or her feelings related to racial identity that emerged in the previous stages. As a result, the individual may seek increased interaction with Blacks; yet, this interaction tends to focus on trying to modify Black behavior so it is more consistent with "White criteria for success and acceptability" (p. 61). During the fifth stage, *immersion/emersion*, Whites seek out more accurate information regarding their roles and responsibilities in a racist society, shifting from a paternalistic stance vis-à-vis Blacks to greater advocacy efforts with other Whites in an effort to promote change. In the final stage, *autonomy*, Whites pursue opportunities to learn from other cultural groups, internalizing a clearer sense of their own racial identity and that of others (Helms, 1990).

Banks's (1994) Typology of Ethnic Identity also consists of six stages beginning with *ethnic psychological captivity*, wherein individuals internalize "negative ideologies and beliefs" about their own ethnic group, resulting in "ethnic self-rejection and low self-esteem" (p. 224). During this stage, the individual feels shame relative to his or her ethnic group, which may lead to avoiding individuals of other ethnic groups or significant attempts to become "highly culturally assimilated" (p. 224). In the second stage, *ethnic encapsulation*, a split emerges in the experience of dominant and marginalized cultural groups, such that groups that are marginalized may become relatively "insular" whereas dominant groups develop "mythical" feelings of superiority. During the *ethnic identity clarification* stage, all groups regardless of ethnicity begin to experience a more objective view of positive and negative attributes relative to their own group affiliation. During stage four, *biethnicity*, individuals are motivated to function in two cultures and acquire the necessary skills in order to do so.

> We can describe such an individual as biethnic. . . many African Americans, in
> order to attain social and economic mobility, learn to function effectively in Anglo-
> American culture during the formal working day. The private lives of these indi-
> viduals, however, may be highly African American and monocultural. (p. 226)

In the *multiethnicity and reflective nationalism* stage, individuals who have developed
cross cultural competencies deepen their understanding of other cultures, moving
beyond an awareness of obvious aspects (holidays, food) to deeper considerations
such as the values and practices of another culture. Finally, individuals enter the *glo-
balism and global-competency* stage, in which they learn to balance their global, national,
and ethnic identities (Banks, 1994).

As a final example, Bennett (1986) argues that to be effective in teaching intercultural communication, the subjective experience of the trainee must be considered.
More specifically,

> Since intercultural sensitivity is not 'natural' to any single culture, the develop-
> ment of this ability demands new awareness and attitudes. As trainers, we need
> to know how the attitude of intercultural sensitivity develops so we can facili-
> tate precise movement in that direction (p. 180).

Understanding where individuals may fall along a continuum of cultural sensitivity
can assist educators in selecting appropriate methods and sequencing certain programmatic elements based on how students might respond to such material. Bennett's
Developmental Model of Intercultural Sensitivity (1986) is offered as a model to assist
in this process, which begins with a period of *denial* by members of the majority
group. Here, individuals are not aware that worldviews exist that are different from
their own as a result of isolation from such cultural differences. During the second
stage, *defense*, recognition of differences occurs, with accompanying efforts directed
to preservation of one's own views through denigration of other cultures and/or the
attribution of superiority to one's own. In the third stage, *minimization*, cultural differences are acknowledged yet minimized, overshadowed by perceived cultural similarities. Individuals in this stage minimize cultural differences through a belief in
certain universal principles that are thought to underlie all of human behavior. The
fourth stage, *acceptance*, is characterized by the recognition that individuals of diverse
cultures have different worldviews and ways of behaving. Here, difference is no longer seen as a "thing" but rather as a "process" (p. 185). During the fifth stage, *adaptation*, behavioral and psychological changes occur in the way that one's own reality is
processed, in one's conduct toward different cultures, and in the capacity to take the
perspective of a culture that is different from one's own. The final stage, *integration*, is
characterized by contextual evaluation, or the ability to evaluate phenomena from
another perspective or within different cultural contexts, and constructive marginal-
ity, in which people are able to stand apart from all cultural perspectives, including
their own, while also engaging in an ongoing process of self-examination vis-à-vis
culture (Bennett, 1986; McAllister & Irvine, 2000; see also Hammer, 2012).

Examining the Effectiveness of Multicultural Education

Informed by such theoretical frameworks regarding how multicultural identity
evolves, it is worth asking if multicultural education actually accomplishes that
which it intends. Despite calls to evaluate the effectiveness of multicultural education

and better prepare multicultural educators, institutions often resist the evaluation of whether their programs are effective as well as the attendant modification to extant curricula (Brown, 2006; Bennett, 2003). Exceptions do occur, however, and we highlight a few exemplars here.

For example, Brown (2006) examined the relative impact of transformative learning strategies on the beliefs and attitudes of preservice teachers regarding issues of diversity and multiculturalism. Participants included 40 educational administration graduate students in a Southeastern university, who were enrolled full time in a 2-year master's program in school administration. The study was designed to evaluate student responsiveness to a diversity curriculum spanning 2 years. During the first year of study, students were required to enroll in a social context course titled *The Social Context of Leadership*. As Brown describes,

> Social context provides a retrospective, contemporary, and prospective evaluation of the social, cultural, political, economical, and philosophical contexts from which the current issues that affect school and schooling have evolved. During this foundations course, students are asked to investigate the trends in educational studies, as well as the social and academic goals of education. (p. 714)

During the second year of study, students engaged in an internship at various school sites, which included a seminar with reflective practices related to the challenges that faced them as educational leaders. Throughout both experiences, students completed weekly reflective analysis journals.

Brown (2006) describes such curricular content as falling under the rubric of transformative learning in that it "can lead to a transformation of one's personal agency as well as deepen one's sense of social responsibility toward and with others" (p. 706). Grounded in adult learning theory, transformative learning theory, and critical social theory, the program employed methods that have been identified by previous researchers including critical reflection, policy praxis, and rational discourse in order to assess whether these strategies can increase student perception of growth in the areas of acknowledgment, awareness, and action toward social justice (Brown, 2006). At the beginning and conclusion of this 2-year program of study, students completed the Cultural and Educational Issues Survey (Version B), a 63-item questionnaire aimed at discerning the attitudes of preservice leaders concerning issues of education and culture. Previous analysis suggested this instrument has strong reliability (Cronbach's alpha 0.92). In terms of qualitative assessment, students completed weekly reflective analysis journals as a component of the social context course described previously; engaged in a structured internship with a seminar component designed to foster integration of theory and practice based on their internship experience; completed a cultural autobiography and life history interview; participated in a 1-day prejudice-reduction workshop; conducted a cross-cultural interview; engaged in an "educational plunge" where they visited a setting they had never been before and reflected on this experience in writing; researched and facilitated a class focused on a marginalized group and their educational experience in the United States; and finally, created policies and practices that fostered equitable education for all students (Brown, 2006).

The results of the quantitative analysis suggest that participating in transformative learning strategies such as those listed may improve preservice teachers' attitudes relative to diversity in education (i.e., posttest scores on the Cultural and Educational Issues Survey Version B were significantly lower than pretest scores at the $p < .001$ level, which suggests preservice teachers' attitudes toward diversity and education can be improved through participation in transformative learning strategies). However, two caveats are offered for these conclusions. First, it cannot be determined whether results are attributable to the transformative learning strategies employed, the instructors' personal style, and/or the course material. Second, the study employed a small sample size and did not utilize random assignment, limiting definitive interpretations of the observed results.

From a qualitative standpoint, students reported growth in the areas of "awareness of self," "acknowledgment of others," and "action" through policy practice. During this 2-year program,

> students wondered, questioned, and hesitated. They reportedly stretched themselves, pushed their boundaries, grew, and developed. Many of the learner responses were emotionally laden. At times, they revealed being amazed, enthralled, awakened, and grateful. At other times, they were afraid, stressed, angry, and guilt ridden. (Brown, 2006, p. 719)

Despite the important caveats (e.g., regarding the etiology of these changes), Brown (2006) argues that such results "can help educational administration programs begin to better understand the connections between leadership preparation experiences and the knowledge, disposition, and skills garnered" (p. 732).

From the standpoint of teacher preparation, McAllister and Irvine (2000) focused on the type of training that preservice teachers receive prior to delivering multicultural education content. Overall, they found that much attention is focused on *content* with relatively little emphasis on the *process* of cross-cultural learning. In other words, theories of change such as those noted previously, which might help understand what is or is not "happening" and why, are de-emphasized relative to the acquisition of content knowledge. Their overarching point is that greater awareness of underlying processes associated with exposure to multicultural education programs (e.g., resistance) can help teachers understand better how to sequence course content and create environments that are more conducive to learning.

Along these lines, some scholars focus explicitly upon intrapsychic processes that are thought to be integral to the effectiveness of multicultural education. For example, in their analysis of the literature, Mildred and Zuniga (2004) found that the relationship between developmental and psychological issues and students' readiness to engage in the necessary components of multicultural education are critical in regard to both process and outcome. Brown (2004a) further evaluated such processes by examining the role of instructor methodology on the resistance of teacher education students to cultural diversity awareness. Study participants included 109 junior-level students enrolled in a required, stand-alone cultural diversity course at a midsized, urban, Midwestern University (only Caucasian students [n = 100] were included in the analysis). This course is taught in two segments; the current study focused on the first 10 weeks of the course, which emphasize diversity in learners (including culture, class, gender, race, ethnicity, and religion). The study employed a mixed methods design. Qualitative data in the form of reflective journals, reaction papers, field experiences, and research projects were collected throughout the semester in order to measure incremental changes in student attitudes, beliefs, and behaviors. In addition, students were administered the Cultural Diversity Awareness Inventory (CDAI) as a pretest and posttest measure in order to examine the effects of instructional methodology on changes in cultural diversity awareness. The CDAI is a 28-item questionnaire, which uses a 5-point Likert scale and reports excellent psychometric properties. For the purposes of this particular study, instrument items were divided into five subtests, including diversity awareness, classroom environment, family/school interaction, cross-cultural communication, and alternative assessment. Previous researchers consistently have identified these areas as essential in preparing informed multicultural educators. Prior to conducting this study, Brown completed observations of, and interviews with, students and instructors in two stand-alone diversity courses, and then implemented a pilot study to determine appropriate test materials and strategies for the current research study. The pilot study (i.e., the modified course which emerged from the interviews and observations of the two stand-alone diversity courses) was focused on "reducing resistance by increasing self awareness and a cognizance of others" (p. 329).

Students were divided into two groups. Group 1 was taught by the investigator and employed all instructional strategies and materials implemented in the pilot phase of the study. Class periods 1 to 8 were focused on creating an understanding of why cultures develop, their interdependence, and resistance to change (Great Fruit Race simulation); self-examination and cultural influence ("cultural puzzle" activity); in-depth examination of cultural bias (role-play activity and "same and different" simulation); and fostering cross-cultural awareness through cooperative groups. Field experiences for Group 1 included three separate interactions with an ethnic culture (minimum of 6 hours); students then were required to discuss their field experience with their group members (four students in each group) and write an individual and group reflection paper. In addition, Group 1 also completed a research project consisting of a 12- to 15-page paper and group presentation designed to examine marginalized cultures, explore educational issues within this identified culture, investigate initiatives designed to minimize impediments to this culture's academic and social development, and develop strategies that can be used in the classroom to meet the needs of all children.

Group 2 was taught by two instructors who had been observed and interviewed during the pilot study and followed their own previous course format. These courses included: viewing videos portraying atrocities against historically marginalized ethnic groups and completing a "cultural worksheet"; reading an article focused on racism in education, viewing a video depicting slavery, and engaging in a class discussion; and participating in a simulation designed to increase empathy for marginal cultural groups. Additional course content included guest speakers, videos, class discussion, and articles concerning religion, gender, language, and ethnic discrimination. Group 2's field experience included three observations (and in a few cases tutoring) of students at an inner-city elementary school. Group 2's research project consisted of a 2- to 3-page reaction paper, which asked students to identify a social problem, describe it, and use five different sources to help explain why this problem exists. It should be noted that the same message and text were used for both groups; however, course goals, instructional strategies, and objectives were not identical as indicated in the preceding.

Quantitative results indicate a significant relationship between CDAI scores at pretest and posttest depending upon course format. Group 1, which followed the modified course format focused on increasing student self awareness and cognizance of others, demonstrated a statistically significant increase in scores on the total diversity and family/school interactions and communication subtests ($p < .001$), and environment ($p < .01$) subtest. Group 2, which followed a course format previously employed by current instructors, demonstrated a statistically significant increase between pretest and posttest scores on the total diversity and environment subtests ($p < .05$). Except for the environment subtest, scores on all subtests improved more for Group 1 compared with Group 2. In terms of qualitative data, the researcher was unable to compile accurate statistics for Group 2 because assignments often were incomplete. Results from Group 1 indicate that by the study's conclusion, 95% indicated a need to raise their cultural awareness and increase sensitivity in multicultural classroom settings as well as in social interactions with teachers, students, and parents. In addition, 65% indicated they would research different cultures represented in their respective classrooms; 83% stated they would get involved in community projects in their school's neighborhood; and 63% indicated they would invite parents and students to informal gatherings throughout the school year. Another finding concluded that the best approach in terms of community/school interaction was to understand the beliefs, values, and traditions of one's students. In addition, 100% indicated they would employ a variety of instructional strategies in order to address the needs of culturally diverse students.

Although instructor variables and learning strategies undoubtedly play a key role in the effectiveness of diversity education, it is equally important to consider other contextual factors, such as message framing and student motivation. Recent evidence, for instance, suggests that the promotion of positive attitudes toward other cultural groups depends on the underlying source of motivation to regulate prejudice (Legault, Gutsell, & Inzlicht, 2011). Using the theoretical foundation of self-determination theory, Legault et al. (2011) developed two prejudice-reduction interventions designed to induce either internally generated motivation to reduce prejudice (autonomous) or externally elicited motivation (controlled). In line with past work suggesting that those with an autonomous motivation to be nonprejudiced also displayed less prejudice and discrimination than those with a controlled motivation (e.g., Legault & Green-Demers, 2012; Legault, Green-Demers, Grant, & Chung, 2007; Legault, Green-Demers, & Eadie, 2009; Plant & Devine, 1998), the authors created two different types of motivational messages. These messages were conveyed in brochures, which were framed as a campus-wide initiative to reduce prejudice and promote diversity. Thus, non-Black undergraduates (N = 103) were assigned randomly to one of three conditions: the autonomy brochure condition, the controlling brochure condition, or the no-brochure condition. The autonomy brochure aimed to promote autonomous motivation toward prejudice reduction by emphasizing the value, importance, and personal significance of nonprejudice and diversity. It outlined the various benefits of diverse and fair classrooms and societies, and also highlighted the ways that diversity and intergroup relating can be meaningful and enjoyable. The controlling brochure, in contrast, targeted controlled motivation by stressing the social requirement to be nonprejudiced. The need for political correctness was underscored and the negative consequences of failing to behave in nonprejudiced ways were described. Students in the no-brochure (i.e., neutral) condition read basic information related to the definition and problem of prejudice, but motivation to be nonprejudiced was not manipulated. After carefully reading the brochures, participants' degrees of autonomous versus controlled motivation to be nonprejudiced and their levels of prejudice were ascertained using the 24-item Motivation to be Nonprejudiced Scale (Legault et al., 2007) and the Symbolic Racism 2000 Scale (Henry & Sears, 2002).

Results indicated that those in the autonomy brochure condition demonstrated significantly less prejudice than those in the no-brochure condition. In other words, supporting autonomous motivation for being nonprejudiced decreased prejudice (Legault et al., 2011). In contrast, promoting prejudice reduction using controlling tactics elicited an ironic effect; those who read the controlling brochure demonstrated more prejudice than those in the no-brochure condition. As the authors noted, an attempt to control prejudice reduction using pressure was worse in terms of outcomes than doing nothing at all. Because the researchers employed an explicit measure of prejudice—which they thought might have alerted subjects to the fact that their level of prejudice was being assessed (thus affecting validity through social desirability effects)—they conducted a follow-up study using more implicit manipulation and measurement.

In this second experiment, 109 non-Black undergraduate students were once again randomly assigned to conditions aimed at manipulating autonomous or controlled motivation to reduce prejudice. However, in this study, motivational priming was achieved more subtly through the use of items embedded in a survey. That is, participants were induced to agree with either autonomous reasons (e.g., "I value diversity") or controlled reasons (e.g., "Prejudiced people are not well-liked") for being nonprejudiced (versus a neutral, no-prime condition). Motivation to be non-prejudiced then was assessed before participants completed the Symbolic Racism Scale and performed the Implicit Association Test (Greenwald, McGhee, & Schwartz, 1998), which is a measure of automatic racial bias. Results suggested that the priming manipulation was successful in targeting differences in the source of motivation to regulate prejudice. That is, those primed with autonomous motivational content displayed more autonomous motivation to be nonprejudiced compared to those primed with controlled motivation or no motivation. Complementing findings from the first experiment, priming autonomous motivation to be nonprejudiced reduced prejudice relative to the neutral, no-prime condition. In addition, priming controlled motivation to be nonprejudiced ironically increased prejudice, relative to no motivational priming. Importantly, these effects held across both implicit and explicit measures of prejudice. Thus, even subtle or implicit messages relating to motivation to control prejudice can exert vastly divergent effects on prejudice and attitudes toward outgroups. Moreover, the source of motivation matters. Interventions that support autonomous motivation to be nonprejudiced appear to be more effective than the controlling approach that is so often used in anti-prejudice programming and policy. Indeed, whether it is explicitly controlled or subtly prompted, Legault et al. (2011) show that external motivation to comply with nonprejudiced standards is more detrimental to the goal of prejudice reduction than doing nothing at all.

Perhaps the most basic conclusion from these findings is that multicultural education programs and courses may "work," but the likelihood of their effectiveness is enhanced substantially if one: (a) adopts a sufficiently sophisticated conceptual framework regarding the underlying mediators of change; (b) takes "who students are" prior to the experience into account; and (c) recognizes potentially powerful priming and motivational processes, which may mediate the degree to which multicultural education is experienced as imposed, congruent, or welcomed.

The complexity of such interacting processes is revealed in a meta-analysis by Engberg (2004), who reviewed related studies in four primary domains: multicultural courses, peer-based interventions, service-based interventions, and diversity workshops and training. Although the overall conclusion was positive in that these various experiences were determined to reduce prejudice, multiple theoretical, empirical, and methodological limitations across studies meant that firm conclusions were not possible. Moreover, four specific limitations were noted: (a) lack of conceptualization or a guiding theoretical framework; (b) insufficient instruments employed to measure racial bias; (c) quasi-experimental designs (e.g., convenience sampling, short study durations, lack of control for confounds, the absence of longitudinal analyses); and (d) the insufficient demarcation of different groups on the basis of important background variables (e.g., race, gender), which may have obscured differences and inflated positive findings. In the context of overall positive findings—by addressing these limitations at the level of theory, methods, and analysis—Engberg believes that research in the effectiveness of multicultural education strategies such as the reduction of racial bias could significantly be enhanced.

The aforementioned literature reveals a number of important suggestions and themes, which we seek to address in the current study. In conducting our analysis, we will touch on a range of issues that were referenced earlier including (a) the processes by which multicultural content is conveyed; (b) the role that differences among students may play in ultimate outcomes of such a course; (c) the relative degree to which faculty and students are or are not prepared for the multicultural education experience they are about to facilitate and encounter; (d) the effect that underlying psychological processes (e.g., affective, attributional) may have in mediating course outcomes; (e) whether the required course (e.g., in this case, a "World Cultures" course) actually achieved its desired impact of enhancing multicultural tolerance and appreciation by students; and (f) any implications that emerge from this analysis for the design, implementation, and understanding of how multicultural education should, and should not, be conveyed. In an attempt to address these questions, we next highlight EI Theory, the EI Self, and the BEVI, an interrelated model, framework, and method that have been in development since the early 1990s, to examine and apprehend the processes by which beliefs and values are acquired, maintained, and transformed.

EI Theory, the EI Self, and the BEVI

EI Theory seeks to explain "the processes by which beliefs, values, and 'worldviews' are acquired and maintained, why their alteration is typically resisted, and how and under what circumstances their modification occurs" (Shealy, 2004, p. 1075). Derivative of EI Theory,

> the Equilintegration or EI Self seeks to represent in pictographic form the integrative and synergistic processes by which beliefs and values are acquired, maintained, and modified as well as how these are linked to the *Formative Variables* (FoVs), *Core Needs*, (CoNes), and *Adaptive Potential* (AP) of the self. (Shealy, 2016, p. 96)

Informed by scholarship in a range of key areas (e.g., "needs-based" research and theory; developmental psychopathology; social cognition; psychotherapy processes and outcomes; affect regulation; theories and models of "self"), the EI Self seeks to illustrate how the interaction between our core needs (e.g., for attachment, affiliation) and Formative Variables (e.g., caregiver, culture) results in beliefs and values about self, others, and the world at large that we all internalize over the course of development and across the life span.

Concomitant with EI Theory and the EI Self, the BEVI is a comprehensive analytic tool in development since the early 1990s that examines how and why we come to see ourselves, others, and the larger world as we do (e.g., how life experiences, culture, and context affect our beliefs, values, and worldview) as well as the influence of such processes on multiple aspects of human functioning (e.g., learning processes, relationships, personal growth, the pursuit of life goals). For example, the BEVI assesses processes such as: basic openness; the tendency to (or not to) stereotype in particular ways; self- and emotional awareness; preferred strategies for making sense of why "other" people and cultures "do what they do"; global engagement (e.g., receptivity to different cultures, religions, and social practices); and worldview shift (e.g., to what degree do beliefs and values change as a result of specific experiences). BEVI results are translated into reports at the individual, group, and organizational levels and used in a variety of contexts for applied and research purposes (e.g., to track and examine changes in worldviews over time) (e.g., Anmuth et al., 2013; Atwood, Chkhaidze, Shealy, Staton, & Staton, 2014; Brearly, Shealy, Staton, & Sternberger, 2012; Hill et al., 2013; Shealy, 2004, 2016; Shealy, Bhuyan, & Sternberger, 2012; Tabit et al., 2011; for more information about the EI model and BEVI method, see Chapters 2, 3, and 4 as well as www.ibavi.org/content/featured-projects).

METHODS AND RESULTS

Study 1: When the Promotion of Cultural Engagement May Not Be Effective

Students enrolled in a midsized, rural, Midwestern University were selected for the following analysis (N = 137), aimed at better understanding the degree to which undergraduate students benefit or do not benefit from participation in diversity courses (i.e., World Cultures). World Cultures is part of a four-course general education requirement that all enrolled students complete during their first 2 years of study. As described in the syllabus, the purpose of this course is to provide students with the necessary tools to understand and appreciate the diverse cultures that they will encounter throughout their personal and professional lives. Study 1 employed a one-group pretest–posttest design, utilizing a convenience sample.

All students who were enrolled in the World Cultures course were included in the analysis. Students registered for one of four sections of the course online; each section was taught by a different instructor. In terms of demographics, 3 students identified as Black or African American, 126 Caucasian/White, 0 Asian or Pacific Islander, 1 American Indian or Alaskan Native, 2 Hispanic/Latino, and 5 Other. The mean age was 18.91 (standard deviation SD = 2.8 years); the number of males was 111 and the number of females was 26.

Students who chose to participate in the research project were provided with a username and password and asked to complete the 336-item BEVI pretest during the beginning of the course. Student participation was voluntary and informed consent was required before completion of the BEVI could commence. At the conclusion of the course, students were asked again to complete the BEVI as a posttest measure. Upon completion, analysis of pre–post data was analyzed across all BEVI scales using repeated measures analysis of variance (ANOVA). This study was exploratory in nature, and as such, research questions focused mainly on whether Time 1/Time 2 differences would be observed, and if so, on which BEVI scales. Given the goals of the course, it was anticipated that some changes would be observed—in a positive or desired direction—particularly on scales that purport to measure sociocultural openness and global engagement.

As indicated in Table 5.1, results overall suggest that the World Cultures course, designed to facilitate learning outcomes including sociocultural openness and tolerance for cultures different from one's own, appears to be associated with the opposite effects. More specifically, upon completion of the course as compared to course entry, students were more rigid in their belief systems, more inclined to endorse simple causal attributions regarding why human beings do what they do, more emotionally aware and activated, and less open to developing a deeper engagement with other

TABLE 5.1
Degree of Worldview Shift

SCALES	TIME			GENDER		
	PRE	**POST**	**F**	**FEMALE**	**MALE**	**F**
Causal Closure	1.229	1.317	7.780 (1, 133)**	1.196	1.351	11.595 (1, 133)***
Basic Determinism	1.718	1.856	9.187 (1, 134)***	1.615	1.958	19.196 (1, 134)***
Emotional Attunement	3.013	3.133	6.920 (1, 133)**	3.257	2.889	13.581 (1, 133)***
Global Engagement	2.647	2.579	4.454 (1, 134)*	2.691	2.535	7.662 (1, 134)**

Note. $*p < .05$, $**p < .01$, $***p < .001$.

cultures. Although it cannot unequivocally be concluded that the course is "causing" these changes—or even that greater "negative" changes might have emerged had the course not occurred—it is striking that theoretically desirable attributes (e.g., openness, engagement) diminished over the duration of the course.

In addition to observed Time 1/Time 2 differences, a second trend emerged with the data analysis in terms of gender differences (see Table 5.1). In comparison to males, females endorsed a greater degree of openness and ability to hold cognitive complexity, as well as a less rigid sense of self, at both pretest and posttest. When looking at each of the BEVI scales included in the analysis specifically, our results indicate that Basic Determinism and Causal Closure, which collectively measure (among other factors) the degree to which individuals prefer basic/simple explanations for why people think, feel, and behave in particular ways indicate that females endorse this way of thinking to a lesser degree at both pretest and posttest. At the same time, scores on the Basic Determinism and Causal Closure scales increase for both genders from precourse to postcourse. On the Emotional Attunement scale, which measures the degree to which an individual is aware of and accessible to affect in self and other, results suggest that females endorse a higher degree of Emotional Attunement as compared to males at pretest and posttest; however, at course completion both males and females indicated a higher degree of emotional attunement. These intriguing results suggest perhaps that both male and female students may be more emotionally activated at the conclusion of the course, but such activation is not experienced as positive, at least when juxtaposed with the overall pattern across the other scales noted previously (which suggests less openness to, and engagement with, "the other" overall).

One hypothesis we propose to explain this finding is the possibility that students begin reevaluating how their own experiences influenced the development of personal belief and value systems, particularly in relation to content disseminated throughout the course, at a time of acute emotional activation (i.e., at the conclusion of the course). Implications for future research emerging from this finding include the following: (a) Re-administer the BEVI after a specified amount of time has elapsed following course completion to determine whether allowing students additional time to reflect on course material would lead to deactivation on this specific scale, as well as across other BEVI scales (e.g., as a Time 3 administration); and (b) Extend the length of such courses over more than one semester. Perhaps providing students with additional structured time to engage in both course material and self-reflection would create a deeper sense of personal understanding regarding the etiology of one's own beliefs and values, as well as allow for more openness related to diverse perspectives and cultural frameworks (e.g., see Wandschneider et al., 2016).[1] Finally, data from the Global Engagement BEVI scale—which measures an individual's level of empathy, emotional openness, the degree to which he or she values respectful relations and healthy traditions within and between cultures, cultural awareness, inclination toward advocacy efforts, and concern for the environment—indicate a decrease on this scale both for males and females upon the completion of this course.

In short, from a programmatic standpoint, a course designed to create deeper understanding of the larger world should theoretically be associated with greater sophistication regarding why humans do what they do as well as greater engagement with the larger world. However, as evidenced by these results, participation in the course appears to be associated with the opposite tendencies, a finding that not only is supported by the statistically significant findings, but also by other trends across various scales, such as Identity Diffusion, which suggests that individuals may feel more unclear or stuck vis-à-vis who they are and where they are going at the conclusion of the course ($p < .08$). Statistical analysis also revealed that females in general appear to be significantly more open than males to the sorts of outcomes that would theoretically be desirable for such a course, not only across the scales listed previously, but on other BEVI Scales such as Socioemotional Convergence, which indicates that females at this developmental stage may have a greater capacity than males to "hold" complexity, in terms of beliefs and values that may superficially appear opposed, but in fact are reconcilable ($p < .001$). In other words, females overall tended to be significantly more open than males to the content and objectives of this World Cultures course, a gender-based finding that receives strong support from other Forum BEVI Project analyses (Pendleton, Cochran, Kapadia, & Iyer, 2016).

In addition to gender, previous research has indicated a multitude of variables that have the potential to impact the effectiveness of multicultural interventions, including but not limited to, instructor characteristics (Banks, 1994; Gay, 2010; Bennett, 2003). Thus, as is discussed next, it would be useful to hone in on the relative contribution of specific variables to such learning processes and outcomes (see Wandschneider et al., 2016).

Study 2: Exploring the Complex Factors That Influence Sociocultural Openness

In conducting this project, the researchers were interested in gaining a better understanding of who learns what and under what circumstances as well as the factors that interact to produce particular outcomes; we also wished to understand *why*, from an explanatory standpoint, these processes may or may not occur. Study 1 was designed to evaluate the "what" of this equation, whereas further analysis (Study 2) was conducted in an attempt to gain insight into the "why" dimension. Findings of Study 1 (i.e., that individuals showed decreases in openness and engagement after completing a course designed to produce the opposite effects) beg an overarching question of

---

[1] Indeed, although such results are striking—particularly in light of the specific goals of this course—they are not without precedent from other analyses of this nature (e.g., see Wandschneider et al., 2016).

why students are responding in this way. On the one hand, experimental and mixed methods approaches could allow for a fine-grained analysis of relevant variables (e.g., potential variation among instructors, the effects of modified approaches to content delivery, examination of qualitative data to ascertain why, and which, students are having negative or positive experiences of this course). Although this sort of research is worthy of pursuit, a more basic and immediate question could be examined from the larger database of which the World Cultures participants are a part. Specifically, as previously described, the Forum BEVI Project is a multi-institution, multiyear initiative designed to understand the processes and outcomes of international, multicultural, and transformative learning. A fundamental rationale for conducting this project was the proposition that human beings learn differently in part because of who they are prior to engagement in the experience itself. Thus, it may be erroneous to attribute the results of a learning experience only to the experience itself, since there is good reason to believe that there is an interaction between who people are prior to the experience with the experience itself. This fundamental proposition is at the core of the Forum BEVI Project, and is highly relevant to the current discussion. Why? Because if students differ in their predisposition to an intercultural experience, and we could identify both commonalities and differences within a specific learning cohort, it might be possible to approach that cohort in a more nuanced and sophisticated manner vis-à-vis multicultural coursework, rather than assuming that all participants are equal. It might even be possible to integrate those very findings (about similarities and differences) into the learning experience itself. To examine these issues, we conducted a series of analyses from a larger dataset of 2,331 participants from 11 universities throughout the United States, who had completed the BEVI under the auspices of the Forum BEVI Project (see Wandschneider et al., 2016; www. ibavi.org/content/featured-projects). ANOVA, regression analysis, and structural equation modeling (SEM) were employed to analyze the results of this exploratory study.

The first set of analyses examined whether and which demographic variables might differentiate the sample at an item level of analysis, with a particular focus on sociocultural and global engagement items. As noted, gender proved to be a highly discriminating Formative Variable throughout this project (e.g., Pendleton et al., 2016). For example, on the BEVI question—*We should try to understand cultures that are different from our own*—significant differences emerged at the level of gender ($p < .01$), accounting for 5.2% of the variation in responding ($R^2 = 0.052$). In short, females appear to believe it is more important to try to understand cultures that are different from their own than do males. Similar gender-based differences ($p < .01$) also emerged for the BEVI question, *I enjoy learning about other cultures*. Females indicated greater enjoyment accounting for 7.0% of the variation in responding ($R^2 = 0.070$). As a final exemplar, for the BEVI item—*We should do more to help minority groups in our society*—both gender and political orientation differences were observed at the $p < .01$ level of significance. Specifically, females endorsed this statement more strongly than males ($R^2 = 0.044$), as did Democrats when compared to other political affiliations including Republicans, Independents, and Other ($R^2 = 0.093$) (see Edmunds, Federico, & Mays, 2016).

SEM examined the relationship between (a) specific Formative Variables, including Negative Life Events on the BEVI (which measures the degree to which individuals report unhappy childhood experiences and difficulties in life), (b) mediators, including Sociocultural Openness on the BEVI (which measures, among other subfactors, the degree to which individuals are inclined toward the beliefs and values of cultures that are different from their own), and (c) outcomes (which, in Figure 5.1, indicates the degree of *interest* an individual expresses in engaging in international

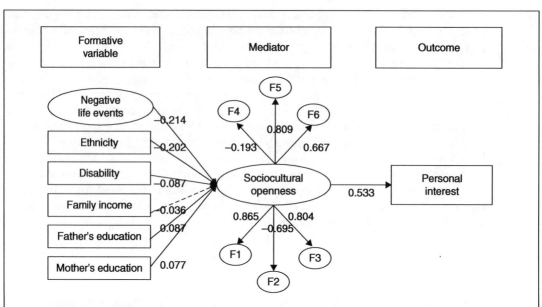

FIGURE 5.1. **The SEM association of Formative Variables (Negative Life Events), mediators (Sociocultural Openness), and outcomes (personal interest in international or multicultural learning) on the BEVI.**

Note. X^2 = 9031.527, df = 1207, p = .0000, root mean square error of approximation (RMSEA) = 0.053, comparative fit index (CFI) = 0.939.

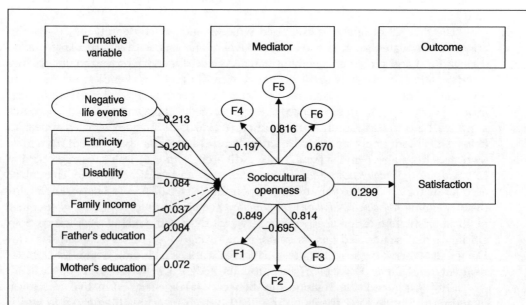

FIGURE 5.2. **The SEM association of Formative Variables (Negative Life Events), mediators (Sociocultural Openness), and outcomes (reported level of satisfaction upon the conclusion of an international or multicultural learning experience) on the BEVI.**

Note. X^2 = 8954.646, df = 1207, p = .0000, RMSEA = 0.052, CFI = 0.939.

or multicultural learning; and in Figure 5.2, indicates the degree of *satisfaction* an individual expresses after participating in an international or multicultural learning experience).[2]

Taken together, these two structural equation models offer a number of intriguing findings. For example, a higher degree of Sociocultural Openness—as well as interest in and satisfaction from a wide range of international and multicultural learning experiences—was associated with a lesser degree of reported negative/unhappy life events, a greater tendency to report non-Caucasian status, a lesser tendency to report "disability status" (e.g., physical, psychological), and a greater tendency to report more education by fathers and mothers alike. From an EI theoretical perspective, such results make sense, particularly in light of the needs-based considerations that are at the core of this framework. Specifically, the greater the degree one reports that their "core needs" were met in a "good enough" manner, the more likely that same individual will demonstrate the capacity and inclination to attend to "other" as well as "the larger world" in addition to the concerns of one's "own self" (e.g., see Chapters 2, 3, and 4).

This tentative proposition receives additional support from a final level of analysis, consisting of correlation matrix data between Sociocultural Openness and other BEVI scales as presented in Table 5.2 on the "long version" of the BEVI[3] (see also http://www.thebevi.com/docs/bevi_scale_pairwise_correlations_and_significance_levels.pdf). Essentially, these correlations suggest that the inclination to be open and accepting of cultural difference is associated with various other belief/value constructs. More specifically—and in full recognition that these are oblique constructs (i.e., statistically overlapping but differentiable factors, derived on the basis of EFA)—individuals who are higher in sociocultural openness tend to report that they had more core needs met (e.g., for acceptance, affiliation) during childhood and adolescence (Needs Closure); are more likely to be concerned about the environment and natural world (Ecological Resonance); are more likely to hold and tolerate cognitive/affective complexity or ambiguity (Socioemotional Convergence); are less likely to deny basic thoughts, feelings, or needs (Basic Closedness); are less likely to feel stuck, lost, or confused (Identity Diffusion); are more likely to be interested in and open to affect in self and other (Emotional Attunement); are less likely to report traditional religious beliefs (Socioreligious Traditionalism); are less likely to insist that they are completely confident and assured about who they are (Hard Structure); are less likely

---

[2] As described in Chapter 4 of this book, Negative Life Events consists of self-report statements regarding one's own upbringing and life history. Among other dimensions, Socioemotional Convergence measures the degree to which individuals demonstrate an overarching capacity to "hold complexity" (i.e., avoid black and white characterizations regarding how the world "is" and "should be"). For more information, see www.thebevi.com.

From an interpretive standpoint, ethnicity is a dummy measured variable; value "0" indicates the respondent is a minority, and "1" means the respondent is a Caucasian. Disability also is a dummy variable; "0" indicates the person is not eligible for services for students with disabilities, and "1" means otherwise. Family income is measured by a series of numbers indicating the respondent's annual family income. It ranges from "1" (Less than $10,000) to "10" ($175,000 or more). Both father's education and mother's education are ordinal measured variables. They range from "0" (Some high school or less) to "8" (Doctoral degree). The dependent variable "Democrat" also is a dummy variable; "0" means not a Democrat and "1" means a Democrat. It is not clear why "disability status" is negatively associated with Sociocultural Openness. Although an empirical and theoretical question, it could be that self-identification as "disabled" (e.g., with a psychological condition) may be associated—at an aggregate level—with less psychological "energy"/capacity to engage with cultural practices and perspectives that are different from one's own, at least as measured by this construct on the BEVI. Finally, we used weighted least squares means and variance adjusted (WLSMV) as the estimator for all the structural equation models because the variables have ordinal or dummy measures.

[3] These findings are derived from the "long BEVI" on the basis of Exploratory Factor Analysis (EFA) findings. See Chapter 4 for more information about the "long" and "short" versions of the BEVI.

TABLE 5.2
Correlation Matrix Findings Illustrating the Relationship Between Sociocultural Openness and Other BEVI Scales

BEVI SCALE	CORRELATION
Needs Closure	–.90
Ecological Resonance	.88
Socioemotional Convergence	.82
Basic Closedness	–.81
Identity Diffusion	–.71
Emotional Attunement	.77
Socioreligious Traditionalism	–.62
Hard Structure	–.58
Negative Life Events	–.57
Divergent Determinism	–.50

to report experiencing unhappy childhood events or experiences (Negative Life Events); and, are less likely to express contrary or argumentative attitudes for the sake of doing so (Divergent Determinism).

DISCUSSION

We are inclined to agree that the goals of multicultural education are worthy, if not necessary and inevitable; these include the promotion of cultural awareness and understanding, inclusion of marginalized social groups, encouragement of students to be active participants in the knowledge construction process, and ultimately, increasing tolerance for diversity (Banks, 1993, 2005; Bennett, 2001, 2002, 2003; Brown, 2004a, 2004b; Gorski,2006). Nonetheless, evidence suggests that the reach of multicultural education often exceeds its grasp (e.g., Banks, 1993; Bennett, 2001, 2003; Gorski, 2006), especially if we do not appreciate that urging individuals to engage in anti-prejudice thought and activity may inadvertently result in more rigid and stereotyped beliefs about the self, the world, and others (e.g., Legault et al., 2011). As the interrelated analyses presented in Study 2 suggest, people bring a range of different attributes and experiences to any international or multicultural experience (such as their experiences of their own life histories). These differences are associated not only with the capacity to be open to different cultures, but may further influence the degree to which people are inclined to engage in and enjoy diversity experiences. On the basis of such findings, we offer the following suggestions to educators, researchers, and practitioners who wish to promote understanding within and between cultural groups, which we believe fall under the rubric of best practices.

First, understand the etiology and nature of beliefs and values. It is important for multicultural educators to appreciate the complex and interacting factors that culminate in how and why people experience society and culture the way they do. For example, we need to understand what prejudice is, how prejudicial beliefs are acquired, and why *all* human beings are capable of such experiences. Moreover, as the data indicates, it is important to understand the cultural self as integrally related to other aspects of self, such as religious or political convictions (or lack thereof), environmental values, and the capacity to attend to affect in self and others. In short, we need to demonstrate a sophisticated understanding of beliefs and values and of human nature—from a theoretical, empirical, subjective, and real world perspective—in order to grasp and convey the complexity of why we are who we are in an informed and accessible manner (Shealy, 2004, 2016; Shealy et al., 2012). Our understanding of such matters should be integrated into all aspects of multicultural coursework and programs in order to enrich and humanize our pedagogy. A lack of sophistication at this level may lead to interventions that are experienced by recipients as superficial and polemical, if not alienating. The types of perspectives that we are offering here dovetail nicely with initiatives that are attempting to increase awareness and competency around multicultural education within teacher training programs as well. For example, the international education organization—National Association of Foreign Student Advisers (NAFSA)—is attempting to integrate international perspectives into teacher preparation programs, including Interstate New Teacher Assessment and Support Consortium (InTASC) criteria. We see the data presented here as having a strong bearing not only on the content that is integrated into these standards, but also aspects of process, as well as education, training, and learning writ large (e.g., see Cultivating the Globally Sustainable Self, 2015).

Second, process is as important as content. When we introduce content that may violate the extant belief/value structure of our audience, we bear a particular responsibility to anticipate and address such processes proactively, in an effective and respectful manner. Because such material inherently is evocative, it stands to reason that participants in multicultural experiences are differentially activated even before the experience begins; such activation may run the gamut from highly favorable to highly unfavorable for reasons that may not be at all clear to the individual who is experiencing the reaction. If we do not recognize that such processes potentially are operative, create time and space for individuals to become aware of what they believe and feel, and normalize such experiences, we unwittingly forfeit the opportunity to focus on what we are trying to accomplish: deepening the capacity and inclination for reflection on self, others, and the larger world. Put in more positive terms, if we do attend to such processes, we are that much more likely to lower defensiveness and heighten receptivity to the content we are about to share. By stepping back from the content of "what we should believe" in order to emphasize process reflection on "why we believe what we believe," we open up a space in ourselves—and others—to reflect openly. In doing so, we may cultivate self awareness as well as the necessary and sufficient competencies to facilitate such complex pedagogical processes and outcomes. In short, whereas most people are able to learn sufficient content knowledge vis-à-vis multicultural education, the capacity to deliver such knowledge with wisdom and care may be the most important competency of all.

Third, appraise worldviews before, during, and after an intervention. Conveying multicultural content to an audience without knowing what that audience already believes about such content is counterproductive at best, and anathema to the respect, growth, and development we are trying to promote. Likewise, assuming that all is going well, or that we achieved our goals—in the absence of any data to affirm such conclusions—is an indefensible practice for any multicultural educator, mainly because the whole purpose of such intervention is to promote deeper reflection and awareness, if not belief/value change. In the pursuit of such goals, it is imperative that educators be flexible in their approach and are willing to modify both content and methodology in order to improve effectiveness through routine assessment of beliefs and values, as well as related personal experiences, before, during, and after interventions. Research repeatedly has demonstrated that effective teachers are those who constantly reevaluate themselves and their teaching methods. As indicated, the BEVI offers one, and by no means the only, method for facilitating such objectives, by helping individuals understand what they believe and value, and how their beliefs and values are similar to, or different from, the group to which they are a part. As interventionists, such awareness helps us develop, present, and sequence content and processes in a more deliberate way in order to foster self awareness and understanding in a more accessible manner.

Ultimately, any type of valid assessment that appropriately ascertains what an audience actually believes and feels is worthy of development and implementation. However, because most people *want* to be perceived by others as being non-prejudicial, it is important that researchers conduct high quality assessments that are psychometrically sound (e.g., reliable and valid) in order to attenuate the likelihood of social desirability response confounds (e.g., should not be face valid). This point cannot be overemphasized. In short, especially with affectively loaded material as is the case in the multicultural realm, it is imperative that we know who our audience is before we intervene, how we are doing as processes unfold, and whether and to what degree we achieved our goals. Ecologically valid assessment is indispensable to pursuing such means and ends.

Fourth and finally, own personal beliefs and values. Individuals who assume a position of authority vis-à-vis multicultural education bear a particular responsibility to know themselves overall as well as their own issues and biases in particular. Along these lines, agitated diatribes by a multicultural educator or scholar about "power and privilege" or "microaggressions" may be cathartic for the presenter and induce guilt in the audience, but the transformational impact of these interventions is questionable. As the aforementioned results suggest, this approach may increase defensiveness, resistance, and dismissal, and possibly a change in one's beliefs in the opposite direction of what was intended. Since people tend to be suspicious of those in positions of power who use their platforms to "work out" issues under the aegis of multicultural paradigms and epistemologies, we contend that it is better to strive for authentic, caring, and sustained engagement regarding multicultural issues and processes.

The capacity for prejudice and misuse of power is part of the human condition, and not the purview of any one group. Wise multicultural interventionists acknowledge and communicate such realities. Their audiences are likely to appreciate and resonate with such self aware candor. In short, as educators, researchers, and practitioners, we must recognize that we are not somehow immune to the same biasing forces and factors that shape all human beings, and should acknowledge and account for these very real possibilities in ourselves, in the roles we assume, pedagogies we develop, and interventions we deliver.

REFERENCES

Allport, G. W. (1954). *The nature of prejudice.* Reading, MA: Addison-Wesley.

Anmuth, L. M., Poore, M., Cozen, J., Brearly, T., Tabit, M., Cannady, M., . . . Staton, R. (2013, August). *Making implicit beliefs explicit: In search of best practices for mental health clients, clinicians, and trainers.* Poster presented at the annual meeting of the American Psychological Association, Honolulu, HI.

Aronson, E. (2012). *The social animal* (11th ed.). New York, NY: Worth Publishers.

Association of American Colleges and Universities. (2000). *AAC&U survey on diversity requirements: Overview of survey data*. Retrieved from http://www.aacu.org/divsurvey/irvineoverview.cfm

Atwood, K., Chkhaidze, N., Shealy, C. N., Staton, R., & Sternberger, L. G. (2014, August). *Transformation of self: Implications from the Forum BEVI Project*. Poster presented at the annual meeting of the American Psychological Association, Washington, DC.

Banks, J. A. (1993). The canon debate, knowledge construction, and multicultural education. *Educational Researcher, 22*, 4–14.

Banks, J. A. (1994). *Multiethnic education: Theory and practice*. Needham Heights, MA: Allyn & Bacon.

Banks, J. A. (1996). The canon debate, knowledge construction, and multicultural education. In J. A. Banks (Ed.), *Multicultural education, transformative knowledge, and action: Historical and contemporary perspectives* (pp. 3–29). New York, NY: Teachers College Press.

Banks, J. (2004). Multicultural Education: Characteristics and goals. In J. Banks & C. Banks (Eds.). *Multicultural education: issues and perspectives*. San Francisco, CA: Jossey-Bass.

Banks, J. A. (2005). Multicultural education: Characteristics and goals. In J. A. Banks & C. A. McGee Banks (Eds.), *Multicultural education: Issues and perspectives* (5th ed.). Hoboken, NJ: John Wiley & Sons, Inc.

Bennett, C. I. (2001). Genres of research in multicultural education. *Review of Educational Research, 71*, 171–217.

Bennett, C. I. (2003). *Comprehensive multicultural education: Theory and practice* (5th ed.). Boston, MA: Allyn & Bacon.

Bennett, M. J. (1986). A developmental approach to training for intercultural sensitivity. *International Journal of International Relations, 10*, 179–196.

Brearly, T., Shealy, C. N., Staton, R., & Sternberger, L. G. (2012, August). *Prejudice and religious and non-religious certitude: An empirical analysis from the Forum BEVI Project*. Poster presented at the annual meeting of the American Psychological Association, Orlando, FL.

Brown, E. L. (2004a). What precipitates change in cultural diversity awareness during a multicultural course: The message or the method? *Journal of Teacher Education, 55*, 325–340.

Brown, E. L. (2004b). Overcoming the challenges of stand-alone multicultural courses: The possibilities of technology integration. *Journal of Technology and Teacher Education, 12*, 535–559.

Brown, K. M. (2006). Leadership for social justice and equity: Evaluating a transformative framework and andragogy. *Educational Administration Quarterly, 42*, 700–745.

Brown, R. (2010). *Prejudice: Its social psychology*. Oxford: Wiley-Blackwell.

Camicia, S. P. (2007). Prejudice reduction through multicultural education: Connecting multiple literatures. *Social Studies Research and Practice, 2*, 219–227.

Council of Graduate Schools. (2012). *CGS International Graduate Admissions Survey Report*. Retrieved from http://www.cgsnet.org/benchmarking/international-graduate-admissions-survey

Cultivating the Globally Sustainable Self. (2015). Paper presented at James Madison University, Harrisonburg, VA. Retrieved from http://www.jmu.edu/summitseries/

Dee, T. S. (2005). A teacher like me: Does race, ethnicity, or gender matter? *American Economic Review, 95*, 158–165.

Edmunds, A., Federico, C. M., & Mays, L. (2016). Exploring the etiology of ideology: In search of the political self through the EI model and BEVI method. In C. N. Shealy (Ed.), *Making sense of beliefs and values* (pp. 303–330). New York, NY: Springer Publishing

Engberg, M. E. (2004). Improving intergroup relations in higher education: A critical examination of the influence of educational interventions on racial bias. *Review of Educational Research, 74*, 473–524.

Feistritzer, C. E. (2011). *Profiles of teachers in the U.S. 2011*. Retrieved from http://www.ncei.com/Profile_Teachers_US_2011.pdf

Gay, G. (2010). Acting on beliefs in teacher education for cultural diversity. *Journal of Teacher Education, 61*, 143–152.

Gorski, P. C. (2006). Complicity with conservatism: the de-politicizing of multicultural and intercultural education. *Intercultural Education, 17,* 163–177.

Gorski, P. C. (2009). What we're teaching teachers: An analysis of multicultural teacher education coursework syllabi. *Teaching and Teacher Education, 25,* 309–318.

Grant, C. & Sleeter, C. (1998). Turning on learning: Five approaches to multicultural teaching plans for race, class, gender, and disability. Upper Saddle River, NJ: Prentice-Hall.

Greenwald, A. G., McGhee, D. E., & Schwartz, J. L. K. (1998). Measuring individual differences in implicit cognition: The Implicit Association Test. *Journal of Personality and Social Psychology, 74,* 1464–1480.

Hammer, M. (2012). The intercultural development inventory: A new frontier in assessment and development of intercultural competence. In M. Vande Berg, R. M. Paige, & K. H. Lou (Eds.), *Student learning abroad* (Ch. 5, pp. 115–136). Sterling, VA: Stylus Publishing.

Helms, J. E. (1990). Toward a model of white racial identity development. In J. E. Helms (Ed.), *Black and white racial identity* (pp. 49–66). Westport, CT: Greenwood Press.

Henry, P. J., & Sears, D. O. (2002). The Symbolic Racism 2000 Scale. *Political Psychology, 23,* 253–283.

Hill, C., Johnson, M., Brinton, C., Staton, R., Sternberger, L., & Shealy (2013, August). *The etiology of economic beliefs and values: Implications and applications from the Forum BEVI Project.* Poster presented at the annual meeting of the American Psychological Association, Honolulu, HI.

Hurtado, S., & Ruiz, A. (2012, June). *The climate for underrepresented groups and diversity on campus.* Los Angeles, CA: Higher Education Research Institute at UCLA. Retrieved from http://heri.ucla.edu/briefs/urmbriefreport.pdf

Legault, L., & Green-Demers, I. (2012). The protective role of self-determined prejudice regulation in the relationship between intergroup threat and prejudice. *Motivation and Emotion, 36,* 143–158.

Legault, L., Green-Demers, I., & Eadie, A. L. (2009). When internalization leads to automatization: The role of self-determination in automatic stereotype suppression and implicit prejudice regulation. *Motivation and Emotion, 33,* 10–24.

Legault, L., Green-Demers, I., Grant, P., & Chung, J. (2007). On the self-regulation of implicit and explicit prejudice: A self-determination theory perspective. *Personality and Social Psychology Bulletin, 33,* 732–749.

Legault, L., Gutsell, J., & Inzlicht, M. (2011). Ironic effects of anti-prejudice messages: How motivational interventions can reduce (but also increase) prejudice. *Psychological Science, 22,* 1472–1477.

Lopez, W. L., & Sabudeco, J. M. (2007). Culture of peace and mass media. *EuropeaPsychologist, 12,* 147–155.

McAllister, G., & Irvine, J. J. (2000). Cross cultural competency and multicultural education. *Review of Educational Research, 70,* 3–24.

Mildred, J., & Zuniga, X. (2004). Working with resistance to diversity issues in the classroom: Lessons from teacher education training and multicultural education. *Smith College Studies in Social Work, 74,* 359–375.

National Center for Education Statistics. (2011). *Digest of education statistics: 2010* (Chapter 3: Postsecondary education). Retrieved from http://nces.ed.gov/programs/digest/d10/ch_3.asp

Nieto, S. (2000). Affirming diversity: The sociopolitical context of multicultural education. New York, NY: Longman.

Pendleton, C., Cochran, S., Kapadia, S., & Iyer, C. (2016). Understanding the gendered self: Implications from EI Theory, EI Self, and the BEVI. In C. N. Shealy (Ed.), *Making sense of beliefs and values* (pp. 261–302). New York, NY: Springer Publishing.

Pettigrew, T. F., & Tropp, L. R. (2006). A meta-analytic test of intergroup contact theory. *Journal of Personality and Social Psychology, 90,* 751–83.

Plant, E. A., & Devine, P. G. (1998). Internal and external motivation to respond without prejudice. *Journal of Personality and Social Psychology, 75,* 811–832.

Sfeir-Younis, L. S. (1993). Reflections of the teaching of multicultural courses. In D. Schoem, L. Frankel, X. Zuniga, & E. Lewis (Eds.), *Multicultural teaching in the university*. Westport, CT: Praeger.

Shealy, C. (2004). A model and method for "making" a combined-integrated psychologist: Equilintegration (EI) theory and the beliefs, events, and values inventory (BEVI). *Journal of Clinical Psychology, 60*, 1065–1090.

Shealy, C. N. (2016). *Making sense of beliefs and values*. New York, NY: Springer Publishing.

Shealy, C. N., Bhuyan, D., & Sternberger, L. G. (2012). Cultivating the capacity to care in children and youth: Implications from EI Theory, EI Self, and BEVI. In U. S. Nayar (Ed.), *Child and Adolescent Mental Health* (pp. 240–255). New Delhi, India: Sage Publications.

Sleeter, C. E., & Grant, C. A. (1987). An analysis of multicultural education in the United States. *Harvard Educational Review, 57*, 421–444.

Sleeter, C. (1996). Multicultural education as social activism. Albany, NY: State University of New York Press.

Stangor, C. (2009). The study of stereotyping, prejudice, and discrimination within social psychology: A quick history of theory and research. In T. D. Nelson (Ed.), *Handbook of prejudice, stereotyping, and discrimination*. New York, NY: Psychology Press.

Steele, C. M., & Aronson, J. (1995). Stereotype threat and the intellectual test-performance of African-Americans. *Journal of Personality and Social Psychology, 69*, 797–811.

Tabit, M. B., Cozen, J., Dyjak, K., Pendleton, C., Shealy, C. N., Sternberger, L. G., & Staton, R. (2011, August). *Sociocultural impact of denial: Empirical evidence from the Forum BEVI Project*. Poster presented at the annual meeting of the American Psychological Association.

U.S. Department of Commerce. (2011). *Back to school: 2011–2012*. (U.S. Census Bureau News, Report No. CB11-FF.15). Retrieved from http://www.census.gov/newsroom/releases/pdf/cb11ff

United States Census Bureau. (2008). *National population projections*. Retrieved from http://www.census.gov/population/www/projections/downloadablefiles.html

United States Census Bureau. (2011). *Overview of race and Hispanic origin: 2010*. (2010 Census Briefs). Retrieved from http://www.census.gov/prod/cen2010/briefs/c2010br-02.pdf

Wandschneider, E., Pysarchik, D. T., Sternberger, L. G., Ma, W., Acheson-Clair, K., Baltensberger, B., . . . Hart, V. (2016). The Forum BEVI Project: Applications and implications for international, multicultural, and transformative learning. In C. N. Shealy (Ed.), *Making sense of beliefs and values* (pp. 407–484). New York, NY: Springer Publishing.

White, S. (2004). Multicultural MPA curriculum: Are we preparing culturally competent public administrators? *Journal of Public Affairs Education, 10*, 111–123.

Whitehead, K. A., & Wittig, M. A. (2005). Discursive management of resistance to a multicultural education program. *Qualitative Research in Psychology, 1*, 267–284.

Wyatt-Nichol, H., & Antwi-Boasiako, K. B. (2008). Diversity across the curriculum: Perceptions and practices. *Journal of Public Affairs Education, 14*, 79–90.

Jessica Spaeth, Seth Schwartz, Usha Nayar,
and Wenjuan Ma

6

IDENTITY DEVELOPMENT AND THE CONSTRUCTION OF SELF: FINDINGS AND IMPLICATIONS FROM THE FORUM BEVI PROJECT

It is only after a reasonable sense of identity has been established that real intimacy with others can be possible.

—Erik Erikson

The concept of "identity" has long occupied theorists and researchers of the human condition. To highlight briefly a few exemplars, the concept of "identity status" (Kroger & Marcia, 2011; Marcia, 1966, 1980) focuses on exploration and commitment as foundational processes of self-development. Narrative approaches (McAdams, Josselson, & Lieblich, 2006) emphasize the constructed sense of identity that manifests through one's subjectively experienced and expressed life story. The idea of "possible selves" (Oyserman & James, 2011) refers to potential identities that one wishes to realize or avoid. Social identity theory (Spears, 2011; Tajfel, 1982) is concerned with how individuals derive a sense of self in relation to their perceived membership in specific social groups. As a final example, role-based identity theories (e.g., Stryker, 2004) focus on how identity emerges from social roles, such as mother or doctor, that one assumes in life (for a comprehensive review of these and other perspectives on identity, see Vignoles, Schwartz, & Luyckx, 2011).

In addition to theories of identity, allied perspectives have focused upon the associated outcomes of particular identity statuses. More specifically, among other sequelae, the relative degree to which individuals are—or are not—able to achieve and express a clear and stable sense of "who they are" has been associated with multiple aspects of human development and functioning, from the selection and pursuit of careers (Skorikov & Vondracek, 1998) and relationships (Beyers & Seiffge-Krenke, 2010) to problem solving, decision making (Berman, Schwartz, Kurtines, & Berman, 2001), and meaning making (Berzonsky, Cieciuch, Duriez, & Soenens, 2011). A clear and coherent sense of identity has been associated with positive self-image and a lower likelihood of externalizing or internalizing symptoms of psychological distress (Schwartz, 2007; Schwartz et al., 2010; Schwartz et al., 2011; Schwartz, Donnellan, Ravert, Luyckx, & Zamboanga, 2012; Schwartz, Klimstra, Luyckx, Hale, & Meeus, 2012). Likewise, when compared to their peers, such "identity synthesized" individuals are more likely to feel positive about, and confident in, their decisions, more likely to engage in enjoyable relationships, and less likely to engage in harmful behaviors toward self and others (Beyers & Seiffge-Krenke, 2010; Beyers & Vansteenkiste, 2005; Luyckx, Goosens, & Soenens, 2005).

On the other hand, a diffused sense of identity—which can take either the form of disinterest in identity exploration (i.e., "carefree diffusion") or a willingness to engage in identity exploration, but not having the psychological resources to do so (i.e., formerly diffused, but currently defined as "troubled diffusion") (Luyckx, Klimstra, Schwartz, & Duriez, 2013; Schwartz, 2001)—is associated with a range of internalizing and externalizing symptoms, such as illicit drug use and sexual risk taking (Schwartz, Mason, Pantin, & Szapocznik, 2008; Schwartz, Zamboanga, Wang, & Olthuis, 2009). Despite much work on the nature of identity, including what it is and the outcomes associated with particular identities, less attention has been directed to questions of how and why identity develops as it does. Thus, we first describe theory and data from a multiyear, multi-institution assessment of learning initiative called the Forum BEVI Project, which may help illuminate the antecedents of identity development in general and identity diffusion in particular.

OVERVIEW OF EQUILINTEGRATION THEORY AND THE BELIEFS, EVENTS, AND VALUES INVENTORY

Although a full explication of the Forum BEVI Project is presented in Shealy (2016), a brief overview of the three main components that are integral to this project—Equilintegration (EI) Theory, the EI Self, and Beliefs, Events, and Values Inventory (BEVI)—may be helpful at the outset. Basically, EI Theory seeks to explain "the processes by which beliefs, values, and 'worldviews' are acquired and maintained, why their alteration is typically resisted, and how and under what circumstances their modification occurs" (Shealy, 2004, p. 1075). Derivative of EI Theory, the Equilintegration or EI Self explains the integrative and synergistic processes by which beliefs and values are acquired, maintained, and transformed as well as how and why these are linked to the formative variables, core needs, and adaptive potential of the self. Informed by scholarship in a range of key areas (e.g., "needs-based" research and theory; developmental psychopathology; social cognition; affect regulation; psychotherapy processes and outcomes; theories and models of "self"), the EI Self seeks to illustrate how the interaction between our core needs (e.g., for attachment, affiliation) and formative variables (e.g., caregiver, culture) results in beliefs and values about self, others, and the world at large that we all internalize over the course of development and across the life span (from Chapter 3).

Concomitant with EI Theory and the EI Self, the BEVI is a comprehensive analytic tool in development since the early 1990s that examines how and why we come to see ourselves, others, and the larger world as we do (e.g., how life experiences, culture, and context affect our beliefs, values, and worldview) as well as the influence of such processes on multiple aspects of human functioning (e.g., learning processes, relationships, personal growth, the pursuit of life goals). For example, the BEVI assesses processes such as: basic openness; the tendency to (or not to) stereotype in particular ways; self- and emotional awareness; preferred strategies for making sense of why "other" people and cultures "do what they do"; global engagement (e.g., receptivity to different cultures, religions, and social practices); and worldview shift (e.g., to what degree do beliefs and values change as a result of specific experiences). BEVI results are translated into reports at the individual, group, and organizational levels and used in a variety of contexts for applied and research purposes (e.g., to track and examine changes in worldviews over time) (e.g., Anmuth et al., 2013; Atwood, Chkhaidze, Shealy, Staton, & Sternberger, 2014; Brearly, Shealy, Staton, & Sternberger, 2012; Hayes, Shealy, Sivo, & Weinstein, 1999; Hill et al., 2013;

Isley, Shealy, Crandall, Sivo, & Reifsteck, 1999; Patel, Shealy, & De Michele, 2007; Pysarchik, Shealy, & Whalen, 2007; Shealy, 2000a, 2000b, 2004, 2005, 2006, 2012; Shealy, Bhuyan, & Sternberger, 2012; Tabit et al., 2011; for more information about the BEVI, including a description of scales, see Chapter 4).

In addition to data from an original exploratory factor analysis, results presented were developed on the basis of a large dataset (N = 2331) collected during 2011 to 2012 from the Forum BEVI Project, a multi-institution, multiyear project examining the assessment of international, multicultural, and transformative learning. Coordinated by the Forum on Education Abroad (www.forumea.org) and International Beliefs and Values Institute (www.ibavi.org), participants primarily included undergraduate students (96.7%) and were recruited through a range of learning experiences (e.g., study abroad, residential learning communities, general education courses with a focus on transformative/multicultural learning). A small portion of graduate students (3.3%) also was included. The sample typically ranged between the ages of 17 and 26, with an average age of 19. However, 3.9% fell into the age range of 26 to 62, with another 9% falling into the age range of 12 to 17. Although the majority of participants reported as U.S. citizens (93.3%), non-U.S. citizens also were included in the sample (N = 156 or 6.7%). Also, participants were drawn from 38 different countries of origin. Of the sample, 79.1% reported as Caucasian with 20.9% as non-Caucasian (6.6% Black or African American; .9% American Indian or Alaskan Native; 7.4% Asian or Pacific Islander; 2.9% Hispanic/Latino; 3% Other). Finally, from the standpoint of gender, 40.8% of the sample was female, with 59.2% male. All participants were required to provide informed consent as determined by multiple Institutional Review Boards processes, and participation was entirely voluntary. Participants were not required to complete the BEVI, and could elect to discontinue participation at any time. Analyses were conducted via Statistical Package for the Social Sciences (SPSS) and MPLUS, and consist of analysis of variance (ANOVA), regression analysis, and structural equation modeling (SEM). More information on the Forum BEVI Project is available in Chapter 4 and at www.ibavi.org/content/featured-projects.

Beliefs, Values, and Identity

Consistent with the EI model and BEVI method, multiple constructs and variables have been invoked to describe or explain identity, including beliefs, values, and goals (Marcia, 1966; Waterman, 1999), self-esteem and reflexive self-evaluations (Kernis, Lakey, & Heppner, 2008), and one's unique and overarching life story (McAdams et al., 2006). Moreover, various theoretical arguments have been advanced regarding the processes by which the "self" is organized. For example, Showers and Zeigler-Hill (2003) describe the process of "self-organization" as including positive and negative self-beliefs, and the way these self-beliefs are compartmentalized or integrated into aspects of overall self-concept. From this perspective, the relative accessibility of self-beliefs guides the formation of self-concept, and influences an individual's behavior, cognitive capacities, and emotional reactions. As may be evident, then, many theoretical approaches to identity focus on the development and composition of "beliefs and values" as well as how such internalized constructs mediate the experience of self, others, and the larger world

Indeed, a number of identity theories assume that beliefs and values represent the foundation of identity. For example, Berzonsky and Neimeyer (1988) and Berzonsky (1990, 2003) conceptualize identity as a self-theory (e.g., Epstein, 1980), which represents an amalgamation of "personal constructs, assumptions, hypotheses, beliefs, schemas, and postulates relevant to the self-interacting in the world" (Berzonsky, 2011, p. 56). Waterman (2007, 2011) defines self-discovery as the uncovering of one's basic talents and potentials, a process, which is linked integrally to the development of core beliefs and values about oneself. A number of theorists have postulated that individuals maintain epistemological self-theories that guide decisions and courses of action. For example, "self-theory" includes acquired knowledge, strategies, and skills that facilitate adaptation to daily challenges; one's effectiveness in this regard is evaluated in relation to subjectively held goals and values as well as the individual's ability to respond and adapt to life situations (Berzonsky, 2011). To adapt to and cope with dynamic conditions and possibilities in our world, Berzonsky (1990, 2003, 2011) describes how existing identity structures both receive stimuli and adjust in order to accommodate information that is incompatible with one's existing sense of identity (Kerpelman & Pittman, 2001). Likewise, as the "theory of planned behavior" maintains, individuals who have a more coherent and flexible sense of identity, more proactive coping skills (Carver & Connor-Smith, 2010; Folkman, 2010), and greater perceived control over their decisions are better able to adapt to and cope with difficult life situations (Ajzen, 2002, 2012; Jopp & Schmitt, 2010; Luyckx, Klimstra, Duriez, Schwartz & Vanhalst, 2012).

Among other processes that influence the development of one's identity—what are called "formative variables" from an EI standpoint—is the *Zeitgeist* in which one's identity develops. Defined as "the influence exerted by the sharing of the values and ideas prevailing in the social environment of each generation" (Vedder et al., 2009, p. 642), one's *Zeitgeist* includes, but is not limited to, the prevailing culture, context, political and religious orientations, and spoken language in which one develops. Such processes interact with other formative variables, such as our life experiences and relations with caregivers, to influence not only the nature and form of the beliefs and values that are inculcated by and within us, but the personal and professional identities we ultimately assume (Shealy, 1995, 2005). Thus, in contemplating the antecedents of identity, it is important to acknowledge not only the specific formative variables that interact to shape what we become, and who we say we are, but the sociocultural structures and dynamics that predominated during such processes of development. As the EI model maintains,

> Beliefs and values are determined by an individual's history, larger culture, and unique Zeitgeist, inculcated over time, and may or may not transcend a specific time and place. Although that which is believed and valued may be relative to a given time or place, the human capacity and need for an organizing worldview is an etic derivative of the self; thus, although the content of our beliefs and values may vary as a function of what is available for acquisition, the processes (e.g., developmental, affective, attributional) by which beliefs and values are acquired are determined by constitutive aspects of the self (Shealy, 2004, p. 1083).

From the standpoint of antecedents, the implications of such a perspective for cross-cultural perspectives on the development of identity should be clear since what we come to believe and value about self, others, and the world at large depends in no small part on what was available for acquisition. For example, young people in largely open Western societies have a great many values and beliefs for potential inculcation whereas young people in hierarchically structured societies are more likely to be expected to internalize values and beliefs from family members or other elders (Bosma & Kunnen, 2001; Schwartz, Montgomery, & Briones, 2006).

Furthermore, the extent to which the prevailing social structures and mores may be challenged varies from one cultural context to the next (Cheng & Berman, 2012; Schwartz, Whitbourne, Weisskirch, Vazsonyi, & Luyckx, 2012; Schwartz, Zamboanga, Meca, & Ritchie, 2012). In short, from an EI perspective, and integral to the Forum BEVI Project (e.g., DeWitt, Mazzoleni, Pysarchik, & Shealy, 2012)—a multi-institution, multiyear assessment project, examining international, multicultural, and transformative learning—these very sociocultural processes must be accounted for when attempting to understand not only *what* beliefs and values comprise identity at an individual and aggregate level, but *why* differences and similarities occur as they do within and between cultures.

The Structure and Process of Identity: Neo-Eriksonian Perspectives

Although there are many frameworks regarding identity, the EI model is most consistent with, and informed by, Erik Erikson and the neo-Eriksonian perspectives, particularly regarding the acquisition, maintenance, and transformation of beliefs and values. By way of brief review, Erikson (1968) characterized identity development as:

> employ[ing] a process of simultaneous reflection and observation [. . .] the process described is always changing and developing: at its best it is a process of increasing differentiation, and it becomes ever more inclusive as the individual grows aware of a widening circle of others significant to him, from the maternal person to "mankind." (pp. 22–23)

Erikson's (1950) life-span theory of identity development inspired the identity status approach (Kroger & Marcia, 2011), which in turn fostered theory and research on more specific models. These developments have included, but are not limited to, social-cognitive accounts of the ways in which identity is constructed (Berzonsky, 2003, 2004, 2008), humanistic perspectives on self-realization and self-discovery (Waterman, 2007, 2011), and sociological perspectives on how identity-related skills and knowledge are used to pursue one's "core needs" as well as roles, positions, and other social resources (Côté, 1996; Côté & Levine, 2002). One common denominator among these various "neo-Eriksonian" approaches is that they focus on the development of a sense of self that is relatively more or less coherent, and which subsequently is ". . .experienced and expressed *by the self*—to the self, others, and the larger world— *as the self*" (Shealy, 2016, p. 107).

Relevant to the current approach, although Erikson (1968) only briefly referred to the concept of "psychological foreclosure" in regard to the process of identity development, Marcia (1966) distinguished four identity statuses based on the degree of exploration and/or commitment in which an adolescent engages. Of these four— achieved, foreclosed, moratorium, and diffused—the current approach focuses on the processes associated with foreclosed, and especially diffused, identity statuses. With identity diffusion, the individual has not yet made identity commitments and may have—or may not have—engaged in an exploration of alternatives (Meeus, Van de Schoot, Keijsers, Schwartz, & Branje et al., 2010). On the other hand, foreclosure represents the enacting of commitments without much prior exploration of alternatives. Foreclosed identity commitments generally are based upon the preferences and values of significant others (Berzonsky, 2008). Expanding upon identity foreclosure, Valde (1996) offers "identity closure" as a fifth category, which represents a "combination of the strength of certainty and the weakness of inflexibility" (p. 253).

Similarly, Meeus et al. (2010) use the term "early closure" to refer to foreclosure among early adolescents. It should be emphasized that in Western societies in particular, foreclosure often is characterized as developmentally inadequate or immature (Kroger & Marcia, 2011). However, in many non-Western contexts—and in ethnic minority families and communities in Western countries—foreclosure may well be the most adaptive resolution to identity issues. In short, foreclosure may be adaptive in many cases, and such status does not necessarily indicate an impaired process of identity development.

Some research has suggested that identity foreclosure carries different psychological meaning depending upon the developmental pathway through which it occurs. For example, Meeus et al. (2010) differentiate between "early closures" and "closures." Early closure individuals begin and stay in a foreclosed status, possess strong identity commitments early on, and do not engage in a process of in-depth exploration of who they are and might become. In contrast, individuals in a "closure" status are considered more developmentally advanced than individuals in "early closure," but have not engaged in a process of in-depth exploration regarding what their current commitments are or might become. With regard to "healthy" adaptation, Waterman (2007) emphasizes the negative relationship between foreclosure and psychological well-being in a Western context. Although the process of making commitments has been observed to operate similarly in Western and East Asian cultures, the process of identity exploration does not appear to progress in the same manner, or be regarded similarly, in East Asian countries as it does in Western cultural contexts (Cheng & Berman, 2012). Although identity achievement (considered to be optimal) and identity foreclosure both involve the process of deriving identity commitments, identity foreclosure does so without a concomitant to, and subjective experience of, autonomy. However, in an East Asian context, the individual agency of commitment making may not be as important to, or adaptive with, the more collectivist sense of self, which appears to predominate.

The process of commitment making is also associated with fundamental aspects of emotional functioning. For example, individuals in the achieved and foreclosed statuses tend to report lower levels of depressive symptoms (Meeus, 1996), anxiety (Berman, Weems, & Stickle, 2006), substance use (Schwartz et al., 2011), and aggression (Crocetti, Rubini, Luyckx, & Meeus, 2008) as well as relatively high levels of emotional stability and self-esteem (Luyckx et al., 2005). However, the enactment of commitments, in itself, does not appear sufficient to establish feelings of eudaimonic well-being in Western societies (Ryan & Deci, 2001). Importantly, the relative autonomy—referred to as "volition" of self-concordant goals—has been shown to be predictive of well-being outcomes in cross-cultural research, suggesting that the autonomy of one's goals may matter, regardless of collectivist or individualist context (Chirkov & Ryan, 2000). In Western societies, however, the strength of autonomous identity commitments has been associated positively with vigilant decision making and associated negatively with procrastination, rationalization, and the tendency to experience self-consciousness (Berzonsky, 1990; 1992). In contrast, for cultures that are more interdependent and relational, the association between self-consistency and psychological well-being is weaker; as such, the goal of Chinese adolescents may tend toward "self in relation" rather than an "autonomous self" (Cross, Gore, & Morris, 2003; Lam, 1997).

Although both foreclosed and achieved statuses show similar variants of contentment and self-esteem, achieved commitments appear to be associated with a sense of purpose, direction, and autonomy. An achieved sense of identity is most important in Western societies where individualized decision making is prioritized over loyalty and obligation to the family or other social groups (Schwartz, Zamboanga, et al., 2012). Indeed, in many Western countries, young people are expected to navigate the transition to adulthood largely on their own. Individuals in foreclosure may rigidly hold their commitments, and this lack of flexibility may not be as adaptive in the face of changing and/or challenging life circumstances (Schwartz et al., 2011). Unlike the achieved and foreclosed statuses, individuals in an identity diffusion status are distinguished by making no commitments and having an undefined sense of self (Kroger & Marcia, 2011). Importantly, Luyckx and colleagues (2008) found two clusters of identity diffuse individuals: troubled and carefree diffusions. Individuals in "troubled diffusion" were marked by higher scores on ruminative exploration, which signals a troubled approach toward identity issues. Those in the "carefree diffusion" cluster appear to have an untroubled approach toward identity and are not distressed by their lack of identity commitments. However, individuals in the traditional "identity diffusion status" scored lowest on a measure of intimacy and were less self-revealing in a situational intimacy task (Kinsler, 1973).

On the basis of overview—and informed by the findings from the Forum BEVI Project—what do the EI model and BEVI method suggest regarding the structure of identity in general and the antecedents of identity in particular? Although a number of BEVI scales have relevance to definitional and etiological matters regarding identity, the scale of Identity Diffusion[1] is most directly related to the neo-Eriksonian perspectives described. Operationally, Identity Diffusion on the BEVI refers to

> the degree to which an individual is undifferentiated from parents, experiences a foreclosed identity, reports a troubled childhood, feels little agency or ability to affect change, reports odd or unusual etiological perspectives, and is searching but feels helpless, lost and confused. (Shealy, 2015, p. 14)

Along these lines, it may be instructive to review a sampling of items that load statistically on Identity Diffusion.

I have to admit that I am just like my parents.
I am the way I am because I was born that way.
I have gone through a painful identity crisis.
I never felt like I was good enough for my family.
Even though we expect them to be, men are not really built to be faithful in marriage.
Being from other planets have helped our species.
Parents should stay together for the sake of their children.

Consideration of this statistically derived constellation of items (from exploratory factor analysis) is instructive at a number of levels. For example, Erikson (1968) describes a period between adolescence and adulthood called "institutionalized moratoria," in which adolescents are granted freedom to explore and experiment with various roles. During this time, young people in Western societies may be able to try out and experience new ways of doing and being without the attendant requirement to accept or choose a specific set of role commitments (Arnett, 2002, 2007). Importantly, emerging adulthood is characterized by a relatively high degree of freedom to explore and experiment with the enactment of different roles—and their corresponding beliefs and values—in areas such as career, partnership, and relationships with

---

[1] The lead author and editor wish to express gratitude to Seth Schwartz, PhD, for his input and suggestions, including the recommendation that this BEVI scale, originally labeled "Identity Closure," be renamed "Identity Diffusion."

one's family of origin (Schwartz, Cote, & Arnett, 2005). If the emerging adult stage is too structured or unstructured, exploration either will be unduly constrained or insufficiently guided (Côté, 2000). That said, it is the case that parents and other authority figures remain important during emerging adulthood, and young people often remain somewhat emotionally and financially dependent on their parents well into their 20s (Arnett, 2011). Moreover, the extent to which young people can "delay" full adulthood varies considerably across cultural contexts (Schwartz, Zamboanga, et al., 2012). In some non-Western countries, young people are expected to take over the family business, marry someone of their parents' choosing, or continue to reside in the familial home well into adulthood. Such cultural constraints will affect the extent to which emerging adulthood—and Erikson's psychosocial moratorium—is possible or feasible (Cheng & Berman, 2012).

As may be inferred from the constellation of sample items that load statistically on Identity Diffusion, an overarching experience of a troubled childhood, feelings of pain and crisis, the sense of "stuckness," and paranormal beliefs, such as, "Beings from other planets have helped our species" seem to characterize a high degree of Identity Diffusion. Interestingly, part of what appears to capture individuals in such a status is that they simultaneously identify what was experienced as undesirable about their upbringing or familial dynamics. However, these individuals still seek to maintain a sense of connection for the sake of family or loved ones, thus tending to adopt beliefs and values that keep them in such an undesirable position and do not threaten their primary relationships. Such a struggle seems reminiscent, in many ways, of the insecure attachment status described poignantly by Bowlby (1980), and is consistent with the frequently observed clinical reality that even children and youth who have experienced "physical or sexual abuse, exploitation, humiliation, and rejection—still remain fiercely loyal to their family of origin, often clinging tenaciously to the hope that things at home can be put right" (Shealy, 1995, p. 575; Shealy et al., 2012).

Correspondingly, Arseth, Kroger, Martinussen and Marcia (2009) found that individuals in the diffuse identity status had the lowest mean proportion of secure attachment when compared to the other three identity statuses and that a diffuse status was negatively correlated with secure attachment. Likewise, as implied by the constellation of items, a high degree of "identity diffusion" on the BEVI also appears indicative of a lack of self-exploration (Valde, 1996), in that such individuals have accepted their fate, even as they recognize the unfortunate implications of doing so, and have eschewed a process of "institutionalized moratoria," not allowing such exploration to occur. Finally, in the development of the diffuse identity status, a trademark characteristic has been a tendency to be "relatively directionless, unconcerned about their lack of commitment, and easily swayed by external influences" (Kroger & Marcia, 2011, p. 34). Although individuals in diffusion may still cling to their caregivers, such inclinations appear intertwined with a recognition that all was not right with one's upbringing or family of origin, even as there was, and is, no other way to exist or move forward in life (Shealy, 1995; Shealy et al., 2012).

The Relationship of Identity Diffusion to Other BEVI Constructs

On the basis of the operationalization of Identity Diffusion, further illumination of this construct is possible by considering its relationship to a range of other constructs on the BEVI. As presented next, from an EI perspective—and on the basis of correlation matrix data[2]—a clear relationship exists between formative variables (e.g., life history; background) and the degree of Identity Diffusion that is reported on the BEVI. Moreover, from the standpoint of developmental psychopathology and its approach toward understanding "mediators" of adjustment (Cummings, Davies, & Campbell, 2000), a high, or low, degree of Identity Diffusion also is associated with other aspects of how the individual experiences self, others, and the world at large. In Table 6.1, we report the relationships of Identity Diffusion to other BEVI Scales, which are derived from correlational matrix data (Spaeth, Shealy, Cobb, Staton, & Sternberger, 2010). Note from Table 6.1 that the internal consistency of Identity Diffusion is .82. Likewise, the "21" refers to the fact that this scale was extracted via promax exploratory factor analysis, using SPSS, as the 21st factor.[3] Finally, the correlated factors (see Table 6.1) on the BEVI are all statistically related to Identity Diffusion, and are listed in descending order of magnitude.

Based upon such correlation matrix findings, the relationship between Identity Diffusion and the constructs from the BEVI helps illuminate how and why individuals interpret experiences and negotiate the meaning and purpose of their lives (Erikson, 1968) including, but not limited to, self-evaluation, self-esteem, life satisfaction, life purpose, personal meaning, and eudaimonic well-being (e.g., Diener, Lucas, & Scollong, 2006; Ryan & Deci, 2001; Ryff, 1989; Waterman, 2007). Although "identity" has been related to many of these aspects of human existence, the empirical linkages among hypothesized causal pathways and outcomes often are not well specified (Harter, 1999, 2012; Shealy, 2016). Thus, we first consider what the correlation matrix data suggest about the antecedents of identity, by focusing specifically on the etiology of Identity Diffusion.

From an EI perspective (Shealy, 2004, 2016), beliefs and values about self, others, and the larger world—including those related to Identity Diffusion—have etiological origins in an interaction between formative variables (e.g., life history; background variables) and core needs (e.g., attachment, affiliation). As with other

---

TABLE 6.1
Correlation Matrix Comparing Identity Diffusion to Other BEVI Scales

Scale 3. Identity Diffusion (.82, SF 21) (undifferentiated from parents, identity is foreclosed, troubled childhood, feels little agency or ability to affect change, searching and lost but feels helpless, confused)

Needs Closure (.84)
Sociocultural Openness (−.71)
Socioemotional Convergence (−.69)
Negative Life Events (.66)
Emotional Attunement (−.63)
Ecological Resonance (−.49)
Hard Structure (.42)
Divergent Determinism (.42)

---

[2] See www.thebevi.com/docs/bevi_scale_pairwise_correlations_and_significance_levels.pdf

[3] Along with other criterion-based strategies for factor reduction, only those factors that had an eigenvalue of at least 2, item loadings of at least .30, and internal consistencies of at least .75 were retained.

BEVI scales, from a life history perspective (Dunkel, Kim, & Papini, 2012; Dunkel, Mathes, & Harbke, 2011), note from the correlation matrix data that Negative Life Events is strongly and positively correlated (.66) with Identity Diffusion. What does Negative Life Events measure? From one perspective, Negative Life Events is akin to an intake interview that was built into the BEVI, and consists of the sorts of questions a clinician might ask a client during an initial interview. More specifically, such items address the client's beliefs about his or her childhood, family, presence or absence of abuse or neglect, early development, schooling, relational history, and so forth. From a correlational standpoint at least, life history (as defined by Negative Life Events) clearly is strongly associated with Identity Diffusion. In short, the greater the degree of life events reported to be "negative," the more likely an individual is to report the sort of conflicted and confused sense of identity that appears to be encapsulated by Identity Diffusion.

As EI Theory and the EI Self specify, the degree to which one's core needs are experienced as acceptable and good by those in a position to do so (e.g., one's care-givers) is related directly to the degree to which such core needs become internalized by the developing human being (i.e., core needs are experienced as integral rather than split off from the self) (Shealy, 1995; Shealy et al., 2012). As noted, the culmination of this internalization process for human beings inextricably is linked to the constellation of beliefs and values that ultimately are internalized and considered as part of one's "version of reality" about self, other, and the world at large (Shealy, 2005, 2016). So how does the degree to which core needs are reported to have been met relate to Identity Diffusion? Although statistically differentiable from Identity Diffusion via exploratory factor analysis, Needs Closure on the BEVI is in fact highly correlated with Identity Diffusion (.84). At one level, this finding is not surprising given that Needs Closure (a powerful, primary factor extracted first on the basis of a Schmid–Leiman transformation, which essentially is a factor analysis of a factor analysis; see Schmid & Leiman, 1957) also taps into aspects of Negative Life Events (e.g., the experience of a bad or unhappy childhood). What is most interesting—and again congruent with Identity Diffusion—is that Needs Closure also includes odd explanations for why things are the way they are as well as thought processes that might be described, from a clinical standpoint, as distorted if not disturbed. In short, the most fundamental observation here is that life history (e.g., beliefs regarding one's childhood and family of origin; the reported presence or absence of abuse or neglect; early development, schooling, and relational history) interacts with the degree to which core needs were believed to have been met, which further appears to be associated with the degree to which beliefs about self, others, and the world at large are closed, contradictory, and confused.

Congruent with the findings, Waterman (1982) identified several interrelated variables that may influence the pathway of identity formation. First, the more an adolescent identifies with his or her parents during the period of identity formation, the greater the chance that meaningful and sustainable identity/life commitments will be enacted. However, if the experience of self, other, and the larger world between parent and child is too strongly linked (e.g., the experience of the child must resemble that of the parent)—or if autonomy and reflection in decision making are limited (e.g., offspring are discouraged from thinking critically about what they do and why)—a foreclosed or diffuse identity may result. In Western cultures, permissive, neglecting, authoritative, and authoritarian parenting styles (Baumrind, 1971) have been linked to identity formation in offspring. For example, more authoritative styles tend to support democratic decision making in which perspectives are solicited and valued regardless of their relative status or power within a system, and the active imagining of multiple perspectives regarding who one is and may become. In the Western world, such a parenting style is associated with a mature and stable sense of identity achievement when compared to individuals with permissive, neglecting, and/or rejecting parents (Berzonsky, 2004; Waterman, 1982). It is important to remember that not all cultural and ethnic groups around the world would necessarily value or promote such outcomes, and that other identities may in fact be more normative in different sociocultural contexts (e.g., foreclosure may in fact be the expectation for various ethnic and cultural groups around the world) (Cheng & Berman, 2012). For present purposes, the emphasis is more about how and why particular identities become established in the first place for human beings (e.g., what are the antecedent variables and processes that appear to impact identity development), rather than whether such outcomes are universally desirable. Even so, it seems plausible that Identity Diffusion, as operationalized, may not be experienced as a "positive" long-term outcome regardless of culture or context, although such a hypothesis remains an empirical question.

The results are also consistent with the literature suggesting that negative family dynamics, including conflicted attachment, poor communication, and low autonomy all impact the healthy development of identity (Cummings et al., 2000; Shealy, 1995; Shealy et al., 2012). Indeed, Erikson (1968) suggested that such family and parental characteristics were in fact associated with caregivers and offspring who experienced identity confusion. More specifically, Erikson maintained that parents who sought to project a façade of wealth, status, propriety, and happiness tended to minimize the experience or expression of honest feelings. For Erikson, such desires for approval and recognition also have been associated with jealousy, hypersensitivity, and criticism toward their children. The net effect of such processes is impairment in the quality of children's decision making, as well as the negation of an authentic experience or expression of emotions and needs. Along these lines, and more empirically grounded, Reis and Youniss (2004) found that poor communication between mothers and offspring was associated with regressed identity. Specifically, students who evidenced a regression in identity also indicated disturbances in their communication with their mothers between 10th and 12th grade. Such relational disturbances included quarreling, becoming very angry, avoiding one another, and feeling that one's mother (or child) is disappointed in oneself. However, in cases where mother–adolescent communication improved, adolescents reported marked improvement in sharing their feelings with their mothers, accepting advice, being able to compromise, and feeling better after talking with their mothers.

Consistent with such findings, from the standpoint of the BEVI, Table 6.2 indicates the strength of the relationship between Negative Life Events and Identity Diffusion by demonstrating that the greater the degree of Negative Life Events, the more likely individuals are to "strongly agree" with items that load statistically on Identity Diffusion (here, the y-axis is the score of Identity Diffusion, ranging from 1 to 4).

From an etiological perspective, a recurring theme in relation to the development of healthy identity is the relative degree to which autonomy, defined as the "promotion of volition" (Soensen et al., 2007) is encouraged in offspring. In a cross-cultural sense, Kagitcibasi (2005) named the "autonomous-relational" self as a way to integrate both the desire for differentiation and the importance of being able to rely on others (e.g., Deci & Ryan, 2012; Ryan & Deci, 2001). For example, Smits, Soenens, Vansteenkiste, Luyckx, and Goossens (2010) found that adolescents in predominantly Western societies who actively are encouraged to explore the validity of information provided to them about the nature of reality, and to critically appraise parental norms, subsequently develop stronger commitments, such as what to study, while also

TABLE 6.2

The Degree to Which Negative Life Events on the BEVI Is Associated With a Tendency to Strongly Agree to Items Loading on Identity Diffusion

SOURCE	SUM OF SQUARES	MEAN	DF	MEAN SQUARE ERROR	F	SIG.
Corrected Model	215.109		3	71.703	504.891	0.00
Intercept	9463.919		1	9463.919	66639.31	0.00
Negative Life Events	215.109		3	71.703	504.891	0.00
Strongly disagree		1.643				
Disagree		1.939				
Agree		2.129				
Strongly agree		2.495				
Error	318.828		2245	0.142		
Total	9998.478		2249			
Corrected Total	533.938		2248			

Note. $R^2 = 0.403$ (adjusted $R^2 = 0.402$).

demonstrating a greater degree of subjectively experienced well-being. Of great importance is the validity to which these statements apply to adolescents outside of the United States, as the majority of samples to which these theories have been tested are from Western, educated, industrialized, rich, and democratic societies (WEIRD) (Arnett, 2008; Henrich, Heine, & Norenzayan, 2010).

Life experiences outside of the immediate family—included as "formative variables" from the standpoint of the EI Self—also may mediate and moderate Identity Diffusion. For example, Duerden, Widner, Taniguchi, and Mcoy (2009) examined the effects of a two-week adventure program on adolescent identity development. Overall, program participants experienced positive psychosocial growth across three of Erikson's stages—industry, identity, and intimacy—as compared to a control group. Moreover, relative to controls, program participants reported increased levels of informational processing, in which the rationale for decision making is more actively evaluated and critiqued (Berzonsky, 1990, 1992). Program participants also reported reduced degrees of diffuse-avoidant processing, which is characterized by procrastination. A diffuse/avoidant style of decision making has been associated with a fragmented self-identity, which is loosely integrated and heavily dependent upon hedonic and situational cues and factors. In contrast, informational processing has been associated with a more coherent sense of self as well as healthy identity development (Berzonsky, 2008).

As further evidence that one's perception of identity is affected not only by early family processes, but may be impacted by formative variables that are operative throughout the life span, Berman, Kennerley, and Kennerley (2008) found that clinically significant improvements in identity exploration and achievement—as well as significant declines in identity distress and foreclosure—could be facilitated by a program that emphasized active reflection on oneself and one's aspirations. Along similar lines, Berman et al. (2008) created a pilot study to evaluate the feasibility of the Daytona Adult Identity Development Program designed to foster positive identity development in adults. During this program, participants became the "experts" through intentionally identifying their problems and engaging in activities to solve these problems. Importantly, group leaders and group participants were not informed as to what to do or how to solve their problems, but instead worked together to generate possible solutions; in doing so, participants were able to develop mastery, which was found to translate into empowerment and positive identity development. Importantly, helping young adults engage in meaningful identity exploration is crucial. Although many youth, both urban and nonurban, experience uncontrollable, systematic burdens, they are not "required to fail" because of these adverse social-structural processes (Côté, 2000). Thus, the development and implementation of programs that increase the ability of youth to be mentored and engaged in extracurricular activities, within the context of social-structural barriers and burdens placed especially on urban youth, may be key to the development of positive identity (Schwartz, Rodriguez, Weisskirch, Zamboanga, & Pantin, 2012). Theoretically then, the highest scoring individuals on Identity Diffusion would be most in need of interventions designed to promote identity exploration, empowerment, and mastery. As such, in future research, it would be interesting to see whether there are differential process and outcome interactions (e.g., pre/postmeasurement) from such programmatic interventions for individuals who score high, medium, or low on Identity Diffusion.

Identity Diffusion and Tolerance of Disequilibrium

Now that we have considered both findings and associated literature that help to explain the antecedents of Identity Diffusion, we focus our attention on the next level of organization from an EI perspective, which addresses the relative ability of individuals to tolerate the experience of disequilibrium (Shealy, 2004). On the BEVI, two scales—Basic Closedness and Hard Structure—address this putative capacity; both are correlated positively with Identity Diffusion (.62 and .42 respectively). Overall, these results suggest that the higher an individual scores on Basic Closedness, the more likely he or she is to report feelings of insecurity, to have difficulty with introspection, to struggle to acknowledge basic emotional states, and to experience difficulty with decision making. Items assessing Basic Closedness include "I am completely at peace," "I never really feel sad," and "Life makes perfect sense to me," which deliberately tap a tendency toward social desirability, and have some consonance with the "Lie Scale" on the Minnesota Multiphasic Personality Inventory-2 (MMPI-2) (Greene, 2010). In short, Basic Closedness appears to be associated with a tendency to dismiss emotional pain and/or identity confusion. The construct of Hard Structure taps into similar conceptual ground by assessing the degree to which individuals are overly settled on, and confident in, "who they are," experience no regrets about their own life, and report that they seldom are caught "off guard." Sample questions include, "I like myself exactly as I am" and "I don't waver in what I think."

From a clinical standpoint, in order to apprehend who one is and what one may do with one's life, it may be necessary to experience and work through sometimes unpleasant emotions as well as inherent paradoxes of life, and then move forward, better informed by these deep and complex aspects of human experience. As such, it should not be surprising that high scores on Basic Closedness and Hard Structure are highly correlated with high scores on Identity Diffusion. Extant literature supports these findings. For example, Waterman (2007) observes that a predilection toward self-reflection and consideration of alternative life paths is associated with identity achievement. The opposite tendencies (i.e., nonreflection and lack of consideration of alternatives) are associated with identity foreclosure and diffusion. At the same time, Waterman notes also that "identity foreclosure" may be associated with a subjective sense of well-being, if the identity that is foreclosed upon is congruent with underlying talents (e.g., who one "really is") as well as strongly sanctioned by individuals and a community that has great personal significance to the foreclosed individual. In other words, identity foreclosure should not always be seen as a "failing," but could simply be the result of a match between who one is and how one is valued within a particular life context. Again, in some cultural contexts, identity foreclosure is a valued identity strategy (Cheng & Berman, 2012). Even so, identity diffusion seems to be associated with a poorly integrated self-concept and view of others as noted. Moreover, the extreme version of identity diffusion has been linked with psychological dysfunction, such as Borderline Personality Disorder (Kernberg & Clarkin, 1993). Recall, however, that two forms of identity diffusion have been identified, which may account for relative differences in clinical profiles among identity diffuse populations. For example, Luyckx et al. (2013) found that troubled-diffused individuals worried about where their lives were headed and which choices were best; however, they struggled to direct these worries toward an active identity search. On the other hand, carefree-diffused individuals did not appear to worry or be interested in identity issues at all (Schwartz et al., 2011; Skorikov & Vondracek, 2011). Therefore, individuals in troubled diffusion may be unable to take proactive steps toward identity development, whereas individuals in carefree diffusion may be unmotivated to engage in identity development at all. Although seemingly plausible, it remains an empirical question as to whether such mental health and emotional functioning outcomes are applicable in non-Western contexts.

Identity Diffusion and Critical Thinking

From an EI perspective, the category of Critical Thinking on the BEVI encompasses scales that address an individual's tendency and capacity to hold complexity and derive attributions about self, others, and the larger world in a relatively sophisticated and nuanced manner. Of the scales in this category, Identity Diffusion is correlated (.42) with Divergent Determinism, which measures an individual's tendency to prefer contrarian (e.g., arguing for the sake of arguing without inductive intent toward some logical endpoint) and nonreflective (e.g., no point in thinking about how things might have been) ways of relating to self, others, and the larger world. Examples of questions on this scale include, "You really can't say that one viewpoint is better than any other" and "What's done is done so forgive and forget." As may be clear, such statements essentially convey a sense that there is little point in thinking critically about competing perspectives or why events happen as they do. Not surprisingly, such a version of reality is likely to be associated with Identity Diffusion, since a predilection toward nonreflection about self, others, and the larger world tends to be associated with a more diffuse sense of identity (Waterman, 2007).

Identity Diffusion and Access to Self, Others, and the Larger World

The three remaining categories on the BEVI refer to the ways in which individuals interact with and think about others, themselves, and the world at large. Consistent with the patterns noted, correlation matrix data suggest that individuals high in

Identity Diffusion also appear to evidence less capacity to attend to inner cognitive and affective processes with depth or complexity, and to be less inclined to care for and/or think about experiences of others or events and needs in the larger world.

For example, Socioemotional Convergence (SEC) has a significant −.69 correlation with Identity Diffusion, meaning that individuals who are relatively high in SEC tend to be relatively low in Identity Diffusion. As a factor, SEC appears to measure an individual's ability to hold complex and potentially contradictory juxtapositions such as the power of self-reliance with the recognition of personal vulnerability; patriotism and multicultural appreciation; self-examination and a "don't look back" sensibility; as well as the ability to remain open to the recognition of personal shortcomings while maintaining a fierce determination to focus on what is positive. To capture the complex and seemingly contradictory nature of this construct, the scale includes items like, "We will eventually accept that men and women are simply different" and "I strongly support equal rights for women." Individuals who are higher in SEC apparently are able to see the potential validity in both items whereas those who score lower appear less inclined to do so.

Identity Diffusion also has a significant and negative correlation of −.71 with Sociocultural Openness (SO), which measures the level to which an individual holds liberal and progressive views and is accepting, culturally attuned, open, and globally oriented. Examples of questions from this scale include: "Homosexuals should have all the same rights as heterosexuals," and "All of us would benefit if women had more economic and political power."

Identity Diffusion is significantly and negatively correlated (−.63) with Emotional Attunement (EA), which refers to an individual's capacity and inclination to experience and express emotions. Individuals who are very emotionally attuned are described as highly sensitive, highly social, needy, affiliative, undifferentiated, and comfortable with emotional expression. Examples of questions from this scale include: "I cry several times a year," "My emotions can sometimes get the better of me," and "I have real needs for warmth and affection."

Finally, Identity Diffusion is significantly and negatively correlated (−.49) with Ecological Resonance (ER), which is associated with a tendency to be concerned about ecological matters, value the rights of all, and contend that spirituality exists in the natural world. Examples of questions from this scale include: "We should think of the earth as our mother," and "I feel closer to God when I am in nature."

Identity Diffusion: Antecedents and Effects

It is one matter to demonstrate that there are strong and compelling relationships among Identity Diffusion and other aspects of psychological functioning. More important is attempting to identify theoretical pathways that specify both the formative variables associated with a tendency toward Identity Diffusion as well as outcomes that are mediated by this construct. Toward such means and ends, we tested several structural equation models (SEMs) to ascertain the extent of empirical support for our theoretical understanding of these associations. In Figures 6.1 to 6.3, we focus on three outcomes that are components of fundamental aspects of identity, particularly for college age students: marital status, educational aspirations, and grade point average (GPA).

For purposes of interpretation, note that all three of these models fit the data adequately using standard fit indexes (e.g., The Root Mean Square Error of

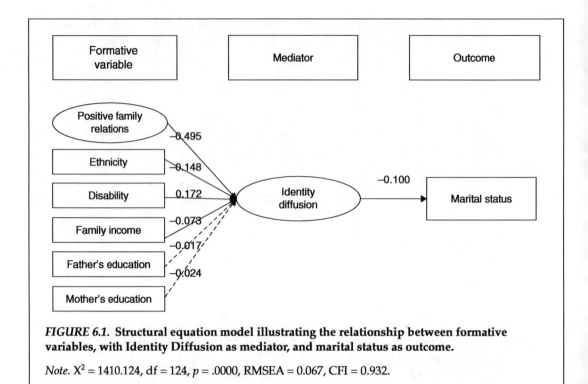

FIGURE 6.1. Structural equation model illustrating the relationship between formative variables, with Identity Diffusion as mediator, and marital status as outcome.

Note. X^2 = 1410.124, df = 124, p = .0000, RMSEA = 0.067, CFI = 0.932.

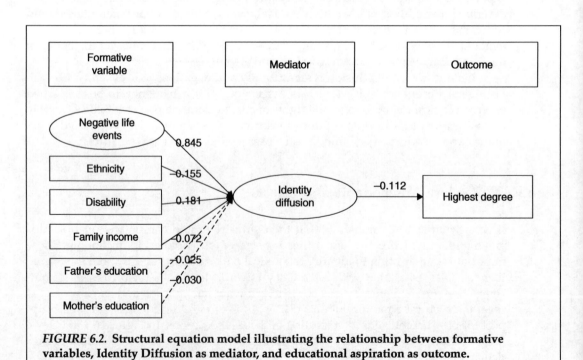

FIGURE 6.2. Structural equation model illustrating the relationship between formative variables, Identity Diffusion as mediator, and educational aspiration as outcome.

Note. X^2 = 2009.398, df = 198, p = .0000, RMSEA = 0.063, CFI = 0.901.

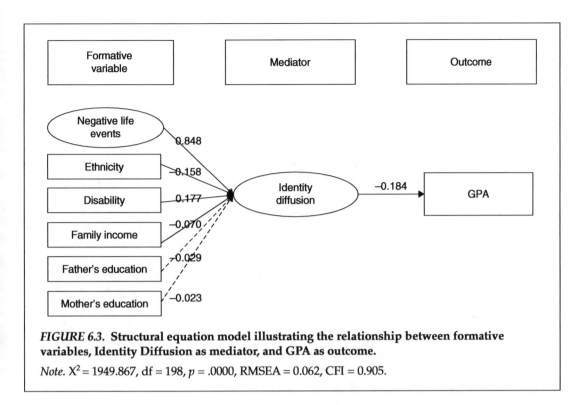

FIGURE 6.3. **Structural equation model illustrating the relationship between formative variables, Identity Diffusion as mediator, and GPA as outcome.**

Note. $X^2 = 1949.867$, df = 198, $p = .0000$, RMSEA = 0.062, CFI = 0.905.

Approximation (RMSEA), Confirmatory Fit Index (CFI)), meaning that the covariance structure in the model approximates the covariance structure in the data. Within each of these models, dashed lines refer to relationships that are not significant, and solid lines refer to significant relationships. From a theoretical standpoint (and SEM basically allows for the empirical evaluation of theoretically derived models), each of these SEMs essentially is asking whether "Formative Variables" (e.g., life history, demographics) are predictive of "Mediators," which from the standpoint of developmental psychopathology are "processes that account for the linkage" between Formative Variables and "Outcomes" (again, we focus here on three fundamental outcomes: marital status, educational aspiration, and GPA) (e.g., Cummings et al., 2000, p. 131). So, how do we interpret these models?

First, consistent with the results, a higher extent of Negative Life Events is *positively* predictive of Identity Diffusion whereas a higher degree of Positive Family Relations is *negatively* predictive of Identity Diffusion across all three models. Moreover, the same patterns apply to three other Formative Variables across all three models: Ethnicity,[4] Disability, and Income. Specifically, being non-Caucasian, having a disability, and reporting lower income were significantly and positively predictive of higher Identity Diffusion. Second, Identity Diffusion also is predictive of these three outcomes. Specifically, a higher degree of Identity Diffusion was (a) negatively predictive of being married; (b) negatively predictive of higher educational aspirations[5]; and (c) negatively predictive of grade point average.

---

[4] Ethnicity is dummy coded, with 0 = minority and 1 = Caucasian.
[5] On the background section of the BEVI, this question is worded as follows: "Please indicate the highest academic degree that you intend to obtain," with response options ranging from no intention of pursuing a degree to the intention of securing a doctoral degree.

DISCUSSION

As discussed at the outset, a high degree of Identity Diffusion is associated with a tendency to be "closed to" the ambiguity and disequilibrium that may accompany exposure to many interrelated aspects of existence, from one's relationship to the emotional world of self and other, to a tendency to accept "gray" versus "black and white" vis-à-vis different cultures, to the relative inclination to care for and resonate with the "natural world." So, Identity Diffusion essentially appears to be a measure of maladjustment, in that individuals who score highly on this scale tend to be less open or attuned to self, others, and the larger world, and less able to tolerate complexity. All of these findings are consistent with, and extend, data and theory from scholarship on the formation and nature of identity. For example, a diffused identity has been associated with uncertainty of self and an intolerance of ambiguity (Berzonsky, Rice, & Neimeyer, 1990; Marcia, 1966) as well as with relative difficulty analyzing and integrating information from multiple perspectives (Read, Adams, & Dobson, 1984). Additionally, individuals in a state of diffused identity may be experienced by others across a spectrum, from "careless or carefree, [and] charming" to "psychopathic, independent or schizoid" (Marcia, 1980, p. 111).

So, how does such a perspective inform results? Let us consider first the correlation matrix data. Using our initial findings as a point of departure—demonstrating that a higher degree of Negative Life Events and Needs Closure are associated with a greater degree of Identity Diffusion—research on the ways individuals adapt to difficult life situations has been dominated by two classic traditions, focusing either on critical life events or on mechanisms of coping. Through such research, several forms of coping have become apparent: problem-focused coping in which individuals identify problems, seek support, and actively problem-solve; emotion-focused coping in which individuals appraise the situation, distance themselves, and seek comfort; and avoidant coping, where an individual uses distractions as a way of not dealing with the problem (Carver & Conner-Smith, 2010; Jopp & Schmitt, 2010). Two additional perspectives from the literature further clarify processes by which individual differences in coping strategies manifest themselves: access to resources and control beliefs (Moos & Holohan, 2003). Specifically, individuals with more resources—such as a greater degree of "physical health, finances, and [supportive] relationships with family members and friends" (Moos & Holohan, 2003, p. 1393)—as well as greater internal control beliefs, defined as "mental schemas," which "have a specific role as they motivate actions, for example, by initiating or hindering the use of specific [coping] strategies" (Jopp & Schmitt, 2010, p. 169), were less likely to report having experienced distressing life experiences. In addition, individuals who experienced more distressing life experiences also reported greater use of coping strategies, which suggests that such formative variables are not destined to result in poorer life outcomes, but may culminate in resilience (Shiner & Masten, 2012; Cummings et al., 2000). The simultaneous consideration of resources, coping strategies, and control beliefs suggests that in the context of handling critical life events, individuals who have more resources, more adaptive coping skills, and stronger control beliefs are more adept at dealing with these difficult situations compared to individuals with fewer resources, less adaptive coping skills, and weaker control beliefs (Jopp & Schmitt, 2010).

From an EI perspective, and based on the correlation matrix data presented, a higher degree of Negative Life Events is associated with greater Identity Diffusion, which on the one hand begs the question of what types of "control beliefs" such individuals possess? The general point to be offered here is that a higher degree of exposure to Negative Life Events may well result in a greater array of control beliefs, but from the standpoint of the BEVI, such beliefs do not appear to be congruent with a higher degree of awareness or openness to self, to others, and to the larger world. Even so, exposure to learning experiences that are very different from those to which one is accustomed (e.g., study abroad), has been found in at least some instances to be associated with changes in how one experiences one's own life history. For example, in one study in which the BEVI was administered twice, with at least 3 months between administrations during which a study abroad experience occurred, Negative Life Events, Needs Closure, and Identity Diffusion all decreased (by a percentage of change factor of 24%, 30%, and 33%, respectively). In other words, following the study abroad experience, scores for the group as a whole were less likely to be elevated on these scales (DeWitt et al., 2012), which suggests not only that one's narrative about one's self may change in a relatively short period of time, but that specific types of experiences may be associated with such changes.

Next, consider the implications of the structural equation models. First, recall that the mean age of this sample is 19. Thus, for these specific findings, it could be that individuals who have experienced a higher degree of specific formative variables—including most significantly, a lower degree of Positive Life Events as well as a non-Caucasian status, lower parental income, and higher tendency to report being disabled—are that much more likely to demonstrate a high degree of Identity Diffusion, which may be a mediating factor in the associations between these antecedents and marital status. More specifically, it may be that such "formative variables" are predictive of a "premature marriage" (i.e., getting married because of external expectations). Importantly, it should be emphasized that factors such as one's ethnic group, socioeconomic status, and education level can impact the decision or necessity to get married (Schneider, 2011). However, in more Western cultural contexts, research conducted on the relationship between identity development and marriage has indicated that marriage can be considered an "identity investment," suggesting that individuals enter into marriage with a certain level of commitment or with a particular mindset (e.g., Helson, 1967; Josselson, 1987; Pals, 1999). Along these lines, four "prototypes" of marriage that correlate with the identity stages proposed by Marcia (1966) have been identified, which include anchored, defined, restricted, and confused (Josselson, 1987; Marcia, 1966). In a follow-up longitudinal study of adolescent young women originally interviewed by Helson, Pals found that a more anchored identity in marriage mediated the link between ego resiliency and identity consolidation (i.e., the more secure women were in marriage, the more resilient they were in terms of consolidating their identity over time). Additionally, women with lower ego resiliency were more likely to get married and, in turn, experienced higher self-doubt and identity uncertainty, which hindered overall healthy identity development. However, the engagement in premature marriage does not necessarily lead to permanent hindrance in identity development. Arnett (1998, 2011) found that individuals who marry early may miss the "emerging adult" experience but, in turn, develop a healthy sense of identity in relation to their new life status (i.e., as parents). Additionally, Arnett also found an inverse relationship between being married and engaging in "risk" behaviors. In one study, the majority of emerging adults who were married, and also indicated higher degrees of religiosity, engaged in less "risky" behavior than individuals who did not indicate religiosity. However, because other identity factors were not investigated, it cannot be concluded that individuals, who also experience identity diffusion, would have the same positive outcomes as Arnett's sample. Although an empirical question, given the SEM pathways specified, and the relationship of Identity Diffusion to other BEVI scales as illustrated by correlation matrix findings, such a marital "solution" to one's historic difficulties may be nonoptimal in terms of identity consolidation over the long term. Moreover, toward the larger goal of clarifying antecedents to identity development, future SEM research might consider whether perceived need satisfaction through the EI framework and related approaches, such as Self-Determination Theory (e.g., Deci & Ryan, 2012; Ryan & Deci, 2001), mediates the linkage between life history and life outcomes, such as marital status.

At another level, the fact that a *higher* degree of Identity Diffusion also is predictive of *lower* aspirations for higher education as well as *lower* academic performance as defined by GPA appears consistent with multiple findings in the literature. In particular, educational aspirations and performance would appear to be determined, at least in part, by the capacity to adapt to and cope with complexity, which is further associated with modification of extant identity structures (Berzonsky, 2011). Likewise, given that greater resources, coping skills, and control beliefs are associated with the ability to manage difficult life situations, it stands to reason that a higher degree of Identity Diffusion would be predictive of lower academic aspirations and performance, particularly in the context of higher education (Jopp & Schmitt, 2010).

Overall, results paint a clearer picture regarding what a "healthier" identity may look like, how Identity Diffusion relates to other core aspects of self (e.g., emotional capacity; engagement with "different" others), and how antecedent variables influence the level to which an individual may experience Identity Diffusion. For example and more specifically, if a young person does not aspire as much as his or her peers to receive more education, and does not do as well in school, he or she may be more likely to report a *higher* degree of Identity Diffusion, at least for a college-aged and eligible population. Moreover, if a young person is non-White, disabled, and of low income, he or she is also more likely to exhibit a *higher* degree of Identity Diffusion. However, if a young person is married, he or she is more likely to exhibit a *lower* degree of Identity Diffusion, which raises the intriguing possibility that such status may be more likely to occur when a young person *is not* experiencing a sense of confusion or uncertainty about who he or she is and/or where he or she is going in life. On the positive side, such assurance of identity suggests the relative absence of upset about who one is or where one is going (Schwartz, Zamboanga, Weisskirch, & Rodriguez, 2009). On the other hand, it arguably is normative for young people to experience uncertainty, confusion, and the like, during the identity exploration phase of this stage of life, which theoretically could be manifesting as a higher degree of Identity Diffusion on the BEVI, for individuals who have not resolved their marital status. In short, although correlation matrix data suggest overall that a high degree of Identity Diffusion is a manifestation of maladjustment (e.g., insofar as it is associated with a lack of Emotional Attunement and interest/caring for others, and the larger world), it may be that higher Identity Diffusion may also be a "symptom" of youth, for selected subsets of this population. Present data do not allow for a detailed examination of this possibility, but future research may productively examine the correlates of Identity Diffusion from a cross-sectional and longitudinal perspective.

In conclusion, on the basis of literature, results, and discussion, we offer three final observations that may be helpful in terms of future theory and research vis-à-vis identity in general and Identity Diffusion in particular. *First, in scholarly examinations of identity, we should focus upon questions of what and how.* More specifically, in addition to examining various categories or phases of identity structure or development (the *what*), it would be helpful to understand further *how*, and under what life circumstances, identity becomes codified as it does. Hopefully, the model and method presented here illustrate how both what and how objectives may simultaneously be pursued, through further operationalization of the Identity Diffusion construct, as well as explication of the antecedents (e.g., life events) and concomitants (e.g., emotional access) that are associated with its formation.

Second, the definition of what we mean by a "healthy" or "developed" sense of identity should be explicated, empirically and theoretically. In the present analysis, correlation matrix data are especially suitable to such objectives, by suggesting for example that a clear, healthy, and flexible sense of identity is associated with a higher degree of having one's "core needs" met, both historically and currently (e.g., Soenens & Vansteenkiste, 2011). Such an adaptive (e.g., open, aware) sense of identity also appears to be associated with a greater capacity to experience and express affect; greater interest in, and concern about, the natural world; greater ability to acknowledge feelings of weakness or insecurity; less of a tendency to be argumentative for the sake of being so; and lesser tendencies toward traditionally religious ways of understanding self, others, and the larger world.

Third and finally, the construct of "identity" should be understood in relation to overarching and encompassing aspects of self. As indicated, the experience of specific formative variables will impact how one's identity becomes structured, even though such processes are mediated by each individual's adaptive potential and unique formative variables, such as culture and context (Shealy, 2004). The resulting experience of self is associated with the version of reality of self that we call real and present as such to ourselves and others (Erikson, 1950; Shealy, 2005). From an EI perspective, verbalized content about one's identity manifests as belief statements, which culminate from an interaction between formative variables (e.g., life history) (Dunkel et al., 2012) and core needs (e.g., attachment, affiliation) (Soenens & Vansteenkiste, 2011). In short,

> identity, as the self's narrative about itself, may productively be understood as a verbal representation of the individual's beliefs about self to self, others, and the larger world, which manifests at any moment in time as the most recent culmination of a complex interaction among core needs, formative variables, and external contingencies. (Shealy, 2016, p. 107)

Hopefully, these findings illustrate how the EI model and BEVI method may help us understand further the fascinating processes by which we humans come to tell a story about ourselves—to ourselves, others, and the larger world—regarding why we are who we are, and who we may become.

REFERENCES

Ajzen, I. (2002). Perceived behavioral control, self-efficacy, locus of control, and the theory of planned behavior. *Journal of Applied Social Psychology, 32*(4), 665–683.

Ajzen, I. (2012). The theory of planned behavior. In P. M. Van Lange & A. W. Kruglanski (Eds.), *Handbook of theories of social psychology* (Vol. 1, pp. 438–459). Thousand Oaks, CA: Sage Publications.

Anmuth, L. M., Poore, M., Cozen, J., Brearly, T., Tabit, M., Cannady, M., . . . & Staton, R. (2013, August). *Making implicit beliefs explicit: In search of best practices for mental health clients, clinicians, and trainers*. Poster presented at the annual meeting of the American Psychological Association, Honolulu, HI.

Arnett, J. (1998). Risk behavior and family role transitions during the twenties. *Journal of Youth and Adolescence, 27*(3), 301–320.

Arnett, J. (2002). The psychology of globalization. *American Psychologist, 57*(10), 774–783.

Arnett, J. (2007). Socialization in emerging adulthood: From the family to the wider world, from socialization to self-socialization. In J. E. Grusec & P. D. Hastings (Eds.), *Handbook of socialization: Theory and research*. (pp. 208–231). New York, NY: Guilford Press.

Arnett, J. (2008). The neglected 95%: Why American psychology needs to become less American. *American Psychologist, 63*(7), 602–614.

Arnett, J. (2011). Emerging adulthood(s): The cultural psychology of a new life stage. In J. L. Arnett (Ed.), *Bridging cultural and developmental approaches to psychology: New syntheses in theory, research, and policy* (pp. 255–275). New York, NY: Oxford University Press.

Arseth, A., Kroger, J., Martinussen, M., & Marcia, J. (2009). Meta-analytic studies of identity status and the relational issues of attachment and intimacy. *Identity: An International Journal of Theory and Research, 9*(1), 1–32.

Atwood, K., Chkhaidze, N., Shealy, C. N., Staton, R., & Sternberger, L. G. (2014, August). *Transformation of self: Implications from the Forum BEVI Project*. Poster presented at the annual meeting of the American Psychological Association, Washington, DC.

Baumrind, D. (1971). Current patterns of parental authority. *Developmental Psychology, 4*(1, Pt. 2), 1–103.

Berman, A., Schwartz, S., Kurtines, W., & Berman, S. (2001). The process of exploration in identity formation: The role of style and competence. *Journal of Adolescence, 24*(4), 513–528.

Berman, S., Kennerley, R., & Kennerley, M. (2008). Promoting adult identity development: A feasibility study of university-based identity intervention program. *Identity: An International Journal of Theory and Research, 8*(2), 139–150.

Berman, S., Weems, C., & Stickle, T. (2006). Existential anxiety in adolescents: Prevalence, structure, association with psychological symptoms and identity development. *Journal of Youth and Adolescence, 35*(3), 303–310.

Berzonsky, M. (1990). Self-construction over the life-span: A process perspective on identity formation. In G. J. Neimeyer & R. A. Neimeyer (Eds.), *Advances in personal construct psychology* (Vol. 1, pp. 155–186). Greenwich, CT: JAJ press.

Berzonsky, M. (1992). Identity style and coping strategies. *Journal of Personality, 60*(4), 771–788.

Berzonsky, M. (2003). Identity style and well-being: Does commitment matter? *Identity: An International Journal of Theory and Research, 3*(2), 131–142.

Berzonsky, M. (2004). Identity style, parental authority, and identity commitment. *Journal of Youth and Adolescence, 33*(3), 213–220.

Berzonsky, M. (2008). Identity formation: The role of identity processing style and cognitive processes. *Personality and Individual Differences, 44*(3), 645–655.

Berzonsky, M. (2011). A social-cognitive perspective on identity construction. In S. J. Schwartz, K. Luyckx, & V. L. Vignoles (Eds.), *Handbook of identity theory and research* (Vol. 1 & 2, pp. 55–76). New York, NY: Springer Science + Business Media.

Berzonsky, M., & Neimeyer, G. (1988). Identity status and personal construct systems. *Journal of Adolescence, 11*(3), 195–204.

Berzonsky, M., Cieciuch, J., Duriez, B., & Soenens, B. (2011). The how and what of identity formation: Associations between identity styles and value orientations. *Personality and Individual Differences, 50*(2), 295–299.

Berzonsky, M., Rice, K., & Neimeyer, G. (1990). Identity status and self-construct systems: Process X structure interactions. *Journal of Adolescence, 13*(3), 251–263.

Beyers, W., & Seiffge-Krenke, I. (2010). Does identity precede intimacy? Testing Erikson's theory on romantic development in emerging adults of the 21st century. *Journal of Adolescent Research, 25*(3), 387–415.

Bosma, H., & Kunnen, E. (Eds.). (2001). *Identity and emotion: Development through self-organization*. New York: NY: Cambridge University Press.

Bowlby. J. (1980). *Attachment and loss*. New York, NY: Basic Books.

Brearly, T., Shealy, C. N., Staton, R., & Sternberger, L. G. (2012, August). *Prejudice and religious and non-religious certitude: An empirical analysis from the Forum BEVI Project*. Poster presented at the annual meeting of the American Psychological Association, Orlando, FL.

Carver, C., & Connor-Smith, J. (2010). Personality and coping. *Annual Review of Psychology, 61*, 679–704.

Cheng, M., & Berman, S. (2012). Globalization and identity development: A Chinese perspective. *New Directions in Child and Adolescent Development, 138*, 103–121.

Chirkov, V. I., & Ryan, R. M. (2001). Parent and teacher autonomy-support in Russian and U.S. adolescents: Common effects on well-being and academic motivation. *Journal of Cross-Cultural Psychology, 32*, 618–635.

Cote, J. (1996). Identity: A multidimensional analysis. In G. R. Adams, R. Montemayor, & T. P. Gullotta (Eds.), *Psychosocial development in adolescence* (pp. 130–180.) Thousand Oaks, CA: Sage Publications, Inc.

Cote, J. (2000). *Arrested adulthood: The changing nature of maturity and identity*. New York, NY: New York University Press.

Cote, J., & Levine, C. (2002). *Identity formation, agency, and culture: A social psychological synthesis*. Mahwah, NJ: Lawrence Erlbaum Associates Publishers.

Crocetti, E., Rubini, M., Luyckx, K., & Meeus, W. (2008). Identity formation in early and middle adolescents from various ethnic groups: From three dimensions to five statuses. *Journal of Youth and Adolescence, 37*(8), 983–996.

Cross, S., Gore, J., & Morris, M. (2003). The relational-interdependent self-construal, self-concept consistency, and well-being. *Journal of Personality and Social Psychology, 85*(5), 933–944.

Cummings, E., Davies, P., & Campbell, S. (2000). *Developmental psychopathology and family process: Theory, research, and clinical implications*. New York, NY: The Guilford Press.

Deci, E., & Ryan, R. (2012). Self-Determination theory. In P. M. Van Lange, A. W. Kruglanski, & E. T. Higgins (Eds.), *Handbook of theories of social psychology* (Vol. 1, pp. 416–436). Thousand Oaks, CA: Sage Publications.

DeWitt, H., Mazzoleni, E., Pysarchik, D., & Shealy, C. (2012, September). *Linking campus internationalization to effective international education outcomes assessment*. Symposium delivered at the annual meeting of the European Association of International Educators, Dublin, Ireland.

Diener, E., Lucas, R., & Scollon, C. (2006). Beyond the hedonic treadmill. Revising the adaptation theory of well-being. *American Psychologist, 61*(4), 305–314.

Duerden, M., Widmer, M., Taniguchi, S., & McCoy, J. (2009). Adventures in identity development: The impact of adventure recreation on adolescent identity development. *Identity: An International Journal of Theory and Research, 9*(4), 341–359.

Dunkel, C., Kim, J., & Papini, D. (2012). The general factor of psychosocial development and its relation to the general factor of personality and life history strategy. *Personality and Individual Differences, 52*(2), 202–206.

Dunkel, C., Mathes, E., & Harbke, C. (2011). Life history strategy, identity consolidation, and psychological well-being. *Personality and Individual Differences, 51*(1), 34–38.

Epstein, G. (1980). *Studies in non-deterministic psychology*. New York, NY: Human Sciences Press, Inc.

Erikson, E. (1950). *Childhood and society*. New York, NY: W.W. Norton & Co.

Erikson, E. (1968). *Identity: Youth and crisis*. Oxford, England: W.W. Norton & Co.

Folkman, S. (2010). Stress, coping and hope. *Psycho-Oncology, 19*(9), 901–908.

Greene, R. L. (2010). *The MMPI-2/MMPI-2-RF: An interpretive manual* (3rd ed.). Upper Saddle River, NJ: Prentice Hall.

Harter, S. (1999). *The construction of the self: A developmental perspective*. New York, NY: The Guilford Press.

Harter, S. (2012). Emerging self-processes during childhood and adolescence. In M. R. Leary & J. P. Tangney (Eds.), *Handbook of self and identity* (2nd ed., pp. 680–715). New York, NY: The Guilford Press.

Hayes, D., Shealy, C., Sivo, S., & Weinstein, Z. (1999, August). *Psychology, religion, and Scale 5 (Religious Traditionalism) of the "BEVI."* Poster session presented at the meeting of the American Psychological Association, Boston, MA.

Helson, R. (1967). Personality characteristics and developmental history of creative college women. *Genetic Psychology Monographs, 76*(2), 205–256.

Henrich, J., Heine, S., & Norenzayan, A. (2010). The weirdest people in the world? *Behavioral and Brain Sciences, 33*(2–3), 61–83.

Hill, C., Johnson, M., Brinton, C., Staton, R., Sternberger, L., & Shealy (2013, August). *The etiology of economic beliefs and values: Implications and applications from the Forum BEVI Project.* Poster presented at the annual meeting of the American Psychological Association, Honolulu, HI.

Isley, E., Shealy, C., Crandall, K., Sivo, S., & Reifsteck, J. (1999, August). *Relevance of the "BEVI" for research in developmental psychopathology.* Poster session presented at the meeting of the American Psychological Association, Boston, MA.

Jopp, D., & Schmitt, M. (2010). Dealing with negative life events: Differential effects of personal resources, coping strategies, and control beliefs. *European Journal of Aging, 7*(3), 167–180.

Josselson, R. (1987). *Finding herself: Pathways to identity development in women.* San Francisco, CA: Jossey-Bass.

Kagitcibas, C. (2005). Autonomy and relatedness in cultural context: Implications for self and family. *Journal of Cross-Cultural Psychology, 36*(4), 403–422.

Kernberg, O., & Clarkin, J. (1993). Developing a disorder-specific manual: The treatment of borderline character disorder. In N. E. Miller, L. Luborsky, J. P. Barber, & J. P. Docherty (Eds.), *Psychodynamic treatment research: A handbook for clinical practice* (pp. 227–244). New York, NY: Basic Books.

Kernis, M., Lakey, C., & Heppner, W. (2008). Secure versus fragile high self-esteem as a predictor of verbal defensiveness: Converging findings across three different markers. *Journal of Personality, 76*(3), 477–512.

Kerpelman, J., & Pittman, J. (2001). The instability of possible selves: Identity processes within late adolescents' close peer relationships. *Journal of Adolescence, 24*(4), 491–512.

Kinsler, P. (1973). Ego identity status and intimacy. *Dissertation Abstracts International, 33*(8), 3946B.

Kroger, J., & Marcia, J. (2011). The identity statuses: Origins, meanings, and interpretations. In S. J. Schwartz, K. Luyckx, & V. L. Vignoles (Eds.), *Handbook of identity theory and research* (Vol. 1 & 2, pp. 31–53). New York, NY: Springer Science + Business Media.

Lam, J. (1997). Transformation from public administration to management: Success and challenges of public sector reform in Hong Kong. *Public Productivity and Management Review, 20*, 405–418.

Luyckx, K., Goosens, L., Soenens, B., Beyers, W., & Vansteenkiste, M. (2005). Identity statuses based on 4 rather than 2 identity dimensions: Extending and refining Marcia's paradigm. *Journal of Youth and Adolescence, 34*(6), 605–618.

Luyckx, K., Schwartz, S. J., Berzonsky, M. D., Soenens, B., Vansteenkiste, M., & Smits, L., & Goosens, L. (2008). Capturing ruminative exploration: Extending the four-dimensional model of identity formation in late adolescence. *Journal of Research in Personality, 42,* 58–82.

Luyckx, K., Klimstra, T., Duriez, B., Schwartz, S., & Vanhalst, J. (2012). Identity processes and coping strategies in college students: Short-term longitudinal dynamics and the role of personality. *Journal of Youth Adolescence, 41,* 1226–1239.

Luyckx, K., Klimstra, T., Schwartz, S., & Duriez, B. (2013). Personal identity in college and the work context: Developmental trajectories and psychosocial functioning. *European Journal of Personality, 27,* 222–237.

Marcia, J. (1966). Development and validation of ego identity status. *Journal of Personality and Social Psychology, 3*(5), 551–558.

Marcia, J. (1980). Identity in adolescence. In J. Adelson (Ed.) *Handbook of adolescent psychology* (pp. 159–187). New York, NY: Wiley & Sons.

McAdams, D., Bauer, J., Sakaeda, A., Anyidoho, N., Machado, M., Magrino-Failla, K., . . . Pals, J. (2006). Continuity and change in the life story: A longitudinal study of autobiographical memories in emerging adulthood. *Journal of Personality, 74*(5), 1371–1400.

McAdams, D., Josselson, R., & Lieblich, A. (Eds.). (2006). *Identity and story: Creating self in narrative*. Washington, DC: American Psychological Association.

Meeus, W. (1996). Studies on identity development in adolescence: An overview of research and some new data. *Journal of Youth and Adolescence, 25*(5), 569–598.

Meeus, W., Van de Schoot, R., Keijsers, L., Schwartz, S., & Branje, S. (2010). On the progression and stability of adolescent identity formation: A five-wave longitudinal study in early-to-middle and middle-to-late adolescence. *Child Development, 81*(5), 1565–1581.

Moos, R., & Holohan, C. (2003). Dispositional and contextual perspectives on coping: Towards an integrative framework. *Journal of Clinical Psychology, 59*(12), 1387–1403.

Oyserman, D., & Jame, L. (2011). Possible identities. In S. J. Schwartz, K. Luyckx, & V. L. Vignoles (Eds.), *Handbook of identity theory and research* (Vol. 1 & 2, pp. 117–145). New York, NY: Springer Science + Business Media.

Pals, J. (1999). Identity consolidation in early adulthood: Relations with ego-resiliency, the context of marriage, and personality change. *Journal of Personality, 67*(2), 295–329.

Patel, R., Shealy, C. N., & De Michele, P. (2007, August). *Environmental beliefs and values: Etiology, maintenance, and transformation*. Poster session presented at the annual meeting of the American Psychological Association, San Francisco, CA.

Pysarchik, D. T., Shealy, C. N., & Whalen, B. (2007, February). *Antecedents to outcomes-based international learning: A new psychometric assessment approach*. Paper presented at the annual meeting of the Association of International Education Administrators, Washington, DC.

Read, D., Adams, G., & Dobson, W. (1984). Ego-identity, personality, and social influence style. *Journal of Personality and Social Psychology, 46*(1), 169–177.

Reis, O., & Youniss, J. (2004). Patterns in identity change and development in relationships with mothers and friends. *Journal of Adolescent Research, 19*(1), 31–44.

Ryan, R., & Deci, E. (2001). On happiness and human potentials: A review of research on hedonic and eudaimonic well-being. *Annual Review of Psychology, 52*, 141–166.

Ryff, C. (1989). Happiness is everything, or is it? Explorations on the meaning of psychological well-being. *Journal of Personality & Social Psychology, 57*(6), 1069–1081.

Schmid, J., & Leiman, J. (1957). The development of hierarchical factor solutions. *Psychometrika, 22*, 53–61.

Schneider, D. (2011). Wealth and the marital divide. *American Journal of Sociology, 117*(2), 627–667.

Schwartz, S. (2007). The structure of identity consolidation: Multiple correlated constructs or one superordinate construct? *Identity: An International Journal of Theory and Research, 7*(1), 27–49.

Schwartz, S., Beyers, W., Luyckx, K., Soenens, B., Zamboanga, B., Forthun, L., . . . Waterman, A. (2011). Examining the light and dark sides of emerging adults' identity: A study of identity status differences in positive and negative psychosocial functioning. *Journal of Youth Adolescence, 40*(7), 839–859.

Schwartz, S., Cote, J., & Arnett, J. (2005). Identity and agency in emerging adulthood: Two developmental routes in the individualization process. *Youth and Society, 37*(2), 201–229.

Schwartz, S., Donnellan, M. B., Ravert, R., Luyckx, K., & Zamboanga, B. (2012). Identity development, personality, and well-being in adolescence and emerging adulthood: Theory, research, and recent advances. In R. Lerner, M. Easterbrooks, J. Mistry, & I. Weiner (Eds.), *Handbook of psychology, volume six: Developmental psychology* (pp. 339–364). Hoboken, NJ: Wiley.

Schwartz, S., Forthun, L., Ravert, R., Zamboanga, B., Umana-Taylor, A., Filton, B., . . . Hudson, M. (2010). Identity consolidation and health risk behaviors in college students. *American Journal of Health Behaviors, 34*(2), 214–224.

Schwartz, S., Klimstra, T., Luyckx, K., Hale, W., & Meeus, W. (2012) Characterizing the self-system over time in adolescence: Internal structure and associations with internalizing symptoms. *Journal of Youth Adolescence, 41*, 1208–1225.

Schwartz, S., Mason, C., Pantin, H., & Szapocznik, J. (2008). Effect of family functioning and identity confusion on substance use and sexual behavior in Hispanic immigrant early adolescents. *Identity: An International Journal of Theory and Research, 8*(2), 107–124.

Schwartz, S., Montgomery, M., & Briones, E. (2006). The role of identity in acculturation among immigrant people: Theoretical propositions, empirical questions, and applied recommendations. *Human Development, 49*(1), 1–30.

Schwartz, S., Rodriguez, L., Weisskirch, R., Zamboanga, B., & Pantin, H. (2012). Personal, ethnic, and cultural identity in urban youth: Links with risk and resilience. In G. Creasey & P. Jarvis (Eds.), *Adolescent development and school achievement in urban communities: Resilience in the neighbourhood* (pp. 216–226). New York, NY: Routledge.

Schwartz, S., Whitbourne, S., Weisskirch, R., Vazsonyi, A., & Luyckx, K. (2012). Converging identities: Dimensions of acculturation and personal identity status among immigrant college students. *Cultural Diversity and Ethnic Minority Psychology, 19*(2), 155–165.

Schwartz, S., Zamboanga, B., Weisskirch, R., & Rodrigues, L. (2009). The relationships of personal and ethnic identity exploration to indices of adaptive and maladaptive psychosocial functioning. *International Journal of Behavior Development, 33*(2), 131–144.

Schwartz, S. J. (2001). The evolution of Eriksonian and neo-Eriksonian identity theory and research: A review and integration. *Identity: An International Journal of Theory and Research, 1*, 7–58.

Schwartz, S. J., Zamboanga, B. L., Meca, A., & Ritchie, R. A. (2012). Identity around the world: An overview. *New Directions in Child and Adolescent Development, 2012*(138), 1–18.

Schwartz, S. J., Zamboanga, B. L., Wang, W., & Olthuis, J. V. (2009). Measuring identity from an Eriksonian perspective: Two sides of the same coin? *Journal of Personality Assessment, 91*(2), 143–154.

Shealy, C. N. (1995). From Boys Town to Oliver Twist. Separating fact from fiction in welfare reform and out-of-home placement of children and youth. *American Psychologist, 50*(8), 565–580.

Shealy, C. N. (2000a, July). *The Beliefs, Events, and Values Inventory (BEVI): Implications for cross-cultural research and practice*. Paper presented at the meeting of the International Congress of Psychology, Stockholm, Sweden.

Shealy, C. N. (2000b, July). *The Beliefs, Events, and Values Inventory (BEVI): Implications for research and theory in social psychology*. Paper presented at the meeting of the International Congress of Psychology, Stockholm, Sweden.

Shealy, C. N. (2004). A model and method for "making" a C-I psychologist: Equilintegration (EI) theory and the Beliefs, Events, and Values Inventory (BEVI). [Special Series]. *Journal of Clinical Psychology, 60*(10), 1065–1090.

Shealy, C. N. (2005). Justifying the justification hypothesis: Scientific-humanism, Equilintegration (EI) theory, and the Beliefs, Events, and Values Inventory (BEVI). [Special Series]. *Journal of Clinical Psychology, 61*(1), 81–106.

Shealy, C. N. (2006). *The Beliefs, Events, and Values Inventory (BEVI): Overview, implications, and guidelines*. Test manual. Harrisonburg, VA: Author.

Shealy, C. N. (2012). *Making sense of beliefs and values*. New York, NY: Springer Publishing.

Shealy, C. N. (2015). *The Beliefs, Events, and Values Inventory (BEVI): Overview, implications, and guidelines*. Test manual. Staunton, VA: Author.

Shealy, C. N. (2016). *Making sense of beliefs and values*. New York, NY: Springer Publishing.

Shealy, C. N., Bhuyan, D., & Sternberger, L. G. (2012). Cultivating the capacity to care in children and Youth: Implications from EI Theory, EI Self, and BEVI. In U. Nayar (Ed.), *Child and adolescent mental health* (pp. 240–255). New Delhi, India: Sage Publications.

Shiner, R., & Masten, A. (2012). Childhood personality as a harbinger of competence and resilience in adulthood. *Development and Psychopathology, 24*(2), 507–528.

Showers, C., & Zeigler-Hill, V. (2003). Organization of self-knowledge: Features, functions, and flexibility. In M. Leary & J. Tangney (Eds.), *Handbook of self and identity*, (pp. 47–67). New York, NY: Guilford Press.

Skorikov, V., & Vondracek, F. (1998). Vocational identity development: Its relationship to other identity domains and to overall identity development. *Journal of Career Assessment, 6*(1), 13–35.

Skorikov V. B., & Vondracek, F. W. (2011). Occupational identity. In S. J. Schwartz, K. Luyckx, & V. L. Vignoles (Eds.), *Handbbok of identity theory and research* (pp. 693–714). New York, NY: Springer.

Smits, I., Soenens, B., Vansteenkiste, M., Luyckx, K., & Goossens, L. (2010). Why do adolescents gather information or stick to parental norms? Examining autonomous and controlled motives behind adolescents' identity style. *Journal of Youth Adolescence, 39*(11), 1343–1356.

Soenens, B., & Vansteenkiste, M. (2011). When is identity congruent with the self? A self-determination theory perspective. In S. J. Schwartz, K. Luyckx, & V. L. Vignoles (Eds.), *Handbook of identity theory and research* (Vol. 1 & 2, pp. 381–401). New York, NY: Springer Science + Business Media.

Soenens, B., Vansteenkiste, M., Lens, W., Luycks, K., Goossens, L., Beyers, W., & Ryan, R. (2007). Conceptualizing parental autonomy support: Adolescent perceptions of promotion of independence versus promotion of volitional functioning. *Developmental Psychology, 43*(3), 633–646.

Spaeth, J., Shealy, C., Cobb, H., Staton, R., & Sternberger, L. (2010). *Life Events, Identity Development, and the Construction of Self: Preliminary Results from the Forum BEVI Project*. Poster Presented at the American Psychological Association Annual Conference, San Diego, CA.

Spears, R. (2011). Group identities: The social identity perspective. In S. J. Schwartz, K. Luyckx, & V. L. Vignoles (Eds.), *Handbook of identity theory and research* (Vol. 1 & 2, pp. 201–224). New York, NY: Springer Science + Business Media.

Stryker, S. (2004). Identity competition: Key to differential social movement participation? In S. Stryker, T. Owens, & R. White (Eds.), *Self, identity, and social movements* (pp. 21–40). Minneapolis, MN: University of Minnesota Press.

Tabit, M., Cozen, J., Dyjak-Leblank, K., Pendleton, C., Shealy, C., Sternberger, L., & Staton, R. (2011, June). The sociocultural impact of denial: Empirical evidence from the Forum BEVI Project. Poster presented at American Psychological Association.

Tajfel, H. (1982). Social psychology of intergroup relations. *Annual Review of Psychology, 33*, 1–39.

Valde, G. (1996). Identity closure: A fifth identity status. *The Journal of Genetic Psychology, 157*(3), 245–254.

Vedder, P., Berry, J., Sabatier, C., & Sam, D. (2009). The intergenerational transmission of values in national and immigrant families: The role of zeitgeist. *Journal of Youth and Adolescence, 38*(5), 642–653.

Vignoles, V., Schwartz, S., & Luyckx, K. (2011). Introduction: Toward an integrative view of identity. In S. J. Schwartz, K. Luyckx, & V. L. Vignoles (Eds.), *Handbook of identity theory and research* (Vols. 1 & 2, pp. 1–27). New York, NY: Springer Science + Business Media.

Waterman, A. (1982). Identity development from adolescence to adulthood: An extension of theory and review of research. *Developmental Psychology, 18*(3), 341–358.

Waterman, A. (1999). Identity, the identity statuses, and identity status development: contemporary statement. *Developmental Review, 19*(4), 591–621.

Waterman, A. (2007). Doing well: The relationship of identity status to three conceptions of well-being. *Identity: An International Journal of Theory and Research, 7*(4), 289–307.

Waterman, A. (2011). Eudaimonic identity theory: Identity as self-discovery. In S. J. Schwartz, K. Luyckx, & V. L. Vignoles (Eds.), *Handbook of identity theory and research* (Vols. 1 & 2, pp. 357–379). New York, NY: Springer Science + Business Media.

ENVIRONMENTAL BELIEFS AND VALUES: IN SEARCH OF MODELS AND METHODS

Sustainable development is development that meets the needs of the present without compromising the ability of future generations to meet their own needs.

—Brundtland Report

As degradation of our climate, resources, and ecosystem continues, the environmental movement strives for relevance and impact. Although there is widespread public support for environmental protection, such support does not translate generally or readily into action. Furthermore, while much scholarly attention has been dedicated to the attitude/behavior gap, such literature is not well connected, lacks definitional and conceptual clarity, and does not sufficiently explicate how and why there are individual differences in the experience and expression of environmental beliefs and values in the first place. As Stern, Dietz, Abel, Guagnano, and Kalof (1999) note, the complexity of such interacting processes too often is reduced to a description of ". . .social-psychological antecedents (sometimes loosely lumped together as 'attitudes') [which] are being put forward as explanatory constructs" (p. 91). Moreover, as Heberlein (2012) observes ". . .attitudes are important but need a more fundamental understanding of the science behind them" (p. 13). In an attempt to find common ground and deepen our understanding along these lines, with the ultimate goal of increasing the coherence and applicability of our theory and data, we first juxtapose a number of models and methods of environmental beliefs and values. We then offer an integrative framework and innovative approach for apprehending and measuring the complex and interacting processes by which environmental beliefs and values are acquired, maintained, and transformed. Finally, we conclude with a practical application of how a proenvironmental model may help transform the beliefs and behaviors of future generations, by highlighting research, education, and practice under the aegis of the global movement in Education for Sustainable Development (ESD) (Center for Green Schools, 2014; McKeown & Nolet, 2012).

More specifically, this chapter is structured in the following manner. First, we overview the following four theories and their accompanying measures: (a) Value–Belief–Norm Theory (VBN) (Stern et al., 1999); (b) Theory of Planned Behavior (TPB) (Ajzen, 1991); (c) Environmental Identity Model (Stets & Biga, 2003); and (d) the Motivation Toward the Environment Scale (MTES) (Pelletier, Tuson, Green-Demers, Noels, & Beaton, 1998). Next, we describe a novel approach to this complex topic—Equilintegration or EI Theory, the EI Self, and the Belief, Events, and Values Inventory (BEVI) (Shealy, 2004, 2016)—which collective examine the formative variables (e.g., life events) that are associated with belief and value mediators regarding the environment as well as a range of interrelated processes (e.g., affective, attributional). Through this juxtaposition of established and emergent models and methods, we hope to facilitate a deeper understanding of the complex idiographic processes that mediate and moderate the relative degree to which individuals are inclined to experience and express care for the living world, as well as the potential application of such theory and data to education and sustainability in the real world, which is our concluding focus.

VALUE–BELIEF–NORM THEORY

Grounded in research on ecofeminism values (Rokeach 1968, 1973; Schwartz 1992, 1994) and norm activation theories (Schwartz, 1970, 1977), VBN suggests a six-stage causal chain of variables that lead to an "ethic of care" perspective. Beginning with (a) *personal values*, to include *altruistic* (e.g., unity with nature), *traditional* (e.g., family), *self-interest* (e.g., control over others), and *openness to change* (e.g., an exciting life); (b) moving to *generalized beliefs*, including but not limited to the New Ecological Paradigm (NEP)—the awareness that human beings are significantly and negatively impacting the natural world; (c) then to *more specific beliefs*, including, but not limited to Awareness of Consequences (AC) (e.g., Do you think that toxic substances in air, water, and the soil will be a very serious problem for the country as a whole?); (d) next, *Ascription of Responsibility* (AR), which refers to the recognition that the individual has a role in mitigating the value under threat; (e) which results in *beliefs about specific actions or personal normative beliefs* (e.g., I feel a personal obligation to do whatever I can to prevent climate change); and finally ending with (f) *types of nonactivist support, defined in three dimensions*: (i) *environmental citizenship* (e.g., Are you a member of any group whose main aim is to preserve or protect the environment?), (ii) *willingness to sacrifice* (e.g., I would be willing to pay much higher taxes in order to protect the environment), and (iii) *consumer behavior* (e.g., How often do you make a special effort to buy paper and plastic products that are made from recycled materials?) (Stern et al., 1999, pp. 95–96).

From the perspective of VBN, values have been found to have both a direct and indirect impact (i.e., values flowing through beliefs) on behavioral intentions (Stern, Dietz, Kalof, & Guagnano, 1995, p. 1630), such that altruistic values were stronger among individuals who participate in proenvironmental behaviors (Stern & Dietz, 1994; Stern, Dietz, & Kalof, 1993; Stern, Dietz, & Guagnano, 1995). Findings also reveal that proenvironmental personal norms are a predicator of all three dimensions of nonactivist support: policy support, private-sphere behaviors, and environmental citizenship (Dietz, Stern, & Guagnano, 1998; Stern et al., 1999). When tested against theories of cultural biases, postmaterialist values, and belief in the sacredness of nature, VBN appears more strongly to be associated with behavioral intentions (Dietz et al., 1998; Stern et al., 1999). Finally, given that VBN was informed in part by the ecofeminism "ethic of care," gender always has assumed a moderating role in this model. More recently, however, other social structural variables (e.g., age/cohort, political ideology, education, race, etc.) have been related to VBN, in recognition that additional social psychological and sociodemographic variables also have considerable explanatory power vis-à-vis the development or magnification of an "ethic to care" (e.g., Dietz et al., 1998; Shealy, Bhuyan, & Sternberger, 2012; Slimak & Dietz, 2006; Stern et al., 1999; Whitfield, Rosa, Dan, & Dietz, 2009).

THEORY OF PLANNED BEHAVIOR

Ajzen's (1991) Theory of Planned Behavior (TPB) is an extension of the theory of reasoned action (Fishbein & Ajzen, 1975) and maintains that attitudes, norms, and perceived behavioral control all lead to behavioral intentions, such that the stronger the intention, the more likely one is to engage in the behavior. In this model, three functions comprise behavioral intentions, including *attitude toward behavior* (referring to an individual's positive or negative evaluations of the behavior); *subjective norm* (social networks that may or may not approve of the behavior); and *perceived behavior control* (the individual's perception of his or her ability to perform the behavior) (Ajzen 1991, p. 188).

In order to evaluate the validity of the TPB in relation to environmental conduct, Kaiser, Hübner, and Bogner (2005) used a five-point bipolar scale. Examples from the measure include: (a) *attitude toward the behavior* ("Refraining from using a clothes dryer—good/bad"); (b) *subjective norms* ("Most people who are important to me think I should refrain from using a clothes dryer—likely/unlikely"); and (c) *perceived behavioral control* ("For me, refraining from using a clothes dryer—simple/complicated"). And finally, to assess actual real world activity vis-à-vis the environment, a fourth dimension of *behavioral intention* also is examined ("I intend to refrain from using a clothes dryer—determined/undetermined") (p. 2155). Results indicate that the TPB accounted for 76% of intention vis-à-vis these three variables and that "subjective norms remain statistically significant in their direct influence on intention" (p. 2167). Furthermore, Kaiser and colleagues also compared the TPB to VBN and found TPB was able to identify behavior and behavioral intention more fully than VBN (see also Oreg & Katz-Gerro, 2006, for another comparison of VBN and TPB). Moreover, in a follow-up study, "intention still determined 43% and 76% of behavior variance" when testing TPB using two different models (Kaiser, Schultz, & Scheuthle, 2007, p. 1539). Overall, in their chapter on environmental attitudes, Gifford and Sussman (2012) highlight TPB and VBN as two of the most prominent theories in explaining the relationship between attitudes and behaviors.

Manning (2009) conducted a meta-analysis with subjective norms broken into two categories—*perceived injunctive*, referring to the motivation "to comply with perceived behavioral expectations of relevant referents" (p. 652) and *descriptive information*, which "functions as a heuristic with regard to behavioral decisions offering cues as to what is appropriate behavior in a given situation" (p. 652)—and found a stronger relationship between descriptive information and behavior. However, more recent studies find that such subjective norms are *not* a significant predictor of behavior, as Marchini and Macdonald (2012) found in research on predicting rancher intent to kill jaguars. Further illustrating the complexity of such relationships, another study measuring carbon offset behavior concluded that reported self-identity was a significant determinant of behavior whereas perceived behavioral control, subjective norms, and attitudes were not (Whitmarsh & O'Neill, 2010).

ENVIRONMENTAL IDENTITY MODEL

Stets and Biga's (2003) Environmental Identity Model, grounded largely in identity theory (e.g., identity theory draws on a symbolic interaction orientation), focuses on prominence, salience, and commitment. More specifically, the dimension of *prominence* taps the reported importance for individuals of relating to or interacting with the natural environment. For *salience*, individuals might be asked how they would describe themselves to a roommate they were meeting for the first time (e.g., worker, environmentalist, friend, etc.). For *identity commitment*, individuals might be asked whether they had met any friends through their environmental activities (via quantitative assessment) as well as how important it was to them to be regarded by others as an environmentalist (via qualitative assessment). Findings suggest that human agency is based on identity rather than attitudinal processes; therefore, identity is seen to be an important construct in explaining motivation for behavior (Stets, 2006; Stets & Biga, 2003). Moreover, when measuring identity with two competing proxies for attitudes, NEP and AC, they found that NEP did not correlate with proenvironmental behavior, whereas AC did, on the social altruism dimension. However, without an identity dimension, both NEP and AC are significantly correlated with proenvironmental behavior, although more strongly with AC. Although studies using the Stets and Biga model of environmental identity are rare, recent scholarship has emphasized the role of identity vis-à-vis environmental behavior. For example, environmental identity was found to be a significant predictor of behavior in the absence of an affective connection (Hinds & Sparks, 2008) and in comparison to TPB variables (Whitmarsh & O'Neill, 2010).

MOTIVATION TOWARD THE ENVIRONMENTAL SCALE

As a fourth exemplar, Pelletier, Tuson, Green-Demers, Noels, and Beaton (1998) developed the Motivation Toward the Environment Scale (MTES), which is grounded in Self-Determination Theory (SDT). According to SDT, people act in the service of basic needs of autonomy, competence, and relatedness, which are facilitated or impeded via intrinsically or extrinsically motivated behavior (Darner, 2009; Deci & Ryan, 1985, 2000). This model depicts three broad levels of motivation—intrinsic, extrinsic, and amotivation—in which *intrinsic* is the deepest and most powerful form of motivation, and is explained as "the innate tendency to engage in an activity for the sole pleasure and satisfaction derived from its practice" (Pelletier et al., 1998, p. 441) and is measured by questions addressing variables such as "for the pleasure I experience when I find new ways to improve the quality of the environment" (Villacorta, Koestner, Lekes, 2003, p. 492). In *extrinsic* motivation, "The goal of the behavior is to bring about positive consequences or to avoid negative ones" (Pelletier et al., 1998, p. 441). Extrinsic motivation consists of four subsets and affiliated sample measurements, which are listed in descending order: *integration* (e.g., "because being environmentally conscious has become a fundamental part of who I am"); *identification* (e.g., "because I think it's a good idea to do something about the environment"); *introjection* (e.g., "I would feel bad if I didn't do anything"); and *external* (e.g., I am environmentally inclined "to avoid being criticized") (Villacorta et al., 2003, p. 492). *Amotivation* is the third level in which "actions are mechanical and meaningless" (Pelletier et al., 1998, p. 442). A measurement example is, "Honestly, I don't know; I truly have the impression I'm wasting my time doing things for the environment" (Villacorta et al., 2003, p. 492).

Findings from this line of research reveal people are behaving proenvironmentally for different reasons (Pelletier et al., 1998), where concern for the environment is aligned most closely with intrinsic motivation. However, social networks (e.g., parents and peers) also influence one's concern for the environment vis-à-vis extrinsic integration (Villacorta et al., 2003, p. 501). In a comparative study, values were found to influence proenvironmental behavior more than self-determined motivational types (de Groot & Steg, 2010). Furthermore, that same study found values to influence motivation. For example, when altruistic or biospheric values were present, so was intrinsic motivation.

THEORY COMPARISONS

In reviewing the preceding theories and measures of social psychological antecedents to environmental behaviors, we highlight similarities and differences in approach (e.g., Oreg & Katz-Gerro, 2006). The theories that appear to offer the most homogeneity in their measurements are Value-Belief-Norm (Stern et al., 1999) and the Environmental Identity Model (Stets & Biga, 2003). For example, Dietz, Stern, and Guagnano (1998) make clear that behavioral indicators include both intentions and actual behavior (p. 454), congruent with Stets and Biga who assess environmentalism through self-reported behaviors and behavioral intentions. Notably, however, current research suggests that using behavioral intentions as a substitute for actual behavior remains problematic (Heberlein, 2012).

Furthermore, Stern and colleagues (1999) and Stets and Biga (2003) both use the NEP and AC to measure environmental attitudes. However, the two theories differ in two ways. First, NEP and AC are only a portion of the Value–Belief–Norm Model, while Stets and Biga use these variables solely as proxies for attitudes. Remember from VBN that the NEP measures a broader spectrum of concerns about the environment, while AC relates to specific beliefs about environmental degradation. For Stets and Biga, AC has three dimensions: egoistic, social altruistic, and biospheric. Furthermore, they measure these three dimensions with a mix of values from Stern and colleagues as well as AC measurements. Moreover, it appears as though Stets and Biga may have blended two variables (values and AC) from VBN and labeled them AC. Finally, Stern and colleagues note that they did not measure identity in their work (p. 89). Stets and Biga, however, describe the structure of identity similarly to the structure of values described by Stern and colleagues (i.e., prominent and salient identities from prominent and salient values). In sum, the distinction between the structure of values and the structure of identity based upon these theories is unclear.

Complicating matters further, of the four subsets of extrinsic motivation described by Pelletier et al. (1998) in the MTES, integration and identification appear consonant with environmental identity theory. Within MTES, the concept of integration is motivated by self-definition, meaning that individuals behave in a way that aligns with their own definition of self. Similarly, within the concept of identification, an individual is motivated by his or her own values, goals, and identities. However, one could argue that self-definition is created through an individual's values, goals, and identities, which effectively erases the line between integration and identification. As with much work in this area, the literature is vague about the distinction between these terms. What is explicit is the congruency between these two constructs (integration and identification from the MTES) and environmental identity. All seem to address the relative degree to which individuals act in ways that are consistent with how they see themselves, which may then coincide with a personal norm, as used in VBN, which is defined as "the expectations people hold for themselves while underscoring that these expectations derive from socially shared norms" (Schwartz, 1973, p. 353).

Another parallel among the literature can be found in the assertion by Pelletier and colleagues (1998)—regarding the MTES—in which environmental motivation is associated with the relative degree of satisfaction about environmental conditions.

Put simply, an individual evaluates the state of the environment as a basis for determining his or her own level of satisfaction; a negative evaluation compels the identification of improvement goals, which is a basis for motivation. This frame is congruent with AC and AR, derived from Schwartz's Norm Activation Theory and expressed through the VBN. Similar to the assertion by Pelletier and colleagues, then, individuals who tend to experience awareness of the consequences of environmental problems likewise tend to ascribe responsibility to themselves to combat such problems.

In addition to multiple problems of definitional clarity and distinctiveness as illustrated, theories may or may not address issues of etiology (e.g., how these constructs form) or individual differences (e.g., how and why people differ) in their environmental beliefs, values, and behaviors (see Chapter 2). Henry and Dietz (2012) acknowledge that such matters are important, but unspecified, vis-à-vis VBN: "The approach assumes that values are the result of early socialization, [and] are relatively stable over time, and are less malleable than either beliefs or norms" (p. 242). Ajzen (1991) makes a similar observation:

> The Theory of Planned Behavior traces attitudes, subjective norms, and perceived behavioral control to an underlying foundation of beliefs about the behavior. Although there is plenty of evidence for significant relations between behavioral beliefs and attitudes toward the behavior, between normative beliefs and attitudes toward the behavior, between normative beliefs and subjective norms, and between control beliefs and perceptions of behavior control, *the exact form* [emphasis added] of these relations is still uncertain. (p. 206)

Finally, regarding issues of etiology and individual difference that are emphasized next, Stern and colleagues (1999) concur that "further work is needed to understand how specific opportunities and constraints act, and also how life histories embedded in gender, race/ethnicity, and community may shape values and beliefs" (Kalof, Dietz, Stern & Guagnano, 1999, p. 91; see also Oreg & Katz-Gerro, 2006).

Recommendations for Scholarship

The preceding overview of prevailing theories of environmental beliefs, values, and behaviors suggests the following five observations and consequent recommendations for scholarship.

First, at times the rationale for selected terminology is not sufficiently defined

In other words, terms used in some of the preceding theories fail to explicate how or why they have been selected. Thus, it is difficult to appraise the thinking that prompted a focus on one term over another.

Second and related, the apparent meaning among selected terms is often identical, even though terminology is not

Thus, it often seems that scholars are focusing on different areas of emphasis when in fact they are studying very similar if not identical phenomena. The opposite confound applies when identical terms are selected, even though the apparent meaning of such terms may be quite different.

Third, problems of terminology are exacerbated further in the development and/or selection of specific measures

Because there is little coherence at the level of terminology, the operationalization of such terminology (i.e., the development of specific items to measure a construct) often is quite divergent, which impedes a direct comparison among studies.

Fourth, fundamental questions of etiology and individual differences that are or should be relevant are neither asked nor answered

Nowhere is this shortcoming more apparent than in the seeming lack of recognition that until we examine the etiology of environmental worldviews—as well as the reasons for differences and similarities among individuals in what they say and do—it will be difficult for us to offer the kind of nuanced and sophisticated explanations, recommendations, and models that can illuminate these complex processes or make a demonstrable difference at an applied level in the "real world."

Fifth and finally, the complex and interacting nature of the "environmental self" should neither be understood nor examined as an isolable and unitary construct

In other words, it is questionable whether an individual's environmental "identity" really operates apart from other aspects of self. Thus, what might we learn if we examined environmental beliefs, values, and other antecedents in a much fuller and richer context, by considering developmental, contextual, cultural, affective, attributional, and nonconscious processes that presumably are no less integral to "self" than are those that relate exclusively to the environment? Likewise, what might we learn about environmental beliefs and values if we examined other processes that mediate and moderate their development and expression?

Nothing in the preceding critique should be construed to suggest that work already done in this area is flawed. As the theories illustrate, much has been learned by attempting to articulate and measure relevant constructs and processes. However, at this point in the evolution of this field, the central contention here is that scholarship in this area may greatly be advanced and enhanced by more focused attention to the preceding observations and recommendations. Toward such means and ends—and eschewing any and all definitive claims—the second half of this chapter focuses on an innovative and integrative model and method that attempt to address these points, and offer findings that appear to have promise in furthering our understanding of these complex and interacting processes as well as attendant matters of real world application.

EI THEORY, EI SELF, AND BEVI

Before providing an overview of the Equilintegration (EI) model and the Beliefs, Events, and Values Inventory (BEVI) method, it may be helpful to articulate how and why "beliefs and values" are defined as they are particularly, because—as we have argued previously—one of the main problems with scholarship in this area is a lack of specificity in this regard. Toward this end, we recall Allport (1961), who defined a "value" as "...a belief upon which a man acts by preference" (p. 454), which suggests that values are grounded in, or based upon, beliefs. Building on Allport's work, Rokeach further elaborates, "Values, like all beliefs, have cognitive, affective, and behavioral components. . ." (Rokeach, 1973, p. 7). Along these lines, Shealy (2016) offers the following observation vis-à-vis belief/value definition and measurement:

> . . . recall for Rokeach that value systems were "part of a functionally inte-grated cognitive system in which the basic units of analysis are beliefs. Clus-ters of beliefs form attitudes that are functionally and cognitively connected to the value system" (Braithwaite & Scott, 1991, p. 662). Because Rokeach was interested in how these value systems were associated with a range of predict-able processes and outcomes, much of his research and measurement work occurred at this level of analysis even as he clearly contended that "beliefs" were the "basic units of analysis." Rokeach was not alone in this regard as other pioneers noted previously also granted the legitimacy of this key point. . .by starting with "belief" as the most basic level of analysis—and specifying its hierarchical relationship to values, schemas, attitudes, and worldviews—we are able simultaneously to differentiate and juxtapose these constructs in order to clarify their relationship to one another. From the perspective of the BEVI, such clarification means that these constructs may be identified and studied empirically, in a manner that is informed psychometrically via factor analysis, and its attendant hierarchical organization. Specifically, a *"belief"* is akin to a single BEVI item, such as "Shame can be a good motivator for children." A *"value"* is akin to a subscale (i.e., a subfactor), which essentially is a cluster-ing of beliefs that are differently worded but occupy similar statistical space. A *"schemattitude"* (from "schema" and "attitude" scholarship, typically engaged in by clinical practitioners and social psychology researchers, respec-tively) is akin to a scale, such as Sociocultural Openness on the BEVI, which is comprised of two or more subfactors, which may be differentiated statistically but are also sufficiently correlated as to "load" on the same scale. A *"world-view"* is akin to all that is represented by the assessment instrument as a whole; using the BEVI, for example, someone's worldview includes the sum total of all scales taken together, which collectively represents (i.e., samples) the "big picture" of how an individual sees self, others, and the world at large. Because "belief" is the most basic building block of this system, it is defined in detail; the remaining three constructs (values, schemattitudes, worldview) are deriva-tive terms that also are empirically (i.e., statistically) verifiable. In summary, then. . .from a definitional standpoint, a *belief:* is an internalized and discrete version of reality (i.e., a mental representation about self, others, or the world at large) that can influence and mediate the experience and expression of needs, feelings, thoughts, and behaviors. . . . (pp. 45, 48)

From this definitional point of departure—and deliberate linkage to measure-ment—it now is possible to consider accompanying matters of theory. Although a full explication is presented in Chapters 2 and 3, a brief overview of the three main com-ponents of this approach—Equilintegration (EI) Theory, the EI Self, and BEVI—may be helpful at this point. Equilintegration (EI) Theory seeks to explain "the processes by which beliefs, values, and 'worldviews' are acquired and maintained, why their alter-ation is typically resisted, and how and under what circumstances their modification occurs" (Shealy, 2004, p. 1075). Derivative of EI Theory (Shealy, 2004), the Equilinte-gration or EI Self explains the integrative and synergistic processes by which beliefs and values are acquired, maintained, and transformed as well as how and why these are linked to the formative variables, core needs, and adaptive potential of the self. Informed by scholarship in a range of key areas (e.g., "needs-based" research and theory; developmental psychopathology; social cognition; affect regulation; processes and outcomes of therapy; theories and models of "self"), the EI Self seeks to illustrate how the interaction between our core needs (e.g., for attachment, affiliation) and formative variables (e.g., caregiver, culture) results in beliefs and values about self, others, and the world at large and internalize over the course of development and across the life span (see Chapter 3; http://www.ibavi.org/content/featured-projects).

Concomitant with EI Theory and the EI Self, the BEVI is a comprehensive analytic tool in development since the early 1990s that examines how and why we come to see ourselves, others, and the larger world as we do (e.g., how life experiences, culture, and context affect our beliefs, values, and worldview) as well as the influence of such processes on multiple aspects of human functioning (e.g., learning processes, relationships, personal growth, the pursuit of life goals). For example, the BEVI assesses processes such as: basic openness; the tendency to (or not to) stereotype in particular ways; self- and emotional awareness; preferred strategies for making sense of why "other" people and cultures "do what they do"; global engagement (e.g., receptivity to different cultures, religions, and social practices); and worldview shift (e.g., to what degree do beliefs and values change as a result of specific experiences). BEVI results are translated into reports at the individual, group, and organizational levels and used in a wide range of contexts for a variety of applied and research purposes (e.g., to track and examine changes in worldviews over time) (e.g., Anmuth et al., 2013; Atwood, Chkhaidze, Shealy Staton, Sternberger, 2014; Brearly, Shealy, Staton, Sternberger, 2012; Hill et al., 2013; Patel, Shealy, & De Michele, 2007; Pysarchik, Shealy, & Whalen, 2007; Shealy, 2004, 2005, 2006, 2012; Shealy, Bhuyan, & Sternbergerer, 2012; Tabit et al., 2011; for more information about the BEVI, including a description of scales, see Chapter 4).

UNDERSTANDING ENVIRONMENTAL BELIEFS AND VALUES THROUGH THE BEVI: THREE STUDIES

As may be clear from the preceding overview, the BEVI explicitly examines issues of etiology and individual differences in environmental beliefs and values—while allowing for consideration of related constructs—through examination of patterns of interrelationship among various constructs on the BEVI. To illustrate how the BEVI examines these processes, we highlight three studies that have attempted to address the nature and origins of environmental beliefs and values.

Study 1: Environmental Beliefs and Values: Who Cares, Who Does Not, and Why?

Patel (2008) examined etiology, maintenance, and transformation of environmental beliefs, values, and worldviews through the BEVI and complementary measures (Patel et al., 2007). A convenience sample of 204 undergraduate students enrolled in general psychology classes at a comprehensive university in Virginia[1] was selected, and data were collected in the following order: (a) online completion of the BEVI,

---

[1] This study was approved through the Institutional Review Board (IRB) in 2007.

(b) completion of the NEP (Dunlap, Van Liere, Mertig, & Jones, 2000), (c) watching advertisements highlighting adverse effects of global warming, and (d) completion of the Global Warming Scale.[2] It should be noted that each of the BEVI's process scales was further developed since this study (based upon Exploratory Factor Analysis [EFA] and later Confirmatory Factor Analysis [CFA]) into subscales that address specific domains (see Chapter 4). A particularly relevant subscale for the purpose of this study is the Ecological Closure (EC)[3] scale, which assesses (among other processes) an individual's beliefs about the environment and human–nature interactions. Sample items from EC of the BEVI include "I feel a deep spiritual connection to the Earth"; "We must do more to protect the Earth's natural resources"; and, "Big corporations often harm the Earth."

The NEP also was included in this analysis as it is a widely accepted scale and used in a number of studies, some of which have been described previously. Dunlap and Van Liere (1978) developed the New Environmental Paradigm scale to measure the extent to which an individual endorses a worldview predicated upon ecological principles; it was revised and renamed the New Ecological Paradigm (NEP) scale in 1990 (Dunlap et al., 2000). Consisting of 15 Likert-scale items, it includes items such as: *We are approaching the limit of the number of people the Earth can support; Humans have the right to modify the natural environment to suit their needs; When humans interfere with nature it often produces disastrous consequences.*

One-way analysis of variance (ANOVA) was conducted to determine differences in NEP and EC scores based on demographic variables. Results with significance for the one-way ANOVAs are presented in Table 7.1.

As shown in Table 7.1, the effect of gender was significant for the NEP, $F(1,189) = 7.88, p = .01$. The NEP was significantly higher for females (M = 52.85) as compared to males (M = 49.19). The effect of political orientation was found to be significant for the NEP, $F(3,187) = 5.20, p = .00$, and the EC score, $F(3,187) = 6.44, p = .00$. Religious orientation was shown to have a significant effect on the NEP, $F(2,188) = 7.08, p < .001$.

Post hoc analyses were conducted using Bonferroni's post hoc criterion in significance for effects of political orientation and religious orientation. These analyses revealed that the NEP score for Democrats (M = 54.07, $p = .00$) was significantly higher than for Republicans (M = 48.88). Similarly, EC for Republicans (M = 43.05) was significantly higher as compared to both Democrats (M = 41.11, $p = .00$) and Independents (M = 40.97, $p = .00$). NEP scores for Christians (M = 50.78) were significantly lower than Atheists or Agnostics (M = 55.74, $p = .03$) and individuals with other religious orientations (M = 56.58, $p = .01$).

Correlation analyses were conducted to determine the relationship between the NEP and all 10 scales of the BEVI.[4] Table 7.2 shows the Pearson's coefficient of correlation for these scales, including significance levels. Results indicated several important relationships.

---

[2] We did not include data on the Global Warming Scale, since this pilot measure did not substantially add to the following findings.

[3] In the Patel (2008) study, this scale was labeled Ecological Closure (EC) and is now labeled Ecological Resonance (ER). Note that a high score on EC in Study 1 would be associated with disagreement on these sample items.

[4] Although the scale labels noted in Table 7.2 should provide necessary information regarding the meaning of various BEVI scales, note that the original 10 scales from an earlier version of the BEVI differ somewhat from the current version of the BEVI. See Shealy (2004) for a description of the original BEVI scales; and Chapter 4 for a current version of all BEVI scales.

TABLE 7.1

One-Way ANOVAs for NEP and EC Based on Gender, Political Orientation, and Religious Orientation

DEMOGRAPHIC VARIABLES		NEP	EC
Gender	F	**7.88****	3.40*
	Male	M = 49.19	M = 41.14
	Female	M = 52.85	M = 42.04
Political Orientation	F	**5.20*****	**6.44*****
	Democrat	M = 54.07	M = 41.11
	Independent	M = 52.08	M = 40.97
	Republican	M = 48.88	M = 43.05
	Other	M = 53.31	M = 41.85
Religious Orientation	F	**7.08*****	1.99
	Atheism/Agnosticism	55.74	41.32
	Christianity	50.78	41.99
	Other	56.58	40.63

Note. *p < .05, two-tailed test; **p < .01; ***p < .001.

The NEP (M = 51.85, standard deviation [SD] = 8.16, N = 191) was found to be significantly correlated with Self Access (SA) (M = 161.75, SD = 6.42), r = −.17, p = .02; Separation Individuation (SI) (M = 45.66, SD = 3.24), r = −.15, p = .04; and Gender Stereotype (GS) (M = 85.37, SD = 4.29), r = .28, p = .00. These correlations are

TABLE 7.2

Correlations Between the New Ecological Paradigm (NEP), Sociocultural Closure (SC), Ecological Closure (EC), Religious Traditionalism (RT), Need For Control (NFC), Emotional Attunement (EA), Self Access (SA), Separation Individuation (SI), and Gender Stereotype (GS) scales on the BEVI

		NEP	GWS	SC	EC	RT	NFC	EA	SA	SI	GS
NEP	Pearson Correlation	1.00	**0.59**	**−0.19**	**−0.31**	−0.04	0.06	−0.05	**−0.17**	**−0.15**	**0.28**
	Sig. (two-tailed)		0.00	0.01	0.00	0.62	0.40	0.49	0.02	0.04	0.00
	N	204	204	191	191	191	191	191	191	191	191
EC	Pearson Correlation	**−0.31**	**−0.23**	**0.58**	1.00	**0.23**	**0.21**	0.03	**0.22**	0.04	−0.05
	Sig. (two-tailed)	0.00	0.00	0.00		0.00	0.00	0.70	0.00	0.58	0.47
	N	191	191	191	191	191	191	191	191	191	191

GWS = global warming scale.

suggestive of a relationship between an individual's ecological worldview (NEP score) and his or her inclination and capacity for understanding or seeking to apprehend "inner" phenomena that theoretically are associated with self-change, growth, and development (SA); the relative degree to which he or she has differentiated from his or her primary caregiver (SI); and gender beliefs regarding roles and relationships (GS). Furthermore, the correlation between the NEP (M = 51.85, SD = 8.16, N = 191) and EC (M = 41.79, SD = 3.03) also was significant, r = −.31, p = .00. Initial evidence for the construct validity of EC is suggested by the significant correlation and direction of relationship among NEP and EC measures.

Additionally, EC (M = 41.79, SD = 3.03, N = 191) was found to be significantly correlated with the Religious Traditionalism (RT) (M = 165.95, SD = 5.71), r = .23, p = .00; Need for Control (NFC) (M = 139.74, SD = 4.80), r = .21, p = .00; and SA (M = 161.75, SD = 6.42), r = .22, p = .00. These correlations are suggestive of a relationship between an individual's EC and his or her core beliefs and values regarding a religious and spiritual worldview, as measured by RT, his or her need to plan, structure, and manage behaviors and emotions, as measured by NFC, and his or her inclination and capacity for understanding or seeking to apprehend "inner" phenomena that are theoretically associated with self-change, growth, and development, as measured by SA.

Study 2: The Relationship Between Ecological Resonance and Other Belief/Value Constructs

For studies 2 and 3, analyses were developed on the basis of a large dataset (N = 2331) collected during 2011 to 2012 from the Forum BEVI Project, a multi-institution, multi-year project examining the assessment of international, multicultural, and transformative learning. Coordinated by the Forum on Education Abroad (www.forumea.org) and International Beliefs and Values Institute (www.ibavi.org), participants primarily included undergraduate students (96.7%) and were recruited through a range of learning experiences (e.g., study abroad, residential learning communities, general education courses with a focus on transformative/multicultural learning). A small portion of graduate students (3.3%) also was included. The sample typically ranged between the ages of 17 and 26, with an average age of 19. However, 3.9% fell into the age range of 26 to 62, with another 9% falling into the age range of 12 to 17. Although the majority of participants reported as U.S. citizens (93.3%), non-U.S. citizens also were included in the sample (N = 156 or 6.7%). Also, participants were drawn from 38 different countries of origin. Of the sample, 79.1% reported as Caucasian with 20.9% as non-Caucasian (6.6% Black or African American; .9% American Indian or Alaskan Native; 7.4% Asian or Pacific Islander; 2.9% Hispanic/Latino; 3% Other). Finally, from the standpoint of gender, 40.8% of the sample was female, with 59.2% male. All participants were required to provide informed consent as determined by multiple Institutional Review Board (IRB) processes, and participation was entirely voluntary. Participants were not required to complete the BEVI, and could elect to discontinue participation at any time. Analyses were conducted via SPSS and MPLUS, and consist of ANOVAs, regression analyses, and structural equation modeling (SEM). More information on the Forum BEVI Project is available in Chapter 4 and at www.ibavi.org/content/featured-projects.

The descriptive information listed for each scale corresponds to the content assessed by the items that load on each scale. In Table 7.2, we present correlation matrix findings examining the relationship of BEVI scales to Ecological Resonance (ER) on the BEVI in descending order of magnitude (e.g., the correlation of each scale by all other scales; all correlations are significant; see http://www.thebevi.com/docs/bevi_scale_pairwise_correlations_and_significance_levels.pdf).

As Table 7.3 illustrates, and recognizing the oblique nature of these factors derived from EFA, numerous correlations exist between ER and other BEVI scales, which help illuminate the theoretical and empirical associations between these constructs on the BEVI. Essentially, items on ER measure the degree to which individuals tend to find spirituality in the natural world, express concern for the Earth, and are open to new experiences. Those scales found to be most strong and positively correlated with ER were those of Sociocultural Openness ($r = .88$), encompassing progressive, liberal, and culturally attuned values; Socioemotional Convergence ($r = .69$), relating to the relative capacity to hold simultaneously complex and seemingly contradictory beliefs; and Emotional Attunement ($r = .64$), which speaks to the affective sensitivity and inclinations of individuals toward self and others. Two scales found to be highly and negatively correlated with ER were Needs Closure ($r = -.72$), which assesses the degree to which individuals report an unhappy childhood as well as odd or reductionistic explanations for why individuals behave or function as they do, and Basic Closedness ($r = -.65$), which measures the degree to which individuals tend to deny basic human feelings and thoughts. Other scales that were correlated strongly and negatively with ER include Socioreligious Traditionalism ($r = -.53$), which measures a predilection for traditional and conventional religious beliefs; Identity Diffusion ($r = -.49$), which measures foreclosed identity and feelings of helplessness and confusion; Self Assurance ($r = -.44$), suggesting unduly high confidence and few doubts or questions about self; Negative Life Events ($r = -.43$), measuring the degree to which individuals report many life conflicts or regrets, beginning in childhood; and Divergent Determinism ($r = -.43$), which measures the degree to which individuals are inclined toward contrarian beliefs and arguing seemingly for the sake of doing so.

Study 3: Antecedents of Environmental Beliefs and Values

Using the same sample as Study 2, we conducted a final examination of how the BEVI may address the preceding recommendations through a series of regression analyses. Tables 7.4 and 7.5 illustrate the predictive relationship between a series of background variables on the BEVI and the ER scale.

TABLE 7.3

Correlation Matrix Data Comparing Scale 17, Ecological Resonance, with Other BEVI Scales

BEVI SCALES	ECOLOGICAL RESONANCE
Sociocultural Openness	.88
Needs Closure	−.72
Socioemotional Convergence	.69
Basic Closedness	−.65
Emotional Attunement	.64
Socioreligious Traditionalism	−.53
Identity Diffusion	−.49
Self Assurance	−.44
Negative Life Events	−.43
Divergent Determinism	−.43

TABLE 7.4
Regression Model Examining the Relationship Between Background Variables and the Ecological Resonance Scale

	UNSTANDARDIZED COEFFICIENTS		STANDARDIZED COEFFICIENTS		
	B	Std. Error	Beta	T	Sig.
(Constant)	3.323	0.082		40.467	0.00
Gender	−0.078	0.032	−0.052	−2.403	0.016
Political orientation is Democrat	0.318	0.031	0.207	10.351	0.00
Has no plan to participate in international experience	0.189	0.046	0.084	4.072	0.00
Previously studied abroad	0.188	0.055	0.073	3.384	0.001
Personal interest in international experience	0.088	0.01	0.202	8.862	0.00
Pays for international activities through other ways	−0.141	0.076	−0.036	−1.853	0.064
Years of foreign language learning prior to college	−0.019	0.007	−0.057	−2.641	0.008
Speaks only English	−0.096	0.031	−0.065	−3.093	0.002
International student	0.087	0.041	0.043	2.121	0.034
College provided orientation for study abroad	0.071	0.038	0.042	1.901	0.057
F	42.658***				
R-squared	0.162				
Adj. R-squared	0.157				

Note. *$p < .05$, two-tailed test; **$p < .01$; ***$p < .001$.

TABLE 7.5

Regression Model Examining the Relationship Between Gender and the Ecological Resonance Scale

ITEMS ENDORSED BY FEMALES	TYPE II— SUM OF SQUARES	DF	F	MEAN SQUARE	R SQUARED	SIG.
Q118—I worry about our environment	30.321	1, 2300	54.603	30.321	.023	0.00
Q176—I worry about the health of our planet	26.243	1, 2295	49.4	26.243	.021	0.00
Q179—Too much land is being developed	20.817	1, 2294	40.032	20.817	.017	0.00
Q284—We must do more to protect the Earth's natural resources	22.869	1, 2279	53.091	22.869	.023	0.00

As Table 7.4 illustrates, nearly all of these demographic variables were predictive of ER ($p < .01$). In particular, variables that were found to be significant included previous participation in study abroad; plans (or lack thereof) to participate in an international experience; personal interest in international experience; years of foreign language learning prior to college; speaking only English; and identification as an international student. Overall, such variables suggest that the intended or actual international or multicultural experiences are associated with a greater tendency to express proecological beliefs and values.

Finally, as Table 7.5 illustrates, and consistent with Study 1, gender also was predictive of ER in that females indicated a greater concern for the environment than males.

"I worry about our environment," $f(1, 2300) = 54.603$, $p < .01$, R Squared = .023; "I worry about the health of our planet," $f(1, 2295) = 49.4$, $p < .01$, R Squared = .021; "Too much land is being developed," $f(1, 2294) = 40.032$, $p < .01$, R Squared = .017; "We must do more to protect the earth's natural resources," $f(1, 2279) = 53.091$, $p < .01$, R Squared = .023.

DISCUSSION

The preceding three studies provide a range of intriguing findings that are of relevance to the research recommendations noted previously. Overall, such findings speak to the overarching need for us to account for the etiology of environmental beliefs and values as well as how a predilection to "care for" the natural world is— and is not—related to other psychological constructs. More specifically, we now discuss six implications of such findings for future research as well as potential relevance for real world application.

Six Implications of the EI Model and BEVI Method for Environmental Research and Practice

1. *Finding Spirituality in the Natural World*

Recall first that individuals who score highly on ER tend to see the earth as one's mother, apprehend spirituality in the natural world, be introspective, open to experience, sexually uninhibited/open, value rights for all, and be liberal/progressive. Among other specific findings, the ER scale, in Table 7.3, was found to be negatively correlated to Socioreligious Traditionalism, which measures adherence to conventional religious beliefs and a strong fear of God. Likewise, as Table 7.1 illustrates, agnostics and atheists were found to be more likely to express environmental concerns when compared to Christians.

The argument that environmental concerns are mediated deeply by religious beliefs and values has been discussed widely. For example, Lynn White (1967), in his seminal article on religion and environment, proposed that Christianity is the most anthropocentric religion in the world. Such a perspective is echoed by Schultz, Zelezny, and Dalrymple (2000) who contend that "Christian doctrines emphasize human supremacy over nature and that people who adhere to these doctrines tend to view nature as something to be dominated, conquered, and subdued" (p. 577). Further empirical evidence has supported the finding that Christians are less concerned about the environment (Eckberg & Blocker 1989, 1996; Guth, Green, Kellstedt, & Schmidt, 1995; Hand & Van Liere, 1984; Kanagy & Willits, 1993; Schultz et al., 2000; Shaiko, 1987; Truelove & Joireman, 2009; Woodrum & Hoban, 1994), albeit with caveats. At the same time, other studies (Hartwig, 1999; Kanagy & Nelsen, 1995; Wolkomir, Futreal, Woodrum, & Hoban, 1997) report no significant effect of religion on environmentalism.

Biel and Nilsson (2005) offer the following insight into such opposing perspectives: "These contradictory views can partly be attributed to which parts of the Bible are emphasized in creating causal links between religious values and environmental concern and behavior" (p. 179). Similarly, Stern and colleagues suggest "different aspects of religious belief affect different types of environmentalism" (Dietz et al., 1998; Stern et al., 1999, p. 91). In the future, it would be helpful to hone in more specifically on which aspects of religious beliefs generally—and Christianity in particular—are associated with a pro/anti-environmental stance, for whom, and under what circumstances. For example, it is a mistake to assume that religious ideation, or a lack thereof, is necessarily predictive of a pro- or anti-environmental stance, since individuals who self-report in either category may be more similar than different from one another at the level of beliefs and values (Brearly, Van den Bos, & Tan, 2016).

2. *Development Processes and Attunement Toward the Natural World*

Table 7.3 shows that Needs Closure (NC), which measures the degree to which individuals report that basic life needs were not sufficiently met, as well as Basic Closedness (BC), which measures the tendency to deny thoughts or feelings that seem to be typical for most human beings, are negative correlated with Ecological Resonance (ER). From the perspective of the EI Self (see Chapter 3), core human needs can be represented along a continuum from the most basic physiological needs (e.g., appetitive) to the most complex psychological needs (e.g., awareness). More specifically, these results suggest individuals whose core needs (e.g., for attachment, affiliation) were *not* met in a "good enough" way, as considered by Donald Winnicott (Greenberg & Mitchell, 1983), appear similarly inclined *not* to express environmental concerns. Furthermore, those who deny basic human feelings and thoughts, as illustrated by BC in Table 7.3, are less like to demonstrate Self Awareness (SA), which measures an inclination to focus upon or wonder about "inner" processes in oneself and others. Moreover, those who are able to tolerate complexity and ambiguity in their thought processes, as evidenced by Socioemotional Convergence, appear to be more concerned about ecological issues than those who evidence less of this tendency. Among other implications, these overall findings are congruent with Villacorta and colleagues (2003) who found that concern for the environment positively correlated with intrinsic aspirations such as affiliation, self-development, and community involvement (p. 501). Also consistent with the EI Self, according to Maslow (1954), those individuals whose basic material and psychological needs are adequately satisfied are more likely to express caring beyond self, including concerns about the natural environment (e.g., Brechin & Kempton, 1994; Shealy et al., 2012).

By way of further illustration that Ecological Resonance (ER) is associated with other fundamental aspects of self-functioning, note from Table 7.3 that Emotional Attunement (EA) is positively correlated with ER. In other words, individuals who are highly emotional, highly social, and strongly affiliative tend to have proenvironmental attitudes. Such empirical findings appear consistent with the basic tenets of ecopsychology, aspects of the Biophilia Hypothesis, and the EI Self, which collectively suggest that humans may be born with an innate sense of empathy and relatedness to nature and the living world (Kellert 1993, 1997; Roszak, 1992; Shealy et al., 2012; Wilson, 1984). In future research, it would be helpful to focus closely on this theoretical question of whether "attunement" with the natural world appears to be a "core human need." Along these lines, Wells and Rollings (2012) provide an authoritative review of research examining the relationship between nature and health, while Russell (2012) examines how wilderness therapy programs have been successful in treating an array of illnesses. Informed by such perspectives, it would be interesting in future research to investigate the relationship between NC and ER on the BEVI in these "wilderness" like treatment programs to see if the correlation between these two BEVI variables becomes less negative via pre/postprogram assessment (e.g., see Holt, Cobb, Shealy, & Harmison, 2010).

3. *Gender and the Environment*

Table 7.1 shows that NEP scores are significantly higher for women compared to men, a finding that is strongly supported by the Gender Traditionalism scale of the BEVI (Pendleton, Cochran, Kapadia, & Iyer, 2016), indicating that gender is a significant predictor of environmental beliefs and values. Such findings are supported by other studies that suggest women on average hold greater proenvironmental value orientations, propreservation normative beliefs (Steger & Witt, 1989), and proenvironmental attitudes and behaviors (Schultz et al., 2000) than men. Among other associations, such behaviors may include consumer behavior (Dietz et al. 1998) and parliament support of environmental treaties (Norgaard & York, 2005).

However, the relationship between gender and environmentalism has not always been clear. In Van Liere and Dunlap's (1980) review of 21 studies from the 1960s and 1970s, a correlation between gender and environmentalism was found in some studies, while not in others. Along these lines, as Table 7.1 illustrates, although females scored significantly higher on NEP than males, such findings are not replicated on this earlier version of environmental beliefs and values on the BEVI (e.g., EC). Likewise, Mohai (1992) also found women to be slightly more concerned about the environment, but men were more likely to engage in environmental activism. In response to findings like these, Stern and colleagues (1993) suggest "gender differences in environmentalism are a result of gender differences in beliefs about the effects of environmental problems" (p. 340). Moreover, women place higher emphasis on altruism than men, and appear to be more "other-oriented" and "socially responsible" (Schultz et al., 2000), perhaps due to differences in socialization and life experiences (e.g., child rearing). Finally, such contradictions may also be the result of social constraints, which differentially impact females depending upon time and place (Mohai, 1992).

In any case, the reasons why females overall appear to resonate more with ecological concerns have received significant theoretical explication, but are not well understood empirically or in terms of etiological factors or individual differences between males and females. In other words, gender per se may neither be necessary nor sufficient as a moderator of Ecological Resonance. As the preceding correlation matrix data suggest, other factors that may be associated with, but not caused by "gender"—such as one's life history and attendant capacity to experience and express an interest in one's own emotional and psychological world—may be more salient than gender in explaining why some human beings are more or less ecologically resonant. Future research examining these relationships in greater detail would help to parse out the relative contribution of gender to the development of a pro or anti-environmental sensibility as well as related causal pathways (e.g., structural equation modeling) (Pendleton et al., 2016).

4. *Political Orientation and the Environment*

NEP scores for Democrats were found to be significantly higher than that for Republicans according to Table 7.1, whereas EC scores for Republicans were significantly higher than for both Democrats. This finding is consistent with past studies that have investigated such a linkage (e.g., Arp, 1994; Daneshvary, Daneshvary, & Schewer, 1998; Dunlap, 1975; Gamba & Oskamp, 1994; Guth et al., 1995; Hine & Gifford, 1991; McCright & Dunlap, 2011; Patel et al., 2007; Samdahl & Robertson, 1989; Van Liere & Dunlap, 1980). Although warranting replication, Dunlap (1975) offered an early and tripartite explanation for this seemingly sturdy pattern. First, Republicans typically support business and industry, which often are resistant to environmental reforms. Second, actions to address environmental issues involve increased involvement of government activities and regulations, to which political conservatives typically are opposed. Third, environmental reforms necessitate substantial policy changes, which often are opposed by conservatives.

However, as with the other demographic variables noted previously—religious affiliation and gender—it is important to understand what exactly is it about the way the "self" is structured that tends to link a conservative (e.g., Republican) political ideology with a relative tendency to be less environmentally concerned (see Chapters 2 and 3). There are a number of questions worthy of pursuit along these lines. For example, as with all of these moderators and mediators, it seems quite plausible that there are greater within-than between-group differences. If so, it would be helpful to study the interactions among multiple BEVI scales, including formative variables (e.g., Negative and Positive Life Events), to see if it is possible to tease apart the interacting factors that are associated with, say, self-reporting Democrats who also are relatively low on ER as well as their Republican counterparts who are high on ER (e.g., Edmunds, Federico, & Mays, 2016).

5. *Openness and the Environment*

As Study 3 illustrated, multiple demographic variables also appeared to be predictive of ER. In this study, many of these appear to be associated with international and multicultural interests and experiences. For example, previous study abroad experience, personal interest in international experience, years of foreign language learning prior to college, and identification as an international student were among the background variables that were associated with greater ER. Indeed, Sociocultural Openness on the BEVI—which measures an inclination to be interested in cultural beliefs and practices that are different from one's own, among other processes—also is strongly and positively correlated with ER. Along related lines, BC (Table 7.3) and NFC (Table 7.2) are negatively correlated with ER.

Overall, such findings suggest that individuals who are inclined to wonder about and be drawn toward belief systems and cultural practices that are different from their own, open to basic thoughts, feelings, or needs that are integral to being human, and have a capacity to tolerate ambiguity and complexity, are more likely to be concerned about the environment. Such findings may be similar to the openness to change value orientation used by Stern et al. (1999) in their Value–Belief–Norm model as well as building on older research suggesting that individuals who are more flexible in their behaviors and beliefs are more likely to show a proenvironmental commitment (Arbuthnot, 1977).

In any case, consistent with other preceding observations is the basic conclusion that environmental beliefs, values, attitudes, and worldviews are associated with and predicted by core definitional components of identity or self, which begs a fundamental question regarding why and how individuals become structured or organized as they are in the first place (Shealy, 2016). Meriting further inquiry, we believe these complex processes may be better understood if the lens through which we see the human condition (e.g., the rich interaction among formative variables, adaptive potential, and core needs as suggested by the EI Self) is sufficiently complex and comprehensive to account for why we become what we become (Spaeth, Schwartz, Nayar, & Ma, 2016).

6. *Education for Sustainable Development*[5]

Although the preceding implications primarily relate to theory, data, measures, and methods, we wish to conclude by placing this work in a broader and applied context that relates not only to research, but also to classroom-based practices as well as larger societal interventions and policies. From our perspective, that optimal framework is Education for Sustainability (EfS) (Center for Green Schools, 2014) as well as Education for Sustainable Development (ESD), a global education reform movement under the auspices of the United Nations Educational, Scientific, and Cultural Organization (UNESCO). As an aspirational framework, ESD "allows every human being to acquire the knowledge, skills, attitudes and values necessary to shape a sustainable future." It also focuses on the integration of ESD concepts into the classroom, such as "climate change, disaster risk reduction, biodiversity, poverty reduction, and sustainable consumption." Finally, it seeks to promote "participatory teaching and learning methods that motivate and empower learners to change their behaviour and take action for sustainable development" through the development of competencies such as critical thinking and collaborative decision making (see www.unesco.org/new/en/education/themes/leading-the-international-agenda/education-for-sustainable-development). As described by Coffman, Hopkins, and Ali (2009), there are "four

---

[5] We acknowledge here that Environmental Education, Nature Conservation Education and ESD have been a part of extensive discourse with related and different meanings. Although clarification would be helpful as noted, delineation within and among such terminology falls outside the scope of this chapter.

major thrusts of ESD—improving the quality of and access to basic education, reorienting existing education to address sustainable development, developing public understanding and awareness, and training" (p. 146). Obviously, any attempt to reorient the world's education systems along ESD lines is an enormous and multiyear endeavor, which will necessitate participation and commitment by all social sectors (e.g., educators, scholars, policy makers, business, media, the public at large). Likewise, multiple perspectives have and will come to bear upon such processes, from technology and agriculture, to government agencies and nongovernment organizations, all pursuing a range of allied initiatives (Center for Green Schools, 2014; McKeown & Nolet, 2012).

Against the wide backdrop, how might a deep understanding of environmental "beliefs and values" help facilitate ESD means and ends? As discussed at the 2012 UNESCO ESD conference in Toronto, Canada, we need to understand not only *what* ESD beliefs and values are and are not, but *how* they may evolve at the individual, group, organizational, governmental, and societal levels, and *why* they are internalized in the first place (Shealy, 2012). In many ways, the extant ESD focus has largely been upon matters of policy and curriculum, foci which certainly are necessary, but perhaps not sufficient for the long-term viability of ESD. That is because adherents of ESD often are preaching to the already converted choir. As if not more important, we need to understand why people are—or are not—predisposed to believe and act along ESD lines in the first place, which is, of course, a central focus of the EI model and BEVI method presented previously.

By extension and pragmatically, from the standpoint of ESD, what should our educational systems be doing now to prepare the next generation and the one beyond? Excellent guidance in this regard is provided by three documents that should be of relevance to all educators and scholars who are interested in promoting a more aware and sustainable curricula: first, the *National Action Plan for Educating for Sustainability* (Center for Green Schools, 2014) (see http://www.centerforgreen-schools.org/sites/default/files/resource-files/National-Action-Plan-Educating-Sustainability.pdf); second, *The Future We Want* (2012) is a report of the Rio+20 United Nations Conference on Sustainable Development (see http://unesdoc.unesco.org/images/0023/002301/230171e.pdf); third, *Shaping the Education of Tomorrow* (2012), is a UNESCO report on UN Decade for Sustainable Development (see http://unesdoc .unesco.org/images/0021/002166/216606e.pdf). The first of these documents is a national, multipartner initiative based in the United States, which has as its aim the "greening" of all schools by 2040—to include a wide array of relevant stakeholders and emphases (from leadership and teacher preparation to policy and research). The second provides a detailed policy statement regarding the likely increasing relevance of ESD perspectives and approaches for the world's education systems, and the attendant commitments from policy makers and educational leaders around the world. The third document articulates a rationale as well as concrete guidance regarding how and why ESD principles and practices can and should be integrated into our local and global curricula. For example, highly relevant to the theory and data presented in this chapter, this report concludes that,

> there is increased recognition that this challenge cannot be solved only through technological advances, legislative measures and new policy frameworks (UNEP, 2011). While such responses are necessary, they will need to be accompanied by changes in mindsets, values and lifestyles, as well as a strengthening of people's capacities to bring about change. (p. 4)

Both at an administrative level in schools and in the classroom, the ESD paradigm is

> leading to reflection on the personal values of both teachers and students, but also of the school as an organization. Critical reflection is encouraged to make those values more explicit and connect them with (un)sustainability. This confrontation can lead to rethinking these values and the practices they support. (p. 43)

From the standpoint of ESD, as Figure 7.1 illustrates, integrating such processes into the classroom requires a fundamental reworking of how we imagine the interdependent roles and responsibilities among teacher and learner. In particular, note the process-oriented interactions among local and global competencies to be acquired, including "values and ethics," "action," "knowledge," "systems thinking," and "emotions." Wals (2012) emphasizes this perspective as follows: "Since

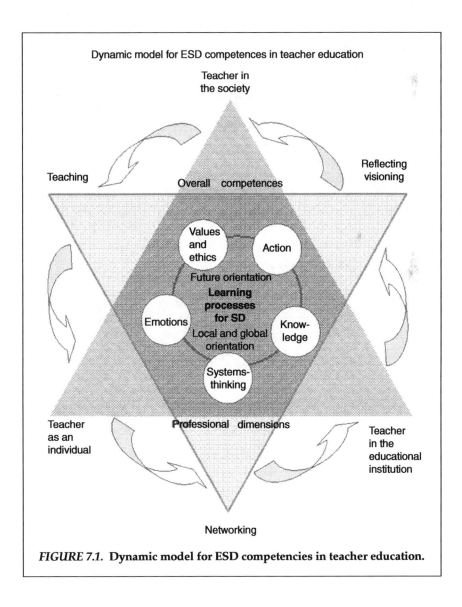

FIGURE 7.1. Dynamic model for ESD competencies in teacher education.

people are less willing to preserve or conserve what they do not appreciate or value, any environmental education program that does not provide learners with nature experiences is likely to fail" (p. 631). Note here that one needs to value and understand nature via experience, since such interactions activate both affect and the senses.

In addition to a focus on broad, integrative, systems-level thinking, both locally and globally, "the person of" the teacher and student is emphasized, with an explicit process-based focus on why we believe, value, and feel what we do. As the data presented in this chapter illustrate, we know something of the formative variables (e.g., life history, demographics, personal characteristics) that are associated with the capacity and inclination to care for self, others, and the larger world (Shealy et al., 2012). It is heartening to see the resonance between extant data and theory and this comprehensive model of how ESD ideally should be expressed and experienced in the classroom.

As this interacting ESD model indicates—and as the preceding data and theory suggest in terms of affective and cognitive aspects of the EI Self as well as correlates of Ecological Resonance on the BEVI—what we must do is create and support educational systems, processes, and curricula that actively cultivate more aware, reflective, and responsive teachers and learners. Ultimately, such individuals may come to understand that they—and our future as a species—are inextricably linked to both an intellectual and visceral understanding of the interconnectedness of all living things as well as our lamentably acquired tendency to deny accountability for who we are and why we believe, value, and behave as we do (Shealy et al., 2012). Wals (2012) emphasizes the experiential importance of ESD and related approaches, noting that the key is "connecting with the world (nature, environment, planet)" (p. 639). Such engagement not only is vital for improving our environment, but may also provide a solution to the "multitude of physical, psychological, and emotional ailments pervasive in modern-day society" (Russell 2012, p. 428; see also Wells & Rollings, 2012).

SUMMARY AND CONCLUSION

In an attempt to understand the origins and nature of environmental beliefs and values, we first provided an overview of four theories and their accompanying measures: (a) VBN (Stern et al., 1999); (b) TPB (Ajzen, 1991); (c) Environmental Identity Model (Stets & Biga, 2003); and (d) the MTES (Pelletier et al., 1998). Based upon this overview, we offered five recommendations for scholarship in this area: (a) offer a rationale for selected terminology; (b) differentiate selected terminology; (c) ensure a linkage between terminology and measures; (d) examine not only what people believe and value about the environment, but why, by considering questions of etiology and individual differences; and (e) understand how environmental beliefs and values are related to the varied ways in which human beings experience self, others, and the larger world.

In an attempt to address these recommendations, we then described Equilintegration or EI Theory, the EI Self, and the BEVI (Shealy, 2004, 2016), which seeks to "go deep," by apprehending and measuring the complex and interacting processes by which environmental beliefs and values are acquired, maintained, and transformed. At this point, we presented findings from three interrelated studies of the BEVI vis-à-vis the environment: Study 1 examined which demographic variables appeared to be most and least predictive of "who cares, who doesn't, and why" about environmental issues; Study 2 examined the relationship between environmental beliefs to other beliefs and values about self, others, and the world at large; and, Study 3 examined the complex etiological factors (e.g., life history) that appear to be associated with the development of pro- or anti-environmental beliefs and values.

In our discussion, we then offered six different implications from such findings that we believe have relevance for future research and practice. These included the need to (a) understand the role of "spirituality" regarding beliefs and experiences of the natural world; (b) further examine how formative variables (e.g., life history, demographics) affect our beliefs and behaviors vis-à-vis the natural world; (c) explicate, theoretically and empirically, why one's gender appears to be predictive of a pro/anti-environmental stance; (d) consider what it is about the underlying belief/value commitments that are implied by one's political orientation, which also appear to be associated with one's attendant environmental stance; (e) examine why greater openness in general (e.g., to one's emotional world, other cultures) also tends to be associated with a greater inclination to express care and concern for the environment; and finally, (f) at an applied level, we suggest that the theory and data presented here have implications, in general, for how we "teach" about environmentalism in the classroom, and more specifically, to the explication of underlying beliefs and values that are relevant to EfS and ESD, both locally and globally. Because knowledge alone, or conventional approaches to environmental education, do not necessarily translate into proenvironmental behavior (Heberlein, 2012), it behooves us to link environmental beliefs and values to the most basic aspects of identity, which likely involve a direct encounter with affect as well as other nonconscious aspects of self. At its core, we believe ESD interventions will be most effective when these complex interactions among beliefs, values, meaning making, life history, and context are all understood and addressed via sensitively designed, appropriately assessed, and skillfully delivered interventions, in the classroom and beyond (e.g., Center for Green Schools, 2014; McKeown & Nolet, 2012).

In conclusion, we observed at the outset of this chapter that although the public at large does demonstrate interest in actions that will protect the environment and preserve the natural world, there is a disconnect both between sentiment and action as well as the role of the academy in promoting such change. Part of the challenge here is a reality that scholarly literature in this area is not well connected, lacks definitional and conceptual clarity, and does not sufficiently explicate how and why there are individual differences in the experience and expression of environmental beliefs and values in the first place. From our perspective, theory and data can and should play a central role in understanding why, and under what circumstances, we humans are—or are not—inclined to care for the natural world. However, we must assume greater responsibility for translating our concepts and findings into a form that is accessible (e.g., to educators, students, policy makers, and the public at large), and can demonstrably impact educational content, processes, and systems, both locally and globally. Toward such means and ends, our scholarship must encounter such matters with sufficient depth and breadth, with a long-term commitment to ecological validity in our measures and methods (e.g., see Cultivating the Globally Sustainable Self, 2015).

Although we deliberately eschew definitive claims in this regard, it is our hope that the juxtaposition of various approaches to examining environmental beliefs and values, including the EI model and BEVI method, have helped clarify one way to conceptualize and evaluate these complex and interacting processes, while pointing a way forward that may increase the depth, clarity, and relevance of our research, and its application in the real world. In the final analysis, the success of transnational efforts to combat the degradation of our climate, resources, and ecosystems will require these sorts of sophisticated models and methods in order to understand why, and under what circumstances, human beings come to care about the environment in the first place. On the basis of such knowledge, we should know better how to "cultivate the capacity to care" (Shealy et al., 2012), not only for the environment writ large, but for all living beings, in thought, word, and deed (Center for Green Schools, 2014; Cultivating the Globally Sustainable Self, 2015).

REFERENCES

Ajzen, I. (1991). The theory of planned behavior. *Organizational Behavior and Human Decision Processes, 50,* 179–211.

Allport, G. W. (1961). *Pattern and growth in personality.* New York, NY: Holt, Rinehart & Winston.

Anmuth, L. M., Poore, M., Cozen, J., Brearly, T., Tabit, M., Cannady, M., . . . Staton, R. (2013, August). *Making implicit beliefs explicit: In search of best practices for mental health clients, clinicians, and trainers.* Poster presented at the annual meeting of the American Psychological Association, Honolulu, HI.

Arbuthnot, J. (1977). Attitudinal and personality variables in the prediction of environmental behavior and knowledge. *Environment and Behavior, 9,* 217–232.

Arp, W. (1994). A triad of environmental concern: Race, party affiliation and political ideology. *Western Journal of Black Studies, 18,* 121–131.

Atwood, K., Chkhaidze, N., Shealy, C. N., Staton, R., & Sternberger, L. G. (2014, August). *Transformation of self: Implications from the Forum BEVI Project.* Poster presented at the annual meeting of the American Psychological Association, Washington, DC.

Biel, A., & Nilsson, A. (2005). Religious values and environmental concern: Harmony and detachment. *Social Science Quarterly, 86,* 178–191.

Braithwaite, V. A., & Scott, W. A. (1991). Values. In J. P. Robinson, P. R. Shaver, & L. S. Wrightsman (Eds.), *Measures of personality and social psychological attitudes* (Vol. 1, pp. 661–753). San Diego, CA: Academic Press.

Brearly, T., Shealy, C. N., Staton, R., & Sternberger, L. G. (2012, August). *Prejudice and religious and non-religious certitude: An empirical analysis from the Forum BEVI Project.* Poster presented at the annual meeting of the American Psychological Association, Orlando, FL.

Brearly, T., Van den Bos, K., & Tan, C. (2016). The nature and etiology of religious certitude: Implications of the EI framework and Beliefs, Events, and Values Inventory. In C. N. Shealy (Ed.), *Making sense of beliefs and values* (pp. 331–369). New York, NY: Springer Publishing.

Brechin, S. R., & Kempton, W. (1994). Global environmentalism: A challenge to the postmaterialism thesis? *Social Science Quarterly, 75,* 245–269.

Center for Green Schools. (2014). *National action plan for educating for sustainability.* Retrieved from http://www.centerforgreenschools.org/home.aspx

Coffman, J. E., Hopkins, C., & Ali, I. M. (2009). Education for sustainable development: Halfway through the decade of ESD and a long way from sustainability. *Beliefs and Values, 29,* 142–150.

Cultivating the Globally Sustainable Self. (2015). Retrieved from www.jmu.edu/summitseries

Daneshvary, N., Daneshvary, R., & Schwer, R. K. (1998). Solid-waste recycling behavior and support for curbside textile recycling. *Environment and Behavior, 30,* 144–161.

Darner, R. (2009). Self-determination theory as a guide to fostering environmental motivation. *Journal of Environmental Education, 40*(2), 39–49.

Deci, E. L., & Ryan, R. M. (2000). Self-determination theory and the facilitation of intrinsic motivation, social development, and well-being. *American Psychologist, 55*(1), 68–78.

Deci, E. L., & Ryan, R. M. (1985). *Intrinsic motivation and self-determination in human behavior.* New York, NY: Plenum.

de Groot, J. I. M., & Steg, L. (2010). Relationships between value orientations, self-determined motivational types and pro-environmental behavioural intentions. *Journal of Environmental Psychology, 30*(4), 368–378.

Dietz, T., Stern, P., & Guagnano, G. (1998). Social structural and social psychological bases of environmental concern. *Environment and Behavior, 30*(4), 450–471.

Dunlap, R. E. (1975). The impact of political orientation on environmental attitudes and actions. *Environment and Behavior, 7,* 428–454.

Dunlap, R. E., & Van Liere, K. D. (1978). The new environmental paradigm: A proposed measuring instrument and preliminary results. *Journal of Environmental Education, 9,* 10–19.

Dunlap, R. E., Van Liere, K. D., Mertig, A. G., & Jones, R. E. (2000). Measuring endorsement of the new ecological paradigm: A revised NEP scale. *Journal of Social Issues, 56,* 425–42.

Eckberg, D. L., & Blocker, T. J. (1989). Variations of religious involvements and environmental concerns: Testing the Lynn White thesis. *Journal for the Scientific Study of Religion, 28,* 509–517.

Eckberg, D. L., & Blocker, T. J. (1996). Christianity, environmentalism, and the theoretical problem of fundamentalism. *Journal for the Scientific Study of Religion, 35,* 343–355.

Edmunds, A., Frederico, C., & Mays, L. (2016). Exploring the etiology of ideology: In search of the political self through the EI model and BEVI method. In C. N. Shealy (Ed.), *Making sense of beliefs and values.* New York, NY: Springer Publishing.

Fishbein, M., & Ajzen, I. (1975). *Belief, attitudes, intention, and behavior: And introduction to theory and research.* Reading, MA: Addison-Wesley.

Gamba, R. J., & Oskamp, S. (1994). Factors influencing community residents' participation in commingled curbside recycling programs. *Environment and Behavior, 26,* 587–612.

Gifford, R., & Sussman, R. (2012). Environmental attitudes. In S. D. Clayton (Ed.), *The oxford handbook of environmental and conservation psychology.* New York and Oxford: Oxford University Press.

Greenberg, J. R., & Mitchell, S. A. (Eds.). (1983). *Object relations in psychoanalytic theory.* Cambridge, MA: Harvard University Press.

Guth, J. L., Green. J. C., Kellstedt, L. A., & Schmidt, C. E. (1995). Faith and the environment: Religious beliefs and attitudes on environmental policy. *American Journal of Political Science, 39,* 364–382.

Hand, C. M., & Van Liere, K. D. (1984). Religion, mastery-over-nature, and environmental concern. *Social Forces, 57,* 265–281.

Hartwig, B. H. (1999). Christianity and the environment in the American public. *Journal for the Scientific Study of Religion, 38,* 36–44.

Heberlein, T. A. (2012). *Navigating environmental attitudes.* New York, NY: Oxford University Press.

Henry, A., & Dietz, T. (2012). Understanding environmental cognition. *Organization & Environment, 25*(3), 238–258.

Hill, C., Johnson, M., Brinton, C., Staton, R., Sternberger, L., & Shealy. (2013, August). *The etiology of economic beliefs and values: Implications and applications from the Forum BEVI Project.* Poster presented at the annual meeting of the American Psychological Association, Honolulu, HI.

Hinds, J., & Sparks, P. (2008). Engaging with the natural environment: The role of affective connection and identity. *Journal of Environmental Psychology, 28,* 109–120.

Hine, D. W., & Gifford, R. (1991). Fear appeals, individual differences, and environmental concern. *Journal of Environmental Education, 23*(1), 36–41.

Holt, J., Cobb, H., Shealy, C., & Harmison, R. (2010). *The effects of an outdoor therapeutic program on the environmental beliefs and values of adolescents with emotional problems.* (Proquest UMI Dissertation Publishing). James Madison University, Harrisonburg, VA.

Kaiser, F. G., Hubner, G., & Bogner, F. X. (2005). Contrasting the theory of planned behavior with the value-belief-norm model in explaining conservation behavior. *Journal of Applied Social Psychology, 35,* 2150–2170.

Kaiser, F. G., Schultz, P., & Scheuthle, H. (2007). The theory of planned behavior without compatibility? Beyond Method Bias and Past Trivial Associations1. *Journal of Applied Social Psychology*, 37(7), 1522–1544.

Kalof, L., Dietz, T., Stern, P., & Guagnano, G. A. (1999). *Race, gender and environmentalism: The atypical values and beliefs of white men* (Unpublished manuscript). George Mason University, Department of Sociology and Anthropology, Fairfax, VA.

Kanagy, C. L., & Nelsen, H. M. (1995). Religion and environmental concern: Challenging the dominant assumptions. *Review of Religious Research, 37*, 33–45.

Kanagy, C. L., & Willits, F. K. (1993). A 'greening' of religion? *Social Science Quarterly, 74*, 674–683.

Kellert, S. (1993). *The biophilia hypothesis.* Washington, DC: Island Press.

Kellert, S. (1997). *Kinship to mastery: Biophilia in human evolution and development.* Washington, DC: Island Press.

Manning, M. (2009). The effects of subjective norms on behavior in the theory of planned behavior: A meta-analysis. *British Journal of Social Psychology, 48*, 649–705.

Marchini, S., & Macdonald, D. W. (2012). Predicting ranchers' intention to kill jaguars: Case studies in Amazonia and Pantanal. *Biological Conservation, 147*, 213–217.

Maslow, A. (1954). *Motivation and personality.* New York, NY: Harper & Row.

McCright, A., & Dunlap, R. (2011). The politicization of climate change and polarization in the American public's views of global warming, 2001–2010. *The Sociological Quarterly, 52*, 155–194.

McKeown, R., & Nolet, V. W. (Eds.). (2012). *Schooling for sustainable development in Canada and the United States.* New York, NY: Springer.

Mohai, P. (1992). Men, women, and the environment: An examination of the gender gap in environmental concern and activism. *Society and Natural Resources, 5*(1), 1–19.

Norgaard, K., & York, R. (2005). Gender equality and state environmentalism. *Gender & Society, 19*(4), 506–522.

Oreg, S., & Katz-Gerro, T. (2006). Predicting proenvironmental behavior cross-nationally: Values, the theory of planned behavior, and value-belief-norm theory. *Environment and Behavior, 38*, 462–483.

Patel, R. (2008). *Environmental beliefs, values, and worldviews: Etiology, maintenance, and transformation* (Unpublished Dissertation). James Madison University, Harrisonburg, VA.

Patel, R., Shealy, C. N., & De Michele, P. (2007, August). *Environmental beliefs and values: Etiology, maintenance, and transformation.* Presented at the annual meeting of the American Psychological Association, San Francisco, CA.

Pelletier, L. G., Tuson, K. M., Green-Demers, I., Noels, K., & Beaton, A. M. (1998). Why are you doing things for the environment? The Motivation Toward the Environment Scale (MTES). *Journal of Applied Social Psychology, 28*, 437–468.

Pendleton, C., Cochran, S. Kapadia, S., & Iyer, C. (2016). Understanding the Gendered Self: Implications from EI Theory, the EI Self, and the BEVI. In C. N. Shealy (Ed.), *Making sense of beliefs and values* (pp. 261–302). New York, NY: Springer Publishing.

Pysarchik, D. I., Shealy, C. N., & Sternberger, B. (2007, July). *Examining outcome objectives for student learning and curricula.* Symposium presented at the meeting of the National Association of State Universities and Land Grant Colleges, Santa Rosa, CA.

Rokeach, M. (1968). *Beliefs, attitudes, and values: A theory of organization and change.* San Francisco, CA: Jossey-Bass.

Rokeach, M. (1973). *The nature of human values.* New York, NY: Free Press.

Roszak, T. (1992). *The voice of the Earth.* New York, NY: Simon & Schuster.

Russell, K. C. (2012). Therapeutic uses of nature. In S. D. Clayton (Ed.), *The oxford handbook of environmental and conservation psychology.* New York, NY: Oxford University Press.

Samdahl, D. M., & Robertson, R. (1989). Social determinants of environmental concern: Specification and test of the model. *Environment and Behavior, 21*, 57–81.

Schultz, P. W., Zelezny, L., & Dalrymple, N. J. (2000). A multinational perspective on the relation between Judeo-Christian religious beliefs and attitudes of environmental concern. *Environment and Behavior, 4*, 576–591.

Schwartz, S. H. (1970). Moral decision making and behavior. In J. Macauley & L. Berkowitz (Eds.), *Altruism and helping behavior* (pp. 127–141). New York, NY: Academic Press.

Schwartz, S. H. (1973). Normative explanations of helping behavior: A critique, proposal, and empirical test. *Journal of Experimental Social Psychology, 9*, 349–364.

Schwartz, S. H. (1977). Normative influences on altruism. In L. Berkowitz (Ed.), *Advances in experimental social behavior, 10*, 221–279.

Schwartz, S. H. (1992). Universals in the content and structure of values: Theoretical advances and empirical tests in 20 countries. *Advances in Experimental Social Psychology, 25*, 1–65.

Schwartz, S. H. (1994). Are there universal aspects in the structure and contents of human values? *Journal of Social Issues, 50*(4), 19–46.

Shaiko, R. G. (1987). Religion, politics, and environmental concern. *Social Science Quarterly, 68*, 244–262.

Shealy, C. N. (2004). A model and method for "making" a C-I psychologist: Equilintegration (EI) theory and the Beliefs, Events, and Values Inventory. *Journal of Clinical Psychology, 60*, 1065–1090.

Shealy, C. N. (2005). Justifying the justification hypothesis: Scientific-humanism, Equilintegration (EI) theory, and the Beliefs, Events, and Values Inventory (BEVI) [Special Series]. *Journal of Clinical Psychology, 61*, 81–106.

Shealy, C. N. (2006). *The Beliefs, Events, and Values Inventory (BEVI): Overview, implications, and guidelines.* Harrisonburg, VA: Author.

Shealy, C. N. (2012, May). *Beliefs, values, and education for sustainable development.* Interest group discussion at the biannual meeting in Toronto, Canada.

Shealy, C. N. (2016). *Making sense of beliefs and values.* New York, NY: Springer Publishing.

Shealy, C. N., Bhuyan, D., & Sternberger, L. G. (2012). Cultivating the capacity to care in children and youth: Implications from EI theory, EI self, and BEVI. In U. Nayar (Ed.), *Child and adolescent mental health* (pp. 240–255). New Delhi, India: Sage Publications.

Slimak, M. W., & Dietz, T. (2006). Personal values, beliefs and ecological risk perception. *Risk Analysis, 26*(6), 1689–1705.

Spaeth, J., Schwartz, S., Nayar, U., & Ma, W. (2016). Identity development and the construction of self: Findings and implications from the Forum BEVI Project. In C. N. Shealy (Ed.), *Making sense of beliefs and values* (pp. 205–232). New York, NY: Springer Publishing.

Tabit, M., Cozen, J., Dyjak-Leblank, K., Pendleton, C., Shealy, C., Sternberger, L., & Staton, R. (2011, June). *The sociocultural impact of denial: Empirical evidence from the Forum BEVI Project.* Poster presented at American Psychological Association, Washington, DC.

Truelove, H. B., & Joireman, J. (2009). Understanding the relationship between Christian orthodoxy and environmentalism: The mediating role of perceived environmental consequences. *Environment and Behavior, 41*(6), 806–820.

Steger, M., & Witt, S. (1989). Gender differences in environmental orientation: A comparisons of publics and activists in Canada and the US. *Political Research Quarterly, 42*, 627–649.

Stern, P. C., & Dietz, T. (1994). The value basis of environmental concern. *Journal of Social Issues, 50*, 65–84.

Stern, P. C., Dietz, T., Abel, T., Guagnano, G. A., & Kalof, L. (1999). A value belief-norm theory of support for social movements: The case of environmental concern. *Human Ecology Review, 6*, 81–97.

Stern, P. C., Dietz, T., & Guagnano, G. A. (1995). The new environmental paradigm in social psychological perspective. *Environment & Behavior, 27*, 723–745.

Stern, P. C., Dietz, T., & Kalof, L. (1993). Value orientations, gender, and environmental concern. *Environment & Behavior, 25*, 322–348.

Stern, P. C., Dietz, T., Kalof, L., & Guagnano, G. A. (1995). Values, beliefs and proenvironmental action: Attitude formation toward emergent attitude objects. *Journal of Applied Social Psychology, 25*, 1611–1636.

Stets, J. E. (2006). Identity. In P. J. Burke (Ed.), *Contemporary Social Psychological Theories* (pp. 88–110). Stanford, CA: Stanford University Press.

Stets, J. E., & Biga, C. F. (2003). Bringing identity theory into environmental sociology. *Sociological Theory, 21*, 398–423.

Van Liere, K. D., & Dunlap, R. E. (1980). The social bases of environmental concern: A review of hypotheses, explanations, and empirical evidence. *The Public Opinion Quarterly,* 181–198.

Villacorta, M., Koestner, R., & Lekes, N. (2003). Further validation of the motivation toward the environment scale. *Environment and Behavior, 35,* 486–505.

Wals, A. E. J. (2012). Learning our way out of unsustainability: The role of environmental education. In S. D. Clayton (Ed.), *The oxford handbook of environmental and conservation psychology.* New York and Oxford: Oxford University Press.

Wells, N. M., & Rollings, K. A. (2012). The natural environment in residential settings: Influences on human health and function. In S. D. Clayton (Ed.), *The oxford handbook of environmental and conservation psychology* (pp. 509–523). New York, NY: Oxford University Press.

White, L. (1967). The historical roots of our ecological crisis. *Science, 155,* 1203–1207.

Whitfield, S., Rosa, E. A., Dan, A., & Dietz, T. (2009). The future of nuclear power: value orientations and risk perceptions. *Risk Analysis, 29*(3), 425–437.

Whitmarsh, L., & O'Neill, S. (2010). Green identity, green living? The role of pro-environmental self-identity in determining consistency across diverse pro-environmental behaviours. *Journal of Environmental Psychology, 30,* 305–314.

Wilson, E. (1984). *Biophilia.* Cambridge, MA: Harvard University Press.

Wolkomir, M., Futreal, M., Woodrum, E., & Hoban, T. (1997). Substantive religious belief and environmentalism. *Social Science Quarterly, 78,* 96–108.

Woodrum, E., & Hoban, E. (1994). Theology and religiosity effects on environmentalism. *Review of Religious Research, 35,* 193–206.

Christen Pendleton, Sam Cochran, Shagufa Kapadia,
and Chitra Iyer

8

UNDERSTANDING THE GENDERED SELF: IMPLICATIONS FROM EI THEORY, THE EI SELF, AND THE BEVI

It is impossible to realize our goals while discriminating against half of the human race. As study after study has taught us, there is no tool for development more effective than the empowerment of women.

—Kofi Annan, UN Secretary General

Arguably, our beliefs and values about "gender" are among the most pressing of our time. Why? Because even a cursory review of headlines any day of the week will reveal that what we believe about gender affects all aspects of existence, from the assumptions we harbor for why men and women do what they do; to our predilection for supporting rights in the name of gender; to our inclination to condone, tolerate, or abhor gender-based violence; to our capacity for experiencing and expressing intimacy in our relationships. Thus, it is important not only to understand *what we believe*, but *why we believe what we believe* about these fundamental aspects of the human condition. Along similar lines, it would be helpful to understand the etiology of our beliefs and values about who males and females are—and are not—since "gender traditionalism" is associated with a range of antecedents and consequences that impact one's relationship to self, others, and the larger world, for better or worse.[1]

Gender traditionalism may be defined as the degree to which an individual endorses traditional, simple, and essentialist views regarding gender and gender roles, while also tending to endorse and promote gender inequity (Davis & Greenstein, 2009). Extant research suggests that certain formative variables (e.g., family socialization) impact the formation of gender traditionalism and that gender traditionalism is correlated with other belief structures and life outcomes (e.g., Bolzendahl & Myers, 2004; Brinkerhoff & McKee, 1988; Ciabattari, 2001; Davis & Greenstein, 2009; Eisler & Corral, 2009; Eisler, Loye & Norgaard, 1995; Fan & Marini, 2000; Hill, 2002). For example, ideologies regarding gender are tied to, and reinforced by, other value-based constructs such as religious ideology and cultural beliefs (Brinkerhoff & McKee, 1988). Because these constructs are difficult to disentangle, it is important to study the

---

[1] Although exceeding the scope of this chapter, we recognize that transgendered individuals may self-identify as male and/or female—or neither—gender. By definition, a "gender traditional" perspective would be inimical to transgenderism. Thus, it is our hope that the literature, findings, and discussion presented here will facilitate greater understanding and compassion regarding gender identity, writ large, including but not limited to transgendered individuals.

interrelationships among them. At a larger and applied level, gender inequity has demonstrable and largely negative outcomes for men, women, and communities, as we will describe throughout this chapter (Eisler & Corral, 2009; Eisler, Loye, & Norgaard, 1995; Men Adrift, 2015).

Thus, it is important to contemplate how our scholarly work on gender may inform policies and practices in the real world. Ultimately, with clearer operationalization of the construct of gender, deeper understanding of the etiology of gender ideology, and greater appreciation of the real world implications of our work, we may be better able to translate such information into applied form in order to facilitate awareness and relations within, and between, the genders. Also, as we will indicate, new measures are needed to examine what we think we know, while helping advance our understanding of these complex processes, and facilitating growth and development at an applied level. Toward such means and ends, this chapter examines the utility of an integrative theoretical, empirical, and applied approach to these issues, by reporting on a large dataset from the Forum BEVI Project, a multisite, multiyear initiative that investigated international, multicultural, and transformative learning (Wandschneider et al., 2016). This project relies on a mixed methods measure—the Beliefs, Events, and Values Inventory (BEVI), and its Equilintegration (EI) framework—to examine the etiology and impact of "gender traditionalism" on a range of processes and outcomes. Specifically, the following questions will be addressed:

1. From a construct validation perspective, do BEVI results correspond with extant literature on gender for males and females?
2. How might the EI theoretical framework and BEVI further our understanding of the role of formative variables on the development of gender traditionalism?
3. Does a higher degree of gender traditionalism on the BEVI mediate specific outcome variables?
4. What are the implications of this theoretical model and assessment method for the facilitation of better understanding and relations within and between the genders?

In order to ask and answer these questions, this chapter is divided into the following seven sections. First, we provide an overview of literature on the construct of gender, by describing various controversies and common themes that tend to characterize this line of inquiry. Second, we turn to the formative variables (e.g., life history, demographics) that theoretically and empirically have been linked to the development of gender identity as well as how our beliefs and values regarding gender have evolved over time. Third, we focus on a dimension of gender that historically has received less attention in the larger field—how and why male gender identity develops as it does. Fourth, at a related level, we then examine why and how men and women are socialized to experience and express affect differently as well as the consequences of such processes for gender relations. Fifth, on the basis of all of the preceding, we illustrate why gender identity matters, by examining the local and global implications of the "gendered self" for actions, policies, and practices around the world. Sixth, to examine how these highly complex and interacting processes may be analyzed simultaneously, we then present results from a multiyear, multi-institution assessment of learning initiative called the Forum BEVI Project, which explores the relationship between antecedents and outcomes of gender traditionalism. Seventh and finally, we show how this theoretical model (Equilintegration Theory) and applied method (the BEVI) may be used in "the real world"—to help the genders understand why they believe what they believe about "who" men and women are and should be, both individually and in their relationships together—before offering a summary and conclusion.

INTRODUCTION TO THE GENDERED SELF

Distinctions between sex and gender have long been studied across multiple academic disciplines. In general, there is consensus that "sex" refers to the biological characteristics associated with being a man or woman, such as genitalia, and for women, menstruation, pregnancy, and lactation. "Gender," on the other hand, refers to the socially constructed understanding of what it means to be male or female, including the roles ascribed to men and women. Kahn (2009), based on the composite work of earlier researchers, defines gender as the "general social and cultural beliefs on the part of individuals and societies about people and what differentiates them. These social and cultural beliefs about gender determine societal expectations about people's thoughts, feelings, and behaviors, otherwise known as gender roles" (p. 52). Notwithstanding cultural variations in approach and intensity, socialization for gender roles is ubiquitous across societies; hence the "learned roles" tend to be regarded as a natural phenomenon (Kapadia, in press). Scholars who support a purely biological or physiological basis for gender differences are termed "essentialists," while those who point solely to social and cultural influences to explain such differences are termed "social constructionists." In short, many theories of gender development exist including biological, cognitive, and social approaches (Blakemore, Berenbaum, & Liben, 2009). At the same time, although gender largely is considered a sociocultural construction, it is important to note that gender development is likely impacted by myriad interactive factors. Blakemore et al. (2009) offer support for this multifaceted, interactional process of gender development noting,

> It may be the case that some aspects of gender development have their roots in evolutionary processes, some in the effect of hormones on the developing brain, some in the reinforcement provided by parents and others, some in the interaction of children's peer groups, some in the observation and imitation of gendered behavior and roles in the child's experience and the media, some in cognitive constructions, and some because of social interaction with others. There is no reason to think that biological, social, and cognitive factors are not all involved in the process of children's gender development. (p. 17)

A majority view of gender scholars likely would grant that some differences among men and women indeed are biologically endowed, although many attributes and roles associated with gender are believed to be learned, constructed, and influenced by sociocultural factors. In fact, evidence supports the impact of biological factors on some aspects of gendered behavior. For example, males and females have differing experiences of hormone exposure across the life span, which results in temporary as well as permanent alterations in brain structure and function (Berenbaum, Blakemore, & Beltz, 2011; Darlington, 2009). Only in the past couple of decades have researchers begun to study the female brain (Darlington, 2009). Mainly, male brains were used exclusively in research and results were generalized across the species (Darlington, 2009). While study of the female brain has helped to determine the impact of hormone exposure and fluctuation on female development (e.g., demonstrating that varying hormone levels impact abilities differently at different times of the month), it seems questionable at best to maintain that brain-based biological influences are the sole cause of male/female differences. As Blakemore et al. (2009) observe,

> The brain is (fortunately) not a static organ; it changes in response to experience. So it is difficult to know if sex differences in the brain produce sex differences in behavior or result from differences in the experiences of men and women. (p. 176)

While certain differences such as anatomical features clearly are sex differences, due to the bidirectional impact of social and biological factors, distinguishing other dissimilarities as either "sex differences" or "gender differences" is challenging at best if not impossible (Hines, 2004). As Berenbaum et al. (2011) note,

> There is a sizable literature examining associations between circulating hormones and gender-related characteristics, primarily aggression, mood, and cognitive abilities. . .most of this work has been conducted in adolescents and adults. Findings are complex and difficult to summarize briefly. Much of the complexity reflects small effects, reliance on observational studies in adults, and bidirectional effects of behavior and hormones (e.g., aggressive behavior can increase testosterone). Hormones do not have simple causal effects on behavior, and the most valuable studies are those that examine the ways in which hormones act indirectly and interact with social factors to change gender typing. (p. 813)

Thus, rather than attempting to reduce gender to essentialist or constructionist explanations, perhaps the most accurate description comes from a melding of, and interaction between, these points of view into a biosocial model where each informs, but neither totally determines, male/female differences (Berenbaum et al., 2011).

So just how different are men and women? The literature on sex and gender differences is vast and at times contradictory. Although an exhaustive review of this literature is beyond the scope of this chapter, some brief context may be helpful. First, the debate in the literature on gender differences across psychological variables,

> ranges from claiming that gender differences are close to zero (Hyde, 2005) to the view that they have been obscured by methodological limitations and are actually very large (Del Giudice, Booth, & Irwing, 2012), and a variety of positions in between (Lippa, 2006). According to Lippa (2006, p. 639), the real challenge for "gender researchers is to explain the complex profile of psychological gender differences and to untangle the myriad social and biological factors that generate both gender differences and gender similarities." (Vianello, Schnabel, Sriram, & Nosek, 2013, p. 3)

Differences commonly cited in the literature include certain visuospatial, mathematical, and verbal abilities, certain physical abilities (such as motor abilities and abilities requiring muscle strength), children's style of play, children's play interests, and aggression. Hines (2004) points to the typically low effect sizes of many of these reported differences (as compared to an aggregate difference in height for example, which is quite large), and describes some of the challenges associated with sex difference research including the tendency to publish studies that display differences in findings (and not to publish studies that yield no sex differences), which leads to an overrepresentation of difference reports; the impact of researchers' stereotypes on perceptions and conclusions; a lack of cross-situational consistency in sex differences; and the fact that few individuals correspond to the average male or female patterns (instead there is a great deal of variation within each sex, with each having representation at the top and bottom of distributions for all characteristics). Even when consistent differences between the modal performance of males and females are found in a certain area, there almost always is significant overlap among male and female groups (Hines, 2004).

Support for gender being understood largely as a social and cultural construction is found in the *gender similarities hypothesis,* which holds that despite the messages of popular culture, more variability can be found within genders than between genders (Hyde, 2005). In lay discourse, males and females often are characterized as being psychologically different, as having different needs, and disparate ways of being and communicating. Popular culture has emphasized these putative differences in well-known books such as *Men Are from Mars, Women Are from Venus* (Gray, 1992). While gender differences may indeed vary a great deal across context and development, as Hyde documents, results from 46 meta-analyses suggest that males and females are similar on most psychological variables. The meta-analysis found that 78% of effect sizes (including most of those often cited in the literature) were small or close to zero. Even so, several exceptions to the gender similarities hypothesis have been identified, including larger gender differences in certain motor behaviors (e.g., throwing), facets of sexuality (e.g., regarding casual sex), and moderate differences in physical aggression. In this regard, Hyde emphasizes the need to consider context vis-à-vis the prevalence or likelihood of gender differences, noting that gender differences in aggression, academic performance, and helping behaviors appear highly dependent on the influence of social norm expectations. For example, when the social context is manipulated, assumed "differences" between the genders can in fact be reversed or magnified. A study by Vianello et al. (2013) found that sex differences in personality traits were reduced to "weak or near zero" (p. 11) when implicit measures of personality were utilized compared to the use of explicit measures (which are partly impacted by social norms and social desirability). Additionally, traits more typically endorsed by males or females were different using implicit measures and explicit measures of personality. These findings suggest that differences derived from explicit measures likely are impacted by social desirability and ideas about how one should be or act based upon his or her gender. Such results suggest that gender differences are neither vast nor stable as popularized accounts suggest, but instead, often are context-driven and perpetuated by conformance to varying social expectations and dynamics.

Thus, it would appear that the psychological needs of men and women are highly similar, but due to social norms and socially constructed gender stereotypes, are attended to and prioritized differently. For example, psychological aspects of self likely are supported or not, and to varying degrees, based upon what we believe boys and girls need. Hyde (2005) discusses the negative implications of overinflated claims of gender differences including perpetuating the sense that men and women should conform to stereotypical gender roles and should not exhibit characteristics associated with the opposite sex. Such stereotypes can negatively impact women's roles in the workplace and men's ability to feel comfortable in nurturing roles, particularly as fathers. Furthermore, reifying gender stereotypes and inflating differences may impact human development and communication. For example, the disproportionate focus on self-esteem deficits in adolescent girls suggests, erroneously, that adolescent self-esteem is somehow less of a problem for males. The result of this stereotype is that the emotional needs of boys at this developmental stage often are relatively unrecognized, as described later in this chapter, with attendant implications for the underemphasis regarding interventions that could be salutary. Over time then, it follows that the differential perceptions regarding gender, mediated by contextually reinforced gender-based norms, may well be associated with different ways of treating males and females across the life span, with further implications for the genders' experience of self, others, and the larger world. At the very least, the construct of gender that is believed to be true or real is closely tied to, and influenced by, a range of formative variables such as one's cultural, religious, temporal, ethnic, racial, societal, and historical background (e.g., Bolzendahl & Myers, 2004; Brinkerhoff & McKee, 1988; Ciabattari, 2001; Davis & Greenstein, 2009; Eisler & Corral, 2009; Eisler, Loye, & Norgaard, 1995; Fan & Marini, 2000; Hill, 2002).

Against the backdrop, "gender" is regarded here in terms of generally understood male and female roles, which largely are prevalent—although by no means exclusively—across cultures and contexts around the world. More specifically, traditional masculine characteristics typically are described as unemotional, aggressive, independent, and strong while traditional feminine characteristics typically are described as dependent, sensitive, caring, and emotional (Enns & Sinacore, 2001; Levant & Kopecky, 1995). In light of such perceptions of difference, another dimension of gender that largely remains constant across contexts is the inequity inherent in gender hierarchies. As Bussey and Bandura (1999) observe, "many of the attributes and roles selectively promoted in males and females tend to be differentially valued with those ascribed to males generally being regarded as more desirable, effectual and of higher status" (p. 676). That said, different individuals—and the societies that they comprise—may show greater or lesser degrees of support for such putative differences. These gender-based beliefs, often termed gender ideology, are described by Davis and Greenstein (2009) as, "the underlying concept of an individual's level of support for a division of paid work and family responsibilities that is based on the notion of separate spheres" (p. 89). Other terms used to describe a relative allegiance to, or justification of, gender inequity include gender traditionalism, gender-role attitude, and gender egalitarianism.

As may be evident, the gender ideologies to which we ascribe often have demonstrable and real world impact on everything from how we understand ourselves, to the ways in which we parent our offspring, to the politics we are inclined to endorse. Moreover, the degree to which we understand the origins of our gender ideologies also may determine whether and how we regard gender-based actions, policies, and practices as good, bad, or indifferent (Eisler & Corral, 2009). Thus, as noted at the outset of this chapter, if we are to address the local and global implications of gender ideology, it is necessary not only to understand *what* individuals, groups, governments, and societies believe about gender, but *how* and *why* formative variables (e.g., life history) mediate the construction and maintenance of belief structures, particularly those that are related to gender traditionalism. For present purposes, this final point is most fundamental, since all of the other elements emphasized—how gender roles are defined; which gender characteristics are privileged over the other; and how such beliefs play out in "the real world"—have their origins in the formative variables that shape us all. As such, a question that is as—if not more—important than *whether there actually are differences between the genders* is *Do we believe that there are differences between the genders and why?* Because our beliefs about gender difference are much more important—from the standpoint of actions, policies, and practices around the world—than are the putative realities of any such differences.[2] To illustrate how interactions among formative variables and gender identity mediate not only what we believe, but why, we examine next how our collective concepts of gender have evolved over time.

Evolving Beliefs About the Gendered Self: The Impact of Formative Variables

Relying upon 24 years of data (1974–1998) on gender-role attitudes collected from General Social Surveys (GSS), and organized by the National Opinion Research Center (NORC), Ciabattari (2001) documents the evolution of gender ideology over time in the United States. Specifically, a sample size of 3,575 participants was divided into cohorts by generation (pre-baby-boomers, baby-boomers, and post-baby-boomers). Because results from prior empirical findings suggest that male gender ideology is influenced by socioeconomic status (SES), family background and composition, personal history, religious and political beliefs, race, ethnicity, regional background, and historical context, such factors were utilized as independent variables. On the one hand, overall results indicate that gender ideologies of men in the United States have become increasingly less conservative since the 1970s. This reduction in gender traditionalism from 1970 to 1990 was seen across cohorts, independent of age. Nonetheless, when examining the interaction of race and gender, interesting trends emerge. For example, African American men tend to be more accepting of women's roles in the workplace than other cohorts. Likewise, Hispanic men, while endorsing support for separate spheres of work, do not endorse the belief that children are impacted negatively by their mother working.

Notwithstanding such reductions in gender traditionalism in the United States, cross-national data on significant indicators of gender equity present a mixed picture. Trends from a 2010 United Nations (UN) report indicate that progress in the area of gender equality has been made in some areas such as health, economic participation, and education. For example, in aspects of literacy and education there has been notable progress; however, globally, women are in a much more precarious position regarding health and well-being. Consider, for instance, the social and cultural factors that increase women's vulnerability to HIV/AIDS in regions such as sub-Saharan Africa, North Africa, and the Middle East. As this UN report notes, in addition to the fact that sex with multiple partners often is culturally tolerated for men more than women,

> Unequal gender relations within and outside the family often limit the ability of women to protect themselves from HIV infection. Refusing unprotected sex is a challenge for women who are dependent on men socially and economically and therefore have limited bargaining power. (United Nations, 2010, p. 32)

The United Nations Development Fund for Women (2007) estimates that worldwide at least one out of every three women will be physically, sexually, or otherwise abused during the course of her lifetime. Women are victims at higher rates than men of sexual trafficking, sexual and domestic violence, and genital mutilation. The U.S. State Department (2007) reports that approximately 12.3 million persons are trafficked annually worldwide (other estimates range from 4 to 27 million), and that 80% of these

---

[2] See www.ibavi.org for more information regarding the mediating role of beliefs on actions, policies, and practices around the world.

victims are women. Consider also that 140 million girls and women worldwide are victims of female genital mutilation (FGM), a dangerous procedure that offers no medical benefits and damaging health risks (World Health Organization, 2013). According to the World Health Organization (2013), "FGM is recognized internationally as a violation of the human rights of girls and women. It reflects deep-rooted inequality between the sexes, and constitutes an extreme form of discrimination against women" (Fact Sheet 241). In 2012, the UN General Assembly published research on the damaging effects of FGM and accepted a resolution for its elimination, yet the practice continues to occur at disturbing rates (Fact Sheet 241). Such realities illustrate the potentially deleterious impact of traditional gender beliefs, which not only promote inequity across societies and cultures, but illustrate why gender-based discrepancies in areas of power, decision making, and violence warrant attention.

To investigate such processes longitudinally, Fan and Marini (2000) examined 8,822 adolescents and young adults from the United States, aged 14 to 22, at three points in time (1979, 1982 and 1987) using the National Longitudinal Survey of Youth (NLSY) (a 90.4% retention rate among participants was reported). Participants were asked to give their level of agreement (strongly agree, agree, disagree, or strongly disagree) to eight different statements regarding the employment of wives, such as, *A woman's place is in the home, not the office or shop* and *Men should share the work around the house with women, such as doing dishes, cleaning, and so forth.* Overall, results indicated that "socialization of gender-role attitudes begins in the family of origin and is influenced by gender" (p. 279). More specifically, sex, family background, and race all influenced gender-role attitudes, while religious ideation did not. For example, young women demonstrated more egalitarian gender-role attitudes than did young men, but the attitudes of both sexes were impacted by family history and background (e.g., mother's employment and higher degree of parental education were associated with a greater degree of egalitarian attitudes). Both male and female participants demonstrated a shift toward more egalitarian gender attitudes as they aged. The attitudes of men changed more than the attitudes of women, although women started out with more egalitarian views. Men tended to move more toward the egalitarian beliefs held by women, such that as men aged, their beliefs became more similar to women's.

So, although gender-based beliefs may change at the individual level, and appear to be changing differentially by gender as well as socioculturally, such changes are by no means globally universal, which begs the question why? As a partial answer, GSS data were analyzed again in a separate study by Bolzendahl and Myers (2004), who concluded that "attitudes towards feminist issues," including gender ideology, are mediated either by *interest-based* or *exposure-based* explanations (p. 761). In the case of interest-based explanations, when an individual's personal goals and interests are impacted negatively by gender inequity, he or she theoretically will be motivated to develop more egalitarian gender beliefs. On the other hand, exposure-based explanations contend that the encounter with ideas, situations, or experiences, which promote gender egalitarianism (e.g., such as education or socialization) is likely to impact and ultimately change beliefs regarding gender ideology. In short, interest-based explanations contend that gender-based beliefs change when individuals are affected by the consequences of such beliefs whereas exposure-based explanations maintain that beliefs may change due to reflection and other forms of experiential learning. Even so, as Bolzendahl and Myers also suggest, this distinction between exposure and interest-based explanations probably should be framed in complementary rather than dichotomous terms since an interplay between the two appears to account best for the formation of gender ideology.

In addition to such mediational considerations, Bolzendahl and Myers (2004) also corroborated Ciabattari's (2001) findings, concluding that "acceptance of feminist attitudes and ideas have steadily grown over the past 25 years" (p. 780). However, they conclude that the rate of such change is slowing. How was such a conclusion reached? Opinions on abortion, sexual behavior, public sphere gender roles, and family responsibilities were used to determine participants' reaction to feminist attitudes. Results suggest that attitudes related to abortion were not consistent with opinions in the other three domains, indicating that beliefs about abortion may occupy a different psychological space than attitudes toward gender equity. Moreover, four formative variables in particular—education, age, religious ideation, and political ideology—appeared to have particular predictive relevance to pro/anti-feminist attitudes for both men and women, even as interesting differences and similarities emerged between the genders. For example, education was a strong predictor of feminist attitudes for both sexes, but was a stronger predictor for women (i.e., greater education was associated with greater pro-feminist attitudes, especially for women). On the other hand, political ideation was not a strong predictor for either sex, but did have a marginally stronger impact on women's attitudes (i.e., political ideation was more predictive of pro-feminist beliefs for women than men). Finally, mother's education was found to have a more consistent effect for men's attitudes than women's (i.e., as mother's level of education increased, their son's level of gender traditionalism decreased).

This latter and intriguing finding, which receives further support from the study described later in this chapter, is bolstered by other international research. For example, in a large-scale study of urban college students in India, aged 18 to 21, the relative degree of mother's education was likened to greater or lesser gender sensitivity. Gender sensitivity refers to awareness of, and concern for, avoiding reliance on traditional gender-based beliefs. Gender sensitivity can be seen, for example, in one's choice of language by substituting gender neutral terms such as chairperson for gender biased terms such as chairman, or in avoiding phrases such as "crying like a little girl" or "don't be such a girl" that evoke and reinforce outdated gender stereotypes. Among multiple sociodemographic variables, mother's education emerged as the significant variable mediating attitudes toward a range of gender sensitivity domains such as gender roles and stereotypes, access to and control over resources, access to health care, power relations, tolerance of violence, and beliefs about sexuality (Kapadia, Shah, & Rajaram, 2007). Furthermore, a study to map the identity anchors of urban emerging adult women in Baroda, India, revealed that the young women perceived education and occupation as enabling factors in developing an identity that is free from rigid gender-role restrictions and impositions of traditional hierarchical family and cultural structures (Kapadia, 2011).

In addition to the preceding formative variables, such as gender and education, do other factors, such as ethnicity, also influence gender ideology? Fan and Marini (2000) discovered that African American participants were found to hold the most gender egalitarian beliefs, whereas Hispanic participants reported the most traditional gender-role attitudes. While African Americans tend to be more egalitarian in terms of gender-role attitudes as compared to other racial/ethnic groups in the United States, a study by Stanik and Bryant (2012) indicated that within-group differences correlated with yet another variable: marital quality. Specifically, in a participant group of African American couples of similar ages and educational backgrounds from the Southern United States, lower levels of marriage quality were reported among couples with husbands who possessed more traditional gender-role attitudes. Additionally, husbands of couples who engaged in traditional divisions of labor reported lower marital quality. Husbands with traditional gender-role attitudes, who also engaged in traditional divisions of labor with their wives, reported the lowest marital quality when compared to all other husbands (Stanik & Bryant, 2012). Overall, such research demonstrates that ideologies about gender do change over time (e.g., becoming more egalitarian), that a range of variables are associated with how gender roles are defined (e.g., ethnicity), and that such beliefs have real life impact (e.g., in reports of marital quality). Along these lines, it is interesting to note that the division of labor according to gender is associated further with stereotypes that rationalize and perpetuate separate labor spheres (Schmitt & Wirth, 2009).

Carter, Corra, and Carter (2009) examined the interaction of race and gender on changes in gender-role attitudes in the United States using data from two composite indexes of gender traditionalism from the GSS from 1974 to 2006. Results indicated that African American women hold less gender traditional attitudes than do African American men or Caucasian men and women. At the same time, differences between African American women and other groups appear to be diminishing, with differences between Caucasian women and African American women converging most. Carter and colleagues posit that women's increased labor force participation has had a significant impact on the evolution of gender ideology in both women and men. Further explanations for shifts in gender ideology point to social changes such as the increase in dual-earner and female-headed households, decreasing degree of gender stratification in the labor market (Cotter, Hermsen, & Vanneman, 1999), and cohort replacement over time (i.e., the rate at which a new cohort, or generation, replaces the current cohort) (Brooks & Bolzendahl, 2004).

Regarding such attitudinal change processes, Brooks and Bolzendahl (2004) point to external circumstances, including experiences specific to one's cohort (cohort effects) as well as social structural change, which affects all adults (period effects). Utilizing data from the GSS, they found that cohort replacement accounted for 55% of the change that occurred in gender-role attitudes from 1985 to 1998. The same study showed that labor force status and marital status accounted for 8% of participant change in gender-role attitudes since 1985. Furthermore, results implicate the proliferation of receptivity to rights-based ideology in the United States as an impetus for changing gender ideology. As these authors note,

> while aggregate trends in gender role attitudes are rooted in cohort and period effects, much of these effects appear to be *indirect:* approximately 34% of the contribution of cohort replacement and 45% of the period effects are mediated by rights-based ideology. (p. 128)

Although the impact of early environmental factors on the formation of gender-role attitudes is influential (Cunningham, 2001), such findings also indicate that gender-role attitudes continue to be shaped by ideological influences and experiences throughout adulthood.

Pampel's (2011) study provides further explanation for changing gender ideologies as well as support for the impact of cohorts on gender-related attitudes. Drawing upon data from the GSS from 1977 to 2006, Pampel compared determinants of gender egalitarian attitudes across 86 English speaking adult cohorts in the United States from 1900 to 1985. Findings supported the diffusion argument, which maintains that structural changes in society (e.g., increasing numbers of women in the paid labor force and higher education; increases in the percentage of women procuring high quality jobs; increases in dual-career families) catalyze the adoption of less gender traditional attitudes as well as widespread societal value shifts. These changes occur first in less traditional groups, and eventually (and perhaps to a lesser degree) in more traditional groups. As Pampel reports, "The early stages of change most affect the attitudes of educated and working women, those in non-traditional positions and with the strongest interests in gender equality" (p. 964). Thus, the strength of determinants of nontraditional gender views increases as pioneering groups adopt more egalitarian attitudes. While this attitudinal evolution may initially have a polarizing effect (as more traditional groups initially resist such change), it inexorably occurs, even among more traditional groups. Likewise, as gender egalitarian views disperse among those with less interest in gender equality, the strength of the aforementioned determinants decreases. In short, the effects of predictors of more egalitarian gender-role attitudes "become stronger across cohorts as attitudes shift from largely unfavorable toward gender equality to favorable among women with greater education and higher commitment to work" (p. 976).

Among younger cohorts, the effects of predictors weaken as gender equitable attitudes become more commonplace in the population and group differences decline in importance (Pampel, 2011). These results are stronger for women than for men, who tend to hold less egalitarian attitudes toward gender and tend to be less responsive to social change. Education for example, tends to impact gender ideology in men in a similar way to women, but the impact may not reach statistical significance. Pampel attributes these findings to evidence that diffusion has occurred at a faster and deeper rate for women than it has for men, which stands to reason since diffusion theoretically is more likely for groups that hold the strongest interests in equality.

In short, regarding the impact of formative variables on gender ideology—a key focus of the analyses presented later in this chapter—Pampel's (2011) findings suggest that certain characteristics (higher SES; lower family and religious involvement; higher levels of education; prestigious jobs and higher salaries) are predictors of more gender egalitarian beliefs. In contrast, Pampel's study found that other characteristics (increased numbers of children and increased church attendance in men; marriage and increased church attendance in women) predict more traditional gender attitudes whereas some formative variables, such as marriage in men, have little influence on gender-related attitudes. In the final analysis, American cohorts over the 20th century progressively have adopted more egalitarian views of gender, suggesting that generational influences are stronger predictors of gender egalitarian attitudes than SES, sex, or education (Brooks & Bolzendahl, 2004). Such findings support prior cross-cultural research on the impact that cohort replacement has on gender equality in industrialized nations worldwide (Inglehart & Norris, 2003).

The Gendered Self of Men

Much attention has been paid to the consequences of gender traditionalism and gender inequity on women, since they are on the receiving end of patriarchal imbalances. However, a focus on women is necessary, but not sufficient, if we are to address the root causes and effects of such inequities while also addressing potential solutions. Gender is a relational concept and hence any understanding of, and action toward, improving women's status must necessarily address men and masculinity. In societies that are suspended between tradition and modernity, an understanding of deeply embedded masculine values is essential in addressing traditional gender attitudes, which may manifest in the extreme as violent practices such as "honor killings." These practices strive to preserve the status quo, including male dominance, through the ultimate control of female sexuality (Chatani, 2011; Shealy, 2010b). Moreover, an understanding of "masculine" values and experiences is helpful in reaching out to men in a way that is more likely to result in engagement than resistance (Cochran, 2005). Such an understanding would facilitate applications focusing on "empower-ment of men," not in the form of power over women, but in terms of achieving free-dom from stereotypical notions of masculinity, embracing apparently "feminine" qualities such as nurturance and empathy, and creating space to articulate anxieties and vulnerabilities (Kapadia, 1999; Khanna, Kapadia, & Dongre, 1998; Men Adrift, 2015). Finally, it would be advantageous if the experience and perspective of men were better understood in order to recruit male participation in dialogue and change efforts, as is the case through organizations such as the Society for the Psychological Study of Men and Masculinity, under the auspices of the American Psychological Association.[3]

In considering gender traditionalism and its negative implications for men, it is important to understand how masculinity is defined in dominant discourse (e.g., Donaldson, 1993). For example, Kahn (2009) supports the position of prior research by suggesting that it would be helpful to identify whether specific characteristics must be expressed within a society in order to assume the role of "man." In this con-text, it is relevant to acknowledge the notion of multiple masculinities, as the concept is a cultural and sociohistorical construction with different cultures privileging dif-ferent attitudes about masculinity at different points in time. And yet, there is a hege-monic form of masculinity in every culture, which is the most visible among the other forms of masculinities (Roy, 2001). Likewise, in some cultures, certain aspects of mas-culinity are considered indispensable, such as the biological ability to have children. For example, a study in rural Maharashtra (India) revealed that men are pressured to prove their virility such that infertile men were referred to as *namard*, meaning, "not a man or lacking in masculinity" (Gujjarappa, Apte, Garda, & Nene, 2002). Along similar lines, a study in urban Gujarat (India) revealed that men who are suspected to have fertility problems may experience social ridicule and/or be pressed by the family to bring about a "solution" to this problem, which often manifests in the trans-fer of blame onto the woman (Mehta & Kapadia, 2008). Such patterns evince the negative implications of normative hegemonic notions of masculinity for both women and men.

One prominent definitional and etiological model of masculinity, based upon David and Brannon's (1976) *Blueprint for Masculinity*, has been adapted by Pollack (1999) as *The Boy Code*, a set of rules and expectations that are internalized by males during development. To understand the content of such internalizations, Pollack conducted hundreds of interviews with boys in which participants of all ages acknowledged adherence to these internalized rules of masculine conduct as well as a concomitant fear of what may occur should they be broken. According to Pollack, while all boys and men may not endorse this masculinity ideology, rejecting it likely results in a negative societal response; thus to some degree, most males conform.

One of the core defining aspects of "the boy code" is that masculinity is defined in opposition to femininity. Boys and men who endorse traits typically considered to be feminine risk being stigmatized and ridiculed. Additionally, masculinity is mea-sured by status and success, which are defined via the assertion of power, domi-nance, and control over others. Along similar lines, Kahn (2009) asserts that this kind of dominance over others occurs along a spectrum, from occupying a leadership role, to asserting dominance, to engaging in physical or sexual violence. According to this

[3] See http://division51.net

model, masculinity is defined further by the ability to be strong, confident, autonomous, and impervious to stress, and correspondingly, to eschew weakness or vulnerability. For Pollack (1999), such tendencies require men to learn how to disconnect from their emotional world in order to remain "a rock" that will hold everything and everyone together. Finally, this masculinity ideology requires men to be brave and aggressive (even violent) in the face of adversity and danger. This theme encourages an ethic of persistence, even at the risk of endangering oneself or others, in order to feel and appear masculine.

A study of men from a low socioeconomic group in urban India provides cross-cultural support for this masculinity ideology. In this analysis, a majority of respondents endorsed characteristics such as helping a woman in distress, engaging in a fight when someone makes a derogatory remark to one's sister or wife, being aggressive, being muscular, and sticking to one's decision even in the face of disapproval from many others as signs of masculinity, whereas crying in times of distress indicated a lack of masculinity (Rajaram, 2001). Along similar lines, another study of Indian young men 18 to 25 years of age revealed a range of behaviors associated with being a "real man," such as being a leader, manager, and breadwinner of the family; being able to fight with others; engaging in substance abuse; being able to dominate and control women, tease girls, and have multiple sexual partners (Pandya, Parmar, & Khanna, 2009). Resonant with such results, and demonstrative of the cross-cultural nature of such gender-role expectations, the Male Role Norms Inventory defines traditional masculine ideology as consisting of seven norms: avoidance of femininity; restriction of emotionality; toughness/aggression; self-reliance; homophobia; nonrelational sexuality; and achievement (Levant et al., 1992; Richmond, Levant, & Ladhani, 2012).

Ultimately, Pollack asserts, even in today's postmodern era, boys and men are still held to these "boy code" conceptions of masculinity to varying degrees, even as they simultaneously are expected to move beyond the traditional male stereotype. Pollack (1999) captures this complex paradox as follows:

> I believe that boys, feeling ashamed of their vulnerability, mask their emotions and ultimately their true selves. This unnecessary disconnection—from family and then from self—causes many boys to feel alone, helpless and fearful. And yet society's prevailing myths about boys do not leave room for such emotions, and so the boy feels he is not measuring up. He has no way to talk about his perceived failure, he feels ashamed, but he can't talk about his shame either. Over time, his sensitivity is submerged almost without thinking, until he loses touch with himself. And so a boy has been "hardened," just as society thinks he should be. Even as we continue to harden our boys the old-fashioned way, we expect them to live up to some very modern and contradictory expectations, particularly in their relationships. We want them to be "new men" in the making, showing respect for girl peers, sharing their feelings in emotionally charged circumstances, and shedding their "macho" assumptions about male power, responsibility, and sexuality. In short, we want our boys to be sensitive New Age guys and still be cool dudes. Is it any wonder that a lot of boys are confused by this double standard? (pp. xxiv)

The juxtaposition of old world masculinity with new age sensitivity is confusing at best, and is implicated in a host of negative outcomes, ranging from frustration, depression, and low self-esteem to failed and violent relationships. Boys and men thus often are caught in a double bind. They either may conform to the traditional concept of masculinity by suppressing certain emotions, thus risking psychological, relational, and physical health concerns, or be emotionally expressive, sensitive, and vulnerable and risk being labeled effeminate (Cochran, 2010; Levant et al., 1992; Levant et al., 2003; Men Adrift, 2015; Pandya et al., 2009; Richmond et al., 2012; Shealy, 2010b).

Masculine ideology is related conceptually to, and strongly correlated with, gender-role conflict (Levant, 1998; Levant et al., 2003). As many facets of traditional masculinity encourage unhealthy behaviors, internalization of such an ideology is problematic at multiple levels (Good et al., 1995; Richmond et al., 2012). Gender-role conflict describes the negative psychological and relational outcomes associated with adhering to, or deviating from, the dominant masculinity ideology. Some men will face significant obstacles in their attempts to conform to traditional masculinity norms and thus will experience a different kind of strain. Patterns of gender-role conflict are the observable and measurable outcomes of Pleck's (1981) gender-role strain as well as the concomitant stress related to experience with a rigidified and contradictory gender role (O'Neil, 2008). The concept of gender-role strain was offered in reaction to, and as a replacement for, the gender identity paradigm. Its proposal was grounded in the following rationale, positing that:

> contemporary gender roles are contradictory and inconsistent; that the proportion of persons who violate gender roles is high; that violation of gender roles leads to condemnation and negative psychological consequences; that actual or imagined violation of gender roles leads people to over conform to them; that violating gender roles has more severe consequences for males than for females; and that certain prescribed gender role traits (such as male aggression) are too often dysfunctional. (Levant & Pollack, 1995, p. 3)

By way of further explication, Pleck (1995) identified three subtypes of gender-role strain. First, the *discrepancy strain* (or gender-role discrepancy) is associated with not successfully conforming to, or failing to fully embody and fulfill the expectations of, the dominant ideology expectations of the traditional male role. Research points to a number of negative psychological and interpersonal outcomes resultant from this discrepancy strain including increased hostility and low self-esteem (Richmond et al., 2012). Even when male gender roles are fulfilled successfully, the socialization process that enables this fulfillment may be damaging and result in long-term negative outcomes. When those subjected to the socialization of a culture's dominant male gender role are traumatized or damaged as a result, the outcome is labeled *trauma strain* or male-gender-role trauma (e.g., Normative Male Alexithymia), the second form of gender-role strain. In other words, successfully conforming to male-gender-role expectations may have deleterious impacts, as many of the characteristics associated with dominant discourse masculinity have fundamentally negative side effects. Third and finally, the *dysfunction strain* describes the negative impact that adhering to culturally dominant gender roles may have at multiple levels of functioning for the individual and his relations with others (Cochran, 2010; O'Neil, 2008). For example men tend to engage in more risk taking behavior and thus sustain more injuries (although this difference among genders is decreasing). Additionally boys tend to be diagnosed with psychopathology more in childhood, which is in part a function of their tendency to externalize distress at a higher rate than females (Blakemore et al., 2009).

To illustrate how such constructs have been operationalized, the Gender Role Conflict Scale measures dysfunction strain by assessing four patterns of gender-role conflict: (a) success/power/competition; (b) restrictive emotionality; (c) restrictive affectionate behavior between men; and (d) conflict between work and family relations—across three contexts: intrapersonal, interpersonal, and therapeutic (O'Neil, 2008). Attendant research suggests that adherence to a dominant masculine ideology is psychologically and interpersonally dysfunctional and produces negative outcomes for men cross-culturally. Although studies on gender-role conflict with diverse populations are less prevalent, overall results suggest that this construct is related significantly to higher degrees of stress, anxiety, aggression, alexithymia, and depression as well as lower self-esteem. Furthermore, studies suggest that older homosexual men experience gender-role conflict, but may do so in different ways and at earlier developmental stages. As O'Neil notes further, when heterosexual men age, some aspects of gender-role conflict may be attenuated. Compounding the difficulties men face at an emotional level, and likely resultant from their tendency to mask emotional hardship, men are less likely to seek mental health services, which only serves to exacerbate the depth of the original presentation. As Cochran (2005) observes,

> . . . traditional masculine gender role socialization often produces outcomes which make seeking psychological help uncomfortable if not prohibitive for many men raised in the United States. Almost thirty years have elapsed since David and Brannon (1976) described traditional masculine values under four headings: "The Sturdy Oak," "Give 'em Hell," "No Sissy Stuff," and "The Big Wheel." Empirical research conducted over the intervening years has tended to confirm the impact that aspiring to live up to these ideals has on men's psychological and physical functioning. (p. 653)

In summary, decades of research on gender-role conflict and related lines of inquiry suggest the following four themes vis-à-vis men and masculinity: (a) men do not innately possess very different psychological needs from women, and in fact are similar in terms of most psychological variables (particularly when social context is manipulated such that men and women do not feel the need to conform to social norms); (b) there is a significant relationship between gender-role conflict and depression, anxiety, stress, low self-esteem, poor psychological well-being, and substance use and abuse; (c) gender-role conflict significantly correlates with depression and low self-esteem across diverse sexual, racial, and cross-cultural samples; and (d) gender-role conflict is related to negative interpersonal problems (e.g., attachment, marriage) as well as dysfunctional outcomes such as negative attitudes toward women, homosexuals, and minorities, and increased endorsement of sexual harassment, rape myths, and violence against women.

Finally, although this "boy code" framework is highly illuminating, it should be noted that such binary views of gender have been criticized for confusing prescriptive norms (explaining the way in which men are expected to act) with descriptive norms (explanation of the way in which men actually act). From this perspective, any binary framework of masculinity is limiting, since it does not fully capture the experiences of all men (Kahn, 2009; Stoltenberg, 2000). Along similar lines, although the ideals of such a "boy code" framework and its concomitant frames are considered to be unattainable, harmful, and antiquated (e.g., Cochran, 2010; David & Brannon, 1976; Men Adrift, 2015; Pandya et al., 2009; Pollack, 1999; Richmond et al., 2012), it is important to attend to individual differences and variability of gender in order to avoid artificially dichotomizing or attenuating the complexity of these processes, a goal that is consistent with the theory and data presented next.

Affect and the Gendered Self

Of all the aspects described previously, one of the most striking "differences" between men and women—and arguably at the heart of the matter—is how males and females relate to the world of emotion, in self and other. And on this point, abundant evidence suggests—including multiple findings from the current study—that males, on average, experience much more difficulty than females in capacity to feel, label, and express what is happening within them and in others at an emotional level. Although it theoretically is possible that genetically mediated factors might account for some portion of the variance in emotional expression, there is little evidence to date that "genes" are the cause of these substantive differences between males and females (e.g., Berenbaum et al., 2011; Blakemore et al., 2009; Darlington, 2009; Hines, 2004; Hyde, 2005; Lippa, 2006; Vianello et al., 2013). As indicated in the literature, a much more parsimonious explanation is that boys—for a range of socio-culturally mediated factors having to do with enduring concepts of what it means to be "a man"—simply are socialized to have relatively less access to their own emotional world and that of others.

In fact, research suggests that from infancy boys and girls are responded to differently, but not necessarily because caregivers intend to do so. Rather, such differential treatment seems mediated by largely nonconscious but internalized beliefs regarding what boys and girls need, who they should be, how they should act, and how they should be responded to. For example, although the reasons are not entirely understood, during the first few months of life, boys appear to display more emotional expressiveness than do female infants. However, by early childhood boys exhibit a far reduced propensity toward emotional expression, particularly vulnerability or distress. Boys are also allowed to whine less, are given different messages regarding emotional expression, are provided with less emotional support, and are pushed to be more independent at younger ages. Finally, research suggests that caregivers respond less empathically to boys on average (e.g., Haviland & Malatesta, 1981; Levant, 1998, 2011; Malatesta & Haviland, 1982; Pollack, 1999).

Again, according to Pollack (1999), the net effect of this process is a restriction in the emotional range deemed to be acceptable for boys to display (e.g., encouraging boys to smile even when they are unhappy). Although women tend to express emotions, empathy, and sympathy more openly and intensely and respond to the emotions of others more frequently, ". . .physiological measures of emotional intensity, sympathy, empathy and interest in babies are much less likely to detect such differences in sexes" (Blakemore et al., 2009, p. 132). Along these lines, mothers tend to discuss sadness with girls, but speak more about anger to boys. Mothers also tend to mirror directly the facial expressions exhibited by male infants, but respond with more dissimilar expressions to female infants. By responding in this way, it appears that females are afforded greater opportunities to observe, develop, and expand their capacity to experience and express a wider range of affect. In follow-up studies, mothers continued to display a greater degree of emotional expressiveness with female children at ages 3 to 6 months and 2 years. Researchers concluded that this difference in exposure to a greater range of emotional expression may in part account for women being better able to decode emotional expression. By 2 years of age boys become less verbally expressive, and by 6 years of age, are less facially expressive than girls (e.g., Levant, 1998, 2011; Malatesta & Haviland, 1982; Richmond et al., 2012).

How do we account for such different processes and outcomes? Pollack (1999) suggests that society pushes male individuation to occur prematurely and more abruptly than is necessary and healthy. This push to individuate prematurely could be in opposition to healthy emotional development from the perspective of attachment theory. By early childhood, boys and girls often begin to expect different responses to displays of sadness and vulnerability. Many boys come to understand that the expression of such emotions is not as acceptable; thus, they begin to display them less frequently. As boys age, they tend to become less and less emotionally responsive and communicative. Thus, boys often turn to anger as a socially acceptable means of expressing a spectrum of emotional experiences (Pollack, 1999; Richmond et al., 2012).

In discovering how difficult it was for American men (both therapy clients and research participants) to describe their emotional states, and that doing so took much practice, Levant (1992) proposed *Normative Male Alexithymia* to "account for a socialized pattern of restrictive emotionality influenced by traditional masculine ideology that he observed in the many American men" (Richmond et al., 2012, p. 63). The term "alexithymia" literally means "without words for emotions," and began to be used in the 1960s to describe the condition of certain psychiatric patients (Levant 2011). Levant theorized that as a result of being systematically discouraged from expressing and discussing their emotions, many boys and men do not develop sufficient awareness of their emotional states or the attendant vocabulary to describe them, particularly emotions that reflect vulnerability. And indeed, a meta-analysis of alexithymia literature concluded that men on average exhibit higher levels of alexithymia (Levant, Hall, Williams, & Hasan, 2009). Furthermore, empirical research supports a relationship between the endorsement of traditional masculine gender ideology and alexithymia in men, even after controlling for demographic variables (Levant et al., 2003). Deficits associated with Normative Male Alexithymia can result in problems such as abuse, addiction, interpersonal difficulties, and relational problems (Levant & Kopecky, 1995; Richmond et al., 2012).

The developmental antecedents and consequences of alexithymia are evident in the fact that boys who have difficulty identifying their own emotions also struggle to read the emotions of those with whom they interact. It is important to note that being unaware of their emotional responses does not mean that males do not have emotional experiences. In fact, Levant & Kopesky (1995) note that early research in this area (Buck, 1977) found that boys display just as many physiological responses to emotional situations as do girls. Boys may feel sadness or shame, but may be less aware of what they are feeling and/or confused as to the form or origins of such emotions. When the sources of these emotions are unknown, the tendency may be to blame others and/or the environment. Because a masculine ideology does not encourage boys to identify and express needs and feelings verbally, aggressive acting out may be the primary recourse to such confusing and overwhelming internal states. As Richmond et al. (2012) observe,

> Male violence is so pervasive that it has to be considered a gender-based epidemic (Kilmartin, 2007). While not all men are violent, most violence is committed by men (Hyde, 2007). Aggression and dominance (which aggression is thought to serve; Sapolsky, 1997) are centrally embedded in male role norms, meaning that to be aggressive and even violent is considered normative for boys and men. Physical aggression is thought to be a result of the way men and boys "should be," or "are," and hence is not regarded as deviant. (p. 62)

The Local and Global Implications of the Gendered Self

Now that we have considered the influence of formative variables on gender ideology, the consequences of gender ideology for males, and the differential development of emotional awareness and expression for males and females, we turn our attention to broader implications of the gendered self for actions, policies, and practices around the world. From a psychological and behavioral standpoint, a high degree of gender traditionalism negatively impacts men as we have seen, but also perpetuates gender inequity. Although the position of power that is afforded men via patriarchy benefits them in certain ways, gender inequality—and the resulting violence against women that it promotes—negatively impacts men, women, families, and communities. So contends Pinar Ilkkaracan, founding president of Women for Women's Human Rights (WWHR), a women's nongovernmental organization (NGO), based in Turkey, which has engaged in a wide range of scholarly and advocacy projects internationally.[4] On the basis of such work over decades, Ilkkaracan describes how and why a traditional masculine gender role can ultimately lead to abuse against women, as well as wide-spread inequities (Shealy, 2010b). Such outcomes include, but are not limited to, violence against women and girls, in the form of discrimination, female feticide, and infanticide (Rajaram & Zararia, 2009); domestic violence, honor killings, sexual assault, trafficking, and rape (Abramsky et al., 2011; Hackett, 2011); other systemic consequences such as illiteracy, poverty, economic, and social injustice (Chhabra, 2008); general and specific subordination and exploitation; restrictions on physical mobility and education; and political disenfranchisement (Keleher & Franklin, 2008).

Echoing themes of Pollack (1999), Richmond et al. (2012), and others cited previously—but from an explicitly international perspective—Ilkkaracan points first to the suppression of emotions such as sadness and fear in men while simultaneously encouraging stoicism, bravery, and strength. As a result of these processes, many boys and men around the world both fear an inability to live up to the socially sanctioned standards and expressions of masculinity, yet experience difficulty expressing or understanding these prohibited feelings (e.g., shame). As such, by exerting control and authority over self and other, the traditionally gendered male seeks to assuage and ward off his own insecurities about prohibited feelings. According to Ilkkaracan, this sense of isolation and disconnection from one's own emotional world (which certainly impacts men's ability to recognize and attend to the emotional experience of others) is the source of much of the emotional disturbance in the male population, which ultimately impacts girls, women, and the community at large (Shealy, 2010b).

Nowhere does this dynamic manifest more dramatically than in the realm of sexuality. In particular, social and cultural construction of male sexuality perpetuates male insecurity, by instilling in men the belief that they should be powerful, with attendant anxiety that they are not powerful enough. For Ilkkaracan, then, controlling female sexuality is understood as an attempt to quell male anxiety. Such tendencies are more pronounced in societies where nondemocratic conditions prevail, and the rights of women are curtailed. The greater the degree of inequality between men and women, the more difficult it will be to achieve present, authentic, and equal emotional connections. This inequity further impacts healthy and pleasurable aspects of sexuality for men and women as well as the ability to establish and maintain trusting, intimate relationships. Ultimately, in societies in which the rights of women are curtailed, men are negatively impacted by the absence of experiencing healthy sexual and egalitarian

---

[4] See www.wwhr.org

relationships, and the mutual enjoyment and connection they entail. Thus, privileging the male experience—sexual and otherwise—actually harms men (Shealy, 2010b).

Such privileging and power-based dynamics—which have roots in the differential capacity and inclination of men and women to experience and express affect, vulnerability, and need—ultimately play out not only at the most basic levels of functioning (e.g., sexual relations), but at the broadest level too in the allocation of resources, which impacts further the health and well-being of families, communities, and societies as a whole (Eisler, Loye, & Norgaard, 1995; Men Adrift, 2015; Shealy, 2010b). Consider, for example, two indexes that track such processes in the form of economic activity: the Gross National Product (GNP) and Gross Domestic Product (GDP). Traditionally, a nation's quality of life has been determined by its relative wealth as measured by GNP and GDP. However, this assumption fails to consider the human and environmental costs associated with the productivity being measured, (e.g., human rights violations and deforestation); fails to account for any activity not included in the formal economy (e.g., much work is performed by women in support of their families and communities, but is not included in GNP or GDP); and does not indicate how resources (e.g., food, water, medication, education) are distributed nor tracks the impact of such distribution on human life (Eisler & Corral, 2009).

Results of data collected from 89 nations as part of the Gender Equity and Quality of Life Project suggest that contrary to popular belief, a nation's level of wealth is not commensurate with the quality of life of its inhabitants. In fact, large discrepancies in quality of life are present among countries with very similar GDPs. Findings from the Gender Equity and Quality of Life Project suggest that women's status, and the resulting level of gender equity, is a more accurate predictor of a nation's quality of life (Eisler & Corral, 2009). Similar results were derived by Arrindell et al. (1997), who examined variations in the subjective well-being of 36 nations using Hofstede's dimensions of national culture (1980). One such dimension, labeled Masculinity–Femininity (MAS), was used to measure the continuum along which nations exist in terms of variables related to gender-role social norms and includes juxtapositions such as the following two examples: *Sex roles in society should be fluid* VERSUS *Sex roles in society should be clearly differentiated* and *Differences in sex roles should not imply differences in power between the sexes* VERSUS *Men should dominate in all settings*. What are the implications for high versus low MAS countries? Overall, low MAS countries

> offer both sexes, especially women, greater opportunities for the fulfillment of multiple social roles (employment, marriage, parenthood) that are associated with good self-rated health status, low morbidity, little restricted activity, infrequent use of medical care, and low drug use for both men and women, and also have additive positive health effects for both sexes (see Barnett & Baruch, 1987; Cleary, 1987; Arrindell et al., 1997, p. 41).

In general, results of this study found that the combination of lower levels of MAS—in conjunction with sufficient financial resources—resulted in nations with the highest levels of well-being. Thus, financial means were deemed necessary in order to achieve the vision and norms that characterize a "feminine society," such as Sweden, which tends to value those traits typically associated with femininity (Arrindell et al., 1997; see also Eisler & Corrall, 2009; Men Adrift, 2015).

Digging more deeply into these global implications of gender-based actions, policies, and practices, consider overpopulation and literacy, two issues that certainly are core to a nation's concept of its own "quality of life." As documented by Eisler et al. (1995), a strong positive correlation (.89) was discovered between prevalence of contraception and national life expectancy. What might account for this finding? As women are afforded control over their own bodies and reproductive rights, their survival increases due to reduced strain on their bodies from frequent pregnancy; fewer deaths from childbirth; less time spent caring for children, with subsequent allocation of their time to paid work, education, and the ability to attend to personal health and skill building. To take another example, a substantial literacy gap between men and women was found to correlate with a lower life expectancy as well as a higher rate of infant mortality. Specifically, as literacy rates among women become more equal to that of men, rates of infant mortality decrease and life expectancy increases (.66). What might account for this finding? Perhaps the most parsimonious explanation is that more educated women are better able to access information, skills, and resources that bear directly on issues of pregnancy prevention and prenatal care, among related processes. Thus, the most cost effective means of controlling the pernicious implications of overpopulation may well be the education of women (Eisler & Corral, 2009).

Ultimately, Eisler and Corral (2009) offer two types of leadership models—domination and partnership—that account for whether or not such outcomes prevail. From a definitional standpoint,

> the domination model is characterized by strong-man rule, rigid male dominance, institutionalized violence, and the devaluation of women and the feminine . . . . In the domination model, caring for those who are not members of one's in-group as well as caring for our environment are not priorities. Rather, the whole system is based on using the environment and people to benefit those that are on top, in terms of power or control over others. Relations conform to in-group versus out-group rankings in which difference—beginning with the most fundamental difference in our species, between male and female—is equated with superiority or inferiority, being served or serving, dominating or being dominated. (p. 33)

In domination models, strict gender roles predominate; stereotypically masculine traits such as domination and power are valued, while stereotypically feminine traits such as empathy and warmth are deemed inferior as they do not lead to the kind of success that this model values. The partnership model, on the other hand, values stereotypically feminine traits, and supports a more egalitarian, democratic social structure and less institutionalized violence. Within the partnership model, "so called feminine qualities and behaviors, whether they reside in women or men, are not only held in high esteem but also are incorporated into the operational values-based systems and structures of the society" (p. 33). This more gender equitable model values difference and collaboration, and acknowledges that both men and women can and should possess characteristics stereotypically construed as "masculine" and "feminine." Thus the partnership model accepts and supports the gender similarities hypothesis (Hyde, 2005). It is important to note the use of the word "stereotypical" when discussing these models. As Eisler et al. (2009) point out, none of these traits are inherent in either sex. There are many men who are warm and nurturing and many women who are not. Likewise, many stereotypically masculine qualities are beneficial to female and male leaders, such as logical thinking and assertiveness.

As Eisler and Corral (2009) document, it is in our collective interest to move toward partnership, and away from domination models around the world. To do so, we need to revisit previously underexamined beliefs and values, such as gender roles. "The shift to partnership leadership is part of a larger shift in beliefs and values—as they are expressed through institutions, relationships, and in many other spheres of life—from the personal to the political" (p. 32). In short, current conceptions of stereotypical masculinity and femininity are outdated, irrelevant, and antithetical to meeting fundamental psychological and sociocultural needs of individuals, couples, families, and societies. In a related sphere, contemporary research in the areas of leadership and management shows also that the domination model is outdated and ineffectual, and suggest that leadership based on mutual respect, responsibility, emancipation, and encouragement is necessary for economic success (see also Dyjak-LeBlanc, Brewster, Grande, White, & Shullman, 2016). As the status of women continues to rise, and partnership models gain popularity, a new conceptualization of power is being offered in which more value is placed on stereotypically "feminine" qualities. It is noteworthy, in this regard, that Finland, a nation representative of the partnership model of leadership, is ranked as more economically competitive than the much wealthier United States. Likewise, Nordic nations, which regularly garner high rankings on the UN Human Development Reports, demonstrate the significant gains that stand to be made when societies shift toward partnership models. For example, these nations,

> . . .pioneered the first peace studies courses. They pioneered laws against physical punishment of children in families. They pioneered a strong men's movement to disentangle male identity from violence. They also pioneered what we today call industrial democracy: teamwork in factories rather than turning human beings into mere cogs in the industrial machine. Environment initiatives such as the Natural Step came out of these nations. And, of course, women in the Nordic nations occupy a far higher percentage of political leadership positions than anywhere else in the world: between 40 and 50 percent (Eisler & Corral, 2005, p. 78).

In short, beliefs and values about gender matter. They have real world impact not only at the level of individual and interpersonal functioning, but in the types of policies and leadership structures that are instituted and enforced, both locally and globally.

Understanding the Gendered Self through EI Theory, EI Self, and BEVI

In the preceding overview, we have considered the nature, etiology, and implications of gender ideology across various levels of analysis, from basic issues of definition (e.g., what do we mean by "gender"); to the relation of specific formative variables on the expression of gender-based stereotypes; to issues of how gender ideology is formed; to the implications of such processes for the "gendered self" of males; to broader manifestations of how such processes play out at the levels of individual, social, and global well-being. These are complex matters to be sure, made more so by the fact that multiple levels of analysis have to be examined simultaneously in order to understand why and how such interactions occur as well as how to translate our findings into real world application (e.g., programs, courses, policies).

Highly consistent with the present approach, Davis and Greenstein (2009) contend in their review of research on the construction and consequences of gender ideology that continued research is necessary on formative variables that impact gender ideology as well as the consequences of such ideologies at a range of applied levels (e.g., on family, work, education). Specifically, "more work can be done to extend the measurement of gender ideology using alternative types of measurement strategies. . .or the construction of open-ended questions that provide context to individual responses" (p. 99). Furthermore, they point to the need for "more data on how gender ideology is constructed" (p. 99). Finally, they observe that "a thorough understanding of the conceptual or theoretical processes by which such factors affect gender ideology is essential" (pp. 99–100). Highly consonant with such guidance, the remainder of this chapter describes a theoretically and empirically derived model and method that are designed specifically to address these sorts of recommendations. After introducing Equilintegration (EI) Theory, the EI Self, and the BEVI, we describe results from a multiyear, multi-institution assessment initiative called the Forum BEVI Project, which bear directly on the complexity of the gendered self. We then conclude with a series of points regarding how this model and method may help further work in this area while contributing to intergender understanding and development at an applied level.

Although a full explication is presented in Chapters 2, 3, and 4, a brief overview of the three main components of the present approach—Equilintegration (EI) Theory, the EI Self, and the BEVI—may be helpful at this point. Equilintegration (EI) Theory seeks to explain "the processes by which beliefs, values, and 'worldviews' are acquired and maintained, why their alteration is typically resisted, and how and under what circumstances their modification occurs" (Shealy, 2004, p. 1075). Derivative of EI Theory (Shealy, 2004), the Equilintegration or EI Self explains processes by which beliefs and values are acquired, maintained, and transformed, as well as how and why these are related to formative variables (e.g., caregiver's level of education, culture), core needs (e.g., for attachment, affiliation), and adaptive potential of the self. Informed by scholarship in a range of key areas (e.g., "needs-based" research and theory; developmental psychopathology; social cognition; therapy process and outcomes; affect regulation; and theories and models of "self"), the EI Self seeks to illustrate how the interaction between our core needs and formative variables results in the formation and subsequent internalization of beliefs and values about self, others, and the world at large (see Chapter 3 and www.ibavi.org/content/featured-projects).

Concomitant with EI Theory and the EI Self, the BEVI is a comprehensive analytic tool in development since the early 1990s that examines how and why we come to see ourselves, others, and the larger world as we do. The BEVI helps to explain how life experiences, culture, and context affect our beliefs, values, and worldview as well as the influence of such processes on multiple aspects of human functioning (e.g., learning processes, relationships, personal growth, the pursuit of life goals). For example, the BEVI assesses processes such as: basic openness to alternate ideas and ways of thinking; the tendency to (or not to) stereotype in particular ways; self- and emotional awareness; preferred strategies for making sense of why "other" people and cultures "do what they do"; global engagement (e.g., receptivity to different cultures, religions, and social practices); and worldview shift (e.g., the degree to which beliefs and values change as a result of specific experiences). BEVI results can be translated into individual and group reports, and used in a wide range of contexts for a variety of applied and research purposes (e.g., to track and examine changes in worldviews over time) (e.g., Anmuth et al., 2103; Atwood, Chkhaidze, Shealy, Staton, & Sternberger, 2014; Brearly, Shealy, Staton, & Sternberger, 2012; Hayes, Shealy, Sivo, & Weinstein, 1999; Hill et al., 2013; Isley, Shealy, Crandall, Sivo, & Reifsteck, 1999; Shealy, 2000a, 2000b, 2004, 2005, 2006, 2015, 2016; Shealy, Bhuyan, & Sternberger, 2012; Tabit et al., 2011; for more information about the BEVI, see Chapter 4 as well as www.ibavi.org/content/featured-projects).

Methods

This study is exploratory in that we are attempting to understand the relationship between formative variables (e.g., life history, demographics), mediators (various scales on the BEVI), and outcomes (e.g., self-reported religious or nonreligious affiliation) in a manner that is consistent with other analytic work with this measure.

Analyses of BEVI results were developed on the basis of a large dataset (N = 2331) collected during 2011 to 2012 from the Forum BEVI Project, a multi-institution, multiyear project coordinated by the Forum on Education Abroad (www.forumea.org) and International Beliefs and Values Institute (www.ibavi.org). Participants primarily included undergraduate students (96.7%), although a small portion of graduate students (3.3%) also was included. The sample ranged between the ages of 17 and 26, with an average age of 19; 3.9% fell into the age range of 26 to 62, with another 0.9% falling into the range of 12 to 17. Although the majority of participants reported as U.S. citizens (93.3%), non-U.S. citizens also were included in the sample (N = 156 or 6.7%). Also, participants for the overall sample were drawn from 38 different countries of origin. Of the sample, 79.1% reported as Caucasian with 20.9% as non-Caucasian (6.6% Black or African American; 0.9% American Indian or Alaskan Native; 7.4% Asian or Pacific Islander; 2.9% Hispanic/Latino; 3% Other). Finally, from the standpoint of gender, 40.8% of the sample was female, with 59.2% male. All participants were required to provide informed consent as determined by multiple Institutional Review Board processes at each institution involved, and participation was entirely voluntary (e.g., participants were not required to complete the BEVI, and could elect to discontinue participation at any time). Analyses were conducted via SPSS and MPLUS, and consisted of analysis of variance (ANOVA), regression analysis, and structural equation modeling (SEM). More information (e.g., institutional participants, methodological issues) from the Forum BEVI Project is available at www.ibavi.org/content/featured-projects.

Results and Discussion

Consistent with the literature regarding how females and males differentially experience self, others, and the larger world, BEVI results demonstrate striking and consistent statistically significant differences across a range of analyses. The following ANOVA results at the item level of analysis on the BEVI illuminate this pattern. Specifically, relative to females, males appear to:

1. *Report a more rigid conceptualization regarding their own masculine identity* (Table 8.1).

TABLE 8.1

Gender Difference for the Statement: "A man should act like a man"

SOURCE	SUM OF SQUARES	MEAN	DF	MEAN SQUARE ERROR	F	SIG.
Corrected Model	870801		1	87.801	142.236	0.00
Intercept	18639.723		1	18639.723	30195.95	0.00
Gender	87.801		1	87.801	142.236	0.00
Male		3.004				
Female		2.608				
Error	1423.476		2306	0.617		
Total	20151		2308			
Corrected Total	1511.277		2307			

Note. $R^2 = 0.058$ (adjusted $R^2 = 0.058$).

TABLE 8.2

Gender Difference for the Statement: "I am a very feeling person"

SOURCE	SUM OF SQUARES	MEAN	DF	MEAN SQUARE ERROR	F	SIG.
Corrected Model	45.657		1	45.657	77.572	0.00
Intercept	19106.613		1	19106.613	32462.33	0.00
Gender	45.657		1	45.657	77.572	0.00
Male		2.763				
Female		3.05				
Error	1353.729		2300	0.589		
Total	20506		2302			
Corrected Total	1399.387		2301			

Note. $R^2 = 0.033$ (adjusted $R^2 = 0.032$).

2. *Be less likely to acknowledge and/or experience awareness of basic feelings, needs, and vulnerabilities* (Tables 8.2–8.4).
3. *Express a relative preference for intellectualization and emotional control* (Tables 8.5 and 8.6).
4. *Are less likely to grant legitimacy to the value of understanding and working through painful emotions* (Table 8.7).

TABLE 8.3

Gender Difference for the Statement: "Sometimes I feel needy and vulnerable"

SOURCE	SUM OF SQUARES	MEAN	DF	MEAN SQUARE ERROR	F	SIG.
Corrected Model	67.638		1	67.638	143.165	0.00
Intercept	17970.404		1	17970.404	38036.89	0.00
Gender	67.638		1	67.638	143.165	0.00
Male		2.658				
Female		3.007				
Error	1080.958		2288	0.472		
Total	19119		2290			
Corrected Total	1148.596		2289			

Note. $R^2 = 0.059$ (adjusted $R^2 = 0.058$).

TABLE 8.4

Gender Difference for the Statement: "I have real needs for warmth and affection"

SOURCE	SUM OF SQUARES	MEAN	DF	MEAN SQUARE ERROR	F	SIG.
Corrected Model	62.909		1	62.909	120.512	0.00
Intercept	19309.418		1	19309.418	36990.34	0.00
Gender	62.909		1	62.909	120.512	0.00
Male		2.757				
Female		3.093				
Error	120.1673		2302	0.522		
Total	20574		2304			
Corrected Total	1264582		2303			

Note. $R^2 = 0.050$ (adjusted $R^2 = 0.049$).

5. *Grant greater legitimacy to violence in terms of pursing goals* (Table 8.8).
6. *Report less interest in learning about or being accepting of different cultures and their practices* (Tables 8.9 and 8.10).
7. *Report experiencing less concern regarding the rights and experiences of women* (Tables 8.11 and 8.12).
8. *Endorse less expressed concern about the environment and natural world* (Tables 8.13 and 8.14).

TABLE 8.5

Gender Difference for the Statement: "I value clear logic above most other things"

SOURCE	SUM OF SQUARES	MEAN	DF	MEAN SQUARE ERROR	F	SIG.
Corrected Model	6.034		1	6.034	13.652	0.00
Intercept	19812.582		1	19812.58	44829.08	0.00
Gender	6.034		1	6.034	13.652	0.00
Male		3.003				
Female		2.898				
Error	998.384		2259	0.442		
Total	20817		2261			
Corrected Total	1004.418		2260			

Note. $R^2 = 0.006$ (adjusted $R^2 = 0.006$).

TABLE 8.6

Gender Difference for the Statement "My emotions can sometimes get the better of me"

SOURCE	SUM OF SQUARES	MEAN	DF	MEAN SQUARE ERROR	F	SIG.
Corrected Model	55.825		1	55.825	105.289	0.00
Intercept	19558.688		1	19558.683	36888.46	0.00
Gender	55.825		1	55.825	105.289	0.00
Male		2.785				
Female		3.102				
Error	1219.487		2300	0.53		
Total	20834		2302			
Corrected Total	1275.312		2301			

Note. $R^2 = 0.044$ (adjusted $R^2 = 0.043$).

Overall, findings from BEVI item analyses are consonant with prominent themes from the literature. For example, central tenets of Pollack's (2009) "Boy Code" (e.g., denial of vulnerability; emotional restriction; reduced capacity to understand the emotional experience of self and other), Levant's (1992) "Normative Male Alexi-thymia," and Eisler and Corral's (2009) "dominance model" all would appear to

TABLE 8.7

Gender Difference for the Statement "It helps to work through painful feelings from the past"

SOURCE	SUM OF SQUARES	MEAN	DF	MEAN SQUARE ERROR	F	SIG.
Corrected Model	18.103		1	18.103	40.698	0.00
Intercept	20261.073		1	20261.073	45550.59	0.00
Gender	18.103		1	18.103	40.698	0.00
Male		2.896				
Female		3.076				
Error	1020.824		2295	0.445		
Total	21300		2297			
Corrected Total	1038.927		2296			

Note. $R^2 = 0.017$ (adjusted $R^2 = 0.017$).

TABLE 8.8

Gender Difference for the Statement "Violence is not a good way to achieve a goal"

SOURCE	SUM OF SQUARES	MEAN	DF	MEAN SQUARE ERROR	F	SIG.
Corrected Model	77.994		1	77.994	150.958	0.00
Intercept	20677.388		1	20677.39	40021.26	0.00
Gender	77.994		1	77.994	150.958	0.00
Male		2.871				
Female		3.249				
Error	1166.618		2258	0.517		
Total	21922		2260			
Corrected Total	12446.12		2259			

Note. $R^2 = 0.063$ (adjusted $R^2 = 0.062$).

predict these very sorts of findings. But can we go further than this descriptive level of analysis to issues of etiology? For example, because the BEVI examines a wide range of formative variables (e.g., life history, demographics), is it possible to determine whether certain variables or scores on specific scales predict a greater degree of gender traditionalism? The short answer is yes, as illustrated by the following ANOVA, regression, and structural equation model (SEM) analyses.

TABLE 8.9

Gender Difference for the Statement: "I enjoy learning about other cultures"

SOURCE	SUM OF SQUARES	MEAN	DF	MEAN SQUARE ERROR	F	SIG.
Corrected Model	82.145		1	82.145	171.67	0.00
Intercept	22200.952		1	22200.95	46396.57	0.00
Gender	82.145		1	82.145	171.67	0.00
Male		2.959				
Female		3.344				
Error	1092.904		2284	0.479		
Total	23376		2286			
Corrected Total	1175.048		2285			

Note. $R^2 = 0.070$ (adjusted $R^2 = 0.070$).

TABLE 8.10

Gender Difference for the Statement: "We should be more tolerant of different cultural practices"

SOURCE	SUM OF SQUARES	MEAN	DF	MEAN SQUARE ERROR	F	SIG.
Corrected Model	45.248		1	45.248	123.541	0.00
Intercept	23292.37		1	23292.37	63595.15	0.00
Gender	45.248		1	45.248	123.541	0.00
Male		3.092				
Female		3.38				
Error	827.382		2259	0.366		
Total	24165		2261			
Corrected Total	872.63		2260			

Note. $R^2 = 0.052$ (adjusted $R^2 = 0.051$).

Consider first Table 8.15, which examines the relationship between Negative Life Events and Gender Traditionalism on the BEVI. Basically, the significant finding here is that the more individuals report that they have experienced negative life events (e.g., a troubled situation in their home environment; conflicts with parents or peers; difficulties in school), the more likely they are to report a higher degree of

TABLE 8.11

Gender Difference for the Statement: "I strongly support equal rights for women"

SOURCE	SUM OF SQUARES	MEAN	DF	MEAN SQUARE ERROR	F	SIG.
Corrected Model	75.290		1	75.29	186.393	0.00
Intercept	25211.171		1	25211.171	62414.54	0.00
Gender	75.29		1	75.29	186.393	0.00
Male		3.177				
Female		3.547				
Error	918.539		2274	0.404		
Total	26205		2276			
Corrected Total	993.829		2275			

Note. $R^2 = 0.076$ (adjusted $R^2 = 0.075$).

TABLE 8.12
Gender Difference for the Statement: "Pornography degrades women"

SOURCE	SUM OF SQUARES	MEAN	DF	MEAN SQUARE ERROR	F	SIG.
Corrected Model	154.517		1	154.517	213.633	0.00
Intercept	16737.955		1	16737.96	23141.69	0.00
Gender	154.517		1	154.517	213.633	0.00
Male		2.49				
Female		3.019				
Error	1650.528		2282	0.723		
Total	18543		2284			
Corrected Total	1805.045		2283			

Note. $R^2 = 0.086$ (adjusted $R^2 = 0.085$).

Gender Traditionalism. Thus we can consider higher levels of accrued negative life events to be predictive of more traditional gender ideologies.

Consider next Table 8.16. Here, regression was utilized in order to examine variables deemed to be predictive of Gender Traditionalism. All of the following variables were found to be significantly predictive (minimally $p < .05$) of participants' scores on the Gender Traditionalism scale: gender; grade point average; whether or not participants were learning a foreign language at home; and the degree to which participants relied on television news programs for news.

TABLE 8.13
Gender Difference for the Statement: "I worry about our environment"

SOURCE	SUM OF SQUARES	MEAN	DF	MEAN SQUARE ERROR	F	SIG.
Corrected Model	30.321		1	30.321	54.603	0.00
Intercept	20514.502		1	20514.502	36943.47	0.00
Gender	30.321		1	30.321	54.603	0.00
Male		2.89				
Female		3.123				
Error	1277.177		2300	0.555		
Total	21822		2302			
Corrected Total	1307.498		2301			

Note. $R^2 = 0.023$ (adjusted $R^2 = 0.023$).

TABLE 8.14

Gender Difference for the Statement: "I worry about the health of our planet"

SOURCE	SUM OF SQUARES	MEAN	DF	MEAN SQUARE ERROR	F	SIG.
Corrected Model	26.243		1	26.243	49.4	0.00
Intercept	20457.564		1	20457.564	38509.18	0.00
Gender	26.243		1	26.243	49.4	0.00
Male		2.895				
Female		3.112				
Error	1219.193		2295	0.531		
Total	21703		2297			
Corrected Total	1245.436		2296			

Note. $R^2 = 0.021$ (adjusted $R^2 = 0.021$).

More specifically, being female, having a higher grade point average (GPA), learning a foreign language at home, and watching news programs on television all were significantly predictive of a *lower* degree of Gender Traditionalism.

Finally, grounded in an EI theoretical framework, we used structural equation modeling (SEM) to test causal relationships among (a) Formative Variables (i.e., Negative Life Events and Positive Life Events scales, as well as background variables

TABLE 8.15

The Relationship Between Negative Life Events and Gender Traditionalism on the BEVI

SOURCE	SUM OF SQUARES	MEAN	DF	MEAN SQUARE ERROR	F	SIG.
Corrected Model	30.281		3	10.094	9.874	0.00
Intercept	58434.624		1	58434.624	57160.54	0.00
Negative Life Events	30.281		3	10.094	9.874	0.00
Strongly disagree		4.906				
Disagree		5.071				
Agree		5.117				
Strongly agree		5.227				
Error	2310.375		2260	1.022		
Total	60773.697		2264			
Corrected Total	2340.656		2263			

Note. $R^2 = 0.013$ (adjusted $R^2 = 0.012$).

TABLE 8.16

Effect of Demographic and Background Variables on Gender Traditionalism: Regression Analysis

Scales	UNSTANDARDIZED COEFFICIENTS		STANDARDIZED COEFFICIENTS		
	B	Std. Error	Beta	t	Sig.
Constant	4.987	0.113		44.175	0.00
Gender	0.646	0.052	0.31	12.507	0.00
Grade point average	0.046	0.01	−0.118	−4.79	0.00
Learning foreign language at home	0.173	0.081	0.053	2.133	0.033
Rely on television news programs for news	0.139	0.049	0.07	2.852	0.004
Hours per week of using cell phone during study abroad	0.018	0.01	0.045	1.799	0.072
F	41.451***				
R-squared	0.124				
Adj. R-squared	0.121				

*Note. *$p < 0.05$, **$p < 0.01$, ***$p < 0.001$.*

including ethnicity, disability, family income, father's education, and mother's education); (b) Mediators (i.e., the Gender Traditionalism scale from the BEVI); and (c) Outcomes (e.g., educational aspirations, political ideology, and religious orientation). Results from all models found both Negative Life Events *and* Positive Family Relations to be significant predictors of Gender Traditionalism, a point that is expanded upon further in the following discussion. Additionally, results identified the status of being married; the relative lack of interest in international or multicultural education experiences; lower educational aspirations; lower GPA; a tendency to endorse a Christian orientation; and a tendency to endorse a Republican political orientation as among the main variables to be significantly associated with a *higher* degree of Gender Traditionalism.

To illustrate the nature of such relationships, consider two sample SEMs. Figure 8.1 examines the causal pathways between Negative Life Events and other formative variables, to the mediating variable of Gender Traditionalism, to the outcome of a relative degree of educational achievement. For purposes of interpretation, note that all three of these models fit the data adequately using standard fit indexes (e.g., root mean square error of approximation [RMSEA], comparative fit index [CFI]), meaning that the covariance structure in the model approximates the covariance structure in the data. Within each of these models, dashed lines refer to relationships that are not significant, and solid lines refer to significant relationships. From a theoretical standpoint (and SEM basically allows for the empirical evaluation of theoretically derived models), each of these SEMs essentially is asking whether "Formative Variables" (e.g., life history, demographics) are predictive of "Mediators," which from the standpoint of developmental psychopathology are "processes that account for the linkage" between Formative Variables and "Outcomes" (Cummings, Davies, & Campbell, 2000, pp. 131).

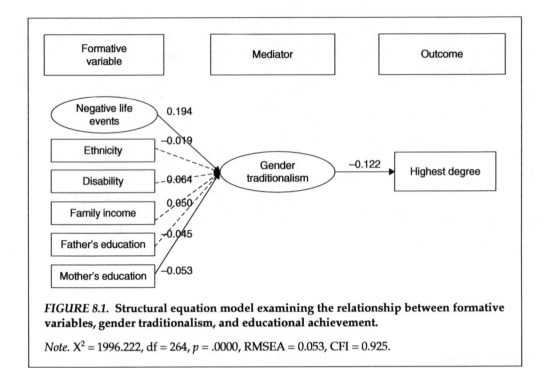

FIGURE 8.1. Structural equation model examining the relationship between formative variables, gender traditionalism, and educational achievement.

Note. $X^2 = 1996.222$, df = 264, $p = .0000$, RMSEA = 0.053, CFI = 0.925.

Overall, results suggest that a greater degree of negative life events and a lower level of maternal education are significantly predictive of a higher degree of Gender Traditionalism. Subsequently, a higher degree of Gender Traditionalism also is predictive of a lower degree of educational achievement. In other words, individuals who report a higher degree of Negative Life Events and lower levels of maternal education are more likely to endorse higher levels of Gender Traditionalism and less likely to report higher educational aspirations.

As Figure 8.2 illustrates, however, the causal relationships among these variables do not always follow the same pathways. For example, with "Republican" as an outcome variable, results suggest that a higher degree of Positive Family Relations, a self-reported disability status, higher SES, and lower level of maternal education all are predictive of a higher degree of Gender Traditionalism. At the same time, the tendency to self-identify as Republican also is mediated by Gender Traditionalism. In other words, a higher degree of Gender Traditionalism is predictive of a greater likelihood of self-identifying oneself as Republican.[5]

Especially noteworthy from such analyses is the finding that both negative and positive life events may be associated with a higher degree of Gender Traditionalism. Thus, it may be that value-based messages regarding the "proper" role of males and females are communicated, and inculcated, in family situations that are experienced as either negative *or* positive, which may be explained—at least in part—by the

---

[5] It should be noted that a higher degree of Gender Traditionalism was significantly and negatively predictive of Democratic (the standardized coefficient is −.222) and Independent (the standardized coefficient is −.051) political orientations whereas it was significantly and positively predictive of a Republican (the standardized coefficient is .309) political orientation.

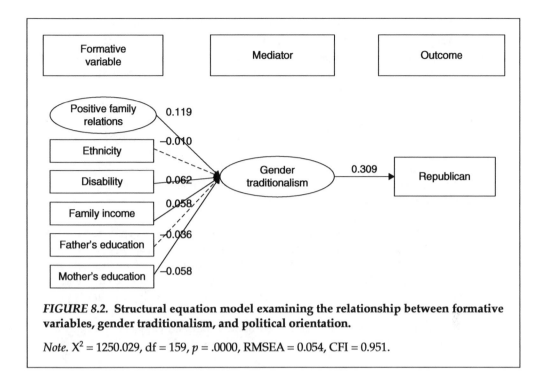

FIGURE 8.2. Structural equation model examining the relationship between formative variables, gender traditionalism, and political orientation.

Note. $X^2 = 1250.029$, df = 159, $p = .0000$, RMSEA = 0.054, CFI = 0.951.

following observation. Note that higher SES was predictive of higher Gender Traditionalism in the Positive Family Relations, but not Negative Life Events models, and that higher SES was predictive of a greater likelihood of a Republican orientation, but not with Democrat or Independent orientations. Note further that in both models, a lower degree of maternal education was predicative of a higher degree of Gender Traditionalism. Although tentative, perhaps it is the case that as one's SES increases, Gender Traditionalism goes up, but mainly for those who self-report as Republican. In any case, across both models, a higher degree of Gender Traditionalism is predictive of a lower tendency to pursue and complete higher education or excel in school. Finally, the fact that negative and positive life events are associated with higher levels of Gender Traditionalism suggests that gender ideology is impacted by formative life events in conjunction with other variables such as peers, culture, and the media.

SUMMARY AND CONCLUSION: TOWARD REAL WORLD APPLICATIONS

In this chapter, we examined a wide range of perspectives and findings across six levels of analysis. First, we provided an overview of literature on the construct of gender, by describing various controversies and common themes that tend to characterize this line of inquiry. Second, we turned to the formative variables (e.g., life history, demographics) that theoretically and empirically have been linked to the development of gender identity as well as how our beliefs and values regarding gender have evolved over time. Third, we focused on a dimension of gender that historically has received less attention in the larger field—how and why male gender identity develops as it does. Fourth, at a related level, we then examined why and how men and women are socialized to experience and express affect differently as well as the consequences of such processes for gender relations. Fifth, on the basis of all of the preceding, we sought to illustrate why gender identity matters, by examining the local and global implications of the "gendered self" for actions, policies, and practices around the world. Sixth, to examine how these highly complex and interacting processes may be analyzed simultaneously, we then presented results from a multiyear, multi-institution assessment of learning initiative called the Forum BEVI Project, which explores the relationship between antecedents and outcomes of gender traditionalism, as part of a larger study of learning processes.

In addition to this summary overview, recall also that we sought to address the following four research questions at the outset of this chapter:

1. From a construct validation perspective, do BEVI results correspond with extant literature regarding gender identity for males and females?
2. How might the EI theoretical framework and BEVI further our understanding of the role of formative variables on the development of gender traditionalism?
3. Does a higher degree of gender traditionalism on the BEVI mediate specific outcome variables?
4. What are the implications of this theoretical model and assessment method for the facilitation of better understanding and relations within and between the genders?

Regarding the first three of these questions, we hope to have illustrated that the EI model and BEVI method indeed are highly resonant with extant literature, while furthering our understanding of the predictors and outcomes of the "gendered self." For example, we have shown how the BEVI may demonstrate that certain formative variables (e.g., such as SES and parents' level of education) impact the development of traditional gender beliefs (Bolzendahl & Myers, 2004; Ciabattari, 2001; Davis & Greenstein, 2009; Fan & Marini, 2000; Hill, 2002), and that a proclivity toward gender traditionalism is correlated with other belief structures (e.g., concern about the environment) as well as specific outcomes (e.g., attunement to one's own emotional experience and the emotional experiences of others) (Brinkerhoff & McKee, 1988; Davis & Greenstein, 2009; Eisler & Corral, 2009 Eisler, Loye & Norgaard, 1995; Men Adrift, 2015). Hopefully, then, the literature, theory, and results presented previously help advance our understanding of the etiology of gender ideology, and provide an empirically grounded assessment tool for examining a wide range of outcomes that are predicted by a higher, or lower, degree of gender traditionalism. However, the fourth question—regarding issues of application—has yet to be addressed, mainly because our focus largely has been on theoretical and empirical questions of interest. So, in closing, we would like to illustrate, briefly, how this model and method may be used in the "real world" in order to facilitate understanding and relations within, and between, the genders. To do so, first we will showcase an example from one of the applied chapters in this book regarding therapeutic assessment (see Coates, Hanson, Samuel, & Cozen, 2016) and second, offer additional implications of this work.

By way of context, the BEVI allows for the development of individual, group, and organizational "reports," which essentially consist of narrative text, scale profiles, and tables, designed to communicate quantitative and qualitative information from the BEVI in an accessible form. The BEVI is well suited to address gender-based issues (e.g., in courses, programs, organizational contexts) not only due to the fact that Gender Traditionalism is a BEVI scale, but because it can provide a breakdown by sex for each of the scales on group reports. In addition, group reports offer a breakdown of the Gender Traditionalism scale (and all scales) by deciles. This reporting feature allows the group to determine the percentage of participants who scored in each decile, and thus to compare the frequency with which certain scores appeared, as depicted in the following example. Moreover, the BEVI contains three qualitative items, which makes it a "mixed methods" instrument, and allows for analysis of thematic content that is subjectively offered in the participant's own words, a specific recommendation of Davis and Greenstein (2009) regarding the study of gender.

Against this explanatory backdrop, the following case study was derived from a military higher education institution and presented in Coates et al. (2016). Although space limitations do not permit a full explication of the case study, the adapted passage illustrates the application of BEVI results toward prompting discussion around issues of gender.

This group of college age students scored very high (82nd percentile) on Gender Traditionalism (which again measures the contention that men and women are built to be a certain way and should occupy "traditional" gender roles). And indeed, most of the individual profiles for this group reflect a strong Gender Traditional predilection. However, interesting and relevant to the group—sparking considerable discussion and debate—was the fact that *not everyone* saw matters in the same way. By way of illustration, consider this excerpt from the "Decile Profile" table, which is derived from the overall group profile, and part of the group report. Note that Gender Traditionalism shows the following spread across the ten deciles of this scale:

Gender Traditionalism Scale for BEVI Group Report

Lowest Decile   **Highest Decile**

5%	5%	0%	5%	10%	5%	5%	5%	14%	48%

How do we interpret such findings? Perhaps most dramatic, approximately half of these individuals in this group preparation session (48%) responded in the 90th percentile on Gender Traditionalism. In other words, half of the group scored as high as possible on this specific scale of the BEVI. What is particularly interesting—especially in this military context—is that one fourth of the group was at or below the 50th percentile on Gender Traditionalism, with two individuals in the bottom twenty percent. Prompted by such findings, key aspects of the discussion dealt with how "gender" was regarded in the military, and how the rights and experiences of women were understood and managed by group members.

Perhaps reflective of these results, the group expressed considerable intensity around the issue of "gender" (e.g., on the one hand contending that it "didn't matter," while also describing—from the women in the session—how "femininity" reportedly needed to be, of necessity, suppressed). As important, the fact that the group did not see itself "the same" at this level, despite strong and unanimous feelings by half of the group, was an illuminating point for the group to consider. However, Gender Traditionalism was *not* one of the most intensely responded to scales for this group (i.e., the group tended, as a whole, to "Agree" and "Disagree" rather than "Strongly Agree" or "Strongly Disagree" to this scale). Such a finding provides context vis-à-vis this group, by suggesting that although views for some were very strongly held, overall, the group tended to be somewhat more moderate in their beliefs along these lines, at least relative to other scales on the BEVI. Overall therapeutic assessment at the group report level provides a way to illuminate beliefs and values; helps individual members to understand who they are as a group with greater depth, sensitivity, and nuance; increases engagement; assesses openness and defensiveness and utilizes a non-pathologizing frame that is designed to facilitate transformative change.

This example elucidates one way in which the BEVI can be utilized to deepen awareness of participants' belief structures and facilitate deep and meaningful discussion in a group setting. If this work is to be used toward the goal of better understanding and even altering gender ideologies, research supports the combination of exposure to new information regarding the predictors and consequences of gender ideology, in conjunction with use of the BEVI across a range of academic, training, and clinical settings. At the academic level, this format could be used in group settings such as process-based college courses designed around the topics reviewed in this chapter, or courses that embed this material as a component of curriculum. The BEVI could be utilized, as shown, to illuminate a deeper understanding of participants' belief structures and facilitate conversation and process around topics related to gender-role attitudes. Additionally, generation of BEVI reports—pre- and post-course-completion—offers a way to measure shifts in attitudes, and thus to better assess the impact of these experiences on ideology alteration. Based on the arguments set forth in this chapter, it would be particularly important that these courses be directed toward males as well as females. One way to do this would be to offer the course in departments including, but not limited to, those focusing on women's or gender studies. Because research suggests that gender ideologies are impacted by modeling, cognitive processes, education, and the influence of others—and because beliefs about gender impact models of leadership—it makes good sense for this material to be incorporated into a range of courses, programs, and contexts in addition to those that traditionally focus on aspects of "gender studies" (e.g., educating the educators in primary, secondary, and higher education settings; management training for business leaders). As another example, this format can be utilized in much the same way to facilitate introspection in a clinical or counseling context in order to promote deeper awareness of self and others via a specific focus on issues of gender (e.g., in individual, couples, and family work; process/psychoeducational groups; intergroup dialogue). Additionally, use of the BEVI at the beginning and end of these experiences provides outcome data and thus a means for assessing change and efficacy of treatment (e.g., see Coates et al., 2016; Cozen, Hanson, Poston, Jones, & Tabit, 2016).

In short, although the primary emphasis of this chapter was theoretical and empirical, it seems fitting to conclude with this applied example, since at the end of the day scholars and practitioners who focus on gender likely are united in their conviction that the "gendered self" is not a mere abstraction, but has a real and demonstrable impact upon us all. Applied measures are needed in real world settings, like mental health, if we are to grapple in tangible form with the implications of the dominant discourse, gender-based conflict and gender inequity (e.g., Davis & Greenstein, 2009). For example, in working with men, Cochran (2005) recommends the following:

By using the best available clinical reports and research evidence and by integrating this with a consideration of the male client's values, a clinician will be better equipped to provide a respectful and collaborative approach to the assessment tasks at hand. (p. 657)

Such guidance is highly aligned with the use of the BEVI report system in a mental health context, with individuals, couples, groups, and families (Coates et al., 2016; Cozen et al., 2016). Thus, whatever we can do—in a valid and reliable manner— to promote better understanding and relations within and between the genders ultimately seems aligned with this shared goal. In doing so, we must recognize the interplay between macro (e.g., policy) and micro (e.g., therapy) levels of analysis vis-à-vis gender roles and relations. The interweaving of macro- and microissues is imperative from the standpoint of psychology, to be sure, but also from an interdisciplinary perspective if we are to address real world problems, such as gender inequity, in a comprehensive and integrative manner over the long term (Cultivating the Globally Sustainable Self, 2014; Kapadia, 2011).

In the final analysis, as Eisler and Corral (2009) maintain, "to build foundations for a less violent, more equitable world, attention must be given to the childhood dynamics that shape people's emotions, actions, and minds, which all culminate in what we believe and value about ourselves and others" (p. 32). Clearly, our acquired beliefs and values about gender represent one of the most important areas of inquiry and practice if we are to create a more sustainable world for us all. Hopefully, the model and method presented here take us that much further toward these essential means and ends.

REFERENCES

Abramsky, T., Watts, C., Garcia-Moreno, C., Devries, K., Kiss, L., Ellsberg, M., . . . Heise, L. (2011). What factors are associated with recent intimate partner violence? Findings from the WHO multi-country study on women's health and domestic violence. *BMC Public Health, 11*, 1–17.

Anmuth, L. M., Poore, M., Cozen, J., Brearly, T., Tabit, M., Cannady, M., . . . Staton, R. (2013, August). *Making implicit beliefs explicit: In search of best practices for mental health clients, clinicians, and trainers.* Poster presented at the annual meeting of the American Psychological Association, Honolulu, HI.

Arrindell, W. A., Hatzichristou, C., Wensink, J., Rosenberg, E., van Twillert, B., Stedema, J., & Meijer, D. (1997). Dimensions of national culture as predictors of cross-national differences in subjective well-being. *Personality and Individual Differences, 23*(1), 37–53.

Atwood, K., Chkhaidze, N., Shealy, C. N., Staton, R., & Sternberger, L. G. (2014, August). *Transformation of self: Implications from the Forum BEVI Project.* Poster presented at the annual meeting of the American Psychological Association, Washington, DC.

Barnett, R. C., & Baruch, G. K. (1987). Social roles, gender, and psychological distress. In R. C. Barnett, L. Biener, & G. K. Baruch (Eds.), *Gender and stress.* New York, NY: The Free Press.

Berenbaum, S. A., Blakemore, J. E. O., & Beltz, A. M. (2011). A role for biology in gender related behavior. *Sex Roles, 64*(11–12), 804–825.

Blakemore, J. E. O., Berenbaum, S. A., & Liben, L. S. (2009). *Gender development.* New York, NY: Psychology Press.

Brearly, T., Shealy, C. N., Staton, R., & Sternberger, L. G. (2012, August). *Prejudice and religious and non-religious certitude: An empirical analysis from the Forum BEVI Project.* Poster presented at the annual meeting of the American Psychological Association, Orlando, FL.

Brinkerhoff, M. B., & MacKie, M. (1988). Religious sources of gender traditionalism. In D. L. Thomas (Ed.), *The religion and family connection: social science perspectives* (pp. 232–257). Provo, UT: Religious Studies Center, Brigham Young University.

Bolzendahl, C. I., & Myers, D. J. (2004). Feminist attitudes and support for gender equality: Opinion change in women and men 1974–1998. *Social Forces, 83*(2), 759–790.

Brooks, C., & Bolzendahl, C. (2004). The transformation of US gender role attitudes: Cohort replacement, social-structural change, and ideological learning. *Social Science Research, 33,* 106–133.

Buck, R. (1977). Nonverbal communication of affect in preschool children: Relationships with personality and skin conductance. *Journal of Personality and Social Psychology, 35*(4), 225–236.

Bussey, K., & Bandura, A. (1999). Social cognitive theory of gender development and differentiation. *Psychological Review, 106*(4), 676–713.

Carter, J. S., Corra, M., & Carter, S. K. (2009). The interaction of race and gender: Changing gender-role attitudes, 1974–2006. *Social Science Quarterly, 90,* 196–210.

Chatani, L. (2011). Culture and honor killing. *WSRC Communiqué,* (1), 1–2.

Chhabra, S. (2008). Sexual violence among pregnant women in India. *Journal of Obstetrics and Gynecology Research, 34*(2), 238–241.

Ciabatarri, T. (2001). Changes in men's conservative gender ideologies cohort and period influence. *Gender & Society, 15*(4), 574–591.

Cleary, P. D. (1987). Gender differences in stress-related disorders. In R. C. Bamett, L. Biener, & G. K. Baruch (Eds.), *Gender and stress.* New York, NY: The Free Press.

Cochran, S. V. (2005). Evidence based assessment with men. *Journal of Clinical Psychology, 61*(1), 649–660.

Cochran, S. V. (2010). Emergence and development of the psychology of men and masculinity. In J. C. Chrisler & D. R. McCreary (Eds.), *Handbook of gender research in psychology.* New York, NY: Springer.

Coates, M., Hanson, B., Samuel, D., & Cozen, J. (2016). The Beliefs, Events, and Values Inventory: Psychological assessment implications and applications. In C. N. Shealy (Ed.), *Making sense of beliefs and values* (pp. 371–406). New York, NY: Springer Publishing.

Cotter, D. A., Hermsen, J. M., & Vanneman, R. (1999). Systems of gender, race and class inequality: Multilevel analyses. *Social Forces, 78*(2), 433–460.

Cozen, J., Hanson, B., Poston, J., Jones, S., & Tabit, M. (2016). The Beliefs, Events, and Values Inventory (BEVI): Implications and applications for therapeutic assessment and intervention. In C. N. Shealy (Ed.), *Making sense of beliefs and values* (pp. 575–621). New York, NY: Springer Publishing.

Cultivating the Globally Sustainable Self. (2014). Paper presented at James Madison University, Harrisonburg, VA. Retrieved from http://www.jmu.edu/summitseries/

Cummings, E. M., Davies, P. T., & Campbell, S. B. (2000). *Developmental psychopathology and family process: Theory, research, and clinical implications.* New York, NY. The Guilford Press.

Cunningham, M. (2001). Parental influences on the gendered division of housework. *American Sociological Review, 66*(2), 184–203.

Darlington, C. (2009). *The female brain.* Boca Raton, FL: CPC Press.

Davis, S. N., & Greenstein, T. N. (2009). Gender ideology: components, predictors, and consequences. *Annual Review of Sociology, 35,* 87–105.

David, S. D., & Brannon, R. (1976). *The forty-nine percent majority: The male sex role.* Reading, MA: Addison-Wesley.

Del Giudice, M., Booth, T., & Irwing, P. (2012). The distance between Mars and Venus: Measuring global sex differences in personality. *PLoS One, 7.* Retrieved from http://dx.doi.org/10.1371/journal.pone.0029265

Department of State. (2007). *Trafficking in persons report.* Washington, DC: Author. Retrieved from http://www.state.gov/documents/organization/82902.pdf

Donaldson, M. (1993). What is hegemonic masculinity? *Theory and Society, 22,* 653–657.

Dyjak-LeBlanc, K., Brewster, L., Grande, S., White, R., & Shullman, S. (2016). The EI Leadership Model: From theory and research to real world application. In C. N. Shealy (Ed.), *Making Sense of Beliefs and Values* (pp. 531–574). New York, NY: Springer Publishing.

Eisler, R., & Corral, T. (2005). From domination to partnership: Meeting the UN millennium goals. *Convergence, 38*(3), 75–94.

Eisler, R., & Corral, T. (2009). Leaders forging values-based change: Partnership power for the 21st century. *Beliefs and Values, 1*(1), 31–44.

Eisler, R., Loye, D., & Norgaard, K., (1995). *Gender equity and the quality of life: A global survey and analysis.* Pacific Grove, CA: Center for Partnership Studies.

Enns, C. Z., & Sinacore, A. (2002). Feminist theories. In J. Worrell (Ed.), *Encyclopedia of women and gender.* San Diego, CA: Academic Press.

Fan, P., & Marini, M. M. (2000). Influences on gender-role attitudes during the transition to adulthood. *Social Science Research, 29*(2), 258–283.

Good, G. E., Robertson, J. M., O'Neil, J. M., Fitzgerald, L. F., Stevens, M., DeBord, K. A., . . . Braverman, D. G. (1995). Male gender role conflict: Psychometric issues and relations to psychological distress. *Journal of Counseling Psychology, 42*(1), 3–10.

Gray, J. (1992). *Men are from Mars, women are from Venus.* New York, NY: HarperCollins.

Gujjarappa, L. H., Apte, H., Garda, L., & Nene, U. (2002). *The unseen side of infertility: A study of male perspective in infertility in rural western Maharashtra, India.* Paper presented at the International Conference on Socio-Medical Perspective of Childlessness, Goa, India.

Hackett, M. (2011). Domestic violence against women: Statistical analysis of crimes across India. *Journal of Comparative Family Studies, 42*(2), 267–288.

Haviland, J. J., & Malatesta, C. Z. (1981). The development of sex differences in nonverbal signals: Fallacies, facts, and fantasies. In C. Mayo & N. Henley (Eds.), *Gender and nonverbal behavior.* New York, NY: Springer.

Hayes, D. J., Shealy, C. N., Sivo, S. A., & Weinstein, Z. C. (1999, August). *Psychology, religion, and Scale 5 (Religious Traditionalism) of the "BEVI."* Poster session presented at the meeting of the American Psychological Association, Boston, MA.

Hill, C., Johnson, M., Brinton, C., Staton, R., Sternberger, L., & Shealy, C. N. (2013, August). *The etiology of economic beliefs and values: Implications and applications from the Forum BEVI Project.* Poster presented at the annual meeting of the American Psychological Association, Honolulu, HI.

Hill, S. (2002). Teaching and doing gender in African American families. *Sex Roles, 47*(11/12), 493–506.

Hines, M. (2004). *Brain gender.* New York, NY: Oxford University Press Inc.

Hofstede, G. (1980). *Culture's consequences: International differences in work-related values.* Beverly Hills, CA: Sage.

Hyde, J. S. (2005). The gender similarities hypothesis. *American Psychologist, 60*(6), 581–592.

Hyde, J. S. (2007). New directions in the study of gender similarities and differences. *Current Directions in Psychological Science, 16,* 259–263.

Inglehart, R., & Norris, P. (2003). *Rising tide: gender equality and cultural change around the world.* New York, NY: Cambridge University Press.

Isley, E. B., Shealy, C. N., Crandall, K. S., Sivo, S. A., & Reifsteck, J. B. (1999, August). *Relevance of the "BEVI" for research in developmental psychopathology.* Poster session presented at the meeting of the American Psychological Association, Boston, MA.

Kahn, J. S. (2009). *An introduction to masculinities.* Malden, MA: Wiley-Blackwell.

Kapadia, S. (1999). Self, women and empowerment: A conceptual inquiry. In T. S. Saraswathi (Ed.), *Culture, socialization and human development: Theory, research and applications in India* (pp. 255–277). New Delhi: Sage.

Kapadia, S. (2011). Psychology and human development in India. *International Society for the Study of Behavioral Development Bulletin, 2,* (Serial No. 60), 37–42.

Kapadia, S. (2011, October). *Identity anchors of emerging adult women in India.* Paper presented at a symposium on Emerging Adulthood: Glimpses from Contemporary India at the 5th conference on Emerging Adulthood, Providence, RI.

Kapadia, S. (in press). Gender across cultures: Sex and socialization in childhood. In L. A. Jensen (Ed.), *The oxford handbook of human development and culture: An interdisciplinary perspective.* New York, NY: Oxford University Press (OUP).

Kapadia, S., Shah, U., & Rajaram, N. (2007). *Gender sensitivity among college youth in Baroda.* WOHTRAC small grants report. Baroda: WOHTRAC-WSRC, The M. S. University of Baroda.

Keleher, H., & Franklin, L. (2008). Changing gendered norms about women and girls at the level of household and community: A review of the evidence. *Global Public Health, 3*(1), 42–57.

Khanna, R., Kapadia, S., & Dongre, L. (1998). *Men's role and responsibility for women's health.* WOHTRAC (Monograph No. 2). Baroda: WOHTRAC-WSRC, The M. S. University of Baroda.

Kilmartin, C. T. (2007). *The masculine self* (3rd ed.). Cornwall-on-Hudson, NY: Sloan.

Levant, R. F. (1992). Toward the reconstruction of masculinity. *Journal of Family Psychology, 5*(3–4), 379–402.

Levant, R. F. (1998). Desperately seeking language: Understanding, assessing and treating normative male alexithymia. In W. S. Pollack & R. F. Levant (Eds.), *New psychotherapy for men* (pp. 35–56). New York, NY: John Wiley.

Levant, R. F. (2011). Research in the psychology of men and masculinity using the gender role strain paradigm as a framework. *American Psychologist, 66*(8), 765–776.

Levant, R. F., Hall, R. J., Williams, C., & Hassan, N. T. (2009). Gender differences in alexithymia. *Psychology of Men and Masculinity, 10,* 190–203.

Levant, R. F., Hirsch, L. S., Celentano, E., Cozza, T., Hill, S., MacEachern, M., . . . Schnedeker, J. (1992). The male role: An investigation of norms and stereotypes. *Journal of Mental Health Counseling, 14*(3), 325–337.

Levant, R. F., & Kopecky, G. (1995). *Masculinity reconstructed.* New York, NY: Dutton.

Levant, R. F., & Pollack, W. S. (Eds.). (1995). *A new psychology of men.* New York, NY: Basic Books.

Levant, R. F., Richmond, K., Majors, R. G., Inclan, J. E., Rossello, J. M., Heesacher, M., . . . Sellers, A. (2003). A multicultural investigation of masculinity ideology and alexithymia. *Psychology of Men and Masculinity, 4*(2), 91–99.

Lippa, R. A. (2006). The gender reality hypothesis. *American Psychologist, 6,* 639–640. Retrieved from http://dx.doi.org/10.1037/0003-066X.61.6.639

Malatesta, C. Z., & Haviland, J. M. (1982). Learning display rules: The socialization of emotion expression in infancy. *Child Development, 53,* 991–1003.

Men Adrift (2015, May 30). *The Economist.* pp. 21–26.

O'Neil, J. M. (2008). Summarizing 25 years of research on men's gender role conflict using the gender role conflict scale: New research paradigms and clinical implications. *The Counseling Psychologist, 36*(3), 358–445.

Pandya, A., Parmar, N., & Khanna, R. (2009, November). Exploring young men's notions about men and masculinity. *WSRC Communiqué, (1),* 4–6.

Pampel, F. (2011). Cohort changes in the socio-demographic determinants of gender egalitarianism. *Social Forces, 89*(3), 961–982.

Pleck, J. H. (1981). *The myth of masculinity.* Cambridge, MA: MIT Press.

Pleck, J. H. (1995). The gender role strain paradigm: An update. In R. F. Levant & W. S. Pollack (Eds.), *A new psychology of men* (pp. 11–32). New York, NY: Basic Books.

Pollack, W. (1999). *Real boys: Rescuing our sons from the myths of boyhood.* New York, NY: Henry Holt and Company LLC.

Rajaram, N. (2001). Masculinity, sexuality and reproductive health in a community of Baroda. In N. Rajaram & V. Zararia (Eds.), *Exploring masculinities: A traveling seminar* (pp. 86–90). Baroda: Department of Sociology and WOHTRAC-WSRC, The M. S. University of Baroda.

Rajaram, N., & Zararia, V. (2009). Translating women's human rights in a globalizing world: The spiral process in reducing gender injustice in Baroda, India. *Global Networks, 9*(4), 462–484.

Richmond, K. A., Levant, R. F., & Ladhani, S. C. J. (2012). The varieties of the masculine experience. In R. Josselson & M. Harway (Eds.), *Navigating multiple identities: Race, gender, culture, nationality and roles* (pp. 59–74). New York, NY: Oxford University Press.

Roy, R. (2001). Introduction. In N. Rajaram & V. Zararia (Eds.), *Exploring masculinities: A traveling seminar* (pp. 6–10). Baroda: Department of Sociology and WOHTRAC-WSRC, The M. S. University of Baroda.

Sapolsky, R. M. (1997). The trouble with testosterone: Will boys just be boys? In R. M. Sapolsky, *The trouble with testosterone* (pp. 147–159). New York, NY: Touchstone.

Schmitt, M. T., & Wirth, J. H. (2009). Evidence that gender differences in social dominance orientation result from gendered self-stereotyping and group-interested responses to patriarchy. *Psychology of Women Quarterly, 33*(4), 429–436.

Shealy, C. N. (2000a, July). *The Beliefs, Events, and Values Inventory (BEVI): Implications for cross-cultural research and practice.* Paper presented at the meeting of the International Congress of Psychology, Stockholm, Sweden.

Shealy, C. N. (2000b, July). *The Beliefs, Events, and Values Inventory (BEVI): Implications for research and theory in social psychology.* Paper presented at the meeting of the International Congress of Psychology, Stockholm, Sweden.

Shealy, C. N. (2004). A model and method for "making" a C-I psychologist: Equilintegration (EI) Theory and the Beliefs, Events, and Values Inventory (BEVI). [Special Series]. *Journal of Clinical Psychology, 60*(10), 1065–1090.

Shealy, C. N. (2005). Justifying the justification hypothesis: Scientific- Humanism, Equilintegration (EI) Theory, and the Beliefs, Events, and Values Inventory (BEVI). [Special Series]. *Journal of Clinical Psychology, 61*(1), 81–106.

Shealy, C. N. (2006, November). *From Falwell to bin Laden: Making sense of why we believe what we believe.* Presented at the Centre for Dialogue, La Trobe University, Melbourne, Australia.

Shealy, C. N. (2010a). *Beliefs, events and values inventory.* Retrieved from http://www.thebevi.com/aboutbevi.php

Shealy, C. N. (2010b). Women's rights are human rights: An interview with Pinar Ikkaracan. *Beliefs and Values, 2*(1), 8–15.

Shealy, C. N. (2015). *The Beliefs, Events, and Values Inventory (BEVI): Overview, implications, and guidelines. Test manual.* Harrisonburg, VA: Author.

Shealy, C. N. (2016). *Making sense of beliefs and values.* New York, NY: Springer.

Shealy, C. N., Bhuyan, D., & Sternberger, L. G. (2012). Cultivating the capacity to care in children and Youth: Implications from EI Theory, EI Self, and BEVI. In U. Nayar (Ed.), *Child and adolescent mental health* (pp. 240–255). New Delhi, India: Sage Publications.

Stanik, C. E., & Bryant, C. M. (2012). Marital quality of newlywed African American couples: Implications of egalitarian gender role dynamics. *Sex Roles, 66*(3–4), 256–267.

Stoltenberg, J. (2000). *Refusing to be a man: Essays on sex and justice.* London: UCL Press.

United Nations. (2010). *The World's Women 2010: Trends and statistics* (Sales No. 10.XVII.11). New York, NY: Author.

Tabit, M., Cozen, J., Dyjak-Leblank, K., Pendleton, C., Shealy, C., Sternberger, L., & Staton, R. (2011, June). *The sociocultural impact of denial: Empirical evidence from the Forum BEVI* Project. Poster presented at American Psychological Association, Washington, DC.

United Nations Development Fund for Women. (2007). *The issue: Violence against women and the international response.* Retrieved from http://www.unwomen.org

Vianello, M., Schnabel, K., Sriram, N., & Nosek, B. (2013). Gender differences in implicit and explicit personality traits (Available at SSRN 2249080). *Personality and Individual Differences, 55,* 994–998.

Wandschneider, E., Pysarchik, D. T., Sternberger, L. G., Ma, W., Acheson-Clair, K., Baltensperberger, B., . . . Hart, V. (2016). The Forum BEVI Project: Applications and implications for international, multicultural, and transformative learning. In C. N. Shealy (Ed.), *Making sense of beliefs and values* (pp. 407–484). New York, NY: Springer Publishing.

World Health Organization. (2013). *Female genital mutilation* (Fact sheet 241). Geneva: Author. Retrieved from http://www.who.int/mediacentre/factsheets/fs241/en/

Adam J. Edmunds, Christopher M. Federico,
and Lauren Mays

9

EXPLORING THE ETIOLOGY OF IDEOLOGY: IN SEARCH OF THE POLITICAL SELF THROUGH THE EI MODEL AND BEVI METHOD

Values and basic beliefs are more polarized along partisan lines than at any point in the past 25 years.

—Pew Research Center, 2012

In the United States, a focus on political partisanship has impacted actions and practices in government as well as public perceptions writ large. For a variety of reasons, various indexes, including voting patterns and survey data, suggest we presently are living through an era of political division far more fractious than the decades of "consensus politics" immediately following World War II (Gallup, 2012a). In addition to considerable scholarship, popularized books—such as *What's the Matter with Kansas?: How Conservatives Won the Heart of America* (Frank, 2004) and *The Political Brain: The Role of Emotion in Deciding the Fate of the Nation* (Westen, 2007)—all are attempting to understand the dynamics of how people interpret and respond to political information across the ideological spectrum. While political partisanship on all sides is recognized to impact political discourse and attendant policies (e.g., abortion, health care, foreign policy, deficit reduction), the etiology of ideology is far less understood, or even discussed. In other words, it is one thing to describe *what* political beliefs and values differentiate us. Far more telling is *why* such differences occur in the first place. A theoretical and empirical exploration of "why" is at the heart of this chapter. This approach is important because political ideology is one aspect of self that influences how one sees and engages the world and yet, this aspect of self is also affected by how the world shapes it through various processes (e.g. life history, genetics, personality). Moreover, how different aspects of self manifest, such as political ideology, on a conscious or nonconscious level, is of particular interest because such aspects may be influenced by different factors, including introspection, affect, and level of openness.

Ideology has been defined as "the body of doctrine, myth, belief, etc., that guides an individual, social movement, institution, class, or large group" (Ideology, n.d.). Jost (2006) notes that the concept of ideology generally has been used in two ways: (a) as a system of belief or meaning regarding society, politics, or economics, and (b) in a propagandistic manner, in which the term or beliefs it is used to describe are distorted. Political ideology similarly has been defined by Erikson and Tedin (2003) as a set of beliefs that explain how society should behave and look as well as how such an end point should be realized. Finally, ideology represents a version of reality that is informed by particular experiences, motivations, affective responses, and cognitive styles (Jost, Federico, & Napier, 2009).

Interest in the psychological foundations of ideology has grown in recent years, with increased recognition that ideological differences have deep motivational roots, which substantively impact social influence and decision-making (Jost, 2006). More recently, the construct of ideology has proved relevant in understanding a range of events and phenomena (e.g., 9/11, wars in Afghanistan and Iraq, gay marriage, abortion debates, partisanship in the United States). Relevant to the study of beliefs and values, Jost, Glaser, Kruglanski, and Sulloway (2003) concluded that particular ideologies emerge from and are related to varying constellations of psychological needs, a central contention also of the Equilintegration (EI) theoretical framework, discussed in this chapter. From their meta-analysis, ideology (e.g., conservatism) was understood as a socially motivated cognition based on situational, dispositional, and psychological factors. From this perspective, individuals are attracted to various ideologies because they meet epistemic, existential, and relational needs.

Political ideology often is understood as existing along a continuum between liberalism (or the political left more generally) and conservatism (or the political right more generally) (Jost et al., 2009). From the standpoint of Merriam-Webster, conservatism is defined as "a political philosophy based on tradition and social stability, stressing established institutions, and preferring gradual development to abrupt change" (Conservatism, 2012). In contrast, liberalism is defined as "a political philosophy based on belief in progress, the essential goodness of the human race, and the autonomy of the individual and standing for the protection of political and civil liberties" (Liberalism, 2012). Two core dimensions distinguish conservatism from liberalism: (a) resisting social change versus advocating for it, and (b) accepting inequality versus rejecting it (Jost et al., 2003). These distinctions were displayed by the 2012 presidential candidates, such as when former U.S. Senator, and conservative presidential candidate Rick Santorum said, "There is income inequality in America. There always has been and hopefully, and I do say that, there always will be," (Detroit Free Press, 2012).[1] Finally, in terms of broad social identifications, conservatives remain the largest ideological group at 40% whereas liberals and moderates are 21% and 35%, respectively (Gallup, 2012b). Nevertheless, this pattern of social identification does mask some underlying complexity and inconsistency in underlying attitudes, as many self-identified conservatives actually adopt broadly liberal positions on many issues (Stimson, 2004).

While many understand liberalism and conservatism to represent opposites on a continuum, some scholars regard this bipolar paradigm as simplistic for purposes of explaining ideology, postulating that these are independent or nondichotomous dimensions, with different underlying mediational processes (Conover & Feldman, 1981; Kerlinger, 1984). For example, Duckitt's dual-process model proposes two distinct continua for social and economic issues because the socially conservative often are distinct from the economically conservative even though both groups tend toward the conservative end of the liberal–conservative continuum (Duckitt & Sibley, 2010; Duckitt, Wagner, du Plessis, & Birum, 2002). According to Duckitt and others, the ideology of social conservatives and economic conservatives may be attributable to different emphases (e.g., law and order/security for social conservatives and social

---

[1] Interestingly, the historic distinction of the "left" (liberal) and "right" (conservative) political wings has its origin in seating arrangements for the French Legislature during the French Revolution in the 18th century; advocates for change sat on the left side of the chamber while supporters of the ruling body sat on the right side (Bobbio, 1996).

inequality/dominance for economic conservatives) as well as different motivational foundations. Along these lines, libertarianism provides a salient example of the complexity of plotting political ideology along a simple continuum between liberalism and conservatism, since this political philosophy includes aspects of both conservatism and liberalism. Specifically, libertarianism focuses on liberty, personal responsibility, and freedom to do what one wants without constraint as long as the rights of others are not infringed (Boaz, 1997). Its emphasis on freedom includes social behavior such as adult consensual sexual relationships, drug use, and civil liberties—all positions on the liberal side of the spectrum. However, its emphasis on economic freedom also embraces minimal government regulation of business practices—a conservative position—with the caveat that individuals should be protected from exploitation or fraud. Libertarians also oppose governmental subsidization (i.e., corporate welfare) of industries and companies (Libertarian Party Platform, 2010). In short, libertarianism is difficult to plot along a liberal–conservative continuum, which suggests the need for a more multidimensional paradigm of political ideology.

POLITICAL PARTIES IN THE UNITED STATES

In the United States, it is important to note that many individuals who endorse conservative, libertarian, or liberal ideologies do not associate with any party. In fact, among U.S. citizens within the United States, 30% affiliate with the Democratic Party, 27% with the Republican Party, and 42% describe themselves as Independent (Gallup, 2012c). From the standpoint of party platforms, the Democratic Party endorses liberal characteristics such as equality for all people, regardless of sexual orientation, gender, or race/ethnicity; adoption of progressive tax policies; advocacy for labor rights and proenvironmental policies; and strong regulation of businesses (Democratic Party, 2012). According to its platform, the Republican Party is mainly socially and economically conservative, advocating for limited social welfare programs; display of religious (particularly Christian) practices in the public sphere (e.g., prayer in school); aggressive foreign policy; limited government regulation and taxation; and fiscal conservatism (i.e., limited government spending) (Republican Party, 2012). Most state and federal government officials belong to either of these parties. While many libertarians may consider themselves to be independent of the Democratic and Republican parties, and vote between the two parties based on a combination of factors, many other libertarians are members of the Libertarian Party, which advocates for whichever perspective emphasizes libertarianism in political discourse. The Libertarian Party is the third largest political party in the United States, with 250,000 registered voters (Libertarian Party, 2012). Although it tends to have more success at local and state levels, individuals who hold libertarian positions have been elected to the U.S. Congress under the auspices of the Republican Party (e.g., House Representative Ron Paul of Texas and Senator Rand Paul of Kentucky).

UNDERSTANDING IDEOLOGICAL DISTINCTIONS

Political affiliation is but one way to differentiate between liberals, conservatives, and to a lesser extent, libertarians. Research has identified several other ways in which these ideologies differ, especially between liberals and conservatives. These factors include moral foundations, personality traits, attitudes about threat and uncertainty, and biology.

Moral Foundations

Through their analysis of the etiology and development of morality, Haidt and Joseph (2004) developed Moral Foundations Theory (MFT) in an attempt to explain the complexities of morality. Haidt and Graham (2007) further refined this framework, positing five different foundations for morality: harm/care, fairness/reciprocity, in-group/loyalty, authority/respect, and purity/sanctity. The first foundation, harm/care, refers to the capacity to feel another's pain and experience compassion for suffering. Second, fairness/reciprocity reflects the cooperative nature of society and the negative emotions experienced when communal camaraderie is violated. The third foundational principle, in-group/loyalty, is seen to be derivative of the evolutionary advantages of trusting members of one's own group, while distrusting outsiders. Authority/respect, the fourth foundation, respects the hierarchical nature of society and devalues insubordination. Last, the foundational principle of purity/sanctity is concerned with physical and spiritual contagion and includes the "virtues of chastity, wholesomeness, and the control of desires" (Haidt, Graham, & Joseph, 2009, p. 112). Cultures and contexts vary in the emphasis they place on each of these foundations; it also should be noted that the associated emotional aspect of these foundations suggests that there may be an underlying evolutionary predisposition for each.

In juxtaposing these moral foundations with liberal and conservative political ideologies, Haidt and Graham (2007) and Graham, Haidt, and Nosek (2009) found that liberals' beliefs and actions are guided by two of the moral foundations (harm/care and fairness/reciprocity) more than the others whereas conservatives base their beliefs and actions on all five of the foundations nearly evenly. In expanding their analysis, Haidt, Graham, and Joseph (2009) further reported that libertarians tended to be low on all five of the principles, and thus were perceived to be more individual-focused overall. Another group was labeled the "religious left," due to its "liberal" focus on fairness and the reduction of harm, combined with a concurrent yet de-emphasized endorsement of the other three principles. Members of this group identified as either neutral or liberally oriented with an embrace of religion similar to that of conservatives.

In addition, further research by Iyer, Koleva, Graham, Ditto, and Haidt (2011) found, perhaps not surprisingly, that liberty is the driving moral foundation for libertarians, who also tended to rely upon reason over emotion, and were more individualistic and independent than liberals or conservatives. Iyer et al. found that while libertarians appear to prioritize the harm/care and fairness/reciprocity moral foundations over the other three foundations, when compared with liberals and conservatives, they scored lowest on each of the five moral foundations, suggesting that they do not base their beliefs or actions on these foundations to nearly the same degree as liberals and conservatives (Haidt et al., 2009). Thus, Iyer et al.'s findings led to a revision of moral foundations to include liberty/oppression as the sixth moral foundation, which accounts for "feelings of reactance and resentment people feel toward those who dominate them and restrict their liberty" (Haidt, 2012).

Other investigations have highlighted the existence of multiple classes of self-identified liberals and conservatives using latent-variable techniques, many of which show different patterns of moral-foundation endorsement despite adopting a common identity label (Weber & Federico, 2012). For example, social conservatives tend to place greater emphasis on in-group/loyalty, authority/respect, and purity/sanctity than other types of conservatives (e.g., those who emphasize fiscal matters). Thus, the simple liberal/conservative dichotomy may obscure more complex patterns of moral intuition in politics.

Overall, when examining these principles in terms of political orientation, liberals and conservatives present and engage differently based upon their conceptualization of what constitutes a "good society" (Haidt et al., 2009, p. 110). For example, the issue of gay marriage illustrates the different applications of moral foundations. Using the MFT framework, Haidt et al. (2009) elucidated these differences as follows:

> the passions and the intractability of the gay marriage controversy make more sense once you understand that the left side sees legalizing gay marriage as a straightforward way to reduce harm (to innocent victims) without hurting anyone else while increasing fairness (including issues of equality and rights). Using just the Harm and Fairness foundations, one simply cannot construct convincing arguments against gay marriage. . .Cultural conservatives, however, are more likely to see gay people as members of a different culture (attacking or infiltrating the heterosexual ingroup) who subvert gender roles (rejecting the authority of church, law, and tradition) while pursuing a carnal and hedonistic lifestyle (including "impure" sexual acts that trigger feelings of disgust). (p. 112)

When evaluating the morality of sexual behaviors, liberals tend to believe that if individuals are not harming themselves or others, then their sexual behavior is not immoral. Therefore, homosexuality is not wrong because it does not cause harm to anyone. In contrast, conservatives perceive homosexuality as wrong because of their emphasis on the purity/sanctity moral foundation (Haidt & Hersh, 2001) as well as their fidelity to established social conventions (Inbar, Pizarro, & Bloom, 2009). At a complementary level, findings by Triandis and Gelfand (1998) illustrated conservatives' and liberals' preference for order and equality, respectively, with conservatives emphasizing social relationships that are vertical in nature, while liberals stressed horizontal social relationships. Moreover, Liu and Ditto (2012) found evidence that liberals and conservatives interpret facts differently in order to line up with their moral positions. In short, given these differences in foundation emphasis, it should not be surprising that liberals and conservatives react to each other differently, with attendant confusion and divisiveness.

Personality Traits

In addition to moral-foundation differences among liberals, conservatives, and libertarians, research also has found variation in personality styles. In particular, these differences have been identified via the "big five" personality traits (openness, conscientiousness, extraversionism, agreeableness, and neuroticism). Overall, liberals score higher than conservatives on measures of openness to experience, suggesting (among other attributes) that they are drawn toward new experiences and creative endeavors whereas conservatives score higher on measures of conscientiousness, indicating a preference for orderliness and structure. Such characteristics have been identified through self-assessment (e.g., Caprara, Schwartz, Capanna, Vecchione, & Barbaranelli, 2006; Gerber, Huber, Doherty, Dowling, & Ha, 2010; Mondak, 2010) as well as analysis of interpersonal interactions, personal and professional working space, and personal possessions (Carney, Jost, Gosling, & Potter, 2008). Moreover, across the "big five," liberals also have been found to be more neurotic and less conscientious, extraverted, and agreeable than conservatives (Thornhill & Fincher, 2007), although these results are somewhat less consistent (see Mondak, 2010). Finally, Iyer et al. (2011) found that libertarians scored similarly to liberals on openness to experience, and to conservatives on neuroticism, but differently to both groups on agreeableness, conscientiousness, and extraversion (McCrae & Sutin, 2009).

System Justifications

System justification is the "motivation to defend, bolster, and justify the status quo" (Jost et al., 2009, p. 309), even "at the expense of personal and group interest" (Jost & Banaji, 1994, p. 2). In this vein, research suggests that people tend to hold positive attitudes toward themselves and others like them, as well as toward existing social systems and the status quo (Jost, Banaji, & Nosek, 2004). In addition, Jost and others posited that not all people engage in system justification to the same extent. For example, conservatives engage in system-justification arguments more frequently than liberals. As such, liberals experience less happiness than conservatives partly because liberals focus on issues of inequality in the world. More specifically, liberals tend to feel that inequality is the product of a system which can and should be restructured, and thus experience more distress than conservatives, who tend to attribute inequality to individual factors for which they are not responsible (Jost et al., 2003; Napier & Jost, 2008).

Uncertainty–Threat Model

The Uncertainty–Threat Model was developed as a theoretical frame to explain the etiology of political conservatism from a "motivated social-cognitive approach" (Jost et al., 2003, p. 340). According to Jost et al., ". . .ideological differences between right and left have psychological roots: Stability and hierarchy generally provide reassurance and structure, whereas change and equality imply greater chaos and unpredictability" (Jost et al., 2007, p. 990), findings which are highly consistent with the basic precepts of the Equilintegration model, discussed later in this chapter. As a result, for those inclined to seek it, conservatism fulfills a psychological need to manage threat and reduce uncertainty. Liberalism, on the other hand, appeals to those who are more open to new experiences, tolerant of ambiguity, and likely to become excited by, rather than fearful of, the unknown. Such qualities also seem associated with a capacity for cognitive complexity, in that those who are less fearful of uncertainty may be simultaneously more capable of tolerating ambiguity and avoiding premature closure regarding that which is "new and different." Along these lines, Jost et al. (2007) demonstrated that uncertainty avoidance and resistance to change independently contribute to political ideology, adding to a literature that political and other ideologies are derivative of an interaction among psychological needs and core beliefs regarding the relative importance of change and equality (e.g., Shealy, Bhuyan, & Sternberger, 2012).

At the same time, external events appear to impact ideology across the spectrum, as evidenced by the fact that the apparent experience of uncertainty and threat led Democrats, Independents, and Republicans to adopt more conservative attitudes after 9/11 than they reported prior to 9/11 (Bonanno & Jost, 2006). Indeed, recent work suggests that the motive to avoid uncertainty may increase conservatism in actual policy attitudes more among those who self-identify as liberals or for whom the liberal side of an issue is more salient (Federico, Deason, & Fisher, 2012). Moreover, Janoff-Bulman (2009) proposed that different political orientations are mediated by motivational predilections toward approach or avoidance: conservatism is driven by an avoidance motivation, whereas liberalism is driven by an approach motivation. Conservatism seeks to identify potentially negative outcomes and experiences, as evidenced by the need to avoid threats and danger, whereas liberalism seeks to identify positive outcomes and experiences, as evidenced by the need to approach the enticing unknown and uncertain. Not surprisingly then, according to Janoff-Bulman (2009), conservatives demonstrate their avoidance motivation through inhibition, as is commonly seen by their resistance to change and preference for social order, whereas liberals demonstrate their approach motivation by their embrace of change and preference for social justice. Nonetheless, and consistent with our observations regarding the complexity of these constructs, Duckitt et al. (2002) and Duckitt and Sibley (2010) observed that social conservatism and economic conservatism are two different sociopolitical constructs, a distinction that is illustrated further by Authoritarianism and Social Dominance Orientation (SDO).

Authoritarianism

In many respects, the modern psychological study of ideology has its roots in the study of authoritarianism. First examined to explain the rise of fascism in Europe during the World War II era, *The Authoritarian Personality* in 1950 by Adorno, Frenkel-Brunswick, Levinson, and Sanford offered early and influential research on authoritarianism, averring that individuals with authoritarian personalities have submissive attitudes toward authority figures and hold prejudiced views toward targeted out-groups while defending the status quo. The empirical cornerstone of their approach was the "F scale," a questionnaire measure of authoritarianism. They explained authoritarianism in psychodynamic terms, arguing that it resulted from the repression of hostility toward idealized, conventional authorities (especially parents), and the projection of this hostility onto various out-groups. Importantly, Adorno et al. (1950) noted that authoritarianism was associated not only with ethnocentrism but with right wing political attitudes and identifications as well, making it an early psychological explanation for ideological differences.

Despite inspiring much research, *The Authoritarian Personality* and the F scale eventually came in for a variety of theoretical and methodological criticisms (Christie, 1954). In particular, Altemeyer (1981) refined research on authoritarianism via the concept of "Right Wing Authoritarianism" (RWA) and the revised measure he developed to assess it. In Altemeyer's (1998) model, RWA consists of three interrelated tendencies: authoritarian submission to legitimate authorities, authoritarian aggression toward "deviants" and out-groups, and rigid conventionalism. Overall, those scoring high on RWA tend to defer to established authority when making decisions, treat others harshly if instructed by authority, express a preference for highly traditional beliefs, values, and practices, and tend toward a conservative political ideology (Altemeyer, 1996). Individuals who score high on RWA tend to agree with statements such as "Our country desperately needs a mighty leader who will do what has to be done to destroy the radical new ways and sinfulness that are ruining us," and "It is always better to trust the judgment of the proper authorities in government and religion than to listen to the noisy rabble-rousers in our society who are trying to create doubt in people's minds" (Altemeyer, 2004, p. 426). Along with submission to authority, those who score high on RWA also tend to be politically right wing, exhibit high levels of prejudicial beliefs such as ethnocentrism and homophobia, condone harsh punishment of extremists, and endorse the limitation of social freedom due to security concerns. They also tend to be fundamentalist in their religious beliefs, and adhere to the religion of their parents (see Altemeyer, 1998, for a review). Interestingly, high RWA individuals tend to endorse beliefs about themselves that are socially favorable; therefore, individuals high in RWA seemingly are unaware of how their prejudice may be experienced by others.

Recent developments in the literature on authoritarianism have refined further the construct by conceptualizing it as an "authoritarian predisposition" that is activated under conditions of social threat (Stenner, 2005). Work in this vein has attempted to measure authoritarianism strictly in terms of child rearing values—that is, whether one emphasizes obedience and conformity versus independence and curiosity in raising children. This approach helps avoid the explicitly political content included in many earlier measures of authoritarianism, such as the F scale and the RWA scale. Even with this tighter measurement strategy, however, authoritarianism is related strongly to ideology, partisanship, and a variety of political attitudes, especially those linked to the maintenance of social order (Barker & Tinnick, 2006; Hetherington & Weiler, 2009; Stenner, 2005).

Social Dominance Orientation (SDO)

Whereas authoritarianism has been associated with social conservatism, SDO has been linked to economic conservatism. Individuals with a high SDO maintain that some groups are dominant over others as a consequence of evolution and the natural order of social stratification (Pratto, Sidanius, Stallworth, & Malle, 1994; Sidanius & Pratto, 1999). Interestingly, RWA and SDO scales are independent predictors of conservative attitudes, with positive but weak correlations between them. For instance, social conformity is strongly associated with higher RWA scores but not with SDO. Moreover, individuals who are more socially conservative score higher on the RWA, whereas those who strongly accept income inequality will score higher on SDO scales (Duckitt & Sibley, 2010). The distinction between RWA and SDO may be ascertained by analyzing the worldviews associated with each. While RWA consists of having a "dangerous world" perspective, SDO has a "competitive jungle" worldview (Duckitt et al., 2002). In other words, higher SDO is correlated with one's opinions with respect to hierarchy and status, while higher RWA is related to one's opinions with respect to order, loyalty, and group affiliation. Despite the differences between the two scales, conservatives tend to score higher on both of these measures than do liberals (Altemeyer, 2004; Duckitt et al., 2002; Roccato & Ricolfi, 2005). Moreover, individuals who score high on both SDO and RWA tend to be more prejudiced than other individuals (Altemeyer, 2004).

FRAMING THE ETIOLOGY OF IDEOLOGY

From the preceding overview, it appears that liberals and conservatives, and at times libertarians, have measurable differences that lead them to experience the world differently from one another. However, the etiology of such differences—what causes them—is on the cutting edge of our understanding. Although correlational research offers tantalizing clues, questions of cause and effect are still underemphasized, perhaps in part due to the complex nature of such inquiry vis-à-vis the political self. For example, although various personality traits may be associated with specific sociopolitical ideologies, etiological pathways are not always clear (i.e., does personality cause ideology, does ideology influence personality, or are both manifestations of similar underlying processes). Moreover, although neurophysiological differences may be evident among various sociopolitical ideologies, it is unclear whether biology is a consequence or cause of differing ideological tendencies. We do not claim to resolve such matters, only to point toward the sort of theoretical and empirical perspectives that may be helpful to such a pursuit over the long term, including those that are described next.

Heredity/Biology

On the one hand, some evidence suggests that political ideology is influenced by genetic and heritable components (Alford, Funk, & Hibbing, 2005; Dawes & Fowler, 2009; Settle, Dawes, & Fowler, 2009). Such research suggests that identical twins are more similar in their political attitudes than are fraternal twins. In an attempt to understand such putative processes, Hatemi et al. (2011) considered how genomes and chromosomal linkages may influence political ideology. Despite such findings, other scholars recognize the potential reductionistic hazards of overstating the biological underpinnings of ideology, given the current state of methodological sophistication; in short, "chicken and egg" questions predominate within such scholarly foci. Moreover, there has been some debate about how exactly genes, personality, and politics relate to one another, with some arguing that the relationship between genes and political attitudes are mediated by differences in personality (Kandler, Bleidorn, & Riemann, 2012) and others arguing that personality and politics are related not from any mediating effect of personality, but merely because politics and personality are influenced by common genetic variants (Verhulst, Eaves, & Hatemi, 2012).

More recently, research has identified differences in neurocognitive functioning between liberals and conservatives. In other words, different parts of the brain appear to exhibit different levels of activity depending upon one's orientation as liberal or conservative (Amodio, Jost, Master, & Yee, 2007; Zamboni, et al., 2009). For example, Kanai, Feilden, Firth, and Rees (2011) observed that people with diverse ideologies exhibited brain-based structural differences. Specifically, individuals who self-identified as liberals had increased gray matter volume in the anterior cingulate cortex of the brain (an area that affects executive control) as compared to individuals who self-identified as conservatives, whereas conservatives had increased volume of their right amygdala (area that processes emotions, such as fear) as compared to individuals who self-identified as liberals. As another example of this emerging area of focus, Oxley et al. (2011) found that individuals who endorsed conservative positions displayed higher physiological reactions to threatening stimuli than individuals who supported liberal positions. The question, of course, is what causes what—are underlying genetic processes and/or environmental experiences responsible for these physiological differences? If previous research is any indication, it seems likely that some interaction between nature and nurture will be necessary to understand the role of neurobiological vis-à-vis the etiology of political ideology (e.g., evidence has accrued regarding the formative variables that are associated with such ideological differences, including the role of socialization and attachment).

Socialization and Attachment

Other programs of research are examining the impact of upbringing and early life experiences on political ideology. For example, Lakoff (2002) postulates that conservatism and liberalism are influenced by family metaphors that are grounded in different approaches to parenting. For instance, conservatives appear to be guided by a relatively "strict-father model" in which rules, order, and discipline are paramount. Liberals, on the other hand, may endorse a more "nurturant-parent model," in which care, kindness, and compassion are emphasized. In evaluating this perspective, Barker and Tinnick (2006) found that the more one adopted a particular parenting metaphor (strict or nurturant), the more consistently liberal or conservative one was. In other words, the ways in which an individual described their own upbringing (discipline versus compassion) was further associated with their political orientation. McAdams et al. (2008) also explored Lakoff's hypotheses, and found evidence for a relationship between a conservative sociopolitical ideology and life history. Specifically, the life narratives of conservatives tended to focus on strict rules, self-discipline, personal responsibility, deference to authority, and group allegiance, whereas the life narratives of liberals were characterized by themes of empathy, openness to new experiences, deep regard for fairness, and sympathy for human suffering. Importantly, however, and differing from the conclusion of Barker and Tinnick (2006), McAdams et al. (2008) observed that these expressed narratives may and may not be a reflection of what actually happened since sociopolitical ideology could influence the recollection of life events in ways that correspond to one's current frame. Nonetheless, the associations that emerge from such lines of research suggest important underlying pathways that may fruitfully be explored.

Along with early life experiences, do caregiver attachment processes differ between liberals and conservatives? In examining this question, early arguments suggested that children raised with relatively strict and punitive parents would develop into more socially conformist individuals who saw the world as dangerous and threatening and endorsed socially conservative positions (e.g., Adorno et al., 1950). Moreover, children who report cold and unaffectionate parents may become tough and independent individuals who view the world as competitive, thereupon endorsing economically conservative positions (Duckitt, 2001; Duckitt et al., 2002; Ross, 1993). Indeed, focusing upon adult attachment styles rather than early-childhood family dynamics, Weber and Federico (2007) found that individuals with an anxious attachment style saw the world as dangerous and threatening, and tended to endorse social conservatism, as measured by the RWA scale. On the other hand, individuals with an avoidant attachment style perceived the world in competitive terms, endorsing economic conservatism, as measured by the SDO scale. Such findings led these scholars to theorize that individuals who are securely attached are less likely to see the world as dangerous and competitive, and more likely to hold a liberal ideology.

Demonstrating the complexity of such processes, Thornhill and Fincher (2007) found that liberals scored higher on scales measuring avoidant attachment than did conservatives, whereas conservatives scored higher on secure attachment. Also, according to their measures, liberals experienced more stress in their childhood than did conservatives (Thornhill & Fincher, 2007). In addition, Koleva and Rip (2009) reviewed research examining the relationship between attachment and political ideology and found liberalism associated with both secure attachment and insecure avoidant attachment, whereas conservatism was associated with insecure avoidant attachment and anxious–ambivalent attachment. They posited that how attachment is conceptualized (i.e., relational need or relational habit) determines whether attachment security or insecurity leads to conservatism or liberalism. Thus, if attachment security is seen as a relational need that is satisfied, then one is more likely to embrace liberal ideology. However, if attachment security is conceptualized as a relational habit that leads to expectancies for future security, then conservatism will be endorsed.

Moreover, Gillath and Hart (2010) found that experimental priming of a secure attachment (i.e., identifying and reflecting on one's relationship with someone who provides love, acceptance, and help—a security providing attachment figure) led to a decrease in the endorsement of conservative foreign policy, which suggests that sociopolitical ideology may be influenced by feelings of security. Taken as a whole, such studies suggest that attachment style is related to sociopolitical ideology, although the nature of such a relationship may be influenced by issues of conceptualization, measurement, and methodology.

Summary

To summarize, at least from the perspectives already discussed, political ideology appears to be a form of motivated social cognition, which manifests in different forms, including liberalism, conservatism, and libertarianism. Among other predilections, liberalism embraces complexity, openness to experience, and tolerance for ambiguity, whereas conservatism is associated with a preference for certainty, order, structure, and closure (Jost et al., 2003). Moreover, libertarianism emphasizes liberty above other considerations, and typically endorses aspects of both social liberalism and economic conservatism (Boaz, 1997). Such processes have prompted an exploration of origins. Among other factors, neurophysiological factors, life history, socialization, and attachment do seem to mediate sociopolitical ideology, although processes of directionality are complex at best. As such, toward the overarching goal of further clarification regarding these complex issues of etiology and outcome, we now turn our focus to theory and data from the Forum BEVI Project, a long-term and multi-institution assessment of learning project that may help illuminate further these processes and outcomes (www.ibavi.org/content/featured-projects). Following an overview of this project model and method, we present various findings, which help identify causal pathways among formative variables (e.g., life history), mediators (e.g., scales of sociopolitical beliefs and values), and outcomes (e.g., self-reported stances on selected sociopolitical issues). Such examination offers additional insight into the possible mechanisms that contribute to development of the self, including aspects of political ideology, and how endorsement of such ideology may be evidenced through endorsed or rejected belief statements about self, others, and the larger world.

EI THEORY, THE EI SELF, AND THE BEVI

Although a full explication is presented in Shealy (2016), a brief overview of the three main components of the present approach—Equilintegration (EI) Theory, the EI Self, and Beliefs, Events, and Values Inventory (BEVI)—may be helpful at this point (for more information, see Chapters 2–4). Equilintegration (EI) Theory seeks to explain "the processes by which beliefs, values, and 'worldviews' are acquired and maintained, why their alteration is typically resisted, and how and under what circumstances their modification occurs" (Shealy, 2004, p. 1075). Derivative of EI Theory (Shealy, 2004), the Equilintegration or EI Self explains integrative and synergistic processes by which beliefs and values are acquired, maintained, and transformed as well as how and why these are linked to the formative variables, core needs, and adaptive potential of the self. Informed by scholarship in a range of key areas (e.g., "needs-based" research and theory; developmental psychopathology;

social cognition; psychotherapy processes and outcomes; affect regulation; theories and models of "self"), the EI Self seeks to illustrate how the interaction between our core needs (e.g., for attachment, affiliation) and formative variables (e.g., caregiver, culture) results in beliefs and values about self, others, and the world at large that we all internalize over the course of development and across the life span (Shealy et al., 2012).

Concomitant with EI Theory and the EI Self, the BEVI is a comprehensive analytic tool in development since the early 1990s that examines how and why we come to see ourselves, others, and the larger world as we do (e.g., how life experiences, culture, and context affect our beliefs, values, and worldview) as well as the influence of such processes on multiple aspects of human functioning (e.g., learning processes, relationships, personal growth, the pursuit of life goals). For example, the BEVI assesses processes such as: basic openness; the tendency to (or not to) stereotype in particular ways; self- and emotional awareness; preferred strategies for making sense of why "other" people and cultures "do what they do"; global engagement (e.g., receptivity to different cultures, religions, and social practices); and worldview shift (e.g., to what degree do beliefs and values change as a result of specific experiences). BEVI results are translated into reports at the individual, group, and organizational levels and used in a range of contexts for a variety of applied and research purposes (e.g., to track and examine changes in worldviews over time) (e.g., Anmuth et al., 2013; Atwood, Chkhaidz, Shealy, Staton, & Sternberger, 2014; Brearly, Shealy, Staton, & Sternberger, 2012; Hayes, Shealy, Sivo, & Weinstein, 1999; Hill et al., 2013; Isley, Shealy, Crandall, Sivo, & Reifsteck, 1999; Pysarchik, Shealy, & Whalen, 2007; Shealy, 2000a, 2000b, 2004, 2005, 2015, 2016; Shealy et al., 2012; Tabit et al., 2011; for more information about the BEVI, including a description of scales, see Chapter 4).

In the present analysis, we draw upon the EI model and BEVI method to explore the etiology of political ideology. More specifically, we are interested in understanding whether specific formative variables (e.g., key aspects of one's life history or background) are associated with the endorsement or rejection of specific belief statements as well as core constructs on the BEVI that are especially predictive of one's political ideology. When viewed through the lens of the EI theoretical framework, the juxtaposition of item and scale levels of analyses on the BEVI may help illuminate why the "political self" becomes organized as it does.

EXPLORING THE ETIOLOGY OF IDEOLOGY

For present purposes, we are interested in exploring the relationship between three interrelated processes: (a) whether specific formative variables (including ethnicity, gender, age, parental education, socioeconomic status [SES], highest level of education completed, primary location where raised) are (b) predictive of various constructs (i.e., factors or scales) on the BEVI, which (c) further mediate specific measurable outcomes (e.g., political affiliation).[2] After providing methodological information, we present two sets of findings: (a) an item level of analysis, which examines patterns of responding by political affiliation to two types of BEVI items; and (b) structural equation models and correlation matrix data, which illustrate the

---

[2] We recognized that partisanship or political affiliation is but one way to differentiate one's political ideology. While party identification and ideology are not conceptually the same thing, due to their relationship in the following analyses, party identification serves as an estimate of one's ideology (i.e., partisanship is an outcome that is strongly related to political ideology).

complex interactions between formative variables, mediators, and outcomes vis-à-vis political affiliation as well as the relationship among various aspects of the self (e.g., affective, attributional, developmental).

Analyses were developed on the basis of a convenience sample from a large dataset (N = 2331) collected during 2011 to 2012 from the Forum BEVI Project, a multi-institution, multiyear project examining the assessment of international, multicultural, and transformative learning. Coordinated by the Forum on Education Abroad (www.forumea.org) and International Beliefs and Values Institute (www.ibavi.org), participants primarily included undergraduate students (96.7%) and were recruited through a range of learning experiences (e.g., study abroad, residential learning communities, general education courses with a focus on transformative/multicultural learning). A small portion of graduate students (3.3%) also was included. The sample typically ranged between the ages of 17 and 26, with an average age of 19. However, 3.9% fell into the age range of 26 to 62, with another 9% falling into the age range of 12 to 17. Although the majority of participants reported as U.S. citizens (93.3%), non-U.S. citizens also were included in the sample (N = 156 or 6.7%). Also, participants were drawn from 38 different countries of origin. Of the sample, 79.1% reported as Caucasian with 20.9% as non-Caucasian (6.6% Black or African American; 0.9% American Indian or Alaskan Native; 7.4% Asian or Pacific Islander; 2.9% Hispanic/Latino; 3% Other). Finally, from the standpoint of gender, 40.8% of the sample was female, with 59.2% male. All participants were required to provide informed consent as determined by multiple Institutional Review Boards processes, and participation was entirely voluntary. Participants were not required to complete the BEVI, and could elect to discontinue participation at any time. Analyses were conducted via SPSS and MPLUS statistical analyses, and consist of analysis of variance (ANOVA), regression analysis, and structural equation modeling (SEM). More information on the Forum BEVI Project is available in Chapter 4 and at www.ibavi.org/content/featured-projects.

Item Level Analyses

In exploring the origins of political ideology at an item level of analysis on the BEVI, perhaps the most basic question is identifying which items to select. Two criteria were developed in that regard. First, we wished to identify items that differentiated statistically between self-identified "Republicans," "Independents," and "Democrats." In other words, political affiliation needed to be predicted well by observing whether belief statements were differentially endorsed or rejected across different political affiliations. Second, we wished to understand whether different "types" of items differentiated across political affiliations. More specifically, we wanted to understand whether items other than those that were relatively face valid (i.e., would seem to be predictive of party affiliation "on the face of it") could illuminate underlying affective and attributional processes that help explain the etiology of ideology. Therefore, two sets of items were selected in that regard: expected predictors and explanatory predictors. As the "expected predictor" items of Tables 9.1 to 9.5 indicate, when compared to Democrats, Independents, or those who indicated an "Other" political orientation, Republicans are more likely to *agree* with the following BEVI items:

> *I am more conservative than liberal on social issues.*
> *Church and state must be separate.*
> *Too many people are looking for a free handout.*

TABLE 9.1

Q306. I Am More Conservative Than Liberal on Social Issues

SOURCE	SUM OF SQUARES	MEAN	DF	MEAN SQUARE ERROR	F	SIG.
Corrected Model	464.289		3	154.763	253.569	0.00
Intercept	13214.633		1	13214.633	21651.33	0.00
Political Orientation	464.289		3	154.763	253.569	0.00
Democrat		1.955				
Independent		2.316				
Republican		3.034				
Other		2.198				
Error	1385.078		2271	0.61		
Total	15065		2275			
Corrected Total	1850.367		2274			

Note. $R^2 = 0.251$ (adjusted $R^2 = 0.250$).

Likewise, they are more likely to *disagree* with the following BEVI items:

Many government programs do a lot of good.
There is too big a gap between the rich and poor in our country.
Church and state must be separate.

TABLE 9.2

Q223. Church and State Must Be Separate

SOURCE	SUM OF SQUARES	MEAN	DF	MEAN SQUARE ERROR	F	SIG.
Corrected Model	65.127		3	21.709	36.517	0.00
Intercept	21465.063		1	21465.063	36106.82	0.00
Political Orientation	65.127		3	21.709	36.517	0.00
Democrat		3.192				
Independent		3.112				
Republican		2.827				
Other		3.296				
Error	1357.81		2284	0.594		
Total	22888		2288			
Corrected Total	1422.937		2287			

Note. $R^2 = 0.46$ (adjusted $R^2 = 0.45$).

TABLE 9.3

Q55. Many Government Programs Do a Lot of Good

SOURCE	SUM OF SQUARES	MEAN	DF	MEAN SQUARE ERROR	F	SIG.
Corrected Model	39.970		3	13.323	36.517	0.00
Intercept	17751.259		1	17751.259	40831.94	0.00
Political Orientation	39.97		3	13.323	30.647	0.00
Democrat		2.94				
Independent		2.753				
Republican		2.631				
Other		2.671				
Error	1000.77		2302	0.435		
Total	18792		2306			
Corrected Total	1040.741		2305			

Note. $R^2 = 0.038$ (adjusted $R^2 = 0.037$).

Again, such findings although striking from the standpoint of consistency, are perhaps not surprising. In other words, patterns of rejection or endorsement of such politically oriented beliefs would be expected to predict political affiliation, and do. But what might we learn about the etiology of ideology by examining belief

TABLE 9.4

Q70. Too Many People Are Looking for a Free Handout

SOURCE	SUM OF SQUARES	MEAN	DF	MEAN SQUARE ERROR	F	SIG.
Corrected Model	102.683		3	34.228	57.541	0.00
Intercept	20766.002		1	20766.002	34910.4	0.00
Political Orientation	102.683		3	34.228	57.541	0.00
Democrat		2.767				
Independent		2.983				
Republican		3.28				
Other		2.976				
Error	1369.315		2302	0.595		
Total	22238		2306			
Corrected Total	1471.998		2305			

Note. $R^2 = 0.070$ (adjusted $R^2 = 0.069$).

TABLE 9.5

Q274. There Is Too Big a Gap Between the Rich and the Poor in Our Country

SOURCE	SUM OF SQUARES	MEAN	DF	MEAN SQUARE ERROR	F	SIG.
Corrected Model	100.037		3	33.346	59.466	0.000
Intercept	13440.273		1	13440.273	23968.193	0.000
Political Orientation	100.037		3	33.346	59.466	0.000
Democrat		3.179				
Independent		3.021				
Republican		2.678				
Other		2.893				
Error	1276.838		2277	0.561		
Total	21328.000		2281			
Corrected Total	1376.875		2280			

Note. $R^2 = 0.073$ (adjusted $R^2 = 0.071$).

statements that would not necessarily be expected to predict political affiliation, but also do? Consider Tables 9.6 to 9.9. Here, Republicans also are *less likely* to agree with the following BEVI items than are Independents or Democrats.

> *I am comfortable around groups of people who are very different from me.*
> *I have wondered about who I am and where I am going.*
> *I am always trying to understand myself better.*
> *I like to think about why things are the way they are.*

What do such findings suggest? Recall that the Equilintegration or EI model essentially is concerned with both interpretive as well as descriptive levels of analysis (see Chapters 2 and 3). That is to say, it seeks to ask and answer questions of *what* (e.g., what do people believe about politics, religion, and so forth) as well as *why* (e.g., why do specific formative variables, such as life events, influence the beliefs and values toward which human beings are inclined). Second, the EI model and BEVI method were derived out of actual utterances made by real human beings in clinical, training, and educational contexts (Shealy, 2004; see also Chapter 4). Thus, by design, we anticipate that the belief/value statements human beings declare to be true or false, and good or bad, for themselves, others, and the larger world are expected to be deeply intertwined with other core aspects of self, such as one's relative degree of access to affect, capacity for introspective, and inclination toward engagement with others.

By extension then, this model and method regard political ideology as a symptom or sign of how the self writ large is structured, and is therefore no more or less salient than other ideological commitments (e.g., toward religion, the environment, issues of gender), which all are deterministically linked to and intertwined with one another. As such, when combined with sufficient information about one's life history and background, to know something of one's political ideology, it is quite possible to derive empirically and theoretically substantiated predictions about other self-structures and

TABLE 9.6

Q364. I Am Comfortable Around Groups of People Who Are Very Different From Me

SOURCE	SUM OF SQUARES	MEAN	DF	MEAN SQUARE ERROR	F	SIG.
Corrected Model	19.516		3	6.505	12.294	0.000
Intercept	12029.800		1	12029.800	22733.674	0.000
Political Orientation	19.516		3	6.505	12.294	0.000
Democrat		2.908				
Independent		2.797				
Republican		2.682				
Other		2.824				
Error	1194.319		2257	0.529		
Total	18958.000		2261			
Corrected Total	1213.835		2260			

Note. $R^2 = 0.016$ (adjusted $R^2 = 0.015$).

processes (e.g., affective capacities; self awareness; gender relations). Third, the EI framework explicitly recognizes that the complex interaction between nurture (e.g., formative variables) and nature (e.g., the genetically mediated "adaptive potential" of the Core Self) ultimately culminates in what human beings come to believe about self, others, and the larger world. In short, then, the present approach seeks to build upon the advances

TABLE 9.7

Q123. I Have Wondered About Who I Am and Where I Am Going

SOURCE	SUM OF SQUARES	MEAN	DF	MEAN SQUARE ERROR	F	SIG.
Corrected Model	6.597		3	2.199	4.571	0.003
Intercept	22846.005		1	22846.005	47494.32	0.00
Political Orientation	6.597		3	2.199	4.571	0.003
Democrat		3.208				
Independent		3.157				
Republican		3,078				
Other		3.166				
Error	1105.398		2298	0.481		
Total	23958		2302			
Corrected Total	1111.995		2301			

Note. $R^2 = 0.006$ (adjusted $R^2 = 0.005$).

TABLE 9.8

Q149. I Am Always Trying to Understand Myself Better

SOURCE	SUM OF SQUARES	MEAN	DF	MEAN SQUARE ERROR	F	SIG.
Corrected Model	11.166		3	3.722	8.744	0.00
Intercept	21970.751		1	21970.751	51613.41	0.00
Political Orientation	11.166		3	3.722	8.744	0.00
Democrat		3.174				
Independent		3.092				
Republican		3.004				
Other		3.089				
Error	976.082		2293	0.426		
Total	22958		2297			
Corrected Total	987.249		2296			

Note. $R^2 = 0.011$ (adjusted $R^2 = 0.010$).

in our understanding of both what political ideology is, and why it manifests as it does, by exploring the dynamic, organismic, and interacting processes that occur over the life span across different levels of self. Toward such means and ends, the complementarity between this approach and the growing literature on psychology and ideology noted previously—including but not limited to lay epistemic theory (Jost et al., 2003), moral

TABLE 9.9

Q372. I Like to Think About Why Things Are the Way They Are

SOURCE	SUM OF SQUARES	MEAN	DF	MEAN SQUARE ERROR	F	SIG.
Corrected Model	3.003		3	1.001	2.626	0.049
Intercept	21793.064		1	21973.064	57173.21	0.00
Political Orientation	3.003		3	1.001	2.626	0.049
Democrat		3.144				
Independent		3.095				
Republican		3.061				
Other		3.145				
Error	859.933		2256	0.381		
Total	22656		2260			
Corrected Total	862.936		2259			

Note. $R^2 = 0.003$ (adjusted $R^2 = 0.002$).

foundations theory (Haidt & Graham, 2007; Haidt et al., 2009), and personality theory (Gerber et al., 2010; Mondak, 2010)—may be evident.

In short, from an EI perspective, it stands to reason that "selves" become structured in ways that predispose them to self-identify with particular political positions. For example, as recent political elections in the United States illustrate, the fact that Republicans tend to *disagree* more than Democrats with belief statements such as, *I am comfortable around groups of people who are very different from me* and *I like to think about why things are the way they are* certainly is informative at a descriptive level of analysis. At an explanatory level of analysis, however, more interesting is what such inclinations suggest about the underlying structure of the self as well as why it is organized as it is. From an EI perspective, it is not that the aggregated Republican "chooses" not to reflect upon such matters, but rather is structured in such a way that such reflection is deterministically less likely to occur. In this regard, such self-structure did not just "happen," but resulted from a complex interaction among different levels of self, including the sum total of all encounters with formative variables through development, which essentially codifies into the belief/value structures that we call our own (see Chapters 2 and 3).

SEM and Correlation Matrix Analyses

In the final set of analyses, we examine this proposition regarding the etiology of ideology more closely. Specifically, we want to understand better how complex and interactive developmental processes largely determine why we experience self, others, and the larger world as we do irrespective of whether we understand or even agree that such processes occurred to and within us (Shealy et al., 2012). To do so, we next present a series of structural equation models (SEM) along with related correlation matrix data. Consistent with the underlying EI framework of the BEVI, the SEM theoretical model posits that (a) formative variables (e.g., life events; ethnic background) (b) mediate the nature of belief/value constructs that are inculcated and codified, for present purposes, as various BEVI scales, which ultimately lead to (c) "outcomes" in the "real world," including but by no means limited to one's political affiliation. Thus, we really are testing a theoretical model regarding how these processes contribute to one another along prespecified paths via standard fit indexes that are appropriate for such analyses (e.g., RMSEA, CFI). Here, we focus on SEMs regarding the relationship between Negative Life Events (NLE) and Socioemotional Convergence (SEC) scales on the BEVI vis-à-vis political ideology.[3, 4] What do we conclude from a review of such models?

---

[3] As described in Chapter 4, NLE consists of self-report statements regarding one's own upbringing and life history. Among other dimensions, SEC measures the degree to which individuals demonstrate an overarching capacity to "hold complexity" (i.e., avoid black and white characterizations regarding how the world "is" and "should be").

[4] From an interpretive standpoint, ethnicity is a dummy measured variable; value "0" indicates the respondent is a minority, and "1" means the respondent is a Caucasian. Disability also is a dummy variable; "0" indicates the person is not eligible for services for students with disabilities, and "1" means otherwise. Family income is measured by a series of numbers indicating the respondent's annual family income. It ranges from "1" (Less than $10,000) to "10" ($175,000 or more). Both father's education and mother's education are ordinal measured variables. They range from "0" (Some high school or less) to "8" (Doctoral degree). The dependent variable "Democrat" also is a dummy variable; "0" means not a Democrat, and "1" means a Democrat. Finally, we used weighted least squares means and variance adjusted (WLSMV) as the estimator for all the structural equation models because the variables have ordinal or dummy measures.

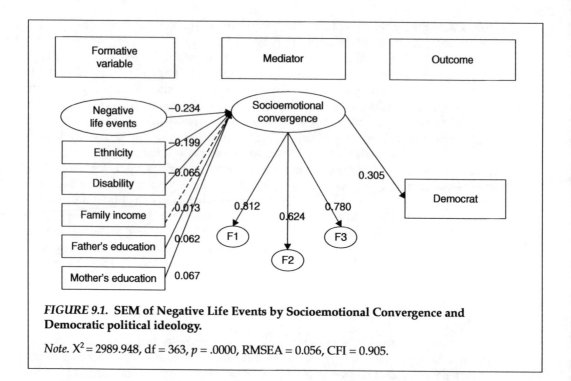

FIGURE 9.1. SEM of Negative Life Events by Socioemotional Convergence and Democratic political ideology.

Note. $X^2 = 2989.948$, df $= 363$, $p = .0000$, RMSEA $= 0.056$, CFI $= 0.905$.

As illustrated in Figures 9.1 and 9.2, it may be helpful to highlight three key findings. First, note that the degree to which individuals report a relatively high degree of Negative Life Events (NLE) is significantly predictive of a lower degree of Socioemotional Convergence (SEC) for both Democrats and Republicans in these SEMs (for purposes of interpretation, solid lines refer to statistically significant findings). In other words, the *greater the degree* that individuals report conflict in the home or origin, unhappy childhood experiences, legal or other life difficulties, and so forth, the *lower the degree* of basic openness, self awareness, and sociocultural interest the individual evidences, from the standpoint of the BEVI. Second, other formative variables (in addition to NLE) also predict SEC. Specifically, those individuals who (a) are non-Caucasian, (b) report that they do not have a disability diagnosis,[5] and (c) who report a higher degree of education for their father and mother all evidence a greater degree of SEC, regardless of whether they are Democrat or Republican. Third, the higher degree of SEC an individual reports, the more likely they are to report that they are a Democrat and the less likely they are to report that they are a Republican. So, taken as a whole, and consistent with that which would be predicted by an EI framework, these findings suggest that the more people report that they experienced particular types of formative variables (e.g., a happy/satisfactory experience during their upbringing and in life, had parents with a greater degree of education), the more likely they were to evidence a capacity and inclination for openness to or engagement with self, others, and the larger world, which further is associated with the tendency to self-report as Democrat.

---

[5] It is not clear why "disability status" is negatively associated with SEC. Although an empirical and theoretical question, it could be that self-identification as "disabled" (e.g., with a psychological condition) may be associated with less "holding of complexity," at least as measured by this construct on the BEVI.

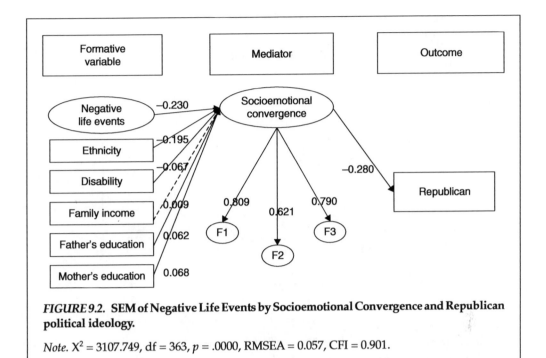

FIGURE 9.2. **SEM of Negative Life Events by Socioemotional Convergence and Republican political ideology.**

Note. $X^2 = 3107.749$, df $= 363$, $p = .0000$, RMSEA $= 0.057$, CFI $= 0.901$.

Finally, to augment and explain further these SEM findings, consider Table 9.10, which was derived from correlation matrix data, based upon an Exploratory Factor Analysis (EFA) of BEVI data, which preceded the Confirmatory Factor Analysis (CFA) used for purposes of SEM.[6]

What do we conclude from such correlation matrix data? First, for interpretative purposes, note that this analysis considers the correlation of SEC to other BEVI scales, which are significantly ($p < .001$) correlated at or above .50 (see http://www .thebevi.com/docs/bevi_scale_pairwise_correlations_and_significance_levels.pdf). Second, consistent with the SEMs and other ANOVAs reported previously, note that the *greater* the degree of Socioemotional Convergence (SEC) individuals report, the more likely they are to report (a) that their "core needs" *were* met (Needs Closure); (b) the *greater* their capacity and inclination for attending to emotions in self and other (Emotional Attunement); (c) the *greater* their degree of interest or engagement in cultures that are different from that which they are accustomed (Sociocultural Openness); (d) the *lesser* their tendency to adopt a "contrarian" viewpoint for the sake of doing so (Divergent Determinism); (e) the more *likely* they are to acknowledge basic thoughts or feelings or tolerate emotional pain (Basic Closedness); (f) the *greater* their tendency to express care and concern for the environment and natural world (Ecological Resonance); (g) the *lesser* degree of confusion or "stuckness" they evidence regarding who they are and where they are going in life (Identity Diffusion); (h) the *less likely* they are to report unhappy experiences during their upbringing and in life (Negative Life

---

[6] More information about the BEVI, including EFA parameters as well as correlation matrix data, is available at www.thebevi.com/aboutbevi.php. See also Chapter 4.

TABLE 9.10

Correlation Matrix Data of Socioemotional Convergence and Other BEVI Scales

Needs Closure (−.93)

Emotional Attunement (.84)

Sociocultural Openness (.82)

Divergent Determinism (−.81)

Basic Closedness (−.79)

Ecological Resonance (.69)

Identity Diffusion (−.69)

Negative Life Events (−.69)

Hard Structure (−.53)

Events); and (i) the *more likely* they are to acknowledge doubts about one's self or one's actions in the world (Hard Structure). The implications of such findings extend beyond the etiology of political ideology, in that it may be helpful to bear such relationships in mind as we continue to explore such interacting processes in future research, recognizing that one's "political self" is inextricably linked to broader aspects of why we experience self, others, and the larger world as we do.

Summary Observations

On the basis of the preceding findings, we offer three summary observations regarding our exploration of the etiology of ideology.

First, depth matters

As our item level of analysis indicates, it is relatively easy to differentiate political ideologies on the basis of expected differences (e.g., regarding the role of government; self-endorsement of conservative or liberal labels). Arguably, a more interesting and illuminating tack examines less obvious aspects of self-organization (e.g., affective, attributional, developmental) that nonetheless also may be associated with political differences from an ideational standpoint. In this regard, the finding that Republicans overall are less likely to wonder "about who I am and where I am going" or to like thinking about "why things are the way they are" may suggest that political affiliation simply represents the "best fit" to how the self is structured rather than a rational process of "deciding" what one does and does not believe vis-à-vis various political considerations.

Second, interactions matter

Results do suggest that the greater the degree of Negative Life Events that individuals report they experience, the *less likely* they are to evidence the sort of construct-based patterns suggested by the preceding correlation matrix data vis-a-vis

Socioemotional Convergence. For example, the more "negative experiences" individuals report at the level of formative variables, the less open they generally appear to be, which makes sense from an EI perspective. Also, the more our core needs are met in a "good enough" manner, the more capacity we appear to have not only to tolerate, but actively care for, self, others, and the larger world (e.g., Shealy, 1995; Shealy et al., 2012). Interestingly, a higher degree of SEC is in fact associated with a greater tendency to report a Democratic political affiliation. However, such a conclusion should *not* necessarily be construed to mean that Democrats experience less "Negative Life Events" than do Republicans, since there is competing evidence along these lines, as reported previously (e.g., Koleva & Rip, 2009; Thornhill & Fincher, 2007; Weber & Federico, 2007). Indeed, two subfindings are especially instructive in this regard. On the one hand, a higher degree of SEC (e.g., an inclination to experience the world in shades of gray rather than black and white) is associated with a Democratic rather than Republican political affiliation. Moreover, a higher degree of NLE also is associated with a lower degree of Socioemotional Convergence. However, a syllogism does not necessarily follow that a low degree of NLE is associated with a greater degree of Democratic affiliation or that a high degree of NLE is associated with a greater degree of Republican affiliation. Although an empirical question awaiting further study, it may be that political affiliation is similar to religious affiliation in that the specific nature of one's identity in this regard may vary depending upon the nature of the formative variables through which such identity was inculcated. Just as there is a difference between "fundamentalist" and "orthodox" Christians (with the former tending toward greater certitude than the latter regarding matters of religious faith), it may be that there are similar differences between "fundamentalist" and "orthodox" Republicans or Democrats. If so, the most important formative variables that may mediate such outcomes may have to do with the relative degree of warmth and responsiveness individuals experienced by caregivers during development rather than some putative rational process that culminates in one's political affiliation (see Brearly, Van den Bos, & Tan, 2016). In short, to understand the etiology of ideology, we should account for within-group variability (e.g., the fact that various subsets of self-identified Republicans may be more open, aware, and engaged than various subsets of self-identified Democrats), by ensuring as researchers that our theoretical models and assessment methods are able to do so.

Third, self-preservation matters

In the final analysis and related to the preceding points, the structure of the self (e.g., the political affiliations we endorse; our inclination to experience and express affect) does not "just happen," but results from complex interactions (e.g., affective, attributional, developmental), which become codified in the beliefs and values about self, others, and the larger world that we call our own. Such processes seem operative whether or not we understand them or even agree that they occurred (Shealy et al., 2012). Thus, as we struggle to move beyond the political divisiveness of our present age, it may be helpful to contemplate the possibility that our political affiliations are deterministically acquired via a complex set of interactions representing the "best fit" for each human being. Ultimately, it may be more difficult to vilify "the other" if we appreciate the possibility that our political inclinations are nothing more or less than an expression of how we are organized at the level of our Core Self. That is not to say that change to our political affiliations is neither possible nor desirable, just that it stands to reason why we fight for our preferred political parties, since we really are fighting to protect and preserve the viability and coherence of underlying psychological structures, of which we may or may not be aware.

CONCLUSION

At the outset of this chapter, we began with the fundamental conclusion of the Pew Research Center (2012) that "values and basic beliefs are more polarized along partisan lines than at any point in the past 25 years." We also observed that in considering political ideology, greater focus typically has been devoted to what divides us in terms of our political ideologies (e.g., the content of our differing beliefs and values politically), with less focus on the etiology of ideology (e.g., why we differ in the first place). Although these are and should remain complementary emphases, our contention is that if we were to give greater attention to *why* rather than *how* we differ politically, the complex phenomenon of political ideology would become more comprehensible and accessible. As Stevens (2012) laments in a recent critique of political science, "many of today's peer-reviewed studies offer trivial confirmations of the obvious," and dwell on quantitative minutiae that should not erroneously be equated with knowledge (p. 6). As a point of contrast to this pessimistic appraisal, we argue that the generation of data and development of knowledge need not be mutually exclusive endeavors. As we have attempted to illustrate, quantitative analysis of individual-level political data may in fact play a crucial, if not indispensable, role in the development of knowledge. In other words, there may be no other way to develop some forms of knowledge, such as those presented here, without empirical studies and statistics (i.e., it is not possible, by theory or argument alone, to have a basis for supporting the conclusions we have reached). That said, generative and ecologically valid outcomes are that much more likely if we integrate the whole human being into our research, which means considering simultaneously complex—and indeed, "messy"—interactions among a wide range of variables that too often are not included in mainstream, macrolevel research on the foundations of ideology (e.g., affect, attribution, life history, context, culture; see also Jost, 2006; Jost et al., 2009).

In the final analysis, as psychologists who are interested in politics and political science, we respectfully offer the framework presented here—including significance findings from a range of analyses—as one way to deepen our understanding and examination of the political animal. There are many reasons for doing so. For example, as the theory and data described here suggest, when human beings report that they have not received "what they need" in their own lives (e.g., during development), their attendant capacity and inclination to see and experience self, others, and the larger world correspondingly appear to be affected. By extension, when many individual human beings share such experiences of self, and come together in groups and societies, it seems likely that political actions, policies, and practices will follow to no small degree, as we regularly witness in our polarized political discourse, not only in recent elections in the United States, but all over the world. Thus, in seeking to comprehend the etiology of ideology, it likely will help if we include an examination of why and how the political self comes to be structured as it does. Likewise, if we focus not only on *what* divides us, but *why*, it seems more likely that our conceptual frameworks, predictive models, and policy solutions will be that much more likely to possess ecological validity and real world meaning, for scholars, policy makers, and the public at large.

REFERENCES

Adorno, T. W., Frenkel-Brunswik, E., Levinson, D. J., & Sanford, R. N. (1950). *The authoritarian personality*. New York, NY: Harper.

Alford, J., Funk, C., & Hibbing, J. (2005). Are political orientations genetically transmitted? *American Political Science Review, 99*(2), 153–167.

Altemeyer, R. (1981). *Right-wing authoritarianism*. Winnipeg, Canada: University of Manitoba Press.

Altemeyer, R. (1996). *The authoritarian specter*. Cambridge, MA: Harvard University Press.

Altemeyer, R. (1998). The other "authoritarian personality." *Advances in Experimental Social Psychology, 30*, 47–92.

Altemeyer, R. (2004). Highly dominating, highly authoritarian personalities. *The Journal of Social Psychology, 144*, 421–447.

Amodio, D., Jost, J., Master, S., & Yee, C. (2007). Neurocognitive correlates of liberalism and conservatism. *Nature Neuroscience, 10*, 1246–1247.

Anmuth, L. M., Poore, M., Cozen, J., Brearly, T., Tabit, M., Cannady, M., . . . Staton, R. (2013, August). *Making implicit beliefs explicit: In search of best practices for mental health clients, clinicians, and trainers*. Poster presented at the annual meeting of the American Psychological Association, Honolulu, HI.

Atwood, K., Chkhaidze, N., Shealy, C. N., Staton, R., & Sternberger, L. G. (2014, August). *Transformation of self: Implications from the Forum BEVI Project*. Poster presented at the annual meeting of the American Psychological Association, Washington, DC.

Barker, D. C., & Tinnick, J. D. (2006). Competing visions of parental roles and ideological constraint. *American Political Science Review, 100*(2), 249–263.

Boaz, D. (1997). *Libertarianism: A primer*. New York, NY: The Free Press.

Bobbio, N. (1996). *Left and right*. Cambridge, UK: Polity Press.

Bonanno, G., & Jost, J. (2006). Conservative shift among high-exposure survivors of the September 11th terrorist attacks. *Basic and Applied Social Psychology, 28*, 311–323.

Brearly, T., Shealy, C. N., Staton, R., & Sternberger, L. G. (2012, August). *Prejudice and religious and non-religious certitude: An empirical analysis from the Forum BEVI Project*. Poster presented at the annual meeting of the American Psychological Association, Orlando, FL.

Brearly, T., Van den Bos, K., & Tan, C. (2016). The nature and etiology of religious certitude: Implications of the EI framework and Beliefs, Events, and Values Inventory. In C. N. Shealy (Ed.), *Making sense of beliefs and values* (pp. 331–369). New York, NY: Springer Publishing.

Caprara, G. V., Schwartz, S. H., Capanna, C., Vecchione, M., & Barbaranelli, C. (2006). Personality and politics: Values, traits, and political choice. *Political Psychology, 27*, 1–28.

Carney, D. R., Jost, J. T., Gosling, S. D., & Potter, J. (2008). The secret lives of liberals and conservatives: Personality profiles, interaction styles, and the things they leave behind. *Political Psychology, 29*(6), 807–840.

Christie, R. (1954). Authoritarianism re-examined. In R. Christie & M. Jahoda (Eds.), *Studies in the scope and method of "The Authoritarian Personality"* (pp. 123–196). Glencoe, IL: Free Press.

Conover, P. J., & Feldman, S. (1981). The origins and meaning of liberal-conservative self-identifications. *American Journal of Political Science, 25*, 617–645.

Conservatism. (2012). In *Merriam-Webster.com*. Retrieved March 12, 2012 from http://www.merriam-webster.com/dictionary/conservatism

Dawes, C. T., & Fowler, J. H. (2009). Partisanship, voting, and the dopamine D2 receptor gene. *Journal of Politics, 71*(3), 1157–1171.

Democratic Party. (2012). *Democratic national platform*. Retrieved November 10, 2012 from http://www.presidency.ucsb.edu/platforms.php

Detroit Free Press. (2012). *Transcript: GOP primary candidate Rick Santorum's speech to the Detroit Economic Club*. Retrieved from http://www.freep.com/article/20120219/PINION05/202190367/Transcript-GOP-primary-candidate-Rick-Santorum-s-speech-Detroit-Economic-Club-

Duckitt, J. (2001). A dual-process cognitive-motivational theory of ideology and prejudice. In M. P. Zanna (Ed.), *Advances in experimental social psychology* (Vol. 33, pp. 41–113). San Diego, CA: Academic Press.

Duckitt, J., & Sibley, C. G. (2010). Personality, ideology, prejudice, and politics: A dual-process motivational model. *Journal of Personality, 78*(6), 1861–1893.

Duckitt, J., Wagner, C., du Plessis, I., & Birum, I. (2002). The psychological bases of ideology and prejudice: Testing a dual process model. *Journal of Personality and Social Psychology, 83*(1), 75–93.

Erikson, R. S., & Tedin, K. L., (2003). *American public opinion.* New York, NY: Longman.

Federico, C. M., Deason, G., & Fisher, E. L. (2012). Ideological asymmetry in the relationship between epistemic motivation and political attitudes. *Journal of Personality and Social Psychology, 103*(3), 381–398.

Frank, T. (2004). *What's the matter with Kansas? How conservatives won the heart of America.* New York, NY: Metropolitan Books.

Gallup. (2012a). *Voters indicate tight race for Congress.* Retrieved from http://www.gallup.com/poll/153047/Voters-Indicate-Tight-Race-Congress.aspx

Gallup. (2012b). *Conservatives remain the largest ideological group in U.S.* Retrieved from http://www.gallup.com/poll/152021/Conservatives-Remain-Largest-Ideological-Group.aspx

Gallup. (2012c). *Record-high 40% of Americans identify as independents in '11.* Retrieved from http://www.gallup.com/poll/151943/Record-High-Americans-Identify-Independents.aspx

Gerber, A. S., Huber, G. A., Doherty, D., Dowling, C. M., & Ha, S. E. (2010). Personality and political attitudes: Relationships across issue domains and political contexts. *American Political Science Review, 104,* 111–133.

Gillath, O., & Hart, J. (2010). The effects of psychological security and insecurity on political attitudes and leadership preferences. *European Journal of Social Psychology, 40,* 122–134.

Graham, J., Haidt, J., & Nosek, B. A. (2009). Liberals and conservatives rely on different sets of moral foundations. *Journal of Personality and Social Psychology, 96,* 1029–1046.

Haidt, J. (2012). *Moral foundations theory homepage.* Retrieved September 16, 2012 from http://www.moralfoundations.org/

Haidt, J., & Graham, J. (2007). When morality opposes justice: Conservatives have moral intuitions that liberals may not recognize. *Social Justice Research, 20,* 98–116.

Haidt, J., Graham, J., & Joseph, C. (2009). Above and below left-right: Ideological narratives and moral foundations. *Psychological Inquiry, 20*(2), 110–119.

Haidt, J., & Hersh, M. (2001). Sexual morality: The cultures and reasons of liberals and conservatives. *Journal of Applied Social Psychology, 31,* 191–221.

Haidt, J., & Joseph, G. (2004). Intuitive ethics: How innately prepared intuitions generate culturally variable virtues. *Daedalus, 133,* 55–66.

Hatemi, P. K., Gillespie, N. A., Eaves, L. J., Maher, B. S., Webb, B. T., Heath, A. C., . . . Martin, N. G. (2011). A genome-wide analysis of liberal and conservative political attitudes. *Journal of Politics, 73*(1), 1–15.

Hayes, D., Shealy, C., Sivo, S., & Weinstein, Z. (1999, August). *Psychology, religion, and scale 5 (Religious Traditionalism) of the "BEVI".* Poster session presented at the meeting of the American Psychological Association, Boston, MA.

Hetherington, M., & Weiler, J. D. (2009). *Authoritarianism and polarization in American politics.* Cambridge: Cambridge University Press.

Hill, C., Johnson, M., Brinton, C., Staton, R., Sternberger, L., & Shealy. (2013, August). *The etiology of economic beliefs and values: Implications and applications from the Forum BEVI Project.* Poster presented at the annual meeting of the American Psychological Association, Honolulu, HI.

Ideology. (n.d.). In *Dictionary.com Unabridged.* Retrieved July 05, 2013, from http://dictionary.reference.com/browse/ideology

Inbar, Y., Pizarro, D., & Bloom P. (2009). Conservatives are more easily disgusted than liberals. *Cognition & Emotion, 23,* 714–725.

Isley, E., Shealy, C., Crandall, K., Sivo, S., & Reifsteck, J. (1999, August). *Relevance of the "BEVI" for research in developmental psychopathology.* Poster session presented at the meeting of the American Psychological Association, Boston, MA.

Iyer, R., Koleva, S. P., Graham, J., Ditto, P. H., & Haidt, J. (2011). *Understanding libertarian morality: The psychological roots of an individualist ideology* (Unpublished manuscript). University of Southern California, California, LA. Retrieved from http://www.moralfoundations.org/

Janoff-Bulman, R. (2009). To provide or protect: Motivational bases of political liberalism and conservatism. *Psychological Inquiry, 20*(2–3), 120–128.

Jost, J. T. (2006). The end of the end of ideology. *American Psychologist, 61*, 651–670.

Jost, J. T., & Banaji, M. R. (1994). The role of stereotyping in system-justification and the production of false consciousness. *British Journal of Social Psychology, 33*, 1–27.

Jost, J. T., Banaji, M. R., & Nosek, B. A. (2004). A decade of system justification theory: Accumulated evidence of conscious and unconscious bolstering of the status quo. *Political Psychology, 25*(6), 881–919.

Jost, J. T., Federico, C. M., & Napier, J. L. (2009). Political ideology: Its structure, functions, and elective affinities. *Annual Review of Psychology, 60*, 307–337.

Jost, J. T., Glaser, J., Kruglanski, A. W., & Sulloway, F. J. (2003). Political conservatism as motivated social cognition. *Psychological Bulletin, 129*, 339–375.

Jost, J. T., Napier, J. L., Thorisdottir, H., Gosling, S. D., Palfai, T. P., & Ostafin, B. (2007). Are needs to manage uncertainty and threat associated with political conservatism or ideological extremity? *Personality and Social Psychology Bulletin, 33*, 989–1007.

Kanai, R., Feilden, T., Firth, C., & Rees, G. (2011). Political orientations are correlated with brain structure in young adults. *Current Biology, 21*, 677–680.

Kandler, C., Bleidorn, W., & Riemann, R. (2012). Left or right? Sources of political orientation: The roles of genetic factors, cultural transmission, assortative mating, and personality. *Journal of Personality and Social Psychology, 102*, 633–645.

Kerlinger, F. N. (1984). *Liberalism and conservatism: The nature and structure of social attitudes.* Hillsdale, NJ: Erlbaum.

Koleva, S. P., & Rip, B. (2009). Attachment style and political ideology: A review of contradictory findings. *Social Justice Research, 22*, 241–258.

Lakoff, G. (2002). *Moral politics: How liberals and conservatives think.* Chicago, IL: University of Chicago Press.

Liberalism. (2012). In *Merriam-Webster.com.* Retrieved March 12, 2012 from http://www.merriam-webster.com/dictionary/liberalism

Libertarian Party. (2012). *Frequently asked questions.* Retrieved from http://www.lp.org/faq

Libertarian Party Platform. (2010). *Libertarian party 2010 platform.* Retrieved from http://www.lp.org/platform

Liu, B. S., & Ditto, P. H. (2012). What dilemma? Moral evaluations shape factual belief. *Social Psychological and Personality Science, 4*(3), 316–323. doi:10.1177/1948550612456045

McAdams, D. P., Albaugh, M., Farber, E., Daniels, J., Logan, R. L., & Olson, B. (2008). Family metaphors and moral intuitions: How conservatives and liberals narrate their lives. *Journal of Personality and Social Psychology, 95*(4), 978–990.

McCrae, R., & Sutin, A. R. (2009). Openness to experience. In M. Leary & R. Hoyle (Eds.), *Handbook of individual differences in social behavior* (pp. 257–273). New York, NY: The Guildford Press.

Mondak, J. J. (2010). *Personality and the foundations of political behavior.* New York, NY: Cambridge University Press.

Napier, J. L., & Jost, J. T. (2008). Why are conservatives happier than liberals? *Psychological Science, 19*(6), 565–572.

Oxley, D. R., Smith, K. B., Alford, J. R., Hibbing, M. V., Miller, J. L., Scalora, M., . . . Hibbing, J. R. (2011). Political attitudes vary with physiological traits. *Science, 321*, 1667–1670.

Pew Research Center. (2012, June 4). *Trends in American values: 1987-2012: Partisan polarization surges in Bush, Obama years.* Retrieved from http://www.people-press.org/files/legacy-pdf/06-04-12%20Values%20Release.pdf

Pratto, F., Sidanius, J., Stallworth, L., & Malle, B. (1994). Social dominance orientation: A personality variable predicting social and political attitudes. *Journal of Personality and Social Psychology, 67*, 741–763.

Pysarchik, D. I., Shealy, C. N., & Sternberger, B. (2007, July). *Examining outcome objectives for student learning and curricula*. Symposium presented at the meeting of the National Association of State Universities and Land Grant Colleges, Santa Rosa, CA.

Republican Party. (2012). *Republican national platform*. Retrieved November 10, 2012 from http://www.presidency.ucsb.edu/platforms.php

Roccato, M., & Ricolfi, L. (2005). On the correlation between right-wing authoritarianism and social dominance orientation. *Basic and Applied Social Psychology, 27*, 187–200.

Ross, M. (1993). *The culture of conflict*. New Haven, CT: Yale University Press.

Settle, J. E., Dawes, C. T., & Fowler, J. H. (2009). The heritability of partisan attachment. *Political Research Quarterly, 62*(3), 601–613.

Shealy, C. N. (1995). From Boys Town to Oliver Twist: Separating fact from fiction in welfare reform and out-of-home placement of children and youth. *American Psychologist, 50*(8), 565–580.

Shealy, C. N. (2000a, July). *The Beliefs, Events, and Values Inventory (BEVI): Implications for cross-cultural research and practice*. Paper presented at the meeting of the International Congress of Psychology, Stockholm, Sweden.

Shealy, C. N. (2000b, July). *The Beliefs, Events, and Values Inventory (BEVI): Implications for research and theory in social psychology*. Paper presented at the meeting of the International Congress of Psychology, Stockholm, Sweden.

Shealy, C. N. (2004). A model and method for "making" a Combined-Integrated psychologist: Equilintegration (EI) theory and the beliefs, events, and values inventory (BEVI) [Special Series]. *Journal of Clinical Psychology, 60*(10), 1065–1090. doi:10.1002/jclp.20035

Shealy, C. N. (2005). Justifying the justification hypothesis: Scientific-humanism, Equilintegration (EI) theory, and the Beliefs, Events and Values Inventory (BEVI). *Journal of Clinical Psychology, 61*(1), 81–106. doi:10.1002/jclp.20092

Shealy, C. N. (2015). *The Beliefs, Events, and Values Inventory (BEVI): Overview, implications, and guidelines. Test manual*. Harrisonburg, VA: Author.

Shealy, C. N. (2016). *Making sense of beliefs and values*. New York, NY: Springer Publishing.

Shealy, C. N., Bhuyan, D., & Sternberger, L. G. (2012). Cultivating the capacity to care in children and youth: Implications from EI theory, EI self, and BEVI. In U. Nayar (Ed.), *Child and adolescent mental health* (pp. 240–255). New Delhi, India: Sage Publications.

Sidanius, J., & Pratto, F. (1999). *Social dominance: An intergroup theory of social hierarchy and oppression*. Cambridge, England: Cambridge University Press.

Stenner, K. (2005). *The authoritarian dynamic*. Cambridge: Cambridge University Press.

Stevens, J. (2012, July 23). Political scientists are lousy forecasters. *The New York Times*, p. 6.

Stimson, J. A. (2004). *Tides of consent: How public opinion shapes American politics*. New York, NY: Cambridge University Press.

Tabit, M., Cozen, J., Dyjak-Leblank, K., Pendleton, C., Shealy, C., Sternberger, L., & Staton, R. (2011, June). *The sociocultural impact of denial: Empirical evidence from the Forum BEVI Project*. Poster presented at American Psychological Association Convention, Washington, DC.

Thornhill, R., & Fincher, C. L. (2007). What is the relevance of attachment and life history to political values? *Evolution and Human Behavior, 28*, 215–222.

Triandis, H. C., & Gelfand, M. J. (1998). Converging measurement of horizontal and vertical individualism and collectivism. *Journal of Personality and Social Psychology, 74*, 118–128.

Verhulst, B., Eaves, L. J., & Hatemi, P. K. (2012). Correlation not causation: The relationship between personality traits and political ideologies. *American Journal of Political Science, 56*, 34–51.

Weber, C., & Federico, C. M. (2007). Interpersonal attachment and patterns of ideological belief. *Political Psychology, 28*(4), 389–416.

Westen, D. (2007). *The political brain: The role of emotion in deciding the fate of the nation*. New York, NY: Public Affairs.

Zamboni, G., Gozzi, M., Krueger, F., Duhamel, J-R., Sirigu, A., & Grafman, J. (2009). Individualism, conservatism, and radicalism as criteria for processing political beliefs: A parametric fMRI study. *Social Neuroscience, 4*(5), 367–383.

*Timothy W. Brearly, Kees van den Bos, and
Charlene Tan*

10

THE NATURE AND ETIOLOGY OF RELIGIOUS CERTITUDE: IMPLICATIONS OF THE EI FRAMEWORK AND BELIEFS, EVENTS, AND VALUES INVENTORY

It infuriates me to be wrong when I know I'm right.

—Molière

In this time of globalization and collision of worldviews, the need for a deeper understanding of religious faith is more pressing than ever. Ideologies and religious systems that seem to contradict one's own beliefs often are perceived as a personal or cultural attack, which may lead to physical or relational violence against the perceived source of this attack (Silberman, Higgins, & Dweck, 2005; Tan, 2009). One does not have to look far to see examples of conflicts where the battle lines are drawn between those of different religious affiliations. A small sampling of recent examples includes the clashes between Protestants and Catholics in Northern Ireland, Jews and Muslims in the Middle East, Christians and Muslims in Bosnia and Sudan, Hindus and Muslims in India, and Muslim extremists' violence toward secularized America and the "Christian West" (Paloutzian & Kirkpatrick, 1995). While it may be argued that these conflicts are also about politics, ethnicity, or economics in addition to religious faith, the question of why differences in religious faith often create the borders between friend and enemy still remains largely unanswered (Yiftachel, 2006). In other words, it seems that differences in religious belief often are linked to conflict between individuals and groups, but the *why* of this association still appears unclear.

In grappling with this fundamental question of "why," we examine a wide range of issues in this chapter including the psychology of religion, the nature of belief certitude, as well as the theoretical associations and empirical correlates that are related to these constructs. We then present findings from a large-scale assessment project, which examines the etiology of beliefs and values. Based upon the accompanying theoretical model (Equilintegration or EI Theory) and assessment method (the Beliefs, Events, and Values Inventory [BEVI]), we offer a series of data-based conclusions and recommendations that address the study of religious certitude specifically as well as the nature of belief certitude more broadly. Chief among these is support of agnosticism, along a larger Continuum of Belief, as an intellectually defensible and interpersonally advantageous framework on matters over which definitive conclusions—those that are empirically, independently, and reliably verifiable—seem untenable. Finally, we translate this perspective into applied form by describing educational and psychological interventions that encourage critical reflective thinking about religious or nonreligious systems of thought, with a specific focus on cross-conviction dialogues. Through this comprehensive approach—which juxtaposes relevant literature with theory, data, and application—it is our hope that this chapter may help advance the overarching goal of facilitating greater understanding of why we believe what we believe regarding transcendental matters while offering possibilities for deeper and more constructive engagement with self and others on these fundamental matters that affect us all.

THE NATURE OF CERTITUDE

Certitude has been conceptualized in a number of ways (e.g., Arkin, Oleson, & Carroll, 2009), but for present purposes, is defined as the absence of doubt, which may result from a complex interaction among affective, attributional, developmental, and contextual processes, and is likewise associated with an inability to contemplate the potential legitimacy of another's perspective much less the potential shortcomings of one's own. The tendency toward certitude requires fidelity to an allied—and often unknown or unacknowledged—epistemological framework with its own set of assumptions (Shealy, 2005). Thus, without digressing too far into philosophical arguments regarding certainty, it may be helpful to highlight the dilemma that is inherent in claiming inviolability regarding one's own beliefs.

The problem of induction, for instance, challenges the assumption that we can deduce from our past experiences what will be certain in the future. For example, if a hot stove burned my hand in the past, I might be certain it will do so again in the future. However, this inductive logic assumes that the laws of nature are constant and uniform, while simultaneously ignoring the fact that additional variables must be accounted for as well (e.g., the fact that a stove burner may or may not be turned on). As an antidote to such linearity, philosophers such as Immanuel Kant, and psychologists such as Rollo May, have emphasized the subjective, phenomenological, and existential nature of human experience (Towler, 1984). From the standpoint of allied scholarship and practice in psychology, an individual may not necessarily "know" the complete and correct interpretation of reality, as if omnipotent, but should instead grant that multiple perspectives may be valid even if the apprehender regards them as improbable or even impossible (May, 1983; Spinelli, 2005).

On the other hand, even if someone may not be able to know something for certain, it does not necessarily follow that one concurrently may not have a high level of confidence that a particular proposition about the nature of reality is true (Van den Bos, 2011; Vickers, 1988). Some religious scholars have gone so far as to aver that one may experience legitimate certainty based on the assumption of supernaturally revealed ("a priori") truth. However, this sort of inductive logic appears sufficient only among those who concur on a particular religious source for their beliefs (Frame, 1987; Shealy, 2005). Though many are unaware of these epistemological nuances, we argue that reflection upon them encourages an informed yet humble approach toward competing perspectives. This line of reasoning has been popularized recently by works tailored to the broader reading public, such as *Being Wrong*, which essentially maintains that one's capacity to embrace the possibility of being mistaken is perhaps better viewed of as a sign of cognitive competence than human fallibility (Harford, 2011; Schultz, 2010).

Moreover, it is not just the religious who are subject to such processes, since the expression of certitude, which so often underlies religious belief, may be observed also in the attitudes and assertions of the avowedly "nonreligious." For instance, Richard Dawkins, a prominent atheist, has declared that the end of religious faith could solve many of the world's most pressing conflicts (2006). In contrast, others have pointed out the "religiousness" of such absolutist claims and their concurrent hostility toward the religious "other" (Haidt, 2007; Himmelfarb, 2012; Jackson & Hunsberger, 1999). Due to the apparent prevalence of these types of claims from a variety of ideological perspectives, some have concluded that the multiplicity of views present in our globalized world has created a "postmodern paradox," which has made the certainty provided by absolutist worldviews especially attractive (Dunn, 1998; Hogg, 2011; Hogg, Adelman, & Blagg, 2010). Regardless, whether the content of one's worldview is religious or nonreligious, it seems that both of these perspectives often are held with a sense of certitude that prompts rejection of or even attacks toward those who hold a conflicting perspective (e.g., Skitka, Bauman, & Lytle, 2009; Skitka & Mullen, 2002).

This situation is rendered even more complex when we consider that many people who hold such views often feel justified by a sincerely held belief that they are creating a better world (Silberman et al., 2005). The philosopher and political theorist Isaiah Berlin appears to have had this dynamic in mind when he observed:

> If one really believes that [an "Ultimate Solution"] is possible, then surely no cost would be too high a price to pay for that? To make such an omelet, there is surely no limit to the number of eggs that should be broken. . .If your desire to save mankind is serious, you must harden your heart, and not reckon the cost. (as cited in Murphy, 2012, p. SR12)

Essentially, then, claims that are certain regarding transcendental matters exist both within and beyond the bounds of organized religion. Why would this be? On the one hand, expressers of certitude—in a religious and nonreligious realm—may experience a high psychological need for closure (Brandt, 2010). From this perspective, closure requires an a priori disregard for the multiplicity of other competing claims, with a lack of sensitivity to the inherently ambiguous nature of truth claims in general, due to the security experienced by envelopment within one's perceived base of factual knowledge. Evidence for this phenomenon is provided by studies, which have found that an expression of certitude often is intimately connected with overt assuredness regarding the nature and impact of "truth" in the world (Brandt, 2010; Hogg, 2005; Van den Bos, Euwema, Poortvliet, & Maas, 2007). For instance, research illustrates that the degree to which one is able to acknowledge uncertainty predicts the amount of negative affect (e.g., anger) toward statements that strongly contradict one's own perspectives, including those of a religious nature (i.e., the higher the degree of certainty, the higher the degree of negative affect) (Van den Bos, Van Ameijde, & Van Gorp, 2006; Van den Bos et al., 2012).

Such findings beg the following questions: Is it possible to coexist peacefully with others who hold beliefs that contradict—sometimes vociferously—one's own? How can someone hold religious or nonreligious beliefs without becoming prejudiced toward those who do not grant legitimacy to one's own version of reality (Shealy, 2005)? Such questions are core to the psychological study of religion, as psychologists ultimately are concerned with increasing "people's understanding of themselves and others. . .to. . .improve the condition of individuals, organizations, and society" (American Psychological Association, 2010, p. 2). From an ethical standpoint, the following rationale for such an emphasis by psychology and psychologists—as well as allied scholars and practitioners should be clear: When people are unable to peacefully coexist with those who hold different or contradictory beliefs, they are motivated to attack the "freedom of inquiry and expression," instead of seeking to increase their understanding of the "other," which psychologists are expected to promote and preserve (p. 2; Silberman et al., 2005; Tan, 2009; Van den Bos et al., 2006). As Cilliers (2002) maintains, "It is only when [people] have a deep understanding of their own religious traditions and are willing to learn and recognize the richness of other religious traditions that constructive cooperation can take place between groups from different faiths" (p. 58). In this chapter, then, we contend that one's ability to tolerate uncertainty—and thus constructively engage those with religious perspectives that are different—is associated with a particular psychological structure, which has been formed over one's life span via an interaction of multiple formative variables (e.g., demographics, experiences, culture). Moreover, this self-structure is expressed through both conscious beliefs and values as well as through the activation of unconscious emotional schemas, which directly affect the holding and expression of one's religious beliefs—or nonreligious beliefs—in relation to others (Shealy, 2016).

PSYCHOLOGICAL PERSPECTIVES ON RELIGIOUS CERTITUDE

Building upon this introduction to the construct of certitude, it may be helpful to consider how the psychological study of religion has informed our understanding of the nature of religious belief. In much of the scholarly literature, the term *religion* refers to "narrow, dogmatic beliefs and obligatory observances" (Wulff, 1996, p. 47). In this sense, *religion* may be distinguished from more intrinsic forms of religious belief (Fischer, Greitemeyer, Kastenmüller, Jonas, & Frey, 2006) as well as *spirituality*, which often refers to the "mysterious realm of transcendent experience" (Wulff, 1996, p. 47). For present purposes, unless otherwise noted, the term religion is used in its broadest sense, which encompasses both religion and spirituality. However, in order to have an accurate view of psychology's historical relationship with religion, while facilitating a more nuanced examination of religious certainty, it may be helpful to overview the major perspectives on religion that have dominated this field of inquiry over the years.

The earliest psychological conceptualizations of religion tended to be critical in nature, often seeing it as a defense against reality (Paragment & Park, 1995). For example, Freud perceived religion to be a form of "wish fulfillment," which was a product of infantile longings for a powerful and protective father figure, as well as an amalgamation of rituals, which were consistent with the obsessive symptoms of neurosis. Although Freud saw religion as being pragmatically useful in its ability to tame destructive human instincts, he also felt it tended to promote psychological servitude (Paloutzian & Kirkpatrick, 1995). Thus, Freud proposed that if people could abandon religion and courageously face the unknowns of their own existence, human civilization would be the better for it. Juxtaposing this perspective with our current focus, one might conclude that Freud believed that religious people needed courageously to accept noncertitude (Wulff, 1996).

In contrast to Freud's dynamic approach, the early behaviorists linked religious belief to environmentally mediated phenomena, such as "superstitious" behavior, which sought to impose order and predictability upon events and phenomena that seemed outside of an organism's control. In other words, they attempted to demonstrate that religious ideation could parsimoniously be explained by naturalistic and behavioral laws. For example, B.F. Skinner conceptualized religion as a product of reinforcement by an individual's religious priests, creeds, and codes. In a well-known experiment to illustrate such processes, he conditioned pigeons to exhibit superstitious behavior in order to elicit pellets of food (Skinner, 1948). Another behaviorist, George Vetter, compared human religious belief to "superstitious behavior" in animals (such as pigeons and rats), which arises as a response to unpredictable or uncontrollable situations (Vetter, 1958). Along complementary lines, James Leuba demonstrated experimentally that he could produce a mystical experience in subjects through the use of psychedelic drugs. On the basis of this work, he concluded that spiritual experiences were naive illusions that are explained through physiological processes. It is interesting to note, however, that Leuba also saw this "spiritual urge" as an essential characteristic of human nature. Resisting the exclusivity of traditional religious expressions, he worked to found religious societies that used ceremony, prayer, and confession apart from the worship of a particular god (Leuba, 1925; Leuba, 1950).

Although some behaviorists might have granted that religion could have social benefits, it was seen as far better for "believers" to lead principled and meaningful lives without needing the proverbial crutch of supernatural beliefs (Skinner, 1987). George Vetter (1958) asserted this viewpoint in his work, *Religion and Magic: Their Psychological Nature, Origin, and Function*:

> The priesthoods of whatever stripe can never live down, nor make amends for, their disgraceful role in retarding the development of modern science during the past millennium in Christendom. . .Supernaturalism is, in its social functions and consequences, a dangerous opiate. And, what is perhaps even worse, it discourages objective attempts at intelligent social trial-and-error, planning, and even research, and undermines man's faith in his own resources. (p. 515)

Although many were quite critical of religion, other early and nonbehavioral psychologists apprehended religion in a more favorable light. For example, in his seminal *Varieties of Religious Experience*, William James (1902) agreed that for some people, religion could be dangerous and a sign of naiveté. However, through his observations of a wide variety of religious persons, he concluded that when religious belief was combined with intellectual rigor (which he referred to as "healthy-minded" religion), levels of "human excellence" could be achieved, which could not otherwise be reached.

From an alternative but no less sympathetic standpoint, Carl Jung saw religious experience as being rooted in "archetypes," which are part of a universal human psyche that he referred to as the "collective unconscious." Such experiences, and their expression through participation in religious traditions, were central to an individual's process of individuation and self-realization. According to Jung, modern humans were vulnerable to experiencing conflicts regarding the complexities and seeming contradictions of religious belief, which might lead to a loss of a transcending perspective on life. This conclusion was due largely to his experiences as a clinician, where he observed:

> It is safe to say that every one of [my patients over the age of thirty-five] fell ill because he had lost what the living religions of every age have given to their followers, and none of them has been really healed who did not regain his religious outlook. (Jung, 1933, p. 229)

As such, Jung proposed that religious experiences should be explored and facilitated in order to promote higher levels of *human consciousness*, which could allow the successful navigation of the individuation process apart from the boundaries of traditional religion. In this way, Jung sought to introduce an inclusive religious system, which would transcend the divisive certitude of traditional religious perspectives. Jung's theory largely has been ignored by the field of psychology due to its esoteric leanings as well as attendant difficulty with the empirical investigation of its central constructs. However, his views have contributed to a more positive valuation, by psychologists and nonpsychologists, of spiritual/religious experience in human development and functioning. (Wulff, 1996)

Like Freud, Erik Erikson (1950) saw correlations between one's religious convictions and early developmental experiences and needs. However, instead of perceiving this linkage as evidence for the problematic substitution of religion for unmet infantile needs, he saw religion as potentially aligning with the most basic yearnings of the self. More specifically, the religious inclination was a manifestation of deep human needs to experience a sense of "trust" that life ultimately is benevolent. Erikson also believed that religion could facilitate wisdom, which was a focus of his final stage of human development—ego integrity versus despair—and relevant to one's ability to accept the inevitability of his or her own death. Like other theorists, Erikson warned that religious belief could be associated with abuse and exploitation; however, he perceived religious experience to be an integral component of mature human development, arguing that healthy adults recognized and nurtured their spiritual inclinations (Kiesling, 2008; Wulff, 1996).

From the perspective of humanistic psychology, Erich Fromm conceptualized the impulse toward religion as an attempt to resolve the existential anxiety, which derives from humanity's experienced separation from other creatures due to our unique capacity for self awareness. Moreover, he defined "religion" as any system of thought or action that was shared by a group, provided an object of devotion, and fostered an orientation toward meaning making. He also separated religions into two broad types: *humanistic* (God as an example of the ideal person; focused on self-realization; loving; joyful) and *authoritarian* (God possesses all of the ideal yet unachievable human qualities; people are limited in their power; guilt is a primary experiential state) (Awad & Hall-Clark, 2009; Fromm, 1950). Fromm's ideas have received some empirical support, including a study, which found that religious commitment was associated with increased levels of personal growth when the death of a close friend was attributed to a loving god (Park & Cohen, 1993). In some ways, Fromm's division of religion into authoritarian and humanistic types parallels the difference between religious convictions characterized by a sense of certitude versus those that are held in the context of a personally empowering quest for spiritual meaning making.

Another important conceptualization of religion from a humanistic standpoint was that of Abraham Maslow (1964), who distinguished between religious people who had experienced a "peak experience" and those who either had not or had become defended against such a state. For Maslow, a "peak experience" was a period of intense feelings of wholeness and fusion with the world in which one feels fully alive and becomes aware of absolute values such as truth, justice, and beauty. According to Maslow, religious people who had not experienced a "peak experience" were looking to a religious system which was meant to preserve the "peak experience" of someone in the past, with the lamentable consequence of preventing present-day followers from actually encountering such an experience for themselves. More specifically,

What happens to many people. . .is that they simply concretize all of the symbols, all of the words, all of the statues, all of the ceremonies, and by a process of functional autonomy make them, rather than the original revelation, into the sacred. . .In [this] idolatry the essential meaning gets so lost in concretizations that these finally become hostile to the original mystical experiences, to mystics, and to prophets in general, that is, to the very people that we might call from our present point of view the truly religious people. (Maslow, 1964, pp. 24–25)

One substantive critique of Maslow was that his views were based in part on the traits of figures that he saw as historical exemplars of self-actualization (such as Martin Luther King and Jesus) without empirical data to support his hypotheses (Wulff, 1996). Nonetheless, Maslow's basic propositions have received considerable interest by psychologists and nonpsychologists. For present purposes, it may be hypothesized that someone who experiences a high degree of certainty in their religious convictions would have less capacity or inclination for the transcendent "peak experiences" that Maslow described.

From another vantage point, aligned with the theoretical postulates and applied interventions of the psychodynamic school, attachment and object relations theorists often maintain that the ways we interact with our experience of God are associated intimately with our historical experiences as well as the ways in which we interact with others. In other words, if our approach to the divine is shaped by an attitude characterized by certitude, then this same attitude may well characterize our encounters with the "other" (e.g., resulting in less capacity or inclination toward understanding and the ability to experience and express a full range of emotions within interpersonal relationships). One exemplar of this perspective was Donald Winnicott (1953, 1971), who saw religion not as a universal neurosis as viewed by Freud, but rather as a relationship with the divine that is tied to an individual's internalized structure for relationships. Therefore, one's relationship with God could either be beneficial or detrimental depending on the level of object relations maturity through which such relationships were experienced and expressed. This hypothesis is still being explored, with at least one study concluding that there is a strong correlation between the quality and maturity of a person's relationship with God and the maturity of his or her relations with others (Hall, Brokaw, Edwards, & Pike, 1998).

Attachment theorists also have hypothesized that religious commitments to God may be a form of attachment relationship. Examples of such putative phenomena include pursuing God through prayer and rituals, using God for comfort during times of distress, and experiencing God as a secure base for approaching the unknown. Furthermore, it has been suggested that individuals with secure attachments experience relationships with a loving god, while individuals with insecure attachments are more likely to perceive God as distant—or to avoid forming a relationship with God at all. Evidence for such processes has been found in cultures where parenting style correlates with the overriding cultural conceptualization of God (Rohner, 1986). Along similar lines, Granqvist (2007) found that experiences with insensitive parents (e.g., rejecting and/or role-reversing) were associated with changes in religious orientation in response to life stressors. Likewise, Davis (2009) found a correlation between attachment anxiety and avoidance vis-à-vis one's experience and perception of God.

Along similar lines, other scholars have found evidence that some may use their relationships with God as a compensation for previous insecure attachments. For instance, Kirkpatrick and Shaver (1990) found that people who grew up in relatively nonreligious families, and reported avoidant attachments with their caregivers, were more likely to be religious as adults (when compared to other attachment styles).

Also, regardless of the religiosity of their parents, those categorized as avoidant experienced the highest rates of sudden religious conversions among the various attachment styles. Regardless of whether one is reenacting or compensating for an attachment experience, such studies seem to support the hypothesis that one's religious experience may be correlated with attachment style, life experiences vis-à-vis caregivers, and the basic human needs that attachment relations are designed to meet (e.g., Shealy, Bhuyan, & Sternberger, 2012).

At first glance, it might seem that a securely attached adult would be certain of his or her relationship with God, whether affiliating or disaffiliating. In deference to Erikson (1950), however, it is important to remember that secure attachment is characterized more by the experience of trust in others and the larger world than is insecure attachment. This observation suggests that a more securely attached individual might be more capable of tolerating a lack of certainty, which may emerge in a variety of spheres (e.g., Spaeth, Schwartz, Nayar, & Ma, 2016). For example, interpersonally, such individuals would arguably be able to tolerate the inherent uncertainties that characterize intimate relationships because they default to a trusting attitude toward the "other" (regardless of whether that "other" is perceived as a physical or a spiritual being). In contrast, an insecurely attached person might be more inclined to adopt a perspective—and seek to experience physical and/or spiritual relationships—grounded in certainty. In some ways, through such relational "foreclosure," they might succeed in freeing themselves from the uncertainty of trusting in the reality of one's spiritual experience by "faith and not by sight" (e.g., as articulated by the Christian apostle Paul in his second letter to the Corinthian church). On the other hand, as Mikulincer and Shaver (2001) found, when one's secure attachment schema is activated by the subliminal presentation of words that exemplify it (e.g., love, support), there is a tendency to exhibit increased tolerance for out-groups, even when the perspectives of such groups challenge one's own belief system.

Historically speaking, Gordon Allport was one of the most prominent and enduring thinkers regarding the conceptualization and psychological study of religion. At the core of his approach was the construct of the "mature religious sentiment," which he described as a well-differentiated and complex faith, which is relatively independent of its origins in childhood needs, and consistently directive of a person's ethical standards, even though it is held with some level of uncertainty or doubt. According to Allport (1969), such a framework "never seems satisfied unless it is dealing with matters central to all existence" (p. 78) and faces this profound calling "without absolute certainty. . .[as] the mature religious sentiment is ordinarily fashioned in the workshop of doubt" (p. 83). A person who holds this "mature religious sentiment" sees his or her faith as a working hypothesis, which gives a basis for values and infuses one's life with energy (Wulff, 1996), a perspective that perhaps is consistent with the Biblical declaration that "faith is an assurance of things hoped for, the conviction of things not seen" (Hebrews 11:1). From this perspective, faith is seen as an end in itself, in contrast with expressions of religious belief that are used instrumentally to attain other psychological, political, or social ends (Flere, Edwards, & Klanjsek, 2008). Allport labeled this first type of religious belief "intrinsic," hypothesizing that it was associated with positive psychological outcomes (Pargament & Park, 1995). Allport regarded the second type of religious belief "extrinsic" or "immature religiosity," which seemed to accommodate psychological needs for security and comfort and/or to legitimate one's particular political or group identity (Awad & Hall-Clark, 2009).

In addition to congruence with other theorists noted previously, echoes of attachment theory resonate here, in that religion is understood again as a means to pursue existential comfort and security. According to Allport (1969), extrinsic religion can address these psychological needs by defining one's particular religious group identity against other groups through an attitude characterized by certainty. Intrinsic religion, on the other hand, sees religious belief as a value unto itself—an appreciation of one's subjective experience of God rather than an investment in ensuring that others validate that subjective experience. Rather than seeking to alleviate the existential anxiety that comes from a lack of certainty, intrinsic religion revels in the experience of faith itself. This extrinsic/intrinsic dichotomy parallels the previous proposal that while certitude may be associated with interreligious conflict, faith results in self aware and humble conviction, which is capable, even desirous, of dialoging with those who hold differing religious beliefs and values (Awad & Hall-Clark, 2009; Pargament & Park, 1995; Wulff, 1996).

Religious Certitude and Prejudice

Consistent with this central proposition regarding intrinsic versus extrinsic religiosity, it also was Allport's (1969) hypothesis that extrinsic religiousness was the source of prejudicial and authoritarian attitudes, which historically have been associated with religion. Although many studies have found a correlation between religion and prejudice in the past, this apparent connection has proven to be complex. For instance, along with nonreligious persons, highly committed religious persons also have been found in some studies to be among the least prejudiced groups in society (e.g., Ford, Brignall, VanValey, & Macaluso, 2009; Gorsuch & Aleshire, 1974; Kirkpatrick, 1993; Laythe, Finkel, Bringle, & Kirkpatrick, 2002). Allport's dichotomy offers plausible illumination regarding this potentially confusing relationship between religion and prejudice. For instance, studies have indicated that intrinsic religiosity is associated with less prejudice toward gays, lesbians, and ethnic minorities than extrinsic religiosity. So, it seems possible both to be highly committed from a religious perspective but also highly intrinsic, and thus less prejudiced toward others. On the other hand, it may be that highly intrinsic religious persons may simply be more motivated to hide their prejudice (Awad & Hall-Clark, 2009).

Although a number of conceptual and psychometric problems with Allport's intrinsic/extrinsic categorization have been illuminated (such as its ambiguity and presupposition of particular religious commitments), his framing of the complex differences in how people experience and express their religious beliefs continues to influence our understanding of these phenomena (Wulff, 1996). In any case, regarding the relationship between religious belief and prejudice, definitive conclusions remain elusive, mainly because it appears that the type of religious engagement people experience (e.g., intrinsic versus extrinsic) may mediate the degree of prejudice that is experienced. Such complexity is compounded further by the fact that religious commitments may range from very strong, to very weak, to nonexistent. Hopefully, the current investigation of such processes vis-à-vis belief certitude will provide a helpful frame for differentiating between religious expressions that impede—or facilitate—authentic intergroup communication and understanding regarding matters of religion.

Religious Quest Versus Religious Fundamentalism

Although Allport (1969) saw intrinsic and extrinsic religious inclinations in dichotomous terms, they have not been shown to be well correlated in this way. In fact, some research has supported the possibility that spiritual, psychological, and social motivations do not necessarily contradict one another (Pargament & Park, 1995). In an attempt to address these complex interactions, Daniel Batson (1976) added a third orientation, "quest," which includes constructs such as doubt, complexity, and openness to perspective change. Reminiscent of the previously mentioned ideas of Immanuel Kant and Rollo May, the quest orientation has been described as "honestly facing existential questions in all their complexity, while at the same time resisting clear-cut pat answers" (Batson, Schoenrade, & Ventis, 1993, p. 166). Thus, those with a "quest" orientation perceive that they may not know the absolute truth regarding spiritual matters; however, they also maintain that asking questions and searching for answers are important aspects in the process of believing. Previous studies have correlated a "quest" orientation with self-acceptance, open-mindedness, flexibility, helpfulness, and responsiveness toward others, while also being inversely correlated with prejudice (Batson et al., 1993; Hunsberger, 1995; Hunsberger & Jackson, 2005). However, such conclusions have been questioned on grounds similar to the intrinsic/extrinsic orientations. For instance, one study found that while the quest scale might be partially valid in Christian settings, it may not be for Muslims (Flere et al., 2008). Another study concluded that the prevalence of a quest orientation declines with age (Wulff, 1996). Regardless, it is not difficult to apprehend the similarities between this orientation and the hypothesis that a relatively open and inquisitive inclination to grapple with one's own religious commitments would be associated with a resistance toward the certainty that "final answers" provide.

As a point of contrast to the quest framework, an orientation toward religious fundamentalism also has been proposed to explain processes of certitude. From this perspective, fundamentalists of various faiths typically are distinguished by the following deeply held beliefs; (a) one's particular religious perspectives are the only inerrant truth; (b) such truth is opposed by evil forces which must be fought; (c) such beliefs must be followed today the way they were perceived to be followed in the past; and finally (d) those who endorse and follow such beliefs have a special relationship with one or more deities (e.g., see Altemeyer and Hunsberger, 1992; McFarland, 1989; Shealy, 2005). In fact, Altemeyer and Hunsberger have found a strong negative correlation between these two orientations. Although someone with a quest orientation may share many of the same doctrinal perspectives as a religious fundamentalist, he or she arguably would differ in the level of certitude with which these perspectives are held. In short, the quest orientation—with its focus on doubt, complexity, and openness to a change—is representative of a less "certain" holding of one's faith. Religious fundamentalism, on the other hand, is aligned highly with certitude regarding the inerrant truth of at least some of its religious teachings as well as resistance toward any change in the way that this "truth" is understood or followed (Tan, 2009).

Some studies have pointed to religious fundamentalism as the religious manifestation of Right Wing Authoritarianism (RWA) (Altemeyer & Hunsberger, 1992; Hunsberger, 1995; Laythe, Finkel, & Kirkpatrick, 2001). Among other levels of analysis, this perspective is interesting in terms of the interface between religion and governance (e.g., how some oppressive Central American regimes encourage Christian missionaries to evangelize in their countries). Such findings are consistent with data demonstrating that people are less likely to question the government after an experience of religious conversion (Pargament & Park, 1995). Of course, such scholarship has strong historical roots. For example, and consistent with Freud and Skinner, Karl Marx saw religion as an "opiate of the masses," which militated against social unrest. Along similar lines, Niccolò Machiavelli emblematically suggested that leaders should maintain the religious structures of their countries in order to keep the people "well conducted" (Silberman et al., 2005). As suggested previously, a religious perspective of certitude generally would be associated with resistance to political changes within authoritarian-leaning regimes, along with their theological concomitants, as well as the inevitable cognitive and emotional disequilibrium that these changes would foster. Although we have highlighted two perspectives of religious "quest" and religious "fundamentalism," it should be noted that these are not necessarily incompatible or mutually exclusive. In other words, overlaps and variations in the two extremes also exist. For example, a believer may hold fundamentalist attitudes in relation to certain doctrines, while remaining open to learning about new or alternative perspectives regarding other doctrines (Tan, 2009).

Religious Certitude and Religious Orthodoxy

As with most psychological constructs that bear on the interaction of religiosity and other attitudinal phenomena, such as prejudice, correlational trends are complex, but discernible. For example, Kirkpatrick (1993) found that religious fundamentalism was associated with five different forms of prejudice, while Christian orthodoxy either was inversely related or unrelated to each of these same scales. For this reason, some researchers have looked to Christian orthodoxy (the degree to which someone has internalized traditional Christian tenants) as a useful measure for differentiating the effects of RWA and/or religious fundamentalism from actual religious beliefs (Ford et al., 2009; Hunsberger, 1989; Laythe et al., 2001; Laythe et al., 2002). Christian orthodoxy has in fact been shown to correlate with less prejudicial attitudes in a number of analyses. For instance, one study confirmed that religious fundamentalism and RWA predicted negative attitudes toward homosexual people. However, the same study found that Christian orthodoxy predicted positive attitudes toward members of this group (Eunike, 2009; Ford et al., 2009). These findings seem to support a central tenet, that prejudice may be related to authoritarian attitudes of certitude, rather than the doctrinal content of one's religious belief. Furthermore, recent work on religious fundamentalism suggests that it too may vary in terms of intensity (i.e., on a continuum from high fundamentalism to low fundamentalism), with associations to related cognitive, emotional, and behavioral processes. For instance, although an individual otherwise inclined toward fundamentalism may not approve of a certain behavior (i.e., homosexual sex), he or she may still express positive feelings toward gay people if able and willing—affectively and cognitively—to "separate the sinner from the sin" (Hunsberger & Jackson, 2005).

Religious Certitude and Identity Closure

Other research has attempted to differentiate religious persons by building on Marcia's (1966) emphasis on exploration and commitment vis-à-vis identity development. In particular, Kiesling (2008) suggested that spiritual identity could be understood through the dimensions of "role salience" (the importance of spirituality to one's sense of identity) and "role flexibility" (the extent to which one has considered changes in his or her spiritual identity). In this study, the "foreclosed" group was composed of individuals who expressed a high commitment to their faith, but without much exploration of other options. For these people, spiritual change consisted of deepening their current faith. Such individuals showed few signs of reflection or doubt, and tended to emphasize their relationships with God as their primary religious motivation. The second, "moratorium" group reported high levels of religious exploration, but had not arrived at a place of commitment. These individuals often reported challenging experiences, which were associated with serious questions and doubts. They saw themselves as arbiters of truth as opposed to authorities, and typically came from families that did not participate in religious practices. The final "achieved" group had navigated a period of religious exploration that had culminated in personal religious commitments. Such individuals were able to describe their spiritual identities clearly and specifically, emphasizing an enhanced capacity to relate with others, which they attributed to their religious experiences and commitments. Such individuals were also highly reflective about their religious ideation in the past, and expected to remain so in regard to their faith in the future. However, they had experienced attenuation of their previous religious crisis, and now understood themselves as being more settled and spiritually at ease (Kiesling, 2008). Thus, among other implications, if high fundamentalism is associated with prejudice, one potential antidote may be the cultivation and valuation of an ongoing open and reflective religious framework as a person develops, rather than seeking to "foreclose" religious identity via the inculcation of unshakable certitude (e.g., Spaeth et al., 2016; Tan, 2009).

It should be emphasized that a belief in spiritually revealed truths or inspired texts may well occur for individuals who otherwise lack a sense of certitude regarding these truths or texts. As studies of Christian orthodoxy have illustrated, one may hold traditional religious beliefs in a fundamentalist/authoritarian manner, characterized by a form of certitude that is associated with prejudice and intergroup conflict. However, one also may hold these traditional beliefs in an open/reflective manner, characterized by an appreciation of the apparent elusiveness of absolute certainty in regard to any truth claim (whether it be "religious" or "scientific"). Furthermore, these reflective beliefs seem to be associated with greater interest in, and acceptance of, those who hold different perspectives. In short, consistent with such scholarship, the fact that James, Leuba, Maslow, Jung, Erikson, and many other thinkers grant that a faith journey and faith commitments have the potential to facilitate generative purposes at individual, group, and societal levels makes a case against throwing the proverbial "baby" of religious belief out with the "bathwater" of certitude.

Religious Certitude and Neuroscience

As a final consideration along these lines, recent perspectives rooted in neuroscience have added an entirely new level of analysis to the study of religious certitude. For example, Bargh and Chartrand (1999) have provided evidence that nonconscious processes, rather than conscious beliefs, mediate much of our behavior, religious and not. In other words, deep emotional responses in the brain, rather than abstract religious principles alone, may more parsimoniously explain why people behave as they do toward others (e.g., Haidt, 2007; Newberg & Waldman, 2006). Such findings lend support to the central contention here that it is necessary, but by no means sufficient, to understand the content of religious belief. Of potentially greater importance, particularly in relation to understanding the dynamics of interbelief conflict, is the certainty with which beliefs are held as well as *why* such beliefs have been internalized with such certainty in the first place. In other words, to understand why some individuals are more inclined to experience and express certitude in regard to their religious beliefs, we may need to account for formative variables (e.g., life history, demographics) that are associated with the likelihood of certitude, or the lack thereof, as well as allied affective, biological, and cognitive processes that may mediate or at least covary with the relative degree of religious certitude that an individual expresses (Shealy, 2005). By accounting for such complexity in real time, taking into consideration individual differences among us, we may be better able to "make sense" of the messy complexity that culminates in a relative degree of religious or nonreligious certitude.

EXAMINING RELIGIOUS CERTITUDE THROUGH THE EI MODEL AND BEVI METHOD

Accounting for the origins of religious certitude—through an interdisciplinary, measurable, and nuanced understanding of the etiological factors associated with religiousness—has been called for in the scholarly literature (e.g., Bloom, 2007; Paloutzian & Kirkpatrick, 1995; Pargament & Park, 1995). By utilizing such an approach, it may become feasible to parse cause and effect vis-à-vis religious certainty, and reliably apply such understanding to the individual case. Consistent with such a call, but eschewing any definitive claims, an overview of the three main components of the present approach—Equilintegration (EI) Theory, the EI Self, and the BEVI—may be helpful at this juncture (see Chapters 2, 3, and 4 for a full explication). Essentially, Equilintegration (EI) Theory seeks to explain "the processes by which beliefs, values, and 'worldviews' are acquired and maintained, why their alteration is typically resisted, and how and under what circumstances their modification occurs" (Shealy, 2004, p. 1075). Derivative of EI Theory, the Equilintegration or EI Self explains the integrative and synergistic processes by which beliefs and values are acquired, maintained, and transformed as well as how they may be linked to the formative variables, core needs, and adaptive potential of the self (Shealy, 2016). Informed by scholarship in a range of key areas (e.g., "needs-based" research and theory; developmental psychopathology; social cognition; affect regulation; psychotherapy processes and outcomes; theories and models of "self"), the EI Self seeks to illustrate how the interaction between core human needs (e.g., for attachment, affiliation) and formative variables (e.g., caregiver, culture) often leads to particular kinds of beliefs and values about self, others, and the world at large, that are internalized over the course of development and across the life span.

Concomitant with EI Theory and the EI Self, the BEVI is a comprehensive analytic tool in development since the early 1990s that examines how and why we come to see ourselves, others, and the larger world as we do (e.g., how life experiences, culture, and context affect our beliefs, values, and worldview) as well as the influence of such processes on multiple aspects of human functioning (e.g., learning processes, relationships, personal growth, the pursuit of life goals). For example, the BEVI assesses processes such as: basic openness; the tendency to (or not to) stereotype in particular ways; self- and emotional awareness; preferred strategies for making sense of why "other" people and cultures "do what they do"; global engagement (e.g., receptivity to different cultures, religions, and social practices); and worldview shift (e.g., the degree to which beliefs and values change as a result of specific experiences).

BEVI results are translated into reports at the individual, group, and organizational levels and used in a variety of contexts for applied and research purposes (e.g., to track and examine changes in worldviews over time) (e.g., Brearly, 2012; Hill et al., 2013; Shealy, 2004, 2005, 2016; Shealy, Bhuyan, & Sternberger, 2012; for more information about the BEVI, including a description of scales, see Chapter 4).

RESEARCH QUESTIONS AND RESULTS

This study is exploratory in that we are attempting to understand the relationship between formative variables (e.g., life history, demographics), mediators (various scales on the BEVI), and outcomes (e.g., self-reported religious or nonreligious affiliation) in a manner that is consistent with other analytic work with this measure. Analyses were developed on the basis of a large dataset (N = 2331) collected during 2011 to 2012 from the Forum BEVI Project, a multi-institution, multiyear project coordinated by the Forum on Education Abroad (www.forumea.org) and the International Beliefs and Values Institute (www.ibavi.org). Participants primarily included undergraduate students (96.7%), although a small sample of graduate students (3.3%) also was included, all of whom were recruited through a range of learning experiences (e.g., study abroad, residential learning communities, general education courses with a focus on transformative/multicultural learning). The sample ranged between the ages of 17 and 62, with an average age of 19; 3.9% fell into the age range of 26 to 62, with another 0.9 % falling into the range of 12 to 17, and the majority falling between the ages of 18 and 25. Although the majority of participants reported as U.S. citizens (93.3%), non-U.S. citizens also were included in the sample (6.7%) resulting in representation from 38 different countries of origin. Of the sample, 79.1% reported as Caucasian with 20.9% as non-Caucasian (6.6% Black or African American; 0.9% American Indian or Alaskan Native; 7.4% Asian or Pacific Islander; 2.9% Hispanic/Latino; 3% Other). Finally, from the standpoint of gender, 40.8% of the sample was female, with 59.2% male. All participants were required to provide informed consent as determined by multiple Institutional Review Boards processes, and participation was entirely voluntary. Participants were not required to complete the BEVI, and could elect to discontinue participation at any time. Analyses were conducted via Statistical Package for the Social Sciences (SPSS) and MPLUS, and consist of analysis of variance (ANOVAs), regression analyses, and structural equation modeling (SEM). More information on the Forum BEVI Project is available in Chapter 4 and at www.ibavi.org/content/featured-projects. Our data analyses for this exploratory study will focus on addressing five interrelated questions: (a) how does the BEVI operationalize religious certitude; (b) who is most likely, from a demographic standpoint, to score highly on the BEVI's measurement of this construct; (c) how does the BEVI's measurement of religious certitude relate to other BEVI scales; (d) what variance in religious certitude exists both within and between religious groups; and (e) to what extent do specific formative variables (e.g., family history) predict religious certitude.

Question 1: How does the BEVI operationalize religious certitude?

On the BEVI, the Socioreligious Traditionalism scale likely is related to "religious certitude" as discussed, as it consists of items indicating strong, traditional religious beliefs, a relatively unquestioning stance vis-à-vis one's faith, assuredness regarding

God's tangible role in this life and the hereafter, and a fundamentalist sensibility regarding sociocultural issues. Sample items include:

> *God's word is good enough for me.*
> *I am a religious person.*
> *Sometimes bad things happen because it's God's will.*
> *Homosexuality goes against God's design.*
> *I know that evil people go to hell when they die.*

Therefore, it is our hypothesis that high scores on this scale will be related to this common form of religious certitude. Such perspective should be delineated from certainty regarding transcendental or spiritual inclinations more generally, since this scale is not a criterion-based measurement of the "religious certitude" construct. Rather, given its Likert-type structure (Strongly Agree, Agree, Disagree, Strongly Disagree), this scale is hypothesized to vary according to the content of one's religious belief as well as the certainty with which one holds such beliefs. In short, for present purposes, the higher the degree of "Socioreligious Traditionalism," the greater the degree of "religious certitude."

Question 2: Who is most likely to evidence a greater degree of Socioreligious Traditionalism on the BEVI?

As Table 10.1 illustrates, for this sample at least, regression analyses suggest that there are a number of significant differences on the BEVI regarding who is most, and least, likely to score highly on Socioreligious Traditionalism.[1] Of particular note, at an initial level of analysis (i.e., other variables also differentiate these groups), individuals who report that they are Republican, Christian, or Islamic all are significantly more likely to endorse a high degree of Socioreligious Traditionalism, whereas

---

[1] Other marital status refers to marital status other than "Divorced," "Married," "Single," and "Widowed." Paying college education by oneself refers to the source of college education payment (1 = paying college education by oneself; 0 = someone rather than oneself paying for college education). Years of foreign languages learning prior to college or university indicates the years the participant spends on learning foreign languages before attending the college. Speak French simply indicates that the respondent speaks French as a foreign language; likewise, to answer how many days of a week the respondent reads a news magazine, or uses an online social network during study abroad, the respondent simply provides an estimation of days or hours respectively spent per week. To ascertain interest in international education or study abroad, the dependent variable is a student's level of interest. The question is as follows: "On a scale of 1-7, with 1 being 'extremely low' and 7 being 'extremely high,' please indicate your level of personal interest in international education or study abroad experiences." The independent variables are demographic and experiential variables. Several of the independent variables are dummy variables: gender (0 = male, 1 = female); "parents paying for international experience" (0 = parents do not pay, 1 = parents pay); "university provides orientation for international experience" (0 = university does not provide, 1 = university provides); "plan to travel abroad" (0 = no plan to travel abroad, 1= plan to travel abroad); "plan to take an internationally focused course" (0 = no plan to take a course, 1 = plan to take a course); and, "speak a foreign language other than English" (0 = does not speak a foreign language, 1 = speaks a foreign language). Another independent variable, the "highest academic degree intended to achieve" is coded from 1 = associate degree, 2 = bachelor's, 3 = master's, 4 = specialist (e.g., Ed.S.), 5 = professional (e.g., law), to 6 = doctoral degree. Also, participants are asked about the number of foreign countries they have previously visited (e.g., respondents indicate the actual number of countries they have visited). Background variables include "mother's education" and "family income." "Mother's education" indicates the highest academic degree of a respondent's mother, which ranges from 0 = some high school or less to 8 = doctoral degree. "Family income" is an ordinal variable that reflects the average annual income of a student's parents/guardians regardless if the student receives financial support from them. Income ranges from 1 to 10, 1 = < \$10,000 to 10 = > \$175,000.

TABLE 10.1

Background Characteristics of Individuals Who Score More Highly on Socioreligious Traditionalism

| | UNSTANDARDIZED COEFFICIENTS | | STANDARDIZED COEFFICIENTS | | |
SCALES	B	STD. ERROR	BETA	T	SIG.
Constant	2.069	0.068		30.547	0.00
Other marital status	−0.302	0.115	−0.044	−2.627	0.01
Political orientation is Republican	0.314	0.033	0.171	9.608	0.00
Religious orientation is Atheism	−0.303	0.062	−0.114	−4.901	0.00
Religious orientation is Agnosticism	−0.398	0.065	−0.139	−6.157	0.00
Religious orientation is Christianity	0.707	0.049	0.387	14.304	0.00
Religious orientation is Islam	0.845	0.177	0.083	4.783	0.00
Personal interest in international activities	−0.026	0.009	−0.051	−2.85	0.004
Paying college education by oneself	−0.061	0.029	−0.035	−2.077	0.038
Years of foreign languages learning prior to college or university	−0.033	0.007	−0.082	−4.605	0.00
Speak French as a foreign language	−0.081	0.036	−0.038	−2.226	0.026
Days of a week read a weekly news magazine	0.041	0.017	0.043	2.478	0.013
Hours per week using an online social network during study abroad	0.011	0.004	0.052	3.033	0.002
F	109.379***				
R-squared	0.373				
Adj. R-squared	0.370				

Note. ***$p < .001$.

individuals who report that they are atheists and agnostics are significantly less likely to endorse a high degree of Socioreligious Traditionalism. Such characteristics, combined with the correlation matrix findings presented next, provide insight into what this particular factor of Socioreligious Traditionalism is measuring on the BEVI.

Question 3: How is religious certitude on the BEVI related to other belief/value structures?

As indicated, one of the more complex but salient dimensions of religious certitude is how it is, or is not, related to other aspects of how people experience self, others, and the larger world. For example, as previously mentioned, there is a distinction between religious fundamentalism and religious orthodoxy, with those scoring high on the latter construct tending to exhibit less prejudice and intolerance than those who express high levels of religious fundamentalism. Given these previous findings, what might Socioreligious Traditionalism on the BEVI illustrate about the relationship of its particular form of religious certitude to other belief/value constructs and processes? As Table 10.2 illustrates, correlation matrix findings from the BEVI show the following relationships between Socioreligious Traditionalism and other BEVI scales.[2]

How do we interpret these findings? Essentially, those individuals who score highly on Socioreligious Traditionalism also tend to be:

- *Much less likely* to be interested in and open to cultures and cultural practices that are different from their own (Sociocultural Openness)
- *Much less likely* to be concerned about environmental processes such as climate change or the degradation of natural resources (Ecological Resonance)
- *More likely* to deny basic thoughts, feelings, and needs that are common or typical for most human beings (Basic Closedness)
- *More likely* to express traditional and conservative beliefs about who men and women are and should be (Gender Traditionalism)
- *More likely* to indicate that basic needs were not met in a good enough way during their upbringing (Needs Closure)
- *More likely* to report that they have few doubts or regrets and are seldom caught off guard (Hard Structure)

TABLE 10.2
Correlation Matrix Findings of Socioreligious Traditionalism and Other BEVI Scales

Scale 15. Socioreligious Traditionalism

Sociocultural Openness (−.62)
Ecological Resonance (−.53)
Basic Closedness (.34)
Gender Traditionalism (.34)
Needs Closure (.31)
Hard Structure (.27)
Identity Closure (.24)
Emotional Attunement (−.20)

---

[2] These data represent interfactor correlations among BEVI scales. More information about the BEVI, including EFA parameters as well as correlation matrix data, is available at www.thebevi.com/aboutbevi.php.

- *More likely* to express confusion or "stuckness" regarding who they are or where they are going in their life (Identity Diffusion)
- *Less likely* to have access, and/or be responsive, to their affect or the affect of others (Emotional Attunement)

Overall then, the *more likely* it is that one experiences certitude regarding the beliefs represented by the Socioreligious Traditionalism scale on the BEVI, the *less likely* it is that this same individual, on average, will be open to or interested in different cultures, environmental issues, and other important aspects of self, such as how and why we and others function as we do.

Question 4: What variance in religious certitude exists both within and between religious groups?

This complex question is perhaps one of the most important to answer if we are to understand the explanatory value of grouping people by their particular religious or nonreligious demographic category (Christian, atheist, agnostic, etc.). For example, as the previously reviewed data suggest (e.g., regarding the differences between self-identified Fundamentalist Christians and Orthodox Christians), groups that self-identify with the same overarching category (in this case Christian) appear at times to differ tremendously from one another in terms of their basic experience of self, other, and the larger world. By extension then, could it be that some individuals who self-report as Christian might have more in common with individuals who do not identify as Christian? For example, might it be possible that some atheists and Christians actually share more in common than they do with agnostics, who presumably are open to the possibilities of either category, and thus are less likely to express certitude regarding transcendental matters? Although preliminary and necessitating further investigation, several BEVI analyses offer intriguing findings along these lines. Consider Table 10.3, which addresses beliefs regarding the economics of social welfare, as well as Table 10.4, which deals with basic openness toward or interest in cultures that are different from one's own.

What may we observe about such findings? Due to their relatively large sample size, let us focus on atheism, Christianity, and agnosticism. First, although mean differences among groups are not large, atheists and Christians from this sample appear to believe similarly on both of these items regarding social welfare and cultural understanding. Second, agnostics are significantly more likely to agree that there is too big a gap between the rich and poor in our country, and that we should try to understand cultures that are different from our own. Such findings are interesting at a number of levels, including the seemingly salient fact that a central tenet of Christianity is that the plight of the poor should be prominent in the thinking of Christians (Singer, 2009). It should be emphasized that all three of these groups for this sample—of university level students—are inclined to agree with both statements. Also, some of the variance in the rich/poor item might also be related to the moral attributions one makes about the existence of a large rich/poor gap (e.g., some might argue that it is not the size of the gap that is immoral, but rather the lack of care for the poor that is morally reprehensible). That said, such findings are surprising nonetheless, and worthy of further consideration. Most notably, the intriguing if not ironic finding that agnostics are more likely to endorse both beliefs, particularly regarding the issue of rich and poor, raises the question of whether this group may be more inclined

TABLE 10.3

Comparisons Among Atheists, Agnostics, and Christians on the Following BEVI Item Regarding the Rich and Poor: "There is too big a gap between the rich and the poor in our country"

SOURCE	SUM OF SQUARES	MEAN	DF	MEAN SQUARE ERROR	F	SIG.
Corrected Model	17.891		7	2.556	4.275	0.00
Intercept	19951.125		1	19951.125	33369.71	0.00
Religious Orientation	17.891		7	2.556	4.275	0.00
Atheism		3.045				
Agnosticism		3.132				
Buddhism		3.189				
Christianity		2.9				
Hinduism		3.154				
Islam		3.176				
Judaism		2.968				
Other		3.019				
Error	1358.984		2273	0.598		
Total	21328		2281			
Corrected Total	1376.875		2280			

Note. $R^2 = 0.013$ (adjusted $R^2 = 0.010$).

toward a basic tenet of Christianity than are self-reported Christians. Likewise, the finding that atheists and Christians are similar in their level of openness toward the "other" (i.e., both groups are less open than agnostics) might be surprising, particularly in light of Dawkins' (2006) assertion that atheism is the solution to many of the world's most pressing conflicts (e.g., we'd be better off and less conflictual if we'd but abandon religion), his negative beliefs about Christianity, and his skeptical views of agnosticism.

Additional context from this perspective may be helpful at this point, since Dawkins (2006) has much to say about agnostics, dividing them into two types. "Temporary Agnosticism in Practice" (TAP) is defined as "legitimate fence-sitting where there really is a definite answer, one way or another, but we so far lack the evidence to reach it" (p. 47). In contrast, "Permanent Agnosticism in Principle" (PAP) "is appropriate for questions that can never be answered, no matter how much evidence we gather, because the very idea of evidence is not applicable" such as whether "you see red as I do." That is because, "Maybe your red is my green, or something completely different from any color that I can imagine...philosophers cite this question as one that can never be answered" (p. 47). Dawkins appears to be arguing that the only legitimate form of agnosticism vis-à-vis a belief in God is the TAP form.

TABLE 10.4

Comparisons Among Atheists, Agnostics, and Christians on the Following BEVI Item Regarding Knowledge of Other Cultures: "We should try to understand cultures that are different from our own"

SOURCE	SUM OF SQUARES	MEAN	DF	MEAN SQUARE ERROR	F	SIG.
Corrected Model	11.601		7	1.657	4.046	0.00
Intercept	26815.29		1	26815.29	65464.98	0.00
Religious Orientation	11.601		7	1.657	4.046	0.00
Atheism		3.382				
Agnosticism		3.578				
Buddhism		3.568				
Christianity		3.378				
Hinduism		3.692				
Islam		3.588				
Judaism		3.563				
Other		3.4				
Error	942.109		2300	0.41		
Total	27769		2308			
Corrected Total	953.71		2307			

Note. $R^2 = 0.012$ (adjusted $R^2 = 0.009$).

Thus, from his perspective, "even if God's existence is never proved or disproved with certainty one way or the other, available evidence and reasoning may yield an estimate of probability far from 50 per cent" (p. 50). Here is not the place for a full exploration of why Dawkins would express such certitude regarding his own presentation of "available evidence"—much less his own "reasoning"—except to say that many scholars from across the interdisciplinary spectrum question absolutist rational atheism of the very form promoted by Dawkins, by noting its unacknowledged assumptions, privileged methodologies, underlying epistemologies, and internal contradictions (e.g., Eagleton, 2006; Keller, 2008; Nagel, 1997; Plantinga, 1993). Setting such ongoing debate aside, it suffices to say that abundant evidence suggests we all should exercise due skepticism of our own reasoning, as it appears subject to many empirically demonstrable biasing factors (e.g., Aronson, 2012; Bargh & Chartrand, 1999). From such a perspective, certitude about the indisputably false status of religious beliefs is no more defensible than certitude about the indisputably true nature of such beliefs. As Shealy (2005) observes, "believing something to be 'the real truth'—even vehemently—has no more power to make it so than nonbelief has the power to make it not so" (p. 84). Moreover, pertinent to fervent believers in religion and nonreligion,

. . .the fact that we all possess beliefs and values is not sufficient to confer legitimacy upon them; that is to say, beliefs and values are not necessarily true, right, or better simply because they are held to be so. . .To insist otherwise is like asserting that English is superior to French simply because you speak the former, as do your parents, children, and most everyone else you know. Although the absurdity of such logic (the non-logic) should be painfully apparent to us all, our history as a species indicates it is not. Instead, what we too often seem to 'know for sure'—with a steely confidence that belies the fanatic in us all—is a tautology that our beliefs and values are right by virtue of the fact that they are ours. (p. 102)

In short, despite all of the emphasis on the putative differences between Christians and atheists (Dawkins, 2006), such differences are not clearly found in the present analysis, thus creating important questions regarding the utility and validity of perceiving entire groups of people (e.g., Christians or atheists) either as ineluctably different or similar in their beliefs and values. Moreover, from the standpoint of religious certitude, it would appear that individuals who theoretically would appear to be least inclined toward certitude—agnostics—are also more inclined to believe there is too large of a gap between the rich and poor, and that there is value in understanding cultures that are different from their own. These findings are consistent with the present correlation matrix data, which suggest that individuals high in Socioreligious Traditionalism—our proxy for religious certitude—are less likely to express a sense of interest in or openness to issues and groups that are different from one's own (e.g., Sociocultural Openness, $r = -.62$).

Question 5: Are specific formative variables associated with a higher degree of religious certitude as expressed via Socioreligious Traditionalism?

Finally, as we conclude our analyses, an even more basic question may be asked, which has to do with the etiological and mediational factors that are associated with a relative degree of openness in general, and certitude in particular. More specifically, what life experiences appear to be associated with a relative degree of socioreligiously traditional certitude or lack thereof? On the one hand, mild to moderate evidence from the BEVI suggests that individuals who report a greater degree of Negative Life Events tend to be more likely to report a higher degree of Socioreligious Traditionalism. Such a conclusion is based in part upon the present correlation matrix data, which indicates a significant (.0001) and positive (.31) correlation between Socioreligious Traditionalism and Needs Closure, a scale that measures the degree to which individuals report distressing life experiences associated with core needs not being met.

Despite such findings, the nonlinear nature of such causal processes should be emphasized, as illustrated by the following structural equation models, which demonstrate that the mediators of Socioreligious Traditionalism and Christian identity are complex and worthy of further study. Consider Figure 10.1, which examines the relationship between Positive Family Relations (the degree to which individuals report a happy upbringing and positive relations with their caregivers), Identity Diffusion (the degree to which individuals report feeling stuck, confused, or lost in

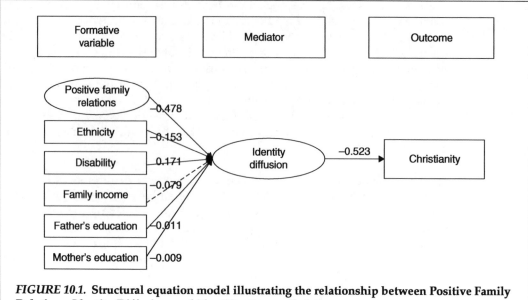

FIGURE 10.1. Structural equation model illustrating the relationship between Positive Family Relations, Identity Diffusion, and identification as Christian.

Note. X^2 = 1964.837, df = 124, p = .0000, root mean square error of approximation (RMSEA) = 0.080, CFI = 0.906.

terms of who they are and whether they have agency to move forward in life), and the outcome variable of Christianity (i.e., those who self-report as Christian).[3]

What do such findings suggest? Essentially, individuals who report that they experienced Positive Family Relations—and report Caucasian ethnic status, a higher family income, and no disability diagnosis—are *less* likely to report that they are confused, stuck, or lost. At the same time, individuals who are high in Identity Diffusion also are less likely to report that they are Christian. These findings are interesting at several levels, but perhaps mostly because they suggest that Positive Family Relations may in fact be associated with a propensity to self-report as Christian when one does not feel a sense of being lost or confused about one's own identity or life. In other words, Positive Family Relations may be associated with a higher degree of clarity about one's own self and life purpose, which may—for families that are inclined toward a Christian orientation—be further associated with such status. But do such findings apply only to Christians in general or also more specifically to those

---

[3] From an interpretive standpoint, Positive Life Events is a Confirmative Factor Analysis (CFA) derived factor comprising items regarding how positively an individual reports their upbringing and family environment were (e.g., a positive value indicates a greater degree of positive life events). Ethnicity is a dummy measured variable; value "0" indicates the respondent is a minority, and "1" means the respondent is a Caucasian. Disability also is a dummy variable; "0" indicates the person is not eligible for services for students with disabilities, and "1" means otherwise. Family income is measured by a series of numbers indicating the respondent's annual family income. It ranges from "1" (Less than $10,000) to "10" ($175,000 or more). Both father's education and mother's education are ordinal measured variables. They range from "0" (Some high school or less) to "8" (Doctoral degree). Finally, we used weighted least squares means and variance adjusted (WLSMV) as the estimator for all the structural equation models because the variables have ordinal or dummy measures.

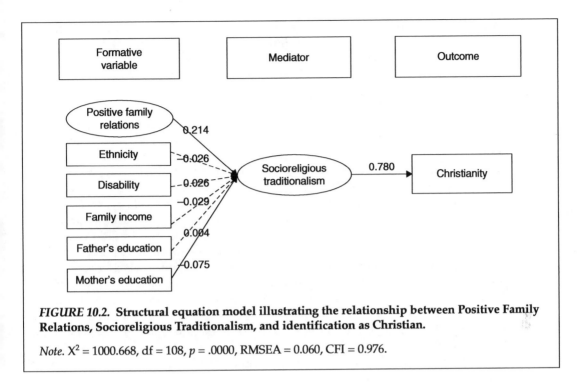

FIGURE 10.2. Structural equation model illustrating the relationship between Positive Family Relations, Socioreligious Traditionalism, and identification as Christian.

Note. X^2 = 1000.668, df = 108, *p* = .0000, RMSEA = 0.060, CFI = 0.976.

Christians who are high on Socioreligious Traditionalism? Figure 10.2 offers an intriguing look at such complexity.

What does this model suggest? Essentially, it appears that Positive Family Relations may indeed be associated with a higher degree of Socioreligious Traditionalism, which in any case, is strongly associated with the tendency to self-report as Christian. Interestingly, from the standpoint of formative variables, it should be also noted that the higher the degree of education the mother is reported to have, the lower the degree of Socioreligious Traditionalism individuals tend to report, which is an interesting variable worthy of further study (e.g., why would mother's education, but not father's, be associated with a lower degree of religious certitude as expressed via Socioreligious Traditionalism?).

CONCLUDING PERSPECTIVES ON RELIGIOUS CERTITUDE

These findings suggest five concluding points. *First, in exploring certitude generally, and religious certitude in particular, it is important to operationalize our definitions.* As with all macrolevel constructs—such as love, intelligence, or certitude—from the standpoint of measurement and research, an item level of analysis should be the first point of inquiry. Much confusion occurs in the scholarly literature due to the fact that different item constellations are used to define similar constructs; therefore, it is important that researchers carefully consider the content of the items used in order to properly contextualize the applicability of their conclusions. Future research investigating the correlations between Socioreligious Traditionalism on the BEVI and other existing measures of religion/spirituality and certitude might help to better elucidate these dynamics and consolidate existing findings. Hopefully, the included sample items will provide a clear understanding of how religious certitude is operationalized on the BEVI, which may facilitate further such research.

Second, psychological constructs may be understood better by researching who is, and is not, likely to embody them. In the current analysis, we learn, for example, that Christian Republicans are more likely to score high on Socioreligious Traditionalism, which would perhaps be expected, and offers important information regarding the meaning and validity of the construct. Along these same lines, however, and perhaps more telling, individuals who self-report as Islamic also demonstrate heightened scores on Socioreligious Traditionalism, suggesting that this construct may capture psychological processes vis-à-vis religion beyond those of a Christian population.

Third, a tendency toward socioreligious certitude appears predictive of a wide range of self-structures. As the correlation matrix data illustrate, if one knows something about an individual's beliefs along the lines of Socioreligious Traditionalism, it is possible to derive empirically informed hypotheses regarding how these same individuals are likely to regard other cultures or be disposed toward environmental issues as well as how inclined they may be to acknowledge basic thoughts and feelings in self or other. Such awareness also suggests that it is important to regard the "self" as a complex and interdependent whole that is greater than the sum of its discrete parts, including but not limited to one's religious faith or lack thereof (see Chapters 2 and 3).

Fourth, within-group differences may be greater than between-group differences, which suggests the need to eschew stereotypes about religious and nonreligious people. On the one hand, the present data do suggest that people who are high on Socioreligious Traditionalism may also be less open to other cultures, less concerned about the environment, and so forth. However, that tentative conclusion is very different from concluding either that all Christians are high on Socioreligious Traditionalism, or that all atheists are more open to other cultures than all Christians. Although this point may seem evident, scholarly and popular discourse (e.g., painting all Christians or all atheists with the same brush) suggests that such affectively laden labels are highly subject to stereotyping if not prejudice, which Aronson (2012) astutely defines as a "negative attitude toward a distinguishable group on the basis of generalizations derived from faulty or incomplete information" (p. 299). From that perspective, popular scholars such as Dawkins (2006) would appear prejudicial *against* at least two groups—Christians and agnostics—and prejudicial *toward* another—atheists—by erroneously ignoring both the differences within all of these groups, and overstating the differences between them. A more sophisticated understanding of the variables that are associated with particular self-referencing categories is likely to go beyond a descriptive level of analysis (e.g., whether one calls oneself an atheist, Christian, or agnostic), instead seeking to understand to what degree, and under what circumstances, such self-reporting labels apply. In short, questions of *how and why we believe as we do* are at least as, if not more, important than questions of *what we believe* if we truly are to apprehend the complex and interacting factors that culminate in "certitude" of whatever stripe.

Fifth, the relative degree of religious or nonreligious certitude an individual expresses may be highly determined, but in a complex, interacting, and nonlinear manner. On the one hand, individuals who are higher on Socioreligious Traditionalism are more likely to report a strong commitment to a religious tradition (e.g., Christianity). Moreover, unhappy life experiences associated with a lack of Needs Closure also are associated with a higher degree of Socioreligious Traditionalism. However, as SEM results suggest, unhappy life experiences are neither necessary nor sufficient antecedents to the development of religious certitude, since a subset of Christians, who also report Positive Family Relations, are inclined to be higher in Socioreligious Traditionalism. Thus, a high degree of Socioreligious Traditionalism may occur in families that are experienced as positive or negative, although such status may be more likely with backgrounds that are of the latter (more negative) variety. At the same time, the tendency to self-report as Christian does not appear to be associated either with a negative life history or a confused or lost sense of self. In short, although a lack of Needs Closure related to early life events tends to be associated with a greater degree of religious certitude vis-à-vis socioreligious traditionalism, such reported experiences are neither necessary nor sufficient in terms of predicting this belief constellation. Thus, in attempting to understand the etiology of certitude, we must account for complex interactions among a range of formative variables, keeping individual differences forefront, and thereby avoiding a "one size fits all" mentality.

AGNOSTICISM AND THE CONTINUUM OF BELIEF

We began this chapter by observing that one's tendency toward certitude regarding religious matters appears to be among the chief causes of conflict between individuals and groups. That is likely because if and when individuals are "sure" of their beliefs and values, they are less able to tolerate the possibility that they may be wrong, or not completely right, thus militating against empathic engagement with another's perspective (Shealy, 2005). In our view, the data that we have presented here affirm and deepen this perspective, by illustrating that we know relatively little about someone based on his or her endorsement of a general term to describe who he or she is, such as Christian or atheist. This observation emerges from the finding that, from the standpoint of the BEVI, religious designations may encompass more differences than similarities among adherents in regard to how they interact with self, other, and the larger world. For example, some Christians ironically may share more in common from a self-structure perspective (e.g., their capacity and inclination to experience and express affect) with their atheist peers than with those who tend to experience less religious certitude, such as many agnostics. This vexing conclusion likely represents an especially exasperating reality for a subgroup of individuals who self-identify as Christians, since from this perspective they may have less in common with their brethren than those who do not self-identify as Christian.

In other words, a lack of certainty in one's belief regarding transcendental matters (whether that belief be most akin to Christianity, agnosticism, atheism, or any other label) seems more predictive of one's ability to interact openly with those who hold other perspectives than any particular religious/nonreligious group affiliation. Thus, although preliminary and subject to further study, it may be that self-identified Christians and other believers in a specific religious system who hold their faith without a sense of absolute certainty (e.g., which could perhaps be referred to as "Agnostic Christians," "Agnostic Hindus," etc.) might in fact be quite open in relation to other members of their religious group. Along the same lines, atheists who avowedly are nonagnostic (which could perhaps be referred to as "Fundamentalist Atheists") may have much in common—from a certitude perspective—with "Fundamentalist Christians" who also are avowedly nonagnostic. Thus and again, it behooves us to be careful about concluding anything regarding the basic psychological structure of individuals who reportedly adhere to a specific religious or nonreligious affiliation without knowing much more about their formative variables and larger belief/value structures, since the differences within such groups may be much larger than the differences between them.

Overall, then, what may we conclude from such an analysis? From our perspective, an agnostic approach that lacks certainty regarding transcendental issues may represent the most intellectually defensible framework on matters over which scientifically definitive conclusions—those that are empirically, independently, and reliably verifiable—appear untenable, while offering an aspirational framework that militates against shrill diatribes and destructive behaviors toward individuals and groups who "believe" differently. As Shealy (2016) observes in relation to belief, religious and otherwise, via the "Continuum of Belief,"

> one may be *sympathetically noncommitted* (i.e., inclined to believe but ultimately noncommittal) or *skeptically noncommitted* (i.e., inclined to disbelieve but ultimately noncommittal). From the standpoint of the Continuum of Belief, then, "agnostic" encompasses any of the "noncommitted" designations, which is consistent with the scope and intent of the term, "agnostic," meaning "without" ('a') "knowledge" ('gnosis'). *Thus, to declare oneself agnostic is to concede the inability to assert unequivocally the certainty of knowledge.* (p. 54)

By way of illustration, consider "Example 3" from the "Continuum of Belief" as it relates directly to our discussion (see Chapter 2).

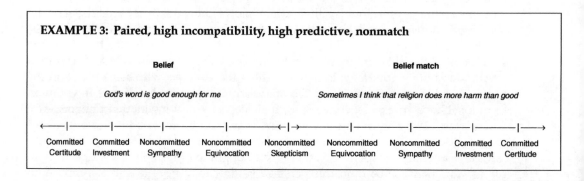

EXAMPLE 3: Paired, high incompatibility, high predictive, nonmatch

From the standpoint of the EI model and BEVI method, recall from Chapter 2 that,

> beliefs typically exist in a synergistic relationship to one another in that a belief stated in one direction typically is matched by one or more counterpart beliefs that exist in relative degrees of opposition to it. Moreover, each belief may be designated as (a) solo or paired (i.e., indicating whether an opposite match has been demonstrated statistically); (b) predictive at the high, medium, or low level (i.e., essentially indicative of correlative strength in the positive or negative direction); and (c) predictive of a match or nonmatch (i.e., whether two beliefs, and two or more individuals holding them, are likely to be "compatible—matched" or "incompatible—nonmatched"—in terms of worldview). (Shealy, 2016, p. 52)

So, one may hold a belief (including, but not limited to religious) with relative degrees of agnostic commitment up until the state of certitude. As previously noted, this point is illuminating in relation to the putative dichotomy between atheism and Christianity because the labels of "Christian" or atheist" offer little by way of explicating where someone actually may fall within these self-reported designations. Since within-group differences often are greater than between-group differences vis-à-vis beliefs and values, it is very important to ascertain where individuals and groups actually reside along the "Continuum of Belief." Revelatory of individual differences among us, and by way of explication,

> consider Example 3 in relation to Huan, Eleanor, and Ana. Recall that the two beliefs of Example 3 are strongly and negatively correlated (i.e., paired, but highly incompatible and highly predictive of a nonmatch between two different believers). Let us say Huan strongly agrees with the belief, *God's word is good enough for me*. Statistically speaking, Huan therefore is highly likely to disagree strongly with the belief, *Sometimes I think that religion does more harm than good*. Likewise, now consider "Eleanor," who represents the mirror opposite of Huan, strongly disagreeing that *God's word is good enough for* me and strongly agreeing that *Sometimes I think that religion does more harm than good*. On the Continuum of Belief, if other item pairings follow this same pattern, which is statistically predicted, both Huan and Eleanor likely fall under "Committed Certitude" on opposite ends of the Continuum of Belief. Now consider a third example from "Ana," who disagrees that *God's word is good enough for me* AND disagrees that *Sometimes I think that religion does more harm than good*. Where would Ana fall along the Continuum of Belief? Probably not under "Committed Certitude," and more likely under "Noncommitted Equivocation." Consistent with BEVI data presented later (e.g., correlation matrix and structural equation modeling), the fact that Ana appears to hold complexity in this way—disagreeing that "God's word is good enough" BUT also disagreeing that "religion does more harm than good"—suggests that she is grappling with fundamental questions regarding her own beliefs vis-à-vis religion and spirituality, and remains open to a range of possible "truths." (Shealy, 2016, p. 53)[4]

Among other implications of this scenario, it is important to understand that both a strong atheist commitment *and* strong religious commitment—that of Eleanor and Huan respectively—are expressions of belief. To be clear, then, "atheism is not nonbelief" (Shealy, 2016, p. 55).

Some atheists may contend, for example, that a belief in God is false, but from the standpoint of the larger definition of belief provided here, such a contention is

---

[4] Of course, all manner of variation may occur along this continuum when we juxtapose beliefs at an item level of analysis. Consider "Luis," for example, who agrees quite strongly that *God's word is good enough for me* AND agrees somewhat less strongly that *Sometimes I think that religion does more harm than good*. Perhaps on further qualitative inquiry regarding how Luis justifies his seemingly contradictory position, he might express his belief that "God's word" contains some real truths, which have stood the test of time, but that difficulties and abuses of interpretation and application have led to situations where religions sometimes seem to do more harm than good. Where would Luis fall along the Continuum of Belief? He seemingly would fall at Committed Investment on one side (*Sometimes I think that religion does more harm than good)* and Noncommitted Sympathy on the other side (*God's word is good enough for me*) of the Continuum of Belief for these paired items.

still a belief that there is no God. For the foreseeable future then, just as proof for the existence of God or some other transcendent reality seems improbable (e.g., empirically, unequivocally), so also does proof for the nonexistence of such an entity or phenomenon. In short, it is our sense that agnosticism most closely approximates the apparent reality that in fact, it is extremely unlikely that the existence or nonexistence of God will be proven in a way that would be empirically and unequivocally valid for all human beings who grapple with this fundamental question. We therefore endorse alignment with agnosticism, broadly defined, as Agnostic Christians, Agnostic Muslims, Agnostic Atheists, Agnostic Agnostics, and so forth.

In the final analysis, there are at least two advantages of such a stance. First, through an attitude of agnosticism writ large, we have the best chance of achieving openness toward the potential truth or goodness contained in a given worldview, while simultaneously not eliminating the possibility of learning from other worldviews that may, on the face of it, seem irreconcilable with our own. Second, this agnostic stance hedges also against the perilous human tendency toward certitude, by granting that the beliefs and values we acquire largely are due to deterministic formative variables and extant contingencies of which we may have little awareness (e.g., Aronson, 2012; Shealy, 2005). By resisting the foreclosed security provided by certitude, we might live more honestly in terms of the complexities we face (i.e., not knowing for sure, "one way or the other"), while simultaneously recognizing that human perceptions inevitably are inclined toward error—thus abiding in accord with Saint Augustine's timeless adage, "I err, therefore I am." In short, experiencing and expressing a spirit of agnosticism along the Continuum of Belief may be the least divisive and most conducive approach to interfaith dialogue, since it declares neither that the other's beliefs certainly are wrong nor that one's own beliefs certainly are right.

Thus far, it has been implied but should be explicit that our support for an agnostic perspective is based in an agnostic theory of knowledge, which subsequently leads to a commitment to agnosticism in our beliefs (i.e., we should recognize that the validity of all knowledge claims rely on a priori assumptions). Moreover, it is our sense—although subject to further inquiry—that "absolute certitude" of a religious variety probably is more akin to a fundamentalist, rather than an orthodox, worldview in most cases. This perspective is supported by the previously reviewed evidence regarding the relative degree of nonprejudicial beliefs espoused by the latter group of religious adherents (i.e., Christian orthodoxy, when separated from fundamentalism, seems to neutralize and in some cases reverse religion's lamentable association with prejudice). Finally, we must neither ignore nor devalue the associations between religious belief and positive statuses at a range of levels (e.g., emotional well-being). In fact, strong convictions regarding religious doctrines that value engagement and appreciation of an individual's experiential self may lead to more positive outcomes related to psychology's goal of preserving individual "freedom of inquiry and expression," broadly defined (American Psychological Association, 2010, p. 2; Silberman et al., 2005; Tan, 2009; Van den Bos et al., 2006). Further, it is also possible that high levels of certitude may actually promote a "believer's" relationship with others, at least within a similar sphere of belief, as the preceding SEM data imply.

So, while religious certitude seems related to intergroup conflict and violence when it propositions against respect for an individual's internal experience and autonomy, such an outcome is not necessarily inevitable. Some less severe forms of religious belief may motivate a believer to avoid shrill diatribes and demonstrate constructive (rather than destructive) behaviors toward people of a different faith.

For example, it is possible for a Christian who strongly believes in the doctrinal impetus to "love your neighbor as yourself" also to be more fervent in this regard than an agnostic who feels less certitude in his or her obligations and affinities toward fellow human beings. Perhaps it is the case, then, that high levels of nonabsolute certitude—when coexisting with an agnostic theory of knowledge—may best be expressed through the term *investment* as indicated in the Continuum of Belief. This term delineates such inclinations from absolutistic certitude, and allows room for the valuing of each human's authentic experiential self, which an absolutistic certitude may see as corrupting of or antithetical to its "truth."

In the end, our preference for an agnostic stance vis-à-vis transcendental matters is bolstered by the fundamental point that it appears possible to be invested in one's beliefs while still retaining a nonrejecting and nonprejudicial stance toward those who believe differently. Certainly, from the standpoint of the BEVI, profiles are not uncommon in which people are very high, or very low, on Socioreligious Traditionalism—a common expression of high or low religious certainty—and still evidence openness or closedness to other ways of experiencing self, others, and the larger world. The existence of these "outliers" is one of the central reasons why it is important not to overgeneralize from religious or nonreligious beliefs. Even though such beliefs are among the most powerful (i.e., highly predictive of other worldviews on the BEVI), it still is common to have all manner of variation at the individual, or even group, level in terms of differences and similarities in worldview, a point that should be recognized when assessing and interacting with people of different religious or nonreligious sensibilities.

Real World Implications and Applications: Toward Cross-Cultural Religious Education

In light of the present theory and data, how do we address such complexity—the promotion of agnostic openness and investment in religious/nonreligious meaning making, as opposed to certitude—in the real world? Overall, we recommend educational and psychological interventions that encourage critical reflective thinking about the religious or nonreligious systems of thought to which each of us is exposed. As noted previously, from our perspective, commitments both to religious (e.g., major religions of the world) and nonreligious (e.g., atheism) systems of thought are forms of faith, to the degree that their adherents profess a belief in the fundamental but nonprovable tenets that underlie them. In other words, both a fundamentalist Muslim and a fundamentalist atheist are expressing their "faith," since in both cases it appears that the system of belief to which they adhere cannot be proved in any definitive and unequivocal manner. Keeping with our emphasis on an agnostic theory of knowledge, as opposed to certitude of whatever stripe, this stance is not meant to discredit or privilege any particular perspective but rather to equip ourselves with the skills for reflecting at a meta-level on why we believe what we believe, in order to facilitate growth, dialogue, and understanding over time. The aim of interventions that align with these goals is to discourage any form of religious or nonreligious certitude (which appears to lead to prejudice and conflict among individuals and groups), while simultaneously fostering a culture of open-mindedness, curiosity, and exploration across the variety of perspectives regarding transcendental matters (Tan, 2009, 2010). Practically, our aim would be to encourage people to "reflect critically on the committed perspective into which they have been nurtured," with the goal of expanding their ability to take on personally authentic convictions (Thiessen, 1993, p. 255). For example, adapting suggestions by McLaughlin (1984, p. 81), an educator, leader, clinician, or parent might consider fostering an environment that supports the following processes and attitudes:

- Encourage people to ask questions, and also be willing to respond to questions honestly and in a way that respects each person's cognitive and emotional development.
- Help people reflect on what parts of their perspectives are a matter of faith rather than universally agreed upon absolutes.
- Encourage attitudes of empathic patience and understanding in relation to religious and nonreligious disagreement.
- Propose that morality is not exclusively dependent upon religious belief.
- Be cognizant of the affective, emotional, and dispositional aspects related to the development of conviction in tandem with the cognitive aspects of that development.
- Respect each individual's experience by encouraging the pursuit of his or her developing convictions, while encouraging reflection on any facets that may not allow space for respecting the convictions of others.

Interventions that seek to foster this type of environment generally benefit from utilizing a dialogical approach that aims to balance both openness and rootedness (Tan, 2010). Consider one such example, as illustrated by the Muslim "Tolerance and Appreciation for Multiculturalism" program, which has been implemented at the Muhammadiyah University of Surakarta, Indonesia (Tan, 2011). This initiative aims to "develop arguments for multicultural Islam based on theological, philosophical and Islamic jurisprudential precepts, using these to legitimate the concept of multicultural Islam, and to promote religious tolerance towards the multicultural society" (Baidhawy, 2007, pp. 22–23). Especially noteworthy, this program is grounded in Islamic teachings that are held firmly by many Muslims. These beliefs include *tawhid* (the unity of the Godhead), which focuses on the unity of humankind that is derived from God; ummah (living together), which teaches the peaceful co-existence of all human beings; and rahmah (love), which promotes caring human relationships based on the attributes of "God the Merciful and the Benevolent." Typically, programs such as these have been advanced within and across communities of religious believers. However, we see every reason for those who adhere to an atheistic worldview to participate as full and equal partners in similar sorts of cross-conviction dialogues, which might be understood as three overlapping and mutually reinforcing levels—preliminary dialogue, practical dialogue, and critical dialogue—which we describe next (Tan, 2010).

First, *preliminary dialogue,* as the name implies, focuses on preliminary or basic inter-religious engagement that does not require direct dialogue or interaction between people of different faiths. Rather, it emphasizes learning about a faith through symbolic acts of interest and support towards another religion, such as visiting a place of worship or observing a religious celebration. This form of dialogue is recommended as an initial step to learning about another faith as it is the easiest to achieve, but is limited in its capacity for promoting inter-religious understanding and correcting misconceptions. To include atheists within such a paradigm, we might suggest that religiously convicted people of whatever faith consider attending various atheistic venues, such as a "freethinkers" (see www.nobeliefs.com) or an "American Atheists" (see www.atheists.org) event. Likewise, atheists might consider respectful engagement with people who profess religious leanings within their various venues.

Second, *practical dialogue* brings believers of different faiths together through social projects that may not be explicitly religious in nature. This provides an opportunity to learn about essential differences in beliefs and practices in an informal and collegial setting (Leganger-Krogstad, 2003). One goal of such dialogue is to decide upon a project that reflects shared values, and then, collaborate together in taking action (e.g., working with a local food bank; participating in a Habitat for Humanity building project). This approach emphasizes that common values (e.g., harmonious living) are core not only to various religious creeds, but are shared also by atheist believers, as exemplified by the "secular humanism" movement, which aspires to be a transcending framework for all these perspectives (e.g., https://www.secularhumanism.org/index.php).

Another example of this type of approach is advocated by an Islamic research center in Britain, which explicates how a "civic morality" may be established between Muslims and non-Muslims, based upon shared principles. This requires a demonstration of civic morality that affirms mutual respect and rejects discrimination against others. As noted in a report by HRH Prince Alwaleed Bin Talal Centre of Islamic Studies (2009), civic morality implies that "Muslims should treat non-Muslim individuals as equal in the domain of social interaction, regardless of religious or doctrinal disagreements" (p. 12). The report adds that this framework, from the Islamic point of view, is premised on the body of principles outlined in the Qur'an and Islamic traditions, including good neighborliness, charity, hospitality, non-aggression, honoring of commitments, and doing good. Such a framework is transitional between practical dialogue and critical dialogue, since the latter perspective respects and values commonalities (as the above center constructively aspires), but ultimately focuses deliberately upon the teachings of a particular faith.

Third, *critical dialogue* involves deliberately planned encounters in which participants discuss religious issues based on theological similarities and differences. This form of cross-conviction dialogue represents the deepest type of encounter among believers of various stripes, as it challenges participants to delve intensively not only into the content of their respective creeds, but also to explicate fundamental issues of meaning and purpose that are associated with them (i.e., why one believes what one believes). Essentially, critical dialogues regarding religion should emphasize the commonalities we share across communities. Such values are integral to, but also transcend any particular religion. These values include humanity, care, respect, trust, and working together for the larger good. Therefore, as previously suggested, it seems that one need not abandon strong religious or nonreligious commitments to avoid prejudice and promote harmony.

One common approach for engaging in critical dialogue is found in "interfaith dialogues," which are based upon the common understanding that diverse moral traditions and legitimate moral differences exist across faiths (Runnymede, 2000). In concert with this theme, the overarching goal of these dialogues is to underline ambiguous and/or controversial aspects of a given belief tradition in order to develop religious literacy, interfaith relations, greater self awareness, and active citizenship (Erricker, 2006; Ipgrave, 2003). Without a direct consideration of the underlying assumptions of various belief traditions—as well as their related commitments, suspicions, and grievances toward other religious and nonreligious traditions—interfaith dialogue exercises remain superficial. Although universal agreement may be reached (e.g., as described under practical dialogue), deeper encounters regarding ethical, metaphysical, anthropological, or theological content likely will remain elusive without an in-depth examination of the most basic convictions of believers across the spectrum (Lindholm, 2004, as cited in Van Doorn-Harder, 2007).

For critical dialogue to be successful, we suggest that religious/nonreligious believers seek to set aside any form of certitude that may hinder interreligious (and nonreligious) understanding. Guided by an attitude of quest (perhaps fostered by the relational connections created via the preliminary and practical dialogues as previously described), participants may be capable of coming together to explore alternative perspectives and interpretations for contested issues in and between various faiths (religious and nonreligious). Examples include, but are by no means limited to, competing claims or beliefs regarding reason, knowing, truth, contemplation, meaning, causation, purpose, love, care, compassion, ethics, morality, science, death, the afterlife, God, salvation, religious conversion, and the need—or lack thereof—of a religious sensibility to live and promote a life worth living for self, others, and the larger world. The objective in these dialogues is to learn and empathize rather than to debate, judge, and "win the argument." To achieve this goal, it is essential for adherents of different faiths to be given the opportunity to share and justify their views, and for all parties to listen respectfully and agree to disagree, if necessary.

In preparing participants to reflect critically on another belief system in a productive manner, it is helpful first to foster a degree of understanding and empathy with that system, which may attenuate critical comments that are based upon false stereotypes or prejudices. While it may be salutary for participants to question and even challenge the assumptions of certain religious beliefs and practices, discussants should avoid inflammatory statements or postures in general. In short, participants need to know that freedom of speech requires responsibility and accountability, and should be provided with guidelines regarding how, whom, and what to question in a socially acceptable and constructive manner, while also avoiding "political correctness" (e.g., hypersensitivity; affective flatness; denial of difference; an "everyone is right" sentiment), since such processes ultimately undermine honesty and depth, tend to be superficial and conflict avoidant, and are unlikely in any case to achieve substantive outcomes at an individual or group level. One specific model that may be useful in this regard is the "intergroup dialogue" methodology, which thoughtfully and strategically brings together equal numbers of "opposing" perspectives and/or representatives of "different" facets of an issue (see http://igr.umich.edu/about/institute). Moreover, explanation and discussion of perspectives articulated earlier in this chapter (e.g., the difference between fundamentalism and orthodoxy; what the "quest" perspective implies; the meaning and implications of the "Continuum of Belief") also may provide the terminological heuristics and conceptual scaffolding that are necessary to facilitate such meta-level reflection. Whatever the method or approach, achieving balance between appropriate sensitivity and honest conviction is key to achieving both depth and integrity vis-à-vis processes of critical dialogue. Concretely, participants may be encouraged to reflect upon the nature of different religious and nonreligious beliefs (e.g., the content of the belief system), the foundation of such beliefs (e.g., the etiology of such beliefs and why they are promulgated), and the perceptions of the adherents to such beliefs regarding their validity (e.g., why believers contend that their belief system is good or true).

For example, in addition to contemplation regarding the various big picture concepts previously noted (e.g., meaning, purpose), participants might bore down further by comparing the various and competing interpretations of "jihad" used by Islamist groups to justify terrorist acts, and by others (Muslims and non-Muslims) who condemn such acts. An exploration of this concept might help participants obtain a more critical and reflective understanding of the varieties of Muslim religious expression. Alternatively, the origins and potential dilemma of the faith-based claim by both Christians and Muslims that their leader (Jesus and Mohammed, respectively) is the primary representative of God, as opposed to any other such figure in the past, present, or future may be a fruitful source of discussion, as can an analogous point of contrast with Hinduism (many gods, but perhaps from one source) or Buddhism (in which the Buddha explicitly disavowed inimitable status, despite such reverence often shown him by devotees). As a final example, an examination of the fundamental atheist belief that there is no God and no need for God—along with an attendant observation regarding how much destruction has been done in the name of God—can be a useful point of contrast and discussion when facilitated respectfully and constructively. Again, the point of such critical dialogue is not to convince others, although such outcomes may occur, but rather to reflect deeply and honestly not only about *what* one believes and values, but *why* such convictions matter in the first place, as well as *how* an experience of certitude may present a source of comfort and/or conflict for self, others, and the larger world.

Reflecting upon the importance of such critical dialogue from an Islamic perspective, Noor (2003) urges fellow believers to "re-learn the norms and rules of dialogue and communication" (p. 325) in a spirit of intelligence, honesty, and compassion:

> Recognizing the multiplicity within ourselves opens the way for us to recognize the multiplicity of the other as well. It would mean that we would be able to look at the West (and the rest) for what it truly is: a complex assembly of actors and agents, interests, beliefs, values, and ideas that may not be completely in harmony with each other. It may also help us realize that in the midst of that confusing and complex heterogeneity that is the other are also values, beliefs, and ideas that are common to ours. . .We need to remind ourselves continually of the fact that the Western world is far from uniform and that there exists a vast array of Western thinkers, leaders, activists, and citizens who care for Muslims as much as they do for their own. These are our real allies and friends, and we must never abandon or disregard them in our pursuit of justice and equity. (p. 327)

The three types of interreligious dialogues previously discussed may be implemented sequentially, progressively, or concurrently, depending on specific needs and objectives. In the end, what seems important is to encourage dialogue in all contexts (i.e., not just formal but also nonformal and informal), while emphasizing authentic relational connections with those who hold differing beliefs and values. If dialogues such as these involve the key stakeholders from all segments of a society—such as schools, religious institutions, social groups, and of course the state and its attendant political structures—outcomes over the long term may be moving and salutary, if not transformative.

SUMMARY AND CONCLUSION

At the outset of this chapter, we proposed that the need for a deeper understanding of religious faith is of great relevance in our increasingly globalized world, as religious systems that seem to contradict one's own beliefs and values often are perceived as a personal or cultural attack, which may lead to conflict or even violence toward the perceived source of this attack. From this point of departure, we considered certitude, a construct defined as the "absence of doubt," in adherents of religious and nonreligious beliefs, whether they be the fundamentalist versions of various religious faiths or the strident truth claims proposed by some advocates of atheism. We then noted that the tendency toward certitude requires fidelity to an allied epistemological framework with its own set of assumptions, before turning to an overview of various psychological theories and theorists, who have expressed negative (e.g., Freud, Skinner), positive (e.g., Jung, Maslow), and contemporary (e.g., the role of human attachment in relation to religious inclination) perspectives regarding religion and spirituality.

From there, we examined the complexity of religious certitude in relation to prejudice, including the intriguing finding that religious belief in itself may not necessarily be associated with antipathy toward "the other," but rather depends upon how beliefs subjectively are held by believers (e.g., the difference between fundamentalist and orthodox experiences of religious ideation, with the former group showing higher, and the latter group lower, degrees of prejudice overall). Along these lines, we considered the various forms in which religious ideation may be held by its adherent, with a specific examination of the broader "quest" orientation, which apprehends religious commitment as an ongoing process that is worked out and understood over time, in concert with the evolution of one's identity (i.e., one may grapple with one's religious/spiritual perspectives over the course of one's life). Among other aspects related to the etiology of certitude, we examined those from neuroscience, which offer tantalizing clues regarding the affectively mediated bias that seems tied to a sense of certainty regarding one's religious or nonreligious beliefs.

At this point, we turned our attention to the overarching model and method that represented the investigative core of this chapter, first by providing a brief overview of Equilintegration (EI) Theory and the EI Self, as well as the BEVI. Following this overview, we offered a series of data-based findings from a multi-institution assessment of learning project, which resulted in five concluding points. First, in exploring certitude generally, and religious certitude in particular, it is important to operationalize our definitions carefully. Second, psychological constructs may be more deeply understood by researching the characteristics of who is, and is not, likely to embody them. Third, a tendency toward socioreligiously traditional certitude generally is tied to a wide range of other belief structures (e.g., regarding other cultures as well as the natural world). Fourth, within-group-differences may be greater than between-group differences when dividing people by religious/nonreligious identification, which suggests the need to eschew surface level analyses of religious and nonreligious people both in scholarly and lay discourse. Fifth, the relative degree of religious or nonreligious certitude an individual expresses may largely be determined by a range of formative variables, but in a complex, interacting, and nonlinear manner. On the basis of such findings, and in light of the original goals of this chapter, we suggest that an agnostic stance along the "Continuum of Belief" may represent the most intellectually defensible framework regarding matters over which scientifically definitive conclusions—those that are empirically, independently, and reliably verifiable—seem untenable, while offering an aspirational framework that mitigates against shrill diatribes and destructive behaviors toward individuals and groups who "believe" differently.

Finally, in rounding out our discussion, we attempted to translate this perspective into applied form by describing educational and psychological interventions that encourage critical and reflective thinking about religious or nonreligious systems of thought, with a specific focus on cross-conviction dialogues, which may be divided into three overlapping and mutually reinforcing levels: preliminary, practical, and critical. By providing descriptive information and examples of each of these types of cross-conviction dialogues, it is our hope that this chapter may help advance the overarching goal of facilitating greater openness, reflection, and understanding among the adherents of various belief systems, whether they be religious or nonreligious.

In the final analysis, what is recommended most is the cultivation of a culture of humble curiosity and respectful exploration in which individuals may interact with those who hold a different religious or nonreligious perspective in an honest, authentic, inquiring, and intellectually responsible manner. Perhaps, if we strive to nurture psyches that are less inclined toward certitude, human beings will be freer to exercise religious faith or nonreligious faith on the basis of a richly earned awareness of why one does or does not believe as one does. By bravely accepting that definitive claims seem untenable—particularly regarding matters that appear to transcend the bounds of empirical reasoning—we may best be prepared for open engagement with self, others, and the larger world. Hopefully, such a caring, candid, and committed stance may help us to navigate more authentically the mysteries that are integral to our lived experience together.

REFERENCES

Allport, G. W. (1969). *The individual and his religion*. New York, NY: The Macmillan Company.

Altemeyer, B., & Hunsberger, B. (1992). Authoritarianism, religious fundamentalism, quest, and prejudice. *The International Journal for the Psychology of Religion, 2*, 113–133.

American Psychological Association. (2010, June 1). *American Psychological Association Ethical Principles of Psychologists and Code of Conduct*. Retrieved November 12, 2011, from http://www.apa.org/ethics/code/index.aspx

Arkin, R. M., Oleson, K. C., & Carroll, P. J. (Eds.). (2009). *Handbook of the uncertain self*. New York, NY: Psychology Press.

Aronson, E. (2012). *The social animal* (11th ed.). New York, NY: Worth Publishers.

Awad, G. H., & Hall-Clark, B. N. (2009). The impact of religiosity and right-wing authoritarianism on prejudice toward middle easterners. *Beliefs and Values, 1*(2), 183–191.

Baidhawy, Z. (2007). Building harmony and peace through multiculturalist theology-base religious education: An alternative for contemporary Indonesia. *British Journal of Religious Education, 29*(1), 15–30.

Bargh, J. A., & Chartrand, T. L. (1999). The unbearable automaticity of being. *American Psychologist, 54*(7), 462–479.

Batson, C. D. (1976). Religion as prosocial: Agent or double agent? *Journal for the Scientific Study of Religion, 15*(1), 29–45.

Batson, C. D., Schoenrade, P., & Ventis, W. L. (1993). *Religion and the individual*. New York, NY: Oxford University Press.

Bloom, P. (2007). Religion is natural. *Developmental Science, 10*(1), 147–151.

Brandt, M. J. (2010). The role of prejudice and the need for closure in religious fundamentalism. *Personality and Social Psychology Bulletin, 36*(5), 715–725.

Brearly, T. W. (2012, August). *The nature and etiology of religious certitude: Implications of the EI Framework and the Beliefs, Events, and Values Inventory*. Poster presented at the annual meeting of the American Psychological Association, Orlando, FL.

Cilliers, J. (2002). Building bridges for interfaith dialogue. In D. R. Smock (Ed.), *Interfaith dialogue and peacebuilding* (pp. 47–60). Washington, DC: United States Institute for Peace.

Davis, E. M. (2009). *Authenticity, inauthenticity, attachment, and god-image tendencies among adult evangelical protestant Christians* (Doctoral dissertation). Retrieved from ProQuest Dissertations & Theses (AAT 3400639).

Dawkins, R. (2006). *The god delusion*. New York, NY: Houghton Mifflin Company.

Dunn, R. G. (1998). *Identity crises: A social critique of postmodernity*. Minneapolis, MN: University of Minnesota Press.

Eagleton, T. (2006). Lunging, flailing, mispunching. *London Review of Books, 28*(20), 32–34.

Erikson, E. (1950). *Childhood and society*. New York, NY: Norton.

Erricker, C. (2006). If you don't know the difference you are living with, how can you learn to live with it? Taking difference seriously in spiritual and religious education. *International Journal of Children's Spirituality, 11*(1), 137–150.

Eunike, J. (2009). The influence of religious fundamentalism, right-wing authoritarianism, and Christian orthodoxy on explicit and implicit measures of attitudes towards homosexuals. *International Journal for the Psychology of Religion, 18*(4), 316–329.

Fischer, P., Greitemeyer, T., Kastenmüller, A., Jonas, E., & Frey, D. (2006).Coping with terrorism: The impact of increased salience of terrorism on mood and self-efficacy of intrinsically religious and nonreligious people. *Personality and Social Psychology Bulletin, 32*, 365–377.

Flere, S., Edwards, K. J., & Klanjsek, R. (2008). Religious orientation in three central European environments: Quest, intrinsic, and extrinsic dimensions. *International Journal for the Psychology of Religion, 18*, 1–21.

Ford, T. E., Brignall, T., VanValey, T. L., & Macaluso, M. J. (2009). The unmaking of prejudice: How Christian beliefs relate to attitudes toward homosexuals. *Journal for the Scientific Study of Religion, 48*(1), 146–160.

Frame, J. M. (1987). *The doctrine of the knowledge of god*. Phillipsburg, NJ: Presbyterian and Reformed Publishing Company.

Fromm, E. (1950). *Psychoanalysis and religion*. New Haven, CT: Yale University Press.

Gorsuch, R. L., & Aleshire, D. (1974). Christian faith and ethnic prejudice: A review and interpretation of research. *Journal for the Scientific Study of Religion, 13*(3), 281–307.

Granqvist, P. (2007). Examining relations among attachment, religiosity, and new age spirituality using the adult attachment interview. *Developmental Psychopathology, 43*(3), 590–601.

Haidt, J. (2007, September 22). *Moral psychology and the misunderstanding of religion*. Retrieved from http://www.edge.org/3rd_culture/haidt07/haidt07_index.html

Hall, T. W., Brokaw, B. F., Edwards, K. J., & Pike, P. L. (1998). An empirical exploration of psychoanalysis and religion: Spiritual maturity and object relations development. *Journal for the Scientific Study of Religion, 37*(2), 303–313.

Harford, T. (2011, April 23). Why we're all far too sure of ourselves. *The Financial Times*. Retrieved from http://www.ft.com/intl/cms/s/2/9219969e-6a28-11e0-86e4-00144feab49a.html

Hill, C., Brearly, T. W., Johnson, M., Brinton, C., Sternberger, L. G., Staton, R., & Shealy, C. N. (2013, August). *Exploring the etiology of economic beliefs and values: Implications from the Forum BEVI Project*. Poster presented at the annual meeting of the American Psychological Association, Honolulu, HI.

Himmelfarb, G. (2012, September 29). The once-born and twice-born. *The Wall Street Journal*, p. C5.

Hogg, M. A. (2005). Uncertainty, social identity, and ideology. In S. R. Thye & E. J. Lawler (Eds.), *Social identification in groups* (Vol. 22). San Diego, CA: Elsevier.

Hogg, M. A. (2011). Self-uncertainty, social identity, and the solace of extremism. In M. A. Hogg & D. L. Blaylock (Eds.), *Extremism and the psychology of uncertainty* (pp. 19–35). Oxford, UK: Wiley-Blackwell.

Hogg, M. A., Adelman, J. R., & Blagg, R. D. (2010). Religion in the face of uncertainty: An uncertainty-identity theory account of religiousness. *Personality and Social Psychology Review, 14*, 72–83.

HRH Prince Alwaleed Bin Talal Centre of Islamic Studies. (2009). *Contextualising Islam in Britain: Exploratory perspectives*. A project by the University of Cambridge in association with the Universities of Exeter and Westminster. Cambridge: Centre of Islamic Studies.

Hunsberger, B. (1989). A short version of the Christian orthodoxy scale. *Journal for the Scientific Study of Religion, 28*(3), 360–365.

Hunsberger, B. (1995). Religion and prejudice: The role of religious fundamentalism, quest, and right-wing authoritarianism. *Journal of Social Issues, 51*(2), 113–129.

Hunsberger, B., & Jackson, L. M. (2005). Religion, meaning, and prejudice. *Journal of Social Issues, 61*(4), 807–826.

Ipgrave, J. (2003). Dialogue, citizenship, and religious education. In R. Jackson (Ed.), *International perspectives on citizenship, education and religious diversity* (pp. 147–168). London: Routledge Falmer.

Jackson, L. M., & Hunsberger, B. (1999). An intergroup perspective on religion and prejudice. *Journal of the Scientific Study of Religion, 38*(4), 509–523.

James, W. (1902). *The varieties of religious experience: A study in human nature*. Cambridge, MA: The Riverside Press.

Jung, C. G. (1933). *Modern man in search of his soul*. Orlando, FL: Harcourt, Inc.

Keller, T. (2008). *The reason for god: Belief in an age of skepticism*. New York, NY: Dutton.

Kiesling, C. (2008). Identity and spirituality: A psychosocial exploration of the sense of spiritual self. *Psychology of Religion and Spirituality, 1*, 50–62.

Kirkpatrick, L. A. (1993). Fundamentalism, Christian orthodoxy, and intrinsic religious orientation as predictors of discriminatory attitudes. *Journal for the Scientific Study of Religion, 32*(3), 256–268.

Kirkpatrick, L. A., & Shaver, P. R. (1990). Attachment theory and religion: Childhood attachments, religious beliefs, and conversion. *Journal for the Scientific Study of Religion, 29*(3), 315–334.

Laythe, B., Finkel, D., & Kirkpatrick, L. A. (2001). Predicting prejudice from religious fundamentalism and right-wing authoritarianism: A multiple-regression approach. *Journal for the Scientific Study of Religion, 40*(1), 1–10.

Laythe, B., Finkel, D. G., Bringle, R. G., & Kirkpatrick, L. A. (2002). Religious fundamentalism as a predictor of prejudice: A two-component model. *Journal for the Scientific Study of Religion, 41*(4), 623–635.

Leganger-Krogstad, H. (2003). Dialogue among young citizens in pluralistic religious education classroom. In Jackson, R. (Ed.), *International perspectives on citizenship, education and religious diversity* (pp. 169–190). London: RoutledgeFalmer.

Leuba, J. H. (1925). *The psychology of religious mysticism*. New York, NY: Harcourt, Brace and Company.

Leuba, J. H. (1950). *The reformation of the churches*. Boston, MA: Beacon Press.

Lindholm, T. (2004). Philosophical and religious justifications of freedom of religion or belief. In T. Lindholm, Jr., W. C. Durham, & B. G. Tahzib-Lie (Eds.), *Facilitating freedom of religion or belief: a deskbook* (pp. 19–62). The Hague: Martinus Nijhoff.

Marcia, J. E. (1966). Development and validation of ego-identity status. *Journal of Personality and Social Psychology, 3*, 551–558.

Maslow, A. H. (1964). *Religions, values, and peak-experiences*. Columbus, OH: Ohio State University Press.

May, R. (1983). *The discovery of being*. New York, NY: W. W. Norton.

McFarland, S. G. (1989). Orientations and the targets of discrimination. *Journal for the Scientific Study of Religion, 28*(3), 324–336.

McLaughlin, T. H. (1984). Parental rights and the religious upbringing of children. *Journal of Philosophy of Education, 18*, 75–83.

Mikulincer, M., & Shaver, P. R. (2001). Attachment theory and intergroup bias: Evidence that priming the secure base schema attenuates negative reactions to out-groups. *Journal of Personality and Social Psychology, 81*, 97–115.

Murphy, C. (2012, February 12). The certainty of doubt. *The New York Times*, p. SR12.

Nagel, T. (1997). *The last word*. New York, NY: Oxford University Press.

Newberg, A., & Waldman, M. R. (2006). *Why we believe what we believe: Uncovering our biological need for meaning, spirituality, and truth*. New York, NY: Free Press.

Noor, F. A. (2003). What is the victory of Islam? Towards a different understanding of the ummah and political success in the contemporary world. In O. Safi (Ed.), *Progressive Muslims: on justice, gender, and pluralism* (pp. 320–332). Oxford: Oneworld Publications.

Paloutzian, R. F., & Kirkpatrick, L. A. (1995). Introduction: The scope of religious influences on personal and societal well-being. *Journal of Social Issues, 51*(2), 1–11.

Pargament, K. I., & Park, C. L. (1995). Merely a defense? The variety of religious means and ends. *Journal of Social Issues, 51*(2), 13–32.

Park, C. L., & Cohen, L. H. (1993). Religious and nonreligious coping with the death of a friend. *Cognitive Therapy and Research, 17*(6), 561–577.

Plantinga, A. (1993). *Warrant and proper function*. New York, NY: Oxford University Press.

Rohner, R. P. (1986). *The warmth dimension: Foundations of parental acceptance-rejection theory*. Thousand Oaks, CA: Sage.

Runnymede, T. (2000). *The future of multi-ethnic Britain: The Parekh report*. London: Profile Books.

Schultz, K. (2010). *Being wrong: Adventures in the margin of error*. New York, NY: HarperCollins.

Shealy, C. N. (2004). A model and method for "making" a Combined-Integrated psychologist: Equilintegration (EI) Theory and the Beliefs, Events, and Values Inventory (BEVI). *Journal of Clinical Psychology, 60*(10), 1065–1090.

Shealy, C. N. (2005). Justifying the justification hypothesis: Scientific-humanism, Equilintegration (EI) Theory, and the Beliefs, Events, and Values Inventory (BEVI) [Special Series]. *Journal of Clinical Psychology, 61*(1), 81–106.

Shealy, C. N. (Ed.). (2016). *Making sense of beliefs and values: Theory, research, and practice*. New York, NY: Springer Publishing.

Shealy, C. N., Bhuyan, D., & Sternberger, L. G. (2012). Cultivating the capacity to care in children and youth: Implications from EI Theory, EI Self, and BEVI. In U. Nayar (Ed.), *Child and Adolescent Mental Health* (pp. 240–255). New Delhi, India: Sage Publications.

Silberman, I., Higgins, E. T., & Dweck, C. S. (2005). Religion and world change: Violence and terrorism versus peace. *Journal of Social Issues, 61*(4), 761–784.

Singer, P. (2009). *The life you can save: Acting now to end world poverty*. New York, NY: Random House.

Skinner, B. F. (1948). "Superstition" in the pigeon. *Journal of Experimental Psychology, 38*(2), 168–172.

Skinner, B. F. (1987). What religion means to me. *Free Inquiry, 7*(2), 12–13.

Skitka, L. J., Bauman, C. W., & Lytle, B. L. (2009). Limits on legitimacy: Moral and religious convictions as constraints on deference to authority. *Journal of Personality and Social Psychology, 97*, 567–578.

Skitka, L., & Mullen, E. (2002). Understanding judgments of fairness in a real-world political context: A test of the value protection model of justice reasoning. *Personality and Social Psychology Bulletin, 28*, 1419–1429.

Spaeth, J., Schwartz, S., Nayar, U., & Ma, W. (2016). Identity development and the construction of self: Findings and implications from the Forum BEVI Project. In C. N. Shealy (Ed.), *Making sense of beliefs and values* (pp. 205–232). New York, NY: Springer.

Spinelli, E. (2005). *The interpreted world: An introduction to phenomenological psychology* (2nd ed.). London: SAGE Publications.

Tan, C. (2009). Taking faith seriously: Philosophical thoughts on religious education. *Beliefs and Values, 1*(2), 209–219.

Tan, C. (2010). Dialogical education for inter-religious engagement in a plural society. In K. Engebretson, M. de Sousa, G. Durka, & L. Gearon (Eds.), *International handbook of inter-religious education* (pp. 361–376). Dordrecht: Springer.

Tan, C. (2011). *Islamic education and indoctrination*. New York, NY: Routledge.

Thiessen, E. J. (1993). *Teaching for commitment: liberal education, indoctrination and Christian nurture*. Montreal & Kingston: McGill-Queen's University Press.

Towler, R. (1984). *The need for certainty: A sociological study of conventional religion*. London: Routledge & Kegan Paul.

Van den Bos, K. (2011). From "is" to "ought": The naturalistic fallacy in the psychology of religion. *Religion, Brain and Behavior, 1,* 242–243.

Van den Bos, K., Buurman, J., De Theije, V., Doosje, B., Loseman, A., Van Laarhoven, D., . . . Veldman, J. (2012). On shielding from death as an important yet malleable motive of worldview defense: Christian versus Muslim beliefs modulating the self-threat of mortality salience. *Social Cognition, 30*(6), 778–802.

Van den Bos, K., Euwema, M. C., Poortvliet, P. M., & Maas, M. (2007). Uncertainty management and social issues: Uncertainty as an important determinant of reactions to socially deviating people. *Journal of Applied Social Psychology, 37*(8), 1726–1756.

Van den Bos, K., Van Ameijde, J., & Van Gorp, H. (2006). On the psychology of religion: The role of personal uncertainty in religious worldview defense. *Basic and Applied Social Psychology, 28*(4), 333–341.

Van Doorn-Harder, N. (2007). Teaching religion in the USA: Bridging the gaps. *British Journal of Religious Education, 29*(1), 101–113.

Vetter, G. B. (1958). *Magic and religion: Their psychological nature, origin, and function*. New York, NY: Philosophical Library.

Vickers, J. M. (1988). *Chance and structure: An essay on the logical foundations of probability*. Oxford: Clarendon Press.

Winnicott, D. (1953). Transitional objects and transitional phenomena. *International Journal of Psychoanalysis, 34,* 89–97.

Winnicott, D. (1971). *Playing and reality*. London: Routledge.

Wulff, D. M. (1996). The psychology of religion: An overview. In E. P. Shafranske (Ed.), *Religion and the clinical practice of psychology* (pp. 43–70). Washington, DC: American Psychological Association.

Yiftachel, O. (2006). *Ethnocracy: Land and identity politics in Israel/Palestine*. Philadelphia, PA: University of Pennsylvania Press.

PART III

MAKING SENSE OF BELIEFS AND VALUES THROUGH PRACTICE: ASSESSMENT, EDUCATION, FORENSICS, LEADERSHIP, AND PSYCHOTHERAPY

Molly Coates, William Hanson, Doug B. Samuel,
Marlana Webster, and Jared Cozen   **11**

THE BELIEFS, EVENTS, AND VALUES INVENTORY (BEVI): PSYCHOLOGICAL ASSESSMENT IMPLICATIONS AND APPLICATIONS

A defining condition of being human is that we have to understand
the meaning of our experience.
                                        —Jack Mezirow

The practice of psychological assessment in mental health settings has been used, historically, to evaluate, diagnose, and guide treatment for clients (Butcher, 2006). Among related applications, modern formal assessment is used to clarify diagnostic questions by comparing individual clients to a normative group. Typically, information is gathered through behavioral observations, clinical interviews, and psychological tests; after which, data are assimilated, and results are presented to the client (Finn & Tonsager, 1992). Aside from providing information in an interview, clients are not usually involved actively in the formulation of clinical presentations or afforded the opportunity to understand how or why conclusions were reached (Curry & Hanson, 2010; El-Shaieb, 2005; Finn & Tonsager, 1997; Rogers, 1954). In contrast to the traditional "information gathering" model of testing, Meyer et al. (2001) contend that contemporary psychological assessment should include the evaluation of current functioning, the confirmation or negation of assumptions about a client, the identification of needs, the monitoring of treatment progress, and the provision of a foundation for an empathic informing via test interpretation and feedback. Meyer et al. likewise distinguish between psychological testing and assessment. Specifically, psychological testing is a categorical and definitive process involving the application of descriptive meaning to scale scores. Psychological assessment, in contrast, includes considerations such as the clinician's interpretation of data, the integration of life history, and the inclusion of other variables and information in order to strengthen nosological scaffolding and address referral questions and recommendations in a rich and ecologically valid manner.

With such a backdrop, this chapter begins by providing the rationale for an assessment method that seeks to elevate and operationalize the ineluctable role of meaning making by clients and clinicians alike. In doing so, we first offer relevant organizational perspectives (e.g., assessment/diagnosis guidelines) before introducing the challenges of attempting to conduct ecologically valid assessments within particular contexts (e.g., schools). Second, we turn our attention to the many value-laden aspects of traditional assessment, including the limitations inherent in rendering diagnoses and conducting evaluations, with a particular focus on how one's culture, beliefs, and life experiences may affect all aspects of the assessment process. Third, we explain the "therapeutic assessment" movement, which recognizes these problems with traditional assessment, and attempts to address them through a different paradigm (e.g., more open, experiential) for working with clients and systems. Fourth, on the basis of these perspectives, we describe a model (Equilintegration Theory) and method (Beliefs, Events, and Values Inventory [BEVI]) for assessment that attempts to bridge traditional and therapeutic assessment approaches by explicating a number of underlying variables (e.g., attributional, affective, developmental) that appear to mediate assessment processes and outcomes. Fifth, we illustrate how the BEVI is used in the "real world" via three different case presentations, including individual-, family-, and group-based interventions. Sixth and finally, in our concluding discussion, we present research regarding how the BEVI appears to be experienced by clients and clinicians, before offering six "best practice" recommendations for engaging in more integrative, exploratory, and collaborative approaches to assessment.

PROFESSIONAL GUIDANCE REGARDING ASSESSMENT

The American Psychological Association (APA)—the key governing body for practicing psychologists in the United States—maintains that psychological assessment should be used as one basis for clinical decision making, and only with instrument scale scores demonstrating sufficient reliability and validity (American Psychological Association, 2010). Moreover, the APA suggests psychologists should consider the purpose of assessment (e.g., why it is being conducted), as well as a broad range of related variables that may mediate functioning and affect interpretations (e.g., contextual, historical, cultural). Likewise, various iterations of the American Psychiatric Association's *Diagnostic and Statistical Manual of Mental Disorders* (*DSM*) typically provide guidelines requiring clinicians to account for cultural, historic, and background factors that could influence the expression of symptomatology and "mental illness" (e.g., Horwitz, 2002). For example, when considering whether or not to assign a diagnosis, the *DSM* advises,

> . . .this syndrome or patterns must not be merely an expectable and culturally sanctioned response to a particular event, for example, the death of a loved one. Whatever its cause, it must currently be considered a manifestation of a behavioral, psychological, or biological dysfunction in the individual. Neither deviant behavior (e.g., political, religious, or sexual) nor conflicts that are primarily between the individual and society are mental disorders unless the deviance or conflict is a symptom or dysfunction in the individual. . . . (American Psychiatric Association, 2000, p. xxxi)

Despite a range of questions and controversies regarding these recommendations (e.g., what is meant by the assertion that "deviance or conflict is a symptom or dysfunction in the individual"), guidelines from both organizations clearly require mental health professionals to consider overarching factors that might affect functioning and the expression of symptoms, rather than focusing solely on test data or diagnostic criteria alone. Such cautionary guidance recognizes that what is labeled "mental illness" may in fact be entirely reasonable, and even expected, reactions to traumatic or distressing life experiences (Cummings, Davies, & Campbell, 2002; Horwitz, 2002; Kleinman, 1988; Szasz, 1960). In other words, behavior that appears to be consistent with diagnostic criteria might, instead, represent an expected reaction to external conditions, rather than an internal state or trait of the individual. For example, the fact that boys are diagnosed with attentional disorders at two to three times the rate of girls might be attributed more parsimoniously to situationally based factors (e.g., conduct that is deemed to be optimal in a classroom setting) rather than some putative genetic anomaly that is "causing" disruptive behavior disproportionately in boys (Armstrong, 1996; Brown, 1995; Centers for Disease Control and Prevention, 2014; Conrad, 1975; Gualtieri & Johnson, 2005; Jones, 2002).

Complicating matters, third-party pressures affect further the integrity and day-to-day practice of assessment. For example, managed care companies may deny reimbursement for psychological assessment even though it may have significant meaning, relevance, and cost-effectiveness for clinicians and clients (Butcher & Rouse, 1996). Likewise, some managed care companies limit the type of permissible interviewing or assessment measures, which restricts the information gathered, and potentially lowers the accuracy of conferred diagnoses (Eisman et al., 2000). Similarly, in some systems (e.g., schools), factors that clearly mediate academic, interpersonal, or behavioral functioning (e.g., events in the home) often are deemed irrelevant or even inappropriate for inclusion in reports or interventions, because they are assumed to fall outside of the school's purview. Thus, disruptive behaviors in the classroom and/or other manifestations of psychological difficulty that might be explained parsimoniously by life events (e.g., abuse, neglect, or conflict at home) are instead attributed to factors (e.g., Attention Deficit Hyperactivity Disorder [ADHD]) more palatable to the school system, mainly because such conclusions locate the "cause" of the problem within the child or adolescent rather within the larger family or community system in which that child is embedded (e.g., Centers for Disease Control and Prevention, 2014; Cummings et al., 2002; Horwitz, 2002; Kleinman, 1988; Szasz, 1960). Such a focus is understandable on the one hand (e.g., if a school were to recognize that the problem was not in the child but in the family, such acknowledgment does suggest that different types of intervention, perhaps involving the family, would be necessary). Nonetheless, reflexively excluding information that may well have etiological relevance to a child's behavior and performance in the classroom seems antithetical to best practice in assessment, if a primary goal of such work is to identify the most likely causes of—and helpful solutions to—extant problems.

In short, whatever the setting or context, our formulations, diagnoses, and recommendations—and the interventions that flow from them—are only as valid as the sources of evidence upon which they are based. Thus, as assessment practitioners, we are obliged not to deny, ignore, or overlook information which reasonably may be key to understanding why our clients function as they do. Likewise, we should be mindful of any underlying beliefs and values (e.g., from our training; from the cultures or systems in which we practice) that may lead us not to experience as problematic the exclusion of such potentially relevant information (e.g., Anda et al., 2006; Chapman et al., 2004; Cummings et al., 2002; Horwitz, 2002; Jones, 2002; Molnar, Buka, & Kessler, 2001; Penza, Heim, & Nemeroff, 2003; Perry & Hambrick, 2008; Shealy, 1995, 2003; Springer, Sheridan, Kuo, & Carnes, 2007; Widom, DuMont, & Czaja, 2007).

THE VALUE-LADEN NATURE OF TESTING AND DIAGNOSING

As noted, psychological testing is, more often than not, under the control of the assessor, therapist, and third parties who wish to gather information about a client's functioning in order to monitor and provide treatment that is informed by such findings. If one's approach does not consider the potential confounds noted previously, the integrity and outcome of the entire assessment enterprise may be compromised. Nowhere are such excesses and confounds more lamentable than in common usage of the American Psychiatric Association's *DSM* (e.g., for information regarding the most current iteration of the *DSM*—the *DSM-5*—see www.dsm5.org/Pages/Default .aspx). Although the formal and informal "diagnosis" of mental disorders has occurred for centuries (Alexander & Selesnick, 1966; Hess, 2011), the validity and reliability of the *DSM*—the most prominent system for the classification of psychological functioning, particularly in the United States—remains mired in controversy (Bradford, 2009, 2010; Horwitz, 2002; Sarbin, 1997).

Formal diagnostic processes and labels have potential value. For example, they may facilitate communication among clinicians, fulfill reimbursement requirements, and allow research within and across categories of mental illness. These and other benefits notwithstanding, the fundamental critiques of the *DSM* are that it: (a) represents a reductionist system of relatively unreliable matching of symptom clusters to diagnoses; (b) minimizes and mechanizes the complexity and richness of the human condition; (c) does not sufficiently take into consideration cultural, historical, and contextual factors that demonstrably mediate the etiology of "symptoms"; (d) all too often produces high comorbidity with other diagnoses; (e) claims to be atheoretical, but actually is aligned with the basic precepts of the medical model; (f) does not provide substantive or reliable guidance in terms of treatment; (g) by dint of its touted objectivity (e.g., simply listing symptoms), such an approach minimizes the inherent subjectivity, potential bias, and power differential of those who render diagnoses on the basis of their perceptions of the existence or prevalence of such listed symptoms; (h) creates financial contingencies that promote the usage of this system of diagnosis (e.g., one often cannot get reimbursed without giving a diagnosis); (i) encumbers human beings with labels that may be stigmatizing and limit opportunities (e.g., immutably defines and delimits those who are diagnosed vis-à-vis other people and systems, such as employment and insurance); and (j) overall, may cause more harm than good to vulnerable human beings whom mental health professionals are bound ethically to protect and help (e.g., Bradford, 2010; Brickman et al., 1982; Eriksen & Kress, 2005; Halling & Goldfarb, 1996; Horwitz, 2002; Sarbin, 1997; Wakefield & Schmitz, 2010).

A number of excellent texts and articles have expounded upon these issues (e.g., see Beutler & Malik, 2002; Duffy, Gillig, Tureen, & Ybarra, 2002; Eriksen & Kress, 2005; Hays, 2001; Horwitz, 2002; Wakefield & Schmitz, 2010). Thus, we focus on three criticisms that have the potential to confound diagnostic assessments and results and, which are especially relevant to the framework presented in this chapter. First, consider the role of culture via assessment and diagnosis (Dana, 2005; Ridley, Li, & Hill, 1998; Solano-Flores & Nelson-Barber, 2000). As early as 1950, assessment researchers such as Raymond Cattell recognized that culture (e.g., age, ethnic background, and socioeconomic status [SES]) could influence diagnostic processes and outcomes because different cultural designations may predict performance on ability measures (Pierce-Jones & Tyler, 1950). Despite awareness of such potential confounds, and concomitant attempts to link such response patterns to dispositional rather than environmental factors, the assessment field in general has yet to account for the fact that one's culture may substantively affect assessment results (Dana, 2005; Hoagwood & Jensen, 1997). For example, Minnesota Multiphasic Personality Inventory-2 (MMPI-2) scale scores have excellent psychometric properties, and the test itself is the most widely used measure of personality and psychopathology in the world (Butcher et al., 2001). However, some MMPI-2 scores have been found to overpathologize on the basis of unique cultural worldviews, such as American Indians and Russians, which creates confusion regarding the interpretation of scores for such groups (Hill, Pace, & Robbins, 2010; Ritsher, Slivko-Kolchik, & Oleichik, 2001). At a broader level, Church (2010) maintains that ". . .directional or reciprocal influences of dispositional traits, characteristic adaptations, and life narratives" affect how various diagnostic presentations manifest across cultures (p. 447).

As a second critique, consider the inadvisability—if not impossibility—of cleaving one's own version of reality, subjective experience, and hermeneutical framework from clinical decision making. More specifically, evidence suggests that personal characteristics of the assessor influences the directionality of assessment, diagnosis, and treatment, even though such value-based perceptions are insufficiently acknowledged vis-à-vis training and practice in the mental health field (Shealy, 2004). For example, as F. Terrell, Terrell, and Taylor (1981) report, African American students with a high mistrust of White/European American people performed better when assessed by an African American examiner. Moreover, children assessed by women had higher scores in verbal comprehension, identifying similarities, and defining vocabulary than when assessed by men (Back & Dana, 1977). Finally, biasing factors are not attributable just to background variables of clients and therapists. For example, Kim and Ahn (2002) found that despite self-reported adherence to an atheoretical diagnostic taxonomy, clinicians nonetheless utilize their own theories and etiological models when assessing symptoms and rendering diagnoses in general and via the *DSM* in particular. Such findings support the contention that categories through which we structure the world shape—and are shaped by—our beliefs and values regarding why we are who we are (e.g., see Chapters 2 and 3; see also Brickman et al., 1982; Kimble, 1984; Shealy, 2005).

As a third critique, consider that the sum total of what makes each individual unique typically is not consistently or methodically assessed when psychological evaluations are conducted (e.g., not only affective, cognitive, and behavioral functioning, but the full range of formative variables, as well as the subjective interpretation of such interactions by both the assessed client and assessor) (e.g., Bradford, 2010). The test is not the problem in this regard, but rather factors including, but not necessarily limited to, the following: (a) the assessor's relative skill and ability to understand and intervene with troubled children, youth, adults, couples, families, and groups; (b) the capacity to differentiate and understand the origins of individual differences; (c) the context in which assessment occurs (e.g., because agencies and contexts differ in what they value, permit, or fund via assessment); (d) population variation, which may bear greatly on the understanding and interpretation of assessment results; and (e) as noted, "who the assessor is" in terms of their professional identity and beliefs, values, and awareness of self (e.g., Shealy, 2004, Shepard, 1992; Watkins, 1993), a gestalt of competencies, which might be referred to as the "person of the assessor" (see also Aponte et al., 2009; Finn, 2007; Finn & Tonsager, 1997; Poston & Hanson, 2010; Shealy, 2016).

ALTERNATIVE AND CONTEMPORARY ASSESSMENT PRACTICE—ASSESSING HUMANS HUMANELY

Among other implications of the preceding discussion, assessment becomes more meaningful when formative variables (e.g., life history, background variables) are linked directly with why and how we experience ourselves, others, and the larger world in the way the we do in order to understand that which is idiographic (i.e., self-referenced) and nomothetic (i.e., other-referenced) about each human being. The result of such assessment, manifesting throughout the process, is that clients have the opportunity to apprehend why they are who they are, why they believe what they believe, and whom they may become. This type of "phenomenological knowing seeks to comprehend how the various dimensions, inner tensions, contradictions, and potentialities of a person coalesce into an integral, invariant organization of subjectivity" (Bradford, 2010, p. 130). Most importantly, as a methodology and philosophy of assessment—perhaps best encompassed under the aegis of Psychological Assessment as a Therapeutic Intervention (PATI)—this approach works (e.g., facilitates treatment progress, improves self-discovery) (e.g., Finn & Tonsager, 2002; Poston & Hanson, 2010; Smith, Handler, & Nash, 2010; Tharinger et al., 2008; see also Hanson & Poston, 2011, and for an alternative perspective, Lilienfeld, Garb, & Wood, 2011).

As Finn and Tonsager (2002) suggest, clients evaluated through an open, collaborative, and reflective process are more accepting of information that could be tied directly to their personal goals and questions about themselves. This outcome makes clinical sense, because the greater depth and breadth evaluators bring to bear in an assessment setting, the more likely they are to consider factors and forces that affect who people are and why (Cummings et al., 2002). Such respect for the inherent complexity and subjectivity of the assessment process, alongside the assemblage of objective data, is more likely to lead to ecologically valid assessment, while affording multiple opportunities for process-based reflections by clients and clinicians alike (Finn, 2008). Moreover, by anticipating and encouraging the unique meaning-making capacities in each client and experiencing clients as more than the sum of their standard scores, clinicians enhance the likelihood that assessment becomes integral to the process of facilitating growth and development, rather than a static audit of how things are and will be. Ultimately, this approach to assessment recognizes ". . .the importance of contextual influences on human behavior" as well as the need to address "larger interpersonal and social systems" (Tharinger et al., 2008, p. 547) in order to promote mutual understanding and mobilize change (Hanson, 2012) (e.g., Cummings et al., 2002). As Mezirow (1997) observes, by promoting transformative learning, we facilitate worldviews that are "more inclusive, discriminating, self-reflective, and integrative of experience" (p. 5). The implications of this approach to assessment extend far beyond the individual case, but also may be applied to couples, families, groups, and other relational systems (e.g., Kubiszyn et al., 2000; Smith et al., 2010).

From a concrete and practical standpoint, there are multiple perspectives on how such assessment should be conducted. Bradford (2010) recommends that the totality of a person be assessed within the context of his or her situation, which means considering individuals as greater than the sum of their parts. From this view, individuals are understood as much more than a series of findings or observations, and always with an appreciation that symptoms may "make sense" (i.e., are not necessarily pathological) in the context of one's unique life situation and context. This approach to understanding human functioning is highly congruent with the perspective of developmental psychopathology, because the etiology of behavioral, cognitive, and affective processes for human beings culminates from a dynamic inter-action among biology, context, life events, interpersonal factors, and innate aspects of personality (Cummings et al., 2002). By implication then, assessment processes and methods that include interviews, standardized measures, and an exploration of one's background and familial history are more likely to capture processes that culminate in pathology, or health, over time (e.g., Tharinger et al., 2008).

ASSESSMENT AS INTERVENTION

As an exemplar of this approach, Finn's model of Therapeutic Assessment (TA; Finn, 1996; Finn & Tonsager, 1992, 1997; Smith et al., 2010; Tharinger et al., 2008) has, as its primary goal, the understanding and facilitation of transformative change through the assessment process. More specifically, the TA model seeks to reduce the power dynamics between evaluator and examinee, thus allowing the examinee to become an integral part of the assessment process. As such, clients are involved in all phases of evaluation, from the initial development of goals, discussion of expectations, con-sideration of different ways that human functioning may be understood, and engage-ment in interactive and inclusive informing processes. Such an approach encourages engaged, clinically meaningful reactions to, and feedback about, assessment results, whether positive or negative; it also has fidelity with the principles underlying informed consent, inviting clients to be active participants throughout the process of their own assessment (Levak, Siegel, Nichols, 2011; Pawlowski, 2002).

As may be clear, the preceding philosophical and applied approach to assess-ment is much more interactive, inclusive, and collaborative—and thereby therapeu-tic—than is the case in practice, traditionally speaking (Meyer, 2001; Nagy, 2011). Many clinicians from an array of theoretical perspectives—humanistic, psychody-namic, systemic, interpersonal, and increasingly, cognitive behavioral—have advo-cated for more integrative, depth-based, and holistic ways of understanding and relating to the human condition. Although multiple factors undoubtedly are at play, as the reductionistic and decades-long fixation with "bad genes" and "chemical imbalances in the brain" continues to accede to the reality of multidirectional causal-ity, the Zeitgeist increasingly appears right for a more sophisticated, empirically sup-portable, and humanistically grounded paradigm of human functioning and the concomitant role of the "mental health professional" in promoting healing, under-standing, and growth (Baughman, 2008; Haslam, 2004; Horwitz, 2002; Lurie, 1991; Pienkos & Sass, 2012; Shealy, 2003). Emergent from this necessary paradigmatic shift, assessors increasingly are seeking to broaden their activities beyond domain-specific fact finding (e.g., intellectual functioning; behavior description) (e.g., Smith et al., 2010; Tharinger et al., 2008).

Overall, then, this strategy moves beyond categorical methods of standardized diagnostic testing to more nuanced and complex ways of working clinically (Nudel, 2012). In such process-based assessment, the goal is not necessarily to render a diag-nosis, although such an outcome may legitimately occur. Rather, data are gathered, first and foremost, to facilitate communication among treatment providers, engage empathically with clients, and promote understanding of the many and varied fac-tors that lead to the presenting situation. Pragmatically, data are also gathered to facilitate change. With this approach, efforts are directed toward an understanding of the whole and complex person to include the value-based experience of self, others, and the larger world (Finn & Tonsager, 1997; Finn 2008). From this PATI perspective, the assessor openly reflects upon his or her own subjective experience of self, actively seeking to understand the client's own version of reality (Bradford, 2010). This approach also emphasizes sharing of assessment methods and perspectives with clients, and active integration of the clients' experience of material that may help deepen an understanding of who they are and why they do what they do (Fischer, 1970, 1994). Ideally, power differentials are reduced and each client's natural curiosity about self is tapped deliberately to enrich and inform the entire process. Done well, such processes enhance the effectiveness and utility of assessment (Tharinger et al., 2008).

Such emphases are crucial to the evolution of assessment research and practice. As Poston and Hanson (2010) observe, "assessment and testing practices are at a critical point in their history. These practices will survive if, and only if, they demonstrate (empirically) their treatment validity and clinical utility" (p. 211). Along these lines, Finn and Tonsager (1992) report that clients who completed therapeutic assessment using the MMPI-2 had significantly lower symptomatology, greater hope for their life situation, and higher self-esteem at 2 weeks after this process than did a control group who simply met with the examiner without completing the MMPI-2 or receiving feedback. Moreover, in their time-series analysis, Smith et al. (2010) found that "families with a preadolescent boy presenting with ODD experienced demonstrable benefits in multiple areas of functioning after participating in TA" (p. 600). Likewise, in their examination of sociocultural variables that may influence assessment findings (e.g., ethnic background, SES), Solano-Flores and Nelson-Barber (2001) report that factors such as "values, beliefs, experiences, communication patterns, teaching and learning styles, and epistemologies" must be accounted for if we are to derive ecologically valid understandings of what students present and why. A recent review suggests that PATI is comparably effective to stand-alone psychotherapy, such as for substance abuse, with outcome-oriented effect sizes hovering around 0.40 (Hanson & Poston, 2011; Poston & Hanson, 2010; see also Tharinger et al., 2008).

Assessment as intervention builds upon more traditional assessment approaches by making them more person-centered and by including the client as an active participant. Some have theorized that the utility of PATI is derived from the activation of deep and sustained reflection on the self (Finn, 2007; Hanson, Claiborn, & Kerr, 1997). Such a focus not only helps clients better apprehend their current beliefs and values, but understand the possible linkage between formative variables (e.g., life history, background) and present functioning (Shealy, 2004). This approach encourages clients to understand themselves and their origins at a deeper level, which correspondingly opens up the possibility that "old ways" of working and relating to self, others, and the larger world may be examined—often for the first time—and perhaps substituted as processes unfold with ways of experiencing and understanding self that are more conducive to the pursuit of interpersonal relations and life goals. In a sense, therapeutic assessment allows clients to write and rewrite their stories and personal narratives (Fischer & Finn, 2008). Again, this way of working is not intended to minimize the demonstrable value of traditional psychological evaluation methods, but rather to suggest that an assessment-as-intervention approach may broaden the types of measures we include and the philosophy and approach regarding their administration and delivery. As we illustrate next, through the EI model and BEVI method, such an approach expands the scope of information we seek in order to understand why our clients are who they are, and what sorts of interventions may productively help them pursue and achieve their deepest life goals (e.g., Bradford, 2010; Meyer et al., 2001; Poston & Hanson, 2010; Tharinger et al., 2008).

THERAPEUTIC ASSESSMENT, THE EI MODEL, AND THE BEVI METHOD

The Equilintegration (EI) Theory perspective—including EI Theory and the EI Self—and the accompanying BEVI, are highly congruent with PATI sensibilities. In development since the early 1990s, EI Theory explains the processes by which beliefs, values, and "worldviews" are acquired and maintained, why their alteration is typically resisted, and how and under what circumstances their modification occurs (see Chapter 2). Derivative of EI Theory, the EI Self explains integrative and synergistic processes by which beliefs and values are acquired, maintained, and transformed as well as how and why they are linked to the formative variables, core needs, and adaptive potential of the self. Informed by scholarship in a range of key areas (e.g., "needs-based" research and theory; developmental psychopathology; social cognition; psychotherapy process and outcome; affect regulation; theories and models of "self"), the EI Self seeks to illustrate how the interaction between our core needs (e.g., for attachment, affiliation) and formative variables (e.g., caregiver, culture) results in beliefs and values about self, others, and the world at large that we all internalize over the course of development and across the life span (see Chapter 3).

Concomitant with EI Theory and the EI Self, the BEVI is a comprehensive analytic tool that examines how and why we come to see ourselves, others, and the larger world as we do (e.g., how life experiences, culture, and context affect our beliefs, values, and worldview) as well as the influence of such processes on multiple aspects of human functioning (e.g., learning processes, relationships, personal growth, the pursuit of life goals).[1] For example, the BEVI assesses processes such as: basic openness; the tendency to (or not to) stereotype in particular ways; self- and emotional awareness; preferred strategies for making sense of why "other" people and cultures "do what they do"; global engagement (e.g., receptivity to different cultures, religions, and social practices); and worldview shift (e.g., to what degree do beliefs and values change as a result of specific experiences). BEVI results are translated into reports at the individual, group, and organizational levels and used in a wide range of contexts for a variety of applied and research purposes (e.g., to track and examine changes in worldviews over time) (e.g., Anmuth et al., 2013; Atwood, Chkhaidze, Shealy, Staton, & Sternberger, 2014; Brearly, Shealy, Staton, & Sternberger, 2012; Hill et al., 2013; Isley, Shealy, Crandall, Sivo, & Reifsteck, 1999; Hayes, Shealy, Sivo, & Weinstein, 1999; Patel, Shealy, & De Michele, 2007; Pysarchik, Shealy, & Whalen, 2007; Shealy, 2000a, 2000b, 2004, 2005, 2015, 2016; Shealy et al., 2012; Tabit et al., 2011; for more information about the BEVI, see Chapter 4 as well as www.ibavi.org/content/featured-projects).

THE BEVI IN ASSESSMENT

Taking a broad-based PATI perspective, the primary focus of this chapter describes usage of the BEVI in real world psychological assessment. As a comprehensive assessment measure, the BEVI is used for an array of purposes, including:

- *To evaluate and understand psychological functioning* (e.g., of individuals, couples, families, groups)

---

[1] For more information about the long and short versions of the BEVI, see Chapter 4.

- *To facilitate intervention planning and processes* (e.g., across different therapeutic schools, configurations, approaches, and perspectives)
- *To promote matching and alignment processes* (e.g., between therapists and clients)
- *To measure treatment outcomes* (e.g., before, during, and after therapeutic interventions)
- *To mobilize change/facilitate growth and development* (e.g., of individuals, groups, organizations)
- *To evaluate learning experiences* (e.g., study abroad; multicultural courses; general education courses and curricula; graduate-level education; professional education/training programs; service learning)
- *To understand learning processes* (e.g., who learns what and why, and under what circumstances)
- *To promote learning objectives* (e.g., increased awareness of self, others, and the larger world)
- *To enhance teaching and program quality* (e.g., which experiences, courses, programs have what impact, and why)
- *To conduct research* (e.g., how, why, and under what circumstances people become more "open" to different cultures)
- *To address organizational needs* (e.g., staff/leadership development; assess organizational climate)
- *To comply with assessment and accreditation requirements* (e.g., linking objectives to outcomes)

Although the BEVI is used for assessment purposes across populations and settings (e.g., business, consultation, education, forensic, mental health, military, research), we focus here on those that relate to mental health interventions, generally, as well as therapeutic assessment in particular (e.g., Finn, 2007, 2008; Finn, Fischer, & Handler, 2012; Finn & Tonsager, 2002; Tharinger et al., 2008). Specifically, the following three case studies—in the context of individual, couples/family, and group work—illustrate how the BEVI may be used to deepen our understanding of who our clients are, broaden our conceptual frameworks, enrich our recommendations, and facilitate larger therapeutic goals.[2]

Case Study 1: Megan Anderson

Evaluation excerpts are presented to demonstrate the juxtaposition of the BEVI with other assessment measures as a component of a larger assessment battery.

PSYCHOLOGICAL EVALUATION

IDENTIFYING INFORMATION
Name of examinee: Megan Anderson
Date of Birth: 4/9/1988

---

[2] The de-identified presentation of clinical material in this chapter, and book, is informed by the March, 2012 Special Section of the journal *Psychotherapy*, entitled "Ethical Issues in Clinical Writing," Volume 49, Issue 1, pp. 1–25 as well as Health Insurance Portability and Accountability Act (HIPAA) regulations, APA ethical guidelines (2002), and other best practices for reporting clinical information. Although assessment results are consistent with clinical events and processes, key information has been modified (e.g., to ensure anonymity; in recognition that this version of the BEVI had 19 scales, whereas the current version has 17; please see Chapter 4 for more information). For space limitations, material is excerpted and adapted in order to focus on usage and interpretation of the BEVI (e.g., via ellipses to indicate that additional content was part of the original report).

REASON FOR REFERRAL

Megan was evaluated due to ongoing difficulties with anxiety in social situations and "just overall." She reports being "an anxious person for as long as I can remember" although her difficulties in this regard have reportedly become more pronounced during her time in college. She wants to understand "why I am anxious," and to become better able to manage social situations and academic requirements. Importantly, Megan describes a negative experience of past assessment processes (e.g., they didn't provide information that helped her understand the source of her difficulties). She also expresses intense guilt about an intimate relationship that "did not go like it should." Finally, Megan reports long-term difficulties in her family or origin, and wishes she weren't "so angry about all that". . .

ASSESSMENT MEASURES

The Wechsler Adult Intelligence Scale, 4th Edition (WAIS–IV)
Woodcock–Johnson—Achievement, 3rd Edition, (WJ ACH), Standard Battery
Minnesota Multiphasic Personality Inventory-2 (MMPI-2)
Beck Anxiety Inventory-II (BAI-II)
Behavior Assessment System for Children, Second Edition (BASC-2)
Beliefs, Events, and Values Inventory (BEVI)
Sentence Completion Test (SCT)
Thematic Apperception Test (TAT)
Life Information Survey (LIS)

BACKGROUND INFORMATION

Megan is a 20-year-old, single, White/European American female from a middle class background in her second year of study, with a 2.75 GPA. She currently is majoring in Art History. Megan's family of origin includes her biological mother and father, both college graduates, who divorced when she was 16, and an 18-year-old brother. She described considerable conflict between her estranged parents as well as a highly "traditional" upbringing. . .

Megan reports an ongoing struggle with anxiety particularly during tests, when studying, and during class participation. However, by report, she also "worries about everything." Apparently, these worries date back to childhood, which she describes as "lots of shouting." By report, her primary symptoms include feelings of dread prior to test taking (i.e., intense fears about failing) as well as chronic ruminative thoughts regarding her intellectual abilities (e.g., she is "not smart enough"), interpersonal relations (e.g., fears that her friends don't like or want to be around her), and family dynamics (e.g., deep difficulties telling her parents what she "really wants or feels"). . .

BEHAVIORAL OBSERVATIONS

Megan was tested over the course of two weeks over three separate sessions, ranging from 3 to 4 hours each. She arrived on time to meetings, and was well groomed. She also was encouraged to reflect both verbally, and in writing, about questions she may have regarding assessment (e.g., what she hoped to learn about herself). Likewise, during the informing process, Megan was provided the opportunity to read and reflect upon her report (e.g., to give her impressions regarding the accuracy of various interpretative points and the relevance of recommendations), and to correct any errors of fact. Her demeanor throughout assessment was open and engaged. . .

TEST RESULTS

Megan was administered the Wechsler Adult Intelligence Scale—Fourth Edition (WAIS-IV), which has mean of 100 and SD of 15, to assess her overall level of cognitive functioning. Megan was administered ten subtests of the Wechsler Adult Intelligence Scale—Fourth Edition (WAIS-IV) from which her composite scores were derived. She achieved a Full Scale IQ (FSIQ) score of 103 (95% confidence interval = 97–105), classifying her overall intellectual ability, as measured by the WAIS-IV, in the Average range. . .

Megan was administered the Woodcock–Johnson Test of Achievement—Third Edition (WJ-III ACH), standard battery—a comprehensive battery of individually administered tests measuring academic areas of reading, mathematics, and written and oral language. The Broad Reading cluster measures reading achievement. Megan's Broad Reading performance is classified in the Average range (SS = 104). . .

Megan's personality and socioemotional functioning were assessed using a number of measures including the Minnesota Multiphasic Personality Inventory-Second Edition (MMPI-2), Behavior Assessment System for Children, Second Edition (BASC-2), Beliefs, Events, and Values Inventory (BEVI), Beck Anxiety Inventory-II, Thematic Apperception Test (TAT), and Sentence Completion Series.

The MMPI-2 is a commonly used measure of adult personality and psychopathology. It has 567 true/false items that are scored for 10 primary clinical scales and a number of validity, content, and clinical subscales. The Beliefs and Values Instrument (BEVI) is a mixed-methods measure that helps individuals understand better why they believe what they believe and value about themselves, others, and the world at large with a particular focus upon learning, personal growth, relationships, and the pursuit of life goals. The BEVI consists of two background information items, two validity scales, 19 quantitative process scales, which are reported as percentiles, and three qualitative experiential items. . .

Megan's scores suggest she reported experiencing significant psychological turmoil and distress (BASC-2, Emotional Symptoms Index T = 74), which is affecting her experience of herself, others, and the world around her. Her scores indicate significant feelings of anxiety including, worry, nervousness, and fear (BASC-2, Anxiety T = 78; MMPI-2, Scale 7 = 72, ANX T = 79). The Beck Anxiety Inventory (BAI-II) also was used to assess symptoms related to anxiety. Megan's overall total score was elevated and clinically significant for the severe range. . .This presentation is consistent with Megan's self-report, and is evidenced by her (Sentence Completion Series) response, "My biggest problem is how anxious I feel around everyone and everything". . .

Megan's score on Negative Life Events from the BEVI (68) is elevated, indicating she reported a relatively high degree of unhappy experiences in childhood and adolescence. Item-level analysis provides insight into the nature of these difficulties, which appear to focus on her perception of hostile relations between her now divorced parents. For example, she Strongly Agreed that "I wish my mother and/or father had done things differently"; "I witnessed a lot of anger or aggression when I was growing up"; "Marital conflict causes problems for children"; "My mother had a bad family situation when she was growing up"; and "Growing up is often a brutal process." Despite these apparent difficulties (and perhaps because of them), Megan scored very high on Emotional Attunement (98), Self Awareness (87), and Basic Openness (73) from the

BEVI, suggesting a strong tendency to focus on emotions in self and other, to be intensely preoccupied with questions of why she and others "work" as they do, as well as the inclination to be quite accepting of basic aspects of what makes human beings human (e.g., she does not deny fundamental thoughts or feelings that are in fact experienced by most people in life). Moreover, she evidences a strong capacity to hold complexity (e.g., to see the world in terms of gray, rather than black and white), as evidenced by her high score on Socioemotional Convergence (75). Although such elevations suggests that Megan would be very open to, and able to benefit from, psychological intervention, such intensive self/affect focus is likely to be all consuming, making it difficult for her to take perspective on her own internal experience or to soothe/calm herself. In short, she likely would be in a constant state of affective arousal and unremitting self-focus. Such scale-level observations are supported further by analysis of items on the BEVI to which she "Strongly Agreed" (as opposed to Strongly Disagree, Disagree, or Agree), including "I am a very feeling person," "I cry several times a year," "I am always trying to understand myself better," and "I need someone in my life to listen to how I feel."

At the same time, her relatively high elevation on Identity Closure (66) suggests that Megan is experiencing considerable confusion regarding who she is and where she is going in her life as well as attendant enmeshment with her family of origin, despite the conflicts she historically reports experiencing. Another pairing of scores, Positive Thinking (PT = 70) and Global Engagement (GE = 80), offer further insight into her basic way of approaching the larger world. In particular, Megan would likely be inclined to adopt an, "I can do it and you should too" attitude toward self and others. She probably would be impatient with people she perceived as "complaining" about their lot in life, who (from her perspective) refused to take responsibility for their lives and actions. Although such a framework has adaptive implications (e.g., may be associated with a tendency to persevere in the face of adversity), such a stance also often lacks a degree of empathy toward self or others when confronted with the complexity of human existence (e.g., there may be reasons why it is very difficult for others to "pull themselves up by their own bootstraps") as well as a relatively naïve assessment of her own ability to affect others and "make a difference" simply through sheer force of will. At the same time, she appears highly motivated to do good works, and may personally feel as though she is responsible for helping to make the world "a better place."

Finally, her score on Gender Traditionalism (69) suggests her general degree of openness would not necessarily extend to this domain in terms of the gender-based actions or inclinations by self or others. It is quite possible that she may experience intense conflict at this level, particularly in light of an intimate relationship she recently severed, as a result of considerable guilt regarding her own sexual behavior, which she described as "wrong." She also is presenting with a somewhat elevated degree of Identity Closure (66). In other words, she may be experiencing a high degree of "stuckness" regarding who she is and where she is going in her life, which is complicated by a basic sense that she should be making the world "a better place," and is not the sort of person who should "be stuck," even as she appears to regard her own internal affective and attributional processes with a sense of deep ambivalence.

This juxtaposition of objective scores and projective responses on the BEVI illustrates the complex and dynamic interaction among different and sometimes contradictory affective, attributional, and developmental processes.

If such dynamics are explored with clients in an empathic, open, and collaborative manner—consistent with the basic principles of therapeutic assessment— the net effect is to help them "make sense of" why they feel, think, and behave as they do. For example, Megan likely would struggle to reconcile the intense depth and extent of herself/emotion focus with strong and simultaneous beliefs that she should be functioning more like a "good girl" who "doesn't complain" about her life or situation. If she could just force herself to "get it right," perhaps the problems she is experiencing would abate. Unfortunately, this strategy does not seem to be working effectively, as her BEVI, BASC, MMPI-2, and BAI-II scores, Life Information Survey, and Clinical Interview all reveal. Moreover, at an item level of analysis, contradictions among Strongly Agree endorsements on the BEVI reveal the struggle Megan is experiencing in her attempts to "overcome" difficulties through force of will, even as she experiences impatience, if not contempt, regarding the depth of her own struggle: "You can't change the past so there's no point dwelling on it"; "I want to find a better sense of balance in my life"; "Someday we will just accept that men and women are simply different"; "Sometimes I feel things too deeply"; "I have gone through a painful identity crisis"; "The best way to get through life is to keep a happy attitude"; "A man should act like a man". . .

Not surprisingly, Megan worries, perhaps obsessively (MMPI-2; OBS = 64), and often experiences guilt and remorse about past deeds (MMPI-2; Pd4 = 75). She perceives herself as more high-strung and sensitive as well as feeling things more intensely than others, which can cause her to feel lonely and misunderstood (MMPI-2; Scale 6 = 74; Pa2 = 76). . .She also struggles with interpersonal connection and relationships, as evidenced further in her Sentence Completion Series response, ". . .I experience stress whenever I am around other people" and ". . .it bothers me that people can tell how I feel." Social interactions can at times consume an enormous amount of energy for Megan, even as she desires greater connection. This conflict is revealed in recurring themes of loneliness, exemplified by her response to one TAT card: "She really wants other people to be in her life, but is always alone. People think she is weird and intense, and she doesn't know how to convince them she's normal." Her Strongly Agree endorsement of the BEVI item, "I have felt lonely in my life," offers final evidence of the intensity of her interpersonal struggles.

Despite internal conflicts and contradictions at a number of levels as noted previously, and the experience of considerable psychological distress, Megan's very high scores on Emotional Attunement, Self Awareness, and Basic Openness on the BEVI all strongly suggest a general lack of defensiveness regarding her own psychological processes, aside from one substantive domain (gender). Also, in general, she evidences a good capacity to persevere in the face of adversity, and to hold complexity in self and other (e.g., she is able to think in shades of gray rather than insist upon a black and white frame of the world, aside from beliefs about gender), even as she experiences a great many internal contradictions regarding what she should be or feel, and why. From a developmental standpoint, such a struggle may help explain her high sense of Identity Diffusion (e.g., she is unclear about who she is and where she is going in life, but is intensely invested in learning more about why she is who she is, and making a difference in the world). As long as these contradictions are appreciated, and the depth of her distress recognized, Megan is likely to be a good and open candidate for psychotherapeutic intervention, which is one of the recommendations included in the following. . .

DIAGNOSIS

Axis I   300.02, Generalized Anxiety Disorder
Axis II: 799.9 Diagnosis Deferred
Axis III: None
Axis IV: Academic Problems; Family Conflict
Axis V: GAF (current) = 60

RECOMMENDATIONS

1. It is recommended that Megan begin individual therapy to reduce her level of isolation, work through intense feelings of anger, fear, and confusion, while improving her awareness of her own functioning. For example, although Megan is highly focused on her own inner world and that of others, she simultaneously appears to feel conflicted about the depth of her own distress, because its intense presence implies a failure on her part to overcome feelings of weakness and vulnerability through force of will. She also appears to be experiencing conflict in her understanding of "who she is and should be" as a female, given the expectations that apparently were conveyed to her in her family of origin. . .It is also recommended that test results be used throughout treatment, not only for discussion purposes, but to monitor progress over time. . .

Megan Anderson: An Informing Postscript

Regarding the preceding evaluation, and the relationship between BEVI findings and the PATI approach, it should be noted that the process of evaluation as well as informing allowed for a rich and engaging initial encounter for Megan throughout (e.g., she was able to pose questions at the outset of the evaluation that she hoped to have answered and to discuss her experience of this evaluation in detail upon its conclusion). When asked, her overall response to the report was "very accurate," and seemed to bring out themes that she had felt, but had not been able to articulate before. In particular, dynamics regarding her feelings of inadequacy vis-à-vis her family were especially salient for her, as she had not made the connection between her chronic experience of insecurity and inadequacy with the intense conflict and criticism she reports throughout her childhood and to the present day. Megan was intrigued particularly by the contradictions in her own experience of self, such as the relatively rigid beliefs she expressed regarding "how things should be" along with her relative degree of expressed contempt for weakness in self or other. The bind presented by such an internal affective and attributional dynamic—feeling contempt toward her own feelings of inadequacy—was both emotionally moving to her (e.g., she cried when describing this struggle) and clarifying regarding the sort of work that may be necessary in therapy (e.g., taking her own emotional experiences more seriously, rather than condemning herself for having such feelings). As discussed with Megan, the "good news" was, all evidence seemed to suggest she had enormous capacity to feel emotion, reflect upon self, and be open to the process of therapy. By toggling back and forth between quantitative scores and endorsed statements from the BEVI, and juxtaposing such findings with other data, it became abundantly clear to Megan that these contradictions in self emerged from, and inextricably were linked to, her own history. Moreover, if she could simply learn to hold her beliefs and feelings, rather than condemn herself for having them (which she automatically had done for so many years, for historical/family reasons that were beginning to become clear), Megan expressed hope she might be able to understand herself better, and move forward in a less "crazy" way, goals that were congruent with her original wishes upon initial presentation. As documented by Cozen, Hanson, Poston, Jones, and Tabit (2016), and as referenced later in this chapter, these sorts of realizations by clients and clinicians occur often with the BEVI, which is a fundamental purpose of the instrument, and consistent with the overarching goals of the PATI approach to therapeutic assessment. The change process was, in this case, clearly mobilized via assessment and feedback.

BEVI Profile: Megan Anderson

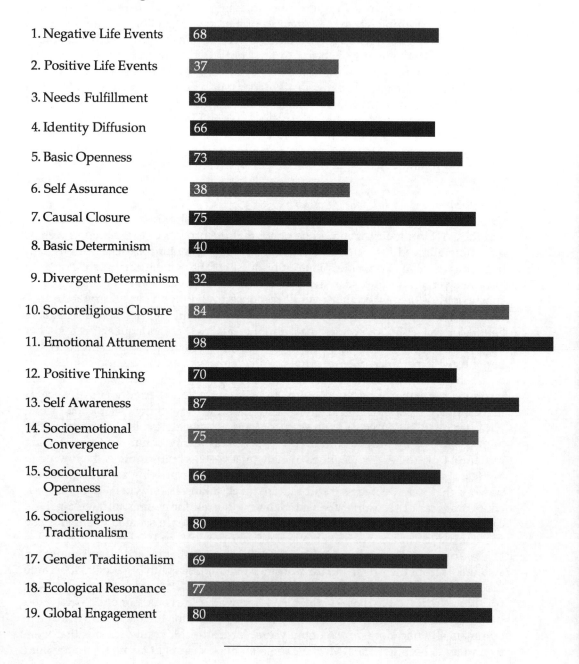

1. Negative Life Events — 68
2. Positive Life Events — 37
3. Needs Fulfillment — 36
4. Identity Diffusion — 66
5. Basic Openness — 73
6. Self Assurance — 38
7. Causal Closure — 75
8. Basic Determinism — 40
9. Divergent Determinism — 32
10. Socioreligious Closure — 84
11. Emotional Attunement — 98
12. Positive Thinking — 70
13. Self Awareness — 87
14. Socioemotional Convergence — 75
15. Sociocultural Openness — 66
16. Socioreligious Traditionalism — 80
17. Gender Traditionalism — 69
18. Ecological Resonance — 77
19. Global Engagement — 80

Case Study 2: David, Cynthia, and Owen Porter

This next case illustrates how the BEVI may be used to help understand dynamics and processes within marital and family systems, and assist with treatment processes, by integrating individual BEVI reports into various therapeutic processes (e.g., Smith et al., 2010). There are many benefits of doing so, which track closely with the guidance provided by Tharinger et al. (2008). For example, as should become evident from the below example, skillful usage of the BEVI is conducive to "helping parents develop a systemic view," "testing out possible interventions," "helping children feel less blamed," "fostering positive family relationship, and "giving families a positive experience of family interventions" (p. 549). Congruent with the philosophy and approach of therapeutic assessment, the goal of BEVI usage is not to "blame" anyone, but rather to illuminate and make accessible underlying processes that often are unknown (e.g., attributions about self or others; value-based similarities and differences within couples, families, and groups; relative variations among individuals in emotional capacity or self awareness), and are driving conflicts and dynamics within couples and families. After providing a clinical overview of this complex case, we juxtapose BEVI scores from the parents and adolescent son in order to show how the BEVI is used in assessment practice with these sorts of configurations.

Marriage and Family Treatment Overview

Owen Porter is a 16-year-old White/European American male, who lives with his biological parents—David and Cynthia. Owen was referred for assessment in an outpatient clinic following his release from hospitalization for suicidal ideation and aggressive acting out. Upon intake, it became clear that the home situation had long been fraught with tension and conflict, including reports of emotional abuse between the parents as well as physical altercations between father and son. Overall, the process was particularly heated between David and Owen, with Cynthia and Owen more or less aligned. Complicating matters, the marital situation between Cynthia and David was marked by deep seated disagreements at multiple levels, from disputes about disciplinary approaches for Owen and their 10-year-old daughter, April, to a marital relationship that was by turns emotionally distant and verbally hostile. In an attempt to understand better the sources and patterns of conflict, both parents and Owen separately completed the BEVI. Before doing so, significant attention was directed to explaining the purpose of completing this measure, and soliciting reactions and questions regarding their goals from this process (e.g., what did they want to learn). Moreover, it was explained that "there would be no secrets" regarding results as long as everyone was comfortable with such a discussion after their individual results were received (e.g., in the form of an accompanying narrative report, which was read privately).

A rule of thumb for BEVI systemic interpretations (e.g., in couples, families, groups) is to focus upon areas of greatest similarities, first—in order to find common ground—and then moving on to areas of difference. This approach with the BEVI is consistent with TA principles and practices (Finn, 2007; Tharinger et al., 2008). Consider just one such comparison on which all three of these individuals appear to see self, others, and the larger world in a similar manner. Positive Thinking on the BEVI measures (among other aspects) a tendency to eschew "negative thinking" and to adopt a stridently cheerful and positive sense of the world and one's place within it. Scores on Positive Thinking are as follows: Cynthia (8th percentile), David (11th percentile), and Owen (35th percentile). From an interpretive standpoint, it would seem that relatively speaking, no one in this system feels particularly optimistic that the current situation can be overcome by anyone involved or that life experience in general is particularly hopeful. Such a sense of apparent futility is important to recognize in terms of potential engagement in therapy and with one another.

Regarding differences, two especially discrepant domains from the BEVI were clear: religion and life history. Specifically, David appears to possess extremely high traditional religious ideation whereas Cynthia appears moderately to mildly inclined in that regard. Specifically, Socioreligious Traditionalism, which measures conventional religious beliefs, and a tendency to be God-fearing—is at the 90th percentile for David and the 46th percentile for Cynthia. At the very least then, one would predict that arguments likely would hinge upon whether, and to what degree, "God" is referenced implicitly or explicitly in terms of how individuals within the family should conduct themselves, as well as why and how behavior is understood and interpreted. Regarding life history, Cynthia also reports a very high degree of Negative Life Events (87th percentile) as compared to David (23rd percentile). Thus, self-referencing that occurs for both of them likely would be radically different in terms of their narratives and interpretations of their own life histories, as well as the meaning and value of taking such processes seriously (e.g., Cynthia self-defines to a great degree on the basis of what she is reporting to be a painful upbringing and history whereas David does not). Now consider Owen's profile on these same two scales of the BEVI. More than either her mother or father, he reports a very low degree of Socioreligious Traditionalism (13th percentile) but a very high degree of Negative Life Events (87th percentile).

Thus, one clear potential source of conflict between Owen and David in particular would be at the level of religious ideation. For all intents and purposes, Owen essentially is reporting no substantive religious affiliations or convictions (and may even be hostile toward the entire subject) whereas David is invested heavily in such a framework. Cynthia's moderate views in this regard place her closer to her son than her husband. Likewise, Cynthia and Owen are identical in terms of their reports of life history/upbringing (both at the 87% percentile), which strongly suggests that both of them would be in accord in their reports of background and its influence whereas David likely would be strongly disinclined to report such a history for himself or to grant potential validity to the effect of such experiences or events on functioning. Consider one other comparison. On Self Awareness—which indicates the degree to which an individual is open to difficult thoughts and feelings, introspective, tolerant of confusion, aware of how the self works, and a feeling person—note the patterns among these three individuals: Cynthia (56th percentile), David (10th percentile), Owen (90th percentile). Here again, we see a substantial difference between father and son, with mother literally "in between." Many other implications are worth noting as well (e.g., relatively speaking, Owen shows a very high degree of Identity Diffusion; David is very high on Gender Traditionalism; David and Owen are highest on Emotional Attunement).

The ensuing processes and discussions during informing were powerful and illuminating as well as affirming of *why* conflicts were occurring as they were. The point was not to demonstrate that anyone was right, wrong, or "pathological," but rather to deepen insight and offer an opportunity for dialogue and greater understanding. All individuals "saw" themselves and each other in the discussions that ensued, and questions and reflections were explicitly encouraged (e.g., regarding the origins of one's own beliefs; how meaning in life was pursued and experienced). As if not more important, the sharing of results facilitated a deeper discussion of how the world is, and should be, as well as why conflict occurred as it did. From a therapeutic standpoint, these results helped identity goals and areas of foci, such as whether Owen had "the right" to question the legitimacy of his father's intense religious sensibilities. Moreover, the question of looking at one's history and its relationship to current functioning also became a central focus (e.g., whether one's history "mattered" or whether people should just "suck it up" and move on). Finally, Cynthia and David were—for the first time in their relationship—encouraged to think seriously about the implications of these fundamental differences in terms of their process of relating with, and understanding, each other, as well as why they each tended to emphasize different "solutions" for Owen's situation. By their own reports, this process helped understand the origins of their conflicts, while also offering specific areas of focus for therapeutic work (e.g., learning how to listen; understanding who feels what, and why; identifying how they wanted the family to work in contrast to its current functioning).

Case Study 3: Group Therapeutic Assessment

As a final exemplar of how the BEVI is used from PATI and therapeutic assessment perspectives, consider assessment results from a group process session under the auspices of a counseling center at a military college in the southeastern United States. Here, we focus upon the Decile Profile, one of the indexes from the BEVI Group Report (see Chapter 4). From an assessment standpoint, the value of such a group profile is it allows individual members of the group to receive and review their own "individual report" (which basically consists of a narrative regarding how an individual sees self, other, and the larger world, as well as the potential implications of such findings). Then, on the basis of this review (which each member conducts in private for him or herself), the group facilitator is able to point out various aspects of difference and similarity among group members. In this way, individuals are able to reflect upon their own worldview (in private) while engaging in a discussion with the larger group about how it sees itself (in public). This process allows for a rich dialogue regarding "who the group is," with a particular focus on differences and similarities that are not understood explicitly early in a group process. Such understanding can deepen appreciation of diversity and nuances that characterize the group, while also facilitating discussion about *why* such differences exist in the first place, as well as the implications for such differences in terms of the group's process together as it moves forward. Consider the findings from Table 11.1.

Space limitations do not permit a full explication of the findings in the table, but a focus on one of the BEVI scales should illustrate how a group therapeutic assessment process occurs. Consider Gender Traditionalism. Overall, the group scored at

TABLE 11.1

Decile Profile for Military College Participants

DECILES	1	2	3	4	5	6	7	8	9	10
1. Negative Life Events	14%	19%	14%	19%	14%	14%	5%	0%	0%	0%
2. Positive Life Events	0%	0%	5%	5%	14%	14%	29%	10%	14%	5%
3. Need Fulfillment	5%	14%	38%	33%	10%	0%	0%	0%	0%	0%
4. Identity Closure	5%	29%	14%	24%	19%	5%	5%	0%	0%	0%
5. Basic Openness	38%	24%	5%	19%	10%	0%	5%	0%	0%	0%
6. Self Assurance	43%	10%	10%	5%	5%	5%	5%	5%	10%	5%
7. Causal Closure	5%	0%	14%	5%	5%	5%	14%	29%	19%	5%
8. Basic Determinism	5%	5%	0%	14%	5%	10%	14%	10%	24%	14%
9. Divergent Determinism	38%	24%	14%	14%	5%	5%	0%	0%	0%	0%
10. Socioreligious Closure	10%	10%	5%	14%	0%	10%	5%	19%	14%	14%
11. Emotional Attunement	0%	0%	0%	0%	0%	33%	24%	14%	19%	10%
12. Positive Thinking	19%	5%	14%	10%	5%	14%	10%	10%	5%	10%
13. Self Awareness	14%	5%	14%	14%	0%	10%	5%	14%	14%	10%
14. Socioemotional Convergence	0%	0%	0%	0%	0%	5%	14%	24%	19%	38%
15. Sociocultural Openness	0%	0%	0%	0%	19%	10%	29%	19%	19%	5%
16. Socioreligious Traditionalism	14%	10%	10%	14%	0%	0%	19%	10%	10%	14%
17. Gender Traditionalism	5%	5%	0%	5%	10%	5%	5%	5%	14%	48%
18. Ecological Resonance	5%	10%	0%	5%	10%	10%	24%	19%	5%	14%
19. Global Engagement	14%	19%	5%	5%	0%	10%	24%	14%	0%	10%
DECILES	1	2	3	4	5	6	7	8	9	10

the 82nd percentile on Gender Traditionalism (from the aggregated profile for this group, not pictured here), which measures the contention that men and women are built to be a certain way and should occupy "traditional" gender roles. And indeed, most of the individual profiles for this group reflect a strong Gender Traditional predilection. However, interesting and relevant to the group—sparking considerable discussion and debate—was the fact that *not everyone* saw matters in the same way. By way of illustration, note that Gender Traditionalism from Table 11.1 shows the following spread across the ten deciles of this scale:

Gender Traditionalism Scale for BEVI Group Report

Lowest Decile   **Highest Decile**

5%	5%	0%	5%	10%	5%	5%	5%	14%	48%

How do we interpret such findings? Perhaps most dramatic, approximately half of these individuals in this group session (48%) responded in the 90th percentile on Gender Traditionalism. In other words, half of the group scored in the top 10% on this specific scale of the BEVI. What is particularly interesting—especially in this military context—is that one fourth of the group was at or below the 50th percentile on Gender Traditionalism, with two individuals in the bottom 20%. Prompted by such findings, key aspects of the ensuing group discussion dealt with how "gender" was regarded in the military, and how the rights and experiences of women in particular were understood and managed by group members. Perhaps reflective of these results, the group expressed considerable intensity around the issue of "gender" (e.g., on the one hand contending that it "didn't matter," while also describing—from the women in the session—how "femininity" reportedly needed to be, of necessity from their perspective, suppressed). As important, the fact that the group did not see itself "the same" at this level, despite strong and unanimous feelings by half of the group, was an illuminating point for participants to consider (i.e., there are strong differences among the group on such matters, even though they apparently are not able to discuss such differences openly). At the same time, Gender Traditionalism was *not* one of the most intensely responded to scales for this group (i.e., the group tended, as a whole, to "Agree" and "Disagree" rather than "Strongly Agree" or "Strongly Disagree" on this scale). Such a finding provides context vis-à-vis this group, by suggesting that although views for some were very strongly held, overall, the group tended to be somewhat more moderate in their beliefs along these lines, at least relative to other scales on the BEVI (we know this information from another index, not pictured here but discussed with the group, called Worldview Intensity). Overall, from the perspective of therapeutic assessment, the BEVI provides a way to illuminate beliefs and values at the group level as well, by helping individual members understand who they are as individuals in relationship to a group of which they are members. The dialectic process of reviewing individual (private) and group (public) reports on the BEVI appears to promote depth, sensitivity, and nuance, increase engagement, assess relative openness and defensiveness, and utilize a nonpathologizing frame that is designed to facilitate transformative change (see Cozen et al., 2016).

DISCUSSION

Against the backdrop of our larger discussion of diagnosis and assessment, this chapter has described the theoretical and professional basis for an innovative and comprehensive measure called the BEVI. We presented three real-world applications that include individual, marriage/family, and group case studies. In the final section of this chapter, we turn our attention to how this measure is experienced by clients and clinicians, as well as our recommendations for therapeutic assessment applications.

The BEVI as Experienced by Clients

As described by Cozen et al. (2016), the BEVI was subjected to a comprehensive analysis of how it is experienced by clients and clinicians. Data were gathered via a range of sources including qualitative responses to the BEVI (e.g., free-response answers by clients to qualitative items built into the measure) as well as two different focus groups of master's and doctoral-level mental health clinicians, in order to identify the most salient themes in terms of real world usage.

First, in terms of qualitative responses by clients, assessment and therapy clients answer three experiential items following the completion of the multiple choice portion of the BEVI. The questions are: (a) *Which event or aspect of your experience had the greatest impact upon you and why?* (b) *Was there some aspect of your own "self" or "identity" that became especially clear or relevant to you or others as a result of this experience?* and (c) *What have you learned and how are you different as a result of this experience?* A representative sampling of client response analyzed for this study (N = 25 from two university counseling centers, two community mental health agencies, and an outpatient private practice) included the following client observations regarding the BEVI:

"It helped me to find out where I stand on many different issues."
"I feel more knowledgeable about myself."
"I liked how this made me think about questions I never would have thought about unless asked."
"I think it is very necessary to look at yourself inwardly."
"I am hoping it will take out counseling to another level. I enjoy learning about myself."
"My faith plays a significant role in how I view others."
"I am learning to be more aware of others' perceptions of any given circumstance."

Such qualitative responses offer a sense of how the BEVI is experienced (e.g., following administration and/or informing) from a "therapeutic assessment" perspective.

Second, in terms of clinician (e.g., assessor and therapist) perspectives, as Table 11.2 illustrates (Cozen et al., 2016), data from two separate focus group interviews regarding BEVI usage in assessment and therapy—involving master's and doctoral-level clinicians—resulted in hierarchically organized series of themes regarding what the BEVI offers to the practice of therapeutic assessment.

As may be seen in Table 11.2, from the standpoint of therapeutic assessment, the BEVI appears particularly well suited to help clinicians: (a) make causal connections (e.g., understand the etiology of particular affective, cognitive, and behavioral manifestations); (b) understand the "big picture" of a client's presentation (e.g., how their current functioning relates to and is explained by past events, and what the implications are of such information for the future); (c) emphasize unique strengths and potential (e.g., illuminate how and why they experience self, others, and the larger world as they do, and offer new ways of reflecting upon such issues); (d) identify information that may have great meaning to people in the real world, but may be de-emphasized in traditional assessment (e.g., religious beliefs or the lack thereof); (e) appraise the degree to which clients are, or are not, relatively open and nondefensive, and capable of self-reflection, thus amenable to and able to benefit from therapeutic interventions; (f) promote engagement with clients by communicating to

TABLE 11.2

Focus Group Themes Regarding BEVI Usage in Assessment and Therapy

PARENT THEME	CHILD THEME	NUMBER OF REFERENCES
Causal Connections		13
	Cognitions, Emotions, and Behavior	4
	Self and Others	3
	Past and Present	2
	Deeper Understanding	6
Big Picture		12
Nonpathologizing and Strength Focused		11
Broader Range of Information		10
Openness, Defensiveness, and Ability to Self-Reflect		6
Increased Client Engagement		5
Sharing Conceptualizations with Client		5
Flexibility		3
Accuracy		3
Increased Therapist Engagement		3

them—via the report system—in a way that they naturally relate to (e.g., in a language that is not overly clinical or jargon-laden); (g) encourage collaboration through sharing of information, demystifying processes, and facilitating joint ownership of respective roles; (h) open up new ways of conceptualization regarding life narratives; (i) capture the complexity of presentations in ways that are experienced as "ecologically valid" by clients; and (j) strengthen the alliance (e.g., by lowering the power-based differential in a way that does not appear to minimize professional credibility, but emphasizes authenticity). These findings are, it should be noted, consistent with, and add to, the growing PATI literature (e.g., Finn, 2007; Hanson, 2012; Hanson & Poston, 2011; Smith et al., 2010; Tharinger et al., 2008).

Ecologically Valid Assessment as Intervention: Best Practices From the Standpoint of the BEVI

By way of summary, and in terms of future directions for assessment research and practice, we offer the following six "best practice" recommendations for ecologically valid assessment as intervention. The following list is meant neither to be exhaustive nor definitive, nor limited only to what we have discovered through our usage of the BEVI generally and therapeutic assessment in particular. Mainly, based upon the literature, findings, and practices, we offer the following recommendations regarding an approach to assessment practice that strives to account for the complexity of the human condition, and does so in a way that is mindful of the powerful implications of conducting assessments, deriving results, and delivering conclusions.

1. Acknowledge Human Complexity

First, individuals who are authorized to conduct assessments in any setting or context must acknowledge that the information that is included and excluded affects the conclusions reached. For example, diagnoses and recommendations for depression credibly should be predicated on a full and comprehensive examination of the etiology and meaning of such symptoms for each human being. That is because two individuals might experience and express identical symptoms that meet *DSM* criteria for a depressive disorder, yet have highly distinct etiologies (Cummings et al., 2002), as well as epistemological frameworks regarding the nature of their "symptoms" (Horwitz, 2002; Kimble, 1984). If a clinician believes that the depressive experiences of these individuals have the same etiology and meaning, the client is on the receiving end of a judgment error (e.g., single-cause etiology), because factors that might reasonably be crucial to understanding and treating a given presentation are ignored or dismissed. Thus, it is essential that a clinician acknowledge the complexity of diagnostic and assessment practices and use equal sophistication in selecting measures and methods in order to produce formulations that are ecologically valid, theoretically grounded, and empirically defensible.

2. Evaluate Formative Variables

Understanding the human condition is possible when buttressed by knowledge of a range of formative variables (e.g., life history, background, systemic factors). This fact remains even if such information merely rules out alternative hypotheses. Indeed, the manifestation of symptoms within the context of standardized assessment practice should be interpreted only after ruling out alternative explanations (e.g., abuse, neglect, conflict, trauma) that might better explain the presentation (Chapman et al., 2004; Molnar, Buka, & Kessler, 2001; Tharinger et al., 2008; Widom, Dumont, & Czaja, 2007). Consider, for example, a client who receives an elevation on Scale 4 (Psychopathic Deviance) of the MMPI-2 as well as Scale 11 (Emotional Attunement) on the BEVI. If one has not examined sufficiently the client's life history and systemic realities, then such scores cannot be interpreted or understood in an ecologically valid manner, mainly because we do not possess the information necessary to help us understand and/or rule out possible explanations for such elevations. In short, mental health professionals must engage in substantive and comprehensive examination of the formative variables that may be associated with the current functioning of the individuals they assess.

3. Eschew Reductionism

Underlying neurobiology must have a role in all aspects of psychological functioning, and certainly interacts with environmental processes throughout the life span to produce phenotypic expression. However, human beings cannot be understood meaningfully and helped if they are reflexively reduced to "bad genes" and "chemical imbalances" (Horwitz, 2002). Portraying clients primarily in genetically mediated and neurochemical terms is unlikely to help them make sense of themselves or locate their symptoms within the context of their histories, relationships, and aspirations. Likewise, if assessment tools are one-dimensional, excessively face valid, and thus prone to response-set confounds (e.g., social desirability), or do not allow the possibility that other phenomena might have etiological relevance to a given presentation, then the forest can be missed for the trees and may communicate a vision of our clients that minimizes their complexity and potential (e.g., Anmuth et al., 2013; Cicchetti & Rogosch, 1996; Fava, Ruini, Tomba, & Wise, 2011; Lachter, 2001; Lurie, 1991; Luyten, Vliegen, Van Houdenhove, & Blatt, 2008). Because an assessor's job is seldom to rule out anything absolutely, care should be taken not to allow epistemological frameworks to limit the questions we ask or answers we seek via our assessment methods and measures.

4. Engage Clients as Collaborators

One great hazard of conducting psychological evaluations is losing sight of the vulnerability that is, in many ways, part and parcel of being assessed. In what other life situations do people place themselves before others who have ascribed expertise and methodologies—and concomitant awareness of self, others, and the larger world—to render definitive conclusions about the deepest aspects of why we are who we are? Although clients may have a basis for selecting the clinicians they do (e.g., a referral), assessors too often forget that this one encounter is likely to be the one and only time clients will ever place themselves in a position to be examined so deeply and definitely—without certainty that the person sitting across from them really is qualified, personally or professionally—to engage in such a process. Our failure in this regard is perhaps the reason why Finn (1996, 2007) strongly recommends that "past hurts" regarding assessment and testing related experiences should fully be queried and processed as needed in the context of any therapeutic assessment intervention.

Along similar lines, perhaps the greatest check on our inherent power as assessors is to regard our clients as collaborators in the assessment process (Claiborn & Hanson, 1999; Finn, 2008; Finn & Tonsager, 2002; Fischer, 2000; Poston & Hanson, 2010; Tharinger et al., 2008). Concretely, this approach obliges us to ask clients to describe who they are, how their lives have been, and what they hope their existence will be in the future. Then, after receiving all assessment information with clarity, competence, openness, and perspective, we are asked to integrate all of our results into a narrative—a version of reality—about the client. Such a narrative must then be shared with the client or clients in a way that is likely to solicit their full and open engagement, an acquired skill that exemplifies why good assessment is good science to be sure, but inevitably, art and craft as well. Such a gestalt of competencies requires assessors to possess legitimately acquired confidence in their own abilities, while also remaining open to the possibility that key information was missed and/or that one's own perspective—one's beliefs, values, attitudes, and worldview—may be inaccurate or in need of modification (Finn, 2007; Hanson et al., 1997, Shealy, 2004). Finally, when the report is completed (e.g., Allyn, 2012) and results are shared, the best of such informing/interpretative processes is deeply felt by the assessment client to be authentic and real, because they recognize their self from the story that is told, and were involved in the narrative process of its development (Smith et al., 2010). It is true that clients may not like aspects of what assessors share with them. Indeed, an assessor's job is neither to deny nor hide realities, but to be open to the possibility that their own hypotheses and interpretations may be wrong. At the same time, clients should be afforded opportunities to react to and potentially shape the final conclusions that are rendered even as they may be changed, in meaningful and measurable ways, by the assessment and informing process (Finn, 1996).

5. Value Meaning Making

As clinicians, if our assessments are devoted exclusively to issues of diagnosis, we forfeit an opportunity to engage our clients empathically in deeper questions that have to do with issues of life meaning and purpose (Finn, 2008; Fischer, 1970). Oftentimes, we hide behind a "referral question" as though what the client tells us is reality. No other health care profession labors under such an other-imposed practice. For example, no physician would accept the patient's diagnosis without at least wondering about alternative explanations for what they, and we, see. We may agree or disagree with what our client says is "the problem," but in the end, we still must render a judgment based upon our experience and knowledge, in full recognition of relevant best practice guidelines. Such a statement may seem contradictory to the spirit of this overall approach, which suggests we listen deeply to the version of reality that our clients provide to us, and involve them in the entire process of assessment. But that is because professional conduct mandates that assessors engage in all such practices simultaneously—listening hard, respecting the perspectives we hear, and rendering judgments based upon a deep understanding of our clients, our field, and ourselves, including the possibility that clients simply are not able or willing to apprehend the origins of their "symptoms," because to do so would be too painful and disequilibrating, at least at the outset of our assessment (see Chapters 3 and 4). Thus, we must consider and present information while simultaneously appraising the level at which our clients are best able to contemplate it (Smith et al., 2010; Tharinger et al., 2008). We all know clients whose presentations are designed—often nonconsciously—to mask or minimize deeper realities that simply and understandably are too painful, complex, or difficult to apprehend, much less describe. So, even as we respect deeply the worth of our clients, we must not also abrogate the responsibility of knowing there may be, and often is, much more to a presentation than meets the eye. In short, the "referral question" is only a point of entry to an intensive and unfettered process of inquiry that must sufficiently be comprehensive in order to rule out, or rule in, any number of possibilities that simply may not be known to us, or our clients, during the initial intake interview (Lillie, 2007; Pope, 1992). Our job is to step back, assess deeply, and wonder about the meaning of what we find. Oftentimes, the qualitative and quantitative data we derive from our interviews and measures reveal a wealth of information about who our clients really are, what they want and need in their lives, and why matters have not been going as they wish. A singular focus on the referral question or diagnostic labels means we risk overlooking crucial issues that may not only have etiological relevance to the symptoms we detect, but may speak to much broader life issues that are of the greatest, long-term relevance to our clients, and therefore should be to us as well (Finn, 2008; Finn & Tonsager, 2002).

6. Own Our Epistemologies

Finally, one of the more epistemologically contentious debates in assessment practice and research is whether objectivity—in any absolute sense—is possible or even desirable. This issue is potently revealed in the exchange between Lillienfeld, Garb, and Wood (2011), on the one hand, and Hanson and Poston (2011) on the other. Among other substantive issues that arose in this fruitful dialogue regarding PATI, Lilienfeld et al. suggest that the validity of assessment as intervention may only be established if "Barnum-like" statements are eliminated from therapist–client discourse. As is widely known, Barnum statements are observations regarding the attributes of human beings that supposedly are unique (and derived largely from psychological tests), but are, in fact, characterized by high base rates of endorsement by almost everyone, thus belying their unique status (e.g., Hanson & Claiborn, 2006). As Lilienfeld et al. maintain,

> it is up to the proponents of PATI to show that the effects of this technique exceed those of a Barnum or "placebo" intervention; if they do not, it might suggest that the effects of PATI have little or nothing to do with accurate assessment feedback. (p. 1052)

Hanson and Poston (2011) grant that "the onus is on PATI researchers, as a whole, to identify, and sort out, underlying change mechanisms" (p. 1060). We affirm strongly such a commitment, as we have attempted to illustrate in the context of the BEVI and its approach to PATI. However, there are at least two questions worth considering in this regard. First, are we really able to guarantee "accurate assessment feedback," or are our findings better understood along a continuum, as empirically and theoretically grounded approximations of a putative, underlying reality (e.g., as "True Score Theory" and "confidence intervals" imply)? Second, have we shown convincingly that it is possible, or desirable, to eliminate "Barnum-like" statements from our conduct as assessors? These questions are not merely postmodern abstractions, but highlight a long-standing epistemological debate among scholars and practitioners that has real world implications (see Kimble, 1984), as the contemporary exchange between Lillienfeld et al. and Hanson and Poston reveals.

In the final analysis, the entire therapeutic enterprise is replete with statements that might be characterized as "Barnum-like," mainly because the act of two or more human beings engaged in a deep process of attempting to understand self and promote healing and well-being inevitably is going to involve a high degree of exploration, speculation, wonderment, consternation, and so forth. Done with depth, honesty, and reflection, as well as efficiency, clients experience such relational encounters as part and parcel of being understood, accepted, cared for, and hoped for—all factors that are associated with positive therapeutic processes and outcomes (e.g., Norcross, 2002; Shealy, 1995). So, the idea that we somehow can or should attempt to strip out the Barnumesque aspects of the psychological assessment and therapeutic intervention is questionable, and reminiscent of the same impulse that has led to the proliferation of manualized treatments, which have merit but also have been criticized for attenuating the very common factors that are integral to therapeutic change (e.g., Nelson, Steele, & Mize, 2006). Even so, there is a demonstrable need to clarify feedback that genuinely is consistent with what is revealed by testing measures, rather than going on an open-ended fishing expedition to match what we "find" with what appears to fit from the client's perspective. Such a call is legitimate and important, as it helps all of us engaged in PATI-like work to be accountable for what it is we say we are doing, and to get better and better at doing it.

In conclusion, even though we should strive for objectivity and all of its worthy concomitants in assessment research and practice, it behooves us to remember three final points: (a) clinicians are potentially no less biased than either the clients they evaluate or the fields in which they are trained and credentialed; (b) worthy standards of objectivity are more aspirational than realizable in any absolute sense; and (c) the privileging of data over engagement may have unintended consequences for the vulnerable people clinicians are entrusted to understand, support, and possibly transform, as we seek to help them cultivate an honest and constructive relationship with their past, present, and future. Through ongoing reflection upon such points in our daily work, it is our hope that the assessments we render and the care we provide first do no harm, evidence humility and integrity in the "realities" we apprehend, and facilitate growth, healing, and meaning making with the human beings we serve.

REFERENCES

Alexander, F. G., & Selesnick, S. T. (1966). *The history of psychiatry: An evaluation of psychiatric thought and practice from prehistoric times to the present*. New York, NY: Harper and Row.

Allyn, J. B. (2012). *Writing to clients and referring professionals about psychological assessment results: A handbook of style and grammar*. New York, NY: Routledge.

American Psychiatric Association. (2000). *Diagnostic and statistical manual of mental disorders, Fourth edition, Text Revision* (DSM-IV-TR). Washington, DC: Author.

American Psychological Association, Inc. (2010). *Ethical principles of psychologists and code of conduct*. Retrieved December 18, 2012 from http://www.apa.org/ethics/code/index.aspx

Anda, R., Felitti, V., Bremner, J., Walker, J., Whitfield, C., Perry, B., . . . Giles, W. (2006). The enduring effects of abuse and related adverse experiences in childhood. A convergence of evidence from neurobiology and epidemiology. *European Archives of Psychiatry and Clinical Neuroscience, 256*(3), 174–186.

Anmuth, L. M., Poore, M., Cozen, J., Brearly, T., Tabit, M., Cannady, M., . . . Staton, R. (2013, August). *Making implicit beliefs explicit: In search of best practices for mental health clients, clinicians, and trainers*. Poster presented at the annual meeting of the American Psychological Association, Honolulu, HI.

Atwood, K., Chkhaidze, N., Shealy, C. N., Staton, R., & Sternberger, L. G. (2014, August). *Transformation of self: Implications from the Forum BEVI Project*. Poster presented at the annual meeting of the American Psychological Association, Washington, DC.

Aponte, H. J., Powell, F. D., Brooks, S., Watson, M. F., Litzke, C., Lawless, J., & Johnson, E. (2009). Training the person of the therapist in an academic setting. *Journal of Marital Family Therapy, 35*(4), 381–394.

Armstrong, T. (1996). ADHD: Does it really exist? *Phi Delta Kappan, 77*(6), 424–428.

Back, R., & Dana, R. H. (1977). Examiner sex bias and Wechsler intelligence scale for children scores. *Journal of Consulting and Clinical Psychology, 45*(3), 500.

Baughman, F. (2008). Psychiatry's "chemical imbalance" fraud: Who killed Rebecca Riley? *Ethical Human Psychology and Psychiatry, 10*(2), 96–108.

Beutler, L. E., & Malik, M. L. (2002). *Rethinking the DSM: A psychological perspective*. Washington, DC: American Psychological Association.

Bradford, G. K. (2009). Revisioning diagnosis: A contemplative phenomenological approach. *The Journal of Transpersonal Psychology, 41*, 121–138.

Bradford, G. K. (2010). Fundamental flaws of the DSM: Re-envisioning diagnosis. *Journal of Humanistic Psychology, 50*, 335–350.

Brearly, T., Shealy, C. N., Staton, R., & Sternberger, L. G. (2012, August). *Prejudice and religious and non-religious certitude: An empirical analysis from the Forum BEVI Project*. Poster presented at the annual meeting of the American Psychological Association, Orlando, FL.

Brickman, P., Rabinowitz, V. C., Karuza, J. J., Coates, D., Cohn, E., & Kidder, L. (1982). Models of helping and coping. *American Psychologist, 37*(4), 368–384.

Brown, P. (1995). Naming and framing: The social construction of diagnosis and illness. *Journal of Health and Social Behavior, 35*, 34–52.

Butcher, J. N. (2006). Assessment in clinical psychology: A perspective on the past, present challenges, and future prospects. *Clinical Psychology: Science and Practice, 13*, 205–209.

Butcher, J. N., & Rouse, S. V. (1996). Personality: Individual differences and clinical assessment. *Annual Review of Psychology, 47*, 87–111.

Butcher, J. N., Graham, J. R., Ben-Porath, Y. S., Tellegen, A., Dahlstrom, W. G., & Kaemmer, B. (2001). *Minnesota Multi-phasic Personality Inventory-2 (MMPI-2): Manual for administration, scoring, and interpretation* (Rev. ed.). Minneapolis, MN: University of Minnesota Press.

Centers for Disease Control and Prevention. (2014). *Attention-deficit/Hyperactivity disorder.* Retrieved June 10, 2014 from http://www.cdc.gov/ncbddd/adhd/data.html

Chapman, D., Whitfield, C., Felitti, V., Dube, S., Edwards, V., & Anda, R. (2004). Adverse childhood experiences and the risk of depressive disorders in adulthood. *Journal of Affective Disorders, 82*(2), 217–225.

Claiborn, C. D., & Hanson, W. E. (1999). Test interpretation: A social influence perspective. In J. W. Lichtenberg & R. K. Goodyear (Eds.), *Scientist-practitioner perspectives on test interpretation* (pp. 151–166). Boston, MA: Allyn & Bacon.

Church, T. (2010). Current perspectives in the study of personality across cultures. *Perspectives on Psychological Science, 5*, 441–449.

Cicchetti, D., & Rogosch, F. A. (1996). Equifinality and multifinality in developmental psychopathology. *Development and Psychopathology, 8*(4), 597–600.

Conrad, P. (1975). The discovery of Hyperkinesis: Notes on the medicalization of deviant behavior. *Social Problems, 23*(1), 12–21.

Cozen, J., Hanson, W., Poston, J., Jones, S., & Tabit, M. (2016). The Beliefs, Events, and Values Inventory (BEVI): Implications and applications for therapeutic assessment and intervention. In C. N. Shealy (Ed.), *Making sense of beliefs and values* (pp. 575–621). New York, NY: Springer Publishing.

Cummings, E. M., Davies, P. T., & Campbell, S. B. (2002). *Developmental psychopathology and family process: Theory, research, and clinical implications.* New York, NY: The Guilford Press.

Curry, K. T., & Hanson, W. E. (2010). National survey of psychologists' test feedback training, supervision, and practice: A mixed methods study. *Journal of Personality Assessment, 92,* 327–336.

Dana, R. H. (2005). *Multicultural assessment: Principles, applications, and examples.* New York, NY: Routledge.

Duffy, M., Gillig, S. E., Tureen, R. M., & Ybarra, M. A. (2002). A critical look at the DSM-IV. *The Journal of Individual Psychology, 58*(4), 363–373.

Eisman, E. J., Dies, R. R., Finn, S. E., Eyde, L. D., Kay, G. G., Kubiszyn, T. W., . . . Moreland, K. L. (2000). Problems and limitations in using psychological assessment in the contemporary health care delivery system. *Professional Psychology: Research and Practice, 31*(2), 131–140.

El-Shaieb, M. (2005). The MMPI-2 and client feedback: A quantitative investigation and exploratory analysis of feedback models (Doctoral dissertation, Colorado State University, 2005). *Dissertation Abstracts International, 66,* 2303.

Eriksen, K., & Kress, V. E. (2005). *Beyond the DSM story: Ethical quandaries, challenges, and best practices.* Thousand Oaks, CA: Sage Publications, Inc.

Fava, G. A., Ruini, C., Tomba, E., & Wise, T. N. (2011). The biopsychosocial factor. *Psychotherapy and Psychosomatics, 81*(1), 1–4.

Finn, S. E. (1996). *Manual for using the MMPI-2 as a therapeutic intervention.* Minneapolis, MN: University of Minnesota Press.

Finn, S. E. (2007). *In our clients' shoes – Theory and techniques of therapeutic assessment.* New York, NY: Routledge.

Finn, S. E. (2008). The many faces of empathy in experiential, person-centered, collaborative assessment. *Journal of Personality Assessment, 91*(1), 20–23.

Finn, S. E., Fischer, C. T., & Handler, L. (2012). *Collaborative/therapeutic assessment: A casebook and guide.* Hoboken, NJ: John Wiley & Sons.

Finn, S. E., & Tonsager, M. E. (1992). Therapeutic effects of providing MMPI-2 test feedback to college students awaiting therapy. *Psychological Assessment, 4*(3), 278–287.

Finn, S. E., & Tonsager, M. E (1997). Information-gathering and therapeutic models of assessment: Complementary paradigms. *Psychological Assessment*, 9(4), 374–385.

Finn, S. E., & Tonsager, M. (2002). How therapeutic assessment became humanistic. *The Humanistic Psychologist*, 30, 10–22.

Fischer, C. T. (1970). The testee as co-evaluator. *Journal of Counseling Psychology*, 17, 70–76.

Fischer, C. T. (1994). *Individualizing psychological assessment: A collaborative and therapeutic approach*. New York, NY: Routledge.

Fischer, C. T. (2000). Collaborative, individualized assessment. *Journal of Personality Assessment*, 74(1), 2–14.

Fischer, C. T., & Finn, S. E. (2008). Developing the life meaning of psychological test data: Collaborative and therapeutic approaches. In R. P. Archer & S. R. Smith (Eds.), *Personality assessment* (pp. 379–404). New York, NY: Routledge/Taylor & Francis Group.

Gualtieri, C. T., & Johnson, L. G. (2005). ADHD: Is objective diagnosis possible? *Psychiatry*, 2(11), 44–53.

Hanson, W. E. & Claiborn, C. D. (2006). Effects of test interpretation style and favorability in the counseling process. *Journal of Counseling and Development*, 84, 349–357.

Hanson, W. E., Claiborn, C. D., & Kerr, B. (1997). Differential effects of two-test-interpretation styles in counseling: A field study. *Journal of Counseling Psychology*, 44, 400–405.

Hanson, W. E., & Poston, J. M. (2011). Building confidence in psychological assessment as a therapeutic intervention: An empirically based reply to Lilienfeld, Garb, and Wood. *Psychological Assessment*, 23(4), 1056–1062.

Halling, S., & Goldfarb, M. (1996). The new generation of diagnostic manuals (DSM-III, DSM-III-R, and DSM-IV): an overview and phenomenologically based critique. *Journal of Phenomenological Psychology*, 27, 49–71.

Haslam, N. (2004). Review of 'Creating Mental Illness'. *Transcultural Psychiatry*, 41(3), 414–416.

Hays, P. A. (2001). Making sense and moving on: Culturally responsive diagnosis and the DSM-IV. In *Addressing cultural complexities in practice: A framework for clinicians and counselors* (pp. 129–149). Washington, DC: American Psychological Association.

Hayes, D. J., Shealy, C. N., Sivo, S. A., & Weinstein, Z. C. (1999, August). *Psychology, religion, and scale 5 (Religious Traditionalism) of the "BEVI."* Poster session presented at the meeting of the American Psychological Association, Boston, MA.

Hess, V. (2011). Writing the history of psychiatry in the 20th century. *History of Psychiatry*, 22, 139–145.

Hill, C., Johnson, M., Brinton, C., Staton, R., Sternberger, L., & Shealy, C. N. (2013, August). *The etiology of economic beliefs and values: Implications and applications from the Forum BEVI Project*. Poster presented at the annual meeting of the American Psychological Association, Honolulu, HI.

Hill, J. S., Pace, T. M., & Robbins, R. R. (2010). Decolonizing personality assessment and honoring indigenous voices: A critical examination of the MMPI-2. *Cultural Diversity and Ethnic Minority Psychology*, 16(1), 16–25.

Hoagwood, K., & Jensen, P. S. (1997). Developmental psychopathology and the notion of culture: Introduction to the special section on "The Fusion of Cultural Horizons: Cultural Influences on the Assessment of Psychopathology in Children and Adolescents." *Applied Developmental Science*, 1(3), 108–112.

Horwitz, A. (2002). *Creating mental illness*. Chicago, IL: The University of Chicago Press.

Isley, E. B., Shealy, C. N., Crandall, K. S., Sivo, S. A., & Reifsteck, J. B. (1999, August). *Relevance of the "EBVI" for research in developmental psychopathology*. Poster session presented at the meeting of the American Psychological Association, Boston, MA.

Jones, J. D. (2002). Plea for a measure of understanding: The importance of intensive psychotherapy in the treatment of children with ADHD. *Psychotherapy: Theory, Research, Practice, Training*, 39(1), 12–20.

Kim, N., & Ahn, W. (2002). Clinical psychologists' theory-based representations of mental disorders predict their diagnostic reasoning and memory. *Journal of Experimental Psychology: General*, 131(4), 451–476.

Kimble, G. A. (1984). Psychology's two cultures. *American Psychologist, 39*(8), 833–839.

Kleinman, A. (1988). *Rethinking psychiatry: From cultural category to personal experience*. New York, NY: Free Press.

Kubiszyn, T. Meyer, G., Finn, S., Eyde, L., Kay, G., Moreland, K., . . . Eisman, E. (2000). Empirical support for psychological assessment in clinical health care setting. *Professional Psychology: Research and Practice, 31*(2), 119–130.

Lachter, B. (2001). 'Chemical imbalance': A clinical non sequitur. *Australasian Psychiatry, 9*(4), 311–315.

Levak, R. W., Siegel, L., & Nichols, D. S. (2011). *Therapeutic feedback with the MMPI-2: A positive psychology approach*. New York, NY: Routledge.

Lillienfeld, S. O., Garb, H. N., & Wood, J. M. (2011). Unresolved questions concerning the effectiveness of psychological assessment as a therapeutic intervention: Comment on Poston and Hanson (2010). *Psychological Assessment, 23*(4), 1047–1055.

Lillie, R. (2007). Getting clients to hear: Applying principles and techniques of Kiesler's interpersonal communication therapy to assessment feedback. *Psychology and Psychotherapy: Theory, Research, and Practice, 80*, 151–163.

Lurie, S. N. (1991). Psychological issues in treatment of the 'chemical imbalance.' *American Journal of Psychotherapy, 45*(3), 348–358.

Luyten, P., Vliegen, N., Van Houdenhove, B., & Blatt, S. J. (2008). Equifinality, multifinality, and the rediscovery of the importance of early experiences: Pathways from early adversity to psychiatric and (functional) somatic disorders. *The Psychoanalytic Study of the Child, 63*, 27–60.

Meyer, G. J., Finn, S. E., Eyde, L. D., Kay, G. G., Moreland, K. L., Dies, R. R., . . . Read, G. M. (2001). Psychological testing and psychological assessment: A review of evidence and issues. *American Psychologist, 56*(2), 128–165.

Mezirow, J. (1997). Transformative learning: Theory to practice. In P. Cranton (Ed.), *Transformative learning in action: Insights from practice. New directions for adults and continuing education* (pp. 5–12). San Francisco, CA: Jossey-Bass.

Molnar, B., Buka, S., & Kessler, R. (2001). Child sexual abuse and subsequent psychopathology: Results from the national comorbidity survey. *American Journal of Public Health, 91*(5), 753–760.

Nagy, T. F. (2011). *Essential ethics for psychologists: A primer for understanding and mastering core issues*. Washington, DC: American Psychological Association.

Nelson, T. D., Steele, R. G., & Mize, J. A. (2006). Practitioner attitudes toward evidence-based practice: Themes and challenges. *Administration and Policy in Mental Health and Mental Health Services Research, 33*, 398–409.

Norcross, J. C. (Ed.). (2002). *Psychotherapy relationships that work*. New York, NY: Oxford University Press.

Nudel, C. (Ed.). (2012). *Firewalkers: Madness, beauty, and mystery*. Charlottesville, VA: VOCAL Inc.

Patel, R., Shealy, C. N., & De Michele, P. (2007, August). *Environmental beliefs and values: Etiology, maintenance, and transformation*. Poster session presented at the annual meeting of the American Psychological Association, San Francisco, CA.

Pawlowski, C. A. (2002). *Effects of MMPI-2 test interpretation feedback favorability on client subjective well-being: A process-outcome study* (Unpublished doctoral dissertation). University of Nebraska-Lincoln, Lincoln, NE.

Penza, K., Heim, C., & Nemeroff, C. (2003). Neurobiological effects of childhood abuse: implications for the pathophysiology of depression and anxiety. *Archives of Women's Mental Health, 6*(1), 15–22.

Perry, B., & Hambrick, E. (2008). The neurosequential model of therapeutics. *Reclaiming Youth, 17*, 38–43.

Pienkos, E., & Sass, L. A. (2012). Empathy and otherness: Humanistic and phenomenological approaches to psychotherapy of severe mental illness. *Pragmatic Case Studies in Psychotherapy, 8*(1), 25–35.

Pierce-Jones, J., & Tyler, F. T. (1950). A comparison of the A.C.E. psychological examination and the culture-free test. *Canadian Journal of Psychology, 4*(3), 106–114.

Pope, K. (1992). Responsibilities in providing psychological test feedback to clients. *Psychological Assessment, 4*, 268–271.

Poston, J. M., & Hanson, W. E. (2010). Meta-analysis of psychological assessment as a therapeutic intervention. *Psychological Assessment, 22*(2), 203–212.

Pysarchik, D. I., Shealy, C. N., Sternberger, B. (2007, July). *Examining outcome objectives for student learning and curricula.* Symposium presented at the meeting of the National Association of State Universities and Land Grant Colleges, Santa Rosa, CA.

Ridley, C. R., Li, L. C., & Hill, C. L. (1998). Multicultural assessment: Reexamination, reconceptualization, and practical application. *The Counseling Psychologist, 26*, 827–910.

Ritsher, J. B., Slivko-Kolchik, E. B., & Oleichik, I. V. (2001). Assessing depression in Russian psychiatric patients: Validity of MMPI and Rorschach. *Assessment, 8*(4), 373–390.

Rogers, L. B. (1954). A comparison of two kinds of test interpretation interview. *Journal of Counseling Psychology, 1*, 224–231.

Sarbin, T. R. (1997). On the futility of psychiatric diagnostic manuals (DSMs) and the return of personal agency. *Applied and Preventive Psychology, 6*(4), 233–243.

Shealy, C. N. (1995). From Boys Town to Oliver Twist: Separating fact from fiction in welfare reform and out-of-home placement of children and youth. *American Psychologist, 50*(8), 565–580.

Shealy, C. N. (2000a, July). *The Beliefs, Events, and Values Inventory (BEVI): Implications for cross-cultural research and practice.* Paper presented at the meeting of the International Congress of Psychology, Stockholm, Sweden.

Shealy, C. N. (2000b, July). *The Beliefs, Events, and Values Inventory (BEVI): Implications for research and theory in social psychology.* Paper presented at the meeting of the International Congress of Psychology, Stockholm, Sweden.

Shealy, C. N. (2003). Creating Mental Illness: Necessary antidote for a reductionistic age. *Journal of Social and Clinical Psychology, 22*, 118–120.

Shealy, C. N. (2004). A model and method for "Making" a combined-integrated psychologist: Equilintegration (EI) theory and the Beliefs, Events, and Values Inventory (BEVI). *Journal of Clinical Psychology, 60*, 1065–1090.

Shealy, C. N. (2005). Justifying the justification hypothesis: Scientific-humanism, Equilintegration (EI) theory, and the Beliefs, Events, and Values Inventory (BEVI) [Special Series]. *Journal of Clinical Psychology, 61*(1), 81–106.

Shealy, C. N. (2015). *The Beliefs, Events, and Values Inventory (BEVI): Overview, implications, and guidelines, Test manual.* Harrisonburg, VA: Author.

Shealy, C. N. (2016). *Making sense of beliefs and values.* New York, NY: Springer Publishing.

Shealy, C. N., Bhuyan, D., & Sternberger, L. G. (2012). Cultivating the capacity to care in children and youth: Implications from EI theory, EI self, and BEVI. In U. Nayar (Ed.), *Child and adolescent mental health* (pp. 240–255). New Delhi, India: Sage Publications.

Shepard, L. A. (1992). Psychometric properties of the Gesell Developmental Assessment: A critique. *Early Childhood Research Quarterly, 7*(1), 47–52.

Smith, J. D.; Handler, L., & Nash, M. R. (2010). Therapeutic assessment for preadolescent boys with oppositional defiant disorder: A replicated single-case time-series design. *Psychological Assessment, 22*(3), 593–602.

Solano-Flores, G., & Nelson-Barber, S. (2000, Owen). *Cultural validity of assessments and assessment development procedures.* Paper presented at American Educational Research Association Meeting, New Orleans, LA.

Solano-Flores, G., & Nelson-Barber, S. (2001). On the cultural validity of science assessments. *Journal of Research in Science Teaching, 30*, 553–573.

Springer, K., Sheridan, J., Kuo, D., & Carnes, M. (2007). Long-term physical and mental health consequences of childhood physical abuse: Results from a large population-based sample of men and women. *International Congress on Child Abuse & Neglect, 31*(5), 517–530.

Szasz, T. (1960). The myth of mental illness. *American Psychologist, 15*, 113–118.

Tabit, M., Cozen, J., Dyjak-Leblank, K., Pendleton, C., Shealy, C., Sternberger, L., & Staton, R. (2011, June). *The sociocultural impact of denial: Empirical evidence from the Forum BEVI Project*. Poster presented at American Psychological Association, Washington, DC.

Terrell, F., Terrell, S. L., & Taylor, J. (1981). Effects of race of examiner and cultural mistrust on the WAIS performance of black students. *Journal of Consulting and Clinical Psychology*, *49*(5), 750–775.

Tharinger, D. J., Finn, S. E., Austin, C. A., Gentry, L. B., Bailey, K. E., Parton, V. T., & Fisher, M. E. (2008). Family sessions as part of child psychological assessment: Goals, techniques, clinical utility, and therapeutic value. *Journal of Personality Assessment*, *90*(6), 547–558.

Wakefield, J. C., & Schmitz, M. F. (2010). The measurement of mental disorder. In T. L. Scheid & T. N. Brown (Eds.), *A handbook for the study of mental health: Social contexts, theories, and systems* (2nd ed., pp. 20–45). New York, NY: Cambridge University Press.

Watkins, E. (1993). Person-Centered theory and the contemporary practice of psychological testing. *Counselling Psychology Quarterly*, *6*, 59–67.

Widom, C., Dumont, K., & Czaja, S. (2007). A prospective investigation of major depressive disorder and comorbidity in abused and neglected children grown up. *Archives of General Psychiatry*, *64*(1), 49–56.

Elizabeth Wandschneider, Dawn T. Pysarchik,
Lee G. Sternberger, Wenjuan Ma, Kris Acheson,
Brad Baltensperger, RT Good, Brian Brubaker,
Tamara Baldwin, Hajime Nishitani, Felix Wang,
Jarrod Reisweber, and Vesna Hart

12

THE FORUM BEVI PROJECT: APPLICATIONS AND IMPLICATIONS FOR INTERNATIONAL, MULTICULTURAL, AND TRANSFORMATIVE LEARNING

The only person who is educated is the one who has learned how to learn and change.

—Carl Rogers

In a diverse portfolio of curricular and programmatic options in colleges and universities, global education has become highly prominent over the past 50 years (O'Meara, Mehlinger, & Newman, 2001; De Wit & Merkx, 2012). To take one of any number of indexes in this regard, the Institute of International Education (2014) reported that a record number of global students, 886,052, studied at U.S. institutions in 2013 to 2014 (up 8.1% over the previous year) and 289,408 American students studied abroad in 2012 to 2013 (an increase of 2.1% over the previous year) (see also International Association of Universities, 2010; Knight, 2006). At a complementary level, institutions of higher education now are interested in "the internationalization of research, offering dual degrees with foreign partners, establishing a branch of campuses abroad," among other areas of emphasis (Marmolejo, 2011). Duru and Poyrazli (2007) contend that these sorts of trends demonstrate the important role that colleges and universities play in training workers for entry into the global marketplace. Likewise, Green (2013) notes that "higher education institutions in the United States are increasingly using the language of 'global citizenship' to describe the skills and habits they seek to cultivate in their students" (p. 52). Against this introductory backdrop, we begin this chapter with an overview of global education in the United States and a review of assessment instruments and approaches. We then will present 15 implications from the Forum BEVI Project, a multiyear, multisite assessment initiative that examined the processes and outcomes of international, multicultural, and transformative learning.

GLOBAL EDUCATION IN THE UNITED STATES

In 2005, the Forum on Education Abroad investigated international education programs in 46 U.S. colleges and universities (Forum, 2005). Results suggested that study abroad programs are intimately related to their curricula and objectives. Most of the surveyed institutions integrated global education into the international curricula of their students; 91% of the institutions usually or always counted credits earned by students while abroad toward major or minor requirements. Moreover, 77% of the respondents noted that credit completed abroad usually or always counted toward general education requirements. Similar to the curricular changes at many U.S. universities, the composition of matriculating students also has changed in the past 50 years. Such students today often have prior international exposure, which is related in part to the fact that transportation to and from other countries is much more accessible. Furthermore, young adults are exposed to the beliefs and practices of different cultures through television, the Internet, and social media. In addition, many students anticipate that cultural competence will be required of them upon graduation from college or university at a level that simply was unimaginable 50 years ago. Thus, it is not surprising that a survey by the American Council on Education (ACE) found that most students studying abroad had prior international experience, with 64% of students polled already having lived in or traveled to countries outside of the United States (Siaya & Hayward, 2003).

Today's students appreciate the importance of grappling with events and issues that are occurring beyond their home borders, in part because of an increasing recognition that global and domestic affairs are inextricably linked. For example, 65% of the students in the 2003 ACE survey concurred that all students should be required to take courses covering global topics (Siaya & Hayward, 2003). Moreover, when entering the global marketplace, graduating U.S. students who have studied abroad arguably possess an advantage over those who have not. Indeed, "students who lack access to cultural capital may not appreciate the significance of study abroad experiences specifically and global understanding in general" (Hu, Pazaki, & Velander, 2014, p. 73). The advantage of study abroad consists of more than cross-cultural experience, and is related directly to the acquisition of knowledge, skills, and attitudes that cannot be acquired without real world experience in another culture. And in fact, many global education programs are designed explicitly to facilitate the acquisition of greater sensitivity toward people from other cultures (O'Meara et al., 2001). As Ramirez (2013) observes, however, such student outcomes are not preordained simply by studying abroad; rather, "the curriculum of these preparation programs needs to intentionally address cultural sensitivity" (p. 8). Thus, it is the responsibility of institutions of higher education to "develop international curricula that foster a student citizenry with stronger global awareness" (Tarrant, Rubin, & Stoner, 2013, p. 2).

THE ASSESSMENT OF GLOBAL LEARNING

As the importance of international education continues to ascend in the United States and globally, a corresponding need has emerged to assess the outcomes and impacts of such learning (Deardorff & Van Gaalen, 2012). In this regard, assessment instruments must be chosen in the context of how a given institution defines internationalization (Coryell, Durodoye, Wright, Pate, & Nguyen, 2012). Knight (2011) observes further that the benefits of global education cannot be measured simply by counting "the number of global students, foreign faculty, institutional agreements, cross-border education programs, research projects, foreign accreditations, branch campuses, and so on" (p. 15). Such indexes may address certain accountability requirements, but they do not reflect the emotional, cognitive, and behavioral impact of globalization. As Zimmermann and Neyer (2013) comment in a study on the personality development of sojourners, "hitting the road has substantial effects on who we are" (p. 527). Although assessment and education, in general, long have been linked in the United States, an emphasis on the assessment of international, multicultural, and transformative learning has been a relatively recent phenomenon, with various attempts under way to define and determine appropriate assessment methods of intercultural competencies (e.g., Deardorff, 2006; Fantini, 2009; Rexeisen, 2012). In this regard, Sternberger, Pysarchik, Yun, and Deardorff (2009) contend that an integrated approach to learning assessment—which includes a carefully planned and well-implemented assessment protocol that is linked to theory and uses multiple methods—may be of considerable benefit to higher education institutions, by helping students develop measurable competencies that are critical to success in an increasingly interconnected world. Along these lines, the Georgia Learning Outcomes of Students Studying Abroad Research Initiative (Sutton & Rubin, 2004), the Georgetown Consortium Project (Vande Berg, Connor-Linton, & Paige, 2009), and the Wabash National Study of Liberal Arts (Salisbury, 2011) are but three large, multi-institutional studies regarding the learning outcomes of education abroad. As summarized in the project Student Experience in the Research University (SERU), "formal study abroad programs. . .bring value-added components to students' intercultural and global competencies that generally meet or surpass the outcomes of other international travel opportunities" (Stebleton, Soria, & Cherney, 2013, p. 15). From the standpoint of assessment, several large-scale initiatives to develop methods and instruments for measuring globalization recently have been pursued in different countries, including, but not limited to, the Association of Commonwealth Universities' Management Benchmarking Program (2012); National Association of Foreign Student Advisers' (NAFSA) "Accessing Best Practices in International Education" (2008); the Netherlands' Organization for International Cooperation in Higher Education's "Measuring Internationalization" or MINT project (2012); "A Guide to Outcomes Assessment in Education Abroad" (2007), from the Forum on Education Abroad; and, the Forum BEVI Project (2015)—the focus of this chapter—which investigates the processes and outcomes of global, intercultural, and transformative learning.

So how has the field of international education approached the evaluation of learning outcomes? Overall, a review of the literature suggests that assessment studies have examined factors such as content knowledge concerning a specific culture or knowledge of global affairs, language acquisition, intercultural sensitivity, competence and communication, and salient personality variables, among other constructs and processes. Recognizing that the relative merits of particular assessment methods depend upon differences in program goals or content as well as realities "on the ground" (Poole & Davis, 2006), typical assessment methods include tests, portfolios, interviews, reflective essays, surveys, and inventories. Although not intended to be exhaustive, it may be helpful to describe a number of these measures and methods in order to illustrate their different applications in research and practice (e.g., see Fantini, 2009).

Some global learning programs are interested in assessing students' knowledge of issues that reflect global awareness and citizenship. For example, the Global Awareness Profile (GAP) is a self-report inventory that includes 126 questions based on common knowledge in two main categories: seven geographical areas (i.e., Asia, Africa, North America, South America, the Middle East, Europe, and Global) and seven subject areas (i.e., environment, culture, politics, geography, religion, socioeconomics, and global) (Corbitt, 2011).

Language acquisition is another significant component of many global learning programs, which requires its own form of assessment. For example, the American Council on the Teaching of Foreign Languages (ACTFL) developed proficiency guidelines in 2012 to assess writing and speaking proficiency levels as well as oral proficiency, using Oral Proficiency Interviews (OPI) and Simulated Oral Proficiency Interviews (SOPI) (ACTFL, 2012). Likewise, the Interagency Language Roundtable (2011) developed a set of skill level descriptions by which language proficiency tests may be developed and scored.

At the same time, there is increasing recognition that such competence involves more than just proficiency in reading, writing, listening, and speaking. As Scarino (2010) notes, comprehensive evaluation of foreign language learning programs should include cultural aspects of learning, because "in any act of learning, people (as young persons and as learners) are engaged in interpreting self (intraculturality) and other (interculturality) in diverse contexts of social and cultural interaction" (p. 326). Along these lines, the European Language Portfolio (ELP) requires students to assemble three components: (a) a language passport that includes basic information about a student's linguistic identity; (b) a language biography that includes language learning goals, progress, and a record of language learning and intercultural experiences; and (c) a dossier that contains a selection of a student's work that is representative of his or her foreign language proficiency (Little, 2002).

Although foreign language and global knowledge are included as part of the content of what is learned, much assessment regarding global learning has focused on attitudinal, cognitive, and affective change. As an early example of such measurement over 50 years ago, Sampson and Smith (1957) attempted to measure "world-mindedness," which was concerned with the problems of humanity rather than the problems of a specific nation or culture. The 32-item World-Mindedness Scale assesses eight dimensions: religion, immigration, government, economics, patriotism, race, education, and war. In an attempt to update this measure and address various psychometric issues, Hett (1993) developed the Global-Mindedness Scale, which reflects attitudes, beliefs, and behaviors, in order to assess "a worldview in which one sees oneself as connected to the world community and feels a sense of responsibility for its members" (p. 143), and consists of five dimensions: responsibility, cultural pluralism, efficacy, global centrism, and interconnectedness (see Clarke, Flaherty, Wright, & McMillen, 2009; Kehl & Morris, 2007). Along related lines, Der-Karabetian (1992) designed the Cross-Cultural World-Mindedness Scale, which consists of 26 items that evaluate attitudes toward race, religion, immigration, patriotism, economics, war, world government, and global education (Der-Karabetian & Metzer, 1993). Likewise, Shaftel and Shaftel (2010) developed the Intercultural Student Attitude Survey (ISAS), a 35-item scale created to assess changes in the attitudes and future plans of undergraduate students who study abroad. This measure focuses on assessing motivational cultural intelligence, which encompasses "the desire to learn about and function effectively in intercultural situations" (p. 12). More specifically, ISAS measures six constructs: cross-cultural open-mindedness, ability to manage stress, adventurousness, self-confidence, disposition toward a global career, and foreign language study.

A number of related measures focus on intercultural sensitivity, competence, and communication. For example, Chen and Starosta (2000a, 2000b) define intercultural communication competence as an umbrella concept composed of cognitive (intercultural awareness), behavioral (intercultural adroitness), and affective (intercultural sensitivity) abilities that impact intercultural communication. Bhawuk and Brislin (1992) argue that intercultural effectiveness requires people to be "interested in other cultures . . . sensitive enough to notice cultural differences, and . . . willing to modify their behavior as an indication of respect for the people of other cultures" (p. 416). Along these lines, Fantini (2000) helpfully sought to organize these levels of analysis by juxtaposing the categories of awareness, attitude, skills, knowledge, and second language proficiency, with four developmental levels of competence under each category: educational traveler, sojourner, professional, and intercultural/multicultural specialist.

Based upon the Developmental Model of Intercultural Sensitivity (DMIS) (Bennett, 1986, 1993; Bennett & Hammer, 2002), the Intercultural Development Inventory (IDI) is designed to measure one's status and progression through developmental stages, including denial, polarization, minimization, acceptance, and adaptation; thus, the stages of DMIS theoretically represent an individual's increasingly sophisticated capacity to apprehend and accurately experience cultures that are different from their own (e.g., Hammer, Bennett, & Wiseman, 2003; Rexeisen, Anderson, Lawton, & Hubbard, 2008). Such stages may be plotted along a continuum representing a person's cultural sensitivity, ranging from monocultural to intercultural mindsets (Hammer, 2012). From the standpoint of DMIS, when people become more interculturally engaged, they are not just becoming more sensitive to a particular culture; rather, their intercultural view and experience will extend to other cultures, including their own.

Regarding processes of navigating different cultures and contexts, the Cross-Cultural Adaptability Inventory (CCAI) assesses an individual's ability to adapt to different cultures. A 50-item self-report measure, the CCAI helps an individual identify his or her strengths and weaknesses within four skill areas of intercultural communication and interaction: emotional resilience, flexibility/openness, perceptual acuity, and personal autonomy (Kelley & Meyers, 1995; Chang, Yuan, & Chuang, 2013). The International Education Survey (IES) has been used "to assess how an international experience impacts personal and intellectual development" (Rexeisen et al., 2008, p. 2). Relatedly, Van der Zee and van Oudenhoven (2000) developed the Multicultural Personality Questionnaire, which measures multicultural effectiveness defined as "success in the fields of professional effectiveness, personal adjustment, and intercultural interactions" (p. 293). This measure has five scales: cultural empathy, open-mindedness, emotional stability, social initiative, and flexibility.

As a final example, the Global Perspective Inventory (GPI) and Global Competence Aptitude Assessment (GCAA) measure three dimensions: cognitive (knowing and knowledge: "how do I know?"), intrapersonal (identity and affect: "who am I?"), and interpersonal (social responsibility and social interaction: "how do I relate?") (see Doyle, 2009). Overall, the GCAA measures dimensions of knowledge, skills, and attitudes as well as internal and external readiness to experience different cultures (Braskamp, Braskamp, Merrill, & Engberg, 2010).

While this overview is not intended to be exhaustive, it should illustrate the types of measures that are being used within the field of international education assessment as well as the main foci of each approach. To be sure, many additional instruments might have been featured. For example, Fantini (2006) profiles 87 such measures under the aegis of "Assessment Tools of Intercultural Communicative Competence" (see also Fantini, 2009). The breadth of this compendium illustrates both the challenge in selecting the "right" assessment measure for a particular purpose as well as an attendant need to specify standards by which measures should be evaluated, research conducted, and practice implemented within the broader field of international, multicultural, and transformative learning. To provide guidance, the *Standards of Good Practice for Education Abroad*, developed by the Forum on Education Abroad, offers a comprehensive system by which the goals and practices of assessment may be evaluated. In this regard, "The Forum *Standards* are intended to be used on an ongoing basis to respond to the practical realities of developing, managing, and assessing education abroad programs" (Whalen, 2011, p. 3). Many of the instruments described previously—the IDI and the GPI, among others—as well as the Beliefs, Events, and Values Inventory (BEVI) described in this chapter, deliberately attempt to align their approaches to measurement with these Forum *Standards* (e.g., Braskamp, Blair, Shealy, & Hammer, 2012).

INTERNATIONAL, MULTICULTURAL, AND TRANSFORMATIVE ASSESSMENT: KEY QUESTIONS

The overview of global learning approaches provides a sense of how scholars and practitioners have attempted to measure the impact of international education, broadly defined. In doing so, many questions emerge. For example: "How do we determine which constructs are most and least salient?" "Whose questions are and are not answered?" "Can we actually measure such complex phenomena in a valid and reliable manner?" In addressing such matters, Sternberger, La Brack, and Whalen (2007) observe the following:

> Increasingly, faculty and administrators within the field of study abroad are taking a closer and more nuanced look at the experiences of study abroad, considering in more detail the cognitive, emotional, and developmental changes that may occur as a result of the experience. (p. 78)

In many ways, the movement to assess multiple dimensions of global learning mirrors what occurred in the U.S. education system 30 years ago, when more sophisticated models and measurement techniques were introduced into U.S. classrooms. Such innovations allowed for the evaluation, monitoring, and improvement of learning over time, while recognizing that students may respond differently to standard instruction in a way that is congruent with their learning and psychological profiles (Lerner, 2003).

Within the field of global education, however, a similar process of understanding and explaining the complexities of the interaction of differences among learners with learning processes and outcomes is a relatively recent undertaking. In all likelihood, that is because accounting for learning differences in a traditional environment is compounded substantially by the realities of living and learning abroad. While such learning is similar in some ways to that which occurs in a traditional classroom, it is qualitatively different on another level since study abroad may be experienced and anecdotally referred to as "dramatic" and "life-changing" (Doyle, 2009, p. 143), in part due to the "high impact" nature of such learning (e.g., Iyer, 2013; Kuh, 2008). Thus, students may not experience such learning in the same way or to the same degree. At the same time, substantial outcome variability also is apparent: some students report changes that are minimal, consisting of increased knowledge of facts regarding the foreign culture they visited, or even negative (e.g., "I couldn't wait to get home"); others emerge fundamentally transformed, no longer experiencing self, others, or the larger world as they did prior to the experience (e.g., Cultivating the Globally Sustainable Self, 2015). Given such variability, then, if we truly wish to understand who learns what and why, and under what circumstances, our approach to assessment research and practice must be sophisticated, comprehensive, and sustained in order to account for the complex interactions that we—as educators, scholars, and administrators—sense in our students but do not necessarily directly apprehend (e.g., Church, 1982; Reisweber, 2008; Sternberger et al., 2007).

Although there is a recent push to measure the affective and cognitive variables that are associated with global learning, assessment research and practice that is designed explicitly to account for such complexity is relatively rare. Instead, much of the scholarship in this area focuses on the acquisition of factual information or attitudinal change in students as well as the mapping of developmental stages such as orientation, study abroad, and re-entry (e.g., Koskinen & Tossavainen, 2003). Such work is very important and highly compatible with aspects of what is reported in this chapter. However, if we are to understand the processes that moderate and mediate change via international, multicultural, and transformative learning, our theoretical models and assessment methods must be able to account for such interacting complexities as they occur for real human beings in real time in the real world. To take but one example, the disequilibrating experience that many students encounter while studying abroad is commonly described as *culture shock*. As Kohls (2001) observed, culture shock results from:

> being cut off from the cultural cues and known patterns with which you are familiar,. . .living and/or working over an extended period of time in a situation that is ambiguous;. . .having your own values. . .brought into question, which yanks your moral rug out from under you; and. . .being continually put into a position in which you are expected to function with maximum skill and speed but where the rules have not been adequately explained. (pp. 93–94)

Although we concur with the validity of such an observation, the underlying affective, cognitive, cultural, contextual, and developmental processes that "cause" an individual to experience "culture shock" to varying degrees are not sufficiently illuminated by a descriptive level of analysis alone (Reisweber, 2008). In short, despite many helpful and productive advances in this area, the complex variables that mediate and moderate global learning processes and outcomes still await precise identification. Hampering our assessment and scholarly efforts in this regard, as noted by Sternberger et al. (2007), "many of the collection methods still do not follow best practices in research design nor do the researchers collect data in ways that are consistent over time" (p. 79). In the final analysis, then, educators and administrators with an interest in these matters must recognize and account for the profound human complexities that interact with a particular international, multicultural, or transformative learning experience to produce the outcomes that we ultimately observe. To achieve such goals, we must become much more methodologically intentional and sophisticated in our assessment research and practice in order to (a) address the overarching questions of who learns what and why, and under what circumstances and (b) translate our understanding into interventions that demonstrably improve teaching, training, and learning both in and outside of the classroom (e.g., Cultivating the Globally Sustainable Self, 2015; Shealy, 2016).

THE FORUM BEVI PROJECT[1]

In an attempt to address these assessment-based complexities, the Forum on Education Abroad through its Outcomes Assessment Committee partnered with the International Beliefs and Values Institute (IBAVI) in 2007 to design and implement a project using the BEVI in order to assess the processes and outcomes of international, multicultural, and transformative learning. There were many reasons for doing so. In particular, the Forum on Education Abroad has a strong and demonstrable record of supporting research-based activities that have the potential to illuminate relevant data, best practices, and appropriate standards for enhancing quality and impact within the field of international education (see www.forumea.org). At a complementary level, the mission of the IBAVI is to "explore beliefs and values and how they influence actions, policies, and practices around the world" (see www.ibavi.org). This partnership therefore was ideally suited to the fundamental goals and purposes of both organizations. Moreover, given the comprehensive nature of the BEVI and its integrated theoretical and applied emphases, this measure was seen as ideally suited to a long-term and large-scale research-to-practice agenda. As such, the overarching goal throughout this multi-institution, multiyear initiative was to identify findings, applications, and recommendations that were of the broadest and deepest relevance to the larger field. From the beginning, then, this project was designed deliberately to speak to these larger issues of assessment research and practice vis-à-vis international, multicultural, and transformative teaching, training, and learning including, but not limited to, the BEVI.

Toward such means and ends, the Forum BEVI Project participants committed—from the outset—to the following principles and practices of assessment research and practice (e.g., Braskamp et al., 2012; Braskamp & Engbert, 2014; Deardorff, 2006; Gerber, Gottlieb, Pysarchik, & Shealy, 2011; Pysarchik, Shealy, & Whalen, 2007a, 2007b; Shealy, 2014; Sternberger et al., 2007):

1. International, intercultural, and transformative learning is highly complex but measurable.
2. Any credible assessment project requires sufficient understanding of relevant theory, measures, design, data, and analysis by all project members.
3. The differences and similarities between assessment practice (what is done in the field) and assessment research (how we understand what is happening through measurement and analysis) must be reconciled.
4. Appropriate assessment standards and practices must be understood and followed (e.g., ethical conduct, Institutional Review Board [IRB] approval).
5. Relevant expertise must be accessed (e.g., research, psychometric, statistical).

[1] A project of this scope could not have occurred without the deep and abiding support from multiple individuals, institutions, and organizations over many years of work. In particular, we gratefully acknowledge the support and engagement of all who participated in various phases of the Forum BEVI Project as well as the indispensable commitments throughout by the Forum on Education Abroad and International Beliefs and Values Institute (IBAVI). We are also grateful for the statistical work of Wenjuan Ma as well as early contributions from Peter DeMichael and Chad Craun, and for the programming expertise of Craig Salee, assisted early on in the project by Todd Broadbent. We also gratefully acknowledge the editorial assistance of Pamela Roy, former Research and Scholarship Associate, and Joy Milano, Research Intern, in the Office of Study Abroad at Michigan State University, both of whom helped address multiple aspects of manuscript preparation. Although our process was highly fluid and intensive, it is our hope that the applications and implications documented here illustrate what may be learned and accomplished through such sustained and collaborative research of this nature.

6. Sufficient institutional support must be secured (e.g., administrative, financial).
7. Processes of project implementation and execution must be consistent with best practices, and monitored throughout.

A final organizational step involved the creation of the Forum–IBAVI Working Group on BEVI Implementation in Research, Education, and Practice. This working group was charged with: (a) identifying and investigating empirical and theoretical questions that may be pursued via the BEVI, which are relevant to international, intercultural, and transformative research, assessment, and practice, broadly defined; (b) providing guidance regarding how the BEVI may best be used to promote learning, growth, and development in various educational, applied, and practical contexts and settings; and (c) specifying best practices for usage of the BEVI's individual, group, and organizational report system.[2,3]

Forum BEVI Project Pilot Phase

As envisioned at the outset, this project would include both pilot[4] and formal phases of implementation. As such, beginning in 2007 and completed in 2009, the pilot phase involved administration of the BEVI to nearly 2,000 international learning participants in the United States and abroad. Statistical analysis narrowed the original number of factors on the BEVI from 40 to 18, and nearly 60 items were eliminated during the subsequent review process. Reliabilities for most of these scales (i.e., factors) were above 0.80 (no retained scale had a reliability of less than 0.75); no factor was retained without an eigenvalue of at least 2; and no item was retained with less than a .30 factor loading. Based upon factor analytic and correlation matrix data, as well as a Schmid–Leiman transformation (essentially a factor analysis of the factor analysis) (Schmid & Leiman, 1957), the 18 scales of the BEVI long version are organized under a series of headings, which correspond with the basic theoretical framework of this measure (discussed in the following).

Despite such advances, a number of institutions and organizations still wished for a shorter version of the BEVI for a number of reasons. First, within the context of higher education in particular, assessment demands already were high and student/faculty time was short. Second, although each scale on the long version of the

[2] We gratefully acknowledge the participation of many faculty, staff, and administrators—and thousands of students in the United States and internationally—who participated in various stages of this project. Lead participants and their accompanying institutions included Kris Acheson, Georgia State University; Tamara Baldwin, University of British Columbia; Brad Baltensperger, Michigan Technological University; Cynthia Banks, GlobaLinks Learning Abroad (ret.); Brian Brubaker, IES Abroad; Stephen DePaul, Terry College of Business, University of Georgia; Jennifer Engel, Loyola University Chicago; RT Good, Shenandoah University; Esther Gottlieb, The Ohio State University; Melanie Harding, University of British Columbia; Wenjuan Ma, Michigan State University; Gayle Nelson, Georgia State University; Hajime Nishitani, University of Hiroshima; Gaby Peschiera-Carl, University of South Carolina; Dawn Pysarchik, Michigan State University; Craig Shealy, James Madison University and IBAVI; Christopher Shirley, Georgetown University; Lee Sternberger, James Madison University; Arnd Wächter, Crossing Borders Education; Christa Walck, Michigan Technological University; Felix Wang, James Madison University; and Elizabeth Wandschneider, Michigan State University.

[3] Selected material in this chapter (e.g., regarding the BEVI, learning implications) has been adapted from Shealy (2014) and Chapters 2, 3, and 4 in the *Making Sense of Beliefs and Values* book with Springer Publishing (Shealy, 2016). Wenjuan Ma, Forum BEVI Project statistician, is responsible for the initial development of the "short version" psychometrics.

[4] The following colleges, universities, and study abroad program providers, all members of the Forum on Education Abroad, participated in the pilot phase of this project: Brethren Colleges Abroad, Dickinson College, IES Abroad, International Studies Abroad, James Madison University, Michigan State University, Saint Mary's College, Saint Olaf College, University of South Carolina, University of Texas, and Wells College.

BEVI assessed different constructs, these were interdependent on one another (i.e., by design, and consistent with the interconnected nature of beliefs, the "oblique" nature of factor rotation parameters allowed items to load on more than one factor) (see Shealy, 2010). Information gleaned from separate Exploratory Factor Analyses (EFAs) during its development did much to illuminate how and why specific "beliefs, events, and values" were associated together as they were. However, we long had recognized the need to move beyond EFA in order to determine by Confirmative Factor Analysis (CFA) if and how the EFA structure of the measure held upon administration to a new and separate sample, and to understand the relationship among more parsimonious versions of each scale construct. Thus, from 2011 to 2013, the developer of the BEVI (Craig Shealy) coordinated a plan and process with the working group to develop a "short version" of the BEVI.

Short Version of the BEVI

Throughout this process, an overarching goal was to determine if a shorter version of the BEVI, with substantially fewer items, could be developed in a manner that did not compromise the fundamental integrity of the measure (i.e., continued to illuminate how and why "beliefs, events, and values" were interrelated as they seemed to be via multiple analyses over the years). As any psychometrician will attest, this process was painstaking and intensive. Following a data-scrubbing process (e.g., ensuring that duplicated or incomplete cases were removed from the database), we identified a sample of 2,331 cases to be used in conducting the CFA. This initial phase was more doable than the next, which required multiple steps to determine which items could be eliminated without sacrificing the integrity of the measure. First, we confirmed which items were loading on which specific scale. Because a number of the long version scales were measuring higher order constructs, it was necessary once again to identify smaller subsets of items (i.e., subfactors) that comprised the larger construct. We used Cronbach's alpha to select the items that could be removed safely without significantly impacting the consistency of a particular factor (i.e., scale) or its subfactors (i.e., subscales). We then used analytic methods aligned with item response theory (IRT) to identify the relative contribution of each item to each scale. Again, the overarching goal of this step was to ensure that the short BEVI extracted information about respondents that was similar to the information extracted on the long BEVI.[5] Although the analyses for this process were relatively straightforward, the challenge lay in the sheer volume of data as well as the need to examine all possible permutations among all items and all scales. Ultimately, we automated these procedures via a "python program," which would stop and output results whenever the Cronbach's alpha coefficient is equal to 0.7 and allow us to compare the respective shapes of the information curve for each version of the BEVI. In other words, to preserve the integrity of the overall BEVI, items loading on the short version needed to evidence a similar capacity to identify the same types of respondents as did the longer version (e.g., regardless of whether someone strongly agreed or strongly disagreed to the items on a particular scale, the short BEVI needed to be able to identify such individuals with equivalent sensitivity to the longer version). The end result of this process was the selection of candidate items for retention and deletion in the development of the short BEVI.

---

[5] Since most institutions, organizations, and settings are now using the "short version" of the BEVI, and because of the extensive analytic process that resulted in this version, it seems likely as of this writing that the "short version" will become the primary version of the BEVI.

But despite this fundamental step forward, we were not done yet. That is because the python program often "spat out" different multiple item combinations of various short BEVI scales. To figure out which combination was best for each scale, we used structural equation modeling (SEM) to test all of these possible combinations based upon theoretical propositions that had emerged over years of research with the measure in order to explain "what" specific BEVI scales were assessing and why. This process also was highly iterative, involving a great deal of back-and-forth dialogue between theoretical and statistical perspectives on this measure. Ultimately, we were able to settle on final solutions for all scales that had good statistical and sound theoretical properties. At the conclusion of this process, 40 demographic and background variables (as opposed to 65), 185 items (as opposed to 336), and 17 scales (as opposed to 18) were retained in the short BEVI.[6] Table 12.1 summarizes core information regarding these scales.

TABLE 12.1
BEVI Scale Summaries

	MEAN	STD. DEVIATION	CRONBACH'S ALPHA	NUMBER OF ITEMS
Negative Life Events	2.889	0.610	0.862	9
Needs Closure	2.646	0.290	0.712	25
Needs Fulfillment	1.892	0.342	0.882	24
Identity Diffusion	2.791	0.322	0.610	13
Basic Openness	2.108	0.417	0.809	12
Basic Determinism	2.887	0.355	0.755	16
Ecological Resonance	2.248	0.524	0.760	6
Self Certitude	2.122	0.357	0.761	13
Religious Traditionalism	2.705	0.782	0.903	5
Emotional Attunement	2.175	0.421	0.814	13
Physical Resonance	2.200	0.429	0.719	7
Self Awareness	1.855	0.358	0.810	12
Socioemotional Convergence	1.908	0.286	0.877	36
Sociocultural Openness	2.058	0.287	0.798	26
Global Resonance	1.719	0.469	0.828	6
Gender Traditionalism	2.275	0.472	0.828	11
Meaning Quest	1.873	0.317	0.831	19

---

[6] It should be noted that we retained one scale—Identity Diffusion—that did not meet this .70 threshold (it had an alpha of .61). Also, a few items progressing through the first steps did not survive SEM, but were retained nonetheless. On both counts, our reasons for doing so were to identify specific combinations of items for the short version of the BEVI that had the best reliability while also retaining as much fidelity as possible to the longer BEVI. Along these lines, one scale—Global Engagement—appeared to be a subfactor of a newly named factor, called Meaning Quest, which explains why the short version of the BEVI has one less scale than the long version. Extensive review of item combinations also resulted in the renaming of several scales in order to better represent the apparent meaning of each factor. Finally, another round of subject matter expert (SME) review of the demographic/background items was conducted as well, which resulted in the elimination of 25 of these items.

TABLE 12.2
Model Fit Information for BEVI Scales

	CHI-SQUARE	DF	P VALUE	CFI	RMSEA
Negative Life Events	428.612	27	0.000	0.977	0.080
Needs Closure	2993.316	225	0.000	0.911	0.073
Needs Fulfillment	2855.248	248	0.000	0.912	0.067
Identity Diffusion	28.973	2	0.000	0.983	0.076
Basic Openness	619.225	54	0.000	0.956	0.067
Basic Determinism	536.465	41	0.000	0.927	0.072
Ecological Resonance	456.526	9	0.000	0.967	0.147
Self Certitude	634.634	62	0.000	0.937	0.064
Religious Traditionalism	166.821	9	0.000	0.995	0.087
Emotional Attunement	654.891	62	0.000	0.960	0.064
Physical Resonance	40.557	2	0.000	0.984	0.091
Self Awareness	598.360	54	0.000	0.948	0.066
Socioemotional Convergence	3523.339	369	0.000	0.901	0.061
Sociocultural Openness	2596.628	225	0.000	0.935	0.067
Global Resonance	93.898	14	0.000	0.994	0.050
Gender Traditionalism	765.686	44	0.000	0.948	0.084
Meaning Quest	836.661	61	0.000	0.925	0.074

CFI, Confirmatory Fit Index; RMSEA, Root Mean Square Error of Approximation.

As noted, to explore scale structure, we used SEM to test the relationships between the items and constructs, a process that was highly iterative. Table 12.2 summarizes the final model fit information, which indicates that these scales have a relatively good model fit and fit the underlying theory adequately well.

In addition to these key aspects of test development described previously, another major activity of the working group was to present findings of our work over the 6 years of this project, which included over 20 publications (e.g., articles, chapters, dissertations), 50 presentations (e.g., symposia, papers, posters), and hundreds of separate analyses. The bulk of this chapter provides a summary of these applications and implications. Before such an overview, however, it may be helpful to include additional explication regarding the theoretical underpinnings, applications, and scale structure of the BEVI.

Equilintegration Theory and the Equilintegration Self

Before describing the BEVI in greater detail (e.g., what it actually measures), a brief overview of its theoretical underpinnings—Equilintegration (EI) Theory and the EI

Self—is needed. Essentially, EI Theory seeks to explain "the processes by which beliefs, values, and 'worldviews' are acquired and maintained, why their alteration is typically resisted, and how and under what circumstances their modification occurs" (Shealy, 2004, p. 1075). Derivative of EI Theory, and informed by scholarship in a range of key areas (e.g., "needs-based" research and theory; developmental psychopathology; social cognition; psychotherapy processes and outcomes; affect regulation; theories and models of "self"), the EI Self seeks to illustrate how the interaction between our core needs (e.g., for attachment, affiliation) and formative variables (e.g., caregiver, culture) results in beliefs and values about self, others, and the world at large that we all internalize over the course of development and across the life span (see Shealy, 2016).

The Beliefs, Events, and Values Inventory (BEVI)

Although we have described various psychometric and development aspects of the BEVI, we have not yet discussed what the BEVI really measures. Concomitant with EI Theory and the EI Self, the BEVI is a comprehensive analytic tool that examines how and why we come to see ourselves, others, and the larger world as we do (i.e., how life experiences, culture, and context affect our beliefs, values, and worldview) as well as the influence of such processes on multiple aspects of human functioning (i.e., learning processes, relationships, personal growth, the pursuit of life goals). The BEVI assesses processes such as: basic openness; the tendency to (or not to) stereotype in particular ways; self- and emotional awareness; preferred strategies for making sense of why "other" people and cultures "do what they do"; global engagement (i.e., receptivity to different cultures, religions, and social practices); and, worldview shift (i.e., to what degree do beliefs and values change as a result of specific experiences). BEVI results are translated into reports at the individual, group, and organizational levels that include a range of scores, indexes, and narratives. Individuals, groups, institutions, and organizations use the BEVI and its report system in a wide range of contexts (e.g., educational, mental health, organizational), and for a variety of applied and research purposes (e.g., to track and examine changes in worldviews over time; to evaluate and improve educational programs or experiences; to cultivate growth and awareness in individuals, couples, and groups; to develop leadership capacity; to enhance organizational functioning; to evaluate whether assessment-based goals are met).

Both the long (336 items) and short (185 items) versions of the BEVI consist of four interrelated components: (a) a comprehensive set of demographic/background items that may be modified for particular projects; (b) a life history questionnaire, which is built into the measure; (c) two validity and 18 (long version) or 17 (short version) scales; and (d) three qualitative "experiential reflection" items. As a web-based and Likert-type inventory with four response options (Strongly Agree, Agree, Disagree, Strongly Disagree), the long version of the BEVI typically requires between 35 and 45 minutes to complete; the short version typically requires between 25 and 30 minutes to complete. Items are balanced deliberately to minimize social desirability and other response-set confounds (see Geisinger, 2013; Robinson, Shaver, & Wrightsman, 1991, 1999). Most importantly, the BEVI is not designed to appraise the debatable correctness or incorrectness of individual responses, but rather to investigate how overall response patterns predict various processes and outcomes, from the beliefs and values associated with ethnocentrism, religious tolerance, partisanship, and gender-based practices and policies to issues of openness, self access, and emotional attunement.

As noted via multiple chapters in *Making Sense of Beliefs and Values*, the BEVI has been used for a wide range of purposes. Research-focused chapters explain how the EI model and BEVI method increase our conceptual sophistication and methodological capacity across a range of areas: culture, development, environment, gender, politics, and religion. Practice-oriented chapters demonstrate how the BEVI is used in the real world across a range of applied domains: assessment, education, forensics, leadership, and psychotherapy. These implications and applications of the BEVI are illuminated by a number of statistical analyses (e.g., analysis of variance [ANOVA], regression, structural equation modeling) as well as the BEVI report system. Evidence of validity is indicated by numerous studies demonstrating that the BEVI is able to predict group membership across a wide range of variables including demographics such as gender, ethnic background, parental income, political orientation, and religious orientation as well as other relevant variables and processes as documented in other chapters of this book (e.g., Atwood, Chkhaidze, Shealy, Staton, & Sternberger, 2014; Brearly, Shealy, Staton, & Sternberger, 2012; Hill et al., 2013; Isley, Shealy, Crandall, Sivo, & Reifsteck, 1999; Hayes, Shealy, Sivo, & Weinstein, 1999; Patel, Shealy, & De Michele, 2007; Pysarchik, Shealy, & Whalen, 2007a, 2007b; Shealy, 2000a, 2000b, 2004, 2005, 2006, 2012; Tabit et al., 2011). For example, EI theory, the EI Self, and the BEVI offer an integrative framework and method for predicting and explaining characteristics that are linked to other global issues such as environmental concerns (Patel, 2008) and intercultural awareness (Reisweber, 2008; see also Shealy, Bhuyan, & Sternberger, 2012).

Although both "long" and "short" versions of the BEVI are available, many users prefer the short version mainly due to time savings, as described previously. Therefore, the following overview of BEVI scales is based upon the "short version," which overlaps substantially with the "long version." Again, the short BEVI consists of 2 validity and 17 process scales. Although there are many ways to present scale scores, they often are presented as a series of colored bars along with a number within each bar. This number corresponds to the percentile score between 1 and 100 that an individual or a group scored on that scale based upon their overall response to the items that statistically load on each BEVI scale (i.e., "loading" refers to which items have been shown statistically to cluster together on a specific "construct" or scale of the BEVI, and therefore comprise the items on that scale). The resulting scores are standardized based upon the means and standard deviations for each scale (see Table 12.1). For group reports, the score is called "aggregate" because it represents the average score for all individuals in the group on a specific scale. BEVI results are presented under nine different domains in the following. A description of each of the BEVI scales, under their respective domains, also is provided along with sample items for each scale (in parentheses).[7] In reviewing the following information, remember that by design, items may load statistically on a given scale in either a negative or positive direction. Thus, if sample items seem to be the opposite of one another, that is both expected and appropriate in terms of the psychometrics of inventories such as the BEVI (i.e., positively and negatively loading items both may comprise a given scale).

I. Validity Scales
- **Consistency**: the degree to which responses are consistent for differently worded items that are assessing similar or identical content (e.g., "People change all the time." "People don't really change.")

---

[7] The BEVI is a copyrighted instrument. BEVI items, item content, scales, or reports may not be modified, copied, disseminated, or published, in whole or part, without the written and express permission of Craig N. Shealy, PhD.

- **Congruency**: the degree to which response patterns correspond to that which would be predicted statistically (e.g., "I have real needs for warmth and affection." "I take my own feelings very seriously.")

II. Formative Variables

- **Demographic/Background Items**: gender, educational level, ethnicity, political/religious orientation, income, and so on (e.g., "What is your gender?" "What is your ethnic background?")
- **Negative Life Events (Scale 1)**: difficult childhood; parents were troubled; life conflict/struggles; many regrets (e.g., "I have had a lot of conflict with one or more members of my family." "My family had a lot of problems with money.")

III. Fulfillment of Core Needs

- **Needs Closure (Scale 2)**: unhappy upbringing/life history; conflictual/disturbed family dynamics; stereotypical thinking/odd explanations for why events happen as they do or why things are as they are (e.g., "I had a wonderful childhood." "Some numbers are more lucky than others.")
- **Needs Fulfillment (Scale 3)**: open to experiences, needs, and feelings; deep care/sensitivity for self, others, and the larger world (e.g., "We should spend more money on early education programs for children." "I like to think about who I am.")
- **Identity Diffusion (Scale 4)**: indicates painful crisis of identity; fatalistic regarding negatives of marital/family life; feels "bad" about self and prospects (e.g., "I have gone through a painful identity crisis." "Even though we expect them to be, men are not really built to be faithful in marriage.")

IV. Tolerance of Disequilibrium

- **Basic Openness (Scale 5)**: open and honest about the experience of basic thoughts, feelings, and needs (e.g., "I don't always feel good about who I am." "I have felt lonely in my life.")
- **Self Certitude (Scale 6)**: strong sense of will; impatient with excuses for difficulties; emphasizes positive thinking; disinclined toward deep analysis (e.g., "You can overcome almost any problem if you just try harder." "If you play by the rules, you get along fine.")

V. Critical Thinking

- **Basic Determinism (Scale 7)**: prefers simple explanations for differences/behavior; believes people do not change/strong will survive; troubled life history (e.g., "AIDS may well be a sign of God's anger." "It's only natural that the strong will survive.")
- **Socioemotional Convergence (Scale 8)**: open, aware of self/other, larger world; thoughtful, pragmatic, determined; sees world in shades of gray, such as the need for self-reliance while caring for vulnerable others (e.g., "We should do more to help those who are less fortunate." "Too many people don't meet their responsibilities.")

VI. Self Access

- **Physical Resonance (Scale 9)**: receptive to corporeal needs/feelings; experientially inclined; appreciates the impact of human nature/evolution (e.g., "I am a free spirit." My body is very sensitive to what I feel.")
- **Emotional Attunement (Scale 10)**: emotional, sensitive, social, needy, affiliative; values the expression of affect; close family connections (e.g., "I don't mind displays of emotion." "Weakness can be a virtue.")
- **Self Awareness (Scale 11)**: introspective; accepts complexity of self; cares for human experience/condition; tolerates difficult thoughts/feelings (e.g., "I am always trying to understand myself better." "I have problems that I need to work on.")

- **Meaning Quest (Scale 12):** searching for meaning; seeks balance in life; resilient/persistent; highly feeling; concerned for less fortunate (e.g., "I think a lot about the meaning of life." "I want to find a better sense of balance in my life.")

VII. **Other Access**
  - **Religious Traditionalism (Scale 13):** highly religious; sees self/behavior/events as mediated by God/spiritual forces; one way to the "afterlife" (e.g., "Without religion there can be no peace." "There is one way to heaven.")
  - **Gender Traditionalism (Scale 14):** men and women are built to be a certain way; prefers traditional/simple views of gender and gender roles (e.g., "Women are more emotional than men." "A man's role is to be strong.")
  - **Sociocultural Openness (Scale 15):** progressive/open regarding a wide range of actions, policies, and practices in the areas of culture, economics, education, environment, gender/global relations, politics (e.g., "We should try to understand cultures that are different from our own." "There is too big a gap between the rich and poor in our country.")

VIII. **Global Access**
  - **Ecological Resonance (Scale 16):** deeply invested in environmental/sustainability issues; concerned about the fate of the earth/natural world (e.g., "I worry about our environment." "We should protect the land no matter who owns it.")
  - **Global Resonance (Scale 17):** invested in learning about/encountering different individuals, groups, languages, cultures; seeks global engagement (e.g., "It is important to be well informed about world events." "I am comfortable around groups of people who are very different from me.")

IX. **Experiential Reflection Items**

The BEVI is a "mixed methods" measure in that both quantitative (i.e., scales) and qualitative (i.e., free response) items are asked during administration and used for purposes of interpretation (e.g., Coates, Hanson, Samuel, Webster, & Cozen, 2016; Cozen, Hanson, Poston, Jones, & Tabit, 2016). The following three qualitative Experiential Reflection Items are included in the BEVI, and completed in written format at the conclusion of administration:

First, please describe which aspect of this experience has had the greatest impact upon you and why?

Second, is there some aspect of your own "self" or "identity" (e.g., gender, ethnicity, sexual orientation, religious or political background, etc.) that has become especially clear or relevant to you or others as a result of this experience?

Third, what have you learned and how are you different as a result of this experience?

The Forum BEVI Project: Applications

Throughout the Forum BEVI Project, a variety of research questions, assessment projects, and applied interventions were examined depending upon the emphases and needs of participating institutions and organizations as well as the overarching goals of the project to understand better the processes and outcomes of international, multicultural, and transformative learning. Overall, these activities fell under one or more of the following eight areas of inquiry and practice:

1. **Evaluating learning experiences** (e.g., study abroad, multicultural courses, training programs, service learning, etc.)

2. **Understanding learning processes** (e.g., who learns what and why, and under what circumstances)
3. **Promoting learning objectives** (e.g., increased awareness of self, others, and the larger world)
4. **Enhancing teaching and program quality** (e.g., which experiences, courses, programs have what impact, and why)
5. **Facilitating growth and development** (e.g., of individuals, groups, and organizations)
6. **Conducting research** (e.g., how, why, and under what circumstances people become more "open" to different cultures)
7. **Addressing organizational needs** (e.g., staff/leadership development)
8. **Complying with assessment and accreditation requirements** (e.g., linking objectives to outcomes)

In the pursuit of such activities, over 500 different analyses were conducted with various subsets of participants, both within and across participating institutions, which included the generation of thousands of individual reports and dozens of group/organizational reports. Although over 8,000 participants completed the BEVI from 2007 to 2013, many of the results given in the following were developed either at the institutional level or on the basis of a large, cross-institutional dataset (N = 2331) collected toward the conclusion of the project, during 2011 to 2012.[8] Participants primarily included undergraduate students (96.7%) and were recruited through a range of learning experiences (e.g., study abroad, residential learning communities, general education courses with a focus on transformative/multicultural learning). A small portion of graduate students (3.3%) also was included. The sample typically ranged between the ages of 17 to 26, with an average age of 19. However, 3.9% fell into the age range of 26 to 62, with another 9% falling into the age range of 12 to 17. Although the majority of participants reported as U.S. citizens (93.3%), non-U.S. citizens also were included in the sample (N = 156 or 6.7%). Also, participants were drawn from 38 different countries of origin. Of the sample, 79.1% reported as Caucasian with 20.9% as non-Caucasian (6.6% Black or African American; 0.9% American Indian or Alaskan Native; 7.4% Asian or Pacific Islander; 2.9% Hispanic/Latino; 3% Other). Finally, from the standpoint of gender, 40.8% of the sample was female, with 59.2% male. All participants were required to provide informed consent as determined by multiple IRB processes, and participation was entirely voluntary. Participants were not required to complete the BEVI, and could elect to discontinue participation at any time. Analyses were conducted via a software package used for statistical analysis (SPSS) and a statistical package used for the analysis of latent variables (MPLUS), and consisted of ANOVAs, regression analyses, and structural equation modeling (SEM).

The Forum BEVI Project: Implications for International, Multicultural, and Transformative Learning

Given the scope of this work, it is challenging to select only a small sample of findings from hundreds in order to identify the most salient "lessons learned." Ultimately,

---

[8] Note that some of the scale names differ from the short and long versions of the BEVI. In addition to the clarification provided in this chapter, please see www.thebevi.com for additional information.

it proved most useful to distill all that we discovered through this project into a series of 15 implications for international, multicultural, and transformative learning:

1. Who we are affects whether, what, and how we learn.
2. Education, broadly defined, is associated with—and likely causes—change in beliefs and values.
3. To understand how effective our interventions are, we must assess who learners are.
4. It is possible to predict who will be interested in—and satisfied by—a learning experience even before the learning experience actually occurs.
5. Specific analyses may be conducted for purposes of outreach and engagement.
6. All educators and educational experiences are not equal.
7. Educational experiences are associated with desirable as well as undesirable processes and outcomes across a wide range of constructs that must be measured to be known.
8. Examining only overall (e.g., aggregate) findings or privileging only a few BEVI scales constitute tempting but counterproductive approaches to comprehensive assessment.
9. Although distinct characteristics of various cross-cultural groups are identifiable, broad-based assessment suggests within as well as between-group variation.
10. As Kurt Lewin (1951) observed, there is nothing so practical as a good theory.
11. It is possible to identify the profile or signature of an institution or organization.
12. Group reports help course instructors, program directors, and administrators understand better the nature of their particular classes, cohorts, or staffs.
13. By jointly utilizing individual and group reports, multiple opportunities for self-assessment, enhanced understanding, and group development may be facilitated.
14. Changes in beliefs and values about self, others, and the world at large appear determined largely by the 7Ds (duration, difference, depth, determine, design, deliver, and debrief).
15. Best practice in assessment requires best practice in research.

We next discuss each of these implications, along with relevant findings, applications, and recommendations.[9]

Implication 1. Who We Are Affects Whether, What, and How We Learn

Formative variables such as life experiences and demographics interact powerfully with the experiences we provide to learners (e.g., study abroad, multicultural coursework, growth/ development workshops, education in general) to influence the learning processes and outcomes that we observe.

Consider Figure 12.1, which is a structural equation model (SEM) regarding the relationship between Formative Variables, Mediators, and Outcomes. Essentially,

---

[9] The presentation of results in the following section of this chapter is informed by the March, 2012 Special Section of the journal *Psychotherapy*, entitled "Ethical Issues in Clinical Writing," Volume 49, Issue 1, pp. 1–25 as well as Health Insurance Portability and Accountability Act (HIPAA) regulations, American Psychological Association (APA) ethical guidelines, and other best practices for reporting such information. In this regard, although all assessment and report results are consistent with original patterns and profiles, key information may have been modified on occasion (i.e., specific scores) in order to ensure the anonymity of respondents and/or consistency across the long and short versions of the BEVI.

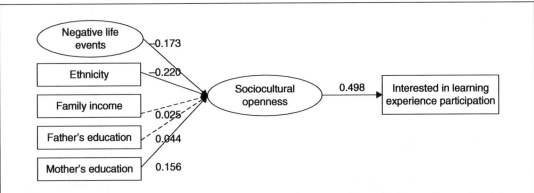

FIGURE 12.1. Sociocultural Openness as a mediator between demographic and experiential variables and interest in global learning experiences (international, multicultural, and transformative).

Note. N = 1016, Chi-square = 9141.328, df = 1257, *p* = .000, RMSEA = 0.052, CFI = 0.938.

SEM is a sophisticated statistical approach that is derivative of various methods for establishing predictive pathways among constructs that are thought to have a relationship with one another. In other words, SEM allows for theory testing, since this approach evaluates the statistical relationship that is theorized to exist between constructs that have achieved a measure of reliability and validity. Thus the "model" of structural equation modeling essentially is the theory presumed to underlie the relationship among a set of constructs (e.g., Kline, 2010). From the standpoint of the EI model and BEVI method, the SEM pictured in Figure 12.1 basically contends that *formative variables* (e.g., antecedent variables that influence why we come to experience self, others, and the larger world as we do) are associated with/predictive of *mediating variables* (e.g., latent variables that help explain underlying psychological processes that contribute to various outcomes that we observe), which further predict *outcomes* (e.g., empirically observable outcomes, such as behaviors or verbalizations regarding one's intention or reality).

So, from this perspective—and grounded in the EI theoretical framework—one's stated "interest" in international or multicultural learning is, in no small part, determined by previous life experiences, which shape our "beliefs and values" regarding self, others, and the larger world. This proposed theoretical model regarding the predictive linkage among formative variables, mediators, and outcomes, receives strong support from Figure 12.1. Here, we used MPLUS with weighted least squares means and variance adjusted (WLSMV) as the estimator. Antecedents in the model are: Negative Life Events; ethnicity measured as a dummy variable (0 = minority, 1 = White/Caucasian); family income as an ordinal measure of the annual family income even if the participant did not receive financial support from them (1 = less than $10,000/year to 10 = $175,000 +/year); and, father's and mother's education levels (each range from 0 = some high school or less to 8 = doctoral degree). The dependent variable is the level of interest in global, multicultural, or transformative learning, which is measured by a single question (1 = extremely low interest to 7 = extremely high interest).

Results show variability in the impact of formative variables on students' interest in international and multicultural learning. Table 12.3 provides the parameters of

TABLE 12.3
Factors Impacting Interest in Global Learning: Structural Coefficients, SEM

		UNSTANDARDIZED COEFFICIENT	UNSTANDARDIZED COEFFICIENT
Negative Life Events ⟶	Sociocultural Openness	−0.166	−0.173
Ethnicity ⟶	Sociocultural Openness	−0.454	−0.220
Family Income ⟶	Sociocultural Openness	−0.007	0.025
Father's Education ⟶	Sociocultural Openness	0.016	0.044
Mother's Education ⟶	Sociocultural Openness	0.061	0.156
Sociocultural Openness ⟶	Global Learning Interest	1.139	0.498

these linkages. Specifically, Negative Life Events and ethnicity are negatively associated with Sociocultural Openness, which means that students experiencing fewer Negative Life Events were more Socioculturally Open, and that Caucasian students are less Socioculturally Open than minority students. Moreover, mother's education is positively associated with Sociocultural Openness, while family income and father's education are not significantly related to Sociocultural Openness. Sociocultural Openness also has a positive influence on students' interest in engaging in international, multicultural, and transformative learning experiences. In short, the experience of particular formative variables (positive life events, being non-Caucasian, and having a mother with a higher degree of education) is predictive of the degree to which one is "open" to the beliefs, values, and practices of other cultures, which is further and strongly predictive of one's interest in engaging with and learning from cultures that are different from one's own.

Implication 2. Education, Broadly Defined, Is Associated With— and Likely Causes—Change in Beliefs and Values

Abundant quantitative and qualitative evidence from different types of learning experiences assessed by the Forum BEVI Project (e.g., study abroad, multicultural coursework, general education) indicates that students are likely to see and experience themselves, others, and the larger world differently following such experiences.

Contemplate, first, the degree to which "education" influences the relative sophistication that students demonstrate in terms of their attributions about self, others, and the larger world, a framework that may generally be grouped—from the standpoint of the BEVI—under the domain of "Critical Thinking." What is meant by this construct? Consider a joint statement presented at the 8th Annual International Conference on Critical Thinking and Education Reform (Scriven & Paul, 1987), in which critical thinking is defined as "the intellectually disciplined process of actively and skillfully conceptualizing, applying, analyzing, synthesizing, and/or evaluating information gathered from, or generated by, observation, experience, reflection, reasoning, or communication, as a guide to belief and action" (see www.criticalthinking .org/pages/defining-critical-thinking/766).[10] According to this definition, critical thinking involves a gestalt of competencies that help an individual assess information (in terms of thoughts, feelings, and behaviors) within oneself and one's surroundings, understand and reason with complexity, and utilize this resulting awareness to understand self, others, and the world in more sophisticated and accurate terms.

Along related lines, Cottrell (2005) regards critical thinking as a meta-thinking skill or cognitive process based on intellectual traits, exposure, educational subjectivity, and the disposition to use such capacities. Another comprehensive definition of critical thinking that emphasizes the "self" is offered by Paul and Elder (2006), which contends:

> Critical thinking is, in short, self-directed, self-disciplined, self-monitored, and self-corrective thinking. It presupposes assent to rigorous standards of excellence and mindful command of their use. It entails effective communication and problem solving abilities and a commitment to overcome our native egocentrism and sociocentrism. (p. 4)

Finally, highlighting the interrelated complexity of this construct, Manaloa, Kusumib, Koyasub, Michitac, and Waseda (2013) observe that scholars have defined the construct of "critical thinking" in any number of ways, to include:

- "Skilled and active interpretation and evaluation of observations and communications, information and argumentation" (Fisher & Scriven, 1997, p. 21)
- "Correct assessment of statements" (Ennis, 1962, p. 81)
- "Identification and evaluation of implicit theoretical assumptions" (Yanchar, Slife, & Warne, 2008, p. 265)
- "An attitude or disposition to recognize when a skill is needed and the willingness to apply it" (Halpern, 1998, p. 452).

The importance of critical thinking, and the relative effectiveness of higher education in facilitating its development and expression, was brought home dramatically by *Academically Adrift* (Arum & Roksa, 2011), which concluded that student advances in "critical thinking" were modest at best, mainly because of a lack of rigor (e.g., limited reading and studying requirements). We appreciate this important contribution to a significant question regarding the efficacy of higher education, noting that such issues often come down to matters of measurement (e.g., from a quantitative standpoint, which items load statistically on a specific scale) and operationalization (e.g., the steps or operations that are assembled to define and demonstrate the construct in question, including "critical thinking").

In this regard, from the standpoint of the BEVI and its underlying EI theoretical framework, the construct of "critical thinking" is resonant with several of these perspectives (e.g., Manaloa et al., 2013; Scriven & Paul, 1987). Specifically, "critical thinking" is evidenced mainly by the degree of attributional sophistication regarding *why* people do what they do as well as *why* various events or phenomena occur as they do, and under what circumstances (Shealy, 2004, 2016). From a construct level of analysis, on the long version of the BEVI, such processes are operationalized via four scales: Causal Closure, Basic Determinism, Divergent Determinism, and Socioreligious

---

[10] Aspects of this section are excerpted and/or adapted from Iyer (2013).

Closure. Among other applications, through the report system described later in this chapter, the BEVI assists students, instructors, and program directors alike in reflecting on these aspects of critical thinking in order to assess and practice greater self-reflexivity toward self, others, and the larger world (e.g., Ethics of International Engagement and Service-Learning Project, 2011; Iyer, 2013). From the standpoint of the Forum BEVI Project, we wished to examine whether the relatively straightforward moderator of "number of years in college" was associated with critical thinking as defined by the BEVI.

Structural equation modeling (SEM) again was chosen to analyze the relationship between the number of years in college and dimensions of critical thinking. As Figure 12.2 illustrates, three of the four BEVI scales that are intended to measure "critical thinking" are in fact statistically associated with years in college. What do such results suggest? Essentially, individuals who score highly on Basic Determinism tend to prefer basic/simple explanations for why people are as they are or do what they do (e.g., are inclined toward simple explanations of complex, biopsychosocially mediated phenomena such as ethnic or gender-based differences among people). Individuals who score highly on Divergent Determinism tend to eschew commonly accepted answers or understandings of phenomena, prefer nonconvergent explanations and nontraditional policy solutions, are unconventional, tend to question authority, may reflexively be contrarian (i.e., for the sake of being so), and resist being pinned down (e.g., will tend to contest the validity or truth of whatever claims are being made). Individuals who score highly on Socioreligious Closure tend to have strong religious beliefs and great faith, believe that God alone provides happiness/health, and perceive little personal control. In short—and mindful of the possibility for correlation/causation confusion—the greater the number of years in college, the higher the overall degree of critical thinking, as evidenced by lower scores on Basic Determinism, Divergent Determinism, and Socioreligious Closure.

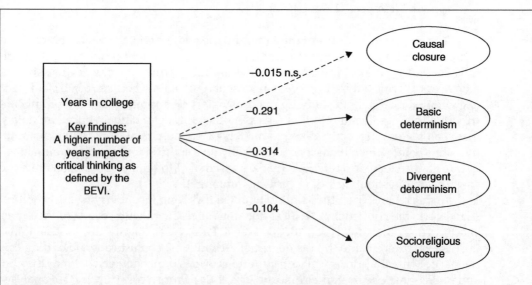

FIGURE 12.2. The relationship of "critical thinking" scales on the BEVI to number of years spent in higher education.

Note. Chi-square = 1579.701, df = 149, p = .000, RMSEA = 0.094, CFI = 0.912.

Consider a more fine-grained analysis by examining correlation matrix findings regarding Divergent Determinism, the scale that is most strongly negatively associated with number of years of college (i.e., lower Divergent Determinism is associated with more years of college). A primary usage of correlation matrixes is to understand the underlying relational patterns among constructs (i.e., scales), which may relate to one another. In doing so, the deliberately oblique factor structure of BEVI scales should be recognized. In other words, as is predicted by the EI theoretical model, and in keeping with the "web-based" nature of "beliefs and values," from a factor rotation standpoint, items are permitted to load on one or more scales, which in fact is key to "making sense" of why beliefs and values are related to each other, and to life events, in the way that they are (i.e., as they naturally occur for real human beings) (Shealy, 2016). In this regard, we examine in Table 12.4 the strongest correlations between Divergent Determinism and other BEVI scales (those at 0.40 or above).

What do such findings suggest? As Table 12.4 illustrates, correlation matrix data suggest individuals who score highly on Divergent Determinism also:

- Are likely to have greater difficulty "holding complexity," tending to see the world in "black and white" terms (Socioemotional Convergence)
- Are more likely to indicate that core needs (e.g., for attachment, affection) were not met in a "good enough" manner (Needs Closure)
- Are less likely to indicate the capacity and inclination to experience affect in self and other, and to value its expression (Emotional Attunement)
- Are more likely to report the experience of a high degree of unhappy life experiences, during childhood/adolescence or generally in life (Negative Life Events)
- Are less likely to be interested in or open to the beliefs, values, and practices of cultures that are different from one's own (Sociocultural Openness)
- Are more likely to deny or ignore fundamental thoughts, feelings, or needs that generally are experienced as "normative" regarding human existence or functioning (Basic Closedness)

TABLE 12.4
Correlation Matrix Findings Above 0.40 Between Divergent Determinism and Other BEVI Scales

SCALES	CORRELATION
Socioemotional Convergence	−0.81
Needs Closure	0.65
Emotional Attunement	−0.58
Negative Life Events	0.53
Sociocultural Openness	−0.50
Basic Closedness	0.45
Ecological Resonance	−0.43
Identity Diffusion	0.42

- Are less likely to be concerned about or invested in matters that have to do with the environment and natural world (Ecological Resonance)
- Are more likely to express feelings of confusion and entrapment regarding their current existence and future prospects (Identity Diffusion)

Taken together, these SEM (Figure 12.2) and correlation matrix findings (Table 12.4) suggest that critical thinking as defined by the BEVI should be understood not only in terms of the relative attributional sophistication of human beings (e.g., the ability to understand the complexities of why we think, feel, and do what we do or why events happen as they do in the larger world). At a more complex level, it also appears that such capacities and inclinations may in fact be associated with our life histories, since a higher degree of Negative Life Events and Needs Closure appears to be associated with a lower degree of critical thinking as defined by the BEVI, an outcome that would in fact be predicted by the basic needs-based postulates of the EI model (Shealy, 2016; Shealy et al., 2012). In any case, the most basic finding here is that the relative sophistication and complexity of attributional tendencies about why people do what they do, or why events happen in the world as they do, increases as people experience more years in college or university. Although subject to further inquiry, and ever mindful of the possibility for correlation/causation confusion (e.g., the role of maturational effects), such results suggest that repeated exposure to complex concepts combined with multiple experiences in which one is required to understand, reflect upon, and justify the rationale for beliefs and values in self, others, and the larger world may in fact be associated with the acquisition of more sophisticated attributional frameworks over time.

Implication 3. To Understand How Effective Our Interventions Are, We Must Assess Who Learners Are

Attributing positive ratings of learning experiences only or largely to the experience itself, without accounting for who students are prior to their engagement in the experience, is neither good practice nor empirically indicated.

To what degree does exposure to international, multicultural, and transformative learning actually change fundamental aspects of an individual's personality or identity, indeed the very "self" of the learner? Put in other terms, does exposure to such learning experiences cultivate the capacity to care in a deeper way for self, others, and the larger world (Shealy et al., 2012)? Such questions are complicated in their own right, and rendered more so by the fact that individuals who self-select to engage in such experiences may already be "in the choir to which we sing" (i.e., they "get" what we are seeking to facilitate even before the learning experience begins). Multiple findings from the Forum BEVI Project suggest that "who we are" prior to the experience in which we engage may interact profoundly with the experience itself to influence outcomes. Consider the following correlation matrix data from one of the "primary" factors on the BEVI, Sociocultural Openness.

What do such findings suggest? Essentially, individuals scoring high on Sociocultural Openness tend to endorse a worldview that may be characterized as liberal, progressive, accepting, culturally attuned, open, concerned, and globally oriented. As Table 12.5 illustrates, individuals who score highly on Sociocultural Openness:

- Are more likely to indicate that core needs (e.g., for attachment, affection) were met in a "good enough" manner (Needs Closure)

TABLE 12.5
Correlation Matrix Findings Above 0.40 Between Sociocultural Openness and Other BEVI Scales

SCALES	CORRELATION
Needs Closure	−0.90
Ecological Resonance	0.88
Socioemotional Convergence	0.82
Basic Closedness	−0.81
Identity Diffusion	−0.71
Emotional Attunement	0.77
Socioreligious Traditionalism	−0.62
Hard Structure	−0.58
Negative Life Events	−0.57
Divergent Determinism	−0.50

- Are more likely to be concerned about or invested in matters that have to do with the environment and natural world (Ecological Resonance)
- Appear more able to experience the world in complex "shades of gray," rather than in black and white terms (Socioemotional Convergence)
- Are less likely to deny or ignore fundamental thoughts, feelings, or needs that generally are experienced as "normative" regarding human existence or functioning (Basic Closedness)
- Are less likely to express feelings of confusion and entrapment regarding their current existence and future prospects (Identity Diffusion)
- Are more likely to indicate the capacity and inclination to experience affect in self and other, and to value its expression (Emotional Attunement)
- Are less likely to endorse a traditional worldview regarding the nature and purpose of religion and its centrality to one's own life (Socioreligious Traditionalism)
- Are less likely to express very strong certitude regarding the correctness of one's own way of seeing self, others, and the larger world, while denying doubts or weakness (Hard Structure)
- Are less likely to report the experience of a high degree of unhappy life experiences during childhood/adolescence or generally in life (Negative Life Events)
- Are less likely to adopt a reflexively contrarian posture regarding the nature of "truth" or "reality" (Divergent Determinism)

In many ways, a high degree of Sociocultural Openness may be seen as "optimal" in terms of the goals that were articulated by various institutions and organizations with which we worked throughout the Forum BEVI Project. Again, however, it should be emphasized that a high—or low—degree of Sociocultural Openness may serve as cause and/or effect. For example, individuals high in Sociocultural Openness may be predisposed toward study abroad or service learning even before the experience occurs, which therefore may function as more of a mediating effect on observed outcomes than whatever experience they encounter. Thus, it is very important to assess such attributes before and after a learning experience in order to be able to "tease out" the degree to which the experience itself—or who someone already was before the experience—is responsible for whatever changes we observe. In any case, multiple findings suggest that the construct (i.e., scale) of Sociocultural Openness is in fact associated with the sorts of outcomes that appear to be at the core of most international, multicultural, and transformative learning interventions (e.g., study abroad, courses, workshops), in that a higher degree of Sociocultural Openness is predictive of a range of real world outcomes, such as those described next.

Implication 4. It Is Possible to Predict Who Will Be Interested in— and Satisfied by—a Learning Experience Even Before the Learning Experience Actually Occurs

If formative variables (e.g., life history, demographics) and mediators (e.g., affective capacity, attributional styles) are assessed with sufficient breadth and depth, it is possible to predict statistically who is, and is not, likely to be inclined toward participation in a learning experience—and who is, and is not, likely to report that they actually benefitted from and/or were transformed by a learning experience—even before the experience occurs.

Such information matters to institutions and organizations for many reasons, including: (a) understanding the "profile" of who was and was not inclined to engage in such experiences; (b) providing outreach to students who historically were not inclined to participate in such experiences in order to try and facilitate their engagement; and (c) identifying which experiences were more or less likely to elicit interest and/or satisfaction. Overall, multiple analyses conducted through different methodologies indicate that we were able to ascertain various profiles—both from background information and BEVI scales—regarding who was and was not likely to be interested in participating in and/or satisfied by such experiences, even before such individuals completed their first course. Consider, for example, Table 12.6, which identifies a set of variables from the BEVI that predict the degree to which respondents will report an interest in specific international or multicultural learning experiences.[11]

Multiple regression analysis revealed that among the demographic and experiential background factors, gender and parents paying for international experiences prove to be the best estimators of students' global interests, based upon the respective standardized coefficients. Specifically, female students are more interested in

---

[11] The dependent variable is a student's level of interest in international education or study abroad. The question is as follows: "On a scale of 1 to 7, with 1 being 'extremely low' and 7 being 'extremely high,' please indicate your level of personal interest in international education or study abroad experiences." The independent variables are demographic and experiential variables. Several of the independent variables are dummy variables: gender (0 = male, 1 = female); "parents paying for international experience" (0 = parents do not pay, 1 = parents pay); "university provides orientation for international experience" (0 = university does not provide, 1 = university provides); "plan to travel abroad" (0 = no plan to travel abroad, 1= plan to travel abroad); "plan to take an internationally focused course" (0 = no plan to take a course, 1 = plan to take a course); and "speak a foreign language other than English" (0 = does not speak a foreign language, 1 = speaks a foreign language). Another independent variable, the "highest academic degree intended to achieve" is coded from 1 = associate degree, 2 = bachelor's, 3 = master's, 4 = specialist (e.g., Ed.S.), 5 = professional (e.g., law), to 6 = doctoral degree. Also, participants are asked about the number of foreign countries they have previously visited (e.g., respondents indicate the actual number of countries they have visited). Background variables include "mother's education" and "family income." "Mother's education" indicates the highest academic degree of a respondent's mother, which ranges from 0 = some high school or less to 8 = doctoral degree. "Family income" is an ordinal variable that reflects the average annual income of a student's parents/guardians regardless if the student receives financial support from them. Income ranges from 1 to 10, 1 = < \$10,000 to 10 = > \$175,000.

TABLE 12.6
Predictors of Interest in Global Learning Experiences[1]: Multiple Regression Analysis

	UNSTANDARDIZED COEFFICIENTS		STANDARDIZED COEFFICIENTS		
	B	STD. ERROR	BETA	T	SIG.
(Constant)	2.864	0.173		16.585	0.000
Gender (0 = M, 1 = F)	0.862	0.094	0.240	9.194	0.000
Parents are paying for international experience (0 = Parents do not pay, 1 = Parents pay)	0.915	0.106	0.238	8.599	0.000
University provides orientation for international experience (0 = No orientation, 1 = Orientation)	0.430	0.105	0.110	4.110	0.000
Family income (1 = <$10,000 to 10 = >$175,000)	−0.073	0.019	−0.103	−3.841	0.000
Plan to travel abroad (0 = No plan, 1 = Has plan)	0.598	0.092	0.165	6.504	0.000
Highest academic degree intend to obtain (1 = Associate degree to 6 = Doctoral degree)	0.114	0.030	0.094	3.780	0.000
Plan to take an international-focused course (0 = No plan, 1 = Has plan)	0.659	0.102	0.167	6.492	0.000
Number of foreign countries visited (actual number)	0.031	0.014	0.056	2.178	0.030
Speak a foreign language other than English (0 = Does not speak, 1 = Speaks)	0.336	0.088	0.095	3.813	0.000
Mother's education (0 = Some high school to 8 = Doctoral degree)	0.074	0.025	0.080	3.030	0.003
F	71.319***				
R^2	0.415				
Adj. R^2	0.409				

[1]*Global learning experiences = international, multicultural, and transformative learning experiences.*

Note. ***$p < .05$.

global learning experiences than males. Intuitively logical, those students whose parents paid for their international experiences also have a greater interest in global experiences. Similarly, students who plan to travel abroad, plan to take an internationally focused course, and speak a foreign language have a greater interest in global learning experiences than those who do not. "Highest academic degree intend to obtain" and "Number of foreign countries visited" also are positively associated with interest in global learning experiences. "Mother's education" is a relatively weak but positive estimator. Finally, "Family income" holds a negative association with a student's interest in global learning, meaning the higher the income, the lower the interest in global learning. The results of this study suggest that a range of BEVI variables can statistically predict interest in global learning, even before such learning occurs (i.e., at the planning stage), a finding with implications for recruitment, orientation, program development, and institutional planning (e.g., if our goal is to "reach" those students who are least likely to study abroad, such data offer perspective regarding who such students are most likely and least likely to be, although specific variability within a given institution or organization obviously should be considered).

In many ways, "interest" in international, multicultural, and transformative learning experiences represents one bookend of a process that is of great relevance not only to the research community, but to program directors, course instructors, and administrators who want to understand whether specific cohorts of students are inclined toward, or against, various learning experiences. But the other bookend of considerable relevance concerns whether students actually are satisfied by the experiences in which they engaged, and whether the BEVI is able to predict such satisfaction even before the learning experience occurs. As Figure 12.3 illustrates, a range of formative variables are statistically associated with such satisfaction. Here, the dependent variable is a student's level of satisfaction across multiple international, multicultural, or transformative learning experiences. Specifically, on a scale of 1 to 7 (with 1 being "extremely low" and 7 being "extremely high"), the question is as follows: "If you have participated, or are currently participating, in international, learning, service, study abroad, travel, or work experiences[12] please indicate your overall level of satisfaction." The independent variables are demographic and experiential variables.

Multiple regression analysis revealed that among the demographic and experiential background factors, the following were most strongly associated with participant satisfaction: a longer length of time participating in one or more of the experiences; previous travel to five or more states in the United States; previous travel abroad; and currently studying abroad. In addition, the variable of "interest" in international experiences—previously living in an international residence hall; and a greater number of years in higher education—all were among the variables associated with a "moderate" degree of "satisfaction." In short, the results of this study suggest that a range of formative variables statistically can predict satisfaction in international, multicultural, or transformative learning—broadly defined—even before such learning occurs.[13] Although the ability to predict "interest" is one matter,

---

[12] For clarification, several of the variables in Figure 12.3 are not part of the "satisfaction" question on the BEVI, but still emerged as relevant for this analysis, albeit moderately (year in university) or weakly (family income, Democrat political orientation, gender, and whether parents traveled abroad). "Satisfaction" options on the BEVI regarding international, multicultural, or transformative learning include the following: (a) completing an internship with a non-U.S. company (in the United States or abroad); (b) living with a roommate from another country or different ethnic background; (c) participation in a course with an international/multicultural focus; (d) participation in on-campus international/multicultural events; (e) service learning in the United States; (f) service learning abroad; (g) study abroad; (h) studying a language other than English; (i) travel to five or more states in the United States; (j) travel abroad; (k) work abroad; (l) living in a residence that is international/multicultural and/or language-focused; (m) participating in off-campus international or multicultural events; (n) have not previously participated in any of these experiences; and (o) other global or international/multicultural experience(s) (please specify).

[13] As indicated by other findings in this chapter, it should be noted that in addition to these formative variables on the BEVI, multiple scales also predict "interest" in and "satisfaction" with international, multicultural, and transformative learning experiences. For example, in one analysis, Sociocultural Openness, Needs Fulfillment, Socioemotional Convergence, Global Engagement, Ecological Resonance, Causal Closure, Basic Determinism, Self Awareness, and Gender Traditionalism all were strongly or moderately predictive of "interest" in such experiences (e.g., Shealy, 2014, 2016).

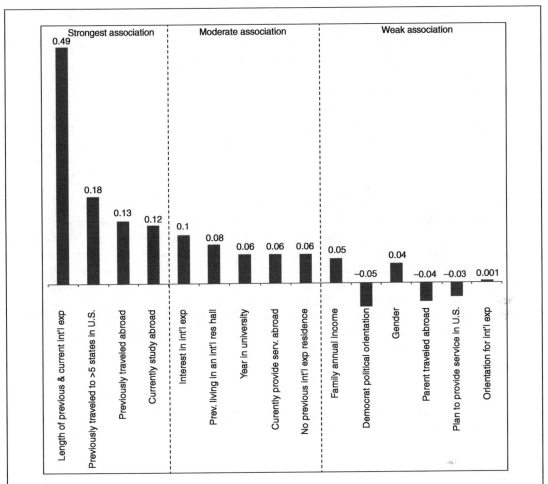

FIGURE 12.3. Satisfaction with international education/study abroad based on demographic variables (strongest, moderate, and no association).

the fact that we also can predict satisfaction on the basis of formative variables may seem surprising. However, such findings are highly congruent with an EI perspective, in that abundant evidence indicates that the kinds of life experiences we do and do not have are associated inevitably with how we experience self, others, and the world at large, including but not limited to, the satisfaction we ultimately report from engaging in a range of learning experiences.

Implication 5. Specific Analyses May Be Conducted for Purposes of Outreach and Engagement

Because we are able to identify subgroups of students who are more or less likely to be inclined toward specific learning experiences, it is possible to offer targeted opportunities or programs for them that are congruent with institutional goals (e.g., to boost study abroad by minority students). Knowing what sorts of learning experiences are most impactful for which sorts of students also helps clarify and refine interventions that are designed to retain and engage students.

One pressing question both within the field of international education—and in higher education generally as well as other performance-based organizational contexts—is whether and how assessment results actually matter in the pursuit of various institutional/organizational goals and objectives. From promoting individual learning at the student or staff level, to enhancing the quality of courses or programs, to evaluating the degree to which institutions or organizations meet their objectives, these "rubber meets the road" issues are not only reasonable, but inextricably linked to the demonstration that what we do as educators and "change agents" actually matters in the real world (e.g., Blair, Latz, Sternberger, & Shealy, 2014; Braskamp & Engberg, 2014). Ultimately, of course, administrators are, or should be, concerned with the justifications for our actions or policies. Such considerations concern matters of learning impact, of course, but also should have implications for matters of quality assurance and cost. For example, presuming the validity of our assessment models and methods, and following best practice efforts to enhance their quality (e.g., Geisinger, 2013; Robinson et al., 1991), it does not seem unreasonable to use data for the purpose of evaluating programs and courses, and indeed, those who direct or teach them. Throughout this project, we have seen enormous variance in the quality of such administration and teaching vis-à-vis program and course outcomes (see Implication 6). Of course, the key is translating the complexity of assessment data into a form that fairly and appropriately may be used to make pragmatic decisions. Given the importance of "effective educational practices" identified by the Association of American Colleges and Universities (AAC&U, 2007), there can be no substitute for valid assessment of such "high impact" offerings to determine how they may be improved and whether they are achieving their potential (see Iyer, 2013; Kuh, 2008).

For example, consider the following finding. In this case, Shenandoah University wanted to ascertain whether there are differences between students who did and those who did not apply for a short-term learning abroad program (N = 57). Such information was of relevance because this institution was interested in knowing why a program that was deliberately designed to be accessible to students (e.g., provided by the institution at no cost to the student participant)—while also serving as a gateway to other international experiences—was not completed by everyone. From the standpoint of the BEVI, one hypothesis is that students who applied were more psychologically predisposed to do so. We used a binary variable (students did or did not apply to participate) to group the participants into two categories and compared the differences between them. As a dependent variable, we ran a Logit Model to detect differences between the two groups. What did we find? Compared to nonapplicants, program applicants were more open to and interested in the attributes and practices of cultures that were different from their own (Sociocultural Openness, b = 7.473, p = 0.039). Results such as these have implications for outreach and engagement with different types of students. That is because it is possible not only to know at the outset of study (i.e., during the first year) which students are most and least likely to take advantage of the learning experiences offered to them (i.e., "the who"), but also to gain a measure of understanding as to the underlying dispositions that mediate for or against engagement (i.e., "the why"). In terms of "best practices" for approaching students who are less inclined to engage in these types of learning experiences, it is important to appreciate that these psychological processes help us to differentiate among students while also offering guidance regarding the kinds of interventions that are more likely to "reach" them. Again, in many cases, we sing to the choir, not recognizing that the students who enroll in various learning experiences are self-selecting to do so. More challenging is reaching out to those students who may not be predisposed initially to such experiences—that is, they are low on Sociocultural Openness—but might be willing to move in that direction if we respond to them in an informed, sensitive, and sophisticated manner that better accounts for who they are at the outset (i.e., thus approaching them where they are rather than where we wish them to be) (e.g., Tabit, Legault, Ma, & Wan, 2016).

Along similar lines, another project partner, Dickinson College, wanted to know if there were differences on the BEVI between students who declared majors in different areas of study. If so, such differences also could have implications for different approaches to engagement and outreach, and help clarify the reasons why students were inclined toward different academic trajectories in the first place. In this analysis of 173 students, interest in global learning experiences was measured by the following question: "On a scale of 1 to 7, with 1 being 'extremely low' and 7 being 'extremely high,' please indicate your level of personal interest in international education or study abroad experiences." Students' academic majors were divided into four categories: social science, arts and humanities, "hard science," and undecided. A one-way ANOVA was conducted to determine if differences existed between students' interest in global learning experiences across multiple academic majors. As Table 12.7 indicates, no significant differences emerged, a finding that was somewhat unique among project participants. Thus, we examined the data more closely. Analysis of the means for each major indicates that all students at Dickinson College have a very strong interest in global experiences, regardless of academic major. Given the very strong historical and current commitment to global

TABLE 12.7
Interest in Global Learning Experiences[1] by Students' Academic Major: Dickinson College

SOURCE	TYPE II SUM OF SQUARES	MEAN	DF	MEAN SQUARE	F	SIG.
Corrected Model	2.865		3	0.955	0.688	0.561
Intercept	6605.555		1	6605.56	4758.89	0.000
Major	2.865		3	0.955	0.688	0.561
Social sciences		6.385				
Arts and humanities		6.313				
Sciences		6.143				
Undecided or other		6.082				
Error	234.58		169	1.388		
Total	6843		173			
Corrected Total	237.445		172			

$R^2 = .012$ (adjusted $R^2 = -.005$).

[1]*Global Learning Experiences = international, multicultural, and transformative learning experiences.*

Notes.
1. Post hoc tests indicate there are no significant differences among the majors.
2. Items are measured on a four-point scale (1 = strongly disagree–4 = strongly agree).

education expressed in Dickinson's mission statement, brand identity, and curriculum, such findings make good sense (i.e., at an institution like Dickinson, "interest" in international learning is not an especially good predictor of differences between students since almost everyone coming to the institution does so with these interests in mind). In combination with other results, such findings ultimately led to another implication, that institutions and organizations have very different "profiles" or "signatures," which should be assessed in order to apprehend the nature and culture of its members (see Implication 11).

Implication 6. All Educators and Educational Experiences are not Equal

The fact that all learning interventions and interveners are "not equal" should promote personal, professional, and institutional development and engagement, as well as a renewed commitment to improvement, rather than discouragement, defensiveness, or denial.

Although intuitively reasonable, and certainly a focus of emphasis within the academy, it would seem that there is a general consensus that those who teach, direct, or lead various learning experiences differ in their relative effectiveness. For example, the fact that we expend considerable energy evaluating the effectiveness of teaching faculty suggests an overarching recognition that such matters are integral to student success, course and program quality, and the pursuit of institutional and organizational goals. Such matters of teacher quality are not just of concern within higher education, but are central to all individuals who assume a teaching role at the K-12 level as well (e.g., Cultivating the Globally Sustainable Self, 2015; Ellis, Lee, & Wiley 2009; InTASC, 2011; Welch, Pitts, Tenini, Kuenlen, & Wood, 2010). Even so, for a variety of reasons, it is difficult to tease apart the relative impact of "teacher" from "learner" much less the interactions between the two that serve to mediate and moderate learning. Thus, one intriguing and consistent finding that we believe has long-term relevance is the apparent differences that emerged in learner outcomes as a function—at least in part—of who was teaching and/or leading a particular learning experience. For example, consider the following juxtaposition between two different Time 1/Time 2 group report profiles by two different individuals who were responsible for leading the same learning experience (see Figure 12.4). How do we interpret such findings? First, it is important to appreciate that this juxtaposition is not based upon truly random assignment to either instructor. Rather, as is often the case with large required courses, these students simply were assigned to one or another section on the basis of a number of factors (e.g., their own course schedules; adviser decisions; and enrollments), which are not controlled for in this convenience sample. Thus, any number of variables might have affected the results we observe. However, in this particular analysis, the basic process for assignment of students to various sections was not predetermined (i.e., was more or less random in a nonexperimental sense, in that there was no specific logic or plan for the assignment of students to a specific section). More importantly, from our review of Time 1/Time 2 BEVI reports across different institutions and programs or experiences, such results do not appear to be anomalous in that we repeatedly see substantial differences in Time 1/Time 2 reports across instructors or directors who are teaching or leading experiences that ostensibly are designed to be "the same." That said, the most fundamental point we offer in this regard—which is at the core of all we have observed throughout this project—is that we simply cannot understand who learns what and why, and under what circumstances, if we do not simultaneously take into account and assess multiple variables, including teacher characteristics (e.g., dispositions), student

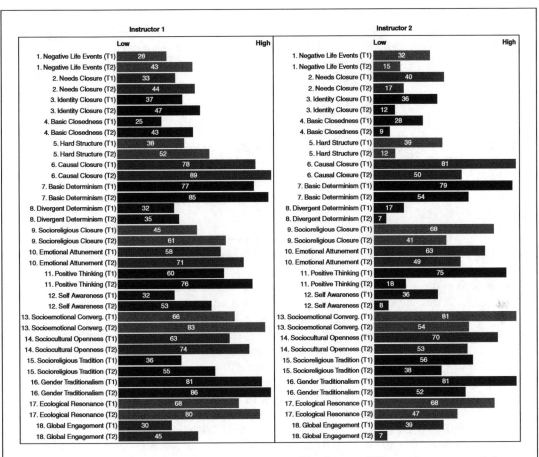

FIGURE 12.4. Comparison of Time 1 and Time 2 profiles for two different instructors of the same course.

characteristics (e.g., life histories), and the quality and nature of the learning experience (e.g., how it is taught/delivered, where, and for what purposes) (e.g., Cultivating the Globally Sustainable Self, 2015). So, we recommend reviewing the patterns revealed in Figure 12.4 not so much as definitive, but rather as illustrative of the kinds of differences that we have observed, and that warrant further study in the years to come. So, in the context of these caveats, let us focus on a few key points of comparison. Specifically, consider differences in Figure 12.5 on Negative Life Events, Self Awareness, and Global Engagement across these two instructors.

Essentially, on these three Time 1/Time 2 comparisons, students of Instructor 1 report, by the conclusion of the course, that they had experienced a greater degree of Negative Life Events, are more Self Aware, and are more Globally Engaged. The exact opposite Time 1/Time 2 profile is associated with Instructor 2 (students report substantially fewer Negative Life Events, much less Self Awareness, and much less Global Engagement). Although hard and fast conclusions are not warranted for the reasons noted previously, since the goals for each section of the course ostensibly were the same (e.g., to produce greater awareness of different cultures), these results should give pause at the very least, as they suggest students are reporting radically different experiences at the conclusion of the course.

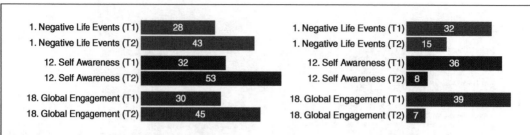

FIGURE 12.5. Comparison of T1/T2 results for two different instructors on the same course across three BEVI scales.

Why? Among other possible hypotheses, the most parsimonious would seem to be the skill through which course content was conveyed and course experiences were facilitated as well as overarching fidelity to the course objectives that were pursued. Such matters of content and process are, of course, at the heart of teaching and learning. As our annual processes of faculty evaluations across higher education institutions indicate, we certainly believe that faculty differ in their instructional competencies, a supposition that would seem to receive at least potential support from such findings. At the same time, many other variables could account for such differences as well, including fundamental differences in the nature of various cohorts (e.g., most faculty who have taught for any duration are likely to experience substantial differences in the makeup or nature of cohorts from semester to semester).

And yet, the dramatic difference in directionality from Time 1 to Time 2 across these three scales—and others—suggest that such phenomena should be studied more closely over time, particularly because we have observed such differences in outcomes across instructors, programs, and institutions. The results suggest not only a deep and largely neglected need to examine differences in the knowledge, skills, and dispositions of those who are in an "instructional" realm, broadly defined, but also how such findings may be used to promote growth and development of instructors and facilitators of change at multiple levels and in various sectors of the educational system. That is to say, if used with care and skill, such findings may help individual instructors understand better the characteristics of their group (i.e., through group reports of their students) as well as what is happening from the beginning to the conclusion of a learning experience. If skillfully facilitated, such findings should help teaching faculty reflect upon and cultivate capacities over the short and long term that are more likely to be effective in terms of facilitating learning, development, and change (e.g., Cultivating the Globally Sustainable Self, 2015).

Ultimately, ensuring instructor competence, effectiveness, and impact is an ever-relevant issue for institutions and organizations. We therefore suspect that using such rich data to analyze the quality of instructors, directors, and leaders could in fact result in significant improvements to course or program offerings over the long term. Moreover, if students or other learners repeatedly are exposed to instructors or directors who consistently achieve results that are below—or above—those of their colleagues, we have a very real opportunity to intervene in a data-driven manner in order to (a) promote the instructional, curricular, or programmatic quality of a specific learning experience; (b) encourage ongoing professional development that may be tracked over time; (c) recognize and explore "excellence" when it repeatedly occurs in terms of "better" learning processes outcomes, to understand what actually is happening in real time between teachers, trainers, and learners; and (d) make changes when all else fails—and after all good faith attempts to improve matters—so that learners are not repeatedly subjected to subpar instructors, directors, or leaders who do not appear to be facilitating acceptable learning processes and outcomes.

At the very least, these findings suggest the need to examine such outcome differences in order to understand what the interactions may be among teacher competencies, student characteristics, and the nature of various learning experiences that are designed to promote "change" (e.g., Cultivating the Globally Sustainable Self, 2015). The need to consider such matters becomes especially important when one realizes that exposure to international, multicultural, or transformative learning may not always result in "good" outcomes at Time 2 (see Implication 7). For example, we have observed Time 1/Time 2 instructional profiles, which may show a much higher degree of Emotional Attunement and Self Awareness, but lower Sociocultural Openness, at Time 2. Contrast that outcome with its mirror opposite of a much lower degree of Emotional Attunement and Self Awareness at Time 2, but higher Sociocultural Openness. Which outcome is better? One's answer probably depends upon one's goals in terms of a course, program, or workshop, but arguably, a higher degree of Emotional Attunement and Self Awareness may actually be a function of exposure to content and experiences that are highly activating of the "self," which may not necessarily translate into greater openness toward the sociocultural "other" (e.g., Tabit et al., 2016) at the conclusion of a learning experience. Over the long term, however, such an outcome may bode better than the opposite outcome, which finds our learner less Emotionally Attuned or Self Aware, but reporting more Sociocultural Openness. As always, the reasons for such discrepant outcomes should be a point of exploration and contemplation—which may be much better interpreted and understood in the context of overall scale scores and qualitative findings—rather than a basis for hard and fast conclusions on their own. Along similar lines, and as explicated in Implication 7, we strongly recommend longitudinal analysis (e.g., Time 3, Time 4 administration), mainly to hone in on what is happening over time. That is because it may well be that an initial decrement on various scales represents the initial "reaction" to an overwhelming experience, which must be metabolized over time in order to ascertain longer term effects.

Implication 7. Educational Experiences Are Associated With Desirable as Well as Undesirable Processes and Outcomes Across a Wide Range of Constructs That Must Be Measured to Be Known

Depending upon the nature and quality of learning, growth, or development experiences— and the life histories, worldviews, and capacities of those who deliver and engage in them— measurable processes and outcomes may or may not be in the anticipated direction. Moreover, "change" may be occurring in ways that are and are not expected. If such processes and outcomes are not measured (e.g., because they are not appreciated or seen as relevant, or because they are assumed to be happening as a matter of course), we may miss information that could in fact be most important about what actually is happening for learners, irrespective of what we think is, or should be, happening. Thus, as educators, researchers, and administrators, we should embrace the fundamentally experimental nature of our work. We may learn as much from what does not work as what does, but only if we measure a sufficient range of relevant constructs.

Oftentimes, understandably, the focus within the larger field of higher education, including international, multicultural, and transformative learning as a whole, is on "what works." Such an emphasis makes good sense, of course, since it behooves us to develop, implement, and promote learning experiences that demonstrably impact our students, institutions, and organizations in a value-added manner. But sometimes the most useful findings that emerged from the Forum BEVI Project involved learning experiences that did not seem to accomplish their intended goals, especially when these unexpected results were discussed openly and productively by project partners. To take one example of several, students enrolled in a course designed to produce greater sociocultural openness and appreciation for diversity[14] were selected for an analysis aimed at better understanding the degree to which individuals do or do not benefit from such a learning experience. As described in the syllabus, the purpose of the course was to provide students with the necessary tools to understand and appreciate the diverse cultures that they will likely encounter throughout their personal and professional lives. The study employed a one-group pretest/posttest design across four sections of the course. Students (N = 137) who chose to participate in the research project were provided with a username and password and asked to complete the long version (336-item) BEVI pretest at the beginning of the semester. At the conclusion of the course, students were again asked to complete the BEVI as a posttest measure. Analysis of pre–post data was undertaken across all BEVI scales using repeated measures of ANOVA. This study was exploratory in nature, and as such, research questions focused mainly on whether Time 1/Time 2 differences could be observed, and if so, on which BEVI scales. Given the goals of the course, it was anticipated that some changes would be observed—in a positive or desired direction—particularly on scales tapping greater Sociocultural Openness and Global Engagement.

As indicated in Table 12.8, results suggest that the course, although designed to facilitate learning outcomes such as tolerance for cultures different from one's own, appears to be associated with the opposite effect. More specifically, upon completion of the course, students appeared to be more rigid in their belief systems, more inclined to endorse simple causal attributions regarding why human beings do what they do, more emotionally aware and activated, and less open to developing a deeper engagement with other cultures than they had been at course entry. It may, of course, be mistaken to assume that these real-time/short-term correlations will bear out over the long term. Moreover, it cannot be concluded that the course is "causing" these changes or even that greater "negative" changes might have emerged had the course not occurred. All that said, however, it is striking that theoretically desirable attributes (e.g., openness, engagement) diminished over the duration of the semester since such outcomes are antithetical to the explicit goals of this course. Moreover, it should be noted that additional qualitative data (e.g., responses on the three free-response items of the BEVI; course evaluations) corroborate these quantitative data, suggesting that at least some aspects of this particular course should perhaps be reconfigured to focus, for example, more on learning process and less on content delivery, especially at the outset of the course (e.g., see Tabit et al., 2016).

This Time 1/Time 2 within-group analysis provided one of our project partners an opportunity to use the BEVI to gauge and compare the relative effectiveness of this required course. Combined with other data, profile results may be used to improve this teaching and learning experience over time, modify extant courses, develop new approaches, and so on. Moreover, such results provide an opportunity for self-assessment and professional development, as group reports may help course instructors, program directors, and administrators better understand the nature of their particular classes or cohorts and their own effectiveness as instructors. For

---

[14] Adapted from Tabit, Legault, Ma, & Wan (2016) from Shealy, C.N. (Ed.) (2016). *Making Sense of Beliefs and Values*. New York, NY: Springer Publishing.

TABLE 12.8
Degree of Worldview Shift

SCALE	TIME		F	GENDER		F
	PRE	**POST**		**FEMALE**	**MALE**	
Causal Closure	1.229	1.317	7.780 (1, 133)**	1.196	1.351	11.595 (1, 133)***
Basic Determinism	1.718	1.856	9.187 (1, 134)***	1.615	1.958	19.196 (1, 134)***
Emotional Attunement	3.013	3.133	6.920 (1, 133)**	3.257	2.889	13.581 (1, 133)***
Global Engagement	2.647	2.579	4.454 (1, 134)*	2.691	2.535	7.662 (1, 134)**

*Note. *p < .05, **p < .01, ***p < .001.*

example, as described in the following, the report system for the BEVI allows instructors to examine group characteristics in detail and to consider how such variables impact the ways in which course content is experienced, which offers an opportunity to modify and/or tailor one's approach to teaching in order to proactively respond to the dynamics of the larger group and its subgroups. Along similar lines, by tracking experience-based outcomes over time, it is possible to identify those educator/leader dispositions that appear to be most and least effective in terms of meeting teaching or program outcomes. Such information may be quite helpful in terms of understanding areas of focus for personal and professional development.

At the same time, as noted, it is also important to appreciate the longitudinal nature of "change" as is suggested by the EI model (Shealy, 2016). That is to say, "negative" results from a learning experience may be due to multiple factors, including but by no means limited to (a) the quality of instruction or facilitation, (b) the nature of a particular cohort, and/or (c) the fact that exposure to content and processes that are "disequilintegrating" may show up on the BEVI in one way at Time 2, but be completely different at Time 3. Research currently under way is following cohorts beyond a Time 2 administration in order to examine both longitudinal processes that occur over time (at Time 3 and beyond) and cross-sectional differences that may characterize cohorts across different years.

Consider, in this regard, Figure 12.6, which juxtaposes Time 1, Time 2, and Time 3 BEVI group report profiles for the same group of study abroad students (N = 20). As this figure illustrates, although some aspects of the T1/T2 comparison move in a direction that presumably would be desirable at the conclusion of a study abroad experience (e.g., Self Certitude drops from the 42nd to the 28th percentile; Gender Traditionalism drops from the 38th to the 27th percentile), other scales move in a direction that presumably would not be desirable, given the goals of the study abroad experience (e.g., Needs Fulfillment drops from the 54th to the 39th percentile; Self Awareness drops from the 78th to the 63rd percentile; and Sociocultural Openness drops from the 76th to the 62nd percentile). As noted in Figure 12.5, T1/T2 administrations occurred between 3 and 4 months after initial administration of the BEVI at the beginning of the study abroad experience. So, what happens if we let at least half

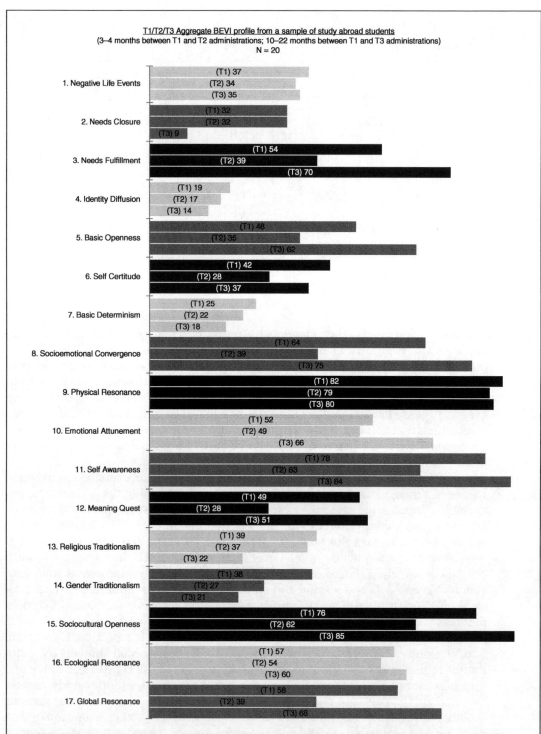

FIGURE 12.6. Comparison of T1/T2/T3 BEVI group report results for the same group of study abroad students.

a year pass before assessing these same students again? Here we see a highly intriguing flip on a number of key scales. For example, in Figure 12.6, consider three scales noted previously that presumably went in the "opposite direction" of what reasonably could be anticipated (or at least hoped for) at Time 2: first, Scale 3—Needs Fulfillment (which measures openness to experiences, needs, and feelings; deep care/sensitivity for self, others, and the larger world); second, Scale 11—Self Awareness (which measures a tendency toward introspection, acceptance of self-complexity, care for the human experience/condition, and tolerance of difficult thoughts/feelings); and third, Scale 15—Sociocultural Openness (which measures progressiveness/openness regarding a wide range of actions, policies, and practices in the areas of culture, economics, education, environment, gender, global relations, and politics). As illustrated, on all three of these scales (among others that might be reviewed as well from Figure 12.6), results now solidly are in the direction of what might be anticipated (or hoped for) at the conclusion of a study abroad experience. How do we explain such findings? From an Equilintegration or EI perspective, the "7Ds" of belief/values transformation (see Implication 14) explicitly acknowledge that multiple factors interact simultaneously to determine how, for whom, and under what circumstances "change" occurs (Shealy, 2016). Moreover, the greater the discrepancy between one's original "Formative Variables" and those to which one is exposed next (e.g., how the individual experiences a culture with which they are deeply familiar as compared to how that same individual experiences a different and unfamiliar culture), the greater the degree of potential "affective/cognitive shutdown" that occurs, as the "self" strives essentially to protect "its self" from the intensely experienced shock of such exposure, which may in qualitative terms be described as "amazing," but nonetheless exerts a toll; thus, the individual simply may need time and space to consolidate and "make sense of beliefs and values" once again in a way that is "equilintegrated" into one's newly reorganized self. Thus, we see a Time 3 profile that largely is a mirror image of Time 2, and in some ways, a poignant reminder of what the human self endures as we all go about the business of living, which is felt that much more dramatically when experiencing "high impact" learning like study abroad (e.g., Iyer, 2013; Kuh, 2008).

From the standpoint of the BEVI and its report system, the basic point to keep in mind here is that the interface between the complexities of being human and the complexities of assessment requires us to adopt measurement strategies that do not wag the dog; in other words, let us first be who we are, and then and only then, seek to capture the meaning of our experience vis-à-vis assessment (e.g., by assessing such evolving human phenomenology over time, rather than "just once," as such an approach is more likely to allow for our human complexity to be apprehended as it naturally manifests in the real world) (Shealy, 2016). At the same time, project results suggest that we cannot assume that "negative" results at Time 2 are due simply to the "disequilintegrating" processes that may occur as a result of challenging learning, growth, and development experiences; it may well be that the two other variables—relative instructional/facilitator quality and/or cohort differences—may in fact account for much of the variance in this regard (i.e., the fact that learners may report qualitatively different responses at Time 3 than at Time 2 should *not* automatically be cited to deflect a focus from instructor/course quality and/or variability among cohorts). In short, our results suggest that if we really want to understand *why* we observe the measurable results that we do over time, our commitment to assessment must occur over the long term, and simultaneously be open to examining a wide range of interacting variables that may well have personal as well as programmatic and institutional/organizational implications.

Implication 8. Examining Only Overall (e.g., Aggregate) Findings or Privileging Only a Few BEVI Scales Constitute Tempting but Counterproductive Approaches to Comprehensive Assessment

Aggregate findings can be misleading because they may mask or wash out "opposing" data for subgroups, which, when compiled, "cancel" each other out and become invisible. Thus, it is essential that the reporting system be able to account for change processes that may be occurring both within (a) demographic subsets of learners and (b) educators who are leading specific types of learning experiences. Likewise, ignoring some of the scales to focus on only a few (i.e., Sociocultural Openness) fails to reveal the rich and complex processes students undergo, the relationships between these processes, and the importance of assessing other aspects of the learning process, which may be as—if not more—important in explaining why we do, or do not, observe particular findings.

It was heartening early on in the Forum BEVI Project to see results that clearly illustrated not only that change was emerging from Time 1 to Time 2 administrations, but in ways that would be expected. Consider, for example, Figure 12.7, a Time 1/ Time 2 analysis (N = 19) from Brethren Colleges Abroad (BCA), which mirrors the Time 1/Time 3 profile from Figure 12.6, and emphasizes a related finding: it is always important to consider one's unique results in relation to the specific instructor, group, and context in which a learning, growth, or development experience occurs. In many ways, this profile of this small N—from students who experienced a range of study abroad programs in different locales—represents what might be seen as optimal. In addition to the interesting finding that (a) Negative Life Events goes down (from the 33rd to the 25th percentile), these students would appear (b) to be "clearer" about who they are and where they are going in life (Identity Closure decreases from the 45th to the 30th percentile); (c) to become more sophisticated and nuanced at the level of attributions made about self, others, and the larger world (e.g., Basic Determinism decreases from the 87th to the 56th percentile); (d) to demonstrate greater introspection and interest in "how people work" (Self Awareness increases from the 28th to the 48th percentile); (e) to report fewer stereotyped notions regarding who males and females are and should be (Gender Traditionalism decreases from the 73rd to the 59th percentile); and (f) to evidence a greater degree of interest in encountering different cultures and practices around the world (Global Engagement increases from the 15th to 39th percentile), from Time 1 to Time 2.

Again, although such a profile may in fact be "optimal," a fundamental problem with such Time 1/Time 2 assessment analyses, no matter what measures are in use, is that such a report may obscure or wash out subgroup differences within the larger group. In other words, aggregate presentations of data do not allow for a more fine-grained analysis of what actually is happening within the group, not only at a scale level, but in terms of multiple mediators and moderators of change (e.g., background/demographic information) that may affect who learns what and why, and under what circumstances. As such, although interesting, a simple Time 1/Time 2 analysis of the group as a whole for any assessment measure, including the BEVI, would probably not be sufficient to understand the complex and interacting within-group factors that ultimately influence the nature and degree of any changes that were observed. Moreover, imagine a Time 1/Time 2 profile that is the opposite of that pictured in Figure 12.7. Would we therefore conclude the learning experience was a complete failure? That could be the case, but at the very least, it would be helpful to do further statistical analysis to determine what exactly is happening within facets of the larger group. It could be, for example, that some groups may share similarities due to self-selection processes that might lead subsets of students to seek a study

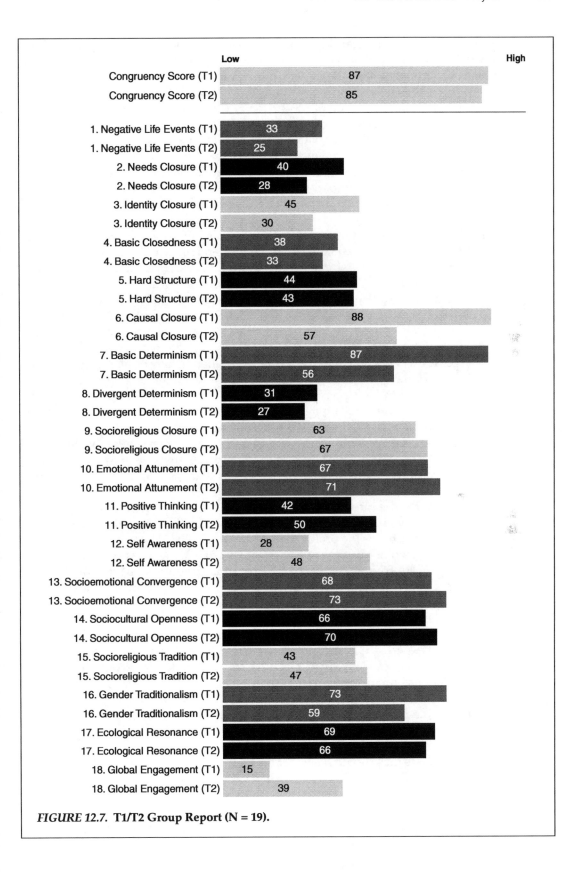

FIGURE 12.7. **T1/T2 Group Report (N = 19).**

abroad or multicultural learning experience whereas others would not. In short, our assumption has been that multiple and substantial differences would characterize various subgroups within the larger group. Hundreds of analyses have confirmed the validity of this most basic proposition, which has substantive implications for the interpretation and application of BEVI Time 1/Time 2 reports, and, we would argue, for the very nature of how Time 1 and Time 2 evaluation of learning processes and outcomes occurs, regardless of which measure(s) are used.

Consider the following analysis, from one of our project partners, the University of British Columbia (UBC) in Canada. Here, in a series of group report juxtapositions (N = 36), we are comparing Aggregate Profile results with those of Profile Contrast. By way of orientation, the description of each of these indexes is as follows:[15]

> **Profile Contrast** illustrates how different and similar the group is across all 17 BEVI scales via the lowest 30%, middle 40%, and highest 30% of full scale scores. The full scale score is summative of scores from the seven domains of the BEVI under which the 17 process scales are clustered: I. Formative Variables; II. Fulfillment of Core Needs; III. Tolerance of Disequilibrium; IV. Critical Thinking; V. Self Access; VI. Other Access; and VII. Global Access (Shealy, 2016). Profile Contrast is "key" to interpreting whether and to what degree groupings by low, medium, and high full scale scores are associated with different elevations on specific BEVI scales. For example, such information may be helpful in interpreting the variability within a specific group, which may range from minimal to substantial. Profile Contrast also may help users comprehend how and why subgroups within the larger group show changes in similar and different directions in the context of learning, growth, and development experiences. Thus, this index is considered a more robust and nuanced measure of the differential impact of specific learning experiences than are aggregated indexes, which may obscure subgroup differences or cancel out changes that are in fact occurring among subsets of the larger group.
>
> **Aggregate Profile** presents aggregated background information and domain scores for the full scale scores of the entire group (i.e., 1st–100th percentile). In other words, this is the profile that we are suggesting is interesting and relevant (i.e., a version of this type of "aggregate profile" typically is relied upon when engaging in group-based Time 1/Time 2 assessment)—but it should not be used alone. It is most useful for Time 1 assessment (i.e., understanding where the overall group is at the outset of a learning, growth, or development experience) and to track group results over time (i.e., from year to year). However, it generally should not be used alone to determine if a learning, growth, or development experience is or is not effective (e.g., at Time 2 assessment) mainly because it may obscure subgroup differences and/or cancel out changes that actually are occurring within various subsets of the larger group. From the standpoint of the BEVI, the best index to determine what is happening in this regard (i.e., between the lowest 30%, middle 40%, and highest 30% of full scale scorers) is Profile Contrast.

To illustrate these points, consider the following comparisons of Aggregate Profile and Profile Contrast results across five BEVI scales for this sample from UBC:

---

[15] The following information for Aggregate Profile and Profile Contrast is excerpted and/or adapted from the "Description of Tables and Indices" section of BEVI group reports.

Negative Life Events; Identity Diffusion[16]; Self Certitude; Religious Traditionalism, and Sociocultural Openness. To facilitate interpretation, in Figures 12.8 to 12.12, we have juxtaposed the three Time 1/Time 2 scale scores for Profile Contrast (lowest 30%, middle 40%, and highest 30%) with the Aggregate Profile score for each respective scale. In this way, it is possible to compare subgroup differences and similarities (Profile Contrast) with the overall score (Aggregate Profile) for each scale in this series of five separate analyses.

Consider Figure 12.8. In the first place, note that Aggregate Profile for Negative Life Events goes up from the 48th to the 55th percentile from Time 1 to Time 2. However, on Profile Contrast, the lowest 30% and middle 40% (70% of the overall sample) actually go down from Time 1 to Time 2 on Negative Life Events. A basic and overarching conclusion from such results is that Profile Contrast is a much more robust and nuanced analysis of what is actually happening within a group than is the Aggregate Profile. So, we must be very careful in our interpretation of Time 1/Time 2 findings on any measure—including but not limited to the BEVI—in order to ensure that we are apprehending what actually is happening within subsets of the overall group, as such subgroups may actually be responding very differently from one another as a result of exposure to an international, multicultural, or transformative learning experience.

Note also the very interesting finding—observed across multiple group report analyses—that the perception of one's life history and background may be differentially affected by one's point of departure prior to engaging in an international, multicultural, or transformative learning experience. This observation is highly

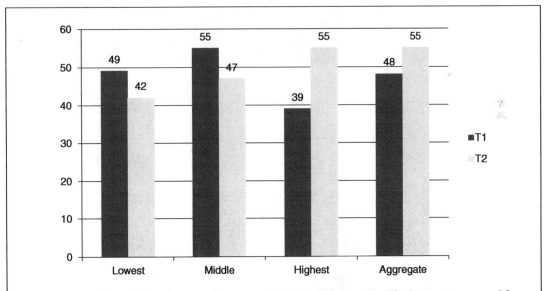

FIGURE 12.8. Comparison between lowest, middle, and highest Profile Contrast scores with the Aggregate Profile score on the Negative Life Events scale from the BEVI.

---

[16] For purposes of clarification, note that some scale names/results are from the "long" version of the BEVI whereas others are from the "short" version of the BEVI. For example, the name of this scale is "Identity Closure" on the long version, but "Identity Diffusion" on the short version. Additional chapters in *Making Sense of Beliefs and Values* (e.g., Chapter 4) provide further clarification regarding processes by which the BEVI and its scales were developed (see Shealy, 2016; http://www.springerpub.com/making-sense-of-beliefs-and-values.html).

congruent with a narrative framework that how we experience ourselves, others, and the larger world is mediated strongly by the life experiences we have and may not "exist" in absolute or inviolable terms (Shealy, 2016). In other words, our memory and experience of our "past" are highly dependent upon events that occur in the present and future. And yet, this process may unfold differently for individuals depending upon their points of departure (i.e., how they are "organized" affectively or cognitively prior to the learning experience). For example, as Figure 12.8 illustrates, individuals who report a greater degree of "Negative Life Events" at Time 1 subsequently show a decrease in such a report at Time 2 (3 to 4 months after the international/multicultural learning experience) whereas individuals who report a lesser degree of "Negative Life Events" at Time 1 subsequently show an increase in such a report at Time 2. What do such findings suggest? Although we emphasize that such findings are common, but not universal, these outcomes suggest that prolonged exposure to radically different "formative variables" (e.g., a different culture, context, language, religion, etc.) interacts with "who we were" at the outset of the experience to produce a sort of "progression to the mean" effect. Such findings imply further that those who experienced their pasts as especially "negative" or "positive" are not so sure that that was the case following the completion of this intensive learning experience (i.e., relative to what they now have experienced via a program, course, workshop, etc., their pasts may now be experienced by them as "better" or "worse" than what they originally believed).

Consider Figure 12.9. From an interpretive standpoint, the Aggregate Profile and Profile Contrast results on Identity Diffusion amplify this point. Recall that "Identity Diffusion" indicates the degree to which individuals report a "painful crisis of identity," and are "fatalistic regarding negatives of marital/family life," and "feel 'bad' about one's self and prospects." If we only reviewed the Time 1/Time 2 Aggregate Profile (which again, takes the average of all participants), we might conclude that no change occurred on this fundamental aspect of how one experiences self from

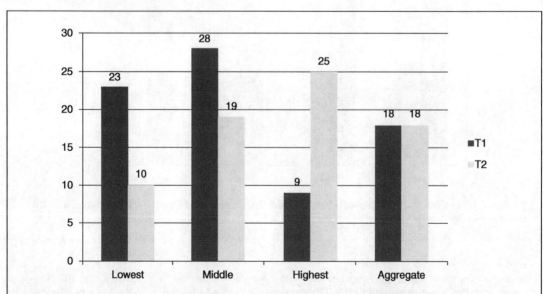

FIGURE 12.9. Comparison between lowest, middle, and highest Profile Contrast scores with the Aggregate Profile score on the Identity Diffusion scale from the BEVI.

the beginning to the conclusion of the experiences (i.e., the Time 1/Time 2 Aggregate Report remains at the 18th percentile). Such a conclusion would be ill-advised as there are clear differences between subgroups on this core construct of the BEVI. Specifically, although none of these subgroups are elevated on this scale—an important point to consider vis-à-vis interpretation of the group as a whole—the lowest and middle "full scale" cohorts would appear to become substantially clearer on who they are and where they are going in life, whereas those who believed they were the clearest on such aspects of self at the beginning of the experience report markedly less clarity by the conclusion of this experience. The reasons for such findings warrant further exploration, but one possibility is that by dint of their exposure to a context and culture that are substantially different from what they were accustomed, each subgroup may "balance" what they previously believed and valued against what they saw in terms of the realities that others faced. Such a process may differentially be associated with greater clarity for those who were relatively unclear about who they were and where they were going versus those who, relatively speaking, felt clearer about such matters at the outset, but became less convinced of their clarity by the end of the experience.

Such tentative conclusions receive additional support via the following comparison between the Aggregate Profile and Profile Contrast for Self Certitude, which measures the degree to which individuals experience a "strong sense of will," are "impatient with excuses for difficulties," tend to emphasize "positive thinking," and are "disinclined toward deep analysis" regarding why they or others behave as they do or why events happen as they do in the larger world. As the findings of Figure 12.10 illustrate—and again, the group overall demonstrates a low degree of this construct —overall findings (from Aggregate Profile) illustrate that individuals report becoming less certain regarding such matters overall following an international, multicultural, or transformative learning event. However, very important differences—at least for this group—emerge, in that those who showed the highest "full scale"

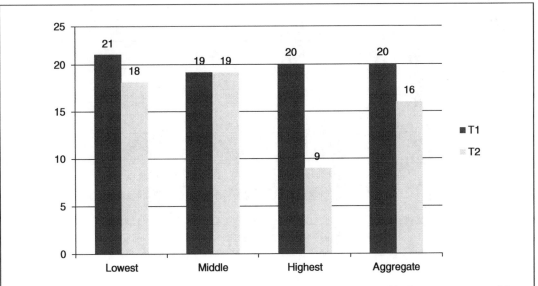

FIGURE 12.10. Comparison between lowest, middle, and highest Profile Contrast scores with the Aggregate Profile score on the Self Certitude scale from the BEVI.

profile (i.e., were the most inclined to be open and engaged regarding the experience they were about to have) showed the greatest drop in certitude by the conclusion of their experience. The lowest full scale group (those that were least inclined) also showed a drop, whereas the middle 40% showed no change at all. Overall, it would appear that these students became "less certain" overall, although those in the middle appeared not to change on this core measure of certitude over the course of their experience.

Importantly, global matters of "certitude" may not apply equally to all belief/value constructs that are integral to one's larger worldview. For example, the following finding also has emerged on several occasions, and has to do with specific subsystems of belief. Consider Figure 12.11, which addresses the degree to which one is "highly religious," tends to see "self/behavior/events as mediated by God/spiritual forces," and contends that there is "one way to the 'afterlife'." Interestingly, here, the Aggregate Profile is a good representation of how the lowest and highest full scale subgroups respond, but does not reflect results for the middle 40% of this group. How do we interpret such findings? Although subject to further inquiry, a preliminary hypothesis is that individuals who are most invested in a traditional religious worldview experience the greatest challenge to the black and white nature of such a framework when exposed to beliefs and values that are markedly different from their own. Interestingly, such a finding does not correspond with an increase in "Identity Diffusion," as noted (quite the contrary), which suggests that such transitions are not experienced as cognitively/affectively confusing in terms of why the world works as it does, but perhaps, are clarifying regarding who we are and who we are striving to become.

Finally, for those engaged in study abroad, service learning, multicultural education, or other educational interventions that are designed to facilitate greater openness to different ways of believing in or behaving around the world, the following findings, from Figure 12.12, are worth noting. Specifically, observe that this group of

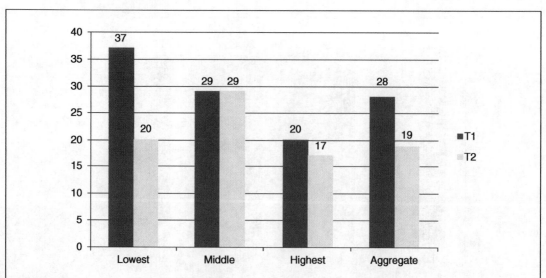

FIGURE 12.11. Comparison between lowest, middle, and highest Profile Contrast scores with the Aggregate Profile score on the Religious Traditionalism scale from the BEVI.

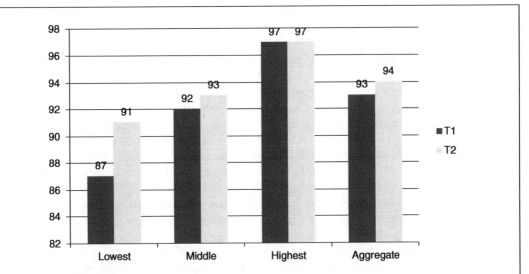

FIGURE 12.12. Comparison between lowest, middle, and highest Profile Contrast scores with the Aggregate Profile score on the Sociocultural Openness scale from the BEVI.

36 students from the University of British Columbia would appear to be extremely socioculturally open at the beginning of their learning experience. Although there is a 10% point difference at Time 1 between the lowest and highest full scale scores, it should be emphasized that this group really is "the choir," in that those engaged in trying to promote the beliefs, values, and practices of a "global citizenry" have a very ready audience. So, looking only at scales on the BEVI that measure such outcomes is not the most relevant area of focus for this particular cohort. In other words, if our goal is "sociocultural openness," this group is already there at Time 1.

Thus, a fundamental recommendation from the Forum BEVI Project is to look far beyond traditional or expected indexes of what we are trying to facilitate, and instead delve much more deeply into the complex interactions that mediate and moderate why and how we experience self, others, and the larger world as we do. That is, as international, multicultural, and transformative educators, scholars, and administrators, we need to include, but look beyond "sociocultural" beliefs, values, and practices in order to understand whether, how, for whom, and to what degree our learning experiences are impacting learners. A focus only on "intercultural" learning would miss the broader implications of the preceding findings, which illustrate that learners are being impacted at multiple levels of self (Shealy, 2016). If we do not ask about these aspects of how self, others, and the larger world are experienced—to include but not be limited to "intercultural" beliefs and values—we miss apprehending the breadth and depth of all that we are impacting via the learning experiences we create. For example, if we only looked at Sociocultural Openness, it would be tempting to observe simply that, "Well, they were open at the beginning and are pretty much the same at the end." Such a simplistic conclusion ignores the rich changes that are in fact occurring—as the other four comparisons reveal—as well as the complex and meaningful interactions that are taking place with subgroups of the larger group. The essential point here is that no specific construct should be privileged above any other, regardless of the primary educational goal we are seeking to promote. Just as our learners are not only "cultural learners," so should our assessment instruments measure much more than "cultural learning" alone.

Along these lines, we have quite often observed the intriguing finding that BEVI participants' reports of their own histories become more "negative" over the course of a few weeks or months (between Time 1 and Time 2 administrations). This phenomenon may occur even while participants simultaneously report a greater degree of Emotional Attunement or Self-Awareness at the conclusion of the experience, which suggests two intriguing possibilities that are reminiscent of several implications. First, consistent with the constructivist paradigm, it may well be that our present experiences alter our past perceptions under certain circumstances such as study abroad. Second, certain experiences may activate emotional arousal or promote self-awareness, but not increase, or even decrease, global engagement. Thus, if we only ask about "cultural" beliefs and values, we may well miss the most important—and perhaps the most interesting and relevant—aspects of what actually is happening within our "learners" when they are exposed to different cultures. In short, we need to examine multiple "parts" and the overarching "whole" simultaneously in order to apprehend the experiential gestalt of learning, both at the individual and group level. In doing so, we are much more able to grasp the underlying interactions within and among various cohorts of learners, which will help us understand what is happening and why, and inform whatever decisions we make regarding changes or developments to pursue (e.g., curricular, staffing, faculty, programmatic, administrative, organizational, institutional).

As a final point under this implication, recall that the BEVI includes three "free-response" qualitative questions—as a mixed methods measure—which allow respondents to offer their perspectives regarding matters of growth and change, or the lack thereof, in their own words. The importance of mixed methods approaches is well documented in terms of assessment best practice (e.g., Creswell & Plano-Clark, 2007; Hanson, Leighton, Donaldson, Terjesen, & Shealy, in press; Teddlie & Tashakkori, 2009), the legitimacy of which has been confirmed to us as well on multiple occasions throughout the Forum BEVI Project. Qualitative responses provide a window into values-based similarities and differences among various cohorts regarding their initial or concluding expectations or perceptions regarding a learning experience. Such information may be very helpful in ensuring that program directors or course instructors are better attuned to what students or other participants are thinking and feeling vis-à-vis the learning experience, while using such information to facilitate more skillful programmatic or instructional interventions. Qualitative data may also provide key insight regarding *why* quantitative data emerge as they do. For example, when profile scores move in directions that are the opposite of what was expected or desired from Time 1 to Time 2 (suggesting that the overall experience may have been more "negative" than "positive"), qualitative responses are crucial to interpreting what may be happening, particularly if several students/participants report similar experiences. Specifically, when responses are relatively "neutral" or open at Time 1 (e.g., "I haven't had an international experience yet"; "I don't know, but look forward to the class")—and become indifferent or negatively toned upon Time 2 BEVI administration, at the conclusion of the experience (e.g., "I've had enough and can't wait to get home"; "This class was terrible")—we gather important information that may help explain the directionality of scale scores. Finally, along similar lines, qualitative responses both help explain quantitative findings *and* highlight the complexity of international, multicultural, and transformative learning processes and outcomes. For example, consider the following three prototypical response excerpts to qualitative question 3 on the BEVI: "What have you learned and how are you different as a result of this experience?":

- I realize how privileged I have been in my life.
- I now see why my country is the best place to live in the world.
- Who I thought I was is very different from what I think now.

When juxtaposed with quantitative scale scores, such responses not only represent a sort of phenomenological shorthand for how a student or participant has experienced a program, course, or workshop, but also offer a window into *why* response profiles may be what they are, particularly if patterns emerge across cohorts. For example, a student who concludes that he or she now knows the "U.S. is best" likely had a very different experience *and/or* was a very different person at the outset of the experience than someone who now recognizes how "privileged" he or she is as compared to how he or she thought or felt at the beginning of the experience. Again, such responses illustrate a fundamental finding of this entire project: There are marked differences between students, faculty, directors, cohorts, and experiences—at the level of beliefs, values, and life experiences—that all interact together to influence the sort of "outcomes" that emerge at the conclusion of a learning experience. In short, qualitative data allow us to "make sense" of the complexity of international, multicultural, and transformative learning in ways that may be highly complementary to, and illuminating of, quantitative data.

Implication 9. Although Distinct Characteristics of Various Cross-Cultural Groups Are Identifiable, Broad-Based Assessment Suggests Within- as Well as Between-Group Variation

A focus on differences between cultural groups is interesting and relevant, but may obscure the fact that greater variability may occur more often within, rather than between, different cultural groups. Such a conclusion has important implications for how we understand "human nature" and make sense of why we become who we become.

One major question of relevance to the BEVI Working Group was the overarching issue of whether and how this measure could be used in countries and cultures different from the United States. That is because the adaptation and usage of "Western" tests and measures in non-Western contexts presents a range of challenges, which center largely on equivalency issues and underlying epistemologies of tests and measures developed in the United States, which may or may not be consonant with those of other countries and cultures. From our perspective, there need not be an ineluctable schism between North/South, Western/non-Western methods and measures. Instead, our "differences" offer a fascinating and rich opportunity for us all to listen and learn from each other, ultimately responding in a collaborative, consensus-based manner that is inclusive, pluralistic, and culturally sensitive as well as methodologically and psychometrically defensible via assessment research and practice (e.g., Hanson et al., in press; Harkness, 2003; Moghaddam, Harre, & Lee, 2007; Wild et al., 2005).

Consistent with such a perspective, five points should be emphasized vis-à-vis cross-cultural usage of the BEVI. First, many BEVI items actually were identified outside of the United States in the context of clinical, research, and educational work with a highly diverse international population (Shealy, 2004). Second, every effort has been made throughout the development and evaluation of this measure to be mindful of cross-cultural issues of usage and application, and to strive for "equivalency" of usage across cultures and contexts. Multiple Subject Matter Experts (SMEs) have reviewed BEVI items at different points in the development of this instrument, including non-English language first/non-U.S. experts in international, multicultural, and transformative learning in order to identify possible issues of bias and/or nonrelevance across countries and cultures. Third, from a theoretical perspective, the BEVI deliberately strives for neutrality regarding the "rightness" or "wrongness" of responses to BEVI items, allowing respondents to answer on a four-point Likert-type scale.[17] As such, the fact that respondents from a "different" culture or context might tend to respond one way or another to various subsets of BEVI items, or even the BEVI as a whole, is precisely what the measure is designed to detect (i.e., differences and similarities between various subgroups). In other words, if such differences emerged across cultures and contexts, the most parsimonious explanation for such differences would be that the BEVI is detecting such belief/value differences rather than being biased toward, or against, one group or another. Fourth and similarly, based upon hundreds of analyses thus far, there is reason to believe that within-group variation on the BEVI will be equivalent or greater than between-group variation. For example, as the following Decile Profiles illustrate, although some culturally salient patterns may emerge on the BEVI, which are indeed relevant and meaningful (i.e., on beliefs/values regarding gender, religion, etc.), the general tendency is for broad-based populations (i.e., from a country) to show greater within- than between-group variation on many of the constructs that the BEVI measures. Fifth, in the final analysis, such matters ultimately are empirical in nature as we have to determine whether there are systematic differences at a population level that inadvertently skew results one way or another. Although further analysis of such issues remains ongoing, evidence thus far suggests that when administered and interpreted in an appropriate manner, the BEVI indeed appears able to be used across cultures and contexts to identify how various groups—even with very different life histories and worldviews—experience self, others, and the larger world.[18]

Consider, for example, the following three Decile Profiles that are drawn from students in three different countries/global regions under the auspices of universities that were part of the Forum BEVI Project.[19] If there are radical differences across these three cultures, they presumably would manifest in patterns of responding across various scales on the BEVI (i.e., would be markedly different and/or skewed in various directions). Take a moment to review these three profiles and the dispersion of responses across the deciles for various BEVI scales (Table 12.9).

Since we are dealing with different countries and regions, it makes sense to look first at Sociocultural Openness, which measures a tendency toward "progressive" and "open" beliefs and values regarding "a wide range of actions, policies, and practices in the areas of culture, economics, education, environment, gender/global relations, politics." Are there differences across these three groups? Consider the percentage of the sample that falls in the tenth decile (e.g., at the 90th percentile or higher on this scale): Country 1 = 46%; Country 2 = 57%; Country 3 = 42%. Clearly, participants from

---

[17] See Chapter 4 in *Making Sense of Beliefs and Values* (Shealy, 2016) for a discussion of the design and structure of the BEVI, including the rationale for not including an "undecided" or "neutral" option.

[18] Reasons for cultural differences and similarities between groups are considered in several chapters in *Making Sense of Beliefs and Values* (e.g., see Tabit et al., 2016).

[19] The Decile Profile essentially divides up each scale on the BEVI into chunks of 10%—deciles—ranging from the basement to the ceiling of each scale. In doing so, Decile Profile illustrates the percentage of individuals from the larger group that fall into each decile, from the lowest (1%–10%) to the highest (90%–100%), for each BEVI scale.

TABLE 12.9
Three BEVI Decile Profiles From Students in Three Different Countries/Regions

COUNTRY/REGION 1

1.	Negative Life Events	17%	20%	13%	8%	6%	14%	3%	6%	9%	4%
2.	Needs Closure	25%	15%	9%	7%	3%	3%	3%	3%	1%	1%
3.	Needs Fulfillment	2%	2%	3%	7%	6%	11%	9%	20%	19%	22%
4.	Identity Diffusion	36%	18%	17%	0%	11%	0%	0%	6%	3%	9%
5.	Basic Openness	6%	8%	6%	11%	7%	11%	15%	8%	18%	12%
6.	Self Certitude	12%	9%	10%	14%	9%	9%	9%	15%	6%	7%
7.	Basic Determinism	20%	17%	19%	9%	8%	9%	7%	2%	5%	4%
8.	Socioemotional Convergence	1%	4%	3%	5%	10%	7%	11%	14%	23%	23%
9.	Physical Resonance	0%	0%	0%	1%	1%	5%	3%	13%	58%	20%
10.	Emotional Attunement	6%	3%	7%	9%	8%	17%	9%	13%	18%	10%
11.	Self Awareness	1%	0%	0%	1%	1%	3%	18%	8%	27%	42%
12.	Meaning Quest	4%	3%	13%	8%	8%	10%	8%	20%	10%	14%
13.	Religious Traditionalism	0%	25%	18%	6%	18%	8%	8%	8%	6%	4%
14.	Gender Traditionalism	24%	15%	18%	5%	7%	9%	7%	6%	3%	5%
15.	Sociocultural Openness	2%	3%	1%	3%	6%	6%	9%	13%	11%	46%
16.	Ecological Resonance	5%	2%	6%	7%	15%	15%	11%	9%	8%	23%
17.	Global Resonance	2%	5%	6%	8%	0%	7%	7%	13%	35%	17%
	Deciles:	1	2	3	4	5	6	7	8	9	10

COUNTRY/REGION 2

1.	Negative Life Events	9%	17%	4%	9%	9%	17%	13%	13%	9%	0%
2.	Needs Closure	30%	13%	9%	9%	13%	4%	13%	0%	9%	0%
3.	Needs Fulfillment	0%	0%	13%	13%	4%	9%	9%	30%	9%	13%
4.	Identity Diffusion	17%	9%	4%	0%	4%	0%	0%	26%	13%	26%
5.	Basic Openness	13%	30%	0%	22%	9%	4%	13%	0%	9%	0%
6.	Self Certitude	0%	4%	0%	9%	9%	17%	9%	17%	0%	35%
7.	Basic Determinism	4%	17%	22%	13%	9%	9%	9%	4%	0%	13%
8.	Socioemotional Convergence	0%	0%	17%	4%	9%	17%	0%	9%	26%	17%
9.	Physical Resonance	0%	0%	0%	13%	4%	30%	0%	39%	13%	0%
10.	Emotional Attunement	4%	4%	13%	13%	26%	9%	4%	13%	13%	0%
11.	Self Awareness	0%	0%	0%	13%	9%	13%	9%	4%	30%	22%

(continued)

TABLE 12.9
Three BEVI Decile Profiles From Students in Three Different Countries/Regions (continued)

12.	Meaning Quest	0%	4%	17%	4%	0%	17%	4%	30%	0%	22%
13.	Religious Traditionalism	0%	0%	4%	4%	0%	9%	17%	17%	17%	30%
14.	Gender Traditionalism	13%	4%	13%	4%	13%	30%	0%	9%	0%	13%
15.	Sociocultural Openness	0%	0%	0%	4%	4%	0%	0%	9%	26%	57%
16.	Ecological Resonance	0%	4%	9%	0%	9%	13%	17%	9%	17%	22%
17.	Global Resonance	0%	0%	4%	4%	0%	9%	17%	13%	39%	13%
	Deciles:	1	2	3	4	5	6	7	8	9	10

COUNTRY/REGION 3

1.	Negative Life Events	4%	25%	12%	12%	4%	12%	4%	12%	8%	4%
2.	Needs Closure	50%	8%	17%	12%	8%	0%	0%	0%	0%	4%
3.	Needs Fulfillment	0%	8%	4%	12%	12%	4%	12%	29%	8%	8%
4.	Identity Diffusion	8%	29%	21%	0%	21%	0%	0%	12%	8%	0%
5.	Basic Openness	0%	17%	4%	29%	4%	4%	12%	8%	8%	12%
6.	Self Certitude	4%	25%	4%	17%	0%	17%	4%	21%	8%	0%
7.	Basic Determinism	21%	12%	0%	21%	4%	12%	12%	4%	4%	8%
8.	Socioemotional Convergence	4%	4%	8%	0%	21%	8%	21%	8%	21%	4%
9.	Physical Resonance	0%	0%	0%	4%	0%	25%	8%	38%	21%	4%
10.	Emotional Attunement	0%	4%	21%	17%	8%	8%	21%	12%	4%	4%
11.	Self Awareness	0%	0%	0%	17%	4%	8%	12%	8%	25%	25%
12.	Meaning Quest	12%	4%	21%	12%	8%	4%	8%	21%	8%	0%
13.	Religious Traditionalism	4%	33%	12%	12%	17%	8%	8%	4%	0%	0%
14.	Gender Traditionalism	17%	17%	21%	0%	17%	12%	4%	4%	8%	0%
15.	Sociocultural Openness	0%	0%	0%	4%	4%	8%	17%	12%	12%	42%
16.	Ecological Resonance	0%	4%	8%	17%	25%	8%	4%	4%	12%	17%
17.	Global Resonance	0%	8%	4%	0%	0%	4%	8%	17%	50%	8%
	Deciles:	1	2	3	4	5	6	7	8	9	10

all three of these countries/regions are extremely high on Sociocultural Openness as measured by the BEVI. How about a couple of other variables, which might reflect underlying cultural dynamics/issues, such as Religious Traditionalism and Gender Traditionalism? What do we see at this level? Essentially, it would appear that Country/Region 2 is the most "conservative" or "traditional" regarding matters of religion and gender. Specifically, 30% of Country/Region 2 participants fall in the 90th percentile on Religious Traditionalism compared to 4% for Country/Region 1 and 0% for

Country/Region 3. And, there is much wider dispersion on Gender Traditionalism for Country/Region 2 than either 1 or 3, which generally shows low levels of Gender Traditionalism. Does it help to know that these BEVI cohorts are composed of individuals from the United States and Central America as well as a highly internationalized group studying in Japan? From the standpoint of religion and gender, which of these three cultures composed of students in higher education (i.e., not the population as a whole) would likely tend to be more "conservative" or "traditional" on average from the standpoint of "formative variables" (e.g., cultural norms)? If you answered Central America, you are correct. Specifically, Country/Region 1 is from project partner Dickinson College in the United States, and consists mainly of U.S. citizens (N = 158). Country/Region 2 is from project partner Georgetown University, which administered the BEVI to English-speaking students drawn from El Salvador and Honduras (N = 23). Country/Region 3 is from project partner Hiroshima University, which administered the BEVI to an older, highly educated, and diverse cohort of English-speaking students who were studying in Japan (N = 24).

Along similar lines, consider another BEVI group report analysis of U.S. citizens who have never studied abroad with a separate group of non-U.S. citizens/dual citizens who all completed the BEVI. Interestingly, on the majority of BEVI scales, these respondents—mostly college-aged students—showed similar scale results on most BEVI scales (i.e., within 5 points of each other). However, as Figure 12.13 illustrates, on three of these scales, differences of over 10% points emerged, which would seem to make sense—and perhaps be predicted—in terms of the capacity of the BEVI to differentiate between these groups. Specifically, the "Non-U.S. Citizen/Dual Citizen" group showed the following BEVI scale elevations relative to the "U.S. Respondents Who Have Not Studied Abroad": Sociocultural Openness (75 versus 58); Ecological Resonance (65 versus 51); and Global Resonance (56 versus 45). At least on these comparisons, it appears that the BEVI is able to identify similarities and differences that are consistent with an intuitive understanding of what would be expected from the standpoint of validity. In short, on scales that are designed most directly to measure "other" and "larger world" concerns, it should not be surprising that the BEVI identified group-based differences that differentiate individuals who, on average, would more likely tend to be nonglobally oriented at present (e.g., U.S. citizens who have not studied abroad) with those who likely have had more globally-oriented experiences overall relative to their U.S. counterparts (e.g., non-U.S./dual citizens).

The point of these two juxtapositions—three Decile Profiles with relatively small sample sizes as well as larger sample sizes across U.S. and non-U.S./dual citizens—is *not* to suggest that such matters of cross-cultural usage are settled, only that—consistent with the processes through which it was developed and evaluated over many years—the BEVI (a) does appear able to identify within-group differences across each of these cultures, illustrating the belief/value diversity therein; and

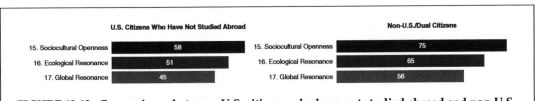

FIGURE 12.13. **Comparisons between U.S. citizens who have not studied abroad and non-U.S. citizens/dual citizens.**

(b) findings that emerged are generally consistent with what would be expected for participants drawn across different cultural and demographic configurations. Of course, as we continue to gather data across cultures and contexts, further analyses will be conducted at a number of levels (i.e., whether reliable differences and similarities emerge across different countries and regions). Such efforts are consistent with other big picture and longitudinal assessment initiatives, such as the exemplary World Values Survey (Inglehart, Basáñez, Díez-Medrano, Halman, & Luijkx, 2004; Inglehart, Basáñez, & Moreno, 1998; World Values Survey, 2009).

Implication 10. As Kurt Lewin (1951) Observed, There Is Nothing so Practical as a Good Theory

The importance of thinking about why learning, growth, or development does—or does not— occur cannot be overemphasized. By specifying what our theoretical understandings and commitments are, and are not, we are compelled to contemplate what our underlying (and often implicit) models and epistemologies are, which bear directly on fundamental questions of assessment models and methods. Without considering such matters, we risk engaging in assessment research and practice that is face valid and superficial as well as lacking in substantive, practical, and real world impact, mainly because we are, perhaps inadvertently, minimizing or ignoring the complexity of these interacting phenomena.

Although we rely on EI Theory and the EI Self in this project—mainly because they are integral to the BEVI—the overarching point is that whatever assessment approach is pursued, the underlying theory should be specified in detail in order to explicate why particular research and practice methods or interventions are recommended and/or specific interpretations justified. In addition to providing guidance regarding *why* we contend that particular interventions *should* impact learning, growth, and development in particular ways, it simply is not possible to conduct high-level types of statistical analyses without a strong theoretical basis for doing so. For example, structural equation modeling requires us to specify the proposed theoretical relationship among various measurable constructs, and was integral to the illumination of various associations among formative variables (i.e., life history, ethnicity), mediators (i.e., various BEVI process-oriented scales), and outcomes (i.e., reported satisfaction upon the conclusion of a learning experience) reported throughout this chapter. Among other benefits, a strong theoretical basis for our measures and methods allows us to

> distinguish between *descriptive* and *interpretive* levels of analysis. That is, we need to examine both what constitutes change (e.g., how we know it is happening), a descriptive level of analysis, as well as why it is occurring (e.g., the rationale for why the changes we observe are in fact occurring), an interpretive level of analysis. We may be wrong or incomplete in our conclusions, but there can be no substitute for engaging in ongoing interpretation or explanation of why we observe the changes—or lack thereof—that we do. (Shealy, 2016, pp. 46–47)

Implication 11. It Is Possible to Identify the Profile or Signature of an Institution or Organization

The aggregate profile of the BEVI may illuminate how a student body at a given institution or organization tends to see self, others, and the larger world. This profile appears to be relatively consistent across years, indicating that the characteristics of an institution's student body may be relatively stable and measurable.

One of the more intriguing findings from the Forum BEVI Project was the emergence of unique BEVI "profiles" or "signatures" that appear to characterize the student body across various institutions or organizations. It is perhaps not surprising that different systems tend to attract different students. Such findings are in fact a central preoccupation of colleges and universities, which keenly are interested in a range of defining characteristics of their student bodies (e.g., entering grade point average [GPA], scores on standardized tests widely used for college admissions such as the Scholastic Assessment Test (SAT) and the American College Testing (ACT), ethnicity, etc.). The fact that such differences extend beyond these standard indexes, and seem to characterize deeper aspects of the aggregate psychological makeup of a student body, is a unique and thought-provoking insight. Consider for example Figure 12.14, which juxtaposes aggregate scores over a 2-year period (2010 and 2011) across all BEVI scales for a stratified random sample of over 600 incoming freshman students from Michigan State University (MSU). Such results illustrate at least two basic findings. First, MSU students demonstrate remarkable continuity on the BEVI across two separate years of administration. In addition to offering further support for the reliability of the measure, what is most intriguing is that the entering MSU student body seems to show a very high degree of consistency in how they experience self, others, and the larger world across different years. Such findings should be of interest at an administrative level, since the student body not only shows stability at the level of traditional indexes (i.e., GPA), but also at the level of underlying life history and psychological variables, such as Emotional Attunement and Sociocultural Openness. Such findings are not mere abstractions, but bear

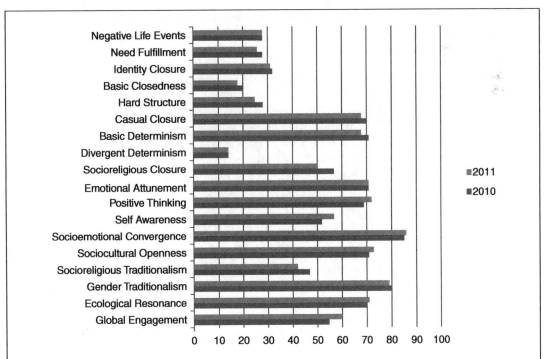

FIGURE 12.14. **Stratified random sample of 2 years of entering freshman students at Michigan State University across all BEVI scales.**

significantly on the overarching "culture" or "feel" of a campus community. More importantly, they may illuminate areas for focus vis-à-vis student programming, communication, and engagement (e.g., in academic affairs, student affairs, etc.), and may help in the interpretation or understanding of various events and dynamics that occur on campus. For example, during one of the years of this study, a racially charged incident occurred at MSU. While the larger community (both on and off campus) engaged in much deliberation regarding whether or not the student body as a whole was "racist," it was possible to observe—at least on the basis of these results—that it does *not* appear that the overall student body at MSU is inclined toward prejudicial beliefs; on the contrary, for the 2 years of this analysis, the entering MSU student body appears to be highly open toward and accepting of cultural differences (e.g., as illustrated by scores on Sociocultural Openness in the 71st and 73rd percentile in 2010 and 2011). However, a more fine-grained analysis of BEVI data by decile (e.g., through a Decile Profile) illustrates that there may well be small subsets of MSU students who are inclined toward racially prejudicial beliefs. Such findings not only put the matter in perspective vis-à-vis the student body as a whole, but may allow for more nuanced and targeted interventions, when appropriately designed and delivered. For example, it is quite common for colleges and universities to implement "sensitivity training" on various issues following incidents and/or as a proactive measure. Group-based data of this sort may allow faculty, staff, and administrators to appraise more accurately the nature and scope of such problems rather than designing and implementing broad-based, one-size-fits-all interventions that may, inadvertently, do harm rather than—and/or in addition to—good (e.g., Tabit et al., 2016).

Second and consistent with these observations, such results offer the possibility of understanding the aggregate makeup of the student body as a whole. More specifically, and focusing on a few key findings in Figure 12.14 across 2010 and 2011, MSU students overall appear *not* to report a high degree of unhappy life experiences prior to matriculation (Negative Life Events = 28th percentile for both 2010 and 2011), and to be quite open/nondefensive generally (Basic Closedness = 20th and 18th percentile for 2010 and 2011). At the same time, the level of sophistication regarding "why humans do what they do" is not especially developed at the outset of their higher education careers (e.g., Basic Determinism = 71st and 68th percentile for 2010 and 2011), which is perhaps not surprising for students who are about to begin an intensive process of examining their underlying assumptions about the nature of reality. Auguring well over the long term in this regard, these students also evidence a high capacity for seeing the world in "shades of gray" rather than black and white (e.g., Socioemotional Convergence = 85th and 86th percentile for 2010 and 2011). Although such openness may not necessarily extend to beliefs and values about gender roles (e.g., Gender Traditionalism = 80th and 79th percentile for 2010 and 2011), they appear very moderate overall regarding their religious inclinations (e.g., Socioreligious Traditionalism = 47th and 42nd percentile for 2010 and 2011). Moreover, they do appear highly open to different cultural beliefs and practices (e.g., Sociocultural Openness = 71st and 73rd percentile for 2010 and 2011) and are highly concerned about the environment and natural world (Ecological Resonance = 70th and 71st percentile for 2010 and 2011). Taken as a whole, such a profile offers important insights about the aggregate psychological makeup of the MSU student body, particularly when compared to the aggregate profile of institutions with quite different missions and traditions. In short, then, the generation of institutional or organizational profiles would seem to have at least five specific usages:

1. Establishing a baseline for each cohort of entering students, which may be followed over time (through re-administration) in order to understand which aspects of the learning experience are associated with the most and least change.
2. Examining interactions among demographic and background variables (e.g., income, acceptance rates), specific learning experiences (e.g., study abroad, participation in a learning community), and outcomes (e.g., BEVI scale changes, GPA).
3. Developing and defining a "brand" (e.g., the relative openness of the student body), which allows for more precise strategic planning (e.g., "We wish to recruit more of X type of student in order to move the institution or organization in particular directions over time.").
4. Helping the institution or organization understand better who and what it is (e.g., what the normal distribution for the student body is as well as areas of greater and lesser variability).
5. Moving beyond traditional demographic tracking by understanding deeper aspects of its identity as an institution or organization, including how the student body experiences self, others, and the larger world.

Implication 12. Group Reports Help Course Instructors, Program Directors, and Administrators Understand Better the Nature of Their Particular Classes, Cohorts, or Staffs

Across a range of different settings and contexts, group reports have been used to help those in a position of leadership understand who their group is, which may help in planning and orientation purposes. Such reports also help assess what may be driving underlying processes of conflict or consensus for the group, which may result in more informed and sensitive leadership interventions. Further administration may allow for an examination of how the group sees itself, others, and the larger world over the long term after particular interventions and/ or experiences occur.

Transformational learning stands as an overarching goal of education writ large; yet the question needs to be asked: to what end and for what purpose (e.g., Cultivating the Globally Sustainable Self, 2015)? In cases where students will engage with vulnerable communities and complex topics, it is critical to establish the clear premise that student learning is not the only consideration; we must also ensure that students are engaging real issues and real people in a substantive manner. Understanding the signature profile of the institution generally—and the group profile of a cohort specifically—can assist instructors and program staff in making ethically sound decisions throughout the process of selection, preparation, monitoring, and support.

One typical usage of the report system in this regard is to compare and contrast various subgroups within a larger institution or organization in order to understand how change occurs over time, while also appreciating the differences and similarities among such groups. Such analysis is important since even strong trends for a group as a whole should not obscure differences within the group as a number of comparative reports from this overall initiative reveal. Consider for example Figure 12.15, which contrasts incoming freshmen students at MSU with a selected group of student leaders, who are especially adept at addressing issues of diversity and multiculturalism (the "Diversity Group"). Presumably, if the BEVI is able to detect differences between groups both currently and across time, substantive differences should emerge in the profiles of these groups. In full recognition that we are examining different groups with different Ns, a number of intriguing differences do exist and are

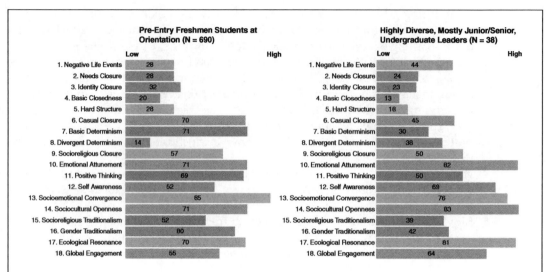

FIGURE 12.15. BEVI organizational profiles between two cohorts of students within the same institution.

worth considering as we contemplate future research. For example, there is a *much higher degree* of Negative Life Events among the Diversity group as compared to the Pre-entry group (Pre-entry = 28th percentile; Diversity = 44th percentile). Moreover, the Diversity group showed a *much higher degree* of attributional sophistication as evidenced by Basic Determinism (Pre-entry = 70th percentile; Diversity = 30th percentile) and a *much lower degree* of Gender Traditionalism (Pre-entry = 80th percentile; Diversity = 42nd percentile) as well as a *higher degree* of Self Awareness (Pre-entry = 52nd percentile; Diversity = 69th percentile) and Sociocultural Openness (Pre-entry = 71st percentile; Diversity = 83rd percentile). The point is, although it is very relevant and informative to look at characteristics of the student body as a whole, it is no less important and illuminating to examine differences among subgroups within the broader population, both to understand differences and similarities between such groups and to map how various cohorts of students become "who they are" over time.

Another area of usage is to understand the similarities and differences between institutions. Consider for example Figure 12.16, which contrasts two BEVI profiles from two project partners: Dickinson College is a highly internationalized, majority female, liberal arts institution; Michigan Technological University (MTU) is not especially internationalized, is majority male, and has a strong engineering focus.

What do we conclude from these contrasting profiles? Among other notable distinctions, observe the differences on scales measuring the relative attributional complexity across the two institutions, as evidenced by percentile scores on Causal Closure (Dickinson = 37th percentile; MTU = 78th percentile) and Basic Determinism (Dickinson = 35th percentile; MTU = 75th percentile). From an interpretive standpoint, Dickinson "first years" from this sample at least evince a much greater tendency to recognize the complexity inherent in making attributions about self, others, and the larger world (i.e., they are much less likely to endorse black and white statements regarding why human beings are the way they are and/or why events happen as they do). To highlight a couple of other examples, Dickinson students from this

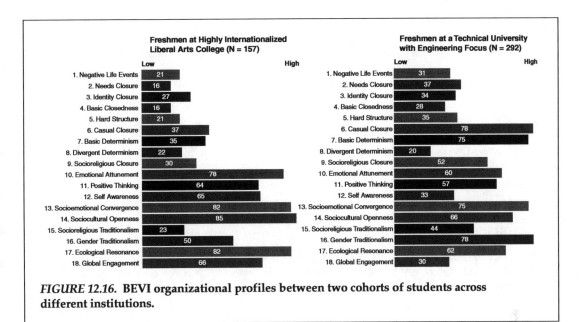

Freshmen at Highly Internationalized Liberal Arts College (N = 157)

	Low		High
1. Negative Life Events	21		
2. Needs Closure	16		
3. Identity Closure	27		
4. Basic Closedness	16		
5. Hard Structure	21		
6. Casual Closure	37		
7. Basic Determinism	35		
8. Divergent Determinism	22		
9. Socioreligious Closure	30		
10. Emotional Attunement		78	
11. Positive Thinking		64	
12. Self Awareness		65	
13. Socioemotional Convergence		82	
14. Sociocultural Openness		85	
15. Socioreligious Traditionalism	23		
16. Gender Traditionalism		50	
17. Ecological Resonance		82	
18. Global Engagement		66	

Freshmen at a Technical University with Engineering Focus (N = 292)

	Low		High
1. Negative Life Events	31		
2. Needs Closure	37		
3. Identity Closure	34		
4. Basic Closedness	28		
5. Hard Structure	35		
6. Casual Closure		78	
7. Basic Determinism		75	
8. Divergent Determinism	20		
9. Socioreligious Closure		52	
10. Emotional Attunement		60	
11. Positive Thinking		57	
12. Self Awareness	33		
13. Socioemotional Convergence		75	
14. Sociocultural Openness		66	
15. Socioreligious Traditionalism		44	
16. Gender Traditionalism		78	
17. Ecological Resonance		62	
18. Global Engagement	30		

FIGURE 12.16. **BEVI organizational profiles between two cohorts of students across different institutions.**

sample are much more likely than MTU students to focus upon "inner" thoughts and experiences in self and other (Self Awareness: Dickinson = 65th percentile; MTU = 33rd percentile) and much less likely to endorse traditional notions of what it means to be "female" or "male" (Gender Traditionalism: Dickinson = 50th percentile; MTU = 78th percentile). *Nothing in such a comparison is intended to illustrate or imply that one group of students is "better" than any other;* the point is rather that we must understand our student bodies in order to appreciate where we are now (i.e., what our baseline is) and where we wish to go. Without such information, it is difficult to ensure that our instructional and administrative goals, methods, and plans are realistic, targeted, and consistent with overarching aspects of our student body and institutional mission.

Such assessment possibilities are aided further by another dimension of the reporting system, which distinguishes among "high," "medium," and "low" full scale scores across subgroups, as described previously. Various indexes and tables on the reporting system address this issue, including Background–Domain Contrast, which illustrates how different or similar the group is at the level of background information and domain scores by the lowest 30%, middle 40%, and highest 30% of full scale scores. Consider the following excerpts of Time 1/Time 2 Group Report results from a sample of participants (N = 101) on Background–Domain Contrast.

Of other highlights that might be emphasized, note from Tables 12.10 and 12.11 that individuals who, at the outset of a learning experience, are at the low, middle, or high end of the "full scale" continuum demonstrate specific profile characteristics, both in terms of "background" variables (i.e., age, gender, education) and "domain" variables (i.e., one of the seven areas under which BEVI scales are clustered). In particular, for this sample of students, those most inclined toward an international, multicultural, or transformative learning experience are:

- Older (average age = 27 versus 19)
- Approximately twice as likely to be female (ratio of females to males of 20:11 versus 16:15)

TABLE 12.10
Sample Findings From Background Information Section of Background–Domain Contrast (N = 101)

Lowest Full Scale	Middle Full Scale	Highest Full Scale
Mean = 41	**Mean = 58**	**Mean = 71**
Background Information	**Background Information**	**Background Information**
Average Age: **19**	Average Age: **22**	Average Age: **27**
Males: **15** Females: **16**	Males: **11** Females: **26**	Males: **11** Females: **20**
Caucasians: **25** Non-Caucasians: **6** ➢ Details:	Caucasians: **26** Non-Caucasians: **11** ➢ Details:	Caucasians: **20** Non-Caucasians: **11** ➢ Details:
Raised in United States: **31** Not Raised in United States: **0** ➢ Details:	Raised in United States: **37** Not Raised in United States: **0** ➢ Details:	Raised in United States: **29** Not Raised in United States: **2** ➢ Details:
Average Years of Education: **2**	Average Years of Education: **3**	Average Years of Education: **7**
Average Parental/Household Income: **$85,484**	Average Parental/Household Income: **$77,162**	Average Parental/Household Income: **$70,161**

- More likely to be non-Caucasian than Caucasian (ratio of non-Caucasian to Caucasian of 11:20 versus 6:25)
- Have more years of postsecondary education (7 years versus 2 years)
- More likely to come from a less wealthy family ($70,000 versus $85,000)
- On the domain section of Background–Domain Contrast (composed of specific BEVI scales), show substantial differences across the seven domains (e.g., 78 versus 32 on the domain of Global Access)

TABLE 12.11
Sample Findings From Domain Section of Background–Domain Contrast

II. Full Scale: **41**	II. Full Scale: **58**	II. Full Scale: **71**
III. Formative Variables • Negative Life Events: **40** • See Background Information	III. Formative Variables • Negative Life Events: **64** • See Background Information	III. Formative Variables • Negative Life Events: **51** • See Background Information

IV. Fulfillment of Core
   Needs: **37**
	IV. Fulfillment of Core
	   Needs: **69**
		IV. Fulfillment of Core
		   Needs: **82**

V. Tolerance of
   Disequilibrium: **36**
	V. Tolerance of
	   Disequilibrium: **52**
		V. Tolerance of
		   Disequilibrium: **68**

VI. Critical Thinking: **35**	VI. Critical Thinking: **51**	VI. Critical Thinking: **73**
VII. Self Access: **57**	VII. Self Access: **76**	VII. Self Access: **78**
VIII. Other Access: **30**	VIII. Other Access: **55**	VIII. Other Access: **78**
IX. Global Access: **32**	IX. Global Access: **54**	IX. Global Access: **78**

From the standpoint of the report system, then, the implications of such findings should be clear. First, differences within groups should not be underestimated but expected (i.e., we should assume that groups may well have important differences both at the level of background and how they experience self, others, and the larger world). Second, for those who are leading learning, growth, or development experiences, reviewing such differences *before* a course, program, or workshop begins may be very helpful in understanding the nature of the group with which they will be interacting throughout the experience. Third, for appropriately trained and skilled facilitators, it may be helpful to share some or all results with participants in order to sensitize them to such differences and similarities among them (i.e., to highlight the fact that there may be very good reasons for why participants react as they do to the experiences they are about to have, as illustrated on several occasions through various projects reported in this chapter). Fourth and finally, such findings may help at the level of interpretation (i.e., the role of the instructor and/or learning experience should be accurately appraised in terms of relative impact) since, most likely, there will be multiple interactions occurring simultaneously that affect learning processes and outcomes. In short, by reviewing such report-based results, more reflective, aware, and skillful learning interventions may be developed, implemented, and appraised since we have a basis for understanding *why* learning processes and outcomes unfold as they do.

Implication 13. By Jointly Utilizing Individual and Group Reports, Multiple Opportunities for Self-Assessment, Enhanced Understanding, and Group Development May Be Facilitated

On many occasions, different cohorts have used the individual and group report system simultaneously in order to enhance understanding of how participants see themselves, others, and the larger world. By juxtaposing individual reports (which are personalized based upon unique scores, and read privately by each individual) with group reports (which show similarities and differences within the group, and are reviewed publicly with the group as a whole), abundant opportunities arise for dialogue, engagement, and growth.

Data from the Forum BEVI Project strongly suggest that the sorts of international, multicultural, and transformative experiences examined in this project *do* influence the amount and degree of growth, development, and learning that occur. But to illustrate such phenomena in real time to administrators, program directors, course/workshop instructors, students, and others who may have strong interests in such matters—but may not have a statistical background—various aspects of the report system are of particular relevance (i.e., to show in clear terms whether and how such "changes" actually occur). Because assessment results from various measures often are not communicated in a way that translates readily into real world usage, the working group devoted particular attention to how the BEVI's report system should be used from the standpoint of accessibility, relevance, and best practice. Consistent with our original charge, we were interested in understanding how the translation of data/scores into accessible report-based systems could be used to promote growth and learning in general, which should have implications for instrument-based report systems including, but not limited to, the BEVI. As such, considerable effort has been devoted to trying to understand how such a "report system" might best translate otherwise abstruse statistical findings into usable findings. In particular, considerable deliberation focused on how feedback from the individual reports of the BEVI should be given to students or staff. Among other conclusions, it was determined that a brief orientation by a trained BEVI administrator was deemed important in order to provide sufficient context for recipients. Moreover, given the comprehensive nature of BEVI reports, it proved important that those in leadership or administrative positions were sufficiently well-versed in matters of interpretation. That is because incomplete or superficial understanding of scales or indexes is contraindicated, especially when contemplating real world implications or applications based upon test scores or reports (e.g., Braskamp et al., 2012). In light of such considerations, it may be helpful to provide additional context prior to presenting actual sample reports that emerged during this project.

Essentially, the BEVI produces reports that may be used at three levels: individual, group, and organization.[20] Individual reports are developed for each participant based upon his or her unique responses to the background information section of the BEVI along with his or her scores on specific BEVI scales. Depending upon the responses, a report is generated under the following headings, which correspond to the theoretical and empirical structure of the BEVI:

1. **Introduction**: Provides an overview of the BEVI.
2. **The Foundation: "Formative Variables" and "Core Needs"**: Provides an indication of what the respondent reports about his or her own life history relative to others.
3. **Tolerance of Disequilibrium**: Describes whether the respondent sees him or herself as "very clear" or "not sure" about who he or she and others "are" under the auspices of how "confident" or "questioning" the respondent appears to be.
4. **Making Sense of Why We Do What We Do**: Indicates attributional tendencies in general (e.g., how and why people do what they do and why events happen as they do).
5. **Access to Yourself and Your Thoughts, Feelings, and Needs**: Describes how the individual deals with his or her own emotions as well as his or her interest in and predilection toward introspection and reflection upon "the self."
6. **Access to the Thoughts and Feelings of Others**: Describes how the person tends to regard and experience issues that are of consequence at a sociocultural level (e.g., beliefs about politics, religion, gender, or the way society "should be structured").
7. **Access to the Larger World**: Indicates one's perspectives on "big picture" issues of the environment (e.g., the degree to which one is or is not concerned about ecological issues) and global engagement (e.g., the degree to which we should or should not be concerned about, or invested in, what is happening outside of our own country, culture, and context).
8. **Conclusion**: Provides context for the preceding report and offers closing thoughts to consider.

Individual reports are designed for application in a range of contexts and settings (e.g., as a teaching tool in classes; predeparture orientation for an international learning experience; to promote growth and development in organizational and other applied contexts), and are intended to facilitate thoughtful and substantive reflection on self, others, and the world at large.

Group/Organizational reports are of two types. First, Time 1 Group Reports describe results from the original administration of the BEVI to a specific group; second, Time 1/Time 2 Group Reports examine how groups change from one administration of the BEVI to the next (Time 1/Time 2/Time 3, etc. reports also may be

---

[20] This section and selected others in this chapter are adapted and/or excerpted from the BEVI test manual.

derived, and are recommended in terms of tracking trends over the long term, as noted). The primary difference between Time 1 and Time 1/Time 2 reports are a few indexes that may be developed only on the basis of comparisons between groups from Time 1 to Time 2 (e.g., Worldview Shift). Each type of report includes a series of tables and indexes that provide information about specific aspects of the group that completed the BEVI. For example, *Background–Domain Contrast* illustrates how different or similar the group is at the level of background information and domain scores by the lowest 30%, middle 40%, and highest 30% of full scale scores. As another example, *Profile Contrast* illustrates how different and similar the group is across all 17 BEVI scales via the lowest 30%, middle 40%, and highest 30% of full scale scores.

Mindful of the overarching goals of relevance and impact of such report-based assessment, including but not limited to the BEVI, questions that emerged consistently during our work with this measure (i.e., those that proved useful in facilitating interpretation and group-based discussion) included:

1. How would you describe the group, organization, or institution overall in terms of the most striking findings?
2. How is the group most different and most similar to itself?
3. Which findings are most surprising, and how can you make sense of such results on the basis of data that are provided?
4. Which findings were expected, and what do they suggest about your group, organization, or institution?
5. Which findings would be most relevant or interesting to a particular group or your overall organization/institution, and why?
6. How could findings inform or shape group-based discussions and processes?
7. What do findings suggest in terms of a particular course, program, or learning experience (e.g., Where might areas of consensus or conflict occur over time? How might patterns interact with a learning, growth, or development experience in terms of overarching goals?)?
8. What might findings suggest about the effectiveness of a particular learning, growth, or development experience?
9. How might findings be used to facilitate the development of new or improved learning, growth, or development experiences?
10. How might findings be used to track changes over time?

There are many other questions to be asked of such report results. Overall, we learned that it was maximally important for users to take sufficient time to review and reflect upon reports in order to ascertain which tables, indexes, or specific findings are most relevant for their specific goals and purposes.

Over the course of this project, the most common usage was a combination of group-based and individual reports (i.e., during a predeparture study abroad orientation program; at the outset of a multicultural course or workshop; in a residence hall at the beginning of the academic year). In this case, individual students would be offered the opportunity to receive their own individual reports, which they (and only they) would read. Then, a group report that had been developed on the basis of the aggregate scores from this group of individuals would be shared with the group. In this way, individuals are able to reflect (in private) upon their own BEVI results with the indexes and other scale information from the BEVI group report (in public). This dialectic process between private and public reflection—which allows for safe internal dialogue and voluntary external dialogue—seems to be integral to the sort of reflection, awareness, and insight that students and staff frequently reported from this process (e.g., "It helped to think about why I am who I am"; "It helps me appreciate why others believe what they do").

At another level, the group reports help program directors or course instructors understand better the differences and similarities of history or worldviews by the members of their group. For example, it was not uncommon for bimodal distributions on various scales (e.g., Gender Traditionalism; Socioreligious Traditionalism) to emerge, which when combined with the breakdown of scale scores by profile, permit the leader or administrator of a learning experience to understand better the makeup of a group even before departing and/or at the outset of a class. From an applied standpoint, such results may be used productively by showing group-based results and asking for volunteers to discuss "why they believe what they believe," a process that can lead to rich dialogue and reflection by participants (e.g., Iyer, 2013; Shealy, 2016).

One common usage of the BEVI report system during this project was to engage students in an examination of the interface between their individual reports and the group report. To illustrate this process, we focus upon a learning community in one of our project partners, James Madison University, called Madison International, which brings together U.S. and international students as part of a living and learning community who complete coursework and participate in other experiences together during their first year at the university (see www.jmu.edu/international/isss/students/get-involved/mi/index.shtml). The following example of individual/group report usage focuses on a subset of these students (N = 22), who completed a course called *Making Sense of Beliefs and Values: A Guided Tour for Global Citizens*. After providing consent and completing the BEVI, individual reports were provided to each student in the course. The first page of a sample individual report is shown in Figure 12.17.

The BEVI trained coordinator then reviews the group report with all members of the cohort. Depending on the goals of a particular BEVI workshop, different sections of the report may be emphasized. In the case of Madison International, most of the focus centered on three components of the group report: (a) Background Information (i.e., descriptive information regarding how the group "breaks down" across a range of different demographic variables); (b) Aggregate Profile (i.e., the aggregate scores for participants across all BEVI scales); and (c) Decile Profile (i.e., the aggregate scores across each scale in increments of 10%, in order to illustrate how the members of a group are dispersed across each of the BEVI scales). Figures 12.18 to 12.20 illustrate these three components of the BEVI group report for the Madison International Learning Community.

How were the preceding three components of the BEVI group profile used with the Madison International Learning Community? After reviewing the background characteristics of the group (e.g., highlighting areas of similarity and difference, from Figure 12.18), the bulk of this session focused on explaining and discussing the results from the Aggregate Profile and Decile Profile. To highlight a number of these scales, and among other findings that might be emphasized, note overall that the group as a whole (from the Aggregate Profile in Figure 12.19):

- Reported relatively positive life histories (e.g., low Negative Life Events, Needs Closure)
- Is quite open to basic thoughts/feelings that characterize the typical experience for most human beings (e.g., low Basic Closedness)

Beliefs, Events, and Values Inventory

You and Your Worldview

A Personal Report from the
Beliefs, Events, and Values Inventory (BEVI)™

User: 9389488   Date of Test: 8/29/2012

The Beliefs. Events, and Values Inventory (BEVI) is designed to help people gain greater awareness of their own beliefs and values. The BEVI also examines how beliefs and values may influence learning, personal growth, relationships, group or organizational processes, and the pursuit of life goals. In addressing these issues, this report contains information about how you see yourself, others, and the larger world. However, because the BEVI takes no position at all on whether the answers you provided are right, wrong, true, or false, neither does this report make any such claims. Instead, this report is designed to promote reflection about issues in life that often are relevant to us all. If you have any questions about the BEVI, please contact the BEVI administrator at your college, university, or study abroad provider. You also may contact us directly at ibavi@ibavi.org. Before reading the following report, you must agree to the three conditions below either by clicking the Agree button or by signing a separate agreement form that will be provided to you prior to reading the report:

1. You (9389488) voluntarily completed the BEVI and subsequently requested this follow up report, which you are reading voluntarily (i.e., you agree that no person, group, organization, or entity is requiring you to read this report).

2. Every effort has been made to communicate information from the BEVI in a way that is helpful and constructive. However, if you experience distress upon reading this report, you agree to contact the BEVI administrator in your organization, the coordinator of a BEVI feedback session, and/or a health or mental health care provider.

3. You are free to keep a copy of this report for yourself. However, because the BEVI and this report are copyrighted, you agree not to photocopy this report or distribute it (electronically or otherwise) to anyone else.

Introduction

Pick up a newspaper or turn on a radio or television anywhere in the world and one fact becomes immediately clear: beliefs and values are integral to the human experience. People have strong opinions about topics from politics, religion, education and the arts, to marriage, family, gender, and sexuality. However, whether a specific belief is "right" or "wrong" is arguably less important than understanding the complex interaction among thoughts, feelings, behavior, life history, and context that results in...

FIGURE 12.17. Sample introductory page from the BEVI individual report.

- Demonstrates a moderate degree of attributional complexity regarding why human beings do what they do and why events in the world happen as they do (e.g., moderate Basic Determinism)
- Evidences a moderate degree of religiosity (e.g., moderate Socioreligious Traditionalism)

Beliefs, Events, and Values Inventory

BEVI Group Report

Madison International

N = 22

Background

Ethnic Group

Black and White	4.55%
Black/African-American	13.64%
Hispanic/Latino	9.09%
Scandinavian	4.55%
White	68.18%

Gender

Female 63.64%

Male   36.36%

Political Orientation

Democrat	31.82%
Independent	31.82%
Philosophical Anarchist	4.55%
Republican	27.27%
Social Democrat (mostly Democratic)	4.55%

FIGURE 12.18. **Introductory excerpt from the background information section of the group report for the Madison International Learning Community.**

- Is highly self and emotionally aware (e.g., high Emotional Attunement, Self Awareness)
- Appears to possess a high capacity to experience self and others in shades of gray rather than in dichotomous terms (e.g., high Socioemotional Convergence)
- Is very open to cultural beliefs and practices that are different from their own (e.g., high Sociocultural Openness)
- Is concerned about the environment and natural world (e.g., high Ecological Resonance)
- Is deeply interested in making a difference in the world (e.g., high Global Engagement)

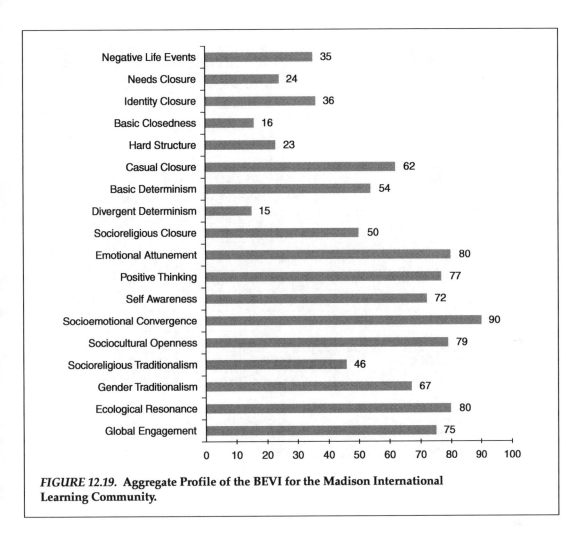

FIGURE 12.19. **Aggregate Profile of the BEVI for the Madison International Learning Community.**

In many ways, such a profile would perhaps be consistent with a group of individuals who have self-selected to be part of an international living and learning community. However, as noted throughout this chapter, it is very important to go beyond aggregated results in order to understand areas of difference and similarity within the group as a whole. To do so, let us focus on one of the BEVI scales, Socioreligious Traditionalism, from the Decile Profile (Figure 12.20), particularly because this scale promoted a great deal of reflection and discussion by community members. As illustrated in Figure 12.21, note first the extraordinary dispersion by the group across this specific scale from Decile Profile.

In particular, approximately 50% of the learning community falls between the 1st and 40th percentile of the scale, whereas the remaining 50% falls between the 70th and 100th percentile (no respondents fall between the 41st and 69th percentile). Note further that approximately one-quarter of the community occupies the lowest 10th percentile on this scale (i.e., is essentially disavowing religion and religious belief). The presentation of this finding sparked a great deal of dialogue by the group. From a thematic perspective, the group seemed fascinated by the

Deciles:	1	2	3	4	5	6	7	8	9	10
1. Negative Life Events	18%	14%	23%	5%	9%	0%	14%	9%	5%	5%
2. Needs Closure	23%	14%	23%	18%	23%	0%	0%	0%	0%	0%
3. Identity Closure	23%	5%	5%	23%	36%	5%	0%	0%	0%	5%
4. Basic Closedness	45%	9%	5%	23%	14%	5%	0%	0%	0%	0%
5. Hard Structure	32%	18%	5%	9%	18%	0%	9%	5%	5%	0%
6. Casual Closure	9%	0%	18%	0%	5%	27%	14%	0%	9%	18%
7. Basic Determinism	5%	9%	18%	14%	9%	9%	18%	0%	5%	14%
8. Divergent Determinism	32%	18%	32%	5%	5%	5%	0%	0%	0%	5%
9. Socioreligious Closure	18%	5%	9%	5%	5%	18%	5%	9%	23%	5%
10. Emotional Attunement	0%	0%	5%	0%	5%	14%	5%	18%	27%	27%
11. Positive Thinking	5%	0%	9%	9%	9%	9%	9%	9%	14%	27%
12. Self Awareness	14%	9%	0%	9%	5%	5%	0%	9%	14%	36%
13. Socioemotional Convergence	0%	0%	0%	0%	0%	5%	9%	18%	27%	41%
14. Sociocultural Openness	0%	0%	0%	0%	0%	14%	14%	23%	32%	18%
15. Socioreligious Traditionalism	23%	5%	9%	14%	0%	0%	0%	32%	9%	9%
16. Gender Traditionalism	5%	5%	9%	0%	14%	9%	9%	14%	23%	14%
17. Ecological Resonance	0%	0%	0%	0%	5%	27%	9%	14%	14%	32%
18. Global Engagement	5%	9%	0%	14%	5%	5%	14%	9%	18%	23%

FIGURE 12.20. **Decile Profile of the BEVI for the Madison International Learning Community.**

fact that such profound differences existed among individual members. They also discussed larger issues, such as the purpose of existence, where beliefs and values come from, and why such questions should—or should not—matter to us as individuals and as a society. In short, the juxtaposition of individual and group reports offers a model for how the individual learner may have a private encounter with "self" regarding one's own worldview, to be followed by a skillfully facilitated dialogue on how the larger group sees self, others, and the larger world. Such a process may well promote a great deal of learning, growth, and development in a manner that is consistent with larger course, program, and institutional goals (Iyer, 2013).

15. Socioreligious Traditionalism	23%	5%	9%	14%	0%	0%	0%	32%	9%	9%

FIGURE 12.21. **The Socioreligious Traditionalism scale from the Decile Profile for the Madison International Learning Community.**

Implication 14. Changes in Beliefs and Values About Self, Others, and the World at Large Appear Determined Largely by the 7Ds (Duration, Difference, Depth, Determine, Design, Deliver, Debrief)

The odds of facilitating effective learning, development, and growth opportunities are enhanced considerably by attending to the 7Ds before, during, and after a learning intervention is developed, implemented, evaluated, and refined.

As noted throughout this chapter, to understand and assess the processes and outcomes of international, multicultural, and transformative learning, it is crucial to both measure and account for the impact of within-group differences on the learning processes and outcomes we observe.

Specifically, the "7Ds" (Shealy, 2016) include the following variables:

1. **Duration** (i.e., how long an international, multicultural, or transformative education experience occurs)
2. **Difference** (i.e., how different the experience is from what the "self" of the experiencer is accustomed)
3. **Depth** (i.e., what the capacity of the learner is to experience all that the intervention is able to convey)
4. **Determine** (i.e., through formal and informal assessment, how well the intervener understands his or her audience)
5. **Design** (i.e., based upon knowledge of the audience and careful deliberation and development, what the quality of the intervention is)
6. **Deliver** (i.e., how well the intervener can fulfill the transformative potential of the intervention)
7. **Debrief** (i.e., before, during, and after the intervention, how deeply the intervener assesses the nature of the learning experience, and uses such feedback to improve planned, current, and future interventions)

Although the 7Ds are based upon a combination of data-driven findings and best practice recommendations, future research could examine specific aspects of each in greater detail. For example, it would be possible to evaluate empirically how a relative understanding of one's audience is associated both with various characteristics of the audience (e.g., from BEVI group scores) as well as differences in learning outcomes (e.g., to what degree congruency between the intervener and the audience is consistent with better learning outcomes, such as higher grades or greater satisfaction). In short, the 7Ds are offered as data/practice-based hypotheses that may help in the generation of specific questions that are worthy of further investigation.

Implication 15. Best Practice in Assessment Requires Best Practice in Research

By attending to data-based findings regarding the mediators and moderators of teaching, training, and learning—and adopting mixed methods approaches to assessment that account for the complexity of the variables at hand—we are much better able to plan for, implement, and evaluate the effectiveness of our interventions. Ultimately, our goals are to: (a) understand the complex interactions between teachers, trainers, and learners as well as the complex processes and outcomes of learning, growth, and development, and (b) use such information to enhance the quality and impact of teaching, training, and learning in the real world.

This fifteenth and final implication really is a take-home message from the entire Forum BEVI Project. As envisioned in the original charge to the working group, we knew that our ability to hone in on very complex and interacting processes of learning, growth, and development would require exquisite attention to myriad issues over a sustained period of time. Several of these "lessons learned" were codified in a symposium delivered at the Association for International Education Administrators (AIEA) in the fourth year of this project (Gerber et al., 2011), which sought to summarize best practice recommendations from four big picture assessment initiatives, including the Forum BEVI Project. These include the following six recommendations:

1. **Assess Deeply** (e.g., encourage innovation; integrate mixed methods; strive for ecological validity; evaluate interactions, mediators, and levels of analysis)
2. **Address Challenges** (e.g., political, time, economic; science/humanities split; not knowing what one does not know)
3. **Secure Support** (e.g., institutional/organizational; develop functional team; identify and pool resources)
4. **Ensure Expertise** (e.g., theory/data link; research design; psychometrics; statistical)
5. **Develop Plan** (e.g., specify assessment goals and outcomes; select measures; assign roles and responsibilities; monitor/correct processes)
6. **Value Collaboration** (e.g., recognize team talents; appraise/meet local needs; facilitate buy-in; solicit input/feedback)

From our perspective, these six recommendations provide a sense of what is necessary to design, implement, and evaluate a multisite, multiyear assessment project in a manner that is more likely than not to generate outcomes of substance and impact. More than anything, beyond the letter of such recommendations, their spirit requires the cultivation of patience, kindness, and humor. That is because the one constant we encountered throughout was change—at the level of direction, approach, method, interpretation, partners, technique, administration, analyses, logistics, and so forth. Thus, there can be no substitute for relying on relational connections and good will toward one another, established through countless phone calls, emails, meetings, and presentations, over many years of collaborative work together.

Forum BEVI Project: Summary and Conclusion

We began this chapter by offering a big picture perspective regarding the *what* and *why* of internationalization within the field of higher education. We turned then to an overview of contemporary efforts in the assessment of international, multicultural, and transformative learning. We next observed that the complex variables that mediate and moderate global learning outcomes still await precise identification. In particular, it behooves scholars, educators, and administrators to recognize and account for the profound and underlying human complexities—affective, behavioral, cognitive, contextual, cultural, developmental, and historical—that interact with a particular international, multicultural, and transformative learning experience to produce the processes and outcomes that we ultimately observe. We then described the partnership formed in 2007 between the Forum on Education Abroad and IBAVI, summarizing the goals and activities of the Forum BEVI Project Working Group. We provided a brief overview of the BEVI and its Equilintegration or EI theoretical framework. We presented specific applications of the BEVI throughout this initiative, and then provided an overview of the analyses and sample characteristics that informed our work. Finally, we discussed the 15 implications in detail.

We recognize fully that the preceding discussion is, to say the least, comprehensive and intensive, which befits a 6-year initiative involving multiple institutions and organizations as well as hundreds of analyses and thousands of participants. Ultimately, it is our hope that this project and its 15 implications contribute, first, to a deeper understanding of the complex interactions and fascinating processes that are associated with who learns what and why, and under what circumstances as well as, second, greater appreciation for the demonstrable fact that such complexities can, and must, be assessed with depth, persistence, and rigor. In this regard, throughout our work, it has been heartening to experience our collective sophistication grow—theoretically, methodologically, empirically, and in applied terms—with attendant and constructive impacts upon a range of programs, courses, activities, and processes in the real world. From our perspective, the *sine qua non* of such work has been realized in the "aha" moments we all have shared. Formerly abstruse dynamics suddenly have been illuminated when we observe, for example, that conflicts or issues in a group actually are revealed via a bimodal distribution on specific scales, which indicate vast differences—or remarkable similarities—among cohort members in how and why they experience self, others, and the larger world as they do, with concomitant implications for group relations and learning processes over the short and long term. Likewise, we no longer get many questions like, "Why are you asking about life events?" as we have shown and learned together that the perception of one's own life history may change, often substantially, following exposure to cultures and contexts that are significantly different from one's own. In short, it seems increasingly to be understood—on the basis of theoretical framing, empirical data, and real world interventions—that who we are prior to a learning experience must be taken into account if we are to understand how and why the "7Ds" interact to produce the learning processes or outcomes that we do or do not observe, including (but not limited to) (a) the learning experiences we create and deliver; (b) what people bring to the learning experience based upon their life histories and worldviews; (c) how we are built and what we need as human beings; and (d) the ubiquitous interactions among these and related levels of analysis. Such findings seem well illuminated by the EI framework—that we inexorably are built to create a "version of reality" in the service of our core needs, the formative variables that shape and define us, and the subsequent beliefs and values that we call our own—which further influence how and why we experience self, others, and the larger world as we do (e.g., Shealy, 2016; Shealy et al., 2012).

As scholars, educators, professional staff, and administrators, we now have a better basis for understanding how our work interacts with the lives and worldviews of those who come before us seeking to learn, grow, and change, even if they—and we—may not apprehend yet what the implications are for them, and us, of engaging in these immersion processes so closely together. The fact that we co-create meaning through our shared lives and experiences is a substantive conclusion of this project that warrants further exploration, as we seek to hone in that much more on the interactions that ultimately are associated with who learns what and why, and under what circumstances (e.g., Cultivating the Globally Sustainable Self, 2015). In short, we must take our responsibilities very seriously, not only because that's "the right thing to do," but because abundant evidence from this project suggests that we may differ substantially in our capacity and inclination to carry out these important obligations as facilitators of learning, growth, and development. From our perspective, such an empirical reality is not, and should not be, an impetus for anxiety or doubt, but rather an opportunity to engage in a deeper exploration of how we may better fulfill our potential as educators, program developers, administrators, and scholars. Just as we expect our students to learn and grow, findings from this project indicate that we can and should expect no less of ourselves, even as we pursue these means and ends with a steadfast appreciation that we never are "done" vis-à-vis our own personal and professional development.

In the final analysis, what has been most gratifying for all of us over the years is to hear so often that what we have been trying to understand and explicate through this initiative has in fact been impactful, meaningful, and relevant. Through our work, we have come to see more clearly that we are—ineluctably—*change agents* who are granted the privilege of transforming the learners who enter our educational institutions and organizations, and are in turn, transformed ourselves. Since we are charged to be agents of change by the next generation of citizens—and compelled by the pressing needs and opportunities of our increasingly interdependent world—it behooves us to answer this call in a manner that is optimally informed and maximally effective. Hopefully, the implications emerging from this project, combined with ongoing collaborative research and practice in multiple local and global settings,[21] will help us all assess international, multicultural, and transformative learning—and apply our insights and understandings—with care, capacity, and commitment in the months and years ahead.

REFERENCES

American Council on the Teaching of Foreign Languages (ACTFL). (2012). *ACTFL Proficiency guidelines 2012*. Retrieved from http://www.actfl.org/sites/default/files/pdfs/public/ACTFLProficiencyGuidelines2012_FINAL.pdf

Arum, R., & Roksa, J. (2011). *Academically adrift: Limited learning on college campuses*. Chicago, IL: University of Chicago Press.

Association of American Colleges and Universities (AAC&U). (2007). *College learning for the new global century: A report from the national leadership council for liberal education and America's promise*. Retrieved from www.aacu.org/leap/documents/GlobalCentury_final.pdf

Association of Commonwealth Universities. (2012). *Research management benchmarking programme*. Retrieved from https://www.acu.ac.uk/focus-areas/research-management-uptake/research-management-benchmarking-programme/

Atwood, K., Chkhaidze, N., Shealy, C. N., Staton, R., & Sternberger, L. G. (2014, August). *Transformation of self: Implications from the Forum BEVI Project*. Poster presented at the annual meeting of the American Psychological Association, Washington, DC.

Bennett, M. J. (1986). A developmental approach to training intercultural sensitivity. In J. Martin (Ed.), Special issue on intercultural training. *International Journal of Intercultural Relations, 10*(2), 179–186.

Bennett, M. J. (1993). Towards ethnorelativism: A developmental model of intercultural sensitivity (revised). In R. M. Paige (Ed.), *Education for the intercultural experience* (pp. 21–71). Yarmouth, ME: Intercultural Press.

Bennett, M. J., & Hammer, M. R. (2002). *The intercultural development inventory*. Portland, OR: The IDI Corporation.

---

[21] Allied scholarship is examined further in Cultivating the Globally Sustainable Self, a 3-year summit series on transformative teaching, training, and learning in research and practice, which began in March of 2015 (see www.jmu.edu/summitseries).

Bhawuk, D. P. S., & Brislin, R. (1992). The measurement of intercultural sensitivity using the concepts of individualism and collectivism. *International Journal of Intercultural Relations, 16*(4), 413–436.

Blair, S., Latz, G., Sternberger, L. G., & Shealy, C. N. (February, 2014). *Assessing global learning: Leadership practices and imperatives for the 21st century academy*. Workshop presented at the annual conference of the Association of International Education Administrators, Washington, DC.

Braskamp, L. A., Braskamp, D. C., Merrill, K. C., & Engberg, M. E. (2010). *Global Perspective Inventory (GPI)*. Retrieved from https://gpi.central.edu

Braskamp, L. A., Blair, S., Shealy, C. N., & Hammer, M. R. (2012). *Which tool does what? Aligning assessment tools to Forum standards*. Retrieved from http://apps.forumea.org/documents/Forum-Denver-2012--WhichToolDoesWhat--Introduction--S.Blair.pdf

Braskamp, L. A., & Engberg, M. E. (2014). *Guidelines for judging the effectiveness of assessing student learning*. Chicago, IL: University of Chicago Press.

Brearly, T., Shealy, C. N., Staton, R., & Sternberger, L. G. (2012, August). *Prejudice and religious and non-religious certitude: An empirical analysis from the Forum BEVI Project*. Poster presented at the annual meeting of the American Psychological Association, Orlando, FL.

Chang, W., Yuan, Y., & Chuang, Y. (2013). The relationship between international experience and cross-cultural adaptability. *International Journal of Intercultural Relations, 37*(2), 268–273.

Chen, G. M., & Starosta, W. J. (2000a). The development and validation of the international communication sensitivity scale. *Human Communication, 3*(1), 2–14.

Chen, G. M., & Starosta, W. J. (2000b). Intercultural sensitivity. In L. A. Samovar & R. E. Porter (Eds.), *Intercultural communication: A reader* (pp. 406–413). Belmont, CA: Wadsworth Publishing Company.

Church, A. T. (1982). Sojourner adjustment. *Psychological Bulletin, 91*(3), 540–572.

Clarke, I., Flaherty, T., Wright, N. D., & McMillen, R. M. (2009). Student intercultural proficiency from study abroad programs. *Journal of Marketing Education, 31*(2), 173–181.

Coates, M., Hanson, W., Samuel, D. B., Webster, M., & Cozen, J. (2016). The Beliefs, Events, and Values Inventory (BEVI). Psychological assessment implications and applications. In C. N. Shealy (Ed.), *Making sense of beliefs and values* (pp. 371–406). New York, NY: Springer Publishing.

Corbitt, J. N. (2011). *Global awareness*. Retrieved from http://www.globalawarenessprofile.com/blog/

Coryell, J. E., Durodoye, B. A., Wright, R. R., Pate, P. E., & Nguyen, S. (2012). Case studies of internationalization in adult and higher education: Inside the processes of four universities in the United States and the United Kingdom. *Journal of Studies in International Education, 16*(1), 75–98.

Cottrell, S. (2005) *Critical thinking skills*. USA: Palgrave Macmillan.

Cozen, J., Hanson, W., Poston, J., Jones, S., & Tabit, M. (2016). The Beliefs, Events, and Values Inventory (BEVI): Implications and applications for therapeutic assessment and intervention. In C. N. Shealy (Ed.), *Making sense of beliefs and values* (pp. 575–621). New York, NY: Springer Publishing.

Creswell, J. W., & Plano-Clark, V. L. (2007). *Designing and conducting mixed methods research*. Thousand Oaks, CA: SAGE Publications, Inc.

Cultivating the Globally Sustainable Self. (2015, March). Retrieved from www.jmu.edu/summitseries

Deardorff, D. K (2006). Identification and assessment of intercultural competence as a student outcome of internationalization. *Journal of Studies in International Education, 10*(3), 241–266.

Deardorff, D. K., & Van Gaalen, A. (2012). Outcomes assessment in the internationalization of higher education. In D. K. Deardorff, H. de Wit, J. D. Heyl, & T. Adams (Eds.), *The SAGE handbook of international higher education* (pp. 167–189). Thousand Oaks, CA: SAGE Publications, Inc.

Der-Karabetian, A. (1992). World-mindedness and the nuclear threat: A multinational study. *Journal of Social Behavior and Personality, 7*(2), 293–308.

Der-Karabetian, A., & Metzer, J. (1993). The Cross-cultural world-mindedness scale and political party affiliation. *Psychological Reports, 72*(3), 1069–1070.

De Wit, H., & Merkx, G. (2012). The history of internationalization of higher education. In D. K. Deardorff, H. de Wit, J. D. Heyl, & T. Adams (Eds.), *The SAGE handbook of international higher education* (pp. 43–57). Thousand Oaks, CA: SAGE Publications, Inc.

Doyle, D. (Fall 2009). Holistic assessment and the study abroad experience. *Frontiers: The Interdisciplinary Journal of Study Abroad, XVIII*, 143–156.

Duru, E., & Poyrazli, S. (2007). Personality dimensions, psychosocial-demographic variables, and English language competency in predicting level of acculturative stress among Turkish international students. *International Journal of Stress Management, 14*(1), 99–110.

Ellis, I. E., Lee, J. M., & Wiley, L. P. (2009). Educator dispositions: A survey of U.S. teacher education programs. *Southeastern Teacher Education Journal, 2*(3), 77–86.

Ennis, R. (1962). A concept of critical thinking. *Harvard Educational Review, 32*(1), 81–111.

Ethics of International Engagement and Service-Learning Project. (2011). *The EIESL project web-based guidebook.* Retrieved from http://ethicsofisl.ubc.ca

Fantini, A. E. (2000). A central concern: Developing intercultural competence. In A. E. Fantini (Ed.), *SIT occasional paper series* (pp. 23–42). Brattleboro, VT: Federation of the Experiment in International Living. Retrieved from http://www.adam-europe.eu/prj/2935/prd/8/1/develop-I-com.pdf

Fantini, A. E. (2006). *Assessment tools of intercultural communicative competence.* Brattleboro, VT: Federation of the Experiment in International Living. Retrieved from http://federationeil.org/documents/AppendixF.pdf

Fantini, A. E. (2009). Assessing intercultural competence. In D. K. Deardorff (Ed.), *The SAGE handbook of intercultural competence* (pp. 456–476). Thousand Oaks, CA: SAGE Publications, Inc.

Fisher, A., & Scriven, M. (1997). *Critical thinking. Its definition and assessment.* Inverness, CA: Edgepress.

Forum on Education Abroad. (2005). *A baseline survey of curriculum integration in education abroad.* Northampton, MA: Author.

Forum on Education Abroad. (2007). *A guide to outcomes assessment in education abroad.* Retrieved from https://www.forumea.org/resources/outcomes/guide

Forum on Education Abroad. (2015). *Forum-BEVI Project.* Retrieved from http://www.forumea.org/research-bevi-project.cfm

Geisinger, K. F. (Ed.). (2013). *APA handbook of testing and assessment in psychology* (Vol.1). Washington, DC: American Psychological Association.

Gerber, T. P., Gottlieb, E. E., Pysarchik, D. T., & Shealy, C. N. (2011). *International program evaluation: The power of collaboration.* Symposium presented at the annual meeting of the Association of International Education Administrators, San Francisco, CA.

Green, M. (2013, November/December). Acting as global citizens: A challenge to U.S. colleges and universities. *International Educator, 22*(6), 52–55.

Halpern, D. F. (1998). Teaching critical thinking for transfer across domains. Dispositions, skills, structure training, and metacognitive monitoring. *American Psychologist, 53*(4), 449–455.

Hammer, M. R., Bennett, M. J, & Wiseman, R. (2003). Measuring intercultural sensitivity: The Intercultural Development Inventory. *International Journal of Intercultural Relations, 27*(4), 421–443.

Hammer, M. R. (2012). *The Intercultural Development Inventory (IDI): Making intercultural competence development a reality.* Paper presented at the 8th annual conference of the Forum on Education Abroad, Denver, CO.

Hanson, W. E., Leighton, J. P., Donaldson, S. I., Terjesen, M., & Shealy, C. N. (in press). Assessment: From psychological testing and program evaluation to feedback, intervention, and positive worldwide change. In C. N. Shealy & M. Bullock (Eds.), *Going global: How psychology and psychologists can meet a world of need.* Washington, DC: American Psychological Association.

Harkness, J. (2003). Questionnaire translation. In J. Harkness, F. Van de Vijer, & P. Moher (Eds.), *Cross-cultural survey methods* (pp. 35–56). Hoboken, NJ: John Wiley & Sons, Inc.

Hayes, D. J., Shealy, C. N., Sivo, S. A., & Weinstein, Z. C. (1999). *Psychology, religion, and scale 5 (religious traditionalism) of the "BEVI."* Poster session presented at the meeting of the American Psychological Association, Boston, MA.

Hett, E. J. (1993). *The development of an instrument to measure global-mindedness* (Doctoral dissertation). University of San Diego, San Diego, CA.

Hill, C., Johnson, M., Brinton, C., Staton, R., Sternberger, L., & Shealy (2013, August). *The etiology of economic beliefs and values: Implications and applications from the Forum BEVI Project.* Poster presented at the annual meeting of the American Psychological Association, Honolulu, HI.

Hu, C., Pazaki, H., & Velander, E. (2014). Evaluating global education at a regional university: A focus group research on faculty perspectives. *Theory in Action, 7*(1), 65–78.

Inglehart, R., Basáñez, M., Díez-Medrano, J., Halman, L., & Luijkx, R. (2004). *Human beliefs and values: A cross-cultural sourcebook based on the 1999–2002 values surveys.* Mexico: Siglo XXI Editores.

Inglehart, R., Basáñez M., & Moreno, A. (1998). *Human values and beliefs: A cross-cultural sourcebook.* Ann Arbor, MI: The University of Michigan Press.

Institute of International Education. (2014). *Open doors data report.* Retrieved from http://www.iie.org/Research-and-Publications/Open-Doors/Data

Interstate New Teacher Assessment and Support Consortium (InTASC). (2011). *Model core teaching standards: A resource for state dialogue.* Retrieved from http://www.ccsso.org/documents/2011/intasc_model_core_teaching_standards_2011.pdf

Interagency Language Roundtable. (2011). *ILR proficiency levels.* Retrieved from http://www.govtilr.org/skills/ILRscale1.htm

International Association of Universities, (2010). *Internationalization of higher education: Global trends, regional perspectives. IAU 3rd Global Survey Report.* Paris, France: International Association of Universities.

Isley, E. B., Shealy, C. N., Crandall, K. S., Sivo, S. A., & Reifsteck, J. B. (1999). *Relevance of the "BEVI" for research in developmental psychopathology.* Poster session presented at the meeting of the American Psychological Association, Boston, MA.

Iyer, C. (2013). *Assessing and engaging beliefs and values in a learning community of U.S. and international students: Implications and applications from the Forum BEVI Project.* (Unpublished doctoral dissertation). James Madison University, Harrisonburg, VA.

Kehl, K., & Morris, J. (2007). Differences in global-mindedness between short-term and semester-long study abroad participants at selected private universities. *Frontiers: The Interdisciplinary Journal of Study Abroad, XV,* 67–80.

Kelley, C., & Meyers, J. (1995). *The cross-cultural adaptability inventory.* Minneapolis, MN: National Computer Systems.

Kline, R. B. (2010) *Principles and practice of structural equation modeling* (3rd ed.). New York, NY: Guilford Press.

Knight, J. (2006). *Internationalization of higher education: New directions, new challenges. Global survey report.* Paris, France: International Association of Universities.

Knight, J. (2011). Five myths about internationalization. *International Higher Education, 62,* 14–15.

Kohls, L. R. (2001). *Survival kit for overseas living* (4th ed.). Yarmouth, ME: Intercultural Press.

Koskinen, L., & Tossavainen, K. (2003). Relationships with undergraduate nursing exchange students: A tutor perspective. *Journal of Advanced Nursing, 41*(5), 499–508.

Kuh, G. D. (2008). *High-impact educational practices: What they are, who has access to them, and why they matter.* Retrieved from https://www.aacu.org/leap/hip.cfm

Lerner, J. (2003). *Learning disabilities: Theories, diagnosis, and teaching practices.* Boston, MA: Houghton Mifflin Company.

Lewin, K. (1951). *Field theory in social science: Selected theoretical papers.* D. Cartwright (Ed.). New York, NY: Harper Brothers Publishers.

Little, D. (2002). The European language portfolio: Structure, origins, implementation and challenges. *Language Teaching, 35*(3), 182–189.

Manaloa, E., Kusumib, T., Koyasub, M., Michitac, Y., & Waseda, Y. (2013). To what extent do culture-related factors influence university students' critical thinking use? *Thinking Skills and Creativity, 10*, 121–132.

Marmolejo, F. (2011). *The future of higher-education internationalization.* Retrieved from http://chronicle.com/blogs/worldwise/defining-internationalization/28615

Moghaddam, F. M., Harre, R., & Lee, N. (2007). *Global conflict resolution through positioning analysis.* New York, NY: Springer Publishing.

NAFSA. (2008). *Accessing best practices in international education.* Retrieved from http://www.nafsa.org/resourcelibrary/default.aspx?id=18067

Netherlands' Organization for International Cooperation in Higher Education. (2012). *Mapping Internationalization (MINT) project.* Retrieved from https://www.nuffic.nl/en/expertise/quality-assurance-and-internationalisation/mapping-internationalisation-mint/background-information

O'Meara, P., Mehlinger, H. D., & Newman, R. M. (2001). *Changing perspectives on international education.* Bloomington, IN: Indiana University Press.

Patel, R. (2008). *Environmental beliefs, values, and worldviews: Etiology, maintenance, and transformation* (Doctoral dissertation). James Madison University, Harrisonburg, VA.

Patel, R., Shealy, C. N., & De Michele, P. (2007, August). *Environmental beliefs and values: Etiology, maintenance, and transformation.* Poster session presented at the annual meeting of the American Psychological Association, San Francisco, CA.

Paul, R., & Elder, L. (2006). *The miniature guide to critical thinking: Concepts and tools.* Dilion Beach, CA: Foundation for critical thinking. Retrieved from http://www.criticalthinking.org/files/Concepts_Tools.pdf

Poole, D., & Davis, T. (2006). Concept mapping to measure outcomes in study abroad programs. *Social Work Education, 25*(1), 66–77.

Pysarchik, D. T., Shealy, C. N., & Whalen, B. (2007a, February). *Antecedents to outcomes-based international learning: A new psychometric assessment approach.* Paper presented at the annual meeting of the Association of International Education Administrators, Washington, DC.

Pysarchik, D. T., Shealy, C. N., & Whalen, B. (2007b, April). *Antecedents to outcomes-based international learning: A new psychometric assessment approach.* Symposium presented at the Undergraduate Assessment Symposium, North Carolina State University, Cary, NC.

Ramirez, G. B. (2013). Learning abroad or just going abroad? International education in opposite sides of the border. *The Qualitative Report, 18*(62), 1–11.

Reisweber, J. R. (2008). *Beliefs, values, and the development of intercultural awareness* (Doctoral dissertation). James Madison University, Harrisonburg, VA.

Rexeisen, R. J. (2012). Study abroad and the boomerang effect: The end is only the beginning. *Frontiers: The Interdisciplinary Journal of Study Abroad, XXII*, 166–181.

Rexeisen, R. J., Anderson, P. H., Lawton, L., & Hubbard, A. C. (2008). Study abroad and intercultural development: A longitudinal study. *Frontiers: The Interdisciplinary Journal of Study Abroad, XVII*, 1–20.

Robinson, J. P., Shaver, P. R., & Wrightsman, L. S. (Eds.). (1991). *Measures of personality and social psychological attitudes.* San Diego, CA: Academic Press.

Robinson, J. P., Shaver, P. R., & Wrightsman, L. S. (Eds.). (1999). *Measures of political attitudes.* San Diego, CA: Academic Press.

Salisbury, M. H. (2011). *The effect of study abroad on intercultural competence among undergraduate college students.* (Unpublished doctoral dissertation). University of Iowa, Iowa City, IA. Retrieved from http://ir.uiowa.edu/etd/1073/

Sampson, D. L., & Smith, H. P. (1957). A scale to measure world-minded attitudes. *The Journal of Social Psychology, 45*(1), 99–106.

Scarino, A. (2010). Assessing intercultural capability in learning languages: A renewed understanding of language, culture, learning, and the nature of assessment. *The Modern Language Journal, 94*(2), 324–329.

Schmid, J., & Leiman, J. N. (1957). The development of hierarchical factor solutions. *Psychometrika, 22*, 53–61.

Scriven, M., & Paul, R. (1987). *Defining critical thinking.* Retrieved from https://www.criticalthinking.org/pages/defining-critical-thinking/766

Shaftel, J., & Shaftel, T. L. (2010). Measuring intercultural attitudes of undergraduates who study abroad. *International Psychology Bulletin, 14*(1), 12–15.

Shealy, C. N. (2000a, July). *The Beliefs, Events, and Values Inventory (BEVI): Implications for cross-cultural research and practice.* Paper presented at the meeting of the International Congress of Psychology, Stockholm, Sweden.

Shealy, C. N. (2000b, July). *The Beliefs, Events, and Values Inventory (BEVI): Implications for research and theory in social psychology.* Paper presented at the meeting of the International Congress of Psychology, Stockholm, Sweden.

Shealy, C. N. (2004). A model and method for "making" a C-I psychologist: Equilintegration (EI) theory and the Beliefs, Events, and Values Inventory (BEVI). [Special Series]. *Journal of Clinical Psychology, 60*(10), 1065–1090.

Shealy, C. N. (2005). Justifying the justification hypothesis: Scientific-humanism, Equilintegration (EI) theory, and the Beliefs, Events, and Values Inventory (BEVI). [Special Series]. *Journal of Clinical Psychology, 61*(1), 81–106.

Shealy, C. N. (2010). *Beliefs, Events, and Values Inventory.* Retrieved September 9, 2012 from http://www.thebevi.com/

Shealy, C. N. (2012) *The Forum BEVI Project: Results, applications, and alignments with the Forum Standards of Good Practice.* Paper presented at the 8th Annual Conference of the Forum on Education Abroad, Denver, CO.

Shealy, C. N. (2014). *Assessing global learning: Implications from the Forum BEVI Project.* Workshop presented at the annual meeting of the Association of International Education Administrators, Washington, DC.

Shealy, C. N. (2015). *The Beliefs, Events, and Values Inventory (BEVI): Overview, implications, and guidelines. Test manual.* Harrisonburg, VA: Author.

Shealy, C. N. (Ed.). (2016). *Making sense of beliefs and values.* New York, NY: Springer Publishing.

Shealy, C. N., Bhuyan, D., & Sternberger, L. G. (2012). Cultivating the capacity to care in children and youth: Implications from EI theory, EI self, and BEVI. In U. S. Nayar (Ed.), *Child and adolescent mental health* (pp. 240–255). Thousand Oaks, CA: SAGE Publications, Inc.

Siaya, L., & Hayward, F. M. (2003). *Mapping internationalization on U.S. campuses.* Washington, DC: American Council on Education.

Stebleton, M. J., Soria, K. M., & Cherney, B. T. (2013). The high impact of education abroad: College students' engagement in international experiences and the development of intercultural competencies. *Frontiers: The Interdisciplinary Journal of Study Abroad, XXII,* 1–24.

Sternberger, L., La Brack, B., & Whalen, B. (2007). How to begin: Key decision points in the assessment process. In M. Bolen (Ed.), *A guide to assessment for international education* (pp. 71–87). Carlisle, PA: Forum on Education Abroad.

Sternberger, L., Pysarchik, D. T., Yun, Z. S., & Deardorff, D. K. (2009). Designing a model for international learning assessment. *Diversity & Democracy, 12*(1), 7–9.

Sutton, R. C., & Rubin, D. L. (2004). The GLOSSARI Project: Initial findings from a system-wide research initiative on study abroad learning outcomes. *Frontiers: The Interdisciplinary Journal of Study Abroad, X,* 65–82.

Tabit, M. B., Cozen, J., Dyjak, K., Pendleton, C., Shealy, C. N., Sternberger, L. G., & Staton, R. (2011, August). *Sociocultural impact of denial: Empirical evidence from the Forum BEVI Project.* Poster presented at the annual meeting of the American Psychological Association.

Tabit, M., Legault, L., Ma, W., & Wan, P. (2016). In search of best practices for multicultural education: Empirical evidence from the Forum BEVI Project. In C. N. Shealy (Ed.), *Making sense of beliefs and values* (pp. 175–204). New York, NY: Springer Publishing.

Tarrant, M. A., Rubin, D. L., & Stoner, L. (2013). The added value of study abroad: Fostering a global citizenry. *Journal of Studies in International Education, XX*(X), 1–21.

Teddlie, C., & Tashakkori, A. (2009). *Foundations of mixed methods research: Integrating quantitative and qualitative approaches in the social and behavioral sciences.* Thousand Oaks, CA: SAGE Publications, Inc.

Vande Berg, M., Connor-Linton, J., & Paige, M. R. (2009). The Georgetown Consortium Project: Interventions for student learning abroad. *Frontiers: The Interdisciplinary Journal of Study Abroad, XVIII,* 1–75.

Van der Zee, K. I., & Van Oudenhoven, J. P. (2000). The multicultural personality questionnaire: A multidimensional instrument of multicultural effectiveness. *European Journal of Personality, 14*(4), 291–309.

Welch, F. C., Pitts, R. E., Tenini, K. J., Kuenlen, M. G., & Wood, S. G. (2010). Significant issues in defining and assessing teacher dispositions. *Teacher Educator, 45*(3), 179–201.

Whalen, B. J. (2011). Introduction. Using the standards of good practice to assess and improve education abroad programs. In *The standards of good practice for education abroad.* (4th ed., pp. 3–5). Carlisle, PA: Forum on Education Abroad.

Wild, D., Grove, A., Martin, M., Eremenco, S., McElroy, S., Verjee-Lorenz, A., & Erikson, P. (2005). Principles of good practice for the translation and cultural adaptation process for patient-reported outcomes (PRO) measures: Report of the ISPOR Task Force for Translation and Cultural Adaptation. *Value in Health, 8*(2), 94–104.

World Values Survey. (2009). *Values survey databank environment, buman & nature.* Retrieved from http://www.worldvaluessurvey.org/

Yanchar, S., Slife, B., & Warne, R. (2008). Critical thinking as disciplinary practice. *Review of General Psychology, 12*(3), 265–281.

Zimmermann, J., & Neyer, F. J. (2013, September). Do we become a different person when hitting the road? Personality development of sojourners. *Journal of Personality and Social Psychology, 105*(3), 515–530.

Vesna Hart and Barry Glick

13

JUSTICE AND THE NATURE OF HUMAN NATURE: WHAT, WHY, AND HOW BELIEFS AND VALUES MATTER

> *We have seen more than once that the public welfare may call upon the best citizens for their lives. It would be strange if it could not call upon those who already sap the strength of the State for these lesser sacrifices, often not felt to be such by those concerned, in order to prevent our being swamped with incompetence. It is better for all the world if, instead of waiting to execute degenerate offspring for crime or to let them starve for their imbecility, society can prevent those who are manifestly unfit from continuing their kind. . .Three generations of imbeciles are enough.*
>
> —Oliver Wendell Holmes, Jr.
Chief Justice, United States Supreme Court
Buck v. Bell, 1927, authorizing sterilization of the "feeble minded"

A fundamental tension within the U.S. justice system is between the need to promote public safety and the need to protect values such as individual rights and freedom, the rule of law, and democratic government.[1] As Cole and Gertz (1998) observe:

> Our laws begin with the premise that all people have rights, the guilty as well as the innocent. Moreover, unlike in some other countries, our laws reflect our concern to avoid unnecessarily depriving people of liberty, either by permitting police to search people at will or by mistakenly punishing an innocent person for a crime that he or she did not commit. Our greatest challenge may be to find ways to remain true to these principles of fair treatment and justice while also operating a system that can effectively protect, investigate, and punish. (p. 3)

Established over centuries of practice and precedent—with the intent to address the tension between promoting order as well as the values of freedom and democracy—courtroom processes ideally seek to provide justice and ensure impartiality.

As a field of practice and inquiry, psychology has played a significant role in contributing to these overarching goals through multiple scholarly programs, journals, and professional activities, such as the work of Division 41, the American Psychology-Law Society, established in 1981. The scope and nature of participation by psychologists is remarkable, including but not limited to conducting psychological forensic evaluations, providing expert testimony, developing and evaluating prevention and treatment programs, and researching various aspect of judicial processes

---

[1] In the development of this chapter, we gratefully acknowledge the suggestions and perspective of Daniel Murrie, PhD, of the Institute of Law, Psychiatry, and Policy at the University of Virginia. Selected content in this chapter has been adapted from materials and/or presentations developed by Barry Glick, PhD.

and outcomes (e.g., the validity of eyewitness testimony; factors that influence jury selection). Furthermore, there is some evidence that the legal system has started reading and using psychological research evidence to formulate policies and procedures (Blumenthal, 2002; Wells, Memon, & Penrod, 2006).

Despite these important contributions, psychologists also recognize that the judicial system is conceptualized, designed, and implemented in a manner that virtually ensures its highest aspirations will not and cannot be realized (Andrews & Bonta, 2010; Fox, 1999; Ogloff, 2000). In other words, the very processes and institutions designed to prevent and decrease criminal behavior may well perpetuate the status quo. For example, our punitive response to criminal behavior too often responds to criminality in a way that is misaligned with what human beings actually need in order to relate to themselves, others, and the larger world in a manner that is less likely to be criminal in nature (Andrews & Bonta, 2010; Cutler, 2011; Fox, 1999; Garland, 2001; Welsh & Farrington, 2007). Thus, rather than cultivating a capacity to care, the net effect of incarceration often is a further brutalization of self, which ironically recapitulates the abusive and neglectful introjects that are correlated with criminality in the first place (Shealy & Bhuyan, 2009; Shealy, Bhuyan, & Sternberger, 2012).

In full recognition of the complexity of the issues at hand, this chapter is divided into three major sections, which focus on the underlying "beliefs and values" that drive so many aspects of the judicial system while also emphasizing how formative variables (e.g., life history, demographics) moderate and mediate criminality. More specifically, we first examine *what* the underlying beliefs and values of our system of justice are, considering along the way its reputed "impartiality" as well as its relative effectiveness, or lack thereof. Second, we address the vexing question of *why* crime occurs in the first place as well as the etiology of our beliefs and values regarding justice through the presentation of data from a large-scale assessment project. Third and finally, we present the results from an intensive workshop, which illustrate *how* the theoretical and empirical examination of beliefs and values may impact the way incarcerated individuals experience and express feelings and needs regarding their past, present, and future, while illuminating attendant implications of such human processes for programs and practices in the justice system.

Across all three sections of this chapter, we strive to ask questions such as the following: Can the justice system really be blind (i.e., impartial), and if not, what are the associated sociocultural implications? What drives the relative degree to which an individual's beliefs about crime are inclined toward punishment or leniency as well as his or her beliefs about the relative merits of rehabilitation? How are other belief systems (e.g., religious) associated with attitudes about crime and punishment? What formative variables are associated with a history of criminality? What are the implications of such processes (e.g., the impact of life history on awareness of and care for self, others, and the larger world) for our understanding and delivery of "justice?" And finally, at an applied level, how might a greater understanding of one's own self—one's beliefs, values, thoughts, feelings, and life history—be integrated into "rehabilitation" in a way that promotes broader societal goals of an effective system of justice?

THE WHAT: BELIEFS, VALUES, AND THE JUSTICE SYSTEM

The United States prides itself on a justice system that claims to be impartial and effective. In fact, when asked "how much confidence" the public has in the U.S. criminal justice system, 70% reported that they had "a great deal/quite a lot" or "some" while 29% reported "very little" or "none" (Sourcebook of Criminal Justice Statistics, 2012). Through the putative selection of impartial juries and appointment or election of impartial judges, engagement of eyewitnesses and expert witnesses, fidelity to the rules of evidence, cross-examination, and other allied practices and procedures, the U.S. justice system seemingly strives to achieve impartial outcomes. However, is impartiality within our justice system even possible? Moreover, could a belief in impartiality actually facilitate injustice at the level of process and outcome? In other words, could our insistence that we have an "impartial" system of justice serve the dual role of perpetuating an unjust system while militating against any credible attempt to address underlying biases and inequities? For if we ascribe to the impression of an impartial system of justice, it stands to reason that we will be neither inclined to apprehend the bias within such a system nor compelled toward reform, especially if reprobate "criminals" are believed to deserve punishment (e.g., Costelloe, Chiricos, & Gertz, 2009). Thus, for policy makers and the public at large, there is good reason to minimize evidence of systemic bias within the justice system, since such acknowledgment would invite cognitive dissonance on a mass scale (Aronson, 2012). Nonetheless, considerable evidence suggests that our justice system is not, and perhaps cannot be, impartial in any genuine sense since deeply held beliefs and values (e.g., stereotypes regarding ethnicity, gender, religion, politics, attractiveness, socioeconomic status) mediate decision making and behavior (e.g., Blandón-Gitlin, Sperry, & Leo, 2011; Carson, Milne, Pakes, Shalev, & Shawher, 2007; Fitzgerald & Ellsworth, 1984; Gobert, 1988; Sanders, 2009; Shepherd, 2009; Solimine & Gely, 2009). Moreover, our beliefs and values about matters such as crime and punishment are mediated by a complex interaction between core human needs, formative variables, and extant contingencies (Shealy, 2004, 2005). Therefore, as a practical matter, all processes and aspects of the justice system are subject to human partiality, from the crafting of laws, to the integrity of their enforcement, to the quality of legal representation, to the selection of juries, to the introduction of various elements of legal proceeding, to decision making regarding guilt, to sentencing and appeal, to rehabilitation, parole, and release, or the lack thereof.

Exemplars of Bias Within the Justice System

Consider first *voir dire*, the process of choosing jury members, in which impartiality is the stated aim. If the system truly were interested in impartiality, jurors would be selected randomly from a valid representation of the entire community (Gobert, 1988). In practice, impartiality is precisely *not* the goal of *voir dire* from the standpoint of legal representation, which ultimately seeks to seat a jury that, in its estimation, is likely to render a verdict in favor of their client. Does such negotiated partiality among jurors matter? Fitzgerald and Ellsworth (1984) focused on this very question, examining juror selection processes vis-à-vis capital punishment. Jurors in capital punishment trials must agree that they would be willing to favor the death penalty in at least certain cases. Otherwise, by rule, the court systematically will exclude any juror who categorically is against the death penalty. Consequently this process then leads to the selection of jurors who are more likely not only to support the death penalty, but to favor the prosecution's case, mistrust criminal defendants, assume a punitive approach toward offenders, and prioritize crime control over due process (Fitzgerald & Ellsworth, 1984).

The assumed goal of a fair trial is frustrated not only by jurors' pre-existing beliefs and values, but also by the lack of basic psychological knowledge that would be necessary and sufficient to the potential rendering of impartial verdicts. For example, jurors may not be able or willing to apprehend the link between psychologically coercive interrogation and the attainment of false confessions. Furthermore, although potentially mediated by the influence of expert witnesses, when making decisions about a defendant's guilt, jurors tend to give more significance to dispositional factors (i.e., traits that are perceived to define the individual) rather than situational (i.e., factors external to the individual that influence their behavior) (Blandón-Gitlin et al., 2011). Such a fundamental attribution error (Ross, 1977) takes a conscious effort to reverse (Gilbert, 1989), even though judicial procedures typically do not incorporate such safeguards (Semmler, Brewer, & Douglass, 2011).

As with jurors, judges also are susceptible to biased decision making regarding their own personal beliefs and values about self, others, and the world at large. For example, Redding and Reppucci (1999) demonstrated bias among state court judges and law students by showing that they more readily accept social science data and testimony that supports their sociopolitical beliefs, while rejecting data and testimonies that appear to challenge them. Findings such as these call the very idea of decisional independence—a judge's assumed ability to make ideology-free decisions, which are based solely on the individual facts and applicable law without political or popular influence—into question.

Judicial independence is supposed to ensure impartiality by insulating federal and state judges from the influence of other branches of government as well as private or partisan interests. For example, according to federal law, "any justice, judge, or magistrate judge of the United States shall disqualify himself in any proceeding in which his impartiality might reasonably be questioned" (28 U.S.C. §§455, 1990). However, such dictates do not shield a judge from his or her own conflicts of interest (Shepherd, 2009; Solimine & Gely, 2009). Given our tendency to favor ourselves, including a tendency to overestimate our own capacity for fairness, such claims about the self are suspect, at best (Aronson, 2012). In the absence of genuinely impartial guidelines or processes vis-à-vis recusal, it should not be surprising to encounter situations in which, for example, Supreme Court Justices Elena Kagan and Clarence Thomas do not recuse themselves from hearing challenges to President Obama's Patient Protection and Affordable Care Act, despite the fact that Kagan was President Obama's lawyer prior to her selection as a justice, and Thomas's wife assumed a nationally prominent leadership role in opposing this health care law (Hume, 2014).

Consider next the role of "expert witnesses." Judges and juries heavily rely upon such individuals, who occupy a unique and powerful position in the judicial process. Expert witnesses are hired to provide allegedly nonbiasing assistance in the identification of facts during court proceedings. Indeed, most forensic clinicians that serve as expert witnesses in courts view themselves as "bias-free" and believe that they "compensate for any biases they might have" (Commons, Miller, & Gutheil, 2004, p. 73). However, research suggests that forensic clinicians are biased when providing evidence from forensic evaluations due to adversarial allegiance as well as the concomitant tendency to form opinions in a manner that supports the party that retained them (Boccaccini, Turner, & Murrie, 2008; Murrie, Boccaccini, Turner, Meeks, & Woods, 2009). Even among experts working on the same side of the case, there tend to be considerable differences of opinion, perhaps due to differences in evaluator opinions, values, and training (Boccaccini et al., 2008; Murrie et al., 2009; Rufino, Boccaccini, Hawes, & Murrie, 2012). Experts can impact jury behavior by utilizing their preferred theories and personal biases, therefore becoming advertent or inadvertent advocates for specific legal outcomes (Loftus, 1980). The complexity of such influence is such that the perceived confidence of the expert can impact the degree to which the expert is perceived by jurors to be credible (Cramer, Brodsky, & DeCoster, 2009). This power to influence the outcome of the judicial process is anything but impartial in means or ends, since expert witnesses who are used to achieve specific outcomes essentially serve as a "partisan source" (Sanders, 2009, p. 67).

Part of the problem here is that many "trait" and "state" factors may interact together to influence the relative capacity for expert impartiality. Consider gender-based perceptions in this regard. When exposed to personally intrusive questioning during cross-examination, the female expert was rated as less confident, trustworthy, likable, believable, and credible than the male expert; likewise, assertive responses to intrusive questions were rated more credible for males than females (Larson & Brodsky, 2010). Complicating matters further, although guidelines have been offered to facilitate an effective balance between idiographic and nomothetic data in relation to forensic risk assessment and testimony (DeMatteo, Batastini, Foster, & Hunt, 2010), a major challenge is generalizing from large-scale studies and aggregate data to a specific defendant (Carson et al., 2007). Because legal procedure is driven by dichotomies (i.e., empirical evidence either does or does not apply to a particular person or situation), the complexities that characterize phenomena of relevance to psychologists (e.g., in which multiple factors may influence behavior) may not be well suited to processes of black and white decision making in courtrooms (Carson et al., 2007). None of this is to say that experts seek to be duplicitous, only that wholesale impartiality is probably not a plausible outcome for anyone who is advocating for an interpretation of phenomena that is designed to confirm their existing version of reality (e.g., Aronson, 2012).

As another example of what might be termed the "fallacy of impartiality," consider literature on eyewitness identification. Pre-lineup instructions, lineup administrator suggestiveness, and multiple presentations in a group format (i.e., when presenting photos of potential suspects) all may influence an eyewitness's ability to identify the actual perpetrator. Furthermore, distance and lighting at the time of an incident, attention to particular stimuli, individual differences in feelings of certitude about one's capacity to be accurate, the amount of time between a crime and the identification of suspects, and the descriptive accuracy of particular details about a suspect, also have been identified empirically as potentially affecting the relative accuracy of eyewitness testimony (Wells & Quinlivan, 2009). Although these concepts have been addressed extensively in research, attendant recommendations to attenuate their biasing effects have not been translated sufficiently into actual practice within the judicial system (Semmler et al., 2011).

In the United States, eyewitness identification is relied upon heavily for convictions. However, to date, at least 305 individuals have been wrongly convicted in the United States due, primarily, to mistaken eyewitness testimony; such individuals ultimately were exonerated on the basis of DNA testing (Innocence Project, 2012). Although DNA testing provides an improved technique for offender identification, eyewitness testimony continues to be a primary feature of criminal proceedings, especially when DNA evidence does not exist. As with expert testimony, it also should be emphasized that other variables may influence the degree to which eyewitness testimony is believed to be valid. For example, the relative degree to which eyewitnesses are perceived to be confident and the corroboration by other eyewitnesses both have significant impacts on judicial process outcomes (Douglass & Pavletic, 2012). Again, despite numerous data-based recommendations that attempt to enhance the impartiality of eyewitness evidence (Pezdek, 2012), jurors, judges, and law enforcement professionals are not necessarily aware of such findings and accompanying best practices (Benton, Ross, Bradshaw, Thomas, & Bradshaw, 2006; Cutler, 2011; Jost, 2011; Semmler et al., 2011; Wise & Safer, 2004; Zimmerman, Austin, & Kovera, 2012).

Particularly telling is the discrepancy between legal and empirical approaches to eyewitness testimony. From a legal perspective, consistency over time is among the most important measures of witness credibility (Fisher, Brewer, & Mitchell, 2009). However, empirical findings provide evidence that although memories become less consistent over time, individuals ironically may believe more strongly that their memories are accurate with the passage of time (Talarico & Rubin, 2003). For eyewitnesses, such phenomena may be caused by interference and transfer effects due to repeated exposure to potential suspects (Pezdek, 2012; Wells & Quinlivan, 2009), repeated interviewing or rehearsal of answers to questions (Shaw & McClure, 1996; Wells, Ferguson, & Lindsay, 1981), information from co-witnesses (Luus & Wells, 1994), or receiving confirmatory feedback about the identified suspect (Bradfield & Wells, 2000). In other words, eyewitness confidence does not necessarily correlate with accuracy (Deffenbacher, 1980), but rather may vary under a range of different conditions (e.g., the amount of time needed to make an identification decision) (Wells, Olson, & Charman, 2002). In short, considerable empirical evidence suggests that human memory about events often is inaccurate and susceptible to manipulation. Despite efforts to increase jurors' knowledge about the accuracy of eyewitness testimony, such an approach alone is not enough to improve the impartiality of jurors' decision making (Magnussen, Melinder, Stridbeck, & Raja, 2010). Indeed, at the most fundamental level, when making decisions throughout the legal system, attorneys, jurors, and judges most likely rely upon the same mechanisms and processes that we all do on a daily basis outside of a courtroom: utilizing quick, automatic evaluations, operating largely outside of conscious awareness, and informed by affective, developmentally and culturally pre-formed cognitions (Aronson, 2012; Buckholtz & Marois, 2012; Haidt, 2001).

Notably, psychological science has made significant progress in identifying factors that improve jury decision making and eyewitness testimony and identification procedures. Most telling of this progress is that psychological research (e.g., the work of APA Division 41) has prompted procedural reforms in some state courts regarding eyewitness interviewing and identification procedures in a number of jurisdictions (e.g., New Jersey, North Carolina, Wisconsin). However, justice systems overall continue to collect and interpret eyewitness evidence in a way that does not take into account the complex interaction of memory and social influence variables that can lead to eyewitness error (Wells et al., 2006). Most salient to the present analysis is that even when fairer legal procedures informed by psychological empirical studies are implemented in eyewitness identification—*voir dire*, and jury decision making, for example—all justice-seeking stakeholders within the process (i.e., police officers, legal representatives, jurors, judges, the public) operate still from their own set of beliefs and values, which impact subsequent decision making and attendant justifications.

Economic Forces in the Judicial System

In addition to these biasing factors and processes, money also influences every aspect of the judicial system. At the most basic level, state-level judges (e.g., trial, appellate, supreme) typically either are appointed or elected (federal judges are appointed and subject to review and confirmation by the legislative branch). Especially for state-level elections, prospective judges may run under the banner of a political party, which necessitates the raising of funds from individuals who support a particular political and sociocultural agenda. Over the past decade, the influence of money on the selection of judges has only intensified (Brandenburg, 2010), with millions raised in support of candidates who represent a particular ideological perspective. Not surprisingly then—and potentially eroding the confidence Americans express in their justice system over the long term (Sourcebook of Criminal Justice Statistics, 2012)—three out of four Americans now believe that campaign contributions can influence courtroom decisions (Justice at Stake, 2002). Criticism of such processes is not confined to social scientists or the public at large. For example, as Liptak (2006) documents from a survey of Ohio state judges, 46% agreed that campaign donations influence the courtroom decisions of some judges. Similarly, as Stephen Breyer, an associate justice of the U.S. Supreme Court, averred, "I believe that it is impossible to be a conscientious judge with one eye on the *U.S. Reports* and the other eye on the latest Gallup poll" (Breyer, 2008, p. 139).

Beyond an influence on the selection and decision making of judges, other aspects of the criminal justice system also are affected by monetary factors, including inequalities in power and material well-being. Such processes manifest in those who run for, and secure, political office (and ultimately make the laws) to the relative prestige of one's educational pedigree. In such cases, the least affluent are most likely to bear the brunt of the most affluent (Agrast, Botero, & Ponce, 2011). Since socioeconomic background also is linked to ethnicity, which further is tied to the likelihood of "defendant status," such variables inextricably are linked to beliefs and values—and attendant laws—regarding crime and punishment. At this big picture level, money factors into the creation and maintenance of the "prison-industrial complex," which emerged from concern over a lack of effectiveness and efficiency within the judicial system, and led to an increasing number of incarcerated individuals. This "complex" refers to the large number of private prisons, as well as businesses that supply goods and services to them, which collectively have incentivized the process of incarceration, since more prisoners lead to more profit (Garland, 2001). Privatization of prisons initially was advocated for by private companies with strong lobbying bases that promised significant savings in operational costs. However, Austin and Coventry (2001) reported that private prisons perform at a similar level of efficiency as public prisons; moreover, such a focus on reducing operational costs may occur at the expense of treatment quality and recidivism reduction.

A final example of the insidious impact of money on processes of justice concerns the relative degree to which defendants have equal access to high quality legal representation. As Agrast et al. (2011) reported in the Rule of Law Index, the U.S. civil justice system is less accessible to disadvantaged groups because of the high cost of high quality legal assistance. In both civil and criminal dimensions of the justice system, wealthy people can afford highly experienced attorneys who specialize in a specific area, whereas those without financial resources must rely on less competent lawyers or public defenders and legal aid. In addition to discrepancies in the amount of access and the extent of utilization, a significant difference in the degree of satisfaction with the justice system has been reported by rich and poor individuals, with the former much more satisfied than the latter (Agrast et al., 2011).

Evaluating the Relative Effectiveness of the Justice System

If considerable evidence exists that the judicial system is not impartial, an allied question has to do with its relative effectiveness in deterring crime, rehabilitating the incarcerated, preventing recidivism, and protecting the public. As Glick and Sturgeon (1998) document, these questions have long historical precedents. To highlight a few examples, perspectives and strategies for dealing with aggressive and violent children are found in the Old Testament (Deuteronomy 21:18–21). In Greco-Roman times, citizens were banished from city-states if they violated the law. Moreover, harsher punishments, such as public whippings or death were given to poor slaves or others who were not part of the privileged class. In the Middle Ages, disputes often were settled by family feuds, duels, and vigilantism. Again, there was little tolerance for aggression, and harsh punishment, rather than deterrence, was the prevailing policy. Such historic precedent for harsh treatment of criminality begs a larger question: Do these strategies work?

Overall, data regarding the effectiveness of "tough on crime" measures to decrease criminal behavior appear disheartening. With the introduction of policies that favor "swift and severe punishment" in the 1980s and 1990s, incarceration rates have increased. The number of incarcerated individuals in the United States has risen fivefold in the period from early 1970s to the beginning of the current millennium, with 1 in 100 adults being imprisoned in the early 1970s to about 5 inmates per 100 persons in 2008 (Bureau of Justice Statistics, 2009). As Bloom (2012) observes:

> The United States leads the world in the rate of incarcerating its own citizens. We imprison more of our own people than any other country on earth, including China which has four times our population, or in human history. And now, a new Pew report announces that we are keeping even nonviolent inmates behind bars for increasingly longer terms…. (p. 1)

But might this high incidence of incarceration be responsible for a general trend toward lower crime rates, which have been documented not only in the United States but globally? As an analysis by *The Economist* concludes:

> There is no single cause of the decline; rather, several have coincided. Western societies are growing older, and most crimes are committed by young men. Policing has improved greatly in recent decades, especially in big cities such as New York and London, with forces using computers to analyze the incidence of crime. . .The epidemics of crack cocaine and heroin appear to have burnt out. The biggest factor may be simply that security measures have improved. . .Many conservatives will think. . .the main reason crime has declined [is] the far harsher sentences introduced on both sides of the Atlantic over the past two decades…This has obviously had some effect—a young person in prison cannot steal your car—but if tough prison sentences were the cause, crime would not be falling in the Netherlands and Germany, which have reduced their prison populations. New York's prison population has fallen by a quarter since 1999, yet its crime rate has dropped faster than that of many other cities. Harsh punishments, and in particular long mandatory sentences for certain crimes, increasingly look counterproductive. American prisons are full of old men, many of whom are well past their criminal years, and non-violent drug users, who would be better off in treatment. (The curious case of the fall in crime, 2013, p. 9)

Moreover, despite dramatic increases in incarceration and attendant spending on prisons, recidivism rates remain high. The United States spends more than $50 billion a year on corrections, yet more than 40% of inmates return to state prison within 3 years of their release (Pew Center of the States, 2011). In short, imprisonment by itself does not seem adequate to address what presumably is a core goal of the judicial system: to decrease criminal activity. In addition, one might wonder whether the emphasis on imprisonment may serve to absolve the public and professionals from being more directly involved in understanding or preventing crime (Ogloff, 2000).

Empirical research evidence suggests also that hiring more police officers does not lead to a reduction in crime rates (Sherman & Eck, 2002; Weisburd & Eck, 2004). Furthermore, prison deterrence programs such as "Scared Straight" could be associated with the opposite effect. For example, juveniles who complete the "Scared Straight" program may be more likely to engage in criminal activity compared to those who did not go through the program (Finckenauer & Gavin, 1999; Petrosino, Petrosino, & Buehler, 2007). Likewise, the school-based intervention, Drug Abuse Resistance Education (DARE), showed trivial or nonexistent effects on decreasing or preventing criminal behaviors (Gottfredson, Wilson, & Najaka, 2002; Shealy & Bhuyan, 2009; U.S. General Accounting Office, 2003). As a final example, the poor impact of boot camps on attenuating recidivism is comparable to the outcomes of imprisonment (Wilson & MacKenzie, 2007).

TOWARD EFFECTIVE PREVENTION AND TREATMENT: BELIEFS, BEHAVIORS, AND THE FACILITATION OF CHANGE

So, does any approach lead to better rehabilitation and recidivism outcomes? The short answer is yes, with specific interventions and populations. For example, social skills training, when implemented with 13 years and older children who already exhibit some behavioral problems—as well as adult offenders—demonstrates some promise in crime prevention (Lipsey & Landenberger, 2007; Lösel & Beelman, 2007). Programs that seem to show promise in the prevention and treatment of criminal behavior are best understood in the context of the historical roots upon which they are based. In particular, Aaron Beck (1976), a psychiatrist working with the mentally ill, first introduced *cognitive restructuring*, a process by which individuals are directed to assess their own thoughts, feelings, beliefs, and attitudes, in order to identify new thinking that reduces risk behavior (Beck, 1961, 1963, 1972, 1976). Likewise, Albert Ellis (1962) developed *Rational Emotive Therapy*, a structured process that helped individuals to rationally deal with problems of living, within their cognitive and affective domain (Ellis, 1962, 1997). Yochelson and Samenow (1977) were the first to apply these principles to the criminal population. They designed a process to help staff and offenders identify those criminal-thinking errors that may cause criminal behavior. Another program based upon cognitive restructuring principles is *Cognitive Self-Change*, developed for the most violent criminal offenders to teach them to replace their risk behaviors by substituting risk thoughts with new thinking (Bush & Bilodeau, 1993). Other early programs based upon this approach include *Rites of Passage* (Preudhomme & Dunston, 1989), *Moral Reconation Therapy* (Robinson & Little, 1988), and *Reasoning and Rehabilitation* (Ross, Fabiano, & Ross, 1986).

Albert Bandura is credited as the father of the cognitive skill programs that are based upon his work in social learning. It was Bandura who introduced the notion that individuals learn by modeling what they see others do, and acquire skills by trying, through role play situations, what has been shown to them (Bandura, 1962, 1971, 1975). Based upon his seminal work, Goldstein, Sprafkin, and Gershaw (1965) designed a series of 60 skills to teach pro-social behaviors to mentally ill patients who were being deinstitutionalized as a result of the public policies of the late 1960s and early 1970s. That early work was later applied to at-risk youth, first by developing a 50-skill curriculum known as *Skillstreaming the Adolescent* (Goldstein & McGinnis, 1997). Such advances later were extended to juvenile delinquents and violent youth (Goldstein & Glick, 1987).

These cognitive skill principles also have been applied to specific behavior issues such as anger management. For example, Meichenbaum and Novaco (1985) developed training procedures to teach a variety of populations how to control angry outbursts. They also developed strategies to reduce anger such as "deep breathing," "counting backwards," and "pleasant imagery." These principles and strategies were then used as components for other programs that deal with aggression and violence. For example, Feindler introduced the *Angry Behavior Cycle* that served as the basis for teaching children the elements that comprise their angry emotions (Feindler & Ecton, 1986). Goldstein and Glick (1987) adapted this intervention as the affective component for their multimodal cognitive behavior intervention. More recent cognitive skill programs based upon Bandura and other cognitive skill programs include *Problem Solving* (Taymans, 2011) and *Thinking for a Change* (T4C; Bush, Glick, & Taymans, 2011).

These two major tracts—cognitive restructuring and cognitive skills—comprise the basis for which cognitive behavior programs have been designed and developed. Implementation of such programs within juvenile and criminal justice, in addition to schools, communities, and mental hospitals, and their effects upon pro-social behavior have been well documented. The skill development, habilitation, and clinical impacts produced for individuals participating in these programs have been analyzed and shown to be an effective intervention for the mental health, juvenile justice, and criminal justice systems (Przybylski, 2008; Welsh & Farrington, 2007).

But what is it about such programs that make them effective in reducing criminal behaviors? Gendreau (1996) analyzed various treatment programs and identified characteristics that influence program effectiveness in changing aggressive and criminal behaviors in offenders: (a) inclusion of services that are intensive and behavioral in nature while targeting dynamic risk factors (i.e., criminogenic needs: antisocial attitudes, styles of thinking and behavior, peer associations, chemical dependencies, and self-control issues); (b) matching characteristics of offenders, therapists, and programs; (c) relating to offenders in interpersonally sensitive and constructive ways; (d) providing relapse prevention strategies; (e) designing structures and activities that disrupt criminal behavior; and (f) advocacy directed toward agencies that provide community-based services.

More recently, the *Risk, Need, and Responsivity* (RNR) model was developed by Andrews and Bonta (2006, 2010). The RNR model postulates that the offender risk level and offender's criminogenic needs should drive the selection of appropriate interventions. Criminogenic needs include antisocial attitudes, styles of thinking and behavior, peer associations, chemical dependencies, and self-control issues. The principles of effective correctional assessment and intervention, according to the RNR model are as follows:

- *Risk principle.* Matching the level of service to the offender's risk of reoffending, based on the assessment of criminogenic needs. The focus is on treatment of the high-risk offenders.
- *Need principle.* Assessing criminogenic needs and targeting them in treatment.
- *Responsivity principle.* Maximizing the offender's ability to experience change by providing evidence-based treatment, while adapting the intervention to the level of motivation, abilities, and strengths of the offender.

One current correctional treatment program—featured in greater detail later in this chapter—is the T4C curriculum from the National Institute of Corrections (NIC) (Bush et al., 2011), an evidence-based, integrated cognitive behavioral change program that is designed to be delivered to small groups of 8 to 12 participants in 25 lessons. This curriculum seeks to change the criminogenic thinking of offenders, and includes cognitive restructuring, social/interpersonal skill development, and the cultivation of problem-solving and communication capacities, all of which aim to address cognitive, social, and emotional needs and realities of the broader offender population. In doing so, T4C uses didactic instruction, role play illustrations of concepts, repeated exposure to relevant material, and homework assignments for the purpose of practicing skills learned in the group lesson. Although this program is used with a variety of offenders (e.g., adults and juveniles, offenders on probation or parole, prison and jail inmates), the effectiveness of the program has been examined primarily with adults on probation (Lowenkamp, Hubbard, Makarios, & Latessa, 2009).

In attempting to develop, implement, and evaluate empirically supported interventions, the challenge is to convince policy makers and public officials of their validity rather than continuing with imprisonment as the primary "solution" to crime reduction (Welsh & Farrington, 2007). The status quo vis-à-vis the justice system seems consistent with Einstein's definition of "insanity" as "doing the same thing over and over again and expecting different results," which begs a question: As a society, why are we so stubbornly devoted to approaches toward "crime and punishment," which do not really seem to prevent incarceration and recidivism? Undoubtedly, there are many potential causes for such policies and practices. However, a prime culprit most likely consists of our vaunted tradition of strong punitive beliefs within American culture (Agnew, 2011; Costelloe et al., 2009; Garland, 2001; Maruna & King, 2004; Payne, Gainey, Triplett, & Danner, 2004; Sims, 2003), a values-based topic to which we turn next in the second section of this chapter.

THE WHY: ORIGINS OF BELIEF AND THE ETIOLOGY OF CRIMINALITY

An overview of literature from psychology and other disciplines (e.g., criminology, sociology, philosophy), as well as popular sources, illustrates how underlying "beliefs and values" drive different aspects of the judicial system, including the etiology of punitive beliefs regarding crime and punishment. Although the fields of psychology and law intersect at a range of levels (e.g., eyewitness and expert witness testimony; jury selection; isolating the predictors of criminal behavior; issues of bias in judicial process), the overarching goals of enhancing public safety, reduced recidivism, and cost control have yet to be achieved in either field (e.g., Carson et al., 2007; Pew Center on the States, 2011). Perhaps that is because a significant focus in psychology has been on research and practice regarding evident partiality within the judicial process, while neglecting more fundamental questions such as, *What drives punitive beliefs and criminal behaviors in the first place?* Complicating matters, as noted previously, the influence of money (e.g., who has access to judicial processes, who assumes political power, free market dynamics driving the prison industrial complex) significantly impacts the beliefs and values of all stakeholders in the judicial process. Ultimately, political and religious beliefs in particular also have been identified as relevant to an overall inclination toward punishment, an overarching "cause" of our current system of justice.

Beliefs and Values About Religion and Politics as Mediators of Justice

In order to survive as a species, *Homo sapiens sapiens* has relied upon social norms and sanctions to maintain pro-social behaviors, order, and safety. Among other sanctions, besides interpersonal or two-party administration of punishment (e.g., "You hurt me, I'll punish you"), a third-party punishment of norm violation (e.g., "I punish you because you harmed him") has long been a foundation of our criminal justice system. The roots of such predilections are complex and multifaceted. For example, Buckholtz and Marois (2012) found that individuals engaged in decision making regarding a punishment (i.e., judges and jury), likely do not make purely factual judgments, but rely upon affective states. Such states are mediated further by sociocultural beliefs and values through which criminality is interpreted and the social order prescribed.

The "string 'em high," "lock 'em up," and "throw away the key" motif cuts deep within American jurisprudence and culture generally, and is attributed at least in part to a backlash against the "penal welfare" system of the pre-1970s, which was perceived to limit our capacity to control criminal activity (Garland, 2001). Subsequent policies of the 1980s and 1990s, in particular, appeared to be grounded in the belief that "swift and severe" punishment will deter offenders from committing crime. Although such an approach has been advocated by some criminologists (e.g., Bennett, DiIulio, & Walters, 1996; Wilson, 1975), the primary proponents of "tough on crime" policies are politicians and their constituents (Agnew, 2011). From an etiological perspective, Sims (2003) observes that how the public defines what causes criminal behavior influences their view toward punishment. Such predilections, when they are operative, are mediated further by the underlying endorsement, within American culture, that human beings have "free will" (Nichols, 2006), despite considerable evidence that such "will" is illusory at best (Aronson, 2012; Hallett, 2007; Shealy, 2016; Soon, Brass, Heinze, & Haynes, 2008; Wegner, 2002). In fact, close to 80% of U.S. citizens believe that "crime is the product of a person's will" (Sims, 2003, p. 23), which predisposes the public at large toward punitive approaches to crime management, since from this perspective, it is possible to "control the will" that is responsible for crime. A number of other studies demonstrate this same suspect conviction, that "criminals have free will" or "choose" whether or not to engage in criminal behavior (Coulter, 2006; Cullen, Clark, Cullen, & Mathers, 1985). Complicating matters, as Sims further notes, those who attribute crime to factors such as a lenient judicial system are more likely to have punitive attitudes toward offenders.

Given the emphasis on a belief in "free will," which has further origins in a Judeo-Christian worldview, it is worth asking if there is a relationship between religious worldviews and attitudes toward crime and punishment. Overall, the associations are complex, mainly because there is great variety in the nature and intensity of religious beliefs as well as methodologies by which these relationships are assessed (Applegate, Cullen, Fisher & Vander Ven, 2000; Grasmick & McGill, 1944; Unnever & Cullen, 2006). For example, Applegate et al. report that scholarship on the relationship between religion and punitive beliefs has followed two paths: (a) a focus on the harsh attitudes present in religious beliefs, which positively predict punitiveness, and (b) a focus on forgiveness and compassion as predictors of less harsh and more rehabilitative attitudes in religious people. Regarding the former area, findings suggest that Christian fundamentalists who interpret the Bible literally emphasize personal salvation, and are passionate evangelists who are inclined toward punitive beliefs (Evans & Adams, 2003;

Grasmick, Davenport, Chamlin, & Bursik, 1992; Greer, Berman, Varan, Bobrycki, & Watson, 2005; Unnever & Cullen, 2006). However, research shows that those who adhere to a "forgiveness/compassion" perspective, and report "a perceived close personal relationship with a loving God are less likely to support capital punishment for convicted murderers" (Unnever, Bartkowski, & Cullen, 2006; see also Brearly, van den Bos, & Tan, 2016).

From a sociopolitical standpoint, findings suggest a positive relationship between conservative political beliefs and a punitive worldview. Overall, scholars attribute this association to a tendency by conservatives to endorse dispositional attributions for criminal behavior (Cochran, Boots, & Chamlin, 2006; Jacobs & Carmichael, 2002). For example, Jacobs and Carmichael (2002) found that the prevalence of conservative values, and a Republican majority in the legislature, increased the likelihood that the death penalty would be legal in a given state. Along similar lines, those who endorse conservative beliefs and derive dispositional attributions vis-à-vis crime have greater difficulty empathizing with criminals (Cochoran et al., 2006; Unnever, Cullen, & Fisher, 2005). As a final exemplar, Gromet and Darley (2011) found that self-identified liberals favored restorative notions of justice, while conservatives favored punitive options.

As the literature suggests, beliefs about crime and punishment—and attendant assumptions about "choice and free will"—ultimately mediate the kinds of actions, policies, and practices vis-à-vis justice that prevail in our society. But, is there any sort of evidence that can be brought to bear on these versions of reality? That is, from a psychological perspective, can we demonstrate empirically, and in a manner that makes sense (i.e., is theoretically grounded), whether human beings, including "criminals," really possess free will as is commonly believed? The short answer is, yes, although the complexities of doing so are not insignificant (Aronson, 2012; Hallett, 2007; Shealy, 2016; Soon et al., 2008; Wegner, 2002). For present purposes, our main contention is that a legal view that dichotomizes criminal behavior as being either voluntary or involuntary is inaccurate as well as obscurantist in terms of the formulation and implementation of legal policies and practices that make sense, given why we do what we do and who we fundamentally are as human beings. To consider these issues more fully, we first must consider what we actually know—as opposed to what we believe is true—about the etiology—or *the why*—of crime and antisocial behavior.

The Origins of Criminality

Overall, and perhaps not surprisingly, literature focused on the etiology of antisocial and criminal behavior suggests an interaction among genetic, biological, psychosocial, and familial domains as an explanatory framework, which shapes the pathways of adaptation or maladaptation throughout the life span (Frick & Viding, 2009; Moffitt, 1993, 2003; Patterson, 1996). In particular, the field of developmental psychopathology has focused on how and why we cultivate a set of beliefs and values that are associated with caring about self, others, and the world at large. In other words, the ways in which we come to experience ourselves and others are a function of how we were experienced and responded to during our own processes of development (Cummings, Davies, & Campbell, 2000; Davies & Cummings, 1994; Shealy, 1995; Shealy et al., 2012).

Research on the etiology of criminality indicates that early disruptive and maladaptive externalizing behaviors are among the best predictors of adolescent and adult criminality (Loeber, Burke, & Pardini, 2009; Moffitt, 2003; Moffitt, Caspi, Harrington, & Milne, 2002). Moffitt (1993, 2003) outlined a taxonomic model that describes developmental trajectories of antisocial behavior, identifying childhood onset and adolescence onset of antisocial behavior. Synthesizing empirical evidence with an emphasis on concepts of equifinality and multifinality in the developmental process (Cummings et al., 2000), Frick and Viding (2009) suggested that there are at least three important pathways through which severe antisocial behaviors in children and adolescents may emerge, with a key distinction between the onset of antisocial behavior in childhood or adolescence. In particular, behavior problems for the childhood-onset group typically exhibit more enduring characteristics through adolescence and adulthood, and may follow at least two different developmental pathways.

One childhood-onset group is characterized by the presence of callous–unemotional traits, which seem to be associated with dysfunctional parenting practices, temperamental deficits in processing negative emotional stimuli (particularly deficits to signs of fear and distress in others), and deficits in responding to punishment cues, which cumulatively lead to disrupted development of empathy, guilt, and other aspects of conscience (Frick & Viding, 2009; Shealy et al., 2012). As children, such individuals often are diagnosed with Oppositional Defiant Disorder or Conduct Disorder, and as adults are diagnosed with Antisocial Personality Disorder (American Psychiatric Association, 2013; Loeber et al., 2009). As Frick and Viding further note, the second childhood-onset group does not exhibit callous–unemotional traits, but rather seems to display cognitive deficits (low verbal intelligence), difficulties in emotional and behavioral regulation (e.g., high anxiety, impulsivity), and ineffective parenting practices (e.g., higher rates of dysfunctional families), which ultimately lead to ineffective socialization across multiple developmental contexts (Moffitt, 2003).

One of the more salient etiological factors in the childhood-onset antisocial behavior group is the linkage between dysfunctional parenting practices and corresponding processes of emotional regulation and functioning (Edens, Skopp, & Cahill, 2008; Oxford, Cavell, & Hughes, 2003; Scaramella & Leve, 2004). In this regard, Patterson (1996) and Moffitt (2003) propose a process of transactional interplay involving a difficult and vulnerable child (e.g., emotionally reactive, impulsive) who experiences inadequate rearing environments (e.g., coercive parenting strategies, poor quality daycare or school), which result in the development of antisocial behaviors. This dysfunctional transactional interaction results in disrupted socialization for a child, which further may be associated with poor social relations with adults and peers in their immediate environment (home, school, neighborhood) (e.g., Cummings et al., 2000). Over time, this process may lead to the formation of enduring dispositional characteristics and maladaptive trajectories across multiple developmental stages (Moffitt, 2003). Besides dysfunctional parenting practices, disadvantaged neighborhoods place children at further risk for early-onset trajectory due to interactions with troubled peers in the neighborhood during middle childhood (Ingoldsby et al., 2006).

The adolescent-onset antisocial behavior group, which begins exhibiting significant antisocial and delinquent behavior corresponding with the onset of adolescence, seems to be characterized by an exaggeration of normative processes of adolescent rebellion, most likely in an attempt to acquire or display a subjective sense of maturity and adult status within an antisocial peer group (Moffitt, 1993, 2003). Because antisocial behavior within this group is an exaggeration of a developmental process in adolescence (e.g., higher levels of rebelliousness and endorsement of unconventional values compared with children without conduct problems) (Dandreaux & Frick, 2009; Moffitt, Caspi, Dickson, Silva, & Stanton, 1996), rather than an enduring vulnerability, their antisocial behavior may dissipate as abruptly as it emerges, unless they experience consequences of their adolescent antisocial behaviors, which follow them into adulthood (e.g., a criminal record, substance use) (Moffitt & Caspi, 2001).

One of the more salient links between parenting practices and adult criminality has been found in individuals who experienced childhood and adolescence abuse and neglect (e.g., Fagan, 2005; Lansford et al., 2007; Shealy, 1995; Smith, Ireland, & Thornberry, 2005; Widom, 1989). However, bearing in mind the complexity of equifinality and multifinality processes (Cummings et al., 2000), it is important to note that not all or even most maltreated children become offenders (Stewart, Livingston, & Dennison, 2008). Furthermore, specific interacting variables must be accounted for in identifying such linkages. For example, paternal criminality, particularly severe conflict or aggression, was found to be a contributing factor to their male child's future criminality. Conversely, in families where mothers were affectionate, self-confident, or where proper supervision was given, paternal criminality was not a predictor of future crime in their offspring (McCord, 1999).

Approaching the question of traits and etiology of aggressive and criminal behavior from a cognitive behavioral theoretical framework, Glick and Gibbs (2011) identify four primary traits that constitute aggression among youth and young adults:

- *Verbal and physical aggression*—characterized by behaviors such as fighting, disruptiveness, profanity, irritability, quarrelsomeness, defiance of authority, irresponsibility, high levels of attention seeking behavior, and low levels of guilt feelings (Quay, 1965; Quay & Hogan, 1999).
- *Skill deficiency*—most behaviorally disordered (aggressive) adolescents have not developed the social skills necessary to successfully negotiate their environments (Glick, 1979).
- *Immaturity*—such behaviors represent patterns that may have been age appropriate at earlier stages of development, but are not acceptable for the adolescent and often lead to alienation with peers, including short attention span, clumsiness, preference for younger playmates, passivity, daydreaming, and incompetence (American Psychiatric Association, 2013).
- *Withdrawal*—these behaviors have variously been labeled as *Personality Problem, Disturbed Neurotic* (Quay, 1964), and *Overinhibited* (Hewitt & Jenkins, 1946), and are characterized by depression, feelings of inferiority, self-consciousness, shyness, anxiety, hypersensitivity, and timidity.

In addition to the previously described internal factors that contribute to criminal behavior, external influences, such as the media, also may have a significant effect on the use of violence and aggression among children and youth. Although the possibility of correlation/causation confusion always should be recognized, excessive television watching in childhood has been associated with long-term antisocial behaviors. For example, following 1,037 individuals from birth to age 26 years, Robertson, McAnally, and Hancox (2013) found that children who watched more television were more likely to have antisocial personality traits in adulthood. Consider also two effects of violence in the media: copycat effect and desensitization effect (Coleman, 2004).

The copycat effect is described as increased violence toward others and/or self for those who watch violence on television. As one exemplar, in the movie *The Deer Hunter* over 40 acts of violence are presented, one of which was a scene in which a group was playing "Russian Roulette." Within 48 hours after viewing the movie, 43 teenagers in the United States reportedly committed suicide (Coleman, 2004); a similar experience apparently occurred in Europe after *The Deer Hunter* was released.

Among demographic variables, race and gender also have been found to be significant predictors of engagement with the criminal justice system. Developmental psychopathology research shows that, in regard to gender, males and females follow similar trajectories in the development of offending behaviors, although females are less likely to engage in criminal behavior than males (Fergusson & Horwood, 2002; Moffit & Caspi, 2001). Likewise, in terms of prison sentencing, the harshness of punishment is greater for males than for females. More specifically, males are more likely to receive long sentences, and also are less likely to receive no prison term when that option is available (Mustard, 2001).

Regarding race, Blacks are more likely than Whites to be arrested, proceed through the criminal justice system, and be imprisoned if found guilty (Keen & Jacobs, 2009). Arrest data show a consistent pattern of overrepresentation by Blacks in prison (Benekos, Merlo, & Puzzanchera, 2011) and a greater likelihood that this population will be more harshly punished than Whites (Johnson, 2003; Mustard, 2001). Furthermore, Blacks are more likely than Whites to receive the death penalty in capital cases (NAACP Legal Defense and Educational Fund, 2006). In reflecting upon such disproportionate outcomes, the role of prejudicial beliefs vis-à-vis gender and race would seem to be implicated. Indeed, the effect of race on treatment of Black individuals in the judicial process has decreased after 1990, compared to 1970, suggesting perhaps that knowing racism is "wrong" makes stakeholders more cautious regarding how they make decisions (Mitchell, Haw, Pfiefer, & Meissner, 2005). Furthermore, when jurors are cognizant of racial issues—during *voir dire*, for example—they also may become less racially biased (Sommers, 2006).

Among other implications of these findings, perhaps most basic is the fact that our systems of justice are developed and implemented by human beings who are highly susceptible to biasing processes. Moreover, the punitive ways in which we apprehend and treat those who are incarcerated tend to recapitulate the very events and dynamics that helped create "the criminal" in the first place, but do little to attenuate recidivism. Such observations should neither be construed as an apology for criminality nor an entreaty for appeasement, but rather a plea for greater understanding at two fundamental and interrelated levels: (a) the inherently biased nature of our entire system of justice and (b) the generative gains we likely would accrue by focusing more on why we humans function as we do, and what the attendant implications are for more effective management of the incarcerated.

As a point of entry into these possibilities, we next introduce the Equilintegration (EI) theoretical framework and the Beliefs, Events, and Values Inventory (BEVI), which have empirical and applied implications for the broader criminal justice system. After describing this model and method, the focus of this chapter turns to research findings regarding the formative variables that are associated with our beliefs and values toward criminal justice. We then link such theory and data to real world practice by demonstrating how the BEVI may be used to promote deeper understanding of self, others, and the larger world by those who are incarcerated, and in a manner that may facilitate the goals and objectives of programs such as T4C, as noted previously.

EI THEORY, THE EI SELF, AND THE BEVI

Although a full explication is presented in Shealy (2016), we next offer a brief overview of the three main components of this approach prior to their presentation in an applied forensic setting. EI Theory seeks to explain "the processes by which beliefs, values, and 'worldviews' are acquired and maintained, why their alteration is typically resisted, and how and under what circumstances their modification occurs" (Shealy, 2004, p. 1075; see Chapter 2). Derivative of EI Theory (Shealy, 2004), the EI Self explains the integrative and synergistic processes by which beliefs and values are acquired, maintained, and transformed. It also explains how and why beliefs and values are linked to the formative variables, core needs, and adaptive potential of the self (Shealy et al., 2012). Informed by scholarship in a range of key areas (e.g., "needs-based" research and theory; developmental psychopathology; social cognition; affect regulation; processes and outcomes of therapy; theories and models of "self"), the EI Self seeks to illustrate how the interaction between our core needs (e.g., for attachment, affiliation) and formative variables (e.g., caregiver, culture) results in beliefs and values about self, others, and the world at large, which are internalized over the course of development and across the life span (see Chapter 3; see also www.ibavi. org/content/featured-projects).

Concomitant with EI Theory and the EI Self, the BEVI is a comprehensive analytic tool that examines how and why we come to see ourselves, others, and the larger world as we do (e.g., how life experiences, culture, and context affect our beliefs, values, and worldview) as well as the influence of such processes on multiple aspects of human functioning (e.g., learning processes, relationships, personal growth, the pursuit of life goals). For example, the BEVI assesses processes such as: basic openness; the tendency to (or not to) stereotype in particular ways; self- and emotional awareness; preferred strategies for making sense of why "other" people and cultures "do what they do"; global engagement (e.g., receptivity to different cultures, religions, and social practices); and worldview shift (e.g., to what degree do beliefs and values change as a result of specific experiences). BEVI results are translated into reports at the individual, group, and organizational levels and used in a wide range of contexts for a variety of applied and research purposes (e.g., to track and examine changes in worldviews over time) (e.g., Anmuth et al., 2013; Atwood, Chkhaidze, Shealy, Staton, & Sternberger, 2014; Brearly, Shealy, Staton, & Sternberger, 2012; Hayes, Shealy, Sivo, & Weinstein, 1999; Hill et al., 2013; Isley, Shealy, Crandall, Sivo, & Reifsteck, 1999; Pysarchik, Shealy, & Whalen, 2007; Shealy, 2004, 2005, 2015, 2016; Shealy et al., 2012; Tabit et al., 2011; for more information about the BEVI, including a description of scales, see Chapter 4).

Criminal Beliefs and Behaviors Through an EI Lens

Although making no definitive claims, EI Theory, the EI Self, and the BEVI offer a model and method that may help advance our understanding of how formative variables (e.g., life history, demographics) moderate and mediate both punitive beliefs and criminal behaviors as well as the etiology of criminal behavior (e.g., who demonstrates criminal behaviors and why, and under what circumstances). From an EI perspective, once belief and value structures are formed, they are "quite stable, if not immutable" (Shealy, 2004, p. 1077). As with all beliefs, those that are "punitive" in nature result from an interaction between "formative variables" (e.g., variables that shape the structure and functioning of "self" both historically and currently, as well as acquired beliefs, values, attitudes, and worldview) and "core needs" (e.g., affiliation, attachment, attunement) (Shealy, 2016).

To illustrate the empirical basis for such a conclusion, we analyzed data from a large dataset (N = 2331) collected during 2011 to 2012 from the Forum BEVI Project, a multi-institution, multiyear project examining the assessment of international, multicultural, and transformative learning. Coordinated by the Forum on Education Abroad (Forum On Education Abroad, 2015) and International Beliefs and Values Institute (www.ibavi.org), participants primarily included undergraduate students (96.7%) and were recruited through a range of learning experiences (e.g., study abroad, residential learning communities, general education courses with a focus on transformative/multicultural learning). A small portion of graduate students (3.3%) also was included. The sample typically ranged between the ages of 17 and 26, with an average age of 19. However, 3.9% fell into the age range of 26 to 62, with another 9% falling into the age range of 12 to 17. Although the majority of participants reported as U.S. citizens (93.3%), non-U.S. citizens also were included in the sample (N = 156 or 6.7%). Also, participants were drawn from 38 different countries of origin. Of the sample, 79.1% reported as Caucasian with 20.9% as non-Caucasian (6.6% Black or African American; 0.9% American Indian or Alaskan Native; 7.4% Asian or Pacific Islander; 2.9% Hispanic/Latino; 3% Other). Finally, from the standpoint of gender, 40.8% of the sample was female, with 59.2% male. All participants were required to provide informed consent as determined by multiple Institutional Review Boards processes, and participation was entirely voluntary. Participants were not required to complete the BEVI, and could elect to discontinue participation at any time. Analyses were conducted via SPSS and MPLUS, and consist of analysis of variances (ANOVAs), regression analyses, and structural equation modeling (SEM). More information on the Forum BEVI Project is available in Chapter 4 and at http://www.ibavi .org/content/featured-projects. For present purposes, we examine how demographic data and quality of family relationships predict punitive beliefs and engagement in criminal activity. Next, we consider three BEVI scales—Needs Fulfillment, Emotional Attunement, and Gender Traditionalism—in order to understand their relationship to the prediction of legal difficulties.

The first set of analyses examined which demographic variables might differentiate the sample at the item level of analyses, focusing on the following two BEVI items: *Punishment can work if it's swift and severe* and *I have had serious legal problems in my life*. The first item was selected because it appeared to capture a core belief vis-à-vis the criminal system[2]; the second item was selected because it allows for an understanding of whether and how life events may be associated with self-reported legal problems. For the first item, we focused on three sample formative variables—gender, political orientation, and residential setting—in order to ascertain whether such "formative variables" were associated with tendencies for or against this belief statement from the BEVI.

First, as Table 13.1 illustrates, on average, males are significantly more inclined than females to believe that swift and severe punishment is effective.

Second, as Table 13.2 illustrates, Republicans are significantly more inclined than those self-identified as Democrats or Independents to believe that swift and severe punishment is effective.

---

[2] BEVI responses may be provided on a four-point Likert-type scale, which includes the following options: Strongly Agree, Agree, Disagree, and Strongly Disagree.

TABLE 13.1
Gender Differences in Punishment Beliefs

SOURCE	SUM OF SQUARES	MEAN	DF	MEAN SQUARE ERROR	F	SIG.
Corrected Model	44.640		1	44.64	80.639	0.00
Intercept	14,248.75		1	14,248.8	25,739.28	0.00
Gender	46.64		1	44.64	80.639	0.00
Female		2.331				
Male		2.616				
Error	1,261.609		2,279	0.554		
Total	1,5555		2,281			
Corrected Total	1,306.249		2,280			

Note. $R^2 = 0.0034$ (*adjusted* $R^2 = 0.034$).

TABLE 13.2
Political Differences in Punishment Beliefs

SOURCE	SUM OF SQUARES	MEAN	DF	MEAN SQUARE ERROR	F	SIG.
Corrected Model	24.710		3	8.237	14.634	0.00
Intercept	14248.75		1	14248.75	25316.75	0.00
Political Orientation	24.71		3	8.237	14.634	0.00
Democrat		2.39				
Independent		2.462				
Republican		2.637				
Other		2.554				
Error	1281.539		2277	0.563		
Total	15555		2281			
Corrected Total	1306.249		2380			

Note. $R^2 = 0.019$ (*adjusted* $R^2 = 0.018$).

Third, as Table 13.3 illustrates, individuals who live in rural areas are significantly more inclined to believe in effectiveness of harsh punishment compared to individuals who live in suburban areas.

As Tables 13.4 and 13.5 illustrate, of these three variables, two—gender and residential setting—were also significantly associated with our second question, *I have had serious legal problems in my life*. More specifically, on average males are significantly more likely to report serious legal problems than are females. Moreover, individuals in urban areas are significantly more likely to report serious legal problems than residents of both rural and suburban settings.

TABLE 13.3
Setting Differences in Punishment Beliefs

SOURCE	SUM OF SQUARES	MEAN	DF	MEAN SQUARE ERROR	F	SIG.
Corrected Model	4.121		2	2.06	3.604	0.027
Intercept	14248.75		1	14248.75	24927.39	0.00
Setting	4.121		2	2.06	3.604	0.027
Urban		2.522				
Rural		2.549				
Suburban		2.453				
Error	1302.128		2278	0.572		
Total	15555		2281			
Corrected Total	1306.249		2380			

Note. $R^2 = 0.003$ *(adjusted* $R^2 = 0.002$*).*

TABLE 13.4
Gender Differences in the Report of Legal Problems in Life

SOURCE	SUM OF SQUARES	MEAN	DF	MEAN SQUARE ERROR	F	SIG.
Corrected Model	19.640a		1	19.64	43.591	0.00
Intercept	5278.33		1	5278.33	11715.11	0.00
Gender	19.64		1	19.64	43.591	0.00
Female		1.405				
Male		1.593				
Error	1034.03		2295	0.451		
Total	6332		2297			
Corrected Total	1053.67		2296			

Note. $R^2 = 0.019$ *(adjusted* $R^2 = 0.018$*).*

To explore such interacting processes more closely, we next conducted a second type of analysis using structural equation modeling (SEM), which allows for the examination of complex relationships among constructs that are hypothesized to exist in a particular theoretical relationship to one another (i.e., the model in SEM). In doing so, we examined the relationship between (a) *formative variables* (e.g., as the EI Self indicates, such variables are those that are associated with how and why we become "structured" as we do from a belief/value standpoint); (b) *mediators* (e.g., on the BEVI, these consist of specific scales, which capture a range of processes, including the belief that "core needs" were met during childhood and adolescence, such as the need for emotional resonance with others); and (c) *outcomes* (e.g., how such formative variables and mediators are associated with specific behaviorally oriented outcomes). For

TABLE 13.5
Setting Differences in the Report of Legal Problems in Life

SOURCE	SUM OF SQUARES	MEAN	DF	MEAN SQUARE ERROR	F	SIG.
Corrected Model	19.628		2	9.814	21.772	0.00
Intercept	5278.33		1	5278.33	11709.86	0.00
Setting	19.628		2	9.814	21.772	0.00
Urban		2.522				
Rural		2.549				
Suburban		2.453				
Error	1034.042		2294	0.451		
Total	6332		2297			
Corrected Total	1053.67		2296			

Note. $R^2 = 0.019$ (adjusted $R^2 = 0.018$).

clarification purposes, each of the following models differ at the "mediator" level of analysis (i.e., specific scales on the BEVI). Both "formative variables" (e.g., Positive Family Relations and other background variables) as well as our "outcome" measure (the BEVI item, *I have had serious legal problems in my life*) remain constant.

First, as Figure 13.1 illustrates, a higher degree of "Needs Fulfillment" (i.e., a BEVI scale that measures the degree to which individuals report core needs were in fact met during development) is *negatively predictive* of a tendency to report agreement that *I have had serious legal problems in my life*; one's non-Caucasian status and reported presence of a disability are *negatively predictive* of Needs Fulfillment; and Positive Family Relations (i.e., a BEVI scale measuring the degree to which caregiver relations and family dynamics were reported to be supportive and constructive) is *positively predictive* of Needs Fulfillment. The model fit indexes for this model are specified as follows: $\chi 2 = 2325.107$, df $= 261$, $p = .000$, RMSEA $= 0.058$, and CFI $= 0.913$.[3]

Second, as Figure 13.2 illustrates, a higher degree of Emotional Attunement (i.e., a BEVI scale measuring the degree to which individuals are inclined to experience and express affect as well as a desire for emotional connection with others) is *negatively predictive* of a tendency to report agreement that *I have had serious legal problems in my life*; one's non-Caucasian status is *negatively predictive* of Emotional Attunement; and Positive Family Relations is *positively predictive* of Emotional Attunement. The model fit indexes for this model are specified as follows: $\chi 2 = 2385.198$, df $= 261$, $p = .000$, RMSEA $= 0.059$, and CFI $= 0.922$.

---

[3] From an interpretive standpoint, ethnicity is a dummy measured variable; value "0" indicates the respondent is a minority, and "1" means the respondent is a Caucasian. Disability also is a dummy variable; "0" indicates the person is not eligible for services for students with disabilities, and "1" means otherwise. Family income is measured by a series of numbers indicating the respondent's annual family income. It ranges from "1" (Less than $10,000) to "10" ($175,000 or more). Both father's education and mother's education are ordinal measured variables. They range from "0" (Some high school or less) to "8" (Doctoral degree). Finally, we used weighted least squares means and variance adjusted (WLSMV) as the estimator for all the structural equation models because the variables have ordinal or dummy measures.

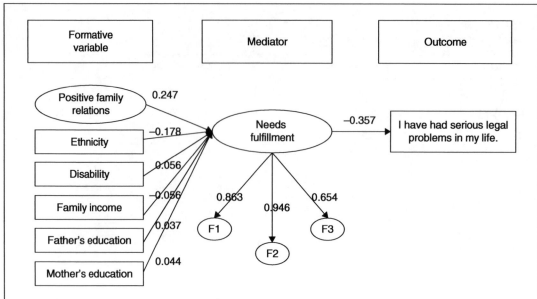

FIGURE 13.1. Structural Equation Model illustrating the relationship between formative variables and outcome with Needs Fulfillment as mediator.

Note. $X^2 = 2325.107$, df $= 261$, $p = .0000$, RMSEA $= 0.058$, CFI $= 0.913$.

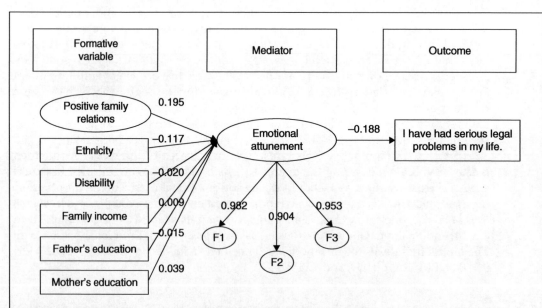

FIGURE 13.2. Structural Equation Model illustrating the relationship between formative variables and outcome with Emotional Attunement as mediator.

Note. $X^2 = 2385.198$, df $= 261$, $p = .0000$, RMSEA $= 0.059$, CFI $= 0.922$.

Interpretation of Findings and Implications for Intervention

These findings suggest a number of intriguing conclusions, which build upon other research presented previously to help illuminate the processes underlying the development of beliefs and values vis-à-vis criminal justice as well as the formative variables and cognitive/affective mediators of criminality. Such results also offer further insight into the sorts of interventions that may be helpful in terms of targeting key areas of emphasis in real world application, as is discussed in the third and final section of this chapter. Regarding interpretation, ANOVA findings presented in Tables 13.1 to 13.3 indicate, perhaps not surprisingly that males, who are Republicans, and reside in a rural setting are most likely to endorse the belief that *punishment can work if it's swift and severe*. Aside from the fact that these demographics are associated with such a belief, what is most interesting is why that would be? In other words, what is it about "being" male, Republican, and rural that are so predictive of this fundamental belief? Harkening back to our attendant and previous discussion of "choice" and "free will," as the SEM data further suggest, such an outcome likely results from a complex interaction among formative variables that largely were determined by external circumstances (e.g., one's caregivers; the nature of family dynamics; one's context; one's gender as it is experienced through development in a particular sociocultural milieu) rather than some putative process of "choice." In other words, we become what we believe for reasons that largely are determined for us, and unbeknownst to us, even as we assume that such outcomes are the result of a "conscious process of decision making." Such a conclusion is not to suggest that reflection and life experience cannot result in fundamental changes to our underlying beliefs and values, as evidence suggests they certainly may, particularly when such experiences are characterized by at least three of the "7Ds," including (a) duration (e.g., the longer length of experience that is discrepant from what we are accustomed), (b) difference (e.g., how distinct the experience is to what we are accustomed), and (c) depth (e.g., our capacity and inclination to apprehend the full affective and cognitive dimensions of the experience to which we are exposed) (Shealy, 2016). In terms of actual outcomes (e.g., whether individuals tend to report that they have in fact experienced serious legal problems in life), such conclusions receive further support from Tables 13.4 to 13.5 presented. Not surprisingly, it appears that males who are urban dwellers also are significantly more likely to report that they have experienced legal problems in their lives.

Delving more deeply into such processes, however, note from the SEMs in Figures 13.1 and 13.2 that the likelihood of one indicating a "positive" life history (e.g., healthy relations with and between caregivers; favorable dynamics in the home) is significantly predicted by one's report that core needs were met as well as one's emotional capacity (e.g., the ability and inclination to experience and express emotions, and to attend to the same in others). This linkage further extends to the likelihood of one reporting that he or she has in fact experienced "significant legal problems" in life. In short, individuals who report that they have experienced a *more negative* life history are *less likely* to report that core needs have been met and *less likely* to experience and express emotions, or to attend to them in others, as well as a *greater likelihood* of reporting that they have experienced "significant legal problems" in their lives.

From an applied perspective, the implications of such findings within a forensic setting with incarcerated individuals may be clear. If we were able to measure and illustrate such processes in a reliable and valid manner, and create a safe and open venue by which such findings could be discussed, it may help those who have engaged in criminal activity to understand fundamental matters of *why* they did what they did as well as what they may need to do in order to change the trajectories that have theretofore defined their lives. Such a prospect is *not* to suggest that such understanding will be sufficient in itself to modify extant self structures, or to ignore contingencies in the real world that also facilitate criminal conduct (and may well prevail upon release), only that such comprehension is a necessary precursor to understanding internal processes that have largely been unknown to the inmate at the very least. Thus, in this third and final section of this chapter, we illustrate how the EI model and BEVI method may facilitate these important means and ends.

THE HOW: WORKING WITH BELIEFS AND VALUES IN THE JUSTICE SYSTEM

Informed by the preceding overview of relevant theory and data, 11 males who were serving their sentence in a residential facility in Virginia (United States)—where emphasis is on securing and maintaining work in a paid job external to the facility—participated in a 3-hour workshop using the EI model and BEVI method. This 5- to 7-month residential facility, a "diversion center," is designed for nonviolent felons who require more security or supervision than is available through community supervision alone. Prior to arriving at the diversion center, a majority of the participants were placed in a detention center, a 5- to 7-month residential program, which emphasizes military drill, discipline, strict hygiene, and limited privileges. In terms of background information, seven participants identified as White, three as Black, and one participant identified as Black and White. Participants' self-identified political orientation varied greatly with three Democrats, three Republicans, two Independents, one with no political orientation, one who did not know his political orientation, and one who did not respond. Participants' self-identified religious orientation also varied with six Christians, two atheists, one Muslim, one undecided, and one who did not respond. As per the Virginia Department of Corrections Human Subject Research Review Committee approval process, the two phases of this intervention—completion of the BEVI and participation in a subsequent workshop 2 weeks later—were completely voluntary. All participants were required to sign informed consent before they were eligible to complete the BEVI or participate in the workshop. Following completion of the BEVI, individual and group reports were generated and presented to the participants during the 3-hour workshop, which was coordinated by the developer of the BEVI.

The goals of the workshop were to engage participants in an intensive process of individual and group-based assessment in order to facilitate a deeper understanding of how and why each of them experienced self, others, and the larger world as they do. More specifically, by completing the BEVI, each participant was given (confidentially, and after signing an additional release) an individual report, which essentially consists of a 7- to 9-page narrative, which is individualized on the basis of specific BEVI scores, and addresses a number of relevant issues (e.g., why do we come to believe what we do; how and why does our life history affect our functioning, and impact why we do what we do; how does a greater understanding of self, emotions, and core needs help us think about our life histories, relationships, futures, etc.). In addition to these individual reports, participants were also able to review a group report, which provides aggregated scores across all group members in the context of five separate group-level indexes (e.g., group profile on the BEVI; dispersion of the group across the group profile; how strongly beliefs and values are held; how similar the group is to itself in terms of beliefs and values; and to what degree beliefs and values change over time). In this way, individuals are able to compare their own results (privately) with the aggregated scores of the group as a whole (publicly). This private/public aspect of the workshop allows each individual participant to review the similarities and differences between themselves and the larger group, while engaging in an intensive process of reflection upon why human beings experience self, others, and the larger world as they do.

In designing this intervention, specific attention was given to identifying how the EI model and BEVI method relate to other program curricula to which participants were exposed. Specifically, as indicated earlier, this workshop was informed by the T4C curriculum developed by Bush, Glick, and Taymans (2011) under the aegis of the U.S. National Institute of Corrections (NIC). Because there was clear synergy between the objectives of T4C—and the approach of the EI model and BEVI method—alignment for purposes of the workshop was accomplished readily. For example, in addition to focusing on cognitive and behavioral changes, T4C emphasizes the importance of awareness and identification of one's own and others' feelings as well as increasing participants' capacity to respond in a more adaptive manner to the experience and expression of affect by self or others. Because the EI model and BEVI explicitly address such issues via individual and group reports—and in the context of in-depth and group-based discussion regarding how beliefs are linked to life history, needs, feelings, and behaviors—the linkage between the workshop and T4C curricula was logically and intuitively apparent.

As noted, the workshop consisted of two sessions: (a) an initial meeting in which the project was described, consent forms were signed, and the BEVI was completed; and (b) an interactive workshop based upon the EI model during which the facilitator engaged participants in a discussion regarding (1) the meaning of beliefs and values, (2) the factors that impact why we believe what we believe, and (3) an in-depth exploration of the connection between beliefs, needs, feelings and behaviors. Importantly, participants readily seemed able to relate to the presented content, and likewise were able to discuss the origins of their own worldviews (i.e., at a subjective level, judging by the quality of their responses and questions, the material appeared to be accessible and relevant for them). After it was clear through group-based discussion that the basic EI model was understood, participants were asked to sign a form allowing them to receive their individual reports (these were identifiable via a code, rather than name, so as to ensure anonymity). At that point, they were given approximately 15 minutes to read these reports privately. Following completion of this process, the group report results were presented and discussed. At the conclusion of the entire workshop, a satisfaction survey was presented, which participants were asked to complete anonymously.

Group Report Results

Raw scores on the BEVI are converted into percentages (ranging from 1 to 100) for all 18 scales of the BEVI. The Aggregate Group Profile is presented in Figure 13.3. As expected, on the two BEVI scales addressing life history, the group report indicated the following scores: Negative Life Events (57th pecentile) and Needs Closure (42nd percentile). Taken together, such scores indicate that this group is reporting a degree of unhappy life experiences, and is reporting that their "core needs" as specified by the EI Self (e.g., attachment, affiliation, etc.) were met less of the time than typically appears to be the case for a nonclinical population. However, on Identity Closure

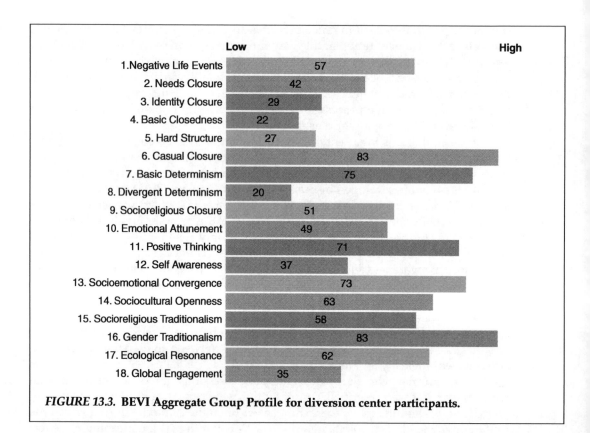

FIGURE 13.3. BEVI Aggregate Group Profile for diversion center participants.

(29th percentile), which measures the degree to which individuals report confusion about life course/path, and little agency or ability to affect change, the group as a whole does not evidence particular elevations.

Moreover and importantly, on three additional BEVI scales—which measure the ability to acknowledge basic human experiences (Basic Closedness, 22nd percentile), the tendency to insist upon the "rightness" of a particular version of reality (Hard Structure, 27th percentile), and the tendency to become argumentative for the sake of being so (Divergent Determinism, 20th percentile)—participants overall displayed a good degree of nondefensiveness in terms of access to feelings and thoughts in self and others.

This general capacity is revealed again by a relatively strong score on Socioemotional Convergence (73rd percentile), a "primary factor"[4] on the BEVI that is associated with the capacity to hold complexity (e.g., the ability to see the world in shades of gray versus black and white). Likewise, a relative elevation on Sociocultural Openness (63rd percentile), another "primary factor" on the BEVI, indicates that overall, this group is quite open to beliefs and practices of groups that are different from one's own. Moreover, as a whole, they are inclined to be concerned about and attuned with

[4] Primary Factor "PF" and Secondary Factor "SF" designations refer to whether the scale was extracted as a "primary" or "secondary" factor, and in which order of extraction (primary factors were derived via a Schmid–Leiman transformation, which essentially is a factor analysis of a factor analysis). Also, in this case, the "long version" of the BEVI was used. Most settings are now using the "short version," which has a number of psychometric advancements over the long version. More information about the BEVI (e.g., factor structure, reliabilities), and its report system, is available in Chapter 4 and at www.thebevi.com/aboutbevi.php.

nature and the "living world" (Ecological Resonance, 62nd percentile), which suggests the potential value of an intriguing and unrealized intervention for this group (e.g., wilderness/nature-based) (e.g., Kelly, Holt, Patel, & Nolet, 2016).

From the standpoint of openness, it also should be noted that overall, scores on both Socioreligious Closure (51st percentile) and Socioreligious Traditionalism (58th percentile) suggest that this group does not evidence intensity or rigidity at the level of religious convictions. Such a gestalt of scores is important because it suggests that this group, as a whole, is likely to be open to the idea and reality of self/other exploration, which bodes well over the long term, provided they are offered sufficient opportunities for constructive and safe reflection on such matters.

At the same time and equally important, the group as a whole tends toward stereotypic and punitive introjects toward self and others (Causal Closure, 83rd percentile) as well as simplistic explanations for why human beings do what they do (Basic Determinism, 75th percentile). Such a conclusion receives further support from the high elevation on Positive Thinking (71st percentile), which is a mixed blessing, since it does suggest an overall tendency to believe one should "overcome obstacles, no matter what," but also is freighted simultaneously with unrealistic beliefs about one's ability to "will oneself" to success, and a concomitant intolerance toward weakness (i.e., "excuses") in self or others. Such tendencies likely are problematic. Why? Although this group would indeed be quite open to what is "really going on" at an affective or cognitive level—a conclusion that is supported further by a solid degree of Emotional Attunement (49th percentile)—their current beliefs regarding how and why they and other human beings "should function as they do" appear to be quite rigid and rudimentary overall.

Complicating matters further, and consistent with this overall pattern, a relatively low degree of Self Awareness (37th percentile), means that the group as a whole is disinclined to reflect introspectively. Moreover, this group shows highly elevated scores on Gender Traditionalism (83rd percentile), which suggests that their beliefs and values vis-à-vis the "proper" roles of males and females, and the relations between them, would be highly stereotyped and rigid. Thus, in this key domain of belief/value functioning, this group is not at all inclined to reflect upon the potential hazards of such an unyielding worldview regarding gender roles and relations. Similarly, as a group, they tend not to be interested in the prospect or possibility of "making a difference" in the larger world (Global Engagement, 35th percentile). Overall, then, complexity and nuance regarding human motives would likely not be discerned readily in self or other, despite the fact that as a group, they would be quite open to learning about such matters, a reality that appeared to be borne out by the overall workshop process.

Although the group report provides an overall (i.e., averaged) profile, an additional table—the Decile Profile—may be as illuminating as the overall group profile, since it offers additional information regarding the similarities and differences among the group as a whole. Such information is key to understanding whether and to what degree the group really is "like itself" and/or if in fact aggregated scores have obscured substantive differences. As the Decile Profile (Figure 13.4) indicates, such is the case with this group, a reality that provided the opportunity for fruitful and evocative dialogue.

In interpreting the Decile Profile, note first that what we essentially are reviewing is a breakdown on the Aggregate Profile (Figure 13.3) by increments of 10% (i.e., deciles). Recall from the Aggregate Profile, for example, that Socioreligious Closure was at the 51st percentile, which would imply, on the face of it, that the group was "in the middle" in terms of whether the actions of self and others could and should be interpreted through a "religious lens" (i.e., whether or not someone was inclined to

Deciles:	1	2	3	4	5	6	7	8	9	10
1. Negative Life Events	9%	0%	0%	18%	0%	36%	18%	0%	0%	18%
2. Needs Closure	0%	0%	0%	36%	64%	0%	0%	0%	0%	0%
3. Identity Closure	18%	27%	9%	9%	27%	9%	0%	0%	0%	0%
4. Basic Closedness	27%	18%	9%	36%	0%	0%	0%	9%	0%	0%
5. Hard Structure	36%	9%	9%	18%	0%	0%	9%	0%	9%	9%
6. Casual Closure	0%	0%	0%	9%	0%	18%	0%	9%	27%	36%
7. Basic Determinism	0%	0%	9%	0%	18%	9%	9%	9%	36%	9%
8. Divergent Determinism	27%	27%	9%	18%	9%	9%	0%	0%	0%	0%
9. Socioreligious Closure	9%	9%	9%	0%	9%	9%	18%	27%	9%	0%
10. Emotional Attunement	18%	0%	0%	18%	9%	18%	18%	18%	0%	0%
11. Positive Thinking	18%	9%	0%	0%	9%	18%	9%	0%	9%	27%
12. Self Awareness	18%	0%	27%	0%	18%	18%	9%	0%	9%	0%
13. Socioemotional Convergence	0%	0%	0%	0%	0%	18%	27%	27%	9%	18%
14. Sociocultural Openness	0%	0%	0%	0%	0%	45%	27%	27%	0%	0%
15. Socioreligious Traditionalism	18%	0%	0%	0%	18%	0%	9%	27%	27%	0%
16. Gender Traditionalism	0%	0%	0%	0%	0%	18%	9%	36%	18%	18%
17. Ecological Resonance	0%	0%	9%	9%	18%	18%	0%	18%	18%	9%
18. Global Engagement	9%	9%	36%	18%	0%	9%	0%	18%	0%	0%

FIGURE 13.4. BEVI Decile Profile for diversion center participants.

agree, or disagree, that one's conduct and the problems of society could best be understood from the standpoint of religious-based convictions). Note that in fact, for this group, 3 of the 11 respondents were at or below the 30th percentile on this scale, which suggests a significant split in the group in terms of whether religious attributions tend to be employed to explain why human beings do what they do.

Moreover, consider the divergence across Self Awareness. As noted, the overall score (37th percentile) indicates that as a whole, this group of individuals does not tend to reflect substantively upon the thoughts and processes of self and other. However, such an aggregate score masks the fact that 4 of the 11 participants actually fell above the 60th percentile on Self Awareness whereas 5 of the 11 participants fell below the 40th percentile; 2 participants were at the 50th percentile.

Similar dispersion also occurs on Emotional Attunement, another very important capacity, which addresses the degree to which one is able and inclined to attend to and be aware of affect in self and other. Although the average score was at the 49th percentile, 4 of the 11 participants fell below the 40th percentile, with two falling in the 10th percentile, whereas 6 of the 11 fell at or above the 60th percentile.

As a point of contrast, consider Gender Traditionalism by recalling first that the group, overall, responded in a highly elevated manner (83rd percentile). As a review of the Decile Profile indicates, there is no real split on this scale within the group. Although there is some variation (ranging from the 60th to the 100th percentile), the majority of respondents (over 70%) are above the 80th percentile on this scale. Thus, in contrast to beliefs and values about religion, the self, and emotion—where the group tends to show a wide spread overall—no such dispersion exists vis-à-vis beliefs and values about gender.

These and other themes comprised substantive areas of dialogue and process for the group. For example, by linking such findings back to our discussion of the EI Self, and in the context of reviewing these profiles, it was possible to consider: (a) the implications of such similarities and differences among group members (e.g., that they as a group may or may not see or encounter the world in the same way); (b) how their very strong convictions about the way the genders are and should be, may be experienced by the women with whom they were involved (e.g., not always well, according to the group); (c) how the relative capacity and willingness to understand one's self and emotional world, and that of others, was directly related to the degree to which they would be able to get their own needs met or accurately interpret the intentions and wishes of others (e.g., many members of the group expressed serious difficulties in these areas as well as a strong desire to be able to talk about such powerful issues, but did not feel they had the opportunity to do so either safely or with any depth during incarceration); (d) what the implications were for cultivating greater capacity to care toward self and others, including their own partners and children (e.g., another strong theme and desire for this group); and (e) how and why access to our own emotions and inner thoughts may be directly related to the kinds of life experiences we have had as well as the striking differences between them at this level (e.g., their variation on Negative Life Events), which may make life and overall functioning more—or less—difficult in the "real world" (e.g., by being relatively able or unable to apprehend and value their own experience, or to facilitate positive social and emotional connections with others, goals that seemed to be shared strongly by the entire group).

Ultimately, the hope here is that by understanding two levels of analysis—both *descriptive* (*what* they believe and value) and *interpretative* (*why* they believe and value that which they do)—these individuals may begin to make better sense of themselves and others as well as the implications for how such knowledge can help them identify risks and opportunities in their lives as they contemplate the world of relationships (e.g., how their rigid ideas regarding gender may affect the experience of them, especially by the women in their lives, and may inadvertently lead to relational conflict that actually can impair their own level of well-being and functionality upon release from incarceration). As is often the case in such group-based discussions, an intense and passionate dialogue ensued regarding the meaning of such findings not only in "the abstract" but at a very real level for them personally, given how important their relationships were to them—particularly with partners, wives, children, employers, and friends—and how badly they wished to "do things right" this time around.

For this workshop, the final area of focus dealt with the qualitative responses group members provided on the BEVI in response to questions which queried them (for example) about how they were—or were not—changed as a result of all they had experienced during their time of incarceration. The mixed methods nature of the BEVI, which facilitates interpretation of quantitative scores by understanding how participants actually are experiencing self, others, and the larger world, in their own words, is an especially illuminating aspect of the overall approach to these workshops (see Chapter 4). Overall, and highly relevant to the perspective presented earlier in this chapter regarding the merits of a punitive approach toward human beings—who already have experienced much by way of punishment in their lives—written responses to these qualitative questions regarding their experience of programs during incarceration were uniformly negative, engendering a great number of agitated if not hostile reactions.

For example, participants reported that the "boot camp" experience (e.g., typically a 6-month stint that occurred prior to placement in the diversion center) had no salutary impact, and was in fact, damaging. Three prototypical qualitative responses are illustrative in this regard. As one individual wrote, *Boot camp had no bearing on me wanting to change.* Another offered the following response: *I have come to realize that not only did it not work on me, but it made me very angry at people who run the program.* Finally, one participant wrote a particularly compelling statement in relation to the difference in facilities that provide rehabilitation (such as the diversion center, where this workshop was conducted) and facilities that do not include a "treatment" component:

> *The fact that within VA DOC, all the talk about rehabilitation is just that TALK. This is the only location I have been that really seems to care about what happens to us once we are released. I feel if other institutions concerned selves more about us as individuals instead of "numbers," release to society would be much more productive as well as successful.*

On the one hand, from the standpoint of corrections, a response to such reactions might be, "Well of course. The boot camp program is not meant to be enjoyable. These individuals are incarcerated, after all, and this program serves as a form of punishment." In granting potential legitimacy to such logic (i.e., we incarcerate individuals first and foremost as a form of punishment), an overarching question remains as to whether or not such programs actually are helpful from a societal standpoint. From the perspective of these workshop participants at least, the net effect of boot camp type programs is the production of even more hostile and alienated individuals, who not only do not gain relevant skills that will lead to better functioning in society, but rather acquire additional and seemingly grounded justifications for their anger at "the system," right or wrong.

At the same time, more than one individual saw the benefit of being "away" from drugs and alcohol, although such benefits appeared simply to be an artifact of incarceration (i.e., it was not that the reasons for their drug/alcohol usage was being addressed and/or that coping strategies were being taught, but simply that they did not have access to substances while imprisoned). Moreover, other individuals indicated that their religious beliefs had changed in a range of ways (e.g., Christianity now was rejected for another religious belief; others felt their religion more deeply). Additional observations had to do with their attempt to cultivate more desirable human qualities (e.g., greater kindness, respect, patience), which may be an intended or unintended benefit of incarceration (e.g., they had time to reflect upon the value of such attributes), but were mitigated against actively within the "boot camp" program (i.e., whatever gains they were able to make personally in terms of thinking about their conduct toward others seemed not to be learned as a result of the boot camp program).

Finally, as a point of contrast, several individuals commented on the value of the diversion center, and the fact that its means and methods—such as exposure to the T4C curriculum—were helpful. As one individual commented, during the whole of his experience of incarceration, the diversion center was the only place that "seems to care about what happens to us once we are released." Even so, many workshop participants voiced a deep desire for many more opportunities for in-depth examination of the kinds of topics and issues that had been discussed in this BEVI workshop.

The last phase of the workshop asked participants to provide written responses to a number of prompts; the opportunity to offer formal and anonymous ratings also was provided. Written responses were provided independently (i.e., time was allotted for each participant to write his or her own responses) and anonymously (i.e., they were requested not to provide their name anywhere on their responses). At the conclusion of this process, participants were invited to share any of their responses if they were comfortable doing so. All participants were also asked to provide a copy of their written responses on a voluntary basis for purposes of better understanding their individual and collective responses to this workshop (i.e., all were willing to do so; photocopies were subsequently made, and the originals returned to the participants). The specific prompts are summarized as follows: (a) reflect upon your understanding of the role and meaning of beliefs and values, including the presentation on beliefs and values, as well as the individual and group BEVI reports; (b) describe your own life priorities in light of all that has been presented and discussed; (c) imagine beliefs and values that you would wish to have about yourself, and others to have about you; and (d) on the basis of all that had been discussed, identify your own future steps for personal change.

Workshop Evaluation Results

In addition to the summary observations noted earlier, a workshop evaluation survey was completed anonymously at the conclusion of the workshop (i.e., they were asked not to provide their names or other identifying information on the survey). From a quantitative standpoint, five items focused on participant learning objectives and three items focused on satisfaction with the workshop coordinator and overall workshop. Two open-ended items focused on identifying best features of the workshop and suggestions for improvement. The first eight quantitative questions were responded to on a 1 to 5 scale (1 being Strongly Disagree, and 5 being Strongly Agree). The results from the workshop evaluation survey are summarized in Figure 13.5.

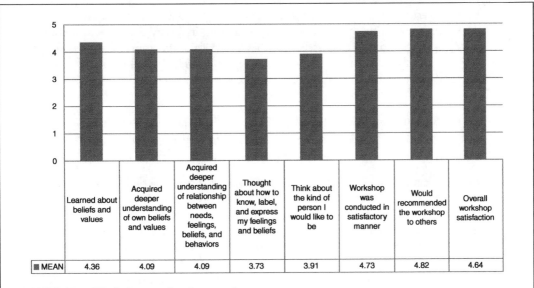

	Learned about beliefs and values	Acquired deeper understanding of own beliefs and values	Acquired deeper understanding of relationship between needs, feelings, beliefs, and behaviors	Thought about how to know, label, and express my feelings and beliefs	Think about the kind of person I would like to be	Workshop was conducted in satisfactory manner	Would recommended the workshop to others	Overall workshop satisfaction
MEAN	4.36	4.09	4.09	3.73	3.91	4.73	4.82	4.64

FIGURE 13.5. **Workshop evaluation results.**

As Figure 13.5 illustrates, participants expressed very high satisfaction with the workshop. The reasons for such ratings are described in the four summary observations presented next, and seem to revolve around the benefits of being able to explore and talk about such crucial matters, which cut to the core of who they are and what they hope to accomplish in their lives. The most frequently mentioned recommendation for improvement of the workshop was to include a one-on-one session to accompany the group session, so that they could speak freely about the depth of their thoughts, feelings, and needs, a recommendation that was forwarded to the head of this facility.

Summary Observations From Workshop Processes and Results

The following four summary observations of the workshop were derived from (a) a review of notes from the group discussion of the workshop along with (b) a review of all written responses to the four prompts described previously.

Observation 1: Participants Very Much Want to Discuss Issues of Beliefs, Values, Needs, and Feelings, as They Are at the Core of Who They Are and Want to Become

In reflecting upon their own beliefs and values, and those of the group, participants seemed highly intrigued by the similarities and differences among them. On the one hand, as noted, they appeared overall to be of a mind that men and women were "simply different," and that there were clear differences between them (e.g., men were to be strong, and women were the feelers). Several individuals recognized the problems, often serious, of this perspective. For example, a number of participants noted that the most significant conflicts they had experienced were with wives and partners who needed them to be better able to express what they were feeling, and how difficult it was for them to do so, which invariably led to fights, including those that ultimately contributed or led to their own recidivistic behavior. Along these lines, if one core finding emerged from this entire process, it likely would be the profound need to help incarcerated individuals understand better how to experience and express what they were needing and feeling in a way that was more likely to be effective rather than destructive to them and their partners, families, employers, friends, and futures. In fact, several participants requested additional services in this regard, a wish that was conveyed to the head of the diversion facility.

Observation 2: The Environments in Which Incarcerated Individuals Are Placed Seem Deliberately Designed to Prevent the Possibility of Any Sort of Meaningful Growth or Development

Participants indicated a deep desire to talk about the nature of, and reasons for, the differences between them. However, the environment in which they were placed made it virtually impossible to create a minimally trusting environment for doing so. As one individual observed, "it's best not to talk about religion because everyone thinks differently, they get upset and arguments occur." On the one hand, this observation is basic— after all, these individuals are in jail or prison, not in a therapy group. But if an overarching goal of incarceration is to lower the likelihood of such an outcome in the future, it seems just as self-evident to wonder why more opportunities for genuine discussion about the issues that appear to occupy these individuals are not offered during most, if not all, of their experiences within such systems (e.g., who they are; whether they can make it "out there"; how to deal with their own internal experiences, needs, and the emotional demands upon them). At that level, the societal impulse to recapitulate harsh and punitive environments through boot camp-like programs, which appear unsympathetic if not hostile toward human "feelings" and "needs," seems counterproductive at best if we truly are interested in lowering rates of recidivism, and releasing fellow citizens into a shared communal space with the skills, awareness, and impetus to engage constructively rather than prey destructively upon one another. At that level, the seeming aversion within the judicial system to the creation of relational environments that are conducive to growth and development seems unwise, since humans are socioemotional animals who depend upon each other, and are born into and for relationships. To work deliberately in opposition to the core needs of these individuals (i.e., attachment, affective, acknowledgment, activation, etc.) simply does not make sense if our goal is at least to try and release individuals who may have a chance of becoming productive members of society (see Chapters 2 and 3).

Observation 3: It is Helpful to Ask, Listen, and Respond to What Incarcerated Individuals Say That They Need in Order to Lessen the Likelihood of Unfortunate Outcomes in the Future

In articulating their own life priorities, participants actually were very clear on what they needed in order to avoid their present fate in the future. In addition to housing and education, as well as freedom from incarceration, the most frequently listed life priorities were: family, significant others (i.e., girlfriend, fiancé), meeting the needs of their children, and employment. More specifically, participants expressed a yearning for stable relationships in their lives and with family members, in particular children, as well as their intimate partners. Likewise, participants expressed a desire to "become a better person," "stay away from drugs and alcohol," experience personal change, and be more successful in life. When asked what they would want others to believe about them, they nearly unanimously answered that they wanted, as one participant stated, for "others to believe that they have changed." Yet, when asked whether they ever talked about such needs with others (i.e., those who cared about them and whom they cared for), the general response was that others would no longer believe in them, so there was no point. Finally, when asked to identify tasks they will have to accomplish in the next 6 months in order to be successful after being released, participants offered responses such as finding and keeping a job; staying away from drugs and alcohol; learning how not to hide emotions; not violating probation; staying devoted to family; and staying away from old friends who were involved in selling drugs. Long-term goals to be pursued over the next 5 years included: completing probation; keeping a job; staying away from drugs and alcohol; and getting married. Although participants were able readily to identify steps needed to lead a more fulfilling, crime-free life, the question they all asked, at one level or another, was how to address both environmental and psychological barriers and obstacles for them personally, so that they had a reasonable chance of success in the real world (i.e., they appeared to recognize how complex, confusing, and intensive such real dynamics were going to be for them to manage).

Again and poignant in that regard, when asked to what degree these fundamental issues had actually been addressed during their incarceration, they responded—to a person—that aside from the T4C program and BEVI workshop in the diversion center, such issues simply had not been raised at any level. Once made aware that these very issues could in fact be a focus of intensive exploration to help them achieve their goals, several participants expressed a desire to engage in deeper self-reflection and possibly psychotherapeutic intervention in order to become better partners to their fiancés and girlfriends, better fathers to their children, to provide in a more successful way for their family, and to break the cross-generational tradition of criminality that had long been the experience for many of them. Moreover, they expressed certainty about what kind of life they wanted to have as well as a willingness to strive toward such goals. Overall, they identified a need to achieve a sense of stability in their lives, and expressed the overarching desire to meet, and have met, their own core needs (e.g., for affiliation, attachment, acknowledgment, etc.), which they acknowledged from experience had insufficiently been met for much of their lives.

Observation 4. If Lower Recidivism Rates, and Greater Family and Community Well-Being, Are at all Relevant to the Goals of Incarceration, Our Current Approaches Are Ineffective at Best If Not Contraindicated

It is difficult to capture, in writing, the hostility and contempt participants expressed toward the experience of being incarcerated. And again, those responsible for developing and implementing such systems might argue, with some justification, that the aversive nature of jail or prison is in fact the point. To be clear, we do not disagree that there is a legitimate need to remove individuals from society who violate established and reasonable laws that are designed to protect individuals and the larger society. At this level, incarceration may represent the last point of recourse for such conduct, and as such, probably is unavoidable at this stage of our societal evolution. Reasonably administered sanctions for inappropriate conduct may be a source or learning that simply cannot be delivered through any other venue. We also wish neither to romanticize the often intractable problems that individuals who find themselves incarcerated face in their personal and interpersonal lives, nor to equate the individuals with whom we worked in this diversion center with all who are imprisoned. As clinicians, educators, scholars, and developers of policy, we have no illusions about the inherent complexity of the life and psychological processes that such individuals display, or the intensive nature of what is required from the standpoint of intervention if such individuals are to have a chance of living and leading constructive versus destructive lives. Ultimately, our plea is less driven by lofty progressive sensibilities or aspirations, and more by the pragmatic and demonstrable recognition that what we currently are doing simply does not work. Bluntly stated, if our goal is to punish, denigrate, crush, and humiliate individuals who have "done bad," we appear to be doing a stellar job. However, if our goal is—or should be—to try and reach these human beings by providing them with information, skills, and opportunities that are necessary if they are to have even a chance of living a relatively normal, pro-social, constructive life when they return to their communities, then there is so much more we can and should do. Moreover, such low intensive efforts were they to be widely implemented seem likely to result in little extra expenditure of public resources, and might even represent a cost savings from more punitive interventions that seem to prevail. Ultimately, we all reap the consequences of the interventions we sow. In this respect, we may feel gratified as a society that our meted punishment was felt to be so by those on the receiving end, but the larger questions we really should be asking are whether we can do better, both morally and pragmatically. Fortunately, both the T4C program and the results of this BEVI workshop indicate that we can provide information, skills, and processes that are deeply desired by those who are incarcerated. Moreover, the principles and perspectives of such interventions have theoretically and empirically salutary implications for how "justice" is conceptualized and delivered.

SUMMARY AND CONCLUSION

We began this chapter by providing a big picture examination of the role of "beliefs and values" in multiple facets of the "justice system" in the United States, writ large. Such considerations included the putative and questionable "impartiality" of the key players within this system (e.g., jurors, judges, attorneys) with a beginning focus on how the reality of bias is recognized explicitly via *voir dire*, the process by which jury members are selected. Other examples of how the concept of "impartial justice" is oxymoronic included the ruling out of potential jurists who are skeptical toward the death penalty in capital cases, thus skewing decisional processes and outcomes; the questionable practice of self-determination regarding recusal by judges, given our well-documented tendency to believe we are capable of greater impartiality than we tend to display; and the kindred shortcomings of "eye witnesses" and "expert" testimony, which demonstrably are biased by all manner of factors that confound the overarching task of discerning what actually happened or is true.

We then turned our focus to larger economic forces that also influence judicial processes, including the suspect system by which state-level judges are appointed or elected, since they may run under the banner of a political party, which inevitably involves fund raising from individuals and groups who are invested in particular legal outcomes. Money also affects fundamental matters of who is able to afford the best quality of legal representation as well as basic conflicts of interest, represented by privately run systems of incarceration, which depend upon a flow of inmates in order to ensure sustainable profits.

Then, there is the overarching question of whether our basic system of justice actually works in terms of crime deterrence, rehabilitation in prison, recidivism prevention, and protection of the public. As documented, the data overall are not encouraging, especially since the United States incarcerates a greater proportion of its citizens than any other country in the world, and continues to evince dismal rates of recidivism. Even so, the field has developed and implemented intervention programs that do work, exemplified perhaps by the T4C curriculum. However, in many programs receiving strong advocacy at a sociopolitical level, such as "Scared Straight" and "DARE," the unhelpful role of underlying punitive ideologies too often is unacknowledged, even when data demonstrate that such programs simply do not work or are contraindicated.

In order to understand better the origins of the worldviews that drive such justice-based policies and practices, we then considered the role of religion and politics. Among other sources for the "string 'em up" mentality that seems implicit in the "tough on crime" ideology is the powerful and largely unrecognized role that putative concepts of "free will" and "choice" play vis-à-vis jurisprudence. These simplistic notions (i.e., abundant evidence indicates that human thoughts, feelings, and actions are driven, to a considerable degree, by forces and factors that are out of our conscious awareness) continue to thrive mainly because they resonate with a Judeo-Christian worldview as well as authoritarian sociopolitical predilections that remain strong within the United States, and in related forms, around the world (e.g., the "eye for an eye" mentality).

If the human dynamics and socioeconomic machinery of the judicial system, and the ideologies that support its programs and methodologies, are inextricably linked to underlying but often implicit beliefs and values, what possible remedy is there in terms of creating a more just justice system? Although there is no one answer to this complex question, the argument offered in this chapter is that until we truly understand and acknowledge the interacting human processes that mediate and moderate crime—and correspondingly incorporate such information into all levels and expressions of our criminal justice system—it is likely that our ideologies and interventions will continue to fall short. Among such processes, as described earlier, early disruptive and maladaptive externalizing behaviors, which largely are linked to disturbed and disturbing familial and community-based processes, are among the best predictors of adolescent and adult criminality. By extension, among the more salient etiological factors in childhood-onset antisocial behavior are dysfunctional parenting practices—including but not limited to abuse and neglect—as well as disadvantaged neighborhoods, which place children at further risk for early-onset trajectory due to interactions with peers. Among demographic variables, race (non-Caucasian) and gender (male) also were found to be significant predictors of an engagement with the criminal justice system.

Following this overview, we then introduced the EI model and BEVI method in order to investigate two interrelated questions that flowed from this research: (a) which variables are predictive of beliefs regarding crime and punishment and (b) which variables are associated with a tendency to report legal difficulties in one's own life. Regarding the former question, through a range of analyses, ANOVA findings were presented, which illustrate that males, who are Republicans and reside in a rural setting, are most likely to endorse the belief that *punishment can work if it's swift and severe*; moreover, urban males also were more likely to report that they had experienced "significant legal problems" in their lives. Delving deeper into such processes, SEM data indicated overall that individuals who report that they have experienced a *more negative* life history also are *less likely* to report that core needs have been met, and *less likely* to experience and express emotions or to attend to them in others, as well as a concomitant and *greater likelihood* of reporting that they have experienced "significant legal problems" in their lives.

From an applied perspective, the implications of such findings within a forensic setting may be clear. If we were able to measure and illustrate such processes in a reliable and valid manner, and create a safe and open venue by which such findings are illustrated and discussed, it may be helpful for those who have engaged in criminal activity to understand fundamental matters of *why* such realities have prevailed, as well as *what* may be necessary for them to understand *who* they are, in order to change the trajectories that theretofore had defined their lives.

Thus, in the third and final section of this chapter, we described a workshop using the EI model and BEVI method that was designed to pursue such means and ends. Deliberately informed by the T4C curriculum, participants consisted of 11 inmates in a diversion center in Virginia, who were presented with the basic EI framework, provided both individual and group reports from the BEVI, and asked to reflect on a range of issues that were relevant to their life experiences, future aspirations, and concomitant beliefs about self, others, and the larger world. In addition to expressing their overall hostility toward the experience of being incarcerated, workshop evaluation results suggest that participants seemed equally appreciative about the opportunity to reflect on these fundamental matters. More specifically, they found it valuable to understand better how and why they experienced self, others, and the larger world as they did—and to consider their aspirations for their future lives, and all that they wished would occur in order to help them along the way—such as the opportunity to examine these issues in greater detail in a safe and confidential manner.

More specifically, as summarized previously, four fundamental observations emerged from this process. First, participants very much want to discuss issues of beliefs, values, needs, and feelings, as they are at the core of who they are and want to become. Second, the environments in which incarcerated individuals are placed seemingly are deliberately designed to prevent the possibility of any sort of meaningful growth or development. Third and related, it may be helpful to ask, listen, and respond to what incarcerated individuals say that they need. And fourth, if lower recidivism rates, and greater family and community well-being, are at all relevant to the goals of incarceration, our current approaches are ineffective at best if not contraindicated altogether.

In conclusion, as emphasized previously, we have no illusions about the complexity of the issues that have been addressed in this chapter. Nonetheless, the theory, data, and applications presented here illustrate strongly that we can and should create a more effective, and humane, system of justice, which will require a fundamental change in (a) *what* we understand about the inherent belief/value underpinnings of our justice system, (b) *why* we possess the beliefs about criminality that we do as well as why criminality occurs in the first place, and (c) *how* we may use information about beliefs and values to help individuals who are incarcerated to have a deeper and clearer understanding of self, others, and the world, while facilitating the acquisition of attendant skills and capacities that are necessary and sufficient for success in the real world.

Is such a transformation at all possible? The 2012 election in the United States offers some hope that we may finally be heading in this direction, as evidenced by the fact, for example, that Californians voted to reform the inequitable "three strikes rule," which imposed a mandatory sentence, including the possibility of life in prison, for the conviction of even minor felony convictions, such as petty theft for the third time. Among other consequences of this rule, originally approved by Californians in a 1994 ballot initiative, was the fundamental fact—supported by the data and intervention described in this chapter—that many of the individuals who end up incarcerated have experienced significant trauma in their lives. As quantitative and qualitative BEVI results illustrate, incarcerated individuals often are experiencing considerable psychological distress, which far too often is neither recognized nor addressed within the justice system. As Staples (2012) observed, the decision by Californians to overhaul the "three strikes" rule that an earlier generation had endorsed, amounts to a,

> . . . referendum on the state's barbaric treatment of mentally ill defendants, who make up a substantial number of those with life sentences under the three-strikes rule. . .Mentally ill inmates are nearly always jailed for behaviors related to their illness. Nationally, they account for about one-sixth of the prison population. (p. X10)

The results presented here, and the experience of workshop participants, are highly congruent with such observations as well as the bottom line conclusion that we all bear some measure of responsibility for the expression of criminality, either by conceptual and applied acts of commission, or by omission vis-à-vis our explanations and interventions in the name of justice. Indeed, the myth of impartiality in our judicial system may serve self-preservation purposes by protecting us from wide scale cognitive dissonance (i.e., since we're "good people," bad things could only happen to "bad people"). The belief in impartiality may also absolve us of responsibility for implementing policies and interventions that address the antecedents of crime and criminality in the first place.

In the final analysis, both locally and globally, we must overhaul not only reductive rules such as "three strikes," but the entire way in which we regard the unfortunate human beings who wind up in our antediluvian jails and prisons in the United States and all over the world. Far too often, our systems of justice justify their activities on the basis of discredited models of human nature, which perpetuate rather than attenuate the very problems they ostensibly are designed to prevent. In the process of dispensing such primitive forms of justice, we do far more harm to criminals— as well as those who subsequently will be victimized upon their release—than any good our collective desire for retribution ever will produce.

REFERENCES

Agnew, R. (2011). *Toward a unified criminology: Integrating assumptions about crime, people, and society.* New York, NY: University Press.

Agrast, M., Botero, J., & Ponce, A. (2011). *WJP rule of law index.* Washington, DC: The World Justice Project.

American Psychiatric Association. (2013). *Diagnostic and statistical manual of mental disorders* (5th ed.). Arlington, VA: American Psychiatric Publishing.

Andrews, D. A., & Bonta, J. (2006). *Psychology of criminal conduct* (3rd ed.). Cincinnati, OH: Anderson.

Andrews, D. A., & Bonta, J. (2010). Rehabilitating criminal justice policy and practice. *Psychology, Public Policy, & Law, 16*(1), 39–55. doi:10.1037/a0018362

Anmuth, L. M., Poore, M., Cozen, J., Brearly, T., Tabit, M., Cannady, M., . . . Staton, R. (2013, August). *Making implicit beliefs explicit: In search of best practices for mental health clients, clinicians, and trainers.* Poster presented at the annual meeting of the American Psychological Association, Honolulu, HI.

Applegate, B. K., Cullen F. T., Fisher, B. T., & Vander Ven, T. (2000). Forgiveness and fundamentalism: Reconsidering the relationship between correctional attitudes and religion. *Criminology, 38*(3), 719–754. doi:10.1111/j.1745-9125.2000.tb00904.x

Aronson, E. (2012). *The social animal* (11th ed.). New York, NY: Worth Publishers.

Atwood, K., Chkhaidze, N., Shealy, C. N., Staton, R., & Sternberger, L. G. (2014, August). *Transformation of self: Implications from the Forum BEVI Project.* Poster presented at the annual meeting of the American Psychological Association, Washington, DC.

Austin, J., & Coventry, G. (2001). *Emerging issues on privatized prisons.* Washington, DC: U.S. Dept. of Justice, Office of Justice Programs.

Bandura, A. (1962). *Social learning through imitation.* Lincoln, NE: University of Nebraska Press.

Bandura, A. (1971). *Social learning theory.* New York, NY: General Learning Press.

Bandura, A. (1975). *Social learning and personality development.* New Jersey, NJ: Holt, Rinehart & Winston, INC.

Beck, A. T. (1961). A systematic investigation of depression. *Comprehensive Psychiatry, 2*(3), 163–170. doi:10.1016/S0010-440X(61)80020-5

Beck, A. (1963). Thinking and depression: Idiosyncratic content and cognitive distortions. *Archives of General Psychiatry, 9*(4), 324–333. doi:10.1001/archpsyc.1963.01720160014002

Beck, A. T. (1972). *Depression: Causes and treatment.* Philadelphia, PA: University of Pennsylvania Press.

Beck, A. T. (1976). *Cognitive therapy and emotional disorders.* New York, NY: International Universities Press.

Benekos, P. J., Merlo, A. V., & Puzzanchera, C. M. (2011). Youth, race, and serious crime: examining trends and critiquing policy. *International Journal of Police Science & Management, 13*(2), 132–148. doi:10.1350/ijps.2011.13.2.231

Bennett, W. J., DiIulio, J. J., & Walters, J. P. (1996). *Body count.* New York, NY: Simon & Schuster.

Benton, T. R., Ross, D. F., Bradshaw, E., Thomas, W. N., & Bradshaw, G. S. (2006). Eyewitness memory is still not common sense: Comparing jurors, judges and law enforcement to eyewitness experts. *Applied Cognitive Psychology, 20*(1), 115–129. doi:10.1002/acp.1171

Blandón-Gitlin, I., Sperry, K., & Leo, R. (2011). Jurors believe interrogation tactics are not likely to elicit false confessions: Will expert witness testimony inform them otherwise? *Psychology, Crime & Law, 17*(3), 239–260. doi:10.1080/10683160903113699

Blumenthal, J. A. (2002). Law and social science in the twenty-first century. *Southern California Interdisciplinary Law Journal, 12*, 1–53. doi:10.2139/ssrn.355280

Bloom, L. (2012, November 23). When will the U.S. stop mass incarceration? *CNN.* Retrieved from http://www.cnn.com/2012/07/03/opinion/bloom-prison-spending/index.html

Boccaccini, M. T., Turner, D. B., & Murrie, D. C. (2008). Do some evaluators report consistently higher or lower PCL-R scores than others? Findings from a statewide sample of sexually violent predator evaluations. *Psychology, Public Policy, and Law, 14*(4), 262–283. doi:10.1037/a0014523

Bradfield, A. L., & Wells, G. L. (2000). The perceived validity of eyewitness identification testimony: A test of the five Biggers criteria. *Law and Human Behavior, 24*, 581–594. doi:10.1023/A:1005523129437

Brandenburg, B. (2010). Big money and impartial justice: Can they live together? *Arizona Law Review, 52*(2), 207–217.

Brearly, T., Shealy, C. N., Staton, R., & Sternberger, L. G. (2012, August). *Prejudice and religious and non-religious certitude: An empirical analysis from the Forum BEVI Project.* Poster presented at the annual meeting of the American Psychological Association, Orlando, FL.

Brearly, T.W., van den Bos, K., & Tan, C. (2016). The nature and etiology of religious certitude: Implications of the EI framework and Beliefs, Events, and Values Inventory. In C. N. Shealy (Ed.), *Making sense of beliefs and values* (pp. 331–369). New York, NY: Springer Publishing.

Breyer, S. (2008). Serving America's best interest. *Daedalus, 137*(4), 139–143. Retrieved from http://www.mitpressjournals.org/doi/pdf/10.1162/daed.2008.137.4.139

Buckholtz, J. W., & Marois, R. (2012). The roots of modern justice: Cognitive and neural foundations of social norms and their enforcement. *Nature Neuroscience, 15*(5), 655–661. doi:10.1038/nn.3087

Bureau of Justice Statistics. (2009). *Prisoners in 2008.* Retrieved from http://bjs.ojp.usdoj.gov/content/glance/incrt.cfm

Bush, J. M., & Bilodeau, B. (1993). *Options: A cognitive change program.* Longmont, CO: National Institute of Corrections.

Bush, J., Glick, B., & Taymans, J. (2011). *Thinking for a change: Integrated cognitive behavior change program.* Washington, DC: U. S. Department of Justice. Retrieved from http://nicic.gov/T4CWeb/

Carson, D., Milne R., Pakes, F., Shalev, K., & Shawher, A. (Eds.). (2007). *Applying psychology to criminal justice.* Chichester: Wiley.

Cochran, J. K., Boots, D. P., & Chamlin, M. B. (2006). Political ideology and support for capital punishment: A test of attribution theory. *Journal of Crime and Justice, 29*(1) 45–79.

Cole, G. F., & Gertz, M. G. (1998). *The criminal justice system: Politics and policies.* Belmont, CA: West/Wadsworth Publishing.

Coleman, L. (2004). *The copycat effect: How the media and popular culture trigger the mayhem in tomorrow's headlines.* New York, NY: Simon and Schuster.

Commons, M. L., Miller, P. M., & Gutheil, T. G. (2004). Expert witness perceptions of bias in experts. *Journal of the American Academy of Psychiatry and the Law, 32*(1), 70–75.

Costelloe, M. T., Chiricos, T., & Gertz, M. (2009). Punitive attitudes toward criminals: Exploring the relevance of crime salience and economic insecurity. *Punishment & Society, 11*(1), 25–49. doi:10.1177/1462474508098131

Coulter, A. (2006). *Godless: The church of liberalism*. New York, NY: Random House.

Cramer, R. J., Brodsky, S. L., & DeCoster, J. (2009). Expert witness confidence and juror personality: Their impact on credibility and persuasion in the courtroom. *Journal of the American Academy of Psychiatry and the Law, 37*(1), 63–74.

Cullen, F. T., Clark, G. A., Cullen, J. B., & Mathers, R. A. (1985). Attribution, salience, and attitudes toward criminal sentencing. *Criminal Justice and Behavior 12*(3), 305–331. doi:10.1177/0093854885012003003

Cummings, E., Davies, P., & Campbell, S. (2000). *Developmental psychopathology and family process*. New York, NY: Guilford Press.

Cutler, B. L. (2011). *Conviction of the innocent: Lessons from psychological research*. Washington, DC: American Psychological Association.

Dandreaux, D. M., & Frick, P. J. (2009). Developmental pathways to conduct problems: A further test of the childhood and adolescent-onset distinction. *Journal of Abnormal Child Psychology, 37*(3), 375–385. doi:10.1007/s10802-008-9261-5

Davies, P., & Cummings, E. (1994). Marital conflict and child adjustment: An emotional security hypothesis. *Psychological Bulletin, 116*(3), 387–411. doi:10.1037/0033-2909.116.3.387

Deffenbacher, K. A. (1980). Accuracy and confidence: Can we infer anything about their relationship? *Law and Human Behavior, 4*(4), 243–260. doi:10.1007/BF01040617

DeMatteo, D., Batastini, A., Foster, E., & Hunt, E. (2010). Individualizing risk assessment: Balancing idiographic and nomothetic data. *Journal of Forensic Psychology, 10*(4), 360–371. doi:10.1080/15228932.2010.481244

Disqualification of justice, judge, or magistrate judge, 28 U.S.C. §§ 455 (1990).

Douglass, A. B., & Pavletic, A. (2012). Eyewitness confidence malleability. In B. L. Coulter (Ed.), *Conviction of the innocent: Lessons from psychological research.* (pp. 149–165). Washington, DC, US: American Psychological Association.

Edens, J. F., Skopp, N. A., & Cahill, M. A. (2008). Psychopathic features moderate the relationship between harsh and inconsistent parental discipline and adolescent antisocial behavior. *Journal of Clinical Child and Adolescent Psychology, 37*(2), 472–476. doi:10.1080/15374410801955938

Ellis, A. (1962). *Reason and emotion in psychotherapy*. Secaucus, NJ: Lyle Stuart.

Ellis, A. (1997). *The practice of rational emotive behavior therapy*. New York, NY: Springer Publishing Company.

Evans, T. D., & Adams, M. (2003). Salvation or damnation?: Religion and correctional ideology. *American Journal of Criminal Justice, 28*(1), 15–35. doi:10.1007/BF02885750

Fagan, A. (2005). The relationship between adolescent physical abuse and criminal offending: Support for an enduring and generalized cycle of violence. *Journal of Family Violence, 20*(5), 279–290. doi:10.1007/s10896-005-6604-7

Feindler, E. L., & Ecton, R. B. (1986). *Adolescent anger control: Cognitive-behavioral techniques*. New York, NY: Pergamon Press.

Fergusson, D. M., & Horwood, L. J. (2002). Male and female offending trajectories. *Development and Psychopathology, 14*(1), 159–177. doi:10.1017/S0954579402001098

Finckenauer, J. E., & Gavin, P. W. (1999). *Scared Straight: The panacea phenomenon revisited*. Prospect Heights, IL: Waveland Press.

Fisher, R. P., Brewer, N., & Mitchell, G. (2009). The relation between consistency and accuracy of eyewitness testimony: Legal versus cognitive explanations. In R. Bull, T. Valentine, & T. Williamson (Eds.), *Handbook of psychology of investigative interviewing: Current developments and future directions* (pp. 121–136). Chichester: Wiley-Blackwell.

Fitzgerald, R., & Ellsworth, P. C. (1984). Due process vs. crime control: Death qualification and jury attitudes. *Law and Human Behavior, 8*(1–2), 31–51. doi:10.1007/BF01044350

Forum On Education Abroad. (2015). *Forum BEVI project: Working group activities in 2010–2011*. Retrieved from http://www.forumea.org/research-bevi-project.cfm

Fox, D. R. (1999). Psycholegal scholarship's contribution to false consciousness about injustice. *Law and Human Behavior, 23*(1), 9–30. doi:10.1023/A:1022370622463

Frick, P. J., & Viding, E. M. (2009). Antisocial behavior from a developmental psychopathology perspective. *Development and Psychopathology, 21*(4), 1111–1131. doi:10.1017/S0954579409990071

Garland, D. (2001). *The culture of control: Crime and social order in contemporary society*. Chicago, IL: University of Chicago Press.

Gendreau, P. (1996). The principles of effective intervention with offenders. In A.T. Harland (Ed.), *Choosing correctional options that work: Defining the demand and evaluating the supply* (pp. 117–130). Thousand Oaks, CA: Sage.

Gilbert, D. T. (1989). Thinking lightly about others. Automatic components of the social inference process. In J. S. Uleman & J. A. Bargh (Eds.), *Unintended thought* (pp. 189–211). New York, NY: Guilford.

Glick, B. (1979). Youth between the cracks. *Behavioral Disorders, 4*(4), 227–230.

Glick, B., & Gibbs, J. C. (2011). *Aggression replacement training: A comprehensive intervention for aggressive youth (revised and expanded)*. Champaign, IL: Research Press.

Glick, B., & Sturgeon, W. (1998). *No time to play: Youthful offenders in adult correctional systems*. Lanham, Maryland: American Correctional Association.

Gobert, J. J. (1988). In search of the impartial jury. *The Journal of Criminal Law and Criminology, 79*(2), 269–327. Retrieved from http://www.jstor.org/stable/1143469

Goldstein, A. P., & Glick, B. (1987). *Aggression replacement training: A comprehensive intervention for aggressive youth*. Champaign, IL: Research Press.

Goldstein, A., & McGinnis, E. (1997). *Skillstreaming the adolescent: New strategies and perspectives for teaching prosocial skills*. Champaign, IL: Research Press.

Goldstein, A. P., Sprafkin, R. P., & Gershaw, N. J. (1965). *Structured learning training for the mentally ill*. Syracuse, NY: Syracuse University Press.

Gottfredson, D. C., Wilson, D. B., & Najaka, S. S. (2002). School based crime prevention. In L. W. Sherman, D. P. Farrington, B. C. Welsh, & S. S. MacKenzie (Eds.), *Evidence-based crime prevention* (pp. 56–164). New York, NY: Routledge.

Grasmick, H. G., Davenport, E., Chamlin, M. B., & Bursik, R. J. (1992). Protestant fundamentalism and the retributive doctrine of punishment. *Criminology, 30(1)*, 21–46. doi:10.1111/j.1745-9125.1992.tb01092.x

Grasmick, H. G., & McGill, A. L. (1994). Religion, attribution style, and punitiveness towards juvenile offenders, *Criminology, 32*(1), 23–47. doi:10.1111/j.1745-9125.1994.tb01145.x

Greer, T., Berman, M., Varan, V., Bobrycki, L., & Watson, S. (2005). We are religious people; we are vengeful people. *Journal for the Scientific Study of Religion, 44*(1), 45–57. doi:10.1111/j.1468-5906.2005.00264.x

Gromet, D. M., & Darley, J. M. (2011). Political ideology and reactions to crime victims: Preferences for restorative and punitive responses. *Journal of Empirical Legal Studies, 8*(4), 830–855. doi:10.1111/j.1740-1461.2011.01242.x

Hallett, M. (2007). Volitional control of movement: The physiology of free will. *Clinical Neurophysiology, 118*(6), 1179–1192. doi:10.1016/j.clinph.2007.03.019

Haidt, J. (2001). The emotional dog and its rational tail: A social intuitionist approach to moral judgment. *Psychological Review, 108*(4), 814–834. doi:10.1037/0033-295X.108.4.814

Hayes, D., Shealy, C., Sivo, S., & Weinstein, Z. (1999, August). *Psychology, religion, and Scale 5 (Religious Traditionalism) of the "BEVI."* Poster session presented at the meeting of the American Psychological Association, Boston, MA.

Hewitt, L. E., & Jenkins, R. (1946). *Fundamental patterns of maladjustment: The dynamics of their origin*. Springfield, IL: State of Illinois.

Hill, C., Johnson, M., Brinton, C., Staton, R., Sternberger, L., & Shealy. (2013, August). *The etiology of economic beliefs and values: Implications and applications from the Forum BEVI Project*. Poster presented at the annual meeting of the American Psychological Association, Honolulu, HI.

Ingoldsby, E. M., Shaw, D. S., Winslow, E., Schonberg, M., Gilliom, M., & Criss, M. M. (2006). Neighborhood disadvantage, parent-child conflict, neighborhood peer relationships, and early antisocial behavior problem trajectories. *Journal of Abnormal Child Psychology, 34*(3), 303–319. doi:10.1007/s10802-006-9026-y

Innocence Project. (2012). *The innocence project*. Retrieved from www.innocenceproject.org

Isley, E., Shealy, C., Crandall, K., Sivo, S., & Reifsteck, J. (1999, August). *Relevance of the "BEVI" for research in developmental psychopathology*. Poster session presented at the meeting of the American Psychological Association, Boston, MA.

Jacobs, D., & Carmichael, J. T. (2002). The political sociology of the death penalty: A pooled time-series analysis. *American Sociological Review, 67*(1), 109–131. Retrieved from http://www.jstor.org/stable/3088936

Johnson, B. D. (2003). Racial and ethnic disparities in sentencing departures across modes of conviction. *Criminology, 41*(2), 449–490. doi:10.1111/j.1745-9125.2003.tb00994.x

Jost, K. (2011, October 14). Eyewitness testimony. *CQ Researcher, 21*, 853–876. Retrieved from http://library.cqpress.com/cqresearcher/

Justice at Stake. (2002, February 14). Justice at Stake National Surveys of American Voters and State Judges. Retrieved from: http://www.justiceatstake.org/media/cms/Pollingsumma ryFINAL_9EDA3EB3BEA78.pdf

Keen, B., & Jacobs, D. (2009). Racial threat, partisan politics, and racial disparities in prison admissions: A panel analysis. *Criminology, 47*(1), 209–238. doi:10.1111/j.1745-9125.2009.00143.x

Kelly, J., Holt, J., Patel, R., & Nolet, V. (2016). Environmental beliefs and values: In search of models and methods. In C. N. Shealy (Ed.), *Making sense of beliefs and values* (pp. 233–360). New York, NY: Springer Publishing.

Lansford, J. E., Miller-Johnson, S., Berlin, L. J., Dodge, K. A., Bates, J. E., & Pettit, G. S. (2007). Early physical abuse and later violent delinquency: A prospective longitudinal study. *Child Maltreatment, 12*(3), 233–245. doi:10.1177/1077559507301841

Larson, B. A., & Brodsky, S. L. (2010). When cross-examination offends: How men and women assess intrusive questioning of male and female expert witnesses. *Journal of Applied Social Psychology, 40*(4), 811–830. doi:10.1111/j.1559-1816.2010.00599.x

Lipsey, M. W., & Landenberger, N. A. (2007). Cognitive-behavioral interventions. In B. C. Welsh & D. P. Farrington (Eds.), *Preventing crime: What works for children, offenders, victims and places* (pp. 33–54). Lowell, MA: Springer.

Liptak, A. (2006, October 1). Tilting the scales?: The Ohio experience; Campaign cash mirrors a high court's ruling. *New York Times*. Retrieved from http://query.nytimes.com/gst/fullpage.html?res=9A06E7D81730F932A35753C1A9609C8B63

Loeber, R, Burke, J. D., & Pardini, D. A. (2009). Development and etiology of disruptive and delinquent behavior. *Annual Review of Clinical Psychology, 5*, 291–310. doi:10.1146/annurev.clinpsy.032408.153631

Loftus, E. F. (1980). *Memory*. Reading, MA: Addison-Wesley.

Lösel, F., & Beelman, A. (2007). Child social skills training. In B. C. Welsh & D. P. Farrington, (Eds.), *Preventing crime: What works for children, offenders, victims and places* (pp. 33–54). Lowell, MA: Springer.

Lowenkamp, C. T., Hubbard, D., Makarios, M. D., & Latessa, E. J. (2009). A quasi-experimental evaluation of Thinking for a Change: A "real world' application. *Criminal Justice and Behavior, 36*(2), 137–146. doi:10.1177/0093854808328230

Luus, C. A. E., & Wells, G. L. (1994). The malleability of eyewitness confidence: Co-witness and perseverance effects. *Journal of Applied Psychology, 79*(5), 714–723. doi:10.1037/0021-9010.79.5.714

Magnussen, S., Melinder, A., Stridbeck, U., & Raja, A. Q. (2010). Beliefs about factors affecting the reliability of eyewitness testimony: A comparison of judges, jurors and the general public. *Applied Cognitive Psychology, 24*(1), 122–133. doi:10.1002/acp.1550

Maruna, S., & King, A. (2004). Public opinion and community penalties. In T. Bottoms, S. Rex, & G. Robinson (Eds.), *Alternatives to prison: Options for an insecure society* (pp. 83–112). Cullompton: Willan.

McCord, J. (1999). Understanding childhood and subsequent crime. *Aggressive Behavior, 25*(4), 241–253. doi:10.1002/(SICI)1098-2337(1999)25:4<241::AID-AB1>3.0.CO;2-3

Meichenbaum, D., & Novaco, R. (1985). Stress inoculation: A preventative approach. *Issues in Mental Health Nursing, 7*(1–4), 419–435. doi:10.3109/01612848509009464

Mitchell, T. L., Haw, R. M., Pfiefer, J. E., & Meissner, C. A. (2005). Racial bias in mock juror decision-making: A meta-analytic review of defendant treatment. *Law and Human Behavior, 29*(6), 621–637. doi:10.1007/s10979-005-8122-9

Moffitt, T. E. (1993). Adolescence-limited and life-course persistent antisocial behavior: A developmental taxonomy. *Psychological Review, 100*(4), 674–701. doi:10.1037/0033-295X.100.4.674

Moffitt, T. E. (2003). Life-course persistent and adolescence-limited antisocial behavior: A 10-year research review and research agenda. In B. B. Lahey, T. E. Moffitt, & A. Caspi (Eds.), *Causes of conduct disorder and juvenile delinquency* (pp. 49–75). New York, NY: Guilford Press.

Moffitt, T. E., & Caspi, A. (2001). Childhood predictors differentiate life-course persistent and adolescence-limited antisocial pathways in males and females. *Development and Psychopathology, 13*(2), 355–376. doi:10.1017/S0954579401002097

Moffitt, T. E., Caspi, A., Dickson, N., Silva, P., & Stanton, W. (1996). Childhood-onset versus adolescent-onset antisocial conduct problems in males: Natural history from ages 3 to 18 years. *Development and Psychopathology, 8*(2), 399–424. doi:10.1017/S0954579400007161

Moffitt, T. E., Caspi, A., Harrington, H., & Milne, B. J. (2002). Males on the life-course-persistent and adolescence-limited antisocial pathways: Follow-up at age 26 years. *Development and Psychopathology, 14*(1), 179–207. doi:10.1017/S0954579402001104

Murrie, D. C., Boccaccini, M. T., Turner, D. B., Meeks, M., & Woods, C. (2009). Rater (dis)agreement on risk assessment measures in sexually violent predator proceedings. *Psychology, Public Policy, and Law, 15*(1), 19–53. doi:10.1037/a0014897

Mustard, D. B. (2001). Racial, ethnic, and gender disparities in sentencing: Evidence from the U. S. Federal Courts. *Journal of Law and Economics, 44*(1), 285–314. doi:10.1086/320276

NAACP Legal Defense and Educational Fund. (2006, Winter). *Death row U.S.A.* New York, NY: NAACP Legal Defense and Educational Fund. Retrieved from http://www.naacpldf.org/death-row-usa

Nichols, S. (2006). Folk intuitions on free will. *Journal of Cognition and Culture, 6*(1), 57–86. doi:10.1163/156853706776931385

Ogloff, J. R. P. (2000). Two steps forward and one step backward: The law and psychology movement(s) in the 20th century. *Law and Human Behavior, 24*(4), 457–483. doi:10.1023/A:1005596414203

Oxford, M., Cavell, T., & Hughes, J. (2003). Callous/unemotional traits moderate the relation between ineffective parenting and child externalizing problem. *Journal of Clinical Child and Adolescent Psychology, 32*(4), 577–585. doi:10.1207/S15374424JCCP3204_10

Hume, R. J. (2014). Deciding not to decide: The politics of recusals on the U.S. Supreme Court. *Law & Society Review, 48*(3), 621–655. doi:10.1111/lasr.12090

Patterson, G. R. (1996). Some characteristics of a developmental theory for early onset delinquency. In M. F. Lenzenweger & J. J. Haugaard (Eds.), *Frontiers of developmental psychopathology* (pp. 81–124). New York, NY: Oxford University Press.

Payne, B. K., Gainey, R. R., Triplett, R. A., & Danner, M. J. E. (2004). What drives punitive beliefs?: Demographic characteristics and justifications for sentencing. *Journal of Criminal Justice, 32*(3), 195–206. doi:10.1016/j.jcrimus.2004.02.007

Petrosino, A., Petrosino, C. T., & Buehler, J. (2007). Scared straight and other juvenile awareness programs. In B. C. Welsh & D. P. Farrington (Eds.), *Preventing crime: What works for children, offenders, victims and places* (pp.87–101). Lowell, MA: Springer.

Pezdek, K. (2012). Fallible eyewitness memory and identification. In B. L. Coulter (Ed.), *Conviction of the innocent: Lessons from psychological research* (pp. 105–124). Washington, DC: American Psychological Association.

Pew Center on the States. (2011). *State of recidivism: The revolving door of America's prisons.* Washington, DC: The Pew Charitable Trusts. Retrieved from http://www.pewtrusts.org

Preudhomme, R., & Dunston, L. G. (1989). *Rites of passage: A program for the New York state division for youth.* Albany, NY: Budget Office of the Governor.

Przybylski, R. (2008). *What works: Effective recidivism reduction and risk focused prevention programs.* Denver, CO: Colorado Division of Criminal Justice.

Pysarchik, D. I., Shealy, C. N., & Sternberger, B. (2007, July). *Examining outcome objectives for student learning and curricula.* Symposium presented at the meeting of the National Association of State Universities and Land Grant Colleges, Santa Rosa, CA.

Quay, H. (1964). Dimensions of personality in delinquent boys as inferred from the factor analysis of case history data. *Child Development, 35*(2), 479–484. Retrieved from http://www.jstor.org/stable/1126711

Quay, H. (1965). *Juvenile delinquency: Research and theory*. Princeton, NJ: Van Nostrand.

Quay, H. C., & Hogan, A. E. (Eds.). (1999). *Handbook of disruptive behavior disorders*. New York, NY: Kluwer Academic/Plenum Publishers.

Redding, R. E., & Reppucci, N. D. (1999). Effects of lawyers' socio-political attitudes on their judgments of social science in legal decision making. *Law and Human Behavior, 23*(1), 31–45. doi:10.1023/A:1022322706533

Robertson, L. A., McAnally, H. M., & Hancox, R. J. (2013). Childhood and adolescent television viewing and antisocial behavior in early adulthood. *Pediatrics, 131*(3), 439–446. doi:10.1542/peds.2012-1582

Robinson, K., & Little, G. (1988). *Moral reconation therapy*. Memphis, TN: Correctional Counseling.

Ross, L. (1977). The intuitive psychologist and his shortcomings: Distortions in the attribution process. In L. Berkowitz (Ed.), *Advances in experimental social psychology* (pp. 173–220). New York, NY: Academic Press.

Ross, R., Fabiano, E., & Ross, R. (1986). *Reasoning and rehabilitation: A handbook for teaching cognitive skills*. Ottawa: University of Ottawa

Rufino, K. A., Boccaccini, M. T., Hawes, S. W., & Murrie, D. C. (2012). When experts disagreed, who was correct? A comparison of PCL-R scores from independent raters and opposing forensic experts. Law and Human Behavior, *36*(6), 527–537. doi:10.1037/h0093988

Sanders, J. (2009). Science, law and the expert witness. *Law and Contemporary Problems, 72*(1), 63–90. Retrieved from www.law.duke.edu/journals/lcp

Scaramella, L. V., & Leve, L. D. (2004). Clarifying parent–child reciprocities during early childhood: The early childhood coercion model. *Clinical Child and Family Psychology Review, 7*(2), 89–107. doi:10.1023/B:CCFP.0000030287.13160.a3

Semmler, C., Brewer, N., & Douglass, A. B. (2011). Jurors believe eyewitnesses. In B. L. Coulter (Ed.), *Conviction of the innocent: Lessons from psychological research.* (pp. 185–209). Washington, DC: American Psychological Association.

Shaw, J. S., & McClure, K. A. (1996). Repeated postevent questioning can lead to elevated levels of eyewitness confidence. *Law and Human Behavior, 20*(6), 629–653. doi:10.1007/BF01499235

Shealy, C. N. (1995). From Boys Town to Oliver Twist. Separating fact from fiction in welfare reform and out-of-home placement of children and youth. *American Psychologist, 50*(8), 565–580. doi:10.1037/0003-066X.50.8.565

Shealy, C. N. (2004). A model and method for making a Combined-Integrated psychologist: equilintegration (EI) theory and the beliefs, events, and values inventory (BEVI). [Special Series]. *Journal of Clinical Psychology, 60*(10), 1065–1090. doi:10.1002/jclp.20035

Shealy, C. N. (2005). Justifying the justification hypothesis: Scientific-humanism, equilintegration (EI) theory, and the Beliefs, Events and Values Inventory (BEVI). *Journal of Clinical Psychology 61*(1), 81–106. doi:10.1002/jclp.20092

Shealy, C. N. (2015). *The Beliefs, Events, and Values Inventory (BEVI): Overview, implications, and guidelines*. Test manual. Harrisonburg, VA: Author.

Shealy, C. N. (2016). *Making sense of beliefs and values*. New York, NY: Springer Publishing.

Shealy, C. N., & Bhuyan, D. (2009). The value of value based education. In M. Mukhopadhyay (Ed.), *Quality school education for all* (pp. 94–113). New Delhi, India: Education Technology and Management Academy.

Shealy, C. N., Bhuyan, D., & Sternberger, L. G. (2012). Cultivating the capacity to care in children and youth: Implications from EI Theory, EI Self, and BEVI. In U. Nayar (Ed.), *Child and adolescent mental health* (pp. 240–255). New Delhi, India: Sage Publications.

Shepherd, J. (2009). Money, politics, and impartial justice. *Duke Law Journal, 58*, 623–685. Retrieved from http://ssrn.com/abstract=1910787

Sherman, L. W., & Eck, J. E. (2002). Policing for crime prevention. In L. W. Sherman, D. P. Farrington, B. C. Welsh, & D. L. MacKenzie (Eds.), *Evidence-based crime prevention* (pp. 295–329). New York, NY: Routledge.

Sims, B. (2003). The impact of causal attribution on correctional ideology: A national study. *Criminal Justice Review, 28*(1), 1–25. doi:10.1177/073401680302800102

Smith, C. A., Ireland, T. O., & Thornberry, T. P. (2005). Adolescent maltreatment and its impact on young adult antisocial behavior. *Child Abuse and Neglect, 29*(10), 1099–1119. doi:10.1016/j.chiabu.2005.02.011

Solimine, M. E., & Gely, R. (2009). Federal and state judicial selection in an interest group perspective. *Missouri Law Review, 74*, 531–554. Retrieved from http://ssrn.com/abstract=1487682

Sommers, S. R. (2006). On racial diversity and group decision-making: Identifying multiple effects of racial composition on jury deliberations. *Journal of personality and Social Psychology, 90*(4), 597–612. doi:10.1037/0022-3514.90.4.597

Soon, C. S., Brass, M., Heinze, H. J., & Haynes, J. D. (2008). Unconscious determinants of free decisions in the human brain. *Nature Neuroscience, 11*, 543–545. doi:10.1038/nn.2112

Sourcebook of Criminal Justice Statistics. (2012, May 4). *Reported confidence in the criminal justice system [Data File].* Retrieved from http://www.albany.edu/sourcebook/pdf/t2112012.pdf

Staples, B. (2012, November 25). California horror stories and the 3-strikes law. *The New York Times*, p. X10.

Stewart, A., Livingston, M., & Dennison, S. (2008). Transitions and turning points: Examining the links between child maltreatment and juvenile offending. *Child Abuse & Neglect, 32*(1), 51–66. doi:10.1016/j.chiabu.2007.04.011

Tabit, M., Cozen, J., Dyjak-Leblank, K., Pendleton, C., Shealy, C., Sternberger, L., & Staton, R. (2011, June). *The sociocultural impact of denial: Empirical evidence from the Forum BEVI Project.* Poster presented at American Psychological Association, Washington, DC.

Talarico, J. M., & Rubin. D. C. (2003). Confidence, not consistency, characterizes flashbulb memories. *Psychological Science, 14*(5), 455–461. doi:10.1111/1467-9280.02453

Taymans, J. (2011). *Problem solving skills for offenders curriculum.* Aurora, CO: National Institute of Corrections.

The curious case of the fall in crime. (2013, July 20). *The Economist*, p. 9.

Unnever, J. D., Bartkowski, J., & Cullen, F. T. (2006). Images of God and public support for capital punishment: Does a loving God matter? *Criminology, 44*(2), 833–864. doi:10.1111/j.1745-9125.2006.00065.x

Unnever, J. D., & Cullen, F. T. (2006). Christian fundamentalists and support for capital punishment. *Journal of Research in Crime and Delinquency, 43*(2), 169–197. doi:10.1177/0022427805280067

Unnever, J. D., Cullen, F. T., & Fisher, B. S. (2005). Empathy and public support for capital punishment. *Journal of Crime and Justice, 24*(1), 1–34. doi:10.1080/0735648X.2005.9721205

U.S. General Accounting Office. (2003). *Youth illicit drug use prevention: DARE long-term evaluations and federal efforts to identify effective program.* (Report GAO-03-172R). Washington, DC: Author.

Wegner, D. (2002). *The illusion of conscious will.* Cambridge, MA: MIT Press.

Weisburd, D., & Eck, J. E. (2004). What can police do to reduce crime, disorder, and fear? *Annals of the American Academy of Political and Social Science, 593*(1), 42–65. doi:10.1177/0002716203262548

Wells, G. L., Ferguson, T. J., & Lindsay, R. C. L. (1981). The tractability of eyewitness confidence and its implications for triers of fact. *Journal of Applied Psychology, 66*(6), 688–696. doi:10.1037/0021-9010.66.6.688

Wells, G. L., Memon, A., & Penrod, S. D. (2006). Eyewitness evidence: Improving its probative value. *Psychological Science in the Public Interest, 7*(2), 45–75. doi:10.1111/j.1529-1006.2006.00027.x

Wells, G. L., Olson, E., & Charman, S. (2002). The confidence of eyewitnesses in their identifications from lineups. *Current Directions in Psychological Science, 11*(5), 151–154. doi:10.1111/1467-8721.00189

Wells, G. L., & Quinlivan, D. S. (2009). Suggestive eyewitness identification procedures and the Supreme Court's reliability test in light of eyewitness science: 30 years later. *Law and Human Behavior, 33*, 1–24. doi:10.1007/s10979-008-9130-3

Welsh, B. C., & Farrington, D. P. (2007). *Preventing crime: What works for children, offenders, victims, and places.* New York, NY: Springer.

Widom, C. S. (1989). Child abuse, neglect and adult behavior: Research design and findings on criminality, violence, and child abuse. *American Journal of Orthopsychiatry, 59*(3), 355–367. doi:10.1111/j.1939-0025.1989.tb01671.x

Wilson, J. Q. (1975). *Thinking about crime.* New York, NY: Random House.

Wilson, D. B., & MacKenzie, D. L. (2007). Boot camps. In B. C. Welsh & D. P. Farrington, (Eds.), *Preventing crime: What works for children, offenders, victims and places* (pp. 33–54). Lowell, MA: Springer.

Wise, R. A., & Safer, M. A. (2004). What US judges know and believe about eyewitness testimony. *Applied Cognitive Psychology, 18*(4), 427–443. doi:10.1002/acp.993

Yochelson, S., & Samenow, S. (1977). *The criminal personality. Vol. 2: The change process.* New York, NY: Jason Aronson.

Zimmerman, D. M., Austin, J. L., & Kovera, M. B. (2012). Suggestive eyewitness identification procedures. In B. L. Coulter (Ed.), *Conviction of the innocent: Lessons from psychological research* (pp. 125–148). Washington, DC: American Psychological Association.

Kelly Dyjak-LeBlanc, Lindy Brewster, Steve Grande,
Randall P. White, and Sandra L. Shullman

14

THE EI LEADERSHIP MODEL: FROM THEORY AND RESEARCH TO REAL WORLD APPLICATION

Why is it so hard to lead yourself? The answer, in my experience, lies in the differences between your idealized self—how you see yourself and how you want to be seen—and your real self. The key to growing as a leader is to narrow that gap by developing a deep self-awareness that comes from straight feedback and honest exploration of yourself, followed by a concerted effort to make changes.

—Bill George

One of the most popular comic strips in the world and surely the most well known about organizations and business is "Dilbert," created by Scott Adams. Adams coined the term the Dilbert Principle (Adams, 1995, 1997) to describe how frequently it seems that the least competent employees instead of being removed from the organization are rather promoted to positions of management. Dilbert is popular and funny because it speaks lamentable truths when illustrating, for example, the bald ineptitude of leaders who are promoted far beyond their abilities, or how systems entangle themselves hopelessly in a senseless web of regulations, or how an organization's culture can promote double-speak and obfuscation instead of authenticity and transparency. Dilbert has been in print for over 20 years, but is still relevant and humorous because organizations and the people who work within them still suffer from these same ills. A Dilbert metric even has been developed through which employees may compare their organizational culture and morale to Dilbert comic strips (Capstone Encyclopaedia of Business, 2003). As Dilbert illustrates, humor is a potent medium through which the toxic repercussions of "bad" leadership may be metabolized by those who are led. It may indeed be cathartic to laugh at the machinations of the conniving boss in the Dilbert strip. However, the fact that such catharsis is so necessary—as evidenced by the enduring and extraordinary popularity of Dilbert—speaks to the hapless experience of so many of "the led" on a daily basis.

THE EI LEADERSHIP MODEL: ORIGIN AND RATIONALE

As a hopeful antidote to such ubiquity, the International Beliefs and Values Institute (IBAVI) has, for many years, conferred its annual *Sustainable Visions and Values (SVV) Award* on leaders who exemplify everything that Dilbert's boss does not—awareness, care, courage, depth, vision, and effectiveness. As a nonprofit organization with a mission to "explore beliefs and values and how they influence actions, policies, and practices around the world," the IBAVI's SVV Award "recognizes a distinguished individual who exemplifies the transformative aspirations that are at the heart of the IBAVI's mission, rationale, and goals" (www.ibavi.org). Although mostly implicit, five fundamental questions seem central to its annual deliberations. First, how do the beliefs and values of leaders impact their leadership (e.g., why do leaders experience and respond to self, others, and the larger world as they do)? Second, are there common beliefs and values among leaders who are deemed to be most effective? Third, how do we evaluate the meaning and impact of interactions between the beliefs and values of leaders and the led? Fourth, how best do we understand the extraordinarily complex variables that influence leadership on a daily basis in the real world? Fifth, which models of leaders and methods of leadership development are most likely to have meaning and relevance across cultures and contexts? In response to such questions, this chapter (a) describes the development of a model of leadership that informs the selection of SVV Award recipients with broader implications and applications for leadership and organizational development in general and (b) illustrates the application and evaluation of this model and its attendant methods with leaders in a real world organization.

Because a number of IBAVI board members had taught leadership or professional development, served in various organizational leadership roles, and/or had been on the receiving end of positive or negative leadership styles and practices, the need to explicate what was meant by "good" and "poor" leadership had both personal and professional resonance. At a parallel level, although the IBAVI has experienced no dearth of worthy candidates over the years, the fundamental attributes of recipients were by no means straightforward. In other words, the board was able to get a good feel for who was appropriate for this award, but had considerable difficulty articulating why. Because the IBAVI has a strong tradition of promoting deeper understanding of self, others, and the larger world through various initiatives (e.g., scholarly, educational, service), not being clear and explicit about "what good leadership is" represented a particular problem. Moreover, the value-based nature of leaders and leadership had become abundantly clear through a multiyear, multi-institution project that had been cocoordinated with the Forum on Education Abroad (www.forumea.org)—the Forum BEVI Project—which examined the assessment of international, multicultural, and transformative learning (see Wandschneider et al., 2016; Chapter 4). The implications of this research and practice for leadership/organizational assessment and development had been evidenced through several applied workshops and other interventions, which suggested an attendant need to ensure clarity regarding what was and was not meant by leaders and leadership. Although a full explication is presented in Shealy (2016), a brief overview of the three main components of the present approach—Equilintegration (EI) Theory, the EI Self, and the Beliefs, Events, and Values Inventory (BEVI)—may be helpful at this point, particularly because the BEVI and EI Theory are integral to the current project on leaders and leadership, as described in the following.

Basically, EI Theory seeks to explain "the processes by which beliefs, values, and 'worldviews' are acquired and maintained, why their alteration is typically resisted, and how and under what circumstances their modification occurs"

(Shealy, 2004, p. 1075; see Chapter 2).[1] More specifically, the "equilibration" half of EI Theory begins with the initial formulation of Jean Piaget,

> who was interested in how and under what conditions knowledge about the larger world was organized mentally and emotionally, and the processes by which these organizational structures developed (e.g., Kegan, 1982; McLeod, 2009; Piaget, 1976, 1977; Wadsworth, 1996). Piaget's robust observations are highly relevant to an understanding of beliefs and values as they impact leaders and leadership processes because, "according to Rokeach (1973, 1979), values are central to a person's *cognitive* organization" (Dollinger, Leong, & Ulicni, 1996, p. 25), which influences how and why we experience self, others, and the larger world as we do (Shealy, 2016, p. 29).

If the "equilibration" half of EI Theory addresses how and why beliefs and values are acquired and maintained, the "integration" half of EI Theory has more pragmatic, though no less ecumenical, ends. Here, the central foci are how these affective, attributional, and developmental processes may be investigated and understood, why it is helpful to do so from a transtheoretical, multidisciplinary, and integrative standpoint, and the attendant implications for training, practice, theory, and research. Such matters are especially relevant in relation to leaders and leadership since we are dealing with highly complex and interacting processes and outcomes among leaders and the led that must be accounted for if we are to understand and intervene in ways that are maximally likely to be meaningful, nuanced, informed, and effective in the real world (e.g., Astrachan, 2004; Barendsen & Gardner, 2006; Burke, 2008; Detert & Burris, 2007; Ford, Ford, and D'Amelio, 2008; George, 2004; Goleman, Boyatzis, & McKee, 2002; Henson, Fulkerson, Caligiuri, & Shealy, in press; Judge, Bono, Ilies, & Gerhardt, 2002; Kets de Vries & Balazs, 2005, 2008; Kouzes & Posner, 2012; Morton, 2013; Wheatley, 2006; White & Shullman, 2010).

Derivative of EI Theory, the Equilintegration or EI Self explains processes by which beliefs and values are acquired, maintained, and transformed, as well as how and why these are related to formative variables (e.g., caregiver's level of education, culture), core needs (e.g., for attachment, affiliation), and adaptive potential of the self. Informed by scholarship in a range of key areas (e.g., "needs-based" research and theory; developmental psychopathology; social cognition; therapy process and outcomes; affect regulation; and theories and models of "self"), the EI Self seeks to illustrate how the interaction between our core needs and formative variables results in formation and subsequent internalization of beliefs and values about self, others, and the world at large (Shealy, Bhuyan, & Sternberger, 2012; see Chapter 3).

Concomitant with EI Theory and the EI Self, the BEVI is a comprehensive analytic tool in development since the early 1990s that examines how and why we come to see ourselves, others, and the larger world as we do. The BEVI seeks to explain how life experiences, culture, and context affect our beliefs, values, and worldviews as well as the influence of such processes on multiple aspects of human functioning (e.g., learning processes, relationships, personal growth, the pursuit of life goals). For

---

[1] For consistency, selected aspects of this chapter, including this section on EI Theory, have been excerpted and/or adapted from Chapters 2, 3, and 4 of Shealy, C. N. (2016).

example, the BEVI assesses processes such as: basic openness to alternate ideas and ways of thinking; the tendency to (or not to) stereotype in particular ways; self- and emotional awareness; preferred strategies for making sense of why "other" people and cultures "do what they do"; global resonance (e.g., receptivity to different cultures, religions, and social practices); and worldview shift (e.g., the degree to which beliefs and values change as a result of specific experiences). BEVI results are translated automatically into individual and group reports, and used in a wide range of contexts for a variety of applied and research purposes (e.g., to track and examine changes in worldviews over time) (e.g., Anmuth et al., 2103; Atwood, Chkhaidze, Shealy, Staton, Sternberger, 2014; Brearly, Shealy, Staton, Sternberger, 2012; Hill et al., 2013; Shealy, 2004, 2005, 2012, 2015; Shealy et al., 2012; Tabit et al., 2011; for more information about the BEVI, see Chapter 4 as well as www.ibavi.org/content/featured-projects).

Of the many aspects of the EI model and BEVI method that are applicable to leaders and leadership, none is more salient than the following: *a complex interaction among core needs (e.g., for attachment, affiliation) and formative variables (e.g., life history, culture) culminates in the beliefs and values we hold to be true, which subsequently impact how and why we experience self, others, and the larger world as we do.* Such theory and data offer a complementary emphasis to the traditional focus on *who* good leaders are and *what* good leadership is. In the larger literature, much less attention has been devoted to questions of *why* leaders differ as they do in their experience of self, others, and the larger world as well as *how* to translate such understanding into effective strategies for leadership and organizational development. Perhaps that is because it is relatively easy to identify instances of effective leadership, and propose attendant and putative characteristics of "good" or "poor" leaders. It is another matter altogether to "delve inside" the leader in order to apprehend complex interactions among affect, cognition, context, and life history, which all theoretically are implicated in leadership behavior. Likewise, the characteristics of well-functioning organizations—what they look like and how they work—also seem more empirically self-evident than the substantive question of *why* organizations evolve to become relatively effective or ineffective in the first place. Finally, it is one thing to try and understand such deep processes at the individual and organizational level, but another task altogether to make them visible and accessible to the members and leaders of organizations for purposes of leadership training or organizational development. Ultimately, of course, such understanding must inform *how* actually to design and conduct interventions for leaders and organizations that result in better processes and outcomes. These emphases—on etiology, depth, assessment, application, development, and impact—are central to the current approach regarding leaders and leadership.

Fortunately, an increasing number of scholars and practitioners are articulating perspectives that address—directly and indirectly—such emphases, by seeking to understand *how* and *why* leaders and organizations function as they do as well as the attendant and real world implications for leadership and organizational development (e.g., Astrachan, 2004; Barendsen & Gardner, 2006; Burke, 2008; Detert & Burris, 2007; Ford, et al., 2008; George, 2004; Goleman et al., 2002; Gostick & Elton, 2012; Judge et al., 2002; Kets de Vries & Balazs, 2005, 2008; Kouzes & Posner, 2012; Morton, 2013; Wheatley, 2006; White & Shullman, 2010, 2012). Complementary to this depth-based perspective, there is growing interest and burgeoning literature exploring the nature of activities, requirements, and competencies of effective global leaders (e.g., Gundling, Hogan, & Cvitkovitch, 2011; Chhokar, Brodbeck, & House, 2007; Henson et al., in press; House, Hanges, Javidan, Dorfman, & Gupta, 2004; Mobley, Li, & Wang, 2011; Shullman, White, Brewster, Grande, & Bhuyan, in press). Even so, at present there is no definitional consensus or unification theory to address the meaning of either "global leaders" or "global leadership," even though many scholars are addressing aspects of these topics, exemplified perhaps by the work of Kouzes and Posner (2012) as well as the Global Leadership and Organizational Behavior Effectiveness (GLOBE) Research Project, a multiyear project involving a wide range of social science/business scholars who study leadership from an international perspective (e.g., House et al., 2004; see also Beechler & Javidan, 2007; Bird, Mendenhall, Stevens, & Oddou, 2010; Campbell, 2006; Dalton, Ernst, Deal, & Leslie, 2002; Javidan & Teagarden, 2011; McCall & Hollenbeck, 2002; Levy, Beechler, Taylor, & Boyacigiller, 2007). As the quest for definitional clarity continues, there appears to be consistent emphasis on the centrality of both context and cultural complexity in understanding global leadership and perhaps leadership more generally (Dalton et al., 2002; McCall & Hollenbeck., 2002).

The present approach is aligned deliberately with these emphases, through the presentation of a theoretically and empirically derived model of leadership, which is grounded in relevant literature and developed in collaboration with a global cohort of Subject Matter Experts (SMEs), and then tested in a real world context. Specifically, this chapter is divided into two complementary parts. Part I begins with an overview of literature, which is followed by a description of the *knowing, doing, being,* and *not being* factors of the EI Leadership Model. Part II reports on the real world application and evaluation of the EI Leadership Model, by describing the results of a three-part workshop conducted with a large organization.[2]

PART I: THE EI LEADERSHIP MODEL—RELEVANT LITERATURE AND FACTORS

Although there is a wide body of research and literature in the leadership field, the subset of scholarship informing the development of the EI Model of leaders and leadership focuses on themes such as awareness, complexity, and transformation under the broader rubric of the nature and origins of beliefs and values. Given this broad backdrop, *the literature presented in the following is meant neither to be exhaustive nor definitive,* but rather illustrative of the sort of theory, research, and practice that has informed the development of the model as well as its real world application as described in the following. As exemplars of such literature, and by way of introduction, consider the seminal work of Margaret Wheatley, Jim Kouzes, Barry Posner, Adrian Gostick, Chester Elton, and Robert Morton.

First, based upon extensive work with leaders and organizations, Wheatley (2006) observes that dominant theories of organizational leadership and consultation have long emphasized themes such as structure, planning, tracking, regulation, and control, while underemphasizing if not ignoring the dynamic and organic complexities of the human beings who lead as well as the systems in which they and "the led" are embedded. As she notes,

> We tried for many years to avoid the messiness and complexity of being human, and now that denial is coming back to haunt us. We keep failing to create the outcomes and changes we need in organizations because we continue to deny

---

[2] The EI Leadership Model should not be confused with Emotional Intelligence (e.g., Goleman, Boyatzis, & McKee, 2002). Although the important and relevant latter literature informs aspects of the EI Leadership Model, these are distinct theoretical and applied frameworks.

that the "human element" is anything but a "soft" and not-to-be-taken seriously minor distraction. . .New technology is purchased; new organizational charts are drawn; new training classes are offered. But most basic human dynamics are completely ignored: our need to trust one another, our need for meaningful work, our desire to contribute and be thanked for that contribution, our need to participate in changes that affect us. . .We are terrified of the emotions aroused by conflict, loss, love. In all of these struggles, it is being human that creates the problem. . .After all these years of denying the fact that we are humans, vulnerable to the same dynamics that swirl in all life (plus some unique to our species), we are being called to encounter one another in the messiness and beauty that name us as alive. (pp. 164–165)

Second, consider the perspective of Kouzes and Posner (2012), who have worked for decades with leaders and organizations in the United States and internationally. Among other relevant insights and recommendations, data from over 100,000 participants regarding the Characteristics of Admired Leaders, consistently indicate—across culture and context—that leaders must be (among other attributes) honest, forward-looking, competent, and inspiring. More specifically, and highly congruent with the results of the EI Leadership Model described in the following, Kouzes and Posner observe that *credible* leaders around the globe are described as follows:

"They practice what they preach"; "They walk the talk"; "Their actions are consistent with their words"; "They put their money where their mouth is"; "They follow through on their promises"; "They do what they say they will do." The last is the most frequent response. When it comes to deciding whether a leader is believable, people first listen to the words, then they watch the actions. . .A judgment of "credible" is handed down when words and deeds are consonant. If people don't see consistency, they conclude that the leader is, at best, not really serious or, at worse, an outright hypocrite. If leaders espouse one set of values, but personally practice another, people find them to be duplicitous. . .Modeling is about clarifying values and setting an example for others based on those values. The consistent living out of values is the way leaders demonstrate their honesty and trustworthiness. It's what gives them the moral authority to lead. (pp. 35–36)

As the third and final exemplar, other practitioner-scholars are explicitly emphasizing the centrality of "belief" vis-à-vis leadership development and organizational processes. In particular, drawing upon their own extensive work as well as insights from specific disciplinary subfields (e.g., social psychology) and individuals (e.g., corporate psychologist, Keven Fleming), Gostick and Elton (2012) contend that the "belief factor" is simultaneously among the least recognized and most important aspects of effective leaders and organizations. Highly resonant with the EI Leadership Model and BEVI method presented in this chapter, Gostick and Elton observe the following:

. . .the first step to becoming a leader who can influence others to believe is to do something very un-manager-like: pause and think about human nature. Why do people believe in the things they do? And how can they be persuaded to change what they think? (pp. 20–21)

Likewise, based upon over 25 years of such work, Morton's (2013) "five principles of leading with belief" offer an innovative and comprehensive framework for understanding why and how beliefs are core to leadership and organizational effectiveness. These principles are as follows: (a) Beliefs Drive Effective Leadership; (b) Successful Leaders Believe in Themselves; (c) Successful Leaders Inspire Belief; (d) Leadership Credibility is Built on Belief; and (e) Leadership Development is Enabled by Belief. As Morton observes,

> The most successful leaders instinctively understood the importance of beliefs and they intuitively leveraged this knowledge to influence new beliefs that would prepare their organizations for change, drive the implementation of their visions, and facilitate the achievement of essential results. The message is simple: If you want to lead in the most powerful and effective way possible, learn how to lead with belief. (p. 1)

From an EI standpoint, foci such as these are at the core of this theoretically and empirically derived model and method of leadership, which we describe and examine in the present analysis. That said, as noted previously and throughout this chapter, we recognize fully that such an emphasis is by no means without precedent. Thus, building upon such acquired knowledge and wisdom, we seek to understand how the most complex and values-based aspects of leaders and leadership—matters of etiology, depth, assessment, application, development, and impact—may be explicated through theoretically and empirically derived models and methods that have local and global utility. Ultimately, such a project must grapple with the inevitable interactions among leaders and the led, while addressing fundamental matters of personal beliefs, values, and purpose. From this perspective:

> The three most enduring questions a leader should ask are: 1) why am I motivated to lead; 2) how is my leadership experienced by others; and 3) is what I am leading worthy of being led. In pursuit of answers to such questions, leaders should lean toward a persistent quest for self-awareness, openness, and integrity regarding the meaning and impact of their lives and work. (Shealy, 2012)

Highly complementary to this perspective, White and Shullman (2010, 2012) offer four additional questions that any global leader should contemplate: (a) What are my strengths (i.e., Why am I successful)? (b) What are my weaknesses (i.e., What are my developmental needs)? (c) In what context will these weaknesses hurt me (e.g., How could my challenges cause me to derail)? (d) What are the biggest differences between globally effective leaders and me (e.g., What might I learn from other leaders who appear to be the most globally effective)?

Such value-based questions emerge from and are derivative of literature that are core to the development of the EI Model, which may be organized under the auspices of the following eight themes, to which we turn next: (a) assessment; (b) awareness; (c) care; (d) complexity; (e) culture; (f) depth; (g) transformation; and (h) vision (Dyjak-LeBlanc, Femac, Shealy, Staton, & Sternberger, 2012; Shealy, 2012).[3]

---

[3] For consistency, this section also will be excerpted and/or adapted for the following and related publication: Shullman, S., White, R., Brewster, L., Grande, S., & Bhuyan, D. (in press). How psychology and psychologists develop global leaders and leadership. In C. N. Shealy & M. Bullock (Eds.), *Going global: How psychology and psychologists can meet a world of need.* Washington, DC: APA Books.

Assessment

Leaders finding themselves in cultures and contexts different from what they are accustomed not only need to be aware of and sensitive to such differences, but also able to assess the beliefs and values of self and others with accuracy, depth, and breadth, and use such findings to enhance their personal growth, development, and effectiveness over the long term. Because value conflicts often are at the core of cultural misunderstandings, a lack of clarification regarding beliefs and values of self and other places the global leader at risk of behaving in ways that are experienced as antithetical to the culture in which one works (e.g., Dyjak-LeBlanc et al., 2012). The complexity of such matters is illustrated by the attitudinal assessment work of Hofstede and colleagues from the 1960s through the 1990s, which compared attitude surveys for IBM across 50 different countries (Hofstede, 2001). Among many other findings, power distance and uncertainty avoidance were two of the most important value conflicts. For example, conflicts tend to arise when leaders have different cultural assumptions regarding the nature and need for organizational hierarchy than do employees. With a low-hierarchical (low power distance) worldview, employees may work around the chain of command to a greater degree than they would in a high power distance culture (i.e., power distance addresses why and how power is distributed as it is within a particular culture). Put simply, people in some cultures accept a higher degree of unequally distributed power than do people in other cultures. Moreover, with a high uncertainty avoidance to leadership, organizations may eschew risk taking and thus conflict when a more entrepreneurial approach is expected by employees or other stakeholders in the organization's mission and activities (see also White & Shullman, 2010) (i.e., uncertainty avoidance refers to the degree to which members of a particular society tend to minimize or accept ambiguity and uncertainty). Rigorous assessment-based models and methods such as these illustrate both the depth of the challenge faced by individuals who serve in leadership roles across multiple countries and cultures as well as the possibility of illuminating dynamics that may be implicit but still have a major impact on the effectiveness of one's work. Such scholarship also speaks to a larger problem within the assessment literature more generally, which has struggled with pure trait-based theories of leadership that do not sufficiently account for the impact of situation and states, much less the interconnected and systemic nature of organizational processes (Judge et al., 2002; Wheatley, 2006).

Fortunately, theoretically and empirically sophisticated approaches that account for and can map upon global contexts are beginning to emerge (e.g., House et al., 2004). For example, Appreciative Inquiry (AI) is a method of assessing people and organizations that mirrors effective anthropological approaches to understanding and operating in different cultures. AI is,

> the cooperative, co-evolutionary search for the best in people, their organizations and the world around them. It involves systematic discovery of what gives life to an organization or community when it is most effective and most capable in economic, ecological and human terms. (Cooperrider & Whitney, 2005, p. 7)

Approaches such as AI exemplify how rigorous assessment methods may illuminate underlying factors that are instrumental to the cultivation and expression of effective leadership. At a larger level, such approaches reveal the importance of psychometrically sound measurement, definitional clarity, ecological validity, and theoretical depth if we are to understand complex processes and interactions that are integral to leadership training and development across cultures, settings, and contexts (Dyjak-LeBlanc et al., 2012).

Awareness

A related and overarching theme is the proposition that effective global leaders should strive to cultivate a deep and sophisticated understanding of self, others, and the larger world, including why we feel, think, and behave as we do, a perspective aligned with Burke's (2008) emphasis on "leader self-examination." The importance of self-examination and understanding can be linked directly to our basic human neurological makeup for survival, activated under the sort of threat from ambiguity that is ubiquitous within the larger global organizational context (White & Shullman, 2010). Along these lines, in contemplating *why* leadership and organizational dynamics manifest as they do, Kets de Vries and Balazs (2005) observe that (a) much of mental life lies outside conscious awareness; (b) nothing is more central to who a person is than the way he or she expresses and regulates emotions; and (c) human development is an inter- and intrapersonal process (pp. 9–10). This perspective is supported further by Kahneman (2011) who suggests that there are many mental biases of which we are minimally aware, and that render our thought processes highly susceptible to systematic error. Cognitive biases, such as the availability heuristic (in which people tend to assess the relative importance of issues by the ease with which they are retrieved from memory) and the role of emotion in intuitive judgments all may create blind spots regarding information to which one should attend (see also Gostick & Elton, 2012). To combat such biasing processes, Mendenhall, Kuhlmann, and Stahl (2001) suggest that the cultivation of inquisitiveness and willingness to learn are the best predictors of success, because they mitigate against the potential for nonawareness that every human is capable of demonstrating.

Likewise, Goleman (2001) maintains that self-awareness and constituents such as self-regulation, motivation, empathy, and social skills all are integral to good leadership. These awareness-based aspects of emotional intelligence ultimately facilitate trust and fairness in the larger organization (Goleman et al., 2002). It should be noted in this regard that the most successful global leaders have attributes that are closely related to the shared human neurology/psychology of the amygdala— inquisitiveness, emotional connection, and empathy—in that they are able to integrate different perspectives, respond proactively to other's needs, and tolerate uncertainty and tension (e.g., Henson & Rossouw, 2013; Mendenhall et al., 2001; Trompenaars & Hampden-Turner, 2010). The ability to manage affectively mediated aspects of ambiguity and uncertainty are increasingly important as the business environment becomes more complex, global, and hypercompetitive (Hodgson & White, 2001; White & Shullman, 2010, 2012). As is discussed next, listening and questioning empathetically are key components of such awareness, requiring a "capacity to care" and attendant inclination to engage in (a) perspective taking; (b) feeling/sensing what is going on in the other; and (c) wanting to help (i.e., "empathic concern"). In short, without sufficient awareness of self, others, and the larger world, leaders may continue to operate within models that are both ineffective and inflexible, leading to the same errors of judgment and decision making time and again.

Care

A leader may be willing to engage in ongoing assessment, and possess a genuine desire for deeper awareness of self and other, but still not be able to build trust, earn respect, and inspire others—the three universally recognized behaviors of charismatic, team-oriented, and human leadership, as indicated by the previously described GLOBE Project. As Kail (2011) observes, followers ultimately are the arbiters of how caring a leader really is; such attributions also are associated with the degree to which leaders are empowered by followers to become influential over them. Kail thus encourages leaders to strive for empathy through listening—rather than waiting to speak—as well as focused attention on what makes each individual unique (e.g., Shealy et al., 2012; Weiner, Kanki, & Helmreich, 1993). Along similar lines, based upon their extensive research and practice, Kouzes and Posner (2012) observe that "leaders foster trust by building trust and facilitating relationships. . .focusing on serving the needs of others, and not one's own, builds trust in a leader" (p. 25). Such a "leadership challenge" requires leaders to (a) model the way; (b) inspire a shared vision; (c) challenge the process; (d) enable others to act; and (e) encourage the heart. Ultimately, as Kail observes, this caring approach allows "everyone to contribute to a goal in a meaningful way," which is preferable to "marginalizing someone for the sake of an imagined better outcome."

Good leaders then—both locally and globally—empower others while simultaneously providing support, mentoring, and coaching. They strive to place others and the bigger picture before themselves, create environments that promote self-actualization, and remain accountable to others for their words and deeds (Kouzes & Posner, 2012). In Western cultures, caring traditionally has been associated with a feminine style of leadership, which has been valued less than a more "masculine" approach, which eschews "care" in favor of "power," "domination," and "control," which all are assumed to be integral to the "strength" of the leader. As Hofstede (2001) notes, however, such a gender-based attribution is not necessarily the case in other cultures (see also Eisler & Corrall, 2009). In particular, the GLOBE study suggests that true leaders around the world reflexively care about the feelings, needs, and experiences of those who are led, and seek to understand how their approaches to leadership actually are being experienced by others, which harkens back to our themes of assessment and awareness (Chhokar et al., 2007). Ultimately, such care facilitates trust, which is fundamental to the effective pursuit of shared organizational goals. Novogratz (2010) observes as much regarding her work with a global nonprofit venture fund with 20 former prostitutes in Kigali, Rwanda. After struggling to apply Western approaches to leadership and organizational management to run a bakery, Novogratz discovered that listening includes a process of asking questions and implementing the ideas of others, which ultimately engendered trust among all team members. In addition to lessons regarding listening and trust, such work also illustrates that truly caring leaders and organizations are, by definition, attuned to the impacts of their lives and work on individuals, societies, and the larger world (e.g., Cultivating the Globally Sustainable Self, 2014; Kelly, Holt, Patel, & Nolet, 2016; McKeown & Nolet, 2013; National Action Plan for Educating for Sustainability, 2014; Shealy et al., 2012).

Complexity

Given the challenges and opportunities of a globally interconnected and rapidly changing world, "operational decisions that once were clear cut are becoming more complicated and ambiguous" since "strategies and plans that should work". . .are more likely to "fall apart yielding (yet again) less-than-expected results" (McGuire, Palus, Pasmore, & Rhodes 2009, p. 3). Not surprisingly, then, effective leaders of today "understand that the command and control techniques of the Industrial Revolution no longer apply" (Kouzes & Posner, 2012, p. 18; Wheatley, 2006), which begs a core question: When the "external reality is unknowable and/or unfixable" (Terry, 2001, p. 13), with paradoxes seemingly untenable, what are those in positions of leadership to do? Through a complexity lens, they are to understand that everything in their world cannot be anticipated much less controlled, while simultaneously cultivating the capacity to tolerate—and even make peace with—the disequilibrium that inevitably flows from such chronic ambiguity. In short, such leaders appreciate the value of a paradigmatic shift from "command and control" to empowerment and partnership approaches wherein groups or teams come together as "learning organizations" in order to address challenges and problems (Eisler & Corrall, 2009; White & Shullman, 2010). In doing so, there is a twin recognition that complexity and ambiguity are not to be avoided but accepted and embraced. Adaptive leaders (Heifetz, Grashow, & Linsky, 2009) therefore are systems-level thinkers, who observe and raise questions, frame issues, interpret context, and challenge norms as needed before intervening. Such leaders must be able and willing to contain and integrate opposing or contradictory thoughts rather than seek to minimize or deny such complexities (Martin, 2009; Dyjak-LeBlanc et al., 2012).

Culture

The GLOBE Project defines culture as "shared motives, values, beliefs, identities and interpretations or meanings of significant events that result from common experiences of members of collectives that are transmitted across generations" (House et al., 2004, p. 15). Such a definition suggests that culture represents one level of mental programming, which may be learned or unlearned based upon group interactions. Two other determining factors include "human nature," which is universal, and personality, which is specific to the individual and both inherent and learned (Hofstede, 2001). Moreover, artifacts, stories, symbols, and customs shared and adopted by members of a group or society are integral to the "culture" construct (e.g., House et al., 2004; Chhokar et al., 2007), which influences the parameters through which groups of people work to address and solve problems.

Given that there are clear differences across different cultures, leaders need to develop the capacity to move beyond their own preconceptions of the "right way to do things" and cultivate openness to the potential effectiveness of different beliefs, perceptions, and behaviors. In this regard, GLOBE research indicates that the most important leadership attribute is an apprehension and expression of local expectations regarding what constitutes a good leader, even more than understanding local cultural values. Likewise, Aycan (2001) contends that a "global mindset" is necessary for effective leadership across culturally different settings in that such leaders have the "big picture" in mind allowing them to balance paradoxes, while trusting process over structure (e.g., they value difference and approach new situations from the standpoint of what needs to be learned rather than what already is known). Again, working cross-culturally requires tolerance for ambiguity, conflict, and uncertainty (e.g., to be risk tolerant) (Osland, 2001; White & Shullman, 2012). So, a global leader does not insist upon the reduction of uncertainty, but seeks to embrace and work with it, unlocking engagement and creativity along the way (Dyjak-LeBlanc et al., 2012; White & Shullman, 2010).

Moreover, if a leader is to assume responsibility for his or her organizational community, the "organized disposition" of a given cultural milieu must be understood (Schmitz, 2012). This goal may be particularly challenging when the beliefs, values, and expected behaviors within an organizational context are unknown or taken for granted by the members of the organization (i.e., they are not sufficiently aware of the cultural dynamics that are operative within the organization). To take but one example, attitudes toward time may differentially impact what is seen as important with an organization. Lorde's (1995) concept of the mythical norm also is illustrative in this regard. Especially relevant within a Western, industrialized context, "This norm is usually defined as White, thin, male, young, heterosexual, Christian, and financially secure. It is with this mythical norm that the trappings of power reside within this society" (pp. 533–534). According to Lorde, we too often ignore how the dominant culture distorts our understanding of difference. Instead of recognizing unique subcultures, which have frequently developed in a dialectical relationship with the dominant culture, we become befuddled by and fearful of these distortions, which impede our ability to appreciate cultural difference. This inability and unwillingness to see ourselves as others see us is related also to discrepancies between what we say we do and what we actually do.

Therefore, from a best practice standpoint, Fouad and Arredondo (2007) recommend that organizational change agents be schooled specifically in the multicultural characteristics of an organization while also cultivating the attendant skills necessary to translate such awareness into sensitive and effective action. Although geared toward psychologists as change agents, their central contention seems salient to all individuals who assume a leadership role, in that we are "cultural beings, making it necessary for us to engage in awareness building about our worldview and experiences that bias, both positively and negatively, our beliefs about ourselves" (pp. 101–102). That is because in an organizational context, culture has tangible consequence. Why? Because cultural proximity (i.e., the closer one resembles or manifests the fundamental beliefs, values, and behaviors of the culture) often translates into greater privileges and fewer obstacles within the organization. Moreover, the complex and interacting nature of such variables means that bias in one cultural domain may override cultural congruence in another. Consider for example the role of gender vis-à-vis culture (e.g., Eisler & Corral, 2009; Pendleton, Cochran, Kapadia, & Iyer, 2016). In an organizational context, depending on the culture at hand, women may face a double-edged sword in that they are not taken seriously if they are considered too "feminine" even as they must not present as too masculine lest they seem "manly" (Morrison, White, & Van Velsor, 1994). Combine this single variable of gender with another of ethnicity, and the complexity of accounting for interactions between such formative variables by leaders and with "the led" becomes readily apparent, particularly in a cross-cultural organizational context (e.g., Dyjak-LeBlanc et al., 2012).

Depth

Consistent with the themes presented thus far, depth-based leaders strive to eschew superficiality and pointlessness in their lives and work, having learned that human beings are not always rational or logical creatures, but driven often by powerful non-conscious, affective, and historical processes of which they may have little awareness. Such understanding of self and other may lead one toward a healthy sense of humor and abiding skepticism regarding one's own motives and those of others, while simultaneously pursuing organizational means and ends that are worthy of pursuit. As Terry (2001) observes:

> Depth, or a sense of agency regardless of position coupled with passion, creates conditions for leadership and change to occur. When you're being bashed and beaten up, from where do you get your hope? It's not enough to do the right thing. You have to find some kind of a home for yourself that provides meaning and a sense of faith and possibility that allows you to remain engaged in life. Cynicism disengages us from life. Leadership engages us. Hope comes from our deepest quest for significance in life. It is the foundation that sustains us. (p. 38)

To apprehend why and how depth-based intrapersonal processes are ineluctably associated with leadership development and organizational change, consider the exemplary work of Kets de Vries and Balazs (2008). These scholar-practitioners describe how an understanding of clinical processes and phenomena may inform organizational consultation in a deep and ecologically valid manner. Specifically, they illustrate how unconscious, interpersonal, and group-related dynamics may exert a profound impact on decisions and policies in organizational life, for better or worse. Without sufficient appreciation of the ubiquity and power of such dynamics, human motivations and actions vis-à-vis leaders and leadership are likely to be incomprehensible or ignored, to the detriment of the organization and its members. Citing real world organizational dynamics and phenomena, Kets De Vries and Balazs (2005) demonstrate how such understanding from a depth-based therapeutic perspective (e.g., object relations theory) may be combined with traditional organizational development methods (e.g., team building, mediation, performance management, total quality circles) in order to effect substantive change. For example, via a particular consulting assignment, the authors illustrate how irrational and largely unconscious processes impact real world dynamics in the workplace, and how a leader's "inner theater" (p. 8) influences cognition, emotion, and behavior. In seeking to normalize the ubiquity of such psychological processes, Ford, Ford, and D'Amelio (2008) observe that the expression of resistance may emerge from underlying and highly legitimate affective underpinnings, such as feelings of injustice or betrayal that may be grounded in real experience both within and outside of the organization. The depth-based notion here is to understand and work with "resistance," since it is inevitable and may have legitimacy, while also offering an opportunity to engage those who may have worthy perspectives and experiences that could help guide and facilitate the change process (Knowles & Linn, 2004).

The construct of cognitive closure elegantly illuminates these "resistance" processes, particularly those that relate to "seizing and freezing" (Kruglanski &

Webster, 1996, p. 265). Kruglanski and Webster identify two fundamental characteristics of cognitive closure: the "urgency" and "permanency" tendency. Specifically, the urgency tendency refers to an individual's inclination to seize upon or grasp hold of information whereas the permanency tendency references the need to "freeze" or safeguard and resist any perceived threats to previously seized information. Understanding the cognitive processes involved in seizing and freezing provides information about why individual differences emerge in relation to the experience of organizational change, and provides an explanatory framework for social cognition generally as well as the development of belief structures more specifically (Aronson, 2012). By understanding such depth-based processes at an individual level, greater sense can be made of reactions to organizational change that manifest at the group level. Ultimately, when seeking to understand why human beings do what they do, including individuals in leadership positions and followers, the importance of attending to the role of formative variables (e.g., life history, background characteristics) as well as individual differences (e.g., how affect and attributions are processed) cannot be overemphasized (Gostick & Elton, 2012; Shealy, 2005).

When such realities of the human condition are expressed through or influenced by cognitive/affective processes such as resistance, the relative capacity of the leader to apprehend or at least intuit what actually is happening, while intervening with wisdom and skill, becomes paramount (e.g., Wheatley, 2006). That is because resistance flows from an interaction between both levels of analysis: the real world experience of betrayal, injustice, or incompetence—*and* unconscious and affective processes, mediated by one's own beliefs, values, and history—an interaction that may be unknown or inaccessible at any given moment in time (Kets de Vries & Balazs, 2005, 2008). In short, the ability to acknowledge that such possibilities may in fact emanate from deep aspects of *one's own self* rather than "the other"—along with the attendant courage to act upon such awareness in the service of the organization and the led—may be the sine qua non of effective leadership as envisioned by the EI Leadership Model described later in this chapter (Dyjak-LeBlanc et al., 2012).

Transformation

James MacGregor Burns (1978), a Pulitzer Prize winning historian, used the term "transforming leadership" to describe positional leaders who use charisma and role modeling to inspire and transform followers to be intrinsically motivated leaders. Grounded in cross-cultural experience, transformational leadership means that leaders must "deal with others as individuals; consider their individual needs, abilities, and aspirations; listen attentively; further their development; advise; teach; and coach" (Bass, 1997, p. 133). Transformational leadership deliberately focuses upon enhancing the "motivation, understanding, maturity, and sense of self-worth" of those who are led (p. 130). Along these lines, Keys (2013) observes that transformational leadership is change-oriented, and that transformational leaders are open to innovation and creativity, and will take risks and adapt to uncertainty and ambiguity. Others are motivated through the words and deeds of transformational leaders, which build trust and commitment (Novogratz, 2010). They foster self-confidence and self-esteem in others to achieve what becomes a shared vision (Kouzes & Posner, 2012). From a global standpoint, a transforming leader will understand and take account of cultural expectations of engagement and motivation. Likewise, transforming leaders will not be overly discouraged by failure, believing they will prevail by sensible adaptation and ongoing cultivation of the capacity of each individual on their team (e.g., Cultivating the Globally Sustainable Self, 2014; Morton, 2013).

In contrast to transactional leadership, which views the relationship between managers and subordinates as an exchange—rewards for good performance and reprimands for poor performance—transformational leaders influence others on the basis of interpersonal processes of caring and trust while facilitating attendant processes of personal growth and development. Not surprisingly, then, leadership effectiveness has been linked to transformational approaches. Specifically, leaders who were rated by their subordinates as transformational were experienced as more satisfying and motivating to the subordinates, were more likely to be associated with subordinates who expressed commitment to their organizations, and were more likely to be rated by the leaders' supervisors as effective leaders (Judge & Bono, 2000, p. 761). Dweck's (2008) notion of a growth mindset illustrates this core aspect of the transformational approach, which believes in the inherent capacity of others, passionately calling upon them to strive for something greater. In contrast, the fixed mindset believes that leaders have "fixed abilities," which are not amenable to change regardless of experience or effort. As an antidote, Morton (2013) contends that leaders must cultivate the capacity and inclination to examine critically such delimiting beliefs, which are antithetical to the transformational potential of the organization and its members.

Finally, it should be noted that Quinn (2009) prefers the term "transformational change agent" over "leader" to emphasize that stakeholders throughout an organization may enact agency in their respective roles. Quinn contends that transformational individuals are inner-directed and other-oriented, valuing "deep change" over incremental change. Such deep change requires a shift of fundamental values, and challenges "productive equilibrium" and the norms that emerge from a tendency to repeatedly confirm that normative beliefs are correct (see also Gostick & Elton, 2012; Morton, 2013). He also distinguished "change leaders" from "normal managers," suggesting "change leaders get outside the hierarchical box" (p. 58), and are not defined or delimited by their position within an organization.

Vision

A final theme of particular relevance to global leaders and leadership concerns the nature and role of "vision" among individuals who assume a leadership role (e.g., vision is a core component of the definition of the GLOBE charismatic leadership behavior) (Chhokar et al., 2007). According to Snyder, Dowd, and Houghton (1994), vision is "more than just a plan or goal" (p. 18), but emerges from a thoughtful conceptualization of what the future of the organization should be or has the potential to embody. In articulating vision, it is necessary for leaders to exemplify and communicate a shared understanding of beliefs and values, which is essential for maintaining unity throughout an organization (Dyjak-LeBlanc et al., 2012; Gostick & Elton, 2012; Morton, 2013). As Kouzes and Posner (2012) observe, "leaders envision the future by imagining exciting and ennobling possibilities" (p. 22). From a longitudinal perspective, Griffin, Parker, and Mason (2010) examined how leadership vision has the capacity to influence change over time. Among other findings, openness to role change and role self-efficacy are both associated with the capacity of a leader to articulate a compelling vision. Moreover, the perception and experience of a leader's vision appears directly related to how the individual employee experiences him or herself (e.g., as effective and relevant, or not) (Griffin, Neal, & Parker, 2007). Overall, findings suggest that vision is essential for setting organizational direction, to be sure, but should be expressed and modeled in a manner that explicitly is supportive and empowering of all organizational members regardless of position or status.

Description of the Equilintegration (EI) Leadership Model

At this point, it may be helpful to recall the original questions and rationale for pursuing the development of this leadership model. The original five questions are as follows:

1. How do the beliefs and values of leaders impact their leadership (e.g., why do leaders experience and respond to self, others, and the larger world as they do)?
2. Are there common beliefs and values among leaders who are deemed to be most effective?
3. How do we evaluate the meaning and impact of interactions between the beliefs and values of leaders and the led?
4. How best do we understand the extraordinarily complex variables that influence leadership on a daily basis in the real world?
5. Which models of leaders and methods of leadership development are most likely to have meaning and relevance across cultures and contexts?

Moreover, recall that the current model of leadership and its application were informed by the multiyear, multi-institution Forum BEVI Project, which examined the processes and outcomes of international, multicultural, and transformative learning as well as why we experience self, others, and the larger world as we do (see Wandschneider et al., 2016). From this point of departure, a review of leadership and organizational development literature was conducted, which ultimately may be grouped under eight themes that continue to inform the model of leaders and leadership we wished to develop: Assessment, Awareness, Care, Complexity, Culture, Depth, Transformation, and Vision. On the basis of the preceding questions, applied research project, and literature, the following four principles were derived in order to provide guidance to the SMEs in the development of the leadership model described as follows.

1. Leadership *models* should have ecological validity across context and culture (e.g., research should demonstrably enhance the quality and effectiveness of leadership, both locally and globally).
2. Leadership *theory* should inform leadership research (e.g., conceptual frameworks must account for complex interactions among affective, cognitive, motivational, and developmental aspects of "being a leader").
3. Third, leadership *research* should be sophisticated (e.g., methodologies should examine the mediating role of formative variables, such as life history).
4. Leadership *practice* should address questions of who, what, why, and how (e.g., why some leaders are experienced as more effective than others, and how to individualize leadership development processes).

Although a number of methodological approaches might have been adopted to develop the leadership model reported next, job analysis was selected mainly because it allows for an in-depth and comprehensive analysis of relevant characteristics of leaders and leadership, with attendant sensitivity to empirical, theoretical, and applied aspects of model development (e.g., Center for Business, 2013; Fine & Cronshaw, 1999; Prien, Goodstein, Goodstein, & Gamble, 2009). Moreover, a similar job analysis approach had early been adopted to understand the characteristics of "child and youth care" professionals, which was readily updated and adapted to the present task (Shealy, 1995, 2012).[4]

Essentially, job analysis allows for the systematic evaluation and specification of what behaviors, knowledge, skills, abilities, and other characteristics are necessary for competent performance of particular jobs or work activities (e.g., Center for Business, 2013; Fine & Cronshaw, 1999; Prien et al., 2009). Informed by the goals of and context for this project (e.g., the four principles listed earlier), 20 national and international SMEs participated in a comprehensive job analysis of global leaders and leadership in order to identify, develop, and evaluate the work behaviors (WBs), knowledge, skills, and abilities (KSAs), and personal characteristics (PCs) of "best" and "worst" leaders. An initial list of possible participants was developed by members of the IBAVI board based upon four overarching criteria: (a) *reputation* (e.g., degree to which the individual has been recognized and experienced as aware, caring, transformative, visionary, etc.); (b) *experience* (e.g., served with distinction in leadership roles across different sectors such as nongovernmental organizations [NGOs], academic, business, etc., both in one's own country of origin and in other countries); (c) *diversity* (e.g., to ensure balance and representation across a range of variables including gender, cultural background, educational background, language, etc.); and (d) *alignment* (e.g., to what degree were participants able and willing to address the fundamental goals of this project).

The final roster of participants appeared highly congruent with these criteria (e.g., well regarded; drawn from 14 different countries; served in over 90 leadership roles; gender balance of 9 females and 11 males; average age of 46, with a range of 27–68). Through four job analysis workshops, subsets of SMEs developed the initial WBs, KSAs, and best (i.e., Highest Optimal) and worst (i.e., Lowest Optimal) PCs as well as accompanying "critical incidents" (e.g., real world examples of behaviors, knowledge areas, characteristics, etc.). All SMEs participated in the final editing, review, rating, and ranking processes through the Job Analysis Questionnaire (JAQ). An example of a WB that emerged from this job analysis includes *"Inspires and motivates others,"* which is defined in part as ". . .empowering and persuading others; sharing values, beliefs, and ideals; by personal example; through story telling in order to pursue a vision and mission and lead change processes." An example of a KSA is *"Knowledge of group processes and their facilitation,"* which is defined in part as "knows how to use groups to make decisions and when not to; how to address group conflict. . .; the importance of fostering healthy relationships and aspirations among the members of the group (e.g., establishing processes of accountability and legitimate goal-setting). . ." An example of a Highest Optimal or "best" PC is *"Insightful,"* which is defined in part as "accurately interprets subtleties and understands nuance; able to put together parts of disparate information into a coherent gestalt; apprehends complexity. . ." Finally, and example of a Lowest Optimal or "worst" PC is *"Arrogant,"* which is defined in part as "lack of understanding and awareness of,

---

[4] The editor wishes to acknowledge the helpful guidance and support of Dr. John Veres III and the Center for Business at Auburn University (www.cbed.aum.edu) for the original and current job analyses, both of which were conducted by Shealy (1995, 1996, 2012).

interest in, or care for the feelings, experiences, and needs of others; aggressively self-promoting; self-absorbed and boorish. . ."

All four of these job components were analyzed by all SMEs across four JAQ criteria in order to ascertain the degree to which each component of the job analysis was essential to leading and leadership: (a) "Rank" (i.e., highest to lowest); (b) "Importance" (i.e., not at all important to crucial); (c) "Frequency" (i.e., demonstrated hourly to yearly); and (d) "Necessary at Entry" (i.e., not important at entry to "definitely" must demonstrate at entry). Data were entered and analyzed via Excel software in order to finalize the EI Model of Leadership, which is divided into four factors (WBs, KSAs, Best PCs, Worst PCs) with two levels for each factor: Level I = EI Leaders "Must" exhibit/possess the respective WBs, KSAs, Best PCs and "Must Not" exhibit the respective Worst PCs. Level II = EI Leaders "Should" exhibit/possess the respective WBs, KSAs, Best PCs and "Should Not" exhibit the respective Worst PCs. More specifically, within the EI Leadership Model, the assignments made to Level I or Level II status; the numeric designations within factors A, B, C, and D; and the relative order of rankings within each of the four factors, all were derived from aggregated data provided by the SMEs from the JAQ. Specifically, to achieve a "must" designation, a job component must be (a) performed very frequently (weekly–hourly); (b) rated in the range of very important to crucial; and (c) rated as "probably must possess" to "definitely must possess" in terms of "necessary at entry."

To illustrate how such information and data were compiled, examine next the EI Leadership Model in Figure 14.1. According to the aggregated data provided by SMEs, in rank order of importance under Level I (the "must" dimension), note that the first three most important WBs a leader *must do* are (a) "demonstrate integrity," (b) "demonstrate understanding of self and other," and (c) "demonstrate critical thinking and reflective decision making." To take another example, according to the aggregated data provided by SMEs, in rank order of importance, note that the three most important Worst PCs that a leader *must not be* are (a) "incompetent," (b) "manipulative," and (c) "corrupt." Likewise, under Level II (the "should" dimension), note that WBs, KSAs, Best PCs, and Worst PCs also are rank ordered on the basis of SME responses to the JAQ. Again, the distinction between "Must" and "Should" is numerical in origin, based upon a cut point assigned to aggregated data for each of the four components of the JAQ (e.g., "must" demonstrate upon entry into the position versus "should" acquire over time within the position). Finally, as may be evident from the previous examples, each of these WB, KSA, Best PC, and Worst PC components is defined in detail, to include "critical incidents"/real world examples, in order to illustrate what specifically is meant by each aspect of the model (Shealy, 2012).[5] To understand the level of detail comprising each of these components, a sample excerpt from the KSAs component of the EI Leadership Model is included as Figure 14.2, which includes the full definition of the most highly ranked and rated KSA. Although space limitations do not permit a full explication, among the many benefits and usages of a comprehensive job analysis are its ability to inform the development of materials and procedures for selection and screening, education and training, certification and credentialing, benchmarking and development, and strategic planning and goal setting. More specifically, as the KSA definition suggests, it now becomes possible to develop and/or assemble all manner of leadership and organizational assessment and development approaches on the basis of the narrative guidance provided within this KSA. Moreover, as illustrated in Figure 14.1, current leaders are able to use definitions like

---

[5] More information about the EI Leadership Model is available at www.ibavi.org

EI LEADERSHIP MODEL

	I. MUST	II. SHOULD	
A. *DO*	1. Demonstrate integrity	10. Understand and care for the larger world	**A.** *DO*
	2. Demonstrate understanding and awareness of self and others		
	3. Demonstrate critical thinking and reflective decision making		
	4. Communicate effectively		
	5. Understand and value the organization and its people		
	6. Embrace complexity		
	7. Facilitate constructive and effective group processes		
	8. Inspire and motivate others		
	9. Facilitate growth and development		

	I. MUST	II. SHOULD	
B. *KNOW*	1. How to communicate honestly, openly, effectively, and persuasively	5. About the organization and its people	**B.** *KNOW*
	2. How to make decisions efficiently and in a thoughtful, fair, and informed manner	9. About management and administration	
	3. How to establish trusting relationships and a healthy work environment	11. About human nature	
	4. About the nature, process, and impact of decision making	13. About group processes and their facilitation	
	6. How to communicate in writing and orally	14. How to manage and administer	
	7. How to facilitate growth and development	15. About leaders and leadership	
	8. How to promote moral and ethical conduct	16. About the larger world	
	10. How to reflect with depth and accuracy about self, others, and the world at large	17. About complexity	
	12. About effective processes of communication in multiple forms, technologies, and modalities	18. How to solicit honest and valid feedback from others	
		19. How to experience and express a wide range of emotions	
		20. How to respond to needs and opportunities within the larger world	
		21. About different ethical, moral, and value-based systems and codes of conduct	
		22. About human growth and development	

FIGURE 14.1. The EI Leadership Model. (*continued*)

C. BE	1. Integrity	10. Insightful	C. BE
	2. Responsible	15. Aware	
	3. Honest	16. Flexible	
	4. Trustworthy	17. Empathic	
	5. Ethical	18. Clear	
	6. Knowledgeable	19. Reflective	
	7. Informed	20. Facilitative	
	8. Effective	21. Innovative	
	9. Smart	22. Authoritative	
	11. Open	23. Caring	
	12. Fair	24. Compassionate	
	13. Visionary	25. Consistent	
	14. Reasonable	26. Inspiring	
		27. Humorous	
		28. Creative	
		29. Passionate	
		30. Forgiving	
		31. Driven	
		32. Inquisitive	
		33. Introspective	
		34. Warm	
		35. Talented	

D. NOT BE	1. Incompetent	8. Arrogant	D. NOT BE
	2. Manipulative	10. Insensitive	
	3. Corrupt	12. Insecure	
	4. Controlling	14. Rigid	
	5. Harassing	15. Unpredictable	
	6. Deceitful	16. Pessimistic	
	7. Dishonest	17. Selfish	
	9. Authoritarian	18. Parochial	
	11. Ignorant		
	13. Obstructive		

FIGURE 14.1. **The EI Leadership Model.**

Note. The EI Leadership Model is divided into two levels and four factors. Assignments to Level I or Level II, and numeric designations within factors A–D, were derived from averaged ratings and rankings by 20 SMEs of all components (i.e., the preceding terms plus their full definitions, which include detailed how/why information as well as "critical incidents") across four JAQ criteria: (1) "Rank," (2) "Importance," (3) "Frequency," and (4) "Necessary" upon job entry. Finally, please note that non sequential numbers that appear in the EI Leadership Model (e.g., from 8 to 10 under Level I, Factor B) resulted from different rating and rank order calculations from JAQ results.

EI LEADERS AND LEADERSHIP:
KNOWLEDGE, SKILLS, ABILITIES (KSAs)

1. **Ability to communicate honestly, openly, effectively, and persuasively** in order to demonstrate vision (e.g., where the organization is, where it is going or should go, and why), integrity (e.g., saying what you mean and meaning what you say), courage (e.g., acknowledging and addressing difficult issues), and clarity (e.g., informed by multiple sources of input, providing a clear path forward for the organization); willingness to consult with others regarding information to be communicated; seeks feedback about the effectiveness of communication and to make modifications as necessary on the basis of that feedback; demonstrably aware that leaders may think that they are communicating effectively or in the "best way possible," but that other members of the organization may also have equally valid or even better ideas and perspectives regarding communication processes (i.e., is open to the possibility that others may be more skilled in communication and/or could substantially enhance the quality of the leader's communication); communicates information that may not be desirable with discretion and in a maximally effective manner; ensures that communication is aligned and congruent with the realities "on the ground"; accurately appraises the amount, content, and nature of information that is necessary for the organization as well as who needs what information, and when; recognizes that communication may be abused and misused by self, others, and the organization; does not necessarily assume that poor communication is due to negative or nefarious intent (but is vigilant to that possibility); anticipates the implications and consequences of communication (positive and negative) and accounts for such perspective and information in developing, delivering, and modifying communication.

2. **Ability to make decisions efficiently and in a thoughtful, fair, and informed manner** by ensuring that information gathered is necessary and sufficient (e.g., accurate, pertinent) for decision making to occur in a just and appropriate manner; engaging in strategic planning; recognizing that. . .

FIGURE 14.2. **Sample KSA excerpt from the EI Leadership Model.**

---

this as a prompt for reflecting upon their own leadership and that of their organizations in relation to the guidance and perspective provided by a distinguished cohort of global leaders. In short, rather than relying on ad hoc or idiosyncratic approaches or perspectives regarding leaders and leadership, a systematic job analysis provides a theoretical, empirical, and applied basis and foundation upon which short- and long-term processes of assessment, development, planning, and tracking may productively be pursued (e.g., Center for Business, 2013; Fine & Cronshaw, 1999; Prien et al., 2009; Shealy, 1995, 2012).

PART II: REAL WORLD APPLICATION OF THE EI LEADERSHIP MODEL

In the context of the preceding overview, rationale, literature, and job analysis, which resulted in the EI Leadership Model, Part II of this chapter describes how this model was applied and evaluated in a real world organizational context.[6] An upper level human resources leader of a medical billing group that oversees physicians' business operations, finances, billing, and collections processes in a large teaching hospital requested the workshop after learning about the development of a new leadership model. This staff person had observed the need for improved communication among upper administrative levels in the organization as well as increased clarity of organi-

---

[6] We gratefully acknowledge the key assistance and support of Janet Hollis in the development and implementation of this workshop.

zational goals. With the endorsement of the organization's chief executive officer (CEO), a workshop based upon the EI Leadership Model was developed to help facilitate greater understanding of the needs and opportunities within this organization.

Workshop Participants and Process

Forty-nine leaders at multiple levels throughout the organization including the CEO, chief financial officer, chief operating officer, various vice presidents, directors, managers, and supervisors participated in the workshop. For the remainder of this section, workshop participants will be referred to as leaders or participants, and the highest levels of the organizational leadership will be referred to as executive leaders. Prior to and in preparation of the workshop, participants were offered the opportunity to complete the BEVI and the EI Leadership Model Grading Form on a voluntary and anonymous basis (i.e., participation was invited but not required, and no record was developed regarding who did and did not elect to participate; individual BEVI reports were distributed directly to each participant based upon an ID that only he or she knew; and no names or other identifying information was associated with any organizational "grades" that were submitted). The instruments were scored and both individual and group results were prepared by the BEVI programmer for distribution during the workshop. The workshop was held in a large training room with a PowerPoint presentation and adequate space to break into small group discussions.

   The goal of the workshop was to use the background and context of the EI Leadership Model as a means to assist participants in their own growth and development while increasing organizational productivity, quality, innovation, and morale. The workshop consisted of the following three sessions:

1. **Beliefs, Values, Leaders, and Leadership.** A 1-hour presentation regarding how beliefs and values are developed, the nature of human need, an exploration of why we adopt the worldviews we do vis-à-vis the Equilintegration or EI framework, and how our beliefs and values influence organizational dynamics and leadership processes. The presentation was followed by 30 minutes of small group discussions in which leaders reflected together upon the content presented using workshop reflection questions. The facilitators collected these documented reflections from each group in order to gain an increased sense about what the participants were learning throughout the workshop.
2. **BEVI Overview and Reports.** A 30-minute presentation of the background and development of the BEVI, the BEVI scales, sample analyses, and sample structure was delivered as well as the results of the BEVI aggregate group report for the leadership team. The presentation was followed by 45 minutes of small group discussions, in which leaders reflected on their BEVI group results using workshop reflection questions and then documented their main reflections, which were collected by workshop facilitators.
3. **EI Leadership Review, Ratings, and Reflection.** This third and final session consisted of a 1-hour presentation of the EI Leadership Model, which was followed by the presentation of aggregate group results "grades" from these leaders on the *doing, knowing, being,* and *not being* factors of the model. The presentation was followed by 45 minutes of small group discussions, in which leaders reflected on their EI Leadership Model "grades" using workshop reflection questions and then documented their main reflections, which were collected by the workshop facilitator.

BEVI Workshop Results

The nature of the first session is described in the brief overview presented earlier. The second session essentially involved a review of individual reports and the BEVI organizational profiles. As customarily is the case in such workshops, this process first offers an opportunity for participants to read their own individual reports, which consists of a narrative discussion of beliefs and values along with individualized perspectives derived from scale scores across a wide range of areas (e.g., attributional tendencies; how affect is managed; inclination to focus on needs and experiences in self/other). Following this process (typically requiring approximately 10 minutes), the BEVI Organizational Report is presented and discussed. In addition to a range of demographic variables that are descriptive of the overall group that completed the BEVI, this report consists of a series of profiles/indexes addressing various aspects of how the group is different and similar to itself. The discussion that follows typically builds upon such characteristics in order to explore and understand more deeply *why* a group functions in the way that it does. Through this process, the underlying reasons for what is working well and what is not becomes more transparent (e.g., relative strengths; areas of potential conflict), with attendant implications for improving functioning and effectiveness (e.g., by working with group dynamics that may be mediated by very different underlying ways of experiencing self, others, and the larger world).

As Figure 14.3 illustrates, for workshop respondents who completed the BEVI in advance of the workshop (N = 24), patterns of difference and similarity emerged in this organizational context as well. As was discussed with the group, the BEVI profile

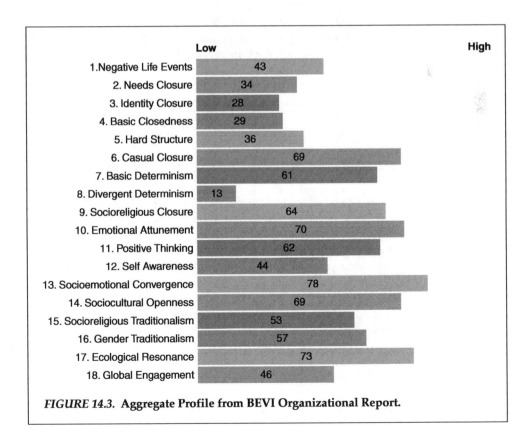

FIGURE 14.3. **Aggregate Profile from BEVI Organizational Report.**

suggests that as a whole, this group of leaders presents as quite emotionally aware and engaged (Emotionally Attunement = 70th percentile); able to apprehend the world in terms of gray rather than black and white (Socioemotional Convergence = 78th percentile); to be quite open to and interested in cultural beliefs and practices that are different from one's own (Sociocultural Openness = 69th percentile); and to express a high degree of concern about ecological issues and the natural world (Ecological Resonance = Convergence = 73rd percentile). On the other hand, as a whole, the group tends to lean toward basic ways of explaining why people or systems work in the ways that they do (Causal Closure = 69th percentile), which may in part be explained by more traditional religious inclinations in general for the group (Socioreligious Closure = 64th percentile).

To interpret more deeply what such aggregate tendencies may imply, it usually is helpful to juxtapose the broader group profile with another BEVI profile, which breaks down each of the scale scores by deciles (i.e., the dispersion of the larger group is illustrated across each of the scales in increments of 10%, from those who score in the lowest 10% of the scale to those who score in the highest 10% of each scale). As is typically the case, groups that are seemingly similar may in fact show quite different dispersions across each of these scales, which illuminate where areas of similarity and difference actually exist. Thus, in many ways, this profile is among the most important of all on the BEVI Organizational Report.

A cursory review of Figure 14.4 reveals very interesting patterns of similarity and difference within the group, which provided a point of departure for rich dialogue and reflection. Consider Emotional Attunement (Scale 10), for example, which essentially measures sensitivity, affiliation needs, and the valuation of affective expression in self and others. Here, evidence suggests that the group is highly similar to itself in that no respondent falls below the 40th percentile, with over two-thirds of the group falling above the 60th percentile on this scale. From an interpretive standpoint, it seems likely that the group as a whole would have a similar sensibility vis-à-vis emotionality, and would be quite comfortable with and desirous of affectively based communication and connection in general (i.e., since no respondents fell below the 50th percentile, and given that a greater degree of Emotional Attunement would generally seem to be desirable within an organizational context). This point generated considerable discussion as will be discussed later.

10. Emotional Attunement	0%	0%	0%	0%	4%	25%	21%	33%	8%	8%

On the other hand, consider the dispersion of the group on Gender Traditionalism, another BEVI scale. Here we see a quite striking pattern of difference across the entire scale, with the group more or less evenly divided. For example, 21% of the sample (5 individuals from an N of 24) falls at or above the 80th percentile on this scale whereas another 16% (4 individuals) falls at or below the 20th percentile on this scale (i.e., there is a substantial division among subgroups within the organization, with one subgroup of 5 leaders endorsing highly traditional beliefs about gender whereas another subgroup of 4 leaders endorsed highly nontraditional beliefs about gender). Since Gender Traditionalism essentially measures the degree to which individuals endorse traditional beliefs regarding why men and women are the way they are as well as whom they are supposed to be, such findings suggest very different beliefs on these fundamental matters, which emerged during discussion of such findings.

16. Gender Traditionalism	8%	8%	8%	17%	4%	17%	8%	8%	4%	17%

Deciles:	1	2	3	4	5	6	7	8	9	10
1.Negative Life Events	9%	17%	25%	12%	12%	12%	4%	4%	4%	8%
2. Needs Closure	0%	0%	38%	46%	17%	0%	0%	0%	0%	0%
3. Identity Closure	21%	33%	12%	17%	12%	0%	0%	0%	0%	4%
4. Basic Closedness	8%	12%	29%	29%	12%	8%	0%	0%	0%	0%
5. Hard Structure	8%	8%	21%	12%	21%	17%	4%	8%	0%	0%
6. Casual Closure	0%	4%	12%	17%	4%	12%	17%	12%	8%	12%
7. Basic Determinism	0%	8%	17%	17%	8%	4%	21%	8%	8%	8%
8. Divergent Determinism	25%	33%	25%	4%	8%	4%	0%	0%	0%	0%
9. Socioreligious Closure	4%	4%	12%	8%	4%	12%	17%	17%	4%	17%
10. Emotional Attunement	0%	0%	0%	0%	4%	25%	21%	33%	8%	8%
11. Positive Thinking	0%	17%	8%	12%	4%	8%	17%	12%	12%	8%
12. Self Awareness	21%	12%	8%	12%	4%	21%	8%	4%	0%	8%
13. Socioemotional Convergence	0%	0%	0%	0%	0%	12%	38%	17%	17%	17%
14. Sociocultural Openness	0%	0%	0%	0%	0%	21%	38%	17%	21%	4%
15. Socioreligious Traditionalism	17%	4%	4%	0%	17%	12%	8%	21%	17%	0%
16. Gender Traditionalism	8%	8%	8%	17%	4%	17%	8%	8%	4%	17%
17. Ecological Resonance	0%	4%	0%	8%	0%	4%	42%	8%	17%	17%
18. Global Engagement	12%	12%	17%	12%	8%	21%	4%	4%	0%	8%
Deciles:	1	2	3	4	5	6	7	8	9	10

FIGURE 14.4. Decile Profile from BEVI Organizational Report.

EI Leadership Workshop Results

Results from the EI Leadership Model Grading Form included each of the four areas of the leadership model: Work Behaviors (WBs), Knowledge, Skills, and Abilities (KSAs), and Personal Characteristics (PCs) of Highest Optimal (i.e., "best") and Lowest Optimal (i.e., "worst") leaders and approaches to leadership. In assigning grades, participants were asked to evaluate the quality of leadership as a whole within the organization. Of the workshop participants, 16 leaders completed the grading form prior to the workshop.[7]

Work Behavior Grades
An excerpt of WBs from the grading form and a chart of aggregate group results are included in Figure 14.5. Participants graded the 10 WBs on a five-point Likert scale with an A (score of 5) indicating a rating of "Excellent, always evidenced across individuals and circumstances" and an F (score of 1) indicating "Failing, never evidenced

---

[7] Additional "grades" were submitted, but not in advance of the workshop, so were not able to be included in the results that were presented to the group.

Complete this form on the basis of your general understanding of what each of the below terms/phrases means and assign a grade based on the following criteria:

A = Excellent, always evidenced across individuals and circumstances
B = Good, frequently evidenced across individuals and circumstances
C = Fair, sometimes evidenced across individuals and circumstances
D = Poor, rarely evidenced across individuals and circumstances
F = Failing, never evidenced across individuals and circumstances

A. Work Behaviors: For your organization, please rate each of the following items, which were determined to be descriptive of what effective leaders must or should DO.

1. Demonstrate integrity	A	B	C	D	F
2. Demonstrate understanding and awareness of self and others	A	B	C	D	F
3. Demonstrate critical thinking and reflective decision making	A	B	C	D	F
4. Communicate effectively	A	B	C	D	F
5. Understand and value the organization and its people	A	B	C	D	F
6. Embrace complexity	A	B	C	D	F
7. Facilitate constructive and effective group processes	A	B	C	D	F
8. Inspire and motivate others	A	B	C	D	F
9. Facilitate growth and development	A	B	C	D	F
10. Understand and care for the larger world	A	B	C	D	F

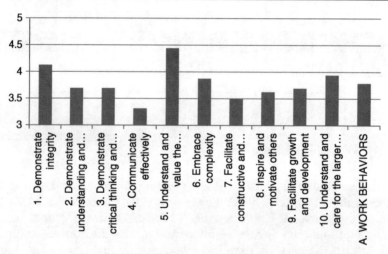

FIGURE 14.5. **Work Behavior (WB) Grading Form and chart of results.**

across individuals and circumstances."[8] Overall, results indicated that leaders were quite capable of understanding and valuing the organization and its people, and demonstrated a high degree of fidelity to behaviors associated with organizational integrity. On the other hand, relative to such important strengths, participants rated

[8] For the full title of each WB, KSA, or PC, please see the excerpt from the "grading form" that accompanies each graph, which shows the actual "grades" that were assigned based upon participant ratings. Please note also that the original terminology of "Best" and "Worst" Personal Characteristics has been amended to "Highest Optimal" and "Lowest Optimal" in order to correspond with the "Highest Optimal" and "Lowest Optimal" Full Scale Score designations from the BEVI.

lower effective communication and the facilitation of constructive and effective group processes. An overarching goal of this process was to identify areas where processes appeared to be going very well as well as areas for potential improvement over the long term. Mean differences of a grade level do offer potential guidance in that regard. For example, as the results illustrate, leaders assigned a B+ (4.4) to "Understand and value the organization and its people" and a C+ (3.3) to "Communicate effectively." Despite seemingly relevant mean differences in this regard, no aggregate rating fell below 3 ("fair") on any of the four competency areas, which suggests the important finding that the organization does not appear—at least from this analysis—to be experiencing significant deficits in terms of the experience of overall leadership quality or effectiveness.

KSA Grades

Likewise, an excerpt of the KSAs from the grading form and a chart of the aggregate results are included in Figure 14.6. Participants rated the 22 KSAs using the same five-point Likert scale from the WBs section. Results suggest a strong degree of confidence in the ability to "manage and administer" and "promote moral and ethical conduct" as well as a high degree of knowledge about "the organization and its people." In other words, KSA 14 (i.e., skill regarding "how to manage and administer"), KSA 8 (i.e., skill regarding "how to promote moral and ethical conduct), and KSA 5 (knowledge "about the organization and its people"), were the highest of all KSAs according to the leaders who graded leadership within the organization. Relative to such very strong competencies, leaders report a greater challenge in the ability to "experience and express a wide range of emotions" (KSA 19), as well as knowledge about "the nature, process, and impact of decision making" (KSA 4), and "effective processes of communication in multiple forms, technologies, and modalities" (KSA 12).

Highest Optimal PC Grades

The 35 PCs of Highest Optimal approaches to leadership mean scores are presented in Figure 14.7. Participants used the same Likert scale from the previous two sections to grade these items. Results indicate the leaders are regarded as responsible, knowledgeable, honest, informed, effective, smart, and talented (Best PCs 2, 6, 3, 7, 8, 9, and 35). Although still strong, characteristics that are seen as relatively less indicative of leadership include a tendency to be visionary, reflective, and creative (Best PCS 13, 19, and 38).

Lowest Optimal PC Grades

Finally, the grading form for the 18 Lowest Optimal approaches to leadership and means for those items are presented in Figure 14.8. Participants used an adapted five-point Likert scale to grade these items to indicate that these characteristics were less desirable. In other words, in contrast to the previous three areas, an A (or 5) for "excellent" means that the characteristic is "never evidenced across individuals and circumstances" whereas an F (or 1) for "failing" means that the characteristic is "always evidenced across individuals and circumstances." Perhaps most important, respondents indicate that leaders are *not* characterized as corrupt, harassing, or deceitful (Least Optimal or "worst" PCs 3, 5, and 6). Relative to such indexes, the most negative attribute of leadership writ large was the characteristic of "controlling" (Worst PC 4), but even there, the aggregate rating fell between "good" and "fair," which suggests a basis for reflection, as noted in the following workshop description, but no major problems in this final area of organizational functioning.

B. Knowledge, Skills, and Abilities: For your organization, please rate each of the following items, which were determined to be descriptive of what effective leaders must or should KNOW.

1. How to communicate honestly, openly, effectively, and persuasively	A	B	C	D	F
2. How to make decisions efficiently and in a thoughtful, fair, and informed manner	A	B	C	D	F
3. How to establish trusting relationships and a healthy work environment	A	B	C	D	F
4. About the nature, process, and impact of decision making	A	B	C	D	F
5. About the organization and its people	A	B	C	D	F
6. How to communicate in writing and orally	A	B	C	D	F
7. How to facilitate growth and development	A	B	C	D	F
8. How to promote moral and ethical conduct	A	B	C	D	F
9. About management and administration	A	B	C	D	F
10. How to reflect with depth and accuracy about self, others, and the world at large	A	B	C	D	F
11. About human nature	A	B	C	D	F
12. About effective processes of communication in multiple forms, technologies, and modalities	A	B	C	D	F
13. About group processes and their facilitation	A	B	C	D	F
14. How to manage and administer	A	B	C	D	F
15. About leaders and leadership	A	B	C	D	F
16. About the larger world	A	B	C	D	F
17. About complexity	A	B	C	D	F
18. How to solicit honest and valid feedback from others	A	B	C	D	F
19. How to experience and express a wide range of emotions	A	B	C	D	F
20. How to respond to needs and opportunities within the larger world	A	B	C	D	F
21. About different ethical, moral, and value-based systems and codes of conduct	A	B	C	D	F
22. About human growth and development	A	B	C	D	F

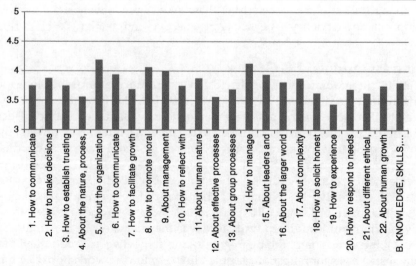

FIGURE 14.6. Knowledge, Skills, and Abilities (KSAs) Grading Form and chart of results.

C. Highest Optimal Personal Characteristics: For your organization, please rate each of the following items, which were determined to be descriptive of what effective leaders must or should BE.

1. Integrity	A	B	C	D	F	18. Clear	A	B	C	D	F
2. Responsible	A	B	C	D	F	19. Reflective	A	B	C	D	F
3. Honest	A	B	C	D	F	20. Facilitative	A	B	C	D	F
4. Trustworthy	A	B	C	D	F	21. Innovative	A	B	C	D	F
5. Ethical	A	B	C	D	F	22. Authoritative	A	B	C	D	F
6. Knowledgeable	A	B	C	D	F	23. Caring	A	B	C	D	F
7. Informed	A	B	C	D	F	24. Compassionate	A	B	C	D	F
8. Effective	A	B	C	D	F	25. Consistent	A	B	C	D	F
9. Smart	A	B	C	D	F	26. Inspiring	A	B	C	D	F
10. Insightful	A	B	C	D	F	27. Humorous	A	B	C	D	F
11. Open	A	B	C	D	F	28. Creative	A	B	C	D	F
12. Fair	A	B	C	D	F	29. Passionate	A	B	C	D	F
13. Visionary	A	B	C	D	F	30. Forgiving	A	B	C	D	F
14. Reasonable	A	B	C	D	F	31. Driven	A	B	C	D	F
15. Aware	A	B	C	D	F	32. Inquisitive	A	B	C	D	F
16. Flexible	A	B	C	D	F	33. Introspective	A	B	C	D	F
17. Empathic	A	B	C	D	F	34. Warm	A	B	C	D	F
						35. Talented	A	B	C	D	F

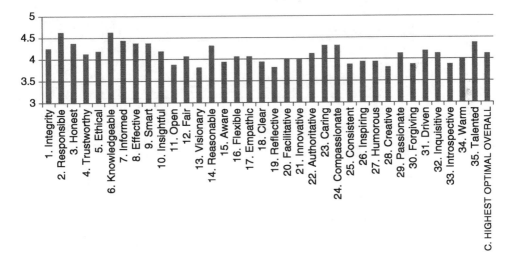

FIGURE 14.7. **Highest Optimal Personal Characteristics (PCs) Grading Form and chart of results.**

Workshop Experience: Small Group Deliberations

For each of the three workshop sessions and small group discussions, a review of the documented responses to the reflections reveals how each session was experienced and what was learned. *During the first small group discussion regarding the nature and origin of beliefs and values,* several of the small groups indicated that they gained

Note that the below rating system is different for Lowest Optimal Personal Characteristics

A = Excellent, never evidenced across individuals and circumstances
B = Good, rarely evidenced across individuals and circumstances
C = Fair, sometimes evidenced across individuals and circumstances
D = Poor, frequently evidenced across individuals and circumstances
F = Failing, always evidenced across individuals and circumstances

D. Lowest Optimal Personal Characteristics: For your organization, please rate each of the following items, which were determined to be descriptive of what effective leaders must or should NOT BE.

1. Incompetent	A	B	C	D	F
2. Manipulative	A	B	C	D	F
3. Corrupt	A	B	C	D	F
4. Controlling	A	B	C	D	F
5. Harassing	A	B	C	D	F
6. Deceitful	A	B	C	D	F
7. Dishonest	A	B	C	D	F
8. Arrogant	A	B	C	D	F
9. Authoritarian	A	B	C	D	F
10. Insensitive	A	B	C	D	F
11. Ignorant	A	B	C	D	F
12. Insecure	A	B	C	D	F
13. Obstructive	A	B	C	D	F
14. Rigid	A	B	C	D	F
15. Unpredictable	A	B	C	D	F
16. Pessimistic	A	B	C	D	F
17. Selfish	A	B	C	D	F
18. Parochial	A	B	C	D	F

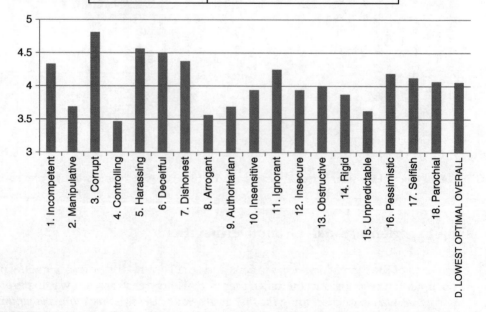

FIGURE 14.8. **Lowest Optimal Personal Characteristics (PCs) Grading Form and chart of results.**

understanding about why humans function as they do; the importance of attending to core human needs; how the environment and life experiences shape a person's beliefs, values, and worldview; and how the EI framework and BEVI help cultivate greater self/other awareness. For example, the importance of "putting yourself in the other person's shoes" in order to understand and embrace differences was emphasized by one group. Another group wrote that they developed greater "awareness of why we are the way we are and how this affects our decision making and leadership." The attendant recognition that a great deal of diversity may make it "difficult to come to agreement on an organization's values" highlighted the importance of "learning more about where our beliefs and values come from and how fundamental they are to our lives and behavior."

During the second small group discussion regarding individual and group BEVI results, a number of groups appeared to engage deeply in discussions regarding belief/value differences and similarities among members of leadership, and the attendant implications for organizational development. At the most basic level, the importance of "values forums" and "education around values" was emphasized as was the need for a "common understanding of values" as well as "definition/clarity" in this regard. Such a focus was felt to be important in part because each individual brought his or her own interpretations to various aspects of the organization and/or his or her role within it; thus, the diversity of management style and communication could lead to confusion regarding expectations, for example, regarding "work–life balance" (i.e., such a value was prized in word but not always in deed). As such, different groups emphasized that it was important for leaders to "practice what we preach" and "walk the talk." As one group wrote, "what we say and what we think are not always aligned." Along similar lines, greater "transparency" and "openness" was desired in order to promote more authenticity and genuine communication among various levels and sectors of leadership. "Compassion for the other person" and "active listening" were additional recommendations in this regard. One group imagined creating an environment where "staff is able to speak freely without feeling it will be held against them." Not surprisingly, then, "trust in leadership (that leadership is trying to do the right thing)" was cited as necessary to "mitigate the tension" that could arise. Including "all parts of the organization" and listening to "input" from everyone—"not just one leader group"—also were seen as key.

During the *third and final small group discussion regarding the EI Leadership Model and accompanying "grades,"* participants observed that upper management was more likely to succeed when they "demonstrated integrity and harness[ed] diversity," worked to "engage all leaders" within the system, and sought to ensure less of a "disconnect between personal values and organizational values." "Communication, awareness, encouragement, and listen[ing] (active)" were among the values emphasized. Problems emerged when leaders "fail to recognize differences in others' beliefs/where they are coming from." The consequences of not attending to such belief/value differences and similarities emerged at several levels (e.g., during initial hiring decisions). Along similar lines, a desire was expressed to "make sure there is as little inconsistency in our working selves [and] our true selves." One strategy for addressing issues such as these could be to "distribute the BEVI to staff members" in order to promote greater understanding of these belief/value similarities and differences. Likewise, the desire to "engage all leaders" within the larger system (not just a subset) was emphasized as was "a shared mission and sense of overall purpose." Greater "communication and vision" were seen as crucial, even while recognizing that the "rapid change" the organization was experiencing may be contributing to difficulties in this regard. Small groups also reported that it is important to seek work–life balance and develop a shared mission as well as a sense of overall purpose.

Overall, qualitative and quantitative feedback indicates that group members especially appreciated the opportunity to (a) learn more about what beliefs and values are, where they come from, and how they may be understood; (b) reflect more deeply upon self and others vis-à-vis the organization; (c) review and discuss belief/ value similarities and differences within and among members of leadership through the BEVI individual and organizational reports; (d) understand organizational strengths, weaknesses, and future directions through the EI Leadership Model and findings; and (e) begin a process of open dialogue with all leaders across varying levels of the organization for purposes of planning, growth, and development over the short and long term.

Discussion: Implications of the EI Leadership Model and Workshop

It is easy to find examples of ineffective organizational leadership. Whether a leader or the led, we all can point to moments or tendencies in organizations of poor decision making, a lack of vision, inattention to morale, ineffective communication, systemic tendencies toward obstruction, and so forth. Similarly, most of us can identify characteristics that we do and do not esteem in the leaders we have known. Ultimately, it is one thing to identify such processes or characteristics on an informal basis, and another matter altogether to make them manifest in a way that obscure dynamics are clarified, strengths and weaknesses identified, and growth and development facilitated. As important, the consequences of not attending to what actually is happening at these deep, complex, and interacting levels can mean the difference between success and failure from a leadership and organizational standpoint. Fortunately, an increasing number of scholars and practitioners are articulating depth-based perspectives in leadership and organizational literature. Highly congruent with such trends, the overarching purpose of applying the present leadership model to a real world organizational setting was to ascertain whether and how such abstruse processes could be illuminated in order to point the way toward practical and substantive change. We conclude that such processes and outcomes are not only possible, but necessary if we are to cultivate leaders and foster leadership that is able to meet the challenges and opportunities of our day. We base this perspective on the following four reasons, which we discuss next and in conclusion: (a) leadership models matter; (b) beliefs and values are integral to leaders and leadership; (c) leadership assessment reveals what is and is not working, and why; and (d) leadership models and assessment methods provide a road map for change.

First, leadership models matter

The fundamental rationale for developing the EI Leadership Model—and the major impetus for real world application—is to illuminate and make accessible leadership and organizational processes that too often are opaque and complex. If such dynamics were mere abstractions, this exercise would primarily be intellectual in nature. But the fact of the matter is, the degree to which leaders understand themselves and others—and are interested in doing so—has a profound impact on other leaders, those who are led, and the organization as a whole. However, the real issue here is what model of human beings is endorsed—explicitly or implicitly—by leadership and the organization. Are humans rational creatures who say what they mean and mean what they say? Or, as the EI Leadership Model contends, are humans highly complex creatures who strive throughout their lives to meet core human needs, the pursuit of which is either facilitated or impeded by the beliefs and values that are acquired vis-à-vis one's experience of self, others, and the larger world? Fundamentally, these are belief/value-based and epistemologically grounded considerations (e.g., Gostick & Elton, 2012; Kouzes & Posner, 2012; Morton, 2013; Shealy, 2005) that determine how and why we interpret and understand actions, feelings, and thoughts—our own and others—as we do. From the standpoint of leaders and leadership, the type of model to which we are drawn likely says a great deal about what we believe human beings are as well as why we do what we do. At a deeper level, data suggest that our inclination toward one type of model or another also says something about our abilities and inclinations toward ambiguity, the world of affect, cultures and practices that are different from our own, and global issues that affect humanity as a whole. The ability to tolerate depth and complexity, in other words, appears directly related to the type of leadership models to which we are drawn (e.g., Kets De Vries & Balazs, 2005; Shealy, 2016; Wheatley, 2006; White & Shullman, 2010).

At the level of research and practice, our lack of attention to issues of complexity and depth impedes our ability truly to understand why leaders and followers—and the organizations in which they reside—function as they do. Moreover, our ability to imagine and actualize effective and ethical organizations may be circumscribed by quick fix solutions and processes of leadership that emphasize control and hiearchy (Wheatley, 2006). In short, fundamental assumptions about the nature and goals of leadership—our models—must be unpacked and unconcealed, especially because there is "a lack of serious and shared meaning embodied in the term leadership" (Terry, 2001, p. 1). At this level of analysis, the current organization is to be commended for its openness to examining these abstruse issues in the first place, which nonetheless had a direct impact at a bottom line level (e.g., morale, productivity, efficiency, innovation).

Second, beliefs and values are integral to leaders and leadership

An overarching strength and benefit from the leadership workshop was the importance of how it helped the participants gain a greater understanding of how beliefs and values develop in individuals, how differences and similarities emerge among leaders and the led, and ultimately how and why people function as they do. Furthermore, a strength and benefit of the workshop was its importance in helping participants begin to navigate and reflect on their own specific differences within the organization, given the results and findings of the BEVI and EI Leadership Model Grading Form. Leaders appreciated the opportunity to learn about how their beliefs and values as a group create work environments with attendant strengths and weaknesses. Accordingly, this learning brought awareness to why individuals are the way they are, and how such human dynamics affect decision making and leadership. This learning also offered a new language for talking about, understanding, and attending to differences, facilitating insight and connection to real life examples within their organization, and grappling with whether and how behaviors are and are not consistent with the shared beliefs and values of the organization as a whole.

As noted previously, Schmitz (2012) argued that leadership is about taking action and responsibility, regardless of position or organizational level, in order to engage the community for the common good. The BEVI and EI Leadership Model appear to have provided participants with tools to assess such matters (e.g., one's own cultural background as well as the backgrounds of others). Furthermore, such instruments and interventions bring to the forefront our assumptions about how organizations ought to be structured, how power should be distributed, and how decisions should be made. By making these implicit assumptions visible, new ways of imagining how individuals interact and organizations operate may emerge or become apparent.

Toward such means and ends, recall that a basic precept of the EI Leadership Model is that human beliefs and values are determined in no small part by a complex interaction among core needs (e.g., for attachment, affiliation) and formative variables (e.g., life history, culture). Those who assume a leadership role are not somehow immune from these same factors and forces that shape how all of us experience self, others, and the larger world (Shealy, 2012). The difference is, those of us in a position of leadership may also subject others to the beliefs and values we hold to be self-evident, whether or not we are aware of, or accountable for, doing so (Gostick & Elton, 2012; Morton, 2013). Thus, any discussion of leaders must recognize the moral implications of leadership, by ensuring, for example, that matters of ethics, authenticity, and motivation are all juxtaposed with the raw instrumentality of leadership (e.g., Bass & Riggio, 2006; George, 2004; Kouzes & Posner, 2012; Terry, 1993; Wheatley, 2006). In other words, we cannot and should not evaluate the quality or effectiveness of leaders or leadership only by examining bottom line outcomes of corporate profit or market dominance. We must also appraise the processes by which such outcomes are achieved as well as the experience of those who are the beneficiaries of its work, for better or for worse. In short,

> individuals who assume the role of leader must acknowledge a moral obligation to be mindful of the forces that facilitate or impede the fulfilment of human potential. Moreover, in word and deed, they should seek to attenuate obstacles, and promote the greater good, by virtue of the fact that they have access to greater resources, and are in a position of relative power and influence, over other human beings. (Shealy, 2012)

We see these belief/value dimensions of leaders and leadership—the need to emphasize depth and complexity as well as awareness and responsiveness toward the "wicked issues" that affect humanity as a whole—as interdependent parts of a larger whole (e.g., Coffman, Hopkins, & Ali, 2009; Cultivating the Globally Sustainable Self, 2014; National Action Plan for Education for Sustainability, 2014).

Third, leadership assessment reveals what is and is not working, and why

As these results suggest, the current organization evinces many positive features. For example, several indexes from the EI Leadership Model suggest that leaders are highly responsible and knowledgeable about the goals and purpose of the organization; moreover, as noted, no aggregate rating on any of the elements of the broader model fell at or below the "fair" (grade of C), and many were at the "good" (grade of B) or higher level. On the other hand, as is likely always the case, there is room for improvement, at the level of communication and transparency, for example. In this regard, it seems evident that one of the paradoxes within the current organization is that leadership as a whole has a great deal of capacity to experience and express affect. And yet, such inclination may not be sufficiently recognized and/or utilized from an organizational standpoint, as evidenced by the seeming misalignment among (a) one of the highest and most uniformly distributed scores on the BEVI—*70th percentile on Emotional Attunement*; (b) the lowest grade given on the 10 WBs of the EI Leadership Model—*Communicate Effectively*; (c) the lowest grade given on the 21 KSAs of the EI Leadership Model—*How to Experience and Express a Wide Range of Emotions*; and (d) the lowest grade given on the 18 Lowest Optimal PCs of the EI Leadership Model—*Controlling*.

Reflect, for the moment, on the "perfect storm" that such a constellation of findings predict and reveal. Essentially, it would appear that there is something of a mismatch between the inclinations and capacities of at least one subset of leaders (individuals in lower level leadership roles) and another subset of leaders (probably executive leadership, at least on the basis of qualitative findings from the small group deliberations), which are experienced as not optimally transparent and overly controlling vis-à-vis communication. Executive (i.e., upper) leadership might argue that the "lower leaders" are simply overly "emotional" or "too sensitive," and therefore overreacting to various decisions and/or processes that were "coming down" from above. But from the standpoint of the BEVI and EI Leadership Model, it really does not matter whether this subset of "lower leaders" is "overreacting" or not. In fact, there really is no way to answer this question in any definitive way, since we are—by necessity—in the realm of subjectively held beliefs and values, which are affectively loaded and experientially based. In short, the point is not whether such an experience by a subset of leaders *should be happening*, but that it *is in fact happening*. Indeed, upon reviewing these findings in the workshop, one member of executive leadership observed that dialogue had occurred at that level about whether and how to bridge the gap between decision making at the highest level with that of the lower level, since they were responsible for matters of implementation in their respective groups. Such honesty and reflection is commendable, and seemed to be experienced as refreshing by participants in the workshop. Most important, the pattern of findings presented here suggests the need, opportunity, and benefits of more such reflection and subsequent actions along these lines in collaboration between executive and lower levels of leadership.

Another finding speaks again to the importance of leadership and organizational assessment. Recall the substantial dispersion across the entire scale of Gender Traditionalism, which indicated that unlike Emotional Attunement, for example, the beliefs and values held by the group regarding matters of gender (e.g., why men and women are as they are; who they are supposed to be) ranged across the entire scale, from the basement (the lowest possible decile) to the ceiling (the highest possible decile). In the real world, such a finding suggests that underlying beliefs and values about the proper role of males and females—including but not limited to matters of leadership—are extremely varied within this group, ranging from what might be called "highly traditional" on one end of the continuum to "highly progressive" on the other. How might such dynamics play out in the real organizational world? When juxtaposed with the fact that this BEVI sample was completed by a strong majority of female leaders (83%), such findings beg the questions—which was explored during the workshop—as to whether such differences show up for women and men in the organization when faced with matters of advancement, review, collegiality, and so forth. Among other aspects of the discussion, it became very clear that these issues were in fact an ongoing process within the system, as a number of women leaders commented on the paradox that they often were their own worst critics and/or obstacles toward one another (rather than necessarily experiencing such dynamics from their male coleaders). The implications for such processes extend beyond the workshop, and may create opportunities for further exploration and dialogue—as well as professional and organizational development—in the months and years ahead if the organization is to avoid getting in its own way, while facilitating the full expression of potential and talent within its ranks, by both genders.

Fourth, leadership models and assessment methods provide a road map for change

Assessing just to say one has done so is pointless at best and counterproductive at worst. Rather, assessment—in leadership, organizational, or other contexts—should always be about gathering information so that better decisions are made. Without some basis for decision making, organizations are rudderless because "it's hard to know where to go, if you don't know where you are" (Shealy, 2012). Knowing where you are requires some form of assessment, which should lead to dialogue, which should lead to change, if the inevitabilities of resistance are empathically understood and skillfully navigated (Ford et al., 2008; Morton, 2013). In this regard, one of the most promising results from the workshop was the promotion of open dialogue among the various levels of leadership in the organization following the review of assessment results, even as upper administration grappled with the implications of various findings. Such a process may break down "the silos" that limit openness and awareness of organizational differences and strengths. Silos create and maintain psychological distance, which undermines efforts to build trust, generate respect, and inspire others (Kets de Vries & Balazs, 2005). Accordingly, opportunities for connection and meaningful discussion as well as openness to discussing an organization's difficulties are crucial, and may be facilitated by such assessment-based processes.

One longer term "road map" implication from this workshop is the benefit of engaging in more frequent process-based interventions, since improved and affectively authentic communication was a principle desire of workshop participants. In doing so, the apparent belief/value diversity within the leadership group must be recognized and addressed. Well-designed models and methods offer the facilitator a means for not only gaining greater insight into individual, group and organizational processes, but also raise the possibility and expectation for participants to engage authentically with themselves and each other. Ultimately, the goal is to create organizational environments that allow for authentic dialogue, reflection on the process in which individuals work, and greater openness toward complexity and ambiguity (George, 2004; White & Shullman, 2010). As Kets de Vries and Balazs (2005) observed,

> . . . it does not take a rocket scientist to realize that organizations that resemble gulags in their repressiveness cannot bring out the best in people; on the contrary, they encourage people to just go through the motions, to present a false self while working—showing a public face to the world that is contrary to how they really feel. Executives in organizations where people can be authentic and feel alive, on the other hand, take every opportunity to minimize the presentation of a false self. Because they themselves have learned to experience a greater sense of authenticity, they help their employees avoid the identity confusion that comes with presenting one image to oneself and another one to others. (p. 13)

In this regard, group facilitation through the BEVI and EI Leadership Model appeared to facilitate the process by which authentic dialogue could occur.

That said, one of the challenges in conducting a workshop that lasts for a day or less is similar to attending only one class or group therapy session. In short, there are limits to what may be accomplished in a single meeting time (e.g., Shullman et al., in press). Moreover, cognitively and affectively, much of the work and learning takes place after individuals have time to consider and reflect on their experiences. So, short-term interventions that are assessment and process based may help identify which directions to travel in the months ahead, and may even facilitate initial steps along the way. But a workshop such as this one really should be seen as part of a longer term road mapping process, which is integrated into the mission and culture of an organization (e.g., to value depth-based assessment using appropriate means and methods). At the same time, it would be quite possible to break up the workshop into two or more days in order to build a deep sense of rapport and engage in the sort of depth-based dialogue that the process and results of this workshop clearly initiated.

At the very least, Griffin, Neal, and Parker's (2007) description of adaptive performance where positional leaders set the expectation that change will take place, outline a compelling vision, and then support all members of the team in pursuing change could provide an environment for change to be pursued even with a one-time workshop or presentation. Likewise, Terry (2001) contends that a compelling vision alone will not necessarily lead to needed change unless and until positional leaders are involved, and such a process is integrated into longer term commitments on behalf of the organization. Thus, a short, 1-day workshop may be advantageous because it provides opportunities for organizational members to define the process and the frames from which to make sense out of the process. Ultimately, organizations should examine their goals and status, insofar as they are known, to determine what timeline and approach makes the most sense, and request adaptation of workshops like this one to meet their unique needs.

Much was discovered during the current workshop, but if such assessment information is not translated into a "road map" form that can contribute to the betterment of the organization over time, then its transformational potential will be underutilized. Fortunately, in the present case, human resource personnel and other key members of leadership appear invested in understanding how to address key findings that emerged, such as how to improve transparency, openness, and flow at a communicative level; how to better apprehend and manage the underlying affective currents within the organization's culture, in order to move toward better alignment between the "work self" and "true self" and promote a greater experience of respect between different leadership levels; and, how to grapple with the vast diversity among female leaders in particular, but inclusive of males in leadership roles, in terms of what the underlying commitments are to the role of women and men as leaders. These sorts of issues and dynamics—revealed through assessment—actually matter to the people who are doing the leadership work of the organization. To aid in that process, assessment data from the current workshop may be seen as a sort of baseline against which to measure future growth and development. The model itself may be seen in aspirational terms, such that leaders may apprehend where they are now on all four dimensions—Work Behaviors; Knowledge, Skills, and Abilities; Highest Optimal Personal Characteristics; Lowest Optimal Personal Characteristics—and contemplate how they might arrive at a better position, demonstrating such arrival empirically through future assessment. As the goal of the original job analysis suggested, we are trying to articulate the who, what, why, and how of leaders and leadership, not because anyone ever "gets there" once and for all, but because the quest to achieve one's potential as a leader is and should be akin to the quest to fulfill one's larger potential in life, and in doing so, to help others do the same. Ultimately, if our assessment processes are aligned with these fundamental goals, which are translated into flexible road maps that lead toward leadership and organizational growth, we and the people who work for and with us, will be the beneficiaries.

SUMMARY AND CONCLUSION

We began this chapter by asking five fundamental questions. First, how do the beliefs and values of leaders impact their leadership (e.g., why do leaders experience and respond to self, others, and the larger world as they do)? Second, are there common beliefs and values among leaders who are deemed to be most effective? Third, how do we evaluate the meaning and impact of interactions between the beliefs and values of leaders and the led? Fourth, how best do we understand the extraordinarily complex variables that influence leadership on a daily basis in the real world? Fifth, which models of leaders and methods of leadership development are most likely to have meaning and relevance across cultures and contexts? In an attempt to provide a theoretical, empirical, and applied basis for asking and answering such questions, we first described the Forum BEVI Project, a multiyear, multi-institution assessment of learning project with broad applicability to leaders and leadership, which illustrated that human beliefs and values are determined in no small part by a complex interaction among core needs (e.g., for attachment, affiliation) and formative variables (e.g., life history, culture). As such, in order to understand *who* leaders are and should be as well as *what* good and bad leadership looks like, we need to focus on *why* leaders differ in this regard as well as *how* to translate such understanding into effective strategies for leadership and organizational development. Fortunately, as noted, an increasing number of scholars and practitioners are articulating depth-based perspectives in various leadership and organizational literature, which we then described under the auspices of eight themes: (a) assessment; (b) awareness; (c) care; (d) complexity; (e) culture; (f) depth; (g) transformation; and (h) vision. On the basis of the preceding questions, applied research project, and literature, the following four principles were derived in order to provide guidance to the SMEs in the development of the leadership model that was described in Part I.

First, leadership *models* should have ecological validity across context and culture (e.g., research should demonstrably enhance the quality and effectiveness of leadership, both locally and globally).

Second, leadership *theory* should inform leadership research (e.g., conceptual frameworks must account for complex interactions among affective, cognitive, motivational, and developmental aspects of "being a leader").

Third, leadership *research* should be sophisticated (e.g., methodologies should examine the mediating role of formative variables, such as life history).

Fourth, leadership *practice* should address questions of who, what, and why, and how (e.g., why some leaders are experienced as more effective than others, and how to individualize leadership development processes).

In the current approach, job analysis was selected (e.g., Center for Business, 2013; Fine & Cronshaw, 1999; Prien et al., 2009). Informed by the goals of and context for this project (e.g., the four principles listed previously), 20 national and international SMEs participated in a comprehensive job analysis of global leaders and leadership in order to identify, develop, and evaluate the WBs, KSAs, and PCs of "best" and "worst" leaders, which culminated in the EI Leadership Model. After providing a description of the model in Part I of this chapter, Part II discussed how it was applied and evaluated in a workshop to 49 leaders in a large organization via three interrelated sessions, each of which included both a presentation and small group discussion: (a) the nature of "beliefs and values" including their role in organizational dynamics and leadership processes; (b) individual and group report data from the BEVI, which illustrated similarities and differences among organizational leadership as well as strengths and areas to address; and (c) presentation of the EI Leadership Model, discussion of the aggregate "grades" leaders assigned to their organization, and implications for leadership and organizational development over the short and long term.

Among many other observations and outcomes, qualitative and quantitative feedback indicates that group members especially appreciated the opportunity to (a) learn more about what beliefs and values are, where they come from, and how they may be understood; (b) reflect more deeply upon self and others vis-à-vis the organization; (c) review and discuss belief/value similarities and differences within and among members of leadership through the BEVI individual and organizational reports; (d) understand organizational strengths, weaknesses, and future directions through the EI Leadership Model and findings; and (e) begin a process of open dialogue with all leaders across varying levels of the organization for purposes of planning, growth, and development over the short and long term. On the basis of all of the above, we offered four final overarching observations from this entire process.

- Leadership models matter.
- Beliefs and values are integral to leaders and leadership.
- Leadership assessment reveals what is and is not working, and why.
- Leadership models and assessment methods provide a road map for change.

In conclusion, we circle back to the beginning of this chapter by observing that working people (at least in the United States) appear to devote over one-third of their lives—the greatest percentage of our daily allocation of life, at 8.8 of 24 hours—to work (Bureau of Labor Statistics, 2012), which adds up to around 90,000 to 100,000 hours of our "lifetime" (e.g., Bennett, 2009). Such data should give pause, since for too many, this expenditure of life is not experienced as optimal either because of poor organizational dynamics and/or individuals in leadership positions who are unaware of, insufficiently responsive toward, or overtly antagonistic toward the needs and well-being of the people they lead (Gillet, Fouquereau, Forest, Brunault, & Colombat, 2012).

At this level, it is remarkable that we would be unaware of such dynamics, given the profound impact organizations and leaders have upon us, and the sheer amount of time we will spend over the measure of our lives in such environments (e.g., Kets De Vries & Balazs, 2005). Juxtapose that perspective with the observation—emerging frequently in the workshop—that our "work selves" and "true selves" may or may not be aligned. That is to say, the work that we do may or may not actually line up with why we are who we are, and what our potentials in life really are. At the biggest picture level, it certainly is the case that there is so much "work" to be done in the larger world that is directly related to addressing the "wicked issues" of our day, which ultimately will affect us all if they have not already

(Coffman et al., 2009; Cultivating the Globally Sustainable Self, 2014; National Action Plan for Education for Sustainability, 2014). Taken together, such considerations suggest that we would do well to reflect more deeply, frequently, and systematically on the nature, quality, and legitimacy of the organizations that we advance and the leaders to whom we report.

In the final analysis, as the SMEs of the EI Leadership Model remind us, leaders must "demonstrate integrity," know "how to communicate honestly, openly, effectively, and persuasively," and be "responsible" and "honest" as opposed to "incompetent" and "manipulative." Moreover, today's leaders must be able to "discern and articulate principles" that are worthy of emulation and/or are the "right thing to do" and "consistently appraise whether and why the mission, activities, and goals of an organization are worthy of pursuit." Such behaviors, knowledge, skills, values, and attributes are not just noble ideals, but pragmatic aspirations if our organizations and those who lead them are able to rise up and help us meet the opportunities and needs of our globally interconnected age.

REFERENCES

Adams, S. (1995, May 22). Manager's journal: The Dilbert principle. *Wall Street Journal*, p. A12.

Adams, S. (1997). *The Dilbert principle: A cubicle's-eye view of bosses, meetings, management fads & other workplace afflictions*. New York, NY: Harper Collins Publishers.

Anmuth, L. M., Poore, M., Cozen, J., Brearly, T., Tabit, M., Cannady, M., . . . Staton, R. (2013, August). *Making implicit beliefs explicit: In search of best practices for mental health clients, clinicians, and trainers*. Poster presented at the annual meeting of the American Psychological Association, Honolulu, HI.

Aronson, E. (2012). *The social animal* (11th ed). New York, NY: Worth Publishing.

Astrachan, J. H. (2004). Organizational departures: The impact of separation anxiety as studied in mergers and acquisition simulation. *The Journal of Applied Behavioral Sciences, 40*(1), 91–110.

Atwood, K. Chkhaidze, N., Shealy, C. N., Staton, R., & Sternberger, L. G. (2014, August). *Transformation of self: Implications from the forum BEVI project*. Poster presented at the annual meeting of the American Psychological Association, Washington, DC.

Aycan, Z. (2001). Expatriation: A critical step toward developing global leaders. In M. Mendenhall, T. Kuhlmann, & G. Stahl (Eds.), *Developing global business leaders: Policies, processes and innovations*. Westport, CT: Quorum Books.

Barendsen, L., & Gardner, H. (2006). The three elements of good leadership in rapidly changing times. In F. Hesselbein & M. Goldsmith (Eds.), *The leader of the future 2: Visions, strategies, and practices for the new era*. San Francisco, CA: Leader to Leader Institute, Jossey-Bass.

Bass, B. M. (1997). Does the transactional-transformational leadership paradigm transcend organizational and national boundaries? *American Psychologist, 52*(2), 130–139.

Bass, B. M., & Riggio, R. E. (2006). *Transformational Leadership* (2nd ed.). Mahwah, NJ: Lawrence Erlbaum Associates.

Beechler, S., & Javidan, M. (2007). Leading with a global mindset. In M. Javidan, R. M. Steers, & M. A. Hitt (Eds.), *The global mindset (advances in international management)* (Vol. 19, pp. 131–169). Bingley, UK: Emerald Group.

Bennett, B. (2009). *How many hours will you work in your lifetime*. Retrieved June 24, 2013 from http://watchingthewatchers.org/indepth/34561/lifetime-piling-up-many-hours-you

Bird, A., Mendenhall, M., Stevens, M. J., & Oddou, G. (2010). Defining the content domain of intercultural competence for global leaders. *Journal of Managerial Psychology, 25*, 810–828.

Brearly, T., Shealy, C. N., Staton, R., & Sternberger, L. G. (2012, August). *Prejudice and religious and non-religious certitude: An empirical analysis from the forum BEVI project*. Poster presented at the annual meeting of the American Psychological Association, Orlando, FL.

Bureau of Labor Statistics. (2012). Charts from the American time use survey. Retrieved June 24, 2013 from http://www.bls.gov/tus/charts/

Burke, W. B. (2008). *Organization change: Theory and practice*. Los Angeles, CA: Sage Publications.

Burns, J. M. (1978). *Leadership*. New York, NY: Harper Collins Publishers.

The Capstone Encyclopaedia of Business: The most up-to-date and accessible guide to business ever! (2003). Oxford: Capstone Pub.

Campbell, D. P. (2006). Globalization: The basis principles of leadership are universal and timeless. In W.H. Mobley & E. Wheldon (Eds.), *Advances in global leadership* (Vol. 4, pp. 143–158). Oxford, England: JAI Press/Elseveir.

Center for Business. (2013). Retrieved June 18, 2013 from http://www.cbed.aum.edu/

Chhokar, J. S., Brodbeck, F. C., & House, R. J. (Eds.). (2007). *Culture and leadership across the world: The GLOBE book of in-depth studies of 25 Societies*. New York, NY: Lawrence Erlbaum Associates.

Coffman, H., Hopkins, C., & Ali, I. (2009). Education for sustainable development: Halfway through the decade of ESD and a long way from sustainability. *Beliefs and Values, 29*, 142–150.

Cooperrider, D. L., & Whitney, D. (2005). *Appreciative inquiry: A positive revolution in change*. San Francisco, CA: Berrett-Koehler Publishers.

Cultivating the globally sustainable self: Summit series on transformative teaching, training, and learning in research and practice. (2014). Retrieved March 19, 2014 from http://www.jmu.edu/summitseries/index.shtml

Dalton, M., Ernst, C., Deal, J., & Leslie, J. (2002). *Success for the new global manager: What you need to know to work across distances, countries, and cultures*. San Francisco, CA: Jossey-Bass.

Detert, J. R., & Burris, E. R. (2007). Leadership behavior and employee voice: Is the door really open? *Academy of Management Journal, 50*(4), 869–884.

Dweck, C. (2008). *Mindset: The new psychology of success*. New York, NY: Ballantine Books.

Dyjak-LeBlanc, K., Femac, C., Shealy, C., Staton, R., & Sternberger, L. (2012, August). *Real world application of the EI leadership model: Working with worldviews in a health care organization*. Poster presented at the annual meeting of the American Psychological Association, Orlando, FL.

Eisler, R., & Corral, T. (2009). Leaders forging values-based change: Partnership power for the 21st century. *Beliefs and Values, 1*(1), 31–44.

Fine, S. A., & Cronshaw, S. F. (1999). *Functional job analysis: A foundation for human resources management*. Mahwah, NJ: Lawrence Erlbaum Associates (Forum BEVI Project). Retrieved November 18, 2011 from http://www.forumea.org/research-bevi-project.cfm

Fouad, N. A., & Arredondo, P. (2007). *Becoming culturally oriented: Practical advice for psychologists and educators: Psychologists as Organizational Change Agents*. Washington, DC: American Psychological Association.

Ford, J. D., Ford L. W., & D'Amelio A. (2008). Resistance to change: the rest of the story. *Academy of Management Review, 33*(2), 362–377.

George, B. (2004). *Authentic leadership: Rediscovering the secrets to creating lasting value*. San Francisco, CA: Jossey-Bass.

Gillet, N., Fouquereau, E., Forest, J., Brunault, P., & Colombat, P. (2012). The impact of organizational factors on psychological needs and their relations with well-being. *Journal of Business and Psychology, 27*(4), 437–450.

Goleman, D. (2001). *Harvard business review on what makes a leader*. Boston, MA: Harvard Business School Publishing Corporation.

Goleman, D., Boyatzis, R., & McKee, A. (2002). *Primal leadership: Learning to lead with emotional intelligence*. Boston, MA: Harvard Business Review.

Gostick, A., & Elton, C. (2012). *All in: How the best managers create a culture of belief and drive big results*. New York, NY: Free Press.

Griffin, M. A., Neal, A., & Parker, S. K. (2007). A new model of work role performance: Positive behavior in uncertain and interdependent contexts. *Academy of Management Journal, 50*(2), 327–347.

Griffin, M. A., Parker, S. K., & Mason, C. M. (2010). Leader vision and the development of adaptive and proactive performance: A longitudinal study. *Journal of Applied Psychology, 95*(1), 174–182.

Gundling, E., Hogan, T., & Cvitkovitch, K. (2011). *What is global leadership: 10 key behaviors that define great global leaders.* Boston, MA: Nicholas Brealey.

Heifetz, R., Grashow, A., & Linsky, M. (2009). *The practice of adaptive leadership: Tools and tactics for changing your organization and the world.* Cambridge, MA: Harvard Business Press.

Henson, C., Fulkerson, J., Caligiuri, P. & Shealy, C. (in press). *Consultation: Who needs psychological expertise around the world and why?* In C. N. Shealy & M. Bullock, (Eds.). Going global: How psychology and psychologists can meet a world of need. Washington, DC: APA Books.

Henson, C., & Rossouw, P. (2013). *Brainwise leadership.* Sydney, AU: Learning Quest.

Hill, C., Johnson, M., Brinton, C., Staton, R., Sternberger, L., & Shealy, C. N. (2013, August). *The etiology of economic beliefs and values: Implications and applications from the Forum BEVI Project.* Poster presented at the annual meeting of the American Psychological Association, Honolulu, HI.

Hodgson, P., & White, R. P. (2001). *Relax, it's only uncertainty: How to lead the way when the way is changing.* London, UK: Prentice Hall.

Hofstede, G. (2001). *Culture's consequences: Comparing values, behaviors, institutions and organizations across nations.* Thousand Oaks, CA: Sage Publications.

House, R. J., Hanges, P. J., Javidan, M., Dorfman, P. W., & Gupta, V. (Eds.). (2004). *Culture, leadership and organizations: The GLOBE study of 62 societies.* Thousand Oaks, CA: Sage Publications.

Javidan, M., & Teagarden, M. B. (2011). Conceptualizing and measuring global mindset. In W. H. Mobley, M. Li, & Y. Wang (Eds.), *Advances in global leadership* (Vol. 6, pp. 13–39). Bingley, UK: Emerald Group.

Judge, T. A., & Bono, J. E. (2000). Five-factor model of personality and transformational leadership. *Journal of Applied Psychology, 85*(5), 751–765.

Judge, T. A., Bono, J. E., Ilies, R., & Gerhardt, M. W. (2002). Personality and leadership: A qualitative and quantitative review. *Journal of Applied Psychology, 87*(4), 765–780.

Kahneman, D. (2011). *Thinking fast and slow.* New York, NY: Farrar, Strauss and Giroux.

Kail, E. (2011, October 28). Leadership character: The role of empathy. *The Washington Post.* Retrieved March 19, 2014 from http://www.washingtonpost.com/blogs/guest-insights/post/leadership-character-the-role-of-empathy/2011/04/04/gIQAQXVGQM_blog.html

Kegan, R. (1982). *The evolving self.* Cambridge, MA: Harvard University Press.

Kelly, J., Holt, J., Patel, R., & Nolet, V. (2016). Environmental beliefs and values: In search of models and methods. In C. N. Shealy. (Ed.), *Making sense of beliefs and values* (pp. 233–260). New York, NY: Springer Publishing.

Kets De Vries, M., & Balazs, K. (2005). Organizations as optical illusions: A clinical perspective on organizational consultation. *Organizational Dynamic, 34*(1), 1–17.

Kets de Vries, M. F. R., & Balazs, K. (2008). Where is the Beef? A clinical perspective on organizational consultation and change. In T. Cummings (Ed.), *Handbook of organizational development* (pp. 79–95). Thousand Oaks, CA: Sage Publications.

Keys, T. (2013). *Leading transformational change: Leadership practices for the 21st century.* Amherst, NY: Trinity Leadership Products.

Knowles, E. S., & Linn, J. A. (2004). The importance of resistance to persuasion. In E. S. Knowles & J. A. Linn (Eds.), *Resistance and persuasion* (pp. 3–9). Mahwah, NJ: Lawrence Erlbaum Associates.

Kouzes, J. M., & Posner, B. Z. (2012). *The leadership challenge* (5th ed.). San Francisco, CA: Jossey-Bass.

Kruglanski, A. W., & Webster D. M. (1996). Motivated closing of the mind: "seizing" and "freezing." *Psychological Review, 103*(2), 263–283.

Levy, O., Beechler, S., Taylor, S., & Boyacigiller, N.A. (2007). What we talk about when we talk about 'global mindset': Managerial cognition in multinational corporations. *Journal of International Business Studies, 38,* 231–258.

Lorde, A. (1995). Age, race, class and sex: Women redefining difference. In M. L. Anderson & P. H. Collins (Eds.), *Race, class and gender: An anthology* (2nd ed., pp. 532–540). Belmont, CA: Wadsworth.

Martin, R. (2009). *Opposable mind: Winning through integrative thinking*. Cambridge, MA: Harvard Business School Publishing.

McCall, M. W. Jr., & Hollenbeck, G. P. (2002). *Developing global executives: The lessons of international experience*. Boston, MA: Harvard Business School Publishing.

McGuire, J. B., Palus, C. J., Pasmore, W., & Rhodes, G. B. (2009). *Transforming your organization*. Greensboro, NC: Center for Creative Leadership.

McLeod, S. A. (2009). *Jean Piaget*. Retrieved from http://www.simplypsychology.org/piaget.html

McKeown, R., & Nolet, V. (Eds.). (2013). *Schooling for sustainable development in Canada and the United States*. Dordrecht, Germany: Springer.

Mendenhall, M. D., Kuhlmann, T. M., & Stahl, G. K. (Eds.). (2001). *Developing global business leaders: Policies, processes and innovations*. Westport, CT: Quorum Books.

Mobley, W. H., Li, M., & Wang, Y. (Eds.). (2011). *Advances in global leadership* (Vol. 6). Bingley, UK: Emerald Group.

Morrison, A. M., White, R. P., & Van Velsor, E. (1994). *Breaking the glass ceiling: Can women reach the top of America's largest corporations?* Reading, MA: Addison Wesley.

Morton, R. (2013, June). The theory of belief-based leadership. *Public Sector Digest*, pp. 1–5. Retrieved March 14, 2014 from http://www.publicsectordigest.com/articles/view/1150

National Action Plan for Educating for Sustainability. (2014). Retrieved March 23, 2014 from http://www.centerforgreenschools.org/sites/default/files/resource-files/National-Action-Plan-Educating-Sustainability.pdf

Novogratz, J. (2010). *Inspiring a life of immersion*. Retrieved March 19, 2014 from http://www.ted.com/talks/jacqueline_novogratz_inspiring_a_life_of_immersion

Osland, J. S. (2001). The quest for transformation: The process of global leadership development. In M. Mendenhall, T. Kuhlmann, & G. Stahl (Eds.), *Developing global business leaders: Policies, processes and innovations*. Westport, CT: Quorum Books.

Pendleton, C., Cochran, S., Kapadia, S., & Iyer, C. (2016). Understanding the gendered self: Implications from EI theory, EI self, and the BEVI. In C. N. Shealy (Ed.), *Making sense of beliefs and values* (pp. 261–302). New York, NY: Springer Publishing.

Piaget, J. (1976). *The grasp of consciousness: Action and concept in the young child*. Cambridge, MA: Harvard University Press.

Piaget, J. (1977). *The development of thought: Equilibration of cognitive structures*. New York, NY: Viking Press.

Prien, E., Goodstein, L. D., Goodstein, J., & Gamble, L. (2009). *A practical guide to job analysis*. New York, NY: Wiley.

Quinn, R. E. (2009). *Change the world: How ordinary people can achieve extraordinary results*. San Francisco, CA: Jossey-Bass.

Shealy, C. N. (1995). From Boys Town to Oliver Twist: Separating fact from fiction in welfare reform and out-of-home placement of children and youth. *American Psychologist, 50*(8), 565–580.

Shealy, C. N. (1996). The "therapeutic parent": A model for the child and youth care profession [Special feature]. *Child & Youth Care Forum, 25*(4), 211–271.

Shealy, C. N. (2004). A model and method for "making" a C-I psychologist: Equilintegration (EI) theory and the Beliefs, Events, and Values Inventory (BEVI) [Special Series]. *Journal of Clinical Psychology, 60*(10), 1065–1090.

Shealy, C. N. (2005). Justifying the justification hypothesis: Scientific-humanism, Equilintegration (EI) theory, and the Beliefs, Events, and Values Inventory (BEVI) [Special Series]. *Journal of Clinical Psychology, 61*(1), 81–106.

Shealy, C. N. (2012, December). *Beliefs, values, and the EI leadership model: The knowing, doing, and being competencies of transformative leaders*. Keynote address delivered at the Leadership Academy Conference, James Madison University, Harrisonburg, VA.

Shealy, C. N. (2015). *The Beliefs, Events, and Values Inventory (BEVI): Overview, implications, and guidelines*. Test manual. Harrisonburg, VA: Author.

Shealy, C. N. (Ed.). (2016). *Making sense of beliefs and values*. New York, NY: Springer Publishing.

Shealy, C. N., Bhuyan, D., & Sternberger, L. G. (2012). Cultivating the capacity to care in children and youth: Implications from EI theory, EI self, and BEVI. In U. Nayar (Ed.), *Child and adolescent mental health* (pp. 240–255). New Delhi, India: Sage Publications.

Shullman, S., White, R., Brewster, L., Grande, S., & Bhuyan, D. (in press). How psychology and psychologists develop global leaders and leadership. In C. N. Shealy & M. Bullock (Eds.), *Going global: How psychology and psychologists can meet a world of need*. Washington, DC: APA Books.

Snyder, N. H., Dowd, J. J., Jr., & Houghton, M. (1994). *Vision, values and courage: Leadership for quality management*. New York, NY: The Free Press.

Tabit, M., Cozen, J., Dyjak-LeBlanc, K., Pendleton, C., Shealy, C., Sternberger, L., & Staton, R. (2011, June). *The sociocultural impact of denial: Empirical evidence from the Forum BEVI Project*. Poster presented at American Psychological Association, Washington, DC.

Terry, R. W. (1993). *Authentic leadership: Courage in action*. San Francisco, CA: Jossey-Bass.

Terry, R. W. (2001). *Seven zones for leadership: Acting authentically in stability and chaos*. Palo Alto, CA: Davies-Black.

Trompenaars, F., & Hampden-Turner, C. (2010). *Riding the waves of innovation*. New York, NY: McGraw-Hill.

Wandschneider, E., Pysarchik, D. T., Sternberger, L. G., Ma, W., Acheson-Clair, K., Baltensperberger, B., . . . Hart, V. (2016). The Forum BEVI Project: Applications and implications for international, multicultural, and transformative learning. In C. N. Shealy (Ed.), *Making sense of beliefs and values* (pp. 407–484). New York, NY: Springer Publishing.

White, R. P., & Shullman, S. L. (2010). Acceptance of uncertainty as an indicator of effective leadership. *Consulting Psychology Journal: Practice and Research, 62*(2), 94–104.

White, R. P., & Shullman, S. L. (2012). Thirty years of global leadership training: A cross-cultural odyssey. *Consulting Psychology Journal: Practice and Research, 64*(4), 268–278.

Wheatley, M. J. (2006). *Leadership and the new science: Discovering order in a chaotic world* (3rd ed.). San Francisco, CA: Berrett-Koehler Publishers.

Jared Cozen, William Hanson, John Poston,
Sarah Jones, and Mary Tabit

15

THE BELIEFS, EVENTS, AND VALUES INVENTORY (BEVI): IMPLICATIONS AND APPLICATIONS FOR THERAPEUTIC ASSESSMENT AND INTERVENTION

Every person is like all other persons, like some other persons, and like no other person.

—Clyde Kluckhohn and Henry Murray[1]

Within the larger mental health field, practicing clinicians are faced with an overwhelming number of therapeutic models and intervention techniques (Norcross, 2005). These approaches often employ different psychological constructs to guide clinical treatment and define therapeutic change (Henriques, 2011; Levitt, Stanley, & Frankel, 2005; Magnavita, 2010; Wachtel, 1997). One schema used to organize the multitude of psychotherapeutic models is the division of theoretical and clinical approaches into three broad frameworks: psychodynamic, cognitive behavioral, and humanistic (Gelso & Hayes, 2007). At the outset, an overview of this "big three" organizational schema may provide context for the integrative potential and therapeutic assessment implications of the Beliefs, Events, and Values Inventory (BEVI), which is the primary focus of this chapter.

FRAMEWORKS OF INTERVENTION

The psychodynamic framework begins with Freud, who developed drive theory, the tripartite model of personality, and the technique of psychoanalysis (Freud, 1909/1961; Freud, 1927/2011). Freud's theory and psychoanalytic method later were modified and expanded upon in what some theorists and historians refer to as the "relational turn" (Elisha, 2011). Major innovations in this movement include Klein's object relations, Winnicott's conceptualization of self, Bowlby and Ainsworth's attachment theory, Sullivan's interpersonal theory, and Kohut's self psychology (Greenberg & Mitchell, 1983; Priel, 2009; Wolitzky & Eagle, 1997). More recently, there has been increased interest in short-term dynamic therapies (e.g., Coren, 2009;

[1] This quotation is derived from Kluckhohn and Murray (1953) and was adapted by McAdams and Pals (2006).

Davanloo, 1980; Luborsky, 1984; Luborsky & Crits-Cristoph, 1998; Mander, 2000; Strupp & Binder, 1984), while also demonstrating the overall effectiveness of psychodynamic interventions (e.g., Leichsenring & Rabung, 2008; Roseborough, 2006).

The cognitive behavioral framework consists of three waves, each of which extends the theoretical and clinical focus of the previous generation (Hayes, 2004). The first wave, classic behavioral therapy, was established by Watson (1913) in his Behavioral Manifesto, further developed by Skinner's (1947) theory of operant conditioning, and implemented clinically by Wolfe's (Wolfe, Brady, Serber, Agras, & Liberman, 1973) treatment model of Systematic Desensitization. The second wave incorporated a cognitive emphasis articulated by Ellis and Harper (1961) Rational Emotive Behavior Therapy and Beck's (1963) Cognitive Therapy. Cognitive behavioral approaches over the past 20 years comprise the third wave, which has expanded beyond a behavioral and cognitive focus to include experiential and mindfulness approaches toward theory and practice. Examples of these new approaches include Linehan's (1993) Dialectical Behavioral Therapy, Hayes's (2004) Acceptance and Commitment Therapy, and Wells's (2009) Metacognitive Therapy.

The humanistic framework has its origins in the work of Adler (1916) and Rank (1952), although Rogers (1951) is thought to be a major pioneer in this orientation, too, with his Person-Centered Therapy. Other approaches broadly considered to fall within the humanistic framework include Gestalt Therapy (Perls, 1951/2010), Experiential Therapy and Emotion-Focused Therapy (Greenberg, 2001), Existential Psychotherapy (May, 1958), and the postmodern, constructivist perspective (Kelly, 1963; Mahoney, 2003; Rennie, 2004).

Four Problems With the Big Three

The usage of the "big three" organizational frameworks begets at least four conceptual and applied problems. *First, despite the heuristic appeal of this tripartite framework, such an approach minimizes the theoretical and clinical heterogeneity within each of these frameworks.* This confound is due to many interacting factors, including the historical processes by which theories have been developed, interpreted, and implemented (e.g., Greenberg & Mitchell, 1983). To take just one example, within the psychodynamic framework, some clinicians assume a neo-Freudian epistemological stance toward constructs such as "the self" whereas others who also would consider themselves "psychodynamic" may adopt a more postmodern and constructivist approach (Elisha, 2011).

A second problem with the "big three" approach is the real world minimization of theoretical and clinical heterogeneity between each of these frameworks. That is because in practice, clinicians may rely upon theoretical structures, processes, or constructs within one tradition (psychodynamic, cognitive behavioral, humanistic) to inform their work while also employing intervention approaches and techniques from another tradition. Such integrative approaches to practice—whether they are deliberate or even acknowledged—are due to a range of real world influences such as theoretical cross-fertilization, theoretical assimilation, pragmatic exigencies of doing the work, and the integration movement (Magnavita & Achin, 2013; Norcross, 2005). For example, consider the theoretical overlap between Linehan's use of "dialectics" in her Dialectical Behavioral Therapy (a cognitive behavioral approach) and Gestalt's Field Theory (a humanistic approach). Both approaches emphasize relational, systemic, and contextual approaches toward conceptualization and intervention (Cain, 2002; Linehan, 1993).

A third problem with the "big three" approach is that such a framework underestimates the powerful role other subdisciplines and perspectives play in informing theoretical and applied aspects of practice in the real world. Among many other candidates, systems theory, attachment theory, evolutionary psychology, and cognitive neuroscience all influence the way therapists think about their clients and their work (Badcock, 2012; Greenberg, 2001; Nichols, 2011). Consider that clinicians routinely conduct intake interviews at the outset of therapy, in which historical information about life/family history is gathered. Such information helps clinicians formulate their understanding of *why* clients present as they do regardless of the theoretical framework to which they ascribe. Also, this approach clearly is consistent with data and theory—if not best practice—from the field of developmental psychopathology, yet another field of considerable relevance to all three frameworks of therapeutic work (Cummings, Davies, & Campbell, 2000).

A fourth and final problem with the "big three" framework is that if a practitioner adheres solely to a specific tradition, such fixedness may produce barriers to conceptualization and intervention, by encouraging myopic fidelity to particular ways of thinking and working. For example, a cognitive behavioral therapist may focus upon maladaptive beliefs, whereas a psychodynamic therapist may emphasize historical processes, while a therapist from the humanistic framework might point to a lack of coherence and meaning in his or her client's narrative (Adler, 2012; McAdams, 2006; Norcross, 2005). Why does such singularity of focus matter? Because in practice, the pure psychodynamic clinician may eschew clinical emphasis on client beliefs that demonstrably are maladaptive, but could be addressed directly *and* empathically to good therapeutic effect; likewise, the pure cognitive behavioral therapy clinician may erroneously believe that the "relationship" between client and therapist—which theoretically is emphasized more within the humanistic or psychodynamic frameworks—is far less important than it actually is in terms of the necessary and sufficient conditions for therapeutic change (Henriques, 2011; Magnavita & Achin, 2013; Norcross, 2005). In short, encouraging strict adherence to a single therapeutic framework ultimately may limit a clinician's effectiveness by inculcating professional prejudices that are neither helpful to clients nor valid in terms of what actually happens within and between the practice areas (Shealy, Cobb, Crowley, Nelson, & Peterson, 2004).

INTEGRATIVE THERAPEUTIC ASSESSMENT: EI THEORY, EI SELF, AND BEVI

Recognition of these problems is not new, and attempts at redress are increasingly mainstream and widespread, most notably through the integration and unification movements vis-à-vis conceptual models and methods of intervention (Henriques, 2004; Magnavita & Achin, 2013; Norcross, 2005; Wachtel, 1997; Wampold, 2010). In light of these important developments, a concomitant question arises: Would it be possible to measure such therapeutic work, and use such measurement to understand and facilitate change through an integrative lens? In other words, it is all well and good to focus on integrative approaches toward therapy. However, might it also be possible to conduct our assessments in a manner that not only facilitates therapeutic intervention across the "big three," but also helps facilitate integrative conceptualization, planning, and intervention (Beutler, Groth-Marnat, & Rosner, 2003; Steele, Steele, & Murphy, 2009)? As has been the case with therapy common factors—"those aspects of treatment that are associated with positive or negative outcomes across all therapies or therapists" such as empathy, acceptance, and understanding (Shealy, 1995, p. 567)—might it be possible to identity "assessment common factors" (Shealy, 2016, p. 105) through an integrative "psychological assessment as a therapeutic intervention" (PATI) lens (Finn, 2007; Finn & Tonsager, 1997; Poston & Hanson, 2010)? In doing so, could we illustrate how the interplay between content (e.g., scores on specific scales) and process (e.g., the experience or expression of affect, or engagement in self-reflection, as a result of discussing such scores) may deepen the therapeutic relationship, clarify relevant issues, and facilitate the pursuit of intervention goals?

Toward such means and ends, we describe Equilintegration (EI) Theory and the EI Self along with the BEVI. After an overview of this model and method, we illustrate how the BEVI facilitates an understanding of five proposed assessment common factors—formative variables, dichotomous thinking, dialectical thinking, emotional awareness, and self-awareness—that we believe are relevant especially to clinicians across the "big three." Finally, we highlight two therapeutic assessment principles in regard to utilizing an EI perspective and the BEVI therapeutically, and present findings from an exploratory study examining the integrative potential of the BEVI in both therapeutic and assessment contexts.

As a model and method, the EI framework and BEVI are highly compatible with PATI sensibilities (Fischer, 2000; Hanson & Poston, 2011; Poston & Hanson, 2010), by seeking to understand the meaning of client and trainee explanations about what is real or true for themselves, others, and the world at large, and engaging them in an attendant process of in-depth clinical assessment and exploration. As a model and method of assessment, EI Theory explains "the processes by which beliefs, values, and 'worldviews' are acquired and maintained, why their alteration is typically resisted, and how and under what circumstances their modification occurs" (Shealy, 2004, p. 1075). Along these lines, we contend that beliefs, values, and worldviews are centrally important constructs within the mental health field, which should warrant in-depth and routine assessment across settings and populations (see Chapter 2 for a full explication of EI hypotheses and principles).

Derivative of EI Theory, the EI Self explains integrative and synergistic processes by which beliefs and values are acquired, maintained, and transformed as well as how and why these are linked to the formative variables, core needs, and adaptive potential of the self. Informed by scholarship in a range of key areas (e.g., "needs-based" research and theory; developmental psychopathology; social cognition; affect regulation; therapeutic processes and outcomes; theories and models of "self"), the EI Self seeks to illustrate how the interaction between our core needs (e.g., for attachment, affiliation) and formative variables (e.g., caregiver, culture) results in beliefs and values about self, others, and the world at large that we all internalize over the course of development and across the life span (see Chapter 3 for more information about the EI Self).

Concomitant with EI Theory and the EI Self, the BEVI is a comprehensive and integrative assessment measure in development since the early 1990s (e.g., Anmuth et al., 2103; Atwood, Chkhaidze, Shealy, Staton, & Sternberger, 2014; Brearly, Shealy, Staton, & Sternberger, 2012; Hill et al., 2013; Shealy, 2004, 2005, 2015, 2016; Shealy, Bhuyan, & Sternberger, 2012; Tabit et al., 2011; for more information about the BEVI, see Chapter 4 as well as www.ibavi.org/content/featured-projects). This instrument examines how and why we come to see ourselves, others, and the larger world as we do (e.g., how life experiences, culture, and context affect our beliefs, values, and worldview) as well as the influence of such processes on multiple aspects of human functioning (e.g., learning processes, relationships, personal growth, the pursuit of life goals). Both the long and short versions of the BEVI consist of four components: (a) a comprehensive set of background information items;

(b) an intake interview that has been converted into a Likert-type format, and integrated into the BEVI via specific scales (e.g., Negative Life Events [NLE]); (c) 18 scales composed of 336 items on the long version and 17 scales composed of 185 items on the short version; and (d) three qualitative items. By design, the BEVI is meant to be a mixed methods measure, whereby both response sets are able to be mixed or integrated when used for assessment and therapeutic purposes (i.e., in a clinical context, both quantitative scores and qualitative responses may be used together in order to understand a client presentation, communicate results to a client, and facilitate interventions) (Creswell & Plano Clark, 2011; Hanson, Creswell, Plano Clark, Petska, & Creswell, 2005). From the standpoint of scales, the BEVI assesses processes such as: basic openness; the tendency to (or not to) stereotype in particular ways; self- and emotional awareness; preferred strategies for making sense of why "other" people and cultures "do what they do"; global engagement (e.g., receptivity to different cultures, religions, and social practices); and worldview shift (e.g., to what degree do beliefs and values change as a result of specific experiences). BEVI results are translated into reports at the individual, group, and organizational levels and used in a wide range of contexts for a variety of applied and research purposes (e.g., to track and examine changes in worldviews over time) (for more information, see Chapter 4).

Assessment Common Factors: Applications of EI Theory, EI Self, and BEVI

Before explicating five proposed assessment common factors of relevance to integrative therapeutic change—formative variables, dichotomous thinking, dialectical thinking, emotional awareness, and self-awareness—an important caveat is in order: from an EI and BEVI perspective, labeling and organizing phenomena into discrete categories for conceptualization may be useful as long as such processes are not done in a reductive or superficial manner, thus overlooking the complex nature of the interactions among these categories. It seems plausible that there always will be a dialectical tension between creating a coherent, logical narrative and capturing the dynamic and complex nature of human experience. At the same time, so long as our models and methods are ecologically valid, there is real merit in attempting to illustrate highly complex processes in a way that is maximally accessible.

Factor 1. Formative Variables: Background Characteristics and Life Events on the BEVI

From an EI perspective, formative variables (e.g., life history and background characteristics) are theoretically and empirically associated with how and why beliefs and values about self, others, and the larger world become structured as they are (Shealy, 2016). On the BEVI, in addition to a comprehensive set of background and demographic variables (e.g., education level, religious/political orientation), the Negative Life Events (NLE) and Positive Life Events (PLE) scales provide an indication of how an individual views his or her life history and formative experiences. More specifically, NLE and PLE include information regarding childhood experiences, the conduct of one's caregivers, as well as perceptions of their relative emotional health and stability, how much conflict individuals experienced in the home, and other life history processes common across the life span (e.g., performance in school, legal problems, relations with peers). By design, these scales essentially comprise a comprehensive intake interview that has been converted into a Likert-type format and integrated into the BEVI.

Although psychodynamic perspectives have long emphasized the relevance of experiences in childhood or adolescence in terms of psychological functioning, in truth, many therapeutic schools of thought and allied programs of research recognize that life experiences affect psychological functioning for better or worse (Cummings, Davies, & Campbell, 2000; Wachtel, 1997). For example, psychodynamic, integrative, and systemic therapeutic models explicitly emphasize the relevance of childhood experiences in understanding adult conflicts (Gold, 2011; Nichols, 2011; Young, Klosko, & Weishaar 2003). Early events and formative experiences also are emphasized in attachment theory and the field of developmental psychopathology, which have influenced clinical practice across the spectrum of models and approaches (Bowlby, 1982; Cummings, Davies, & Campbell, 2000; Shealy et al., 2012). According to attachment theory, children develop internal working models of relationships, which essentially are cognitive/affective schemas that are derivative of relational experiences with early caregivers. These models then serve as templates for relating to others, which may be responsible for chronic struggles later in life (e.g., interpersonally, emotionally). Indeed, attachment style, with its origins in childhood, is associated with a wide array of psychosocial outcomes in adulthood (see Mikulincer & Shaver, 2007 for a review). Thus, a central emphasis for many psychodynamic and integrative therapies is for the client to develop insight into the nature of his or her early experiences as well as how such experiences relate to current functioning (e.g., relational and emotional processes) (Gold, 2011; Young et al., 2003). Similarly, many therapeutic approaches to assessment view increased insight and self-understanding as important outcomes (Finn & Tonsager, 1997; Fischer, 2000). Although cognitive behavioral and humanistic interventions may not focus on formative variables to the same degree as psychodynamic approaches, the former models often recognize that early life experiences are integral to the development of the self, emotional regulation strategies, and interpersonal coping skills (e.g., Linehan, 1993).

Finally, as noted previously, the fact that mental health clinicians typically conduct some form of an intake interview, which includes questions about life history and family functioning, illustrates that we implicitly, if not explicitly, recognize that the experiences we have early in life (e.g., in our families of origin) affect our functioning in ways that may have direct relevance to therapeutic interventions, regardless of theoretical fidelity or predilection, even if our focus tends toward the present and not the past. At the very least, then, it stands to reason that building an "intake interview" into the BEVI is logical because, by doing so, we are acknowledging the relevance of such experiences to "here and now" functioning, as well as their potential linkage to other affective and cognitive processes that are relevant both to practitioners and scholars (e.g., Shealy, 2004). Moreover, such inclusion helps socialize and, in essence, prepare clients for subsequent assessments and interventions (Claiborn & Hanson, 1999).

Factor 2. Dichotomous Thinking: Basic Determinism on the BEVI

Our second proposed assessment common factor is captured by the construct of "dichotomous" (i.e., "black and white") thinking, a manifestation that therapists across the "big three" encounter in their clients. A number of BEVI scales measure various aspects of an individual's cognitive style and attributional system—constructs central to behavioral change in cognitive therapy models. BEVI scales that are particularly relevant to assessing such constructs include Basic Openness, Self Awareness, Basic Determinism, and Socioemotional Convergence. For example, the Basic Determinism Scale measures the degree to which an individual "prefers basic/simple explanations for why people are as they are or do what they do" (Shealy, 2016). A sample item that statistically loads on this scale, *People don't really change*, appears to illustrate a form of dichotomous thinking, in which an individual tends to view self, others, and the world through a simple, binary, and mutually exclusive polarity (Napolitano & McKay, 2007; Oshio, 2009).

Dichotomous thinking may be beneficial in certain contexts, such as when time is limited and a quick decision is needed (Oshio, 2009). However this "all-or-nothing" style of thinking may be also associated with negative interpersonal and psychological outcomes. For example, in Beck's (1995) *The Basics of Cognitive Therapy and Beyond*, "all-or-nothing thinking" is considered a form of cognitive error (p. 119). Dichotomous thinking has been also linked to psychopathology, including personality and eating disorders, as well as personality traits such as perfectionism (Byrne, Cooper, & Fairburn, 2004; Linehan, 1993; Napolitano & McKay, 2007; Oshio, 2009). Moreover, such either/or thinking is related to the psychodynamic construct of "splitting," which refers to the tendency to evaluate oneself, others, and interpersonal relationships through extreme positions such as "all good" or "all bad" (Oshio, 2009, p. 731). This polarized style of thinking and feeling may be associated with maladaptive patterns of emotional and behavioral functioning, which further impair interpersonal relationships and self-regard (Linehan, 1993).

Factor 3. Dialectic Thinking: Socioemotional Convergence on the BEVI

As a mirror opposite to dichotomous thinking, therapists also encounter clients who (mercifully) seem to have the capacity to think complexly in that they are able to apprehend self, others, and the larger world in "shades of gray" rather than black and white. On the BEVI, Socioemotional Convergence assesses these fundamental characteristics of an individual's experience of self, other, and the larger world, including whether and to what degree an individual apprehends "complex and seemingly contradictory" beliefs about matters that really do not resolve themselves to "one way or another" thinking (Shealy, 2016). Among other possible examples, items that load highly on Socioemotional Convergence include beliefs that too many individuals do not take sufficient responsibility for their own lives while simultaneously agreeing that we should help those who cannot help themselves. A low Socioemotional Convergence responder may agree with one statement but not the other; those who score higher appear to understand that both statements could be true, which is both an acknowledgment of the complex nature of reality and consistent with the capacity to tolerate disequilibrium, a fundamental proposition of the EI framework (Shealy, 2004). Dialectical thinking parallels this construct, in that seeming contradictions actually represent "opportunities to. . . .create new, more complex systems" (Wu & Chiou, 2008, p. 240).

Consistent with an EI framework, the dialectical position has both cognitive and affective aspects. The cognitive component involves an emphasis on the dynamic nature of knowledge whereas the affective component involves "the emotional tensions of the creative process, which include holding opposing views simultaneously, sustaining uncertainty, breaking away from established ways of seeing things, and tolerating ambiguity" (Wu & Chiou, 2008, p. 240). Dialectical thinking has been also associated with models of creativity, cognitive development, and adaptive coping (e.g., Basseches, 1980; Chen, 2009; Riegel, 1976; Vukman, 2005). From the standpoint of intervention, attempts to facilitate a dialectical stance is exemplified by Linehan's (1993) Dialectical Behavioral Therapy, in which the dialectic of acceptance and change is emphasized while instruction in dialectical thinking is applied to the skills of mindfulness, interpersonal effectiveness, emotional regulation, and distress tolerance.

Factor 4. Affective Capacity: Emotional Attunement on the BEVI

As with the other assessment common factors, therapists regardless of theoretical predilection inevitably will contend—directly or not—with the relative capacity of their clients to experience and express emotion. On the BEVI, the Emotional Attunement scale is related to such capacity, assessing the degree to which individuals are "highly emotional, highly sensitive, highly social, needy, [and] affiliative" (Shealy, 2016). An example of an item from this scale is *I have real needs for warmth and affection*. Across all major therapeutic approaches, emotional awareness is considered central to well-being (Burum & Goldried, 2007; Warwar, Links, Greenberg, & Bergmans, 2008), regardless of how such capacity is encountered in practice. It is also central to therapeutic assessment processes and outcomes (Finn, 2007).

From an EI perspective, emotion serves multiple functions, including providing information regarding what is most important in one's interpersonal and social field and self-access to one's own internal sense of well-being, while providing motivational impetus for taking action in order to meet the "core needs" as described in the EI Self (see Chapter 3). As fundamental mediators of motivation, emotion guides interpersonal communication and interactions, and is pivotal to ongoing existential processes of meaning making in life (Warwar et al., 2008). Because emotion plays a central role in our adjustment and adaptation, the inability to tolerate, process, experience, or express affect is thought to be core to many psychological disorders. As Greenberg (2007) maintains in the Emotion-Focused Therapy model, three aspects of emotion are integral to well-being: emotional awareness, emotional acceptance, and emotional attention. Highly consistent with such emphases, the Emotional Attunement scale of the BEVI focuses explicitly on how a client's emotional awareness may be evaluated and communicated in the context of therapeutic assessment and intervention.

Factor 5. Access to Self, Others, and the Larger World: Self Awareness on the BEVI

As a final exemplar, therapists inevitably must grapple—to one degree or another—with their client's relative interest in and capacity for encountering and understanding who and why they, others, and the larger world are as they are. The BEVI measures different aspects of such processes via several scales. For example, Self Awareness measures the degree to which an individual is "open to difficult thoughts and feelings, introspective, [able to] tolerate confusion, [and] aware [of] how the self works" (Shealy, 2016). A sample item from this scale is *I like to think about who I am*.

As with all of these constructs, part of the difficulty is understanding—and operationalizing—what exactly we mean by "self," a question that is considered through definitional and pictographic aspects of the EI Self (see Chapter 3). From an integrative therapeutic standpoint, the construct of self presents several challenges. First, there have been changes over time in the construct of self within various psychotherapeutic paradigms. For example, from a Freudian perspective, the self is largely unconscious, in conflict, and ruled by mechanistic, deterministic, and bioenergetic properties (e.g., drives/instincts) (Freud, 1927/2011; see also Elisha, 2011; Greenberg & Mitchell, 1983; Wolitzky & Eagle, 1997). With contributions from the British object relations theorists such as Klein, Winnicott, Guntrip, and Fairbairn, as well as Bowlby and Ainsworth's attachment theory and Kohut's theory of self psychology, the emphasis in psychoanalytic schools shifted toward the relational aspects of the self in terms of its development and properties (Elisha, 2011; Wolitzky & Eagle, 1997). Within the more relational and intersubjective models of psychoanalytic theory, the clear dichotomy between self and other breaks down such that self-awareness cannot be separated completely from the individual's relationships with significant others, both in the development of the individual's sense of self, and in the therapeutic treatment and healing of the self (Elisha, 2011).

A second difficulty in examining the concept of self and self-awareness is that these constructs not only evolved over time, but also were influenced, in part, by theoretical cross-fertilization between the different frameworks (Magnavita, 2010). That is, theoretical plurality has begun to characterize each of the schools. Therefore, when examining the construct of self vis-à-vis self-awareness, distinctions blur among psychodynamic, humanistic, and cognitive behavioral frameworks. For example, there are many postmodern and humanistic strains within some of the current psychodynamic and psychoanalytic models (Elisha, 2011). Some contemporary psychoanalytic theorists interpret Freud's concept of self from a constructivist and postmodern point of view in which self constructs are most effectively viewed as a dynamic narrative that is interpersonally, socially, and culturally constructed. In this light, "false" and "true" selves are viewed "less as structured layers than as evolving processes, as two diverse forms of being in time. . .True-self processes imply an open, flexible, temporality, whereas false-self processes are characterized by a static and. . .rigid. . .past oriented. . .(mode of being)" (Priel, 2009, p. 494). Along these lines, it should be noted that this descriptor of self-awareness is highly congruent with the dialectic cognitive/affective processes noted earlier and measured by the Self Awareness, Basic Determinism, and Socioemotional Convergence scales on the BEVI.

Closely related to self-awareness, the constructs of self-understanding and self-discovery also have been integral to therapeutic change in several studies that examined the perspectives of both psychotherapists and clients (e.g., Binder, Holgersen, & Nielsen, 2010; Gibbons et al., 2009; Levitt, Butler, & Hill, 2006; Levitt & Williams, 2010). Additionally, enhancing self-understanding and self-discovery also are an integral part of assessment interventions (Finn, 2007; Fischer, 2000). Even so, most of these approaches focus more on the overarching goal of enhancing self-understanding through interventions, rather than doing so in the context of measuring this construct in a valid and reliable manner, or illustrating its relevance to other aspects of the human condition. Correlation matrix and other predictive analytic data from the BEVI clearly illustrate that self-awareness not only is relevant to other constructs, it also is mediated by life experiences and other formative variables (Shealy, 2010). In particular, it appears that the greater degree of Negative Life Events (NLE) reported by an individual, the lower the relative degree of Self-Awareness, a finding that has important implications for how individuals in therapy are understood and where the focus of our interventions might be directed.

The BEVI in Practice

Assessment as a Therapeutic Intervention

Although "assessment as intervention" increasingly evokes professional attention and discourse (Hanson & Poston, 2011; Lilienfeld, Garb, & Wood, 2011), the fundamental issue at stake is captured by Riddle, Byers, and Grimesey (2002), who identify two methods by which assessment measures are used in therapy. The traditional perspective tends to emphasize objective classification, which largely regards the client as a passive agent. Here, test results are not readily shared with the client, but rather used to diagnose, select a treatment approach, and predict outcomes. The role of therapist is that of expert and the role of client is that of service recipient. The "human science" perspective, on the other hand, regards the assessment process as potentially transformative and empowering (p. 33). Here, the therapist shares test results with the client and seeks interpretation within the interpersonal frame of the therapeutic relationship. Various terms have been used to describe this framework, including "Therapeutic Assessment. . .collaborative/individualized assessment. . .collaborative consultation to psychotherapy. . .and brief personalized assessment feedback" (Poston & Hanson, 2010, pp. 203–204).

Along these lines, Finn and Tonsager (1997) regard assessment as consisting of both information gathering and the facilitation of integrative interventions. From this perspective, assessments should function primarily as a therapeutic intervention, and be characterized as nonpathologizing, noncategorical, individualized, and collaborative. To date, substantial empirical support has accumulated, theoretical explanations of benefit have been offered, and key variables have been identified, such as how much feedback should be delivered and how to deal with discrepancies between assessment findings and self-representation (Claiborn & Hanson, 1999; Finn, 1996, 2007; Finn & Tonsager, 1997; Hanson & Claiborn, 2006; Hanson & Poston, 2011; Ward, 2008). In real world usage, the BEVI is deliberately aligned with such an ethos and way of working. There are two fundamental principles, in particular, that are relevant to the BEVI's use in therapeutic assessment. Described next, these principles consist of moving beyond a diagnostic framework and of working within a collaborative context.

Principle 1: Broadening the Framework of Who Clients Are— Moving Beyond Diagnoses

A central ethical tenet of psychotherapy practice is to do no harm, as stated in Principle A of the Ethical Principles of Psychologists and Code of Conduct (American Psychological Association, 2012). For this reason, many humanistic therapists decry the use of psychological assessments because they perceive it as "dehumanizing. . .and judgmental" (Finn & Tonsager, 1997, p. 377). Fischer (2000) has observed that "assessment processes and the resulting reports were often destructive to patients' self-respect" (p. 7). The prevailing diagnostic role of psychological assessments may bear partial responsibility for this experience (Quinn & Chaudoir, 2009). Negative feelings of embarrassment, shame, fear, and guilt may arise when one is given a psychological diagnosis. From the client perspective, receiving a diagnosis may feel as though one's core sense of self is being sentenced and judged (Corrigan & Wassel, 2008).

In reality, of course, the real world situation vis-à-vis diagnosis is complex, as a number of first person accounts attest. For example, *Firewalkers: Madness, Beauty, & Mystery* documents the experiences of individuals who received some of the most serious diagnoses the mental health field may confer (see www.vocalvirginia.org). On the downside, one of the book's authors, who was diagnosed with chronic undifferentiated schizophrenia, observed: Rather than a diagnosis, "what I needed was for someone to trust that my mind was intact" (Spiro, 2010, p. 20). On the other hand, as *Firewalkers* also illustrates, there are times when receiving a diagnosis may serve a beneficial function for an individual in distress. For example, relief may be experienced when a coherent explanation is attached to suffering, which was previously inexplicable (Frank & Frank, 1991; Perry, 2011). In addition, a diagnosis may guide a clinician toward an effective empirically based treatment or provide an avenue for a client to obtain funding for much-needed services.

Despite the potential benefits of diagnostic labels, the experience of receiving a label from an external authority often feels alien, disempowering, and demoralizing (e.g., Spiro, 2010). As such, Fischer (2000) has long advocated that clinicians move beyond "classification assessment" (p. 3) through a process of open and collaborative formulation between client and therapist. Recognizing the epistemologies that inadvertently shape what we know to be "true" as assessors and therapists (Kimble, 1984), Fischer warns against the imposition of "artificial, categorical clarity" (p. 7) because putative "knowledge" always is influenced by subjective perspective and contextual influence. Therefore, clinicians should respect the complexity and ambiguity inherent to the therapeutic process, viewing assessment as a hermeneutic process of "circling repeatedly from an observation back to context or to larger prior comprehensions, (and) then back again to observation" (p. 13). As an added feature, this approach enhances multicultural awareness, knowledge, and skill (Ridley, Li, & Hill, 1998). Finally, from a clinical perspective, traditional classification also may imply that therapeutic struggles are fixed and immutable, which may create a self-fulfilling prophecy for clients, who come to identify with a label, therefore reductionistically truncating the complexity and potential of their lives (Perry, 2011; Pouchly, 2011; Quinn & Chaudoir, 2009). In short, therapeutic assessment emphasizes dynamic processes over rigid classification, goals that are core to the intent and structure of the BEVI and its EI framework.

More specifically, the BEVI seeks credibly to privilege unique elements of a client's presentation while embedding such specificity within an empirically based, normative frame. Such an approach is not without precedent. For example, Finn and Tonsager (1992) developed a structured, empirically based, and individually tailored assessment procedure—a Therapeutic Assessment—which is influenced by the humanistic framework, self psychology, and relational psychotherapy (Finn, 1996, 2007; Finn & Tonsager, 1992). Core to such an approach, and consistent with the BEVI, is what might be called an ideographically centered, but nomothetically grounded assessment designed to help "…clients generate questions they would like answered/addressed by the assessment and testing, collecting background information related to their questions, exploring past assessments—and/or testing-based hurts,…answering as much as possible clients' initial questions" (p. 204).

In the final analysis, the BEVI recognizes both the potential hazards and benefits of a "traditional" method of assessment and diagnosis. As such, this measure is not "anti-diagnosis," but rather directed toward a deeper understanding of the underlying formative, cognitive, affective, and contextual variables that ultimately relate etiologically to the manifestation of "symptoms" that become the basis for such a diagnosis. By explicitly linking the BEVI to processes of therapeutic intervention—and by deliberately attempting to use assessment approaches to help understand "where clients are" while facilitating understanding and the therapeutic alliance—the BEVI offers an illuminating and constructive function vis-à-vis the process of intervention. In this sense, it deliberately sides with the hope and potential that is—or should be—a central focus for therapists, because such aspects of the therapeutic relationship have been shown empirically to be ameliorative (Horvarth & Bedi, 2002). Moreover, by including complementary aspects of self (e.g., culture, religion) that may be as, if not more, important to clients than the foci that traditionally are considered paramount by clinicians (Dana, 2005; Pouchly, 2011; Ridley et al., 1998), the BEVI seeks to include the client's experience of his or her own world more deliberately in the therapeutic process.

Principle 2: Facilitating Collaboration and Connection

The processes by which BEVI feedback is gathered and shared with clients is oriented deliberately toward a collaborative approach, which is meant to bring the client into the process of understanding self, others, and the larger world, and thereby promoting connection between the therapist-assessor and client, as well as the broader context in which they both are embedded. Commitment to such collaborative work has been prized by practitioners and scholars, because this approach has been linked to reduced feelings of isolation, increased feelings of hope, decreased symptoms, greater insight, increased self-esteem, increased positive rapport with the therapist, and a higher level of agency and motivation as described and/or reported by therapists and clients alike (e.g., Allen, Montgomery, Tubman, Frazier, & Escovar, 2003; Finn & Tonsager, 1997; Fischer, 2000; Hilsenroth, Peters, & Ackerman, 2004; Norcross, 2002). Because the strength of the therapeutic alliance is among the most predictive variables of therapeutic outcomes (Norcross, 2002), it should not be surprising that "collaboration is one of the key features of the alliance concept" (Horvath & Bedi, 2002, p. 59). Such collaborative and relational processes extend to, and are perhaps exemplified by, the usage of assessment data within therapy, because such processes require a therapist to share his or her professional expertise with clients in a way that is open, honest, and coherent (e.g., Lambert, 2010). Indeed, a positive and collaborative relationship with an assessor is associated with clients experiencing greater gains in new self-understanding from an assessment intervention (Poston, 2012). Consistent with such collaborative and egalitarian practices, APA ethical guidelines maintain that,

> results are given to the individual or designated representative unless the nature of the relationship precludes provision of an explanation of results (such as in some organizational consulting, preemployment or security screenings, and forensic evaluations), and this fact has been clearly explained to the person being assessed in advance. (APA, 2012)

Along these lines, it should be noted that providing feedback is not merely a recommendation, but an explicit ethical mandate, even with the most widely used psychological measures in the field. Thus, it is important that test feedback is given in a manner that maximizes its therapeutic potential for clients. For example, in his Minnesota Multiphasic Personality Inventory-2 (MMPI-2) manual, Finn (1996) maintains that:

Clients become most engaged in taking the MMPI-2 when they are treated as collaborators, whose ideas and cooperation are essential to the assessment. Clients become most invested in an MMPI-2 assessment when the results will be used to address their personal goals. When an MMPI-2 assessment addresses clients' goals and clients are treated as collaborators, they are more likely to give accurate and useful information when completing the test. When MMPI-2 feedback is given to clients in an emotionally supportive manner, they often feel affirmed, less anxious, and more hopeful, even if the test feedback seems likely to produce painful emotional reactions. (pp. 5–6)

Finn also observes that although such guidelines were prepared for the administration and interpretation of the MMPI-2, they may be applied to other assessment measures. Further explicating this approach, Finn and Tonsager (1997) specify three overarching areas of foci when introducing assessment data into the therapeutic realm: (a) the client's subjective experience of the assessment, (b) the assessor's own subjective experience, and (c) the dynamic interplay between the client and the assessor (p. 379). In regard to feedback, they suggest that information aligning most closely with the client's worldview be shared first, with more opaque results saved for later in the process. Wholly consistent with these mandates, guidelines, and practices, the BEVI seeks to prioritize and illuminate the client's experience—their questions, feelings, reactions, interpretations, contradictions, complexities, and hopes. As such, as we hope to illustrate next, the BEVI provides a method for collaboratively channeling rich and relevant content into therapy, which opens the process to deeper exploration, interpretation, and meaning making.

Methods and Design

This study of the BEVI is grounded in a social constructionist theoretical framework, which postulates that the derivation of "meaning" is constructed within, and mediated by, sociocultural processes and contexts (Merriam, 2009). This theoretical framework aligns well with the fundamental propositions of the EI model and BEVI method, which are designed to examine how and why human beings make sense of self, others, and the world at large as they do (Shealy, 2016). Using a basic qualitative design as described by Merriam, the following study is multimethod, using data from three sources: clinician focus groups, client written responses, and a transcribed therapy session in order to examine and understand the experiences of both clinicians and clients vis-à-vis the BEVI. More specifically, the study focused on the following research questions:

1. Is the BEVI ecologically valid (e.g., are profile results consistent with clinician observations and the phenomenological experience of clients)?
2. Can the BEVI be useful to clinicians for purposes of facilitating case conceptualizations?
3. When used clinically, does the BEVI correspond to best practices for therapeutic assessment (e.g., Finn, 1996; Fischer, 2000).
4. How specifically might the BEVI add value to various assessment and therapeutic activities?

5. Do the hypothesized "assessment common factors" (formative variables, dichotomous thinking, dialectical thinking, emotional awareness, and self-awareness) emerge thematically when clients and clinicians discuss their usage and experience of the BEVI?

Participant Population

Client Participants. Fourteen clients participated in this qualitative study. One of them participated in the videotaped and transcribed therapy session; the other 13 completed the BEVI, and their written qualitative responses were analyzed. These clients were selected by convenience, and included undergraduates seen for individual counseling at a senior military college; individuals, couples, and families seen in an outpatient private practice; individuals and families seen at a community mental health clinic; and individuals seen for counseling at a community mental health clinic.

Clinician Participants. Ten clinicians participated in this qualitative focus group. Because we were interested in issues of both training and practice, we took a nontraditional sampling approach. Specifically, focus groups included doctoral students across the spectrum of training, as well as licensed master's- and doctoral-level clinicians working in different settings. All participants had to participate in an orientation process for the BEVI, to be actively engaged in its usage, and to have at least a master's degree in a mental health field (all were licensed at the master's level prior to matriculating in the doctoral program). Thus, participants included three second-year doctoral students, two third-year doctoral students, and one doctoral-level intern; all of these individuals were licensed at the master's level prior to doctoral-level matriculation. In addition, two doctoral-level, licensed psychologists participated (one for each of two focus groups) along with another licensed master's-level clinician. Of the ten clinicians, one was male and nine were female; nine self-identified as White/European American; and one self-identified as African American. Although clinicians ascribed to various theoretical leanings, all classified their theoretical orientation as integrative. They deliberately were not told to interpret the BEVI through a particular framework (e.g., including, but not limited to, "therapeutic assessment"). Two of these clinicians also served as researchers in this study. The first author (a second-year doctoral student) and the developer of the BEVI (a professor, who participated in the development of focus group questions, but did not participate in focus group processes, discussions, or coding) are the primary researchers in this study. Another second-year doctoral student cofacilitated the focus groups, and also served as a researcher in this study. Three other doctoral-level students and one doctoral-level intern assisted with the coding and analysis for the focus groups.

Focus Groups

To appraise matters of inter-rater reliability, the two focus groups were conducted according to the basic guidelines advocated by Barbour (2005). Both focus groups consisted of clinicians and lasted approximately 45 minutes. The same written protocol was followed for both focus groups, which included a brief introduction and a list of questions read from a script (see Exhibit A) that addressed both the clinicians' experiences, as well as the clients' reactions to the BEVI. Summary descriptions of the BEVI scales were distributed to the participants in order to help them remember and identify relevant scales. The protocol material was e-mailed ahead of time to the participants for their review.

Focus group 1 consisted of five clinicians, two of whom participated through phone conferencing and three of whom participated face to face. Focus group 2 consisted of three clinicians, two of whom participated through phone conferencing and one of whom participated face to face. To ensure balance and perspective, each of the focus groups deliberately included doctoral trainees and licensed psychologist participants. The same researchers co-facilitated both focus groups, and were responsible for recording process and reflection notes.

Both focus groups were audiotaped and transcribed; participant names were eliminated from the transcripts to maintain anonymity. The transcriptions were then consensus coded in three stages. The first stage consisted of reviewing the transcripts and identifying emergent themes relevant to the research questions. The second stage consisted of narrowing these themes down to the most salient and developing a code book with the code names, criteria, and exemplars (see Exhibit B). The third stage consisted of using this code book to code the responses in the two focus groups. All stages were exercised through consensus (e.g., Schielke, Fishman, Osatuke, & Stiles, 2009).

Clients' Qualitative Questions

The BEVI contains three open-ended questions regarding the clients' experience of taking this measure. Thirteen sets of these responses were collected, analyzed, and coded by the principle researcher through a process of analytic coding (Richards, 2009).

Videotaped Therapy Session

As a final check on focus group findings, and to evaluate further the ecological validity of study methods, a therapy session was recorded and transcribed in which BEVI results were cointerpreted with a client. Sections of the transcript were then analyzed and interpreted in relation to the themes that emerged from the other two data sources.

Sequence of Analysis and Interpretation

Although the analysis and interpretation of the qualitative data involved an iterative process among these different data sources, in order to best answer the research questions, the following sequence of coding was followed:

1. Analyses of the focus groups for main themes.
2. Analyses of client responses embedded in the BEVI measure.
3. In-depth analyses of a therapy session to compare and contrast with the other data sources.
4. Blending of all three data sources to create a complex, coherent, and rich framework in which the research questions could be addressed.

This sequence of analysis and interpretation is represented graphically in Figure 15.1.

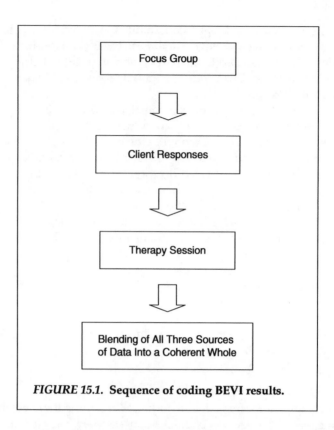

FIGURE 15.1. Sequence of coding BEVI results.

More About Emic Positioning

With the support and knowledge of other members of the core faculty in the first author's APA accredited doctoral program, this project was undertaken in order for extant doctoral students to have the opportunity to participate in real world clinical research on a measure—with therapeutic assessment potential—that had been in development since the early 1990s. Nonetheless, six of the clinicians (including the first author) are currently in a doctoral program, of which the developer of the BEVI is a core faculty member and adviser; two of the clinicians were former advisees of the developer prior to graduating from the program. Thus, 10 of the clinicians are in emic positioning in terms of having multiple relationships with the developer of the BEVI and having had prior exposure to the BEVI measure. The two primary researchers are in emic positioning in regard to the data in that both researchers are currently using the BEVI as a conceptual aid and intervention tool with clients. As noted, one of the researchers is the developer of this instrument. Such emic positioning potentially could threaten credibility by inhibiting critical feedback from the participant clinicians and/or bias the researchers toward the BEVI. As such, a number of steps were taken to attenuate possible risks.

First, we recruited a separate faculty-level researcher and faculty member with etic positioning, who is an expert in qualitative analysis, to oversee this project and the interpretation of data. Specifically, the methodology for this study, its implementation, and data analysis all were developed, reviewed, approved, and conducted deliberately under the auspices of this same separate researcher and faculty member's mixed methods course. Second, by design, the test developer had no role in conducting either of the focus groups, transcribing either session, developing the coding system, or coding data from the focus groups, client feedback, or therapy session. Third, no names or identifying information of focus group participants were associated with any transcribed observations from either group. Fourth, as noted, data were integrated directly from clients (qualitative responses and observing therapy sessions) so as to triangulate the evidence and offer multiple viewpoints (Creswell & Plano Clark, 2011; Richards, 2009). Fifth, the first author engaged in a technique of bracketing while also explicitly tracking processes of collecting, coding, analyzing, and interpreting data (Merriam, 2009). Sixth and finally, the first author reevaluated and revised the overarching emphasis of this research from "Does the BEVI work?" to "Can the BEVI work?," a paradigmatic shift that should reduce the threat to credibility because the purpose is more descriptive and exploratory than evaluative.

Results

Focus Groups

After reviewing the transcripts of the two focus groups, 65 themes were identified initially. Through a process of consensus, these themes were merged and reorganized into 11 final themes. Table 15.1 (see Exhibit C) shows the final result. The codes are displayed in a hierarchy with parent codes listed on the left column, child codes listed in the middle column (when applicable), and the number of references or responses that were categorized within the code listed on the right column. The sequence of codes listed is determined by the number of references within the text. In the following section the criteria, relevance, and relationships between the themes are described, and examples of responses that align with each of the 11 codes are provided. The focus groups from which the responses were taken are identified by the labels "FG1" and "FG2" for the first and second focus groups administered, respectively.

Theme 1: Understanding Causal Connections

The most common theme to emerge from the focus groups was "Understanding Causal Connections." This theme refers to how the BEVI may be used to help the therapist and client gain a deeper understanding of the underlying causal connections between forces and elements that may have been viewed previously as disconnected and disparate. Because this theme is somewhat broad, it was divided further into four subthemes (called "child themes" in the vernacular of qualitative methodology). The four child themes include three types of causal connections; the fourth referred to the increased understanding or insight that is the outcome of deriving these causal connections. The first subtheme, "Cognitions, Emotions, and Behavior," refers to how the BEVI helped highlight causal relationships between a client's beliefs, emotions, and behaviors, as is reflected in the following focus group response:

> I think it was particularly helpful. . .in terms of explaining. . .what was going on with her, some of the reasons that she might be internalizing a lot of her emotions. . .For example, [her] beliefs about how a woman should be, not expressing anger, holding everything in, that type of thing. (FG2)

The second subtheme, "Self and Others," refers to the causal relationships between the client's own behavior and the behavior of others. The response following indicates this type of connection:

> One client started thinking about it and reflecting on his relationship with his mother and how she has different beliefs than him and how his beliefs match with that and how he can use that understanding in being able to connect with her more. (FG1)

The third subtheme, "Past and Present," refers to the causal relationship between the client's past and his or her current life:

> The BEVI certainly opens up discussion for how maybe you were this way, and became this way. (FG2)

The apparent outcome of "making causal connections" is to increase insight and understanding. In several therapeutic approaches, as well as in change process research, insight is a central step toward change (Gibbons et al., 2009). Even in therapeutic approaches that de-emphasize the necessity of client insight, such as some behavioral and family systems techniques, the clinician still must understand how causal connections are established by a client in order to plan appropriate interventions (Nichols, 2011). That said, many theorists within the humanistic tradition contend that gaining greater insight about oneself and the world is not only a means toward change, but a central human need in itself (Pervin, 2002). According to this tradition, which is aligned with the EI framework underlying the BEVI, we are meaning-making creatures; psychological well-being is thereby predicated on the relative ability to develop a rich and consistent narrative regarding one's self and the world (Adler, 2012).

The final subtheme under the parent theme of "Causal Connections" is labeled "Deeper Understanding." There were many references in the discussion group to this subtheme. A sample response reflecting the BEVI's potential to facilitate client understanding includes the following:

> Using the framework of the BEVI and going over some of that data with her she was better able to make sense of herself, and her life, and how she had gotten to where she was in her life. (FG2)

Theme 2: Big Picture

The second most common theme that emerged from the two focus groups was the BEVI's utility for developing a broad, holistic, and integrated framework through which clients may be understood and therapeutic processes facilitated. We labeled this theme "Big Picture." The theme of "Big Picture" does overlap with the theme "Causal Connections," and specifically, the subtheme of "Deeper Understanding." All of these share the core element of integration, of "fitting things together" into a cohesive narrative or picture, of "making sense of the world." However, the responses within the code of "Big Picture" specifically emphasize breadth, and the broadening or widening of both the therapist's and client's viewpoint and understanding of self, others, and the larger world, which is wholly consistent with a therapeutic assessment framework. Some of the responses that are included in this code are included in the following:

It just seemed . . . to expand on the frame. (FG1)

It provides a more holistic frame. (FG2)

It brought it together . . . in a picture that created some more pockets to understand her at a bigger picture level. (FG1)

It helps me to be more mindful of really seeing the client . . . holistically. There are times where I find myself getting really focused . . . on one piece of the picture. . .[and] it helped me to be more mindful of broadening the lens that I was looking through and being able to really meet the client's needs and meet them where they're at. (FG2)

Theme 3: Nonpathologizing

The third most frequent theme that emerged was labeled "Nonpathologizing." This theme refers to how the BEVI is useful in developing a nonpathologizing framework that allows the therapist and client to focus on strengths and resources as well as areas of difficulty. This attribute of the BEVI aligns well with the therapeutic assessment model outlined by Fischer (2000), Finn (1996), and others. Some of the responses in this category included the following:

It was able to capitalize on some areas of the strengths where things could go differently for clients. So they may be able to capitalize on these strengths even though they have a number of negative life events and show resiliency. So I like its ability to do both. (FG2)

And it's such a nice frame . . . to explore . . . in that non-threatening way [helping them in] thinking about their beliefs and values. (FG2)

We were talking about the MMPI the other day and how it tends to be pathologizing and I thought that the way he interpreted [the BEVI], while it was honest, it also was supportive and it didn't make them feel bad. (FG2)

It isn't pathologizing and it isn't necessarily threatening but it feels so informative as opposed to labeling. (FG2)

Although problem-focused tests like the MMPI-2 can be remarkably helpful, especially in therapeutic assessment contexts (Finn, 1996), other tests, like the BEVI can be equally helpful and complementary. Along these lines, it should be noted that because BEVI scales are reported along a percentage-based continuum (very high to very low), any given scale could be interpreted in terms of strengths or weaknesses (e.g., a very high degree of Emotional Attunement generally would be advantageous for purposes of therapy whereas a very low degree of Emotional Attunement could indicate that a client may experience considerable difficulties dealing with emotions not only in therapy, but in relationships more generally). In any case, presenting both types of information—relative strengths and areas for improvement—appears to be experienced as helpful by clients (Hanson & Claiborn, 2006).

Theme 4: Sharing the Conceptualization With the Client

Although each of the three broad therapeutic frameworks (psychodynamic, cognitive behavioral, and humanistic) leads to different and often conflicting frames for conceptualizing a client's presentations and problems, all three approaches stress the critical task and question of how to share the therapist's conceptualization and test results with the client in a therapeutic manner (Wampold, 2001). The BEVI's usefulness in this crucial therapeutic task emerged as a common theme within the two focus groups. Following is an example of a response which fell into this category:

> Helping with the conceptualization of your client for yourself and then also how to share that with the client in a way that is going . . . to create movement and be therapeutic for them. (FG1)

Theme 5: Broader Range of Information

The theme we labeled "Broader Range of Information" refers to the BEVI's ability to capture information regarding different domains of the client's life and experience, which traditional measures may not access. These different domains include the client's perception of his or her early experiences (Negative and Positive Life Events Scales) as well as beliefs and values regarding religion (Socioreligious Traditionalism); nature and the living world (Ecological Resonance); different societies and cultures (Sociocultural Openness); what roles and responsibilities we have toward the larger world (Global Engagement); and what males and females should be, and how they should act (Gender Traditionalism). Although topics like these may emerge in therapy, or undergird key aspects of functioning, they often are implicit despite the fact that such matters are often at the very heart of daily life and the experience of self, others, and the larger world. Thus, once such issues are brought into the room via discussion of quantitative scores and qualitative responses on the BEVI, the therapist and client often are surprised at how these basic beliefs and values can be highly relevant to core aspects of how the client organizes his or her experience, and in fact may open up new ways of relating to the overarching therapeutic or assessment process. Thus, this theme includes the BEVI's capacity both to capture this additional information while also using it to catalyze discussion of these domains within the therapy session. The comments following fall into the first category:

> It really does sort of flush out other factors that may not show up in other measures. (FG2)

> It was a nice springboard to allow her to speak about certain areas that may not have come up in a typical informing not using the BEVI, like her views of what it means to be a woman, that kind of thing, sort of her religious views and where those came from. (FG2)

> [It was] providing an opening for talking about those things. Some things that maybe wouldn't come up otherwise, like issues of religiosity, of gender traditionalism, things like that that aren't accessed on a, at a very easy level otherwise, unless it's within the context of something like this. (FG1)

Theme 6: Assessing Openness, Defensiveness, and the Ability to Self-reflect

Another theme that emerged was the measure's value in helping the therapists to access and assess the clients' capacity for openness and self-reflection, another key area of relevance across therapeutic traditions, generally, and therapeutic assessment, specifically. Because clients may experience a range of reactions to test feedback, BEVI scores can be used to anticipate, and subsequently enhance, feedback processes and outcomes. Following is a comment that represents this category:

> At a foundational level . . . it . . . does inform the way that they really see the world, their defensiveness, ability to even trust, and that helps a lot especially with a therapy client that I'm seeing now. And the BEVI really caught that. (FG2)

At a related level, the client's capacity for self-reflection may be a good indicator of how successful he or she can be in therapy (e.g., Dimaggio, 2011), as indicated by the response following:

> We've had several cases of this very rigid way and approach of thinking and yet the openness is still there. . .so it was helpful to. . .see and to make sense of . . . (that) . . . in the therapeutic relationship. (FG1)

The measurement of a client's openness, defensiveness, and self-reflective capacity can be useful in deciding what treatment approach to use—essentially an issue of matching approach to client readiness and style—and where to begin, or transition, treatment, as indicated in the responses following, which reflect common processes for therapists in the context of understanding and furthering therapeutic interventions:

> [Is] this person ready and able and at capacity to handle some kind of deep therapy work or does more work need to be done at that building trust and alliance level before you can move on? So I think it [BEVI]. . . .provides [this in a] more tangible [way] and ties it to where we need to go from here. (FG2)

> I think that fundamentally the BEVI really assists in better understanding the clients so that you can get a sense of where really to begin or what they're able to hold. (FG2)

Theme 7: Client Motivation and Engagement

Another theme that emerged in the focus groups was the use of the BEVI to increase client motivation and engagement in therapy. The theme of client motivation can be divided conceptually into two sections. First, some clients were immediately positively motivated by the idea of the assessment. These cases can be seen in the following responses:

> She was looking forward to the opportunity and particularly because we're talking about terminating soon. She thought that this would be a perfect way to kind of encapsulate everything that we have been working on. (FG1)

> Actually she was pretty excited about the idea and she's like "Yeah this will be great. This will be wonderful." (FG1)

Second, the motivation of some of the clients increased as a by-product of the measure and receiving feedback. In effect, it mobilized the change process and empowered clients. Examples of these cases can be seen in the following responses:

> Something about them having entered the information themselves and having it reflected back to them kind of without my filter . . . was helpful. It almost seemed more unbiased that way. . . . They bought into it a little bit more. (FG1)

> One particular young man who initially came in . . . was not a very good therapy client . . . [However] by the end, shortly after the BEVI his insight had increased and he was also sharing information about other aspects. (FG1)

Theme 8: Flexibility

The BEVI's integrative, nonpathologizing, and broad framework appears to promote flexibility in a number of different domains including theoretical orientation, clinical population, and therapeutic application. Moreover, focus group participants also identified a number of other domains (besides therapy and assessment) that would be relevant for the BEVI. Responses that refer to the BEVI's flexibility in this regard include:

> It can be used within several different frameworks, several different theoretical kinds of orientations. (FG1)

> It would be really great for the Peace Corps volunteers to take this kind of thing. Any kind of international corporation that might be sending the employees abroad to. . .optimize their experience and hopefully . . . have a happy and productive employee on the other end. . . . (FG2)

> I also wondered even about the. . .military in a similar . . . sense. I wonder if there would be any way to help particularly people who might be vulnerable to PTSD through some kind of measure like this. (FG2)

> For us in higher ed, I think . . . it's a helpful thing. . .I think for programming purposes and just trying to get a deeper understanding of the population that you're serving, and then how to target certain programs to address some of those needs. (FG1)

Theme 9: Accuracy

The effectiveness of a measure depends upon its validity and reliability in both a psychometric and real world sense. In other words: Can the measure accurately and appropriately capture usable information (e.g., is it ecologically valid)? The BEVI's accuracy in this regard was evaluated in the following manner. The developer of the assessment measure gave blind interpretations of various BEVI profiles. In other words, he read, analyzed, and interpreted profiles "blind" without any knowledge of whom the profile referred to. His interpretations were then given to clinicians who were participating in the focus groups. When asked later during the focus group processes about the accuracy of such interpretations, and how they converged with the therapist's clinical assessment as well as the client's own perspective, feedback was uniformly positive. Some examples of responses that fell into this category are included in the following:

> I think that looking at the scale is providing a very accurate analysis of this individual. (FG2)

> For the assessment client that I was working with, I mean, it was pretty spot on actually. (FG2)

> They were very insightful. They were right on target. (FG1)

> He was really able to sort of nail the two or three main pieces of her personality structure that are contributing to a lot of her distress. (FG2)

Theme 10: Validating for the therapist

In addition to enhancing client engagement, a final theme that emerged was how using the BEVI helped increase the therapist's motivation and engagement. Essentially, it appears that the process of giving, interpreting, and discussing the BEVI tends to reinforce insights, illuminate an underlying clinical sense or intuition, or clarify ideas the therapist had about the client but was unable to substantially articulate or justify. Moreover, the therapist's increased motivation also appeared to result from the measure's ability to identify areas of struggle or challenge (e.g., through the pattern of high and low scale scores; qualitative responses; review of "strongly agree" and "strongly disagree" items), while also emphasizing areas of client strength, growth, and development potential. These results renewed hope in the therapist for a successful outcome while also validating the work that already had been achieved with the client. An example of the therapist's increased motivation and engagement as a result of using the BEVI, is reflected in the response following:

> I think sometimes you get exhausted . . . But . . . I think being able to see that there are some areas that are making growth possible, I think for me it was kind of a little like, because I think sometimes we can get real jaded when we're working with clients week after week so seeing particular scale of openness for me with that one particular client when I was started to feel like Lord she's never going to make much progress but . . . for me it was a rejuvenation afterward. (FG1)

Three Qualitative Questions Embedded in the BEVI[2]

As discussed in the methodology section, the BEVI deliberately is a mixed methods instrument, because in addition to its quantitative scales, it also includes three qualitative items. When the quantitative scale scores are combined, or integrated, with the open-ended qualitative responses, a traditional mixed methods approach emerges, seemingly as an explanatory or embedded approach (Creswell & Plano Clark, 2010; Hanson et al., 2005). By combining the data strands vis-à-vis dialogue with clients, the overall experience of therapy and assessment is enriched. Along these lines, the basic structure of client feedback (e.g., during the post-assessment discussion) as well as therapist review (e.g., prior to meeting with a client) also is "mixed methods," including both a written narrative, as well as scale scores and critical items that are presented from the BEVI reports. Regarding the qualitative items, at the conclusion of answering quantitative items, the client is asked three questions regarding his or her experience either in taking the BEVI (if he or she had not yet engaged in assessment or therapeutic work) or in the context of a therapeutic or assessment experience that was already under way. The questions are as follows:

1. First, please describe which aspect of this experience has had the greatest impact upon you and why?
2. Is there some aspect of your own "self" or "identity" (e.g., gender, ethnicity, sexual orientation, religious or political background, etc.) that has become especially clear or relevant to you or others as a result of this experience?
3. Third, what are you learning or how are you different as a result of this experience?

A sample of 13 BEVI profiles were collected and reviewed for this aspect of the project. This was a sample of convenience, which included therapy clients from four different venues: a counseling center from a university; a counseling center from a military college; an outpatient community clinic; and, a private outpatient practice. The 13 sets of answers were coded and analyzed by the first author for emergent

---

[2] The de-identified presentation of clinical material in this chapter, and book, is informed by the March, 2012 Special Section of the journal *Psychotherapy*, entitled "Ethical Issues in Clinical Writing," Volume 49, Issue 1, pp. 1–25 as well as Health Insurance Portability and Accountability Act (HIPAA) regulations, American Psychological Association (APA) ethical guidelines, and other best practices for reporting clinical information.

themes regarding the clients' experience in taking the BEVI, and how this experience may have been therapeutically useful. Responses were related for the most part to the clients' reactions to taking the BEVI assessment measure because those experiences also appeared to have therapeutic meaning. It should be noted that our procedure for using the BEVI as a therapeutic intervention was informed by Finn's (1996) model as described in his manual on how to use the MMPI-2 as an intervention tool, and involved a sequence of four steps:

1. Orienting the client to the BEVI measurement and developing a referral question or questions for which the results can be applied.
2. Having the client take the BEVI inventory.
3. Analyzing the results.
4. Presenting the results to the client and collaborating with the client on a meaningful conceptualization and interpretation.

After coding and analysis by the principle researcher, 17 themes related to the research questions were identified, which then were organized hierarchically under four major headings: Aspects of Self; Values; Self and Others; and No Impact. The themes are listed in tabular form (see Table 15.2, Exhibit D), with the number of references within the text to these themes listed on the right. Based upon analysis of this initial organization of content, these 17 themes were then collapsed further into the following 5 overarching themes, which appeared to encompass and account for these qualitative data from clients.

Theme 1: Identity and Self Worth
In response to the BEVI qualitative questions, the themes related to Aspects of the Self were the most common. The most common of these themes were responses related to self-image and self-worth. These included responses that reflected a disparity or incongruence between the ideal and perceived self:

I would like to be a better person than I am in reality.

It also included responses that related to a positive identity:

I am a naturally happy person and I have a good relationship with my family. I've learned to be strong and I am better person after military school.

Finally, it included responses that related to one's social or public self:

People think that I am gay here in America because I like and do different things from them.

Theme 2: Ability to Self Reflect
Examples of client responses that related to this theme—"the ability to self-reflect"—are included in the following:

I liked how this made me think about questions I never would have thought about unless asked.

I believe everything I need to understand is deep inside me, but it needs more excavation and integration.

Theme 3: Complexity

Another theme common to the experiences of therapists and clients is the notion of discovering complexities and contradictions within the self. Client responses that reflect this theme are included in the following:

> I am hoping it will help to take our counseling to another level. I enjoy learning about myself, [and I am] more complex then I originally thought.

> Realizing I hold some seemingly conflicting views, such as on social issues.

Theme 4: Values and Religion

Within the category of values, the theme of Religion was among the most frequently referenced, which perhaps is not surprising, given the focus on such matters by many therapy clients, whatever their inclination, from devout to atheist. Even so, mental health professionals often struggle to address such matters as part of practice, despite long-standing best practice recommendations to do so (e.g., Shafranske, 1996). Thus, the BEVI appears to offer an accessible and nonactivating way to address such issues, when salient for clients, within a therapeutic context. Some examples are given in the following:

> My faith plays a significant role in how I view others.

> The aspect that has affected me the most was religion. I had never tried in the past to answer any of the questions about my religion that this assessment has.

> The questions about religion showed me my strong views

Theme 5: Self in Relation to Others

The theme relating to learning about oneself in relation to others was also one of the most frequently referenced, a finding that is consistent with results from "contrast cases" and personalized normative feedback studies (Hanson & Poston, 2011). This theme included responses in which clients reflected on how their values related to others around them:

> It seems to me that I am more liberal than I think other people are around me.

It includes reflections regarding intimate relationships:

> Learning how . . . different spouse's perceptions of identical situations can be.

This theme also included reflections relating to the client's desire to become more involved with others:

> My world is currently small and without influence. I potentially could make a small influence somewhere even at this stage of life.

Individual Therapy Session

Finally, in order to determine whether the themes identified in the preceding results emerge in real time interactions between therapists and clients, we include portions of a therapy session that was conducted by one of the authors of this chapter. In doing so, we use the BEVI as a therapeutic assessment in accordance with guidelines outlined in Finn's (1996) manual for using the MMPI-2 as a therapeutic intervention. Sections of the de-identified transcripts (see footnote 1) are reproduced with brief summaries of the related themes that emerged. In the following transcript, the therapist has just given the client her BEVI results and they begin discussing the client's results regarding various scales.

TH: The other thing it [BEVI results] said was that you were very attuned to your emotional world.

CT: Yes.

TH: And that felt like it was....

CT: It was very, very right, yes, very much so. I react a lot on emotion.

TH: And you're very aware of your emotion, what you're feeling. . .it's a big part of your life. . .and it's a big motivator.

CT: Yes. It's true. Maybe that's not a good thing.

TH: Well I'm sure there's difficulties about being sensitive.

CT: Yes, I'm pretty sensitive to what's going on around me.

TH: And inside of you.

CT: Mmmhmmm.

TH: And one thing that we've talked about before is difficulty tolerating a lot of painful emotions.

CT: I really don't have . . . I can't do that....

The accuracy of the BEVI appears valid in this case, in terms of how it resonates with the client and validates her own internal experience. This aspect of herself and experience is then linked to an area that had been a focus in previous sessions, that of feeling vulnerable, which led to further discussion and reflection:

TH: So the emotion part. The problem is the control? You feel things very deeply but the problem is that once something touches you, you worry about how you will be flooded with emotion and you will not be able to....

C: See even talking about it makes me emotional.

TH: And it makes you feel vulnerable.

C: Yeah.

TH: Vulnerability is one of the big things we've talked about even in terms of....

C: But if I'm vulnerable I'm going to get burned.

In this phase of the session, sharing the BEVI results led the client to disclose one of her core beliefs: "If I'm vulnerable I'm going to get burned." Thus, the process of reviewing the BEVI scores with this client appeared to have uncovered a core conflict for her. On the one hand, she feels that she is a sensitive and emotional person; on the other, if she allows herself to feel and express this emotion, she believes she will get "burned." In short, the BEVI results provide an opening for the therapist to directly address the client's pessimistic or cynical belief system, by focusing on other aspects of the client's BEVI profile:

TH: Well, the other thing that I noticed was the positive thinking, the skepticism and tell me how you feel . . . this thing about if you're vulnerable and you're hurt. That lesson or that belief seems to go into that. You don't go into that positive thinking business. You're skeptical.

CT: What's his name. Scientology. The power of positive thinking. That's bullshit. (Laughs)

TH: But even beyond the cult thing just talking about you know when we talk about . . . when you talk about the ability to change, writing yourself off "Well maybe [he] . . . can but me, no, it's too late. What's the point?" Is that right?

CT: That's what I said.

TH: What's the point? Because we can't change it. It's the way it is.

CT: Yeah.

TH: That part of your belief of who you are and how you think about things . . . I wonder if that applies to vulnerability . . . like what's the point of showing vulnerability? I'm not going to get what I need anyway?

CT: Well all of that which you just said. You probably hit the nail on the head to use such a cliché term. I think that probably is how I deal with things.

In this portion of the session, the BEVI is used to open up and discuss a central conflict for the client in a way that is nonpathologizing, validating, and experience-near. The client appears to be able to feel understood while she grapples with a belief system that may be maladaptive and ultimately painful for her. Addressing the client's belief system through a discussion of the measure allows for a nonconfrontational, matter of fact, and collaborative approach. This collaborative stance allows the client to approach core issues in a more open and reflective manner.

TH: . . .the thing [score on the Positive Thinking scale of the BEVI] that is smallest of all is positive thinking. This is really a huge bit of skepticism.

CT: It really is, isn't it?

TH: . . .very . . . like, almost sort of jaded about the world.

CT: It's funny that you should say that, because Sam tells me that all the time. He just said it to me the other day.

TH: Well then....

CT: He says, "Why don't you believe in me? Why are you so negative? Why can't you be positive? Why can't you think it's gonna be okay?"

TH: Because you learned very early that the way to avoid disappointment is to be very cynical and skeptical. That way you don't get disappointed, or even worse, you don't get hurt.

CT: Yes!

TH: And, it's hard for Sam, kind of, sometimes, when that part of you, that part of how you to deal with life....

CT: Well, I'm sure it's probably not more . . . Seeing that on paper is scary.

TH: Is it scary?

CT: Yeah. I didn't realize I was that negative.

From a process standpoint, at this point in the session, it was important to validate the client's emotional experience and explore her reaction to experiencing an aspect of how she sees self, others, and the larger world as it was represented through her BEVI scale scores. Later, it would be valuable to explore the source of this belief system and associated attitudes toward her own emotions and relationships.

In conclusion, the preceding excerpt illustrates many of the themes that have emerged from other sources (e.g., the focus groups, client reports) in this examination of the BEVI: Deeper Understanding; Nonpathologizing; Openness, Defensiveness, and the Ability to Self Reflect; Increasing Client Engagement; Sharing Conceptualization; and Accuracy. In short, the exchange also illustrates how the BEVI can be used as a therapeutic intervention in a collaborative, experience-near, and client-centered manner.

DISCUSSION

This chapter considers the EI model and BEVI method from the standpoint of therapeutic assessment and intervention. It also presents results from an exploratory study, which addressed the following five research questions regarding the use of the BEVI measure in a therapeutic context:

1. Is the BEVI ecologically valid (e.g., are profile results consistent both with clinician observations and the phenomenological experience of clients)?
2. Can the BEVI be useful to clinicians for purposes of facilitating case conceptualizations?
3. When used clinically, does the BEVI correspond to best practice principles for therapeutic assessment (cf., Finn, 1996; Fischer, 2000)?
4. How specifically might the BEVI add value to various assessment and therapeutic activities?
5. Do the hypothesized "assessment common factors" (formative variables, dichotomous thinking, dialectical thinking, emotional awareness, and self-awareness) emerge thematically when clients and clinicians discuss their usage and experience of the BEVI?

In order to examine these questions, three qualitative data strands were collected, examined, and interpreted. These strands included two focus groups that consisted of participant therapists, qualitative responses from clients, and a transcript from a therapy session that addressed BEVI findings.

In relation to the first research question, the accuracy of the BEVI was a common theme that emerged from the focus groups. As noted, responses vis-à-vis BEVI results such as, "They were very insightful" or "They were right on target" referred to the perceived accuracy by clinicians of the blind interpretations they received regarding the measure. Support for the ecological validity of the measure was illustrated by a number of clinician responses regarding the "real world" nature of BEVI findings, as well as the client's reaction to the BEVI results as detailed in the preceding therapy session. In short, although additional research should be conducted and is under way, results from the present study suggest that the BEVI appears to map closely to the realities, complexities, possibilities, and objectives that are inherent to the clinical enterprise. Perhaps that is because this measure was developed in large part on the basis of actual client and trainee verbalizations (e.g., belief statements) over many years and in multiple contexts (Shealy, 2004, 2015, 2016).

Regarding the question of whether the BEVI assists in case conceptualization, several emergent themes appear to speak directly to this point. For example, from the focus group processes, Theme 1, "Understanding Causal Connections," Theme 2, "Big Picture," and Theme 3, "Nonpathologizing," all concern matters of how we help ourselves as clinicians, and our clients, understand the *what* and *why* of case conceptualization (e.g., what is happening conceptually and why a particular cognitive/affective/behavioral configuration came to be). Moreover, Theme 2, "Complexity," and Theme 3, "Values and Religion" from qualitative client results also provide conceptual information that enriches our understanding of how our clients experience self, others, and the larger world, which certainly are relevant to processes of developing and refining our client conceptualizations. On the question of best practice, leaders in the field of therapeutic assessment have advocated for a wide range of changes in our approaches toward clients, including a move toward less pathologizing approaches to assessment, a greater degree of openness regarding what we "experts know" and the bases for such status, and a deeper commitment to collaboration and inclusion, among other recommendations (e.g., Finn & Tonsager, 1997; Fischer, 2000; Poston & Hanson, 2010). Of particular relevance to the current approach, an adapted version of the following principles promulgated by Finn (1996) vis-à-vis therapeutic assessment and the MMPI (see pp. 5–6), also appear highly consistent with how the BEVI is used in therapy and assessment, and may serve as an initial basic best practice framework for this measure:

1. The BEVI's nature and purpose should be explained before giving the measure to the client.
2. Results should be shared in a collaborative spirit with the client, while avoiding an authoritarian stance.
3. Results should be related, if possible, to the client's presenting problems, initial questions, and current conflicts.
4. Results should be discussed in a jargon-free manner using the client's language when possible.
5. The client should be given an opportunity to explore his or her own reactions to the results.
6. The client's process of reacting to the results can further add to the clinician's conceptualization of the client's unresolved conflicts and coping style.
7. The interpersonal process between the client and therapist during the reviewing of BEVI results should be explored and worked through if salient and relevant—conflicts, ruptures, wounds, positive connections, and other issues and dynamics may be considered.
8. Intrapsychic process, interpsychic process, transference, and countertransference may all be explored within the context of co-evaluating the BEVI results.

From our perspective, all of these "best practices" were followed in relation to how the BEVI is used and experienced in the real world by clients and clinicians alike. For example, the process of sharing results with clients necessitates a "collaborative spirit" as well as an exploratory approach, as clinicians essentially appear to be using the BEVI to try and understand—*with clients*—how to make sense of their presentations, symptoms, processes, struggles, and hopes vis-à-vis BEVI results. Thus, although it may be used in this manner, the BEVI is not intended to be a vehicle for "giving feedback" to clients who are meant passively to receive it, but is rather a method for engaging clients in depth-based exploration about how emergent results may help clinicians and clients understand better what the realities and possibilities are for the clients, in terms of how and why they experience self, others, and the larger world as they do, and what the potential implications of such an organizational self-structure may be. For example, as the preceding transcript illustrates, by encouraging the client to generate her own examples or links to BEVI scores and content, she was able to assume a level of collaboration, and indeed ownership, of the therapeutic process (Hanson, Claiborn, & Kerr, 1997). Such an outcome seems highly congruent with the preceding principles as well as the letter and spirit of therapeutic assessment (e.g., Finn & Tonsager, 1997; Fischer, 2000; Poston & Hanson, 2010).

On the fourth and broader question of whether and how the BEVI might facilitate additional goals and activities that are inherent to therapy and assessment, these points (e.g., regarding usage as a conceptual tool; relative degree of congruence with the best practices of therapeutic assessment) speak to the apparent "value-added" nature of the BEVI. However, based upon the themes that emerged earlier, some additional explication may be in order. For example, focus group findings suggest that the BEVI (a) helps therapists identify "core" or underlying issues that are most relevant; (b) expands the frame of conceptualization, to include domains that are not usually addressed but are central to the lives of our clients, including their beliefs about gender, religion, or other cultures, among other foci; (c) facilitates a more comprehensive, integrative, and holistic frame, which helps therapists understand conflicting aspects of the client's personality and character structure; (d) enables therapists to assess a client's relative capacity and inclination for openness and self-reflection; (e) assists therapists in understanding better how to engage their clients, moving therapeutic processes forward in a constructive manner; and (f) facilitates the cultivation of nonpathological and nonreductionistic perspectives of their clients.

Finally, there is the question regarding the putative "assessment common factors" (Shealy, 2016, p. 105) that were hypothesized to be measured by the BEVI and underlying the processes of therapeutic change. These five proposed common factors—formative variables, dichotomous thinking, dialectical thinking, emotional awareness, and awareness of self—were drawn from the literature regarding the three traditions of clinical psychology (Psychodynamic, Cognitive Behavioral, and Humanistic) as well as from common factors theory and related data and the broader integration/unification movements, and were associated with specific scales of the BEVI. Fully granting the preliminary nature of such a process, for present purposes, we reviewed the content that both clinicians and clients generated to see if the themes that emerged appeared consistent with such factors.

First, consider the proposed assessment common factor of "formative variables," which is operationalized on the BEVI via Negative Life Events (NLE), Positive Life Events (PLE), and Needs Closure. How salient were such processes? From our reading, the first "parent theme"—Causal Connections—is directly related to such factors. Recall the previous examples of thematic content under this theme from the focus groups:

> One client started thinking about it and reflecting on his relationship with his mother and how she has different beliefs than him and how his beliefs match with that and how he can use that understanding in being able to connect with her more. (FG1)

> The BEVI certainly opens up discussion for how maybe you were this way, and became this way. (FG2)

In short, clinicians appear to value that the BEVI "brings out" these connections between *what* individual clients say about who they are, and *why*, from an etiological standpoint, they are inclined to do so.

Regarding the proposed "assessment common factors" of "dichotomous thinking" and "dialectic thinking"—which correspond respectively with (among other scales) Basic Closedness and Socioemotional Convergence on the BEVI—focus group processes also seem to offer confirmatory evidence. As noted, these perspectives essentially represent mirror opposites (a reality that is illustrated further by the following correlation matrix data: http://www.thebevi.com/docs/bevi_scale_pairwise_correlations_and_significance_levels.pdf).

From the focus groups, the "Big Picture" theme that emerged speaks to the importance of "putting it all together" in a meaningful way. Consider, for example, the following representative observations that emerged along these lines:

> It brought it together . . . in a picture that created some more pockets to understand her at a bigger picture level. (FG1)

> It helps me to be more mindful of really seeing the client . . . holistically. There are times where I find myself getting really focused . . . on one piece of the picture. . . .[and] it helped me to be more mindful of broadening the lens that I was looking through and being able to really meet the client's needs and meet them where they're at. (FG2)

As another example, the parent theme of "Assessing Openness, Defensiveness, and the Ability to Self Reflect" also seems to tap directly into the factor of "dichotomous thinking." Consider the following focus group observations:

> We've had several cases of this very rigid way and approach of thinking and yet the openness is still there . . . so it was helpful to . . . see and to make sense of . . . (that) . . . in the therapeutic relationship. (FG1)

In short, regarding these two proposed assessment common factors, it would appear that the BEVI helps to explicate the relative degree of complexity that is there to be apprehended in clients, which would seem to be congruent with the "dialectical" framework, and by definition, mitigating against dichotomous thinking, which tends to be associated with reductionistic or linear ways of apprehending our clients in therapy and assessment (e.g., Cummings, Davies, & Campbell, 2000; Horowitz, 2002; Spiro, 2009).

Fourth, the proposed assessment common factor of "emotional awareness" also emerged consistently both for clinicians and therapists as a key factor in understanding client presentations and how to intervene. Recall, for example, the following excerpt from the clinician/client exchange given earlier, during review of the client's BEVI profile, with a particular focus on the Emotional Attunement scale.

TH: The other thing it (BEVI results) said was that you were very attuned to your emotional world.

CT: Yes.

TH: And that felt like it was....

CT: It was very, very right, yes, very much so. I react a lot on emotion.

TH: And you're very aware of your emotion, what you're feeling . . . it's a big part of your life . . . and it's a big motivator.

CT: Yes. It's true. Maybe that's not a good thing.

TH: Well I'm sure there's difficulties about being sensitive.

CT: Yes, I'm pretty sensitive to what's going on around me.

TH: And inside of you.

CT: Mmmhmmm.
TH: And one thing that we've talked about before is difficulty tolerating a lot of painful emotions.
CT: I really don't have . . . I can't do that....

Fifth and finally, the potential of the BEVI to explicate the proposed "self-awareness" assessment common factor also appeared salient in a number of thematic areas. From Causal Connections, for example, consider the following focus group observation:

> Using the framework of the BEVI and going over some of that data with her she was better able to make sense of herself, her life, and how she had gotten to where she was in her life. (FG2)

It should be emphasized that all five of these proposed assessment common factors are not conceptualized as orthogonal in nature, as each may share an affective and cognitive component with the other. For example, on the BEVI, Self Awareness theoretically is subsumed under a broader rubric of "Self Access," which includes Emotional Attunement, Positive Thinking, and Self Awareness. Arguably, then, to be "self-aware" a client or clinician must be able to tolerate the sort of disequilibrium that results from experiencing aspects of self that disconfirm our preferred ways of experiencing what we believe we are. Such an ability to accept contradictions and hold complexity is akin to the skill of dialectical thinking. As measured by Socioemotional Convergence on the BEVI, then, dialectical thinking may be a precursor or facilitating condition for increased self-awareness, an empirical question that could be investigated in the future. Likewise, the role of formative variables in producing a relative degree of "self-access" is further suggested by the following focus group observation:

> The BEVI certainly opens up a discussion for how maybe you were this way, and became that way. (FG2)

As a final consideration, the difference between content and process alluded to at the outset of this chapter should be explicated more fully. Specifically, it is one thing to capture "where" a client is vis-à-vis his or her specific BEVI profile. That content focus may be contrasted with a more process-oriented usage of the BEVI to promote various therapeutic and assessment means and ends, such as greater awareness of self, others, and the larger world. That said, it should be recognized that these two domains (process and content) are intricately connected. For example, in the case vignette outlined previously, the client becomes aware of her tendency to be skeptical and avoid positive thinking (i.e., content-based findings). Then, by engaging in process-based discussion of these findings, the client appears to become more aware of these self-tendencies, and how they affect her larger relationships, which leads to clarification of future therapeutic goals. Consistent with the PATI model, then, content and process on the BEVI are interwoven in the integration of measurement, collaborative interpretation, and therapeutic intervention, which all are designed to facilitate the clarification and pursuit of therapeutic processes and goals.

LIMITATIONS

Convenience Sampling

One limitation of the study is that participants were recruited through convenience sampling, as opposed to purposeful sampling (Creswell & Plano Clark, 2011). As a result, the sample is more heterogeneous than usual. Typically, qualitative studies involve highly homogeneous samples. Consequently, we may have lost meaningful, culturally rich data. In any case, in future research, it may be useful to study specific, closely aligned subsets of clinicians and clients, as well as diverse types of clinicians who are committed to different theoretical perspectives.

Sample Size

Another limitation is the small sample size. Although not unusual for qualitative research of this nature, the themes derived from client qualitative responses from the BEVI were extracted from a sample of 13 different clients. It would be important to note if an examination of a larger sample of responses, where saturation was clearly reached, led to similar themes.

Coding Reliability

A difficulty that emerged from the thematic analysis of the source material was the conceptual overlap between some of the codes. For example, the response that follows could be reasonably coded within either Causal Connections (Deeper Understanding) or Big Picture code.

> It brought it together . . . in a picture that created some more pockets to understand her at a bigger picture level. (FG1)

The conceptual breadth of the thematic codes, the subjective nature of thematic analysis, and the difficulty in establishing effective inclusion and exclusion criteria led to some difficulties with inter-rater reliability. Part of this difficulty stemmed from the tension between two goals in the coding process. First, there was a necessity to impose a conceptually clean and orderly structure upon the material. Second, there was a desire to stay close to the participant's wording and logic in order to capture the lived-in experience of the therapists and clients who used this measure. The dialectic between these sometimes competing objectives was difficult to navigate.

In order to counteract any variance between the researchers' coding choices, responses that appeared to satisfy criteria for more than one code were coded for all relevant categories.

In the end, although there was some variability in terms of determining the exact frequency of references to individual codes, there was overall consensus in regard to the coding categories. Thus, greater emphasis should be given to the themes—and data "trustworthiness" (Morrow, 2005)—than to the number of references each theme received.

SUMMARY AND CONCLUSION

In this chapter, we have attempted to describe the EI model—and BEVI method—against the backdrop of traditional and emerging approaches to intervention, with a particular focus on therapeutic assessment. More specifically, we began with a brief overview of the "big three" frameworks for intervention, psychodynamic, behavioral, and humanistic, before articulating four problems with the "big three": (a) minimizing heterogeneity *within* these frameworks; (b) minimizing heterogeneity *between* these frameworks; (c) underestimation of the powerful role of subdisciplines in informing practice; and (d) the problem of myopic fidelity to particular ways of working. We then provided an overview of the EI model and BEVI method, with a particular emphasis on their congruence with the PATI approach. Along these lines, we offered five putative "assessment common factors" that seemed to be indicated by the current approach, and consistent with an integrative approach toward therapeutic assessment: (a) formative variables, (b) dichotomous thinking, (c) dialectical thinking, (d) emotional awareness, and (e) self–other awareness. From our perspective, two overarching principles seemed to capture the essence of the present PATI approach—"broadening the framework of who clients are" and "facilitating collaboration and connection." Against this theoretical, empirical, and applied backdrop, we posited five specific questions to be examined in the current study: (a) Is the BEVI ecologically valid? (b) Can the BEVI facilitate case conceptualization? (c) Does the BEVI correspond to best practices of therapeutic assessment? (d) How specifically does the BEVI add to assessment and therapy activities? and (e) Do the hypothesized "assessment common factors" emerge thematically for clients and clinicians vis-à-vis BEVI usage?

To examine these questions, methods for this study drew from three sources of information: (a) two independent focus groups; (b) a review of qualitative questions by clients; and (c) analysis of a videotaped transcript. Results emerged in the form of two sets of themes for clinicians and clients. From the perspective of clinicians, the BEVI appeared to: (a) promote an understanding of causal connections; (b) allow for a "Big Picture" focus; (c) emphasize nonpathologizing findings and observations; (d) facilitate sharing of a conceptual framework with clients; (e) broaden the range of information that was gathered and presented; (f) allow for the assessment of openness, defensiveness, and the capacity for self-reflection; (g) promote client motivation and engagement; (h) be applied flexibly not only to therapy and assessment, but in other areas of inquiry and practice; (i) provide perspective that clinicians and clients experienced as accurate; and (j) validate and support the work of clinicians. From the perspective of clients, the BEVI appeared to (a) clarify matters of one's personal identity and self-worth; (b) appraise and promote one's capacity for self-reflection; (c) capture the real world complexity of one's presentation and life situation; (d) allow for inclusion of one's personal values and religious (or not) convictions; and (e) emphasize the relationship of self to others. Finally, to demonstrate how such processes actually manifest in the context of a therapeutic assessment approach, we provided a transcript of a videotaped session to show the iterative and dynamic way in which BEVI results are experienced by clinicians and clients alike in the furtherance of clinical processes and goals.

Overall, these results point to the many potential benefits of the BEVI in a clinical context generally, and toward the therapeutic assessment paradigm and approach, more specifically. Other potential uses of the BEVI within the therapeutic context may be explored in future studies, including but not limited to usage of the BEVI as a screening tool for therapy readiness; for matching therapy clients with specific approaches, interventions, or therapist styles; as a therapy outcome measure; to facilitate different types of therapeutic interventions (e.g., couples, family, group); and to facilitate training processes for students, who may complete the BEVI to understand their own beliefs and values vis-à-vis self, others, and the larger world. As focus group findings suggest, there are many other uses of the BEVI (e.g., for psychological assessment; in military settings; for organizational and leadership development locally and internationally; in higher education), which also may help inform and enrich usage from the standpoint of therapeutic assessment and intervention. In the final analysis, a gap certainly exists between the need and supply of integrative, depth-based, process-oriented, and comprehensive assessment measures that can effectively be used across a range of clinical applications, contexts, and populations. This chapter points to the BEVI's potential to help meet these important needs, while opening up a wide range of issues, processes, and foci that are of considerable relevance to clients, therapists, and the broader mental health field.

REFERENCES

Adler, A. (1916). The origins and development of the feeling of inferiority and the consequences thereof. In A. Adler, B. Glueck, & J. E. Lind (Trans.), *The neurotic constitution: Outlines of a comparative individualistic psychology and psychotherapy* (pp. 1–34). New York, NY: Moffat & Yard. doi:10.1037/10671-001

Adler, J. M. (2012). Living into the story: Agency and coherence in a longitudinal study of narrative identity development and mental health over the course of psychotherapy. *Journal of Personality and Social Psychology, 102*(2), 367–389.

Allen, A., Montgomery, M., Tubman, J., Frazier, L., & Escovar, L. (2003). The effects of assessment feedback on rapport-building and self-enhancement processes. *Journal of Mental Health Counseling, 25*(3), 165–181.

American Psychological Association (APA). (2012). *Diagnostic and statistical manual of mental disorders* (4th ed., pp. 807–813). Arlington, VA: American Psychological Association.

Anmuth, L. M., Poore, M., Cozen, J., Brearly, T., Tabit, M., Cannady, M., . . . Staton, R. (2013, August). *Making implicit beliefs explicit: In search of best practices for mental health clients, clinicians, and trainers.* Poster presented at the annual meeting of the American Psychological Association, Honolulu, HI.

Atwood, K., Chkhaidze, N., Shealy, C. N., Staton, R., & Sternberger, L. G. (2014, August). *Transformation of self: Implications from the Forum BEVI Project.* Poster presented at the annual meeting of the American Psychological Association, Washington, DC.

Badcock, P. B. (2012). Evolutionary systems theory: A unifying meta-theory of psychological science. *Review of General Psychology, 16*(1), 10–23. doi:10.1037/a0026381

Barbour, R. (2005). Making sense of focus groups. *Medical Education, 39,* 742–750.

Basseches, M. (1980). Dialectical schemata: A framework for the empirical study of the development of dialectical thinking. *Human Development, 23,* 400–421.

Beck, A. (1963). Thinking and depression: I. Idiosyncratic content and cognitive distortions. *Archives of General Psychiatry, 9*(4), 324–333. doi:10.1001/archpsyc.1963.01720160014002

Beck, J. S. (1995). *Cognitive therapy: Basics and beyond.* New York, NY: Guilford Press.

Beutler, L. E., Groth-Marnat, G., & Rosner, R. (2003). Introduction to integrative assessment of adult personality. In L. E. Beutler & G. Groth-Marnat (Eds.), *Integrative assessment of adult personality* (2nd ed., pp. 1–36). New York, NY: The Guilford Press.

Binder, P., Holgersen, H., & Nielsen, G. H. (2010). What is a "good outcome" in psychotherapy? A qualitative exploration of former patients' point of view. *Psychotherapy Research, 20*(3), 285–294.

Bowlby, J. (1982). *Attachment and loss: Volume 1. Attachment* (2nd ed.). New York, NY: Basic Books.

Brearly, T., Shealy, C. N., Staton, R., & Sternberger, L. G. (2012, August). *Prejudice and religious and non-religious certitude: An empirical analysis from the Forum BEVI Project.* Poster presented at the annual meeting of the American Psychological Association, Orlando, FL.

Burum, B. A., & Goldried, M. R. (2007). The centrality of emotion to psychological change. *Clinical Psychology Science and Practice, 14*(4), 407–413.

Byrne, S. M., Cooper, Z., & Fairburn, C. G. (2004). Psychological predictors of weight regain in obesity. *Behavior Research and Therapy, 42,* 1341–1356.

Cain, D. J. (2002). Defining characteristics, history and evolution of humanistic psychotherapies. In D. J. Cain (Ed.), *Humanistic psychotherapies: Handbook of research and practice* (pp. 3–54). Washington, DC: American Psychological Association.

Chen, C. (2009). Dialectical thinking and coping flexibility: A multi-method approach. *Journal of Personality, 77*(2), 471–494.

Claiborn, C. D., & Hanson, W. E. (1999). Test interpretation: A social influence perspective. In J. W. Lichtenberg & R. K. Goodyear (Eds.), *Scientist-practitioner perspectives on test interpretation* (pp. 151–166). Boston, MA: Allyn & Bacon.

Coren, A. (2009). *Short-term psychotherapy: A psychodynamic approach* (2nd ed.). New York, NY: Palgrave Macmillan.

Corrigan, P. W., & Wassel, A. (2008). Understanding and influencing the stigma of mental illness. *Journal of Psychosocial Nursing & Mental Health Services, 46*(1), 42–48.

Creswell, J. W., & Plano Clark, V. (2011). *Designing and conducting mixed methods research* (2nd ed.). Thousand Oaks, CA: Sage.

Cummings, E. M., Davies, P. T., & Campbell, S. B. (2000). *Developmental psychopathology and family process: Theory, research, and clinical implications.* New York, NY. The Guilford Press.

Dana, R. H. (2005). *Multicultural assessment: Principles, applications, and examples.* New York, NY: Routledge.

Davanloo, H. (1980). *Short-term dynamic psychotherapy.* New York, NY: Jason Aaronson.

Dimaggio, G. (2011). Impoverished self-narrative and impaired self-reflection as targets for the psychotherapy of personality disorders. *Journal of Contemporary Psychotherapy, 41*(3), 165–174.

Elisha, P. (2011). *The conscious body: A psychoanalytic exploration of the body in therapy.* Washington, DC: American Psychological Association.

Ellis, A., & Harper, R. A. (1961). *A guide to rational living* (3rd ed.). Hollywood, CA: Melvin Powers Wilshire Book Company.

Leichsenring, F., & Rabung, S. (2008). Effectiveness of long-term psychodynamic psychotherapy: A meta-analysis. *Journal of the American Medical Association, 300*(13), 1551–1565.

Finn, S. E. (1996). *Manual for using the MMPI-2 as a therapeutic intervention.* Minneapolis, MN: University of Minnesota Press.

Finn, S. E. (2007). *In our client's shoes: Theories and techniques of therapeutic assessment.* New York, NY: Routledge.

Finn, S. E., & Tonsager, M. E. (1992). Therapeutic effects of providing MMPI-2 test feedback to college students awaiting therapy. *Psychological Assessment, 4,* 278–287.

Finn, S. E., & Tonsager, M. E. (1997). Information-gathering and therapeutic models of assessment: Complementary paradigms. *Psychological Assessment, 9*(4), 374–385.

Fischer, C. T. (2000). Collaborative, individualized, assessment. *Journal of Personality Assessment, 74*(1), 2–14.

Frank, J. D., & Frank, J. B. (1991). *Persuasion and healing: A comparative study of psychotherapy* (3rd ed.). Baltimore, MD: Johns Hopkins Press.

Freud, S. (1961). Five lectures on psycho-analysis. In J. Strachey (Ed. & Trans.), *The standard edition of the complete psychological works of Sigmund Freud.* New York, NY: W.W. Norton & Company, Inc. (Original work published in 1909).

Freud, S. (2011). *The ego and the id* (J. Riviere, Trans.). Mansfield Centre: Martino Publishing. (Original work published in 1927).

Gelso, C. J., & Hayes, J. A. (2007). *Countertransference and the therapists inner experience: Perils and possibilities*. Mahwah, NJ: Lawrence Erlbaum Associates, Inc.

Gibbons, M. B., Crits-Christoph, P., Barber, J. P., Stirman, S. W., Gallop, R., Goldstein, S. A., . . . Ring-Kurtz, S. R. (2009). Unique and common mechanisms of change across cognitive and dynamic psychotherapies. *Journal of Consulting and Clinical Psychology, 77*(5), 801–813.

Gold, J. (2011). Attachment theory and psychotherapy integration: an introduction and review of the literature. *Journal of Psychotherapy Integration, 21*(3), 221–213.

Greenberg, J. R., & Mitchell, S. A. (1983). *Object relations in psychoanalytic theory*. Cambridge, MA: Harvard University Press.

Greenberg, L. (2001). *Emotion-focused therapy: Coaching clients to work through feelings*. Washington, DC: American Psychological Association.

Greenberg, L. (2007). Emotion and cognition in psychotherapy: The transforming power of affect. *Canadian Psychology, 49*, 49–59.

Hanson, W. E., & Claiborn, C. D. (2006). Effects of test interpretation style and favorability in the counseling process. *Journal of Counseling & Development, 84*, 349–357.

Hanson, W. E., Claiborn, C. D., & Kerr, B. (1997). Differential effects of two test interpretation styles: A field study. *Journal of Counseling Psychology, 44*, 400–405.

Hanson, W. E., Creswell, J. W., Plano Clark, V. L., Petska, K. S., & Creswell, J. D. (2005). Mixed methods designs in counseling psychology. *Journal of Counseling Psychology, 52*, 224–235.

Hanson, W. E., & Poston, J. M. (2011). Building confidence in psychological assessment as a therapeutic intervention: An empirically based reply to Lilienfeld, Garb, and Wood (2011). *Psychological Assessment, 23*, 1056–1062.

Hayes, S. C. (2004). Acceptance and commitment therapy. In S. C. Hayes, V. M. Follette, & M. M. Linehan (Eds.), *Mindfulness and acceptance* (pp. 1–29). New York, NY: Guilford Press.

Henriques, G. (2004). Psychology defined. *Journal of Psychology, 60*(12), 1207–1221.

Henriques, G. (2011). *A new unified theory of psychology*. New York, NY: Springer Science and Business Media. doi:10.1007/978-1-4614-0058-5

Hill, C., Johnson, M., Brinton, C., Staton, R., Sternberger, L., & Shealy. (2013, August). *The etiology of economic beliefs and values: Implications and applications from the Forum BEVI Project*. Poster presented at the annual meeting of the American Psychological Association, Honolulu, HI.

Hilsenroth, M. J., Peters, E. J., & Ackerman, S. J. (2004). The development of therapeutic alliance during psychological assessment: Patient and therapist perspectives across treatment. *Journal of Personality Assessment, 83*(3), 332–344.

Horwitz, A. (2002). *Creating mental illness*. Chicago, IL: University of Chicago Press.

Horvath, A. O., & Bedi, R. P. (2002). The alliance. In J. C. Norcross (Ed.), *Psychotherapy relationships that work: Therapist contributions and responsiveness to patients* (pp. 37–69). New York, NY: Oxford University Press.

Kelly, G. A. (1963). *A theory of personality: The psychology of personal constructs*. New York, NY: W.W. Norton & Company.

Kimble, G. A. (1984). Psychology's two cultures. *American Psychologist, 39*(8), 833–839.

Lambert, M. J. (2010). *Prevention of treatment failure: The use of measuring, monitoring, and feedback in clinical practice*. Washington, DC: American Psychological Association.

Levitt, H. M., Butler, M., & Hill, T. (2006). What clients find helpful in psychotherapy: Developing principles for facilitating moment-to-moment change. *Journal of Counseling Psychology, 53*(3), 314–324.

Levitt, H. M., Stanley, C. M., Frankel, Z., & Raina, K. (2005). An evaluation of outcome measures used in humanistic psychotherapy research: Using thermometers to weigh oranges. *The Humanistic Psychologist, 33*(2), 113–130.

Levitt, H. M., & Williams, D. C. (2010). Facilitating client change: Principles based upon experience of eminent psychotherapists. *Psychotherapy Research, 20*(3), 337–352.

Lilienfeld, S. O., Garb, H. N., & Wood, J. M. (2011). Unresolved questions concerning the effectiveness of psychological assessment as a therapeutic intervention: Comment on Poston and Hanson (2010). *Psychological Assessment, 23,* 1047–1055. doi:10.1037/a0025177

Linehan, M. M. (1993). *Cognitive-behavioral treatment of borderline personality disorder.* New York, NY: Guilford Press.

Luborsky, L. (1984). *Principles of psychoanalytic psychotherapy: A manual for supportive-expressive treatment.* New York, NY: Basic Books.

Luborsky, L., & Crits-Christoph, P. (1998). *Understanding transference: The Core Conflictual Relationship Theme method* (2nd ed.). Washington, DC: American Psychological Association.

Magnavita, J. J. (2010). Methods, components, and strategies of unified treatment: Using evidence and personality systematics to enhance outcome. In J. J. Magnavita (Ed.), *Evidence-based treatment of personality dysfunction: Principles, methods, processes* (pp. 253–285). Washington, DC: American Psychological Association.

Magnavita, J., & Achin, J. (2013). *Unifying psychotherapy: Principles, methods, and evidence from clinical science.* New York, NY: Springer Publishing.

Mahoney, M. J. (2003). *Constructive psychotherapy: A practical guide.* New York, NY: The Guilford Press.

Mander, G. (2000). *A psychodynamic approach to brief therapy.* New York, NY: Sage.

May, R. (1958). The origins and significance of the existential movement in psychology. In R. May, E. Anger, & H. F. Ellenberger (Eds.), *Existence: A new dimension in psychiatry and psychology* (pp. 3–36). New York: NY: Basic Books. doi:10.1037/1132-001

McAdams, D. P. (2006). The problem of narrative coherence. *Journal of Constructivist Psychology, 19*(2), 109–125.

McAdams, D. P., & Pals, J. L. (2006). A new big five: Fundamental principles for an integrative science of personality. *American Psychologist, 61*(3), 204–217. doi:10.1037/0003-006X61.3.204

Merriam, S. B. (2009). *Qualitative research: A guide to design and implementation.* San Francisco, CA: Jossey-Bass.

Mikulincer, M., & Shaver, P. R. (2007). *Attachment in adulthood: Structure, dynamics, and change.* New York, NY: Guilford Press.

Morrow, S. L. (2005). Quality and trustworthiness in qualitative research in counseling psychology. *Journal of Counseling Psychology, 52*(2), 250–260. doi:10.1037/0022-0167.52.2.250

Napolitano, L. A., & McKay, D. (2007). Dichotomous thinking in borderline personality disorder. *Cognitive Therapy and Research, 31,* 717–726. doi:10.1007/s10608-007-91234

Nichols, M. P. (2011). *The essentials of family therapy* (5th ed.). Boston, MA: Allyn & Bacon.

Norcross, J. C. (Ed.). (2002). *Psychotherapeutic relationships that work: Therapist contributions and responsiveness to patients.* New York, NY: Oxford University Press.

Norcross, J. C. (2005). A primer on psychotherapy integration. In J. C. Norcross & M. R. Goldried (Eds.), *Handbook of psychotherapy integration* (pp. 3–23). New York, NY: Oxford University Press, Inc.

Nudel, C. (Ed.). (2009). *Firewalkers: Madness, beauty & mystery.* Charlottesville, VA: VOCAL.

Oshio, A. (2009). Development and validation of the dichotomous thinking inventory. *Social Behavior and Personality, 37*(6), 729–742. doi:10.2224/sbp.2009.36.6.729

Perry, B. L. (2011). The labeling paradox: Stigma, the sick role, and social networks in mental illness, *Journal of Health and Social Behavior, 52*(4), 460–477.

Perls, F. (2010). Self, ego, id, and personality. *International Gestalt Journal, 33*(1), 115–132. (Originally published in 1951).

Pervin, L. A. (2002). *Current controversies and issues in personality* (3rd ed.). Danvers, MA: John Wiley & Sons, Inc.

Poston, J. M. (2012). *Path analysis of attachment style and therapeutic assessment outcomes* (Unpublished doctoral dissertation). Purdue University, West Lafayette, IN.

Poston, J. M., & Hanson, W. E. (2010). Meta-analysis of psychological assessment as a therapeutic intervention, *Psychological Assessment, 22*(2), 203–212.

Pouchly, C. A. (2011). A narrative review: Arguments for a collaborative approach in mental health between traditional healers and clinicians regarding spiritual beliefs. *Mental Health, Religion & Culture, 15*(1), 65–85.

Priel, B. (2009). Bakhtin and Winnicott on dialogue, self, and cure. *Psychoanalytic Dialogues: The International Journal of Relational Perspectives, 9*(4), 487–503.

Quinn, D. M., & Chaudoir, S. R. (2009). Living with a concealable stigmatized identity: The impact of anticipated stigma, centrality, salience, and cultural stigma on psychological distress and health. *American Personality and Social Psychology, 97*(4), 634–651.

Rank, O. (1952). *The myth of the birth of the hero: A psychological interpretation of mythology* (F. Robins & S. E. Jelliffe, Trans.). New York, NY: Robert Brunner. (Originally published in 1914).

Rennie, D. L. (2004). Reflexivity and person centered counseling. *Journal of Humanistic Psychology, 44*(2), 182–203. doi:10.1177/0022167804263066

Riegel, K. F. (1976). The dialectics of human development. *American Psychologist, 31*(10), 689–700.

Riddle, B. C., Byers, C. C., & Grimesey, J. L. (2002). Literature review of research and practice in collaborative assessment. *The Humanistic Psychologist, 30,* 33–48.

Ridley, C. R., Li, L. C., & Hill, C. L. (1998). Multicultural assessment: Reexamination, reconceptualization, and practical application. *The Counseling Psychologist, 26,* 827–910. doi:10.1177/0011000098266001

Richards, L. (2009). *Handling qualitative data: A practical guide* (2nd ed.). Thousand Oaks, CA: Sage.

Rogers, C. R. (1951). Where are we going in clinical psychology? *Journal of Consulting Psychology, 15*(3), 171–177. doi:10.1037/h0059653

Roseborough, D. (2006). Psychodynamic psychotherapy: An effectiveness study. *Research on Social Work Practice, 16*(2), 166–175.

Schielke, H. J., Fishman, J. L., Osatuke, K., & Stiles, W. B. (2009). Creative consensus on interpretations of qualitative data: The ward method. *Psychotherapy Research, 19*(4–5), 558–565.

Shafranske, E. P. (Ed.). (1996). *Religion and the clinical practice of psychology.* Washington, DC: APA Books.

Shealy, C. N. (1995). From Boys Town to Oliver Twist: Separating fact from fiction in welfare reform and out-of-home placement of children and youth. *American Psychologist, 50*(8), 565–580.

Shealy, C. N. (2004). A model and method for "making" a combined-integrated psychologist: Equilintegration (EI) Theory and the Beliefs, Events, and Values Inventory (BEVI). *Journal of Clinical Psychology, 60*(10), 1065–1090.

Shealy, C. N. (2005). Justifying the justification hypothesis: Scientific humanism, Equilintegration (EI) Theory, and the Beliefs, Events, and Values inventory (BEVI). *Journal of Clinical Psychology, 61*(1), 81–106.

Shealy, C. N. (2015). *The Beliefs, Events, and Values Inventory (BEVI): Overview, implications, and guidelines.* Test manual. Harrisonburg, VA: Author.

Shealy, C. N. (Ed.). (2016). *Making sense of beliefs and values.* New York, NY: Springer Publishing.

Shealy, C. N., Bhuyan, D., & Sternberger, L. G. (2012). Cultivating the capacity to care in children and youth: Implications from EI theory, EI Self, and BEVI. In U. Nayar (Ed.), *Child and adolescent mental health* (pp. 240–255). New Delhi, India: Sage Publications.

Shealy, C. N., Cobb, H. C., Crowley, S. L., Nelson, P., & Peterson, G. (2004). Back to our future? The consensus conference and combined-integrated model of doctoral training in professional psychology. *Journal of Clinical Psychology, 60*(9), 893–909.

Skinner, B. F. (1947). "Superstition" in the pigeon. *Journal of Experimental Psychology, 38,* 168–172. Retrieved from http://psychclassics.yorku.ca/Skinner/Pigeon/

Spiro, L. (2009). Lauren's story. In C. Nudel (Ed.), *Firewalkers: Madness, beauty, & mystery* (pp. 14–33). Charlottesville, VA: VOCAL.

Steele, H., Steele, M., & Murphy, A. (2009). Use of adult attachment interview to measure process change in psychotherapy. *Psychotherapy Research, 19*(6), 633–643.

Strupp, H. H., & Binder, J. L. (1984). *Psychotherapy in a new key: A guide to time limited dynamic psychotherapy.* New York, NY: Basic Books.

Tabit, M., Cozen, J., Dyjak-Leblank, K., Pendleton, C., Shealy, C., Sternberger, L., & Staton, R. (2011, June). *The sociocultural impact of denial: Empirical evidence from the Forum BEVI Project.* Poster presented at American Psychological Association, Washington, DC.

Vukman, K. B. (2005). Developmental differences in metacognition and their connections with cognitive development in adulthood. *Journal of Adult Development, 12*(4), 211–221.

Young, J. E., Klosko, J. S., & Weishaar, M. E. (2003). *Schema therapy: A practitioner's guide.* New York, NY: The Guilford Press.

Wachtel, P. L. (1997). *Psychoanalysis, behavior therapy, and the relational world.* Washington, DC: American Psychological Association.

Wampold, B. E. (2001). *The great psychotherapy debate: Model, methods, and findings.* New York, NY: Routledge.

Wampold, B. E. (2010). The research evidence for common factors models: A historically situated perspective. In B. L. Duncan & S. D. Miller (Eds.), *The heart and soul of change: Delivering what works in therapy* (2nd ed., pp. 49–81). Washington, DC: American Psychological Association.

Ward, R. M. (2008). Assessee and assessor experiences of significant events in psychological assessment feedback. *Journal of Personality Assessment, 90,* 307–322.

Warwar, S. H., Links, P. S., Greenberg, L., & Bergmans, Y. (2008). Emotion-focused principles for working with borderline personality disorder. *Journal of Psychiatric Practice, 14*(2), 94–104.

Watson, J. B. (1913). Psychology as the behaviorist views it. *Psychological Review, 20,* 158–177. Retrieved from http://psychclassics.yorku.ca/Watson/views.htm

Wells, A. (2009). *Metacognitive therapy for anxiety and depression.* New York, NY: Guilford Press.

Wolfe, J., Brady, J. P., Serber, M., Agras, W. S., & Liberman, R. P. (1973). The current status of systematic desensitization. *American Journal of Psychiatry, 130*(9), 961–965.

Wolitzky, D. L., & Eagle, M. N. (1997). Psychoanalytic theories of psychotherapy. In P. L. Wachtel & S. B. Messer (Eds.), *Theories of psychotherapy* (pp. 39–96). Washington, DC: American Psychological Association.

Wu, P., & Chiou, W. (2008). Postformal thinking and creativity among late adolescents: A post-Piagetian approach. *Adolescence, 43*(170), 237–251.

EXHIBIT A

BEVI FOCUS GROUP:
INTRODUCTION AND QUESTIONS

INTRODUCTION

Today we are hoping to gather some information about your experience thus far in using the BEVI in clinical practice, including both therapy and assessment cases. Over the next 30 to 60 minutes, we are going to ask you to tell us about what this process has been like for you, as well as what you think it may have been like for the client based on feedback they provided to you, their responses to the BEVI, and your experience with them in the room. There are no "right" or "wrong" answers. The responses you provide will be confidential in the sense that the researchers will only identify you by number and not by name. We ask that you be as open as possible in providing your responses and are respectful of the other group members.

QUESTIONS

Prior to Administration

1. Prior to administering the BEVI to your clients, how did you frame the instrument to them and what was their response to this possibility?
2. *If you administered the BEVI to a therapy client.* . .How did the BEVI relate to your own understanding of therapeutic work? In other words, what aspects of the BEVI relate most to the actual process of preparing to conduct therapy?
3. *If you administered the BEVI to an assessment client.* . .Based upon your understanding of the BEVI, what information were you hoping to gain from adding this measure to an assessment battery?

After Administration

Administer a handout with each of the BEVI scales and/or direct them to explanatory information at www.thebevi.com.

Please take a minute to read this document, which reviews each of the BEVI scales. Because you are participating in this focus group, you have discussed the BEVI and its interpretation with the developer of the BEVI, have engaged in the administration of the BEVI, and have attempted to use the BEVI in assessment and/or therapy with your client.

1. For those of you who received a "blind" interpretation of the BEVI by its developer (in other words, the developer of the BEVI did not know anything about the client except the scale profile), what was your experience of the blind interpretation you received?
2. How helpful and relevant was this "blind" interpretation to understanding your client in assessment and/or therapy?
3. How did you use information from the BEVI in your work with clients?
4. What was the clients' reaction to the BEVI?
5. From your perspective, how is the BEVI similar, different, or complementary to other forms of assessment in the context of therapy and/or assessment?

6. What seem to be the main contributions of the BEVI to your therapeutic and/or assessment work?
7. From the standpoint of education and training, has the BEVI and its underlying theoretical and empirical framework helped you reflect upon or further your own process of growth and development as a mental health professional?
8. From an interprofessional standpoint, how might the BEVI facilitate collaboration (e.g., case formulation, treatment planning) across different providers or disciplines?
9. Are there other settings, populations, or applications that you think would be particularly well suited to the BEVI?
10. In summary, what do you think are the major themes or points that have emerged from our discussion? Is there anything else you would like to add regarding your experience of the BEVI and its usage in practice?

EXHIBIT B

CODE BOOK FOR CLINICIAN FOCUS GROUPS

Causal Connections

Child Theme 1—Cognitions, Emotions, Behavior

Criteria: The measure's usefulness in providing an understanding of the causal connections between cognitions, emotions, and behaviors.

Example: I think it was particularly helpful with the assessment client that I'm working with now in terms of explaining some of what was going on with her, some of the reasons that she might be internalizing a lot of her emotions. . .For example, beliefs about how a woman should be, not expressing anger, holding everything in, that type of thing. (FG2)

Child Theme 2—Self and Other

Criteria: The measure's usefulness in providing an understanding of the causal connections between the client's beliefs, values, and attitudes and his or her relationships.

Example: Another person has used it in interpersonal relationships in trying to reflect on why at times he can trigger certain responses in people. (FG1)

Child Theme 3—Past and Present

Criteria: The measure's usefulness in providing an understanding of how the client's past affects his or her present self and experience.

Example: The BEVI certainly opens up discussion for how maybe you were this way, and became this way. (FG2)

Child Theme 4—Deeper Understanding

Criteria: The BEVI's use in helping the therapist and client to "make sense" of the client's experience, to create a coherent picture.

Note 1: What differentiates responses that fall into this code from those that fall into "Big Picture" is that these responses focus solely on coherency and understanding whereas the responses that belong to "Big Picture" focus both on coherency and breadth.

Big Picture

Criteria: The measure's helpfulness in developing a broad, holistic, and integrated frame. The two main elements contained in these responses are breadth and integration.

1. Breadth: It is a big picture and covers a broader range of information (the idea of breadth emerges again in the theme "Broader Range of Information").
2. Integration: It fits together as a whole. It is a coherent picture that "makes sense" (the idea of coherency emerges again in the theme "Causal Connections").

Example: It was just really interesting to see how those things fit together in. . .a visual graphic. (FG1)

Note 2: The reason this code is a child code of "Making Causal Connections" and not a separate code altogether is that these notions are logically intertwined. It is difficult to imagine gaining insight *without* making causal connections. This conclusion is borne out by the fact that most of the responses that included understanding either implicitly or explicitly refer to the causal connections between different factors.

Example: Using the framework of the BEVI and going over some of that data with her she was better able to make sense of herself, and her life, and how she had gotten to where she was in her life. (FG2)

Nonpathologizing

Criteria: The measure's usefulness in developing a nonpathologizing frame that allows the therapist to focus on the client's strengths and resources as well as areas of difficulty.

Example: It isn't pathologizing and it isn't necessarily threatening but it feels so informative as opposed to labeling. (FG2)

Openness, Defensiveness, and the Ability to Self Reflect

Criteria: How the measure helps to assess the client's openness, defensiveness, and the ability to self reflect.

Example: (The results) didn't fit my own conceptualizing, I would be like "oh!" I didn't know if I would find that person necessarily. . .open in the ways that. . .(the BEVI). . .reflected and showed. (FG1)

Client Engagement

Criteria: How the measure can be useful in increasing the client's motivation and engagement with the therapeutic process.

Example: I think it was helpful for them to kind of see, because it's something about them having entered the information themselves and having it reflected back to them kind of without my filter. (FG1)

Sharing the Conceptualization

Criteria: How the measure can be useful in framing the conceptualization for the client in a therapeutic manner.

Example: Helping with the conceptualization of your client for yourself and then also how to share that with the client in a way that is going. . .to create movement and be therapeutic for them. (FG1)

Broader Range of Information

Child Theme 1: Capturing the Information

Criteria: How the measure can capture a broad range of information. The theme of breadth was also covered in "Big Picture." The difference here is that the factor integration/coherency is not as emphasized (i.e., emphasis is not solely on the breadth aspect).

Example: It really does sort of flush out other factors that may not show up in other measures. (FG2)

Child Theme 2: Using the Information

Criteria: How the measure can be used to bring this information into the therapy process.
Example: (It was) providing an opening for talking about those things. (FG1)

Flexibility

Criteria: How the measure is flexible. This flexibility may occur on multiple levels (e.g., theoretical approaches, different populations, different functions).
Example: I've also seen the potential of using it with couples as well, who we don't get to work with a lot. But I do think that would be a tremendous tool to put two steps together, to kind of compare and contrast, I'm sort of moving on a little bit. . .(inaudible). . .within the different family systems, umm, different relationships as well. (FG1)

Accuracy of BEVI Blind Interpretation (Validity)

Criteria: The ability of the blind interpreter to review the profile resulting from a BEVI administration and accurately capture the client's presentation.
Example: Well for the assessment client that I was working with, I mean, it was pretty spot on actually. . .for the most part 95% she really resonated with. (FG2)

Validating for the Therapist

Criteria: How using the measure can be validating for the therapist and useful in increasing the therapist's motivation and engagement in the therapy process.
Example: I think sometimes you get exhausted. . .But. . .I think being able to see that there are some areas that are making growth possible, I think for me it was kind of a little like, because I think sometimes we can get real jaded when we're working with clients week after week so seeing particular scale of openness for me with that one particular client when I was started to feel like Lord she's never going to make much progress but umm for me it was a rejuvenation afterward. (FG1)

EXHIBIT C

TABLE 15.1
Emergent Themes of Focus Groups 1 and 2

PARENT THEME	CHILD THEME	NUMBER OF REFERENCES
Causal Connections		13
	Cognitions, Emotions, and Behavior	4
	Self and Others	3
	Past and Present	2
	Deeper Understanding	6
Big Picture		12
Nonpathologizing and Strength-Focused		11
Broader Range of Information		10
Openness, Defensiveness, and Ability to Self Reflect		6
Increased Client Engagement		5
Sharing Conceptualizations with Client		5
Flexibility		5
Accuracy		3
Increased Therapist Engagement		3

Note. Some references may have met criteria for coding in more than one "child theme" (i.e., the number of references to "child themes" may add up to more than the total references for a "parent theme").

EXHIBIT D

TABLE 15.2

Emergent Themes of Client Responses

CATEGORY	THEME	NUMBER OF REFERENCES
Aspects of Self		28
	Self-Image/Self-Worth	7
	Affirming/Validating	3
	Complexity	4
	Self-Reflection	4
	Discomfort	3
	Changing Aspects of Self	3
	Emotional Self	2
	Self-Knowledge	2
Values		14
	Religion	8
	Environment	3
	Where I stand	2
	Politics	1
Self and Others		11
	Self-in Relation to Others	9
	Effects of Family of Origin	1
	Community Involvement	1
No Impact		5
	No aspect of Self-became clearer	3
	Did not learn anything	2

PART IV

IMAGINING A WORLD WHERE BELIEFS AND VALUES MAKE SENSE

Craig N. Shealy

IMAGINING A WORLD WHERE BELIEFS AND VALUES MAKE SENSE: FUTURE DIRECTIONS AND FURTHER REFLECTIONS

Love recognizes no barriers. It jumps hurdles, leaps fences, penetrates walls to arrive at its destination full of hope.

—Maya Angelou

The preceding 15 chapters of *Making Sense of Beliefs and Values* are intensive to say the least, from the implications, nature, and measurement of these belief/value constructs in Part I, through the research chapters in Part II (culture, development, environment, gender, politics, and religion), and the practice chapters of Part III (assessment, education, forensics, leadership, and psychotherapy). By way of summary and conclusion, then, a two-track approach is adopted in Part IV, this final chapter, which includes (a) consideration of research questions and practice applications that are in progress or could be pursued in the future and (b) a big picture view of how the world might look if we were to adopt a habit of "making sense of beliefs and values" as a matter of course.

In terms of future directions, as of this writing, multiple projects are under way in the United States and internationally that build upon the work described in this book, including, but not limited to:

- An examination of the beliefs and values of established and aspiring leaders via the Beliefs, Events, and Values Inventory (BEVI) and Equilintegration (EI) Leadership Model (e.g., young leaders in the Middle East)
- Comparing cross-country/regional predictors and processes of belief/value change across a range of populations, settings, and contexts (e.g., Asia versus North America)
- University-wide and longitudinal assessment that samples the entire student body, which juxtaposes the BEVI with other institutional measures, allowing us to focus deeply on a wide range of mediators and moderators of learning, growth, and development over time
- Interpretation of BEVI "full scale" and "domain" scores—in addition to scale scores—with different populations (e.g., examining the interaction between Time 1, Time 2, and Time 3 group reports, and high, medium, and low full scale scores)

- Seeking to operationalize—theoretically and empirically—what is meant by the construct of "global identity"
- And as a final example, continuing usage of the BEVI in the mental health and forensic realms (e.g., to inform comprehensive psychological evaluations; to understand and further various therapeutic goals via the BEVI report system for individuals, groups, and couples)[1]

In contemplating other such future directions, it may be helpful to review the recommendations that emerged from the six research and five practice chapters that were discussed in Parts II and III of this book. Of course, the four chapters of Part I—which include *Our Belief in Belief* (Chapter 1), *Beliefs, Needs, and Self: Three Components of the EI Model* (Chapter 2), *The EI Self: Real World Implications and Applications of EI Theory* (Chapter 3), and *Beliefs, Events, and Values Inventory (BEVI)* (Chapter 4)—inform the chapters that follow in Parts II and III. As such, in this final chapter, we first review the summary recommendations for research and practice that were presented in these chapters, which should be considered food for thought rather than an exhaustive listing of all "future directions."[2]

MAKING SENSE OF BELIEFS AND VALUES: SUMMARY OF RECOMMENDATIONS FOR RESEARCH

In **Chapter 5—*In Search of Best Practices for Multicultural Education***—Tabit, Legault, Ma, and Wan (2016) analyze Time 1/Time 2 BEVI data from a required multicultural education course, which appears to be associated with findings that significantly move in the opposite direction of what was intended (e.g., less Global Engagement as measured by the BEVI at Time 2). Although acknowledging correctly that multiple factors could be responsible for such findings, the four concluding recommendations they offer seemingly would apply to multiple interventions, which seek to "change" worldviews and are worth reviewing at this point: (a) understand the etiology and nature of beliefs and values; (b) process is as important as content; (c) appraise worldviews before, during, and after an intervention; and (d) own one's beliefs and values. Among other potential "future directions," on the basis of such guidance, it would be interesting to design, implement, and evaluate the effectiveness of multicultural education courses or programs that strive for fidelity with these four guidelines (the *Making Sense of Beliefs and Values* course, described later in this chapter, offers one possibility in this regard). Among other implications, such a course would include a strong self/group assessment and process-based component that is focused not so much on *what* beliefs and values are "correct" or "preferable" vis-à-vis matters of race, ethnicity, or culture, but *why* we come to acquire the beliefs and values that we do regarding such matters. Ideally, such a focus would facilitate both sustained personal reflection and group-based dialogue. The overarching goal here would be to normalize the fact that we differ in our beliefs and values, while discussing why that is so, not to condone such differences when they manifest in racist or otherwise prejudicial beliefs, but to use

---

[1] Individuals who are interested in the possibility of BEVI usage should contact us directly at bevi@thebevi.com

[2] To ensure fidelity with the original conclusions and/or recommendations, aspects of the following "future directions" are excerpted and/or adapted from the content of respective chapters in this book.

such observations as a point of departure for larger processes of reflection and discussion throughout the duration of the learning experience. As Tabit et al. (2016) note, this type of process is likely to unfold in a more constructive manner—consistent with the good and necessary objectives of such learning experiences (e.g., courses, workshops, seminars)—if instructors are able and willing to acknowledge their own motives regarding such experiences (e.g., why they are interested in serving in such a role) as well as their own life histories, backgrounds, and beliefs (as appropriate, of course), that reasonably could explain such interests. To quote from the conclusion of their chapter,

> the capacity for prejudice and misuse of power is part of the human condition, and not the purview of any one group. Wise multicultural interventionists acknowledge and communicate such realities. Their audiences are likely to appreciate and resonate with such self-aware candor. In short, as educators, researchers, and practitioners, we must recognize that we are not somehow immune to the same biasing forces and factors that shape all human beings, and should acknowledge and account for these very real possibilities in ourselves, in the roles we assume, pedagogies we develop, and interventions we deliver. (p. 200)

Chapter 6—*Identity Development and the Construction of Self: Findings and Implications from the Forum BEVI Project*—offers an in-depth and data-based examination of the processes and outcomes through which "identity" is constructed, with a particular focus on Identity Diffusion from the BEVI, which appears to measure,

> the degree to which an individual is undifferentiated from parents, experiences a foreclosed identity, reports a troubled childhood, feels little agency or ability to affect change, reports odd or unusual etiological perspectives, and is searching but feels helpless, lost, and confused. (see Chapter 4)

Among other implications of this work, Spaeth, Schwartz, Nayar, and Ma (2016) offer a theoretically and empirically grounded framework for understanding "what a 'healthier' identity may look like, how Identity Diffusion relates to other core aspects of self (e.g., emotional capacity; engagement with 'different' others), and how antecedent variables influence the level to which an individual may experience Identity Diffusion" (p. 224). In addition to other research implications, one clear "future direction" is articulated by these authors as follows:

> although correlation matrix data suggest overall that a high degree of Identity Diffusion is a manifestation of maladjustment (e.g., insofar as it is associated with a lack of emotional attunement and interest/caring for others, and the larger world), it may be that higher Identity Diffusion also may be a "symptom" of youth, for selected subsets of this population. Present data do not allow for a detailed examination of this possibility, but future research may productively examine the correlates of Identity Diffusion from a cross-sectional and longitudinal perspective. (p. 224)

More broadly, Spaeth et al. (2016) offer three additional conclusions regarding future research possibilities, which are excerpted and summarized as follows: (a) in scholarly examinations of identity, we should focus upon questions of *what* and *how* (e.g., our emphasis should not only include what differentiates individuals in terms of identity outcomes, but the process-based variables that are associated with how such identity becomes codified as it does); (b) the definition of what we mean by a "healthy" or "developed" sense of identity should be explicated, empirically and theoretically (e.g., if in fact we are saying that some identity codifications are "more" or "less" "healthy," it behooves us to describe how and why such conclusions may be reached); these authors begin to do so, but more work in this regard is necessary, perhaps initially by comparing and contrasting high versus low full scale scorers on the BEVI; and (c) the construct of "identity" should be understood in relation to over-arching and encompassing aspects of self (e.g., this point, emphasized in Chapter 2 and at various points throughout this book, suggests that a core organizing construct such as identity must include an emphasis on multiple aspects of functioning, includ-ing but not necessarily limited to affective, behavioral, cognitive, contextual, and developmental variables).

Chapter 7—*Environmental Beliefs and Values: In Search of Models and Methods*—begins, as its title suggests, with an overview of prominent models and methods for assessing environmental/ecological beliefs and values by noting (as do many authors in this book) that there is a deep need for greater clarity, consistency, and coherence at fundamental levels of definition and assessment. More specifically, on the basis of their review, Kelly, Holt, Patel, & Nolet (2016) provide,

> five recommendations for scholarship in this area: (a) offer a rationale for selected terminology; (b) differentiate selected terminology; (c) ensure a linkage between terminology and measures; (d) examine not only what people believe and value about the environment, but why, by considering questions of etiology and individual differences; and (e) understand how environmental beliefs and values are related to the varied ways in which human beings experience self, others, and the larger world. (p. 254)

Through three studies, the authors focus next on how the EI model and BEVI method may help address such recommendations "by apprehending and measuring the complex and interacting processes by which environmental beliefs and values are acquired, maintained, and transformed" (p. 254). Based upon these findings, Kelly et al. offer six implications that may be of relevance to research and practice in the future. These are as follows:

> (a) understand the role of "spirituality" regarding beliefs and experiences of the natural world; (b) further examine how formative variables (e.g., life history, demographics) affect our beliefs and behaviors vis-à-vis the natural world; (c) explicate, theoretically and empirically, why one's gender appears to be pre-dictive of a pro- or anti-environmental stance; (d) consider what it is about the underlying belief/value commitments that are implied by one's political orien-tation, which also appear to be associated with one's attendant environmental stance; (e) examine why greater openness in general (e.g., to one's emotional world, other cultures) also tends to be associated with a greater inclination to express care and concern for the environment; and finally, (f) at an applied level, we suggest that the theory and data presented here have implications, in gen-eral, for how we "teach" about environmentalism in the classroom, and more specifically, to the explication of underlying beliefs and values that are relevant to Education for Sustainability (EfS) and Education for Sustainable Develop-ment (ESD, 2013), both locally and globally. (p. 255)

It is difficult to imagine an area of emphasis that is of greater import to us all than protecting the viability of the natural systems that sustain life. Perhaps ongoing research along these lines may help us understand better how, why, and under what circumstances proenvironmental beliefs, values, and behaviors may be operationalized and facilitated in research and practice as well as inculcated and expressed in the real world.

Along with the environmental and ecological issues summarized earlier, **Chapter 8**—*Understanding the Gendered Self: Implications from EI Theory, the EI Self, and the BEVI*—represents another top priority emphasis, both locally and globally, if we are to "make sense of beliefs and values," and translate such understanding into more sustainable actions, policies, and practices around the world. Pendleton, Cochran, Kapadia, and Iyer (2016) maintain as much when stating, at the outset of their chapter, that

> beliefs and values about "gender" are among the most pressing of our time. Why? Because even a cursory review of headlines any day of the week will reveal that what we believe about gender affects all aspects of existence, from the assumptions we harbor for why men and women do what they do; to our predilection for supporting rights in the name of gender; to our inclination to condone, tolerate, or abhor gender-based violence; to our capacity for experiencing and expressing intimacy in our relationships. (p. 261)

In the comprehensive discussion that follows, Pendleton et al. (2016) focus on seven interrelated levels of analysis: (a) an overview of literature on the construct of gender; (b) the formative variables (e.g., life history, demographics) that theoretically and empirically have been linked to the development of gender identity as well as how our beliefs and values regarding gender have evolved over time; (c) how and why male gender identity develops as it does; (d) why and how men and women are socialized to experience and express affect differently as well as the consequences of such processes for gender relations; (e) examination of the "gendered self" vis-à-vis actions, policies, and practices around the world; (f) presentation of results from the Forum BEVI Project in order to explore the relationship between antecedents and outcomes of gender traditionalism; and (g) how the EI model and BEVI method may be used in "the real world"—to help the genders understand why they believe what they believe about "who" men and women are and should be, both individually and in their relationships together. Of the many research and practice "future directions" of such work, we need to understand better the formative variables that are associated with relative degrees of "gender traditionalism." We then need to translate such knowledge into accessible (i.e., minimally threatening and maximally constructive) educational and process-based interventions that may help the genders understand *why* they "become what they become" and *how* we might better raise "the gendered self" in a manner that is more congruent with what we actually need as human beings, irrespective of gender.

In **Chapter 9**—*Exploring the Etiology of Ideology: In Search of the Political Self through the EI Model and BEVI Method*—Edmunds, Federico, and Mays (2016) delve deeply into the partisan morass that presently characterizes political life in the United States and in many countries around the world, beginning with the following data-based perspective from the Pew Research Center: *Values and basic beliefs are more polarized along partisan lines than at any point in the past 25 years.* In their thoughtful analysis of such matters, Edmunds et al. (2016) review a range of literatures including theory and research on the construct of ideology, a comparison of various political ideologies, and a range of research programs regarding the nature and etiology of such ideological preferences before presenting as series of empirical findings. On the basis of such literature and analyses, their three "summary observations" provide a number of possibilities for future research as well as opportunities for real world dialogue and engagement across partisan aisles. First, *depth matters* (e.g., essentially, from the standpoint of theory and assessment, it is important to go beyond basic differentiating variables such as "the role of government," to focus on underlying affective and attributional processes, which speak to matters of how, and why, political identity becomes structured in the way that it does). Second, *interactions matter* (e.g., it is not sufficient, and may be inaccurate, to conclude that Democrats or Republicans are inclined toward specific ideological commitments; rather, as with religious orthodoxy versus religious fundamentalism, it is quite possible empirically that there may be greater within- than between-group variability, an outcome that will not be revealed unless interacting factors, such as formative variables, are taken into account in our approach to research assessment and design). Third, *self-preservation matters* (e.g., related to the preceding two points, in research on political ideology, and in the service of grappling more constructively with political divisiveness, it may be helpful to remember that political affiliations are determined by factors that largely are outside of our conscious awareness). As Edmunds et al. (2016) conclude,

> it may be more difficult to vilify "the other" if we appreciate the possibility that our political inclinations are nothing more or less than an expression of how we are organized at the level of our core self. That is not to say that change to our political affiliations is neither possible nor desirable, just that it stands to reason why we fight for our preferred political parties, since we really are fighting to protect and preserve the viability and coherence of underlying psychological structures, of which we may or may not be aware. . . Thus, in seeking to comprehend the etiology of ideology, it likely will help if we include an examination of why and how the political self comes to be structured as it does. Likewise, if we focus not only on *what* divides us, but *why*, it seems more likely that our conceptual frameworks, predictive models, and policy solutions will be that much more likely to possess ecological validity and real world meaning, for scholars, policy makers, and the public at large. (p. 325)

Chapter 10—*The Nature and Etiology of Religious Certitude: Implications of the EI Framework and Beliefs, Events, and Values Inventory*—examines yet another defining issue of our day, by examining the factors and forces that are associated with one's relative degree of "certainty" vis-à-vis religious beliefs and values. In a wide-ranging exploration of such matters, Brearly, van den Bos, and Tan (2016) follow their review of theoretical and empirical literatures and subsequent analyses with five concluding recommendations. First, in exploring certitude generally, and religious certitude in particular, it is important to operationalize our definitions (e.g., to avoid confusion and promote discourse, scholars should be explicit regarding item loadings as well as the conceptual and empirical relationships among related measures). Second, psychological constructs may be understood better by researching who is, and is not, likely to embody them (e.g., to understand the nature and validity of our constructs, it is important to conduct a detailed analysis of self-report characteristics). Third, a tendency toward socioreligious certitude appears predictive of a wide range of self structures (e.g., it is important to apprehend beliefs about religion as one manifestation of a larger network of inclinations toward other matters, such as the environment, while also examining the predictive role of life history and other formative variables in the interplay of such convictions). Fourth, within-group differences may be greater than between-group differences, which suggests the need to eschew stereotypes about religious and nonreligious people (e.g., it may well be that some subgroups of self-reported "Christians" actually have more in common with subgroups of self-reported "atheists" or "agnostics" than with other subgroups of "Christians"—thus, in research and practice, one should avoid stereotyping members of a self-reporting group as all being like-minded). Fifth, the relative degree of religious or nonreligious certitude an individual expresses may be highly determined, but in a complex, interacting, and nonlinear manner (e.g., congruent with the preceding point, in research on the etiology of religious certitude, it is important to account for a wide range of interactions among formative variables, in recognition that similar outcomes may be due to different combinations of factors).

Based upon their work, another "future direction" could be the further exploration of self-reported "agnosticism," since preliminary evidence from this chapter suggests that such an affiliation may be associated not only with a greater tendency to see the world in shades of "gray" (as opposed to black and white), but ironically, also to evidence greater expressed care for issues that typically are seen to fall within the purview of a Christian orientation (e.g., caring for the poor). At a related level of analysis, it would be interesting to examine whether the same dichotomy discussed by these authors between "fundamentalist" and "orthodox" Christians might show alignment with an "agnostic" sensibility (e.g., are orthodox Christians psychologically organized—from the standpoint of the BEVI or other measures—in a manner that actually is more congruent with the organizational structure of self-reported "agnostics," in contrast to fundamentalist "Christians" or for that matter, individuals who strongly align with an "atheist" worldview).

A final and real world implication from this chapter emerges from its focus on cross-cultural religious education. From the standpoint of research, it would be very interesting to examine whether a religious education program that is designed in a manner that is recommended (e.g., exposing people to religious perspectives while also encouraging critical thinking and open-mindedness) would result in outcomes that are "better" than traditional, single-religion education programs. Obviously, it would be necessary to operationalize what is meant by "better"—and the authors do provide considerable guidance in that regard—not only at the level of content, but how such content is delivered. From the standpoint of the EI model and BEVI method, a related study could investigate whether there are self-selection and other predictive variables that not only influence who is and is not inclined toward the cross-cultural or single-culture approach to religious education, but whether such pretest "interest" variables actually predict posttest "satisfaction" indexes. Looking around our world, which so often is inflamed by strident adherence to one religious tradition or another, it is worth reflecting upon the following perspective from their conclusion, which has implications for how we design and assess religious education and interfaith dialogue programs:

> what is recommended most is the cultivation of a culture of humble curiosity and respectful exploration in which individuals may interact with those who hold a different religious or nonreligious perspective in an honest, authentic, inquiring, and intellectually responsible manner. Perhaps, if we strive to nurture psyches that are less inclined toward certitude, human beings will be freer to exercise religious faith or nonreligious faith on the basis of a richly earned awareness of why one does or does not believe as one does. By bravely

accepting that definitive claims seem untenable—particularly regarding matters that appear to transcend the bounds of empirical reasoning—we may best be prepared for open engagement with self, others, and the larger world. (p. 365)

MAKING SENSE OF BELIEFS AND VALUES: SUMMARY OF RECOMMENDATIONS FOR PRACTICE

One of the overarching goals of this book was to try and create a synergistic relationship between research and practice in order to inform each of these domains through the values and epistemologies of the other. So, research chapters would include practice implications (e.g., recommendations for how to apply findings to real world settings and populations) and practice chapters would include a research component (e.g., by gathering and/or presenting actual quantitative or qualitative findings that illuminated practice implications). In discussing "future directions," then, moving from Part II (Research) to Part III (Practice) chapters, our focus will remain on possibilities for moving forward in this reciprocal manner, beginning with **Chapter 11—*The Beliefs, Events, and Values Inventory (BEVI): Psychological Assessment Implications and Applications*.** In their detailed analysis of how the BEVI has been and may be used within the domain of psychological assessment, Coates, Hanson, Samuel, Webster, and Cozen (2016) follow a review of multiple aspects of assessment (e.g., professional guidelines, the value-laden nature of testing and diagnosis, alternative assessment practices and interventions) with an overview of how the BEVI has been used in "the real world." Specifically, they focus on three case studies of individual, couples/family, and group-based assessment, in order to link this approach to assessment activity in the real world. As was the case with research chapters, practice chapters also sought to include a set of recommendations that may be considered in the future by practitioners and scholars alike. Coates et al. (2016) offer six such "best practices," which could inform further inquiry and application, and are as follows. First, *acknowledge human complexity* (e.g., when conducting evaluations and assigning diagnoses, clinicians should be mindful not to assume that the reasons for the same presentation—such as depression or anxiety—are at all similar in terms of the reasons for such presentations, and therefore must gather sufficient information to ensure that the reasons for, and treatments of, such presentations are tailored to the realities and needs of the individuals before them). Second, *evaluate formative variables* (e.g., related to the previous point, it is imperative that a detailed examination of life history and events is conducted as part of any evaluation that results in formulations, diagnoses, or recommendations; without such information, human beings presenting with various concerns will be de-contextualized, which could well impact the validity and appropriateness of the "treatment" that follows). Third, *eschew reductionism* (e.g., because human beings are complex, the onus is on those in a power-based position of evaluation to apprehend such complexity in order to ensure that it is not artificially reduced for whatever reason; thus, simplistic explanations such as "chemical imbalances in the brain"—which do not at least consider the possibility that real world experiences and events may more parsimoniously account for a given "symptom cluster"—are contraindicated from the standpoint of practice). Fourth, *engage clients as collaborators* (e.g., our ethical mandate to "first do no harm," is that much more likely to be realized if we strive, insofar as possible, to include our "clients" and "patients" as collaborators with us when identifying what their challenges are and how they may be addressed, in full recognition, of course, that we are educated and trained to apprehend the psychological phenomena that emerge during the course of assessment, and should not abrogate our essential role in that regard). Fifth, *value meaning making* (e.g., if we are not considering how and why our "clients" and "patients" are interpreting their situations and symptoms, we forfeit the opportunity to engage with them at this fundamental level of human existence, which has to do with why we are here and what we are doing with our lives, which may or may not bear upon the "referral question" that they bring before us). Sixth and finally, *own our epistemologies* (e.g., especially within the realm of mental health assessment writ large, it is essential that we understand and acknowledge the epistemological commitments that we inherit from the educational and training models that were emphasized during our process of professional identity development; without such awareness and accountability, we risk seeing our "clients" and "patients" through a lens that may be incomplete or biased in a manner that affects, sometimes profoundly, the diagnostic and treatment recommendations we deliver over the course of our professional lives). As Coates et al. (2016) conclude,

> even though we should strive for objectivity and all of its worthy concomitants in assessment research and practice, it behooves us to remember three final points: (a) clinicians are potentially no less biased than either the clients we evaluate or the fields in which we are trained and credentialed; (b) worthy standards of objectivity are more aspirational than realizable in any absolute sense; and (c) the privileging of data over engagement may have unintended consequences for the vulnerable people we are entrusted to understand, support, and possibly transform, as we seek to help them cultivate an honest and constructive relationship with their past, present, and future. Through ongoing reflection upon such points in our daily work, it is our hope that the assessments we render and the care we provide first do no harm, evidence humility and integrity in the "realities" we apprehend, and facilitate growth, healing, and meaning making with the human beings we serve. (pp. 399–400)

Chapter 12—*The Forum BEVI Project: Applications and Implications for International, Multicultural, and Transformative Learning*—is one of the most comprehensive chapters in the entire book, and for good reason. That is because it seeks to summarize 6 years of research and practice from the Forum BEVI Project, an initiative involving multiple institutions and organizations, which examined the processes and outcomes of international, multicultural, and transformative learning. The applications and implications of this work—reported in detail by Wandschneider et al. (2016)—offer numerous "future direction" opportunities for scholars and practitioners alike as well as administrators, educators, policy makers, and others with a stake in such matters. Because the processes and outcomes of education writ large are integral to multiple chapters in this book (e.g., dealing with culture, environment, gender, religion), the best way to summarize such work may be to list the 15 implications that arose from this initiative:

> *Implication 1. Who we are affects whether, what, and how we learn.*
> *Implication 2. Education, broadly defined, is associated with—and likely causes— change in beliefs and values.*

Implication 3. To understand how effective our interventions are, we must assess who learners are.

Implication 4. It is possible to predict who will be interested in—and satisfied by—a learning experience even before the learning experience actually occurs.

Implication 5. Specific analyses may be conducted for purposes of outreach and engagement.

Implication 6. All educators and educational experiences are not equal.

Implication 7. Educational experiences are associated with desirable as well as undesirable processes and outcomes across a wide range of constructs that must be measured to be known.

Implication 8. Examining only overall (e.g., aggregate) findings or privileging only a few BEVI scales constitute tempting but counterproductive approaches to comprehensive assessment.

Implication 9. Although distinct characteristics of various cross-cultural groups are identifiable, broad-based assessment suggests within- as well as between-group variation.

Implication 10. As Kurt Lewin observed, "there is nothing so practical as a good theory."

Implication 11. It is possible to identify the profile or signature of an institution or organization.

Implication 12. Group reports help course instructors, program directors, and administrators understand better the nature of their particular classes, cohorts, or staffs.

Implication 13. By jointly utilizing individual and group reports, multiple opportunities for self-assessment, enhanced understanding, and group development may be facilitated.

Implication 14. Changes in beliefs and values about self, others, and the world at large appear determined largely by the 7Ds (duration, difference, depth, determine, design, deliver, debrief).

Implication 15. Best practice in assessment requires best practice in research.

Each of these implications offers opportunities for further research and practice, and a number of such initiatives presently are under way. To contemplate specifics, given its comprehensive and detailed nature, it is recommended that the particulars under one or more of these implications be reviewed directly in their chapter. At a more general level, Wandschneider et al. (2016) offer the following big picture perspective regarding "future directions":

> In the final analysis, what has been most gratifying for all of us over the years is to hear so often that what we have been trying to understand and explicate through this initiative has in fact been impactful, meaningful, and relevant. Through our work, we have come to see more clearly that we are—ineluctably—*change agents* who are granted the privilege of transforming the learners who enter our educational institutions and organizations. Since we are charged to do so by the next generation of citizens—and compelled by the pressing needs and opportunities of our increasingly interdependent world—it behooves us to answer this call in a manner that is optimally informed and maximally effective. Hopefully, the implications emerging from this project, combined with ongoing collaborative research and practice in multiple local and global settings, will help us all assess international, multicultural, and transformative learning—and apply our insights and understandings—with care, capacity, and commitment in the months and years ahead. (p. 478)

In **Chapter 13**—*Justice and the Nature of Human Nature: What, Why, and How Beliefs and Values Matter*—Hart and Glick (2016) provide a wide-ranging examination of beliefs, values, and the justice system via three interrelated levels of analysis: (a) whether our system of justice really is or reasonably could be "impartial" in any genuine sense ("No," would seem to be the answer, based upon a review of multiple biasing factors, from the ways in which juries are selected to the influence of money on every aspect of the legal system); (b) beliefs about, and the etiology of, criminality (e.g., from the relationship between fundamentalist religious beliefs and a punitive approach toward criminals to all that we have learned about the sorts of historical variables and developmental trajectories that are associated with "who" engages in criminal conduct, and under what circumstances); and (c) how it is possible to work with beliefs and values in a constructive and depth-based manner within the justice system (e.g., working with 11 male felons in an intensive workshop that employed the EI model and BEVI method, and in a manner that deliberately was integrated with the *Thinking for a Change* curriculum). In terms of "future directions," the four observations that these authors provide on the basis of workshop data and feedback—against the backdrop of the larger literatures that they reviewed—bear repeating, as they suggest the need for further interventions along the lines of this workshop as well as potential directions for reform-based programs and practices, which will need accompanying evaluation strategies.

> *Observation 1: Participants very much want to discuss issues of beliefs, values, needs, and feelings, as they are at the core of who they are and want to become.*
>
> *Observation 2: The environments in which incarcerated individuals are placed seem deliberately designed to prevent the possibility of any sort of meaningful growth or development.*
>
> *Observation 3: It is helpful to ask, listen, and respond to what incarcerated individuals say that they need in order to lessen the likelihood of unfortunate outcomes in the future.*
>
> *Observation 4. If lower recidivism rates, and greater family and community well-being, are at all relevant to the goals of incarceration, our current approaches are ineffective at best if not contraindicated.*

In this regard, after encountering this chapter, it is difficult not to conclude that the entire system needs an overhaul, to say nothing of systems of justice in other parts of the world, which may be less just than our own. Ultimately, from the standpoint of beliefs and values, how we regard and treat those members of our society who simultaneously are among the least admired and most in need speaks volumes about our fundamental morality as a people. As Hart and Glick conclude,

> . . .we all bear some measure of responsibility for the expression of criminality, either by conceptual and applied acts of commission, or by omission vis-à-vis our explanations and interventions in the name of justice. Indeed, the myth of impartiality in our judicial system may serve self-preservation purposes by protecting us from wide scale cognitive dissonance (i.e., since we're "good people," bad things could only happen to "bad people"). The belief in impartiality may also absolve us of responsibility for implementing policies and interventions that address the antecedents of crime and criminality in the first place. In the final analysis, both locally and globally, we must overhaul not only reductive rules such as "three strikes," but the entire way in which we regard the unfortunate human beings who wind up in our antediluvian jails and prisons in the

United States and all over the world. Far too often, our systems of justice justify their activities on the basis of discredited models of human nature, which perpetuate rather than attenuate the very problems they ostensibly are designed to prevent. In the process of dispensing such primitive forms of justice, we do far more harm to criminals—as well as those who subsequently will be victimized upon their release—than any good our collective desire for retribution ever will produce. (p. 522)

Worlds away from the realities of incarceration, Dyjak-LeBlanc, Brewster, Grande, White, and Schullman (2016) offer in **Chapter 14—*The EI Leadership Model: From Theory and Research to Real World Application*—**a comprehensive analysis of leaders and leadership, with multiple implications for future research and practice. Following a description of the rationale for an EI Leadership Model, these authors describe the literature-based framework that undergirds this model, consisting of eight thematic areas: (a) assessment; (b) awareness; (c) care; (d) complexity; (e) culture; (f) depth; (g) transformation; and (h) vision. In addition to illuminating the letter and spirit of this approach, such a framework also offers a sort of meta-analysis of "future direction" theories, findings, and applications. As Dyjak-LeBlanc et al. (2016) observe, this work was motivated by the pursuit of five interrelated questions, which would seem to be highly salient to the development and implementation of further studies on leaders and the led:

1. How do the beliefs and values of leaders impact their leadership (e.g., why do leaders experience and respond to self, others, and the larger world as they do)?
2. Are there common beliefs and values among leaders who are deemed to be most effective?
3. How do we evaluate the meaning and impact of interactions between the beliefs and values of leaders and the led?
4. How best do we understand the extraordinarily complex variables that influence leadership on a daily basis in the real world?
5. Which models of leaders and methods of leadership development are most likely to have meaning and relevance across cultures and contexts?

Four principles also had been developed on the basis of these eight themes and five research questions in order to provide further guidance to the 20 Subject Matter Experts from around the world who participated in the development of the EI Leadership Model. These principles also have reflective implications for future research and practice, and are as follows:

1. Leadership *models* should have ecological validity across context and culture (e.g., research should demonstrably enhance the quality and effectiveness of leadership, both locally and globally).
2. Leadership *theory* should inform leadership research (e.g., conceptual frameworks must account for complex interactions among affective, cognitive, motivational, and developmental aspects of "being a leader").
3. Leadership *research* should be sophisticated (e.g., methodologies should examine the mediating role of formative variables, such as life history).
4. Leadership *practice* should address questions of who, what, why, and how (e.g., why some leaders are experienced as more effective than others, and how to individualize leadership development processes).

After describing the specifics of the EI Leadership Model, the remainder of this chapter presents the processes and results of an in-depth workshop with a real world group of leaders, which was conducted in three sections to include the presentation of content to be followed by small group discussion. On the basis of findings that were presented, analysis of small group process content, and workshop feedback, Dyjak-LeBlanc et al. (2016) offer four concluding points, which have additional implications for research and practice.

- *First, leadership models matter* (e.g., "From the standpoint of leaders and leadership, the type of model to which we are drawn likely says a great deal about what we believe human beings are as well as why we do what we do." [p. 562])
- *Second, beliefs and values are integral to leaders and leadership* (e.g., "An overarching strength and benefit from the leadership workshop was the importance of how it helped the participants gain a greater understanding of how beliefs and values develop in individuals, how differences and similarities emerge among leaders and the led, and ultimately how and why people function as they do." [p. 563])
- *Third, leadership assessment reveals what is and isn't working, and why* (e.g., ". . . the pattern of findings presented here suggests the need, opportunity, and benefits of more such reflection and subsequent actions along these lines in collaboration between executive and lower levels of leadership." [p. 565])
- *Fourth, leadership models and assessment methods provide a road map for change* (e.g., ". . .if our assessment processes. . .are translated into flexible road maps that lead toward leadership and organizational growth, we and the people who work for and with us, will be the beneficiaries." [p. 568])

In summarizing such perspective, these authors offer the following concluding thoughts:

> . . .in the final analysis, as the SMEs of the EI Leadership Model remind us, leaders must "demonstrate integrity," know "how to communicate honestly, openly, effectively, and persuasively," and be "responsible" and "honest" as opposed to "incompetent" and "manipulative." Moreover, today's leaders must be able to "discern and articulate principles that are worthy of emulation and/or are the "right thing to do" and "consistently appraise whether and why the mission, activities, and goals of an organization are worthy of pursuit." Such behaviors, knowledge, skills, values, and attributes are not just noble ideals, but pragmatic aspirations if our organizations and those who lead them are able to rise up and help us meet the opportunities and needs of our globally interconnected age. (p. 570)

Finally, in **Chapter 15**, our last in Part III of this book—*The Beliefs, Events, and Values Inventory (BEVI): Implications and Applications for Therapeutic Assessment and Intervention*—Cozen, Hanson, Poston, Jones, and Tabit (2016) examine the uses of the BEVI with a range of therapeutic settings, contexts, and populations. Multiple opportunities for future research and practice emerge. Through the lens of "therapeutic assessment," these authors begin with a brief overview of the "big three" frameworks for intervention—psychodynamic, behavioral, and humanistic—before articulating four problems with the "big three": (a) minimizing heterogeneity *within* these frameworks; (b) minimizing heterogeneity *between* these frameworks; (c) underestimation of the powerful role of subdisciplines in informing practice; and (d) the problem of myopic fidelity to particular ways of working. In their own right, each of these problems warrants additional consideration, particularly for those who are interested in advancing a more integrative approach to research, training, and practice in the mental health field. Another proposition, worthy of further investigation, consists of five "assessment common factors" that seem consistent with an integrative approach toward therapeutic assessment: (a) formative variables, (b) dichotomous thinking, (c) dialectical thinking, (d) emotional awareness, and (e) self–other awareness. As with therapeutic common factors, the basic idea here is that these five "assessment common factors" might also cut across various approaches that are aligned with the precepts of "therapeutic assessment."

Against this theoretical, empirical, and applied backdrop, Cozen et al. (2016) posit five specific questions to be examined in the current study: (a) Is the BEVI ecologically valid? (b) Can the BEVI facilitate case conceptualization? (c) Does the BEVI correspond to best practices of therapeutic assessment? (d) How specifically does the BEVI add to assessment and therapy activities?, and (e) Do the hypothesized "assessment common factors" emerge thematically for clients and clinicians vis-à-vis BEVI usage? To examine these questions, methods for this study drew from three sources of information: (a) two independent focus groups that reviewed clinician observations regarding BEVI usage; (b) a review of responses to qualitative questions by clients; and (c) analysis of a videotaped transcript. Results emerged in the form of two sets of themes for clinicians and clients. As the authors note, all of the following findings warrant further examination in the future. Specifically, from the perspective of clinicians, the BEVI appeared to: (a) promote an understanding of causal connections; (b) allow for a "big picture" focus; (c) emphasize nonpathologizing findings and observations; (d) facilitate sharing of a conceptual framework with clients; (e) broaden the range of information that was gathered and presented; (f) allow for the assessment of openness, defensiveness, and the capacity for self-reflection; (g) promote client motivation and engagement; (h) be applied flexibly not only to therapy and assessment, but in other areas of inquiry and practice; (i) provide perspective that clinicians and clients experienced as accurate; and (j) validate and support the work of clinicians. From the perspective of clients, the BEVI appeared to (a) clarify matters of one's personal identity and self-worth; (b) appraise and promote one's capacity for self-reflection; (c) capture the real world complexity of one's presentation and life situation; (d) allow for inclusion of one's personal values and religious (or not) convictions; and (e) emphasize the relationship of self to others. To demonstrate how such processes actually manifest in the context of a therapeutic assessment approach, Cozen et al. (2016) provide a transcript of a videotaped session to show the iterative and dynamic way in which BEVI results are experienced by clinicians and clients alike in the furtherance of clinical processes and goals. That methodology suggests another opportunity for future research, as it would be good to juxtapose multiple sessions of this nature in order to deepen our understanding of the meaning and potential of such Psychological Assessment as a Therapeutic Intervention (PATI)-like interventions via BEVI results. Their final conclusion is worth excerpting, as it too offers several possible areas for research and practice in the future.

> Overall, these results point to the many potential benefits of the BEVI in a clinical context generally, and toward the therapeutic assessment paradigm and approach, more specifically. Other potential uses of the BEVI within the therapeutic context may be explored in future studies, including but not limited to usage of the BEVI as a screening tool for therapy readiness; for matching

therapy clients with specific approaches, interventions, or therapist styles; as a therapy outcome measure; to facilitate different types of therapeutic interventions (e.g., couples, family, group); and to facilitate training processes for students, who may complete the BEVI to understand their own beliefs and values vis-à-vis self, others, and the larger world. As focus group findings suggest, there are many other uses of the BEVI (e.g., for psychological assessment; in military settings; for organizational and leadership development locally and internationally; in higher education), which also may help inform and enrich usage from the standpoint of therapeutic assessment and intervention. In the final analysis, a gap certainly exists between the need and supply of integrative, depth-based, process-oriented, and comprehensive assessment measures that can effectively be used across a range of clinical applications, contexts, and populations. This chapter points to the BEVI's potential to help meet these important needs, while opening up a wide range of issues, processes, and foci that are of considerable relevance to clients, therapists, and the broader mental health field. (pp. 608–609)

MAKING SENSE OF BELIEFS AND VALUES: MORE FUTURE DIRECTIONS

At this point, we have extracted and summarized key aspects of six research chapters (culture, development, environment, gender, politics, and religion) and five practice chapters (assessment, education, forensics, leadership, and psychotherapy) for the purpose of highlighting possibilities regarding how researchers and practitioners might build upon such recommendations in the future. But as we look ahead, questions worth deliberating that transcend the preceding areas of focus—broad as each is—include, but are not necessarily limited to, the following:

- *Could we imagine a world in which "making sense of beliefs and values" was an expected dimension of human learning, growth, and development?*
- *In practical and aspirational terms, what would it mean—what would it look like—to visualize our world through this lens?*
- *How could such a focus help us apprehend and address the most pressing issues of our day, both locally and globally?*

To be sure, big picture questions such as these are addressed at least implicitly, and often explicitly, in the preceding chapters, but usually via applications and implications within a particular topical area. As of yet, we really have not stepped back to imagine the implications of a world where "making sense of beliefs and values" became normative. Why would it matter to do so? Because as referenced throughout this book, innumerable findings and applications demonstrate that the beliefs and values we acquire throughout development fundamentally impact how and why we experience self, others, and the larger world as we do, and correspondingly influence our behavior, including whether or not, and to what degree, we apprehend such interactions in the first place. In this regard, consider the following "real world" examples of how beliefs and values are expressed on a daily and routine basis across a myriad of settings and contexts:

- A teacher who emphasizes particular value-laden content in a class in order to amplify a certain point
- A police officer, attorney, or judge who exercises belief-based discretion when interpreting whether and how a specific law may apply to the actions and motives of the accused
- A journalist who selects a preferred topic on which to focus in a particular manner
- A parent who disciplines his or her child in a way that comports with his or her understanding of how best to shape human nature, which may largely and nonconsciously be determined by the parent's own life history
- An erstwhile partner who cannot sustain a relationship because early and unresolved life trauma inevitably compels him or her to believe that human intimacy is not to be trusted
- An administrator, manager, or business person who must juggle competing value-based systems such as worth, potential, profit, loss, quality, and the greater good
- A clinician who is drawn toward one explanation rather than another for what ails a client or patient, and therefore selects this versus that treatment, which impacts processes and outcomes of healing for better or worse
- A religious leader who emphasizes one of several possible interpretations of a specific passage in a preferred religious text to address a particular issue
- A politician who elects to support, or not, an action or policy for reasons that are determined by multiple factors, both known/conscious and unknown/nonconscious, and which have predictable and unpredictable consequences for those to whom the action or policy applies
- And so on. . . .

The point is, in the work we pursue, relationships we seek, and lives we lead, the beliefs and values we hold to be self-evident—whether or not they are consciously known to us—profoundly impact who we are, what we do, and how we engage people and systems around us and in the wider world. As such, it may be helpful to offer five broad-spectrum "future directions" that may help us not only "make sense of beliefs and values" over the long term, but apprehend how and why to apply such understanding to the most pressing issues of our day. These "future directions" include the following: (a) Practice Patience; (b) Engage Opposition; (c) Oppose Extremism; (d) Explore Etiology; and (e) Cultivate Capacity.

Practice Patience

Because of the dialectic relationship between worldviews (e.g., religious/nonreligious; conservative/liberal), it is important to reflect upon the obvious fact that a "traditional" stance today may well have been "nontraditional" years ago, and vice versa. Thus, even as we work to create change, we should recognize that changing beliefs and values may take time mainly because of the complex processes by which beliefs and values are acquired, maintained, and at times and under specific circumstances, transformed (see Chapters 2 and 3). Consider, for example, support for interracial marriage, a proposition that not only would have been experienced as "liberal," but radically so in the 1950s. As Kristof (2014) observes, "In 1958, 4 percent of Americans approved of black-white marriages; today, 87% do" (p. A21). Likewise, the majority of Americans believed "separate" schools for Blacks and Whites could indeed be "equal" in 1954, at the time when the *Brown v. Board of Education* Supreme Court decision concluded otherwise. As Aronson (2012) documents,

> In 1942, only 30 percent of the whites in this country favored desegregated schools; by 1956, the figure rose to 49 percent; in 1970, to 75 percent. Finally, in 1980, as it became increasingly clear that school desegregation was inevitable, the figure approached 90 percent. (p. 341)

In short, the vast majority of Americans appear to believe now exactly the opposite of what they believed over seven decades ago. Thus, what once was a mainstream consensus now would be considered addle-brained if not racist by the vast majority of Americans. Imagine how stunned Americans would have been to be authoritatively told—let us say by a booming voice from the sky that—*Your primordial belief that separate is equal is wrong, if not evil, and will be repudiated 70 years hence*—and you have some sense of the "disequilintegration" (e.g., the affective/attributional struggle we humans may experience) when the belief/value content of our Ectoselves (i.e., the "shell self" that contains our beliefs and values) is challenged in dramatic form (see Chapter 3 for a discussion of these issues). Really, we do not need to invoke a booming voice from the sky; just witness the societal conflagration following the U.S. Supreme Court's decision in 1954, and the attendant reverberations for decades afterwards. In fact, every time the Supreme Court renders a decision, especially on a highly divisive sociocultural issue, the outpouring of fury and despair on the one side—and praise and elation on the other—may be understood from this perspective as a bimodal distribution of Ectoselves, residing at different points along the "Continuum of Belief" (see Chapter 2), reacting to the subjective experience of having their belief/value structure either spurned or affirmed.

Moreover, this ineluctable and dialectic relationship appears to prevail across culture and time, as evidenced, most basically, by the fact that all societies that allow for some version of political organization and expression will tend to cleave along their version of liberalism/conservatism among other belief/value continua (e.g., Inglehart, Basáñez, & Moreno, 1998; Inglehart, Basáñez, Díez-Medrano, Halman, & Luijkx, 2004; Schwartz & Bilsky, 1987, 1990; Schwartz, 1992, 2012). The bottom line then, is that if an organization like "The Traditional Values Coalition" (discussed in more detail in the next section) did not exist, some group likely would create a version of it since such an entity speaks to the beliefs and values of millions who apparently believe that there is a need for such expression, given the realities they experience "in the world." In short, we conservatives, moderates, and liberals are sort of stuck with each other, at least until the dialectical tension shifts in another direction among one or more "continua of belief." A prime example of such a process involves shifting beliefs about the nature of marriage. As documented by the Pew Research Center:

> Support for same-sex marriage has increased dramatically over the past decade, but there are substantial differences in opinions across generations. Currently, 68% of Millennials favor allowing gays and lesbians to marry legally, compared with 55% of Gen Xers, 48% of Boomers, and 38% of the Silent generation. (see Gay Marriage, 2014)

The point is, the center of gravity on gay marriage has shifted dramatically over the past decade, but at a differential rate for various subsets of the larger population. And even with such changes, we are still stuck with each other's beliefs and values, but at a different dialectic juxtaposition (i.e., at a different place) along the

Continuum of Belief, just as we are *now*—versus *then*—on the question of whether "separate" is or is not "equal." What are the implications of such realities? Ultimately, from the larger goal of "making sense of beliefs and values," it is much better for us to try and understand worldviews other than our own, rather than simply decrying them as stupid, harmful, or wrong, even though they may well be. Such worldviews will be there anyway, and must be, in relation to our own beliefs and values; and they have their purpose by giving expression to perspectives that are in fact genuinely held by a portion of any given populace anywhere in the world, for all of the reasons of belief/value acquisition, maintenance, and transformation that were described in Chapter 2. Thus, on this first "future direction," patience vis-à-vis the beliefs and values of others truly is a virtue worth cultivating by us all (e.g., see also Brooks, 2015).

Engage Opposition

Recall from our discussions in Chapter 2 on EI Theory, and Chapter 3 on the EI Self, that the "Ectoself" or "Shell Shelf" contains the beliefs, values, schemas, and attitudes that collectively comprise a person's worldview. Based upon hundreds of analyses conducted for this book alone—not to mention thousands of allied studies, many of which are referenced in various chapters—affiliates of various competing organizations (e.g., conservative versus liberal, religious versus nonreligious, etc.) are composed largely of like-minded Ectoselves. For example, it is difficult to imagine that the average "Tea Party" member in the United States will be signing up anytime soon to support the work of "Democratic Socialists of America," and vice versa. Remember also our discussion of beliefs, needs, and self via EI Theory and the EI Self in Chapters 2 and 3. From this perspective, the fact that such organizations likely are composed of members who occupy opposite end points along the same Continuum of Belief is inevitable. That is to say, as our paradigm of "belief match" would predict, the beliefs held to be self-evident by the average member of these "conservative" and "liberal" organizations are likely to be strongly and negatively correlated with one another. This process is an "ineluctable and dialectical reality" because "conservatism" can only know that it is "conservatism" when contrasted with "liberalism," and vice versa. Thus, the ironic fact of the matter is that liberals need conservatives, conservatives need liberals, and moderates need both in order to know "one's own self" in relation to "the other."

So, the understandable fantasy that each of these worldviews has about "the other"—"you liberals/you conservatives/you moderates are wrong and annoying, so please just go away"—will not and cannot happen. If the inability to realize this fantasy seems unbearable whatever your leanings, think again about the dialectic processes of "equilintegration," which were discussed in Chapter 2 (e.g., via the acquisition, maintenance, and transformation of belief/value change) as well as the push/pull interplay among the four levels of the EI Self as discussed in Chapter 3 (e.g., between meeting Core Needs at the Endoself level and that which is available for acquisition via the formative variables of the Exoself level). Remember that once established, beliefs and values can and do change, but typically under specific circumstances (e.g., the 7Ds) and only from a particular point of departure at the Ectoself level (e.g., what specific beliefs and values are, how firmly they are held, at which specific point in time, and for whom). As the Continuum of Belief specifies, one point of departure typically may be juxtaposed with a different point of departure as with our prototypical "liberal" or "conservative" members of contrasting advocacy-based organizations. Because we learn about our own Ectoself by encountering Ectoselves that are organized in a relatively similar or different manner to our own, it would be difficult for us to learn how to experience self—much less others and the larger world from a belief/value perspective—without such encounters.

Oppose Extremism

On the other hand, it is all well and good to "practice patience" and "engage opposition," but are there ever times in which abiding "the other's" beliefs and values is futile if not contraindicated? The obvious answer to this rhetorical question is "of course." At the very least, beliefs that are acted upon in a way that leads to bodily harm against others should be seriously challenged if not outright opposed. For example, when beliefs and organized in such a nonreflective and destructive manner at the Ectoself level that Core Needs may only be met by fidelity to some fanatical individual and/or ideology, an attempt to engage such Hard Structure may not only be futile but foolhardy (see Chapters 2 and 3). Two exemplars of hundreds, if not thousands of such ideologies historically, include the most ardent adherents to Nazism in the 20th century and the "Islamic State of Iraq and Syria" (ISIS, also known as ISIL) in the 21st century (e.g., see Aronson, 2012; Bongar, Brown, Beutler, Breckenridge, & Zimbardo, 2007; Staub, 2013). The cardinal characteristic of Ectoselves that cannot and will not be reasoned with are those that experience the mere existence of different beliefs and values to represent an existential threat to their own self structure, which therefore means there is no alternative but to destroy "the other."

That said, we all must be mindful—particularly when policy decisions of life and death are involved (e.g., going to war)—that (a) not all adherents to a given ideology will share the same degree of Hard Structure and (b) we too may be reacting out of our own Hard Structure, which regards "the other" as an existential threat, when it may or may not be. Again, our capacity and willingness to reflect upon such possibilities is key in this regard (i.e., that "the other" may be experienced as an existential threat not because it is, but because we experience it as such). Moreover, such processes do not exist in a vacuum since the sociocultural, economic, judicial, religious, and political milieus in which such reflection occurs may differ enormously. In a society where clear contingencies are operative and internalized—along with the mechanisms to enforce such contingencies—we are looking at very different realities on the ground. For example, in the United States, the "right to free speech" is a fundamental belief at the heart of our constitution, which subsequently has been internalized at the core of our national identity. Growing up in such a culture, we do not tend to reflect upon the fact that this belief was inculcated in us throughout our development (but might not have been), and now is considered sacrosanct. In fact, we could have been born into a society where such a belief was seen as anathema to the existence of other beliefs (e.g., the supremacy of particular religious teachings, which must prevail over all other beliefs). At a complementary level, now imagine that we neither had a wide range of legal rulings that supported the "right to free speech" nor comprehensive enforcement mechanisms (e.g., police, judges, jails) to ensure that this fundamental belief was honored in practice. Under such circumstances—as is the case presently in many parts of the world—it seems quite likely that our vaunted free speech would be curtailed seriously if permitted at all, depending upon the content of one's speech (e.g., public criticism of a repressive government or opposition to deeply held religious beliefs that are sanctioned by the state). The point is, as the EI Model maintains, we must look not only at what the beliefs are in a given culture or context, but why they are—or are not—expressed in the manner that they are. So, in the United States—and in other societies that share this web of enforcement-based contingencies wrapped around Enlightenment-era beliefs, presuming they do not materially (e.g., physically) harm others—we typically have the relative luxury of allowing our citizens to hold and express beliefs and values that are extreme and even violent because we have (or should have) the contingency/enforcement-based means to deter and punish their expression if and when they may result in harm to others.

By extension then, from the standpoint of beliefs and values, whether or not a "potential perpetrator" (e.g., individual, group, nation) represents a genuine threat, which therefore might be acted against, at least three "test questions" probably ought to be answered in the affirmative:

1. *Attribution Test*: Do we have reliable evidence that the potential perpetrator believes that (a) "the other" represents an existential threat, (b) is the cause of subjectively experienced distress, and (c) therefore is deserving of harm?
2. *Deterrence Test*: Are prevailing environmental contingencies and enforcement mechanisms *insufficient* to deter the potential perpetrator from acting upon such beliefs?
3. *Means Test*: Does the potential perpetrator have the means to act upon such beliefs?

If the answer to all three questions is "Yes," it may well be that some sort of action may be necessary to attenuate the risk such an individual or group represents. However, and again, history is replete with examples of *the other* "other" being deemed a threat worthy of "acting against" when the answer to one or more of these proposed "test questions" would be "No." The Iraq War represents a case in point. In fact, these questions could only have been answered in the affirmative if one had reliable reasons to believe that Saddam Hussein actually possessed "weapons of mass destruction," a possibility that charitably remains in dispute to this day, depending upon definitional and related issues (e.g., Iraqi Weapons Inspections, 2013; Kessler, 2009; Murphy, 2014). In contrast, on the basis of the tragic events of September 11, 2001, all three of the "test questions" demonstrably could have been answered in the affirmative for Osama bin Laden and his al-Qaeda followers, which suggests that perhaps bin Laden and al-Qaeda rather than Hussein and Iraq should have been our primary focus (e.g., Gunning for Saddam, 2001).

Explore Etiology

In contemplating "future directions," a core contention is that we must include, but move beyond a focus on "what" our beliefs and values are or should be, in order to emphasize "why" we hold beliefs and values to be self-evident in the first place. In this regard, it bears asking if there are movements, systems, initiatives, or organizations that already focus on both the "what" and "why" of beliefs and values? The short answer is, "yes, to a degree," although such activities are not necessarily aligned with the broader goal of "making sense of beliefs and values" in order to facilitate deeper awareness of self, others, and the larger world. Consider, for example, the Traditional Values Coalition (www.traditional values.org), mentioned earlier, which is "America's largest non-denominational, grassroots church lobby, speaking on behalf of more than 43,000 allied churches and millions of like-minded patriots." Its mission and purpose are described as follows:

> For more than 30 years, Traditional Values Coalition (TVC) is a leading voice in the halls of Congress for the Bible-based traditional values that created and preserved our nation and our prosperity for over two centuries. These values include:

- Promoting religious liberty and a free society;
- Uncovering wasteful spending in Washington;
- Championing Judeo-Christian values in the public square;
- Protecting traditional marriage and family as the cornerstone of society;
- Securing the Constitution against the growing threat of Islam and Shariah law;
- Defending human life from its earliest moments to natural death; and
- Ensuring the economic security of future generations of Americans as a moral issue. (see www.traditionalvalues.org)

Along similar lines, the "Values Voter Summit" (www.valuesvotersummit.org) occurs annually in the United States, and is sponsored by the Family Research Council, a conservative Christian lobbying organization based in Washington, DC (www .frc.org). In describing its purpose, the Values Voter Summit website provides the following information:

> Values Voter Summit was created in 2006 to provide a forum to help inform and mobilize citizens across America to preserve the bedrock values of traditional marriage, religious liberty, sanctity of life and limited government that make our nation strong. It has drawn as many as 3,000 plus attendees from around the nation and foreign countries. Garnering national and international media attention, CNN named it "one of the conservative movement's marquee annual events" and Sean Hannity called it "the premier conservative event now in the country." (see www.valuesvotersummit.org)

As a point of values-based comparison and contrast, consider the International Association for Human Values (IAHV; www.iahv.org/us-en). Based in Washington DC, the IAHV has as its mission to ". . .foster the daily practice of human values—a sense of connectedness and respect for all people and the natural environment, an attitude of non-violence, and an ethic of social service." It also includes the following "we believe" statements:

> All human beings are equal. Responsibility and an attitude of selfless service are the foundation of true empowerment. Peace, happiness and compassion are the intrinsic nature of human beings. Socio-economic development must be built on human values to be sustainable. Incorporation of human values into all aspects of life will ultimately lead to a more peaceful, just and sustainable world. (see www.iahv.org/us-en/about-us/#sthash.jHPvrMBD.dpuf)

For a related example, consider the following mission and purpose of the "Earthvalues Institute," based in Quebec, Canada (www.earthvalues.org):

> A fundamental guiding principle of the Earthvalues Institute (EVI) is the premise of Nature as our teacher and guide. EVI staff creatively weave Nature themes into school curricula, leadership trainings, and all other programs. We see Nature as a vehicle for teaching and learning across curricula and learning modalities, allowing for access to the artist, musician, scientist, and writer in each program participant. Nature is portrayed as the timeless and limitless source of inspiration for all kinds of human endeavours. The relevancy of today's environmental issues and the role Nature can play in individual and group leadership is highlighted in all EVI educational programs. (see www.earthvalues.org)

Relative to our overarching goal, it seems evident that the first two organizations really are not in the business of *making sense of beliefs and values*, but rather are designed to promote a set of economic, political, sociocultural, and religious beliefs and values that are aligned with a conservative or traditional worldview. Likewise, the third and fourth organizations also are promoting a particular worldview via their missions and activities that might reasonably be aligned with a liberal or progressive worldview. From the standpoint of all we have discussed in this book, such organizations exemplify *the what* of beliefs and values in that each of them is seeking to promote a particular paradigm that their adherents contend is good and true. As has been stated throughout, *the what* is necessary, but for our purposes, not sufficient if we truly are trying to make sense of beliefs and values—*the why*—rather than only advocating for a particular worldview, worthy though it may be. To be clear, it is not that these organizations might not have *why* answers at the ready, just that their explicit focus appears to emphasize *what* beliefs and values are to be fostered and revered.

Recall from Chapter 1 that *the what* is concerned with matters of content—what do human beings actually say that they believe and value. *The why* wonders why such content is internalized in the first place. Both levels of analysis—what and why—are necessary if we are to make sense of beliefs and values (i.e., we need to know what the belief/value content is as well as how it comes to be internalized). From the standpoint of advocacy, organizations that grapple with beliefs and values may emphasize *the what* or *the why* for particular values-based reasons. For example, the "Traditional Values Coalition" described previously emphasizes *the what* in declaring emphatic support for "Bible-based traditional values that created and preserved our nation and our prosperity for over two centuries" (www.traditionalvalues.org).

To state the obvious, there is nothing inherently wrong with advocating for *the what* (i.e., the content of one's beliefs and values); the very essence of democracy depends upon free-flowing debate regarding *what* beliefs and values are or should be at the heart of national identity. But to evaluate the merits of competing ideas, we must ask ourselves—and others—to do much more than simply reiterate *what* we hold to be true and good as opposed to false and bad; we also must create a space for others, and ourselves, to articulate *why* we hold the beliefs and values that we do. To imagine a world where why is asked alongside what, we will need movements, initiatives, and organizations to do both if we are to "make sense of beliefs and values," and apply such understanding to a myriad of issues, both locally and globally. Are there such organizations? Yes, and mainly those that are affiliated with colleges and universities—which have as their focus the creation of forums by which ethics and values may be contemplated,[3] sometimes but not always through a specific disciplinary, professional, or thematic lens. To take just a few examples, such centers and institutes include, but are not limited to, the Center for Law, Philosophy, and Human Values at the University of Chicago http://www.law.uchicago.edu/centers/lawphilosophyandhumanvalues); the Dali Lama Center for Ethics and Transformative Values at the Massachusetts Institute of Technology (http://thecenter.mit.edu); the Center for Values and Social Policy at the University of Colorado at Boulder (www.colorado.edu/philosophy/center/links.shtml); the University Center for Human Values at Princeton University (http://uchv.princeton.edu/index.php); The Values Institute at the University of San Diego (https://www.sandiego.edu/cas/phil/affiliations/Values_Institute.php); the Consortium on Law and Values at the University of Minnesota (http://consortium.umn.edu); the Center for Ethics and Values in Business at the University of Notre Dame (www3.nd.edu/~ethics); and the Center for the Study of Culture and Values at The Catholic University of America (www.crvp.org/cscv/index.htm). The work of organizations such as these illustrates how and why beliefs and values can offer rich opportunities for engagement not only within the scholarly community, but with the public at large.

One such organization that recognizes the importance of *what*, but also focuses intensively upon *why*, is the International Beliefs and Values Institute (IBAVI; www.ibavi.org), which has been referenced on several occasions throughout this book. That is because its fundamental mission—*to explore beliefs and values and how they influence actions, policies, and practices around the world*—is aligned highly with the overarching goal of "making sense of beliefs and values." By way of context and background, wishing to examine and understand the underlying psychology of September 11, 2001—and dissatisfied with the proclaimed explanations of etiology at the time (e.g., "they attacked us for our freedom")—an interdisciplinary group of academic colleagues at James Madison University in Virginia began meeting to discuss how our scholarly and professional activities were relevant to these and other real world events.[4] As our conversations evolved, it seemed to us that far too much of our research was intended for consumption by a relatively narrow group of like-minded colleagues in still smaller subfields within our individual academic disciplines. Rarely did we seek out the perspectives of colleagues from fields other than our own; seldom did we attempt to engage the public or policy makers in anything approximating open dialogue, where we had as much to learn as we did to teach.

Throughout our conversations, the broader global context loomed large, encompassing not only 9/11, but a wide range of issues and concerns, including—but by no means limited to—climate change (and related evidence of environmental degradation across the planet), the international actions, policies, and practices of the United States (often mediated by implicit and unspoken beliefs and values), and our conflictual standing and status as a nation (illustrated by global polling data and our actual experiences during international travel). Although we lamented the apparent

---

[3] In particular, the Center for Values and Social Policy at the University of Colorado at Boulder offers a comprehensive listing of relevant centers and institutes, with a particular focus on those with an "ethics" dimension (see www.colorado.edu/philosophy/center/links.shtml). As is the case throughout this book, it is possible that websites and/or organizations may change over time. If so, it may be necessary to conduct a web-based search to locate and/or ascertain the status of a website.

[4] Aspects of the following section have been adapted and/or excerpted from Shealy, C. N. (2007). *Giving Away a World of Psychology*. Retrieved from www.apa.org/international/pi/2007/09/shealy.aspx, on May 7, 2014. For a recent overview of IBAVI activities, please see Shealy, C. N. (2015). *Still Giving Away a World of Psychology* from http://www.apa.org/international/pi/2015/03/world-psychology.aspx

conclusion by nonacademics that the academy was often removed from such "real world" issues and concerns, we eventually concluded that this perception was largely of our own making. The formation of the IBAVI was our attempt to grapple with these issues and concerns through an interdisciplinary, international, and cross-college forum that was designed to:

- Address the great interest in beliefs and values by academics, policy makers, and the public at large
- Counter a perception that the academy is biased, irrelevant, or elitist
- Highlight the crucial role of higher education in producing an accountable, reflective, and enlightened citizenry
- Facilitate interdisciplinary dialogue among colleagues who share an interest in "beliefs" and "values," broadly defined
- Build upon related and extant scholarly, grant-based, educational, professional, and outreach activities
- Illustrate how beliefs and values mediate national and international actions, policies, and practices across multiple domains (e.g., religion, politics, gender, culture, environment)
- Translate research and theory into accessible form and relevant action for a real world audience
- Define and make better sense of beliefs and values (e.g., issues of etiology, maintenance, transformation)
- Promote respectful and meaningful civil discourse that is pluralistic, critically minded, self-reflective, and grounded in sound scholarship

To accomplish these goals, the IBAVI encourages the international academic community—in concert with allied individuals and organizations in the public and private sectors—to become much more proactive and deliberate, organize and direct its vast analytic capacity toward an understanding of these real world issues, and translate what we discover and assemble into terms that may readily be apprehended by the academy, policy makers, and the public at large. More specifically, the IBAVI maintains that we must establish a more just, equitable, rational, and sustainable world order, by focusing on five overarching areas of emphasis: (a) conflict resolution, (b) human rights, (c) sustainability, (d) global education, and (e) religious and cultural understanding.

Since its formal inception in 2004, the IBAVI has pursued a wide range of scholarly and practice-based activities, including the promotion of interdisciplinary and cross-cultural research on the etiology and maintenance of beliefs, values, and worldviews, dissemination of research in accessible media and materials, development of web-based resources, and cosponsorship of scholarly events. Complementary to this scholarly emphasis, the IBAVI engages in a range of educational initiatives designed to promote a greater understanding of the "what," "how," and "why" of beliefs and values—that is, how, why, and under what circumstances human beliefs and values are acquired, maintained, and/or transformed. Of these emphases, a most important consideration is *why*. For reasons articulated throughout this book, until we understand this fundamental question of etiology—*why* we hold the beliefs and values we do—it will be very difficult to take the next logical step: the usage of such information to help us cultivate a greater capacity for understanding why we believe what we believe, and what the attendant implications are of such knowledge for actions, policies, and practices, both locally and globally. In short, as the IBAVI and allied organizations contend, it is very important that we explore the etiology of beliefs and values, while seeking to cultivate our full capacity as human beings, another "future direction" to which we turn next.

Cultivate Capacity

As may be clear by now, in the final analysis, we are not seeking to "make sense of beliefs and values" as an end in itself, but as a means to facilitate greater awareness and care, which subsequently is expressed in thought, word, and deed toward self, others, and the world at large. Such a goal may sound unduly ambitious, but we are doing so anyway on a daily basis, whether we recognize it or not, from the parenting and education we provide, to the laws and services we develop, to the programs and policies we pursue. In this regard, a central argument of this book is that we need to be much more explicit and deliberate on all fronts, making sense of beliefs and values on the one hand, and translating our subsequent awareness processes by which we "raise ourselves" as a species in a way that is aligned with what we need in order to fulfill our full human potential. Many of the advocates, educators, leaders, scholars, and practitioners cited in various chapters are engaged in this very sort of activity through their lives and work. Likewise, these organizations that focus on "beliefs," "values," and "ethics" often seek to pursue such goals directly through their missions and activities. As such, on the basis of such work—and all that we have discussed in this book—the concluding question before us is a follows: *How do we cultivate a more globally sustainable self—which is to say, a greater capacity to care for self, others, and the larger world—in a manner that is* informed *(e.g., by theory, data, and applications that are necessary to "make sense of beliefs and values"),* measurable *(e.g., to demonstrate the relative impact, or lack thereof, of our interventions), and* generalizable *(e.g., thereby contributing to a broader process of social and global change)?*

Innumerable examples of such informed, measurable, and generalizable work have been cited throughout this book, including, but by no means limited to, the Forum BEVI Project—a multiyear, multisite partnership between IBAVI and the Forum on Education Abroad—which focused on the assessment of international, multicultural, and transformative learning (see Chapter 12). Likewise, to see examples of how one may "walk this talk" in life and in work, one need only review the activities and accomplishments of those who have received the Sustainable Visions and Values Award, which recognizes a distinguished individual who exemplifies the transformative aspirations that are at the heart of the IBAVI's mission, rationale, and goals. Through their lives and work across one or more of the IBAVI's five areas of emphasis—conflict resolution, human rights, sustainability, global education, and religious and cultural understanding—these extraordinary individuals embody "Sustainable Visions and Values" (www.ibavi.org/content/about-svv-award-0).

Deliberations regarding this annual award were among the reasons for the development of a 2-year job analysis of international leaders under the auspices of the IBAVI, which ultimately culminated in the development of the EI Leadership Model (see Chapter 14), which is another example of an attempt to translate our understanding of "beliefs and values" into measurable and generalizable form in a real world context.

As another way to "cultivate capacity," consider findings from an analysis of the following IBAVI-inspired course—*Making Sense of Beliefs and Values: A Guided Tour for Global Citizens*—which is designed to be taught at different levels (e.g., high school, undergraduate, graduate) either by an individual instructor or in a team-taught format. Depending upon student educational level and ability, course content may be adapted or presented in lecture format, which is supplemented by additional learning and experiential activities (e.g., films, service learning, group projects). One version of this course has been taught for a number of years, primarily to freshmen students at James Madison University, as part of the Forum BEVI Project (see Chapter 12), and under the auspices of the Madison International Learning Community (see www.jmu.edu/international/isss/students/get-involved/mi/index.shtml for more information and to access a copy of this syllabus).

From the standpoint of our three "capacity cultivating criteria" (i.e., *informed, measurable, generalizable*), how is this course experienced by students? To find out, Iyer (2013) conducted a comprehensive examination of student experiences and reactions via a mixed methods study, which involved both qualitative and quantitative analysis (e.g., identifying prominent thematic themes of student reactions; usage of BEVI individual and group reports/scale scores). Adhering to recommended practices for mixed methods and qualitative analyses (e.g., Creswell & Plano-Clark, 2007; Strauss & Corbin, 1990; Tashakkori & Teddlie, 2009), and using an axial coding process along with NVivo software (Charmaz, 2006; QSR International Pty Ltd., 2012), Iyer and the reviewers/raters working with her extracted 8 main themes and 19 subthemes from their analyses, which were based upon responses to written essays that were incorporated into midterm and final exams for this course. Along with descriptive/definitional information, these themes (in bold) and subthemes (underlined) are listed in Table 16.1.

As may be evident, such themes suggest that this course, in the context of a larger learning community, was associated with a wide range of outcomes, including but not limited to a greater degree of "critical thinking," a tendency toward "deeper learning," and increased "emotional involvement," "identity clarification," "self-awareness," and "understanding and acceptance of others and the world." Thus, it would appear that our first two "capacity cultivating criteria"—*informed and measurable*—may be met, although additional research certainly is indicated to determine whether such outcomes are in accord with the third criterion, *generalizability*. As Iyer (2013) concludes,

> evidence suggests that a course designed to "make sense of beliefs and values"—when grounded in robust theory and data, and taught thoughtfully and well—has considerable potential to facilitate transformative learning, broadly defined. In replicating and adapting this course in other institutions of higher learning, to the K-12 environment, in other public and private organizational contexts, and settings and situations at home and abroad, much of worth is likely to be learned and accomplished. If our goal is creating a citizenry that is more caring and aware, while promoting the knowledge, skills, characteristics, and values that are necessary for success in our increasingly interconnected world, it is hard to imagine a more direct approach than making sense of beliefs and values. (p. 112)

Such perspective is complementary to our final example—which deliberately seeks to meet all three "capacity cultivating criteria" (i.e., *informed, measurable, generalizable*).

TABLE 16.1

Final Themes Extracted From Making Sense of Beliefs and Values Course Essays

THEMES AND SUBTHEMES		DESCRIPTION
1	**Critical Thinking**	Intellectual ability to actively and skillfully conceptualize, apply, analyze, synthesize, and/or evaluate information gathered from, or generated by, observation, experience, reflection, reason, or communication, as a guide to one's beliefs and actions.
A	Engaging in Big Questions	Ability to actively challenge and question long-held beliefs and values, arguments, logic, day-to-day practices and assumptions about self, other, and the world rather than passively accepting them as they are.
B	Increased Reasoning Skills	Ability to draw logical inferences through reasoning processes in order to make sense of self, others, and the world. It includes the ability to grasp complexity regarding human behavior as well as the multidimensional nature of beliefs/values, which collectively inform judgments, decision making, and problem solving.
C	Problem Identification and/ or Problem Solving	Ability to identify problems and generate possible solution(s) for them.
D	Understanding Cause and Effect Relationships	Ability to think in terms of cause–effect or effect–cause relationships (e.g., to be aware of how and why they or others come to believe, feel, or act in the way that they do). Such capacity for thoughtful reflection is considered to be another form of evidence for higher order thinking.
2	**Deeper Learning**	Ability to make interdisciplinary, intellectual, and affective connections regarding course content, which leads to new insights as well as applications to one's own life.
A	Ability to Make Connections with Own Life	Ability to apply concepts discussed in class to his or her own life, and to make sense of one's own life events and experiences. This ability also pertains to the capacity and inclination to put theory into practice (e.g., see relevance to one's own life).
B	Ability to Integrate Learning from other Sources and Facts	Ability to develop, make, recognize, and evaluate connections among disparate concepts, fields, or contexts. Such an ability includes engaging in interdisciplinary thinking.
3	**Emotional Involvement**	Increased receptivity toward a range of feelings and affective experiences, behaviors, or emotions in oneself and others.
A	Affective Arousal or Activation	Experience characterized by an emotional reaction toward self or other.
B	Affective Closure/ Reconciliation	Process of avoiding, blocking, or shutting off feelings and emotional reactions, and the use of defensive strategies to safeguard oneself, especially when presented with conflicting belief and values, worldviews, and versions of reality; simultaneously, there may be a tendency to try and reconcile conflicts in order to move forward in more integrative or consolidated manner.

(continued)

TABLE 16.1

Final Themes Extracted From Making Sense of Beliefs and Values Course Essays **(continued)**

THEMES AND SUBTHEMES		DESCRIPTION
4	**Future Orientation**	Ability to think about and plan for the future (may or may not include specific goals).
A	Future Sightedness	Ability to reflect on the future, which is not related to career (e.g., references to their families or personal lives).
B	Ideas about a Career Path	Idea about a career choice or career versatility as well as reflections regarding how knowledge about beliefs and values may relate to further career goals and activities.
5	**Identity Clarification and Self Awareness**	Refers to an increased knowledge about oneself in terms of who one is and one's relative awareness about one's own needs, beliefs, and values, including the reasons why one is the way he or she is.
A	Identity	Refers to an understanding and commitment to who one is as a person and a member of a group. It concerns how one defines him or herself in relation to others, the world, and his or her understanding of self.
B	Increased Insight and Self Awareness	Refers to an increased capacity for introspection regarding one's own thoughts, emotions, and behaviors. This process involved an ongoing process of self-reflection and self-assessment of one's beliefs and values regarding self, other, and the world. It is an ongoing process of understanding "why I do what I do."
C	Openness	Refers to a lack of cognitive/affective rigidity, presence of permeable boundaries regarding beliefs/values, the ability to experience conflicting information without forcing closure, and a concomitant ability to tolerate ambiguity.
D	Self Actualization/ Becoming Change Agents	Inclination to change one's thoughts, opinions, beliefs/values, and behaviors following a process of self-assessment and reflection. It requires recognition of the need for change and commitment to work toward it.
6	**Increased Knowledge About Beliefs and Values, and BEVI**	Increased knowledge about the content covered in class. This includes an understanding of formative variables, core needs, belief/value formation and maintenance, EI Theory/EI Self, the BEVI, and their interrelationships to one another.
A	Increased Knowledge About Beliefs and Values	Increased knowledge about the content areas covered in class, including definition and formation of belief and values, the role of formative variables in belief/value formation, and factors that maintain beliefs and values.
B	Increased Knowledge About the BEVI	Increased knowledge about the BEVI scales and how the instrument may be used to understand beliefs and values in self, others, and the world.

(continued)

TABLE 16.1

Final Themes Extracted From Making Sense of Beliefs and Values Course Essays (continued)

THEMES AND SUBTHEMES		DESCRIPTION
7	**Increased Understanding and Acceptance of Others and the World**	Increased inclination to accept others as who they are, which follows from a deeper understanding of why others believe, value, and do what they do.
A	Increased Appreciation of Others	Increased appreciation for others (individual or community) for who they are, with a corresponding valuation of them, irrespective of the similarities or differences between self and others.
B	Increased Tolerance of Diverse People and Opinions	Ability to tolerate plurality or diversity among individuals and societies/cultures that vary in thoughts, practices, belief/values, assumptions, worldviews, and ways of living, thinking, feeling, and behaving. Tolerance does not imply that one likes or agrees with others, but reflects the ability to acknowledge that others are different and worthy of respect.
C	Increased Understanding and Empathy for Others	Ability to understand and experience sensitivity toward another's worldviews, thoughts, feelings, and experiences. It includes an ability to put oneself into another person's reality and understand his or her experience.
8	**General Knowledge and Sociocultural Awareness**	Increased, deeper, and substantial understanding of a number of religious, political, environmental, gender-based, artistic, cultural, and sociopolitical issues, and events that are relevant to global citizens.

Specifically, *Cultivating the Globally Sustainable Self: Summit Series on Transformative Teaching, Training, and Learning in Research and Practice*[5] is a 3-year initiative that brings together stakeholders across four groups: (a) leaders from a range of organizations that are seeking change across the IBAVI's five thematic areas (conflict resolution, human rights, sustainability, global education, and religious/cultural understanding); (b) experts in matters of assessment, program evaluation, and research design; (c) leading theorists/researchers/practitioners in various aspects of "the self"; and (d) "big picture" global thinkers and leaders regarding a range of educational, policy, and related matters. The rationale for convening such stakeholders is

---

[5] Although the following text describing this summit series was authored by Shealy, multiple individuals and organizations have participated in the conceptualization, development, and execution of this initiative, including but not limited to past and present steering committee members and conveners—Drs. Michele Estes, Teresa Harris, Craig Shealy, Lee Sternberger, Tim Thomas, and Phil Wishon—along with members of the IBAVI Executive Board and Summit Council. For more information, please see www.jmu.edu/summitseries

informed by two fundamental observations: *Observation 1: Learning from Allied Trans-formational Movements* and *Observation 2: Understanding and Demonstrating Transforma-tion*. Because these observations are fundamental to the summit series, some additional explication may be in order.

Observation 1—Learning From Allied Transformational Movements

Much may be gained by encountering the methods, goals, and activities of allied individuals, groups, organizations, and movements that also are attempting to pro-mote widespread local and global change across complementary and interrelated areas of emphasis. However, such cross-movement engagement seems relatively rare. More specifically, from the perspective of this summit series, scholars, educa-tors, practitioners, leaders, and others who are affiliated with these and related movements too often (a) do not encounter one another at the level of research or practice, (b) may not even know of the existence of such movements, and (c) do not realize that much of what is thought to be "unique" to their movement actually overlaps considerably with related initiatives at the levels of mission, values, and activities. Why does this lack of awareness matter? Because it is not an efficient use of resources to be engaged in activities that are thought to be unique when in fact many other individuals, groups, and organizations are engaged in similar activities that are known by different names. Moreover, at the level of interprofessional col-laboration, there is simple logic to the proposition that we may accomplish more by working toward common means and ends rather than pursuing objectives on our "own," particularly if we are doing so under the mistaken assumption that "our movement" is the only or primary initiative that is charged with the pursuit of a particular set of values or goals (e.g., D'Amour, Ferrada-Videla, San Martin Rodri-guez, & Beaulieu, 2005; Johnson, Stewart, Brabeck, Huber, & Rubin, 2004). By com-ing together and learning from each other's models and methods, we may discover a great deal about how to approach our respective activities in ways that are more effective, while also finding synergy and magnifying our impact beyond that which we could accomplish alone.

Observation 2—Understanding and Demonstrating Transformation

From the perspective of this Summit Series, many of these movements are much more similar than different in terms of their most fundamental goal: transforming human beings at all levels of education (K-20+), both locally and globally, and across cultures and contexts to be more open, aware, caring, and responsive to self, others, and the larger world (e.g., Cranton, 2006; Dirkx, 2012; Mezirow & Taylor, 2009; Shealy, Bhuyan, & Sternberger, 2012; see an example of the Transformative Learning confer-ence series, at http://transformativelearning.ning.com/2014conference; Education for Sustainable Development, at www.unesco.org/new/en/education/themes/ leading-the-international-agenda/education-for-sustainable-development; see also the Center for Green Schools, 2014, *A National Plan for Education for Sustainability*, at http://www.centerforgreenschools.org/sites/default/files/resource-files/ National-Action-Plan-Educating-Sustainability.pdf as well as the work of the Ameri-can Psychological Association's "Society for Environmental, Population and Conser-vationPsychology" atwww.apadivisions.org/division-34/interests/ecopsychology/ index.aspx). Such goals not only are laudable, but perhaps essential, if we are to cre-ate a world of sustainable visions and values, rather than actions, policies, and prac-tices that ultimately lead to the diminishment and destruction of each other and the living world. The challenge is, such movements may focus much more on matters of content than process. That is, the emphasis often is on *what* educational content should be developed and implemented. Far less attention typically is devoted to *why* human beings are inclined toward, or against, such content in the first place, which may be as, if not important, in understanding who learns what and why, and under what circumstances—that is to say, who is and is not "transformed" by exposure to such content, and why (e.g., Wandschneider et al., 2016). To be clear, these matters of content and process are interdependent, which illustrates why this summit series seeks to identify exemplary curricula, programs, organizations, systems, and policies that are in the business of developing and disseminating such content for purposes of transformation across these five overarching areas of emphasis (conflict resolution, human rights, sustainability, global education, and religious and cultural under-standing). As important, we want to understand—through an examination of semi-nal and cutting edge theory, research, assessment, and application—why, for whom, and under what circumstances such transformative content is, and is not, effective, and what the practical implications of such findings might be across a range of applied sectors and settings (e.g., education, nonprofit, scholarly, policy). Thus, in the context of the preceding two observations, *Cultivating the Globally Sustainable Self* brings together key stakeholders—researchers, educators, students, advocates, administrators, and policy makers—to participate in a series of research and practice summits in order to pursue the following two goals: Goal 1: Understanding the Con-tent and Process of Transformation and Goal II: Transforming Understanding into Research and Practice.

Goal I: Understanding the Content and Process of Transformation. In pursuit of the first summit goal, representatives from major traditions that seek to promote human transformation are asked to offer examples of their "best" interventions for review and discussion by participants. By interventions, we seek any method or approach that is designed to promote learning, change, or growth within or across one or more overarching thematic areas—conflict resolution, human rights, sustainability, global education, and religious and cultural understanding—in a manner that is (a) measur-able (e.g., qualitatively and/or quantitatively) and (b) values-based (e.g., consistent with the fundamental goals or principles of the change-oriented movement). Exam-ples of such interventions might include programs of study, specific courses, educa-tional workshops, service learning, training programs, community projects, advocacy efforts, marketing campaigns, immersion experiences, and so forth. In other words, we are seeking exemplars that—from the perspective of their designers, implement-ers, evaluators, promoters, and/or recipients—seem to be especially powerful in terms of achieving means and ends that are at the heart of what the movement is striving to achieve. But as the preceding criteria indicate, the intervention must not only be congruent with the values of the change-oriented movement; qualitative and/or quantitative data also must be provided to support the contention that the intervention is demonstrably effective, for at least a subset of those who experience it.

At a deeper level, summit participants then are asked to offer their best under-standing—theoretically—of *how* and *why* the intervention is in fact effective. In other words, from the perspective of the Summit Series, it is necessary but not sufficient to identify effective interventions. We also must strive to understand how and why our interventions are—or are not—having the impact we intend them to have. In contem-plating such matters, we are not seeking definitive or absolute conclusions, but rather a deeper, more substantive, and collective understanding of what actually is—or is not—being "impacted" (e.g., affectively, behaviorally, cognitively, socioculturally) as a result of our interventions. We want participants to delve inside the hearts and minds of those they are seeking to transform in order to understand better why their interventions appear to have the impact that they do. In this way, it is our hope that we will emerge with a much deeper appreciation of the complex interactions within and among human beings that ultimately mediate and moderate the effectiveness of our interventions. Such information should help us imagine, design, implement, and evaluate more meaningful, relevant, and effective interventions in the future, which is the basic purpose of Goal II described next.

Goal II: Transforming Understanding into Research and Practice. Once we are clearer on the relationship between content (e.g., what we attempt to convey through various transformative movements) and process (e.g., the complex affective, attributional, and developmental interactions that influence who learns what and why, and under what circumstances), it becomes much more possible to develop theoretically robust and empirically grounded studies that actually can inform what we can and should do in practice. If we go about developing and implementing interventions without sufficient attention to such fundamental matters (e.g., regarding the basis for concluding that what we do actually has an impact), we risk wasting a lot of time, energy, and resources on activities that "should work" but may or may not. In this regard, Kurt Lewin's maxim that "there is nothing so practical as a good theory" is deeply relevant to the goals of social change movements, as is the inextricable linkage between theoretical models and applied methods (e.g., Greenwald, 2012). Not knowing, or not caring, that robust theoretical models and defensible empirical methods may in fact be essential for the development and evaluation of effective social change interventions simply is not acceptable, either from the standpoint of time and resource expenditure, or in terms of demonstrating the value of what we do to the many stakeholders who are the recipients and/or funders of our efforts. In short, we do not have the luxury of "just doing stuff" because it seems like it makes sense or should work. We can and must do better as we hope to illustrate through this Summit Series.

Finally, in the context of the preceding overview and goals, *we anticipate the following outcomes from the Cultivating the Globally Sustainable Self Summit Series:*

1. Bring together scholars, educators, students, practitioners, and leaders from a range of transformation-oriented global movements across five thematic areas—conflict resolution, human rights, sustainability, global education, and religious and cultural understanding—in order to learn from and contribute to each other's missions, methods, goals, and activities (Goal I).

2. Develop a draft agenda for a global program of research-to-practice on the basis of summit presentations and deliberations (e.g., regarding theory, data, models, methods) (Goal II).

3. Develop a plan for furthering and monitoring progress regarding the ongoing pursuit of Goals I and II.

4. Provide an opportunity for interdisciplinary stakeholders to showcase, describe, and discuss their interests, activities, and plans.

5. Identify the means and methods by which participants may participate in and propose future activities and pursue/develop further collaboration as part of the planning and preparatory process for the next two research-to-practice summits.

6. Pursue identified scholarly, professional, and organizational venues through which the outcomes, activities, and plans of *Cultivating the Globally Sustainable Self* may be disseminated and furthered over at least the 3 years of this series of summits.

In short, as may be evident from review of the preceding rationale, observations, goals, and outcomes, *Cultivating the Globally Sustainable Self* is designed deliberately in response to our three "capacity cultivating criteria." In this regard, recall the overarching question that began this section:

> *How do we cultivate a more globally sustainable self—which is to say, a greater capacity to care for self, others, and the larger world—in a manner that is informed, measurable, and generalizable?*

Although our results await future dissemination, a shared hope by participants is that we will be able to develop a credible response to these three criteria by offering multiple examples of how we may "cultivate capacity" in an ecologically valid manner with real world implications and applications.[6]

MAKING SENSE OF BELIEFS AND VALUES: FURTHER REFLECTIONS

As we bring this chapter and book to a close, some further (and final, for now) reflections are in order. Specifically, as believing and valuing creatures, the merits of focusing more deeply and persistently on the origin, nature, and impact of beliefs and values are many and varied, which might be summarized via the following five benefits.

Increased Awareness of Self, Others, and the Larger World

As discussed in the opening chapter of this book, and arguably most imperative, by making sense of why we believe what we believe, it becomes more difficult to claim that our beliefs and values are true, right, or better simply because they are our own. That is because if and when we accept that our beliefs and values—and those of others—are determined, in no small part, by formative variables over which we all had little initial control, it becomes plausible to contemplate that we might well have "ended up" with an entirely different worldview if the events and experiences of our lives had been other than what they were.

More Reflective, Authentic, and Empathic Discourse

Second, and by extension, rather than our customary practices—where we engage in conscious and/or nonconscious debate with others over the relative merits of our own beliefs and values, and the demerits of the other—we might be more inclined at least to contemplate taking an additional step whereby we describe and

---

[6] To review the process and progress of *Cultivating the Globally Sustainable Self* over time, please see www.jmu.edu/summitseries

reflect openly upon the origins of our worldviews, before scrapping with others who apparently "believe" differently. In discussing this hopeful fantasy with my own students over the years, I often conjure up a television concept that is perhaps complementary to CNN's *Crossfire*[7]—let us call it *Crossinquire*—in which the purpose is not to throw a red meat topic onto the debate table (e.g., abortion, climate change, death penalty, gay marriage, immigration, war on drugs, etc.) and release the sociopolitical krakens to tear into each other. Rather, we would invite an additional and preliminary step—which theoretically could occupy the entire show—by asking our would-be combatants to begin by deeply and authentically reflecting upon why they believe what they believe vis-à-vis the issue at hand. What might the effect be? Well, among thousands of potential exemplars, rather than a fisticuffed Newt Gingrich—who has frequently sparred on *Crossfire*—leaping into the ring to fight, to cite just one instance, for the placement of children from "welfare mothers" in orphanages to disincentivize out-of-wedlock births,[8] *Crossinquire* would offer an opportunity for Newt first to reflect openly about why such a policy was personally appealing, not just in abstract terms, but personally, in terms of his own life history, background, knowledge, and experiences. And, consistent with the current format, answers would be probed deeply—and in a spirit of genuine and empathic inquiry—in order to humanize and make real the underlying reasons for such policy recommendations in the first place.

Most importantly, and entirely congruent with the fundamental premise of this book, the ultimate goal of *Crossinquire* would not be to prove or disprove the legitimacy or worth of the actions, policies, or practices that Newt—or anyone else—has proposed. That is, we would not privilege any one sociopolitical perspective over another as there is no shortage of strongly held beliefs along any number of liberal/conservative continua. Along these lines, to take another example of thousands, those primarily on "the left" who in principle oppose military intervention to prevent the killing of unarmed and innocent human beings by religious zealots or political despots might also be invited on to *Crossinquire* to explore the origins and implications of their own convictions in this regard. In short, the point of this (somewhat) tongue-in-cheek example, is that rather than the gladiator-like spectacle of two or more differently organized Ectoselves (see Chapter 3) bashing into one another—as is the case with CNN's *Crossfire*—we instead would promote the values and processes of authentic and empathic civil discourse by opening up a space whereby human beings could reflect upon *the why*, in addition to *the what*, of the beliefs and values they hold to be self-evident. And of course, we do not need *Crossinquire* to do so; everyday life provides multiple occasions for such reflection, which also may be codified more formally into a wide range of programs and interventions, as is discussed in the research and practice chapters in this book as well as the *Making Sense of Beliefs and Values* course and *Cultivating the Globally Sustainable Self* summit series, described previously.

---

[7] Retrieved from http://crossfire.blogs.cnn.com on August 14, 2014.

[8] Yes, this anecdote is factually based. Newt Gingrich was the former Speaker of the House of Representatives from 1995 to 1999 and a candidate for U.S. president. For more information about this chapter in our nation's history from a perspective that is aligned with the basic premises of this book, see Shealy, C. N. (1995). From Boys Town to Oliver Twist: Separating fact from fiction in welfare reform and out-of-home placement of children and youth. *American Psychologist, 50*(8), 565–580.

Deeper Understanding of the Human Condition

A third benefit of inculcating the habit of making sense of beliefs and values would be acquiring a much deeper understanding of the human condition. As illustrated across multiple chapters in this book—and as a central focus of the EI Model presented in Chapters 2 and 3—when we understand not only what we believe and value, but why, it becomes that much easier to understand why we do what we do. In short, we all would benefit by apprehending ourselves as creatures who: (a) are destined to pursue our own core needs as an essential expression of human nature; (b) will strive to do so whether or not people and circumstances in our world are responsive to this quest; and (c) will reap the consequences—for better or worse—of the degree to which these core needs are in fact met to a "good enough" degree. By making sense of the local and global implications of our human nature in this way, it becomes that much easier to make sense of that which seems incomprehensible (e.g., the "crazy" feelings, thoughts, and behaviors that humans may exhibit as a result of a chronic and/or extreme exposure mismatch between our core needs, and how we actually are experienced and treated by others early in development and throughout our lives).

Enacting More Sensible Actions, Policies, and Practices

A fourth and related benefit of such a world—where beliefs and values make better sense—would find us imagining, developing, and implementing actions, policies, and practices that actually correspond with who we are, and what we need, as human beings. All of these chapters focus on these points to one degree or another, from the fundamental point that "boot camp" programs may do more harm than good to the relative failure of our "war on drugs" (see Chapter 13); to the personal motives and potential downsides of forcing humans to reflect guiltily upon "privilege," White, Black, or otherwise, without corresponding and ongoing processes of self/other assessment (see Chapter 5); to the great damage inflicted upon boys and men—and thereby women, families, and communities—as a result of how we socialize the experience of affect vis-à-vis gender (see Chapter 8). The point is, the degree to which our actions, policies, and practices are *not* based upon sufficient understanding of who we actually are as a species—and what we need in order to fulfill the potential that is ours—is the degree to which such initiatives will, of necessity, fail. At that level, it really does not matter whether we believe some sociocultural stance should be good, right, or true (e.g., "just saying no" to drugs, sex, or whatever); what actually matters is whether what we propose, develop, and implement is in fact aligned with who we are and what we need as thinking, feeling, and behaving human beings. Until we apprehend such fundamental realities, we will continue to scratch our heads in bewildered exasperation while simultaneously squandering our resources on superficial, counterproductive, and just plain foolish actions, policies, and practices that are designed to ameliorate sociocultural ills, but instead will fail to do so and/or make matters worse, by dint of their disconnection from the nature of human nature (e.g., a perfect illustration of this disconnection is the foolish—and immoral—way in which we perceive and treat those we incarcerate, as documented in Chapter 13).

Striving to Live a Life Worth Living

Fifth and finally, in an attempt to grasp this weighty gauntlet from Socrates—*The unexamined life is not worth living*—I will juxtapose two aspects of living that inevitably arise from trying to "make sense of beliefs and values" in one's head (e.g., *What happens when we die?*) and heart (e.g., *What am I supposed to do until then?*). I will do so through the admittedly unorthodox, if not perilous, approach in an otherwise theoretically and empirically minded tome, by citing a couple of verses from the Christian Bible with which I always have resonated, even though I am no theologian and make no claim to being either "Christian" or "non-Christian." That is because whatever one's leaning along the "Continuum of Belief" (e.g., certitude, investment, sympathy, equivocation, skepticism, from Chapter 2), it may be possible to glean wisdom and insight via the following passages, respectively from *Corinthians* 13:12 and 13:13, which seem highly compatible with much of what we have been discussing throughout this book, although with some interpretive musings that I hope are experienced in sympathetic terms by "believers" and "nonbelievers" alike:

For now we see through a glass, darkly; but then face to face: now I know in part; but then shall I know even as also I am known.

And now abide faith, hope, love, these three; but the greatest of these is love.

From my perspective, the first passage deals with "the head" (e.g., *What happens when I die?*), and calls upon us to ponder imponderables throughout our life; the second passage deals with "the heart" (e.g., *What do I do with my life?*), and calls upon us to be mindful of how we allocate our time, attention, and resources while we are here on Earth. From an applied standpoint, when "making sense of beliefs and values," head and heart must both be engaged. Specifically, to live a life worth living, we must (a) ponder imponderables and (b) cultivate globally sustainable selves, as I attempt to illustrate in these final two reflections.

First, to live a life worth living, we must ponder imponderables. At the outset, I will spare any lingering suspense by acknowledging that alas, I do not "know" what happens to us when we die. What I do know is that by striving to make sense of beliefs and values—our own, others, and in the larger world—some highly intriguing questions arise. Consider two that have occupied theologians, philosophers, and physicists for millennia: *How did matter come from nothing?* and *Why did the universe begin?* We know something about the nature of matter on Earth at least, as well as how elements combine into larger organisms and systems. We also have good reason to believe that the universe began approximately 13.7 billion years ago, as a consequence of the "big bang," a moment in which all matter was concentrated into a single point before exploding to create what became all that we observe—including us—in the cosmos today. But despite such extraordinary scientific advances, we still do not know *why* the universe happened. Although some may contend this question is irrelevant or has been answered, others—like myself—are not so sure, even as we find the answers offered to date both fascinating and compelling (e.g., see Hawking, 1998; Krauss, 2012). At the very least, such imponderables—regarding the origins of matter and the universe—are inescapable considerations for anyone wishing to "make sense of beliefs and values," since so much of what we claim to be "true" is linked inextricably to how we apprehend and investigate these fundamental questions of matter and reality.

Another quintessential imponderable—*Is there life after death?*—bears pondering as well, through both a theological and scientific lens. Of course, multiple religious traditions contend that the answer is an emphatic "Yes." But, is there any evidence from a scientific perspective? Consider the putative phenomenon of "near death experiences" (NDEs). Essentially, NDEs refer to the state in which humans are clinically dead (e.g., no heart or brain activity), but report all manner of phenomena when they are "brought back to life" (e.g., encountering a great light, meeting long-dead relatives, the ability to report on conversations or events that were occurring in places other than the room in which they technically had died). In addition to the pioneering work of Raymond Moody and Elizabeth Kübler-Ross in this regard, others who routinely encounter processes of death and dying (e.g., physicians) increasingly are describing such phenomena, which reportedly number in the thousands all over the world (e.g., Alexander, 2012; Kübler-Ross, 2008; Long & Perry, 2011; Moody, 2001). Although various three-dimensional hypotheses exist (e.g., NDEs are simply the chemical sequelae of a brain in the process of dying), the sheer scope of such reports—not to mention the transformational and real world impact on humans who have survived them—beg further questions, which are not easily dismissed. That is, these reporting authorities—and the human subjects that are their focus—either are (a) mendacious or deluded, which is possible, but seems unlikely given the sheer number of credible authorities reporting on such phenomena from around the world as well as the relative degree of consistency across such reports; (b) misapprehending the etiology of such phenomena (e.g., the "dying brain" hypothesis, which deserves a hearing, but does not seem to account for various aspects of NDE phenomena, such as being able to recount events or conversations that occurred in places other than where the death occurred); or (c) describing a dimension of experience that actually may occur after life on Earth has ended. If one claims to be scientifically minded, it simply is not responsible to dismiss reliably reported phenomena just because they do not comport with one's a priori beliefs regarding the nature of reality. Instead, one must endeavor to study the phenomenon in an impartial manner, and transparently report what has been found, whether or not such findings are consistent with prevailing theories. In addition to NDEs, the basic rules of the science game must be applied fairly to all manner of phenomena which may be regarded as "paranormal." In any case, whatever we discover over time, the imponderable question—*Is there life after death?*—is likely to remain so for now since such "findings" portend profound implications for our beliefs about the nature, meaning, and purpose of existence.

Along these lines, other related imponderables include: *Why are we here? Does existence matter? Is any of this real? Why would we spend our lives learning to live if all we do is die?* Existential thinkers and students of the human condition grapple nobly with such questions, such as Irvin Yalom's "four givens of existence"—freedom, death, aloneness, meaninglessness—and so should we, if our goal is to strive to live an examined life (e.g., Frankle, 2006; May, 1969; Yalom, 2012). Because such enduring questions seem worthy of ongoing contemplation, the harsh certitude of strident atheism—"we awaken each day, kick the can of life further down the road, eventually die, and that's all there is"—seems perfunctory at best for many (e.g., Brearly et al., 2016; De Waal, 2013). In fairness, of course, prominent atheists like Richard Dawkins likely would agree that there is love, laughter, art, and beauty in the world; that we explore, we wonder, we yearn; that we are moved deeply by one another and the experience of being human. But in the final analysis, to conclude so unequivocally that even these vital aspects of subjective human experience may be understood merely as adaptively selected sequelae of our evolutionary heritage seems premature and unimaginative, if not downright unscientific. That is because we presently have no agreed upon methodologies for defining, measuring, and testing whether or not "God exists," not to mention any data one way or another, unless one is willing to admit the previously mentioned NDE findings, which although preliminary and in need of much further study, could seem to suggest that "God might not be a delusion, after all" (Dawkins, 2006).

In the final analysis, when pondering such imponderables—*Why did the universe begin? Is there life after death?* and *Why am I here?*—it must be acknowledged that religious faith indeed does seem to shine light through a glass darkly, giving liminal form to a shimmering destiny upon a perceptible horizon, for billions around the globe. As a clinician, I have seen this light in believers with whom I have been privileged to work. And, in truth, when conducting therapy with believing and nonbelieving individuals, couples, and families, all of whom are in crisis at one level or another, I often have felt a deep sense that I am engaging in activity that encompasses but extends beyond the here and now. If and when I am able to reach that bleak, frightened, or chaotic space within another, and permitted to sit with them long enough, we often are able to find a way out of their darkness, although the meandering path we follow may be arduous for sure. During such journeys, I sometimes have felt that I am in the company of something that is holding us in time—a possibility and hope that this life or these lives are not yet lost, that together we still may find our way into the light. There is an exquisite poignancy to that place—abiding with another soul or souls who are bound so tightly to their hell on Earth—that feels deeply humbling, like a great privilege and responsibility, like I am part of, or a conduit for, some presence, force, or purpose that is much bigger than I. For me, those moments are deeply spiritual. At such times, I feel infused with a sense of assurance and peace that this painful yet hopeful space makes sense, is necessary, and part of a much larger process; that we are here just for a little while; and that we are meant to do all we can to help each other heal, learn, and grow along the way.

That said, my own "spirituality" is not of a religious sort, in that I have not been able to bring myself to endorse one creed over others. Lord knows I have tried in years past, through study and practice, including but by no means limited to, reciting the "Apostles' Creed" eons ago, and the "sinner's prayer" even earlier at the urging of well-intentioned relatives, all to no effect, as far as I could tell. In addition to investigating the world's religions, I have also had the honor of encountering believers of many faiths through travel around the globe—as a clinician, researcher, teacher, and student—and do not question the transformative impact that religious devotion has in a very real way on their lives. The dilemma for "religiously unaffiliated" people like me—and there are a lot of us, with our numbers growing (Pew Research Center, 2012)—is not that I cannot believe that "there is something more" than our three-dimensional world (I do, actually). It's just that the "evidence" for such a world is not at all clear from the truth claims made by adherents to one creed or another, especially when each of these doctrines seems to possess a central tenet that "their system" or "their leader" is the only one worth following. How can it be that multiple religious systems all are correct when simultaneously claiming that theirs is "the one true faith?" The only way such truth claims make sense for me is if they are apprehended as an expression of core human need through the medium of a specific religious system that was developed in a particular time and place. In other words, established religious systems appear to represent the codification of historically emergent responses to core human need. Although such systems may differ in terms of prescribed and proscribed beliefs—which is where, lamentably, conflict arises—all were intended originally to accommodate the expression of core need (e.g., for transcendence), and subsequently strive, with varying degrees of success, to remain responsive to such need over time and in the present day. From this perspective, the human need for "transcendence" is real (e.g., as illustrated via the EI Self), but transcends any specific religious creed, and in fact, is not even dependent upon a religious medium for its expression and fulfillment (e.g., the need may be met through an experience of nature, one's work in the world, and so forth), a point on which Dawkins (2006) and I may well be in accord.

For now, however, "nones" like me—if that is what I am—must be contented by "evidence" for a spiritual dimension to life that seems meaningful, in both an ecumenical and nondenominational sense, as I attempt to describe via my work as a psychotherapist. So in conclusion, and by returning full circle to *Corinthians* 13:12, I do not "know" which face I might face, when "then" arrives, as it surely will, although I remain open to any good and hopeful possibilities in that regard, for myself and others. Whatever that outcome, our vision surely would be improved if we knew more about "why we know as we do"—and "are known as we are." In short, by making sense of beliefs and values in self, others, and the larger world, perhaps we may see more clearly "through a glass darkly" right here on Earth, which should facilitate our overarching quest to live a life worth living.

Second, to live a life worth living, we must cultivate globally sustainable selves. Recall again the two passages from *Corinthians*:

For now we see through a glass, darkly; but then face to face: now I know in part; but then shall I know even as also I am known.

and. . .

And now abide faith, hope, love, these three; but the greatest of these is love.

As noted previously, from my perspective, the former passage deals with "the head" (e.g., *What happens when I die?*), and calls upon us to ponder imponderables throughout our life; the latter passage deals with "the heart" (e.g., *What do I do with my life?*), and calls upon us to be mindful of how we allocate our time, attention, and resources while we are here on Earth. So, as a summary point regarding all we have discussed throughout this book—with a specific focus on how we may strive to live a life worth living—recall a principal conclusion from multiple sources of data: *As a species, we reap what we sow.* In striving to lead a life worth living, then, a central question before us is, *What sort of human selves do we wish to reap?* Those who lack empathy are indifferent to the consequences of their actions upon others, and do not apprehend the systemic, dialectic, and interconnected nature of human existence with the living world? These reap–sowing linkages are not theoretical abstractions. Every day, we bear witness to the blunt end points of such cultivating processes, personally and impersonally, locally and globally, and for better or worse. Fortunately, as illustrated on multiple occasions throughout this book, it is within our power to bend human nature in order to shape such self-cultivation processes. We do such bending daily regardless of whether we do or do not acknowledge that fact.

As may be evident by now, in bearing witness to daily events at home and abroad, we need to experience and express this triptych of capacities—faith, hope, and love—more than ever, and in ways that are complementary with their original meaning. Specifically, from the perspective of "making sense of beliefs and values," the "faith" we need is in our innate (e.g., "God-given" and/or "adaptively acquired") ability to believe in all we are meant to be and become as a species. Others may, but I do not see the need for incompatibility between this perspective and my understanding of how a Christian regards such faith. That is because so much of what we see and experience around us that is dark, hateful, or even evil is the inevitable consequence of inadequate responsiveness over a prolonged period of time to the core needs that define who we are and whom we become. Perhaps that is a notion that most "believers" and "nonbelievers" could embrace. To have faith then is to believe in our potential, not out of mawkish sentimentality, but for robust theoretical and empirical reasons at the very least, which have been tested mightily within a myriad of historical, contemporary, and real world contexts. So, *we have faith* in whom we may become because we have seen what happens when our core needs are—and are not—responded to in a minimally sufficiently manner. Thus, our *faith* is borne of the knowledge that our *fate* is a function largely of how we were experienced and cared for by others *as well as* our own resilient capacities interacting with the "formative variables" that shape us throughout our lives.

Likewise, *we have hope* that we and our fellow humans may create a world that is truly sustainable in the deepest and broadest sense. That is, our faith gives us hope that we may acquire the inclination—and muster the courage—to think, feel, and act toward self, others, and the larger world in a manner that nurtures and uplifts rather than neglects and dispirits. Ultimately, we must do so not only for ourselves and those humans who arrive on this planet after we depart, but for the living creatures and systems that also depend upon us to experience and express such sustainable faith, and see it manifest in the real world.

Finally, *we have love*—"the greatest of these"—which may be understood as *the experience and expression of sufficient responsiveness to core need in self and others as well as an abiding commitment to protect, create, and nurture the conditions by which such need may sustainably be met in the larger world.* In this sense, love is not some soppy utopic ideal, but our birthright as members of this species, for the love we are able to express is a direct consequence of the love we have experienced, especially at the outset of our development, but in truth, throughout our lives. Although we may transcend a lack of such love to a degree, through native resilience, force of will in the service of need, and the acquisition of wisdom over time, we tend on the whole to love as we were, and are, loved, a poignantly stark truth that is beautiful and brutal in its consequence, for better or worse. Arguably then, there is no higher—perhaps no other—purpose to our existence than to love and perchance, to be loved. When we are so, that is because the core essence of the good potential that we are, is known, felt, seen, and spoken by another, which verifies and strengthens its presence within us, and means we are likely to become that much more able to do the same for another. And sadly, it must be acknowledged, when such native potential is not known, or is denied in us, that often is because the neglecting individuals—or the abusive system that is composed of such individuals who are in positions of unchecked power—often did not themselves sufficiently experience love as defined previously, and therefore can neither express it, nor tolerate its expression by others. Such deterministic realities regarding the human condition neither excuse the attendant manifestations of malevolence— nor relieve responsibility on us all to create contingencies that attenuate the emergence of such dark forces—but may offer a measure of understanding regarding the steadfast persistence of evil in our world.

Perhaps that is what is meant by the following expressions of the "Golden Rule," from Buddhism: *Hurt not others in ways that you yourself would find hurtful;* Christianity: *Love your neighbor as you love yourself;* Confucianism: *What you do not wish for yourself, do not do to others;* Hinduism: *One should never do that to another which one regards as injurious to one's own self;* Humanism: *people should aim to treat each other as they would like to be treated themselves—with tolerance, consideration and compassion;*

Islam: *As you would have people do to you, do to them; and what you dislike to be done to you, don't do to them*; and Judaism: *Whoever destroys a soul, it is considered as if he destroyed an entire world. And whoever saves a life, it is considered as if he saved an entire world.* [9] And so, our concluding faith and hope is that we may learn to cultivate globally sustainable selves, by realizing our nascent potential to love as we were meant to be loved; in doing so, we may save ourselves by saving each other. For our capacity and inclination to love will determine the fate of our species, and all who whirl together with us on our lovely orb of aquamarine, round a merciful star that lights the endless night just beyond our shore.

REFERENCES

Alexander, E. (2012). *Proof of heaven: A neurosurgeon's journey into the afterlife.* New York, NY: Simon & Schuster.

Aronson, E. (2012). *The social animal* (11th ed.). New York, NY: Worth Publishers.

Bongar, B., Brown, L. M., Beutler, L. E., Breckenridge, J. N., & Zimbardo, P. G. (Eds.). (2007). *The psychology of terrorism.* New York, NY: Oxford University Press.

Brearly, R. W., van den Bos, K., & Tan, C. (2016). The nature and etiology of religious certitude: Implications of the EI Framework and Beliefs, Events, and Values Inventory. In C. N. Shealy (Ed.), *Making sense of beliefs and values* (pp. 331–369). New York, NY: Springer Publishing.

Brooks, D. (2015, April 11). The moral bucket list. *The New York Times.* Retrieved from http://www.nytimes.com/2015/04/12/opinion/sunday/david-brooks-the-moral-bucket-list.html?_r=0

Center for Green Schools. (2014). *A national plan for educating for sustainability.* Retrieved March 6, 2014 from http://www.centerforgreenschools.org/nationalactionplan

Charmaz, K. (2006). *Constructing grounded theory: A practical guide through. qualitative analysis.* London: Sage.

Coates, M., Hanson, W., Samuel, D. B., Webster, M., & Cozen, J. (2016). The Beliefs, Events, and Values Inventory (BEVI): Psychological assessment implications and applications. In C. N. Shealy (Ed.), *Making sense of beliefs and values* (pp. 371–406). New York, NY: Springer Publishing.

Cozen, J., Hanson, W., Poston, J., Jones, S., & Tabit, M. (2016). The Beliefs, Events, and Values Inventory (BEVI): Implications and applications for therapeutic assessment and intervention. In C. N. Shealy (Ed.), *Making sense of beliefs and values* (pp. 575–621). New York, NY: Springer Publishing.

Cranton, P. (Ed.). (2006). *Understanding and promoting transformative learning: A guide for educators of adults.* San Francisco, CA: Jossey Bass.

Creswell, J. W., & Plano-Clark, V. L. (2007). *Designing and conducting mixed methods research.* Thousand Oaks, CA: Sage.

Cultivating the Globally Sustainable Self. (2015). Retrieved May 31, 2015 from http://www.jmu.edu/summitseries/

D'Amour, D., Ferrada-Videla, M., San Martin Rodriguez, L., & Beaulieu, M. D. (2005). The conceptual basis for interprofessional collaboration: Core concepts and theoretical frameworks. *Journal of Interprofessional Care, 19*, 116–131.

Dawkins, R. (2006). *The god delusion.* Boston, MA: Houghton Mifflin.

De Waal, F. (2013). *The bonobo and the atheist.* New York, NY: W.W. Norton and Company.

Dirkx, J. M. (2012). Self-formation and transformative learning: A response to "Calling transformative learning into question: Some mutinous thoughts," by Michael Newman. Adult Education Quarterly, *62*(4), 399–405.

---

[9] Although most of these verses are drawn from widely known religious texts, the "humanism" quotation was retrieved from Think Humanism, at www.thinkhumanism.com/the-golden-rule.html

Dyjak-LeBlanc, K., Brewster, L., Grande, S., White, R., & Shullman, S. (2016). The EI Leadership Model: From theory and research to real world application. In C. N. Shealy (Ed.), *Making sense of beliefs and values* (pp. 531–574). New York, NY: Springer Publishing.

Edmunds, A. J., Federico, C. M., & Mays, L. (2016). Exploring the etiology of ideology: In search of the political self through the EI Model and BEVI Method. In C. N. Shealy (Ed.), *Making sense of beliefs and values* (pp. 303–330). New York, NY: Springer Publishing.

Education for sustainable development (ESD). (2013). Retrieved February 8, 2013, from http://www.unesco.org/new/en/education/themes/leading-the-international-agenda/education-for-sustainable-development/

Frankle, V. (2006). *Man's search for meaning*. Boston, MA: Beacon Press.

Pew Research Center. (2014). *Gay marriage*. Retrieved September 15, 2014 from http://www.pewresearch.org/data-trend/domestic-issues/attitudes-on-gay-marriage/

Greenwald, A. G. (2012). There is nothing so theoretical as a good method. *Perspectives on Psychological Science, 7*(2), 99–108.

Gunning for Saddam. (2001). Retrieved from http://www.pbs.org/wgbh/pages/frontline/shows/gunning/

Hart, V., & Glick, B. (2016). Justice and the nature of human nature: What, why, and how beliefs and values matter. In C. N. Shealy (Ed.), *Making sense of beliefs and values* (pp. 485–530). New York, NY: Springer Publishing.

Hawking, S. (1998). *A brief history of time*. New York, NY: Bantam Books.

Inglehart, R., Basáñez, M., Díez-Medrano, J., Halman, L., & Luijkx, R. (2004). *Human beliefs and values: A cross-cultural sourcebook based on the 1999–2002 values surveys*. Mexico: Siglo XXI Editores.

Inglehart, R., Basáñez, M., & Moreno, A. (1998). *Human values and beliefs: A cross-cultural sourcebook*. Ann Arbor, MI: The University of Michigan Press.

CNN. (2013*). Iraqi weapons inspections fast facts*. Retrieved from http://www.cnn.com/2013/10/30/world/meast/iraq-weapons-inspections-fast-facts/

Iyer, C. (2013). *Assessing and engaging beliefs and values in a learning community of U.S. and international students: Implications and applications from the Forum BEVI Project*. (Unpublished doctoral dissertation). James Madison University, Harrisonburg, VA.

Johnson C. E., Stewart A. L., Brabeck, M. M., Huber, V. S., & Rubin, H (2004). Interprofessional collaboration: Implications for Combined-Integrated doctoral training in professional psychology. *Journal of Clinical Psychology, 60*(10), 9995–1010.

Kelly, J., Holt, J., Patel, R., & Nolet, V. (2016). Environmental beliefs and values: In search of models and methods. In C. N. Shealy. (Ed.), *Making sense of beliefs and values* (pp. 233–260). New York, NY: Springer Publishing.

Kessler, G. (2009). Saddam Hussein Said WMD Talk Helped Him Look Strong to Iran. Retrieved from http://www.washingtonpost.com/wp-dyn/content/article/2009/07/01/AR2009070104217.html

Krauss, L. M. (2012). *A universe from nothing*. New York, NY: Simon & Schuster.

Kristof, N. (2014, August 28). Is everyone a little bit racist? *The New York Times*, p. A21.

Kubler-Ross, E. (2008). *On life after death*. Berkeley, CA: Celestial Arts.

Long, J., & Perry, P. (2011). *Evidence of the afterlife: The science of near-death experiences*. New York, NY: Simon & Schuster.

May, R. (1969). *Love and will*. New York, NY: W.W. Norton.

Mezirow, J., & Taylor, E. (Ed.). (2009). *Transformative learning in practice: Insights from community, workplace, and higher education*. San Francisco, CA: Jossey Bass.

Moody, R. (2001). *Life after life: The investigation of a phenomenon—Survival of bodily death*. San Francisco, CA: Harper.

Murphy, T. (2014). *This leading GOP congressional candidate insists we found Saddam's WMD program*. Retrieved from http://www.motherjones.com/politics/2014/06/steve-russell-saddam-hussein-oklahoma-congress

Pew Research Center. (2012). *Nones on the rise*. Retrieved from http://www.pewforum.org/2012/10/09/nones-on-the-rise/

Pendleton, C., Cochran, S., Kapadia, S., & Iyer, C. (2016). Understanding the gendered self: Implications from EI Theory, the EI Self, and the BEVI. In C. N. Shealy (Ed.), *Making sense of beliefs and values* (pp. 261–302). New York, NY: Springer Publishing.

QSR International Pty Ltd. (2012). NVivo qualitative data analysis (Version 10) [Computer software]. Doncaster, Victoria, Australia: QSR International Pty Ltd. Retrieved March 9, 2013 from http://www.qsrinternational.com

Schwartz, S. H. (1992). Universals in the content and structure of values: Theoretical advances and empirical tests in 20 countries. In M. P. Zanna (Ed.), *Advances in experimental social psychology* (pp. 1–65). New York, NY: Academic Press.

Schwartz, S. H. (2012). An overview of the Schwartz Theory of basic values. *Online Readings In Psychology and Culture, 2*(1). http://dx.doi.org/10.9707/2307-0919.1116

Schwartz, S. H., & Bilsky, W. (1987). Toward a psychological structure of human values. *Journal of Personality and Social Psychology, 53,* 550–562.

Schwartz, S. H., & Bilsky, W. (1990). Toward a theory of the universal content and structure of values: Extensions and cross-cultural replications. *Journal of Personality and Social Psychology, 58*(5), 878–891.

Shealy, C. N. (1995). From Boys Town to Oliver Twist: Separating fact from fiction in welfare reform and out-of home placement of children and youth. *American Psychologist, 50*(8), 565–580.

Shealy, C. N., Bhuyan, D., & Sternberger, L. G. (2012). Cultivating the capacity to care in children and Youth: Implications from EI Theory, EI Self, and BEVI. In U. Nayar (Ed.), *Child and adolescent mental health* (pp. 240–255). New Delhi, India: Sage Publications.

Spaeth, J., Schwartz, S., Nayar, U., & Ma, W. (2016). Identity development and the construction of self: Findings and implications from the Forum BEVI Project. In C. N. Shealy (Ed.), *Making sense of beliefs and values* (pp. 205–232). New York, NY: Springer Publishing.

Staub, E. (2013). Building a peaceful society: Origins, prevention, and reconciliation after genocide and other group violence. *American Psychologist, 68*(7), 576–589.

Strauss, A., & Corbin, J. (1990). *Basics of qualitative research: Grounded theory procedures and techniques.* Newbury Park, CA: Sage.

Tabit, M. B., Legault, L., Ma, W., & Wan, K. P. (2016). In search of best practices for multicultural education: Empirical evidence from the Forum BEVI Project. In C. N. Shealy (Ed.), *Making sense of beliefs and values* (pp. 175–204). New York, NY: Springer Publishing.

Tashakkori, A., & Teddlie, C. (2009). Integrating Qualitative and Quantitative Approaches to Research. In D. J. Rog & L. Bickman (Eds.), *Handbook of Applied Social Research Methods* (2nd ed., pp. 283–317). Thousand Oaks, CA: Sage.

Wandschneider, E., Pysarchik, D. T., Sternberger, L. G., Ma, W., Acheson-Clair, K., Baltensperger, B., . . . Hart, V. (2016). The Forum BEVI Project: Applications and implications for international, multicultural, and transformative learning. In C. N. Shealy (Ed.), *Making sense of beliefs and values* (pp. 407–484). New York, NY: Springer Publishing.

Yalom, I. D. (2012). *Love's executioner.* New York, NY: Basic Books.

INDEX